CRITICAL ACCLAIM FOR PETER MANSO'S EXTRAORDINARY NATIONALLY BESTSELLING BIOGRAPHY

"Try dipping into Mr. Manso's interviews without at once becoming addicted. Try just skimming the text without getting hooked in the stage-by-stage unfolding of Norman Mailer's career. You can't."

—*The New York Times*

"A sort of sprawling, late-into-the-night party, *Mailer* gives you an enjoyable time."

—*The New Yorker*

"The triumph of this book is its sound . . . a stunning commotion and variety."

—*Los Angeles Times Book Review*

"One thing about Mailer: he's got as many lives as Nixon. And he's a lot more entertaining."

—*The Village Voice*

"Reading this book is an exciting, irresistible experience."

—*Publishers Weekly*

"No one can read this account—page upon page of recollections by people famous and unknown, grave literary personages and trivial sycophants and social climbers, beings up the greasy pole and ignorant of its existence—without noting Mailer's bedrock of decency. . . . Call the collective effect love: for Mailer, and if not for Mailer for what he has tried, and if not for what he has tried, for what he has made others wish to try."

—*The Washington Post*

"Manso skillfully weaves his narrative, cutting this way and that, back and forth, with one person often contradicting another in the manner of a good argument at one's favorite bar late at night."

—*Penthouse*

ALSO BY PETER MANSO

Ptown: Art, Sex, and Money on the Outer Cape

Brando: The Biography

*The Shadow of the Moth: A Novel of Espionage with
Virginia Woolf* (with Ellen Hawkes)

Faster! A Racer's Diary

Running Against the Machine: The Mailer-Breslin Campaign

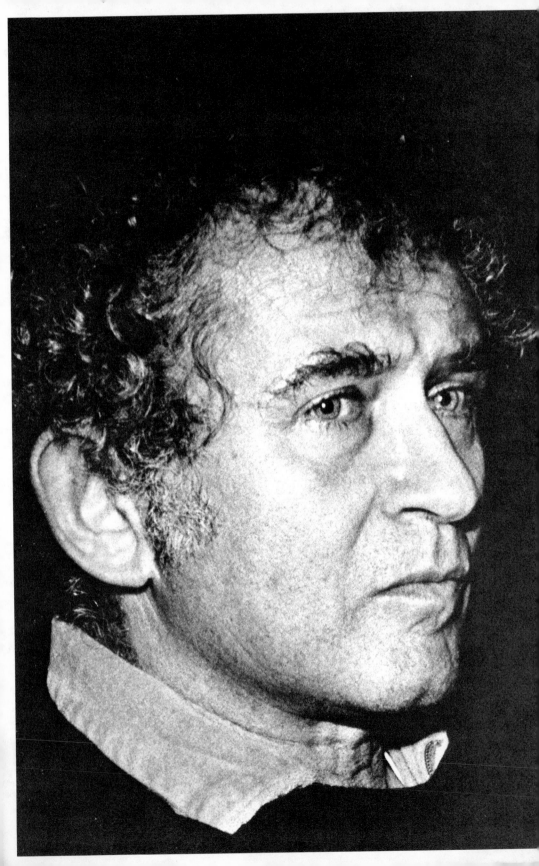

MAILER

His Life and Times

by PETER MANSO

W

WASHINGTON SQUARE PRESS
New York   London   Toronto   Sydney

Washington Square Press
A Division of Simon & Schuster, Inc.
1230 Avenue of the Americas
New York, NY 10020

First Washington Square Press trade paperback edition November 2008

WASHINGTON SQUARE PRESS and colophon are registered trademarks of Simon & Schuster, Inc.

For information about special discounts for bulk purchases, please contact Simon & Schuster Special Sales at 1-800-456-6798 or business@simonandschuster.com

Manufactured in the United States of America

10   9   8   7   6   5   4   3   2   1

ISBN-13: 978-1-4165-6286-3
ISBN-10:   1-4165-6286-9

For permission to reprint excerpts, the author is grateful to the following:

The Atlantic Monthly for the review of The Deer Park, November 1955. Copyright © 1955 by The Atlantic Monthly Company. Reprinted by permission.

Frederick Busch for the review by Frederick Busch of Ancient Evenings, Chicago Tribune Book World, April 10, 1983. Reprinted by permission.

Commentary for the review by Richard Poirier of An American Dream, June 1965. Reprinted by permission; all rights reserved.

Commonweal Foundation for the review by John Garvey of The Executioner's Song, Commonweal, March 14, 1980. Reprinted by permission.

Grosset & Dunlap, Inc., for the ad for Marilyn, New York Times Book Review, December 9, 1973. Reprinted by permission.

Emma Clara Gwaltney for the letters of Francis Irby Gwaltney to Norman Mailer. Reprinted with permission.

Harper's for the review of An American Dream. Copyright © 1965 by Harper's Magazine. Reprinted from the April 1965 issue by special permission.

Harvard Alumni Association for "25th Anniversary Report, Harvard, Class of '43." Reprinted by permission of the President and Fellows of Harvard College.

Walter Karp for the review by Walter Karp of The Executioner's Song, Esquire, December 1979. Reprinted by permission.

Kirkus Reviews for the review of The Deer Park, August 15, 1955. Reprinted by permission of Virginia Kirkus' Service.

Library Journal for the review of The Deer Park, October 1, 1955. Published by R. R. Bowker Co., a Xerox company. Copyright © 1955 by Xerox Corporation.

Life magazine for: the review by Wilfred Sheed of "The Deer Park" play, February 24, 1967, copyright © 1967 Time Inc., reprinted with permission; and the review by Webster Schott of Why Are We in Vietnam?, September 15, 1967, copyright © 1967 Time Inc., reprinted with permission.

The London Sunday Times for: front-page editorial, March 1949, copyright 1949 Times Newspapers Ltd.; and the response to letters defending The Naked and the Dead, May 8, 1949, copyright 1949 Times Newspapers Ltd., reprinted with permission.

For the writings of Norman Mailer:
Little, Brown and Company for the excerpt from Of a Fire on the Moon, copyright © 1970 by Norman Mailer.

(continued at back of book)

To Ellen Hawkes

CONTENTS

I: BROOKLYN (1923-39)

<u>FANNY SCHNEIDER MAILER</u> The family? My father—Norman's grandfather—was a rabbi, and the family ran a grocery store in Long Branch, New Jersey. My father couldn't speak English very well, and once, when we were given a summons for keeping the store open on Sunday, I went in his place to court, shaking in my boots. I was sixteen. I had to come up on the stand and explain it wasn't a "subterfuge." The man who was questioning thought I wouldn't understand, but I did, and I told him we had a separate meat department that was closed completely on Saturdays, and that we were open on Sundays but just in the morning, and even so, with the shades drawn. I told him that we were religious and that our clientele had to be served. I said we were most certainly not in "flagrant disregard" of the law. My father wasn't there, my mother wasn't there, it was just me, the champion, to represent the family. I had a lot of spunk, I guess, and they let us stay open.

My father wasn't the official rabbi, but as far as knowledge goes he was, and a scholar too. He would stay up night after night studying the Torah from one end to the other, and even in his later years we'd find him in the morning still at the table in the dining room. He did a lot with the *shul*. In Long Branch the

*(Left) Grandfather Chaim Yehudah Schneider, unofficial rabbi of Long
Branch, N.J., who never wanted a congregation "because he said that rabbis
were* schnorrers *and he wouldn't live that way."*   *(Right) The Schneider
sisters. From left to right: Rose, Rebecca, Jennie, and Fanny.*

Jewish community wasn't large and didn't have a paid rabbi, so he gave his
services for nothing. On High Holidays a cantor came, but my father would do
the services. He wouldn't think of taking money for that. It was his pleasure.
He was looked up to as the rabbi.

My mother had nothing to do with the store. It was just the girls, one after
another as we progressed out of high school. There were four of us plus my
brother Joe. I was the youngest. My sister Rose became a teacher because she
never wanted anything to do with the store and steered away from it. Which
elected me to come next. Money was tight all the time—*tight, tight*—and I
imagine that's where my sense of business came from. Once, for example, my
father and I were going through the accounts to see who owed us, where we
could use pressure to collect in order to pay our own bills, and when I mentioned
one account he said, "And what's her name?" I said, "Why do you ask me the
names? Her name is sixty-five dollars." He was very soft and would let people

go for months without paying, so we always had the headache of putting our creditors off. He counted on people's honesty. His kindness overpowered his practicality, whereas I was practical, very practical, and I felt, Why is all this wished on me when the others should have taken care of it? But I guess they were soft too.

There was also my sister Beck, whom I loved very much. She was my favorite, more like a mother than a sister. She was at least ten years older, the eldest, and she was my crutch. When she met Louie Shapiro, it was immediately a love affair. My mother didn't favor it. She expected her daughter to marry a doctor at least. My father was more on Louie's side. He said, "Look, he's handsome, they're in love." As religious as he was, he understood it. And Beck was really a very special person. She had that quality of making things easier for everybody. Work meant nothing to her.

MARJORIE "OSIE" RADIN Both sides of the family were Oslite and originally came from Anikxt. The town is no longer in existence but it was near Vilna and Kovno. Both were cities, also regarded as counties, and Anikxt was in one of them, either Vilna Guberniya or Kovno Guberniya, but don't ask me which. I don't know if the Schneiders were known as Schneiders in Anikxt, since a lot of immigrants were just assigned names at Ellis Island.

I was Beck's first daughter, and her father, my grandfather—Chaim Yehudah, lovingly known as Chaimudah—that's where all the brains and talent came from. His mother died when he was very young, and when he was four his father remarried and he was sent away to a yeshiva, one of the two best yeshivas in Russia. Twelve years later, at the age of sixteen, he was ordained as a rabbi.

When he came to this country he became the unofficial rabbi of Long Branch because the community was too poor to support a rabbi full time. Although he was ordained, he never wanted a *shtetl*—a pulpit or congregation—because he said that rabbis were *schnorrers*, and he wouldn't live that way. So he was not only serious and well educated and brilliant but also honorable and principled. He was a Talmudic scholar all his life.

Since I was the first and eldest of the grandchildren, I can remember visiting at my grandparents' home. My grandfather would sit at the dining room table and read to the family in Yiddish. He wasn't political, and even though he was religious, he had his doubts. A very unusual man, who was highly revered and respected in the community; people would come to him with their problems. Not only that, but rabbis would come from all over to speak with him too. I don't know if all his reading was Talmudic, but he did a lot of that. There was a Torah in the house—I don't know how he acquired it, but that in itself was most unusual. He was also very excitable, and he would flare up. Cy, my brother—Charles Rembar—used to be that way as a youngster too. So was Norman.

The store was a large grocery, a family business that had been passed on to my grandfather. But Chaim Yehudah was no businessman. A scholar and a dreamer—yes, Fan's right. It was the girls who took turns running the store.

My mother, Beck, was the eldest, but she married very young. My father, Louis, had been visiting his sister in Long Branch, met my mother when she was fourteen, and fell in love with her. They married when she was about eighteen or nineteen. But she was the hub of the family. All the sisters clung to her, turned to her with problems, and so did the nieces and nephews, including Norman.

I used to hear my mother say that a lot of my grandfather's friends who stayed in New York City, the ones who didn't go out to the sticks like Chaim Yehudah, made it big and became tremendously wealthy while my grandfather was absorbed in his study of the Talmud. But all his daughters were extremely ambitious, especially Fan and my mother. Both terrific businesswomen. Fan was a human dynamo. She could work ten to twelve hours a day. My mother too. I can recall seeing her just exhausted, when she'd lie down crosswise on a bed for less than ten minutes, then jump up, refreshed, and go again. Boundless energy.

Fan married comparatively late, when she was twenty-eight, I think, although the problem is that none of us knows exactly how old she is. But I don't think there were remarks about her becoming a spinster. She wasn't the type. She was too animated, too vivacious, even though maybe now she resents the things she feels were dumped on her as the youngest.

FANNY SCHNEIDER MAILER   When Barney decided to take the free ride to America—he'd been in the South African Army in England during WW One and had the choice of returning to Johannesburg or coming here—his brother-in-law, Dave Kessler, was already quite prosperous. Dave had emigrated with his wife, Anne, and made a lot of money during the war—he had a candy factory that made chocolate-covered cherries. So when Barney first came over, he was living with Anne and Dave on President Street in Brooklyn. Anne had had the flu and wanted a place to rest. That winter my folks were running a small boardinghouse in Lakewood, New Jersey, a winter resort, and Barney made a reservation. The first weekend I wasn't there, but when I got home, Anne said to me, "Oh, Miss Schneider, I'm sorry you didn't see my brother." To me he was just a guest, but I said, "I hope he'll come out again." Which he did, and that was the beginning of it.

Barney had been trained as an accountant, and in 1922 we got married in a hotel somewhere downtown in Manhattan, a big wedding. A hundred people came, most of them from Long Branch. Very few of Barney's relatives were there, only Anne and a few cousins from Brooklyn. But Barney was very fond of my family. He didn't talk about missing his own relatives, maybe because I didn't know them, and I didn't meet them until years later when we took a trip to South Africa.

We went to Atlantic City for our honeymoon—only a week—then we lived with my parents until moving to Flatbush when Norman was one or two. Barney had enlisted in South Africa and had made a good connection with the American shipping board. His superior was a very fine man, a gentleman. I had him once for lunch when Barney applied for a job with the government, and he offered

Barney a good job, which probably I should have agreed to. But I didn't want to go south or west. I was so close to my family I didn't want to go far away.

Norman was born in Monmouth Memorial Hospital in Long Branch on January 31, 1923. I went to the hospital in the early evening, and he was born the next morning. My doctor was in New York at a show, so he took the first train back and showed up in evening clothes. I sent Barney, everybody, home. "I only want a nurse," I said, because I figured I could give vent to my aches and pains with no family around. It was a very difficult birth, at least twelve hours. I said to myself, "No more babies for me. No more." But, of course, I had one more, a very fine one, Barbara, who was born four years later in 1927.

When I brought Norman home I had a nurse for two weeks, then, when the nurse left, I was afraid I'd break the baby if I picked him up. I was the youngest in my family, remember, and I thought to myself, How do I take care of a baby when I've never even touched one? So then each of my sisters came for two weeks.

I thought Norman was perfect, a really lovely baby. He weighed about seven pounds at birth.

Barney would get up about six o'clock in the morning to make the train to New York, where he was working, then he'd leave the office early, about four-thirty, to be back before seven. The dinner was ready-made at the hotel, I had nothing to do with it. We would all eat together as a family if I felt well enough. To be having a baby seemed the biggest job in the world, and I really couldn't understand how people had more than one child. I never dreamt of having five or six children like my parents. But, you see, my mother's generation and my generation were more than one generation apart. Although we were very close-knit and what touched one touched everybody, my mother was more European. I was American.

NORMAN MAILER "Mailer" is an English name, given to my grandparents when they went to South Africa from Russia. Nobody knows what the name was originally. Mailorovski? Mailorovich? Yeah, something out of Dostoevsky! Norman Isaacovich Mailorovski!

FANNY SCHNEIDER MAILER Norman was named Nachum Malech. "Nachum" is "Norman." "Malech" is "king" in Hebrew. We named him—he was our king. Maybe I was more versed in Hebrew names and words than Barney because of my father, although "Kingsley" is what appears on his birth certificate.

CHARLES REMBAR My sister, Osie (pronounced "Ossie"—also called Jorie, my young children's attempt at Marjorie, her first name; Osie is short for Asenath, her middle name), felt that "King" would be silly. She suggested "Kingsley." She was a young admirer of Charles Kingsley, the author of Water Babies. There is a mistaken impression that Norman was named after the summer cottages his mother and aunt operated as a hotel. It was the other way around: the cottages were named Kingsley Court for Norman.

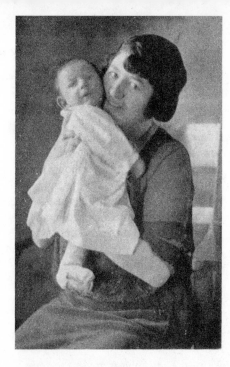

Fanny Mailer with her two-month-old Norman: "It was a very difficult birth, at least 12 hours. . . . He was named Nachum Melech. Melech *is 'king' in Hebrew—and that's what he was, our little king."*

FANNY SCHNEIDER MAILER Barney was still working in downtown Manhattan, and living in Brooklyn was cheaper and much easier than commuting from Long Branch. Anne and Dave were still in Flatbush, and that's how we came to settle only a block away. It was a four-room apartment in the area of Cortelyou Road, a nice neighborhood, mainly Jewish but all English-speaking—middle-class people making their way up—merchants, professionals, office workers. Barney was with a big firm. His references were very good and his appearance was always a hundred percent in his favor. He was very conscientious about his clothes, always very neat and fastidious. Too fastidious, in fact. It took time, and I always figure you can't think so well when you're bothered with your clothing. But that was his nature. No matter how little good clothing he had, he always appeared well dressed.

NORMAN MAILER Very elegant, very fastidious, that was my father. He wore spats. He seemed English to people who met him.

FANNY SCHNEIDER MAILER When Norman started school I would walk him in the mornings, and even in the first grade his teacher recognized his talent and let him write whatever he wanted to. One day she met me outside and I remember her saying, "Mrs. Mailer, you have to realize that your son's pleasures in life are going to be solemn ones."

I was pleased, of course, but it didn't surprise me, because he had already started to read and his nose was always in a book. He didn't start talking earlier than most kids, but he had that quality of making people interested and always had a circle around him, everybody, all the relatives. On Barney's side, since Anne and Dave didn't have any children, Norman was their little pet. He got so much attention from the family that it was like he was a little god.

After my parents died I stopped keeping kosher because I didn't believe it was that important. Barney's family was kosher too, but when he was in the army he'd lost it. What was the point? All that cleaning before Passover, even in the back of the closets in case there was a crust of bread there? I never served pork, but I didn't stick to having separate plates, silver, and pots for *milchigs* and *fleishigs*. I remember our family tugging two barrels of dishes up from the basement for the holidays. It was such a bother, and expensive too. It meant money, and money wasn't plentiful. Beck and my other sisters didn't keep kosher in their homes either, but the hotel was kosher.

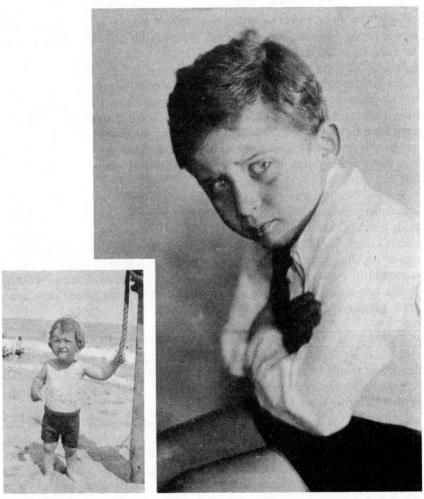

(Left) At age two, Long Branch, New Jersey   (Right) "Even in the first grade his teacher recognized his talent, and I remember her saying, 'Mrs. Mailer, you have to recognize that your son's pleasures in life are going to be solemn ones.'"

We moved to 555 Crown Street when Norman was nine. I wanted to move from Flatbush because I'd be able to have company more often if I was nearer to New York. Also, Crown Heights was more Jewish than Cortelyou Road. Flatbush had cheap *goyim*, more Irish. Crown Heights was different. Our building, 555, was all Jewish, middle-class. There were a few rich Jews, just a few.

I knew Mrs. Samish, the owner of 555, because Anne lived in the lower apartment of this woman's two-family house in Flatbush. Which reminds me: One time Norman was bringing a magazine to Anne, and when he got there Mrs. Samish said, "Oh, Norman, so now you'll be selling magazines." He said, "I won't sell them, I'll write them."

This was earlier, mind you, when he was only six! And he wasn't showing off—he just always aimed high. You can attribute it to the love he got, because love is encouragement. Norman was so secure in his idea of himself because he knew from his heart the way he was loved. I don't think he ever had a spanking. Maybe a pat on the tussie from Barney. But no, Barney wanted to retain his love too, and I don't remember either of us punishing him. I always felt he was a very sensitive individual, and to spank him, I knew, would hurt him. I always felt you give children freedom. Once his Aunt Anne looked at something he'd written and said, "Norman, your handwriting is terrible." He put it away and didn't write anything all evening. After she went home I told him that it didn't matter about his handwriting, that it was what he had to say that was important.

Anyway, Norman shared a room with Barbara. I remember buying him a big square desk. He also had a chemistry set. Whenever Norman was doing something it was heart-whole, he gave everything and it was serious, so his room was always a mess. But I didn't care. I figured if the room is upset, he's accomplishing something. But Barney was fussy and very meticulous, and at first he would come out of Norman's room and say, "Look at the mess he made." I'd say, "Leave him alone. He's going to be a great man." I knew that. Absolutely. Even as he was growing up.

MARJORIE "OSIE" RADIN   Norman started with model airplanes when he was about ten. He was serious, so serious that his Aunt Anne and Uncle Dave decided he should be an aeronautical engineer, and his parents went along with it. Everybody was very impressed with the building of those airplanes except me. Why? I thought. What good is it?

I remember the models hanging in the living room. Anything that he did had to be on display. Compared to Barbara, Norman was more demanding, but the two of them were extremely devoted as brother and sister. That kind of relationship had been fostered between my brother and myself, and Fan did the same thing. It was insisted on. There was always great devotion, and we were all close-knit, the entire family.

RHODA LAZARE WOLF   My family lived in the same building on Crown Street, Barbara and I were best friends, and I remember being aware that Norman was never really scolded by either of them. Barney was just a shadow. The mother

completely took over, nursed all of Norman's narcissism, and made him feel that whatever he did was okay.

LARRY ALSON   I've always thought of Fanny as the protective lioness with her cubs. One story I heard was that when Norman was in grade school he came home with a C on his report card. Fan took the report card and went back to see the principal, insisting "There's some mistake here. My son isn't capable of doing mediocre work. There's no way he could get a C." "What difference does it make?" they said. "It isn't going to appear on his high school transcript when he goes to college." Her reply? "I want him to be acknowledged for what he is, a superior person. I want you to give him the A he deserves." And she got them to change the grade.

FANNY SCHNEIDER MAILER   Yes, I did have an argument with his teacher. It was when he was in the third grade. I felt he deserved an A by the reading he did at home, his conversation, and everything. I even felt that he should be put in the next grade. He was above most children, and if he didn't pay attention, it was because he already knew it all. So I said to her, "Perhaps he was only nervous." She said, "What do you mean?" I said, "You're his teacher and you're a big woman. He's a little boy." She said, "Why would he be scared of me?" I said, "Because you're the boss, and my son is a respectful child." She was big and fat, and I said, "It's your authority." I don't recall if she changed the mark, but I had him taken out of her class. She was just mean and didn't understand him at all. Partly it was anti-Semitism. A big fat Irishwoman. To this day I hate her.

RHODA LAZARE WOLF   Mrs. Mailer saw that Barbara was always properly dressed, always this lovely, proper girl, with her Peter Pan collars and white gloves. My mother would take me to A&S and Martin's, so in that sense the Mailers were more sophisticated.

FANNY SCHNEIDER MAILER   When I'd go shopping with Barbara, two dresses were the limit. We went to Klein's on Fourteenth Street—where else? I couldn't afford anything else. But Rhoda was a shy girl. Her father was a hardworking man, and I guess he didn't want company—he'd come home from his office, have supper, and go to sleep, so Rhoda would come down to see us. She felt at home. I liked her. She and Barbara were very good friends.

In the summertime, though, Norman and Barbara would stay at my sister Jenny's hotel in Long Branch, which was about three blocks from the Scarboro, Beck's hotel. My sister Rose was a schoolteacher, and she used to make up plays for the children to entertain the guests at the hotel. There's a photograph of Norman dressed like a Scottish shepherd in a kilt with a tam-o'-shanter and Barbara as a peasant girl in a plaid dress and babushka. They're so cute. Other children would be in the plays, but I never took their pictures—for them I had no use.

(Left) Isaac Barnett "Barney" Mailer with his children: Barbara, 5, Norman, 9, both in theatrical costume, Long Branch, New Jersey, 1932: "Barney was a sweet, well-mannered man who adored his children. He was mad about Barbara and he'd say that Norman could do no wrong because he was a genius and people had to understand that geniuses were special."
(Right) Barbara at home in Brooklyn, 1938.

It was a very active life for the children those summers. I would be in New York taking care of business, Barney too, and we'd come out for weekends, so my sisters, my nieces looked after them. Anne and Dave used to go down to the hotel for the summer and sort of keep an eye on them too. Norman loved the sea, and he always liked the idea of being with his cousin Cy, Beck's son. Cy's name used to be Shapiro, but he changed it to Rembar—I think when he was in college. That wasn't a big thing to Beck. Cy always had her backing and encouragement too.

But Norman and Barbara didn't grow up at the Scarboro. They were there a few summers, but earlier they were at the place we ran, which my father had a share in—three cottages—which I think I ran for two summers. They also spent a summer with my sister Jenny, who had another hotel, a block from the Scarboro. She and Rose, everybody showered attention on Norman and Barbara. Rose didn't have any children, so Norman was her one and only. We were always family, which has had a lot to do with Norman's taking such good care of his own family. He thinks the family is important. He had an example early.

MARJORIE "OSIE" RADIN Fan talks about Norman's sweetness and perfect manners, but he was normally wild. He used to pull Barbara's hair. They'd spend

Cousin Charles "Cy" Rembar. For Mailer, "the closest to an older brother I will ever come. . . . All through my childhood I worshiped him."

Hotel Scarboro, directly on the Atlantic Ocean, West End, New Jersey.

Passover week with us, say, and he'd chase her in the front door and out the back. She'd scream and cry. He was *always* energetic. You had to keep him occupied. One summer he didn't know what to do with himself, and Fan bought him a pad and gave him a pencil and said, "Here, write something."

CHARLES REMBAR   The original Scarboro was built in the late 1870s, partly from timbers used in the 1876 Centennial Exposition in Philadelphia. It was built by the Dobbinses, a Philadelphia family. My father rented it from them for a few years, and then, in 1920, bought it. In 1923 he entirely rebuilt it. The new hotel had a two-story lobby, a large dining room, a miscellany of smaller rooms, and about two hundred bedrooms that flanked wide corridors. What had been a gabled Victorian wooden structure became a much larger, L-shaped terra cotta and stucco building, which looked very grand to me and probably was. It had a magnificent view of the ocean. There was the beach, a bluff, the boardwalk, the boulevard, and then the property on which the hotel stood, considerably higher than the shoreline. It had a large, pleasant, very green front lawn with flower beds in it, and the space in back was big enough for softball games, though once in a while, on a long, high fly ball to left field, the left fielder had to open the gate to the tennis court, run inside, and dodge the tennis players and the tennis balls to make the catch. Talk about coordination! Not to mention bearing with dignity the outrage of the tennis players. If the ball reached the privet hedge on the far side of the tennis court, it was, of course, uncatchable, a legitimate homer, like one to the left-field bullpen in Yankee Stadium.

In the late nineteenth and early twentieth centuries Long Branch had been a famous resort. Presidents Grant and Garfield summered there, and Wilson conducted one of his campaigns from Shadow Lawn, a huge estate. Then, after the First World War, Long Branch went downhill. Most of the summer visitors were now Jewish. Given the degree of anti-Semitism of the time, it is hard to tell whether the coming of the Jews caused a social decline or whether the Jews moved into an already declining resort that could no longer afford to be exclusive.

South of Long Branch proper was Elberon, different in name and ambience but actually part of the municipality of Long Branch. Elberon contained the large and handsome summer homes of wealthy Jews. South of Elberon was Deal, with even larger homes—many of them palaces—of even wealthier non-Jews. South of Deal was Asbury Park, the up-and-coming middle-class resort.

Long Branch is in Monmouth County, which was, until sometime after the Second World War, an especially lovely bit of land. Away from the ocean were dark-soil truck farms, orchards, small towns, rivers, and winding country roads. The trees were hardwoods, delicately pretty in the spring and gorgeous in the fall. The orchards of course produced blossoms in the spring, and in September the best peaches and apples I've ever eaten, probably because they were tree-ripened and freshly picked. The greenery ran right to the ocean's edge. At the edge, through most of the county, the land ended in a high bluff. Below the bluff were good beaches and a good surf. It was quite different from South Jersey, which began just about at Asbury Park. South Jersey was flat and sandy and low, with small scrub oak and scrub pine. That kind of terrain has its own kind of good looks, but to my young and locally patriotic mind the United States was the best country, New Jersey was the best state, Monmouth was the best county in the state, and South Jersey was meager and colorless compared to where we lived. Even now, when Monmouth County has become mostly a mediocre exurb, with concrete cutting through old orchards, if you travel down the Garden State Parkway you can see the sharp line where the hardwoods end and the sandy pine begins.

In 1923 my father, a man of excellent judgment in every other way, made a disastrous business decision. He poured all his money (he apparently had a fair amount at the time) into building that fine hotel in what was a dying resort. The reason was that he loved the place and had an obstinate faith that Long Branch would make a strong comeback. This was in the face of a plea from the Dobbins family, who evidently liked him a lot, that he move to California and put his money into real estate in the Los Angeles area, as the Dobbinses were doing. My mother favored the idea, but my father made the decision. The mistake gave us a sort of distinction; we lost our money before the Depression. I've sometimes wondered what would have happened if we had become rich in California and Norman had spent his summers there. But we didn't and he didn't.

RHODA LAZARE WOLF　Mrs. Mailer was running things—no question—and it wasn't because Mr. Mailer wasn't functioning as a breadwinner. She was simply top dog in the house. I adored Mr. Mailer because he was much more accepting of people. She had all the problems and pressures of course, but she always seemed to have a slightly furrowed brow, and for a kid to see a furrowed brow is uncomfortable. I was aware that what was important wasn't what Mr. Mailer thought about me—I liked him, we talked about baseball, since I knew all the statistics—but rather what Mrs. Mailer thought. The impression she gave me, and still does, is that she felt herself special, even before Norman became famous, way back then. And then, lo and behold, she gets a son who's *very* special.... But I remember Barbara and Norman telling all these funny stories about her, funny things she said and did. All I could see, though, was this terribly tough, strong woman whom I was afraid of.

BARBARA MAILER WASSERMAN　For a while both my mother and father worked for Sunlight Oil Company, my Uncle Dave's company. I remember in the middle of winter my mother would get phone calls late at night. I'd hear her arguing with customers trying to convince them that they didn't need fuel until the morning or that the problem was their furnace, all of it to avoid the overtime of taking the truck out on a late delivery.

FANNY SCHNEIDER MAILER　Barney didn't like the oil company. It was Dave's money that started the business, and Barney worked there in the beginning to get new customers, but he and Dave couldn't make it, so then I stepped in and ran the office. I used to give orders to the boys to deliver fuel while I was still in bed in the morning. For a while Barney had been the outside man, but then he figured he could step out, which he did, and then opened an office with a cousin of mine who was a CPA.

I'd leave early in the morning and come back at five or six at night. It was a big load, but I managed since I had help at home, Agnes, whom Norman loved. I used to cook boiled fish in the morning before I left. Norman loved it, and he'd ask Agnes if she'd left anything for herself, because he adored her. And she adored him. Who wouldn't, when a child asks you if you've left something for yourself?

But Norman was a poor eater. He was picky. He liked plain food. Barbara wasn't a very hearty eater either. I didn't have much time to cook, so I took the line of least resistance and made them whatever they liked.

MARJORIE "OSIE" RADIN   Dave was a very enterprising businessman. I heard the story that at the start of the First World War he had a lot of sugar on hand and made a killing because sugar was very scarce. His candy company made chocolate-covered cherries and also the pineapples you'd see all over in variety stores, which cost a nickel apiece—a lot of money in those days. It's also possible that he started Sunlight Oil as a tax write-off so as to supply the chocolate company with oil. It was a big factory, and he was a very shrewd businessman.

Barney wasn't a world-beater, but there was nothing crude about him, nothing coarse. My father was elegant, but Barney was extremely fastidious, very neat and clean, a sweet, gentle man, while Fan could be difficult. Fiery, very set in her opinions, very competent and oriented to performance, and certainly Barney was dominated in terms of personality. Fan was also the chief provider. He had his accountant's license from Johannesburg but never got licensed here in the United States. I remember one of the cousins saying, "Why doesn't Barney take the exam and get his certification?" Yet he was a proud man and horrified at the idea—to take the exam was beneath his dignity. That's not to say he was lazy, although certainly he didn't have Fan's or Norman's energy, and Norman, as I say, was full of energy from the minute he was born.

Still, Barney was a sweet, well-mannered man and a devoted husband and father who adored his children. He was mad about Barbara and always used to excuse Norman. Years later, after *The Naked and the Dead*, he'd say that Norman could do no wrong because he was a genius, and people had to understand that geniuses were special. He was very proud of Norman and basked in his success. He loved the parties and the celebrities, and Norman made him a part of it.

But I suppose he and Fan were affected by the Depression, though not to the same extent as my father, who lost all his money. When he and Fan were married he had a good job, I think with General Motors; Barney didn't look Jewish, so there was no show of anti-Semitism. But during the Depression it was impossible. He couldn't get a job. I remember hearing stories about him going out and looking, but there was nothing to find. Every day he'd come home and the kids would ask if he'd found something, because they saw he and Fan were worried. There was no recovery until the Second World War, and I guess he didn't really have a job until the war started.

RHODA LAZARE WOLF   I didn't know anything about Barney's not having a job until Barbara told me years later. It was the kind of information that was conveyed with such pain that I didn't want to remember it, and then, when I read of Norman's telling an interviewer that he used to ask Barney, "Dad, did you get a job today?" I was very impressed. I thought this was one of the first times he was opening up. It was so real.

I think I have a sense of how Fan felt about Barney when she married him, because when he died in '72, she talked to Barbara. In spite of the fact that their relationship was so crummy, there was a real sadness, and she cried. Barbara said it was very sweet, and despite all the hardships and the nonsense, Mrs. Mailer had real feeling for him. She spoke about how much she'd loved him, and I think she really saw him as a prince, a knight in armor. He was extremely good-looking, he had his English act and this whole manner, so she had this fantasy, this dream...then what she had to endure. That's what makes her human. She loved this man even though very early the dream was destroyed.

FANNY SCHNEIDER MAILER   I still have Norman's bar mitzvah invitation. It was held at the temple on Eastern Parkway, two or three blocks from where we lived, and the reception was back at the house. The rabbi and his wife came and all my relations too. I did the cooking myself because it was cheaper, but I hired two waitresses to set up the tables while we were at the temple, and they made everything look nice.

The snow was knee-deep that day, and Norman said, "Mother, nobody'll be here." I said, "To *your* bar mitzvah everybody's going to come, even from Long Branch." And they did. It was an all-day affair, people came and went. Norman gave his speech at the temple beautifully. He had a Hebrew teacher, private lessons, and I paid.

MARJORIE "OSIE" RADIN   Norman went through the usual thing and then gave a surprise speech on Spinoza, which offended the whole congregation, because Spinoza was excommunicated. I don't know who coached him, but evidently the man was a progressive, a liberal.

Actually, it didn't really offend the congregation, they were just shocked. Fan must have known beforehand, but she didn't care. My grandfather was a great admirer of Spinoza, and as my mother used to say, he had his doubts about religion in general.

ARNOLD "EPPIE" EPSTEIN   I don't remember if Norman and I went to each other's bar mitzvah, though it's possible I did if he was bar mitzvahed at the Shaare Zedek over on Eastern Parkway. But I think he told me, "I hate going through with this," meaning the bar mitzvah itself. We'd had a number of conversations about how he didn't really care about being Jewish, and once, outside on the street, he brought out that he felt he was an atheist and didn't believe in religion. I never asked why, but I know for a fact that he felt strongly about it, that he wasn't thrilled about being Jewish and disliked the whole thing, maybe because he felt his parents were forcing it on him.

ALAN KAPELNER   Eastern Parkway is so long that if you take a car from the Brooklyn Public Library and go to Utica Avenue, it's miles. Crown Heights is the district, but I came from Borough Park, which was wealthier. I'm quite familiar with Eastern Parkway, though, because our baseball team would play Eastern Parkway teams on Sunday mornings.

The old neighborhood of Eastern Parkway was almost entirely Jewish. All the kids were sons and daughters of immigrants, first generation—and how do you escape from your mother and father and all their *hazerai*, their fears about the new world, brought over from Russia or wherever? You play ball, every possible game of ball. Each street had its own team, and most of the games were played more for money than for the sport of the thing. Like touch football, a nickel a man. If you didn't play ball, you were done for. Thus, years later, when I heard (rightly or wrongly) that Norman wasn't allowed to play because his mother was afraid he'd be hurt, I figured they were priming him, coddling him. Post-immigrants would do that. I suppose in their eyes Norman was smart and looked like Cary Grant, so he was coddled, as any other "American" or first-generation boy was. We all went through it and at first rather liked it, then it became a skin you had to jump out of, a way of rejecting your parents, rejecting the neighborhood.

Everything in the neighborhood was kosher—the butchers and the delica-tessens, everything. For all I know, the movie house might've been kosher. There were no Hasidim then, but Eastern Parkway had about twenty synagogues, and on holidays they were packed. There were also Yiddish newspapers—the *Jewish Morning Journal*, the *Forward*, also the Communist paper, *Freiheit*, which was all over the place but didn't sell as well as the other two.

Money always played an important part, and there was constant talk about which families had what. And also moving, in terms of neighborhoods: to move from Hester and Rivington streets to Crown Heights was considered a marvelous move because Crown Heights was more middle-class. In Crown Heights there were usually two-bedroom apartments in four- or five-story walk-ups. Borough Park was like the golden mountain. Men who had really made it took their families there—to single-family homes. It was considered the very rich world.

Social life was either at the synagogue or something like the Workmen's Circle, the tradition brought from either Europe or Russia. There were social events and dances, but primarily lectures by Socialists and Communists and people in the theater, like Adler and Carnovsky, because there was a Yiddish theater somewhere around Pitkin Avenue. If you belonged to a Reform synagogue you had lectures—anything to make Jews more cultured. Also, weather permitting, mothers would sit outside and talk—kind of coffee klatches—talk, talk, talk.

ARNOLD "EPPIE" EPSTEIN When we were in grammar school I lived at 510 Crown Street, which was at the far end of the block from Norman, on the other side. Number 555 and the building directly opposite—it must have been 556—were two relatively big apartment houses. In between, in the middle of the block, there were private homes, almost like town houses. But most of the kids lived in the apartment houses, at 510, 520, and then 555 and 556.

I think there was only one other fellow who lived in Norman's building, but Arnold Wolfson and his older brother were in the building across the street, and Murray Schorr too. In my building the only fellow I can remember was Jerry Riemer. Then in 520, in the middle of the block, there was Larry Wittlin and

At 11, with one of his many model airplanes: "Norman was so serious about his planes that his Aunt Anne and Uncle Dave decided he should be an aeronautical engineer, and his parents went along with it."

his older brother Seymour, the first guy in the neighborhood to play golf, which was the most esoteric thing we'd ever heard of—it was social climbing, they were the richest kids on the block, and their grandfather owned the building, I think. Harold Kiesel also lived in 520, but Martin Kalish was in one of the town houses. William Fried lived maybe one or two blocks down Crown Street toward our grammar school, P.S. 161. All the kids, with one or two exceptions, literally lived on the same block.

We were all athletically minded and used to play all kinds of ball games, mainly stickball with a broomstick and a tennis ball—a tennis ball because you could make it do so many things, like curve three feet or make it drop. We'd throw the ball from one side of the street and hit it over the little town houses; sometimes it went through a window, sometimes it landed on a roof, but when the windows would break you'd run. The police were there just about every day, but we got along pretty well with them.

Norman wasn't too involved with this. He was busy building his model airplanes, and built some of the best models any of us had ever seen. He had one where everything worked, the rudder pedals, the controls, everything very complex. The largest was maybe three, four feet long. Big. Other kids made models, but Norman always did the best ones, and this more or less set him apart. He seemed kind of aloof. He had the reputation of being more of a studier and didn't spend that much time hanging out.

When I met him we were in fifth or sixth grade and we got along pretty well, but there was this feeling that he was more subject to doing what his parents said. None of us obeyed our parents; he did. His father wasn't around that much, but his mother was kind of old-fashioned and would appear to tell him it was time to come in or something. He seemed to be on a shorter leash, more obedient, kind of quiet.

I was one of the wilder kids, and Harold Kiesel and I were really the troublemakers. Kiesel was blond and didn't look Jewish at all, probably the best-looking kid on the block. Great build, strong as an ox, but the shyest kid in the world, who'd literally faint when he had to get a shot. I was a little peewee runt, probably smaller than Norman, although he was pretty thin in those days too, and Kiesel and I used to do all kinds of weird things. Like when we got into high school and got involved with chemistry, we used to mix potassium chlorate with sulfur and put it on the trolley tracks. The trolley cars would ride over it, there'd be a tremendous explosion. Then there was this one lousy man on the block who'd always chase us away when we played stickball in front of his house. So one day we wrote "Rat" or "Louse" with potassium chlorate on the sidewalk, then set it on fire, which burned the word into the concrete. The guy had to get the sidewalk dug up. Norman was the only kid on the block to have a chemistry set and he might've mixed the chemicals or even thought up the prank.

When we were fourteen or fifteen we started a trio. I played the drums, Kiesel was on the trumpet, and Norman had a clarinet. I began the band because I was already playing the drums and wanted company. I'd picked up my drums secondhand from a hockshop with my allowance, then talked Kiesel into doing it—I could usually talk him into anything—so he got somebody to buy him a cheap trumpet. Then Norman decided to get involved, and his parents bought him a new clarinet with a case. I don't know if he had lessons, he was probably learning out of a book too, but I remember he could hardly get a note out of the instrument. The idea was that we'd form a trio and go up to the Catskills. He wanted to do it to get girls, but I wanted to make a fortune.

Mailer must have practiced at my house, because my mother didn't care. I was allowed to play the drums as long as my father wasn't there, and, thank God, he never got home until about six o'clock. So it was just terrible cater-wauling. Norman seemed very happy with the whole thing, maybe because he was one of us and it was a swinging thing to do, or maybe because he usually didn't associate with me and Kiesel in the things we ordinarily did when we were screwing around.

So we would get together and listen to records. We'd read Downbeat, which was the hot magazine in those days, and we'd practice. For me it was simple: with the drums I could keep beat with anything. But Kiesel and Norman had to get tunes out of their instruments, and I think they were equally bad. We'd laugh and giggle and like fall on the floor. It was great.

We practiced over one winter, but I don't remember ever practicing at Mailer's. First, because I could never have schlepped the drums up there, but also because the atmosphere at his house was different from the rest of our families. I don't think his parents were that thrilled about him being part of the trio, maybe because they found out about our going to the Catskills, but soon Norman just seemed to drop out. He was the first to go, so the trio just died a natural death.

I visited the Mailers' apartment quite a few times, but I don't remember ever eating there. His father was very standoffish, but his mother seemed pleasant enough, although there was this protectiveness, like he shouldn't do anything wrong, and he had to have good manners. In those days none of the kids had *any* manners. Norm had manners, and he was different from the rest of us, who were like hooligans, real terrors.

Another thing, and maybe it's part of it, was that we thought the Mailers were among the wealthiest families on the block. My father was a building contractor and was in the used-brick business, so he was probably a hundred times wealthier than Norman's father, but if anybody had claimed that the Mailers weren't rich, I would've said they were crazy. Somebody had said, "Well, Norman's father is in the oil business," so we all had the idea that he was an oil executive. Looking back, it was because of the front they presented. His father used to dress in suits and wore a hat and carried an umbrella. He was a real dapper guy, maybe one of the nicest-looking men on the block.

Norman himself was always better dressed than the rest of us too. In fact, he once brought me up to his room to show me two new sports jackets his parents had bought him. I'd never seen a sports jacket in my life! I certainly didn't have one—I probably had one suit that was dirty ninety percent of the time. He also had equipment that we would have loved to have—like the new clarinet, and then when we started playing baseball he was one of the first to get a real leather glove.

What I'm saying, I suppose, is that his family was very proper. Over at Kiesel's place it was like being part of the family; his parents were friendly and we were up there all the time talking to them. The same with Arnold Wolfson's family, like everyone was part of one big clan. But when you were invited to Mailer's house it was like being invited to royalty. You had to act more or less like they acted, and you felt ill at ease. They were too polite, there was no joking. Norman's father wouldn't slap him on the back of the head, or his mother wouldn't be grabbing his arm. You'd walk in and his father would be sitting there reading the paper, his mother would be in the kitchen, and it would all be very quiet— a completely different, genteel kind of atmosphere. The house was always very neat, spic and span. Norman's room—maybe he shared it with his sister, I'm not sure—had things in it, and they were arranged, so my impression was that these people were neat freaks.

RHODA LAZARE WOLF   The Mailers' apartment was usually meticulous, and I think they moved twice in the building. Mrs. Mailer was always trying to upgrade them.

ARNOLD "EPPIE" EPSTEIN   The other thing that impressed me was that Norman had a real middle name: Norman *Kingsley* Mailer. He was one of the few people I knew who had a middle name, and "Norman Kingsley Mailer" had a fancy sound to it. He always seemed to have money in his pocket as well, more than the rest of us. If we had to buy a ball or something, somebody would get out a nickel, another guy a quarter, but Norman always had a few dollars, and he was always generous. Also, another thing that made him seem rich was that every summer they went out to Long Branch. I didn't know where Long Branch was, but it sounded romantic, and the fact that they would go to the same place year after year sounded very exotic to me, like people going to Palm Beach. Norman would just mention it. He used to say he had a good time there, but he never asked me to come and visit.

We were all in Boys' High, just about everybody was. Sometimes, if it was bad weather, we'd take the trolley or train, but usually we'd walk, a couple of miles, usually in groups. But you never had the feeling there were hostile neighborhoods to go through, except that the next block was Carroll Street, and we used to play stickball with them occasionally, and there was some hostility because of that. But I never saw Norm in a fistfight, even though we'd fight among ourselves. Kiesel would get mad at me, or Jerry Riemer. But Jerry Riemer was an epileptic, and if you touched him he'd go into a seizure, and once, for example, he started punching the hell out of me, and I couldn't punch him back.

I think Norm was pretty close to him and also to Joseph Slipyan. Slipyan didn't live on the block, but he became friends with Norman at school. He was a little of the study wart, a little of the athlete, and in a way, perhaps, he was Norm's connection to our ball games, because he was more athletic. Norm wasn't the athletic type, so I guess when Slipyan played, Norm played. Slipyan was an odd-looking guy, kind of chubby, but he could run so goddamned fast he could outrun everybody. He was also one of the quietest people I ever met. You couldn't get two words out of him. Maybe Mailer could, but again, he might've had different ideas about things.

I was really little in those days, so I had to fend for myself with my brain, and I was more verbal than Norman. We used to discuss things at night, and I was like the leader of all the talking about what the world should be doing in the next twenty years. Sometimes I'd see Norm get a little angry at school, maybe in an argument, and then he'd say, "You're wrong, you don't know what you're talking about"—something like that. He was smart and, I think, very competitive, and I'm sure he had great grades. But there were some real brains at Boys' High. It was all boys, mostly Jewish. About 25 percent real bright, serious, ambitious people.

After school we'd hang out at the candy store near where I lived, on the corner of Crown Street. The owner's name was Dubin, and like it was *the* meeting place. We also had meetings at night after dinner, especially in the summer. We'd go outside and stand on the street and talk. Norman wasn't around, since he was out in New Jersey, but even so, like in the spring he always seemed a little withdrawn. He was never a big swearer, although all the kids used to swear, and I don't think that really started until he came back from college.

We started drinking beer around this time, but nobody drank very much, at least I didn't. We started smoking too, come to think of it, although I don't think Norman started until his first year at college. Still, he was an experimenter, and this extended to girls too.

For all of us the sex thing came in stages, like first watching girls undress in front of windows. There were a few good-looking girls on the block, one of whom had the nicest ass and later became "Miss Subways," plus her several older sisters, who put on the greatest act in front of the window every night with the lights on. There was also a girl across the street from Norman, a very pretty blonde. Her last name was Pashman, and she used to get involved in talking about sex with us, which was very exciting. In that same house was a nurse or dental assistant who either lived or worked there, and she used to wiggle up and down the street, and we used to whistle at her. She knew exactly what was going on.

The usual routine was that we'd tease girls on the street. A girl would walk by, you'd walk alongside her and say, "How'd you like to come to bed with me?" though naturally we didn't know what we were talking about. But on Crown Street near Nostrand Avenue there was a group of girls who were kind of forward and had the reputation of being easy to grab and play with. There was also a pretty blonde on Montgomery Street, and you could always go over there and put your hands in her pockets. She'd say, "What are you doing?" and you'd say, "Nothing, I'm just looking for something in your pocket," and meanwhile you're feeling her up. We never went to the movies with girls, though, and we weren't aware of whores.

The other thing was going to the burlesque theater, the J Street Opera House— the Star Burlesque—about once a week. We'd go Saturdays, seven or eight of us and Norm too. After a while we got over to Manhattan, whereas before that Manhattan had seemed like another planet. We'd go to see Margie Hart at the Grady Theater on Forty-second Street. Mailer didn't just tag along either. He was there and didn't want to miss it.

But even though I don't remember Norman being out on the street that much, I had the feeling he was more advanced. I mean, for example, Larry Wittlin's brother. He was a little bit older and would carry condoms around and show them to you. The older fellows carried them, and you'd see them all around, like in a backyard. But *we* didn't carry them, although I can imagine it might've been something Norman did, because I think he spent more time with older fellows, or at least he wouldn't pal around with younger guys the way Kiesel and I would.

Also in our bull sessions, I have the impression that Norman mentioned more advanced things about sex than anybody. He seemed to know more about it. He knew about masturbation before anybody else because he had a friend who lived in a private house at the other end of Crown Street whom he visited quite a bit. Once, when I was about twelve, the guy took me up to his attic and showed me a handkerchief he'd masturbated into. He showed it to me with pride, and as I recall, it was possible that Mailer had taught him, or he had taught Mailer. But then later on, in high school, toward the end, Mailer wasn't doing that much talking. We'd be standing around and he'd be gone, and we just assumed he was off having fun somewhere, up on the roof, who knows where. There was a girl—I think her name was Phyllis—although I don't know what, if anything, went on between them.

RHODA LAZARE WOLF When Barbara and her friends asked me to join their afterschool club, the "Grigs," I felt it was a real honor, even though they were terribly unsophisticated. None of them knew anything about sex. I had been brought up in a lower-class neighborhood, not Crown Heights, where you stood on the corner and told dirty jokes; you didn't know what the hell was going on, of course, you just made up stories, but these girls knew nothing, which was where the problem came in. I introduced sophistication and discord. There was a rape case in the papers, I remember, and I was astonished that Barbara had no idea what the word meant. She was about twelve at that point, I was twelve, and there I was trying to explain the meaning of rape.

At one point Mrs. Mailer told Barbara she was troubled by our relationship. She told her to be careful what she said, not just to me but to anyone, like "Don't trust Rhoda's friends." Barbara was so upset until she finally told me. There's actually an entry in my diary, dated May 31, 1940: "I've read *Studs Lonigan*, and Barbara isn't sure she wants to read it. Mrs. Mailer said, 'You should read it. It'll put you on your guard.'"

But before he went off to Harvard, Norman was usually in the back room of the apartment studying chemistry, and he was always the voice from the rear. He'd call out, "Barbara, who's that?" She'd announce my name and he'd say, "Okay." He approved of my coming downstairs, but he didn't particularly like her other friends visiting, like he was monitoring who was there. That he was bright I had no doubt. At his eighth-grade graduation the principal announced, "Norman Mailer, IQ of 165, the highest IQ we've ever had at P.S. 161."

In the apartment, though, I was once sitting in a chair he liked and he made a gesture with his thumb for me to get off. I didn't budge, so he yanked me and I hurt my hand. Another time he hit me with a tennis racket and I socked him. I hit him hard, and I remember feeling I'd hit him *too* hard. It was the same as now: when you act in an aggressive way toward Norman he gives you that look, and he gave me that look, saying, in effect, "You've gone too far."

At the time he had a girl friend named Phyllis Bradman who was lovely, but I hated her because I was jealous. She was about my height, with a very feminine quality about her, large, soft brown eyes, aquiline nose. She had long black hair and used to wear powder and lipstick. The impression I got was that it wasn't consummated, as they say, and that that was a big frustration for him. He didn't want to go to college a virgin. But it was always put in terms of what he was "doing for her," and even then Norman had an amazing influence on women. Barbara was the first, I was the second, and Phyllis was probably another.

He would tell us things—like I once asked him what a "boner" was. Barbara didn't think I had the nerve. Norman explained that a boy gets hot, his penis becomes erect, and "boner" is just a slang expression. I told him I knew about that but I'd never heard the word before. He even demonstrated with his hands. That's Norman.

I was always grateful that I could talk to him, clear up questions about how one behaves toward a man, attitudes toward the world, toward society. If there hadn't been Norman to talk to and listen to I might've wound up in Queens. What he did was allow me to separate myself from a world that I couldn't tolerate. I was reading books like Dos Passos' *U.S.A.*, and at the time everyone said it was the man's fault if a girl got in trouble, but Norman said, "It's the girl who spreads her legs," and that meant so much to me. He made me think about how people act, about hypocrisy. He was telling me that you can move away, reach a point in your life where it's you who are controlling things.

FANNY SCHNEIDER MAILER Barbara and Norman were brought up to trust each other. I know there were times when they had things between them that I didn't know about, but I didn't delve into it, because I figured if they needed my help they'd come to me. When they were children Norman was very nice and protective, a big brother to Barbara. He always went out of his way to help her.

BARBARA MAILER WASSERMAN Bruce Mazlish, the historian, once asked me what it was like growing up with Norman. He was amazed when I said Norman was the best older brother I could have had, but it's true. He encouraged me when I was going around thinking I was dumb, fat, and klutzy. He kept saying I was beautiful, just as he did when his daughter Kate was an adolescent and all hunched over and self-conscious.

RHODA LAZARE WOLF Barbara once spoke to me of her profound dependence on him, like when Norman, at seventeen or eighteen, talked to her, his fourteen-year-old sister, when she was worried that her boobs were too big. He would spend a lot of time telling her how beautiful she was, and I remember that,

Rhoda Lazare Wolf and Barbara on Crown Street, Brooklyn.

because I felt so awful, kind of skinny with dark hair, and wanted someone to say that to me.

But Norman was a proselytizer. By talking to Barbara and encouraging her, he was helping her break from her mother. Even though there was never any need for Norman himself to break away, he appeared to, with all his incredible experiences—only with every experience he never really broke communications with his mother. Whatever he did was still all right with her. The language in his books, that was all right because it was in book form; and whenever Norman would act outrageously in public, Mrs. Mailer thought he was the victim. Norman would give public readings, the dirtiest goddamned stuff— this is later, obviously—and she'd come out smiling because "my son has performed."

Still, Norman was always trying to start a process of change in a direction he thought was liberating or expanding, like taking us up on the roof and teaching us how to blow smoke rings. Then he tried to give kissing lessons. He showed Barbara in front of me and his parents, and it wasn't presented as a joke. I remember him saying, "Don't press too hard." Barbara went along with it, and he did the same thing with ballroom dancing, the same exhibitions. I didn't trust my reactions and wouldn't let him try it with me, probably because I was scared silly.

He knew that I was terribly shy, but he tried anyway because he thought it would be good for me. I wanted him to leave me alone, not put me into this position of having to make a choice and face myself, but he was absolutely right. The argument was that if I believed in certain things, I should follow through. That's why the conflicts he arouses in people are so extraordinary. You start thinking about things you might never have thought of before. When I talked to him when I was older, sometimes I felt that he didn't really see the human being. But he does see other things, and in the process you realize the abstractions aren't wrong even if he's wrong about *you*, which is why I've always described Norman as one of the kindest people I've known, one of the most noble. I say this knowing that a lot of people would look at me and not know what the hell I'm talking about.

FANNY SCHNEIDER MAILER   I never questioned about Norman going to Harvard. I mean that was the place for my son. My sister—I loved her very dearly and credited her with so much good sense—sent her son to Harvard, so I wanted my son to go there too. First Cy, then Norman. We certainly felt that he would fill the bill, and I figured that no matter what he'd do after he graduated, being a Harvard graduate is very good. He got into MIT too, but I forget who really made the decision—probably Norman himself.

I also took it for granted that Barbara would go to college, to Radcliffe, and I felt I could see her through. I was in business and I could manage, and she was very, very saving in her expenses. I never in any way showed that I favored one above the other. Each was going to stand on his and her own two feet. Each got what was coming to them.

Uncle Dave Kessler and Aunt Anne.

<u>ALAN KAPELNER</u> Norman's going to Harvard would have been an exception. All the Jewish boys I know were going to CCNY or NYU or Columbia. My uncle sent his two sons to Harvard, but he was worth a million. What did Norman's mother know from Harvard to begin with? I'm only guessing, but it must have been in the genes, that ambition—"Beg, borrow, or steal, I'm going to send my boy to Harvard." In high school I'm sure he got A's—more than A's if it was possible—but still, to push your son to go to Harvard would have been totally different from other families in the neighborhood.

<u>RHODA LAZARE WOLF</u> Harvard was an important goal. Fanny was competitive—her sister's son, Cy, had gone to Harvard, so Norman had to go too. And I think Norman accepted this. Both he and Barbara accepted their parents' values, but Barbara would talk to me about her resentment; it wasn't only their parents but another set of grown-ups, Anne and Dave, whose feelings and expectations had to be considered too. Remember, Dave was the one with the money. Several times Barbara took me to have dinner with them. They looked more like well-to-do grandparents. They used to go to Miami, Aunt Anne had good jewelry, and by this point they'd left Brooklyn and lived in Manhattan at the Mayflower Hotel.

<u>LARRY ALSON</u> Early on I found out that Uncle Dave was respected. He subsidized Norman at Harvard, and later, Barbara at Radcliffe. He was one of those rare entrepreneurs. When he was seventeen, in South Africa, he had a bicycle

shop, and then he rented the local opera house and put on big-name performers. On one show he made five thousand dollars, and it kept going. In New York he and Anne lived at the Mayflower Hotel on Central Park West after moving from the Towers Hotel in Brooklyn Heights, which was when he had the George Washington Chocolate Cherry business, after Fanny had taken over the Sunlight Oil Company, the fuel-delivery business in the Heights.

Uncle Dave wasn't regarded as the cultural one, but what he had was a lovely sense of humor, and he was respected as a strong man with money, the provider. What was important about Dave was that his generosity toward Norman was a foreshadowing and would be reflected in the way Norman himself behaved toward talent. Whether or not Norman consciously arrived at it, he reached a determination that he ought to help people, and Dave, I believe, served as some kind of model.

FANNY SCHNEIDER MAILER   Dave was show-off generous. He had good clothes, and, sure, he made good money. But helping Norman and Barbara through school? That should be cut out of the story completely, because the money came from the oil company. It came through my efforts. For years I worked very hard, and I had the right to draw money, and Dave permitted me to sign checks as I needed to. I was drawing a salary, so it was me who paid for Norman's tuition, and for Barbara too, because I wanted my children to have that advantage. That was how my checks were used. Barney was working, so we lived on what he made. But Dave just bragged. He didn't do a damned thing for the family, he only talked a lot. He preached and was always telling everybody how to live. He was flamboyant and he gave the impression that all the money came from Sunlight Oil because he owned the company. But he and Anne went off to Africa for a year and left me in complete charge. I also did all the work to keep the accounts of the chocolate company and see that they were getting as much oil as they needed, at least a thousand gallons a day. Right from my bed, in the morning, before seven o'clock, I'd send off the truck with the delivery. But Dave was ready to tell God how to regulate everything, and no one ever dared to fight with him because he was holding the purse strings.

I don't know why the Kesslers didn't have any children of their own. It never happened, that's all. But they were supposed to really admire Norman, al-though—I think about it very often—were they jealous? They treated me with respect because I was Norman's mother and of course I was running the business. But I think in a way Anne and Dave wanted to retain the love of the children through me. Then, after Anne died, Dave married Lillian, in 1959. She's a "respectable" middle-class woman. She knew how, so when Dave died she got everything—lock, stock, and barrel. Why didn't he give me a share? Or Barney? I worked for the company for years and he gave me zero. He married her at the end of 1959 and died in 1960, so it was only a few months, but I wasn't going to step in and make a big case of it and get nothing.

RHODA LAZARE WOLF   I never met Cy in those years, but I sure as hell was aware of him, because Norman and Barbara as well as their parents used to talk about "Cousin Cy" glowingly. The impression was that he was somehow special, very different from the rest of the family, because he'd gone off to Harvard and had reached a level of worldliness.

I didn't sense any resentment on Norman's part, but I had the impression that Mrs. Mailer had to get Norman to Harvard because Cy had gone there. My God, yes, like, "If Cy got the best, my son will get the best too." That was very clear to me. Even I accepted it, and I thought it was absolutely right. Then, I think, Norman displaced Cy in the family's importance, not simply because he went to Harvard but with the success of *The Naked and the Dead.*

Cy and Norman had similar mothers who were both making sure their sons succeeded. But while Cy moved away from the family, made his own world, Norman never let go of Fan. I think that's because Cy is different from Norman. I like Cy because he's smart and knows what to say and when to say it, but he's more remote as a human being. In the early years, though, he cut a trail for Norman. When you're young you need somebody who goes into the water first so you see you won't sink. Cy did that for Norman. Norman did that for me, and I did that for my whole goddamn family.

What's funny, though, is that when Norman was going off to college, I knew he was smart and serious but also thought he was the great man. When I remember what he was like, what life was like in Crown Heights, I have to remind myself that he was just a kid of sixteen. Only someone with a hundred percent self-confidence could have done what he did, and then—what?—only six or seven years later he pulled off that first novel. It's as if Norman's been a professional all his life.

CHARLES REMBAR When it came to the choice of college, I was involved only to the extent that I had been to Harvard and provided a model. The Kesslers— Barney's sister Anne was married to Dave Kessler—were very much in favor of MIT, probably because Norman's intelligence had been manifested in mathematics and because he was interested in aeronautical design. Osie and my mother favored Harvard, Osie because she thought that Norman ought to have a well-rounded education, and my mother, a wise woman, probably because she felt sure that aeronautical engineering was a passing fancy and not Norman's destiny. I don't recall Norman's own thoughts about the matter, but I remember that he came down to Washington, where I was working as a lawyer for the government just before I went into what used to be called "the service," and it was one of the things we talked about.

As for the influence of Dave Kessler: He helped the Mailers financially, probably to a substantial extent but probably also not to so great an extent as he, or rather his wife, Anne, suggested. Remember that Fan was working very hard during this time and earning money. In addition to his financial help, Dave tried to give emotional support. Dave was as avuncular as an uncle-by-marriage can get. He even acted that way toward me, whose relationship to him was distant. Somehow Norman and I were paired in his mind. "Those two boys will go far," he said. Since his wealth came from manufacturing chocolate-covered cherries (they consisted of what may once have been a cherry with sweetened wallpaper paste between the ex-cherry and the chocolate), I sometimes puzzled over what wonderful future he had in mind for us.

Not that Norman needed any additional emotional support. No child of Fan's would. And, despite the disagreements they had, there was a deep affection between Barney and Norman. Barney was enormously likable, the kind of man hatcheck girls remembered and gave a greeting to. And Barbara was a beautiful and adoring kid sister. Not to mention the aunts—the rest of the attractive and formidable Schneider girls, Fan's sisters. The Schneiders, in order of age, were Joe, Beck, Jenny, Rose and Fan. The greatest influence among these relatives came from Norman's Aunt Beck, my mother, who, in her paradoxically tender, soft-spoken, courteous, extremely powerful way, had considerable influence on everybody who came in contact with her. In addition, there was the influence of her husband, my father, Norman's Uncle Lou, who gave off waves of strength and manliness. Obstreperous children in the hotel were silenced by a hard stare from Lou's light-blue eyes. Once, when an employee went wild and could be controlled no other way, Lou knocked him out with one right-hand punch. Norman, considering his later interests, had to be impressed.

MARJORIE "OSIE" RADIN   Even though Dave and Ann were pushing for Norman to go to MIT and become an aeronautical engineer, Dave couldn't say, "I'm paying the bills," because he wasn't paying. Fan was running Sunlight Oil. Although Barney was up and down in terms of jobs—don't forget, during the Depression years nobody needed an accountant—it was still Fan who was paying Norman's tuition, six hundred dollars, I think. Dave had nothing to do with it, and I want to say in justice to Fan and Norman that Dave Kessler never paid for a goddamned thing. He only talked big. He was a show-off who wanted to get all the credit, and it used to burn my mother up. She would talk to Fan and say, "You shouldn't allow yourself to be put in that position, because no money is worth it." You see, Fan and Barney thought that Norman and Barbara would inherit the Kessler money. They put up with the Kesslers' *meshugas*, which my mother never approved of, and it was a bad bet.

ARNOLD "EPPIE" EPSTEIN   It was the talk of the street, Norman going to Harvard. I mean, who the hell was Norman Mailer in those days? He was just one of the guys, and nobody from Crown Street had ever gone to Harvard. So we were surprised, but then our second reaction was, "Well, if anybody would go to Harvard, it would have to be Norman." There were no real dummies on the street, and most of us were going to college—me, to Brooklyn College because my father said, "You go to a place where you don't have to pay"—but Harvard was more the social thing, and, again, we'd all been under the impression that Norman's family had money. We just figured, Norman the brain, with his family connections, is going to the right school, and he's gonna become a big shot, a very wealthy, well-educated guy—a businessman, like his father the oil executive.

II:
HARVARD
(1939-43)

<u>HARRY LEVIN</u> The year I received tenure I was publicly congratulated at the annual meeting of the Modern Language Association as an example of Harvard's broad-mindedness. Lionel Trilling, at Columbia, received tenure the same year, 1939, but Lionel was seven years my senior. The feeling was that you had to be of Anglo-Saxon blood to be an adequate interpreter of English literature. In the twenties Abbott Lowell, Harvard's then president, attempted to enact a *numerus clausus*, and even though the faculty turned him down, he still got his way: Jewish enrollment was limited to about 10 percent, and Jewish students were assigned Jewish roommates. Day to day, one was made to be aware that one was a Jew. University files indicated certain categories; "A&E" meant Andover and Exeter, but there were other notations, including that one was Jewish. Norman therefore came at a crucial time. Before the war Jews at Harvard tended to be assimilation-oriented. The war brought about a new Jewish consciousness and pride that, if anything, brought the issue out into the open.

<u>KINGSLEY ERVIN</u> I don't think people realize how rigid and elegant and scary the atmosphere at Cambridge was before the war. Very eighteenth-century, a mixture of Boston Brahmin and the literary faculty's elegance.

39

MARVIN BARRETT   I was a year ahead of Norman, and in my freshman year I was assigned to Weld, which was the pits. Grays, where Norman was assigned, was a cut or two above Weld but still not the authentic pre-Revolutionary dormitory of the Yard, like Wigglesworth, where all the rich boys were. Your freshman room assignment had to do with how much money you had. The rooms were given as a supplement to your scholarship. I had a room that cost me 80 bucks a year, on the fifth floor. You were beginning with eight strikes against you to be in such an atmosphere. To be assigned to Grays—and Norman's room was 11–12—was sort of neutral, I think, since it depended on how high up the room was. The cost of rooms started at $40 and went up to $500 a year, so that my room in Weld was one of the real cheapies, although it was luxurious compared to what they live in now. Back then you had maids who came in—it was part of the gentlemanly style. But still, there was a ranking among freshman dorms.

RICHARD WEINBERG   I was from Memphis, Tennessee, and went to public high school. We were Jewish, a family of small shopkeepers, and though we were never rich, we were never really poor either.

I arrived at Harvard a couple of days early, and I vividly remember my first impressions. I'd been preassigned to Grays Hall, so, with a suitcase in each hand, I followed the map to the dormitory. On the bulletin board I saw that I'd been assigned to Grays 11–12 along with one Maxwell Kaufer and one Norman Mailer. I'd arrived before either of them, so when I went up to our suite on the second floor I took the room with the one bed, overlooking the Yard. The two rooms were both large, with a bathroom between, and the walls were covered with Japanese grass cloth, which I'd never seen before. There was a working fireplace—all the dormitories had them then—and even though the furniture was old, it was in good repair, and the place was fairly clean.

I don't know why I was there so early, but two days later I walked into the room and there was Norman, alone. His parents hadn't come up with him, and I remember finding him a smiler. He seemed a pleasant guy, though I sort of put him in the category of being a New Yorker since I was working with some southern prejudice. It wasn't real hostility, but people in Memphis looked on Brooklyn as a place where the tough and underprivileged lived. Also, we were repelled by the accent.

So Max Kaufer and Norman shared the other room, the larger one, overlooking Massachusetts Avenue. We were total strangers, but although we were from different parts of the country, we had all gone to public schools, we weren't from rich families, and we were all Jewish. It was the Harvard method that if you were Jewish, your roommates were Jewish, and as far as I was aware, Norman's social world was entirely Jewish, as if that was the only thing he could relate to. He was friends with a guy named Marty Lubin, who was in either Weld or Thayer, and then became his roommate at Dunster junior year. Also Dick Sisson, who's now a doctor in St. Louis, and Peter Ruderman, who was also from New York. Ruderman was our equivalent of the sixties rebel—there was no one else like him. He was anti-establishment and would wear dungarees to the Harvard

Union for meals, which no one else did, so he stood out as a kind of embarrassment to me, because he too was Jewish.

Which is not to say Norman or I arrived dressed in the usual Harvard, Ivy League way. Both of us went through the same transformation. I came dressed in a bright green tweed suit because I thought tweed meant college, and I had to choose from what was available in my family's clothing business in Memphis. After a while I think Norman and I both realized there were definite rules about dressing: certain kinds of shoes and socks, gray flannel pants, a three-button, single-breasted—as opposed to double-breasted—muted tweed sports coat with a vent in the back and natural shoulders, what today would be described as "preppie." If you didn't wear that, you were immediately classed as an outsider, someone who didn't understand Harvard's ways.

It took me a long time actually to make the switch, although I recognized it immediately, since I was expected to get all my clothes from the family business. I was stuck, because there were no "preppie" clothes in our Memphis store. My family couldn't understand what I was wanting in a sports coat, for example, because no one wore natural shoulders in Tennessee. I could've gone to J. Press and for a few hundred dollars become an instant Harvard man, but that was too expensive. Still, I did manage to buy one of the articles of the preppie uniform— a velvet-collared chesterfield, which everybody wore on Saturday nights. Max and I were dying to have one, so we rushed down to Filene's Basement and each bought one for fifteen dollars. I don't know why Norman wasn't part of that or even if he realized you should have a velvet-collared chesterfield. He was in the same boat, though, and while his wardrobe was skimpy, he soon enough picked up on what was expected.

He didn't present himself and his family as poor, or poorer than Max's and mine. There was the sense that we were all middle-class, and he seemed serious about his studies. We used to discuss engineering from time to time, and although it wasn't expressed as a great passion—he wasn't out to design a new airplane or anything—he was serious in the sense that we all felt we were at college to prepare ourselves for something. Call it parental influence, but college represented a great sacrifice on the part of one's parents.

So Norman and I both worked very hard, Max less so. Max was very bright and made good grades, but he was less single-minded about it. I had to work hard that first year to stay on the Dean's List and keep my scholarship, so I didn't go out much and neither did Norman. We'd work, eat our meals at the Harvard Union every day, and then go to sleep. The experience of just being at Harvard was overwhelming for us.

I didn't go out on dates, and I don't recall Norman going on dates either. But one of the first things he did when he moved into the suite was to put up pinup posters over his desk, the Betty Grable kind of thing, and certainly we talked about girls. He was obviously interested in girls and at some point in our conversations he mentioned a girl friend back in Brooklyn, someone whom we never saw. He wasn't coming on as "Mr. Experience" or admitting that he'd tried to go to bed with her or that he'd succeeded. Most of the residents of Grays were extremely innocent of sex, and in fact I remember we were talking to the guys who lived in the entryway below us—we used to socialize with them, probably the few non-Jews we'd see in our rooms—and that's when it came out that I was the one with sexual experience; the three of them were very innocent and were actually shocked at the idea of touching a woman's breasts. But not Norman. I remember we used to make remarks about our proctor, the older law student who lived in Grays to oversee discipline. But he himself used to have frequent female guests, so we joked about it constantly, probably because we weren't allowed that privilege ourselves. And that proctor was none other than Caspar Weinberger, now Reagan's Secretary of Defense.

Most of these late-night bull sessions were given over to talk about our work, our backgrounds, our classes and teachers, and what we planned to do in the future. We also talked about Harvard as we were getting to know it. As time went on we were getting more and more filled with the mystique of the place and how we were associating with people who were going to end up being President of the United States, senators, directors of banks. But it took us a while to understand what was really going on—what the club system was about, for example. The literature Harvard sent to freshmen didn't cue you in, and the preppies were very polite and didn't come out and tell you directly that you're not invited to the Hasty Pudding Club, the eating clubs, the ranking social clubs. We would read little things here and there in *The Crimson*, but only gradually did we become aware of the fact that we were living in a culture that was more or less unique. I'm not sure Norman ever really perceived what the Harvard social scene was about. That first year he barely had a speaking acquaintance with anyone outside a circle of metropolitan New York Jews, and it wasn't until later, when he got on *The Advocate* and was living and eating at Dunster, that he began to meet non-Jews and gradually learned the social standards—what you're supposed to do and not do in the club system.

Was there much anti-Semitism? I don't know that we perceived it as such. Perhaps we were aware of it below the surface, and I've wondered if this was the reason for what I now recall as a combination of naïveté and privacy on Norman's part. Compared to kids from Andover and Exeter, he wasn't a person of the world, a sophisticate at all. The typical preppie had probably been abroad and gone to deb parties, been part of the Boston social scene and was familiar with what Harvard was all about. His parents were in the mainstream, he might be the son of the ambassador or governor and so forth. I don't know what Norman did or didn't know, but I have the impression that while Max and I only dimly perceived it, he saw it even less clearly than we did. He'd never been anywhere outside of New York. The only phrase I can use is "a little boy from Brooklyn," and whatever else I may be in doubt about, that was clearly my sense of him.

And perhaps too that was part of what I remember as his privacy. It's a characteristic I've seen in other people who've grown up in the old neighborhoods of Brooklyn, that difference between family and others, between private and public. With their neighbors pressing in upon them, they maintain their privacy by taking this attitude. I think Norman still has it despite his sophistication and worldliness. He's vulnerable in many areas, almost defenseless, and back then I think he was protecting himself.

Looking back, I realize that there were many things we didn't know about, that he chose not to tell us. He talked very little about his family. He'd mention his mother and father of course, and I dimly recall his mentioning an oil company, but I didn't know what his father did or even that his mother worked. I never met his mother. My parents visited, and it was a routine thing for parents to take their son and his roommates to lunch. But that never happened with Norman, so either his mother never visited or she came and I never knew anything about it because there was the connection to Marty Lubin. Besides his girl friend back in Brooklyn the only other person he mentioned was his cousin who'd been at Harvard before him.

But he never talked about anyone else in the family, and I had the impression there were areas that he just didn't invite us into. Again, this guarded privacy. The relationship that existed in the suite was a two-and-one kind of situation. Max and I tended to be more communicative and closer. Not that we were hostile to him or he to us, but it was apparent that he had his own world. He didn't really reach out to us. He was kind of a loner in the room.

ALICE ADAMS Years later Norman told us a lot of stories about making a fool of himself as an undergraduate, like the wonderful one about his first day at Harvard. Before arriving in Cambridge he'd gotten a letter from Phillips Brooks House, saying, "When you come to Harvard, come to see us first." So Norman arrived and rushed pell-mell to Phillips Brooks House. Taking the letter literally, he found some very brown-tweedy, pipe-smoking person and said, "I'm here!" Of course the letter was one of those perfunctory things they sent to all freshmen, and the Phillips Brooks House, a charitable institution, wasn't a society or an eating club or anything of the sort.

MARJORIE "OSIE" RADIN He had wanted to go to college with a new wardrobe. Fan's position was "Why don't you wait till you see what the other boys are wearing?" But he insisted, and he bought all the wrong things.

FANNY SCHNEIDER MAILER I must have found someplace that was reduced. I was always looking for a bargain because money wasn't plentiful. So I went with him to the store, but he selected his own clothes. They were terrible—loud, outlandish. Trousers with orange stripes. It was his idea of how one should dress at Harvard, and it was in very bad taste, not the subdued colors people go to Harvard with. I couldn't argue with him about it, he wanted it that way. I said, "You're making a big mistake, but although money is tight, I'm indulging you so you can find out your own mistakes." After a month or two he found I was right. He realized that he was singled out for his peculiar outfits, so we had to buy additional clothes. I was unhappy, because the family blamed me for permitting it. After that he changed quite quickly and wore subdued clothing, but he didn't have a big wardrobe. Who could afford it? Are you kidding? He must have had one suit and one sports jacket and an overcoat.

Agnes, the colored woman, was still working for us, and Norman used to send his clothes home to be laundered once a week. There used to be those special suitcases—you'd put everything in and put it in the mail.

I usually made one visit to Norman every term. Eva Lubin, Marty's mother, and I would go together on the midnight Saturday train. We'd sleep on the train, four or five hours, arrive in Boston at six o'clock in the morning, and hire a roomette at the station so that we could wake up with a shower. We didn't want to disturb the boys too early, so we'd have breakfast and then take the subway to Cambridge. That first year Marty and Norman were in different dorms, so I'd spend the day with Norman, she with Marty. We'd take a walk, maybe I'd sew a few buttons, then we'd have lunch in the college. He showed me all over. He introduced me to some of his friends, but I wasn't eager for that. We both wanted it to be just the two of us, so we could talk about things that were private. Family. He wanted to know everything about everyone, and when I came home I had to fill in everyone here.

I don't know, maybe Norman did feel the lack of rich friends, coming from Brooklyn. But at Harvard he had rich friends. One was very rich, a millionaire— I can't remember his name. But Norman used to get a monthly check for his expenses. He knew that money was tight and he never wrote that he was in need of cash. I'd be a speck ahead of him and send a small extra check sometimes, and the same thing with Barbara, who never wanted me to give her an extra dollar. I said, "Look, dear, give me the pleasure of knowing you'll buy something." And she'd buy a present for me. On the other hand, I was aware that money counts. I'd say to them, "What do you mean, money doesn't matter? Where'd you get that idea? Money always comes out on top. You have money, everybody looks at you different."

It was something new for Norman to be with all those rich boys, but it didn't confuse him. He maintained his mission very well. Maybe he did tread his way very carefully. The point is that my children aren't show-offs. They might have been showing off if they wanted to, but if they couldn't produce the real stuff, they didn't care about what was going on around them. They could free themselves. I don't know whether that's one's nature or upbringing—I don't know where to place the cause—but one loses one's importance when you begin to think you know everything.

RHODA LAZARE WOLF   When he'd come home on visits he was much more sociable, his attitudes more pronounced. He'd make his ideas known about how to behave in the world and would talk to me almost like he was a parent. Except that he wanted everyone to be less inhibited, more open in language and sexual conduct. His parents would tell him to stop swearing, and he'd just giggle and argue with them about it philosophically. He was a kid really, very good-looking and poised, now home from college, but Barbara and I thought he was absolutely correct.

What he was trying to do was shock his mother. But he couldn't possibly rebel, there was nothing to rebel *against*. Whatever he did was perfect. Mrs. Mailer would be annoyed, but her protests were shallow. Like one night they asked me to dinner, we were having lamb chops and were all cutting our meat, and Norman starts pretending that he's not cutting his chop but cutting his penis.

He was grinning—he'd always do these things with this dirty-little-boy look: "I'm not serious, I'm just a dirty little boy"—but underneath he *was* serious. Mrs. Mailer got a real grumpy look on her face and said, "Oh, Norman, stop it," but my feeling was that Mr. Mailer was more disturbed than she was. She was just going through the motions.

And of course Barbara and I loved these shows because we agreed with his protest. Like his language. I have an entry in my diary that he used the expression "son of a bitch" in front of his parents, out loud. That same visit he and Barbara were dancing, I made a crack, and Norman said, "It's good enough to use in my story." "That's Norman's way of complimenting you," I wrote in my diary.

Another entry, dated March 1940: "Norman home, I went to visit Barbara. Norman opened the door and said, '*Entrez*.' The desk was open, with a chair blocking the way, and he said, 'Let me fix the chair,' but I ignored him. Later he was going out, and he said to Barbara and me, 'Goodby, children.' So I said, 'Goodby, infant.' PS: Norman is becoming an author. He wrote two stories so far. The second one is a sort of dirty story. He wants to write like James Farrell, author of *Studs Lonigan*."

RICHARD WEINBERG I suppose we were all true to type—three industrious Jews, although we never talked about ourselves that way, we just more or less accepted it. But Norman kept a low profile that first year and talked only about engineering. He mentioned that he'd been accepted at MIT, and it was just accepted at face value that he was going to be an engineer. If he was writing, it was kept a secret. In fact my impression was that he *wasn't* writing. I've always felt that the big turnaround came at the end of the year with our final assignment in English A.

When you first entered, you had to take a writing exam to determine whether or not you had to take English A. My feeling was that no matter how well you wrote, if you hadn't gone to Andover or Exeter you were going to be in English A. It wasn't exactly remedial so much as it was supposed to make up for the disadvantage of going to a public high school, and you learned by reading examples of good prose and pulling apart the techniques. Norman and I were in different sections, but I think we had the same section man, whose name, I think, was Simpson. Our final assignment was a novella. Neither of us had ever written anything like this, and we were to work on it over a month. It was the big assignment of the year, our last, and we took great pains to present professional manuscripts. I can still remember Norman typing on his little black Remington.

When Norman got his novelette back, he'd received an A+, which absolutely flabbergasted us. Up to that point we hadn't realized that he had that kind of writing ability. But that was the turning point. Either he then got the idea he could be a writer, or, if he'd been writing and we hadn't known, it must have confirmed something for him. It was as important for setting him off on a writing career as winning the *Story* prize the following year.

NORMAN MAILER I wrote my first short stories at the end of my freshman year, having discovered in English A that I wanted to be a writer. I had read *Studs*

Lonigan and got terribly turned on. Then I asked my English A teacher—I still remember his name, Mr. Simpson—if I could write a short story for my final paper. He demurred because the course was supposed to be on how to write expository English but finally gave in. I think I received a *B* +, but in any event the grade itself wasn't the turning point. It was Farrell.

I have no idea now of how much idea I had then of what it means to be a writer. It was romantic for sure, but I wasn't thinking, How am I gonna support myself being a writer? Don't forget, the war was coming on, so we really didn't plan ahead. Also, I was a very impractical, starry-eyed young fellow. Freshman year, I'm not even sure I knew I was at Harvard. I mean, I knew I was in a wonderful place, but I had no idea what Harvard was until long later. . . . But this is novel material—which is why I can't characterize it and don't want to get started. There are states of consciousness that are hard to define without writing about them, and I feel uneasy going anywhere near it.

RHODA LAZARE WOLF   When I graduated from P.S. 161 Norman was back after his first year at Harvard, and he signed my yearbook: "We both graduated from 161, but I went to Boys' High and you will not. I'm going to Harvard and I doubt if they'll let you in. That's still all right. You don't have to follow exactly in my footsteps to be famous, too. Until they burn 161, Norman Mailer, Babbie's brother."

After the phrase "in my footsteps" he drew two small footprints. But at the end is added another line, saying "Normie Mailer," even though I never called him that and neither did Barbara. Only the fellows called him "Normie." But in the previous line, where he put "Norman Mailer," he added a question mark. That's because he said he was going to be a writer and was always wondering what name he should use. Norman Kingsley Mailer? N. Kingsley? Norman K. Mailer? Or Kingsley Mailer?

FANNY SCHNEIDER MAILER   The Scarboro Hotel burned down in '41 or '42, but before that we went out there the summers after Norman's first and second years at Harvard. There was a big cottage on the grounds, and Beck gave Norman a room where nobody should bother him and where he could work on his own time. He would disappear in the afternoon, write through the night, and sleep late. I imagine it was born there in my father, being scholarly, maybe it was bred in the family, that respect, and everyone lent their approval, their encouragement. Usually he'd stay up all hours. Sometimes he might go out during the night to take a walk on the boardwalk, which was right across the street.

MARJORIE "OSIE" RADIN   The family occupied rooms on the ground floor of the hotel because we had to be available to the guests. Sometimes these rooms were noisy, and I'd often say to my mother, "Mama, give me a room upstairs," to which she'd reply, "When you get married I'll give you a room upstairs." But when Norman was seventeen he got a room and took up his typewriter. I wouldn't say he spent the whole summer locked up there, but he had quite a bit of discipline, spending a goodly part of every day there, and he turned out a considerable amount of work.

CHARLES REMBAR   Osie had a large influence on Norman during this time. She was very well read and a good writer herself. So Norman thought of her as someone who understood literature and understood what he was trying to do. He showed her everything he wrote and asked for her opinion.

Norman had been a center of attention before he was five years old. I had lived through the same sort of thing eight years ahead of him. You had highly appreciative audiences, and in later years you got to hear the clever things you had said as a very young child (and usually couldn't remember). It was probably a bad thing for both of us.

After a while Fan—the indomitable, loving Fan—had the oil business and during the summers she and Barney either commuted to Brooklyn from the Scarboro or just came down to the hotel for weekends—I'm not sure which. At any rate, my parents looked after Barbara and Norman when their parents weren't there. My mother set Norman up in an empty room where he could write undisturbed; she valued writing very much. She even had meals sent up to him so that he wouldn't have to interrupt his work.

MARJORIE "OSIE" RADIN   He showed me everything he did, and I remember our talking about his stories. But it wasn't only me. My mother felt that writing was the greatest art of all—she had a love for literature, she was well read, the intellectual thirst was there. All the Schneider sisters were well read, Rose particularly; she and my mother used to foster my own reading interests even though I was a musician. When I was a little girl I used to write jingles. My family called it poetry, but they were just little rhymes, which were published in the Long Branch paper. Everybody in town accused my mother of having written them, which of course wasn't true. But my mother used to leave a pencil and paper at my bedside because sometimes I'd wake up in the middle of the night and write something down.

NORMAN MAILER   That summer I wrote my first half-decent story. Then, in the fall, 1940, I enrolled in Robert Gorham Davis' writing class.

The story was set at a resort in the Catskills, and the bellhops take care of the wives who are staying at the hotel while their husbands are in the city during the week. One night, about one-thirty A.M., a few guys are sitting outside talking about "who's getting what" when a car drives up; one particular bellhop has been with one wife regularly, and at this moment he's upstairs. Out of the car steps the woman's husband and goes up in the elevator. The other bellboys are alarmed. One of them starts to run upstairs to warn his friend, but by the time the bellboy reaches the top of the stairs he hears two terrific shots. The husband emerges from the room, hands over the gun, and the bellboy, the narrator of the story, runs inside and sees that the husband has shot the guy and his wife.

At this point I went into a Hemingwayesque description, I suppose influenced by "The Short Happy Life of Francis Macomber." The narrator-bellboy notes that his friend has been shot through the back of the head, with the bullet exiting through the front, blowing his face away. The face has disappeared. Atomized. The narrator-bellboy is panic-stricken, thinking, Am I breathing his face? Is it floating in the air? Or is it in little clumps on the carpet that I'm now stepping on? He gets sick and throws up. End of story.

I submitted the story to Robert Gorham Davis for my first assignment, and he read it aloud to the class, talking about restraint and understatement. He said the story was good but grievously damaged by my ending, and as he reread it the class cracked up. Paroxysms of laughter. Gorham Davis can be dour, but even he started giggling. I didn't know what to do. My first impulse was to leave, but I couldn't, since then everyone would know I was the author—stories were always read anonymously. My next impulse was to kill Davis.

Later I picked up the story from the cubbyholes and discovered he'd given me an A−. When I had my first tutorial with him, he apologized and told me he'd had no idea what would happen or he wouldn't have read it aloud, which sort of saved me, and I've been grateful for his sensitivity ever since.

ROBERT GORHAM DAVIS   I first started teaching at Harvard in 1933 and was there until 1943, teaching the first rank of composition courses, called English A-1. I first met Norman when he was in his second year and taking the course from me, a year-long course consisting of forty to fifty students, in which you were pretty free to write as you liked. Very frequently I read students' work aloud. They were expected to write about six typewritten pages every two weeks.

My impression was that Norman wasn't awfully well educated. He was taking engineering courses, and I wondered whether he was also taking courses to get himself reading seriously in history and philosophy. That's been my continuing sense about Norman. I once wrote a review for *Story* magazine of something he'd written, and I made the point that his references to works of art, philosophy, history, and so on were of a limited character. He is, on the whole, obsessed with the present. His knowledge of the major figures of the past is pretty slight or superficial, a lot taken from secondary sources, because he's very brilliant and quick at picking things up. But his spottiness was obvious back then, plus his habit of not reading deeply or systematically when he got interested in something.

I didn't wonder about his being in engineering, and, in fact, at first I may not have known. I'm pretty sure Latin was required for a Harvard BA, though, and not for a BS. That's a significant difference, and it might've occurred to me as an explanation for his doing engineering.

BOWDEN BROADWATER   Although I never had any classes with Norman, we had the same teachers along the way, and I had the feeling that he was a Matthiessen admirer. Ted Morrison I thought was an old bore. Hillyer was quite a nice old dodo—civilized, pleasant, gave enjoyable classes. He was very much an American of old stock, not an Anglophile. Ted Spencer was the Anglophile.

Robert Gorham Davis was a very odd duck who was quite sensitive to prose and poetry. He was one of those people you didn't much like, but he was sort of good at what he did, one of the few. I believe he was a former party member and then sang, though I don't know about that for sure. He had connections outside the university. I remember he had a wonderful party name, like Odette Loves or something.

HARRY LEVIN   I can tell you something about Norman's writing teachers in those years.

Robert Gorham Davis: A pretty good teacher, a Yankee sort of fellow who became a Communist but then found that he had to live a double life. For several years he was a regular book reviewer for the *New Masses* under some New England pseudonym, like Gerard Brooks or something. The double life got him down. He wrote a number of stories for *The New Yorker* which weren't outstanding, just highly competent. He went to Smith after Harvard, then to Columbia.

Robert Hillyer: He accused Dos Passos of having used him as a model in *U.S.A.* for the character of Richard Ellsworth Savage, the young Harvard poet who sells out. Dos Passos was quite embarrassed and said he'd only used a few details, but it's the same story, of course, even if Hillyer didn't go into public relations. Hillyer taught composition in a very honorific post, the Boylston Professor of Rhetoric and Oratory, but he wasn't really up to it. He was a conventional if accomplished poet, very antimodernist, and his *bête noire* had been T. S. Eliot. He used to give a party on Queen Elizabeth's birthday—that was the sort of person he was: a thorough traditionalist, a real Anglophile, very genteel.

Theodore Morrison: Not a great writer, although he published a novel or two. A very nice, easygoing man. It was he who, as director of the Freshman English Program, originated the Briggs Copeland Assistant Professorships, the position that Delmore Schwartz, Wallace Stegner, and John Berryman held, and, in more recent years, Kurt Vonnegut.

By the end of the thirties there'd been a real shift politically at Harvard. It came with the Communist party's position on America's nonintervention, the so-called war issue. There were Communists who caucused, one of the most ardent of whom was Daniel Boorstin, who was one of the most cooperative witnesses for McCarthy and then was appointed Librarian of Congress by Nixon. There were others, most notably Robert Gorham Davis, who tried to recruit me for the Communist party.

About the time when the war started, or perhaps earlier, with the Spanish Civil War, we were increasingly concerned with the state of the world and decided to give a course called "Literature and Democracy"—principally F. O. Matthiessen, Perry Miller, Theodore Spencer, and myself. The department looked at us with some superciliousness, so we agreed to do it on our own time. I. A. Richards and Richard Wilbur, the poet, helped, and we conducted it as a conference group. The first time around we found that the brightest students were Marxists, then within a year or two it changed. This was Norman's freshman or sophomore year.

Aside from the social clubs there were the periodicals, *The Advocate* and *The Lampoon*, and there was also the Signet, which was the one club concerned with the arts. The more interesting undergraduates belonged to the Signet.

ROBERT GORHAM DAVIS   I knew *The Advocate* group less well in Norman's years than I had in the late thirties. I'd married in '39, and my political views were changing rapidly during this period. Up until 1940 I'd been very close to the group around F. O. Matthiessen. He was a significant figure in every respect, nationally significant as well as heading Harvard's American Studies Program and the Program in History and Literature which attracted a lot of brilliant young teachers.

HARRY LEVIN   When I read *The Naked and the Dead* I recognized an episode from the course Norman took from me. It was somewhat elaborated, of course, but many years later we met at a cocktail party in Provincetown and I reminded him. His reaction was quite characteristic. He said, "Well, you owe me a smack." The course was "Proust, Mann and Joyce." He just sat in, as did Arthur Schlesinger, Jr.

Was there much awareness among undergraduates of European authors and traditions then? Yes and no. The person who represented it to me—and I was one of his last students—was Irving Babbitt. Walter Lippmann was one of his students and T. S. Eliot too. Harvard was the first university to offer comparative literature courses, though Hemingway and Edmund Wilson were really the undergraduate models, especially when Norman was around. And James T. Farrell too.

MARVIN BARRETT   Like Norman, I lived in Claverly my second year. It was the pits. In fact, Norman and I may have had the same room, number 24. It was right next to the elevator, and when I was there a rich South American was next door. He played a record called "In Spain They Say Si, Si," and he tap-danced interminably. Claverly was part of the Gold Coast. J. P. Morgan probably lived there in the 1900s. It had an indoor swimming pool that was unspeakable. You'd take your friends downstairs and stand there staring at its incredible green slime. No one swam in it.

I don't know why Norman lived there before going to Dunster. The most likely explanation is that he didn't get into a house right away, although if his grade point average was good, that shouldn't have been a problem. It could be that since all the houses had their own sort of community, maybe he didn't want to commit himself or didn't want any part of the house's social life, which may have been some sort of inverse snobbery.

SEYMOUR BRESLOW   I'd known Norman—in those days we called him "Norm"—when we were all freshmen at Grays, and when he and I and Marty Lubin didn't get into our houses, we shared a suite at Claverly our second year.

My background was fairly similar to Norman's and Marty's, though Marty might have had a little more money than the two of us. Sometimes, if a check was late, I'd lend Norman a couple of bucks, and vice versa. I knew there was somebody in his family—his uncle—who had money, but how much I really didn't know. He was the guy who gave Norman the old coupe that kept us all broke. We chipped in for gas, maintenance, parking, all that jazz. Norman put a mattress in the trunk, which was huge—I suppose partly for sex—but if we'd go out with more than one couple we had to really squeeze into that thing.

I think we each had our own room in the Claverly suite, but we all had the sense we were in a holding pattern, not having gotten into houses, and we were pretty unhappy, irked to be in Claverly, because that conferred second-string status.

But that didn't stop us from going out and doing things. Although I'd known Norman our freshman year, I got to know him much better in Claverly, and we got to be pretty close friends. I didn't meet his mother when she visited, but I had dinner with his family a few times in Brooklyn during vacation. Also, he stayed at my house in Connecticut once. He seemed more self-confident that year, partly because we were all more at ease with Harvard. Freshman year we were all dying to leave at Thanksgiving. Second year we had our friends, our life in Cambridge, and we weren't in a big rush to get out of there.

We all worked very hard. Marty and I were both in the sciences and had to spend a lot of time in the lab. But we'd sit around and talk at night—not about politics, none of us was heavily into that, and we probably would have agreed in our views, so there wasn't much to discuss. We'd talk about girls, of course, and also our work—which for Norman meant talking about writing, not about being an engineer. I remember running into him in front of University Hall after a physics exam and asking him how he'd done. He said, "Somebody just asked me how I did on the rotation problem, and I said, 'What rotation problem?' I've gotta become an English major instead of this engineering." Whether he actually did change I'm not sure. He would've gotten a BS in either case, because whatever your major, you needed Latin for a BA, which I know he didn't have.

He'd gotten on *The Advocate* the beginning of sophomore year, so as the year went on he was spending more and more time over there. I never met any of that crowd—he didn't bring them back to the room at all. But we didn't feel squeezed out by his new friends. He showed me several of his short stories. He was quite open about his ambition and let on to me that he wanted to write the Great American Novel, and while he was talking about it in terms of art, there was also fame, money. Dos Passos and Hemingway were not only authors whom he enjoyed reading, they were famous, and later, when he won the *Story* prize, it was wonderful, because it made him feel that his lot in life was to be a writer. His reaction was probably more pronounced among the people at *The Advocate* than with us, though. His life over there was separate, and as the year went on, that became more important to him, not in the sense that he was private or guarded about it, just that we were all working toward our own goals.

GEORGE WASHINGTON GOETHALS   Martin Johnson, a friend of mine, was aware of Norman because of his literary activities. Martin himself was an extremely gifted undergraduate writer and had made *The Advocate* as a freshman, which is unusual. The two of us lived in the same dorm, and Martin, who admired Norman, said to me, "This man is very talented." Norman, I think, had already submitted manuscripts to *The Advocate* as a freshman, but he and I didn't make *The Advocate* until our second year, which was when we met. We would talk about Faulkner and Hemingway, and I can clearly recall Norman on Hemingway, saying things like, "Look at the way this guy uses the visual structure of a sentence to have impact." That sort of thing, very perceptive, very aware of style.

In the fall—this is 1940 now—the two of us wrote our initiation play for *The Advocate*, a parody of *For Whom the Bell Tolls*, which we called "For Whom Your Balls Squall." The title was Norman's, the characters' names mine—like Iram Soreloins from Saroyan, Martha Getshorned, Ernie the Hernia Kid. I played Martha, Ernie Roberts played Hemingway, and Norman played Iram Soreloins. It took an afternoon to write and was about twenty minutes long. It went over great. In those days I weighed about 149, had long, blond, curly hair, and as Martha I was wearing high heels, silk stockings, and a snood. Before the performance I was in the john taking a piss, with my dress up. John Crockett came in and literally fell over on the floor in a dead faint. And in the play when Martha "gets horned" I got horned by Norman, who was using a large baloney sausage.

One of the lines in the play was "Second Act Golden Boy," and I think this tied in with Norman's Rocky Graziano fantasy. At the time he had a great interest and passion for the acting of John Garfield, who did the remake of *Golden Boy*. He used to call him by his real name, Julie Garfinkel. It was his admiration for Garfield and the boxing world that led him into those fantasies about being a fighter.

We saw each other a lot at *The Advocate* office—not in our rooms—and through our discussions I quickly became aware that even at age seventeen Norman was presenting himself as a professional writer. This took two forms. He was a craftsman, he'd say, and was going to write 3000 words every day, come hell or high water—which in fact he did—so that after he'd written a million words of shit, then he'd be ready to write for real. Second, he would assign himself a theme—encounters on a subway with sexual overtones, say— and he'd proceed to ride the MTA and watch people, then come home and write it up. It was like an anthropologist going after field data. He was as disciplined as a West Pointer, and as I come from a long line of West Pointers, I know what I'm talking about. Or take the worst stereotype of the Jewish kid bucking for medical school—Norman's fixity of purpose was that to the nth degree.

MARVIN BARRETT A lot of people at Harvard then were rich kids; there was money all over the place. I was a scholarship student and on a real shoestring, but I made an effort that Norman did not, like sacrificing to get a suit or jacket that I thought would make me look like the rich boys. But I don't think Norman was into that. His dress wasn't fashionable, and with the rich kids during that period there was a lot of concern with fashion. Someone like Bowden Broadwater, the leading aesthete on *The Advocate*, who was quite formidable—he didn't have any money, not a bean, yet he'd spend whatever he had on clothes, then not eat. But Norman didn't care. He wasn't into social climbing or hobnobbing with scions.

One good friend of Norman's was a rich kid, Bruce "Pete" Barton, Jr., the son of Bruce Barton, one of the originating partners of Batten, Barton, Durstine and Osborne, the leading advertising firm. But Bruce was a very special example of the rich boy: he wasn't interested in social things. He was a sweet man and a very good friend. I never called him Pete, like his family or prep school buddies would, because he was named after his father and was always in his shadow. Barton senior was in politics and had also written a million-dollar best-selling book, *The Man Nobody Knows*, in which he claimed, among other things, that if Jesus were alive he would've been an account executive in the advertising agency. Bruce had a real problem with his father.

It was usually through him that I heard what was going on with Norman. In fact, Norman wrote about him at some length in his piece on *The Advocate*, the reminiscence he published in *Esquire*. Bruce was president of *The Advocate* then, and also we were all together in the Signet. The Signet was the intellectual club; it skimmed the top off *The Advocate*, *The Lampoon*, and *The Crimson*, mainly people in art and music. It was a luncheon club, with an occasional dance or formal dinner banquet that required wearing a tuxedo, although I don't remember ever seeing Norman in one. As for the few "gentlemanly" formal aspects of *The Advocate* and the Signet, like dressing for a dinner or whatever, it was a trip for someone like me, coming from Des Moines. To me it was tourism, a combination of getting an education and staring out the window, watching the telephone poles go by. There were plenty of people around who wouldn't have been caught dead in "final" clubs, and Barton was vaguely in revolt against it. Perhaps Norman didn't even know about the "final" clubs. I found out about them in my sophomore year because of the "rat houses" and people being hazed. I asked, "What are those people in the black shirts doing?" and I'd hear about DKE, Porcellian, Fly, Owl, Spee, Delphic. But only one fifth of the college belonged, perhaps a tenth.

There wasn't so much a coterie among the twenty or so people on *The Advocate*. It was more generational, without too much of a split within each class, although Norman's class may have been more divided. He may have had a strong reaction to the aesthetes, so he wanted to separate himself from them. I think of Norman as being socially and politically concerned, so his coterie might have been more outside the university than inside *The Advocate*. In fact, one of Norman's first pieces for *The Advocate* was on the so-called "Negro question." That was an issue definitely in the air, and at the Signet, for example, they wanted a black person, a parade black, and I would imagine that Norman had a concern about that. Also, didn't his story "The Greatest Thing in the World" have an ethnic flavor? It was about an Irish kid, wasn't it? And it's interesting that Norman was exploring Boston and was fascinated with the Irish, since the other group at Harvard would've been exploring a different aspect of

Boston—Beacon Hill and the Cambridge intellectual life. Norman wasn't interested in that at all. He was interested more in the common man.

NORMAN MAILER   Arturo de la Guardia, our *Advocate* artist, detested me. Not because he was an anti-Semite, he just detested all lower-class types. He did the illustration for my first *Advocate* story, "Left Shoe on Right Foot," and was obliged to depict black people. He gave them bulbous noses and fat lips.

BOWDEN BROADWATER   I arranged to have Arturo de la Guardia do the drawings for "Left Shoe on Right Foot." He was in science but very smart and drew marvelously. His family was in and out of power over the years in Panama, but his politics never came up at *The Advocate*. He was good-looking and in a funny way was more like Norman than anyone else. They were both small and wiry and stood out for their large degree of energy. They each had more tooth in them, more bite, and a lot of unformed talent. I don't know what happened to Arturo, but I think he became somewhat important in the Panamanian government in Paris.

But in those days I thought he was a fine illustrator with a lot of sensibility, so I asked him to do the illustration for Norman's piece. I didn't think it was racist drawing at all. I had hoped that Norman would like it. But what, because Norman was a "realist" he'd gone to the Ivory Coast and seen the real ones? Arturo was no racist. I don't know where in the world Norman could have gotten that idea.

ORMONDE de KAY   The issue of discrimination against blacks was very much in the air among *The Crimson* editorial board. But for the generality of undergraduates it was probably not a big concern. To our shame. There were only four blacks in our class, out of a thousand males.

GEORGE WASHINGTON GOETHALS   Norman would talk about the Boston Irish as if he'd found another way of life. What fascinated him was their clannishness, their collective strength. I heard him talk about their being right, saying things like "They may be exclusionary, but they're close." On the other hand, I don't think he had any Irish friends here at Harvard, and contrary to what many people think, there were a lot of local Irish here as students.

ROBERT GORHAM DAVIS   It may be surprising, but Norman was not demonstrative enough in his class behavior for me to remember it. On the other hand, I was well aware of his talent very early on. In fact, my wife and I invited him to our house for dinner certainly once if not more. This was before his *Story* magazine prize, so it wasn't in recognition of that. We invited him alone, and as far as I can remember he was the only student we invited that year. It wasn't commonly done at Harvard, so I must have established a personal relationship with him during conferences. I liked him and valued him—his personality as much as his writing. There were many literary young men who were supercilious and condescending, most of them from fashionable schools. But there was none of that in Norman; he was quiet and modest and very impressive within that modesty. There was a self-contained quality to him, and I had the impression that he had very few friends. I was aware of student groups then, and I knew he wasn't part of any of them. The one group I knew best was more or less homosexual, with a preciousness about them that was very different from Mailer's manner. It had something to do with their social background, the schools they'd gone to, and certainly Mailer wasn't a preppie.

HOPE GORHAM DAVIS   He made a remarkable impression. When his eyes looked at you, you just melted. He was the first student I'd entertained as a faculty wife, and of course I understand now that's what he's always been fighting ever since—that he's a nice Jewish boy. He had beautiful manners in a nice, natural, kindly way. He seemed to be comfortable, not brash or acting overconfident. He was grateful to be invited, and he was just right—easy but respectful and tactful. He knew he was privileged at that moment, but he wasn't unduly nervous or shy.

BOWDEN BROADWATER   He was very thin and short and had a triangular face and very black, oiled, wavy hair. He used to wear a shiny green gabardine jacket—I suppose having gone through the usual Harvard clothes progression of throwing away your old clothes and getting some new ones in Cambridge. He struck me then as a preppy Frank Sinatra. He was quite distinctive among the more stolid members of *The Advocate*, and he stood out for me because of his vitality, in his person as well as in his prose.

NORMAN MAILER   Getting on *The Advocate* was the watershed, and so much happened to me that it's almost like "before *The Advocate*" and "after *The Advocate*." In a sense, my Harvard life began then.

"Getting on The Advocate *was the watershed, and so much happened to me that it's almost like "Before* The Advocate" *and "After* The Advocate." *My Harvard life began then." (First row, second from left.)*

That year there was an *Advocate* anniversary dinner, it may have been the fiftieth anniversary dinner. Roy Larsen, who was something like executive editor of *Time* magazine then, had read my story, "The Greatest Thing in the World," which had been published in *The Advocate* that spring. He came up to me, this beetle-browed, black-haired executive, and said, "I just want to tell you, Mr. Mailer, I liked your story a lot." Even in those days I didn't like *Time* very much, so I got all stiff and said, "Well, thank you, Mr. Larsen." That was all that was said, but then the president of *The Advocate*, Marvin Barrett, rushed up and said, "Roy Larsen likes your story."

Then at the end of the year I met Ted Amussen of Rinehart and Company. I think he'd been told to get in touch with me by Larsen, whom he knew socially. Larsen was much older than Ted and had said, in effect, "Amussen, there's a really talented writer. Why don't you look him up?" It's my impression that I got a letter from Ted saying he wanted to see any work I did, and then we had a drink together.

The following summer I was back at the Scarboro, with my own room again, and was emboldened to start my first novel. It was called *No Percentage*, and ran, I think, about 80,000 or 90,000 words.

I think the beginning of my existentialism is right there, in *No Percentage*. It's about a rich kid who can't get himself together and decides to go hitchhiking to discover what the world's all about. The concept of the novel hangs on whether or not he'll have the moxie to jump onto a boxcar, and he can't do it. The novel ends in failure. I called it *No Percentage* because at the beginning somebody's playing solitaire and somebody else comes up and says, "Why don't you move this card over here?" and the guy says, "It'd be cheating." The other guy says, "Yeah, but who's to know?" The first guy looks at him in disgust and says, "No percentage."

I was out on a hitchhiking trip about a week that summer. I think I'd started the novel first, got stuck, and *then* went on the hitchhiking trip in order to get the experience for the second half of the book. I left with about five bucks in my pocket and went south. I got down to Leesburg, Virginia, then I crossed over to Elizabeth City, North Carolina. I was picked up by a redneck who'd been up for two nights fucking. He thought he'd give me a ride so that I could help to keep him awake by talking, but I was appalled at the things he was telling me, I was such a prude.

All the same, I finished the novel when I came back. It was written in about two months, and I showed it to Ted Amussen. He liked it and showed it to John Farrar of Farrar and Rinehart, who I think just said to himself, "Well, this is a very young editor's enthusiasm for a very young writer's book. It's really kind of silly and not worth publishing." I expect he was right.

FANNY SCHNEIDER MAILER   Norman's hitchhiking trip made me sick. But I always indulged him, because if he felt he was going to write about it, I figured it can't all be imagination, some of it has to be real. So while I worried, I didn't make a fuss. He was sleeping out in the open on the grass, and he didn't even have a warm sweater with him, just the clothes on his back. I remember he wrote about brushing his finger in ketchup, and in fact he hated ketchup at that time. But the mere taste of something different encouraged him to act the way he did, and with Norman, when he used to want to do something, he'd do it. I just had to place my trust in God.

MARJORIE "OSIE" RADIN I remember when he came back his mother wouldn't let him come inside until he took his clothes off. He had to come in through the basement—she wanted to make sure he was deloused. For him, though, it was an experience, something to write about. He was consciously training himself.

GEORGE WASHINGTON GOETHALS He wrote me a very moving letter in which he described being picked up by a fundamentalist type who tried to convert him, which led to a short story, "Pamphlets for Jesus." In the story he described taking the pamphlets and stuffing them into his shoes because his soles were so thin.

That was also the summer he first got laid, when he was eighteen. He was back in Long Branch and wrote me a vivid, hilarious description of going to a prostitute; she was an old bag, but he figured he might as well get it over with. It was a hilarious letter, filled with genuine good humor, and he described how he had to wash off with Lysol afterwards. About 50 percent of the people I knew had gotten laid, but that was because of the times. The war was coming on, people were screwing their fiancées. Of the *Advocate* men, though, I'd say no more than 15 percent. I'd been laid before coming to college, but I never talked about my sex life. Norman, on the other hand, was always very candid about wanting to have a lot of women.

NORMAN MAILER In Brooklyn we called kissing a girl "getting to first," touching her tits was "second," and putting your hand up her crotch was "a three-bagger." I remember one night I went back to my room after a date in Cambridge. My roommate, Marty Lubin, was at his desk studying, and I went by, putting my fingers under his nose. "Get a whiff of this!"

KINGSLEY ERVIN Any undergraduate who could visibly make it with a woman had quite a bit of cachet, and on *The Advocate* probably no more than 5 percent of us would have qualified.

SEYMOUR BRESLOW He started going out of his way to use four-letter words around this time, and there was a greater tendency on his part to emulate what was supposed to be virile and masculine, like smoking and drinking, though none of us did all that much drinking since we couldn't afford it. I do remember, however, visiting him in Dunster when he was sharing his suite with Marty, and he explained that he had a bottle of gin on the mantelpiece because that was what Hemingway drank.

Without getting into specifics, I can say that we were all wound up about sex, about getting laid. Claverly had been pretty lax about rules, depending on the time of day, but Norman didn't meet Bea until the middle of his junior year, so Dunster House was probably more the locale for screwing around. Bea was a music major at Boston University. He met her, I think, at the Friday afternoon Boston Symphony concerts. When the two of them were going out I used to go out with a very good friend of hers, Roz Halper, and we double-dated quite a bit. Marty tended to do this less, but occasionally, like after a football game, we'd all go out together. We didn't have much money, so we'd go to a movie or something.

GEORGE WASHINGTON GOETHALS   He still had his old car, so he could go out and screw. It was a DeSoto coupe hardtop with a bulbous trunk that was large enough, though naturally he had to do without a spare tire. The arrangement was completely functional, even for a man of six feet three and a half like myself. My lady at the time, later my first wife, was at Wellesley, and I was without wheels, and I remember Norman saying, "George, any time you want to use my car, let me know." At the time he was very into Bea, but I never met her, not once. I was aware of her background, but Norman didn't disclose very much. I just knew he'd leave campus and go off into Boston.

ORMONDE de KAY   There was also another side of Norman and it was a little bit like the figure he's come to cut over the years. The bad boy. He had this famous girl friend, later his first wife, and God, she was luscious. *Zaftig*, desirable. The impression was that Norman was sexually very precocious—it was part of his reputation—though as far as I know, only with Bea. I'm not talking about a

Beatrice Silverman, the first of Mailer's six wives: "She was ebullient, gay. Her sexiness was camp, and what I remember was her talking dirty at Dunster House. Norman would act mock-shocked but was really delighted. No question about it, her debunking Harvard stiffness appealed to him."

roué. I think he was awfully pleased to possess a person of such enormous sexual excitement. Bea was arousing—not beautiful but wonderfully earthy, and she wasn't your proper Radcliffe girl. She was a proud woman, very much her own person and ahead of her time in terms of independence and women's rights. She played the piano seriously. She had a lot of temper, a sassy intelligence and character of her own, and at the beginning the two of them started out as companions. Norman was dead serious about his work, and she liked him for that. She could become strident and ideological, but after a few drinks we all did. It was a big ideological period. Bea was definitely with Norman when I met her our junior year. They were already lovers.

FANNY SCHNEIDER MAILER   Bea's father was an accountant, and her mother worked in the office with him. Her mother was a very bright, capable woman, but if she had arranged to be more of a mother and housewife maybe the family wouldn't have fallen apart the way it did. There was no divorce, but there was no binding attraction. A family has to have love, that has to be the main thing. But Bea's mother wanted to be in the limelight in the Jewish army. She was very aggressive, more than Bea even. But with that family it was no wonder. Everybody pulled in a different direction.

ROBERT C. HARRISON   *The Advocate* was a good deal more social back then, and Norman didn't laugh much. You would go into the office at odd moments and he'd be sitting there writing, obviously because the place offered a refuge. We had keys to the building, and if there wasn't anything happening, like a board meeting, it was very quiet. Norman used the board room.

MARVIN BARRETT   Norman came to Dunster in his junior year, where I too was living. My impression was that Dunster was neither distinguished nor fashionable—not an intellectual house like Adams or Lowell, nor a social house like Eliot, which was number one socially, or Winthrop with its jocks and prep-school boys. It was a party house, filled with people in government, economics, and history. Physically it was very handsome in a stage-setting way. A beautiful library, nice dining room—altogether opulent. It was recommended that I apply to Dunster because I would be sure to get in there, unlike Eliot, which was where my parents wanted me to go.

ROBERT C. HARRISON   Dunster wasn't an "intellectual" house at all. "The Dunster Funsters" was the campus tag, and I remember Norman played house football, but that wouldn't have been a big deal or even terribly competitive. In no way is it emblematic, say, of early machismo.

ALICE ADAMS   My ex-husband, Mark Linenthal, and Norman were fairly good friends, and Mark had talked about Norman before I met him in Paris after the war. Funnily enough, the one remark that comes to me of all the things Mark said about Norman is: "Of all the people I've ever known, the two who most wanted to be writers were you and Norman Mailer."

MARK LINENTHAL   I got on *The Advocate* my junior year and I was also in Dunster with him. As a freshman I'd been in Weld Hall, but my grades were terrible, so it cost for me to get into Dunster my sophomore year—via my taking a more expensive, single room. Dunster wasn't a very distinguished house, but it was varied and lively without having a single, unitary reputation, which gave it a freer atmosphere than other houses.

I also had a group of friends who were in American History and Lit, like Adam Yarmolinsky, Lou Pollak who became dean of Yale Law School, and Ralph Siegler, an advertising man in New York. Norman wasn't close to any of them. I was, but I was also a friend of Norman's, and I think some of them were mildly critical of our friendship. They thought Norman was self-dramatizing, striking attitudes, always being something. They were the serious intellectuals, and here was Norman as a sort of literary tough guy, something like a Hemingway knock-off—the opposite of Bowden Broadwater, say, who was outrageous in his elegance, mythically so.

But to me Norman was charming. I remember him and Bea at Dunster House horsing around and talking dirty, and that was fun. Norman didn't fit comfortably into an elevated Harvard social scene, so I think the raffish behavior was a kind of prudent response, since it gave him another thing to be. Also, it was probably meant to have exactly the effect it had on me, which was to charm. It was energy and playfulness, combative but sweet. He was *playing* at being combative, and he was making fun of himself too, with a spectacular sense of humor, which is what nobody perceived.

Part of the charm was that Norman was such a great narrator. He told stories with a kind of outrageous sexual content, like about his experiences during a one-night visit to a Jewish summer camp when he was a teenager, about the girls' camp across the lake, and how he and the other kids were in their tent and the counselor came back late at night and told them about his exploits. Norman acted out the parts. He would characterize himself comically, presenting himself as a kind of impressionable, wide-eyed, fumbling kid. There we'd be, he'd have us as his audience, a few people, and there was always this self-effacing element that gave the stories enormous charm. He was the center of attention of course, but it was still personal experience he was recounting, something that was quite real.

I didn't see Norman's attraction to WASPs then. He probably picked that up at Harvard, but at the time he was asserting his own identity. Gentility was not something he would've admired. His awareness of it may have taken the form of complete rejection—I remember he used to say about one guy and others like him on *The Advocate*, "He writes poems about spring."

Overall, though, he treated his Harvard education the way I'd later see him reading books—to help himself as a writer. He read aggressively, furiously, as a writer reads, looking for what is usable. He didn't read to become influenced. He read to discover possibilities. The program was Norman Mailer, not Kierkegaard. He didn't major in something that was serious, because that would've been subjecting himself to somebody else's discipline. He was trying to subject himself to his own discipline. In order to cultivate himself, he withdrew and cut his own path.

NORMAN MAILER I never switched from engineering to English for the very good reason that I wasn't that interested in eighteenth-century English poets. If I stayed with engineering I'd have more time to write. Also, I never took courses that demanded much work. I once calculated I wrote a million words, not before I got out of Harvard but before I started *The Naked and the Dead*, at least if you count various drafts of *A Calculus at Heaven*, *A Transit to Narcissus*, and all the short stories. Maybe not a million words, but probably three quarters of a million, and a fair amount of this was done while I was still in college.

MARK LINENTHAL On *The Advocate* he was constantly writing. He wanted to be a great writer—he was quite explicit about that and was willing to push more conservative, more prudent concerns aside. I don't remember specifically, but I recall trips into Boston and his taking notes, which was totally in character— Norman taking himself seriously. I wasn't dazzled so much as charmed, and also fascinated. Others sort of looked askance—"Who does he think he is?"— but I didn't react to it as a stereotype. I saw an audacity that was energizing, that had the effect of making *me* better, more perceptive and smarter—and the charm was that it wasn't a contrivance.

He was younger, the baby of our class, but when I talk about his vulnerability, clichés about his being a Jew from Brooklyn keep getting in the way. They're simplistic. It's glib psychology, kind of Cliffs Notes bullshit. Everybody who came to Harvard was in awe. Both George Goethals and I, for example, went to Roxbury Latin School, an intellectually—not socially but intellectually— elevated prep school in Boston, and at Harvard I'd never seen so many bright people. Never. My father had gone to Harvard, my brother too, and my school deliberately aimed at Harvard. But I still felt it was overwhelming. Norman went to Boys' High, granted, but there were a lot of Jewish boys from Brooklyn who became important writers and thinkers, and in one way or another I suppose they felt as overwhelmed and dwarfed as we did. . . . It's possible, of course, that Norman was acting out in order to test people's responses, but I think he needed to be at Harvard because he needed something big and impressive against which to define himself. You can't dismiss the fact that he was a Jew from Brooklyn, but it's too glib to say that his background made him insecure.

There's a poem by George Oppen in "Five Poems About Poetry" that would absolutely apply here:

> The little hole in the eye
> Williams called it, the little hole
>
> Has exposed us naked
> to the world
>
> And will not close.

> Blankly the world
> Looks in
>
> And we compose
> Colors
>
> And the sense
> Of home
> And there are those
>
> In it so violent
> And so alone
>
> They cannot rest.

That's Norman at Harvard—"so violent/And so alone/They cannot rest."

GEORGE WASHINGTON GOETHALS Norman had a habit of segregating his friends. He made it clear that I, as a *goy*, could never understand a Jew. There was none of his fascination with WASP power that came later, even though it was all around us, and what was poignant was that while he saw me as the consummate WASP, it was on his side that the barrier went up, not on mine. One time we were saying goodbye for the summer, exchanging addresses, and all of a sudden he went into "Well, I enjoy writing to you, George, and I enjoy your letters, but of course you can't understand a poor Jewish boy from Brooklyn." And I said, "Fuck off, Norman," because it confused me. He would pull the same number on Jewish classmates—"You can't understand me because I'm *poor* Jewish"—and he would lay this on any Jewish classmate he saw as having a clear and evident different status than his own. I never knew what he hoped to accomplish with this. Now, my reading is that it's some God-knows contorted form of the following: first, a streak—at the time I saw it as apolitical—of identification with the proletariat, because remember, at the time he was talking about Dos Passos and Farrell; and second, partly his vulnerability, since by saying it straight out—"I'm Jewish, I'm Jewish"—he created a kind of barrier so he couldn't be humiliated publicly.

ADELINE LUBELL NAIMAN I imagine that at Harvard he was keeping himself under wraps, playing a gentleman. This was the outgrown skin he'd shed as he would grow. I think he was trying to learn how to be a Harvard man without realizing he could be himself and still conquer, both playing a part and trying to master the game at the same time.

ROBERT C. HARRISON It was clear that Norman was incredibly diligent and determined, presenting himself as wanting to become a professional writer. The other perception was that he was a bore. Everybody found him boring because he spent most of his time claiming that he was just a poor Jewish boy from Brooklyn and the only reason he was at Harvard was because of a rich uncle who believed in him as a writer and was putting him through. You'd be talking to him and somehow it always seemed to come into the conversation: "Well, of course I wouldn't be here with all you rich people, because I'm just a Jewish boy from Brooklyn. The only reason is my rich uncle..." It was almost obsessional.

There wasn't exactly a lot of anti-Semitism around, but jokes about "Abie and Sarah" were commonplace. You'd go to the Old Howard, a burlesque theater in Scollay Square—I'm sure Norman must have gone there, Gypsy Rose Lee worked there—and they did all these numbers. Hence I think he was acknowledging his status outright, sort of "If I tell people, then I won't be embarrassed." He took it to such an extreme that it had to be directly related to his discomfort. He wanted to be sure there wasn't going to be any misunderstanding.

JOHN "JACK" MAHER   When I look back at the people who were on *The Advocate* I realize that Norman might have felt there was a lot of anti-Semitism, though perhaps more than actually existed. He once told me that he'd never had a non-Jewish friend before coming to Harvard and that he'd found it quite difficult moving into what at least then was a largely non-Jewish world.

GEORGE WASHINGTON GOETHALS   Nor did he celebrate Jewish holidays or talk about his family. Also, for all his emphasis on being poor, I never heard him make any comment to the effect that he couldn't do something for lack of money. The only thing he mentioned was going into engineering because his family sent him there, that he felt not wholly unobligated to their aspirations.

ADELINE LUBELL NAIMAN   If Norman was constantly presenting himself as a Jew, then it was probably a way of forestalling an attack, of buying off the critics. But it's also mythmaking, which was very easy for him to do. It was his standard riposte, playing the slum child—even though I wouldn't have taken it seriously, because he wasn't a slum child.

ANNOUNCEMENT IN SEPTEMBER 1941 ISSUE OF *THE ADVOCATE*   *Mother Advocate takes pleasure in announcing Norman Mailer won the National Short Story Contest sponsored by* Story *magazine last June. The story, "The Greatest Thing in the World," appeared in the April issue of this year. This is the fifth time in eight years that a member of* The Advocate *staff has won this distinction.*

ROBERT GORHAM DAVIS   I would guess that Norman had written "The Greatest Thing in the World" in the fall of 1940, then at my suggestion he submitted it to *Story* magazine in the spring of '41, and the prize was announced that fall. The *Story* magazine prize was important, a national contest.

NORMAN MAILER   The prize paid a hundred dollars, and I really started writing after that. My family had wanted me to be a doctor or an engineer—"Norman, why don't you write as a hobby?"—but with the prize they did a 180-degree turn and suddenly saw me as a writer. For my mother it was confirmation that the whole thing was possible.

FANNY SCHNEIDER MAILER Dave believed in Norman too. He went up to Harvard alone, got drunk, and then threw up in the restaurant where he took Norman for lunch. But Dave wished Norman was his son, don't you see? He spent money as was needed, but he was generous only when he could show off. This was after Norman won the prize, and Dave was always there to receive honors. He was not a literary man; he got by on little education. The whole point was to go to Harvard so he could talk about it afterwards. That was his name, "Show-off."

ROBERT C. HARRISON Norman's winning the *Story* magazine contest was a great honor for *The Advocate* and justified the fact that we were a literary magazine, not just a club. We actually had somebody who had done something. But at the same time Norman took very much a back seat in *The Advocate* administration, unlike Jack Crockett and Bowden Broadwater, who ran the meetings, jockeying for control and dominance. Possibly he may have looked on the rest of us as dilettantes, and maybe he was right. I don't think any of us had ideas of making literary careers—certainly I didn't.

ORMONDE de KAY Almost invariably *The Advocate*'s deadline would arrive and there was nothing to publish, so Norman would just sit down at the long refectory table in the room that stank of beer in *The Advocate* office, and within an hour he'd have written a marvelous 1500-word story that would go in without any changes at all. Just extraordinary.

As for *The Lampoon* and *The Crimson*, they were more competitive to get on. *The Advocate* was easy. Also, there was a definite odor of homosexuality there. But I was awestruck by Norman's discipline, his daily output. He presented himself as a professional writer as opposed to the amateurs surrounding him. I bought it, and I think a lot of us did, if only because it was so impressive when you saw him sit down and knock off a publishable story. Just his sheer determination to be a writer—I mean he was so very sure of himself. He knew how to be a sociable human being, he knew very well, and he could be easy and friendly and charming too if he felt like it, though he wasn't habitually charming. I never saw him be rude, but he never sucked up to anybody and intentionally put himself off stride.

JOHN "JACK" MAHER He talked about his mother and father and also about his uncle. But my impression from what he said was that his mother was a very strong woman, his father weak. Not in so many words. I just had the feeling in some unspecified way that his father was a sort of gray, failed man.

BARBARA MAILER WASSERMAN I remember once when Norman was home from college, he took me into the bedroom and said he had to tell me something about our father. He had an air of drama about him, and I felt I was going to be told something very important. "Our father is an unusual man," he began, and my thought was, Who's our father?, since I didn't think this could be Barney. Then he announced that Barney was a gambler and had run up huge debts.

MARJORIE "OSIE" RADIN   Norman always defended his father, but I thought the gambling was crazy. Barney used to come to my mother to get money, and I know she used to help him out on the q.t. Neither Fan nor Norman knew.

I don't know when he started gambling or if this was the beginning of it. In fact, I didn't learn about the gambling until after my marriage in 1949. My mother would never talk about it.

RHODA LAZARE WOLF   Mrs. Mailer had the pressure of her husband, what a deviate he was with his gambling, which had to be kept a secret. God knows what she had to do in the Sunlight Oil office to protect him against Aunt Anne and Uncle Dave. I don't know how much they actually knew, but the fact is that he would disappear, sometimes not show up, and Fan had to cover for him. My cousin worked at Sunlight Oil as a stenographer and told me about it.

They kept it a secret for so long, then finally said the hell with it and let it go open—it was such a big jam he got himself into. I know it had something to do with loan sharks, and there was something about taking his wife's money.

What's amazing is how Mrs. Mailer was able to cover up for all those years, not only about the gambling but that Barney was a failure. But I think Norman loved his father when he found out about his gambling: his father suddenly had a life of his own. He had found a road to freedom and independence. It was like he had developed his own selfhood, and Norman began to see him in a totally different way.

But one thing to remember about the crazy emotional stuff with Norman and his family: what you've got here is a mind that's rather extraordinary. Norman makes so much more out of these situations than really existed. Both he and Barbara had a way of converting Barney and Fan into more interesting people than they actually were, so their versions are more titillating than the truth. Like with Barney's drinking: Barney drank heavily, but he wasn't an alcoholic. Nor was he a womanizer, as far as I know.

JOHN "JACK" MAHER   Norman is exactly ten days younger than I am, but at Harvard he was two years ahead of me. On the train going to Harvard from Minnesota, where I grew up, I had been reading *Story* magazine, the issue in which they published that year's prize-winning piece of undergraduate fiction. It was "The Greatest Thing in the World," by somebody named Norman K. Mailer, an undergraduate at Harvard. I thought, Well, it's a good story, and it'll be interesting if I happen to meet this man. The first semester I was enrolled in Professor Raphael Demos' Philosophy A, a big lecture course in which we were seated alphabetically, and after a few days I noticed the name "Norman K. Mailer" on the notebook of the boy seated next to me.

I remember Norman as being about my size, wiry and curly-haired, but my lasting impression was of an absolutely fabulous talker who kept churning out ideas, some of which seemed to me at the age of eighteen to be absolutely brilliant, some of them absolute nonsense. He had an ability to extemporize on almost anything, to look at some object and use it as a basis for describing the culture of this country for the past fifty years. I don't remember his talking in his later mystical vein, but I always found it incredible that he was majoring in aeronautical engineering. By the time I got to know him, though, he was going to be a writer.

GEORGE WASHINGTON GOETHALS   Sometimes he was a bad judge of character, like his hostility toward John Blum, who I thought was one of God's most decent people. It was directed at anybody—low tolerance, a quick decision that so and so was "an asshole."

On the other hand, Norman and I, Ernie Roberts and Bruce Barton, we all had a distaste for anything Oscar Wildeish, and our feeling was that under Crockett and Broadwater this was going to permeate the magazine and turn it into *petites lettres*.

MARK LINENTHAL   Certainly, while some of the people on *The Advocate* found him charming, others did not, and largely because he was too subversive of established values. Not Establishment or conservative values, but *their* values. It was Norman's habit to break icons even then, to be contrary, like making a crack about Emerson, putting Emerson in a modern context and making fun of him. The image I have is a kind of challenging smile, ironic, independent, sometimes distant, so the stereotypes people come up with—Norman the poor Jew at Harvard, the penniless boy from Brooklyn—are totally wrong. There was some of the Farrellesque realist waging war against the preppies, sure, but it wasn't an unremitting war. It was a seductive role, and I see much more continuity between Norman then and Norman now. The stereotypes make him monolithic, and he was more interesting than that. He was also capable of great intimacy, which those monolithic versions totally overlook.

With Seymour Breslow, Harvard graduation.

BOWDEN BROADWATER   The split between the "aesthetes" and the "realists" wasn't all that simple. There were aesthetes, like Howard Brown, the poet, and myself, but the other camp was really made up of stodgy Andover-Exeter types, like Thornton Bradshaw, who represented the most pompous period of *The Advocate*, and were very much unlike either Norman's wildness as a realist or the goofiness of the aesthetes. They were just all bores, and since we were in the opposing camp, we were fighting. There were others too, like Billy Abrahams who did well-made but boring stories.

But the point is that Norman didn't fit into any of these groups, because he clearly had a narrative gift and his stories had life. They were quite startling— some were even gangster stories—and so much better than the stodgy, well-made "creative writing" kind of story that it didn't matter that he was a so-called "realist." Everyone jumped at the chance to publish his stories because they were so different from the heavy things that were usually pushed at you.

GEORGE WASHINGTON GOETHALS   In our junior year Norman and I were in Ted Morrison's Advanced Composition class, and Norman was even more the professional writer—I emphasize it purposefully—not the "literary figure" or "artist." He said his aspiration was to be a good enough professional to go to Hollywood and write scripts, make some good bread, and screw a different woman every night. Thus on *The Advocate* he was the anomaly, the maverick, in contrast to the Bowden Broadwater, Oscar Wilde *poseur* types. He'd say, "George, I'm gonna be a hell of a good commercial writer. You're the artist."

JOHN "JACK" MAHER   There was a sort of floating group around *The Advocate* and the Signet. I knew Linenthal, I'd known Kingsley Ervin from Minneapolis, where he grew up, but I don't think he and Norman were particularly close, nor was Ormonde de Kay either. But Ormonde was a great deal of fun when he got drunk, and also incontinent. One night he passed out on somebody's couch and wet his pants. Norman didn't drink very much. In fact, he put me to bed after my *Advocate* initiation.

ORMONDE de KAY   I was carried back by Bowden Broadwater and other people after my disastrous initiation at *The Advocate*, carried up four flights of stairs, drunk out of my mind. Broadwater had me drink half a bottle of Scotch, and even though I've been in two wars since, it was the closest I've ever been to death. A horrible business.

GEORGE WASHINGTON GOETHALS   It wasn't that Norman was drinking a lot— he just couldn't hold his liquor. He was a thimble belly. One night I'd been at dinner with friends at Lowell House and we were coming back to Leverett to play bridge, about nine or ten. Norman had this fantasy of being Rocky Graziano, and he was coming from Dunster, drunk as a skunk, and in a playful way he said, "George, I'm gonna whip the shit out of you. Put up your dukes." I remember pushing him on the chest and saying, "Norman, forget it." And his friend laughed like hell, put his arm around him, and they walked off. That was his fantasy life, and now I'm speaking as Professor Goethals, Clinical Psychologist.

He never talked much about his private life, and in all the time I knew him in Cambridge I went to dinner with him at Dunster only once. My grandfather built the Panama Canal, and I had a legacy of the Porcellian Club, the most prestigious club in the U.S., through my maternal line, but I refused to punch for it. I'd had it up to my eyeballs with being the general's grandson, and I told Norman that if it was any club it would be Signet, because that was a meritocracy, and eventually he and John Blum put me up for it. But as I perceived Norman, he was a self-defined loner. He wasn't friendless, but judging from our relationship, while there was genuine closeness, on his side it was metered. He was his own person, with an abiding sense of priorities. He was training himself quite explicitly, and anyone who knew him thought of him as *sui generis*, always an individual with a sense of mission. He was thought of as exceptional but too controlled, *too* disciplined. He already had national recognition—the *Story* magazine prize—but he wasn't cashing in on it. He was an enigma. He had a secret life in the sense that you knew only so much about him and there was an aura you couldn't penetrate. On the other hand, if he'd chosen to run a salon on creative writing at Signet or at Dunster, believe me, it would've been attended.

KINGSLEY ERVIN   He was divided between realism—e.g., Farrell, whose work he was sympathetic to—and the more rarefied view of literature, the aesthetic camp represented by someone like Broadwater. There was a gentlemanly tradition at *The Advocate*, certainly, but we also thought of ourselves as dedicated to some kind of literary priesthood. Mark Linenthal and I thought we were guarding literature from proletarian realism, and Norman was guarding it from the influence of the effetes. He was trying to learn how to describe things, to create the experience of ordinary working-class people in their own context. No dilettante he. And again, this distinguished him from the rest of us.

NORMAN MAILER   I don't think I was that calm or confident about myself in those years. It was more an adolescent's approach to writing, which was much like an adolescent's approach to sex: Am I a great lover? Do these experiences that I think are so incredible really amount to anything?

On the other hand, I didn't have enough taste to see how great the gap was between me and fine professional writers. Also, I was very careful not to read things that would demoralize me. I knew that instinctively. There's a navigator in us—I really do believe that—and I think this navigator knew I wanted to be a writer and had an absolute sense of what was good for me and what wasn't. If somebody had said, "Go read Proust," I'd say, "No, not now." I remember reading *Dubliners* and being bored by it because the concerns were really too fine-meshed for my crude brain. I loved Farrell because Farrell's experience was like mine—hearty, tough. Don't forget, I grew up on pot roast. I like writers I can understand, who are right there. There was also Steinbeck and then Dos

Passos, and it was only later that I began to like Hemingway and Fitzgerald. Faulkner came much further along. But if I've had one instinct over the years that's probably stood me in good stead, it's that I never fall in love with a great writer until I'm ready to. Which may be why I've never fallen in love with Joyce. He's just too damn great. It's the kind of thing where I say to myself, "If I read any more of this, I'll stop writing forever."

JOHN "JACK" MAHER I'd gotten onto *The Advocate* my first year, 1941–42, and it was still a fairly precious literary magazine, with very little undergraduate material. The stuff had been coming from faculty and postgraduate people, people who wrote for the little magazines, litterateurs, hangers-on. Some of it was perfectly good, but there was a nucleus of us who felt that we ought to publish more pieces by writers and poets at Harvard. We'd started to turn it around, Harold Smith, Pete Barton, and I, but then Pearl Harbor happened, and people were switching majors and getting into concentrated programs and then disappearing into the navy and the army. My sophomore year started two weeks after my freshman year, that summer. *The Advocate* folded up during the summer, and I was one of the few people in Cambridge the last few weeks before the first issue our group put together, and I did a lot of it by mail.

When September of '42 came along and we got *The Advocate* going again, it just wasn't like being in college anymore. Every few days somebody you knew would be called up or joined the air force or something. Despite the war, though, that fall the Signet had its election, and through Norman and Mark Linenthal and a few others, I was elected.

My clearest memory of Norman and the Signet was my initiation. You had to write a long, funny speech—which is one of the many talents I *don't* have. So Norman and Mark and four or five others helped, and with some contribution from me, we put together a speech with excerpts from *The Waste Land* and God knows what else. Then they managed to get me thoroughly drunk so that I could go through with it.

GEORGE WASHINGTON GOETHALS Norman seemed quite apolitical, both before Pearl Harbor, when a lot of Jewish undergraduates were militantly trying to join the Canadian Air Force, and afterward, when a number of classmates were going off into the army.

MARK LINENTHAL We didn't discuss the army, and I'm not sure how he got to stay right on to graduate. Maybe it was his age. Maybe his number didn't come up. But my sense was that he wasn't that involved. He was sympathetic but somewhat ironic and on the outskirts of that kind of thing. As always, he was being the writer.

ROBERT C. HARRISON We had what we called "nannies" who cleaned the rooms, and in the dining room waitresses waited on you. Then came Pearl Harbor. All of us streamed into the Yard and were looking up into the sky, we saw a plane, and there was a big rumor, "The Japs are coming." Some people joined up immediately. Others were getting into war work. Everything changed by the fall of '42. They had trays for food, cafeteria style, and the maids and waitresses all disappeared over the next six months.

NORMAN MAILER   The summer after my junior year I stayed up in Boston and took a job at Mattapan, Boston State Hospital, because I wanted the experience. I suspect it came through the grapevine that you could get jobs there, and so another fellow named Doug Wolf, a very talented writer, and I went out there. Doug quit even before I did, he couldn't stand it. I mean, I can't tell you what a shock it was to go from Harvard to that mental hospital. On my fourth day the attendants tackled a black kid, an inmate who had gone berserk, and in fact I was the one who caught him, so I felt responsible. Because after they caught him, they beat him up. When I complained, they moved me to a ward for old people who were senile, where my work consisted of cleaning bedpans and washing old butts. So I quit. I was there a total of seven days.

FANNY SCHNEIDER MAILER   I almost went crazy. He called me and I said, "Where are you? I'm going out of my mind." He said, "The grounds are beautiful." I said, "Look, Norman, don't feed me 'grounds.' I want to hear what's going on. Give it to me all in one lump sum, not piecemeal." Then he said he was going to give it up because it was so bad, so vicious, the way they took care of the crazy ones. He couldn't take it. I suppose his desire to write made him stay there a few more days, but when he realized I was going out of my mind, worrying that he should get out of there alive and in one piece, he came back to New York.

NORMAN MAILER   The rest of the summer I spent writing a play about that mental hospital. I called it "The Naked and the Dead," and then I didn't do anything with it for another year or more until the play got transmuted into my second novel, A Transit to Narcissus. I wrote it first as a play because I was interested in the Harvard Dramatic Society. In those days you'd write things for very little, and I might've talked to somebody in the Drama Society, and they said, "Gee, we're looking for student plays." That's all I had to hear. I sat down and did a play. If they'd taken it—and it wasn't that bad a play—I might have moved in the direction of being a playwright.

JOHN "JACK" MAHER   That fall I realized how seriously he took his "excursions" for his writing. At the end of the football season was the famous Coconut Grove fire, and early in the morning the college awakened us, instructing us to call our parents to reassure them we were not among the dead. Then Norman called me that morning. He wanted to go see the bodies they'd laid out in a public place for identification, and he tried to convince me to go along with him, arguing that it was the kind of event that doesn't happen very often and that we should take advantage of it. I wasn't sure why—I guess for whatever emotional experience he thought it would be. I think he believed that you should grasp every experience that came along—whether for your development as a writer or for the development of your soul or God knows what. But I said no thanks.

I don't know for sure, I don't have proof he actually went. I suppose he could have changed his mind and not gone, but my impression was he'd actually seen what he later told me about. What fascinated him was how shrunken the bodies of adults are after they've been thoroughly charred. He described spending several hours going from one body to the next, and he kept talking about how small the bodies were. And also that a lot of the victims weren't that badly burned, that they'd gotten trapped at the revolving doors and some of them had been literally torn apart as they'd tried to fight their way out. I heard all about it— dismembered bodies, trampled bodies, charred bodies.

NORMAN MAILER ("A CALCULUS AT HEAVEN," FEBRUARY 1943) *All day and night, for three days and nights he had been seeing men fighting and dying, and perhaps it had all happened too quickly, but all he knew was that it had no emotion or meaning to him. He remembered the burnt body of a man that he had looked at for quite a time. It had seemed a terrible degradation, as if the man in burning to death had reverted to a prehistoric type. He had been blackened all over, his flesh in shriveling had given the appearance of black fur, and his features, almost burnt off, had been snubbed and shrunken, so that the man's face in death had only registered a black circle of mouth with the teeth grimacing whitely and out of place in the blackness of the ape. . . .*

JOHN "JACK" MAHER I didn't meet Bea Silverman until the fall of '42 one football weekend after a dance, and subsequently we went out to her family's house, a dreary frame house in Chelsea, to see her sister. I had the impression of Bea as a very warm, vibrant, fun person who was sort of half waif, half mother to Norman—mother in the sense that whenever he'd get wildly enthusiastic about whatever passing enthusiasm was striking him she'd be more amused than take it seriously. "There's my little boy having another one of his crazy ideas"— that kind of thing, understanding it but being more tolerantly amused than absorbed. Back then, at the beginning, she wasn't at all competitive with him, and I thought she was tremendous.

MARK LINENTHAL She was ebullient, gay. Her sexiness was camp. She was like a little girl, wide-eyed and playful at the same time, and what I remember was her talking dirty at Dunster House. She would make a sexually explicit remark, and Norman would act mock-shocked but was really delighted. She was willing to make fun of it all, not in any way that was compensatory or defensive—that would somehow have spoiled the fun—and her debunking Harvard stiffness appealed to Norman, no question. One felt she was his companion in *épater le bourgeoisie.* They encouraged each other, although I think he took special delight in the fact that she would spearhead a project.

What seems funny is that people either turn her into a *femme fatale* or a proletarian ideologue, while in fact there was too much irony there for her to be an ideologue. I suppose Norman calls her the world's first feminist because she'd do those self-assertive, outrageous things, the kind of stuff that made him say, "Oh, Bea." But they were a team, and Norman encouraged it. That was what was so wonderful, aside from the fact that it was totally innocent and not done at anyone's expense.

ADELINE LUBELL NAIMAN   I don't remember it, but Barbara tells me that when Norman was a senior he brought her up to Cambridge to see Radcliffe. I was a freshman, a big party girl having a wonderful time, and she came to a party at Dunster House—the Princeton-Harvard weekend, I think. Then and there she decided she was going to Radcliffe.

I didn't meet her until the fall of '43. That term Phyllis—"Sliver"—Bea's younger sister, who was also at Radcliffe, asked if I'd like to room with her the next term. She said she was in Edmonds House, a co-op, and I thought that might be fun, so I said, "What the hell." The day we moved in, there was Barbara. She and Phyllis were going off to a wedding right away—we hadn't even unpacked. That was the day Bea married Barbara's older brother, Norman. It was January 1944, and soon afterward Norman went off to the army.

Even though we didn't really know each other, Norman and I began to write, just as I wrote to many boys who went off to the army—pen pal letters to keep morale up, so to speak. I knew people at Harvard, like Myron Gladstone, who were part of the nongay, every-bit-as-good-as-gay, would-be-Oxford-missing-lost-generation, though just a little too late. Anglophile, literaryphile, potatoes-in-the-mouth. Not witty but appreciating it. Yet I was a wit—the Cambridge style, verbal barrage without real intent to hurt, simply deflating the inflating. In hindsight I can say that during the years Norman and I wrote before we met, my sense was that he wasn't one of the real ones, the ones that interested me, those who counted.

I know he sometimes says he should have married me. It goes back to that cocktail party that Barbara remembers every minute of. Norman saw me as representing all those bright, sassy, glamorous, confident Radcliffe women with style and so-called chic, the ones who were unobtainable. I suppose that's why he chose Bea. So in saying that about me he's wanting to fulfill a fantasy left over from those days. He lived a lot interiorly—which is not to deprecate the conscious person.

MARJORIE "OSIE" RADIN   When my Aunt Rose met Bea she said to Norman, "She's a selfish young woman." He said, "Oh, no, she's not." Nobody liked her, not even Barney. A number of years ago she was passing through New York and went to see Fan. I happened to call, and she answered the phone. She said to me, "I'd really like to see you." I said, "Thank you," and she said, "Not because I want to see you. I just want to see what you look like now." That's typical.

But Norman married her. Only there were two marriages: after they had married secretly, Fan insisted that they be remarried by a rabbi.

FANNY SCHNEIDER MAILER   I didn't want Norman to marry her. I didn't know about the first marriage, but when I heard about it I stood by him because I always stood by him—he's my child. Maybe I was too easy with him because I loved him so much. I figured if he has faults, probably it's my fault.

I had felt Bea wasn't good for him. Afterwards... well, I don't want to talk about that, because I never approved of her. I just didn't know how to handle it. She wasn't trustworthy, and right from the start she wanted to be top banana. Her mother had been top banana, and that's where she learned it. She took over and wanted to direct everything.

SEYMOUR BRESLOW   We were still close enough that the year after Norman graduated he asked me if I knew a doctor in Brooklyn because he wanted a physical. This was months before he went into the army, and I told him about an uncle of mine, who at the time must have been about ninety years of age. I'd see this uncle once every six years, so it happened that I saw him shortly after our conversation, and he told me that Norman had come to him. I asked, "What for? A physical?" "No," he said, "a blood test. He was getting married."

I called Norman at home, and he was very reticent until I finally said, "Do your parents know?" He said, "No." I asked if they were there, and he said "Yes." So I said, "Okay, then I won't talk to you now," and he hung up. It seems to me that he then went through another ceremony, a religious ceremony, for his parents.

Later, when Norman was in the army, I came up from Philadelphia to New York and had a drink with Bea a few times. We'd sit around and talk and she'd bring me up to date on what was happening. It was during one of these visits that she said Norman looked at being in the army as a way of getting experience. For what, specifically? For what he was going to write afterwards.

III:
THE ARMY, PARIS, THE NAKED AND THE DEAD (1944-48)

NORMAN MAILER ("25TH ANNIVERSARY REPORT, HARVARD, CLASS OF '43") *To put it briefly, I had two years in the Army after Harvard, most of it with the 112th Cavalry from San Antonio, Texas. Was tacked onto them at the end of the Leyte Campaign, then saw some modest bits of action in Luzon as a rifleman in a reconnaissance platoon. After the war, in the occupation of Japan, I rose so high as sergeant technician fourth Grade, T/4, a first cook. The occupation inspired me with shame, however, Harvard snobbery being subtler than one expects, so picked a contretemps one day, and was busted. Left the Army a private.*

CLIFFORD MASKOVSKY   In 1948 I was out of the army and in college, it was final exam time, and I was flipping through the back pages of *Time* magazine and saw a picture of Norman with a smoking cigarette in his hand—a sort of sophisticated picture—and my first thought was, Oh, my God, Norman's been arrested for rape.

I laugh when I recall this, but my response wasn't completely crazy, I assure you, because when I'd first met him in basic training at Fort Bragg, North Carolina, he was going around the barracks asking all the men about their sex lives. This was the first or second week, and he was taking notes, operating like an interviewer, going from individual to individual asking the same questions as if conducting a research survey. He was asking if they went in for foreplay, and, as I recall, most of them said they didn't. In fact, that's why I remember another guy in the group who'll go unnamed, an Italian, who told Norman, "I just get on and off my wife," which was probably the consensus of everybody he talked to, that sex in those days was tapping your wife on the shoulder and saying, "I'm gonna jump on you."

Nobody got angry at him. It was like a matter-of-fact type of thing—"Here's this guy asking me these questions." He wasn't far out about it or showing off, and he wrote people's responses down on what I remember was more like a yellow pad than a notebook. Now, after all these years, I assume he was doing it to get information for something he was going to write, to get the feel of people's attitudes. He hadn't talked about his own wife, Bea, but sex always seemed very much on his mind. Hence my reaction to the *Time* photograph. Obviously this didn't make any sense given the kind of picture it was, so then I turned back a page and saw it was a review of *The Naked and the Dead*.

There were two contingents in our barracks at Bragg. The New York City contingent on the second floor, and the New England contingent on the first. Neither group liked the other. The sophisticated New Yorkers looked down on the yokels from New England; the New Englanders saw New Yorkers as big-mouth, wise-guy types. Since I was from Torrington, Connecticut, I was in the New England group.

But Norman and I were rather close for several reasons. First, both contingents, both floors, were above-average IQ, and we were trained to be forward observers for artillery. But I'd had a year at college, I was eighteen, and here was Norman at twenty or twenty-one, a graduate of Harvard, and while he wasn't a role model as such, I was interested in him. He was intelligent and seemed to know what he was doing. Second, our names are close, M-a-i and M-a-s, so we pulled details together, like guard duty and KP. Maino and Malakoff were in there too, but I think he had more in common with me. Al Maino was older, and Malakoff wasn't a regular kind of guy. There was also Virgilio Mori, whom I remember as dark-complected and a very quiet type of guy. He might not have been college, even though about 95 percent of our group were college men.

So Norman and I met that first week and got to be friendly over the next seventeen weeks. He had a contingent of fellows there, like Frederick Crippen from Brooklyn, and they'd sit and talk about jazz a lot. These guys gravitated to Mailer, and maybe he looked at his surroundings and said to himself, "Instead of a shy young kid, I'm as good as they are, maybe better," so he took on some brashness, probably fairly quickly. It takes a little bit of nerve to go around to each individual and say, "Let's talk about your sex life." If he was shy he sure didn't show it.

He made a big deal of Harvard, not often, but he let it be known. But he *never* let it be known that he was a writer or that he'd won the *Story* magazine contest, even though I would've known about the magazine and known it was a big deal.

He wasn't that good at physical things, though, kind of a weakling almost, a scrawnyish type of fellow and not really strong. But this really wasn't a problem in our group, because our ages ranged from eighteen to thirty-five, so he didn't have the same problems as some of the older guys. Like a guy named Rosenblum, the poor man weighed 250 pounds, and he'd huff and puff. Or the professor from Fordham, Broderick.

There were a fair number of Jews in our contingent, including myself. A lot of the guys had gone to college and were from New York, so I don't think that ever became an issue. Neither Norman nor I presented ourselves as Jewish, because there was no need to.

Still, I don't think that Mailer's Jewishness was the reason for his bravado either. The only thing I can attribute it to is that he looked around and said, "Hey, I'm better than anybody else here," and "I don't have to take shit from anybody." Maybe that's why he had such a feeling about officers. It wasn't so much an authority problem as wanting to test the system. He hated officers. The feeling is pervasive in *The Naked and the Dead*. I don't know what the genesis of that feeling was, but it comes out in his book, and when we were sent out to Fort Ord it was once directed at Bea, and then later, at the end of the war, at me.

But in basic I never saw him in a beef with an officer, even though later I heard that in Japan there was a hassle and he lost his stripes. At Bragg our officers were southerners but not Texans. He didn't meet the Texans until later, in the Philippines. Sergeant Mann, our sergeant, was one hell of a good guy, more like a marine drill sergeant than regular army and the kind of guy you never had a beef with. If you did, you paid a stiff price. The other sergeant I remember was Ernest Aud. He had all the superpatriotic lines, was a little bit of a shit.

Later, when I read *The Naked and the Dead*, I recognized people and felt a great deal of the book was really autobiographical. For example, a guy in our group, Joseph "Joe" Heiman, fits the description he gives of Buddy Wyman in the book. Tall, blondish. Also the personality is similar. I think he also used a guy named Rappaport. A very nice guy but very, very heavy. I remember looking at *The Naked and the Dead* and thinking: Here they are, dammit. These are the guys from basic.

SIDNEY TEITELL   It was an instrument and survey battalion—Fourth Platoon, Able Battery, Twelfth Battalion, Fourth Regiment, and we were at Bragg April 9 to August 5, and all of us had these qualifications on the basis of the examination we'd been given. The emphasis was primarily on mathematics, and I suppose Norman was there because he'd studied engineering. Even though I'd studied political science at Brooklyn College, I'd gone through the New York City educational system, so I'd had geometry, and that's basically what they wanted—trig and geometry for surveying.

Our platoon was definitely the "smart guys" platoon of the battalion, so there was bound to be some antagonism. Most of us had never met southerners before.

To me they were almost mythical figures, so it took me a couple of weeks to believe they were for real. The other platoons were filled with them, and my gut feeling was that they were all rednecks. Some of them may not, in fact, have been from the South but from Pennsylvania or Wisconsin, but as a New Yorker, I felt you could hardly tell them apart from the southerners. I mean, they'd never seen a Jew before in their lives, so you'd overhear remarks like "Ah, those smart Jewboys from New York," that sort of thing. We were alien to them, they to us.

So our outfit wasn't particularly liked. We were enlisted men and had no rank at all, and there was common resentment of all officers. But we also had the feeling that nearly all of the noncommissioned officers were southern rednecks. The one everybody remembered was our first sergeant, Ernest Aud, from Nashville, Tennessee. He was as much a cracker as one can get, a twenty-year man, who had come up through the ranks during peacetime. There was a resentment on his part that here were "intellectuals," quote, end quote, who were coming in and were gonna tell him how to run the place, so he made us toe the line. In essence, we were still going to school and were learning to be soldiers.

Yet nobody there was a soldier, we were all civilians. The greatest compliment you could pay any of us was, "Hey, you'll never make the grade." We'd salute and say, "Thank you very much." But it was a case of having to survive, and that's why I remember Norman Mailer. We had the impression that he was a *Luftmensch*, unaware of where he was and what had to be done.

It happened after the first few weeks, when we'd just worked our butts off. One morning we were inspected and they found demerits as a result of Mailer's bunk. Either his toothbrush was out of place or his bed wasn't a hundred percent right, something or other, and the entire floor was gigged, penalized and our weekend passes were taken away.

Now, part of the training in basic was to make you understand that everybody was dependent upon everybody else, and everybody else dependent upon you. Mailer's infraction was minor, of course, but one of those things the officers made a big to-do about in order to impress us. As a result a couple of other guys and I very quickly decided that for the benefit of the whole platoon the two or three of us, in rotation, would take care of Norman. I wouldn't say he was conspicuously sloppy, just disorderly, distracted. But we had to pass inspection, so it was a question of mothering him. He responded all right, but in fact it happened again on two or three occasions—not as bad, though, because we kept him in line.

I think we were somewhat aware that he was writing, although what I remember was that he did a lot of reading. He seemed to be reading constantly in his sack time. Other guys would be reading too but Norman particularly so. There was nothing wrong with that, I thought it was great, but it was like he wasn't with us. It was like he was on another plane, somewhere else.

Of course nobody liked pulling KP or the discipline. None of us were soldiers. Nobody wanted to be there. You just wanted to do what you had to and then get the hell out. So there was no real speculation about him, just the awareness

RTC
12A

PHOTO NO 2091
RELL CLEMENTS

4TH PLAT. BTRY. A 12TH BN
F.A. R.T.C. FORT BRAGG, N.C.

4th Plat. Btry. A 12th Bn. 4th Tng. Regt. F.A. R.T.C. Fort Bragg, N.C. 11th cycle 8/2/44 (Mailer, 2nd row from bottom, 3rd from right; Clifford Maskovsky, aide de camp, bottom row, 4th from left).

that he didn't seem to be with it. Harvard and all the rest, that didn't matter. Instead it was, "We've gotta clean this place up for inspection," and Norman would drag his ass. He'd be doing the job, but you'd have to say, "Let's move it, boy." In the first situation, when we lost our weekend pass because of his bunk, he may have made some kind of perfunctory apology, but that was beside the point. That abstracted quality stayed with him. He improved as time went on, but so did everyone else.

CLIFFORD MASKOVSKY   There were thirteen of us that were to go to the Pacific, including Norman. We had what we call a delay en route, which means that while we didn't get a furlough, we had ten days to report at Fort Ord in California. We weren't traveling as a group, we could go out there alone.

Norman said to me, "Why don't you come into Brooklyn and we can go out to Ord together?" I did that and met his wife, Beatrice, whom I liked. I didn't get any vibes that they were overly hot for each other or overly cold to each other, just a normal couple. Norman's brashness came out, though, when he decided we should turn in our coach tickets for pullman because in each coach you sat up for several days, plus it involved a change of trains in Chicago. We

1 TNG. REGT.
CYCLE. 8-2-44.

tried, but the price difference seemed exorbitant, something like forty or sixty dollars.

When we got into San Francisco, Norman said, "Hey, we don't have to report to Ord directly. Let's be a little late." Again, his brashness, and I went along, even though by being a "little late" we were really what you call AWOL. So we took a day or two in San Francisco, probably staying at the "Y" or someplace. We went to see *Porgy and Bess,* which I remember because that was the first time I'd ever been to an operetta. We probably also went to a few bars and just wandered around, then took a train down to Ord, where I was surprised to find that Norman was right. Nobody mentioned a thing. No repercussions. Nothing.

Fort Ord was supposedly to be a nine-day stay and then you'd go overseas. But because of our "Military Occupation Specialty"—Forward Observer for Field Artillery—they didn't know what to do with us. One minute we were gonna go to Alaska, another minute we were gonna go to Europe. They didn't train that many of us in those days, so because we were a commodity needed all over, they just kept us at Ord for three or four months before sending us to the Pacific. And during that time Norman and I again pulled details together.

Norman wasn't so much an operator as he just wanted to do things, and I went along with him. For example, every Tuesday, Wednesday, or Thursday we'd have an all-night, twenty-five-mile hike around the Ord reservation and get in at seven in the morning. By the fourth week Norman said to me, "Hey, did you notice where they route this walk? Why don't we fall out and pick 'em up on the way back?" Because he had influence over me I said, "Okay," and we did it. We'd walk maybe a mile or two, and then, because they'd draw a line, a big circle around the reservation, they'd come back to that same point, and we'd pick them up again. We'd lie down in the bushes and put our heads on our packs and sleep or we'd talk some. We got away with this for a couple of weeks because nobody ever took a roll call till you got back. But one night at midnight, when they always served doughnuts, some asshole decided to take a count, and we were caught. We were put on permanent KP, full time.

When I say Norman had that kind of brashness and was constantly testing the system, I'm also saying he was smart about people psychologically. Once, for example, I found myself playing Ping-Pong with the champion of the post. I won the first game, so there was a lot of betting on the second. I was playing over my head, I knew that, but Norman, instead of giving me encouragement, said, "Hey, you can't take this guy, you're out of your league." Why? Because he was betting on the other side. He was working on me psychologically, and I thought to myself, What kind of buddy is this? I lost. But smart him, he won his bet.

It was also during our time at Fort Ord that Bea became a WAVE, and I think he was angry that she'd enlisted in the navy. What he was saying was, "She's an officer, dammit!" Again his thing about officers. He had absolutely no use for them, and he seemed to be laying it on Bea.

ISADORE FELDMAN   I don't remember him making any cracks, but since we'd just come through basic, all of us felt officers lived in another world, and a lot of guys were curious in the case of Mailer and his wife how two people of different worlds got together. A remark like "Mailer, do you have to salute before you screw your wife?" wasn't meant viciously. It was more curiosity, and he'd handle these remarks with a smile, although you couldn't tell whether he was angry or laughing.

Before shipping out we were at Camp Stoneman for about three weeks being equipped with winter clothing and equipment, so we thought for sure we were being sent to Europe. It was so crazy—the only thing I can believe is that they were worried about spies keeping track of who was going where and how many, so this was probably a ruse, because when we finally boarded the *Sea Barb* for the Philippines we were all issued sunglasses and suntan oil.

CLIFFORD MASKOVSKY   It was a very small troopship, a month-long trip to New Guinea, and again Mailer was testing the system. In those days they'd get you up at dawn, everybody up on deck, because that's when you were supposedly most vulnerable to attack from submarines, and after a few days Mailer said to me, "Why don't we sleep in?" Now, that's brashness, and we got away with it for maybe a week until somebody came down to find us. Mailer ran up one gangway, I ran up another. He got away, but they collected my dog tags and called me in, and for the rest of the trip I had to guard the garbage and chip paint.

Again, though, when I read *The Naked and the Dead* I said, "That son of a bitch!" Because quite often he'd just disappear aboard ship, and I'd ask him, "Hey, Norman, where were you?" He'd give me some excuse, throw me off, like "Oh, I'm studying" or "I'm reading." But he must have found some secluded spot and was writing down details. Because when I read the beginning of the novel, when he describes the troopship and talks about the lighting and guys shooting craps, it was all stuff I recognized, stuff you don't necessarily remember unless you capture it while you're there. He had been doing it all along, and even though I didn't know he had ambitions as a writer, I realized later that he thought of all of his experiences, the whole bit, as material he should write down for later use.

GLEN NELSON When we crossed the equator it was really hot, and we just passed the time. I think he was one of the guys teaching people to play chess, he and another guy, Jerry Le Francois. We landed in New Guinea, Hollandia Harbor, on Christmas Day, 1944. We just sat in the harbor, and it was just about the hottest Christmas ever.

ISADORE FELDMAN We didn't even disembark. We were picking up a frigate that was our escort to Leyte. Then, on the way over, I remember sitting up on deck with Mailer, also a young guy named Star, someone named Spur, two or three other fellows. I'm not sure but I think Red Matthewson was in our group too, the guy who became Red Valsen in *The Naked and the Dead*. Just like he was depicted in the book, Red had been a hobo during the Depression and told stories about hopping the freights, and we would just sit around listening to him.

Once we reached Leyte we were all assigned work details. It was the beginning of the mopping-up action, so we were still catching fire. As a matter of fact we had a couple of night attacks, and one morning when we were eating breakfast in the dark we heard a Washing Machine Charlie above us—a Jap fighter, a Zero. Suddenly he opened up, firing at nothing, and pandemonium broke out. That was our first actual fire.

GLEN NELSON There were also reports of paratroopers on the other side of the mountain, but we never saw them. Since we'd gone over as replacements, we were unprepared at that point and didn't have any guns or ammunition.

We'd set up temporary tents and slept on folding cots. Mailer's tent was next to mine, or at least close enough so that I could see him, because I remember him sitting on his cot under the mosquito netting. The terrain was very low and wet, and since there'd been fighting on the island, there were shallow foxholes filled with water, because it rained every day. It was warm and humid with lots of mosquitoes, and there wasn't really much duty.

ISADORE FELDMAN   After about two weeks we were assigned to the 112th Cavalry Regiment. The reorganization took no more than a week, and then we boarded another troopship and sat around the harbor at Leyte before we got the order to move on to Luzon.

The 112th had started as horse cavalry in Texas. They'd actually left the States for the South Pacific with horses, which had been left on the island of New Caledonia. The original cadre of men had been pretty badly shot up, so although it had started out as a hundred percent Texan under the command of a Texan, Brigadier General Julian Cunningham, it was perhaps less than a fourth Texan by the time we went in as replacements. The survivors of the original nucleus were battle-hardened guys. Most of them were older and had really been through it. They were quiet and reserved and didn't make friends easily, part of which had to do with their ranking: most were sergeants, staff sergeants, and master sergeants, whereas all of us were buck privates, pfc's, or whatever. All together, including the artillery battalion, there were around 2000 men in the 112th, which was broken down into first and second squadrons and headquarters squadron. Those of us who were in communications were in headquarters squadron, which was divided into troops, with 30 or 40 men in each. Mailer and I were in the same troop.

There was a whole flotilla that sailed to Luzon, thousands of us coming off onto the beach at Lingayen Gulf. We could hear the 158th RCT in the hills, two miles off the beach, going at it—artillery, small-arms fire. On Leyte we hadn't seen much action, and, like all the other green ones coming over, I was scared. We didn't know what to expect. All we knew was that the initial landing had been made about ten days earlier.

We spent the next two days there on the beach, then at sunset the second day the order came to mount up, so we started down the main highway in trucks and made a 125-mile advance in one night, bypassing all the action in the hills with the 158th, and headed right down to the town of Santa Maria, about 35 miles north of Manila on the main highway. It was a MacArthur gamble, and he gambled the whole column. If the Japs had figured it out and cut in behind us, I wouldn't be here today.

GLEN NELSON   Soon Norman was put in a different outfit. Al Maino, Jerry Le Francois, and I were all sent to the 121st Artillery Battalion, 32d Infantry Division, each to different batteries. Norman was in another division, so we didn't see him. But since he went into Luzon at the same time, in January or February, he must have been part of the same nine-month effort. It was a mop-up operation designed to get the Japs out of the mountains, which was difficult because they'd gotten themselves into the caves. We had air superiority, which was the biggest factor there, but they did a lot of infiltration at night to try to get rid of our artillery because we'd harass them all night long. The mountain Mailer described in *The Naked and the Dead*—what was it? Mount Anaka?—I don't think there's any question, it had to be based on the mountains in Luzon.

ISADORE FELDMAN We didn't have much to do with the Texans, but I know Mailer didn't get along with them. His first job on Luzon was as a telephone lineman, which meant he would have to climb poles, lay wires, and so on. That lasted only a short while, though, because the wire sergeant began to feel threatened by him, his background and education, and got rid of him. Then they put him in the kitchen. But there too it wasn't long before the mess sergeant began to feel threatened and got rid of him as well. So he wound up being a rifleman.

He'd come around and spend time with us. At first I hadn't realized the cause of his transfers, but one afternoon he dropped in at our tent and he was wearing that whimsical smile of his. He had his head down and just grinned, explaining that they'd taken him out of the kitchen. Then he just shrugged his shoulders. It was a mixed group of guys in the tent, and there was someone there who'd just volunteered for General MacArthur's personal guard unit, so Mailer couldn't really open up and go into particulars. But we read into it. The problem was that the sergeant was getting scared for his stripes and saw Mailer as competition. I doubt Norman had mouthed off. He knew better, he knew that they could get him for that. But the resentment was there anyway. We were all rubbed the wrong way by some of the brainless authority among the officers, and some of them, the Texas guys, could be pretty surly, and not just to Mailer but to anyone of lesser rank.

Anyway, he had more combat with his superiors than he did with the enemy. But you could see that he was hurt, his pride and his morale, by having to take that kind of abuse. I could understand his frustration, but I couldn't understand why he stood for it when he could have gone to OTS—Officers' Training School—anytime he wanted. I mean there was his background and education, and I wondered about this.

I wasn't bothered as much by that kind of junk because by being a radio operator I could keep away from it. Part of it was that in the army rank is God almighty. Part of it was also anti-Semitism. With the noncoms, particularly, if they knew your name was Feldman or Mailer or something like that, then you were in for it. There was a guy named McNutty, a switchboard operator, and one night he began to complain about us replacements—"All you come-latelies who don't know what it's all about"—then he made some slurring remarks about my religious beliefs, and I went after him. The anti-Semitism was there by innuendo and also took the form of asides. Remember, there was a lot of Nazi propaganda, anti-Jewish propaganda saying that Roosevelt was Jewish, like "His real name is Rosenfeld." But our own guys would make jokes about it, none of which was pleasant to hear.

Norman, I think, got more of this than I did, and he was more vulnerable to it. First of all, in the radio section there were certain things I had to do and certain things I wasn't supposed to do, and as long as I stayed within my bounds there wasn't too much they could do to me. The fellows in the radio section weren't as crude as the guys Norman was with. Also, I finally made T-5, which meant, thank God, I couldn't be assigned anymore to KP or guard duty. I may be wrong, but I don't think Mailer ever made corporal, which meant he was fair game.

Which only kept me wondering why he never got himself reassigned. Maybe he couldn't have, or maybe he didn't want to permit himself an easy way out because he had a lot of pride. You could see that in the way he made a joke of these incidents instead of crying about them. But I always said to myself, "With his obvious intelligence he could've gone for OTS and made it. Why, oh why doesn't he do that?"

NORMAN MAILER   The whole thing in the army was never to show any expertise. Between patrols, whenever we were in rest camp, they continued to train us on Luzon. They'd go over everything we'd already had in basic just to keep you busy, like drills on the nomenclature of a machine gun. It was totally useless unless you were a supply sergeant. But the trick in any event was to play dumb. One day we were getting a lecture on map reading, I was nodding off in class when the instructor called on me: "Mailer, what're the coordinates here?" He was tapping at a place on the map with his pointer. Now the usual routine was to stumble around for five minutes and then he'd call on someone else. But I jerked my eyes open and in a daze blurted out, "013.75—224.90." I got it right on the nose. But in fact I'd fucked up completely. I'd broken the rules, and all the other guys turned around and glared at me.

ISADORE FELDMAN   None of us knew he was a writer or that he was collecting information for a book, so *The Naked and the Dead* was really a bolt out of the blue. I read it in the early fifties and immediately recognized little pieces of everybody, composites of people who'd been in our outfit. There was a lot of Red Matthewson in Red Valsen, for example. Red even looked the way Valsen's described in the book—a rawboned guy of Swedish extraction. His face was always like a boiled lobster because he was very fair and the tropical sun played heck with his skin, so whenever we'd get any salve, it went to Red. He wasn't big, just about five ten, thin and wiry. He was homely but so homely that he was actually pleasant-looking. He was older than the rest of us by about ten years—a real character who had been around.

I don't know if there was a sergeant exactly like Croft, but there was a guy I heard talked about in Norman's platoon who was what you'd call a redneck. He wasn't very tall, five eight or nine, and I heard he was very belligerent and hard to get along with. He was someone Norman knew as a rifleman. His name, I think, was Gallagher.

There was a little Mexican kid we knew too, like I think there is in the book. A fantastic guy—he won everything, whenever there was a drawing, a lottery, or something. We called him Poncho and he was from Texas. He thrived on luck, but then he got it through the head one night when his patrol was digging in at one of the outposts. The Japs heard them and from four hundred yards away opened fire in the dark. It was just blind luck that they got him right through the helmet.

I knew Francis Gwaltney, who became Mailer's buddy, but I can't really say if there was a character in the book based on him. There's the southerner, Ridges, but he's more of a redneck, and Gwaltney wasn't a redneck. I didn't know much about his background, only that he was from Arkansas. I felt he was kind of a snob—Francis Irby Gwaltney *the third*. He made that point real quickly, and he gave the impression that his family owned half of Arkansas, while I later found out that in fact he was real poor. He came along a little later to Luzon and joined us there, also as a radio operator. He took an immediate liking to Mailer, but it was a while before Mailer seemed to take to him. He was tall and kind of lanky, but I don't think he was a tough guy. He had a certain sophistication about him, but there was a condescending tone in the way he talked—at least when he talked to me. I thought he was a snob and looked down his nose at people.

The one thing in his favor, though, he wasn't a bigot. He told me once that he didn't have much to do with his sister because she was a bigot, not only against blacks but against Catholics and Jews. I didn't realize he and Mailer were talking about writing and books, but I thought of them as buddies, close friends. I wouldn't say Fig was his *best* friend because I don't think Mailer had a best friend; my impression was that, although he'd stop by and join our conversations, he more or less kept to himself.

In fact, when I read the conversations between Goldstein and Roth in *The Naked and the Dead*, they reminded me of some of the talks Norman and I had when I told him personal things that later came out of Goldstein's mouth. Of course Goldstein is a composite, but there are little pieces of me in him, real similarities—like I too was blond with blue eyes, was married and had a son, and I'd been a welder in a welding shop, after the war putting in thirty years as a welder at McDonnell Aircraft.

Also the differences between Roth's and Goldstein's religious attitudes: I would guess there's a little of Norman in Roth, although it was such a composite I think he took three or four Jewish fellows and stuck them under one helmet. But it's true, in that passage I thought of him when Roth says, "God is a luxury I don't give myself. Personally, I'm an agnostic." Roth is the cynic, and the cynicism fits Norman. Like Goldstein, I was raised Orthodox, but Norman was on the verge of being a rebel, and I can understand that maybe part of his being a rebel was not feeling comfortable as a Jew.

Anyway, when I read the book I wasn't bothered by recognizing myself, and I didn't resent Norman's using stuff from our talks. In fact I marveled at his memory, that he had remembered such things. Maybe he initiated our talks, although they just seemed to happen. We talked in private, on a personal level, but even so he didn't talk about his wife. He wasn't speaking as someone who was more experienced or sure of himself, and, if anything, there was a certain amount of covering up, because we were all feeling our way. In his case it was done in a humorous fashion. But there were personal things that we discussed about sex that I don't want to go into now, the conversation about how "women don't like it as much as we do."

He didn't talk about his mother and father either, or whether he had brothers and sisters. He didn't talk about his home life at all, really, so it was hard for me to recognize him in any of the other characters except in that one scene with Roth. But I think he was involved in a piece of action where he and some other guys actually had to climb a mountain like the one in the book. I wasn't in combat with him—when we were in the mountains we went through the valleys to set up our perimeter of defense—but I think I heard Mailer was involved in a climb, and maybe that's where he got the idea of having Roth fall off the mountain.

As I remember, there was very little combat in the book. My feeling was that there was a peppering of real incidents, though, and the situation we were in north of Manila, in and around Santa Maria, was obviously put to fictional use. We were west of the Agno River, about six kilometers, and there was a two-division outfit of Japs on the side, to the east, in a banana plantation. We were strung out in outposts about 2000 yards apart. Every day we went out in patrols of six to fifteen men on foot, making a sweep and then returning at the end of the day to report. If you made contact with the enemy, you were supposed to deal with it. We only stayed on our side of the river, which was a no man's land. The other side was solid Japanese. The river was about 500 yards wide, not very deep but too deep to wade, and with no bridges at that point. Our one little cavalry regiment was patrolling the area, and we were stretched out very thinly, but the men were active, and later our intelligence found out that the Japs had reported that we had two divisions there instead of only one. In *The Naked and the Dead*, in the scene where the Japanese come across the river, I would guess that's probably based on the Agno River where we were patrolling.

There were casualties, in particular one young fellow from New York named Sachs. I don't know if Mailer knew him, but he'd gotten into a tiff with his captain, some disagreement, and he'd stood his ground. So the captain saw to it that he went out on every patrol. He'd come in from one and go right out on the next one. That meant he was condemned to death, and eventually he caught one in the butt, and it ranged up through his stomach. He died two days later. I saw him when they brought him in. Just pitiful.

But that was quite common, to be sent out on patrols as punishment, which of course presents another parallel to *The Naked and the Dead*. Once my friend Blessing and I were up on an outpost with the first Squadron, and we'd just dug in for the night. We were talking in whispers, relieving the tension a little. The Captain was in a foxhole fifteen feet away. He said, "If you guys don't shut up, I'm gonna have you out front." In other words, in front of the perimeter of the fence. Believe me, we shut up.

EMMA CLARA "ECEY" GWALTNEY   Fig and Norman met in '45, I think, when Fig was attached to the same Texas outfit. Somebody made a derogatory remark about Jews, and Fig blurted out, "I'm Jewish. Can't you tell by my nose?" That amused Norman. They'd probably talked before, probably about reading, because I know Norman was the one who told him, "Being from the South, you ought to read Thomas Wolfe."

Fig was already a reader, but with his background in Charleston, Arkansas—having no father and having to work, running a movie projector at the little movie theater from the time he was fourteen—Norman was more educated, more the scholar and thinker, and he had a whole area of experience Fig would have been unfamiliar with.

In contrast to Norman, though, Fig would be sort of untamed, freewheeling. Not at all a redneck, but a totally refreshing, primitive type of person. He was quick-tempered and at that point probably more physical than Norman. He was six feet tall, real thin, but strong. What brought them together was the total disparity in their backgrounds, and Fig's experience growing up in the country complemented Norman's. For example, sex. The small-town boy or girl growing up back then had all kinds of opportunities—behind a barn, parking in the country. They were like puppies, they played. You had heavy necking sessions, and whether or not you went all the way didn't make any difference, you just sort of slid into it, and I think Fig first had sex when he was fourteen. So you compare him with Norman at fourteen—they're so different you can't imagine. The other things you'd do in the South, you went fishing and hunting or you went to the redneck bars and had fights, or to jukin' joints.

In some ways—the supreme irony—Fig would feel like a protector to Norman, kind of a big brother. For instance, he'd say to Norman, "Now, you never been fishin'," or he'd talk to him about guns and hunting. He wasn't wild about that sort of thing, but in the South you grew up with it, so he'd tease Norman, "You poor city boy, you don' know anything." Norman accepted that, and later, when he'd come down here to Arkansas after the war, there'd be Fig teaching him, 'cause he'd never really been immersed in life the way Fig had, what with Fig's father dying when he was two and his mother being considered half crazy because of what we know now were a series of small strokes. Fig was on his own so early, and compared to that, Norman was protected. It was almost as if Fig was teaching Norman what life was really like.

But I imagine all of that was as exotic to Norman as Norman was to Fig. Both of them were curious and eager for any kind of different experience, and both wanted to be writers, although by the time of the army Norman was already a writer. But Fig—just as he later wrote about in *Idols and Axle Grease*—was a great prankster, and he'd tell stories about how as kids they'd take apart an outhouse or break down a car and reconstruct it on top of the bank in Charleston. Hours were spent on such things, and it must've seemed to Norman at once idiotic, small-towny, and yet wonderful.

But Fig never discussed his brotherly role overtly. Norman was much more willing to talk like that, and I think at times it really irritated him that Fig wasn't willing to sit down and be analytical. Still, that wasn't Fig. It either made him uncomfortable or it was painful or he just thought it was too much bullshit, but he'd never sit down and analyze a relationship. He operated much more by instinct.

In the army, though, he was outspoken and insubordinate. He didn't like authority. He hit an officer once—I don't know what for—and he was sent to the stockade and almost court-martialed. In some ways he liked the army, but he kept saying he hated the principle, the idea of it; he hated General MacArthur and he hated the Red Cross—they were "phonies." In fact, he made Norman mad a time or two by saying he was a poor soldier, but to Fig that was a compliment, meaning Norman wasn't the type to be a good military man since that meant blind obedience. And Fig absolutely despised that kind of discipline. He felt that Norman was temperamentally unsuited and had done just what he was supposed to do. Norman had been a duck out of water in the army, and I think that's why he defended him by saying, "I'm a Jew myself."

Still, he admitted later that the army meant a lot to him. "I would've been working in a filling station to this day if I hadn't joined the army"—that sort of thing—and when he came back he went to college on the GI Bill. I don't think Norman had a direct influence on that, but probably some.

I don't know how much combat Norman was in, but one incident Fig wrote about in his novel *The Day the Century Ended* was when he was surrounded on a patrol and ran into a Japanese soldier. I don't know if he killed him or not—he never did tell me—but somehow Fig got away, ran through a jungle, broke his ankle, but just kept going. I know he was under fire a lot because when we'd be watching a war movie he'd tell me about the mistakes, like how grenades would sound, or how they'd throw the grenade, or the sound of firing, or Japanese yelling stuff at you. He'd say, "I know, I know, you don't want to hear this, but that was a mistake."

I don't know if Norman and Fig talked about combat, then or later. But when they were in the Pacific they'd sit and talk for hours about writing. They were kindred souls in among a bunch of rednecks. Other guys would be talking about Betty Grable and they were talking about Thomas Wolfe, say. And Fig had always felt like an outsider growing up because he wasn't part of any social structure, because he just had nobody whatsoever. He had that feeling in the army too, even though he was thoroughly at home and knew Texans. Remember, Charleston's not twenty miles from the Texas line.

FANNY SCHNEIDER MAILER   I was worried when Norman went into the army, but he had to go, didn't he? My hands were tied. You go day by day, minute by minute, and hope for the best. I would scan the newspapers until it made me sick to read what was going on. He wrote me short letters, but he wrote long letters to his father about the fighting. Barney was in Washington and didn't share the letters with me because he and Norman wanted to leave me in the dark as much as possible. I could imagine it, though, and I suppose because I was brought up in an Orthodox home I placed my trust in a higher being that it can't happen to my son.

Earlier, though, I was worried when he was sent to the South and to California for training. I knew what he'd have to put up with, like the fact that he's Jewish. I knew those Texas drunks would make life miserable for him. And we couldn't talk on the telephone. It was expensive, but even more, I was afraid that somebody would overhear conversations that might hurt him.

I heard about one friend, Fig Gwaltney, who was a very nice man. I met him and his wife later and told them that they could stay in the apartment on Willow Street. It was '49, after we'd moved to the Heights and then to the big apartment upstairs. He was a nice young man, a schoolteacher, a professor from Arkansas, and I don't think he'd met a Jew until Norman. They weren't uncomfortable; we didn't make it uncomfortable and they didn't either. We sort of hit it off. After the war he was writing, but I didn't know what.

Once I came home from the oil company office and stopped for the mail downstairs. There was an official-looking letter to Barney, and I was afraid to open it. We lived two flights up, and I walked upstairs and sat down. I turned the letter around a few times to see if I could tell anything from the envelope. Finally I mustered up enough courage and opened it. It was from South Africa, telling Barney his mother had died. While I had a fond feeling for her, truthfully I was relieved.

During this period Bea was in Vermont or New Hampshire attending college to become an officer in the navy. I went up there to visit her once, and occasionally she'd come down. I made no demands on her because she's a person who wanted certain things very private. And I respected that, although I figured she's lonesome, a young woman, you know, just married and the war comes along. I had my own heartaches, but I felt for her too.

Norman would occasionally mention the men he was overseas with—which ones drank, which ones would fight, how they treated the two Jewish boys. He puts on his Texas accent now, but he didn't have it before he went in the army, and when he came back something was lost. A certain kindness, his softness. Because those Texas men were wild. He wasn't accustomed to it. He had to learn to adjust to their drunken periods, and it was sort of an eye-opener for him. Because of his upbringing he wanted to push it aside, but he couldn't.

I never really delved into it with him because, again, I figured it was such a sad part of his life that the more he could forget, the kinder it would be. Maybe I was guarding myself, that I didn't want to hear all the sordid details. Of course I recognized it in *The Naked and the Dead*. Croft—you wondered if he was a real live person. I figured he was just a no-good drunk. And in writing about the two Jewish boys, he handles that well. He draws sympathy. You feel while they are not brash and brave, they are good people. The army as it was there— the drunks, the *goyim*—couldn't possibly understand them.

But the army will never be out of his system. It scarred him. It's not Norman's nature to take things in a flighty way, so it had to affect him, and while he was overseas I always worried that he would have too many heartaches. I never pumped him about what was going on because I figured it would be punishment for him to have to repeat it. I felt that he's so sensitive that his nature was affected by all the brutality he had to witness.

BARBARA MAILER WASSERMAN   Bea once told me that Norman wanted to go into combat so he'd be able to write the Great American Novel. The arrangement was that he'd be writing her long, long letters, so that even if he was killed, then at least there'd be the book.

NORMAN MAILER   I was in basic training at Fort Bragg when, June 6, 1944, the invasion force landed on Normandy. I was ready to cry. I'd always thought I'd be in the first wave on the beaches, but there I was out in the North Carolina pine barrens on a goddamn march while my destiny, my literary destiny, was taking place in Europe.

So as far as my conscious scenario for myself goes, I would say it was misdirected. I'd wanted to go to Europe, and it was only in retrospect I realized that I was lucky. Because I wouldn't have been able to handle Europe. Mind you, it wasn't clear to me that I was going to write a long war novel. In fact, when I started *The Naked and the Dead* I was just going to do a short novel about a patrol. Everybody always makes me too much of a formalist. Like my "arrangement" with Bea that my letters were to be saved. In the course of writing I probably said to her a couple of times, "Hey, babe, save these letters. They might be good for a book someday." Then after a while I began consciously writing them out as notes for a book, no question about that. But it was like keeping a diary, only this was safer, since I could lose a diary or it could rot, mildew, whatever.

NORMAN MAILER (THE LANGUAGE OF MEN, 1951)   *The war was over, Carter had a bride in the States (he had lived with her for only two months), he was lonely, he was obsessed with going home. As one week dragged into the next, and the regiment, the company, and his own platoon continued the same sort of training which they had been doing ever since he had entered the army, he thought he would snap. There were months to wait until he would be discharged and meanwhile it was intolerable to him to be taught for the fifth time the nomenclature of the machine gun, to stand a retreat parade three evenings a week. He wanted some niche where he could lick his wounds, some army job with so many hours of work and so many hours of complete freedom, where he could be alone by himself. He hated the army, the huge army which had proved to him that he was good at no work, and incapable of succeeding at anything. He wrote long, aching letters to his wife, he talked less and less to the men around him, and he was close to violent attacks of anger during the most casual phases of training—during close-order drill or cleaning his rifle for inspection. He knew that if he did not find his niche it was possible that he would crack.*

So he took an opening in the kitchen. It promised him nothing except a day of work, and a day of leisure which would be completely at his disposal. He found that he liked it. He was given at first the job of baking the bread for the company, and every other night he worked till early in the morning, kneading and shaping his fifty-pound mix of dough. At two or three he would be done, and for his work there would be the tangible reward of fifty loaves of bread, all fresh from the oven, all clean and smelling of fertile accomplished creativity. He had the rare and therefore intensely satisfying emotion of seeing at the end of an army chore the product of his labor.

A month after he became a cook the regiment was disbanded, and those men who did not have enough points to go home were sent to other outfits. Carter ended at an ordinance company in another Japanese city. He had by now given

Japan, 1945: "He didn't have his Texas accent before he went into the army, and when he came back something was lost. A certain kindness, his softness."

up all thought of getting a noncom's rating before he was discharged, and was merely content to work each alternate day. He took his work for granted and so he succeeded at it. He had begun as a baker in the new company kitchen; before long he was the first cook. It all happened quickly. One cook went home on points, another caught a skin disease, a third was transferred from the kitchen after contracting a venereal infection. On the shift which Carter worked there were left only himself and a man who was illiterate. Carter was put nominally in charge, and was soon actively in charge. He looked up each menu in an army recipe book, collected the items, combined them in the order indicated, and after the proper time had elapsed, took them from the stove. His product tasted neither better nor worse than the product of all other army cooks. But the mess sergeant was impressed. Carter had filled a gap. The next time ratings were given out Carter jumped at a bound from Private to Sergeant T/4.

On the surface he was happy; beneath the surface he was overjoyed. It took him several weeks to realize how grateful and delighted he felt. The promotion coincided with his assignment to a detachment working in a small seaport up the coast. Carter arrived there to discover that he was in charge of cooking for thirty men, and would act as mess sergeant. . . .

This was the happiest period of Carter's life in the army. He came to like his Japanese K.P.s. He studied their language, he visited their homes, he gave them gifts of food from time to time. They worshipped him because he was kind to them and generous, because he never shouted, because his good humor bubbled over into games, and made the work in the kitchen seem pleasant. All the while he grew in confidence. He was not a big man, but his body filled out from the heavy work; he was likely to sing a great deal, he cracked jokes with the men on the chow line. The kitchen became his property, it became his domain, and since it was a warm room, filled with sunlight, he came to take pleasure in the very sight of it. Before long his good humor expanded into a series of efforts to improve the food. He began to take little pains and make little extra efforts which would have been impossible if he had been obliged to cook for more than thirty men. In the morning he would serve the men fresh eggs scrambled or fried to their desire in fresh butter. Instead of cooking sixty eggs in one large pot he cooked two eggs at a time in a frying pan, turning them to the taste of each soldier. He baked like *a housewife satisfying her young husband; at lunch and dinner there was pie or cake, and often both. He went to great lengths. He taught the K.P.s how to make the toast come out right. He traded excess food for spices in Japanese stores. He rubbed paprika and garlic on the chickens. He even made pastries to cover such staples as corn beef hash and meat and vegetable stew.*

It all seemed to be wasted. In the beginning the men might have noticed these improvements, but after a period they took them for granted. It did not matter how he worked to satisfy them; they trudged through the chow line with their heads down, nodding coolly at him, and they ate without comment. He would hang around the tables after the meal, noticing how much they consumed, and what they discarded; he would wait for compliments, but the soldiers seemed indifferent. They seemed to eat without tasting the food. In their faces he saw mirrored the distaste with which he had once stared at cooks.

The honeymoon was ended. The pleasure he took in the kitchen and himself curdled. He became aware again of his painful desire to please people, to discharge responsibility, to be a man. When he had been a child, tears had come into his eyes at a cross word, and he had lived in an atmosphere where his smallest accomplishment was warmly praised. He was the sort of young man, he often thought bitterly, who was accustomed to the attention and the protection of women. He would have thrown away all he possessed—the love of his wife, the love of his mother, the benefits of his education, the assured financial security of entering his father's business—if he had been able just once to dig a ditch as well as the most ignorant farmer.

Instead, he was back in the painful unprotected days of his first entrance into the army. Once again the most casual actions became the most painful, the events which were most to be taken for granted grew into the most significant, and the feeding of the men at each meal turned progressively more unbearable.

So Sanford Carter came full circle. If he had once hated the cooks, he now hated the troops. At mealtimes his face soured into the belligerent scowl with which he had once believed cooks to be born. And to himself he muttered the age-old laments of the housewife; how little they appreciated what he did. . . .

Harmony settled over the kitchen. Carter even became friends with Hobbs, the big Southerner. Hobbs approached him one day, and in the manner of a farmer, talked obliquely for an hour. He spoke about his father, he spoke about his girl friends, he alluded indirectly to the night they had almost fought, and finally with the courtesy of a Southerner he said to Carter, "You know, I'm sorry about shooting off my mouth. You were right to want to fight me, and if you're still mad I'll fight you to give you satisfaction, although I just as soon would not."

"No, I don't want to fight with you now," Carter said warmly. They smiled at each other. They were friends.

Carter knew he had gained Hobbs' respect. Hobbs respected him because he had been willing to fight. That made sense to a man like Hobbs. Carter liked him so much at this moment that he wished the friendship to be more intimate.

"You know," he said to Hobbs, "it's a funny thing. You know I really never did sell anything on the black market. Not that I'm proud of it, but I just didn't."

Hobbs frowned. He seemed to be saying that Carter did not have to lie. "I don't hold it against a man," Hobbs said, "if he makes a little money in something that's his own proper work. Hell, I sell gas from the motor pool. It's just I also give gas if one of the G.I.s wants to take the jeep out for a joy ride, kind of."

"No, but I never did sell anything." Carter had to explain. "If I ever had sold on the black market, I would have given the salad oil without question."

Hobbs frowned again, and Carter realized he still did not believe him. Carter did not want to lose the friendship which was forming. He thought he could save it only by some further admission. "You know," he said again, "remember when Porfiro broke up our fight? I was awful glad when I didn't have to fight you." Carter laughed, expecting Hobbs to laugh with him, but a shadow passed across Hobbs' face.

"Funny way of putting it," Hobbs said.

He was always friendly thereafter, but Carter knew that Hobbs would never consider him a friend. Carter thought about it often, and began to wonder about the things which made him different. He was no longer so worried about becoming a man; he felt that to an extent he had become one. But in his heart he wondered if he would ever learn the language of men.

ISADORE FELDMAN   At the end of August we left Luzon for Japan. Norman and I were on the same boat, and I know the date we arrived—September 2, 1945—because we were two troop ships away from the *Missouri*, where the signing took place, and we watched the whole thing through binoculars. We went in the next morning and were bivouacked on an airstrip outside the town of Tateyama on the Chiba peninsula, which is the arm of land that surrounds Tokyo Bay.

Mailer and I were close by each other but not in the same tent. I was at headquarters radio and on eight-hour duty, but we'd see each other in the evenings. Gwaltney and Red Matthewson would get together with us too. There was gambling going on, and the young bucks ran around and made their contacts in the nearby Japanese town, but the married men, including Mailer, stuck pretty close to camp. For amusement and relaxation we played cards or swapped stories. If Mailer screwed around in Japan, I didn't know about it, and my guess was he didn't.

We were there for about six months, and while I still had no idea that he was writing, I thought I saw changes in him. When I'd met him in California he'd seemed more or less a happy-go-lucky fellow. In Japan he was kind of quiet. He kept to himself a lot and also he seemed bitter—maybe bitter about life in general, maybe bitter about the way fate had treated him in the service, going back to the very beginning in the wire section, then his transfer to the kitchen. I'd lost track of him when he'd been made a rifleman, but now I felt that his sense of humor was more caustic. He smiled, but it wasn't real.

There was also the swearing. In Japan he used to take a personal relish in the way he'd roll curse words off his tongue. He loved swearing, just the pleasure of saying those words and getting away with it. I could understand his bitterness though. The army left its mark on all of us. There was a loss of innocence, and the army took something out of your personal esteem, your self-confidence. But Norman had battled it, so maybe his bitterness and his anger and frustration affected him more than most.

CLIFFORD MASKOVSKY   During the months that Mailer and I had been separated, Jerry Le Francois—a guy I knew well and who unfortunately died recently—was the interisland correspondent and used to write to all of us, including Mailer. At one point Le Francois wrote me saying Mailer had stopped responding to his letters, though this didn't keep him from continuing to write Mailer, so when I was in heavy combat and missing for a few days he'd written Norman to tell him but had heard nothing back.

Finally I was reunited with Norman when I got my orders to go back to the States and was sent to a large naval air base on Yokohama where American soldiers were staging. It must have been September or October '45.

I had become a battalion sergeant major. I had my stripes and was wearing them, walking through the barracks, carrying a duffel bag. Suddenly I hear somebody calling, "Maskovsky! Maskovsky!" I knew it had to be somebody who knew me fairly well to use my name that way, so I turned around and there was Mailer. He was running towards me, then he saw my uniform and stopped, and the first thing out of his mouth was "Whose ass did you kiss to get those stripes?"

It wasn't a joke; he meant it. It was his attitude about officers again, and it really pissed me off. He hadn't seen me for a year, and I know he'd heard from Le Francois that I'd been missing. It wasn't "I'm glad to see you're alive," not even "Geez, I'm glad to see you after all this time." No, it's "Whose ass did you kiss . . ."

Eventually we were on the same ship coming back, the U.S.S. *Grant*, a large troopship compared to the *Sea Barb*. Because of my stripes I was a sergeant of the guard and had to give guard duty. There were twenty-nine posts, and I had to segregate the ship. There were all these people who didn't know each other, who were from different organizations within the army and air force who had enough points to go home, and when I first started to assign guard posts, nobody would acknowledge his name. So I said, "Okay, there's only one way to make sure of this." They'd all settled into their tiers, three high, but I ordered them to get the hell up on top deck, where I reassigned bunks and singled guys out for guard assignment.

Mailer just cursed me up and down—he was furious. Then he asked if I could give him something special instead of guard duty, so I put him in charge of candy distribution, because we didn't have a commissary on ship. I gave him the light detail even though I was pissed at him. Why? I'm not sure, except probably I was also still in awe of him. Besides, I felt some loyalty and warmth even though he wasn't loyal to me.

We landed in Seattle, Washington—Fort Lawton, I think—and were there for a couple of days before being shipped east on a troop train. This was after

Christmas, maybe February or March. The troop train was wild—full of soldiers going cross-country, coming home from the war. Guys were selling their mess kits, clothes, whatever, and buying booze whenever we passed through a town, totally plastered, getting on and off the train. The MPs, the supervisory personnel, were having a difficult time controlling us.

Norman was on the train, and it was strained, because he was still pissed about my stripes. For my part, I think I'd begun to reconsider giving him that easy detail on the U.S.S. *Grant*. I was hurt and felt betrayed, the same way I'd felt betrayed when I was playing Ping-Pong at Fort Ord. I didn't tell him so, I just didn't want any more to do with him. He'd written himself off as far as I was concerned, not only because of that choice crack—"Whose ass did you kiss?"—but because I realized he didn't do anything without forethought. He wasn't the kind of guy who just jumped into something, although he liked to give that impression, so it raised the question for me—I mean, who was this guy? Had there ever been the real Norman Mailer, whoever that was?

Obviously I hadn't been aware of this in basic, and really not even on the way back home, but when *The Naked and the Dead* came out, things started to add up. Like the sex survey. Why else would he take a survey? Or the fact that he'd disappeared for like two weeks on the *Sea Barb* and you wouldn't see him except at mealtimes. He'd never told me he was a writer, but looking back, I assume he was doing everything at that stage to develop a novel. It was all centered on him. Maybe that's what it takes—I don't know.

FANNY SCHNEIDER MAILER When Barbara was in college just after Norman had graduated—she started Radcliffe at the beginning of the summer, 1943— I was still running the oil-delivery business. I used to commute every day from Crown Heights, and I remember feeling very tired, so we moved. Anne and Dave were already living in the Mayflower Hotel in Manhattan, and Brooklyn Heights seemed the answer.

I got myself all dressed up and went to a house on Henry Street, near the St. George Hotel. I sensed immediately that the woman was anti-Semitic, and I thought to myself, I'll fix her. So after looking at the apartment I said, "I'll tell you, Madam, I'm looking for an apartment much nicer than this one. I wouldn't consider this apartment." I felt I had to give her a parting shot, I just couldn't leave without telling her she's a bum. The feeling that someone's anti-Semitic comes very easily. It's the way they look at you, it's the questions they put, and I thought to myself: You dirty slob. My children are tops and you object to them?

Then I went to 102 Pierrepont. The man who owned the house looked me up and down as if I was to be examined for something like a disease. I said to him, "My daughter is entering Harvard, my son is a Harvard graduate and is going into the army to defend his country." That kind of shut him up for a while, and he knew I was under stress, so he showed me the apartment. I told him it was just my husband and me, so there wouldn't be any wear and tear, so, grudgingly, he gave it to me. We lived there until 1949. It was a very nice apartment—two bedrooms with a large living room so Barbara could entertain her friends when she was home from college. It was a third-floor walk-up, but the stairs never bothered me. It was expensive—seventy-five dollars a month.

Since Norman was in the army, Barney working in Washington, and Barbara at college, I had extra food-rationing coupons. Luckily the man who gave them out never asked about them. I would send the extra ration tickets to Barbara since she was in a cooperative, Edmands House, where they cooked their own meals.

ADELINE LUBELL NAIMAN Barbara and I spent a lot of time together the spring of '44. She talked a great deal about Norman, her big brother and hero. She wanted to please him, and he gave her incentive. She was obviously under his shadow, but this came from inside her own head more than from other directions.

During the years we roomed together I'd go down to Brooklyn to visit, and I got along very well with Fan. In fact, I adored her. She was the sort of mother I would've loved to have had, and I thought we were really very much alike. Everything she said struck me with absolute delight. She never really understood Bea, whereas I was no threat either to Norman's marriage or to her ownership of Norman. I was okay, the nice Jewish girl.

MARK LINENTHAL When I got back to Harvard after the war Barbara lived in the co-op where I knew some other girls. My sense of her would have been colored by my sense of Norman, his eminence, so I'm probably not a very trustworthy observer, because I would read her through him to some extent. But I don't see how she could have avoided that. I think it took the form of extreme modesty, a very low profile. She seemed a quiet, serious girl committed to values that one could easily associate with Norman—his literary, economic, social attitudes.

JOHN "JACK" MAHER I got a furlough after my basic training and visited Cambridge in June or July of '44. I remember Bea's sister was rooming with Barbara in Edmands House. It was ten or twelve girls with a housekeeper, and Phyllis was one of them. But I don't remember her very clearly. I was obviously more interested in Barbara.

RHODA LAZARE WOLF Barbara was involved with a man who'd been at Harvard with Norman, Jack Maher, a midwestern Catholic. There was talk of love and marriage. In '44 he left and went into the service, and later there was a plan for Barbara to go away with him for a weekend, but Mrs. Mailer found out.

What happened eventually was Mrs. Mailer had a heart attack, or pretended to. Barbara told me about it, and just seeing her face, I realized how trapped she was. Mrs. Mailer wouldn't get up from the floor until Barbara promised she'd never see Jack again. It was horrifying. While Mrs. Mailer was totally involved with Norman, she was just as involved with Barbara, although in a different way.

Norman was on Barbara's side when all this happened, but he also realized it was more dangerous to encourage her to rebel, to play with her life, because of what it would do to their mother. Barbara, though, doesn't make public displays. If she had any kind of fight with her mother, it was never while I was there.

ADELINE LUBELL NAIMAN Jack Maher was a friend of Norman's, and Norman kind of delegated him to Barbara, and Barbara accepted that delegation. But Fan's wasn't the only objection. Jack's parents laid down the law too. It was during the period Norman was overseas, '44–'46. Barbara was badly pained, yet I think she romanticized the relationship, partly because Jack came to her as the appointed suitor. Norman had introduced them, which was a loving thing to do, but maybe there was an element of provocation. Norman always has this slight bitchiness in his head. He's done the same kind of thing to himself as well—gotten into relationships that people he respects have in a sense provided and defined for him. It's a kind of procuring with love, what's best described in Yiddish as being a *shadchen*.

FANNY SCHNEIDER MAILER I was against Jack Maher because he was a *goy*. I didn't know him much, but I knew that his mother was a very staunch Catholic, and I said to Barbara, "If you want to embrace the Catholic Church, you might retain some kind of small happiness. But if you don't want to embrace the Catholic Church, keep away from Jack Maher." She knew it was causing me grief—I didn't have to tell her.

I met Jack Maher, and once I got him to go on the subway with me for a long ride so we could talk and no one could listen. I made it very plain to him that in the long run he would be unhappy, Barbara would be unhappy, his mother would be unhappy, and so would I. I said, "It entails everybody's unhappiness." He didn't give me a reply, but he didn't argue the point with me either, so I didn't press it too hard, because I figured if he's not arguing, he's agreeing with me. I just felt I was giving up my daughter to the Catholic Church.

Bea approved of Jack Maher, but Barney agreed with me. He pushed me to the forefront and told me to be the spokesman. I imagine Barbara was angry with me, but she respected my stand. Maybe she mulled it over in her own mind, that it could never work, and to this day I don't feel guilt for interfering, because I figured I saved her life. I don't know if Norman introduced them. But of course to Norman it wouldn't have made much difference whether he was a *goy* or Catholic or anything, whereas to me it made all the difference in the world. But Barbara and I have never talked about it in the following years. I don't want to prove anything to her, and she doesn't want to prove anything to me. Some things are better left to die a natural death. If you don't touch it, it doesn't hurt anybody.

BARBARA MAILER WASSERMAN In the relations of children and parents, the only rule of thumb I've ever come up with is that their perceptions of each other's motives and feelings are almost always 45 to 180 degrees askew. It's true that my mother and I never again discussed what happened. But I also didn't forgive her or have an intimate conversation with her for the next fifteen years. In fact, I only forgave her when I divorced Larry, my first husband. She hated my doing it and spent the better part of an hour trying to talk me out of it until finally I said, "It's no use, Mother. My mind is made up, and if you love me you'll accept it." There was hardly a beat before she said, "You know Larry really failed you." Which of course wasn't true. But I loved her for her loyalty. I also felt awfully dumb because it had taken me all these years to realize that all I'd ever had to do was to present her with a *fait accompli*. Norman of course had always known that.

KINGSLEY ERVIN   I'd known Jack from Minneapolis, where we both grew up, and Jack's mother definitely played a role in the breakup too. She wasn't pleased with the idea of her son marrying a Jew from New York, and Norman may not have realized this, that in fact it was both mothers who were responsible.

BARBARA PROBST SOLOMON   Fan may have been the Rock of Ages, but she's not a mellow woman. There's something really puritanical about their family expectations, not much potato love or sympathy, and Barbara always said that Norman was the shy and vulnerable one when they were kids. It was all tap dancing and performing. A lot of ego and a lot of "My child before the rest of the world," and for the kids themselves it was perform-or-else. There was support, certainly, but no empathy, no recognition of ephemeral things like a kid's feeling blue or put down. Inchoate emotions weren't validated. Like Fan's busting up Barbara's romance because the boy was *goyishe*. It was pretty late in the day to be that insensitive and willing to break your daughter's heart. But on some level Barbara was taught you couldn't get your heart's desire.

MARJORIE "OSIE" RADIN   When Norman came back from the army I can't remember seeing any great changes. All I remember is he didn't come back immediately but had to stay in Japan, and Fan kept fulminating, saying, "What's the matter with the government? Why don't they let Norman come home?" She was very angry, dying to see him.

NORMAN MAILER   When I got back to Brooklyn in '46 Bea told me she'd met this author in the neighborhood, Norman Rosten. I thought there might have been something between them and started to get uptight, but she said, "Oh no, wait'll you meet him."

He was a poet and a friend of Arthur Miller's—the most easy, decent man, totally relaxed and affable. More important, Norman Rosten was the first published author I'd ever met. There had been Robert Gorham Davis at Harvard, and I'd been impressed that he'd published, but he was a professor. Rosten *supported* himself as a writer. He'd had two books of poetry published and a play produced, and he made an indelible impression on me. For years afterward

Norman's manner was one of the models of behavior for me—until I started going off my tracks in the fifties, and even then, internally, he was a model. His manner was like Henry Miller's. Henry was a guy who'd treat the postman with the same dignity as a world-famous author.

Also when I returned, my neighbor was Arthur Miller. Unknown to me, Arthur Miller was writing his masterpiece while, unknown to him, I was slogging away at *The Naked and the Dead*. If anyone had told me that this tall, middle-class type was writing something as powerful as *Death of a Salesman* I wouldn't have believed it. Seeing him get his mail downstairs day after day, the two of us exchanging small talk, I can remember thinking, This guy's never going anywhere. I'm sure he thought the same of me.

NORMAN ROSTEN   Norman and I had met in the hall of 102 Pierrepont because Arthur Miller lived in that same building; the connection through Miller makes sense because I was close to him and was often over at his place. I'd known Miller since the late thirties from the University of Michigan and knew that Miller would run into Norman occasionally. They didn't exactly love each other. Miller's not the kind of guy who would meet someone and immediately become friends. He's cautious, and temperamentally they were a little suspicious of each other.

If Norman remembers thinking of me as the first "real writer" he met, I suppose it was because I'd published a book of poetry in 1940, my first book, issued in the Yale Younger Poets Series, and I was making a living writing, doing radio plays for shows like *Cavalcade of America*, plus magazine stuff. I'd read his novella *A Calculus at Heaven* in *Cross Section* in 1944 because I had a long poem in the same issue, and when he came back from the army we had talks. While he was away, though, I'd run into Bea in the neighborhood, and I think she may have mentioned he was working on a book. I knew that she was working on a book too. I didn't see her that often, but we'd sometimes have coffee, and once she said, "I'm also writing a novel." She seemed serious about it. Why else would she mention it? I was no one she had to impress.

ADELINE LUBELL NAIMAN   In the summer of 1945, nineteen, fresh out of Radcliffe and full of the nerve of ignorance, I had convinced Little, Brown and Company to hire me as an editor. This was a bargain for them since they had been paying me ten dollars per manuscript reading as a free lance, and my salary was twenty-eight dollars a week. The only woman editor had announced her intention to leave and resume family life with her naval officer husband due back from the war, and a slot was being held for a returning GI. I, therefore, did the work of several people and learned a great deal from my boss, Angus Cameron, the editor in chief, a great editor and mentor and a left-winger.

Later that summer I gave an afternoon tea party at my house in Cambridge when I knew Norman and Bea would be in town. I wanted Norman to meet my friend Pearl Kazin who worked at *Harper's Bazaar*. I thought she might take a story of his, but they didn't get along. It was a funny afternoon, the first time

Adeline Lubell Naiman (just right of center), "Little Miss Little, Brown," who fought in vain for The Naked and the Dead.

I'd really talked to Bea. Her sister Phyllis was the first real woman friend I'd had, but Bea was a disappointment. I never was very interested, since I was a woman who talked to men, so I wasn't looking at her, and she had to be looked at, like a little kid saying, "Look at me." And she couldn't stand it—with some justification I can see now—that Norman and I talked almost incessantly and didn't pay any attention to her. There was no way for her to hold her own in the glitter of discourse. So that afternoon she started showing off, dancing or acting drunk.

I remember feeling that this was a really boring person with a lot of power that I didn't understand, power to compel Norman's sexual addiction to her. Partly it was because she was his first real woman. He was nineteen and she was twenty when they got together and she made possible all those fantasies he'd talked about—going out and getting laid. Yet she was always angry, even before the success of *The Naked and the Dead*. People paid attention to Norman because he was more charming, articulate, and fun, and she resented it. But I don't think she took Norman's and my infatuation seriously. It wasn't an affair. She may have seen me as competition, but in a funny way I don't think she really did, since she was so wrapped up in herself.

I also thought Bea's own ambitions as a writer were spurious; it was another way of competing with Norman and asserting herself: "I'm somebody, pay attention to me." She clearly wasn't a writer in the sense of having a *raison écrire*—if there is such a thing—and her politics didn't interest me either. Most everyone I knew was politically left or thought they were, and I wasn't aware of Bea as being outstandingly active, even though there was a sense of her being an outspoken ideologue.

SANDY CHARLEBOIS THOMAS   Part of his attachment to Provincetown goes back to writing *The Naked and the Dead* there. P-Town's his spiritual home. It embodies a great natural beauty and quality of light and incredible evil, all in the same narrow spit of land.

NORMAN MAILER   I didn't have much literary sophistication while writing *The Naked and the Dead*. I admired Dos Passos immensely and wanted to write a book that would be like one of his. My novel was frankly derivative, directly derivative. A lot of the techniques, like the Time Machine, came out of Dos Passos, and while I was writing I kept saying to myself, "Gee, this isn't nearly as good as Dos Passos. I just don't have his gift."

I had four books on my desk all the time I was writing: *Anna Karenina*, *Of Time and the River*, *U.S.A.*, and *Studs Lonigan*. And whenever I wanted to get in the mood to write I'd read one of them. The atmosphere of *The Naked and the Dead*, the overspirit, is Tolstoyan; the rococo comes out of Dos Passos; the fundamental, slogging style from Farrell, and the occasional overrich descriptions from Wolfe.

The book wrote itself, but there was a set of problems that were not small. I couldn't do the officers. The original Lieutenant Hearn was terrible, a weak, silly man, and he had no life. I think I was having trouble with him because he was some extension of myself, a despised image of myself. The hatred of officers went over to the minor characters, the minor officers, but I had always asked, "What if I had been an officer?" and my imagination was stirred by that. People thought that I was Hearn, that he was some idea of myself. Never. It was the first time I made the move, choosing a character who was physically stronger and more handsome than myself—which is a very hard step for a serious young writer. Of course there is a direct parallel between Hearn's refusing to pick up a cigarette and my losing my stripes when I was in Japan. The scene definitely came out of my own humiliation; it was a real use of something that had happened to me.

Croft came out of the woodwork, though, straight out of my mind. I'd had a sergeant in basic training, Sergeant Mann, who was very tough but fair. Croft was a model of that sergeant, the toughest noncom I'd ever met and the best, the fairest—only Croft wasn't fair. Croft was an amalgam of this guy plus a lot of the tough Texans I knew, some of whom were crazy, truly very tough men who shot up whorehouses, things like that. So Croft came naturally, like Red Valsen and the other men. But Hearn and Cummings drove me crazy.

I wrote 200 pages that summer, 50,000 words in sixty days. I probably worked every day, but I wrote fast, and I don't think I worked more than about three hours a day. This was in Provincetown, at the Crow's Nest cottages out at Beach Point. I'd thought of going to P-Town all through the war. Bea and I had an idyll there in '42 and loved it, and we both wanted to come back.

Then at some point I went with Bea to visit her family in Chelsea, and since we were in Boston we just called up Adeline. I'd met her, she was virtually my sister's roommate, and she'd told me, "Please bring the book to Little, Brown." I had 200 pages done, and all along I'd thought I'd show it to her.

ADELINE LUBELL NAIMAN   I'd written him, having heard from Barbara that the book was progressing, and offered to read it in my position at Little, Brown. No response. I repeated my generous offer through my former roommate. Again no response. Finally I wrote directly to him again and eventually was given 184 thumbed pages of the rough first draft.

This was also the beginning of our renewed correspondence. I kept a file of those letters, a file that somebody swiped from Little, Brown, and what's missing from the file in particular are the letters with lots of dirty language in them. I was infatuated with Henry Miller, and I remember once both of us sitting in a room, typing at each other in Miller fashion.

But what I don't have either, alas, is the brief report I wrote in white heat the day I read the manuscript. I remember that it was a paragraph long and that I threw off my flossy language for something pungent and efficient like, "This is going to be the greatest novel to come out of World War II and we must publish it." I also did what I had been moved to do only a couple of times in my brief tenure as an editor: I filled out a Blue Card with publishing recommendations, estimated sales, price, advertising budget, and the like. I think I said we might sell 7300 copies, but it may well have been 3700; nonetheless, we must publish. I do, however, remember the look of my report, because I sent a carbon off to Norman sub rosa, and his father carried it around in his wallet for the rest of his life, pulling it out at parties whenever I was around and telling a story that grew larger, more heroic, and more sentimental at each telling. I became something like Little Miss Muffet—small, delicate, and courageous, doing battle with the great spiders of the publishing empire. That is not how I saw myself at twenty, but it's true, a turmoil ensued at Little, Brown.

I went in to Angus Cameron and said we had to publish the book. He said, "Tell me about this guy." I explained that Norman was my friend, the brother of my former Radcliffe roommate, and Angus said he'd take the manuscript home that night. The next morning he said, "It makes me nervous, but I'll back you." Then there was a huge fight. Our executive vice-president, Ray Everett, didn't like the book very much but was willing to back Angus. Mr. McIntyre, the president and really an archconservative Boston Tory, didn't like the language and refused to have it. The man was a tyrant, and he later offended me by sending a furious memo scolding me for kissing my husband goodbye in front of the office on Beacon Street.

Anyway, with *The Naked and the Dead* we got down to a battle. Our editorial board included McIntyre and Arthur Thornhill, Sr.—a sort of businessman and treasurer whom I hated—Everett, Angus, and myself. Our meetings weren't heated—there's no such thing as "heated" in that world—but even though it wasn't an out-and-out confrontation, I was shocked by their attitudes. Mr. McIntyre almost never talked to me. Somehow I was an affront, being female and articulate and also not knowing that one should shut up. Still, I was enormously good at what I did, I was a bargain, and he knew it. Angus was a genius, a great editor and a mentor for me, and he continued to back me. He saw what I saw, and he would have published the book had it been just him and me. Ray Everett, the vice-president, was very bright and, though conservative, he trusted Angus and agreed to go along with our enthusiasm if the book's language was changed. Snotty letters flew between Miss Little, Brown and the lowly but intransigent Mailer about the boon LB was bestowing on him by potentially offering him an option contract. Angus wrote to Norman too and got a good argument back. Then our president, McIntyre, came into the picture and refused to publish unless the language got cleaned up.

Stalemate. I said it would be a terrible mistake not to take Norman's book, and that I'd bear the brunt of the work, and so on. Finally the decision was made to let it stand or fall on the say-so of one outside authority whom I would agree to. Names were bandied about; Howard Mumford Jones was suggested, and I said no—for a feminist reason. He'd wanted me to become his literary assistant, and I was told that he really just wanted to screw pretty girls. I'd had him in one course at Radcliffe and I thought he doddered. Then someone mentioned Benny DeVoto, and I leaped at that for two reasons: one, Angus or someone had said he was one of the foulest-mouthed men in town, and two, my brother had studied with him at Harvard and had a high regard for him as a litterateur. So they gave him *The Naked and the Dead*, and a week later he produced the document that I still have. It's seven or eight pages long and begins: "All other considerations which this book presents are subsidiary to the problem posed by the profanity and obscenity of its dialogue. In my opinion it is barely publishable..."

It was a brilliant exegesis and dead right, but of course it was all wrong. I was felled by the voice of the god and wrote to Norman urging him to purge his manuscript of excessive profanity and consider our option contract and the munificent $300 advance. Meanwhile, though, Norman had done the unthinkable and taken the book to another publisher. He was tired of the time we were taking, but he was also angry at the discourse of Little, Brown. He could go from one minute being supplicant and humble and shy to the next minute provoking a fight because his ego was insulted. In any case he got a much better deal from Rinehart—a $1250 advance instead of $300.

At Little, Brown there was a sigh of relief. He didn't have to be dealt with. I didn't have to be dealt with. There was also the suggestion, very Boston, "If we don't have it, it isn't worth having."

The last item in my bowdlerized Little, Brown file is a note I wrote to Angus

Cameron, dated November 14, 1946. Two weeks earlier I had turned twenty-one, earned my first hangover, and realized I was disenchanted with the glamour of publishing. Now I typed, "I received a letter today from Norman Mailer, informing me that he has a contract with Rinehart for *The Naked and the Dead* with a $1250 advance. He stresses the point that they took only a week and it was read by only two people."

The rest is somebody else's story.

NORMAN ROSTEN   After our initial meeting we hadn't sought each other out. But Norman was staying at his mother's, so we'd bump into each other on the street. He was warm and pleasant but a little cryptic in the sense that he wasn't the kind of guy who'd ask, "What are you doing? What are your problems? How's your work?"

One afternoon I ran into him at the corner of Remsen and Henry, and he told me he was having trouble. He explained about Little, Brown and the problem of language, and he said he wanted to show the book elsewhere. That's when I said, opening my big mouth, "Hey, I know a publisher, a top editor at Rinehart." Rinehart had published a book of mine, so he jumped on it and said, "Can we go up there?"

Now, at the time he saw me as a professional; I was living comfortably, and the fact that I knew this editor, Ted Amussen, must've looked like a powerful entree. It's possible that he already knew Amussen, but I must've made a phone call to him, because what I remember vividly is getting on the subway with Norman and then walking into Ted's office. Ted liked the book immediately, and within two days Norman called to tell me they wanted to do it but that there was still a problem with language, a serious problem that could threaten publication.

NORMAN MAILER   I had met Amussen when I was at Harvard, and he'd read my first novel, *No Percentage*. Ted was always very enthusiastic, and with *The Naked and the Dead* I remember he said, "Norman, I really want to see this book"—very positive and dramatic—to which I replied, "Well, Ted, you know I do have this offer of an option contract from Little, Brown." They were offering $250 or $500, my recollection being $250, but at any rate when the book was done they'd then decide whether they wanted it, which I thought was dreadful. I realized I'd be writing in a state of anxiety, never knowing if they'd take it in the end, so I said to Ted, "It's gotta be accepted as is." He said, "Oh, sure, we'll go on that basis." I said, "All right, I want a real contract." He said, "That too." So then they read it and said yes in about a week. But if I hadn't run into Rosten that day on the street, I don't think I would've gone back to Amussen.

Little, Brown hadn't rejected the book. They'd come forward with an option contract. Originally Angus Cameron had wanted to give me a straight contract because he was a gentleman. He wanted to give me the fairest treatment he could. In fact, if he had come back with an option contract when they'd first said they wanted to do it, I'd have seized it. But Angus was too decent for that. He wanted a face-off with Little, Brown from the word go—would they do the book or wouldn't they? So then the firm went through the bends over the book's so-called obscenity. They gave it to DeVoto, who confirmed the opinion that many people held of him privately, which was that he was a consummate ass. He wrote back a letter saying, "Why doesn't this young fellow rewrite this book with a grander, more noble, more exalted conception? Why all this silly obscenity?" This was after a prelude where he had gone on about how "I swear, my wife swears... But... !"

CHARLES REMBAR   While he was writing *The Naked and the Dead*, Norman fed me pieces of the manuscript. In the original the opening sentence was "Nobody could sleep on the night before the invasion of Anopopei." It sounded clumsy to me, like the lead sentence in a newspaper story that tries to get in a lot of information all at once. It seemed to me awkward and ineffective. (Of all his books, only *The Naked and the Dead* has had universal applause, but in my opinion Norman became a better writer later on.) "What would you do?" Norman wanted to know. "How about starting," I said, "with 'Nobody could sleep.' It's a nice short sentence, and then you can go on and tell what they were about to do and why they couldn't sleep." We had this conversation in an Italian restaurant on Mulberry Street, behind the New York Supreme Court building, where I was working as a law secretary to a New York Supreme Court judge. It was an excellent restaurant named Antica Roma (which came to be called, affectionately, "Old Stink").

The Naked and the Dead had a language problem, one that wouldn't exist today and that would indeed seem incredible to anyone who reached the age of reading after the *Lady Chatterley* case was decided. World War Two soldiers used the words "fuck" and "fuckin'" a lot—verb, noun, adjective, adverb. ("I don't fuck with no fuckin' USO.") Norman was writing about the war, writing the dialogue of soldiers. The book was published in 1948, the same year that the Supreme Court affirmed a criminal conviction of Doubleday for publishing Edmund Wilson's *Memoirs of Hecate County*. The *Ulysses* case had not had much effect on the law; after it was decided, two Boston booksellers were convicted of crime for selling Dreiser's *An American Tragedy*. It's hard now to recall, after the decisions of *Lady Chatterley*, *Tropic of Cancer*, and *Fanny Hill*—or, if you're younger, to imagine—how things were for authors before those cases were decided. There was a real possibility that *The Naked and the Dead* would be kept out of the mails or barred from shipment across state lines, or that the author and publisher would be prosecuted. Norman and I talked about it, and the words "fug" and "fuggin'" came into being. I'm not sure which of us produced it. Each thinks he did, generously accepting the blame. But, considering the time, it was not too bad a solution. Pretty safe from a legal point of view and not bad phonetically; GIs often gave the words a guttural sound, somewhere between *ck* and *g*.

NORMAN MAILER   Once and for all this has to be cleared up forever: I never used the word "fuck" in *The Naked and the Dead*. It was "fug" from the beginning. Adeline knows that—the original manuscript had "fug," *f-u-g*. Absolutely. Nobody could print "fuck" at that point, and I never considered it. I used to rationalize it to myself, right from the word go, saying to myself, "They didn't really say 'fuck' in the army, they say 'fug.' Even if I could use 'fuck,' I wouldn't. 'Fug' works better. It's closer to the deadness of the word the way we used to use it, 'Pass the fuggin' bread.'" So "fug" was it from the beginning. If I had used "fuck," it would've been hopeless. The story that's been around forever is that they broke my balls on it. It's not true. My balls, if you will, were broken before I began the book. So were everyone else's in the publishing world.

Now, I might have had a conversation with Cy at one point very early in the writing where I said to him, "Hey, listen, I wish I could use the word 'fuck.'" I might've swung back and forth, testing it, and he might've said, contemplating the problems, "'Fug' is better." And maybe at that point I said, "Gee, thanks, Cy, I agree with you." So he may have thought he changed my mind. It's not so, though.

NORMAN ROSTEN   After a while I introduced Norman to Charlie Devlin. Oh God, a strange man! Devlin had heard me speak someplace, knew I was a writer, and had attached himself to us. He was very much a loner, very isolated. He was a mooch but had definite talent and wanted me to read the novel he was writing. He was a lapsed Catholic and wrote domestic fiction, stuff about the poverty and infighting of families, very Farrellesque, none of which was ever published. I know Mailer was attracted to him, to his critical capacities. He was a very bright guy, well read on his own. He could be mean, but he really got at the thing of the writing, and that's why Norman asked him to go over the manuscript of *The Naked and the Dead,* to suggest cuts or whatever.

Devlin was the kind of guy who would read your work and say, "I think the whole thing's gotta be redone." He'd say it very quietly, and I once rewrote an entire play because he told me he didn't like it. He could look at you and say something very cruel, very destructive. Still, he was a writer, not a faker, and at the time Norman may have been exhausted.

The way they met, though, is exactly the way Norman described it in *Barbary Shore.* Devlin had gotten me a room at 20 Remsen Street, where he lived, and in the summer of '47 Norman mentioned to me that he needed a place to write. I was going away for the summer and suggested he take over my room. So we trudged up—it was an attic area, three flights up. He said, "Jesus, this is great," because it wasn't far from his folks' place. That's when I must've introduced him to Devlin. The timing was right, because Mailer finished the manuscript in September. He must have had to cut the book over the summer and realized that Charlie was not only a good editor but was looking for work.

He never told me he'd hired Devlin; Charlie mentioned it. Norman was determined to get his book published, and beyond that to make it as good as possible. Don't forget, he wasn't a famous writer yet. Maybe he showed Devlin some of the manuscript, Devlin suggested things to cut, and Norman felt he was in control of it the way an editor can be and a writer can't. Devlin must have made him feel that he knew what he was talking about, telling him where the book was too long or repetitive or clumsy. Norman's never been averse to criticism. He's a professional, and he must have trusted Charlie to let him have a crack at it.

RHODA LAZARE WOLF   My impression was that Charlie was a writer, or wanted to be a writer, and that he lived in that famous rooming house. I can still see Charlie so clearly: He was Irish, he sat in a wing chair in the living room and talked in a funny little voice. He had a slightly nasal New York accent, and I felt he was poor as could be, as poor as a church mouse, and that maybe he did hack work to get money. He was about five feet nine, skinny, wiry, with very piercing blue eyes and wispy, sandy-colored hair. He wasn't a tough Irishman; he was a sedentary type, not at all athletic. Norman would introduce him in a way that let you know that he thought he was pretty special.

DON CARPENTER   I met Charlie Devlin much later in San Francisco when Norman suggested we get together. That's where I became aware of his having edited *The Naked and the Dead*.

My then wife and I went to dinner at his place in Pacific Heights. He showed me his copy of the book—it was the most tattered thing I'd seen in my life. He must have read it ten thousand times, and it was signed. For me the problem was that here was an older guy, and this young kid had come along needing help with his book, but meanwhile Charlie himself couldn't get published. His devotion to Norman was so great that it was almost pathetic. He could've taken the easy route and been anti-Mailer, but he did the other thing, which was more heartbreaking, saying, "Mailer has greatness and I don't. I don't have the talent." Charlie loved writing and would very much have loved to be published. In those days there was still a memory of the attitude toward writers which is now dead: that it is an honorable profession somehow connected with leftist causes and straightening out the human race. That if you're a writer, you're a fighter in the trenches. And Charlie had a lot of that in him.

But he never published anything, even though I believe what Norman says about him being the greatest editor he ever had. Devlin agreed too. He talked at great length about going over *The Naked and the Dead*. But I don't know at what point Norman brought him in. I never had the guts to ask.

NORMAN MAILER   Devlin didn't do any rewriting. He edited it for about four weeks, intensively, about fifty hours a week. He showed me cuts all over the place. We'd go over it. In those days I learned very quickly, so he'd be starting to give a long, detailed, highly sardonic description of why something was wrong, and I'd say, "I got it. I agree." He didn't have to tell me more than two or three times, "Don't use 'very's'"s before I was running ahead of him cutting out "very's." He could be abrupt, sometimes cruel in his criticism because he had a thoroughgoing, ongoing, viable philosophy that he wrapped about himself. There was never anything wanton in what Charlie would do, other than that this philosophy had some very cruel edges. So you'd get cut up, because he was like a lawn mower. He'd cut through, cut a swath with his thinking, and he was a very powerful thinker in his way.

FANNY SCHNEIDER MAILER   Of Barney's family the only one that was a big success was Louie, who made a fortune in the stock market. When Norman was bar mitzvahed he had sent a check of five hundred dollars, which was a lot of money in those days. Then he came here on a business visit. We were all in a restaurant on the East Side, and he pulled out two checks, a thousand dollars each for Norman and Barbara. Norman pushed it aside, saying, "Uncle Louis, I can't take this. I thank you, but I can't take it because it'll make me weak and I'd always come running to you for money, and I don't want to do that." I was flabbergasted. I was hoping he'd take it.

This was in the spring, right after Barbara's graduation, and she took the thousand dollars. It was a graduation present, and she went to Europe on it. But Norman returned the check and I was dumbfounded. I thought to myself, You can take it and put it in the bank to have. But I didn't say a word. I figured, It's his life—if he wants to begin it that way, I honor it.

BARBARA MAILER WASSERMAN   I gave a New Year's party at Pierrepont Street at the end of 1946. Norman was there, so was Alison Lurie, who was a classmate of mine, with William Gaddis; in other words, it was a writers' party. I remember Alison saying afterward how she was surprised because Norman seemed happy, whereas all the other writers she knew were intense and depressed. To all of us, of course, Norman was already a success since he had the contract from Rinehart. The fact that he was going to publish a book seemed to me at the time both miraculous *and* totally expected.

The book was finished in September '47, and after turning in the manuscript he and Bea left for Paris, where he said he was going to study at the Sorbonne on the GI Bill.

ALICE ADAMS   Mark Linenthal, my then husband, and I were living in the Place d'Italie, a working-class neighborhood on the Left Bank but fairly far from the Sorbonne. We had come back to Paris after Salzburg since Mark was Alfred Kazin's assistant the first year of Harvard's Salzburg seminar, and one afternoon he came home from registering for classes and brought Norman and Bea. Of course I'd heard about Norman from Barbara Mailer, whom I'd known slightly at Radcliffe—there was a lot of talk about her wonderful brother—and Mark too had talked about him in the year that we'd been married. I was very much looking forward to meeting him, although I think Mark was surprised to have run into him.

I think I'd actually met Bea before when she'd come to visit Mark in Cambridge at his parents'. I have some memory of her saying words like "shit" and "fuck," because the Linenthals were annoyed and it was awkward.

I met Bea's parents only after Paris. We went to their house in Chelsea, one of those lower-class places you're not supposed to live in. The Linenthals had moved to Cambridge from Roxbury, so you can imagine their snobbery toward Jews from bad neighborhoods. Mrs. Silverman was fat and rather noisy and awfully nice to me, as opposed to Mark's mother, and I liked her. I don't remember Mr. Silverman at all. We went out there for Bea's younger sister's wedding, which was the only Jewish wedding I'd been to.

When I first met Norman in Paris, they were staying at a hotel. Then they found an apartment on Rue Bréa. I don't really remember what it looked like, though. The rooms were small. I can visualize a party there, and I know it was very crowded. But still, to have an apartment in those days seemed so remarkable.

I do remember that they brought along the chambermaid from the hotel to be their maid, which they were quite apologetic about. Norman said, "Of course I wouldn't let Bea have a maid if I didn't know she could handle it all herself." In effect, he wasn't going to let her have a maid unless he knew she was a competent housewife. Even then he was very strong on his notion of "women's work." I don't know what she was like as a housekeeper since I wasn't too keen on housekeeping myself, but I do remember that she was a very good cook.

I didn't find her shrill or nagging. That's revisionary, for people to describe her that way. It was my view that she and Norman were enormously fond of each other. She was a fairly "liberated" woman, but even so she once described herself as a *natansika*—Yiddish for "someone who dances behind." The stuff of their relationship, I think, was sex. She wasn't beautiful, really, but she was very pretty. She used a lot of so-called dirty words, but in a programmatic way, and it was part of their act. Norman, in fact, told us that when they were going together as undergraduates Norman would say something, then it was a competition, back and forth. She also talked about being in the WACS or WAVES in Vermont, and she talked about masturbating—that being apart from Norman made her so frustrated. People didn't talk that way then; it seemed a little exhibitionistic.

I met Mrs. Mailer when she came over to France with Barbara. She used to translate Yiddish for me. I was usually the only gentile in the room, and they were all speaking Yiddish, partly to tease me, and there was a great deal of that that year. Mark and Norman used to trade stories about their mothers—who'd got the worst Jewish mother. Mark's mother was Russian, incredibly stupid and selfish, selfish in that it never occurred to her not to say something that came into her mind. She was monstrously ugly, and it's not good for a person's character to be that ugly. She was a horror, with none of Fan Mailer's redeeming qualities. In the course of our conversations about mothers Norman told us how Fan broke up Barbara and Jack Maher—the fake heart attack. But Mark had his own joke. Before he even thought of marrying me, his mother had said, "If you marry that girl, I'll die." And that's why he married me—hoping for her death.

When I saw Barbara in Paris she seemed rather subdued. Both Norman and Bea were so much noisier and more flamboyant, but Bea seemed very fond of her. I thought they were good friends, and I felt a certain envy for that sort of sisterliness, although in those days I envied all Jews for being Jewish.

We saw Norman and Bea almost every day. We'd sit around, have coffee together at places like the Café Flore or at their apartment. For a while Mark and I lived on the Right Bank, Rue de Courcelles, cent soixante-dix-neuf, and I remember Bea and Norman came to a party there. Ken Lynn, the history professor, came too, also Kingsley Ervin, both of whom had been at the Salzburg seminar. There was also a guy named Nick Arnold, real name Rhodes Arnold, who was a friend of Kingsley Ervin. He was a Virginian, and as it turned out, a distant cousin of mine—all southerners are really kin. He was exceptionally good-looking, and he was married to a beautiful Corsican girl named Lucette.

Mark and Norman were both going to a class at the Sorbonne, a wonderful thing called "Cours de la Civilisation Française," which was really a GI Bill special. I was writing. It's a little harder to say what Bea was doing . . . In effect being a housewife, being Norman's wife, and happily. That's my impression— they both seemed extremely happy. But I was already beginning not to be happy, so I may quite easily have overestimated what was going on with them.

Norman was interested in learning the language, and his French became quite good. Bea's was better, and her accent became extraordinary. It was amazing and funny that her character changed completely when she spoke French: she became elegant and rather haughty, less proletarian, whereas in English she made a point of being vulgar. She had a rather literal mind and she was very, very doctrinaire.

I also think Norman had already started the book that later became *Barbary Shore*, because he talked a lot about his friend Charlie Devlin, whom I didn't actually meet until 1950 in Provincetown—although in Paris we knew Jill Mangraviti, who later married him. He also started something about Carmel, reading us a few pages about everything in California being pink. I was dazzled, knocked out by his extraordinary talent.

All in all, it was very loose, a very unstructured social life. We were all broke, living on the GI Bill, though Norman and Bea had more money than we did, perhaps because he'd already had an advance for *The Naked and the Dead*.

The other people I remember were Stanley and Eileen Geist. They were quite snobbish about Norman and Bea at first and thought they were rather lower class, which they later lived to regret. Stanley was bizarre, a strange guy. I don't know what their source of money was, but they seemed to have much more than the rest of us; they were renting an expensive apartment on the Right Bank. Stanley was going to be a great critic, everyone assumed. He had very snotty things to say about *The Naked and the Dead* when he first read it. In effect, crudely rendered, he said: "If I felt like taking the trouble to recount that sort of minute experience, it would be quite easy to do." It was general snottiness, and my impression—which could be cruel and unfair—is that the Geists didn't come around until it was apparent that Norman was going to be a great success.

Unlike the rest of us, though, they definitely had a purpose in Europe. They were intellectual star-fuckers. They were very, very consciously meeting postwar European writers, and so it was through the Geists that Norman met Jean Malaquais at Harold Kaplan's. Kaplan was the Paris correspondent for *Partisan*

CARTE DE SÉJOUR DE
RÉSIDENT TEMPORAIRE

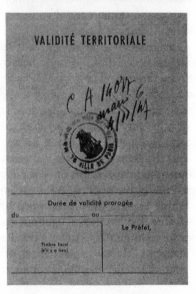

"We'd sit around the Left Bank and talk about books. He was reading
Stendhal and measuring himself against the great writers, reading furiously,
essentially on vacation after making the final changes on The Naked and the
Dead."

Review, had a wonderful apartment in Montparnasse, and knew a lot of people.
The Geists knew *him*, and he served as their great stepping-stone.

MARK LINENTHAL   Norman and Bea weren't poor and struggling. They'd saved
money during the war, and Norman, I know, had a book allowance on the GI
Bill, and he'd often sell the books—I think at Shakespeare and Company. A lot
of people did that as a way of supplementing their income.

His parents were welcoming. I didn't find them suspicious, and I remember
feeling that it was warm and very *en famille*, though they weren't totally approving
of Bea, which surprised me. Either Norman or my then wife Alice explained it
as an instance of a deliberate strategy on his part: he used to pick on Bea, rag

her in his parents' presence so that they would fly to her defense. And that's how he recommended her to them—invertedly, as it were.

The two of them were living in Montparnasse, a little furnished apartment—a bourgeois apartment, not a bohemian pad. Bea, contrary to what a lot of people thought, was not a bohemian. She just said outrageous things, much as she had at Harvard. What sticks in my mind was a party they had. We were just leaving, and there was another couple, whose name I don't remember—non-Jewish, rather austere, a southern boy writer who never showed anybody his work—and Bea, who was sloshed, came out of the bedroom holding up this diaphragm, saying, "This isn't mine, I can't get it in my pussy." Now that's a little girl, the kind of stuff that Norman would respond to by saying, "Oh, Bea." It was an arbitrary moment, a joke, not something the scene called for, and she wasn't trying to grab center stage or compete with him. She was just being outrageous, and he'd benignly disapprove.

That southern guy, though, was the kind Norman was often drawn to and overestimated, I think, simply because he was not available. I remember he once said to me, "The *goyim* know how to live." We were attending lectures at the Sorbonne and there were all these Smith girls in the balcony, these pristine blond *shiksas*, and I remember him commenting.

At other times, though, we'd sit around the Left Bank and talk about books. He was reading Stendhal, and I always had the sense of his measuring himself against the great writers. He was reading furiously, essentially on vacation after making the final changes on *The Naked and the Dead*, and I don't have much of a sense of his working, not there, not then.

I think I was at the Geists' when he met Malaquais. It was already winter. I was aware that Norman sought out mentors, but I was surprised that Malaquais became so important, since I don't remember their first meeting as all that momentous. Malaquais was offbeat, of stature but known only to the cognoscenti. He was an intellectual, Norman an activist, and then when Norman really got into Marxism it was a drag. It made conversation impossible. Alice and I thought, Oh, fuck this, it's dreadful. Again, it was his tumbling to authority, to Malaquais and politics.

JEAN MALAQUAIS   Eileen Finletter and Stanley Geist were married then, and they introduced us at their small apartment on Avenue Gabriel on the Right Bank. My former wife, Galy, a painter, was there; so was Boris Souvarine, one of the fathers of the French Communist party, who broke with Stalin in '24 and published, in 1935, a classic historical survey of Bolshevism in which he cut the Georgian down to size. Immediately Norman and I started talking politics. He was in the Wallace movement, what you might call a fellow traveler—naïve, a kind of Boy Scout intellectually and politically, a "liberal with muscles," to use Dwight Macdonald's expression.

That winter I saw him maybe a dozen times. One afternoon Bea, Norman, Galy, and I went to the Barnum and Bailey circus. Because the show, booming simultaneously over three rings, distracted our attention, we started discussing politics there and then. I said that in my opinion the Wallace movement was more or less infiltrated by the Stalinists, often by proxy, using people like himself, and that in the last analysis there would be no difference between a Truman and Wallace administration except one of style. He reacted as if I were talking gibberish.

We'd meet at cafés or at my place, and our discussions were theoretical— about labor, socialism, the idea of a classless society. We never talked war, concentration camps, being Jewish, art, or literature. Politics and political economy was our fare. He seemed eager, touching, romantic. Also—how do you say?—uncouth? His manners were those of a young Brooklyn boy, not eccentric, not bohemian, with fuzzy notions and no culture, as far as I was concerned. Even then he had this talent for expatiating about philosophers he didn't have the vaguest understanding of, like Kierkegaard, whose work he knows only secondhand. He couldn't speak French, either. He would coin a French sentence, then mimic himself. I did like him.

EILEEN FINLETTER   He spoke quickly, just the way he does today, full of ideas, very excitable. His head looked the same too, with his cute ears. He was very slim, slight, but not in any way frail, because he always gave the impression of being alive and filled with energy. When we introduced him to Jean there was an immediate symbiosis: Malaquais was attracted by Norman's energy, what he thought of as his talent, and Norman was fascinated by Malaquais and his Trotskyism.

KINGSLEY ERVIN   I had been involved in helping to organize the first International Seminar in Salzburg, and Norman gave me the galleys of *The Naked and the Dead* early on in Paris. It staggered me. It was clear he'd produced the thing he wanted to, and if it wasn't *the* Great American Novel, then damned close. I was excited, delighted he'd done it, and thinking back to the way he'd been in Cambridge, I know that I wasn't really surprised.

MARK LINENTHAL   Norman's toughness was still at work, but this was Paris, not Harvard. Harvard had been something to measure himself against; Paris was different. He wasn't beleaguered in France, France was where writers go.

His mood was exhilaration when the book was about to be published. But he was infuriated by the prepub ads, which read: "My name is Croft. I'm one of *The Naked and the Dead* and you can meet me on ———," giving the publication date. He wrote to Rinehart about it, sending back a parody: "My name is so-and-so. I'll fuck you, I'll embrace you on such and such a date." His feeling was that the ads were cheap with their undercover sexual come-on, and I recall his asking me as a literary person, "If you saw that ad, would you read the book?" He wanted classy readers. He resented the pandering.

Then I read the book in galleys and it blew me away. Alice too, and we talked to him about it. I was reading Stendhal for the first time, and that's why I said, "This is better than *The Red and the Black*." I thought there was probably too much Dos Passos in it, but so what? Norman was proud, self-congratulatory but not unpleasantly so. He felt that after all the dedication, the seriousness and embattled work, this was the natural result, and if people were impressed, well, why not? It was a self-affirming, self-confident thing, which was why he was so angry at the ads.

ALICE ADAMS We'd all read *The Naked and the Dead* in galleys. I'm sure of this, because when we took our trip to Mont-Saint-Michel we were already playing a game called "The Naked and the Dead." Bea was usually Wilson, and Norman always wanted to be Croft.

MARK LINENTHAL We took the trip, Norman and Bea, Alice and I—and Barbara too, I think—in the Citroen or Simca they had. Norman did all the driving, Alice and I were in the back, and we caught crabs. It had to have been from the car because it was the only place we'd been. Also because it had mohair seats, something like that.

We stayed at a hotel in Mont-Saint-Michel, walked around, and ate omelets. I remember Norman was flush with success, and he was doing a southern accent. We stopped in Normandy along the way and went out on the rocks, where we played "The Naked and the Dead," acting out specific scenes, but what I remember most is that Norman, doing Croft, was running around yelling, bullying. It was all in jest, but it gave him the chance to be a southern son of a bitch.

JEAN MALAQUAIS Bea was an ideologue, and even though her ideas were really the same as Norman's, she spoke as a self-appointed proletarian. She was sharp, had a more mechanical approach, and threw around terms like "working class" and "lumpen," and she was also rather strident. A couple of years later she and I translated a hundred-page paper entitled "Socialism or Barbary?" I've wondered if that was the source for Norman's title *Barbary Shore*, because my guess is that he was already working on his second novel.

EILEEN FINLETTER She would go on and on with a lot of proletarian rhetoric, and I remember her in the subway once screaming, "Oh, you're all a bunch of capitalist shits," with Norman standing there rolling his eyes, just giving her a shrug. He often looked like a henpecked husband, and she was yelling all the time. She had no imagination, no class, just one idea in her mind, and what I remember most clearly is her going on and on about communism. She'd read the literature, but she was boring, and she must have bored the hell out of him too.

FANNY SCHNEIDER MAILER Barbara and I had gone to Paris in 1948, in April, I think. Barney was going to meet us there from Poland, where he'd been working. On the boat I met Mrs. Probst and we had a nice time together. I'm not very quick on making close relationships, but I saw she was a very nice woman, and she told me somebody else on the boat had a copy of Norman's book. So I said,

"Oh, it's the publisher's wife." I'd already found out she was on board, but I didn't plan to speak to her. I respected her position. But we got to know each other through Mrs. Probst, who told Mrs. Rinehart I was Norman's mother. We still didn't discuss the book. Maybe I was a little shy, like I might say something I wasn't supposed to.

BARBARA PROBST SOLOMON   I was with my mother on the *United States*, traveling first class, and shortly after leaving New York I noticed that at the next table there was another mother with a daughter my age, also named Barbara. Naturally we started to talk. I was eighteen; Barbara, I think, twenty. She'd just graduated from Radcliffe; I was a year out of Dalton. She was going to Europe for a vacation, and unlike myself, she wasn't planning to stay. Her father had gone over two months before as an accountant for a Jewish relief agency in Poland, and they were going to join him in Paris, where they'd taken an apartment. Her brother, Norman, was there too with his wife.

Soon we began to make connections. My brother had gone to Harvard, where he was a close friend of Mark and Alice Linenthal. Mrs. Mailer explained that Norman was a writer and that she was carrying with her a prepublication copy of his first novel. She insisted my mother read it, saying, "He's a genius," which she kept repeating, and I remember responding sarcastically, "Sure, another Jewish boy who's going to be a great American writer."

The amazing part was that a day or two later my mother was up on deck reading the book when a stranger, another woman, stopped and asked her how she came to have the galleys. My mother explained, adding, "It's a brilliant book," and the woman said, "I know. My husband is publishing it." The woman was Mrs. Stanley Rinehart. My mother took her over to meet Mrs. Mailer.

In due course the boat arrived in Cherbourg. Norman and Bea were there to meet Barbara and Fanny, and what struck me was how close they were, that it seemed a wonderful marriage. You could see this right away, there at the dock. My mother and I were met by a limousine arranged by my father, so we all had to split up, but we exchanged addresses and agreed to get in touch with one another.

Norman and Bea lived in Montparnasse, and by now it had sunk in that he was a novelist, and I felt shy. Part of it was that my older brother had been at Harvard with him, in Signet, but Bea may have intimidated me too. I was also struck by how many people were there. Norman had already surrounded himself with a vivacious group of Europeans (remember, this was before the book came out), and a lot of them were Spanish politicos. He introduced Barbara and me to Odette and Robert, one of the last people to be in the Maquis, and also to Enrique Cruz Salido, a kid whose father was a well-known Spanish Socialist. It was through Enrique that Norman had met Paco Benet. Paco had gone to Barcelona with the Linenthals and the Mailers, not only to meet people but to help arrange prison escapes. Norman wasn't politically sophisticated, but everybody was taking the Spanish Civil War to heart—everybody, that is, except the extreme right. As for the Linenthals, of all the people around they were probably

*Barbara Probst Solomon,
Paris, 1948*

the closest to Norman and Bea. Norman and Mark, who'd been on *The Advocate* together, had worked it all out: Mark was going to be the critic, the new Edmund Wilson; Norman, the new Hemingway.

But Bea was very much part of the family in a way that I don't think any wife has been since. She was the *macher*. You know how Fanny kind of pushes the family together? Well, Bea was like that too. She was strong. It wasn't Norman and his little wife, it was Norman and *Bea*. And in Paris Bea was far more intimidating than he was. When you were introduced, you felt you were being introduced to both of them, a definite twosome, and I've never seen Norman with any of his wives act so "couple-y" again.

She was committed to Norman but also overbearing, and she would argue. She was competitive because at that point she'd decided she wanted equal time. Alice Linenthal, now Alice Adams, the writer, was the sexy, smart southern girl up north at Radcliffe; Bea was the quarterback. Physically she had good features, but it was her style—"I'm the butcher's daughter, the smartest girl on the block"— which, by comparison, made Norman into the spoiled boy. She'd come out with lines like "Tough shit, Norman" or "Don't be ridiculous," and as a result she didn't leave him much room to be unconventional. Her goal was to put him in his place, to puncture any pretense, and it was almost like she was his conscience.

She could also be very scary and come on like a commissar, taking the line that she was the true-blue Henry Wallace Progressive. She wanted everybody to know she was tough. She'd wear black turtleneck sweaters and skirts that didn't fit well, like some of those Communist girls who made themselves look awful in order to confirm their political commitments.

FANNY SCHNEIDER MAILER   That was a miserable time when they were in Paris because Bea is the world's worst housekeeper. I didn't see her competitiveness, because Norman hadn't reached fame yet, but it was still there, and later she became impossible.

We had a lovely apartment near the Trocadéro, an elevated apartment which Norman and Bea had found for us. But they wouldn't have lived there—Bea would never take an apartment like that, never. She needed *dreck*. It was always mishmash, and I would have them over for a meal as often as they could come, because she never planned for anything. I don't say she had to clean their apartment herself, but she could have afforded to bring in help if she'd wanted.

For me Paris was like a big vacation. I'd been working for the past fifteen years. Barbara had her friend, Barbara Probst, so I didn't interfere much. I didn't have to hold her hand, and I didn't monopolize Norman's time either.

NORMAN MAILER   Barbara, Bea, and I were having dinner with my parents one night and my father was complaining about my dirty language at the dinner table. Next day when we were alone, my mother asked me to stop. I agreed if, just once, she would use the words herself, literally tell my father to fuck himself. At the table that evening I kept it up until I heard her sort of whisper, "Barney, go fuck yourself." But I knew my father hadn't heard her, so I said, "That's not good enough," and let out another string of profanity. My father looked at me and then turned to my mother: "Fan, I think the boy's lost his mind." That's when she shouted at him, *"Barney, go fuck yourself!"* He couldn't believe it. He blinked his eyes. "Why, Fan!" he said in a mild little voice. My sister and I howled like demons.

BARBARA MAILER WASSERMAN   He loved to swear. We were all back in New York the following winter when Norman bought himself a tape recorder and was playing around with it one day in the Pierrepont Street apartment. My mother was preparing dinner when all of a sudden Norman came into the kitchen and said, "Ma, I have a very important question I want to ask you and I need your considered opinion." And she said, "Yes, dear?" He said, "Which of these five words do you think is the strongest—fuck, piss, cock, shit, or cunt?" My mother went up in smoke. "You promised, you promised!"—just shrieking her head off. Me, I thought to myself, Why does he do these things? And Norman sort of slunk back in the living room with this funny little grin on his face. A moment later he turned on the tape recorder and the whole conversation started coming back at us, including my mother's incredible shrieking. The two of us crept into the kitchen to see what she was doing, and there she was, bent over the sink, doubled over with laughter.

BARBARA PROBST SOLOMON   In Paris, though, Norman and Bea used to go to a place called the Bal Nègre, which I found a little shocking—whether because Bea danced with blacks or whether somebody was naked, I'm not sure. I remember Norman saying to me that he envied my generation's postwar freedom, that we weren't oriented toward marriage. His generation married, he said; they must scream "Fuck you," to be shocking, but they got married, had a proper apartment, three meals, and nice conventional clothes. His unconventional side was to seek out the kids who'd been affected by the war—Odette, Robert, Enrique. He certainly wasn't seeking out the chic French, he was more interested in people like the Spaniards.

MARK LINENTHAL   Alice and I had met these expatriate Spaniards when I was teaching at Salzburg. They were anti-Francoists, expatriates who lived in France but regularly crossed into Spain even though the border was officially closed. They had contacts there, so they gave us names and we went.

We smuggled in propaganda in the spare tire of the car. Norman had gone to Geneva and changed our money into pesetas at a much better rate, and we rolled the money up in tight wads and put them into condoms, which we shoved into the bottom of tubes of toothpaste or shaving cream, thus getting more money into Spain than was allowed. We went because we wanted to see the inside of a fascist country, and Norman, I think, was just as affected by these Spanish politicos as we were. They were in jeopardy when they were in Spain because their families had fought against Franco, some of their friends and families were in prison, and I suppose that's how the later prison break came about, the one involving Norman's sister and Barbara Probst after Norman had gone back to America.

ADELINE LUBELL NAIMAN   What effect the success of *The Naked and the Dead* had on Norman or Bea I didn't know, because they were still in Europe. But here in America, even before publication, it was already clear the book was going to be a best seller. Rinehart did a fantastic advertising job, totally unprecedented. The only real problem was the book's unheard-of price, more than any other novel up until that point. They had the nerve to charge—what was it?—four dollars?—when other books cost two ninety-five.

BARBARA MAILER WASSERMAN   In June we'd left Paris, Norman, Bea, mother, and I. We stopped in Rome and ran into Barbara Solomon, who was staying at the Hassler Hotel with her mother. My mother went back to Paris, and the three of us then drove to Capri, came back along the coast, and stopped at the American Express in Nice. Norman went in for our mail and came out carrying a stack of letters—reviews, notes from friends who'd read the reviews, congratulatory cables. We sat in that hot, stuffy car sweating and reading until Norman suddenly said, "Gee, I'm number one on the best-seller list."

It was totally unreal, a sense of intense pleasure and disbelief that here he'd created all this commotion three thousand miles away.

Later that afternoon we drove to Cap Camarat to meet a friend of Norman's and Bea's who'd taken over a bombed-out villa. That night we slept in sleeping bags. We stayed about three days, then went back to Paris, where everybody had heard about it too. Norman and Bea left for New York in the middle of July, after Norman had given Barbara Solomon and me driving lessons and transferred ownership of his car so we could go to Spain.

NORMAN MAILER I had no intimation at all of what this was going to do to me, no more than if you're told you have to have a serious operation and your first reaction is, of all things, merriment. Then it sinks in step by step over the next sixteen hours, forty-eight hours, the next two weeks. As I remember it, we were all hooting in the car, laughing and making jokes like "What'd I do wrong?" and all that. There was a great excitement to it, but there was also great gloom, yes, because I knew I was going off into uncharted waters and I wondered, how much of an explorer was I?

Before the book had become a success I'd had two feelings about it: while I thought of it as a big book, I wasn't seeing it as a commercial book. I used to go in and bleat to Ted Amussen: "Do you realize that if this book doesn't do reasonably well, I'm going to be reduced to writing historical novels?" I mean, my idea was: Here I am, this wonderfully talented young writer. If you guys don't take care of me properly I'm gonna have to write potboilers, and that'll be a catastrophe.

So I really did have mixed feelings about it. Part of me thought it was possibly the greatest book written since *War and Peace*. In fact, I remember that when Irwin Shaw's *The Young Lions* came out, Leland Hayward, his agent, was trying to overcome *The Naked and the Dead*, which was already out, and he said, "*The Young Lions* is the greatest war novel to come along since *War and Peace*, and it may be that when I reread *War and Peace* I may have to change my mind in favor of *The Young Lions*." And I remember reading his comment and saying to myself, "Jesus Christ, Shaw must feel about *The Young Lions* the way I feel about *The Naked and the Dead!*" On the other hand, I also thought: I don't know anything about writing, I'm virtually an imposter, I've had incredible good luck, I don't belong here. I'm not a literary writer. That's why, later, when Malaquais began translating the book into French and marking the copy to give me lessons on style, I didn't resent it. I knew I was no stylist. I think one of the reasons I became a stylist was precisely because I had so poor a sense of style to begin with.

EILEEN FINLETTER I remember when they came back to Paris, we'd already heard that the book was on the best-seller list. A group of us were in our living room, and at one point Norman said, "I must have done something wrong. Did I hedge on the truth so that they could swallow it? They shouldn't like the book this much, they ought to be angry."

MARK LINENTHAL Norman took Bea and Alice and me to the Tour d'Argent. He was suddenly a famous man and already had some money. A very festive, happy evening, just whoopee—I think it was the first celebration of the book's success. My menu didn't have the price on it, and I saw some *champignon* dish, I forget what it was, but the waiter took a pencil and wrote down on a piece of paper how much it was, to warn me off. Norman, though, wasn't intimidated. The Tour d'Argent can be intimidating, awesome, but I remember he was enjoying the role of Big Daddy.

He and Bea stayed on for a month or so after that. He was looking forward to returning to New York, to his reception there, but also regretted having to leave. Even then that was what was important to him—to be "violent and alone," because that's where the vitality is.

EMMA CLARA "ECEY" GWALTNEY Norman sent us a copy, and Fig was so excited, absolutely thrilled, almost as if it were his own brother who'd written it, like he was naïvely proud of him.

BARBARA PROBST SOLOMON Barney was cast in the role of the conventional Jewish man, and everything was "medium" about him, no razzmatazz, except that he had a lot to say when word came out that *The Naked and the Dead* was a best seller. At dinner one night he had turned to Bea and said, quite unkindly: "You're going to go back to America, Norman's going to be famous, and you're going to have a lot of competition." Bea paled visibly. The handwriting was on the wall—or in Barney's mouth, as it were. He then told her she had to dress better and look more glamorous.

MARJORIE "OSIE" RADIN But instead of basking in Norman's success, Bea was jealous. When they came back from Paris, reporters were waiting for Norman, but she pulled him aside and they went out a back way. She didn't want him to see the reporters or the reporters to see him, which gave him a black eye with the press.

Then another time, after the money started coming in, Bea and Fan went into a store where she was going to buy something, only she wouldn't give her name. She told Fan, "I don't want to be known as Mrs. Norman Mailer." I don't know if she gave her name as Bea Silverman, but that's a real *meshugas*. I mean, why didn't she enjoy his fame and new-found wealth, this new world he was able to enter? Why? Because she didn't want any part of it. The family wasn't giving her any heat, none whatsoever. Everybody was nice to her because she was Norman's wife. Later that summer I asked him, "Norman, how are you enjoying this new fame?" His response? "I love it."

CHARLES REMBAR They came down to visit us in Deal, near Long Branch, where my mother had rented a house for the summer. Norman and I talked, and my rather strong recollection is that he had an extraordinary detachment about his success and celebrity. It's what every young writer wants, dreams of, and it happens very seldom, yet even though it had happened to him he was not overwhelmed by it. He was able to stand aside, to look at it from some distance.

FANNY SCHNEIDER MAILER   When I'd read *The Naked and the Dead* I was very impressed, and I thanked God it's my son, I was so impressed with the greatness of its writing. I might have cringed at a few expressions, but I figure I'm old-fashioned.

I was so elated, so proud, and when one of the friends we had in Paris came to the house to congratulate me—she'd just been to the library or a bookstore—I said, "Well, Norman deserves it. He wrote it."

Barbara and I had come back in September, but Barney had to stay until the end of the year when his work was finished, but because of the book, oh boy, I was wined and dined by the family. The temple, everybody. It was a very, very wonderful event in my life. Unforgettable, as it should be.

Norman did get the freedom to do his writing. Maybe a couple of times before, I said, "Norman, the language—will it be published?" And he would tell me I shouldn't worry. My only concern was it should be a success, because I knew he worked hard on it. Because then he would have money and be a recognized author and go and write other books.

IV: HOLLYWOOD, POLITICS, AND <u>BARBARY SHORE</u> (1948-51)

MAY 1, 1949—LONDON *SUNDAY TIMES* FRONT PAGE EDITORIAL . . . *generally their talk, reported at great length, is incredibly foul and beastly. . . . In our opinion,* The Naked and the Dead *should be withdrawn from publication immediately.*

MAY 8, 1949—LONDON *SUNDAY TIMES* *Response to letters defending* The Naked and the Dead: *. . . it is wholly against the public interest that beastliness should be offered for sale.*

MAY 13, 1949 *Rinehart's sales of* The Naked and the Dead *total 169,000 copies.*

MAY 17, 1949 Newsweek *reports that due to the* Sunday Times *furor in England,* Wingate Press's *"first impression of 10,500 copies of* The Naked and the Dead *has been sold out before reaching bookstores, and 20,000 more copies yet unprinted have been subscribed in advance."*

BARBARA PROBST SOLOMON   When I returned to New York in the fall of '48 Norman said that if he'd known Barbara and I were going to have our great prison-escape adventure he'd have stayed and done it himself. Originally it was Norman, you see, who'd suggested the idea.

When Mark and Alice Linenthal had moved, I took over their room in Paris. The first night I noticed bedbugs, fled, and got locked out. In a panic I went to Barbara's and stayed with her and her parents for about a week. That's when Norman approached me—he and Bea had already decided to go back to New York—and asked if I could drive. I told him I could, so he announced, "You and Barbara will go to Spain to help this friend of Enrique's who's in prison." The idea had come from the Spaniards, who, it turned out, were copying the methods of the Maquis, the French Resistance.

A few days later he took Barbara and me out in his new Citroen to test our driving. It was the first time Norman and I really talked. We went to Chartres, and he was combining his driving instructions with comments about "the most incredible cathedral in the world." He and Mark had already gone to Mont-Saint-Michel, and even if Norman hadn't read Henry Adams—which I don't think he had—Mark would have talked about it, and Norman picks things up viscerally. He didn't just cruise out to Chartres and say, "Here's the car, here's the Revolution." He had to *show* me Chartres.

He forged his driver's license for us, pasting in Barbara's photo, I think, and gave us the car. He and Bea went back to New York, and on August 1 Barbara and I set off for Madrid.

We had planned this crazy scheme to get two guys out, Nicholas Sanchez Albornoz and Manuel la Mananna, and we just waited in the car while the prisoners were being led from prison to a church for Sunday Mass. Our two guys were at the end of the line, as arranged, and they just fell into our car and we drove off. We had to go back by way of Barcelona, and the plan was to leave them off in the mountains, and they'd walk across the border to France, where we'd pick them up on the other side.

The Spanish had guards at four points along the mountain road, and at the first checkpoint they gave us a piece of paper saying four people were in the car. After we passed our third set of guards the two Spanish guys jumped out, leaving Barbara and me to figure out how to get through the last checkpoint with our ticket marked four people. At first we thought we'd try to drive the car right on through, crash-out style; we were young and obviously not thinking clearly, or I suppose we had a grand sense of our immortality. Then we decided to play dumb, like we didn't know any Spanish, just bullshit it. We figured a true American tourist would act outraged, so we stuck to our attitude. Two nice American girls—I mean, somebody would call the President, right? The guy knew something was amiss, but he couldn't figure out what, and finally he had us leave a certain quantity of money with him, which naturally we never saw again.

Once inside France we drove to the little town where we'd arranged to meet the two guys coming out of the mountains. But they didn't show up, so after three days of hanging around and waiting, feeling dreadful that we'd lost them forever, we drove to Perpignan and got in touch with the Spanish Resistance. They told us not to worry, that they'd find them in the mountains, which eventually they did. Barbara and I went back to Paris, and very soon thereafter Barbara went home to New York.

The reason the escape became famous was that it was the first time anyone had been busted out of that prison. But Barbara and I were in on it together every inch of the way; I was no more the heroine than she, even though she downplayed her role. I just decided to make something out of it, to write about it. And after my book came out, Spanish journalists interviewed Norman as a way of introducing my book in Spain, and he stressed that it was both our doing and that he admired us—he used the typical American phrase, stressing our "cool." Of course there's really no equivalent for that in Spanish, so the journalists translated it according to their notion of Hemingway and had him saying, "I thought their balls were well hung." Barbara and I just cracked up.

But only in retrospect did the whole thing take on more aura than it had for us at the time. That was certainly Norman's reaction when Barbara got home to America and told him the story. He saw it as a great adventure, an experience he was sorry he'd missed, and he told her that if he'd known it was going to be such a big deal, he would've stayed in Europe and done it himself.

I don't think he realized, however, that the Spaniards we were helping were definitely the Orwellian, non-Communist contingent, although I doubt that would have made any difference, since he didn't particularly care about the internal splits on the left. Remember, the Spanish had the hearts of everybody except the extreme right, because Spain was the one country that was still left with its fascists after the war. Nonetheless I think Norman had to go back to America when he did, not only because of his book's success but also because he really thought America was the political center of things with Henry Wallace running for President.

ADELINE LUBELL NAIMAN   In July he was going to give a party to celebrate at 49 Remsen Street, his studio. For some reason he had been up at my house in Cambridge a week or so before, and he said he wanted to fix me up with his friend Dan Wolf. I remember he seemed full of that sort of sexual anger he had toward me at that time because I wasn't his, and he socked me, something he's not forgotten either. I was black and blue on my thigh—if I develop cancer, it's his fault—and he said, "Are you coming to the party? The address is very easy to remember—it's *soixante-neuf* minus twenty, Remsen Street." He was always so anxious to be the *enfant terrible*, to shock, *épater la bourgeoisie*.

EMMA CLARA "ECEY" GWALTNEY   In August he and Bea visited us in Fayetteville. We had a little three-room apartment, they were coming for two weeks, and I worried about it being boring for them. As it happened, they were just back from France and didn't care.

Fig and I both thought that Norman was being real careful not to let the success go to his head. If anything, he was eager to prove it wasn't going to affect him. He didn't talk about it. He didn't talk about the money either, and when Fig'd bring it up I think he was embarrassed. We lived across the street from a schoolyard, and there was this boy who was tossing around a football one afternoon. Norman went over there—the fellow was maybe twenty or twenty-one and had no idea who Norman was—and then every day the boy would come by and ask if Norman was around. Fig would say yeah, and Norman would go out and eagerly toss the ball as if he wanted the kid's approval. It was like he was wanting to be one of the boys, wanting to do well. He'd go out there and try so hard, like he was consciously trying to fit in.

We really didn't have anything to do, so we were reading, Bea was drawing some, and we were absolutely loafing, just going to the swimming pool or on picnics some. Or Norman would go stream fishing up in the mountains with Fig and a friend of his. Otherwise we'd play cards or just flop on the couch. They met some of our friends, like Willie and Fletcher Smith. They'd drop over, and Willie would just quietly visit with Norman. One time she dropped by and he was on the couch in his underwear shorts—he'd often sit in his shorts because of the heat—and he started to jump and leave. But she said, "Oh no, it's all right," and paid no attention at all. It didn't bother Willie any. We're used to that, and I think it sorta pleased Norman. It was almost as if he was escaping from all the commotion and attention in New York, like coming back to roots, because Fig had known him before the big success.

Norman and Bea, Brooklyn, 1948: "I really did have mixed feelings about the success of The Naked and the Dead. *Part of me thought it was possibly the greatest book written since* War and Peace. *On the other hand, I also thought, 'I don't know anything about writing, I'm virtually an imposter.'"*

This was a different world, and here Fig was the guide. He was the mentor and Norman the student, learning about the country. For instance, climbing a tree. One time Fig challenged him to climb a tree, saying, "You've probably never climbed a tree, have you?" Norman hadn't, of course, so they went outside, and I thought, Well, that's how men are, they just gotta do that. From the time they're little boys.

Norman also asked questions and made comments about the South. One day, after we'd been driving around and Fig'd pointed out the sheriff, Norman said, "You know, one thing that strikes me are the mean faces. They're scary, hard, unforgiving faces." He meant dangerous, really kind of a tough look, cops who seemed unpredictable. He was puzzled more than anything. How to act with them. He also said, "It's sometimes insulting the way you southerners talk, the way you answer people." The abruptness of the northerner sometimes seems rude to me, I told him so, but he said, "It's a different kind of rudeness. In a way the southerner who says, 'W-e-l-l, I don't know 'bout that,' is a lot more insulting, because it's a kind of an insolent, *slow* arrogance." He claimed you could never tell whether a southerner liked you or not. "You're polite to people you don't like," I remember him saying, and this worried him a little, and it worried him more as the years went by.

At that point, though—this was his first visit to Arkansas—everything was new and interesting, and one night we got into an argument about small-town churches. "There's some validity to this kind of life. It's peaceful, it has a certain stability and standards," he said, but Bea argued with him, and I remember her response: "Norman, they think fucking is a sin." Still, she was mostly deferring to him, trying to put up with this enormous thing that was happening to him. She'd sort of pet him and say, "Are you unhappy? When we get back to New York I'll give you some pleasure." By which she meant sexual pleasure, because we had a little three-room apartment and it was hard to pull out the bed. They were having to restrain themselves and she was being solicitous.

One thing she said to him seemed so strange, though. We were lying by the swimming pool and Norman had his horn-rimmed glasses on. Bea came running up and said, "Oh, Norman, you look like a jerk with your glasses on." He didn't like that, but he sort of deferred to her because he didn't want to create a scene. But she did get a kick out of shocking people down here. One of my friends said to her, "You have such pretty eyes." She said, "What the fuck, you do too." Of course we'd never heard talk like that, it just wasn't allowed. She said the same sort of things when we had a party for them in Fayetteville and invited what university professors we knew. Norman knew I wasn't used to that kind of language, and he went out of his way to be careful about it. But Bea wasn't. Once she had a stomach upset and complained, "My asshole hurts."

Norman was also working on his southern accent. He'd say, "I think I've got it figured out. All you have to do is put 'little ol'' in front of everything—'That little ol' chair, this little ol' plant.'" He'd practice and exaggerate everything. Also, he'd say, "Fig, you could play Croft. You've just got that mean look that says 'Boy, get in here!'" and he'd imitate the way he thought Croft sounded. He never equated Fig with Wilson, it was always Croft, and I'm telling you, sometimes it's amazing we understand each other at all.

The other thing was, Fig and Norman would go out and have beers or play cards. To Norman, Fig was very cool, but one night the two of them had a little set-to over a card game. Norman was playing a lot better than Fig and doing it aggressively, slapping the cards down, playing them fast, and they were snapping at each other. Norman was goading him and saying things like, "What's the matter with you?" Fig said, "Well, you goddamned—" and he stopped himself. It was dramatic, like in a movie. Norman said, "Go ahead and say it, go ahead." And real slow Fig said *"Jew."* Norman replied, "Okay, you needed that, didn't you?" That seemed to satisfy him, as if he had to hear Fig say it. I don't know why, maybe he was testing him. . . . I mean, you could really see this when they'd be drinking. Norman was a jackhammer, *boom, boom, boom.* And Fig'd be more *rrr, rrr, rrr!* It was probing, probing, probing on Norman's part, parrying, parrying, parrying on Fig's.

NORMAN MAILER   In September or October, somewhere in there, the first royalty check came for *The Naked and the Dead* and it was for $40,000, which in 1948 was something like $300,000 today. I walked into the Bankers Trust branch in Brooklyn wearing a combat jacket and scuffed shoes, and I presented the check to a teller, who immediately sent me over to the manager, saying to him only that there was a fellow who wanted to make a deposit. The manager was a stuffed shirt, and we got into this ridiculous conversation. He didn't even look at the check, just said, "Now, wait a moment, you say you bank at Bankers Trust in Manhattan? Which branch, if I may ask?" I said, "Oh, Fifth Avenue, I think Forty-third, Forty-fourth Street—I can't remember." He says, "Who do you bank with there?" I said, "I don't know, whoever takes my money. I go to the window." It went on and on like this, and I'm enjoying it hugely. He still hasn't looked at the check. "Well, who do you know there?" he asks. I said, "Well, it's some Italian fellow, I can't remember his name." "Would it be Mr. DeAngelo?" he asks, and I said, "Yeah, that might be it." So he calls up and says, "Mr. DeAngelo, we have a young fellow here—what's your name?" I said, "Mailer, Norman Mailer," and he says, "A fellow named Norman Mailer is here who says he has an account with you, and he just wants us to deposit a check as a courtesy to him, a check in the amount of . . . forty . . . thousand . . . dollars. Ohhh, oh!" He hangs up and says, "I hear your book is doing well."

CHARLES REMBAR   After the book had become a huge success we were negotiating with Stanley Rinehart about Norman's next book or books. At that time 15 percent was the absolute maximum on royalties. (It still is, except for rare cases.) I suggested that if the book sold more than a hundred thousand copies, the royalties should go to 17½ percent. Rinehart said that this simply wasn't done. I went through some arithmetic with him to show that if that many copies were sold, he would still be making a handsome profit even with the higher royalty. Book prices then, of course, were lower, but manufacturing costs were even lower, compared with the present period. Rinehart thought a bit, then said that it was important for publishers to make some extra money on big-selling books so that they could afford to put out worthwhile books that did not sell many copies and on which the publisher generally took a loss. Norman, who, if he chose, would make an outstanding lawyer, suggested to Rinehart that the extra 2½ percent be put in a trust fund that he would manage and allocate the royalties paid to struggling authors who did good books that publishers hesitated to put out because they might lose money at the normal royalties.

LILLIAN HELLMAN   At some point I took an option on *The Naked and the Dead*. It seemed to me I could make a play of it, so I used my own money, five hundred dollars, which was the usual option money. I dealt with Cy Rembar; I remember meeting him, although I don't remember the dealings very much. There was no thought that Norman and I might work together on it. I couldn't work with anybody. He might have asked for control, but I don't remember. He's always speaking of it, so he may have asked for things, I may have signed them, and there may be existing documents.

I sat down and started the play, and about six or eight weeks into it I realized I couldn't do it. One of the things that stumped me was how I was going to do the flashbacks, also the large number of characters. I don't know if Norman was disappointed. He may have been, but I don't remember any fuss or anxiety from either one of us.

Norman and I dispute the date—but his must be right and mine wrong—when *The Naked and the Dead* galleys were sent to me in Pleasantville, New York—which was how we originally met. Perhaps it was at the very end of '46, because I was writing *Another Part of the Forest*, and I remember putting the play up to read the galleys of his book. I was stunned by its brilliance, thought it was just wonderful, and never having heard of Norman Mailer in my life, I wrote an immediate blurb and sent it to Rinehart. Norman thinks we saw each other when I wanted to take the option. That's not how we met. We met because when he got back and saw my blurb he telephoned to thank me. Then he brought up to Pleasantville one of his two hundred and fifty brides, Beatrice. Hammett was living, and I think they stayed overnight. I do remember Beatrice needed a safety pin for her petticoat because it was hanging below her dress. Nobody can shake me on what I believe I can remember.

At our first meeting he was a very pleasant, interesting young man. I liked him immediately. So did Hammett, whom I had asked to read Norman's book, and he thought it was just as good as I did.

I can't describe how he was "handling" his success and fame at twenty-five because I don't think of people that way. I know how they affect me, and he was a very interesting and charming man who was good company. I know other people will say they think Norman "handled" himself with great immodesty, some people think he "handled" himself with great bravery, and other people think he "handled" himself with great weakness and cowardice. I don't think of people that way; I never thought of how I "handled" myself, in fact.

After our first meeting we saw each other fairly frequently, and one of the times, again in Pleasantville, he brought his sister, Barbara. I remember that because Hammett made a pass at her. Hammett was very, very drunk and not subtle about it. He pulled her down on his lap. He was not a subtle man when he was drinking and trying to make ladies. But Norman was charming about it. I was standing at the front door and I said to him, "I'm deeply sorry if he offended you." Norman said, "He didn't offend me, for God's sake. Who doesn't make passes?" He could easily have been angry or tried to make points, but he was just charming.

JEAN MALAQUAIS   I'd moved from Paris and was teaching at the New School and NYU. Norman sought me out, probably through Dan Wolf, who was a student of mine. He came to my apartment on Montgomery Street in Brooklyn (found for me by Bertram D. Wolfe, the man who wrote *Three Who Made a Revolution*) and suggested that I translate *The Naked and the Dead*. Later he asked me to give him a reading list. One day he brought over someone by the name of Devlin, who spoke as if he were reading me the most hackneyed brochures of the Communist party. We argued for hours. The man was a drudge, and I believe Norman was embarrassed by his bureaucratic bent of mind— nothing but clichés. Devlin, by the way, became McLeod in *Barbary Shore*. In the winter of '48 I visited the Mailers in Jamaica, Vermont—they'd moved up there. I'd agreed to translate *The Naked and the Dead*. The French publisher was going to pay $2000; Norman didn't think that was enough, so he put in another $1000 of his own. His inscription in my copy read: "To Jean and what has been a pleasant relationship until now and will continue, I hope, for years. Norman Mailer, Dec. '48." "Until now...," I'm not sure what that means. Perhaps he was still balking at my analysis of Wallace and the Progressive party.

IRVING HOWE   Malaquais didn't have a very great reputation as an intellectual figure, like André Gide coming to New York, say, and when he arrived on the scene I found him opinionated, cocksure, and dogmatic. I thought it was a joke until I realized it wasn't, but he said there were only two real Marxists left in the world, himself and somebody else in France, and even then he wasn't so sure about the man in France. But I admired his *War Diary*—I reviewed it in a left-wing paper during the war years, his dogmatism notwithstanding.

NORMAN MAILER   At the age of twenty-five I was working for Wallace. There weren't that many celebrities in the campaign, so suddenly I had prominence in those circles. Of course, I didn't know what to do with it. On the other hand, a lot of Progressive party types got behind *The Naked and the Dead* and gave it a tremendous push.

MARJORIE "OSIE" RADIN   Norman first became politically active, I think, when Henry Wallace was running. It was the fall of '48 and he spoke at the Ninety-second Street "Y," and the whole family went to hear him. He was a very poor speaker in those days, sort of faltering, because he was just beginning to speak in public.

We weren't surprised that Norman was on the left. I don't know about Cy, but my mother and I both voted for Wallace. My mother had come full circle. When women had gotten the franchise in '20, I think, she immediately became a Republican county committeewoman, which was an important thing, but after Hoover had served one term the Republican party called a caucus and said they were going to renominate him. My mother stood up and said, "If you nominate Hoover, he will be the last Republican President you will see for years to come." So she was always liberal. I don't know, maybe our side of the family were the progressives.

Then Norman became ultraprogressive. Fan wasn't political, nor was Barney. If anything, Barney was conservative. Which was why, several years later, it was such a joke that he had that security-clearance trouble and Norman and Cy had to come to his defense. But I don't think Norman's swing to the left bothered anybody.

ADELINE LUBELL NAIMAN   It's interesting that quite early on Angus Cameron, the editor at Little, Brown and a left-winger, thought Norman's ideas could be dangerous. This was when Angus was Massachusetts state chairman for the Progressive party and I was the publicity chairman, when all of us were campaigning for Wallace. He thought that Norman, for all his claims to being a radical, was really dangerously on the edge of being fascistic. He saw a kind of mysticism there which could allow him to go either way and which wasn't trustable—since by mysticism I mean the reverse of being a materialist, not being embedded in pragmatic events or cause-and-effect relationships. To be a mystic was to believe dangerously in magic, to go beyond casual relationships, to set up the individual against society as a collective entity.

MICKEY KNOX   In October 1948 Norman came out to Hollywood to speak at a Wallace meeting at Gene Kelly's house, and somebody brought him over to my place in the Valley, near Universal Studios. We hit it off immediately—both of us from Brooklyn, the whole bit. It was social, not political, and we became better friends when he came back out in the spring to work on a screenplay.

He met a lot of people but didn't seem to have too many relationships. He usually wore a shirt and slacks, and even in Hollywood his shoes were mostly undone, the laces untied, and his socks always hung down at his ankles, which was a particular sloppiness that lasted for years. When he was doing a lot of TV in the sixties he was always pulling his socks up, and I'd tell him, "For Christ's sakes, Norm, wear socks over your calf." He wasn't fastidious at all, largely because he didn't care.

He had bags of cachet, though, and was welcomed by the left-wing group out there. Gene Kelly was then married to Betsy Blair, who was actually more left than Gene, and I know the three of them became friends. The Blair-Kelly group included people like Fredric March, John Huston, and Bogart. During the

Wallace election there was an enormous meeting of all the progressives, and while I was under the impression that Norman was a Wallace-ite, he was pretty far left on the spectrum. The two of us, I remember, drove to the meeting together, and on the way over he said, "Let's not talk," meaning, in effect, "I've gotta think about what I'm going to say." He was nervous. The speech was a turning point—he said everything Malaquais had been telling him, which shocked a lot of the people there who were either Communists or fellow travelers. It was the Trotskyite line, Malaquais' notion that both the East and the West were cold warriors and that the Soviets were as monstrous as the West. The horrors of the gulags, Stalinism, the whole thing, but he'd never once before indicated to me how anti-Soviet he'd become. After that a lot of people felt that he was Malaquais' captive, that he was being indoctrinated. He'd been leaning toward communism, but then his politics totally reversed.

SHELLEY WINTERS   When Norman came out, there were two political meetings, the one at Gene Kelly's and then a big rally for Wallace given by the Arts, Sciences and Professions Committee. That's where he met Marilyn Monroe. I know he says he never met her, but he's wrong. I was there, and I'll explain in a minute.

The party at Gene Kelly's was for people to endorse Wallace. Gene was still married to Betsy Blair, and Farley Granger and I went. Farley had done only the Hitchcock picture, and I had done *Double Life*, so we were just starlets. The people there were sort of MGM—Garfield and his wife, also both Hustons, father and son. Mickey Knox too. Burt Lancaster didn't come because of his wife, because he must have known I'd be there.

Norman had come from New York to make an appeal. I thought he was very good-looking, very cute with his big ears, and he didn't seem like a writer to me. Burt had given me *The Naked and the Dead*—he was always trying to educate me—and I read it twice, very slowly, to let it sink in. I thought it was the greatest war novel, and I said to him, "Are you sure you're Norman Mailer?" Because a writer to me was very important and had to look it, and in Hollywood they looked like writers, like Thomas Mann and Brecht, both of whom I'd met.

When Norman spoke he was very arresting, brilliant even. He said we'd won the war but were going to lose the peace unless we turned to Wallace, that unless we built a strong middle class and saw that people had democratic governments we were in trouble. He spoke for an hour, and afterwards he was socializing, mainly with the directors and writers like Harry Brown—I think he already knew him. Everybody had read his book and they were courting him. They wanted him to come and be a screenwriter. He was the East Coast intellectual, and Burt, I know, was very much in awe of him and even then wanted to do *The Naked and the Dead*. But he was nice to all the young actors too. In Hollywood there's a real class system: the actors who make $100,000 a picture won't talk to the ones who make $25,000, and the contract players and the young sexpots are the lowest level—they go to the buffet last. But Norman didn't seem to talk to the big movie stars. He talked to us, the kids.

I was always very nervous around so many stars because I felt inadequate, so Farley and I signed the petition and left. We assumed everybody else would be signing too because they all screamed and gave money. All these years Farley and I wondered why we didn't get into trouble or were never bothered by McCarthy. Then a few years ago I ran into Norman in the Polo Lounge, and we were talking about Reagan. He reminded me of the petition: "You know that thing you and Farley signed?"

"Yeah, gee, and we never had any trouble."

"That's because I tore it up," he said. "Nobody else signed it but you and Farley."

But to come back to Marilyn: Contrary to what everybody thinks, contrary to what *he* thinks, he actually met her. Either he doesn't remember or he didn't realize who she was. But Farley Granger saw it happen too, and he remembers it.

It was at the big event for Wallace given by the Arts, Sciences and Professions Committee at the Pan Pacific Auditorium. Marilyn and I had been sharing an apartment on Hollywood Drive. We were starlets and supposed to be ushers. We were wearing halterlike dresses, very high heels, and red, white, and blue straw hats, boaters. Marilyn was very pretty, just gorgeous. She always used to wear size 12 on the top and size 10 on the bottom, and in those days size 12 was like size 8. I think she may have just done *Asphalt Jungle*.

Anyway, we snuck around backstage to see the big movie stars. Norman was backstage, stage right, holding a clipboard. He was a kind of stage manager for the rally. We stood there while Louis B. Mayer was screaming at Katharine Hepburn that if she went out on stage he was going to tell Louella Parsons about her affair with Spencer Tracy. He didn't want her to speak in favor of Wallace and was threatening to destroy her career, which he could have done, because Parsons and Hopper destroyed Ingrid Bergman's career a few years later. But Hepburn just put her head down, and then Norman said something to her—I don't know what—and she went on out. Norman then turned to Mayer and said, "Here's a pair of scissors. Now you can cut off your nose to spite your face." I don't know if Mayer knew who Norman was, but he said something like "Shut up, snotnose."

Then Norman saw us and said, "You're supposed to be out front." He kicked us out of there and told us to go back out and be ushers—me and Marilyn, both of us.

I know Norman doesn't remember, but it's funny, because the whole hype of his Marilyn book was that he'd never met her. I told Milton Greene the story when I saw him in California, and he agreed with me, saying, "I think Norman's making that up, that he didn't know Marilyn."

But Marilyn knew more about Norman than I did. She said to me, "You know, he's the one who wrote the book that you have." I don't know if she actually read *The Naked and the Dead*, but she carried it around, I remember, because it was a big, big book.

In my autobiography I told the story of the lists Marilyn and I used to make, the people we'd like to have as lovers. Well, we'd both had unhappy love affairs and were in misery, so at one in the morning we used to listen to Frank Sinatra and Billy Eckstine and make our lists. What I left out of my account was that Norman was on Marilyn's list. I'm positive. I may even have the list somewhere. But I remember looking at her list and Einstein was on it, and so was Norman. She always liked the intellectual types. Me, I always liked the pretty actors.

ALICE ADAMS   The first fall we were at Stanford, Norman came up from Hollywood and stayed with us for the Harvard-Stanford football game. He came alone, and we gave a party for him, which was where he met Lois Wilson. Lois Mayfield Wilson. Her husband, Graham Wilson, was a graduate student at Stanford, and how she persuaded him to stay home that day I'm not sure. She's an exceptionally attractive blond from Kentucky. Another southerner, a bright woman, and I really liked her, although we never became friends because she mistakenly believed I had an affair with her husband. Anyway, she had a tremendous crush on Norman, just from reading *The Naked and the Dead*. She'd never met him before, and at the party they spent a lot of time together and then went off for a walk, leading to a lot of speculation as to whether or not they had made it. I rather think not, even though they came back very late.

Mark and I were very fond of Norman, and while we gave the party because we wanted him to have a good time, it was also a show-off gesture. I'm not sure Mark would've felt this, but it was a little bit of thumbing our nose at the academic Establishment, particularly Wally Stegner, who was head of the Stanford Creative Writing Program. Stegner, I remember, came and was rather condescending, saying things about Norman's brashness. "Brash, brash, brash"— he used the word over and over, and then it was quite funny, because he invited Norman to come up and see him the next day. To lay some bricks, he said.

NORMAN MAILER (LETTER TO FRANCIS IRBY GWALTNEY, NOVEMBER 16, 1948)
Dear Fig and Ecey—

I been fuckin' off on writing to ya cause I was workin' hard up to elections and after that I was recooperatin'...

I didn't get any movie stars to go on the radio for us as you may have heard in the election eve broadcast, but I did have a good time in Hollywood. L.A. is probably the ugliest city in the whole world, but I love it. Did Lollypop Parsons really say that I was in Hollywood to form a Communist cell? Are you sure of this, kid? Cause if she did I'll sue her for a million bucks. I read in the papers where she said that I had gone out there to talk to prominent left-wingers, and that's true, but Communist cells I did not form.

Bea's gut is no longer a-growlin'. Workin' on the Wallace campaign got her straightened out. Now we got to go find another lost cause to support.

The New Yorker was cute rather than kind. The girl who interviewed me was a nice kid but she made me sound like a fucking character in an Odets play.

If you like the books, thank Bea for them. She went out and bought them all and sent them away—my little organizer.

If you do go to Stanford, Fig, I got a couple of good friends there, but hell I'll see you long before then.

Our own plans now are indefinite as hell. I'm going to start work on a new novel in a couple of weeks after I block it out in my mind. We can't figure out where we're going to go next, but it may be around Chicago or it may be France again. If we go around Chicago we may be able to get down around Arkansas again for a few days. . . .

NORMAN MAILER (LETTER TO FRANCIS IRBY GWALTNEY, JANUARY 1, 1949)

Dear Fig and Ecey—

If I hadn't answered soon I'd be beginning to think as much as you that your Uncle Norm was going highhat on you. I don't know why I didn't answer sooner except that I don't like writing letters, and you two do, you white-haired sons (and daughters) of bitches. (Just my Jewish chauvinism—in Brooklyn now they're calling me the Jewish Horatio Alger.)

After a lot of hanging around and wondering what to do, Bea and me finally decided to rent a house in Vermont. I decided I wanted to get into isolation and really come to grips with the new novel. For a long time we played with the idea of going to the Middle West, but didn't, cause we hate the Middle West. This way, chilluns, it looks like we won't get to see you until the late spring for we got a lease on a place from January 7 to May 7.

I've been running around purposelessly in New York without getting much done, just generally wasting my time. The play of the book won't be ready to go on until next fall. I'm getting kind of scared about the new novel, but for the first time I'm getting interested in it too which cheers me a bit. . . .

We're leaving for Vermont January 5. Our address up there will be Box 140, Jamaica, Vermont. Write me as Kingsley Mailer cause I'm going to stay incognito to avoid all the village literary teas. . . .

JEAN MALAQUAIS   Prior to the peace conference at the Waldorf Astoria in March '49 I'd conveyed to Norman that this and all so-called peace conferences—the one in Stockholm with Russell and Sartre or the one earlier in Amsterdam in '36 included—were but screens: the closer a war, the louder the international-peace balderdash. In fact, a year later there was Korea. Again we argued. He was scheduled to speak at the conference and sat on the dais among Shostakovitch, Fedeyev, F. O. Matthiessen, and some lesser beacons. The place was jammed; the liberal Establishment had come in a body—Macdonald, Robert Lowell, Irving Howe, Lionel Abel, Mary McCarthy, Arthur Miller—you name it. On the sidewalk, watched by a few weary cops, dozens of idiotic America-Firsters were picketing. When Norman's turn came to speak, there was a thundering ovation. He was, remember, the Horatio Alger of the time; *The Naked and the Dead* was the big book on the war. Suddenly he became white as a shroud, then burst out with what had been the substance of our conversations, attacking the

The Cultural and Scientific Conference for World Peace ("Waldorf Conference"), March 25, 1949. Left to right: A. A. Fedeyev, Secretary General of the Union of Soviet Writers; Mailer; Composer Dmitri Shostakovitch; Arthur Miller; and Dr. William Olaf Stapledon.

conference for what it was—a fraud. Quite brave of him. I didn't have the slightest inkling he was going to do so. Lionized for starters, he was now viciously booed: he'd become an enemy. He walked off, and we all surrounded him, afraid he'd be assaulted.

IRVING HOWE   I was covering the Waldorf peace conference for *Partisan Review*. Norman, I knew, was sort of a fellow traveler with the Wallace movement, and when he got up and made his speech, which shocked the sponsors of the conference—advancing the theory of state capitalism, that the world was moving toward capitalism everywhere—I was familiar enough with the lingo to spot the probable source—namely, Malaquais, whom I'd known for two years already.

The speech was pure left-wing sectarianism, the line that both sides are no good and moving toward an increasing concentration of state power. God knows what being a committed Marxist means, but I don't think Norman ever qualified in any doctrinal sense.

Afterwards I went up and introduced myself. A kind of characteristic exchange occurred. I said, "I thought that was a very honest speech," which was an indirect way of saying I agreed with it, at least with the general drift. Norman balked at that, saying, "Well, nobody's honest." We agreed to meet, but some time went by and we didn't see each other again until '52, when we began to organize *Dissent*.

BOWDEN BROADWATER   I hadn't seen Norman since Harvard, and Mary McCarthy, my then wife, and Dwight Macdonald and a few others, like Robert Lowell, went to infiltrate, because we were quite interested in joining the opposition to the group that had organized the conference. Norman, I suppose, was pretty dubious about that group too, but his speech came as a surprise. I was even more surprised when he asked us to the party afterward at the Hotel Sutton. We were supposed to be in the opposition, and there were definitely a lot of people there whom we didn't want to speak to. We were pretty dazed and excited after all the factionalism at the conference—like Sidney Hook taking a room at the Waldorf to hold his own briefing—but we went anyway, for which, of course, we were roundly criticized. Norman, Mary, and I talked, though not about *The Naked and the Dead*, because Mary happened to prefer Jones's first book to Norman's, which she thought was too stylized. Still, even with his success and just having given his speech, I found Norman quite agreeable, quite affable. He was a little cocky, but that's always been his style, even though he was more bantam league than he is now.

LILLIAN HELLMAN   I don't remember our talking about politics, but I'm certain we did since I was very involved in the Wallace campaign and so was Norman, although to a lesser degree. I was aware of Malaquais, that Norman talked to him a great deal, and I thought that he was probably a phony. I'd read one of his books and didn't like it, but Norman would quote him frequently, and I remember thinking, I wish he weren't so influenced by him.

At the Waldorf conference I wasn't on the panel and was sitting in another room, reading or something, when somebody who worked on the committee came running in and said, "Guess what? Come quick, Norman Mailer is denouncing all of us!" I didn't hear the speech; I read it and was shocked by it.

I had no idea why Malaquais had such an influence on him, but Norman had picked a very unfortunate time to give the speech, because it led to more red-baiting. I'm sure he didn't realize this, because, God knows, Norman was not a red-baiter, and I don't believe for one minute that he was playing anybody's game except his own. He truly believed what he was saying. However, the total effect of that speech—because it was anti-Russian—was to play into the hands of red-baiters. No question, he got us into trouble he had not even thought about. There's also no doubt in my mind that he got himself *out* of trouble, although I don't believe that was his intention. But that speech was undoubtedly the reason why he was never called before HUAC: he had announced to everybody that he was not a Stalinist and no longer had any sympathy with Communists, proto-Communists, pro-Communists, or even anti-Communists. He was a Trotskyist.

NORMAN MAILER (LETTER TO FRANCIS IRBY GWALTNEY, 1949)

Dear Fig and Ecey,

We're taking off from here the seventh of May and going to New York for a couple of weeks. Then we'll be going to Chicago and then to Conway or Fayetteville. (Rather, I will alone. Bea'll be too far along to travel by car, and so she'll fly to Chicago, rest with friends there, and then fly to L.A. (where we're ending up) to join me.) Anyway I'll hit y'all somewhere around June 10. Will you drop me a line at 102 Pierrepont St. before June 1 to let me know whether you'll be in Fayetteville or Conway, and what the address'll be, etc. etc.

Keep writing that novel, Fig.

Love and all,
Norm

ADELINE LUBELL NAIMAN   In the summer of '49, when Norman was going back out to Hollywood, my husband and I were living in Chicago, and they stayed with us on the way to the West Coast. Bea stayed with me for a short time while Norman went out to get things set up. Actually she and I got along very well then. She was in her radiant prime, pregnant, and I suppose she felt the baby was going to hold everything in place. Still, I couldn't get closer to her than the face she wanted to present, although I remember giving her one of my dresses.

NORMAN MAILER (LETTER TO FRANCIS IRBY GWALTNEY, AUGUST 8, 1949)

Dear Fig and Ecey,

It's a crime I haven't written in so long, but it's just been laziness, not loss of love. And too, I've been working hard as hell all through July on the new masterpiece of which I may finish a first draft in a couple of weeks. We found us a house high above Sunset Boulevard in the hills west of Hollywood, and can see half of that horrible city that lies below us. Bea is fine, round as a barrel, big as a house, and is having a beautiful pregnancy. The him-her ought to be born in a couple of weeks. Out here everything is kind of depression hit and the writers are walking around on their hands and knees, not knowing where their next job is coming from. We don't exactly adore this place but like all writers, the first thing that occupies me is can I write here? And that anyway has been going along okay. The book is going to run to about 230 pages or so first draft and I don't know whether I'll be able to rewrite it in four months or two years. It's that kind of thing, experimental, tricky, and I have to feel my way all through it.

I had a good time in Arkansas, damn good. It was sort of the high spot of the trip, you nice people. Say hello to Frank for me. And answer soon, huh kid?

I've been wondering Ecey, if you've been able to get ahold of a copy of volume I of Kapital *in Fayetteville. If you haven't, let us know and we'll send you one from here. And if you want the second and third volumes, which I imagine will*

be impossible to find in Fayetteville, we can help you out on that too. The same
goes for any other books for both of you.
   Tell me about your book, Fig.
   Fat Beatty sends her love.

> *Love from Lotus Land,*
> *Norm*

JEAN MALAQUAIS   Norman asked me to join him in Hollywood to work on a
movie. I had some experience as an assistant director and scriptwriter, both in
France and Mexico. Sam Goldwyn wanted Mailer to do an original screenplay.
After I arrived, Norman's agent arranged a meeting for us with Goldwyn at his
mansion. What happened was high comedy.

The living room was huge, lined with dummy books, and Goldwyn met us
in his bathrobe. The agent had told him that we—or rather, I—had a story, so
it was up to us to do the talking. Goldwyn stood there making comments, all
the while pushing his false teeth back in place, all the while speaking with a
lisp. Then he told us to write a two-page outline. I refused, knowing all too
well how things are done out there, and a few days later we got the contract for
$50,000 to write an original screenplay, with Montgomery Clift and Charles
Boyer in view: $5000 for the first draft, then three times $15,000 for each revision.
We were given three offices, one for each of us, plus the secretaries. The studio
people asked if we wanted them to be French, Spanish, or Italian, almost as if
to cater for our amorous fancies. The day after the contract was signed a notice
appeared in *Variety*, and I became overnight a VIP of sorts, trailing in Norman's
shadow: doors swung open, and there I was, invited to all the parties. Brother,
I told myself, do this one script, then get the hell out of here.

At first we lived in the house Norman and Bea had taken earlier in the
Hollywood Hills. Bea wasn't resentful at being in California, at least not at first.
She was painting. She'd written a novel but couldn't get it published. Girls were
flocking around Norman. He never confided to me about his activities, but I
think he was quite responsive. Bea didn't have any friends of her own, though,
and everything, of course, was centered on him. They quarreled mightily; whenever they did, I'd leave. And they quarreled a lot because he can quarrel a lot.
She gave back, though, and they even fought physically. It was like an outlet
for them—the explosions—and they used foul language almost joyfully, which
set my teeth on edge, if only because Norman held the theory that four-letter
words were somehow invested with "subversive" attributes. After a time Galy
and I moved out; I was writing a book and working on the translation of *The
Naked and the Dead*, and needed privacy. Also, things weren't easy between
Galy and Norman, either. She was inordinately proud, and there were aspects
of his familiarity she didn't like—not that he made passes, not at all, but he
would tease her, stroke her cheek, things like that.

SANDY CHARLEBOIS THOMAS   I don't know if Norman understands why he needs
an audience for what he used to call his "stunts." It appears to be something

he's had since he got famous in his twenties. Something happened to him out in Hollywood. He's talked to me about being corrupted out there. He was young, suddenly very famous, and he was wined and dined. He discovered if he did cutesy little things people just fell all over him. He also talked about this in the context of his breakup with Bea, how the time out there had been very bad for their marriage.

EMMA CLARA "ECEY" GWALTNEY   They'd written us those letters saying that Bea was big and uncomfortable, and I think that was the beginning of their trouble. She sat around while he was lionized; later she told me that herself and said that she couldn't live like that. I remember she said that while everybody was making over him, "There I sat in Hollywood, big as a barrel..." It was almost an amused but resentful detachment: "I was just not going to be in that position. I just didn't like it." I said, "I think I could put myself in the background." She said, "You mean if Fig got famous and it changed your life, changed him, you could stand it?"

SHELLEY WINTERS   As far as I could see, Norman never sucked up to the power guys. Nor was he acting or dressing like a Hollywood person. In fact, his clothes were a disaster area. The same with the house he and Bea took—not typical at all. When I first went up there in a cab I had an argument with the driver because I was sure, just looking at the place, he hadn't found the right address.

I remember Charlie Chaplin used to have a Sunday-afternoon salon type of thing. He was newly married to Oona, and for these luncheon things the only admission was talent. Down below the house was a tennis court, so Norman and I decided we'd learn—I don't think either of us knew how to play. I had a gingham romper on, not sexy shorts or anything, and blue sneakers instead of white ones. Norman was wearing brown pants and a plaid shirt and basketball sneakers. Everybody else had whites, but we didn't give a shit. We played tennis the way you play stickball—no sportsmanship, just swatting the ball around, yelling and laughing, having a good time.

GENE KELLY   We just had fun, laughs. I saw Norman quite a bit socially with mutual friends like Harold Hecht, Burt Lancaster, Shelley and Farley, and Michael Gordon, the director. We were always in groups, in bunches, and during that period there was sort of a New York group that usually met at my house—everybody that came from the New York theater, the New York artistic establishment. Garfield was around, and we also saw a lot of Monty Clift.

Salka Viertel and her son, Peter, a novelist and screenwriter, had a famous salon of expatriates. Bertolt Brecht, Thomas Mann, the Feuchtwangers all gathered at Salka's house, and Charlie Chaplin was there two or three nights a week. Salka wrote screenplays for people like Greta Garbo. She'd been an actress, Polish origin, a very lovely, charming lady whom we all adored, and she and Peter had the intellectual European salon, while we had the fun salon for New Yorkers at our house. That was about the way it was divided up. Ours was more the type where there would be Frank Sinatra, Judy Garland, Lena Horne, and all the piano players like Lennie Bernstein, Oscar Levant, and Johnny Green, who'd drop in and make music.

Our group was predominantly liberal and left-wing, so there was naturally a lot of political discussion. The same was true of Salka's. The town was very divided at that time. Unlike New York, where you could sit in Ralph's on Forty-fifth Street and discuss something, Hollywood had hard lines drawn up.

I don't know whether Norman and I actually spent that much time together at the Viertels', so I don't know whether his reaction was the same as mine. I can only say I was playing mostly the part of a listener because I was so awestruck by those guys. It was a Golden Age. The list of people in Hollywood at that time was overwhelming. There was a resident genius every few blocks, so even Norman didn't cut as wide a swath as you might think, not when there was Thomas Mann, Bertolt Brecht, Charles Chaplin, and Greta Garbo. He was young, a guy who'd just come on the scene. I had been in New York theater as an actor, choreographer, director for several years, the usual kind of personal history that goes with coming up through the theater. So there was a kind of clustering; we were the huddled masses out here in Hollywood who missed New York, and Norman was seen as the latest emissary from the East. He was conspicuously New York. He had "Brooklyn kid" written all over him. He had a quick, staccato manner of speaking and spoke very spontaneously, off the cuff. He didn't adopt any so-called "Hollywood ways," he didn't have time.

KEVIN McCARTHY   Monty Clift introduced us, and in retrospect the relationship between the two of them made sense. Clift and I were good friends—this was before he made his big hairpin turn down skid row. He was a very promising, bright, funny, articulate, imaginative, artistic guy. He probably sized Mailer up and said, "Hey, this is interesting," because he also spent a lot of time getting to know Thornton Wilder and was always latching onto writers to write him scripts. Monty, remember, was very independent—Monty, Marlon, Jimmy Dean, there were several of them, and they all tried to carve out a future for themselves. None of them was just your standard good-looking model type with personality, and they weren't going to go the Hollywood way.

Monty, in fact, saw Hollywood as a factory. He always complained about working with directors who didn't have anywhere near the grasp of the material he did, and very rarely was he under the kind of contract where you can be forced to do x number of pictures yearly. Mailer, therefore, probably found him damn interesting, and Monty would have reinforced Mailer's own aversion to the system. Clift was saying the same things Mailer was, and on top of that he would have had an awful lot of glitter that Mailer would have found only by reading Fitzgerald.

It's hard for me to talk about their roles in relation to each other, because I was just another actor, not a star. I was pretty well known in New York as a stage actor—Kazan, Robert Lewis, and George Kaufman all thought well of me and would give me intriguing assignments—but looking at Mailer and Clift, I was saying, "Gee, Clift's palling around with this very important, successful new writer who's probably going to write for him. Wow, wouldn't I like to be in the same boat!" But I wasn't. Mailer and Clift were just a little hotter than I was.

Clift, though, spoke of Mailer, and there wasn't any deference either way. Monty knew a lot of the same people as Mailer—Chaplin and Gene Kelly— and I think he first took me over to Kelly's house, where I remember playing volleyball. Chaplin and Monty, I know, used to hang out and feed at the Viertels'. Norman was there, and occasionally Lancaster and Harold Hecht too. It was a salon, like these were the people in Hollywood who were conducting some sort of cultural or civilized aspect of life.

SHELLEY WINTERS Norman, Burt, and I were having dinner at a Mexican restaurant, and Burt left me alone with Norman. I started talking about my career, that I wanted the role in the upcoming Dreiser movie. I'd read *An American Tragedy* and I knew I understood the part—I'd once worked in a factory—but George Stevens, the director, wouldn't test me because I had a reputation as a blonde bomb shell. That's what they were building me up for, and Stevens had seen me in *Double Life*, where I played this frowzy, dumb waitress.

Norman encouraged me to try to get the part anyway, but he couldn't tell me how to get an interview with Stevens. Nobody cast George Stevens but George Stevens.

So he came back to my apartment. I had a leopard couch, the whole thing, and I think he liked me, plus I knew that Lancaster was being unfaithful to me with his wife. Norman had great, piercing blue eyes—they're faded a little now—but back then they were like Paul Newman's. But he sensed that I needed to be encouraged intellectually, so he put himself on hold and went through the book with me, explaining that it was *the* American success story, which was why it was being called *A Place in the Sun* instead of Dreiser's title, *An American Tragedy*. This is the way he explained it: that it used to be that if you were a farmer, say, and raised your children respectably and they had a good education, then you had a good life. But that was slowly changing, he explained. People had begun to feel that unless you were rich and famous or a celebrity, life was meaningless, without value.

I'd thought that Norman was a protégé of Dreiser because he knew the book so well. He wasn't, of course, but he taught me how to read, not just the plot but how to figure out what the writer is saying, what the theme is. Actors don't always know that, they just go to the line. Anyway, Norman said, "Dreiser is saying that the boy doesn't know if he's drowned this girl or not. She doesn't have to be an ugly little girl. The other girl, Elizabeth Taylor, could be equally pretty. But the boy has the opportunity to be rich and live in an elegant house with her." We went through the book section by section, especially the boat scene. Norman explained why it was important that you didn't know whether the boy consciously kills the girl or just lets her drown because although he's a nice, moral kid, the drive for money takes over. He wants to be up there in the sun, he's trapped. He's already gone to the license bureau with her, so the drowning is unconsciously the solution to his problem, and when his mother asks, "When the boat turned over, did you try and help her?" he can't answer.

When he was all done explaining this Norman said, "Tell George Stevens you understand this. Read the book again, very, very slowly, with that in mind." We had talked till daylight, and now he left. I was almost a little offended, you know. Here I was the sexpot and nothing had happened.

But the point was Norman talked to me like I was his equal. I wasn't just the blonde bombshell, the nitwit.

The next morning I got Greg Bautzer on the phone. He was the most famous, chic lawyer in Hollywood. He's still there. He wears gray sharkskin suits and is the epitome of Don Juan. I said to him, "Can George Stevens meet me anywhere?" He said, "You're so wrong for the part of a little factory girl." I said, "It doesn't matter. Just let me show him I understand things about the book that I think he would like to know." He said, "Why would you?" and I said, "Because I talked to somebody who was Dreiser's protégé." Then Bautzer called Stevens and told him I was very bright and knew things about the book that he should know if he was going to do the picture. That intrigued George, and he agreed to meet me at the Hollywood Athletic Club at five o'clock. Immediately I dyed my hair brown—I was in the middle of another movie and they had to bleach it back again—and I went to the Firestone Rubber Company to watch the factory girls because I already knew something about Method work. I spent the rest of the day reading every scene that Alice, my character, was in. Then I fixed my hair very flat with little bobby pins and borrowed some clothes from my sister, who was a nurse, and went over to the Athletic Club. I sat there with a sandwich and a paper bag in the corner of the lobby and didn't move, didn't say a word when George Stevens came in at five, knowing he was looking for a blonde bombshell. He picked up *Life* magazine and waited until five-thirty, then mumbled, "Fuck it, she's not showing," and started to go. Then he sees me and looks and looks, comes over and says, "If I test you and you get the part, will you let me photograph you like this?" That's all he said, that bear of a man. And I said, "If I get this part, you can photograph me any way you want, Mr. Stevens."

I stayed up all night rereading the book from beginning to end, putting bobby pins on the pages of my scenes and writing in the margins. I think I told the studio I was doing the other picture for that I was sick, and then I went to see Stevens and told him my understanding of the book, especially the ending— all the while, of course, parroting Norman. But I didn't tell him that Norman had worked with me. Finally he said, "You're very bright. Why are you letting them sell you the way they are, the blonde bombshell?" I said, "Well, you know, my father was making seventy-six dollars a week and they give me two hundred."

The test was wonderful. I got the part, but it wasn't until the end that I told Stevens Norman had worked with me and had told me that I should lay on the poverty.

Looking back at it, and at other times I've talked to Norman, I think he believes that people are basically good, and he won't accept the weakness of other people's decisions about themselves. He makes you expect more of yourself. During our session that night—and it went on for hours and hours—what he was saying was, "You, Shelley, are better than you think you are, and you can get the role." And that changed my life. Forget the Oscar. It gave me great respect for myself as an actress, and it gave others respect for me as an actress too.

But I do think Norman had ambivalence about Hollywood and its values. For example, he's not capable of sleeping with a starlet and using her and then just saying, "That was great, kid. Goodbye." Unlike most men in Hollywood, he's actually a feminist. He sees women as people, not just sex objects. He reveres women. He feels there's a kind of respect they must have. Like when he was working with me on Dreiser, he didn't treat me like a dumb starlet, he just couldn't do that. In fact, I remember times when he was in a restaurant with me and Burt Lancaster. Pretty, sexy girls would come over and sit down and be introduced to "Norman Mailer, the writer." And Norman would cool it. He wouldn't be rude or anything, he'd be charming, and with that funny little grin he has, he'd flatter them and compliment them. But as far as I could see, he wouldn't make dates with them. Now maybe he tells people different, but from what I saw over the years in Hollywood and New York, my impression—from a woman's point of view—is that he never treated a woman like a hunk of meat.

Still, there was that ambivalence about Hollywood. He just couldn't compromise and become a Hollywood writer, where he would've made a half million dollars—and after the success of *The Naked and the Dead* he had every opportunity. The average writer with a hit book like that would've made the best financial deal and done what they told him as best he could. Scott Fitzgerald did, didn't he? But Norman wasn't able to. He couldn't surrender to the glamor of that world. Why had he gone out there in the first place? Not to be a Hollywood writer but because he was involved in the Wallace campaign. The fact that when he came out the second time he was writing a script for Sam Goldwyn was another sign of his ambivalence, of his not letting the left hand know what the right hand was doing.

MARK LINENTHAL   When we visited him in Hollywood, I didn't feel a big change. That's what was nice about it—the sense of an old friend, somebody you could really talk to. You were not in the public light as he was, but he would sort of report to you on what it was like, serve as an intermediary.

We went to hear him on a panel discussion, "The Reel War vs the Real War"—the war as seen by movies versus the war proper. John Howard Lawson and some of the Hollywood Ten participated too, and Norman was terrific. I thought: There's our boy. He's really doing it right. Then I remember we went back to their house in the Hollywood Hills, and it was a continuation of that—taking himself seriously but not throwing his weight around. He was inside his own skin. He wasn't being pulled out of shape by any of this. His sense of scale was terrific. I remember he told me that Goldwyn had said, "Norman, get a haircut or people will think I'm not paying you enough money." He laughed about it.

Either *Homage to Catalonia* or *1984* had just come out and he urged me to read it. He said, "This is a good book for liberals. There's an anti-Soviet element." He meant that it criticized liberal piety, although not in the same sense that he spits out the word "liberal" now, meaning lily-livered and glass-balled. What he was saying was that liberals were trying to do good things but *1984* shows the shit that results, the world in which socialism had arrived at its horrible end, the world that liberalism was tending toward. It was like he was saying to me, "You're a liberal and that's okay, but this book will have a chastening effect." It wasn't an unfriendly remark or an accusation, and, in fact, I think he was saying that he too was a liberal and that Orwell would call all our thinking to account.

Malaquais was still translating *The Naked and the Dead*, and Norman told me he'd said that there wasn't a live line in the novel, and what struck me again was Norman's little-boy quality, like his trips into Boston to do research when he'd been at Harvard. It was a kid's approach to the world. Just because Malaquais had told him that, he'd started keeping a copy of the *Oxford Book of English Verse* on the table in order to improve his prose style. He was like a student, a freshman learning to write. "I'll read these great poets and make my writing vivid." It was both funny and touching.

ALICE ADAMS　Bea was pregnant, and Norman was being courted by the Hollywood CP, being treated like a star, and what she felt about it, I don't know. It's a kind of perception that I would've repressed at the time since I had just started psychoanalysis and was shaken up by it. Still, it seemed to me that Bea was by then a little overwhelmed. Mark and I would say to each other, "It really would've been better if Norman had never quite had a success. Bea doesn't. . ." But the baby was quite imminent, and I remember Norman saying to us rather touchingly, "This is the last time we're ever going to be alone together." We were there for the weekend, and they threw a party for us. A lot of Hollywood Communists came, but I don't remember who except Albert Maltz and John Lawson. Mickey Knox was around and Dorothy Parker. Norman and she were friends. She had a huge dog, and she and some guy—her lover, I think—came for a drink one afternoon.

MICKEY KNOX　Bea's reaction to Norman's celebrity in Hollywood was twofold— she enjoyed sharing the limelight but also resented it. I always thought she was rather sharp with him—and remember, Norman was still a vulnerable guy. She never humiliated him in public, she was just difficult. You gotta remember, she was still a dominant factor in his life and a very strong lady.

Meanwhile Norman was writing his novel and getting to know Hollywood. He visited me on the set a few times when I was doing *Western Pacific Agent*, a small-budget picture made by Robert Lippert. It was shot in Hollywood and was Morris Carnovsky's last picture before he was blacklisted, and I had to pull a trick to get him into it. I think Norman went out to Warner Brothers' *The Flame and the Arrow* to see Lancaster too.

Then I had the part of a lightweight champ in a movie called *Killer McCoy* and went into training at a weight-lifting gym in Santa Monica. Norman and Malaquais came along one day, and Norm said, "Jesus, this is terrific, let's work out." Jean injured his back seriously and had to give up. Norm came with me three times a week, maybe for a month or more.

This was around the time Susie was born—August, I think—and I don't know what effect it had on him. We were both—what—twenty-six? We didn't think about those things, at least I didn't. I mean, he had a baby. Big deal. He behaved like most fathers, because at this point he was totally different from what he was ten years later. The timid side of him was predominant—there was something very sweet about him.

It was also around that time that I brought Norman together with Garfield, Burt Lancaster, and Harold Hecht. Hecht and Lancaster had the first real independent film company, and they were interested in *The Naked and the Dead*. Garfield wanted to play Sergeant Croft, which prompted me to say, "You mean 'Kraft.' If you play it, it'll be called 'Sergeant Kraft'!"—which at the time didn't exactly endear me to Norm.

NORMAN MAILER (LETTER TO FRANCIS IRBY GWALTNEY, 1949, HOLLYWOOD)

Dear Fig and Ecey:

Long time no write, but the last couple of weeks have been sheer raving crazy. Susan got born three and a half weeks ago, and since then I've been running to the hospital, dicking around, getting bawled out by my wife who acts infinitely superior to me now, and just generally suffering.

Anyway, today I got in gear, wrote a letter to my lawyer (not for a divorce) and feeling just generally productive, I thought I'd discharge a couple of obligations. So obligations here's the news.

I finished my novel (first draft) about a month ago, and now I'm going to let it lay around for a few months before I get back to work. It's a short one and it has to be just perfect. In the meantime I sit around waiting for a job.

Naked was sold to an independent company called Norma Productions which is owned by Burt Lancaster. He is going to play Hearn, and I have a script approval, so they can't fuck up the movie too much. Nobody yet is picked to play Croft. When you said you could do it better than Lancaster I began to think of you, old eagle nose with your vinegar puss, and I thought to myself, well maybe he can at that. Did you ever do any acting? We'll make a movie star out of you yet.

I've been waiting for a letter from Feldman, but nothing appears. I think he probably recognized himself in N. and is mad at me. On ne sait jamais.

Et qu'est-ce qui passe (how did you ever spell in French) avec ton roman? Did you finish it yet? Did you send it to Bill? Did he answer? Are you going to send it to me? Are you willing to put up money on the ten errors? I'll accept any bets.

If it's available, send it to me. I want to see it, kid.

Ecey, you never did tell me if you got a copy of Kapital. Let me know, honey. You know I've always wanted to make a revolutionary out of you.

I go to a gym now three times a week, and how the muscles swell on me. You wouldn't stand a chance with me now, you po-o-or white-headed baboon. Bea says I've finally achieved my ambition, and I look like a truckdriver. 185 pounds of muscle and shit.

My pore flabby wife sends her love in a tired little voice. . . .

Say hello to Frank, and all the lese-intellectualese.

Norm

HAROLD HECHT　*The Naked and the Dead* was such a strange, difficult book for film that probably Burt and I were the only ones in Hollywood interested in doing it, so that's why Mailer wanted to go with us. I had seen Burt in a play in New York and become his agent, but basically we both wanted to produce pictures. At the time, we hadn't yet done any. We had no reputation, no importance, and we paid Mailer just a minimum amount of money—we were optioning it.

Mickey Knox had brought us the property. He knew Norman and I knew Mickey because he was Burt's friend. We had several conversations with Mailer, and Lancaster and I both felt he was brilliant. He thought well and he knew what he was talking about, although I don't think he knew anything about films—but neither did we.

Mickey was acting as a friend, but I believe we did pay him something. I don't know if he was getting anything from Norman. I seem to recall that Charles Rembar, Norman's cousin, was involved in our negotiations. I don't think Norman was going to write the screenplay, but he had certain creative control and insisted that we couldn't do anything that departed significantly from the philosophy and attitudes.

CHARLES REMBAR　What I did out there in Hollywood was confined to dealing with Hecht and Lancaster and their lawyers. Norman wanted script approval and we got it. They were never able to produce a script he liked, and he gave them back—he didn't have to—their initial payment.

MICKEY KNOX　Cy Rembar was there a month or two, mainly socializing, I think. But he never talked to me. I never liked him, never trusted him. He was operating in the role of big brother, living with Bea and Norman, and my impression was that he and Bea didn't get along, possibly because Cy always had a superior attitude. Norman seemed to be taken in by it, though, and all through the years he permitted it. He wouldn't talk to me about it. He knew what I felt, and once, when I brought it up, he accused me of "attacking" Cy. Even then his attitude was: Cy's my lawyer, he handles my affairs.

JEAN MALAQUAIS　Norman and I had been working on our script for Goldwyn. As things progressed, we would discuss the story at night, and each of us would write scenes during the day. The main idea for the script came from West's *Miss Lonelyhearts.* Our hero, whose sponsor was a coffin manufacturer, gave "heartfelt" advice to people over the radio, then went out on the sly to actually visit them. Eventually he publicly denounced the hoax, upon which the audience came and destroyed the radio station. We had some sort of justification for the action—it was the right thing for the character to do— and after about a month we had 90 pages ready. But when we gave them to Goldwyn it was a catastrophe.

Goldwyn obviously objected to the script's "seditious" implications. He came over to me and started to preach what a movie is supposed to be, lisping all the while: "Uth Americanth, ith in our hearth when we make a movie!" He had grabbed a button on my jacket and was twisting it, standing there lecturing me, until suddenly it came off. "But when you Frenthmen make a movie ith dry and intellecthual. Good thentimenth mutht be rewarded. Bad thentimenth *mutht* be punithed!" Then he pushed his denture back in again. I was laughing, it was so funny. We hadn't punished the bad guy in the script, so he was telling us to rewrite it his way. We refused.

"All right," he said. "You'll get five thouthand dollarth, I'll get the thcript."

"Nothing doing," I said. "You'll put it in the hands of hack writers."

The next day *Variety* reported we'd broken the contract, and that was that: no more invitations to parties for me. Needless to say, I never stopped sobbing throughout the few months I remained in Hollywood. As for Norman, who was working on *Barbary Shore*, he was still invited all over the place: he was Norman Mailer.

MICKEY KNOX Norman was still thinking about *Miss Lonelyhearts*, and he intended Monty Clift to play the lead; ironically enough, Clift later played the role, but Norman had nothing to do with it. He was tempted by the whole idea of Hollywood, no question, but even though he had a lot of concrete offers, he didn't want to stay. He was already at work on *Barbary Shore*, which was going to be different from *The Naked and the Dead*, and he was absolutely imbued with Malaquais' teaching. He wasn't angry at Goldwyn when they got canned, he was amused. He kept talking about it, and whenever he repeated Goldwyn's line "There'th not enough hearth," I remember he'd almost fall over laughing.

NORMAN MAILER (LETTER TO FRANCIS IRBY GWALTNEY, 1949, HOLLYWOOD)

Dear Fig and Ecey,

...I had a job for awhile with Sam Goldwyn writing a movie for him, but Malaquais and I got fired, or that is we were going to, and so we resigned, and worse still, bought back what we had written. Now we're trying to promote it into some kind of big deal somewhere, and getting nowhere fast.

Hollywood stinks. I'll probably stay here the rest of my life and weep into my beer about what a writer I used to be. Alas, alack. The only good thing that's happened is the funny stories I can tell about Sam Goldwyn, and those I'll tell you when I see you. (Don't take me for serious about staying here all my life. I hate Los Angeles too much. Now if you'd ever seen New York, you'd understand why.)

Susan is cute, and laughs a lot, and looks a little bit like me in spite of being cute. Bea has become the Mother. Never sleeps at night, pushes me around. I just carry a fucking guilt complex all the time....

FANNY SCHNEIDER MAILER   Barney and I went out to visit them when Susie was born. Norman was famous, they would be invited to all the top name parties in Hollywood, but Bea never wanted to go. I said, "Bea, you have to go. You're Norman's wife, people will ask for you. You have help"—they had a real nurse taking care of Susie—"and I'm here too." But Bea was the unhappiest woman in the world because all the praise was for Norman and nothing for her. She just couldn't take it.

Jean Malaquais was out there at the same time and I despised him. He's a balloon, all blown up. He was taking advantage of Norman at every step. Norman would write the screenplay, and he would find fault with it. He lived on everybody, a sponger. He does nothing but blow his horn. Norman was young when he met him, and once Norman forms a good opinion of somebody he can't change it. I have no use for Jean. Norman and I can each have our separate ideas about him. My idea of Malaquais as a man is mud.

And Jean and Mickey Knox didn't get along. Jean hated Mickey. It just occurred to me why: they're both false characters. They see themselves in each other.

JEAN MALAQUAIS   After the Goldwyn fiasco we worked on a comedy. Someone puts an ad in the paper saying, "Reader, if you don't bring one million dollars before tomorrow noon, you're a dead man." Next day a gent knocks on the door, pushes in a suitcase, and leaves in a hurry. And there's a million dollars in that suitcase. We had Bob Hope in mind. A crazy kind of story, a million dollars in a suitcase. The idea had come to Norman, and we embroidered on it with great glee.

After Susan was born Norman's parents came out to visit, and his sister Barbara too. She became angry because I wasn't mincing words with Norman over the sloppy writing in *The Naked and the Dead*. She knew all about the textual markings I was making in my own copy of the book—underlinings, arrows, and circles around phrases to show him the repetitions and improprieties of his prose. We never really discussed his family, but I knew that his mother disliked me for a while quite strongly for what she thought was my disrespect of her son. For her he was *the* genius, and she was very, very protective. But she didn't dare voice her annoyance, because the genius happened to like me.

As for Barney—he was the South African colonel. He wasn't actually a colonel, of course, but Norman would say he looked like a colonel from the Bengal Lancers. I remember him pinching girls' behinds at parties. Later Norman told me about his father's gambling and said that he'd had to pay off his debts.

MICKEY KNOX   True, when they came out Barney was pinching all the girls. He made a play, as I recall, for my wife Georgette and in later years for my second wife, Joanne, too. There was a dinner party in Hollywood when he grabbed Georgette in the kitchen—a mild move, an embrace.

I didn't know about his gambling and didn't find out until later. Norman told me when I had a problem of my own with a poker game in '53. He'd been covering Barney's debts, and he told me as if to say, "Don't pull that same shit on me."

SHELLEY WINTERS   I think he and Bea were a little intimidated by Hollywood. Like the Christmas party they gave, when they just sent out invites to everybody. That was at the house they rented on the edge of a cliff, which I thought was strange because of all the rain you get, so you can hardly go out. The house wasn't lavish, just sort of interesting—modern, with a view from the cliff.

Anyway, Norman admits it: he sent wires from left to right to everybody. Everybody wanted to meet him, so the party was chaos. Elizabeth Taylor and Monty went, John Ford, McLaglen, Cecil B. De Mille. Burt didn't come because he knew I was going to be there with Marlon.

It was raining very hard, and Marlon couldn't drive yet, so I drove us in my little red Pontiac. We couldn't get up the steep hill, so we got wet walking up. Marlon was wearing a borrowed tuxedo because he didn't own a suit, and it was much too small for him. There was a black bartender there, and Marlon just stood behind the bar and talked to the bartender in his little suit. I was trying to talk to people, trying to be sexy and everything, but my dress was soaked. Monty was having a fight with somebody. Then Mickey arrived afterwards in his big old car, came in, and put his raincoat down.

Everybody was late because of the rain. Bea had made some kind of tequila drink or sangria, which the bartender thought was terrible. Then all of a sudden she started setting up little TV tables and putting out a big spread—big hams and turkeys—stuff like Norman still serves at his parties—baked beans, potato chips. It was good but like a picnic, not elegant food like squab and quiche that was usually served in Hollywood.

I was very hungry—I hadn't eaten since breakfast—but Marlon suddenly grabbed me and Mickey's raincoat and wanted to go home because everyone was having serious political disagreements. He said something like "This party's making me nervous," so I grabbed Elizabeth's coat—we both had the same blond beaver coats we'd bought wholesale when they were just coming back in style—and it was a size too small.

Norman stopped us at the door. Marlon had only talked to the waiter and Bea, not to anybody else, even though everybody wanted to meet him because he'd just done *Streetcar*. Norman said, "Where are you going? You didn't meet anybody." That's when Marlon said, "What the fuck are you doing here, Mailer? You're not a screenwriter. Why aren't you in Vermont writing your next book?"

I don't care what Mickey Knox says—that's exactly what Marlon said. I swear to God, so help me. I was standing right there at the door with both of them. I was so embarrassed I ran out and didn't hear Norman's response. That's also how Marlon came to have Mickey's raincoat with Mickey's car keys in the pocket—which caused all the problems later that night when Mickey's car was blocking the driveway. Nobody could get out. Hal Wallis, Mickey's and Burt's boss at Paramount, called me at three A.M. and sent a police car over to retrieve Mickey's keys.

I suppose Norman himself had mixed feelings about being in Hollywood. I know they had a long lease on the house, but they left that spring, in May or June.

MICKEY KNOX   I don't remember Marlon Brando telling Norman to get out of Hollywood and go back to Vermont to write his novel. Brando did take my coat with the keys, but I think he came back pretty soon. I don't remember that there was any problem about it, and the party certainly didn't go on until three in the morning. For the most part Shelley's dead wrong. Like Norman's supposedly inviting people out of the *Players' Directory*—that's thoroughly untrue. Also, the implication that she was somehow involved with Norman—I doubt it. Nobody knows who's really fucking whom out there, but I don't think she would have been his cup of tea.

What actually did happen at the party was that Malaquais attacked Chaplin. Chaplin wasn't a Communist, but, like a lot of people, his sympathies were with Russia—and you know Malaquais, he really bored in. Norman was just a spectator. My sympathies were with Chaplin, and at one point Norman stopped me when I said, "I'm gonna drag Malaquais outside and beat the shit out of him." He was in his role of peacemaker. He wasn't taking sides, didn't say, "Hey, c'mon, you're full of shit" to either me *or* Malaquais.

JEAN MALAQUAIS   The parties were always a mixture of people. Some of the Hollywood Ten—Albert Maltz, Howard Fast, others. But at the time, the Stalinists and crypto-Communists were losing their following, so they fastened onto people like Norman, and even after he'd disavowed them at the Waldorf peace conference they were still trying to hold onto him.

One night Norman was giving a party. Both Chaplin and Oona were there, Chaplin at the center of quite a crowd. If anyone left the circle, Chaplin's face became wooden, as though, "I'm not funny anymore if people want to go and take a leak." After a while I'd moved away and was in a heated argument with some crypto-Communists. There were twenty of them on my back, and Mailer, the host, was just listening. Chaplin, on his way out, stopped to break in: "We in the West have our sphere of influence; let the Russians have theirs." I turned to him and said, "You may be the greatest comedian ever, but who gives you the right to dispose of people, to decide their fate for them?"

He didn't answer, and at the door he asked Norman who I was. Two weeks later Bea, Galy, Norman, and I were invited to his house for dinner. He kept telling hilarious stories, acting out each of them. Like the account of when he was drafted to sell war bonds in 1917 and was on a platform with Mary Pickford and Douglas Fairbanks. As he told it he got up on the piano in his living room, explaining that he'd gesticulated so much he'd fallen off the platform right on top of Roosevelt, then the undersecretary of the navy. And right there and then, as he waved his hands to illustrate, he actually fell off the piano.

Soon after that Galy and I left Hollywood. We had an odd car accident in Arizona—the rear axle came off—and we almost got killed. The garage told us the car had been tampered with, that some bolts and pins had been taken out. Galy thought the Stalinists had done it, and because of Mickey's antagonism, she felt he had sabotaged our car. I must say I don't buy that line.

MICKEY KNOX   That's so outlandish, so unreal, but I'm telling you, I found Malaquais very hostile and aggressive. He might've won me over if he'd used another tack. True, there were many times when I got angry, when he'd start all that anti-Stalinist shit—we're talking about a time when few people knew what the hell was really going on in Russia—but he was walking around like the little professor. For someone like me who was at least physically on the left ever since he was a kid, it was a fucking pain in the ass. But Jean certainly convinced Norman—and he did have the facts, I guess, since it's now proven, although at that point the feeling was that these were all anti-Communist lies. For him to suggest that I tampered with his car, though—that's just so stupid. How the hell can you sabotage a car to break down six or eight hours later anyway?

NAT HALPER   During the summer of 1950 Norman and Bea were living in the Hawthorne house in Provincetown. I'd read *The Naked and the Dead*, and having been in the army for five years, I was impressed by the characters' conversations. His book was the only one about the war in which the GIs sounded to me like the GIs I knew, and so somehow I got him on a panel at the Art Association to talk about new stuff in music, art, and literature. Joe Hawthorne and a nephew of Morris Davidson, a kid named Waxman, talked about music. Waxman raved against modern novels using four-letter words, looking very significantly toward Norman.

Despite the success of *The Naked and the Dead*, Norman still felt he was just a young man in the world. I was older, had some stature because of *Commentary*, knew about Joyce, and so for a year or two he was very respectful. He was writing *Barbary Shore*, and he would ask me things that now sound very naïve, like "How do you work parallels in correspondences?" Structural questions. And he was very interested in the special meanings of words, much as Joyce was. It was like he really wanted to know; maybe he'd use it, maybe not, but he wanted to know.

He seemed in good shape that summer. In fact, when Waxman attacked him he didn't react with fury. It was almost with a little bit of worry, like "Why are people saying these things?" It was as if he was telling himself, "You're a Jewish boy, you may have gone to Harvard, you were a cook in the army, but no matter if you're the greatest genius in the world, you're not high on the social scale." Or "You may be a success, with fan letters and money, but you have to meet people and see the way they act with you before it rubs off." He might've been more impressed with himself if he'd stayed in New York City and been taken up by the literary crowd, but instead he was up here in P-Town, where they're more interested in painting. Also, there'd been other guys here—Dos Passos, O'Neill—so here's a guy who's a kid and doesn't sound like a genius when he talks. There was no aggressiveness, no hostility.

ADELINE LUBELL NAIMAN   His nonrationalistic speculation, noncausal thinking really surfaced when he was writing *Barbary Shore*. I'm trying to remember the year when he made me nervous—the summer of '50, I think, when he was living up on Miller Hill Road in Provincetown. He was moving into places that my system wouldn't allow me to follow. Malaquais had turned his head, and he was sounding like, forgive me, a Trotskyite. Also, the mysticism that Angus Cameron, as an orthodox Marxist, had anticipated was emerging: Norman wasn't going to listen to anybody, although, in fact, he was listening to Jean without always acknowledging it.

NAT HALPER   Rightly or wrongly, I thought of Bea as one of those semiaggressive Brooklyn girls—I've always had a feeling about Brooklyn girls as opposed to Bronx girls—who are righteous about social causes, and although she wasn't my type, she was good-looking. I saw the two of them fairly often. At the time I thought everybody was a married couple, but then someone told me there were all kinds of things going on and that Norman felt she was going around saying he was no good in bed. This is just curbstone analysis, but before that I'd never heard him make any claims to prowess, so I think Bea punctured his feeling of "I'm a man" and may have done some real damage.

FANNY SCHNEIDER MAILER   When Barbara returned from California she met Larry Alson. Jack Alson, his father, was just mad about her and used to say, "If only some of the people in my office"—it was a big accounting firm—"had the same head for figures."

MARJORIE "OSIE" RADIN   I gave a party for Barbara when she was leaving for Europe in the summer of 1950. She brought Larry, and then she left for Europe alone. But he followed her almost immediately, and they were married over there. I don't know, but maybe it was a reaction to all the success of Norman and *The Naked and the Dead*.

LARRY ALSON   I had been living in the Village trying to write and met Barbara after she returned from the West Coast. The following summer, in July or August of '50, we decided to go to Europe. I had some extra bucks from my family's summer camp, the Casals Festival was taking place, and after touring around for a while we planted ourselves in St.-Tropez. We were sharing an apartment, and given the times, Barbara was afraid her parents would find out, so we got married to explain the mailing address. Our friends, Pat and Buddy Richmond,

Back in New York, 1949.

came up from Italy, and we had the ceremony in Nice.

My father was the national treasurer of the Anti-Defamation League—a minor figure with some power in the Jewish community. He was a CPA like Barney, but the difference was that he was very successful. My parents lived on Fifth Avenue, and in Fan's eyes I was proper middle class, no question.

My parents sent us home on the *France*, first class, and after we got back I met Norman and Bea. He was very friendly, welcoming. I liked Bea, even though at some point, I don't know when, I began to feel she had a chip on her shoulder. I was totally innocent and didn't understand anything about their relationship, but I didn't feel uncomfortable with it either, since they had a new baby, Susie, and their attention was focused on her as much as on me and Barbara.

NORMAN MAILER (LETTER TO FRANCIS IRBY GWALTNEY, 1950, NEW YORK)

Dear Fig and Ecey,

. . . Bea and I have been up in Provincetown, a kind of glorified fishing town, for the summer, and by dint of moderate sweat and deep depression I've finally finished a second draft of the albatross. It's nothing extraordinary as a book, but at least it's a book, and maybe with three more months of good work I'll be done with the cocker. What a relief that'll be.

Then I got another novel which I think will be better and bigger too. This one's just a little fart, about two-hundred fifty pages.

Susie is now almost a year old and has decided to celebrate by walking. I'm still not much of a father, but she is a cute bugger and I guess I'm fond of her. She looks like me which is more to her misfortune than otherwise, for she's a funny looking character. Also, going domestic all the way, we got a two month old puppy who's jealous as hell, and goes into a tizzie every time she sees us be nice to Susie....

Are you writing now, Fig? If so, what about? Bill Raney who's gone over to Henry Holt and Co. was asking 'bout you the other week. And how's school?

Answer this you white-haired baboon. We don't forget ole Fig the town idiot.

Bea sends voluptuous love.

Norm

P.S. We bought a house in Putney, Vermont. (That address will reach us.) But we don't move into it till October 1....

FANNY SCHNEIDER MAILER   I think they both agreed to live in Vermont, which was a mistake. They were having a hard time. Norman was very sad, very depressed, but I didn't want to talk about it with him because I figured he's a grown man. Susie was left with me a great deal of the time. I felt the child shouldn't suffer, so I agreed to keep her.

NORMAN MAILER (LETTER TO FRANCIS IRBY GWALTNEY, 1950, PUTNEY, VERMONT)

Dear Fig,

I been a cactus-backed albeit limber dick for not writing in so long, but I got an excuse, a good one anyway. I've been finishing my second novel, to be titled Barbary Shore, *and in a couple of weeks I'll be through editing it. The writing is pretty much done. I think it's a good book and it's sure been a son of a bitch writing it, but I'm beginning to feel pretty cheerful at the thought of having a second novel, cause the last one was just murder.*

We bought a house in Vermont as I think I wrote you, and we've been settling into it. It's a big house, eleven rooms, but it isn't fancy, and there's a big barn behind it which is better looking than the house. I like the setup, though, and would be in heaven if only it would snow...

Naked *isn't going to be made into a movie. The story is too long and too complicated to go into, but the short of it is that the War Department let go a Colonel's Request to the effect that they would be happiest if said film property, blah, blah, were finally not to be made. And since without their approval nobody can raise money, and the guy who was going to make it was a small producer, the thing ended up with no money for me and the producer spending lots of dough on scripts, none of them good, for the No man's land between the War Dept. and myself was pretty rough. I'm kind of relieved in a way because I have a sort of affection for* Naked, *and I'd of felt pretty cheap to have seen it fucked up on the screen....*

Susy is kind of cute. She walks now, has a red nose like a drunk....

My new book, between you and me, is going to raise a shit storm. It's a symbolic novel, but the message is clear enough; both the state capitalism of Russia and the monopoly capitalism of America have internal contradictions which make war inevitable for each of them, and the only answer is revolutionary socialism. So heaven help me when the rain starts.

Thank god there'll still be Arkansas to hide in and Gwaltney to slip food through the door. Vive the ring-nosed eagle. I just hope to hell your students don't find out they can spell better than you.

> *I'd like to see you both,*
> *Norm*

<u>MICKEY KNOX</u>   *The Naked and the Dead* couldn't be made without army assistance, Hecht was having trouble. Then, in 1951, there was a $20,000 payment from Hecht still due, but Norm told him, "Forget it. Just give me the rights back." Hecht owed that $20,000, it wasn't just an option payment, and I said to Norman, "Jesus, $20,000!" He said, "It's better that I get the book back." Then about four years later he sold the rights to Charles Laughton. The two of them had a lot of conversations and felt they were on the right track, but whatever the problems, they couldn't solve them. Eventually the property passed over to Warner Brothers and Norman had no say whatsoever.

<u>NORMAN ROSTEN</u>   The great success of *The Naked and the Dead* was astonishing, but to be good, to be excellent, meant that he was going to stay with it. He was always working, and I realized how hard when I went up to visit him in Putney, Vermont. He knew I liked to ski even though I wasn't very good, and he was sort of half-assed into skiing himself. He met me at the Brattleboro station, and we drove to their house, a farmhouse, ten or fifteen miles away. We did a little skiing, I ran into a tree once or twice, I stayed overnight, but I remember the next morning when I got up he was already at his typewriter, doing revisions on *Barbary Shore*.

<u>GEORGE WASHINGTON GOETHALS</u>   You know Norman's description of how he'd been changed by *The Naked and the Dead*—that the book's success had "lobotomized" his past, forced him to come up with a public persona? Well, it's dead on. Even I was surprised by his transformation, the extent of his "over-determination"—to use a word from my field. Analytically, the seeds of its enormity just weren't apparent in Cambridge. But even if *The Naked and the Dead* hadn't been a success, there's no doubt in my mind, absolutely none, he would have kept on writing.

<u>NORMAN MAILER</u>   What nobody has ever understood is that *Barbary Shore* is my most autobiographical novel.

<u>NORMAN ROSTEN</u>   Of course, when I read *Barbary Shore*, I recognized 20 Remsen Street as well as the models for McLeod and Guinevere. I believe Norman had worked on the book in Hollywood, but I have the sense that before he'd gone out there he'd come back to work at 20 Remsen, since the novel's setting was so similar to that boarding house, the room he'd taken over from me the summer of '47, when he first met Charlie.

The house itself had four stories. There was a long stoop and then a narrow stairway to the top. All the rooms up there were small, about nine by twelve, except one larger room facing the street. There were three sort of dormer rooms, cut up out of the top floor, which was the attic area, and in each of the rooms was a bed. A common bathroom stood down the hall. People who wanted to could live there, like Charlie—there was a hot plate—but Norman and I were there only during the day. All the views but one were to the south, not to the river, and you saw only the backs and courtyards of other buildings.

And there *was* a landlady. I never knew her real name, but Norman called her Guinevere, not only in the book but at the time he was working there. She was in her late twenties, early thirties. She was stacked, and she was slovenly. She was also flirtatious and would come up and make the beds just as Norman describes in the book. We'd kid around, and Charlie was always saying to her, "When are you going to get rid of the kid?" Because she had a little girl about seven who never seemed to go to school and who followed her around all the time. Charlie said to me once, "You know why that little kid's following her? She's protecting her. None of us are going to jump her with that kid there." A lot of Charlie's conversation, like McLeod's in the book, was about how he'd been trying to get at her.

I think it was just Guinevere's attitude that was provocative, more than her actually sticking her ass in your face while she made the beds, say. She was good-looking, very loquacious, and always willing to involve us in conversation—like "What are you guys writing?" Norman originally met her exactly the way he describes: He wanted to sublet my room, and so I took him down to the basement, where she lived. The rent was the same—four dollars a week. I'd told him it would be the same because I'd spoken to her already.

I know he was taken with her because I'd see him chatting with her occasionally downstairs. But as for screwing her, I doubt it. That's probably the writer's fantasy. Charlie would have had the better shot because he was there night and day, but I don't think she'd take him on. As for me, she wasn't quite my style; she was too intimidating, if that's the right word. She was an attractive, strange lady, and we used to wonder if the child was hers. None of us ever saw the husband. The kid made the whole mystery. And, of course, Guinevere is presented just that way in *Barbary Shore*.

There were apartments on the lower floors, but we didn't bother with anyone down there. We just walked up to our rooms, went to work, and then beat it back home at the end of the day. We didn't talk to anyone—we were writers, going to work, living the real life, working hard. Guinevere would make cracks about "you writer guys," and maybe because we were so busy she thought we weren't going to take her too seriously. She used to wear sort of a housecoat. She wasn't dressed scantily, just loosely, so maybe she was overflowing a bit. Her work took ten minutes. She'd make the bed, then kibitz a bit. Even if Charlie or any of us wanted to bang her, it was difficult, because she'd never come up without the daughter. A saucy lady, sassy, lively, with an Irish quality.

Charlie had the room next door, maybe two doors down from my room, which then became Norman's. Devlin was certainly the model for McLeod in *Barbary Shore,* no doubt about it. I sensed there was something very close between him and Norman, perhaps because of his help with *The Naked and the Dead.* From what he said, Norman had found his editing valuable, and Charlie was proud of having done it. He was also interested in Norman's ideas. Devlin was interested in politics in his own funny way, but he wasn't CP or a Stalinist. I suppose some of McLeod's moral and political confusions were based on Charlie, enough of him so that you could say that he was capable of all that. I don't know if he was offended by being portrayed as a shadowy, undercover guy, but as I remember the character, McLeod was always a little bit devious, and Devlin had that air of mystery about him too.

I don't know what happened between them, but after *Barbary Shore* Devlin would hear nothing about Norman. I don't think it was because Norman had used him as the basis for McLeod, but I do know that Norman became the bad guy for Charlie, who implied there was some kind of betrayal.

HEDDA ROSTEN   Also, I remember Devlin was very jealous of Malaquais' influence on Mailer. I don't remember what he said, but I think he felt in a way that Norman had chosen Malaquais over him.

NORMAN ROSTEN   I never actually met Malaquais, but I heard a lot about him, and I can imagine Malaquais being appalled by Devlin's political views, if only because Charlie's ideas were fairly scrambled.

The split between Norman and Charlie happened about the time Charlie married Jill—Jill Mangraviti—and moved out of the Heights to San Francisco, where I think they lived with her rich grandmother. They were married for something like eighteen years and had two kids. Charlie wasn't an alcoholic, but he sure could put the liquor away, and then Jill's grandmother died and she inherited a lot of money, and the minute that happened Charlie was given his walking papers. In some ways she dumped him. On the other hand, she'd put up with him for so long.

After that Charlie vanished, and in 1982 I tried to track him down because his niece was also trying to find him. After Jill and he separated, she moved to New Jersey, then to New York, but I couldn't locate her either. There was also a woman he lived with for a couple of years in the Heights, but that ended badly too. She vowed—and I believed her—that she didn't know where he was. Reportedly he was on welfare, living at the Chelsea Hotel, then he moved to a room around Twenty-fourth Street, but the building was torn down, so he just vanished. Which I'm sorry about, since we were friends, even though we'd had run-ins, like when he borrowed money from us, then asked to borrow more money to give to a poet out on Staten Island.

But coming back to the McLeod character in *Barbary Shore*—the description of McLeod playing head games with Lovett is almost a reverse image. That's something I think Norman would more likely do. It works in the story for the McLeod character, and the novel is autobiographical in the sense that he puts you through all the political formats, trying to find out where you are. In that way the book was a little confusing—you didn't quite know who or what anything was. But it had a magnetic, mysterious appeal at the time because in '51 everyone was screwed up that way. No one quite knew what one was doing.

NORMAN MAILER   I had begun *Barbary Shore* in Paris, calling it *Mrs. Guinevere.*

It's true, though, McLeod is an intensified version of Charlie Devlin. McLeod's style of speech came from Devlin. That dry laugh, the idea of talking about yourself with absolute contempt. Peeling away, peeling away. That was Charlie, that was his style of mind.

Charlie was half pleased with the early section, of course. Amused and titillated, just as we are when our portrait's painted. But he hated the end because it violated his philosophy—it was Malaquais' philosophy in Devlin's body. That's why we had the break. It was as if we'd been priests in a seminary together and I suddenly went over to Islam.

JOHN LEONARD   Mailer—posing as the bad boy—invented himself as though everyone before him, the people who wrote about American culture and society in the thirties and forties, hadn't written, as though they hadn't thought they'd solved certain problems or had it under control.

On the one hand, you consider yourself a child of the Enlightenment—and Marx can be considered a child of the Enlightenment. On the other hand, modernism in literature and the arts wants to break things into fragments; the irrational is coming out all the time. What do you do with Freud put together with the way you think social arrangements should change? That's the problem. And what made Mailer so wonderful, particularly for my generation—I'm forty-four—is that he was doing the same kind of thing better than we were. In *Barbary Shore*, despite the second half's being a disaster, he was reinventing Marx all for himself, personalizing him.

I once talked to him about the book, much later, in 1969. We'd run into each other on the Metroliner coming back from Philadelphia to New York. We sat together, and I told him I thought the first half of the book was brilliant but that the second half suffered. He explained that he'd been interrupted, that he was in a dream when he was writing the first half, and couldn't recover the mood. He indicated that he was interrupted by the disaster in Hollywood—I don't know what the terms of that or his personal life were—but that when he tried to come back to the novel, he didn't know what he wanted to do. His rhythm had been broken, he said, adding, "To this day I can't figure out how I should've ended the book."

Four or five years later, when I was editing *The Times Book Review*, I called Scott Meredith to ask Norman to review an important book about Vietnam. Scott wouldn't put me through to him, explaining that he was working on a novel and couldn't be interrupted. I said, "Shit, I wouldn't be calling if I didn't think this was a book he'd really want to review, so at least you can tell him." Then Norman came in on another line. We talked briefly until he had to take another call. But finally Meredith—who was taking his calls and fending people off—concluded things by saying, "Norman says to tell you, yeah, he should probably review this book, but he can't. You remember what he told you about *Barbary Shore*? Well, he doesn't want to be interrupted again." I just sat there thinking, What kind of memory is this? He'd made incidental remarks to me about finishing *Barbary Shore*, and four years later he remembered them and said, "John will understand. I don't want this to be another *Barbary Shore*."

IRVING HOWE   When I reviewed *Barbary Shore* in *The Nation*—it was an unfavorable review—I didn't make a specific connection with Malaquais. You see, many people when they broke through the Stalinist milieu still wanted to remain leftists and fell into a kind of fundamental Marxist position because it was comfortable. Having done it myself, I know what I'm talking about. And no question, Norman did fall into it for a time, which was what a number of critics, including myself, saw in the book.

THE NATION   *Mailer has come to his radicalism a little late: he does not really know in his flesh and bones what has happened to the socialist hope in the era of Hitler and Stalin, and that is why he can refer so cavalierly to democracy and carry on like a stale pamphleteer. He is sincere and he is serious; I admire his courage in writing a book he must have known would bring him grief and attack. But I can only say that his relation to his material, like his presentation of it, is not authentic. Otherwise he would not seem so sure.*

NEW YORK HERALD TRIBUNE   *Dull, in execution if not conception, it wraps itself in a billowy atmosphere of dreamlike unreality.*

THE NEW YORK TIMES   *At best, the result is not unlike a good modern painting, a yellow mist through which the reader sees only the essential shape and line, and in which a guilt similar to that informing* The Trial, *is felt. At worst, Mailer can be very dull and, in his insistence on the lost purity and nobility of the Communist Left, sentimental and untrue.*

THE NEW YORKER   *An odd book, a political tear-jerker, delivered to the reader with its pages already blurred by its author's own tears of self-pity.*

MAXWELL GEISMAR, SATURDAY REVIEW OF LITERATURE   The Naked and the Dead *was a solid job of realism and social criticism in one of the main traditions of American writing. Mr. Mailer's second novel is a drama of ideas that is held together by a symbolic framework of complete human frustration. It is fashionable, it is literary by current standards, it is well done, but I think it is a mistake.*

TIME   *Norman Mailer has a bad case of moral claustrophobia. Viewed through his polarizing spectacles, all the dice are loaded, all the cards are marked, all the wheels are rigged. All the world's a cage, and all its men and women merely slayers. His first novel,* The Naked and the Dead, *had enough of the juice of life to disguise this sophomoric fatalism. The only juice in* Barbary Shore *is embalming fluid ... Paceless, tasteless and graceless.*

NORMAN MAILER (ADVERTISEMENTS FOR MYSELF)   Barbary Shore *showed its face in the worst of seasons, just a few months after the Chinese had come into the Korean War and set us off on another of our clammy national hysterias. It would have taken a good novel to overcome that bad time—obviously* Barbary Shore *was not good enough. . . .*

What I sensed (to my deep depression) was that I was working my way toward saying something unforgivable, enough so that most readers were already agitated—or what is worse—bored, by their quick, uneasy sense that my vision— what little I had of it—was leading toward the violent and the orgiastic. I do not mean that I was clear about where I was going, it was rather that I had a dumb dull set of intimations that the things I was drawn to write about were taboo . . .

What can be underlined is that the direction I took in Barbary Shore *was a first step toward work I will probably be doing from now on. For I wish to attempt an entrance into the mysteries of murder, suicide, incest, orgy, orgasm, and Time.*

V:
GREENWICH
VILLAGE
AND
THE
DEER PARK
(1951-55)

ADELINE LUBELL NAIMAN There was a change in him—not abrupt, but a growing braggadocio, lots more real confidence and an ability to spar, the realization that he didn't have to try to please anybody. I doubt he understood it, but probably he sensed he'd gotten himself into a bind with Bea, that he'd mistaken the door into the closet for the door into the world. And having seen what the world could offer him, he wanted out.

KINGSLEY ERVIN I saw him at a party, and it was a shock: people were sitting on the floor worshiping him. I have an image—a gentle gurulike voice, holding court, as it were, and I remember thinking, How is this affecting Bea?

RHODA LAZARE WOLF Steve Sanchez was a Mexican radical and a good friend of Dan's from the New School, and the marriage was pretty much over when Dan introduced Steve to Bea. Bea was quite aware that it was over because Norman had basically said, "Let's have sex with other people." One of Norman's ways of getting rid of a wife is to say, "You go out and fuck and I'll fuck."

I first saw Adele in '51 at a big party given by Barbara when she and Larry lived on Riverside Drive. I think that was when I first met Dan too. Adele came in with Norman. God, was she stunning! I spent most of the evening sitting on the floor talking to her. But the situation seemed very tense because Bea was also there with Steve Sanchez. Steve was something. Not big but dark-skinned and intense, and when he looked at a woman you really flipped. I don't know why Barbara would have both Bea and Steve and Norman and Adele there, although Barbara would never have a party without Norman.

LARRY ALSON   Steve was very handsome and there was something nice about him, but he had qualities that we North Americans don't understand—pridefulness, machismo, storming around about particular slights. At three A.M. he insisted we have toasts. I had a bottle of vodka. It was a situation I really didn't want to get caught up in because he was full of so much fury and intensity.

MICKEY KNOX   Norman and Bea had spent the summer in Provincetown and in the fall had gone back to Vermont, but then he started spending more time alone in New York. I still thought their marriage was in better shape than mine, but obviously I was wrong. I was with him when he drove up to Putney to get his things. Bea had taken the house over, but she wasn't there when we went up. He was despondent, suffering. Eva Marie Saint, whom I was dating, came with us, and she remarked, "Norman's so quiet," and that evening we sat around the fire quite some time in silence. He was depressed, withdrawn, and gloomy.

Right after the breakup he was living in a fourth-floor walk-up, filthy halls, a horrible place. It was barely furnished. He was desperate. His mind wasn't on the apartment, which was only temporary, and I think he knew that Fan was going to take a long time to adjust to the divorce.

BARBARA PROBST SOLOMON   Things had been ambiguous when I'd see Norman in New York—comments like "Bea's in the country," "Bea's away." Then later in '51 I was at a party at Barbara's, and Norman arrived with another girl. He took me aside to tell me he and Bea had broken up. I was upset and started to cry, not because I liked Bea but because I'd assumed that all these marriages and love affairs were going to last forever. The girl he was with was Adele.

After Bea, though—or maybe even before the breakup—Fan set up a system that applied to all of Norman's divorces: no matter what, she was going to maintain the Mailer family structure.

ED FANCHER   Dan Wolf and I had been taking courses at the New School on the GI Bill right after the war, which is where I met Adele. I met Norman through Dan, and Dan met Adele through me, and then she met Norman through Dan. When I first met Adele she was quite young, twenty or twenty-one, a nice girl, still living at home in Brooklyn.

ADELE MORALES MAILER   I had been taking any esoteric course that caught my eye, mostly art appreciation, that kind of thing, when Ed picked me up in the New School cafeteria and we started going out together. I was twenty-one, going on twenty-two, so it was in '47. Ed got me an apartment in the building next to his on Sixteenth Street, and I remember feeling that Manhattan was like another planet for me, taking courses at the New School, meeting people at

With Adele at The Copacabana, New York, 1951.

Village coffeehouses like San Remo's. The scene in *Saturday Night Fever* when the boy and girl have a great sense of exhilaration, of freedom and adventure, as they drive across the Brooklyn Bridge into the city? That's the way I felt when Ed picked me up at my parents' house in Bensonhurst and drove me and my few sticks of furniture to the apartment. Our two buildings were connected by the roof. It was like that scene in the movie *Seventh Heaven*, where they go over the rooftops. He lived on the top floor, I lived on the fourth floor, so I used to go over the roof, and I was spending more time in Ed's apartment than in my own. I had a roommate, but I never saw her; we used to leave each other notes, because she was living with someone too. Ed and I were together off and on for three or four years. Dan was a close friend of Ed's, and also Norman and Dan were excellent friends, so I'd vaguely heard about Norman for a long time. At that time, though, he was with Bea.

I was seeing Jack Kerouac while I was still with Fancher, since we both sort of did our own thing. I'd met him at a folk dance, again at the New School, where he came over and started talking to me. I was wearing a white off-the-shoulder blouse, and he told me I looked very beautiful. He was always very courtly, very gentlemanly, almost shy in fact.

I guess I saw Jack over a period of a year but he was still a merchant seaman, so he'd be away at sea and I wouldn't hear from him for months. He said he was in love with me, and I think I was among the first of his friends to see the manuscript of *On the Road*—at any rate probably the first woman.

RHODA LAZARE WOLF   I think she met Dan one night when he was over at Ed's and she called up to tell Ed she'd just slashed her wrists—like Elena Esposito in *The Deer Park*. Norman must have heard the story from Dan.

After Bea, though, Norman was depressed, and one night Dan mentioned Adele. Norman called her and sent a cab over to bring her back to his apartment, and they stayed up all night talking.

ADELE MORALES MAILER   It was a Saturday night, I didn't have a date, so I'd gone out with my cousin Margie, then gone home and was all settled in with my *Times*, nice and comfy. I had my nightgown on, was really in a good mood, and the phone rings. It's Dan. I said, "Goddammit, it's one-thirty. What do you want?" He said, "Listen, you know I know Norman Mailer. He's a great guy, and we're here in his apartment. Why don't you come up?"

Norman had borrowed an apartment from a guy on Sixty-fourth Street, between First and Second Avenues. I said, "Are you crazy? I'm tired and I'm in bed. I don't want to come out."

"Oh, come on, you'll have fun. He's a nice guy."

"But I don't want to, Dan. And besides I don't have the money for a cab."

"Forget it, he'll reimburse you. Just get a cab."

Finally this voice comes on the phone: "This is Norman."

I said, "Oh, hi, Norman."

"Look, why don't you come up for a drink," he insisted. "Get a cab, I'll pay for it."

I started to object, but then he quoted a beautiful line from Scott Fitzgerald— I wish I could remember it exactly—about adventure and getting up and going out into the night, and that did it. I laughed and said, "Gee, that's nice. Okay, I'm coming up." He was so charming that I got dressed and took the cab drive that changed my life.

I got there about two in the morning, and both of them were high. Norman has always told me he was terrified of me that night: "I was frightened to death when I saw you. There you were, so beautiful, with this beautiful neckerchief around your shirt. And a mustache." I always laugh at that—I guess I hadn't bleached it in a while, so I must've had a slight shadow. And there he was, this nice little guy, wearing a plaid shirt, sort of looking into his drink, very shy, saying "Hi." We all sat down, and Dan and I threw our arms around each other. Norman later told me he thought something was going on between Dan and me, but it was just a fond greeting. Dan and Ed and I had been very close.

Bea and Norman were breaking up and I guess it just took me to make it happen. That first night I think I fell in love with him for the way he talked. He told me later he had a theory that he wasn't attractive to women, physically attractive, but I thought he was enormously sensitive and good-looking. Very slender, and he had a nice body.

MICKEY KNOX   Then he moved and was living in the railroad flat at 37 First Avenue, with Adele next door and Dan in the flat upstairs. He probably got the place through Dan, and he put in all the plumbing and heating himself. He had plenty of money, but he wanted to do it himself, maybe to take a breather from writing. My first impression of Adele was that I liked her. She had something very nice and natural about her. It wasn't the feisty, tough Adele of later, when she gained a lot of muscle through Norman. I'm just guessing, but the fact that she was exotic and unlike Bea, who was Jewish, probably had a lot to do with Norman's attraction.

Adele's father, Al, with his dark chiseled features and high cheekbones, looks like an Indian who's walked out of the mountains of Peru, which in fact he did. He's in his mid-eighties now, still vital, and plays handball every day in Brooklyn. A tough little guy who used to be a boxer, and in fact he had over a hundred fights as a kid and then became a typesetter at the *News*. He and Norman liked each other, and they used to box a lot.

But Adele's mother, May, was a horror. She's now dead, died in '81, but both Norman and I thought she was nuts. She was born of Spanish parents who were on their way to America from Galicia and stopped off in Cuba, where Adele was born. The first time I met her was when Joanne—Adele's sister, later my second wife—brought them over to have dinner with us in the Village. Afterwards we walked them down to get a taxi, and out of the blue May said to me, "You're an ex-con, aren't you?" There was only one response and that was to put her on, so I said, "Oh, sure. How'd you know?" She said, "I can tell, I can just tell." The woman was impossible. High-strung, nervous, and she could also be mean and insulting. She wasn't handsome either. Both Adele and Joanne got their looks from Al. Both sisters got along terribly with their mother, and both left home early, with Joanne getting married at eighteen just to get out of the house.

MARIA IRENE FORNES   Adele was kind of beautiful and fiery and powerful, with a lot of energy, so she wouldn't have been intimidated. Ed Fancher, I would say, was important to her even though they fought a lot, and it was like the way they loved each other. What they did in private I don't know, but they fought in public. Not nasty, but more like *Carmen*, the opera. I remember one time at a party at Ed's, Ed said something, and she threw a piggy bank at him. I didn't know English too well, so there was a lot I didn't pick up, but I think she was angry at Ed's being stingy or she wanted him to pay for something. But it wasn't like venom. She's still kind of like that, demonstrative. You wouldn't go "Oh, my God!" You would laugh, and they would laugh.

Adele and I were never really friends, though. One time later Norman told me he was glad I was Adele's best friend, that he liked me as Adele's best friend. I was kind of shocked. I never said, "Why do you say I'm her best friend?" because that would seem nasty. But I thought, I don't know why he thinks we are best friends. I always liked Adele and she liked me, but she was always involved with, first Ed, then...well, she was not then the type of girl who would just go out with the girls or friends. I think it always had to be a man.

But with Ed and Dan and Adele it wasn't that daily thing, "What are you doing tonight? You want to come over?" which is almost like family. There had to be an event, like if there was a brunch we would invite them. By that point Dan was already a friend of Norman's. He'd never talked to me about Norman, but I remember at some point Norman appearing. He seemed very hectic, talked very fast but was sort of sweet, a nice kind of person, and later he and Adele would be coming to some of these brunches in the Village, which were usually a result of some party. The parties didn't go on all night—we'd just decide to meet the next day at somebody's apartment.

I don't know whether there was a change in Adele when she took up with

Norman. If he pushed her, drove her, it was that he is a driver. He can't sit in one place without driving himself or people around him. The thing is, what I felt was that Norman lived a lot in his imagination. Like later, his saying to me, "You are Adele's best friend." How can one person tell another "I'm appointing you . . ."? Adele was always a fiery person, but her fieriness was like a street kid. "Hey!"—and they'd go on, screaming, then laughing. What I perceived in Norman—and I don't claim to know him that well—is that he's a very passionate person. Something starts in his life, and then he starts theorizing on it and then believing that it's so. And practicing it, creating a situation. Which is how you begin to write, of course. It's almost as if he writes you, that he can sort of describe you. And that is flattering—Oh, I am that kind of person, you feel, because after all Norman is a celebrity, he's not just a guy going around making it up. So he creates a person, and if the person subjects himself, if the person is vulnerable to that, he or she accepts it.

So to Norman, being a person of a certain upbringing where perhaps shouting wasn't done, perhaps there may have been something different and interesting in the way Adele behaved. The idea that Latin people are any more passionate or sexual than Jews is not so, of course, but, still, it was like he was doing an investigation of this kind of passion, something that he was going to practice—practice the hundred ways in which he and Adele could have a fight.

I think it was Dan more than Adele who introduced Norman to the Village. But Norman didn't defer to Dan, not in public when I'd see them. They were friends. I never saw them fight. But I never saw Dan fight with anybody. Dan doesn't fight.

ADELINE LUBELL NAIMAN   I always separated Norman's success from our relationship, so I saw his change differently and not as he describes it in *Advertisements*. I just felt he grew up, though events precipitated his growing up in an extravagant form. He'd married Bea as a boy with all these yearnings and drives, a sense of himself that mixed ambition and despair, perhaps with a fear of failure at the edge of it too, then events proved his self-estimation to be what it ought to be. So I think the two coincided. But I also think there was the thing of life and experience, war and success—and, quite simply, growing up. There wasn't a movement from Bea to Adele. There was a gap.

I had been living in Chicago when he'd split from Bea. He must've been upset by it, of course, but he also itched to be out of it, so I doubt he was profoundly shaken. I was in New York right after Dan Wolf fixed him up with Adele, and it was obvious he was already looking for engagement.

ADELE MORALES MAILER   We'd met just at the time *Barbary Shore* was finished, and I was around when it came out, and that was a tough time. The reviews not only attacked the book, they attacked him. They were very personal, people would froth at the mouth. Hateful reviews, and it was as if the reviewers had been laying for him. I used to get even more upset than he did. I would cry.

NORMAN MAILER   There was a party for *Barbary Shore* at the home of John Lamont, my editor, and everyone was stricken because the reviews were so bad.

At Rinehart they knew it wasn't going to do as well as *The Naked and the Dead*, but they hadn't expected reviews this savage. They were shocked. I was the only one who was merry that night. I remember walking around smiling and saying, in effect, to people, "Hey, look how merry I am!" Do you recall that line in *The Naked and the Dead*, "He had the kind of merriment men have when events have ended in utter disaster"? Well, it's true! Now I could get back to something I knew something about, because I was off the big board.

The delayed reaction came when I realized that people take these reviews seriously. I had been thinking of the advance I'd made in style, and I thought my loyal readers would come through, saying, "He's really talented, we've gotta take him more seriously." I thought that the serious readers I'd wanted to like *The Naked and the Dead* hadn't read it because it was a best seller, and conversely, I now thought the best literary critics would love *Barbary Shore*. Well, I had no idea what a bad review was; I hadn't really tasted bad reviews, nor did I realize how personally insulting a bad review can be.

Still, my glee that night was like a guy who goes into the ring, he's over-matched, gets into a slugfest with his opponent, and is knocked out in the first round. They wake him up, and he's real happy even though everybody's looking at him like he's nuts. Yet he's happy because he's discovered he had more guts than he thought he did. He'd walked into the ring scared shitless, but for that one minute he was fighting the other guy even to even. So when the boom hit and I discovered I could take it, that meant more to me than that the reviews were bad. Because I still felt optimistic. Like the kid gets knocked out, everybody else is saying, "Let's get him out of here, he doesn't belong in the ring," but the guy himself is saying, "Wait til I get my next fight, now I know I can do it."

I wouldn't say that the book's failure made me see myself differently, however. If one insists on talking about the "phenomenon of Norman Mailer," that didn't exist for me then, not the phenomenon as such. That came years later, about '54, '55, when I started smoking pot and seeing myself from the inside and the outside both. The inside and the outside: I could go back and forth every five or ten seconds in my head.

ADELE MORALES MAILER   Norman had had an apartment on Pitt Street, where I sometimes stayed, but when Dan left his apartment, which was next door to mine, Norman moved in, and we renovated both of our places to make them into one large apartment. We plastered and painted, and when Norman did the plumbing himself, a wonderful job, our landlord used to say, "So why is this? You're a nice boy, you're Norman Mailer, what do you want to live here for?"

NORMAN MAILER   That railroad flat was something. When I moved in I started to go to work on the place, renovating it top to bottom. I took down the wall dividing my place from Adele's, working maybe for three full days before I asked myself how I was going to get rid of the plaster and brick. Then I began sneaking it out every night in cardboard cartons. I'd leave it in the trash cans out on the street, and they became very heavy to empty, and of course the garbage men didn't appreciate it. The superintendent of the building, a great old Ukrainian guy, was impressed with what I was doing and in fact would later lend me pipe-cutting tools, but one night as I was depositing a load of brick I was stopped by a Sanitation Department dick—the guy was wearing a suit, if you can believe it. He'd been tipped off by neighbors, people up the street. But he couldn't prove anything. Fortunately it was toward the end of the job, so I think Adele and I got rid of the last few cartons by taking a cab to the West Village.

I redid the place, though—the wiring, the plumbing, everything. I put the bathtub in the kitchen, off to one side, and the Ukrainian super showed me how to thread pipe, which I worked on out in the hallway. The feed pipe for the tub came off the kitchen sink. We had a big party one night, and Lillian Hellman came up to inspect my work. Studying my bathtub, she said with a great grin, "Norman, I respect you more for this than for *The Naked and the Dead.*" God, how Lillian loved men who could work with their hands.

ADELE MORALES MAILER   Looking back on it, I suppose it was a real question why Norman was doing all the work himself. He had money at that point, but he wanted the bohemian life. And I just went along, I suppose because I'm one of those people who just does that. Sometimes I look back and say what a dope I was, but I was in love with the guy.

Still, I was an artist, and I wasn't into the bourgeois life either. The loft was big enough for me to work there, and I think Norman had a studio in Brooklyn where he wrote. I was also going to the Hofmann School, and I studied with Hofmann four or five years, both in New York and then on the Cape.

I'd started painting as a kid in public school and majored in art at Washington Irving, at that time one of the best high schools for painting. But until Hofmann I had never done abstract painting, so it was a whole other language, and he made me discover that was the direction I wanted to go in. And God, Hofmann taught me *to see.* It wasn't only painting. He was one of the four most important men in my life, men who changed my life—Hofmann, Lee Strasberg, Frank Corsaro, and Norman.

But Norman and Hofmann couldn't communicate. First, because Hofmann had such a thick Dutch accent that even in class I felt I needed an interpreter, but more importantly, there was no real meeting, because they were on totally different planes. Up until Norman met me he really had had nothing to do with painters. A few years ago Dan Wolf was interviewed in *Esquire* and he mentioned that he thought I'd been very good for Norman, that I'd opened up Norman's world. And I think that's probably true. He'd been away, living up in Vermont, and I introduced him to the whole Village scene and all my painter friends.

FANNY SCHNEIDER MAILER   Why he picked Adele I never could understand. She was no inspiration for anything. He was very unhappy in his private life, lonely and sympathetic, and she came along to receive his sympathy, which he could shower on her. Which she took very, very easily. But she didn't give him what he really needed—sympathetic understanding, encouragement, support in his ideas, his need for order. She's chaotic. And how! But he stayed with her.

She was the kind that knew how to cry. But she was destroying him by not nurturing what was most dear to him, his work. I interfered very little because I figured there was nothing I could do. I'd just have to wait and see. But I felt Adele was no good for him, except she was good to sleep with and to give sympathy. But you can always find a good-looking woman to sleep with. That's really being brusque, isn't it?

BARBARA PROBST SOLOMON Adele was gorgeous, and of all his wives she was the most interesting. She had her own quality. It wasn't just that you could make her up to look like the most perfect woman on Madison Avenue. She had a fire, a sexual kind of heat.

EMMA CLARA "ECEY" GWALTNEY The summer of '51—in August, I think— we came up to New York to visit and stayed in Norman's parents' apartment. They were out in Long Branch, and Susie was with them.

Bea was visiting in New York for some reason and staying in Norman's folks' apartment too. Norman was with Adele, living in their miserable cold-water flat, but I guess he and Bea were faking it for his parents before the official split-up. Bea's sister, Phyllis, was also around a lot.

Norman had told us in a letter that he and Bea were splitting up, but he didn't say she'd be staying with us, so the situation was unexpected. The die was cast, though, as far as the split-up went. I don't know why Bea was hanging around, because surely she didn't care about propriety, so I guess it was Norman's power. Plus the fact that she was still on good terms with his parents, and, of course, Susie was with them. And all the while Norman was trying to keep up appearances with this little intrigue going on.

At first it seemed so exotic, so foreign that we thought the split was temporary, that Adele was a fling, an aberration or some sort of heady experience. Maybe Bea thought that too. She seemed slightly contemptuous, also puzzled—"This is ridiculous. What does he see in her?"—that sort of thing. She was acting sort of rebellious, and she blurted out that part of the reason for their breakup was that the sex had gone bad after the birth of Susie. She also said she'd slept with fifty men before Norman and that Norman had had no previous experience and that that had always been a little bit of the problem. Basically, I think she felt more worldly than him, politically and sexually. She thought he'd been naïve.

She also felt he was changing, which was what she did not intend to put up with—to sit back and watch him, as she thought of it, play the famous writer putting on a show for people. At the time, she said he was a little bit like a politician—everybody who wanted his time got it, whether they were worthy or not. She claimed he was dissipating his energies, not concentrating with the same dedication he'd shown while working on The Naked and the Dead, and she was presenting herself as the wife who devotes herself to a project and is serious, and I had the feeling that she envisioned an austere writer's existence. She had previously felt ahead of him, and it could be that she was jealous too. We, of course, hadn't seen these changes because he never changed with us.

So she was angry, and she didn't make any bones about it. One afternoon

Norman and Fig and Bea and Jean Malaquais were having a political discussion. I was pregnant with my daughter and very sleepy, so I put my head in Fig's lap and sort of dozed off. It was real hot and there was no air conditioning. All of a sudden Bea stripped off her blouse. She had a slip on, but Norman was offended and said, "Bea, why don't you just take out one of your tits and show us?" He was furious. Later Adele came in to pick up a little package she'd left and Bea cracked, "Oh, she forgot her Ortho gel." Then, when we were on our way to Long Branch, Bea said, "I don't need this Adele who has fifteen orgasms at one time." She was really bugging him, letting him have it, and he just sort of took it because he was suffering, taking the breakup pretty seriously.

I felt she was trying to shock people in general, not just get back at Norman. One night she wanted to show us the Bowery—Danny Wolf, Fig, and her sister Phyllis. Norman, I guess, was with Adele. Bea had gotten herself a new red dress, short and strapless. There was no way she could wear a brassiere with straps, and she didn't want to wear a strapless bra, so she put the dress on without a bra. She was pretty big-bosomed and the dress was too tight, too revealing, and we went down to the Bowery, and some young thug came up and tried to make a pass at her. She kind of parried with the guy until Fig stepped forward and said, "Get out of here" or something, and later, when we told Norman about it, he was upset and said it could've been very dangerous.

Looking back, though, I don't think we realized what a traumatic time that was for Norman. We'd met his sister Barbara, and I thought she was so cute, just darling and so friendly, so open, and obviously Norman and she were crazy about each other. But I don't remember her being with us that often, maybe because she had deliberately chosen not to be with Adele and wanted to stay out of the whole situation.

For Norman, though, maybe Adele was a way of breaking with his family, although I got the feeling he was totally protective of his mother. Adele was such a beautiful, exotic creature. She liked Frederick's of Hollywood lingerie, and was so different from anything he'd experienced before. It was almost as if he was enjoying the rebellion—he'd rebelled and gone to this cold-water flat in a bad part of town. Living there, keeping Adele pacified, it was a balancing act, a show, a game. "Keep Adele over here, and Bea's over there, and even though we have all this infighting, we'll keep up appearances for Fan." It seemed to me it was the kind of tension that part of him found enjoyable. I'm not sure Adele really picked up on what was happening. She wasn't like Bea, who knew everything.

Bea, though, was always one of Fig's favorites, probably because she was almost a female Norman. He admired her forthrightness. She tickled him, and she *was* funny. And maybe because she was so honest and forthright, Norman enjoyed teasing Adele. Sometimes when I'd hear them I'd think it was like they were starring in each other's pornographic movie. It was like a play, with Adele coming on as the temptress. I asked Norman once, just for fun, "She shaves her legs, why doesn't she shave under her arms?" "Cause it gets me hot," he said.

FANNY SCHNEIDER MAILER   Fig and Ecey stayed in my apartment on the fifth floor on Willow Street. I gave them the key for two weeks or so. These were the first *goyish* friends of Norman that I knew, but I approved because they were nice, honest people. We didn't put on airs, they didn't put on airs. And I had heard the story about the *goyim* in the army who wanted to break up the friendship, but Fig had stood up for Norman.

ALLEN GINSBERG   I think I first met Norman when I went with a friend, Carl Solomon, to a loft on Monroe Street on the lower East Side. I think he was supposed to be living with a group of other writers and painters in a big communal apartment, the nature of which was "subterranean" in the same way we were using the word, Kerouac and I, and the way Kerouac used it later for the title of his novel *The Subterraneans*. I remember either getting a glimpse of Norman there or a rumor of him.

It was about a year after *Barbary Shore* had come out, and the loft had the same atmosphere as the book, that kind of Dostoevskian man-of-the-underground quality, which I thought was great. I haven't read the novel since, so I don't know whether it's more political, more sharp, than I realized then, but at the time he was hanging around with Jean Malaquais or a group of refugee non-Stalinist leftists. So, in fact, I may have met him earlier, maybe in the late forties, at a party for Malaquais given by Mrs. Lazarus, who was a Quaker pacifist. I remember Dwight Macdonald was there. I was then editor of the *Columbia Review*, my mother was a Communist, my father a socialist, so I was interested in Macdonald and read *Politics*.

TULI KUPFERBERG   I had known he was around and must've met him when he was living on Monroe Street, which I think was like '51. I'd read *The Naked and the Dead*, and I knew people in the kind of bohemian building where he was a presence. The area was in transition, with the Jews moving out and the Puerto Ricans and some hippies moving in. Other people in the building were Jiggs, a blond schoolteacher from Brooklyn, a sort of legendary, beautiful homosexual, and a grand old lady poetess, who was possibly a girl friend of Norman's.

I think Mailer actually made that building. It was special because it was one of the first buildings that bohemians were taking over on the East Side. It never developed into a real focus, but it was kind of like a premonition of what the culture of the sixties was going to be. A lot of people were living in one place, but I don't know that they were interacting that much—maybe it was just a reflection of housing problems. But Norman wanted to live there, and the other people had to live there too. It was a tough neighborhood, so there was good reason to be frightened. Now it seems idyllic.

ADELE MORALES MAILER   We had taken a loft on Monroe Street, right in the shadow of the Manhattan Bridge, and, God, I don't know how we found those places. Today I'd die living in that neighborhood. Maybe I took it as a challenge.

Or maybe I took one look at all those windows, fourteen of them, and thought, Oh boy, this is great. Not all the windows were over the water, but the place was huge. You could ride a bicycle from one end to another. It was bare, and we said we were going to fix it up. We never did, though. I didn't like having to be picked up at the subway. Norman would meet me carrying a rolled-up newspaper that he said was his club. We just weren't there long enough, and then that incident at our big party, when Norman got hit with a hammer—that did it.

I don't really remember everyone who was at the party, but Monty Clift stands out in my mind, and maybe Brando. But if Brando was there, he didn't stay long. It was two in the morning. The party was in full swing and there was a knock on the door—a bunch of street kids who used to hang around the candy store, sort of a neighborhood gang. I think Jean told them to leave, then he turned to Norman and said, "There's going to be trouble." But it all happened so fast, without warning. The kids barged in, and one of them had a hammer. Maybe Norman pushed one of them, I don't know. But before he knew it this guy banged his scalp with the hammer. He looked sort of dazed, but he wasn't unconscious, and while he may have gone down on one knee, he got right up again, the old fighter. I saw he had quite a cut, and the blood was streaming, and I got hysterical, screaming, "Oh, my God, look at you, he cut you." It was like general screaming and scuffling, and then I guess the kids ran away—they saw what they'd done—because when the cops arrived they were already gone. I don't know where Clift was throughout all this, probably off drunk somewhere, but he certainly didn't jump in to help.

RHODA LAZARE WOLF   Like a lot of parties at the time, it was big and crowded with a lot of aspiring young writers and a lot of talk going on. I don't know if Vance Bourjaily was there that night, but usually he was around. Calder Willingham used to be around too. But at Norman's parties there'd also be movie stars, and that night Marlon Brando came in with Rita Moreno. All the women thought, Ahhh—just swooned.

JEAN MALAQUAIS   There were about fifty people there. Marlon Brando was sitting with a girl on his lap—he looked like a Buddha, like the man he'd impersonate in *Apocalypse Now*—never smiling, never saying a word, as if he'd been taught that if you don't say a word you never pass for a fool.

Anyway, around midnight there was a knock at the door. Three or four punks in leather jackets asked for a girl. I was nearby and told them to get lost, remembering that a woman downstairs had been raped a few days before. They wouldn't leave, and I went over to Norman to tell him, but they'd already barged in. Then the fight started. Brando never budged. Norman got hit in the head with a hammer, and when they saw the blood they ran. It was only afterwards that we found out they'd made a pass at the girl they'd come to ask for; she'd slapped one of them, and they were out to punish the bitch. Norman had a bandage for a week. Some business.

KEVIN McCARTHY   To get to Norman's party everybody from uptown had to go to the lower East Side, down to an area where you didn't know what the hell was going on. Norman was way ahead of everybody, getting into the loft thing, because then it was against the law to use lofts to live in, yet somehow he'd found this place. You had to enter by means of a fire escape. He had everybody there, the Plimpton types, Monty Clift, the this, the that. Uptown café society. Black tie, a lot of liveliness, excitement.

Then suddenly the invasion took place. The door burst open and you didn't know what to do and it was scary as hell. These guys were screaming, and Jesus, it was a wild melee. You didn't know who was hitting whom, who was attacking, or what was going to happen, or even whether you should get out and call the police. And suddenly this guy's hitting Norman on the head with a hammer. *Bang, bang, bang.* Maybe six, seven times. There was no warning—they just came through the door—and Norman didn't even fall, which was the god-damnedest thing. He was still conscious and fighting.

EMMA CLARA "ECEY" GWALTNEY   There were a lot of people at the party, and I was impressed with Montgomery Clift even though everyone was trying not to pay attention to him. He wasn't drunk, and he looked really great. He was beautiful.

Calder Willingham was there too. I had loved his novel *End as a Man*, but that night I didn't like him. I was serving some sort of purple punch from a washtub, and a girl came up to get some. Pouring her a glass, I said, "Do you want some ice?" Some people standing nearby sort of giggled, something about the way I pronounced "ice," and they said, "Is she serious?" Calder Willingham said, "Unfortunately she is." Just trashy, I thought. If he'd been any kind of southern gentleman, he could've said, "Well, certainly, a lot of people say 'ice' that way."

Later I overheard Norman say to another friend, "I want you to be nice to them," meaning us. This fellow was very abrasive, very Yankee, and he said, "Why should I?" Norman said, just quick, "Because they're my friends." I thought, Bless his heart—that's nice, he doesn't have to do that. Fig was more gregarious and sociable, he'd talk to anybody, so he was probably over here, over there, talking to this one and that one, and he didn't hear Norman make the remark, which was just as well. He would have gone to Norman and said something like, "What the hell're you doing, telling them to be nice to us? We don't have to be protected!"

Still, we didn't really see the lionizing that Bea had talked about, and he almost devoted himself to us. I think the only change Fig noticed and wondered about was why Norman wanted to live in such an uncomfortable place. As for the fight, I didn't actually see it. But I know Norman was bleeding, and Montgomery Clift went over and was very solicitous. I thought, Well, they must be really good friends. Maybe Montgomery Clift had a crush on him at that point.

Two or three days later Norman drove Bea and us out to Long Branch to visit Susie and his parents, leaving Adele in the city. On the way out he said he was going to tell his mother he was in a taxicab accident and hit his head, because he didn't want her to know how he got his head wound. We said, "Oh, sure," although it seemed strange, and I remember thinking, Well, as famous as he is already, he feels he has to tell his mother a story. Bea agreed, which seemed to be her only concession. Being angry and rebellious about the split, she was otherwise making no concessions whatsoever.

I suppose Norman's mother was mollified by the story of the cab accident, because it never came up. But it seemed to me we were making polite conversation over tension, things that were going on underneath. Norman was tense about how Bea was going to behave—whether she was going to blow their cover story, like possibly announcing that the two of them were no longer living together—but she was being the Jewish wife, and before dinner she and Norman's mother were in the kitchen quietly chatting and seemed to have a lot to talk about. It was two women working together on the salad, and I thought, Well, they're still close. Isn't this a shame, now that Bea and Norman are breaking up? Then it crossed my mind, I wonder if Bea and Fan will remain friends?

This was the first time we'd met Norman's parents. Mrs. Mailer received us very graciously, sort of like a queen mother, regal and ladylike, but I had no idea that she was such a power in the family. Fig and she got along well, Fig being the kind of personality who established an immediate rapport. Before this Norman hadn't really told us anything about his parents except for a slight sort of laughing, reluctant embarrassment about his father. He said something like, "Oh, he puts on a big show. He's quite a talker, some kind of dresser, very dapper. Quite a—" I don't know that he said "ladies' man," but that was in my mind. Not a braggart, but it just seemed to me there was some little hostility somewhere in Norman's feelings about him. Or perhaps it was disappointment. But mostly I was surprised that Norman came from such a conventional set of parents. I thought they'd be more artsy, more intellectual, because to me he was already pretty daring. I thought, They could be from Russellville, from Arkansas, wherever.

Dave and Anne were there for dinner too, but I don't really remember them, because my memory is that Bea dominated the table. Even though she was keeping up appearances, she used shocking language in front of his parents to embarrass him. In fact, later he referred to what she was doing in a letter. It was like the way she'd done everything she could, even taking off her blouse, to disrupt the seriousness of the conversation with Malaquais. I remember, just before dinner Susie came walking in, and she was scratching herself. Bea said, "What's the matter, honey? You got sand in your pussy?" Everyone pretended not to hear her. But Norman suffered. I'd never seen him suffering from that kind of thing before.

NORMAN MAILER (LETTER TO FRANCIS IRBY GWALTNEY, FALL 1951)

Dear Fig and Ecey,

Here y'ams (however you illitearates spell it—Fig's spelling is contagious) back in N'Yuk. (New York accent.)

Right now I'm slightly depressed for I don't know what to do about the loft.

It's beautiful in the daytime, spacious, airy, light, what-all, and big enough to make me feel like an emperor, yet cheap enough to appeal to my pocketbook. The rub is of course the neighborhood. Adele is terrified of it, and I can't quite blame her, for I feel a trifle uneasy myself. Yet the thought of finding a new place, and fixing it up, seems even worse. Sometime in the next couple of weeks I've got to make a decision, for it'll be getting cold soon and I'll have to invest in some heating apparatus or give the joint up. The gang who hammered me are rarely in evidence, and look the other way when I go by. Apparently they all have prison records, and are not eager to be fingered by me to the police. So I think there'll be no trouble, but on the other hand it's annoying to live in such a way that you think twice about going out for cigarettes at eleven o'clock. Eh, bien. . . .

I saw the letter you wrote my uncle, Fig. A masterpiece. My whole family is on a Gwaltneys for President kick, and if they don't stop praising you soon, I'll start knocking you both down out of my basic contrariness to my family.

I think you know how much I enjoyed your visit, and you both discovered New York to me, rather than the other way around. I only wish that the party-fight and the dramatic entrance of Bea hadn't spoiled the lustre just a little.

I hope your work's going well, Fig, and Ecey's work I know is going well. She's going to give birth to a twenty-nine pounder and I'm taking book on that. Adele is fine. You were absolutely right, Fig, about the answer she'd give to the question. It's like olives. Takes knowing. But she was wonderful up in Provincetown.

Now that summer's over there's nothing for me to do but wait for skiing.

I spoke at a forum up in Provincetown, and when somebody in the audience asked me if I didn't think the writer should affirm values, I shrieked back that everybody affirmed values, parents, teachers, ministers, editorial writers, govt. officials, and the artist was the only one who could and should destroy values. Never a dull moment with Mailer. I was tempted to invite the audience to storm the town hall with me, and start the revolution.

A big hug, back, Ecey. I shore admire you, face.

The white eagle never had it so good.

> Love,
> Norm

<u>ADELE MORALES MAILER</u> The first summer Norman and I went up to P-Town together was '51, and he was so excited about showing me the place.

Harry Engel was part of my introduction, and I loved it. Harry was a pretty good painter and sort of Mr. Nice Guy, one of the crew. He and the woman he was going with, someone named Perry, also a painter, would give nice parties, and Harry made wonderful clams for dinner. He didn't offend anybody either, and that's the way I remember those first times in Provincetown. I liked everybody. I felt accepted, as opposed to New York.

I think Norman was fascinated by the painting scene. He didn't know much about art, but he does have a sensitivity and a kind of perceptiveness. Up in P-Town he didn't get along with Jan Muller, though he liked his work and later bought a painting. The two of them were sort of intrigued with each other, but Jan was so shy and tortured that you couldn't really get to know him. Still, I was going around with a lot of painters, and, of course, we went to all the P-Town parties—Miles and Barbara Forst, Tony Vevers, John Frank, Franz Kline, Fritz Bultman, Larry Rivers, and Mike Goldberg were around along with lots of unknown painters. There was also the music scene. Larry Rivers and Mike Severin used to have jam sessions with Gerry Mulligan, and Zoot Sims and Stan Getz too. God, those were wonderful days. I want those days back. But later I began to get more and more into the literary field, we went to more and more of those parties, and I kind of lost touch with the painters.

FAY DONOGHUE   Adele was much better known in Provincetown than Norman. He'd written *The Naked and the Dead*, but given what was in the air, the whole Beat thing, her cachet was that she had been involved with Kerouac. Norman was terrific, an absolutely delightful guy, great fun to be with but by no means the most famous writer in P-Town. Tennessee Williams was around, and people were far more impressed with him because, remember, this was also the time of *Streetcar*.

DR. JACK BEGNER   In the summer of '51 Harry Engel had been asked by his university, the University of Indiana, to look up Norman, which he did, and then later in August Harry came to me and said, "I have a friend here who's sick. Would you come over and give me a hand with him?"

We walked over to Norman's—he had a place in the guest house that later became a restaurant, Don's Café, now Pucci's—and there was Norman asleep. Harry woke him and had to remind him who he was. I don't know whether he'd been potheaded or drunk or a combination of both because I didn't examine him. But he kept looking down at the floor. He was very quiet. Whatever was bothering him was evident in his face, but he wasn't communicative. Then Harry said, "Norman, do you think you'd like to play tennis this afternoon?" Norman sort of lifted his head and said, "Yeah, that'd be a good idea." I was amazed to see him on the court either that day or the next.

The rest of the month, if he came down from his room and we saw him, it was accidental. We didn't get social until later. He was being very quiet, and I suppose I realized it was because it was such a hellish year for him.

NANCY MACDONALD   I'd met Norman on the Cape when he was with his first wife the summer before. Dwight and I had bought a house in Truro, and I vividly remember playing tennis with Norman. He had a peculiar serve. It would come over the net, then jump sideways. Very tricky. Also Dwight organized a softball game, and Cy Rembar used to come and play too.

Mary McCarthy was in Wellfleet with Edmund Wilson, and the atmosphere was almost an extension of New York—a lot of political discussion and the like—and I remember it was a big nudist thing on the beach in those days—people went swimming in the nude—and Freda Utley was once standing next to Dwight, nude except for a little bra to hold her hearing aid in, discussing some issue at great length. It was never flat or dull when Dwight was around. He was always poking somebody, setting things off, and I think Norman really enjoyed this in him.

KURT VONNEGUT   That same summer Norman and I met through Cy Rembar. My son used to play with Cy's son, Lance, and Cy had talked about Norman, so it was bound to happen, and it did. I don't remember either Bea or Adele. My only memory is of Norman. He'd be down on the beach or walking along Commercial Street, and it was always an accidental encounter, typical Provincetown, and we'd have supper or just get together for drinks.

He was unbelievably young, as was I. He had had that extraordinary shock of becoming a world literary figure and had begun hanging out with Edmund Wilson and Mary McCarthy and that bunch up in Truro, the great literary tastemakers of the time, who were courting him. So sometimes he was confused, I would think, sort of feeling his way about how to act. I'm just extrapolating from what it is to be human, what it's like to have that happen to you at the age of—what—twenty-five?

He wasn't shy but rather quite convinced that he was entitled to be an important literary figure—I don't think he had any doubts about that. It's quite customary to run into authors who have decided that a book that's been praised is actually a piece of shit. They can be right, of course, but I sensed none of that in Mailer. *Barbary Shore* was out, and while a lot of people hadn't read it yet, the assumption was that it was the next great Mailer book, the reviews notwithstanding. If Norman himself was going through a great deal of self-doubt, though, I was in no position to sympathize, since I was just writing my first book, *Player Piano*, and we are the same age.

At that point anybody who'd published a book—even a book on how to maintain a tidy cat-litter box—was an astonishing figure to an unpublished writer. So my feeling was, it's sad, it's maddening about the reception of Mailer's new book, but as far as I was concerned, anybody who had published was at the top of the world. That was the big trick, to actually get your artifact published. I'd published about thirty slick stories in *Collier's* and *Saturday Evening Post*, and I'd quit doing PR for General Electric because I made so much more money from the short stories than GE was willing to pay me.

But Norman was always most courtly to me, almost like an English gentleman. It was as though I were visiting Henry James, someone considerably older and better established than I. Yet he wasn't condescending, it was just nice manners. The big reputations as far as I was concerned were Edmund Wilson, Mary McCarthy, Dwight Macdonald—all in Truro. But there was no reason I'd be rubbing ass with them. I was a *Saturday Evening Post* writer, why would they talk to me? I was working, not socializing, and I certainly wasn't going to tell people I was a writer either, because it was by no means certain I was.

I remember once, though, my mother-in-law was visiting when he came over for dinner. She was a midwestern lady and trying to take the proper attitude, but she saw Norman and me as competitors and felt that eventually I would beat him. At one point, when he wandered out on the porch overlooking Commercial Street, my mother-in-law was standing in front of an open kitchen window with the shade pulled, which was in fact only three feet from him. She said to me, "I think you're much cuter than he is." To this day I don't know whether Mailer heard her. At the time he certainly didn't say anything.

As far as any competitive thing between us, I remember thinking *The Naked and the Dead* an extremely good book, though I thought it was an extension of Dos Passos' *U.S.A.*, too derivative, which isn't true but true enough. I mean, you carry things like that around in self-defense. Then, as I say, when I read *Barbary Shore* I was in no mood to care for it. I remember I talked to Knox Burger about Mailer one time. As my career went on I'd keep running into Norman here and there, and I said to Knox that there was sort of a formal distance between us which I never expected to bridge. I wondered what had caused it, what the geography of the division was. Knox said, "He doesn't think you're in the same game." That was just Knox's guess, though.

But that's something I would never confront Norman with. I wouldn't even kid around with him about it. I'm still very careful with him. I value his good opinion, everything's all right now, and I leave it at that. I did, however, write him a letter after *Player Piano* was published in '51 or '52 and asked him how he was and if he'd seen it. Not for a blurb, because the book was already published. I simply valued his opinion, and I wanted a little feedback. There hadn't been any, and, my goodness, I knew Mailer, so I wrote him. He'd read the book and said he liked parts of it, but I remember he said the sociology was a little weak. I don't know quite what he meant by that, probably not much.

But that summer, even after I'd read *Barbary Shore*, there was no ideological or political identification between us. He wouldn't have thought of it, probably because New Yorkers don't like to think of a socialist tradition in the Middle West, which is where I'm from. Also maybe because it's not Jewish. It seems alien to them that these flaxen-haired people should be out there, and the Eugene Debs tradition, the United Mine Workers, and all that—they haven't thought about it, it's confusing to them.

Norman was playing tennis that summer. I wasn't, but my then wife, Jane, was, and she was a good tennis player. She watched Norman playing with the pro, who was saying Norman's name over and over again—the normal tennis talk, but the pro never left off Norman's name—"Oh, Mailer, that's just like you!" "Oh, Mailer, you're gonna try that again." I don't know if Norman was taking lessons or just killing time. A couple of years ago, though, I said to him, "Norman, how's the tennis?" He treated the question with the utmost scorn and, in fact, denied he'd ever played tennis.

Still, even then there was some sense of his having a public persona. It was almost a talk-show persona, like he'd have ready answers to frequently asked questions. I remember I asked him if he had a psychoanalyst, and he said, "No, I'm not ready to get married yet." I assumed he'd given the answer many times before. I don't blame him for that. He was an authentic, admirable literary figure, and he could have any manners he wanted.

EDITH BEGNER   I think he started going down to Baltimore to see Robert Lindner in '52, right around the time of the divorce from Bea. He was so depressed then. I think there's something in Lindner's book *The Fifty-Minute Hour* about Norman, and I think Norman may actually have helped him with the writing. I know he thought Lindner was brilliant. He never admitted he was actually in therapy, and whether he was is anybody's guess.

ADELE MORALES MAILER   Norman met Bob Lindner, I don't remember where, but it was probably around the time of *The Fifty-Minute Hour*, and he told me about him and then brought him home to our apartment. He and Bob were crazy about each other. Norman loved him, and I liked him too, though they didn't seem to pay much attention to me. Norman went down to Baltimore regularly, and I went along a couple of times. It was mainly social, but also Lindner was writing something and Norman was working with him on it. But it had nothing to do with therapy. Norman in therapy? Anyone who thinks that has got to be kidding. Norman always hated the idea of therapy, and probably still does.

LARRY ALSON   Lindner died in 1955 or '56—died because he mistrusted surgeons, just as Norman does, and refused to undergo open-heart surgery.

ADELE MORALES MAILER   I knew that Norman was very generous to Harvard, making annual contributions, but he also told me that he'd suffered there and felt like a fish out of water. It was probably a combination of his family not having much money and being Jewish, but also his feeling that he was unattractive—physically unattractive—and so he was always worrying about being accepted.

He also talked to me a lot about the army. There were those wonderful stories about him being a cook, trying very hard, but also his feeling that the other guys still never accepted him. Most of his stories were about nonacceptance. I think that's one of the very crucial keys. He may have picked up those mannerisms, the Texas accent, because he's an actor, but he never used it with me until many years later. In the army, though, I think it was a part of not feeling accepted, just as he said he never felt accepted at Harvard, and just as he had a theory that women didn't find him attractive.

SHIRLEY FINGERHOOD   After graduation from law school I first worked for Felix Cohn in Washington, but because of McCarthyism there was such an atmosphere of strain I decided it wasn't worth it. Friends of mine who worked for the government would say, "Don't read *The New Republic* on the bus, someone will see you" or "You're endangering us by talking out loud in a restaurant." So I wrote Victor Brodney, who teaches at Harvard, and he mentioned me to Cy, who was looking for a recent graduate. Within days I was interviewed, gave notice, and came to Cy's firm, which was then Levine and Rembar. B. J. Levine had a practice in California—theatrical, movies, movie-star clients like Judy

Garland. Perhaps Cy had met him when he was out there in '49 visiting Norman, I don't know.

Cy and Norman, though, seemed very close, more like brothers than cousins, and if I suppose there was anything competitive, they seemed to have worked out areas of superiority. Norman looked to Cy for business and legal direction. I also suspect Cy had something to do with Norman's divorce from Bea, but I know he was handling his money from the time it started coming in from *The Naked and the Dead*. He was investing it. Cy himself knew about the stock market, but I also suspect that people like Seth Glickenhaus were advising him. Seth was absolutely fantastic. He made a million dollars by the time he was thirty or forty. I think he was in the tax-deductible bond business.

Cy was *the* lawyer of the family, the way one has the doctor of the family. Or like in Italian families, the lawyer who assumes responsibility for the family's many business and legal problems. Except with Cy it took on a different style. He wasn't that much older, he wasn't Norman's father. Like Norman, he was regarded as a *Wunderkind*. His mother, Beck, would've died for him. This family is filled with mothers who would die for sons, Fan and Beck both.

Still, Cy did have a slightly paternal attitude, not only toward Norman but to the family as a whole. In fact, I met Fan because Cy was representing her nursing agency. Somebody was suing them, they were suing somebody, and I was their lawyer.

But the first time I met Norman I was literally under a desk. I'd spilled a file folder, and he came in and helped me pick up the papers. Here he was, a household name at the age of twenty-five, and he was just as nice and pleasant and straight as anybody, and within months of meeting him I was invited to his parties. Cy would be at the parties too, and there was this general sense that I was part of Norman's orbit. He had a group of friends whom I met at his apartment, like Dan and Rhoda Wolf, as well as all the people who later were involved with *The Village Voice*. Barbara at this point was already married to Larry, but we didn't become friendly until they moved down to Bleecker Street and I was living on Charles Street and we had a dropping-in relationship. We took to each other immediately.

Barbara told me that Bea and Norman's divorce had a fantastic influence on her. Her relationship with Norman had always been wonderful—"the two of us against the world" feeling—and then he marries Bea, a woman who was dynamic and terrific. They take Barbara into their circle, invite her to stay with them in Europe, have her into this and that. It's an exciting and permanent thing, there's a baby, then all of a sudden, *bang*, it's over. Barbara's young, and it's now not her brother and his wife, it's over, and it's shattering—the idea that marriage isn't forever, that this is your family—it was a real eye-opener for her. From that point on the idea that everything was permanent disappeared.

Why did Norman take up with Adele? I don't know, but it seems to me that people who are married to very efficient, managing wives and who are put down by them deliberately go out and marry the opposite type with the notion that they will be in charge. After Bea, who was his intellectual equal—she could think straight and could outthink Norman in certain ways—he probably decided he was going to marry someone who wasn't competitive with him. Adele couldn't win an argument with Norman except by screaming. She certainly couldn't challenge him intellectually, and that may have been part of the attraction.

What she did have was a lot of self-confidence as a woman. She thought she was the cat's meow, and she bore herself as somebody who could throw her body around. I went skiing with them fairly early on, I think at the end of 1951, someplace in Quebec, just the three of us. I remember one incident that I think was typical of their fighting for dominance. We were having dinner at the inn where we were staying, and Norman was criticizing Adele for something petty, like the fork she was using or what she'd ordered. Adele said, "Why do you always pick on me, nag me?" He was in very good spirits, and with a big smile on his face he said, "I pick on you because Bea picked on me."

NORMAN MAILER (LETTER TO FRANCIS IRBY GWALTNEY, JANUARY 9, 1952)
Dear Fig,—and dear Maw Ecey,

I've been missing you both even if I haven't written in a couple of months. What the hell, writing letters is a busman's holiday for all of us.

The book I started last summer just wouldn't go at all, and I gave it up, probably permanently. I've done some short stories since then, nothing extraordinary, and Cy Rembar, my lawyer, is now out trying to get them sold. No acceptances, no rejections yet, so I wait. I wish I had a novel to write on, or even the desire to write a novel. I just don't seem to feel any drive. Oh, well, let time pass.

Adele is still fine, and things between us are about as good as they can be for me with a woman. I've decided that at bottom I'm just a sadist, and no damn good for any woman. The reason—I can beat them up. Only with men do I act decently cause I'm scared they'll whop me. Isn't human nature depressing? . . .

I went skiing with Adele for a week last week, and had a good time. That's one thing in life you got to miss, Gwaltney, if you insist on staying down South.

How far along are you now, Ecey? You going to be a good mother? I guess you are. If not you, then who? I still think you're the smartest girl I know.

Bea is still in Mexico, and is going to get married to Steve Sanchez. She's also studying medicine. Our divorce will probably go through about the beginning of February. . . .

SANDY CHARLEBOIS THOMAS   He told me he was very bitter that Bea had taken Susie and run off to be with Sanchez in Mexico, a place that he loathed. He went down there several times, and he said the poverty was just so bad he couldn't bear it.

BARBARA PROBST SOLOMON   In the summer of '52 I looked Bea up in Mexico. She was already studying medicine, living with this crazy Mexican, Steve Sanchez, in a rather proletarian section of Mexico City. Fan had already been down to visit and wasn't going to let go of Susan, the first grandchild. I remember I was with Carlos, a friend of mine, and Bea and her guy took us to some low-down place and Sanchez got in a terrible fistfight. Carlos, who was Spanish, had known Norman and Bea in Paris and was appalled that she should be living with this man, truly shocked that this is what it had come to. Bea eventually married Sanchez. She made her point by living in sin, then she married and had a son with him. They were together seven or eight years. Bea will have nothing to do with Norman now, though once in a blue moon she's stayed at Barbara's.

NORMAN MAILER (LETTER TO FRANCIS IRBY GWALTNEY, MARCH 11, 1952)
Dear Fig,
. . . Adele is fine, and things go on pretty much the same. Bea and I are now divorced, and she's about to marry Steve in Mexico. Feels funny now to think of myself as ever being married.
I've been busy trying to get a novel into the works. Right now, I don't know. I'm keeping my fingers crossed. . . .

WILLIAM PHILLIPS Norman's participation in *Partisan Review*'s panel, "Our Country and Our Culture," was, I think, a political act. He had never been a strong anti-Communist prior to giving his talk at the Waldorf conference two or three years before, and by contributing to the symposium alongside people like Lionel Trilling and other *P.R.* contributors, he was indicating, I suppose, he was part of our community, as it were, though he was critical of the symposium.

It's not for me to say, but *Partisan Review* was generally regarded as *the* magazine of the New York cultural scene in those years, 1948 to '52. The Hitler-Stalin pact in '39 only corroborated our view, since Rahv and I and the others had always been anti-Stalinist. By '45 Morris, Mary McCarthy, and Fred Dupee had dropped off for personal reasons, and of the original group only Dwight Macdonald, besides Rahv and myself, remained. There were political differences with him. It may or may not be accurate to say he felt we were too far to the right, but he also felt we were becoming too literary, which he saw as a departure from the magazine's original purposes. Specifically, Dwight was becoming something of an anarchist, and while we weren't Marxist, there were still remnants of Marxism in our thinking. It wasn't a honeyed departure, but it wasn't violent either. Dwight then started *Politics*, which became a competitor, but I think only a minor competitor. *Dissent* hadn't yet been founded, and *Commentary* wasn't a central part of the political and intellectual scene the way it would be later.

In any case, in '52 I don't know what our readership thought upon opening up the magazine and finding Norman Mailer juxtaposed to Lionel Trilling. Norman was very famous of course, but he was not a part of our particular community. I say this tentatively, since all the terms are so loaded, but it seems to me that there were fewer crossovers then than now between the worlds of the highbrow literary community and the more popular writers. People like the Trillings and Steven Marcus were perhaps—I suppose—more intellectual than the people Norman had been seeing. They were theoretical critics, very serious, and while I'm guessing, I *think* that may be what they represented to him. Irving Howe as well. And we were distinct from the semi-Stalinist community too—

Hellman, Hammett, Howard Fast, the Hollywood Ten, all the fellow travelers. The difference was that they were touting some kind of ideological line—a wobbly line, granted—and there were varying degrees of conformity, but we were decidedly critical of that. We were independent. We felt we weren't captive of some false ideology.

There was another difference too. When *The Naked and the Dead* came out *Partisan Review* didn't relate to it properly, which was an error. In conventional, critical terms, we saw it as a naturalist or realist book while at the time we felt more involved with the more modernist, more symbolic tradition. (At the beginning, Rahv and I were close to Farrell, for example, in our social and literary sympathies, but then we drifted apart.) Farrell wasn't Joyce, Proust, or Mann, but he had a certain power—though *The Naked and the Dead* was very good, it was in another tradition. Also, it had been a huge popular success. One tries not to let oneself be influenced by that, but it does have some negative effect. That doesn't mean we are automatically critical of any book, then or now, that's a success, but a little bit of bias can creep in because one tends to identify, often enough, with the minority culture.

My feeling about Norman was that there were a lot of different people inside him. On the one hand, he was a very serious writer; on the other, he was very worldly. He was a maverick, an outsider. He's always been an outsider, and I felt he was quite unpredictable.

The symposium "Our Country and Our Culture" raised the question: If you were no longer a Marxist-internationalist and felt that the Soviet Union constituted a threat to our values, then what was your relation to your country? We weren't Russians, we weren't Dutchmen, we were Americans, but not uncritical ones. Hence the question, which we raised politically, intellectually, and especially from a literary point of view.

The symposium was published at the height of McCarthyism. Norman's and Howe's were the most disaffected voices on the panel, Norman's more than anyone's. But his argument that the artist must be alienated—he quoted the famous Joyce passage about "silence, exile, cunning"—had nothing to do with McCarthyism. The issue he raised is, of course, an important one and a permanent dilemma, and it seems to me that people who can't think intelligently simply become ideologues of the right or left without realizing the dilemma of keeping your distance, being critical without at the same time jumping into some crazy ideological camp. It's a dilemma that requires constant balance. Part of the problem is that we're all leading middle-class lives yet maintain some radical opinions—when I say radical I'm not identifying with the crazy left— so we're all caught in these contradictions. André Gide was alienated but that doesn't mean he didn't become anti-Russian. If you're alienated from certain things in the quality of the atmosphere in which you live, that doesn't mean you don't care whether America is Communist or not. There are distinctions that have to be made, and dumb people who think they're intellectuals can't think straight on these things. I didn't know what Irving Howe's and Norman's relationship had been before, but I assume apparently they became closer at about the time of the symposium.

NORMAN MAILER   I was invited to the symposium "Our Country and Our Culture" by *Partisan Review* because the one thing *Barbary Shore* established was
that I was a figure of the left, and as a result of the symposium Howe got in
touch with me when he was starting *Dissent*. We had a very funny first meeting,
because his bad review of *Barbary Shore* was there implicitly between us, but
we didn't speak about it, although I think in his letter to me he wrote something
like "We may have had differences in the past," but "I was impressed with your
piece in the symposium because I thought someone was speaking out forth-
rightly."

The other people involved were Fred Dupee, Lionel Trilling, Delmore
Schwartz, Mary McCarthy, Philip Rahv, Dwight Macdonald, Phillips, the whole
gang. I guess it was my first real introduction to these guys. I might've met them
at various literary gatherings but I didn't really know them. In a funny way the
symposium was my coming out.

My voice, I think, was as dissenting as any on the panel. I believe I was one
of the three most militant voices—not militant, because that's not the word,
there was nothing to be militant about; disaffected is what I mean. It was Dwight
Macdonald, Howe, and myself. We were very much opposed to the status quo,
and even though I wasn't surprised at how disaffected I was, I was startled that
there was anyone near me. I thought I'd be all alone. I had had an idea that
Partisan Review was pro-Establishment and didn't amount to much more than
the Committee for Cultural Freedom. Macdonald and Howe notwithstanding,
I wasn't that far off.

IRVING HOWE   We talked about *Dissent*, and Norman was very friendly and
agreed to be part of the venture. Subsequently he wrote some pieces and came
to editorial board meetings, but after a while some of the editorial staff began
to sense there was going to be a divergence. It wasn't yet totally clear, but the
feeling was that what Norman was doing didn't have much political significance,
that he was just being fanciful, playful, that writers are as they are.

JEAN MALAQUAIS   Norman was never persecuted by HUAC, but his father was,
nominally because of his association with Norman. There was a letter from the
government, at which point Norman and Cy Rembar became involved, and the
two of them sent the hounds packing.

CHARLES REMBAR   Barney's difficulty with the Civil Service Commission was
part of the hysteria of the early fifties. The government made loyalty checks on
its employees and if you failed their test—a very tough test to pass—they fired
you. Or if you worked for Hollywood, they could get a lot of publicity out of
congressional investigations. But what could they do about individual writers—
go around to publishers and say, "Don't publish his books"? Even at that time
it would have been too clumsy a violation of the First Amendment. That didn't
happen to Norman or anybody else I know of.

Barney had been working for the U.S. Army as an accountant and mainly
his reaction to the charge that he was a loyalty risk was that it was preposterous.
Fan thought it was an outrage. The notice he received from the Civil Service

Commission claimed that there was "reasonable doubt" as to his loyalty, created by the fact that he had a "continuing close association" with a "concealed Communist"—namely, Norman.

I don't know if it was a veiled attempt to get at Norman. It was possible to get a hearing before the Loyalty Board, and we asked for one, but before that happened Norman and I decided to submit an affidavit and collaborate on it. (Usually, the lawyer writes the affidavit on the basis of what the client tells him.) We also decided to try to end on a comic note with the hope that it might dredge up, from somewhere deep inside the people who would be judging it, a sub-merged suspicion of the silliness of the case. Barney's reaction was, "Well, if the two of you think this is the way it ought to be done, then that's the way." Norman and I each wrote paragraphs, and each rewrote parts of what was written by the other, and argued a bit—not much—about the final revision. This is what we came up with:

State of New York   )

                          : *ss.:*

County of New York)

                          Norman Mailer, being duly sworn, deposes and says:

Since there is no direct charge against my father other than he is my father, it seems to me that I must offer a statement about myself and my relationship with my father before he can clear himself.

I understand that the standard to be applied is whether "there is a reasonable doubt as to the loyalty of the person involved." This extraordinary inversion of the normal standards of justice, coupled with the weight which is attached to the parental-filial association, requires that the government employee take extraor-dinary measures in his defense. Among such measures is his establishment not merely of his own innocence, but also—unless he is that psychological and social abnormality, the man who has completely dissociated himself from his family— the innocence of members of his family. The result is that persons who, in the language of lawyers, are "strangers to the proceeding," must come forward with a statement of their private views. This, it seems to me, can be a hardship and a serious invasion of personal liberties. In my own case it happens it is not. My political views have already been given repeated public expression.

It seems to me that any "defense" must be separated into two compartments: (1) have I ever influenced my father—directed, cozened, implored or otherwise sought to control him by our "continuing close association"? (2) does the "reliable information" that I. B. Mailer's son is a "concealed Communist" possess any reliability or information? . . .

My father is a man of conservative stable temperament, and though we have many of the relations proper to a father and a son, I think I may say with assurance that he has never had any political influence upon me nor I upon him, nor for that matter have I ever made any attempt to so influence him. He is not in the habit of ever speaking about the details of his work, nor have I ever had any interest in asking him about his work. Our political ideas are in great disagreement, and I should like to submit to the members of the Loyalty Board the notion that disagreement between fathers and sons is a human phenomenon which has been long remarked. To put it another way, may I be so forward as to ask any member of the Loyalty Board who has children to consider whether his children possess sufficient influence and control over him to be able to lead him into activities or attitudes unnatural or repugnant to his own outlook or temperament?

Now to the charge that I am a "concealed Communist." . . . Nothing could give me more pleasure than to be able to confront my accuser or accusers. I suspect, however, it is not nearly so simple to clear oneself of the charge that one is a concealed Communist. The questionnaire submitted to my father contains the following sentence: "For your information, a concealed Communist is one who does not want himself known as a Communist and who would deny membership in the Communist Party." (My underlining.) Gentlemen, I must ask you . . . to consider how difficult it is for any individual once accused in this manner to avoid being judged automatically as one kind of Communist or another. For notice: if the accused admits being a Communist, he is a Communist; if he denies being a Communist, his denial is irrelevant to the issue, since the heart of the accusation is that the accused is in the habit of making such denials . . .

For it is a very serious matter to be called a "concealed Communist," more serious I should judge than simply to be called a "Communist." A concealed Communist is in effect a spy. Thus by the doubtful virtue of an accusation which feeds upon itself, there is imposed upon me the burden of establishing that I am not guilty of an offense which carries the gravest consequences.

The irony is that I am one of the few people (apart from that rare creature, the candid professional politician) whose political beliefs have been made entirely a matter of record. . . . The result of my writings so far as I have been able to determine them is that I have influenced exactly no one. Nonetheless I have been open to misinterpretation. The Communists for some years now have been calling me a Trotskyist; the Trotskyists call me a "so-called splinter Socialist"; the splinter socialists call me an anarchist; the anarchists call me a capitalist; and that representation of capitalism which to whatever extent is embodied in my accuser or accusers sees fit to call me a Communist . . .

I would ask the Loyalty Board to consider whether, in the light of my own written record, it is conceivable that I should be a concealed Communist. Let us suppose that a young writer publishes a novel which makes him a figure of some importance in the literary world, and that the Communists thereupon woo and win him. Presumably he could serve them in one of three ways: he could declare himself openly to be a Communist, and thereby lend his limited prestige to the Communist Party; or he could secretly commit himself to the Communist Party and, more or less subtly, slant his writings so as to make Communism appear attractive: or he could secretly commit himself to the Communist Party, and seek to achieve a literary or journalistic status where he could exercise some influence on editorial policy and public opinion. But is there any sanity in the assumption that the Communist Party would have him do none of the three? Can it be said rationally that he would openly espouse political ideas which could only serve to persuade his readers that Communism was bad, and which at the same time, by its dissident and unpopular nature, would destroy any chance of his being accepted in the policy-making circles of influential publications? Is it conceivable that the Communists should want to accept his public damning while he disables himself from rendering them any private service?

So, gentlemen, the situation as I see it is exactly this: is my father, who has no political agreement or sympathy with me at all, to be deprived of his means of making a livelihood within the government (and the government is to be deprived of the services of an experienced and competent professional) because his son is—not, as the charge claims, a "concealed Communist"—but admittedly and openly a dissident from the conventional and generally accepted attitudes about America and its position in the world today? . . .

If further evidence of my parent's patriotic allegiance to this country is necessary, I would suggest that some secret recording device be installed in my parents' home. On those occasions when I continue my "close association" with my parents, such as those evenings when I visit for dinner, the following conversation could probably be heard between my father and myself:

THE TIME: (one of those rare times when politics is discussed.)

NORMAN MAILER: I think the whole thing in Korea is hopeless. It's a pilot-light war. Ignorant Americans and ignorant Orientals are just butchering each other.

I. B. MAILER: I don't know where an intelligent boy like you picks up such idiotic rubbish.

FAN MAILER (the mother): Don't call him an idiot.

NORMAN MAILER: Well, he's not so smart himself.

I. B. MAILER: I never talked to my father the way you talk to me.

Sworn to before me
this 7th day of
January, 1953

[signed] Norman Mailer
_____

[signature and seal
of the notary public]
_____

The affidavit, which probably was startling to the officials involved in those morbid times, led them to clear Barney without even holding a hearing.

_____

VICTOR NAVASKY   What happened to Mailer's father isn't surprising. That kind of absurdity was not uncommon, especially when you're dealing with government security checks. The FBI always maintained that it didn't evaluate files, but it most definitely did, in the sense that they would summarize supposedly derogatory information. They'd say, "We're not evaluating this information, but so-

Lillian Hellman, after attempting the stage adaptation of The Naked and the Dead.

and-so associates with politically questionable..." They would include things like "Has Negroes in his home" or they'd list what books you had in your library. That Mailer could be the cause of his father's grief is a great irony, but in that period it's not singular. If *Barbary Shore* had had a commercial success like *The Naked and the Dead*, he might have gotten into some kind of political trouble himself. They could have found some reason to call him up, sure. But take Arthur Miller's case. He got called up in connection with passport hearings as distinguished from hearings into subversion in the entertainment industry. It was at the point when he was about to marry Marilyn Monroe, and they were always in it for publicity.

LILLIAN HELLMAN Hammett would never have gotten in Dutch if it weren't for the Bail Fund. Norman's time in Hollywood was very brief-lived, and as far as I know, HUAC only called people who were employed by Hollywood and belonged to some organization. What were they going to call Norman on? They couldn't call him on the Progressive party—that would have been *really* unconstitutional. They didn't call me for it, and I was one of the vice-chairmen of the Wallace effort and spoke for Wallace all over the place.

EDITH BEGNER The summer of '52 Norman and Adele were back in Provincetown, and despite what I remember as his drinking he was marvelous to me. I didn't publish my first book until '59 or '60, but I'd had one or two short stories published, and he was giving advice, not in a snotty or condescending way but gently. He was worried I wasn't the type to get enough publicity and would ruin my career all by myself, so he told me I should go and get undressed in Macy's window. I remember it quite clearly, "You gotta get your ass kissed in Macy's window."

That summer they gave a big party over at the Brewster Street studio, where he may have been trying to work. It was a marvelous party, but Adele was trying to get people to fight with her. She got drunk and was telling everyone that she was part colored, trying to get a rise out of people, then she said she was part Indian. I don't think she was trying to aggravate Norman by coming on to guys— that came later. In fact, that summer I think she was trying to get Norman to marry her.

RUTH E. FRIEDMAN   The fifties in Provincetown was an extraordinary time. Jan and Dodie Muller, Mary and Robert Frank, John Grillo, Bob Beauchamp— painters, sculptors, filmmakers—an accumulation of truly talented individuals, most of whom came from New York. There was almost a pipeline from Eighth Street. We all thought Hofmann was preparing the top echelon of the future, and it was like what was going on with Stella Adler; the energy and commitment was awesome, and we also had terrific parties. Most of us worked like hell during the day, and the parties were all about getting loose, getting laid.

I'd already started with Hans Hofmann in '48, working as his model. Wolf Kahn was the monitor. I had no money, but eventually I prevailed on Hofmann to let me be a student, and I studied with him both on the Cape and on Eighth Street.

I had met Adele "on the job," the job being window displays in Williamsburg, Brooklyn, during the winter of 1949–50. She was living between Fifteenth and Sixteenth streets on Ninth Avenue, and the only word to describe her is "vibrant." She was very beautiful—a Latino look—and the sexuality just flowed out of her. Her personality was very pliant, however. She was terrifically affected by others, really spongelike, and she only began to paint after she'd met people.

Enter Norman. At parties Norman was always *deadly* serious, which made him one of the greatest bores going—a large floppy fish among people who were much freer. Jan Muller made him look "like a cream-faced loon," to quote Shakespeare, and although Norman had money and success, in Provincetown he had little status. His connection for something to smoke was always a black guy, never a white, and that was part of his act. Everyone knew it. But Adele didn't have much of a life outside of him. She did some painting, but she hadn't had the time or sense of possibility to explore who she could be. Inside herself she was lost. Norman was so bravura, always on stage like Sinatra. Adele got fed into this machine, then she got spit out, and at the end I doubt whether she knew her middle, last, or even first name.

NAT HALPER   In '52 Norman was living in an apartment in the red house catty-corner to the Patrician Shop, what recently became Prudy's. We had a place on the water and invited him to go swimming off our deck, and he came around very humbly to ask if it was all right if he brought Adele. He thought Marge and I would object to meeting her. I was a little taken aback, then realized there was always a certain courtliness with us. Why? I don't know. But there was a part of him that was still a young boy even as he was consciously becoming a public macho figure. He felt you shouldn't intrude on people, that you should always ask. It was like a different tradition, back to Lord Fauntleroy.

Another instance: Some guy told me that he was waiting to use the pay phone near the Ice House, and someone was in the booth talking and talking, making several calls. It was Norman, and the guy was struck because Norman apologized so abjectly, saying he was sorry that he had so many calls to make, on and on. It's something I've often seen in him—he feels you don't do things to disoblige people. It's as if that's part of the past he's otherwise discarded. That summer, asking if he could bring Adele, maybe he felt that I, being respectably married, would object to him bringing a woman who wasn't his wife.

Having met and heard about Adele, though, I was aware she was important. Bea had punctured his feelings of being a man, but Adele had a reputation of being very, *very* good in bed. Norman picked her up, and that was a restoration. The story was that she'd been the girl friend of a number of guys in the Village, most notably Kerouac, and given the fact that there's always been an open line between P-Town and the Village, people had talked about it. In simple terms, it was the nice Jewish Brooklyn boy moving away from the proper, intellectual Jewish soul mate to the exotic sexpot, especially as Adele had pretensions to secret, primitive knowledge, though no one knew exactly in which field.

During the summer I remember he was also seeing a lot of Dwight Macdonald, people like that, in Wellfleet. After parties we'd go out to some restaurant in Provincetown, and what I noticed was that he was aware of his own celebrity. One night he and Macdonald were kidding around and decided they ought to collaborate and set up a celebrity telephone service, secret numbers, that sort of thing. Both thought of themselves as celebrities whose telephone numbers people would want to know.

Norman never struck me as erudite. He once said to me that guys like myself and Macdonald "soaked up culture." I didn't think it applied to either one of us, but it indicated that he thought culture was simply one big indivisible thing that you went out and somehow absorbed. He's a Renaissance man, but a World Book Renaissance man, and as a result he acted like a guy who trusted his infallible instincts. He was more given to telling you what the score was and to hell with what the artists or critics might say; more often than not the line was "I, Norman, know better."

But when it came to words and etymology he couldn't do that, because they're factual. I remember his being interested in the meaning of words, hoping that he'd find some big revelations there. He asked me if I could suggest a book, and I told him about Buck's work, in which he'd taken a thousand key words and shown that they were in every one of the Indo-Aryan languages. The work was out of print, so I got a bookseller friend to find a copy. But I suppose Norman's interest petered out—I never heard about it again. Then at some point I needed the book and offered to buy it back at a profit. Norman said, "No, but you can borrow it." It was an example to me of how he never lets go of things, either the idea or the material thing.

NORMAN MAILER (LETTER TO FRANCIS IRBY GWALTNEY, SEPTEMBER 2, 1952)

Dear Fig and Ecey,

I'm back from two weeks of bathing, sunbathing, tennis and what all at Provincetown and thought I'd better write before I settle back to work. I'm now one-hundred and forty pages into a novel so I guess it'll stick. God, I hate writing. Wish I could find an easier racket. Anyway, I may have a respite, for I have a bad case of piles and they get no better sitting on this hard chair...

I thought of a place where you could send some stories. There's a new Pocket Book anthology put out by a friend of mine named Vance Bourjaily, also John Aldridge who wrote After the Lost Generation. *It's called* Discovery, *and I believe the plan is to put it out twice a year in pocket book form although at bottom it will be a magazine of short stories. They pay 3½ cents a word which isn't too bad considering that they have no publishing taboos. Will even print fuck in a story, I believe. And you can write about buggering your grandmother if it's good enough. Anyway the address is c/o Vance Bourjaily, 381 Central Park West, New York, N.Y. You can say I told you to send stuff. But send only one or two, and your best cause their standards are high. I remember a story about a guy named Willie (was it) who works as a mechanic and has a happy marriage which I liked very much. Or whatever you like better. . . .*

Where in Tophet is Russellville? There's an odd chance I'll see you in the fall.

Don't get excited yet cause it's all problematical, and as a matter of fact, unlikely. My hope is that Bea will bring Susy here for a month or more since I kind of dread the idea of going down to Mexico and being at close quarters with Bea for a long time. It always leaves me very depressed. Anyway, let me know about Russellville and how work goes there.

I transmitted your praise to Adele and her eyes sparkled. So, good enough.

> *Love,*
> *Norm*

JOHN ALDRIDGE   My first book, *After the Lost Generation*, came out in '51, and in it I'd written about Norman. At the time I was teaching at the University of Vermont, my first teaching job, and Vance Bourjaily and I were starting a paperback literary magazine called *Discovery*. Vance was in New York; he'd cull the manuscripts, then box them and send them to me for my opinion. We received an awful lot of material because in those days it seemed like a great opportunity for youngish writers, a chance to get published. *New World Writing* was just beginning, and they became our chief competitor, though after our first issue Vance and I fell out over the choice of material and I left the magazine, which went on for six issues.

Vance wanted to get Norman and me together, so he had a party. Norman stayed on afterwards, and the two of us spent most of the night talking. He was alone, and we had one of those airy, very young conversations about whether it was possible or not to write novels: I was holding out for the idea that you had to have some sort of social structure, some sort of hierarchy of manners, a social milieu, and Norman was saying in effect, "I can see how that would be a problem, but I still think it's possible to write good novels in a society in flux, a society like our own."

At the time we didn't have the perspective to see the irony of our conversation. *Barbary Shore* had come out the same week as my own book, and because the editors at *The Times Book Review* weren't pleased with *Barbary Shore* they'd sort of buried its review. The review of my book, *After the Lost Generation*, was on the front cover. I don't think there was any competition between Norman and me when we met, although it may have been there, way down below. It was only later that my bad timing became evident to me—Norman had taken a fall for writing a book about an atomized, anarchistic world, and there I was saying, "Hey, you cannot write novels about such a situation." Also it was only later that it became obvious to me that this was a difficult time for him, that he was in a depression.

That night, though, Norman and I talked, and Vance played host. I don't think the two of them were terribly close, but Vance thought there could be a community of writers in New York, centering perhaps on *Discovery*, and he wanted to bring people together. He tried to institute a once-a-week Sunday meeting, the idea being to create a kind of salon situation—and indeed, the soirees at the White Horse were more his doing than Norman's. There was a lot of nostalgia at the time for the writers in Paris in the twenties, that whole scene, and the feeling was that maybe all that could be duplicated in New York. We'd grown up with a tremendous envy of that wonderful sense of community, of everybody helping one another get published without jealousy or competitiveness, and here we were, young, talented people just starting out. A writer's status wasn't linked to money back then, and almost nobody had any money, although Norman had made quite a bit from *The Naked and the Dead*.

So there was a lot of trading around of our work and a lot of contributions to *Discovery*. Later on we realized it might not work, but in '52 there were so many people in New York, just by chance, that for a short time it looked as though something like this would be possible.

JEAN MALAQUAIS   He had never discussed *The Deer Park* with me, but I had the feeling he was going to write something about his experience in Hollywood. He doesn't like to speak about his problems, impressions, or ideas while working on a book, so I never pressed him.

ADELE MORALES MAILER   In '52 he went out to Hollywood to see about writing a screenplay. I couldn't go because I was working, but he wrote me letters all the time he was away.

EMMA CLARA "ECEY" GWALTNEY   Mickey and Norman stopped in Fayetteville on their way out to California. I was visiting in Conway, and Fig called and said Norman had come through and brought his friend Mickey Knox. I said, "Who's that?" And Fig reminded me that when Bea and Norman had been down in '48 we'd gone to a movie called *City Across the River* because Norman said he had a friend in it, Mickey, who was playing alongside Tony Curtis.

MICKEY KNOX   We drove from New York in a Chevy I'd just bought, the two of us. He was already with Adele but not yet married, and he felt he had to get away. He was hooked on her, but they'd had a slight falling out, and he was concerned about their growing involvement. He was also still brooding about the reviews of *Barbary Shore*, so he was down, unlike his earlier self, which was lighter, friendlier. Plus the fact that he was shaky, worried about the new book he was writing.

The trip took six or seven days because we detoured to see his army friend Gwaltney, in Arkansas. We got into a fight just at the point we had to turn off Route 66 to make our detour. I was driving, he had the map and was giving directions, and we went a hundred miles the wrong way. I thought it was his fault since he was the navigator. He claimed that I was the pilot and so the fault was mine. We didn't speak for two days.

Gwaltney was a very nice fellow. Country-boy nice, easy to talk to. Polite, intelligent, not abrasive. Medium height, medium handsome. Teaching at the University of Arkansas. We stayed overnight, and Gwaltney barbecued steaks. We drank, they talked about writing. It was their night, so I left them alone.

But when we were on our way again Norman waited until Arizona to ask, "Is Palm Springs much of a detour?" He'd never been there and wanted to drive through. I knew he was planning a book and that he wanted to get to California because he was writing about Hollywood people. But he didn't mention Palm Springs until we were almost to California, though I think it had been in his mind all along. And later, in *The Deer Park*, lo and behold, he had everything right—the architecture, the vegetation, everything. He described Palm Springs perfectly. We couldn't have spent one hour there.

In Hollywood we checked into a hotel, and I introduced him to Lois Andrews, my then girl friend. She was the famous child bride of George E. Jessel when she was fifteen. She's now dead, but back then she was a very beautiful chick, and Norman was intrigued by her and the whole relationship, so we all spent a lot of time together. He also saw a lot of Betsy Blair and looked up some of his other friends. I can't think of anyone who became exactly one of the characters in *The Deer Park*, but I suppose the closest model for Eitel was John Huston— a model in the sense of style and class, the kind of character he had. Huston was part of the Gene Kelly group, so Norman had run into him occasionally back in '49.

NORMAN MAILER (LETTER TO FRANCIS IRBY GWALTNEY, JANUARY 15, 1953)
Dear Fig and Ecey,
*   . . . Did I tell you in writing how much I enjoyed the couple of days with you? It was really swell, how swell I think maybe you can't know (about my feelings that is) since with your generosity all the two of you must have thought about was how swell it was for you.*
*   Anyway, I've been back and am kind of weary of Christmas-partying, and I haven't done any work, and now I'm going to go skiing for two weeks in Canada which of course is one of the things I live for. Then when I get back I hope in a month or so to start re-writing* The Deer Park. *After much thought on it, and*

even reading it once I've found that I'm not really satisfied with it, and the worst of it is that I don't see any way to change it. So I think I'm going to write another Deer Park with somewhat different characters and what have you. Don't argue with me cause my mind is made up for the time, and I can always go back to the first if I can't pick up the second.

Have you been working, Fig, on "The Yaller-Headed Summer"? . . . John Huston was in town and I tried to see him but failed to make contact. Probably he'll be passing through again, and I could talk to him about a movie on it, but since it's such a long-shot, I wouldn't think about it too much for the time being, especially since your book might never get done in the process. . . .

Adele is fine, sends love to you, and at present we're both planning to drive to Mexico for a couple of months. Can you come with us for all or part of that time. At the very least we'll want to stop off with you for a week or so. . . .

NORMAN MAILER (LETTER TO FRANCIS IRBY GWALTNEY, APRIL 15, 1953)
Dear Fig and Ecey,

Well, I've been working now for two weeks on the new version of The Deer Park *otherwise known as "At the Feet of Wild Horses" or "In the Crack of the Mare," and it's been brutal. I work all day, go home at night, brood over what I've done, and remain depressed until I decide to tear it up. It's all hell, I swear. Maybe in a month or two I'll get straightened out, but right now I just hate writing. . . .*

Adele is going to art school full time now, and her canvases are really something to see. They're very modern—you won't be able to make head or tail of them— just color and gobs of pigment on a canvas, really weird, but so far as I can judge the quality of avant-garde painting, I think she's improving.

At the moment the sun is out and it's hot in my studio—it reminds me of summer, and that blessed day when I'll stop work for a couple of months and start driving out to Arkansas, and then Mexico. These are our plans for the moment. We want to spend a week with you in Arkansas, unless you can come along with us to Mexico. In that case, a day or two ought to be enough, and we can all pull stakes and continue the journey. But for Christ's sakes, Fig, be a good guy and answer my question for once. When does your vacation come? And can you go with us to Mexico? Incidentally the expense will not be great. We'll be driving down of course so that won't cost for birds, and Mexico itself is very cheap, much less than the States. There is a possibility that you'd have to take the bus back from Mexico City—about a two day trip to Little Rock—because Bea wants me to sell the car to her down there, but I don't know if I will because I want to keep the car for the city. Anyway, let me know, huh?

EMMA CLARA "ECEY" GWALTNEY   I think he usually came down to Arkansas to relax. In fact, at the end of his time in Hollywood he'd even written that Bea and he were thinking about moving down south for a year. Then in the spring of '53 he and Adele rented a little place in Russellville for two weeks. They weren't married, but Norman said, "Adele will have on a wedding ring for your friends." I could never figure out when he was going to be conventional and when he wasn't.

With Adele, and Ecey and Fig Gwaltney, Hot Springs, Arkansas, 1953.

They were studying Spanish because afterwards they were going to Mexico to see Susie. He was a much better student than she was, and I remember one time they were studying at the table and she said something he didn't like and he kind of bopped her on the arm a little bit. I was shocked because we just never touched each other in anger. Nobody in our set would hit anybody.

One time they drove over to Conway, where we'd moved, not far from Russellville, and he read the tarot cards for us. They also saw some of our friends who knew about *The Naked and the Dead* and they took it in stride. Later on, when there'd be something in the paper about some trouble Norman had got into, people in Conway just couldn't imagine, and they'd ask about him. We'd say, "That's not the side of him we would ever see at all," the point being that when he was here he slowed down and was trying to be like a southern gentleman.

Later, on their way back from Mexico, they came back through with Susie. She and my daughter Mary Lee stayed with my mother while Adele and Norman, Fig and I went to Hot Springs. I remember they had Susie in dresses all the time. Our kids were wearing those little pants you pull on to play in, so we bought Susie her first pair of little blue jeans. She was thrilled. Norman was very solicitous, worrying about her a good deal, and he told her to call us "Tia Ecey" and "Tio Fig."

It was Norman who wanted to go to Hot Springs because he'd heard about the gambling and the baths. He was very curious too because he'd heard there was Mafia there. It was Adele's first visit, and she wasn't nearly as at ease as Bea had been. Self-conscious, a little bit on the defensive, and perhaps she felt uncomfortable in the South because she's dark. On the other hand, she eased up a bit when the four of us were alone together.

She always emphasized sex and asked me questions like "How old were you when you first had sex?" She asked if I'd had an abortion; she asked if Fig and I had had sex before we were married, and then at one point she said, "Fig's got hair on his chest too. It's more blond than the hair on his head. Don't you like that?" I said, "I guess," and she said, "Oh, that just sets me on fire."

I remember all those little remarks because it seemed so gratuitous to me. Down here we just do it, we don't talk about it, and I suppose that's what Norman meant about the hypocrisy we grew up with. I don't know whether or not I was getting a little test, but when we went to Hot Springs and she said something about her period, Norman said, "You're always worried about your fucking period. Let's don't talk about your period all the time."

There were times when Fig would react to what Norman was saying as another piece of foolishness and say "Okay" and leave it there. You know, just hanging. He wouldn't get involved. For example, Norman and Adele drove through in a real sleek, low-slung Studebaker. Norman was very proud of the car, and he was walking around it, sort of giving a disquisition: "You know, I've figured it out..." Again all Fig said was "Okay..."

NORMAN MAILER   On our way down to Mexico we also stopped in New Orleans. At a party we met Patti Cozzi and a guy named Woody, a TV or radio announcer.

His voice was so resonant, he spoke as if he lived in the bowl of his voice, and he introduced me to mescaline in peyote form. I can remember Woody shouting in my ear, "Keep it in, keep it in," when I wanted to vomit. I was sick as a dog for twenty-four hours. I kept seeing Aztec human sacrifices.

ADELE MORALES MAILER   Norman kept talking about his hallucinations—a lot of little men, very colorful and interesting. I remember we were driving back from Patti's to the hotel and were so stoned we had to abandon the car. There was an awful red light outside our hotel room, and all night the whole world turned red, off-and-on, off-and-on, and I thought I was in hell. I said, "Oh God, never again." Of course Patti and her boyfriend got very spiritual about peyote, but it was terrible.

PATTI COZZI   Woody Leafer had been a radio announcer at WQXR in New York, but in New Orleans we both worked at WDSU, the television station. We had a show called *Mr. Brown Around Town*, and we'd get into the Brown's Velvet Ice Cream truck—that was our sponsor—and go over to some nightclub. Anyway, the idea was to bring the television audience to a place and give them a taste of what was going on, so probably we ran into Norman and Adele while we were doing a show and asked them over. It's hard to remember because Norman wasn't outstanding to me then. He was as he is to me today—he's Norman. I loved Adele. She was very sweet, a nice person.

So I guess they came to our place—we were living in the French Quarter. We'd gotten involved with peyote—not mushrooms, peyote's a round cactus—after we read in *Time* that all the canned pineapple and canned fruits were disappearing from the grocery shelves because the North American Indian Church was having peyote sessions. Peyote reduces your blood sugar to practically zilch, which is why a lot of people feel they're dying when they take it. The Indians always have a supply of fruit in heavy syrup to replace the blood sugar.

In those days you could buy peyote in little pots at Woolworth's—it wasn't illegal. The plant has a part that grows on the surface of the earth, which, after you cut the root off, is a bluish green, teal cap with tufts on it. You take the tufts off and cut the cap up in chunks and that's what you swallow. We kept our peyote in a big box, and Norman must have asked to try it. We weren't dispensing it. Woody must have talked about it, because we were involved in it that year, so it was probably just the four of us. We didn't usually have crowds if we were going to let someone have peyote, and we were very careful about who we gave it to. Your relationship is always spiritual. It's not a quick high, it's not having a drink. It's a mystical experience, a William James thing, a real religious experience.

NORMAN MAILER (LETTER TO FRANCIS IRBY GWALTNEY, JULY 1953, MEXICO CITY, MEXICO)
Dear Fig and Ecey,
I feel like a bastard for not having written in so long, but we've been on the

move almost constantly, going from New Orleans to Mexico City, and since then travelling the last couple of weeks with Barbara and Larry through parts of Mexico. This country is beautiful, really fabulously beautiful with jungle, mountains, valleys, and the long lonely vistas of the Southwest. Some of the towns are incredibly beautiful, better even than similar places in Europe. One of the ironies is that it's cool as hell here in Mexico City. We're at seven to eight thousand feet altitude and it rarely gets above eighty in the day, and at night you have to wear blankets. By the way, Fighole, the mountain driving here is fantastic. There's a stretch of road on the way to Mexico City where for a hundred miles you just ascend through mountains (from sea level practically to the high plateaus of Mexico City) and it's a fabulous drive through deep canyons, hairpin curves, terrific descents and ascents, etc. The thing about it though which wears you out is that for one hundred miles (and I'm not kidding) there is no single straightaway longer than say two hundred yards. You get a stroke passing some of those trucks.

At the moment we're living at a place called the Turf Club which is a couple of miles out of the city limits of Mexico City in a pretty little canyon. We got a weird house. It's got a kitchen, a bathroom, a living room shaped like a semi-circle with half the wall of glass, and a balcony bedroom. It looks out over a beautiful view and is furnished in modern. This for Fifty-five bucks a month. It's really cheap here once you get away from the expensive hotels—like a bottle of Canadian Club whiskey for $2.50 or a bottle of tequila for what it costs to get two quarts of ginger ale.

We went touring all around (no need listing hundreds of names and places) but we went with Barbara and Larry to Acapulco for a few days. It's a great place for a resort, and again fabulously beautiful. High jungle cliffs falling from rocks into the sea. We all went deep-sea fishing, and I caught the first fish I ever pulled in with a rod and reel—as a matter of fact it was the first time I ever used a rod and reel. It turned out to be a sail-fish, weight eighty-five pounds, length eight and a half feet. Hard work m'boy, not for stripling fishers like you and John R. (Actually it's damn hard work—all you do is pull up on the rod, and reel in line, and then the fish runs it out again. It felt like half an hour on a bicycle pump. By the time the fish was in, I couldn't have cared less. There is a bang though when those monsters fly into the air trying to throw the bait. Anyway, eat your heart out.)

We had a fine time in Russellville. Adele and I agreed often that we hadn't been as relaxed and at ease with the world in a long long time. And we just adored Mary Jane. On the trip back I'm looking forward to stopping off for a day or two with you while we let Susy water, so to speak. She by the way is terrific, but there's something sad about her. She has enormous pixie charm when she gets going, but there are long sad hours when she looks off into space with her thumb in her mouth. I adore her. You can have no idea what she's like till she'll be in the house for a few hours. And her English accent. "I like dees and dees and dat vairy mooch." Her Spanish is excellent and she corrects everyone's pronunciation including Bea's.

When we're coming back we have no idea yet. It'll probably be two months anyway and maybe more. So far I've done almost no work on the book (none except what I did in Russellville, and it all depends how work starts going.) If it goes well we may stay longer.

Give Mary Lee a kiss for us. What a little pudding. Adele sends her love, and I do too. Give our regards to all your friends—you know the ones we liked, and take it easy. Have you sent out "Yaller-headed" yet?

EMMA CLARA "ECEY" GWALTNEY   Norman would always write Fig about his writing, and over the years he sent some absolutely great critiques. He'd say, "You're a natural-born writer, but you're sloppy. You just write something, and, by God, if it isn't right you just go on anyway." Fig's method was just to get it out, not mess with it too much, but as the years went on I think he accepted the advice. I don't know if he would acknowledge it, though. He wouldn't say, "I owe Norman. I should give him credit for the fact that I've learned to be more self-critical and take criticism better and work more carefully."

NORMAN MAILER (LETTER TO FRANCIS IRBY GWALTNEY, DECEMBER 1953)

Dear Fig,

...I don't know if I wrote you, but I finally got the damn second draft done, and since then I've been fixing up our apartment. The second draft seems pretty good to me, but there's a stretch of eighty or ninety pages which have to be pretty much re-done, and what with one thing and another, I probably won't be able to finish it before the Spring.

Are you going to come up to New York for Christmas? You can stay with us of course. We have either a double bed or twin beds at your disposal. My place is sort of one big room without separate bedrooms, but if either of us feel the desire to bed with our women we can arrange special hours or whatever. Adele and I hope you both come, and it may be a very good thing for you to talk to Loomis directly and meet the people at Rinehart. In any case, I think you'll have fun up here, and if you come by the 24th, Vance Bourjaily is having a big Christmas Eve party where you'll meet lots of stupid writers. Anyway, let me know. Get that Southern shit out of your ass, boy, and come on up. I know Ecey would love to come. New York is just extraordinary around Christmas and New Years. What I failed to say is: we would love to have you come and stay with us.

Susy is getting more like Grandma every day. It's really funny to see the two of them together. Same determined mouths, same stubborn little chins. She's getting a little spoiled to my taste what with the relatives all gushing over her, so that the other day at the dinner table, hearing her perform like a little trained pig, I said: Susan, do me a favor. SHUT UP.

Susan: You are too serious, you make me sad.

Norman: (furiously) You heard what I said.

(Silence)

Susan: (after three minutes) Why do you say "shut up?" Why do you not say "Keep quiet?"

NORMAN MAILER (LETTER TO FRANCIS IRBY GWALTNEY, JANUARY 5, 1954)

Dear Fig and Ecey,

. . . You write: "if respectability and love for family are one and the same, I'm both."

For Christ's sakes, I was trying to tell you just the opposite in that French restaurant. I'm perfectly aware that you love Ecey and Mary Lee, more than you'll ever know, but I'm just a little sick, Fig, of the defensive way you protest it, as if I won't believe you, and as if to say it makes you therefore "respectable," and so fuck anybody who looks down on a respectable man. You're respectable enough without going out of your way to be respectable. As a matter of fact I have nothing against respectability as such. It's a very legitimate way to lead one's life, and the only danger in it is when the word becomes a symbol. I feel the danger in you is that if you don't keep the word within reason, you're going to feel duty-bound never to touch a drop, go to church every day, and persecute the young with sermons. I wish I could express it, Fig. One of the reasons I've admired you so much, Ecey, is that you're "open," and therefore you're ready to receive any new experience which comes your way on its merits. And frankly, Fig, as an old friend, you're that way too, and nobody's asking you to change except you, yourself. Look what a good time you had at your party once you got drunk and became your own charming self, the self, indeed, which Ecey married.

What I'm trying to say in one sentence I suppose is live your life anyway you want, but don't start judging people adversely if they lead different lives. Everybody's got the right to bumble into whatever life they can make. In my best Yiddish—so now who's giving sermons?

Bea is back from Chelsea, same as ever. She got drunk last night at a family gathering, and said fuck piss cock shit cunt all over the place. Anne and Dave, me mother and father looked like they'd just grown faces of stone. Poor everybody. My family by the way, Kesslers and Mailers, were both enormously pleased by your letters to them. Bea misses her husband Chavo and wishes she were back in Mexico.

Adele is working and looking fine. Tonight, I bring Susy over to sleep with us.

NORMAN MAILER (LETTER TO FRANCIS IRBY GWALTNEY, FEBRUARY 16, 1954)

Dear Fig and Ecey,

Your letters are in hand, so I can answer them both at the same time. Reverse of the old Norman Rosten line when asked by John Selby if he, Rosten, was hard at work on a book for them. Old Rosten said, I'm working on two books at the same time—one with my left hand, one with my right hand. So there, old fertile fart, top that . . .

I'm close to the end of The Deer Park. *I still have half the manuscript to go through for prose which means I'll be on that for a couple of weeks yet, and then there's a last chapter to write which may be very hard, but outside of that I'm okay. Except that I have very little elation at the thought of finishing it because where the hell do I go from there? What, indeed, will the next book be. Sometimes*

I wish that I suffered from your problems, Fig, of having too many books at once that you're dying to do...

By the way, Ecey, you had cause for self-pity. That man of yours came up, stuck out his chin Gary Cooper style to all the temptations of Noo Yawk, and it all rolled over his head. If it'd been you, you'd of had wild affairs, salacious drunks, orgies, dope and what-all. I know the wild-cat in you, Ecey. Isn't it just the injustice of life that the wrong one comes up here?...

NORMAN MAILER (LETTER TO FRANCIS IRBY GWALTNEY, FEBRUARY 23, 1954)

Dear Fig and Ecey,

...I've been puttering along with mine, and I think I'll have a rough final draft done in a couple of weeks. I had to take time out to write an article for Dissent, *the Socialist magazine of which I'm a contributing editor, and that took awhile, and now that all the springs are run down I just crawl forward bit by bit. I suppose what it is is that I don't want to finish the damn book because where next O muse?*

Adele has finally hit a productive period in her painting, and has turned out about five lovely canvases. (All strictly abstract.) I sort of miss not having Fig there to look at it distrustfully, his nostrils sniffing with a kind of Wuzzat-Boss?-look. At the moment we're planning to get married in the next month or two, sort of whenever we get around to it. The littler the ceremony the better....

NORMAN MAILER (LETTER TO FRANCIS IRBY GWALTNEY, APRIL 3, 1954)

Dear Fig,

...I've held off writing because I didn't know, and still don't know about the Spring visit. There's even a chance we won't be able to go out at all. What's happened is that I've gotten very interested in working in a woman's prison for awhile, and if I can get such a job I'd have to go to work right away on it. Since there's that, plus the weeks of work left to accomplish on The Deer Park, *anything is possible at the moment. We may go to Mexico, we may not, I might go to work soon, I might not find such a job—it's just too complicated to go into all the possibilities.*

The news on Century *sounds very good, and I'd love to read it—except perhaps it might be a good idea for me to keep my heavy hand off it. Only one thing worries me—the line of yours "there'll be much in it that you won't agree with because you don't think the way I do." What bothers me is that I get the feeling you've put a lot of speeches into the thing about what you believe, etc. etc. I don't give a damn what an author believes, provided his view is expressed in the total shape of the book, in his view-of-life which is implicit in the material, but there're very few authors who can get away with having a mouthpiece make a speech for them, and neither you nor I belong to that select group. Anyway, if we can't get out to visit and you can't come to visit us, maybe, if you still want me to read it, you could mail it to me, and we could have a long discussion by mail about it.*

At the moment, Adele and I are planning to get married toward the end of

April, probably in New York. What I'd like to do is just clear out with her for a few days and skip all the family crap, but for the moment that looks as complicated as any other way.

I've been reading some of my contemporaries. Lie Down in Darkness *was magnificent I thought. What a writer Styron is. I've come to know him pretty well since he's gotten back to New York, and he's a hell of a nice guy too. Other reading:* The Grass Harp *by Capote.*

Then The Caine Mutiny *which I thought was about the best slick novel I ever read until I got to the last fifty pages which were pretty godawful. The thing about it is that the whole book is a terrible cheat. If he means what he says about obeying authority, then he should have had the guts to write his novel all the way, and have Queeg triumphant and Maryk convicted. This way he satisfies the reader who is pulling for Maryk, and then satisfies authority and himself by reversing it all and attempting to give his own ideas. Ah well, a life, a wife.*

It's good to hear that you're all better, Ecey. I hope you'll like the new Deer Park. *I think it's got all the merits of the old one, and has added a few, but in a couple of months I may have it ready to show you, and then you can decide for yourself. . . .*

SHIRLEY FINGERHOOD   I met Styron and his wife Rose at Norman and Adele's marriage party. I don't know when they'd met, because Norman hadn't known Styron in 1952. I remember that when I'd gone on that skiing trip he'd asked me to bring up a paperback collection in which he had a story. When I arrived he asked, "Did you read it?" I said, "Oh yes, and there's the most fantastic story in it—'The Long March' by someone named Styron." He was furious. He was asking me how I liked *his* story. But then he read Styron's story and said, "You're right. It *is* the most terrific story."

MICKEY KNOX   I think Norman had met Jimmy Jones in '51, and by '53 the three of us were hitting the bars on Eighth Avenue fairly regularly. Billy Styron used to join us, and one night we came out of a bar—Julius' or the White Horse—and Billy put his arms around Jim and Norman—he was really high—and gleefully he said, "Here we are, the three best young writers in America!" Camaraderie? Who knows.

We used to play liar's poker quite a bit. You get used to it, it's a tough habit to break, and Jim lost almost constantly because his personality wasn't suited to it. He was too emotional. I was good, I'd played it a lot, and I taught Norman and Jim both, and Norman got to be a whiz. So there was Jones, sandwiched between two good players. I can't remember him ever winning, and he'd say, "You damned Jewboys!"

We also went in for arm-wrestling. Norman was good there too—he has strong shoulders—but Jim wasn't bad either. One time, real late in the evening, Norman got Jim's hand to about three inches off the table. Now, it's practically impossible to come back from that, but Jim had a look on his face of sheer determination, of fear, a wild kind of look, either close to death or close to violence, and by Christ, he put Norman's hand back up. The two of them stood that way for a minute or two, maybe five minutes, which is a *very* long time, and then they had to call it a draw. It wasn't pleasant, and suddenly things got very quiet.

It's hard to describe, but I felt something negative was happening on both sides. Maybe the arm wrestling was a germ that grew and came out later in Norm's essay about Jones in '59, but something went out of their friendship right there and then. The effort was too powerful, the energy expended was too much for either of them to accept. Not just physical energy but psychic energy. Both of them must have thought, Why spend all this energy with no result, no conclusion? Norm admired Jim's ability to come back from virtual defeat—it *was* extraordinary—but the whole episode, well . . . We weren't crazy drunk, I'd just sort of pushed them into it—"Come on, fellas, this is the showdown," that kind of bullshit—and it was pretty awful to watch.

GLORIA JONES   Jim was very competitive, and I'd heard about the arm wrestling, but I don't think Jim was competitive with Norman. His letters to Norman don't show that. In fact, later on—in '54, I think—Jim tried to help him get *The Deer Park* published. He'd said that *Barbary Shore* was an allegory, which he liked, whereas he felt that Norman was on the wrong track with *The Deer Park*, but still he went to bat for him at Scribner's. So I honestly don't think the competitiveness came from Jim, because he was pretty much his own man and went on about his business.

As for Jim's hanging out at the White Horse, all I can say is that when we were living in Illinois, he'd come back from a trip to New York exhausted and frightened. He loved going out, and as long as there was a bar open, he'd stay. He'd stay until four, then get up at six, which was pretty exhausting for him, so he'd come back to me frightened and once even said, "You gotta keep me out of there. I'm not able to work in New York."

I think Norman saw Jim as a real article in terms of the army, though. Jim came from a very good family, but he was a soldier and was wounded by shrapnel in the leg in Guadalcanal, and in New Georgia he was shot in the head and was decorated. *The Thin Red Line* is really autobiographical. He went all through that and saw a lot of combat, and when he first came home from the war he got in a lot of fights. But I don't think he ever had a fight with Norman. I think Jim could've beat the shit out of Norman, 'cause he was big and he was a boxer in the army. Norman knew that, so he wasn't going to start anything.

I never heard about that particular arm wrestling episode, but that kind of will power was part of Jim's character. I've seen him do that—be down like that and come back—like even when he was broke with money. In '72, I think it was, we were in debt up to our ass—this was when we were living in Paris—and we drove to Deauville for two weeks. Jim took $10,000 and gave himself credit for another $5000. Me, I was praying. We put up in a dump ten blocks from the casino. Every night Jim would put on his tuxedo, go off and play chemin de fer with a lot of big guys like Sam Spiegel, then come back wet with sweat. I used to take the tuxedo to the cleaner's every day, then at about ten at night we'd go back to the casino, and come home at four or five. I was scared but I loved it, and Jim pulled $35,000 out of there.

So I've seen him do that a lot. Like when he was sick. I'd once said to him, "If you're ever really dying, I'm gonna give you a drink"—because he couldn't drink. So when he was dying—seriously, bells were ringing—I started pouring whiskey down his throat, straight bourbon. And they couldn't believe it—he came to and lasted three months after that. The nurses, the doctor, told me never to do it again, they were so terrified. But Jim was tough, he had that sort of will that was beyond belief.

NAT HALPER   What I always admired in *The Naked and the Dead* was his ability to imitate the way the guys talked. I had known army guys, and he had their lingo down pat, but then he decided it was too damn easy, and he'd always tell me it was really Jones who'd done it. In those years he thought Jones was wonderful. I said to him, "Norman, I never knew a goddamned GI who talked like James Jones." But he'd argue, "Jones was regular army." I tried to tell him that I'd been regular army too and never heard corporals and sergeants talk like they do in Jones, but he wouldn't hear it. He was completely hooked on Jones, as if Jones somehow had the secret.

NORMAN MAILER (LETTER TO FRANCIS IRBY GWALTNEY, APRIL 29, 1954)
Dear Fig and Ecey,

Well, there's a couple of pieces of news. First of all, Adele and I got married last April 19th at City Hall with my parents in attendance. Since then, in order to cultivate the impression that we're still living together (that is, to ourselves) we've been going along same as always, and as a matter of fact went to work the next day. Danny gave us a party which was a good one, and Toby Schneebaum (the artist who lives next door) also gave us one, and my sister will give us one the Saturday after this. So, all in all, it feels like Christmas. . . .

The other news is on my book. I'm really almost done with it, they like it at Rinehart, and after one more week of going through it for sentences, I guess I'll type it up. My hope is to have a copy along when I visit you so that you both can read it. . . .

James Jones has been in town, and we've been seeing a bit of him. He's really a hell of a wonderful guy, and I know that you and he would be nuts about each other. If you're ever up near Marshall, Illinois, look him up. (It's a small town, and you could find his house by asking.) I know you'd enjoy him. Old Bull Jones. He's taken to Mickey Knox a great deal, and much to the ladies' disgust, parties are spent now arm-wrestling à la Hemingway thirty-six hour style. To my amazement, I discovered I'm stronger than I thought I was. (Jonesie is like Casey in "Y H Summer.") . . .

SHIRLEY FINGERHOOD   At the party to celebrate their marriage Norman said to me, "Now that I'm getting married, things are going to be different between you and me." I didn't understand at all. We'd always been affectionate, but I'd never thought there was anything sexual between us. He did, though. When they got married he knew the relationship of dominance had shifted toward Adele, so that if she said, "We're not going to see Shirley Fingerhood anymore," he couldn't say anything. Naturally she wasn't going to say, "We're not going to get along with Barbara anymore," because that would have been impossible, but on minor things, such as a relationship with me, he knew the dominance had shifted. Of course afterwards I realized it was because Adele always hated me, which I learned later that year.

Paul Jacobs was in town, and together we dropped in on this gathering at Carol Greitzer's. Norman and Adele were there, and it turned out that Norman and Paul knew everybody in common from California; they even had some special interest in a woman they both knew out there. Paul and Norman, of course, are exactly the kind of people who adore each other, and they went at it. Norman was going on to a party up in Harlem, and he invited Paul to come; Paul was with me, so I went along. Afterwards Paul was absolutely furious because Adele had said to Norman in Spanish, "Do we have to bring that bitch along?" He was angry because I was his friend and angry because Adele was so arrogant as to think that he wouldn't understand Spanish.

ADELE MORALES MAILER   Even though Norman and I moved in together in '51, we didn't get married until '54 because he was reluctant. I wanted to get married, but he might've been afraid of it, though I don't think he had lingering feelings about Bea. Finally I said I wanted to get married, and he said, "Oh hell, let's do it." It was as casual as that. I don't even remember the exact date. We both thought it was excess baggage and never celebrated anniversaries. Flowers and candy—that was for the bourgeoisie.

I don't want to say a word about Fan's attitudes. She was a little removed but never mean or nasty, though she insisted I call her "Mother," and that kind of got my back up. But, really, I think she accepted me as a member of the family. I remember once she took me to Saks to buy a hostess gown. Here I was, this bohemian, but I said, "Okay, so she wants to buy me a gown." In the fitting room I took my dress off; I never shaved under my arms, and she had a fit, she was absolutely horrified. But I suppose she felt that if her son was happy, she was happy. She'd accept anything from him including . . . well, a lot of things. Her mother love has no bounds, no limitations. But if that's true mother love, I must be lacking in it. I can't accept that kind of unlimited love.

I got along with Barney very well, though. He used to tease me and laugh. He would do his Spanish dance for me, a little flamenco, which I thought was funny. We'd be talking about Spain and my being Spanish, and he'd go into this little flamenco number—this little round body tapping his heels—and he loved that song "Never on Sunday." He had one phrase of French from his time in Paris—"*petit peu.*" He'd always pronounce it in a funny way, and we'd all laugh. Barney was ultrarespectability except for his gambling. I know Norman was kind of upset about that, probably because he had to shell out; I don't know, though, I just heard about it. But that was what was so funny about Barney: despite his secret gambling he was the soul of respectability, and he'd put down anybody who was at all off base, anyone he didn't think was proper.

LARRY ALSON   There were some very heavy discussions about Barney's gambling when, more than once, he was heavily in hock. He lost some clients' money—quite a bit, as I recall—and then there was some episode in Mexico City when he and Fan went down to see Susie.

SHIRLEY FINGERHOOD   While I was working for Cy, Barney was unemployed, and he was using our office to do Norman's accounts, perhaps others' too. But I didn't know about his gambling until several years later. It was very important and one of the reasons Anne and Dave had such a role in Barbara's and Norman's life. It's also one of the reasons why Fan had the kind of relationship with the children. Barney was a very sweet man, nice and pleasant, but by the time I met him he was somewhat broken. His family role was subsidiary, and when Barbara and I became friends she discussed his gambling and the problems it created—not so much when they were children but that as adults they were always running around protecting him from himself.

ADELINE LUBELL NAIMAN   Norman swore me to secrecy. It was part of his telling me why he was angry with his father. Barbara may have told me too, and I know I was shocked. It was something I'd never encountered and couldn't understand, like drunkenness, and I couldn't forgive Barney. Up till then I'd been sorry that he was sort of a braggart and so forth, and I was fond of him as the father of somebody I loved. But after that I couldn't feel the same way about him and didn't understand how they could feel the same way, because the things he'd done to their lives—certainly to Fan's life—seemed unforgivable.

FANNY SCHNEIDER MAILER   When I took over the Miss Baltimore Agency I had about twenty nurses working for me and I was in complete charge. Barney made out the statements, but I would give him the information. I took it for granted that where I needed help—information and keeping records—he would give it. It wasn't an awkward situation because I didn't make it awkward. I was simply running a successful business and bringing in most of the money.

What was more a problem was Barney's gambling, which he probably picked up from certain friends after he was here in America, before the Second World War. That was Barney's ruination, it really was. Because at heart he was very honest and good and always treated me like a lady.

BARBARA MAILER WASSERMAN   Actually I've been told my father was told by his family in South Africa during WW I that he had to enlist if he wanted them to pay off his gambling debts—it was the army or jail. Sometimes I wonder if they were hoping he'd never come back—and, indeed, he didn't until forty-odd years later.

FANNY SCHNEIDER MAILER   But it reached a point where he didn't have the means to meet it. If he came to me, I said, "The hell with this." I wouldn't give him a nickel. It was so distasteful to me, so foreign to my nature, that I couldn't take it. We argued a lot, and maybe he got money from Norman. But he just couldn't stop. He meant well, but he was weak. So I took over. I found out who these people were. I can't remember how I did it, but I'm a good sleuth and I found out from phone calls that came in. I told these people that if they didn't stop I was going to a lawyer and would put them in jail. In plain words I said, "I'll put you all in prison. I'm not kidding, I'm tough." I said this on the telephone, and then it eased up. I was ashamed of it, but it needed toughness, so I told them, "I mean what I say," and I think they were really afraid of me. I was afraid of them, but I put on this tough cloak and asserted my rights and told them I would report the whole thing to the government.

I guarded the family from Barney's gambling, although Norman was smart enough to know. Dave knew too, but they all dumped it in my lap, as if I was the mother. I didn't know what he was betting on because I didn't care to know, I just hoped and prayed it would stop. I didn't know when Norman started gambling either—maybe in the army—but he must have gotten it from Barney.

MICKEY KNOX   The only time I borrowed money from Norman was in '53, when I got involved in a crooked poker game along with a friend of mine who was being held responsible for the markers. Some people were threatening to break his legs, so I told him I'd pay half. I went to Norman and he loaned me the money, as if to say he'd had the same troubles with his father.

ADELE MORALES MAILER   From the first time I met him, it struck me that Norman was always generous with money, like he was embarrassed at having so much. Most of it was from the success of *The Naked and the Dead*, and he never thought twice about spending it or giving loans to friends who needed help.

NORMAN MAILER (LETTER TO FRANCIS IRBY GWALTNEY, MAY 28, 1954)
Dear Fig and dear Ecey,

I've held off writing, trying to figure out when we'd be taking off, and the way it looks now, we won't be on the road till somewhere between the fifteenth and the twentieth of June. I still have my book to type up, and once I get done with that I have to spend a week arguing it out with Stan Rinehart. The situation now is this: Ted Amussen is very high on it, but Stan hates it, and I have a hunch the rest of the house is going to divide down the middle. So, wish me luck. I've already had an argument with Stan, and the sole consolation is that Ted is squarely in my corner. . . .

At the moment I'm on a diet. For the last year or two I've been dragging ass in the morning, and feeling generally run-down, and so I went for a general check-up and discovered that I've got a lousy liver. (Probably a follow-through from that yellow jaundice I had in the Philippines.) So now I've got to lay off drinking for thirty days, and drink milk, and eat boiled and broiled meats and fishes, and stuff like that. I don't mind because it's an easy diet, and I've been starting to drink a little too much anyway, but I mention this just to tell you not to buy a bottle specially for us when we arrive. If you want a drink yourself, it won't hurt me to watch (on the contrary, makes me feel noble, etc.) but if I'm a good boy for six months or so, I'll probably be able to restore my liver completely.

ADELE MORALES MAILER   We went to Mexico two summers in a row, '53 and '54. In '54 we lived a good long while, more than just the summer, in the town of San Angel Inn, a beautiful place. There were other Americans around, and Norman was finishing up *The Deer Park*.

We both became involved with bullfighting. Betty Ford, the lady bullfighter, was there, and when we were living in the suburbs of Mexico City we'd drive out to the bullfights every Sunday. Norman was reading a lot about it—I guess Hemingway sparked some of his interest—and he knew all the passes. The two of us used to fool around with it. He'd get out the cape and practice, and at one point he wanted to fight a bull at a farm and I got hysterical. I begged him not to do it, I just wouldn't let him go ahead with it.

When we were there, though, he had a liver problem—the ulcer came a year or two later—and he had to go on a bland diet—in Mexico! What a rough period that was.

JOHN ALDRIDGE   Given the trouble with *The Deer Park*, someone at Rinehart had asked Norman if he would like an outside opinion, and he recommended me. I wrote to Rinehart saying I'd do it but they'd have to understand I would try my best to forget that I'd met Mailer, although in fact I hadn't seen him since our first meeting at Bourjaily's two years before. I was very right-minded in those days and wanted it known that I'd write as objective a response as I could.

I read the manuscript and submitted a three- or four-page single-spaced report. There were a lot of reasons why I didn't like the book, but the big one was that it was dramatically empty, perhaps because it was empty of ideas. There was a bit of straining, of reaching for effect. I felt Norman had gotten all his characters together, but what they did was not made significant, so that a reader might easily say, "I'm not interested in what happens."

Five or ten years later I would have handled it differently. I would've called Norman before writing the letter and said, "I can only write a negative report, so what do you want me to do?" But in those days it didn't occur to me. I'd met Mailer once, and maybe in some strange way I thought I was being helpful. "Culture" and "Literature" all had capital letters for me in those days, and also there was the notion that we were in it together—writers, critics and publishers alike.

As it turned out I wasn't being helpful at all. The implicit antagonism between publishers and writers wasn't nearly as severe as it is now, but I hadn't any real conception of Norman's situation at Rinehart. The people there took my letter and went running back to him, saying, "You see, Mailer!" And the next thing I knew I had a very long letter from Norman telling me they'd shown him my report and that he was clearly distressed by it. He was right—it was not the kind of letter that would be helpful to a writer, though it wasn't written with that in mind. But Rinehart had violated their contract by showing it to him. There was a further exchange of letters between us, with me defending what I had to say and Norman attacking. But Norman isn't a person who holds grudges. By the third exchange he decided to drop the whole thing, saying, "Clearly, we're not meeting on this question. Let's leave it," and then he goes on to talk about skiing or whatever, becoming quite friendly.

I learned later that my reader's report had led finally to the breach with Rinehart. I remember too that Norman then did several revisions of *The Deer Park*, trying to find a new publisher.

NORMAN MAILER (LETTER TO FRANCIS IRBY GWALTNEY, NOVEMBER 30, 1954)

Dear Fig and Ecey,

I'm afraid I've got some upsetting news. About two weeks ago, out of the blue, Stan Rinehart suddenly decided that he would not and could not publish The Deer Park. *So now I'm looking for a new publisher.*

The whole thing is cockeyed. The book was in page proof. Ted Amussen was behind it, everything was just swimming, and then Stan went off his rocker. The details are too long and too dull to go into now, and I'll tell you them when I see you, but at present suffice it that I'm not particularly worried. For one thing Stan owes me the advance, for another I'm quite confident of finding another publisher fast. It's mainly annoyance. I wanted to settle down and work, and now I have to go looking for a publisher. I spoke to Bob Loomis and he was terribly upset, and Ted was upset and said he thought it was the worst mistake Stan ever made. And so forth. The big thing as far as you're concerned is that I honestly think, Fig, that you're in a better position now. I also know you're such a good friend that you'll find this small comfort, but really and truly it is good news for Century, I think, because they'll be more likely to get behind it now and really do a job since they now need a new tailback. So just sit tight, and don't start having wild thoughts. In about a year Stan is going to retire, and then Ted will really be running the business, and it'll be one of the best publishing houses around. All I wish is that Stan had picked last year to retire instead of next year.

CHARLES REMBAR   Since I wrote about what happened in *The End of Obscenity*, it's probably best just to quote it here:

After the manuscript had been set in type, the company came to the conclusion that it was unpublishable because it was obscene. A contract to perform an illegal act is not enforceable, and Rinehart, strongly convinced of the illegality because of one passage in particular, felt relieved of its obligation to publish. On the author's behalf, I disagreed, and offered to test the issue in a suit for the advance of royalties. Rinehart held to its position, but, faced with the suit, paid Mailer for the privilege of not publishing his book. Despite the obvious desirability of adding an extravagantly gifted writer to their list, six other houses had turned the book down before Walter Minton celebrated his ascension to the presidency of Putnam's by taking a chance on it.

The lawyer for one of the other publishers had presented me with a memorandum of over a hundred excerpts from the book, arranged under headings such as "must be deleted," "must be changed," "should be changed." Nowhere in his catalogue was the passage that Rinehart thought fatal.

If Rinehart had chosen to fight the issue instead of making a handsome settlement, I would have got into obscenity litigation about five years before *Lady Chatterley's Lover* came along.

ADELE MORALES MAILER   It was a terrible time. The book used to come back, and Norman would get very upset. One after another, I don't know how many publishers turned it down. Norman would say, "Those motherfuckers. I'll show them."

Walter Minton was the one who finally took it, and he was very supportive. Of course after *Barbary Shore* Norman knew he was on the firing line. *The Naked and the Dead* was a tough act to follow—the Boy Wonder, the fantastic money and fame—so a lot of people were waiting for him to fall on his face. There were others, though, who wanted it to be as good as his first book, but they didn't understand that he couldn't repeat himself, that he had to write a different kind of book. Obviously all that stress wasn't too good for him.

NORMAN MAILER (ADVERTISEMENTS FOR MYSELF)   *The eighth house was G. P. Putnam's. I didn't want to give it to them, I was planning to go next to Viking, but Walter Minton kept saying, "Give us three days. We'll give you a decision in three days." So we sent it over to Putnam, and in three days they took it without conditions, and without a request for a single change. I had a victory, I had made my point, but in fact I was not happy. I had grown so wild on my diet of polite letters from publishing houses who didn't want me, that I had been ready to collect rejections from twenty houses, publish* The Deer Park *at my own expense, and try to make a kind of publishing history. Instead I was thrown in with Walter Minton, who has since attracted some fame as the publisher of* Lolita. *He is the only publisher I ever met who would make a good general. Months after I came to Putnam, Minton told me, "I was ready to take* The Deer Park *without reading it. I knew your name would sell enough copies to pay your advance, and I figured one of these days you're going to write another book like* The Naked and the Dead," *which is the sort of sure hold of strategy you can have when you're not afraid of censorship.*

WALTER MINTON   Up until '55 I was advertising manager at Putnam's. My father was president of the company, but at the time he was very sick, and I took over. Peter Israel worked for me, and one afternoon he said, "Do you know anything about this Mailer book that's around town?" I talked to Ted Purdy, Putnam's editor in chief, and told him to go after it. Purdy was a very bright man, a good editor, but he didn't call Cy Rembar. I did. I hadn't known Cy, but I started bugging him. He was very forthright and told me that the book had to go to

Scribner's because Norman had promised to show it to Jim Jones's editor. Then he said, "Norman may even put it away," and immediately I said, "I guarantee Scribner's won't take it. Just let me see it."

Within a couple of weeks it came in. We knew that some publishers were afraid of it—the censorship issue—but I never thought there'd be any legal problems, nor did Ted. Ted Purdy wasn't the kind of man who'd necessarily consider something like that or be intimidated by it, and as soon as we read the manuscript both of us wanted it.

Cy was the only one I dealt with, and in short order we sent him a contract. There was very little money paid, $10,000, though in 1954 that wasn't an inconsiderable amount, since a first novel by an unknown author might have gotten a thousand.

Apparently the scene that gave Rinehart the chills was where what's his name— Teppis—has the girl on his lap and he opens his legs and she slides to the floor. It's not explicit, but the implication is that she blows him. It's the scene that scared everybody, but for the life of me I couldn't see what the fuss was about. Bennett Cerf called me just before publication and said, "Walter, I hope you won't take offense, I know you're new in the business"—all the standard bullshit— "but I must counsel you against publishing 'The Deer Park.'" I said, "Thank you very much, Mr. Cerf, I'll really consider it, but..." Random House had already turned it down, but what he was saying was that the book was bad for the industry. In that sense he was trying to prevent its publication.

It's true that I said to Norman, "Any book those five publishers turned down we can sell." But what bothered me were our ads that said "The book five publishers were afraid to bring you." From where I stand now it probably was a stupid thing to do. Had the book not arrived with that stigma of notoriety, the reviews might've been different, and the sales could have been twice, maybe three times as big. But the idea was to face the controversy head on since word was already out.

Norman then decided to revise the book in galleys, or maybe even page proofs, and publication was postponed from spring to fall. Norman has a penchant for rewriting, of course, but now, looking back on it, I wonder if people, knowing about the controversy, didn't think the book was postponed so we could chop out the dirty parts. As things turned out, we sold 50,000 or 55,000 copies, which I think hurt Norman. If *The Deer Park* had sold two or three times better, who knows, he might've been more inclined to go on with novels.

NORMAN MAILER (LETTER TO FRANCIS IRBY GWALTNEY, DECEMBER 28, 1954)

Dear Fig and Ecey,

Just a quick note to catch you before you're off to Hollywood. I know you're excited, and I suspect you're scared, and I'm glad you're having the trip. Just enjoy it. I mean it. Think of it as something you'll learn something from. And try to do the thing I failed to do for a whole year. Which is enjoy Hollywood and keep your detachment. Because you're going to meet whole hordes of characters, and some will be monsters and some will be nice and a few will seem wonderful. But always bear in mind that people who work in Hollywood are like Stalinists.

Personally, individually, they may be nice, tactful, decent, sensitive, generous, what-have-you, but never depend upon them publicly—what I mean is that because you like one of them, and he or she likes you, don't depend upon them when the chips are down, because their decisions can never be made on the basis of friendship alone. They have a public life more real than their private life.

But on the other hand don't go out like a country boy determined to hate the big city slickers because you'll find a variety of people and experiences there which will make you write better about anything you choose to write about, even if it has nothing to do with Hollywood. Sort of like my idea that to write a novel about a monastery maybe one ought to be a ditchdigger for a year. And forgive all this advice. I know you two feel as protective toward me and mine as I do toward you, but you have the good manners not to be flinging it in my face all the time the way I do you. . . .

EMMA CLARA "ECEY" GWALTNEY   Fig had sold the movie rights to his novel *The Day the Century Ended* for $35,000, which to us was a lot of money in those days. He was asked to come out to Hollywood and write a synopsis, was paid $600 a week plus expenses, and since it looked like the money was coming in, he quit his job.

NORMAN MAILER (LETTER TO FRANCIS IRBY GWALTNEY, FEBRUARY 15, 1955)
Dear Fig,

Congratulations and commiserations on the dough. I think (I'm probably wrong) that I know how you're feeling, because what the hell I remember how scared I was when Naked *hit. It's something you have to be inside of to know because I always felt too ashamed to tell people who had money worries how funny and frightening and isolated it made me feel not to have money worries. And it's taken me a number of years to realize that indeed I was lucky because finally you save time for yourself by not having to give more than half of your life to work you don't really want to do.*

But as for quitting your job, I can imagine what a difficult decision it is. I have to tell you that you're no more a three-book author than Balzac or Zola, and I can no more imagine you drying up or being unable to write than I could them. I also know that it's easy for me to say, but you're the one who has to do the writing and I know this because all those years when I found it so difficult to write and thought of doing something else, people were always saying to me, "Ridiculous, you're a born writer," and it would just get me angry because I felt it was easy for them to say, even if they were right, but that I was the one who had to sweat out the piles and the depressions.

I know I've wasted whole days at my studio to do an hour's writing, and that bad writing, because I felt that it was my duty to write, that I did nothing else and so I had to justify myself by work, work, WORK! And when one's first big book hits it's a very tough time. You feel like an imposter, you feel that if people ever find out what a dope you are they'll pull you off the peak. And you go through days where you decide you're a great man and even though the reviews were good they weren't good enough, and then there're days when the reverse is true, and one moment you want to be a celebrity hound and the next moment a celebrity and then a hermit—you know all this. It was not only true for me but for all the writers of our generation that I know who hit suddenly, Jonesie, Styron, Mac Hyman, Calder Willingham, every one I can think of.

What I want to communicate, Fig, is that if you find these are very tough times for you, full of all kinds of switch of mood, don't feel guilty about it or think there's something out of whack in you. Success is tougher than failure for awhile, I swear, and sometimes it takes a year to hit your new keel. So ease up on that fucking puritanical conscience of yours just enough to feel that whatever you're feeling and no matter how contradictory it may seem you're entitled to it, and instead of fighting it, accept it. (I'm becoming a Hindu mystic.) . . .

As usual, I've ended up writing a pompous letter when I wanted to say things I felt very much. I'd love so much to see the two of you and talk to you. These have been big months for Adele and me and very good ones. The funny thing about The Deer Park *odyssey was that it got me fighting mad and it feels good to be mad. I began to realize how much I had been needing a kick in the ass, and the result is that I've been liking myself better because I discovered I was still a fighter. And what a fighter Adele was. So it was very good for us. Instead of getting depressed we found ourselves enjoying the whole thing, ready to take on the world—as indeed we may have to come next August or September when* The Deer Park *reviews hit the fan.*

The journal is something I enjoy. I haven't felt like starting a novel, but I have been teeming with ideas, odd ideas, big ideas, tiny ideas, it's been a sort of intellectual ferment. So I figured what the hell I wouldn't fight it but would follow my inclination and not worry about when I started my next book. I've been a worrier and a self-punisher for so many years that it took all my energy and all my depression to turn out a few pages a day on those days I could work. Now with the journal I write twenty to twenty-five absolutely unpublishable pages any day I work on it. But that's good too. I've found that I'm finally able to stop worrying about the effect or the purpose or the success or the moral value of what I do and instead just concentrate on the work. So for the first time in seven or eight years I enjoy working, and I imagine although I don't even much care for the moment that things may grow out of the Journal. If nothing else I'll get stuff out of my system. And too for the first time in years I really have three or four real possibilities for novels. . . .

[Do] the two of you want to come in for a week to New York in the next month? How about it? You both deserve a vacation, and you got the dough now. Remember the wise old Jewish saying, "Spend money. It's good for the soul."

Adele sends her love. I send a goose for Fig and geese (five fingers) for Ecey.

Signed by his hand. (The orgiast.)

Norm

ADELE MORALES MAILER   Looking back, we always seemed to be moving in those years. God, did we move a lot! It was probably as much my doing as Norman's. We had something like five apartments in ten years, not counting the house in Connecticut. We were looking for something, I guess.

Even though we were constantly in and out of Provincetown, we never bought a house there, again because I suppose we didn't really want to settle anywhere, either of us. It was partly fear of commitment. I'm talking about myself—I don't want to get into his motivation because I don't really know. And I don't know what the hell we were looking for. Anyway, I went along with it. I was one of those women, you love a man, you go along with everything he does.

I don't think I ever thought about getting a house in Provincetown, though at certain times Norman may have put out feelers about property. Material things were unreal to me. I liked nice things, but I was terribly impractical. If I had been more practical I might have said, "Let's settle down, let's buy a house, buy property." But I never did. Fan thinks a lot about money because she had a hard life, she had to struggle at an early age. I never wanted for anything as a child, even in the Depression, and so money was unreal to me.

But it wasn't for lack of money that we didn't buy a house. In fact, Norman told me that when *The Naked and the Dead* made enormous amounts of money he had a lot of anxiety about it. All this money, he kept saying. Maybe he was worried he'd turn into a capitalist. Maybe it was guilt, the feeling that he didn't deserve it. Anybody could ask him and he'd give loans, anybody who came to him in need. He wasn't a soft touch or a sucker, but he wasn't petty and small either, and that was one of the things I adored about him.

The closest I got to fixing up a place was on Fifty-fifth Street, which I'd found through a broker in the fall of '54. It was owned by some fag. Below us was that black singer who sang "Old Black Magic"—Billy Daniels. It's still there, a narrow little house, and we had the upper duplex. Two bedrooms upstairs, a tiny living room and a kitchen downstairs, and two baths. We went out and bought new stuff. We decorated. We'd finally gotten married and moved from the lower East Side—all those dumps we'd been living in with stuff we'd picked up, mostly junk.

RUTH E. FRIEDMAN   The place was very proper. Swedish modern, neat, unused, Bloomie's window. It represented money, success. One night my ex-husband and I had dinner there. The meal was okay, but afterwards we were talking in the living room and something about the scene was uncomfortable. You just felt it—something was odd. I didn't know why, or what, until I heard a distinct click. I asked Norman, and he said nothing. Five or ten minutes passed and then he reached down under the couch to reverse his tape recorder. He started joking about it. He admitted he'd been taping us all evening.

Why? Possibly three reasons. One, he's a writer and was collecting stuff. Two, he had problems with my ex-husband, whose behavior was more black than white; my ex-husband had had a whole life with jazz musicians, which Norman envied. Norman could never reach him, could never quite authentically say, "Fuck you, motherfucker," and my ex-husband, you see, didn't give a damn. Norman's investment in being black was enormous, and that year he was constantly talking about drugs. He wanted to *know* about drugs, but he was scared out of his wits to use them, worrying what they'd do to him. Ergo, he chose this moment, with the tape recorder, to get information. Third, our relationship as couples. My ex-husband and I were heavy-duty. We knew a lot of people, and Norman at that time was jealous and acquisitive, very possessive about Adele, but he also fancied himself as a swinger. If the evening had gotten sexual, he would have had it on tape. I thought it was heinous, a total lack of friendship.

EDITH BEGNER   He'd just finished *The Deer Park* when he and Adele came up during August of '55. They were in the middle apartment at Eldred Mowery's, the Waterfront. We were upstairs, right above them. I'd brought up a big long kosher salami from New York and took two or three slices and hung them through a crack in the floor—his ceiling of the deck—and every time they sat outside they'd smell it. This went on for a week and got to smelling terrible until finally he looked up and saw it, though he didn't say a word. About noon one day we were sitting in our living room with some friends, there's a knock on the door, and a voice we didn't recognize calls, "Is Dr. Begner in?" The voice was disguised, so Jack, thinking somebody was sick, went and opened the door. There's Norman, very dark-faced, frowning, looking mad. All of a sudden out comes a gun.

DR. JACK BEGNER   Right, and I said to myself, "Jesus, maybe he's crazy enough to shoot me," so I turned sideways to the left so maybe he'll hit a nonvital organ. I'm talking very fast, he held his pose for fifteen seconds, and finally I said, "Norman, was there something else you wanted?" Then he breaks into a big grin and squirts me in the face—it's a water pistol. He's laughing, getting back at us for the salami.

EDITH BEGNER   Adele was gorgeous then. Norman was very fat, a wreck, and part of it was his steeling himself for the reviews of *The Deer Park*, which was scheduled to come out in the fall.

NORMAN MAILER   I hadn't thought about *The Deer Park* when I was out in Hollywood, and, in fact, I left Hollywood feeling I didn't get enough out there. What I did learn was that the war's the war, and that's a kind of experience that's primal, while all other experience is secondary; that is, you can spend ten years in a social milieu and you won't learn as much as you learn in one year in the army. You don't even have to go to war. A single year in the army, one year of involuntary experience like that or prison, is equal to ten years of social life where you pick your friends, pick your situations, steer your career. I'm talking about myself now. I spent a year in Hollywood and I got less than I got from any two or three weeks in the army.

I probably started *The Deer Park* in the winter of '51–'52, after I took the trip out West with Mickey. I wrote the first draft, then a second, then I went through two galley drafts. Those galleys were changed so prodigiously that they were reprinted, and then I went through the second set. Then I think they had to reprint again, so maybe in fact there were three sets of galleys. It wasn't that the book was a permanent shift for me so much as I was getting more art, that I was learning how to write. Actually, looking back on it, *The Deer Park* has rather a nice style, but it's an in-between style, an interim style. I don't really feel that I had my own style until *Advertisements.*

Of course the change in style in *The Deer Park* extended to my being aware that I was in a totally different place than I'd been five, six, seven years before. I'd gone through *Barbary Shore*, for God's sake, and *The Naked and the Dead* had changed my life—it was like having a major surgical operation, if you will, because it was so very complex. It was so good and so bad . . . let's say it was equivalent to marrying a movie star—that's closer to it—with all that's horrendous and wonderful about being married to a movie star at the age of twenty-five with no previous experience.

I warrant that the description in *Advertisements* of doing the last draft of *The Deer Park* is the most accurate account I've ever written of myself. It's true, I virtually had a nervous breakdown. I was hooked on Seconal and smoking a lot of pot, trying to keep my head clear despite the fact that I was drugged, and I was down to the point where my major exercise for the day was to walk two blocks to the corner for a milkshake, which was all I was capable of. I don't think I was changing fifty words a day, yet I was working sixteen-hour days. I'd started off at a huge rate of speed, but it was like a car when you're burning up the clutch, I was so overdramatizing myself. Finally I knew where to taper off when I read *The Magic Mountain.* That brought things down to a proper measure again.

JEAN MALAQUAIS   I sent Norman a letter about *The Deer Park*; he didn't like it. It hadn't been easy for me to write, the more so since my reaction regarding his *Barbary Shore* had been quite negative. I told him I wasn't out to hurt him nor did I want to jeopardize our friendship, but then I am hopelessly incapable of sugarcoating my words. Norman usually takes criticism rather badly; still, I'm possibly the one person from whom he will take a beating. Our relationship is, I believe, the oldest enduring one in his experience, and if it has survived, it is all his desert, not mine. He does know that, no matter what my criticisms, I never mean to put him down. In any event, he responded first with two brief notes, then a long letter. The first note was dated 22 November: "If I say seriously that I think there is more thought in *The Deer Park* than in anything else I have written, you'll pause and consider what I have said." The second note, a week or two later, simply stated: "I intend to answer your letter in great detail." Which he did, sometime in January, I believe, though the letter itself is undated:

I find I don't know exactly what to say. It's not that I simply disagree with your criticism. It is more that I believe that what you said about my work in process was just not psychically true for me. I guess I would agree that Munshin and Teppis are far and away the most successful characters but I don't know that they are novelistically as exciting as Eitel and Marion and for that matter Elena and even Lulu. I tried most conscientiously not to impose my thoughts on the characters. In places I even bent over backwards, as with Sergius, who being 23 and uneducated, would have opinions, one cannot call them philosophical fancies, which I myself might have had at 23, and this is the heart of what I mean when I call The Deer Park *the most philosophical of my books; he's fumbling toward the vein which I in my own way with my different character may also be fumbling toward. I would say, Jean, that very few people have gotten even a little bit of what I believe, and it is in* The Deer Park. *I do believe it is the first book I have ever written where I could defend every sentence. Defend it at the very least on the grounds that I considered it carefully and relinquished it to the printer only when I was exhausted with the effort to express it more finely.*

Hell is not only paved with good intentions, there are 500,000 novelists today who indulge in such inner life in their books that they feel they have created masterpieces of one sort or another, whereas the only masterpiece was the autoerotic gratification of their egos. This may well be true for me, and yet I doubt it. Time, however, is going to answer all this. I feel DP is the first "new" book I have written. The first book where I really have felt consciously that I was so ahead of my time. If I'm right, the proof will come over the next 10 or 20 years. And if I'm wrong, I hope there will be 2 or 3 other novels in between to console the ravages to my vanity. At any rate, dear old friend, it's really pointless to discuss it further. When I see you I do want to talk about The Deer Park *more, and perhaps we shall thrash out more exactly some lines of disagreement.*

ALFRED KAZIN   I remember *The Deer Park* seemed to me utterly ridiculous—the idea that sex brought knowledge. Of course I saw a connection here to Norman's bizarre flight from being a lower-middle-class Brooklyn Jew, since I've always thought the clue to the Jewish American novel was the fact that we were the first Jews to get divorced, the first ones to have sex.

Years ago Jules Feiffer and I were talking about Norman, and someone asked, "How come these Jews get married so often?" Jules replied, "Because they can afford it." And he was exactly right. Saul Bellow with his greater conservativeness would never have been able to marry four times if he hadn't had the money, and I wouldn't have married three times if I, to my surprise, hadn't been able to afford it either.

I've been married three times and had what I suppose is a normal amount of sexual experience. But as I say in my book *New York Jew*, the big event in my life was a love affair I had in the Village in 1943 with a well-known character called Mary Louise Peterson. Despite my happiness, it was a great shock to me. I felt very guilty, very bad, and it was typical of my relationship with my then wife, who wouldn't divorce me. Later on, thinking about Mailer, Bellow, Herb Gold, and Bernie Malamud—whom I always thought of as being too good to be true, even though he's had the normal amount of extramarital sex, which he wrote about in one of his bad novels—all of that convinced me that the sex thing was related to the Jewish thing. The Jewish religion is really a family religion, it's ancestor worship. Breaking up a family—which is what happens with these things—it's breaking up the Tradition.

In any case, I remember once Norman invited me to have lunch with him in the Oak Room at the Plaza. There was a fashion show going on, but he was so intent on the conversation that he ignored the models sweeping up and down before us. I thought it was very funny, but I couldn't help thinking that here it is again, a typical Jewish attitude towards sex—that sex can be turned into a concept, the way Freud did. Except Freud never really meant it, Freud was looking around for something to make him famous, and he hit on sex, whereas Mailer, I think, really believed it. And there's always anxiety, fear involved. If you grow up with a Russian Jewish mother you fear you're going to be punished for fucking too much. By definition, fucking is opposed to having a wife. Orthodox Jews consider it a special *mitzvah* to make love to your wife on a Saturday, while "fucking" is extracurricular and something else entirely.

JUDY FEIFFER   Norman was very upset by the reviews of *The Deer Park*, which he expected to be great—as they should have been. Instead they were mixed. There was a lot riding on that book, and he was upset, angry, and depressed.

KIRKUS   *I felt on reading* The Deer Park *originally that it was a catastrophe, good neither for author nor publisher. Now, on second look, some of the too obvious crudities have been eliminated, the book brought into better focus. But I still think it a bad book and a dull one.*

LIBRARY JOURNAL   *Over-long, over-serious, sometimes boring...*

THE NEW YORK TIMES   *Though it is not a wholly successful novel, it is studded with brilliant and illuminating passages and, by and large, it is good reading. If it lacks the impact of* The Naked and the Dead, *which still stands as probably the best fictional account of the war's actual fighting, it is far better than* Barbary Shore.

WILLIAM HOGAN, SAN FRANCISCO CHRONICLE   *Norman Mailer has established a new par for the modern writing course: He has succeeded in making sex dull ... What is the point of* The Deer Park? *I suspect Mailer started out to write a shocker only. The ingredients are here, but Mailer is too undisciplined a craftsman to make an interesting shocker from this almost sure-fire material.*

MALCOLM COWLEY, NEW YORK HERALD TRIBUNE   *In this book Mailer has made a real advance over* The Naked and the Dead, *which must have been a comparatively simple novel to write... In* The Deer Park *the characters are treated more in depth, the structure of the novel is more complicated, and the author had to make up his own rules as he went along. He has taken risks and made mistakes, but not cheap or shameful ones, and he has avoided artistic temptations, as Sergius O'Shaughnessy tried to do. The book leaves us with the feeling that Norman Mailer, though not a finished novelist, is one of the two or three most talented writers of his generation.*

ATLANTIC   *While Mailer's hatred of dishonesty is exhilarating up to a point, it contains a hint of paranoia.*

VI:
THE
VILLAGE
VOICE
(1955-56)

NORMAN MAILER (ADVERTISEMENTS FOR MYSELF) *All I felt then was that I was an outlaw, a psychic outlaw, and I liked it, I liked it a good night better than trying to be a gentleman, and with a set of emotions accelerating one on the other, I mined down deep into the murderous message of marijuana, the smoke of the assassins, and for the first time in my life I knew what it was to make your kicks. . . .*

ADELE MORALES MAILER Norman was still having problems sleeping. Mickey had introduced me to a doctor, a guy who fancied himself among the literati, and he prescribed Seconal, which Norman used to wash down with bourbon. He's lucky it didn't kill him, and later he got very mad at the doctor for hooking him on the pills. Of course Norman got mad at a lot of people toward the end there.

MICKEY KNOX I never liked dope—pot gave me a hangover, and I thought he was smoking it too much. Later, I know, he blamed the doctor because it got so he couldn't sleep without pills. The man had an office in midtown. He admired Norman, he admired writers in general. You'd go up there and he'd quote Shakespeare.

After that there was a definite change. Norman would spring an accent as though it came out of thin air. He became a student of himself, trying to find out what the fuck he was, who he was, where he was going. He said he was practicing self-analysis, and I once saw him do it: at Barbara's one night he went into a deep, personal state—like he disappeared. He sat there for hours. I don't know if there's any real connection, but this was also the period when he had an orgone box, not an orgone box really. He built it himself and it had no zinc lining. He soundproofed it with carpeting. Said he went into it to scream. He was screaming before the psychiatrists were talking about the primal scream for therapy.

He wouldn't write fiction for ten years, and I know he was very hurt about *The Deer Park*, running scared. He hired me to make the rounds of bookshops in New York, posing as a buyer, a guy coming in off the streets, in order to find out what salespeople felt about the book. Sort of market research. I took notes. He was desperate to know why the fuck it wasn't selling better.

JOHN ALDRIDGE   After the Rinehart debacle I came back to New York to see Vance Bourjaily, and we went to a party at Norman's. Malaquais was there, Vance, God knows who else. I may even have written Bourjaily about this, because I remember writing it down—that Norman was surrounded by too many people who were encouraging him in whatever he wanted to do. There were too many sycophants, but through no fault of Norman's. He simply draws people. My feeling was that it was unhealthy for him.

ADELINE LUBELL NAIMAN   It was after the publication of *The Deer Park* that I felt a different thing was happening to Norman's life. In a word, he was beginning to play the role of a host to succubi.

But *The Deer Park* brought on our first intellectual argument. Up till then I could go with whatever he did. I wrote him about the book, telling him what it needed as a novel, and I hurt him. He'd regarded me as the best editor in publishing, but he wouldn't accept what I said because he heard it as critical— my saying that I wished he'd stop trying to shock the churchgoers, always doing battle, always taking on unseen enemies.

I knew it was a very hard time for him. On a second novel you always make a mistake, but this was his third and it should have been a success. He was scared, and I suppose one explanation for those painful years, and eventually the stabbing, was *The Deer Park*'s failure. I think the impact of the public on the private was both a desired event and a torment for him. Trying drugs and being a bad boy was myth-building. It was experimentation, yes, but also a way of saying, "Look at me, look at me." Paradoxically, though, Norman is really very clean and straight inside. Not too many people grow up saying they want to be "good." In his case the impulse was hard to eradicate and doesn't ride well with the public... "Mediation" implies too much rationality. I think it's more

Norman's jockeying between the impulses of the boy still imprinted on his soul and the image of the man he hadn't quite achieved.

DR. JACK BEGNER   During that winter they were living on the East Side, not too far from us, and one night Adele phoned. She said Norman had taken their two poodles out for a walk about ten-thirty, and it was already an hour later and he hadn't returned. I said I'd come over, and by the time I got there, there was Norman. His left eye was almost out of his head. Someone had obviously hit him, and I knew that if you hit the orbital ridge or the bone above, you cause a collapse of the orbit itself, and the eye can pop out. Norman's eye was popped a little bit, but I didn't know how much.

I phoned my friend Sigmund Schutz, an eye doctor. The eye wasn't that bad, and Siggie told me to put a bandage on it and to instruct Norman not to use it for forty-eight hours. Norman, though, was on cloud nine. He was in ecstasy, saying, "You know I feel just the way I felt when I was in the army." He loved it, the danger. What had happened was that he'd gone out with the two dogs, stopped in a bar, and started to argue with two sailors, who took him outside and beat him. I think he knew he'd asked for it, but he was getting off on the violence, almost as if he needed it. And it was a hell of a beating he took.

ADELE MORALES MAILER   When he'd come home with the dogs he said, "Now don't get excited, but I got hit on the head again." In those days he stayed out eternally, and I waited and worried, but that night he said, "I got into a fight because this guy accused my dog of being queer."

The absurd thing was that he'd turned to one of the two guys and handed him the dogs' leashes. Here are these two big beautiful poodles with their handsome clips, enough to make any street guy crazy, and Norman gives them to the guy to hold while he's squaring off with his buddy. He was also mad because Tibo didn't jump to his defense. Poor Tibo! But the guy fought dirty and tried to gouge his eye out. I was worried about the eye, so I called Jack. Later Norman had surgery for a detached retina, but I don't think it had anything to do with that fight. But I loved him asking the guy to hold the dogs. He wasn't embarrassed about getting in another fight. I just asked him why he hadn't kept walking, and he said, "Nobody's gonna call my dog a queer."

JEAN MALAQUAIS   Norman wrote me about it, and I wrote back from Paris, "If I'd been one of them I'd have beaten you up too—two o'clock in the morning, a bourgeois stinker walking two prize poodles." They probably said something about the dogs and Mailer turned cocky. *Mon Dieu*, I told him that part of him *wanted* to be beaten up, but naturally he never recognized that. Such things he represses very strongly.

NORMAN MAILER ("THE COMMENTARY COLUMNS")   *On those occasions when we do not know if it's God or the Devil we must fear, do we not have insomnia with Angst, does not madness insinuate itself? There is a suggestion to go out on the street and look for the adventure One or the Other is demanding. Most of us stay home. All right then, so we die of cancer, goes the sigh in the wind of our small depleted courage.*

FANNY SCHNEIDER MAILER   Greenwich Village and *The Village Voice* and all of that was a whole new thing, because he attributed too much truth and importance to everything he did. He did nothing in a light way. And so after *The Deer Park*, I think, was the worst period, because Adele is *meshugge*, real *meshugge*. Barney didn't assert himself about it. Maybe he felt he couldn't win. Neither of us talked about it because it wasn't worth wasting our breath. I figured the less you talk about some things, the weaker they get.

JUDY FEIFFER   The Village was a fabulous place in the fifties. The Cedar Bar and the White Horse—hangouts for Dylan Thomas, De Kooning, Kline. Norman wasn't living in the Village, but he would wander in and out of the scene at any moment.

One afternoon he called me and said some friends and he were starting a sort of revolutionary magazine or newspaper. They needed a photographer and would I come to this meeting? So I went and talked to Dan Wolf and Ed Fancher. My impression was that Norman had a close, very trusting friendship with Dan. They were chums, in sync. I think he admired Dan's political and ideological savvy. It was the time of McCarthyism, and *The Voice* was to be an uncensored forum for writers and intellectuals, a kind of great underground, the equivalent of a European newspaper of intellectual expression. Dan was a brilliant editor because he didn't edit. Every writer was crazy about him.

ED FANCHER   The idea behind *The Voice* wasn't an original one. The existing paper, the *Villager*, didn't represent the cultural side of the Village at all, and at every party someone would say, "We oughta have a newspaper in the Village." Finally Dan said, "Why don't we actually do it?"

We began to have discussions the winter of '54–'55. Dan and I were close friends, we'd met at the New School right after the war, and Dan was quite friendly with Mailer. My grandfather had left me a small amount of stock against which I could borrow, so I put in $5000. Norman put in another $5000. Dan didn't have any money but was a partner nonetheless.

I was living in the Village but commuting to a clinic in New Jersey where I worked as a psychologist, and when we decided to start the paper I arranged to work half time. It wasn't long before we exhausted the first $10,000, and then Norman and I put in an additional $5000 each, and a friend of mine from the New School, Howard Bennett, brought in another $15,000. Dan had an equal share, but in labor. He was working eighty hours a week.

Dan and I had two goals in mind. From the very beginning we saw the Village as a place to start, a base where there was a strong cultural tradition from which we could build a general readership beyond the Village. We didn't have a polemical position, we certainly weren't Marxists, but we saw ourselves as "the outs" as opposed to *Partisan Review*, which was the Establishment. We wanted the paper to be nondogmatic, and we were at least as interested in the cultural scene as we were in politics. *The Nation, The New Republic*, and *Partisan* were all boring. Ideology bored us—not simply the Communist line but the anti-Communist line too.

As for Norman's role: We didn't particularly want him to be a silent partner, but he was busy revising *The Deer Park*, so he'd come around only occasionally to help with circulation or something. The only one of us who knew anything about putting out a newspaper was Jerry Tallmer, and *The Voice* couldn't have been launched without him. I'd met him at a party and called him up to see if he'd work with us. First he said no, then he came back with a sheet of movie listings, and I knew he was hooked.

The choice of the name *The Village Voice*, I gather, is a bone of contention. Norman thinks he chose it. My recollection is that we were gathering a list and a schoolteacher I knew in New Rochelle suggested it, and I simply put it on the list with the others. Norman may have been the one who decided it was the best name on the list.

JERRY TALLMER   I'd been free-lancing, trying to write. This was the summer of '55, I was twenty-four, and after Ed called me I told him no, that I needed to earn money. Also I hadn't liked *The Naked and the Dead*, one of the reasons being that the two Jews in the book were so sad and morose and *so* Jewish. I was all psyched up about Jews in those days, as were a number of us.

Then he called back a second time, and I walked over to 22 Greenwich Avenue, where Ed said they were meeting, upstairs one flight to a floor-through apartment that was becoming a newspaper office, and I knew I was home. It was so ratty and beat up. They'd picked up three or four ancient typewriters from some hock shop, Ed had found three or four old desks, since he was also in the moving business in the Village, and the minute I laid eyes on Dan I thought we were alike. We looked alike, thin New York Jews. He was even more cynical than I was. Remember, this was the depth of the Eisenhower era, the silent generation and all that shit, and Dan and I both hated the Establishment. There was also an English journalist, John Wilcock, out of the Rupert Murdoch school before there was a Murdoch. We all went to lunch, and everything was very vague, but they said Norman was an old friend and that he and Ed would be the investors.

A few days later they produced Norman. John Wilcock, Ed, Dan and Rhoda, Norman, and I went to lunch. Norman was quite affable. He was also quite cagey about committing himself. His terms were that he was simply investing to make money: he wouldn't write for the paper, he wouldn't interfere editorially, he'd just be a silent partner. And I think it's fair to say he was watching me, watching everybody, the way he does. I'd been curious about meeting him, but because I hadn't liked *The Naked and the Dead* I was being careful. Also, Norman was already a rather tough guy, with a budding reputation. He wasn't fat but he wasn't thin—like the jacket photograph on *The Naked and the Dead*, where he's very slim, dark, finely boned. I remember Rhoda telling me, and later too, with stars in her eyes, how beautiful he'd been as a boy back in Brooklyn. Handsome, sensitive, talented. The *Wunderkind* of the neighborhood.

Assembling the paper was a long, slow process, especially since none of us had very much experience. Ed was studying to be a psychiatrist at the New School and had taken one course in journalism; I'd worked as a kid editor at *The Nation* for three or four years; but Dan knew nothing about journalism— he'd worked for the *Columbia Encyclopedia*, then for the Turkish Information Service. It wasn't until November that we brought out our first issue, and the paper started losing like a thousand dollars a week. Neither Dan nor Ed was braced for quite as much as that, but it was Ed's worry, not mine. He used up the money he'd saved for a trip around the world, they got a little bit more out of Norman, and then started looking for investors, like Howard Bennett, the son of a wealthy Hartford or New Haven dentist. He was Ed's friend, only Ed's friend.

I was separated then, we were working ninety to a hundred hours a week, and my whole life was *The Voice*—but there were lots of girls, for me, for everybody. There was also a succession of parties. I think one was in Norman's apartment uptown. Norman had very little to do with the process of publishing the paper in the beginning. He stayed away, basically, but he and I had had conversations the few times he came to the office before he started his column in January '56. I remember, though, at the Christmas party in '55 he and I were sitting on the floor together. I was wearing old dirty white bucks from another generation. He looked at them and said, "When are you going to stop being a college boy?" Then that New Year's he invited me to go to a party up in Harlem. I'd met a German girl and we followed him uptown. Me, Norman, the girl, the only white faces. I don't think Adele was there. I remember Norman carrying on—exaggeratedly talking like a bad movie, using the southern accent. The scene was very hip but getting more and more weird, wacky, and nutty, and soon I drove the German girl home. Norman stayed. The girl I was with couldn't believe it. She said, "That's Norman Mailer? Norman Mailer doesn't behave like that, I've read Norman Mailer."

Anyway, the first year was terrifically exciting because we were all trying to find our way. We'd sit in the office talking for hours—it wasn't just fights and arguments. In fact, I remember once in those first months I came into the office and there was a strange young girl, maybe seven or eight years old, sitting on top of Dan's desk. It was Susie, Norman's daughter, visiting from Mexico. Everybody was gathered around, as usual, talking about politics, the paper, whatever, when suddenly Susie looks around the room and pipes up, "What I want to know is, who's the big boss?" Everybody cracked up.

As *The Voice* continued, we all had our roles. Dan stood in the back room and talked brilliantly hour after hour. But he was a catalyst. He wanted a sophisticated, liberal, as well as antiliberal paper. He was against cant. He was very much anti-Communist, even though we were dismissed by the downtown business community as Commie Jews.

Each of us had his own idea about the kind of paper we wanted, including Norman, and this is where he and I had our falling out. My concept, unlike Ed and Dan's, was to restore the "I" in criticism, in my own writing as well as in other people's. Norman's idea, I think, was for the paper to be a hip shock sheet. He didn't invent the word "hip" but he promoted it. He wanted *The Voice* to deal in a *Daily News* way with the new subjects of drugs, jazz, the swinging black scene, and sexuality, all under the aegis of "anti-Establishment." As a result of our different concepts a war started in the office.

Norman was deadly serious in those days, and it's my belief that this was a black and terrible time for him. He was deeply into marijuana—he said so and wrote so—and it distorted his vision. He tried to work under the influence of pot but at long last found he couldn't. Whereas in the beginning he stayed away, in '56 he was starting to be a buttinsky and wanted everything to be a certain way, his way. We challenged him, Ed, Dan, and I, and there were arguments. Dan would scream at him and Norman's counterargument was "You aren't winning, you're losing money." Then his other line was that he was hip and we were square: I was an intellectual square, Ed was a small-town *goyisher* square, and Dan was a reactionary.

The payoff thing to me was saying to Norman "You have no taste." Nell Blaine, quite a fine painter and typographer, had designed our layout and logo. But Norman took it into his head that one of the reasons *The Voice* was failing was the logo. He said he knew a lot about art because he was married to a painter, and he locked himself in one of the back rooms for three days and applied that knowledge to the logo. He came out and showed it to everyone. He'd changed the letters and had little, teeny, diddly line drawings between the letters—little sketches of somebody shooting dope, somebody pushing a baby carriage, all the things people supposedly did in the Village. He held this thing up like he'd produced *War and Peace* or another Matisse and asked what we thought of it. I looked at it a long time, and then, remembering his remark about my shoes and being a college boy, I said, "I guess it's all right, but I think it's a little high-school." His response was to give me a silent, baleful look. Black hatred. I think from that instant he decided there was going to be trouble between us, but the logo stayed as it was.

This was in January '56, around the time he started his column. Looking back on it, I'd guess he started doing the column for two reasons: one, he was trying to boost circulation, because any column by Norman Mailer was going to be an attraction; and two, he had certain bullshit inside his system that he wanted to get out. I suppose also the middling success of *The Deer Park* had something to do with it, especially after he'd put together that famous ad in November '55. We had all been amused by the ad but he took it with deadly seriousness.

So in January he began the column, writing at home and sending it in. I was copy-editing every fucking thing from headlines to the stories down to the six-point agate in the classifieds, the display ads, everything. I was obsessed. Dan wrote some of the headlines, but everything went through my hands, including

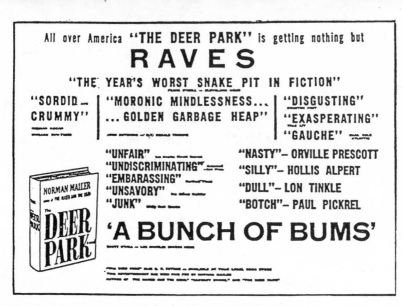
"This advertisement was paid for by Norman Mailer."

Norman's column, which I thought was basically turgid and unreadable. Remember, though, this was Mailer of '56, and while he has become a great many other things since, at the time he was under the stress of drugs, there was *The Deer Park* crisis, and whatever was going on in his marriage.

Dan also opposed the kind of writing in Norman's columns, but the agreement had been made and Dan wasn't going to go back on it, even though there was evidence that the column was offending some readers. A guy named Kenneth J. Schmidt, on Greenwich Avenue, sent a letter to the editor after Norman's fourth or fifth column, then sent about three or four more, signing them "Normal Failure." They were funnier than hell—Dan and I both thought so—and we printed them. They were getting to Norman, beginning to bother him even though he could never concede as much, much less object to their publication. There were all kinds of letters, some stupid, some not so stupid. Schmidt's were the best. Thinking back, I realize I should have recruited him as a writer. Maybe I didn't because I didn't have the guts, because I didn't want to make more trouble.

Norman was tolerated because he was a founder of the paper, an investor, and because he was Norman Mailer. But he never trusted me. I don't think to this minute he trusts me, and if he reads this he'll probably trust me all the less, although I'm trying to be as correct as I can. And what triggered our real blowup was the episode of the typos. First, though, I should explain our method for getting the paper printed. After our printer down on Canal Street got tired of our craziness, we'd found another guy in Washington, New Jersey, next to the Pennsylvania border. Two days before going to press we'd literally work twenty-four hours straight, with an occasional nap, then pile into a battered old car I'd provided—five or six of us, Ed, Dan, me, John, one or two girls to attend to the classifieds—and we'd drive two or three hours to the printing plant to put the paper to bed. Once, even, we almost had an accident. I hit a patch of ice, the car spun around and almost went off the road.

Now, among Norman's terms for writing the column was that we couldn't change a period; we were just supposed to print it as is. But he was consistently late, and it would always be twice as long as the space allocated. We'd scream back and forth, especially me because I had to do the shit work of tearing the paper apart, patching things together, forcing things in with a shoehorn at the eleventh and twelfth and twenty-fifth hours. Then I had to get into the car and drive to the printer, then proofread it, and from time to time amidst this chaos, this miasma—and believe me, we were pretty bleary—a typo would sneak in, just as he reported in his last column.

The typo that blew the thing was Norman's phrase "the *nuances* of growth" in a column "The Hip and the Square," April '56. This came out unbeknownst to me or anybody else as the "*nuisances* of growth." Now, between those two words there's a difference of an *i* and an *s*. The phrase makes sense when read either way—and I'm of the old school of proofreading, where one person reads out loud to another. Anyway, we were all there and didn't catch it. We left the printers and drove back with another triumph, another issue, and as usual I fell into bed and slept fourteen or fifteen hours. We always treated the next day like a Sunday, so usually I'd be alone in the office, as I was that afternoon when the phone rang. It was Norman. Without explanation he says, "Tallmer, why don't you get your finger out of your ass!"

He was cold sober and furious. I still didn't know what particular typo he was talking about—I didn't find out until later—but I said something like "You don't talk to me like that," something real square, and then I must have asked what he was so upset about, because he yelled, "Typos! Typos!" Raving.

There then followed a big scene in the back room between Ed, Dan, and Norman that night. Closed door. I think he was saying "It's Jerry or me," and they stood up to him. I also know that sometime in this period—maybe not just then—Dan said, "Norman, you're acting like the worst cartoon caricature of a capitalist with a high hat beating the slaves." Which I always thought was very funny, very true, although it certainly didn't improve the atmosphere in the office.

So in his last column Norman announced his departure from *The Voice*. But he also chose to write about a current production of *Waiting for Godot*. Now, one of the early people in *The Voice* was Howard Fertig, who'd seen the play in Paris, and he came in with a brilliant, original piece. His line was "To say that *Waiting for Godot* is about tramps waiting by the roadside is to say that *Moby Dick* is about a whale." Anyway, I wrote a review of Herbert Berghof's production with Bert Lahr and E. G. Marshall. Howard rather bitterly felt he'd discovered *Godot*, and it was true, he had. Norman began his farewell column by saying, "I have not seen *Waiting for Godot*," and then criticized it, calling it a "poem to impotence" and announcing that he doubted he would like it since he—like Joyce—didn't believe we are doomed to impotence.

After the *Godot*-"nuisances" column, a shame-faced Norman came in a week later with a huge, long article that would have filled the entire paper, his *second* piece on Godot—he'd since read the play and seen the production and felt he'd been unfair to Beckett. But we told him we couldn't print it as a column. So he said, "What would it measure in agate?" We figured it out and told him we could get it into one page. He said, "All right, I'll buy the page." Ed was so desperate for money he agreed, and Norman ran the *Godot* piece as a full-page ad in classified-size type, a paid ad, with a note above saying "Advertisement." Which I suppose is where he may have gotten the idea for the title *Advertisements for Myself*. It was definitely an experience that struck home—humbling—some sort of learning or recognizing on his part, which he admitted when he wrote that Adele had told him, "Baby, you fucked up."

The great occasion for the blowup, the trigger, was the meeting after the typo business. Ed and Dan have since told me so, and this was what caused the legal battle with them. I have a certain amount of guilt about it. Norman and Howard Bennett were the most uneasy allies that ever existed—like Soviet Russia and Nazi Germany, for God's sakes. It got very nasty, but it ended with a legal arrangement, a document stipulating that Ed and Dan were president and vice-president, whatever, but if the debt on the books fell below a certain line, they'd lose control and the paper would automatically go over to Howard and Norman, though Dan and Ed might still hold their stock.

ADELE MORALES MAILER   When Norman wrote that I'd told him "Baby, you fucked up," he was right. I probably said that a few times over the years. He was never reluctant about telling me how I'd fucked up, so what the hell, I wasn't shy about telling him the same. But the break with Dan was very upsetting. Norman had been very close to Dan, and I was very upset because I loved Dan. I don't know if it could have been avoided. Things had been blown way out of proportion. Also, Dan wouldn't have tried to approach Norman—come back to square one and start over—because Dan's not the type.

ED FANCHER   He felt the paper was too middle-class, too conservative. To us, though, this was academic since we were on the verge of bankruptcy and it was seven years before we broke even.

The blowup came when there had been typos for three or four weeks running. I know we really knocked ourselves out to avoid them, but Norman felt it was half deliberate, even sabotage. I wasn't at the meeting, but Dan told him to go to hell, which was when the freeze set in. About that same time, April or May, we also had a blowup with Howard Bennett. He and Norman barely knew each other, but they temporarily became allies. We had to deal with the two of them and their lawyer—Cy Rembar, of course—and we had a reorganization of the paper. Norman and Bennett retired but enjoyed financial benefits as long as *The Voice* showed a profit or its loss didn't exceed a set limit. If we went beyond that limit, we either had to put in more money or give them controlling interest. I put in additional money. Dan and I each had 30 percent, 60 percent total, to Norman and Bennett's 40 percent.

EMMA CLARA "ECEY" GWALTNEY   We went up to New York to visit again, in June '56. Norman and Adele were in their nice apartment—white walls—and one of the things he was worried about was being "cool." That was his thing, and to him Fig was very cool. *All* southerners were cool. What I was beginning to see was that he envied what he construed the South to be—namely, a certain kind of freedom.

At that point Fig was worried about Norman, and he didn't particularly like Adele. But we were their guests, and he was trying. We felt something was going on. Norman had a great big loud hi-fi and was playing a lot of jazz. He and Adele had a fight, and the next morning she said to me, "Don't take last night seriously. We're not going to break up. We just do that for kicks." I thought, How stupid, but okay.

We also went over to someone's house—I forget whose, but a guy who was showing a documentary he'd made. It was supposed to be important, about downtrodden people, but it was real boring. What I remember, though, was a very good-looking, dark, sultry woman who was there. I think her name was Irene something. Very dramatic-looking. And she was very obvious, very overt, coming on to Adele. We joked about it afterwards, and Adele laughed and said, "Did you notice that? She made me uncomfortable looking at me that way."

Of course we'd heard about the problems with *The Deer Park*, the big to-do with Bennett Cerf at Random House, but while we were visiting, Bob Loomis, Fig's editor, invited us to a party. I forget whether Norman wasn't invited or just refused to go. Maybe it had something to do with Loomis not supporting him at Random House, or perhaps it had something to do with Loomis being Styron's editor. Styron was Norman's friend then, so maybe he felt Loomis had betrayed him. I don't know. Maybe it was just that Norman was uncomfortable with people. Whatever the reason, Norman and Loomis were on the outs.

But again, even though he wasn't going, Norman insisted we go. Loomis was married to a dark-headed girl, and they had a nice apartment off Washington Square. Fig's agent, John Shaffner, was there too. It may be that Norman helped him get Shaffner as an agent, 'cause unless Fig wrote directly he would have had no other avenue to the New York literary world. It's amazing, all of what Norman did for Fig. I think that weighed heavily on Fig—it's bound to have. He must have always wondered, Could I have done it by myself? Which he might have—I don't know. But it must have been horrible, and there was probably guilt on both sides.

In fact, it was during this period that Norman was really pushing for Fig to come to New York. I imagine there are very few writers, two egos, who stay friends over thirty-five years, particularly when one is world-famous and the other struggling and not very well known except in his little area. But Norman truly wanted Fig to make it big, with all his heart. That's why he kept saying "Come to New York."

What I remember about our stay, though, was that Norman said, "I have something to tell you. Dan Wolf will want to see you. You should know we're not speaking, but you go ahead and have a visit with him and Rhoda." Norman used to tease Fig about his "Gary Cooper image," always fair and square and so forth, but Norman was always fair too, and he was being very fair about this.

Fig said we wouldn't see them if he and Dan were having trouble, but Norman insisted: "I know they want to see you, so you should go."

So we went, and they told us they were concerned about Norman. It was said very politely: "We don't want to say anything against him or sit here and gossip behind his back, but we're genuinely worried." We were talking almost like four relatives. "He's gone off on tangents. He's turned against some of his friends. We don't understand."

Thank God, at the time the phrase "where he's coming from" hadn't surfaced, but that's what they meant. Rhoda obviously really cared about him, and she was almost in tears. She said, "I really think he's a very sick man. I think he needs help. He gets in fights, he gets mad at people for no reason." They didn't go into details, it didn't have hard edges. What they were saying was "We just don't understand," and though they didn't say so specifically, I think in an unspoken way they were worried that he was having a breakdown.

Dan was very gentlemanly. He didn't seem angry so much as crushed, or hurt. Maybe he was being polite because it was a touchy situation; I mean, there we were, Norman's old friends, visiting but not cognizant of exactly what was happening.

Fig was very open about it. He said, "I'm sure as hell worried about him too. Still, he's got good sense, he'll come out of it. But is he working? Is he doing good work?" And Dan said, just bits and pieces. Fig tended to blame Adele. Probably unjustifiably, but he thought at least she aided and abetted. Maybe she did, but I also thought Fig was too prejudiced, absolutely one way against her.

Edwin Fancher, Jerry Tallmer, and Dan Wolf, co-founders of The Village Voice, 1955.

RHODA LAZARE WOLF   One incident I think of in trying to understand those difficult years was the earlier time he came to brunch to meet my friend Zola and her friends. Adele was with him. He was slim, good-looking, this guy who'd written the great war novel. But these girls who had wanted to meet him were visibly disappointed—in his manners, in his physical appearance, because they expected someone more intense. Afterwards Norman said something about it because he realized what had happened: that they'd seen him for what he really was, the nice Jewish boy from Brooklyn who'd gone to Harvard. He was aware of letting them down, which wasn't exactly unsymptomatic either, because I remember him speaking about the response he'd been getting from people in general. Everyone expected so much of him, so maybe he was trying to break out of it, the mid-fifties being the turning point.

When he'd been planning *The Deer Park* he'd started picking people's brains for their insights into the unconscious. He was doing it with Lindner, the psychiatrist, also with Dan, trying to get information about psychoanalysis. I was in Reichian therapy, and he was asking me all sorts of questions, maybe because he was turned on by Reich. This was back in '53 and '54, but then, as I observed it, he seemed to be getting nuttier and nuttier. Suddenly he switched from student to master. He got involved with all kinds of primitivism, and since he was very aware of the impression he was making, my feeling is that he deliberately got wild with drugs—marijuana, then peyote and mescal.

There was a definite pattern to it. Adele was both follower and leader, and as things were getting bad, it was a dangerous situation. It had started before they had founded *The Voice*, so by the time Norman and Adele had moved to Fifty-fifth Street in '54 he was smoking pot like crazy, keeping his ears next to the loudspeaker. He was being the stage director, telling us how we were supposed to listen to music and what our responses had to be. He was also recording his own voice with a tape recorder, listening to himself over and over, and then he'd have us listen too, to analyze his accent and inflection. He'd say, "Isn't this interesting, it's coming out like a Texan." Or "I'm doing this, I'm doing that... listen!" He was seeing how far he could push himself, how far he could extend the boundaries, and of course no one dared laugh at him to his face.

Adele never told him to stop, either. She may have thought he was ridiculous, but she was also willing to go very far with him, though obviously at a price. During the nine years with her he made this tremendous change, went through all this shit—what he did to himself, other people, his parents. Those nine years were the most important years of his life, good or bad. Still, Adele couldn't have stopped him. Nor could Dan. Dan is very strong, but he couldn't get him off the crazy track either. That's why they couldn't be friends anymore, why they had their break. Norman was absolutely sure his way was the correct way. He'd bully you. He was bullying everybody in those days, especially after *The Deer Park* and his columns in *The Voice*.

VII:
THE HIP
AND THE
SQUARE,
<u>ADVERTISE</u>-
<u>MENTS</u>
FOR
<u>MYSELF</u>,
AND
"THE
TROUBLE"
(1956-60)

<u>ADELE MORALES MAILER</u> After he left *The Voice* in the spring of '56 we went to Paris, my first trip to Europe. It was sort of like a delayed honeymoon, and we didn't see a hell of a lot of people—Jean and Galy Malaquais, maybe Eileen Finletter, and we ran into Harriet Sohmers from Provincetown in some café playing pinball. We also saw Jimmy Baldwin, and this was at the time he'd had the trouble with the cops, when they beat him up very badly and threw him in jail. He told us about it when we went out to see him at his apartment, I think in Neuilly.

Norman was doing some reminiscing about his previous time in Paris, but mostly he was very nervous. He was drinking and couldn't sleep. The insomnia was terrible. Jim Jones and Norman had been bosom pals of course, but I didn't get along with Jones, so we didn't see him. He was like a parody of the chauvinistic macho type, and I thought he was adolescent and silly, almost laughable.

NORMAN MAILER ("A WANDERING IN PROSE: FOR HEMINGWAY," SUMMER, 1956)

Why do you still put on that face
powder which smells like Paris when
I was kicking seconal and used to
get up at four in the morning and
walk the streets into the long wait
for dawn (like an exhausted husband
pacing the room where you wait for
the hospital to inform you of wife
and birth) visions of my death seated
already in the nauseas of my tense
frightened liver. . . .

and I sicker than I've ever been,
weak with loathing at all that I had not done,
and all I was learning of all I would
now never do, and I would come back
after combing the vistas of the Seine
for glints of light to bank in the
corroded vaults of my ambitious and
yellow jaundiced soul and there back
in bed, nada, you lying in bed in hate
of me, the waves of unspoken flesh
radiating detestation into me because
I have been brave a little but not nearly
brave enough for you, greedy bitch,
Spanish lady, with your murderous
Indian blood and your crazy purity
hung on courage in men as if it were
your queen's own royal balls. . . .

JAMES BALDWIN   My first encounter with Norman was at Malaquais' apartment.
The Deer Park had come out, and I was finishing *Giovanni's Room*. I'd probably
met Malaquais through the *Paris Review* crowd, and by and large I wasn't
comfortable with intellectuals, French *or* American, since they seemed to leave
so much out of account. I knew that Malaquais was displeased with *The Deer
Park*. Malaquais is the French rationalist, and *The Deer Park* is anything but
rational—*Norman's* anything but rational—and that evening I thought Malaquais patronized him enormously, something Norman didn't see. Perhaps I was
entirely wrong, but I took Norman very seriously as a writer, and it seemed that
Malaquais didn't. I was a little offended by that.

JEAN MALAQUAIS   They were very competitive as writers, and I had the feeling
that Baldwin was a confounded snob. He would throw names around, he was
more "elegant" than Norman, more "European," as you say here in the States.
Adele was there too, but it was really just the two of them. They were drinking
a lot, two bottles of whiskey, arguing, I remember, and the meeting lasted until

James Baldwin (front).

two or three in the morning, when they left together. It was a love-hate relationship from the start.

EILEEN FINLETTER I was living in Europe through the fifties, and the stories that had been reaching us in Paris about the kind of life he was living were unbelievable. Nobody could quite connect it with the Norman they'd known. But when he and Adele visited, I wasn't shaken up by any major changes. He was more self-assured, trying to convince us that pot was the only way, and maybe he was a little more aggressive in trying to prove a point, but not belligerent. It was only later, when he published "The White Negro"—which signaled that he was taking on the whole Establishment—that I heard things through the grapevine and I began to wonder what the hell he thought he was doing.

MARIA IRENE FORNES I spent the most time with Norman and Adele when they came to visit me on Ibiza. Norman got a car—I guess in Barcelona—and we went to see a man who was a pornographer or who was collecting pornography in the south of France, and then we drove to Italy together too.

At that time I had no idea he was suffering. I wasn't a writer then, and I didn't know exactly what was the significance of his books not being big sellers like they were before. He may have been talking about it, but not to me. I didn't understand the drama of it, and I was also naïve about what American ambition is.

But they came to Ibiza definitely to rest. They stayed in a hotel facing the Mediterranean, a gorgeous place, and it was the part of the year when there wasn't anyone else staying there. I was very surprised, though, when he wanted me to have a party. I'd told Norman that a number of people had wanted to meet him—the artists, people who were perhaps not very active as writers but who were in some way trying to find their own identity. I thought that since somebody like Norman, a celebrity, was always recognized, he'd want just to be quiet and not have so much fuss made over him. But Norman said, "No, I'd like to meet these people, I'd like a party."

I do have a feeling, though it's more like a shadow of memory, that he said he hadn't been able to sleep as well as he did there at the hotel for a long time. It was very calm, quiet, not wild the way it got in the summertime, so you didn't have to get hysterical about what was happening in town either.

It was a short stay, about a week, before we went to the south of France, then to Florence. Adele was enjoying being in Europe, and I felt I'd never enjoyed the two of them as much. They were relaxed, very tender talking to each other. Norman was the camp leader, and in that way Adele and I were passive. But to me it was *them*, and during this trip Adele was being very sweet to Norman too. One time he started laughing and said to me, "When she sleeps, she says, 'Norman, I love you. Norman, I love you.'" He wasn't saying it arrogantly. It was like always having your puppy by your side, and he's always faithful, and even when you push him away he stays with you. He was laughing, being tender with her, because at that moment he was enjoying that kind of love. I use the example of the puppy not to say that he was boasting or really saying "Look at her, she's mine, I can do anything with her." It wasn't that. It was a good moment, with a kind of tenderness to it.

He didn't say anything about his fight with Dan until later, when I came back from Europe. Then he said, "Dan is not the same person he used to be." Dan, though, never said anything to me. Our relationship was more that he was like my teacher, and he listened, then he would tell me things that had to do with some kind of alternatives for things rather than telling me about his life or his problems. Still, I recall that when I came back there was some sort of gesture from him, as if to say "It's not the same with Norman." Some kind of thing like "Norman," with raised eyebrows.

ADELINE LUBELL NAIMAN   Ever since our big fight in '56 I've always tried to stay away from the public Norman. I don't like some of the things he's done as a public person, because when he puts on his public role it makes him uncomfortable and inaccessible. The other thing is that Norman is somebody whom I guess I've truly loved for thirty-five years but whom I never wanted to marry— unlike other women, I suppose—because I had me and didn't want to give that away. It would have been awful, and also that isn't the way I love him.

Of course it's hard for people to see him as I do since they see someone who paints so flamboyant a self. It's hard to see or care about his other identity, even to recognize it, because of just how thorough a trade-off he's made taking on that public mantle. Bergson, the French philosopher, once wrote that you can see all the individual pieces, but you can never reconstruct the whole; you'll get an approximation, but you won't get the totality or the infusing vitality, the *élan vital.* And that's very true of Norman. You have to understand who all the people are who are talking about Norman. Norman responds to that, it's part of his persona.

Myself, I'm coming from a kind of willful innocence, a sort of after-the-fact girlishness; I held myself in a small place out of sheer intent, for safety, out of cowardice and comfort—which doesn't seem to me especially bad since I haven't seen the joy of the alternate route. I perceived Norman as a Gestalt, as the whole person rather than fragments or an articulation of lines. But seeing the alternate route in him scared me. In fact he scared me and hurt me very deeply, so much so that we are now no longer as close as we once were. It was the only real fight we've had, and it happened because of his tendency not to accept the fact that he was in love with a particular kind of woman for herself. His intellect would get embarrassed and he'd be the one to get competitive.

It was at a party at the duplex he and Adele had on the East Side. Their relationship was failing. Norman was stoned. I didn't like drugs, I didn't like drunks, I didn't like people being out of control. Norman got boiling mad at me. He remembers it still. He'll comment, "I drove my closest old friend down the stairs. That was when I was in love with marijuana."

What really happened is he accused me in his stupor of hating Adele, of scorning her, of feeling that she was intellectually shallow and inferior. All of which was so far from anything I felt that I knew it must be something that he was battling in himself. For him I was still the token of the brilliant intellectual, so he projected on me the snobbery that he was sure people must have been feeling toward Adele. But that's not how one relates to people, and it's not how I related to her. Adele was a person of a certain kind in her own right. I was sort of shy with her because she was a different kind of person from me and it was hard to connect, but I did try to get inside her head sometimes, and I liked her. But Norman didn't think so, and he was setting me up as his fantasy conscience; the word "fantasy" is important here because that's not who I was in any way. But it was after that fight that I said, "I'm never going to see him again. This is an end."

Up until then I had trusted him as I trusted my life. But then I realized we were working at odds, and I started to protect myself. I went back to my friend's place where I was staying, and I was shaking and crying and I felt I couldn't take it. It was partly the violence, because I don't deal well with violence, and partly too what I felt was real rage. Punching me years before on the thigh was sexual anger—it was saying "I'm angry at you, but it's because I can't have you." This was different. This was another person or force taking over Norman. He was no longer one of my closest intimates to whom I could say anything, and this is where I saw the real shift of identity—not in previous years, not earlier. He'd always been extraordinarily tender with me, protective in a nice and generous way, but this was the disruption. I thought I'd never see him or talk to him again, which I didn't for almost five years. I remember saying to my friend, "For me he's dead." I'd thought that we'd be together all our lives, in the head, that we would grow old together, but that night he was suddenly dead for me, and I thought I'd never go back.

EMMA CLARA "ECEY" GWALTNEY   Norman came through one night that summer. Fig was in a painful period when the writing wasn't going well, and maybe Norman wasn't aware of it, because he seemed abrasive and deliberately wanted to shock us.

He'd been with somebody, a woman, and kept telling us about it even though we really didn't want to hear. "Nothing happened the first night, it just didn't work," he said. "But oh, the second night! Adele and I may really have a marriage, but I think this'll be the test."

Yet he also got irritated, maybe because Fig made a little remark about Adele. Fig had always been just sort of polite to her, but Norman blew up and said, "You know why you don't like her? It's because you're afraid of her. You know that she's too much woman for you." Norman could always find the most cutting things to say, and this made Fig real mad.

We were drinking, but not excessively, and Norman wasn't on anything as far as I know. But he kept talking about sex, asking a lot of questions—"Do you folks do this or that?" and he named all kinds of things. To Fig this was a new side of Norman, which he didn't understand at all, and he kept saying, "It's really none of your fuckin' business." Norman had gained weight and looked bloated, and I was aware he was taking pills to sleep, Seconals, as well as pills to wake him up in the morning, and that night, that lacerating evening, he really looked bad.

But Norman was throwing down the gauntlet. Oh, boy, was he. Telling Fig he had to come to New York: "You could get a teaching job up there. If you stay here, you're just going to get more and more small-town, more and more conservative. I'm afraid you're just going to bog down." That was his program for us: Come to New York, get in a different atmosphere, test ourselves.

I have an awful facility to see the validity of some things Norman says—I'm more objective—and I thought maybe he was right, and I actually would have been willing to go up to New York. But I could see Fig's point of view too. First, he hated New York. He said it was dirty, and maybe it also made him uncomfortable. I think of a passage by Thomas Wolfe in which he says a lot of southerners are afraid of New York, that they go and think they'll conquer it but come home defeated. More than this, though, it was a bad time for Fig—after Hollywood and things not happening for him as he had expected. And Norman in a sense confirmed the things he was worrying about, although Fig would never have acknowledged it to anybody, and certainly not to Norman.

But most of all Fig felt you just don't come to somebody's house and spend the whole evening attacking. You just don't do that. And since Fig wasn't equipped the way I am to deal with that kind of thing, he absolutely took it to heart. He didn't blow up, he was just kind of sad, totally exhausted by it. We both were, but Fig more than me. Norman was leaving the next morning, and at one point he and I were in the kitchen. I said, "Well, Norman, don't think it hasn't been fun, 'cause it hasn't." That's an old joke, what you call a southern insult, but he hadn't ever heard it before and took it real seriously and said, "Oh, well…" What a traumatic evening! He just put us through the wringer.

It was after he left that he sent a letter referring to "clearing the air." Norman was a great believer in clearing the air. Fig wasn't. My natural bent is more like Norman's: talk it out, let's be analytical, calm, reasonable. Still, Fig took the risk of responding to Norman's letter because Norman had been telling him how to live. Over the years Norman had given Fig a lot of advice, but this was when it reached a crescendo; maybe he'd been doing it to a lot of other people too— neither of us knew. But Fig's point was: Don't talk down to me. Norman must have mentioned giving him help because Fig wrote, "I have publicly given you credit for what you've done for me."

Which was why I thought it was a great letter. It's what I mean about Fig being visceral. Totally. I was never prepared to give somebody up, and I admired him for that. He knew he'd never be famous the way Norman was, but he was a writer, and he said to himself, "I'll be a writer on my own terms." Why do people torture themselves? He felt he simply had to do it his way, and he never learned to play the smart game. Of course the letter also shows that Norman and Fig had a very special relationship, and I think different from any other Norman's had. Many people have indulged him—I have—but not Fig.

But that evening injured Fig, and after the letter he would never bring it out and talk about it. We were worried about Norman, the experimentation with drugs and sex. He told us about marijuana and having taken mushrooms and seeing little men. Fig was also worried that he was losing his idealism, his literary commitment.

Still, looking back, I can see all the knotty dissension that would arise because of Norman's advice over the years. Even before *The Naked and the Dead*, Norman had given Fig advice about agents and publishers. Fig was totally ignorant of that world, and maybe he never realized how much trouble Norman went to, the hassle it was in New York to go to this one or that one and talk about Fig's work. I suppose he made an instinctive comparison of being Norman's guide down here, and for Fig that was no bother—like introducing Norman to some old codgers who Norman thought were exotic characters, or going fishing or going to the swimming hole. That required energy all right but of an entirely different kind.

But there is also a tone in the letter that harks back to some other things he'd said about his own work methods. At first Fig didn't have any objection to Norman's advice; he took everything and tried to learn from it. So Norman sent do's and don'ts, like his letter about prepositions. I'm also sure Norman got impatient with Fig's work methods—his writing spontaneously. Fig felt, If it doesn't work right now, I'll just write it till it does work. And of course that was anathema to Norman.

FRANCIS IRBY GWALTNEY (LETTER TO NORMAN MAILER)
Dear Norman:

I was under the impression that you knew I was writing a book. If you were aware of it, I want you to know that I keenly resent your letter. If you weren't aware of it, it doesn't make much difference.

It's about time you realize something: I am not a student and am specifically not one of your students. I don't like your kind of writing and I do not intend to learn to like it.

I also find myself unimpressed by your attitude. You seem to think that anything you say—no matter how insulting and crassly adolescent it is—must be taken for an utterance of God. You displayed some of the same attitude when you were down here the last time, namely that you were doing me a wonderful favor by condescending to visit. I don't like that. I am a writer in my own right and I would have been one without you, although I have publicly given you credit for what you have done for me. So let's just stop this second-coming-of-Christ routine. It bores me. It certainly doesn't have the effect intended.

And don't try to be funny. You're goddamn right I'm going to be a major novelist. I wouldn't have started writing if I hadn't thought I could. Please don't be so surprised to find yourself thinking the same thing.

Let me put it this way. I am aware of my own limitations and I am sure I can overcome them. I don't need your help. I don't want it. I need only your friendship, but I don't want it on your terms. I don't like to be insulted. Any friendship can stand only so much of that. Your rather naive remark, that your behavior "cleared the air," strikes me as being outright silly. I don't like things like that and you have been aware of my likes and dislikes on the subject of friendship for some twelve years now.

You asked for an honest reply. You have it, right in your goddamn teeth. You've pushed hard enough. Now you owe me an apology.

LARRY ALSON   From '51 to '55 our social circle had been independent of Norman's. Then after they came back from Paris in '56 Norman and Adele moved out to Bridgewater, Connecticut, where a bunch of writers were attempting to create a salon like they'd tried at the White Horse back in '51 or '52. Only it was claustrophobic, a closed community. Styron, for example, had invited John Aldridge up and found a house for him. A whole bunch of people were up there, part of the group, and then Styron somehow put Aldridge into coventry, so ostracized him that he was forced to leave.

Barbara and I had known Styron in the Village through the New School and suggested that Norman look him up. The two of them had had some connection before, but it was up in Connecticut that they started spending time together. It's likely there was a kind of competitiveness, each bad-mouthing the other's work, but I know that Norman's generosity is an enormous part of his character. I remember once Jim Jones and Norman were discussing Styron—it may have been at a party at Lillian Ross', where all the writers were talking in terms of a Hemingway competition, as if you get into the ring, ready to knock out the existing champ. Jones was saying, "I'm not sure Styron's in our class," while Norman insisted, "Yes, he is, he belongs there."

MICKEY KNOX   Jones was competitive—I suppose most writers are—but I think he was less competitive than Norman. For instance, Jim's friendship with writers was much more lasting than Norman's, and Billy Styron was his friend up till the end. Irwin Shaw too.

In contrast, I once saw Norman be very rude to Shaw. We were at Frankie and Johnny's, the steak place, and three or four tables away Shaw was with an actress I'd once auditioned for Actors Studio; she was married to a psychiatrist, we'd sort of had a fling, so I waved to them. Norman just nodded. When we were leaving I stopped at their table to say goodbye, Norman kept right on walking. The next time I saw Irwin he was furious. "What the fuck's the matter with him?" he said, "why couldn't he say hello?" I said, "Shit, why couldn't you say hello?" He said, "Well, I'm older. But not that much." I don't know precisely when that *shtick* started. I don't know if there was rancor because *The Naked and the Dead* reached the best-seller list one month before *The Young Lions*, but I'd heard that the two of them had even been in competition about who could lose weight faster. Norman certainly did when he was out in Bridgewater, when he gave up smoking several times—but even there that was grounds for another contest.

ADELE MORALES MAILER   Neither of us had roots, that was the problem, and I guess we thought we'd finally settle in Connecticut. The house we bought was beautiful, old and white, and Julien Levy, the art dealer, was on the other side of the ridge from us. I painted and Norman built me a studio, like an upper attic that he renovated after putting in new windows. We brought our furniture from Fifty-fifth Street, but after the initial push we never fixed the place up, and it looked like a bohemian loft, like every other place we'd had.

Still, we'd have guests every weekend, a full house. Howard Fertig, I think, was working for Norman part of the time, doing secretarial work, and Norman sort of fathered him. Susie also came and spent time, probably most of the first fall.

Norman was still having his sleeping problems, but one thing he did was set up a workshop. He went out and bought power tools—he loves to work with his hands—and he also tried being an inventor, which was funny. I'm not being a bitch—this is a stirring memory. I know he and Nat Halper talked about inventing a game, but Norman was also going to invent something involving Joannie, my sister, though I can't remember what it was. He was also trying to give up smoking, off and on, though he never really succeeded until after we broke up, when they started talking about the connection between smoking and cancer.

That first year I was pregnant, and I loved it. I wanted a baby and so did Norman. He was very pleased, crazy about it, in fact. I went into New York Hospital to have Dandy on March 16, 1957, and I remember driving back up to Connecticut with her. Fan and Barney of course were delighted—the Jewish mother, my son's child sort of thing. She and Barney would take the train up and stay weekends, almost regularly.

There were other people in the area we'd see, like John Aldridge and Bill and Rose Styron. Norman had a falling out with Aldridge—whether about *The Deer Park*, though, I don't know. But Rose Styron? What can I say? She's a very strange gal. I didn't like her and didn't get along with her. She was a pain in the ass, that's all.

We'd often go into New York for parties, drive back late half crocked, like three in the morning, and it's a wonder I'm still alive. After Dandy was born, though, we went less and less, and I began to feel isolated. I had my studio and was starting acting classes in the city but, still, the winter did it. Norman felt it too. In fact, he was more insistent than I that we move back.

But while we were there Norman also set up a gym, a punching bag. My father might've gotten him interested in boxing, but not until the mid-fifties, because when we were first living together I didn't see my people. I couldn't get along with my mother. After we got married we got together with them a little, and that's probably when Norman started thinking about boxing. My father had about eighty-two bouts. He was a featherweight, a club fighter on the way up, very promising. But he didn't want it enough. My mother certainly didn't want it. She was worried he'd get hurt and nagged at him to quit. So he wound up working at the *Daily News* for forty-five years.

MARIA IRENE FORNES   When they were living in Connecticut I went to visit them a couple of times. It was just the three of us, nobody else, and I remember I felt Norman was getting a little odd. There was a barn, sort of set up like a gym, where he had weights. Or maybe it was a room with a punching bag. He told me he had boxed with somebody, a big boxer, who had said that he wasn't bad for a nonboxer, then he asked me if I wanted to put on the gloves. I can't remember if Adele was practice-punching too. But Norman was teaching us, showing us, and there was something misdirected. I didn't feel he was in a state or odd in any large, overt way, but there was something that wasn't there before.

JOHN ALDRIDGE   I'd just come back from a year in Italy and had a one-year teaching job at Sarah Lawrence, was newly married, and we were casting around for a place to live. Styron was well ensconced on his acres up in Connecticut, and Leslie, my then wife, had known him at Duke and also gone out with him in Paris. We had a little bit of money and thought it would be great to move up into literary country, so we went up to visit Styron and look for property. Through a realtor we found Arthur Miller's house, which he and Marilyn had vacated to go to England to make *The Prince and the Showgirl*, and we bought it.

Norman was already settled, living a few miles away. Styron was about three miles away from where we were, so it was a kind of triangular arrangement with us roughly midway between the two of them. Old Van Wyck Brooks lived in Bridgewater too, along with Lew Allen and also Ed Gilbert, who had written for films and later wrote a novel based on the literary life up there. The community was a satellite of New York, and the idea of the writer living in the country seemed to be part of the mythos, almost like going to Paris at one time would've been. If you felt you wanted to achieve something, you wanted to move to the country, where it would be very quiet but you'd also be in proximity to other literary people.

William and Rose Styron, Roxbury, Connecticut: "Styron began to see Mailer as the force, the center, and that would bother ol' Billy, Norman usurping his turf."

So we began to see Norman and Adele socially. There were occasional times of serious talk, but for the most part it was play. Our talk usually had to do with agents, advances, editors, that sort of thing. Everybody was drinking a lot, Norman included, and in the winter the evening would close in very quickly. In fact, the winter was so bad, so very bleak, that by the following spring my wife and I had had enough and moved out. Norman lasted two years, but then he couldn't take it either, though he never actually told me he disliked the winters. He was writing, also doing carpentry work. He had a shop in his basement with power tools, and he had these objects he'd work on, little wooden spheres, very polished. Precisely what they were I never found out.

In the warm months the two of them would come over and swim in our pool, which was the damnedest thing since it was undrainable. Arthur Miller's cousin had put in this concrete-lined pit and forgotten to put a drain at the bottom, so we'd have to call the fire department to pump it out, and it would get beautifully green before we'd get around to it. Once Norman brought Chandler Brossard over to swim, and he also had somebody up working with him on the play version of *The Deer Park*, but I don't remember who that was, though I do know that the play was giving him problems.

I remember Adele only in relation to him, although I think I was aware that she was painting. She and Norman had a very strange, combative relationship, which I gather was very tense, but I couldn't tell whether this was just play on Norman's part, whether he treated all women like that, or whether there was something really going on between them. It wasn't easy to say. Adele was very exotic, and it was possible that she was sort of Norman's entrée into a freer sexual life. She was clay to be molded.

We'd also see Bill and Rose Styron, whose house was nice and big with a lot of acreage, although none of the places up there were working farms. It was more comfortable than gracious in the beginning, but then they began to fix it up. They had a second little house, as you often have in those places, with a little living room, a fireplace, and a loft, which was where Bill did his work. I assume they were living almost entirely on Rose's money—she's the heiress of the Burgunder fortune, Burgunder department stores in Baltimore—because although Bill's first novel, *Lie Down in Darkness*, sold respectably and received a great deal of critical acclaim, he wasn't making money in those years.

I felt, and I think Norman did too, that Styron was being very, very calculating in his efforts to ingratiate himself with people who might matter to his career. He used to have weekend gatherings at his place and always managed to have people who could be counted on to help him, like Bennett Cerf. Scarcely a weekend went by that they didn't have a houseful of weekend guests. Bob Loomis was one who'd come up there quite often, along with a number of similar people, and Rose was the perfect hostess.

Styron was working on *Set This House on Fire*, which, given how fast he works, was about ten years in the doing. Mailer was in a trough at the time, feeling in a state of real crisis. I knew he'd been very badly troubled by the *Barbary Shore* failure, and then *The Deer Park*, but we didn't talk about it. He was too defensive. He had a way of holding people at sufficient distance because they were both frightened of him and respected him, and you never knew what he was going to do next. He'd keep you off balance by what he calls counter-punching—introducing an idea or argument out of nowhere, yet remaining in control, while throwing you these unpredictable curves. Which does not invite the question "What's wrong?"

There was a big personal investment in Norman on the part of all of us. Norman does that; and even though we had Styron, Styron was not Norman. Norman's being there justified our being there. In the sense that there was a pack and there was a leader, Norman was the leader, and again, this may be greatly unfair, but I have a feeling that Styron was enjoyed from time to time without really being liked. He was so damned pleasant, the good ol' boy, that there was a kind of impenetrability about him. He was originally king of the roost and seemed to have taken Mailer's arrival in good stride, probably because he felt there wasn't all that much threat from Norman. But by the time I arrived Mailer felt distinctly competitive and quite quickly became the center of energy in a way that Styron never was. Maybe that created the tension or helped to create the tension that developed and apparently crescendoed, after we left, into their final encounter.

I know very little about this encounter except that it had something to do with Adele and was accompanied or preceded by some challenge Norman made to Bennett Cerf, asking him outside, where they were going to beat each other up. I'm not sure, but I think it had something to do with Cerf's turning down *The Deer Park*. Anyway, Styron apparently broke it up. I heard that then, later in the evening, Styron supposedly made a remark about Adele. I don't know what the remark was, nor did Norman ever say. It was apparent, though, that Rose Styron and Adele never got along. . . . I don't know, perhaps it was something about Adele being a lesbian. I'm not sure where I got that from, perhaps remarks that Norman made in some sort of half-joking way that she liked boys *and* girls, something like that, but Styron talking along those lines makes sense because he was quite capable of it, a sort of "get 'em any way you can" feeling. There was that growing tension between them plus the fact that as time went on—again, I'm theorizing—Styron began to see Mailer as the force, the center. That would bother ol' Billy, Norman usurping his turf.

CHANDLER BROSSARD   We seemed to know the same people, so Norman invited me up to Connecticut for a weekend, the plan being for the two of us to do an interview up there. No sooner did I arrive, however, late Friday, when I met Adele.

Now, people like Adele have a metaphysic of skin response which is so shallow that, in her case, it seemed that if you indicated you weren't interested in her she had no use for you. Her whole attitude was: Aren't I divine? I wasn't interested, and when she saw she couldn't reach me she was upset, all of which amused Norman enormously.

He showed me around the house, showed me his gym out back, and in the course of the tour I saw a copy of my novel *The Bold Saboteurs* lying on a table, at which point he said, "Yes, I bought a copy, but I haven't gotten around to reading it." Okay. We sat down and started our interview, soon getting drunk, and as Norman got drunker he stopped at one point and said, "I wasn't telling you the truth. I really have read it. I read it through"—contrary to what he later claimed in that essay of his, "A Quick and Expensive Look," or whatever it's called—"and I liked it enormously."

"Why did you tell me you hadn't read it?" I asked.

"Well, you upset me. People I envy upset me."

"Oh?"

"Yes. I've heard about you from Calder Willingham. He told me about your other book, *Who Walk in Darkness*."

I shrugged and let it pass. The next morning we played the tape back, and do you know, for the first ten minutes I couldn't tell myself from Norman—he had been imitating my voice. Without knowing it he had mimed my whole speech pattern, my accent, and I mean perfectly. When we got to know each other better he used to unconsciously imitate Calder too. There was an English accent as well, and one time I asked him where he'd picked it up. He laughed and said, "I don't know, watching old Charles Laughton movies maybe."

Anyway, this was the first time we spent any time together, and I realized that there were labyrinths in this sweet boy, this Huckleberry Finn, and I told myself, "Be wary." He and Adele had a number of fights all during the second day—I mean constant, loathsome bickering—until he got rid of her and the two of us went over to see John Aldridge. We then wandered around for a while, Norman telling me who lived here, who was there, until we got to the topic of Styron.

I had known about Styron many years before because a friend of mine was from Baltimore, like Styron's wife. In fact I'd spent an unpleasant evening with Styron out in the Hamptons, and it was quite clear to me, Detective Brossard, that this weak, bullshit southern boy had gotten himself a Jewish heiress. So I mentioned this to Norman, explaining that I'd tried to talk to Styron but that when the conversation had gotten too deep for him, he'd taken his bottle of Pinch down to the beach, sat and drank all night.

Later that night there's an enormous party, the whole literary scene. Styron was over in the corner lecturing to a bunch of dummies, Norman is interested in getting drunk and having some action, and Adele meanwhile is aching for some awful scene, I can just tell. I'm talking with someone else, and soon she comes over and says, "I like juicy, fuckable men. You're dry and unfuckable."

"Adele," I said, "if I were juicy and fuckable, the last person I'd want to fuck is you. You bore the shit out of me."

"Go fuck yourself," she said, walking off. But I knew she'd be back, so I went over to Norman and said, "Norman, you've gotta get this woman away from me. I don't want to get involved. Something's the matter."

All of this is to describe a weekend. Norman and I had only just met, and there was a kind of instant candor, something I rarely go in for. I had been around a lot, and he liked that. Part of the explanation too was that I preferred *Barbary Shore* to *The Naked and the Dead* and told him as much, which obviously pleased him.

But my boxing clearly interested him and he kept coming back to it. I was leaving the next morning, but I had to tell him again that he didn't know what he was doing. I'm probably just a little bit better than most people because I went to this gym and was trained by George Brown, who trained Hemingway, but he had this fantasy because Adele's father was a boxer, and I said, "Norman, let's not go a step further. You don't know how to box, you don't know how to hold your hands, and what's gonna happen is I'll cut your face up terribly, but the law of averages says pretty soon you're going to break my rib or something, because you don't care how much punishment you sustain."

But he pursued it, and I had to repeat myself: "No, Norman. What you really want is for us to fall into each other's arms and cry and hug, covered with blood. That doesn't give me the slightest fucking kick at all and I'm not gonna do it."

"You're very funny, Chandler," he replied.

"That's it, Norman. I'm not gonna do it. You have some need to do it, I don't," I told him. "It's a strangely primitive notion. It kind of repels me because I don't like blood, and also it seems kind of homosexual to me."

He laughed. He always fielded those things, you see. He heard you, but he never came back with a direct answer.

NAT HALPER He invited me and Marge up to Bridgewater too, but Marge couldn't come, so I took the train up alone and he met me at the station. His house was old and spacious, though I've never had the feeling that Norman has any need to make a pleasant or homelike or even aesthetic atmosphere for himself; all his places have been more or less functional. I also felt that moving out to Connecticut wasn't so much to escape the city as to go to a place where there were all sorts of people who were in the public eye, like Styron and Julien Levy.

The guy fleeing New York City flew to a place where there were other people in the arts, not just so he could talk to them but because he was already in public life and liked being a public figure.

Nonetheless, Adele was at the house, and she and I had always been friendly, so it was "Hi," chatting about this and that. She wasn't playing the gracious hostess, but she made dinner and then faded into the background. Afterwards Norman and I drove over to see Styron. This was the year there was a rumpus about *By Love Possessed*, which had become a terrific best seller and everybody said would win the Pulitzer. But there was a hitch. Dwight Macdonald had written a really poisonous review in *The New Yorker*, which I thought was outrageous since it seemed to start with the premise that Cozzens was a conservative, but Macdonald, knowing that wasn't good enough to make a book lousy, then pointed out that Cozzens wasn't as good as Faulkner. After that, word got around that Cozzens was through.

Anyway, I defended Cozzens, and Norman and Styron ganged up on me, especially Styron when Norman told him I was interested in Joyce. Styron was contemptuous—you know, "Joyce is no good because people can't understand him." My impression was that in terms of other writers, especially the older generation, the two of them were lined up: Against our enemy, we're brothers— that sort of thing. But then riding home afterwards Norman started making remarks about Styron being a goddamned politician, that his wife was taking care of his career and that he was getting places because of her. It was strange, almost a turnabout. That night I was aware that more and more he was getting into the game of literary politics.

RUTH E. FRIEDMAN   My family knew Styron's people in Virginia. The point, though, is that Rose Styron was rich and Jewish. Styron is a real, dyed-in-the-wool southern aristocrat and a snob. Adele Mailer was neither rich nor Jewish.

BARBARA PROBST SOLOMON   It was clear that there were a lot of his old friends he wasn't going to be seeing anymore. One was very much aware of his experimentation, like he and Adele were playing with fire. There was a sense of sexual limits being pushed, and since I was peripheral I couldn't tell whether it was Adele pushing Norman or Norman pushing Adele, but it was plainly the world in which they were living.

LARRY ALSON   There was a rumor that Styron was making allegations about Adele, but it was a very bad time for Norman in general. There was great tenseness, which was observable to everyone who cared about him, and I know that Barbara tried to persuade him to see a therapist. Once he called me on the phone and said, "Is my wife there?" I said, "What?" He said, "Is Barbara there?" I was flabbergasted, speechless.

NORMAN PODHORETZ   I grilled both Norman and Styron but never discovered what, exactly, it was about. I heard the story that there was an orgy or that Styron accused Adele of being a dyke, but that seemed very anticlimactic.

GEORGE PLIMPTON   I think Norman moved up to Connecticut really *because* of Bill Styron. They became very close. They're both great conversationalists, great storytellers... the kind who sit around the kitchen table until four A.M., night people, and it must've been like one of those literary friendships you read about in books—Emerson, Thoreau, Hemingway and Fitzgerald—that sort of thing. Then somebody said something, and in this case it was much worse than the episode that broke, for example, Hemingway and Fitzgerald apart. I heard there was a bitter argument in Styron's kitchen. Personal references had been made about wives.

Jones was in Paris at the time, a close friend of both, and it seems there was a play to pull him into one camp or the other. Norman wrote him a little letter or something. Jones sided with Styron, and then, of course, Norman ripped them in the essay that appeared in *Advertisements*, and then again in the *Esquire* piece, "Some Children of the Goddess," where he said of Styron, "I liked the boy in him, disliked the man." It didn't help to heal matters when he referred to *Set This House on Fire* as a "maggoty novel."

GLORIA JONES   Jim and I were living in New York for about six months, and we went with them to a party at Victor Weybright's, the guy who was head of New American Library. We were all dressed up, very spiffy, and this was really high-steppin'. The Weybrights were very elegant, and everybody you'd ever heard of was there—Erskine Caldwell, James Farrell, the whole lot.

Adele and I supposedly had a fight, but we didn't. She wanted to smoke some pot, and I said "No," because I didn't know how to do pot. I said I wanted to be very proper, because I always had my eye on a buck, you know, and I didn't want to screw up anything at Weybright's. Still, she didn't throw a tantrum or anything, that was all blown out of proportion. Both of them acted very well around us, and maybe we went to P. J. Clarke's afterwards. This was before Norman wrote his essay of course.

NAT HALPER   The morning after the visit to Styron's we drove over to see Julien Levy, whom I'd met in Provincetown. Levy had a beautiful Max Ernst chess set out on the lawn, and at the time I was running the HCE Gallery, and people had the impression both of us were big wheels. Julien had never gotten over the fact that his father had left him money in a foolproof trust, a spendthrift trust, on which he could draw only interest, so in fact we were both living from day to day.

Aside from Provincetown, the other connection Norman and I had was through my chess playing. He'd watched me play at the Marshall Chess Club, a team match, and was fascinated by the atmosphere, the outward calm, the tension underneath. He'd gotten the idea I was a great games player—he overrated my abilities, I'm good but not tops—and since he needed money he wanted to invent a game. He came to me with the idea—it was a variant of Success, one chose careers, or "life gambles," as he put it—and he wanted me to be the consultant.

I suppose he needed money because of alimony, and *The Deer Park* hadn't been a huge success, and at the time board games like Monopoly were a craze. He was serious, it was a straw he was groping for, and he began to design it. It went on for a month or two. He'd mention it, I'd make objections, and then he'd come back with modifications. The problem was that it wasn't clear-cut enough, it could never work as a game that would sell.

WALTER MINTON   I'd heard that there was some money from *The Naked and the Dead* that had been used to buy government bonds on margin. You used to be able to do that, and for close to ten years it produced a pretty decent amount of money for him to live on. Then, in the tenth year, *boom*, it all went. This was somewhere around '58 or '59.

From '56 to '61, about once a year or so, Barney would come in to the Putnam's offices to go over the books—not really to audit them so much as talk about what money was here, what money was coming in from anything else. He was a guy who was street-smart, no bullshit, dollars and cents, but always polite, calling up and asking if he could come in. The first time I think Norman said, "My dad's going to call you. He does my accounting."

Beyond this Norman never talked about his parents. But you could tell that his mother came on pretty strong. He was the absolute apple of her eye, and she felt he wasn't getting the recognition he deserved. She never actually said anything, but you knew what she wanted to ask was, "Why can't you do better for Norman?"

MICKEY KNOX   During this time he was still writing constantly, which he does even during his worst personal periods. I don't know if he was worried about not writing fiction, but looking back on it, I suppose the reception of *The Deer Park* was much more painful than anyone realized. I sort of sensed it, though, because he talked a lot about it after he had me do the bookstore survey.

Through this time I could see that Fan Mailer was doting. It really went beyond her being the Jewish mother. I know Jewish mothers, having had one myself, and I was surprised that such a woman could countenance what was happening to him. Just what he was writing, like "The White Negro." My God! Then I realized that in her eyes he could do no wrong.

SOL STEIN   In 1957 I was a founding member of the playwrights' group of the Actors Studio. The organizing force was Molly Kazan, and there were ten of us originally, including Bob Anderson, Arnold Schulman, Tennessee Williams, Bill Inge, and then it broadened to include more people. The purpose was to have writers stage their work, using Studio actors and directors, so we'd learn what the direction process was. We had weekly meetings, but I don't think Norman came regularly, just off and on. For the rest of us, though, there was this feeling you could miss church, you could miss an anniversary, but you didn't want to miss this group. From the actors' side of the Studio, there was Rip Torn, Geraldine Page, Tony Franciosa, and Kevin McCarthy, I think, and if I'm not mistaken, this was where Norman first met these people. The Studio sort of opened up new territory.

MICKEY KNOX   Norman had been working on adapting *The Deer Park* for the theater. I hadn't brought him into Actors Studio, but we did some scenes as a project with Frank Corsaro directing, with Kevin McCarthy and Annie Bancroft. At first there was another person playing Eitel, who, oddly enough, was let go, so McCarthy came in while we were rehearsing.

Norman was there every day during the three or four weeks, but he wasn't playing much of a directorial role. Adele sometimes came, but she wasn't yet an actress. He and Corsaro got along. He was also friendly with McCarthy and he liked Annie Bancroft. Strasberg's relationships with everybody were very cool, always, but I don't think he ever did anything to Norman. Norman was aware of what he did to actors, though, and I think he felt that he was sucking Marilyn's blood, which is why he later wrote about him as such a son of a bitch.

But the Actors Studio was a perfect place for him to break in the play, to give a couple of acts a dry run. Plus they had Annie Bancroft, who was bright and funny and very good in the part, and in the course of the production Norman really began knowing and understanding the actors. He'd written a play before, much earlier, and I vaguely remember it was called "The Naked and the Dead," which he told me was where he got the title for the novel. But we never talked about putting that on, we just did those scenes from *The Deer Park*, where I first did Marion Faye, then Munshin.

FRANK CORSARO   I'm not sure how Norman's script of *The Deer Park* came to me, but it was after I'd done *A Hatful of Rain* in '57, which was the first of the big projects and really galvanized the Actors Studio into a theater company. I think it was through Mickey Knox. Mickey's an inveterate interloper, he comes in and out, and I'd known him. He brought me the script and said he wanted to play one of the characters, Teppis, the producer, a wonderful character.

So I read it, and while Norman is very gifted—and at that time we were interested in getting people like him—I felt he didn't know how to write for the stage. He had a theatrical vision and his characters were vivid, but the script had a lopsided, sloppy form, or perhaps no form at all. Still, there was a lot of material that would be interesting to try to shape, to infuse with some kind of dramatic cohesion.

I also felt emotional realities were missing. Usually I would have taken the actors and worked them a little bit, as I'd done for *A Hatful of Rain*, but I thought it was necessary for Norman to hear his words, so I got some actors— Anne Bancroft, who was fascinated with the part of Elena, Kevin McCarthy, Mickey, Patrick O'Neal, the others I can't remember—and I set up a series of semistage readings.

Over the next month the two of us would get together and I'd try to indicate where I thought there were holes that needed to be attended to in rewriting. Of course, Norman hadn't written a novel since *The Deer Park*, which was a couple of years already, and a number of us at the Studio wondered about that—the typical question, "Why isn't he writing a book?" There was the notion that he was a typical one-book writer, that he'd written one tremendously successful novel and that was it. Plus the impression that he was trying to break into the theater, that he was "slumming" in order to find a new attitude, that he was stagestruck.

In general he was fascinated by what was going on, and when he and I were together, or with the actors, there was always a sense of him wanting to participate, like he was enjoying the possibility of what all this might mean, since a lot of theater people were paying attention to him, a kind of attention he'd probably never gotten before. We thought we were going to get good results, but the sad thing was that he tightened up, either out of fear or lack of knowledge. Months would go by in which I'd hear nothing, so I'd call him to check on what was happening, and he'd say, "Well, I'm working on it." So I'd suggest getting together again, and then we'd rehash things, he'd write things down, some kind of outline, in an effort to give the material some form. I always had to start with the premise that I had to get through all that shit of his belligerence, and by the end there was the feeling, He's going to do it, he's come around.

Meanwhile there were the actors. At first he was rather impressed with the fact that he was able to get Anne Bancroft interested in his material, but finally he didn't like her in Elena's role. One night, I remember, he and I went over to her apartment in the Village. The ostensible reason was that the three of us— she was living alone—were going to talk about the play, yet it was obvious he was trying to make her, and she said, "No way. Sorry, buster." He was fulminating. We were there for about an hour and didn't get much into the play at all. There was nothing subtle about it—I was supposed to get the picture and leave. But it was apparent that he'd be rejected, and it was almost as if that was really what it was about—courting rejection. Anne Bancroft was very peasant-smart, with a good shit detector. She wasn't an unknown, she'd done *Two for the Seesaw*, and while she hadn't yet done *The Miracle Worker*, she was living well. Anyway, he then insisted that Adele play Anne's part even though she hadn't had enough experience.

Looking back on it, I saw that the problem was related to what had first attracted me to the material—the kind of melding of sex and politics. The play was a metaphysical melodrama, with all kinds of real issues trying to balance themselves—specifically, the nature of failure, both social and private. Yet somehow he was mixing up the elements. He rationalized the characters and manipulated them in the same way I sometimes think Arthur Miller gives a theory of what it's all about but doesn't actually carry out the drama. It's a kind of intellectualization. With a character like Eitel, the director, you have a marvelous element of personal anguish and despair, but instead of dealing with that in the character, he retreated from Eitel and took refuge in pyrotechnics and phony drama, in generalizations.

I felt that his throwing himself into the theater was a kind of diversion, no question, but Mailer speaks from a kind of visceral frustration, so there was a genuine attraction to working within the dramatic form too. Sometimes one is attracted either to the form or to the showboating—it depends on what talent is there—but with him I'd say it was both, just as I saw the same thing in Tennessee Williams. Both these guys often didn't have a home. Norman's had lots of homes, but I felt that in his own being he wasn't satisfied with whatever it was he had at hand. You often see that in people in the theater—what I call the child in the theater who wants the adulation, the acceptance on a vast, immediate scale. You can't just dismiss that. It's part of the fascination, and in a funny way, in the books Mailer did later on, the reportorial essays, he found a voice and a release for his imagination because everything he wrote about was a kind of theatrical event, grand-scale demonstrations of power, and in a funny way the irony he intended in the essays anatomized his own peculiar failure to visualize on a metaphysical level.

SHELLEY WINTERS I think Norman felt Corsaro was a very good director, even though they fought a lot. Frank had been in analysis and was one of the most successful analysands I've ever seen, which was really the source of their conflict: Corsaro was doing a psychoanalytic interpretation of the play, which Norman was resisting.

I liked *The Deer Park* and was mad at Norman when he didn't cast me, but I felt he had the same problem as Irwin Shaw. They're both good writers, but a playwright has to leave space for the actor—you've gotta write the dialogue and then let the actor supply the emotion. But Norman tries to tell the actors what to think, and we actors haven't lived Norman's life, haven't had his Harvard experience, his first sexual experience, what he ate. Frank would try to make him cut that stuff, and Norman was coming on tough and having terrible fights with everybody. He had fine actors to do his play, but he'd fragment rehearsals. He'd talk, interrupt, and wouldn't let anyone function.

FRANK CORSARO I'm not sure exactly how it happened, but Adele called me about acting classes. I didn't know whether she'd been interested before Norman came to the Studio, but she talked a lot about acting, the "I'm-perfect-for-the-part" sort of thing. Maybe she'd said it before and in his fantasy Norman thought, Well, why not? Maybe he paved the way—I don't remember—but when she called it seemed like a logical thing.

She hadn't had any experience and wasn't very good. She was full of tension, and there was tremendous hostility against the world, a "Don't fuck with me" attitude, which made her unpleasant onstage. She was obviously a very sensual lady, and while she wasn't relying on that, she exuded what I call dirty sex, like "Tie me to a bed." So we began to work together, and the moment she tried to get personal with her stuff, it became clear that there was built-up animosity— anger, resentment, confusion. She wanted to take acting classes, and I think maybe it had to do with getting into Norman's play, which she felt exiled from.

We worked once a week for several hours. She'd do scenes from material I'd given her that was usually modern, never classic, things that would allow her to bring out her animosity. Finally she began to go with it, by which I mean she started to become a presence with some real power. She had always had that cloud of a voice, but gradually that and her fluttery innocence began to go, and I saw that they were part of the mask. I'm quick to see through that—I hear a nervous laugh, I know behind it she wants to kill somebody. I remember I told Norman she should be encouraged.

She worked hard, and then it was steady progress. I would give her things to do that would open her up. For example, something in which she had to believe she was drunk. When you get somebody like Adele with conflicted emotions, you don't go for the emotions, you go for things that seem emotionless, such as "What are you drinking, what does it taste like?" She suddenly began to flow, to emerge in a way that was inimitable, and I felt if she could go on and really harness it, she'd make a very impressive figure. Of course what happened is that after the stabbing she just stopped. But with the divorce she came back, picked up on it again.

ADELE MORALES MAILER   I began in '57. What happened was that Norman got involved in the Actors Studio through Mickey Knox and Danny Mann, and after meeting Frank Corsaro, he introduced us. I studied with Frank for almost three years.

I hadn't thought about acting, but Norman came back and said that he'd told Corsaro I had talent. I said, "What? I'm a painter, not an actress." "But you're always acting, you love to act," he said. "You're so dramatic, why don't you put it to work?"

I didn't feel he was forcing me into anything, but he's always liked actresses, and he was very encouraging. So I went, and I loved it, and I was still going when that thing—the incident—happened in '60. I used to commute once a week from Bridgewater. Also when we were in Provincetown, in that house on the hill in '59 and '60, I'd work my scene out, memorize my lines, and fly into New York once a week.

I was also in *The Deer Park* project. Norman was having terrible fights with Corsaro over the direction, and with Anne Bancroft, who was going to play Elena, and finally he and Annie had a big blowup. "You know what you can do with this part?" she told him. "Get Adele to play it. That's what you've wanted all along." Norman's reply? "Fine, because you'll never amount to anything anyway." Good ol' Norman.

FRANK CORSARO   I would see Norman and James Baldwin together at the Actors Studio, and, in fact, I'd gone to high school with Baldwin, so I knew him well. What I witnessed in their meetings was an enormous rivalry, on both sides.

At Actors Studio I was supposed to do Baldwin's play *Blues for Mr. Charlie*, which was flagrantly antiwhite, although there were intimations of something more, because Baldwin was trying to balance the budget. Strasberg and I went over it. Inevitably, though, it was unconsciously racist—it had to do with the biggest *schlong* in the world, that kind of horseshit—so we got together with Baldwin, and because on the other side of his paranoia Baldwin was astute enough to see the value of our suggestions, he agreed to rewrite it. Every night I went around to meetings at Baldwin's. The Movement was going on, and he was living it up like a pasha, fucking these blond college kids, but then he moved, and I found myself tailing him around trying to get the work out of him. Finally I got the point: He wasn't doing it. Then I heard that he'd shown up at Strasberg's house and said, "The play has to be slanted the way it is. If Frank Corsaro doesn't want to direct it, don't let him direct it." So I backed out, and that was the end of it.

As long as blacks were fighting the whites, it was easy for Baldwin to write *The Fire Next Time,* and I think that tension entered into the complexity of Norman and Baldwin's relationship. Whenever I was together with them Jimmy was a combination of coquette, preacher boy, and arrant wit, all in one—in other words, a cunt. And when he and Norman were together it was like the two of them were wrestling for position, but always with a smile on Norman's face. They never went at it openly, but I knew Baldwin hated him with a passion. Norman didn't express hatred for Jimmy, just a kind of ironic sense of the occasion, because Norman occupies a much bigger space in Baldwin's world than Baldwin does in Norman's.

But the same thing affected both of them. It's a disease of our time: the image, the media, becomes your *raison d'être.* If you don't belong in a society that craves winners and losers, you're fucked up somewhere. All of us fight that battle, and it particularly affects you in the theater because theater reaches an enormous public and puts you in the limelight. You're front and center, your face is recognized, whereas if you're an author your name is on a book but who the hell knows who you are?

EDITH BEGNER   When Dandy was just a baby, in the summer of '57, Norman wouldn't let her be vaccinated or have any shots. Jack was furious, and that's when their real differences started.

DR. JACK BEGNER   He was gonna fight it, and I said, "You're not only a menace to yourself, you're a menace to your child. You have no right to do this." He dismissed this by giving me all his holistic medicine stuff about doctors not knowing what they're doing.

EDITH BEGNER   Adele was very upset, and eventually she went and had it done anyway.

DR. JACK BEGNER   What we most often talked about were the fights. I'd seen a lot of matches he'd only heard about, and he hadn't met Roger Donoghue yet, so the two of us got along—at least until I began lecturing him about his drinking, since I thought he was headed for an alcoholic psychosis. That was the beginning of the end. I was too bothered by what he was doing to himself, not to mention his crazy demands. I thought he was nuts in those years, going through several breakdowns.

IRVING HOWE   We decided to do an issue of *Dissent* on New York City, scheduled to come out the summer of '57, and Norman sent us "The White Negro." I was overwhelmed, delighted to have the piece, but I should have fought with him about that one passage—the existential analysis of those hoodlums beating up the storekeeper—which I now think is pretty much nonsense. My concern was intellectual and moral, because that passage was an endorsement of violence.

Would he still defend that sentence about the eighteen-year-olds "daring the unknown" by murdering a fifty-year-old storekeeper? That seems to me crucial. That's where it begins, you see. With Bellow, how well or how badly he behaved with his wife has very little to do with his writing, but with Mailer that passage has everything to do with his life, and it's crazy for him or anyone else to try to make the distinction—I think finally impossible.

JOHN ALDRIDGE He had shown me a draft of the essay in Connecticut, and I really didn't understand how important it was. I suggested that maybe he'd want to go back over the prose, tone it down, cut some of the verbiage, because it seemed to me grossly inflated, which he took in good grace. He had initiated showing it to me and he wanted criticism.

At that time I didn't say anything about the essay's self-reflectiveness. I took that for granted, knowing Norman as I had come to know him, even though he hadn't written anything like this before. Later, when I read the whole of *Advertisements for Myself*, I thought it the best possible thing that could happen—his finally coming to grips with himself as sufferer, victim, alleged failure, et cetera. He was making creative capital of it, making it work for him. I wrote something right after the book came out, saying that in telling us about the extent of his failure and suffering he'd managed to come forth with some of the best prose he'd ever written. I know it took him a while to find a style, but then he found one that later became *the* Norman Mailer.

NORMAN MAILER Writing "The White Negro" emboldened me to raise more questions. In the act of forcing myself to do that piece—and I wrote it with tremendous fear and agitation and great difficulty—I was emboldened later, for instance, to write *Advertisements*. It gave me the courage to make remarks of the order of "I shall attempt to answer the question of"—the oft-quoted sentence in which I list all those things—"murder, suicide, orgy, orgasm, incest," and so forth. My true purpose as a writer, I recognized, might be to tackle questions like that. They were going to be my frontier, and if I had any chance at all of becoming a great writer it was to move in that direction. I was never going to be a greater poet than James Joyce or a greater mystic than Yeats or a greater sociologist than John Dos Passos or a greater stylist than Hemingway. I wasn't going to get near any one of them on their terms. If I wanted to be a great writer—and by then being terribly fortified both by success *and* failure, I absolutely wanted to be a great writer—then I'd found a place where perhaps I could do it. I felt I had perceptions about these matters that I'd never read in anyone else's literature.

JEAN MALAQUAIS "The White Negro," I think, was a forerunner of Norman's Manichean ideas. In time he would become the high priest of a fringe ephemeral constituency, as if he were uttering holy writ. That's why I used the phrase "hip theology" in my reply. I was then in Switzerland, and I wrote Norman directly, not to *Dissent*, and he was the one who had my letter published. What I said was that he bestows on the Negro a messianic mission, that he romanticized the black man. It was a seasonal thing, a romantic extrapolation of what came to be known as the guilt complex among American liberals.

I wondered why Norman was jumping into all this hipster nonsense, and my answer was not very flattering: "hip" and "square" were all over the place, it was *à la mode*, and Norman jumped into it. Aside from the erotic myth—that Negroes are good fuckers—there seems to be a thread running through Norman's life that drives him to be on the first rung, the center of attention. Suppose spinsters go down the street and start singing lewd songs—Norman will be there with a theory. He'll try to blow up the occasion into some momentous event. Why? Because, lacking a proper philosophical background, he aims at building a system of his own. To pick things out of the air and mark them with his own stamp is an especial talent of his. It's instinctive, and he always finds the opportunity.

Perhaps "The White Negro" gave him something topical to latch onto, as *The Deer Park* hadn't fulfilled his expectations. Also, there was this big thing spilling out all over the place—the sit-ins, the blacks who were going to conquer America . . . In Paris—it was 1956—Baldwin had asked me to introduce him to Mailer. A year later, after "The White Negro," Baldwin felt that Norman didn't understand a thing about black people, the argument being "You have to be black to understand them." Well, that's questionable, to say the least.

Looking back, it is difficult to say whether I was worried about him. Temperamentally, I'm not the worrying type. I took his distress as being part of his inner existential chemistry. I didn't think it was anything terminal, but, as I saw it, he could do with a tongue-lashing *à ma manière*, and I knew he'd take it without rancor.

NED POLSKY   Don't forget, *Dissent* had a lot of people who were politically radical but culturally and socially very conservative—staid academic, socialist types—so there was a lot of flak over "The White Negro." The hipster stuff, the violence, they felt was too far out.

I wrote my reply to Norman's piece because I'd known the kinds of people he was talking about, and after it was published Irving Howe called to say Mailer wanted to meet me. Norman likes to know his "enemies," but also he's flattered by attention, and at the time I was doing a lot of work for *Dissent*, so he and I had lunch before an editorial meeting. I'd been a little worried since I'd attacked him, but it was a pleasant meeting, and from time to time thereafter we'd run into each other at the White Horse or at parties.

Part of the White Horse crowd was a crazy guy, part Indian, part Irish, named Harley O'Hara. His father had been a collegiate athlete, and just for kicks he wrote a novel about his childhood in the backwoods of Wisconsin, which became a best seller. I'd known Harley when I was a graduate student. He was fascinated with violence, and once when some guy swiped his girl friend, he went over to their apartment and shot up the place. Luckily no one was home, but there were bullet holes all over, he was arrested, and his father, who was a big shot, spread hundred-dollar bills around to get him released on the condition of psychiatric treatment. But at the time he got friendly with the local cops and decided to make police-training films.

One day in '58 we were sitting around the White Horse, and he announced that his parents, who were away in Europe, had a big estate in Danbury, and we all went up there for the weekend, with booze and a lot of good Algerian hash. I ran into Norman, perhaps in the town of Danbury itself, and invited him over that night since he was living nearby in Bridgewater. Adele and Julien Levy came with him, we were all very stoned, and at one point Harley told Norman that the cops had a particular way of holding a nightstick—taught to them by a World War Two marine judo instructor—so that no one could take it away.

It was already pretty late, we were all drinking and smoking, and Norman didn't believe him. Harley produced a nightstick that one of the cops had given him, and he held it with two hands, six inches from his chin, pushing out. Norman kept coming at him, Harley kept poking at him, clobbering him, and Norman was getting woozier and woozier. It didn't go further than that, though— there was no climax—because then we realized that this other friend there, a guy who'd been lying under a sunlamp totally stoned, had burnt himself, and we had to rush him to the hospital.

It was the same evening I turned Norman on to Ray Charles, whom he'd never really heard before. I played "I Got a Woman," and he just went wild. It surprised me a little since Ray Charles wasn't exactly an unknown in those days.

WILLIAM PHILLIPS   The mood was different then, and while one may have felt he'd gone too far, one accepted it. There was a feeling in the air that fiction writers are allowed anything, so while "The White Negro" was considered intellectually nonacceptable, it was still acceptable for purposes of fictional exploration. It was assumed, as with Lawrence, that the thinking of a man who's wild was interesting, not as a device because that implies he didn't believe what he was saying, whereas I always assumed Mailer believed or half believed all those things about analism, cancer, and God. Those were ideas that he was willing to play with, but play with seriously. In someone else such notions might indicate a *meshugge* personality, but with Mailer, no, not necessarily.

ALLEN GINSBERG   *On the Road* was published in '57, and in '58, when Norman was living on Perry Street, Jack Kerouac was going over to see him, and I went along because I already knew Norman, while Jack and he hadn't met. I'll try to remember details of that meeting; I won't try to characterize it since I don't think characterizations are helpful.

I think Jack was a bit withdrawn and shy, while Norman was friendly, although I had the feeling Norman was very busy and was sort of taking time off for the meeting. They weren't competitive, that wasn't the issue. It was that each of

Gregory Corso, William Burroughs, Allen Ginsberg, and Peter Orlovsky.

them was in a slightly different world. Mailer was out front, in the sense of the public world, Kerouac extremely private and shy. Jack just wanted to be—what?—a French Canadian. But he was very proud of being the greatest writer in America—that's what he thought, which he may well have been. So it was an odd meeting, because Kerouac was respectful. They also had had this mutual girl friend, Adele.

I think Kerouac said something about being a poet, that his prose was really poetry and that he was interested in the novel as a poet might be. They didn't get into any really deep talk about the process of writing itself, which was what I was interested in seeing. *The Village Voice* was somewhat on my mind, and I think I asked Norman what was going on there or why he was out of it.

Whatever, I think Norman loved Kerouac. Although he'd have difficulty showing his love, I think he really liked him and saw him as a great big softie, as a great innocent. I think he felt more hard and sophisticated and worldly, somewhat "I know the business" kind of thing, whereas Kerouac had written in total privacy and solitude, written about fifteen books that weren't published until later, and Kerouac wasn't thinking at all in those terms. He was thinking in Buddhist terms, because by that time he was already sick of the world—not so much of the attention being paid to him, just disappointed in the quality of the attention, realizing it was ashes and viciousness and spite, that nobody was really learning anything, and that America was hardhearted, and that it was going to do itself in, do him in and everybody else. I'm not talking about a man in a state of depression, I'm talking about a saint. It was like exaltation. He already felt beyond hope or fear. He'd already burnt out the world, while perhaps at this time Mailer was just beginning to try and seize the world.

The meeting was also affected by Kerouac's reaction to "The White Negro." I don't mean to be presumptuous, but I thought the essay was very square, and Kerouac thought that Norman was being an intellectual fool. The whole point of On the Road, plus his fifteen or twenty other books, as well as all of Burroughs' writing, all of mine, and everything else going on with the Beat thing had to do with American tenderheartedness. Norman's notion of the hipster as being cool and psychopathic and cutting his way through society with jujitsu was a kind of macho folly that we giggled at. We giggled at it because it's silly and misses the point. In '45 and '46 Burroughs was experimenting with what it was like to be a thief, rolling drunks. In the early forties Burroughs, Kerouac, Herbert Huncke, and I spent a good deal of time in Times Square with the criminal population. In '48 I was busted for being part of a large gang of thieves and was characterized as either the evil Columbia University genius behind this gang or the intellectual dupe, the victim being held captive with drugs.

By '50 Burroughs had already manslaughtered his wife, and before that we had earlier tragedies among our friends—suicides and deaths. So the whole notion of being smarter, more psychotic, beating the world at its own game was no longer of interest. Coolness, reserve of any kind, was the opposite of the sort of warmhearted, open, Dostoevskian Alyosha-Myshkin-Dmitri compassion that Kerouac and I were pursuing. Our figure of fun was Burroughs in the form of W. C. Fields or Old Bull Lee in On the Road.

So Norman's distinction between the hipster and the beatnik was leading the whole situation in the wrong direction. It was just more desensitization. Kerouac had a comment about it in his '58 article called "Origins of the Beat Generation," where he made a distinction between the hot beatnik and cool beatnik; he was saying the cool thing is very charming, sort of like Dostoevsky's Kirillov or Stavrogin, but for art you need a little bit of that hard, gemlike flame. Also, what it would be like in America with people rushing up and confronting each other totally, sincerely, frankly, with open faces and stammering. So the proposition of an image of manhood or hearthood in America as chill, calculating, and jujitsu seemed funny and naïve. Naïve because you're trapped in the world-mind when the whole scene is much vaster and more interesting.

I think Kerouac also felt that anybody who spoke in this area was stealing his thunder, but he wasn't thinking in terms of turf, because turf is all that macho heterosexual bullshit.

Norman was coming out of the straight world, and since I'd first met him in the subterranean scene of Monroe Street, I had a different view of his passage. Despite his naïveté, I thought it was great that he had entered the lists, that he had gotten into the cultural battle. It was a tremendous insight on his part. I wrote a little thing around that time saying that the great thing about Mailer

It was the first poetry reading I ever gave. A lot of people, maybe a hundred. Allen and me, Rexroth, Kerouac, Lamantia, Gary Snyder, Phil Whalen. I'd already met Lamantia and Ginsberg and was associating with Robert Duncan, who was away in Majorca at the time, and I'd been introduced to the poetry of Creeley and Olson.

Looking back, I'd say that the undertext of what we were part of was essentially an environmental movement, although we didn't know it then. People like Gary Snyder, Ginsberg, myself were interested in the mind-as-biology, in consciousness. San Francisco is the center of numerous approaches to nature and biology: whether you go inland to the desert, north to the Sierras, west to the seashore, to Big Sur, it's really all part of nature. And living in San Francisco, while we look somewhat to Paris and New York, as much or more we're looking to China and Japan; we see ourselves as part of the Pacific rim, part of the rim of fire, the volcanic part of the world. We were looking to nature and to the east as the logos, the source. We'd also been reading Pound's *Cantos*, and so when we look to China we can look as easily to ninth-century A.D. China, to the Tang dynasty as well as to the modern China. But it wasn't until the mid-sixties that I realized what we were actually doing—that we were nature/consciousness/mind/biology-oriented.

But I do think that reading at the Six Gallery started the sixties, turned our stance toward politics around. I don't want to give us sole credit, like "Hey, we did it," but that was the moment: we were the literary wing of an environmental movement that has among its various wings the high point of rock 'n' roll in the early and mid-sixties and has at the other end 900,000 people in Central Park speaking out for the nuclear freeze. *Howl* was the trigger. Afterwards none of us could step back and say, "I didn't mean it. It's just too fuckin' frightening out there."

Like Brecht, our poetry was going to have to become part of the culture. People might not see that one poem was responsible for the next twenty years; maybe it's hard for me to see because I'm caught in the middle. But you've got Allen reading *Howl*, you've got the whole group of us, which meant that we all had to take this liberation and assume our stances. Maybe we would have anyway, but it's as if you have a swirl and you drop an enzyme in and it catalyzes a reaction. *Howl* was the trigger. I'm sure Norman wrote his "Ode to Allen Ginsberg" because of that. The second part goes:

> I sometimes think
> That little Jew bastard
> That queer ugly kike
> Is the bravest man
> In America.

That's good, because I think Allen standing up there reading—putting himself on the line—was one of two of the bravest things I've ever seen. Remember, it was '55. People had crew cuts, and they looked at you like you were misplaced cannon fodder. The country was being run by Luce publications. It was a dangerous, cold, ugly time, and it was scary.

ALLEN GINSBERG   I'm basically a coward, and my behavior has been dictated by the path of least resistance. Mailer's poem, his interpretation—"You're one of the most courageous people I've met"—comes from naïveté. I'm flattered—it's friendly and very tender and very sweet—but I suppose he calls me a "queer ugly kike" because he thinks that it's such a big deal to say someone's queer. Which is extremely naïve.

BARBARA PROBST SOLOMON   People like James Baldwin were saying, in effect, "Come on, Norman, you Harvard Jewish baby, you heterosexual, you ain't out in the big world of experience. We got something you ain't got—we know about crime, about being black, about being poor, about being homosexual." But Norman is also very shrewd. He knows when he's on the wrong train. It wasn't easy to get caught short being a leftover Dreiser or Dos Passos—which is what he'd set himself up as—so when he looked over his shoulder and there was the Beat Generation, he knew he had to do something to compete.

He wasn't seeing many of his Harvard friends then, and of course too he was drinking heavily. The academics weren't yet enthralled with him, and I remember he once advised Diana Trilling to go to porno films for the sexual turn-on. She said to him, "Norman, at my age there is no sexual turn-on." He got flustered, he was that embarrassed.

DIANA TRILLING   I met Norman at a dinner party at Lillian Hellman's. Steven and Gene Marcus were with Lionel and me, and Norman and Midge Podhoretz were there as well. In fact that was Podhoretz's first meeting with Mailer too. Was that 1957 or early '58? It suddenly occurs to me that everything went very fast. We all got to know each other so quickly.

Anyway, it was a big dinner party. I was seated at Norman's left, and on the other side of him was Constance Askew, the wife of Kirk Askew, an art dealer. She was a big dowagerlike lady with an ear trumpet—or that's the way I remember it—a bit forbidding, and I was enormously taken with Norman's behavior because he was so mannerly. He gave her his full attention. I was used to literary people who didn't spend five seconds speaking to anyone who wasn't recommended to them by their public achievement. But Norman wasn't only correct by traditional social standards, he was even courtly. Then, when we'd got through the first half of dinner, almost as if he'd been given a signal at a Cambridge dinner party, he turned to me on his left and said, "Now, what about you, smart cunt?"

Ordinarily I'd have frozen out anyone who took that line with me: "You respectable lady, I'll see if I can shock you." But with Norman I burst out laughing. It was such a challenging greeting, so boldly flirtatious, it was so outrageous and funny applied to me and coming right after this beautiful display of manners with Mrs. Askew, talking into her putative ear trumpet. The contrast was wonderful, and we were friends at once. I thought of him coming out of his Village world—the drugginess, all that hyped-up life—and sitting at a dinner party between two such Establishment figures as Mrs. Askew and me. It could've put him under a strain, but it didn't seem to at all. He was very much in charge of himself, and he had his own style for handling the situation. I admired this. He was challenging the Establishment, the different kind of culture I came out of, and it must've interested him that I burst out laughing.

Either that same evening or on another occasion at Lillian's, Glenway Wescott and I were talking and Norman came over to sit next to me. We got into one of those who-could-outstare-the-other games, the eyeball competition, and Glenway put a dollar on me. We were about to start, and I asked, "Does smiling count?" Norman leaned over and took the money. "That's cheating," I said. "The game hasn't started."

"The game started and it's already finished."

I was very annoyed and I said, "You're a cheat. This isn't honest." But he didn't give in. He insisted on what he thought were the literal terms of the agreement, but they weren't the terms to which I'd agreed, but Norman didn't care about that.

If we gave Norman some kind of legitimacy in the midst of all his *meshugas*,

Diana and Lionel Trilling, and son, Jim, 1958: "The New York intellectual group thought Mailer was incredibly smart, and so did Trilling too. And Diana even more so, meshuggeh *but brilliant."*

it's no more than we did for a lot of other people as well. I'm talking now about Lionel and me. Cultures change, tides turn, and Lionel no longer stands for what he then did, but in the period that we're talking about he represented a kind of consciousness of his time, or maybe I should say a kind of conscience of his time. He was the father figure to end all father figures. Whether it was Allen Ginsberg or others, they all came to our house to collapse, to go crazy, to say they weren't crazy. Lionel was Big Papa; and if you're married to the Big Father, you're the Big Mother. If someone could win my friendship and respect, then he got some of the paternal blessing, if only at second hand. That was true for so many younger people we knew—but it was Lionel, not I, who was the important figure for them. I was sort of dragged along in his wake. That wasn't true of our relation with Norman, though. I was the primary person. Norman wasn't primarily drawn to Lionel. I wasn't the path to Lionel, nor, on the other hand, was he interested in diminishing Lionel, but I think he liked being in relation to us as conscience figures of the time. Not Village figures, not pot figures, but sobersides. Norman always cared about this particular corner of the universe, what I call the superego corner—responsibility, values, conscience.

He came to our house frequently, and Lionel always enjoyed seeing him but never made any move toward having a friendship. It was I who mapped the friendship. Norman knew this as well as I did. I think he had regard for Lionel. He was perhaps a little frightened of him—Lionel's manner was so deceptive, so quiet and sort of gentle. He knew Lionel was awfully smart, and I had the impression that he was always a little on guard with him. When he came to our house he behaved beautifully. Never, never did he misbehave. There was none of this stuff I used to hear about—the fighting and insulting people.

MIDGE DECTER   "The White Negro" had been published the summer before, and it was November or December of '57, the party at Lillian Hellman's, when Norman P. said to him, "I'm working on an essay about you right now." Mailer said, "I'll bet you ten dollars I can tell you what you're going to say." Norman P. said, "I'll bet you ten dollars you can't." That was the beginning of their relationship.

Mailer was not in the least bizarre. He was dressed properly in a suit, because you didn't come dressed bizarrely to a Lillian Hellman party. He came with Adele, who was, of course, the most noticeable woman there.

I couldn't say whether he was drinking heavily, since we all drank heavily in those days, but he wasn't truculent. He was Mailer. He has a way of looking at you and being extremely curious, making enormous demands on you. You hardly know him and he's already somehow exerting the demand that you be better than you are, braver or tougher or one thing or another. He's one of the few novelists—and by now I've known many novelists—who is, not only at his typewriter but also in his being, genuinely open and curious about everybody around him. It's a quality novelists are supposed to have—I know almost none who have it. If you're an insurance salesman from Sacramento, Mailer's just as interested in you as he would be in a literary critic. There's always that curiosity—

who you are, what you're like, what you're good for, and how good you actually may be.

In any event, I didn't talk to him that much, but I still have a vivid impression of him at that party—which was a big party. I was tremendously impressed with his presence, his energy, and openness to everybody in the room. He and Norman P. got on very well. They'd been having this conversation about their bet—a bet that Mailer was eventually to lose—and we left the party feeling that we'd see him again.

He and Adele then moved back to the city, we went to their apartment on Perry Street, and the relationship between the two Normans accelerated very quickly. Mailer would call, the two of them would go for walks—that kind of thing. With me it was a little different. The only way I can put it is that he was always making demands on you—"You have to be your best"—which always made me slightly tense. He was making me anxious in other ways too, like looking you in the eye and saying, "You know who you are? You're really a general, a lieutenant." He was always translating you into something, perhaps as a form of parlor games, but as Willie Morris used to say, "He was really writin' all the time." The demand was real. He made it on himself too, so it wasn't as if he was picking on you, but it was a kind of contest, not so very different from the thumb-wrestling games he'd play.

But he never engaged in any of this with Norman P. That wasn't their style. When it was the two of them, they'd discuss ideas. They argued about "The White Negro" and hipsters. Mailer was committed to that stuff, Norman P. was against it but still took it seriously, and that was the point: he didn't dismiss it. He didn't say, "Oh, come on, this is a lot of tired old bullshit." Which is really what people had said about *Barbary Shore*, like Will Barrett, who reviewed the book and said, "Oh, ho-hum, now Mailer's taking up this stuff." It was none of that. Podhoretz was saying, "I'm against this, this is bad news," and Mailer was saying, "No, you don't understand." The two of them would go back and forth. The relationship developed, each of them taking the other seriously.

NORMAN PODHORETZ   Norman and I just hit it off and saw each other several times within weeks of that first meeting. I remember going around the Village one night with him and Adele and perhaps his sister Barbara too. It was thick from the beginning, and fundamentally, like all friendships, it was based on sympathy. Part of it was Brooklyn. I've long believed that people from Brooklyn single each other out in later life because Brooklyn is a real place, a real culture, and there is something about growing up there that has a lasting effect.

Beyond this, I admired and was intrigued by Mailer, though I think I came as a surprise to him. I wasn't at all sure what he expected from having read my work, but of all the people in the so-called literary world, or, to use Terry Southern's term, "the quality lit biz," I think he found me the most simpatico. This was a difficult time for Norman, culminating in the stabbing of course, and in fact he once called me a "foul-weather friend," which is a clever observation, since I was always a better friend to him when he was in trouble than when he was up. I was fascinated by him, by his life and work, but not his craziness, and fortunately very little of that was ever directed toward me. Why, I'm not sure. He was always very careful around me, which was just as well, because I wouldn't have tolerated any of that shit from him. I suppose he knew that. Whether he was monitoring himself, though, I can't say.

The friendship was relaxed, not competitive. I could never take most of the people in his entourage, his court, and there was never any of the arm-wrestling stuff when the two of us would go to bars, for example. I also didn't like the drugs. I was a heavy drinker in those days, but Norman was always trying to turn me on to pot. I'd actually smoked marijuana when I was a kid, never liked it, and I thought the mystique of pot in the late fifties was simply silly. I remember one night at a party at Mailer's when the whole crew was solemnly, almost religiously passing around a joint, and somebody just threw up all over the place. On the other hand, I found it interesting that a guy with Mailer's gifts was caught up in that kind of foolishness. From the beginning I had made a distinction between Norman and Allen Ginsberg, and certainly Kerouac. I thought Mailer was better, more intelligent and more serious, more critical of both his own ideas and prevailing cultural tendencies, and to the extent that he slid into all that stuff, I found it a disappointment.

In any case, if it sometimes got to be difficult to see him without his gang, I just wouldn't see him. We were drinking buddies, we confided in each other, and we read each other's writing. He often read things to me because he liked reading aloud, and once, in '59 or '60, I remember he spent a few hours at our house reading to Midge and me what was supposed to be the beginning of a big novel—it was never published—that began with him before conception, as a seed.

The night we first met at Lillian's I was already working on my essay about him, the *Partisan Review* piece. I had always thought more highly of him than most of the serious literary world did, and at the time I was planning a book on postwar American fiction, which was going to be framed by my essay on Mailer and another I later wrote on Bellow—a book I never managed to finish.

By the time I'd finished the piece on him, though, Norman and I had become good friends, and I remember showing it to him—he was living on Perry Street in the Village then. He was pleased with it and happy that it would be coming out in *Partisan Review*. What he may not have realized, though, was that the editors of *PR*, Philip Rahv and William Phillips, were reluctant to publish it because they felt I was overrating him. They thought Mailer was merely a middlebrow—a term used a lot in those days—who wasn't in the same league as Faulkner, Hemingway, or Fitzgerald. Rahv in particular argued with me, and he was surly about publishing the piece. But as a young critic they wanted to encourage, I had a special clout. Otherwise I doubt they would have published so respectful a piece about Mailer. They certainly wouldn't have published it if it had just come in over the transom.

Most of my literary friends, not all, but most, were equally skeptical about Mailer. But I think the Trillings, Lionel and also Diana, appreciated the essay.

I don't want to make claims that aren't justified or to claim a larger role for myself than I really had, but while I'm vague about it, my memory is that if I wasn't exactly a go-between, I was sort of Mailer's sponsor, not only with the Trillings but others who had given me a hard time about him, people like Jason Epstein.

The Trillings, however, liked him very much and were sort of fascinated by his "wickedness." Norman, though, was very much on his good behavior with them. He was charming, especially with Diana. I think in the end she was much more interested in him and his work than Lionel ever was.

Another thing. I remember Norman practicing his accents, making a project of himself. I considered that side of him foolish and inferior, yet I was always surprised by how little damage it did to his writing. I used to say this in defending him to friends of mine who didn't have sympathy for him. I insisted he was someone who had to go his own way, because there was no persuading him or forcing him to learn from anybody else's mistakes or experience. He was absolutely determined to do it all for himself, invent the world anew, which I thought was admirable and courageous. How does he put it—"Don't understand me too quickly"? Well, I was careful not to judge him too quickly, because while there was a lot of nonsense involved, my feeling was that his antics might turn out to be not so silly or crazy after all.

From his point of view I was part of the so-called literary Establishment, the youngest member, I suppose the *Wunderkind*, and I was having some influence on my elders in pushing them to the left both culturally and politically; and Mailer, obviously, was part of that too, which made us allies. Beyond this, as a critic I felt a certain proprietary interest in Mailer. Norman was my tiger. I had a stake in the work he was doing not only as a critic but as a contemporary, in the sense that he was acting out in public the radical mode I believed in then.

WILLIAM PHILLIPS   Rahv and I had reservations about Podhoretz's essay, but the situation was complicated by the fact that Rahv didn't like anybody praised too much. Still, I don't believe Podhoretz's claim that we'd never have published the piece if he hadn't been Lionel Trilling's protégé. We asked for changes, but we always asked for changes; the particular changes were necessary to mute his praise for Norman.

During those years, '58 to '64, the relationship between Mailer and Podhoretz didn't surprise me, partly because back then Norman Podhoretz wasn't the Norman Podhoretz you see today. He was much more bohemian. Between the two of them there was a rapport in interests and in their interest in experience— Podhoretz had interesting experiences and Mailer had consummate experiences—plus the fact that Mailer represented a grand talent. You could never pin him down. There were pulls and drives towards all kinds of fixations, all kinds of psychological theories. As with Lawrence, one was slightly aware that he was interested in all kinds of psychological and morbid kinds of experience, the Reichian stuff, and to some extent this made up the richness of his mind, its complexity and contradictions. Talking with Mailer was never as simple and easy as talking with Steven Marcus or Lionel Trilling, say, because you never knew what direction he'd take, and I don't mean in a skitterish way, but probing different depths, exploring different directions.

IRVING HOWE He was moving away. He'd lost interest in *Dissent*, but we maintained an amiable distance. He'd invite me to a party twice a year, we'd meet once or twice at the Trillings'. Then we'd meet once a summer on the Cape—sort of ritualistic occasions, like remembering to see your aunt. But intellectually there was really no longer a strong connection between us.

I wouldn't know about his increased drinking, but he may have had a development uphill, downhill, both ways. With people like me and Trilling, though, he kept the skill to present his Howe face, his Trilling face. The day before seeing either of us he might have been on a terrible drunk, and he might repeat it the day after, but when he came to us he was able to show himself just as he wanted to—suit, tie, vest, the whole stylized deal straight from Oxford.

It was clear to me the distance was growing between where I was and where he was going—I'm not sure I knew where he was going—but let's say between what category I fitted into—rationalist, liberal socialist—and what I saw in Norman, namely, Emerson. And I don't know if he realized this, just how much Emerson was in him—simply the deification of self, the celebrator of self. There were elements of Rimbaud and Verlaine too, and of course I can now see why he was fascinated by Malraux. The energy, the adventure.

He spoke with a certain impatience, a mild contempt of the tradition of which Trilling and I were part. I remember he kept talking about breaking the last barrier of sexual inhibition. I've never known what the last barrier is, but he used a phrase like that, and I kept thinking, What the hell do you do afterwards? That was the problem, you see. From simulated shock you have to go to real shock, and there was a sense that this could only lead to some kind of explosion, the particular nature of which we couldn't say.

WALTER MINTON I don't know whether Norman pushed at Adele the way he later did with Beverly, but Peter Israel told me a story. In '58 or thereabouts we had a party up here in Saddle River for a lot of publishing people, and afterwards Peter and his then wife Nancy didn't have a ride back to the city, so they went with Norman. Norman got caught behind a slow-moving car in the Lincoln Tunnel, and Adele told him to pass anyway, yelling, "You're chicken, you're scared. You're always telling me not to be afraid. Now you're scared!" So Norman goes out and around. *Zoom!* I guess the on-coming truck gave way or something. Peter said he was petrified. She was goading him, and I've always thought of that story when I think of what happened a few years later. I can almost see her—I swear to God—whatever happened, whatever brought that on, saying, "You haven't got the guts."

I think a good part of what happened was that he was unwilling or unable to write. Norman was, is, and always will be primarily a novelist. But he was in a position where he wasn't making a living. Whatever source of income he had from his investments dried up. *The Deer Park* wasn't the success either he or I expected it to be, and he was sort of left in limbo. He didn't get the readership and therefore didn't write, maybe because he wasn't sure of himself. It all tied together, and what happened had an awful lot to do with money.

Norman is one of those writers who has to write about himself, not in the sense of ego but in the sense that he is either unable or unwilling to write about anything he hasn't personally experienced. Now, during this period he was drinking pretty good. He held his booze better than most, but he was also getting involved in the fight thing and was also into pot. The fact that one cannot or will not write about anything one hasn't experienced can lead you into a lot of problems. Like where does it end? My father used to define a gentleman as someone who may make a few mistakes but doesn't marry them. Norman marries them, maybe because he has to. The same with his books. He's never written anything that he hasn't investigated, known, and experienced, so during this period he initiated a very conscious search for experience. He got himself into situations and took outrageous positions for the sheer joy, the test, of getting himself out of them.

JULES FEIFFER   I suppose it was a special time, because we were moving out of the period of Eisenhower suppression. Mailer was earlier than anybody to pick up advance notes on what was coming—he clearly foresaw the sixties, though I don't remember him talking about it at great length. What I do remember from him at parties were short bursts, little short takes, observations, many of which thoroughly confused me. I had no trouble with "The White Negro," say, but in social conversation the connections seemed to be missing.

Norman Podhoretz was very much around Mailer, he had a clear crush on him, and he also played a very important role for Mailer in terms of the literary community; he legitimized him, made him okay to the *Partisan Review* crowd because Mailer was the outlaw. Podhoretz had his credentials as a Trillingite, and then, of course, he wrote about Mailer and was one of the first to do so. Remember, in the fifties and even early sixties novelists were thought of as very important people. This died out in the seventies, but back then one still thought of Hemingway and Fitzgerald and Sinclair Lewis as having incredible stature, and Mailer was one of two or three Americans clearly destined to follow in their footsteps. And one treated him that way. He was also one of the few novelists who had a political philosophy, who was an original and radical political thinker. There was Paul Goodman and perhaps Norman O. Brown, but these guys weren't novelists, and even if you counted them, there just weren't that many others who were taking a radical stance.

Why was there such an intense social life? Primarily, I think, because the people in that group, which later became known as the New York literary Establishment, were all pretty much in the business of putting themselves on the map. As individuals they were fiercely competitive, energetic, ambitious, many of whom liked each other and turned each other on. Take George Plimpton. It seemed there was something going on at his house almost every week.

You never got a sense of George arranging things or hosting, although he did introduce people and you thought of these functions as *Paris Review* or Plimpton parties. There was always a very expensive buffet, tall, beautiful girls—East Side models—and then there'd be Mailer, Styron, Bruce Jay Friedman, Philip Roth, plus people like Bob Silvers, Jason Epstein, John Marquand, Donald Ogden Stewart, Terry Southern, as well as Doc Humes. There may have been official guests of honor, but who remembers?

ROGER DONOGHUE   I first met him in '58 at Danny Stradello's restaurant on the East Side, at a celebrity-type operation where there was a party going on for a new Dean Martin movie. Norman was at the bar, and at one point I said, "Oh, yeah, you're the fella who wrote *The Deer Park*." He was with Mickey Knox, and later on I had dinner with him and Adele in the Village, and we started palling around together, going to the fights.

Norman's interest in boxing really got going with me, 'cause I was giving him lessons and we sparred a lot. I taught him my way, which was more facing sideways. Later my influence went out the window when he took up Torres' "peek-a-boo" style, which Jose got from Cus D'Amato. He was a good amateur. Like Hemingway and Schulberg, it was part of that macho thing, writers liking to be with fighters, fighters liking to be with writers. One day I saw Schulberg and his nose was all over his face. He said, "I'm not gonna spar any more with that black kid from Trenton." Budd backed off after that, but the problem with Norman was that while he'd box intelligently, he'd get aggressive, get out of hand when he was drunk.

Norman likes tough guys, like Jimmy Reardon, the ex-NYC cop who took the fall with Harry Gross, the gambler, in the early fifties. One time he was helping Reardon with a book he was writing, took a night off to read 300 pages, and every time he'd make a comment Reardon would interrupt and say, "But, Norman, later on it does so and so." I kept kicking him—"You dumb Irish son of a bitch, listen to this man. You're gettin' a million dollars' worth of advice, just keep your fuckin' mouth shut." But he couldn't. Reardon *is* a tough guy, he *has* stood up, but he's got all this ego shit too. He and Norman have the same bravado—one kosher, the other pig-shit Irish. It's all the same.

EDITH BEGNER   Norman gave me a hard time once that summer of '58. I suppose he was doing it to most women he knew, mistaking those times when you wanted to talk for a sexual pass. He kept drinking heavier and heavier, and I kept refusing, and he got sullen and insulting. It went on for hours. I kept saying, "You'd better go now," but he kept trying to convince me that I shouldn't refuse because of Jack. He and Eldred and the others thought that I'd come up to P-Town alone to have affairs. Basically, what angered him was the turndown. He told Eldred and the gang that I was a cocktease, that I'd provoked him and then turned him down. The rest of the summer they called me Saint Edith.

SEYMOUR KRIM   I was driving up to Provincetown with Nancy Macdonald, Dwight's ex-wife, early in the summer of '58, and we stopped for gas on the

Cape, and there was Norman, alone, in his Triumph. Nancy introduced us, and then a few days later he and I and Nancy had dinner in P-Town. That first night I remember he said he couldn't get started on a new book unless he had a good fistfight. This was meant seriously, and it scared me because he had this taunting look in his eye, and little old Seymour didn't want to get into it with this wild man. He was snorting and weaving when we got up from the table, there was no real communication, so for me it was an unsatisfactory meeting. I never had any more difficulties after that, although Chandler Brossard, a close buddy of mine at the time, told me that once when he was visiting Norman at his house in Connecticut, Norman asked him to step into the backyard and fight barefisted. Chandler had a violent streak equal to Norman's, but he felt Norman was naïve, unaware that you can break your hands doing it barefisted, so he declined the offer of Normie the Hun.

In the summer of '59 I was back up in P-Town as an editor of the *Provincetown Review*, staying with Bill Ward and Harriet Sohmers, and somewhere around that time I made up my mind to put together a collection of my essays—*Views of a Nearsighted Cannoneer*—which Norman gladly agreed to do the introduction to.

That summer I got to know him. He enjoyed hanging out with the Washington (D.C.) beatniks—Bill Walker, Lester Blackiston, Dick Dabney—and those guys would be arm-wrestling all the time, jumping on each other's backs at parties—all that summer-camp horseshit—and I couldn't see the point of Norman, this brilliant intellect, fooling around with them as if everyone was thirteen. But I underestimated his locker-room macho.

I remember he was going over the galleys of *Advertisements for Myself* that summer, and one night he invited me up to the house he rented on the hill, the Hawthorne house, to see some old black-and-white dirty movies. We were about halfway through when the projector broke, and he got so frustrated he began to make a big meal for all of us—chop suey, all in one huge pot! I didn't realize he'd been a cook in the army, but he was throwing everything into this stew—roast beef, vegetables, chop suey—an improvised mélange of crud, which I took as some kind of metaphor. I found it uneatable, he found it fine, so the thing that struck me was he had a cast-iron stomach, much tougher than mine and in some ways less discriminating. Like his point of view—he's capable of great nuances, subtleties, remarkable and immediate understandings, while on the other side there's his bluntness, a rawness and even grossness on occasion—and I found all this in the meal which I couldn't eat but which he consumed with relish. What was interesting too was just how certain he was that he'd created some small culinary masterpiece. Talk about confidence!

But Adele was a pisser then. An attractive, flirty girl, playing games with an insistence I've not usually seen. She chased me around the room with scissors, trying to cut off a tie my sister had sent me from Italy. I didn't find this amusing, so I kept saying, "Come on, Adele, stop it or I'm gonna get sore." Finally Norman told her to stop. There was a perversity there, not necessarily sexually, though more than once I had the thought that Norman may have been pushing her into all kinds of bizarre shit. By "perverse" what I mean was her attitude toward life, her ways of getting attention. Like chasing me with scissors or getting into a hair-pulling, wrestling match with Harriet Sohmers, as she did the following summer.

During this period, though, Norman didn't strike me as being out of control. Myself, I was quite in control then, since I'd flipped in '55, paid my dues, and was very much together. It's funny, when Norman wrote the introduction for my collection he didn't read my essay about flipping out; I thought he had, but a half dozen years after the stabbing he said he'd only then read it. "So you went all the way with this?" he asked, like a younger brother. It made an impression on him and may have led to his being more relaxed about talking about his own crack-up. With me he switched from a philosophical defense of his behavior—the cancer metaphor—to a more human approach.

HENRY GELDZAHLER   I took a place at the Waterfront, where Norman was either living or had a room for writing, and we'd have a drink sometimes, just stop and chat. Everyone used to hang out at the bar at the Old Colony, and Norman had a kind of protective feeling about me, a little paternalistic, somehow a little bit sibling. I was a graduate student at Harvard, very impressed and accepting, very loving, but I also knew there were some elements of bullshit. Still, this was pre-gay lib, and while we never discussed it, I made clear that this was the case, and he threw protection around me. Maybe I was instinctively asking for it, but he would signal people who entered our circle at the bar that this guy, meaning me, wasn't territory.

He also talked about how I ought to learn to defend myself in fights. We were standing at the bar one night and he says, "Now, if someone comes up to you and is very rude, the first thing you should do is take your drink and throw it in the guy's eyes." I said, "Norman, first of all, I drink water, so it would just be refreshing. Second of all, the only person I have to protect myself from is you!" He roared with laughter. He always loved that story and told it for years. It was a popular party piece after that.

I remember he and Adele had a big house up on Miller Hill Road both summers, '59 and '60. I used to go to parties up there, and it was extremely sticky. You had the feeling that when the two of them were together you had to choose sides, which I had no intention of doing.

Part of our relationship, though, was that he liked my *chutzpah*. For example, we were in the Old Colony and a woman came up to him and said, "Oh, Mr. Mailer, it's such a pleasure to meet you, I've heard so much about you and your books." He said, "Thank you very much." After she left I asked him, "Did you hear what she said?" He said, "Yeah, that she'd heard so much about me and she loves my books." "No," I said, "she hasn't read your books. She's just *heard* about them." And we both cracked up. Here I was, twenty-two or something, pointing out to him that he'd changed the story to his benefit and that the woman had actually been an asshole. He loved it.

He was very generous to me when I took the job at the Met. Before I went to New York the next year he told a lot of people about me—like Jean Vanden

Heuvel, Dru Heinz, and Dwight Macdonald. It was like he was a PR flack for me, telling people that there was this guy coming from Harvard, he's bright, you'll like him, which really did a lot of ground-breaking for me. Part of it was having a common Yiddish intellectual connection. For example, he had been writing an essay about Picasso, and he wanted me to look at it, to read it, even though I was just a graduate student. The essay I saw was about 100 pages, much longer than the way it appeared in the *Provincetown Review* or in *Cannibals and Christians*, which came out later. But after reading it I looked him in the eye and said, "You know a lot about a lot of stuff, but you don't know much about this." I thought he was going to get furious, but he didn't. He just went ahead and published it anyway.

WALTER MINTON   I never edited Norman; I'd be surprised if he allowed anyone to edit his work. We had only one editorial discussion about *Advertisements for Myself*—specifically, that I didn't think he should include the play version of *The Deer Park*. I tried to talk him out of it and I couldn't.

You hear of writers and editors, or writers and publishers, having great personal relationships. I'm sure they exist, but I myself have never really gotten involved. My father worked with Maxwell Perkins for twenty-four years. After he read the book *Editor to Author* he told me, "I think somebody had to go through every letter Perkins wrote to find these, because this isn't what he did at all." Perkins' classic line was "This is great, give me more." And he said it to the right people. So I know Norman's work, I dealt with him. But I wasn't that involved with writers. Part of it was me, my personality, and part of it was my idea of publishing.

What I remember was that we discussed the jacket photograph. Norman had a thing about what kind of picture of himself ought to appear, and the one he wanted to use for *Advertisements* had him in a sailor's hat, which I thought was ridiculous. He had three or four others showing him in different stages of growth for the back cover, but this one was for the front and it was all wrong. We argued. He prevailed.

Originally, when he'd come in with the idea for *Advertisements*, though, our response was, "How much do you want?" and we gave him $10,000. No one at Putnam's thought it was an unseemly book, and I guess if I had any negative thoughts about it, my feeling was why spend six months to a year putting together a collection when he could be writing another novel? Norman, though, saw *Advertisements* as more eccentric, more *outré* than it actually was. Commercially the book proved to be pretty much of a bomb.

NORMAN MAILER   The idea for *Advertisements* had been growing all the time. On the one hand I wanted to do a serious work, "The Psychology of the Orgy," but I'm making it too simple by saying that "The White Negro" was fructifying for such projects; it had also been desperate. Because if the essay hadn't worked, I would've been in a lot of trouble. The big books I wanted to write at that point in my life—there was never any point in my life when I wanted to write larger books—just weren't coming. One of the reasons was I was so spaced out on pot that I was getting visions of great works at night but by morning would find only fragments, scratchings on pieces of paper. It was like I burned out my brain in those years, let's say from '54 or '55 through '60. Of course, the stabbing took place after that, but still, I think probably by the time of "Superman Comes to the Supermarket" I had begun to make a certain peace with what one can accomplish. In other words, give up the large dream, and then you will do an awful lot. I've never been psychoanalyzed, but that's what psychoanalysts apparently manage to do with their successful patients. They're saying, "Give up the largest dream and I will help you make something of yourself."

There wasn't any model for *Advertisements*. I just kept finding it. I'd started off with the idea of a collection of stories and articles but discovered that my collection would have no meaning unless I threw in a lot of the worst pieces. Because where I had failed often offered the most interesting revelations. Unconsciously I was trying to take inventory. I was trying also to end a certain part of my literary life and begin anew. I wanted to declare myself, put myself on stage firmly and forever.

I'd assumed the book wouldn't be very commercial, and it wasn't, although it sold 9000 copies hard-cover and went into paperback. Walter Minton got his money back and more. But when I proposed it, I think Walter said to himself in his usual fashion, "God, Norman really gives you some lalapaloozas. What the hell am I gonna do with this?" I suppose he was going to indulge me, he was my good publisher. Then I think he was bewildered when people really liked it afterward, when it became a fairly important title. Occasionally a critical piece would pass his desk, talking about this serious book, and he'd just shake his head and say to himself, "They're all nuts, they don't know what a good book is. A good book *sells!*"

Again, though, I didn't have to think about *Advertisements* commercially. Cy was making money for me on the stock market, enough so that I think we really lived on the investments. I didn't have to worry about money. I never did, not until the late sixties. I had a charmed economic life for the first half of my literary career.

ALFRED KAZIN   As a literary historian I've been fascinated by the prima donnas among American novelists. Mark Twain put himself forward, and he was the first novelist to see the way modern literature sells in this country. But what I'm talking about is something else. The super egotist. Styron, Mailer, and Baldwin fit that category, and I think Mailer was the worst of the lot. I know the history of Fitzgerald, who went crazy trying to keep up—his drinking, his crazy wife. Also Hemingway. And I followed Bellow through four marriages. But I've never known anyone whose career was always in public and who constantly put himself forward the way movie people do so much as Mailer.

ADELE MORALES MAILER   Mickey told us that when he was in Paris he had the worst fight with Styron and Jim Jones, practically a fistfight. This was after

Advertisements where Norman criticizes everyone—the essay called "Quick and Expensive Comments on the Talent in the Room." The two of them had Norman's article out and were going over it, screaming with laughter, then getting angrier and angrier. Jones was in an absolute rage—"That son of a bitch, how could he do this to me?" Norman had gone public, put down three other writers in one fell swoop.

GLORIA JONES Jesus, that essay was enough to make you mad at him forever, 'cause not only did Norman publicly accuse Jim of being the biggest sellout, it just wasn't true, and so Jim was deeply hurt and angry.

One way Jim had of dealing with this was that he would have people sign the book and write marginalia. Someone would visit, and Jim would read the part about that person, and then they'd get mad and sign the book, write comments in the margin. We had a large bookshelf near the dining room table, and Jim kept the book where he could reach it, and eventually I think we had comments from everyone except Kerouac. Some of the comments were long, but sometimes they'd just write, "Fuck you," or "Up yours," because we might be drunk at that point. By the end Jim was reading not only Norman but what the writers had written in the margins, which was part of the fun. This went on until '74, when we left Paris. It might have taken that many years for everybody whom Norman had written about to come through. But Jim didn't pull it out with people who weren't mentioned. The fun was the people who were in the book.

This aside, there was an incredible camaraderie among these guys despite their fights. Bill would give money to Jimmy Baldwin if he needed it, and I think Bill would even have gone to Norman's side if something happened. There was that kind of closeness because these guys were very special and understood they were smarter than most people, plus they knew that as novelists they were the best around. They saw themselves as part of the same very special club, a club that you had to be real good to get into. They were mean and used to laugh like hell at certain people, and laugh about each other too—I've heard stories about Bill Styron and Norman reading Jim's *Some Came Running* and making fun of it, somebody told Jim, and he was hurt and mad about that— but still there was that bond. There was that sense of "us against them." For example, once our servant got really drunk (two days later he was picked up and put in the slammer as a jewel thief). But that night at our house Jimmy Baldwin, Nelson Algren, Bill Styron, and the servant, a bearded Indian, all got very drunk, and the servant said to Jim, "And I don't like your writing, sir." And Jim said, "Who do you like, C. P. Fucking Snow?" And after that they'd all laugh about "C. P. Fucking Snow." That kind of person they'd make fun of. C. P. Snow wasn't in the club. He was an outsider.

MICKEY KNOX Gloria Jones is now friendly about Norman, but when *Advertisements* came out she was just as furious as Jim. Oh boy, and how, and I suppose mainly because Jim himself was so upset about it, even more than Styron. I'd see him in Paris and he'd go on and on about it. They'd already been drifting apart—I suppose the Styron feud helped it along—but Jim kept saying, "The printed word! He printed it!" He never spoke about getting even, he was just hurt. He felt betrayed and also that the break was now for eternity because it was published.

I know that in the earlier years Norman felt his friendship with Jones was important, and Jim was very loving to Norman. He genuinely loved him. He was so deeply hurt not only because of what Norman had written but because he'd lost the friendship, and friendship in general was something very important to him. That's one of the reasons he and I remained friends despite the fact that I was still a close friend of Norman's.

Later I arranged to bring the two of them together, at Norman's insistence. Norman was in Paris and wanted to see Jim, and he asked me where he could meet him. I was leery about it, but he insisted, "No, you gotta do this for me." So I took him to a private club on the Left Bank where I knew Jim and Gloria might be. They were sitting at the bar, but even though they saw each other, there was no contact. Neither of them could go over and say "Hey..."

Jim continued to say things to me about Norman. He'd haul out that damned essay, all marked up, and it came to a head one memorable night in Jim's house. Bill and Rose Styron, Jimmy Baldwin, and I all gathered around Jim's famous bar, which was an old, antique altar, and I became the surrogate because Norman wasn't there. "Look," I said, "I didn't write it. It's between you guys and Norman." Jim finally said, "It's gotta be him or me." Styron and Baldwin jumped in and Jim ran and got his famous copy of *Advertisements*, saying, "Lemme read you what he wrote about my good friend Billy!" And he read, "Bill Styron wrote the prettiest novel of our generation, *Lie Down in Darkness*." He kept repeating it over and over, gleefully. Bill started twitching, getting very nervous and unhappy, and finally he asked Jim to stop. It went on till four or five in the morning. We ended up at Les Halles, but the night was a disaster.

Irwin Shaw was another one who'd pull the same thing with me, probably because he was such a close friend of Jim's. I resented them all, and nowadays Gore Vidal too. Nobody's going to get me to say Norm's a shit. What do they want from me? They have a problem, they can go to Norman direct.

<hr>

GEORGE PLIMPTON One of the great disappointments was when Hemingway came to New York and I tried to get the two of them together. Hemingway had an apartment opposite the Knickerbocker Club on Sixty-second and Fifth, and a group of us gathered there one evening before going out to dinner—A. E. Hotchner, Miss Mary, one of the Hearsts, George Brown, Antonio Ordonez, the bullfighter, and a beautiful girl I had brought named Jean Scott. I remember asking Papa if he would like to have Norman Mailer join us. He said he would, so I called Norman, and since plans weren't set, I told him to hang around— if he wanted to come—until I got back to him with final arrangements. Norman was very eager. But then something happened. Hotchner stepped in and said no. He thought the chemistry wasn't right, something would go wrong with the evening, something to the effect of "I don't think we ought to do that, Papa, we've got reservations," and Papa nodding his head. Perhaps he didn't want the excitement and the challenge—but what I especially remember is that I never called Norman back. Awful of me. Perhaps I couldn't think of an easy way to explain why the evening was off. I suspect Norman was upset. He probably sat by the phone waiting.

FRANCIS IRBY GWALTNEY (LETTER TO NORMAN MAILER, NOVEMBER 6, 1959)

Dear Norman:

My admiration for Advertisements for Myself *is not tainted by what I called "an occasional gleam of dishonesty." Five or six times a year I am asked by various academic groups in Arkansas to lecture on "the novel." There isn't really much I can say during the course of an hour, but I try to overcome that by recommending something like Forster's* Aspects of the Novel. *But Forster is, like his novels, essentially a cold man who understands the novel in much the same manner a scientist might understand a formula. In the future—and I am preparing another one of those speeches now—I intend to strongly recommend* Advertisements *as the best thing yet published which shows the novelist at work with both his conscience and his distractors. I realize that it is a recommendation of considerable proportions, but having taken two degrees in comparative literature—or "literary criticism" if you want to call it that—and my reading in the field is broad enough that I feel qualified and safe.*

So, you may see, my objection to the book was both small and limited.

The dishonesty in the book was this: you sometimes felt sorry for yourself. The alteration of a fact doesn't strike me as being particularly dishonest. Facts are, after all, either cold or sensational, with sketchy middle ground, and can be used in writing only if they illustrate. But when you alter a fact to excuse yourself, you're indulging in self-pity and that is deeply dishonest. Fortunately, you were rarely guilty and I am eager to judge guilt by degrees because I am probably more dishonest than you are, ever have been or ever will be.

I objected to your use of your liver. I don't remember your ever having suffered with a liver ailment when you were in the Philippines. And, after the publication of The Naked and the Dead *and during the writing of* Barbary Shore, *you were glowing with solid health. Your liver problem arrived, if I remember correctly, only after you started living it up for fast. So it seems to me that you were using the excuse of physical exhaustion and illness to excuse something that you thought you failed to do.*

And for Christ's sake, stop letting yourself be a victim of those people you call shits. Dorothy Kilgallen and Paul Gregory aren't likely to sit in judgment of your work. Those people are merely the jazzy scum skimmed from tinsel. The real critics, the ones who have thus far managed to prevail, take your work seriously and they all consider The Deer Park *a far better book than the one upon which your popular reputation rests.*

As for my remarks about your mental health, I apologize if you're hurt, but I will not take back a word of it. And I am sorry that I am not suave enough to tell you about it in the manner you suggested. I can write only in my own way and anything I say about your health is said only because it breaks my heart to know you're sick. (That, itself, is probably sick too, which does, after all, permit me to say that I can judge from a personal point of view.)

Ecey has never been as hard on you as I have: she sends her love.

NORMAN MAILER (LETTER TO FRANCIS IRBY GWALTNEY, NOVEMBER 13, 1959)

Dear Fig,

I'm glad we got into this because I think part of our unspoken disagreement and slow if finally dramatic estrangement, was due to a good bit of mutual misunderstanding. Maybe I can take the most doubtful step of taking a bit of credit for my instincts when I asked you what you meant by an "occasional gleam of dishonesty." The book is necessarily filled with all sorts of small dishonesties. This kind of book makes that inevitable. But they had no gleam, they were generally in the form of shitty little compromises where to have told more of the truth would have taken 10,000 words and then not have been satisfactory. I feel the same way about fact that you do, I mean I'm not hipped on it but I am respectful of it, and something which has a gleam of dishonesty is an attractive lie. To my knowledge there were none such in the book. Only the offering here and there of two general facts instead of twelve specific ones, which sort of narrative leaves me feeling flat—what I call the shitty dishonesties.

On the liver, you just happen to be wrong. I came down with jaundice in late January or early February of 1945, and spent as I remember 10 or 12 days in a First Cavalry Hospital on the outskirts of Manila while the city was being taken. As you say, I was healthy enough after The Naked and the Dead *and during* Barbary Shore, *but I most certainly did get a bad liver while I was writing* The Deer Park *when it was still a Rinehart book, and I was living a reasonably slow life at the time, certainly slower than the life I was leading in Hollywood. You may remember that time I passed through Arkansas and spent I think 10 days with you and Ecey, when I couldn't drink and indeed was not allowed to drink for a month. I was in poor shape then and it was only in Mexico when I started smoking pot that the liver began to get a little better. You may remember how when we came back with Susie I turned on one night and we sat around watching Walter Huston in "Rain" on television. So you see, I think I was accurate on those particular facts.*

Anyway, I think we might as well now shake hands upon the end of the feud. When we see each other again, which I would like, I think we can become friends once more, maybe better friends than before, but we must give each other the right to argue violently and to disagree passionately. This was what began to pinch our friendship with intolerably muffled irritations on both sides.

Give my love to Ecey.

Yours,
Norman

P.S. If the last full paragraph is too abrupt, well forgive my Yankee manners.

NORMAN MAILER (LETTER TO EMMA CLARA GWALTNEY, JANUARY 14, 1960)

Dear Ecey,

Okay, great, I guess we're all still standing, as anyone could have told us. People don't die that easy.

Listen, I liked getting that letter from you, and the only thing I wish is that you'd really let go on me sometime. I don't think you or Fig ever really understood the differences between us. I like a fight between friends, I mean a quick honest one. Maybe I'm pugnacious, but it's the only thing that relaxes me, and what I used to dislike about the people in Arkansas, you included most of all Ecey, was that everybody was so fucking polite. For what? It's bad for the blood and it's bad for character because people end up false—they become more and more sweet all the time and all the while they get more pent up. And they were good people down there—still are I suppose—but it got to the point where I was always tense around both of you because I felt I couldn't say anything without damaging your nervous systems irreparably. And so then I finally blew a gasket that night. But I did apologize to Fig, one way and another, and then when the correspondence went sour I began to think that Fig really and truly wanted to tear it, as if I had become a psychic luxury he could no longer afford. And of course I had been pissed off at both of you because of your trip to New York the summer before when I was trying to finish The Deer Park. *Now that you read* Advertisements *you can see what a state I was in, but at the time I was so fucking hurt and mad that all Fig could come up with was something on the order of, "If Norman don't watch himself, he's gonna have a nervous breakdown." Which was a real boon from a friend, I suppose.*

Anyway, the point is not to yammer gripes back and forth in letters, because that would take forever. It would be better to see each other, and then we can all have a fight or two if it turns out that way, certainly we can clear the air. . . . I may go to lecture for two days at the Univ. of Texas in Dallas, and if I do, then I'll stop off on the way back if you'd care to have me. Or if I don't do that— I've been lecturing too much lately and not writing enough—then maybe you'd be interested in driving up to Provincetown this summer. We'll have a house there from May to September, and I think I even know how to have a good time when I'm up in Provincetown—you'll see. It's the most beautiful seaport in the East, and yet it's a honkytonk with tourists from Boston and the crowd from the Village—reread the pages on it in "Advertisements for Myself on the Way Out."

As for the book, I wish you would unload on it—tell me everything you don't like. I feel kind of easy about it. I mean I did my best, and I learned a lot about myself, and I think I'm stronger today, although a bit duller—there's nothing like writing about yourself to waste some of the possibilities of the unconscious. So I feel interest in the reactions of others which I never felt before, I mean objective interest. In the past the reactions of reviewers and friends would either nourish me or wound me, but this time I think I've learned a bit, and better still only one or two reviews got under my skin.

Personal news. We have another daughter, Betsy Ann, 3½ months old now, and as cute as her father. Dandy is now close on 3, and Sue is very much 10—

*a great kid, tough and cool with an air of pleasant gravity about her. She knows
more about a lot of things than I'll ever know. Adele is fine, changed quite a bit,
but not in looks. . . .*

> *So love, kind of love,
> Norman*

ALLEN GINSBERG   I thought *Advertisements for Myself* was good prose because
it was personal—maybe too stylized but still personal—and it connected his
private life with his public personality.

It didn't seem he was more confused than me or Kerouac. We were all
foundering. Kerouac was drinking himself to death by then. Burroughs was
coming out of junk. The odd thing was the graciousness about Mailer's effort
to keep in constant communications with the ongoing spiritual battle over the
American soul, to include the world and its response in his art. Perhaps it wasn't
graciousness so much as grace, and you saw this in *Advertisements*.

Kerouac disapproved of what some people called Norman's grandstanding,
but I think Norman's got a spiritual motive for his public address. I recognized
it because I have public address too—it's the awareness that there is a living
world and mind outside that is influenceable and influencing, and that if you
talk directly to it you can break through and communicate, actually alter the
attitude of mind or human consciousness through a work of art. The work of
art therefore becomes Shelleyan, an unacknowledged legislative act, which can
work in a lot of different ways—as Kerouac did it, in total saintly privation,
writing all his works knowing that they're never going to be published except
maybe after he's dead; or you can try, as Norman and I have tried, to address
the public directly.

But I didn't think—don't think—Norman's celebrity was a problem. If you're
smart enough, and by that I mean transparent-hearted enough, you can go
anywhere and do anything and there will be no problem with either celebrity
or the law. If Mailer can talk about himself as a victim, then he's aware and has
become transparent, and that nullifies all dangers.

H. L. "DOC" HUMES   The press media-ized Norman, played a lionizing game
that nobody understood back then. They got Ginsberg, they got Kerouac, they
even got Fitzgerald back in the thirties, but nobody understood the full weight
of the publicity engine and what it could do to talent.

MICHAEL McCLURE   People talked about Norman being crazy or truculent, but
I call that period "the dark night of the soul" for myself too, lasting from about
'55 to the autumn of '63, when I was in serious grief due to psychedelic drugs.
I wasn't sleeping, and I wrote enormous amounts of poetry, writing a book of
poems, which Grove published but which at the time I didn't even *know* I was
writing, typing constantly in this intensively turned-on, visionary state, and I
was probably institutional. Joanna and Janie, my wife and daughter, somehow

managed to hold me together. Maybe a lot of people were falling apart all over—1959–60 was a great year to fall apart. In San Francisco it would have been drugs; in New York I don't know what.

In '59 I'd gotten scared because of an article on the Beats in *Life* magazine. I was running a gym here in San Francisco, the only job I could get, practicing Tantric yoga, hallucinating, and living in a building full of painters. Paul O'Neill, the *Life* writer, had come out and interviewed me, and when he left I said, "That guy's gonna fuckin' kill us, that slimy bastard is gonna stomp us out." I refused to have my picture taken, but they got one from a school photographer at Princeton, where I'd given a reading, and sure enough, they went after Ginsberg, after Lamantia, six or seven of us.

The article was called "The Only Revolution Around" and even included a snide photo of a beatnik mother and father with a baby on the floor with beer cans. A real hatchet job, and the subtext plainly invited Americans to catch all the Beats and hang them from the nearest lamppost. It was an open invitation—"Get these weirdos"—so we were fair game for the cops, and Luce publications obviously approved of any local DA grinding us under. Not only was I shook but my stepfather phoned from Tucson and said, "I just want you to know that you killed your mother." It didn't occur to them that the article was absolute raving horseshit. That's what was so scary about it—no one did.

In retrospect, though, when I think about California vis-à-vis the late fifties and then think about Norman, the first thing that comes to mind is Norman's connection to Mallarmé, who said the book is a spiritual instrument, a sacred means by which one speaks of his spirit and conceivably changes the "consciousness of the race." Now, other people do not have the right to tell us how large our experiences or feelings or perceptions are. They're timeless, sizeless, proportionless, and monumental. Norman didn't realize this in *The Naked and the Dead*, but he certainly realized it in *Advertisements*. The passion and perception there, the willingness to be absurd, the willingness to take a position that I call "biological" is connected with Mallarmé—and I'm not talking about vision here, or metaphor, I'm talking about biological experience, about real feelings. To be concrete: If Norman has a powerful feeling that one can only be listened to if one is irreverent, then he will write an irreverent book and take the consequences for doing so. When somebody says "You've got to moderate your irreverence," he says "Hey, I *feel* irreverence, and there's truth in the irreverence." It's not allowing social modifications of his perceptions. It's what led him away from that laid-back, cool hipsterism of late bop. It made him idealize the outlaw.

The other thing we have in common is that we all became what Gertrude Stein called "media saints." To this day if I want something in the newspaper I can get it in without cultivating it. Norman has the same power—and fuck 'em, those who say this shouldn't be the concern of an artist. If you don't play on the media, no one will know your work. I realized that when I was in the theater, that I had to play the media like a keyboard, otherwise people wouldn't have known I had plays around. And Norman's indeed the master of that.

NORMAN PODHORETZ   I thought that Ginsberg, Kerouac, and the Beats were discrediting the whole radical impulse that I was hoping would come to something good and important. Norman and I differed here.

I was looking for a certain combination of qualities, and for me Mailer had it, as did Norman O. Brown and Paul Goodman. Unlike the Beats, he brought mind and discipline to bear on the eruption of instinct. If there was to be a revolution in consciousness, Mailer's was the way to make it. But I don't think his turning to the Beats was a result of his feeling he had nowhere to go after "The White Negro." It had more to do with his being impressed by the impact they made, by the fact that the Beats were getting attention, like that *Life* cover story. To him the attention the Beats were getting was proof positive they were onto something, and he wanted in on it. Of course they *were* getting attention, but that didn't necessarily mean what Mailer thought it meant. The problem is that the meretricious very often gets attention, an obvious fact that Mailer tended to overlook.

NED POLSKY   In the Beat scene, as it were, people didn't really have much to do with Norman. He was recognized and admired from a distance, but you'd rarely run into him at Beat parties and so on, apart from what he may have organized on his own. I'd see people like Paul Krassner and Ed Sanders of the Fugs who later started the Peace Eye Bookstore and then put out a magazine called *Fuck You, A Magazine of the Arts*, which published a lot of Beat stuff, including Ginsberg. Kerouac had been around earlier, but by the time I was in the Village he was off the scene.

By the late fifties the Village had become a much bigger junk scene. A lot of the early Beats were also shooting up, and I saw a lot of that mostly through Alex Trocchi, who was a friend of mine. This is also the time when blacks were first beginning to come down to the Village, whereas before, it was worth their lives, because Italian hoodlums would beat them up. The first bar that admitted blacks was called Johnny Romero's on Minetta Lane, which opened, I think, in '57. A friend of mine, John Ross, used to go there; he was a white guy but a real white Negro—you'd never see him without his shades on. When I came back from Mexico he told me that the bar had become blacker and blacker until finally when he went in he was usually the only white guy in the place. One time there was one other white guy at the end of the bar, and he went up to him and said, "Dr. Livingstone, I presume?" and they threw him out.

When I'd come back to the Village the White Horse was sort of *the* place, and one of the regulars I hung around with was Marshall Allen, the second richest guy in the Village. He supported a lot of people, including Delmore Schwartz, and I know Marshall knew Norman. The other people at the White Horse were Bob Wheeler, a history teacher, Annie Truxel, a painter, and Paddy and Tom Clancy—not Liam—before they formed their group, though Paddy was already putting out records of Irish folk music. And Delmore Schwartz too, of course, who was much older than the rest of us and sort of looking for the lost Village of the forties. I don't remember any of the *Evergreen* crowd, like Barney Rosset or Dick Seaver. Maybe they were at the Cedar. But LeRoi Jones was around, living with Hettie, a nice Jewish girl from the Bronx whom he married before doing his black nationalist number. Jimmy Baldwin too. It was *the* place in the late fifties—only then some people moved up to the Corner Bistro at West Fourth and Jane, I think.

The Village in those days was an intensely social scene, really two scenes: the White Horse, and the other was at Marshall Allen's, because he had the biggest pad, which was sort of an open house. I don't recall Norman hanging out at either, probably because he'd moved up to Connecticut. But even when he came back to Perry Street, in '58, I didn't see him much. In fact, by then, though, some of the really poor Villagers, Beat types, were being driven out by the higher rents and were moving over to the lower East Side, what's now called the East Village.

TULI KUPFERBERG   Norman was one of the people who organized a party specifically to celebrate the "End of the Beats." It was in some place on West Fourth Street, near Sixth Avenue. Ted Joans was there, James Baldwin, Robert Cortelyou, not the art dealer, a Frenchman, and it may have been his apartment. I got my first and lasting distaste for the French when he got up on a chair and made an incredible speech at the top of his voice, ending up shouting. As soon as he finished, you realized he'd said nothing.

Actually, there was some kind of manifesto that came out of it. I'm grinning now that I think back on that time, and I sort of question the value of going over this ground, as I often have before.... He who does *not* know history is *not* condemned to repeat it. Like maybe the adage should be changed, huh?

But I would never say "Normie's my pal." I was always in awe of him, and you don't know quite how to act. A mixture of awe and envy, a terrible mixture that doesn't really lead to deep friendship. At parties you had to fight your way into it just to talk to him. I remember, for example, a European countess who used to give parties at the Dakota, and Norman went to three or four of these, always the center of attention.

MARIA IRENE FORNES   What I found curious was that he liked power and fame, and the fact that people would seek him out more than other people who were just as famous. He'd go to a party and immediately be surrounded by ten or fifteen people. Someone would say "I love your work," and Norman would say something to engage that person. Then another person would come up, and Norman would talk to him without dismissing the first person, so everyone would feel comfortable standing around him in a circle. It was as if he was playing a game of Ping-Pong, only with ten people instead of one, and his admirers didn't mind being juggled. They could enjoy standing there, being spectators, and all the while Norman would be choreographing it.

I remember I saw it happen with Norman and Jimmy Baldwin at an event that either Norman himself or both of them had organized. It was called "The Burial of Hip," or "The Funeral of Hip," and Norman and Jimmy were the speakers. They were burying hip, prematurely perhaps, and Jimmy was saying to Norman "I'm a Greek, you're a Roman," meaning that he was a private person and Norman wasn't and that the essence of hip was in private life, not in a movement. Other people spoke too. Susan Sontag and I went because Alfred Chester, the writer, invited us to come. It wasn't a public or official meeting, and it just turned out that Norman and Jimmy were the main debaters. But you could feel there was tension because Norman got more attention.

Most people seek fame, including myself, but I see it as terrible and dangerous. But for Norman fame was power, and this was the time he was starting to capitalize on it. It had to do with the boy thing in him, admiring the heroes and adventurers, the very male thing, the boxer, Hemingway. You see yourself one way, and then that self becomes institutionalized, something public. With Norman the world cared about what he said and did, so he created himself, and the world responded.

But what I found peculiar was that he was also in search of this same kind of adulation privately, and while he had friendships with his equals, he also surrounded himself with ass kissers. Maybe he was testing himself. But what kind of test is it if the dice are fixed? It's like if you're boxing and you knock someone out, but then it turns out your opponent was cheating, falling down to make you feel good, so then you go out and test yourself by hitting a wall, and you break your arm. People can make themselves crazy that way.

But I never felt there was a division between Norman in private and what he was like in public. He never violated his private sense of integrity by giving a different image in order to show himself in public. He may have been a little more tense, because he was wondering if this was going to be another boring party or whether there'd be something worth while, but he didn't go to a party to conquer it. He went with a kind of nervousness and excitement, because he was going to do this juggling of wits when he was standing in the middle of a circle of people. But when he did that, he wasn't just relaxing, he was testing. The testing, though, always came back to his private values.

EILEEN FINLETTER   Norman's ambition had always been to be a great writer, but then he started talking about writing "the big one," which I considered ridiculous. It's the old Hemingway crap. And here again, I don't think it would have taken hold quite as much if Norman hadn't been living in New York, where the power machine is so strong that he felt: I can do my work and at the same time get into that power structure. I mentioned this once, and he said, "I need the city."

WILLIAM PHILLIPS   The prejudice against Mailer on the part of some people that he was lowbrow or middlebrow because he'd had a huge popular success was gradually being wiped out, partly by the obvious intellectual concerns in *Advertisements for Myself* and partly because the whole question of middlebrow and highbrow was beginning to evaporate. The atmosphere was beginning to change, with the popular media opening up to the more serious figures. *Atlantic*, *Harper's*, *Playboy*, the better-paying publications like *Life* and so on, all of them were publishing writers whom they'd more or less excluded in the past. *Commentary* fed into it a little bit too, and certainly the development of paperbacks was also narrowing the gap. Norman was thus a true crossover figure, publishing in *Partisan Review* and *Playboy* both, and I can't think of anybody who did it quite the same way.

MIDGE DECTER   I can't remember who was on whose side in those days, but the general attitude toward Mailer was based on the fact that he had been a best seller, even though by then highbrow writers had become best sellers too, so that the "quality lit biz," as Terry Southern used to call it, was already accustomed to the idea that accepted members of the community could be big successes. But the stigma clung longer to Mailer because he was not only a best seller, he was a celebrity too. He was in gossip columns. *Ipso facto*, he was a middlebrow.

Paradoxically, perhaps, with the publication of *Advertisements for Myself* Mailer had begun to be introduced into literary society—not fashionable but highbrow society. Mailer certainly wasn't campaigning for it; I've known writers campaigning, particularly that *Paris Review* crowd, and you would go to parties and Terry Southern would be crawling up to everyone. Still, Mailer was very pleased—he'd never had such treatment. He and Norman P. had a lot of arguments about this or that pertaining to the *Partisan* piece, but remember Mailer's mode—he makes these very, very graceful jokes that back then would have been his way of saying he liked it.

NORMAN PODHORETZ   I realized quite early, certainly by the time of *Advertisements for Myself*, that Norman was, as I once wrote, "the only man in America . . . capable of perfect honesty on the subject of success." For him success was a goal unto itself, overwhelmingly so, and it wasn't—isn't—to be thought of as opposed to moral or spiritual purity. I don't mean that he was operating as a careerist, since the term presupposes a distinction that didn't occur to his imagination. One of the reasons he was controversial—and, incidentally, why I was controversial—was that he had no false piety or hypocrisy about success. The idea of making an impact was indistinguishable from the intrinsic value of his work. He saw himself as making a revolution in the consciousness of his time, and the progress of that revolution could be measured by the progress of his career as a writer. In effect, he himself was the barometer.

DIANA TRILLING   Between those two performances, *The Naked and the Dead* and *Advertisements*, he had many things happen to him. There were great problems which could be seen either as problems of style or problems of life, depending on who was putting the questions.

In *Advertisements* he described two hoodlums jumping an old man and stomping him to death, two delinquents who in that very act supposedly experienced more love than they'd known in their entire lives. When I wrote my essay about Norman—that wasn't until a year or two after *Advertisements for Myself* was published—I found I couldn't talk about that statement of Norman's. It's not the kind of thing that a literary critic is used to dealing with. There's too much an absolute of personal urgency. Stomping somebody to death is not the way love is achieved, not even metaphorically. That was bad writing because it was bad thinking because it was bad being.

I'm reminded of an encounter I had with Norman O. Brown when he came to speak at a Columbia Phi Beta Kappa ceremony. It was the same occasion on which Robert Lowell read a new poem in manuscript, his "For the Union Dead." Brown made a speech much like his book *Life Against Death*, calling on us to move into madness as a way of transcending the dull actualities of life. A few days later I sat next to him at a luncheon at Barnard, and I said something about having found it very striking that he was exhorting us to madness from the same platform with Lowell, who had to use so much of his energy trying to stay sane in order to do his work. Brown pushed his chair back in amazement—he hadn't known about Lowell's mental difficulties. He said, "If I'd known that, I wouldn't have spoken that way."

To me that's one of the quintessential remarks of our literary times. I recall it with some horror. Why? Because the world is full of mad people with or without Lowell's talents who are struggling to stay sane to do their work, live their lives, and it's hard for me to understand why Brown needed this information about Lowell in order to recognize that his statements couldn't meet the test of reality. The issue is one of metaphor. Beyond that, license. What are we allowed to get away with by calling it literature rather than life? Was Norman's hipster, his "White Negro," entirely a figure of speech? I'm not at all sure, and I don't think Norman himself has quite figured that one out either. I'm taking here the same line I took in my essay, that for Norman the rebellious imperatives of the self finally connote a distrust of the artwork itself; it's as if there were a universe that belongs to art which is separate from and inconsequential to the universe of actuality. It's a significant problem, and I would be hard put to say whether Norman's confusion is a clue to his success or to his failure as an artist. Is it a limitation of a man's success as a writer if he overrides the boundaries between art and reality in the way that Norman has? I'm not sure, but I know that the question remains central.

IRVING HOWE   I always thought he was incredibly smart, and so did Trilling too. And Diana even more so—*meshugge* but brilliant. The feeling we had—Trilling and I talked about it—was that we were essentially rationalistic people for better or worse, and while Mailer was crazy and sometimes dangerous—which I still believe—he was still able to get at certain things we could not. We admired it, I think even envied it. He was our genius, "our" meaning the New York intellectual group. We weren't novelists, we weren't poets. He was a novelist, and we felt it was good to have a putative genius, even a possible genius. Diana, I think, was more tolerant of Norman's "craziness," more interested, finally, in Norman than Lionel. On the other hand, it's a very complicated matter, because sometimes one felt that Diana was Lionel's advance guard. She'd express things that he wasn't quite ready to say, take risks that he wouldn't, so I think her attitude was to a good extent Lionel's too, only she was the one saying it. So when I reviewed *Advertisements* and wrote that people "found it easier to regard him as a hostage to the temper of our times" rather than "confront him seriously as an intellectual spokesman," it was the Trillings I had in mind.

NAT HALPER He and I were riding on a bus together in New York, down Broadway, and he turned to me and said he'd gotten interested in religion. At first I thought he was being satirical, but he asked me, "Why don't you believe in God and make him a better God by believing in him?" I suppose it had to do with his existentialism—what comes through in *Advertisements*, the notion that God is no better than us, and if we're better, God will be better. He had always assumed I was a complete relativist, and that day he said, "Isn't it possible that you're wrong? Isn't it possible that there can only be *one* right?"

One of us had to get off the bus, unfortunately, but I had the feeling these were ideas he was wrestling with, that he was testing himself, doing a dry run.

DIANA TRILLING I wonder if Norman didn't begin to make a religion of his ideas and then decide that he really cared about religion—that he likes codification, that he was looking for a ruling doctrine, something to which he could really submit. I think there's a great need in Norman to combat a fundamental passivity. I'm of course talking in very psychoanalytical terms, but I think Norman's hipster, his assaultive male, represents a need to overcome the fear of passivity—not passivity in actuality but the fear of it.

I've often wondered what Norman is like in bed. One thing is for sure, he doesn't take any chances of rejection, he's a very wary seducer. He puts out the smallest possible feeler, and if that isn't met at once with some kind of reassurance, he retreats—he wants the woman to take the chances. Well, then, if you can build yourself up into enough of a sexual personality, the way Norman has, you can seem to come on as someone who says, "Oh boy, am I hard to get." Where it all actually starts is with self-protection. Nobody is that concerned with his masculine inviolability who isn't unduly worried.

Norman's early relation to Lionel and me was complicated, I think, by his feelings about Adele. You must remember that that was the marriage in which we first met him, yet I don't recall his ever coming to dinner with her. The first time we had a date with them was when they invited us to their apartment on Perry Street—I think it was Perry Street. It was a wonder Adele didn't drop all the dishes, she was so nervous. It was perfectly clear that Norman had said to her in advance something along the lines of, "Now, these are special people, this is a lady and a gentleman, and we're going to have a proper dinner." Adele was very pleasant and cordial, but it happened that just at that moment I thought I had an ulcer; I had been misdiagnosed. Before I left home I had a big glass of milk. When we got there I saw that Adele was serving something like steak *au poivre*, something I couldn't eat, so I said, "I'm terribly sorry, I'm not going to be able to eat dinner," and I explained why. Norman was very quick and responsive. He was always responsive to anything that required the exercise of restraint, control of will, some dominance over appetite. I had the sense that it made a big impression on him that while a delicious meal was being served I could drink my glass of milk and not seem to be bothered. I guess he felt that this represented self-command, which represented breeding—which in a sense it does, I suppose.

But what bothered us, Lionel and me, was the two of them together, that anybody would act that way in relation to us. At one point, I remember, Adele started to put something on the wrong plate and Norman corrected her, and I caught him giving her one of those looks that a husband might give his wife in some story in a woman's magazine in which the boss comes to dinner and she's not performing properly—that old scenario that he's not going to get his promotion. That's the way we were being treated. I felt it was Norman's insecurity about social behavior, but of course it also had to do with curiosity, with the traditional social curiosity and sensitivity of the novelist.

Some time later I recall a curious homosexual scene with Adele at a party at William Phillips' house. Lionel was away on a fishing trip, and I went to the party with the Marcuses. Adele had been drinking, I had been drinking, everybody was drinking. She had been making some kind of movement toward me that I was perfectly well aware of, but I was trying not to pay too much attention. Then she sat down in a chair across from me and said she'd like to paint me. I told her that several people had tried, but it usually wasn't very successful. Finally she got closer to what she was after. She started to talk about some extraordinary experience she had had—she and Norman, I suppose. It was obviously some sexual experience she was describing: it involved a second woman, and she was suggesting that it could be reproduced for me. With me. She said it had been surreal—I remember her using that word—and she wanted to know if I'd ever had such an experience. I said I hadn't, and I said that she should tell me about it. From my own unconscious, perhaps from some need for self-protection, that came out with a kind of unpleasant edge; I hadn't meant to be cruel. Adele began to cry. Norman was at the other end of the room, and I'm sure he was conscious of what was going on, but he didn't give any sign of noticing us. He saw she was crying, but he didn't pay any attention. William Phillips took her home. When he came back William told me that they'd been talking about me on the way home and that Adele had said she was frightened of me because I was an intellectual. In some odd way she saw that as a threat.

NORMAN PODHORETZ I've always found Mailer's taste in women incomprehensible. Not just Adele, all of them. He always romanticized these women, falsified what they were to an incredible degree. That Adele was Indian or Spanish, for example. She was neither. She was just an American girl. But she was what Brooklyn boys used to call a "boss chick." She was very beautiful and mean, and it's easy enough to understand why a Jewish boy from Brooklyn who probably wasn't all that sure of himself with girls would want to tame a creature like Adele. It's so obvious it's boring.

IRVING HOWE In April 1960, when I was in bad shape for personal reasons, I'd gotten an award from the National Institute of Arts and Letters for fifteen hundred dollars, which meant a lot to me. Norman and Adele were at the ceremonies, and they both saw that I was really very shaky. Norman didn't quite know how to cope with it. He was warm and sympathetic, but she was terrific. She sort of took me by the arm and marched me in. It's over twenty years now, but I've always felt a sort of gratitude to her for that gesture.

One of the things I like about Norman—and I like many things—is that he doesn't hit you when you're down. He'll hit you when you're up, he'll hit you if you're bigger than he is, possibly so as to get himself smacked around. I've seen him get nasty—get that way when, as it struck me, I didn't know why or didn't understand the reason for it. It was a kind of cocky, very taunting rage, but never with me. He's always treated me with a lot of gentleness.

I think there's an ambivalence and confusion in his mind about his private life made public—he can hardly ask people not to talk about his life after he's been so public about it. I've always thought of him as being divided into—I don't know how many—maybe four or five parts. Parts of him were beyond my reach, parts of him I couldn't bear, but the parts he was willing to show me or those I saw, I liked.

The position out of which people like myself come entails a good deal of skepticism, and Norman didn't seem to have that. Yet there was something attractive about his willingness to take chances and even be a little foolish in public. I grew up poor, and so did Alfred Kazin. Trilling was at best lower middle-class. We're Jewish, Norman's Jewish, and I—not Alfred—always thought about Norman's being spoiled. I think the Trillings spoiled him, I think maybe I did a little bit too.

MARTIN PERETZ   Norman came to give a lecture at Brandeis, and it turned out to be a Norman Mailer performance, with a great deal of agitation in the audience, because this was a hundred years ago culturally and Norman cursed a bit. There was a man in the audience, Joseph Israel Cheskis, who'd been dean of Brandeis' predecessor institution, Middlesex University, a professor of romance languages and a real Yiddisher, an old Jewish socialist, by then in his seventies. His brother had been rector of Moscow State University and disappeared during the purges, so he had a kind of sharp view of life. Norman was talking about orgasms or whatever, and Cheskis, all five feet one of him, got up and mumbled to his wife, but in such a dramatic way that everyone heard, "Esther, this kissing, shitting, fucking, and sucking, it's an old business. Let's go!"

That was the first and last time I ever really saw Norman thrown, and it took him a moment to recoup. But he did, because I had the feeling, clinging to him after the event, that I was clinging to a triumphant star. We went to a bar and pizza place in Waltham, Norman, me, and a group of other hangers-on who wanted to bask in whatever he would allow us to bask in. Afterwards we went back to someone's house, probably a Brandeis student's, and what struck me was that despite all the *meshugas* of his life at that point, he was very gentle. He understood that what people wanted was to be reflected in his celebrity. Our attention flattered him, but he reciprocated and kind of let us in.

I remember him talking about Jean Malaquais, and I think it was also that night when he laid out to me his ideas in "The White Negro." I hadn't read it, even though it had been published in *Dissent* and I thought of myself as part of the *Dissent* crowd, since Irving Howe, Lewis Coser, Bernie Rosenberg, and Michael Walzer were all at Brandeis. It must've been shortly before a university vacation, because as Norman and I left each other, he gave me his Perry Street address and phone number and said, "Call me in New York." Which stunned me. Wow! "Call me in New York"!

A few weeks later I called, and he invited me over. I remember using that invitation as a way of impressing my friends, because I invited one or two guys to come with me. I was this awkward, slightly bookish, socially nervous twenty-year-old, and Norman Mailer was inviting me to call him!

I think I visited Norman twice during that vacation, and there was nothing prepossessing about his place at all, just an ordinary apartment. Adele was there, and I had the feeling that she must have been wondering, What the hell are all these people doing here?—like it was an intrusion. Norman, though, was ever so gracious, just as he'd been when he gave me his phone number. I was trying to be bright and entertaining, and my memory is that he had to help the conversation out a lot. He was teaching about life, but I didn't think of him as the rabbi, never.

ADELE MORALES MAILER That summer of '60 we were back in P-Town, living up on Miller Hill Road. A lot of people, a lot of drinking. Drinking runs through this whole story . . . drinking, drinking, drinking. There's not as much anymore. We're all older. But then there were a lot of parties and a lot of drinking and a lot of grass. I think the foundations of Provincetown are bales of grass.

I suppose I put up with it because I was insecure and unsure of myself. I didn't know who I was. I was Norman's wife, I went along. I'm not saying I was

Provincetown waterfront.

a passive dishrag—I wasn't. I gave as good as I got. I presented a strong image on the outside, but inside I was really feeling, What do you want from me? I've blocked a lot of it out because it was a very rough period. At the time, though, I didn't think it was that bad.

Of course the most dramatic thing was the "Taxi, taxi" incident and then Norman's arrest and trial.

PATROLMAN WILLIAM SYLVIA, A.K.A. "COBRA" I arrested Mailer that night 'cause he was drunk and loud. I was in the patrol car with Sergeant St. Armond, and we came up through the center of town, patrolling early in the morning, since the clubs had let out. We'd made our sweep, gone up to the West End, and then we came down again. In the center by the wharf there you had the A-House and the Surf Club, the Lobster Pot, and also the Ace of Spades, which was gay, mostly for females. Also the Old Colony, where people would spill out onto the street and go across to Sammy's place or down that alleyway to the Sea Dragon. The taxis used to be there too. It was like one-thirty in the morning, and we'd warned him the first time by. The second time when we came back, I think maybe he was with some friends, he started yelling at the cruiser, "Taxi, taxi." So we just took him the hell in.

The station was only a couple of blocks away, and I drove. He was in back with the sergeant. When we came up on Ryder Street, by the time I got out of the car is when it happened. The sergeant was on his ass on the ground. Mailer had shoved him and was trying to take him out. I came around and grabbed him, and you know what he got—he got the blackjack, he got the stick on his head. It didn't knock him out or anything, just calmed him down.

Then his wife came down to bail him out. We gave him a drunk test, and Dr. Hebert gave him some stitches, fifteen or so, I think, and afterwards he went home. In our opinion he was loaded, and in the doctor's opinion too—you know what I mean? Everybody comes to Provincetown, a lot of them come to let their hair down, then they end up in trouble. Afterwards they're sorry, but what the hell can you do?

The thing is, on the way over to the station he wasn't acting up inside the cruiser. Just like anybody else, he went all right, no trouble. Then, *bingo*. I mean he wrestled with me over to the door, and he's a little taller than me, not a hell of a lot, but heavier. Sometimes people with liquor, see, I don't know if you call them wiry or what, but they're harder to handle. And his injury—he's got a hell of a heavy head of hair, so he could've just got a bruise on the car bumper—sometimes you get a bruise and then later it splits open. But I tell you, right afterwards he walked himself in, he quieted down. I mean, what the hell. Some of these guys, you'd like to punch 'em in the mouth.

CHIEF JAMES MEADS Our cop, Billy Sylvia, said Norman had hit his head on the cruiser's bumper. Norman said he was blackjacked. Knowing Cobra, Norman was blackjacked. That Cobra! He used to stand in front of Town Hall, his arms crossed, and when some tourist would ask directions he'd shrug and say he was from out of town. He'd be on duty, wearing his uniform!

<u>ADELE MORALES MAILER</u>   There were a lot of people at the trial, and Norman was up on the stand, wearing his best Brooks Brothers blue suit. Maybe suspenders too. I remember he had his hands either holding his suspenders or his thumbs hooked into his vest pockets. And he kept calling the cop "Cobra," which was really funny. Norman was good at it, grandstanding, very dramatic. He could have been a marvelous actor if he'd just gotten rid of the ham. Then he said, "Will Adele take the stand?" I got up, I thought I was the heroine of the scene. I'm an actress too—throughout our life this has gotten me into trouble too—and I thought I was very good. Later Norman scolded me, though. When the prosecuting attorney asked me what he'd had to drink, I said, "Just gin and tonic," thinking I was making things better. Norman said that was a mistake. "You didn't know, you couldn't help it, but tonic just helps alcohol move through your bloodstream faster."

<u>NAT HALPER</u>   At the trial Norman would say, "Cobra this and Cobra that," and Marshall, the then chief of police, would say, "You mean Mr. Sylvia?" Norman would say, "Oh, I beg your pardon—Mr. Sylvia," and then a few minutes later he'd say "Cobra" again. He was patting himself on the back how he was putting it over on the stupid cops.

Looking back, it was a very strange time, and I mean specifically that summer. There was the Sun Gallery show, where Tony Vevers had a nude drawing with pubic hair displayed in the window, and the police went in and said they'd close the place if it wasn't withdrawn. Everybody got in on that protest too. There were also the parties. I'd hear about them up at Norman's place on Miller Hill Road. He was spending time with Rick and Barbara Carrier, who had taken a place at Mary Mowery's at the Waterfront. There was a party out on the deck right after he came back from covering the convention and interviewing Kennedy in Hyannis. Baldwin was there, and Carrier, and the photographer who'd gone with him to Kennedy's and the photographer's wife, and Roger Donoghue too. It was the first time I'd met Donoghue, and since Fay had met him only the month before, she was asking me what I thought of him. Baldwin just seemed to be sitting off in the corner and was noticeable as the only black person around.

That was also the time Norman and I had our big argument. He was trying to con me into showing Adele's picture at HCE. I guess she decided to be somebody known—she tried acting, she tried painting. Norman came into the gallery, bought a Jan Muller painting, talked about buying another, and then tried to sell me on the idea that she was good. So he brought in a painting and I agreed to hang it in the next show.

The painting was all right, it really wasn't bad. We would always hang shows in terms of wall space, and where it fitted amazingly well was between a Motherwell and a Hartley. But this happened to be in the second, smaller room of the gallery, and at the opening Adele came in, looked around, and couldn't find her painting. She began to look like a complete spitfire, and when she walked into the little room and spotted it, she stalked out.

About fifteen minutes later Norman arrived, took me aside, and said, "I suppose I'm allowed to withdraw the picture?" I said, "Yes," to which he replied, "I just don't understand it. You're trying to sell art, I'm a guy with some sort of reputation and it would be good for you to have my support. I've already bought one picture, I'm talking about buying another, and you won't play ball."

He didn't actually take the picture off the wall, not then. I'm sure he'd heard of rich guys like Riesenfeld getting a show at Wildenstein's, and he thought there were unstated rules like in politics. But it was at this point I made the remark that became notorious around town and caused him not to speak to me for about four or five years. I said, "Norman, little did I think that you would ever turn out to be an artist's wife." He came back with "I don't know what crazy neuroses you have"—like it was supposed to be neurotic on my part that I wouldn't play ball. And that's when *he* stormed out. We got Adele's painting back to her and hung an Avery in its place.

ADELE MORALES MAILER   Of course a lot of other things happened that summer besides Norman's trial. First, Jimmy Baldwin came up and visited for about a week, and Jimmy drank as much as anybody else. I know he hadn't liked "The White Negro," and he and Norman had a terrible fight over that, but it was still a friendly time. He was very nice to me, never rude. And he used to listen to me, for a change.

I remember I was doing my first musical, *The Pirates of Provincetown*, at the Provincetown Playhouse. I danced in the chorus, and it was a difficult part, because I have two left feet. But Jimmy came to the opening and was very complimentary. I had the feeling that he was a loner. He and I went out to Long Nook Beach with a couple of other people, and there was something very moving about Jimmy, this little figure, short and very thin, in a bathing suit. I felt a deep unhappiness in him. Lonely, so lonely. It was like seeing this spidery little black figure against an enormous white dune.

I don't think he felt he belonged, he felt uncomfortable and out of place. I don't know if it had to do with his homosexuality, I don't know what his hang-ups were. He wasn't coming on like the preacher boy, he was quiet and not terribly sure of himself, very articulate but shy.

I doubt that Norman realized this. Norman is a steamroller and was so involved with himself that it tended to block off some of his perceptions. I used to wonder if he was really able to put himself in another person's place. I don't know if he does it more or less now, but back then I felt that even though he gets into his characters, they're feeling what he's feeling.

At the same time, he intellectualizes incredibly—I mean everything. But I sometimes wonder if anything is ever simple for him. He loves to complicate. The simplest sentence you say to him, he'll take it and turn it around instead of just accepting it for what it is. He'd say to me the next day, "That conversation last night..."

But again, it was a real scene. I remember we went to a cocktail party at Dwight Macdonald's. We got out of the car and there was everyone standing around nude. All these intellectuals, the whole bunch. It was just so cute.

Norman and I looked at each other and shrugged and took off our clothes. No, I think Norman left his shorts on. And I think that was when this woman came over to him, and she had the most incredible bush—tiger-striped or purple or something. Norman didn't know where to look. He was sitting down and she was standing right there in front of him.

Then the incident with Nat and his gallery, which was so unpleasant and dumb on our part. As I say, being married to Norman is like being married to a steamroller. In a way I was so unsure of myself I went along with whatever he talked me into, so I went along and allowed him to walk into the gallery, and take my painting out of the show. Today I would be so grateful and happy that they'd taken the painting. But I went along with Norman's delusions of grandeur. It was ridiculous, the whole thing was silly and childish, and I hope Nat came to understand that I realized that.

JAMES BALDWIN   Norman was working on his "Supermarket" piece, I was in and out of their house, in and out of other people's houses, such that it's all a tremendous blur. I loathe P-Town. The scene was crazy—touristy, cheap, filled with bellicose cops.

But when I wrote the *Esquire* piece on Norman, specifically when I said that "Norman still imagines he has something to save whereas I have never had anything to lose," I wasn't talking about his innocence per se but about the innocence of all American writers who don't have any sense whatever of what it means to be a black boy in this country.

One of the irreducible difficulties of being an American artist lies in the peculiar nature of American fame, the system of rewards and punishments. It's very difficult, even in my own case, not to become show business. What can occur in a boy like Norman, and with great force in a boy like me, is that you are removed from the people who produced you, from your nourishment, your contact. You are in a drawing room where no one disagrees. You find yourself in limbo. I walked out of the cocktail parties several years ago because I can't make it, can't spend the rest of my life dealing with people who do not know who my mother is. My mother who has worked for them all their lives...

I was aware that Norman had to break out, free himself from his background, from his family. I thought his infatuation with hip was embarrassing, but I recognized it as something compensatory. It's a little painful to say this—I'm talking about someone I care about—but nowadays Norman and I do not get along for a very peculiar combination of reasons, probably involved with his ego, possibly involved with mine. Let's not circle around the question of the *shvartzer*. The American public is really doomed by its avoidance of the question of the *shvartzer*. The American Jew is in a very particular place since so much more was expected of the Jews; the fact that he is, in essence, an American white man is a very bitter thing to deal with. But not for me. I'm almost sixty. But I am the *shvartzer*. Perhaps I expected something from my countrymen when I was twenty-five. No longer. Not even from Norman.

I came up being a *Wunderkind* too, but not Jewish in Brooklyn and not being white. I always thought of him as being very valuable, and therefore I'm very worried about him. I know the pressure he's under, the pressures I'm under. For the intellectual the moral life involves a certain kind of responsibility, a moral responsibility, which has been balked and choked in this country by the problem of color. When it's a white man who calls himself an artist, I look for a witness. Can I get a witness? No one's fulfilled this, or maybe just a couple of people, but I'm not going to name names. There are things that I regard as unforgivable. I'm now doing a book about three friends of mine who were murdered. They were not friends of the white intellectual community. They were symbols, an opportunity to wash your conscience and nothing more . . . and Norman got bored with the struggle when the struggle came north.

But I'm not even talking about Norman, not really. Norman is as Norman does. It would be unfair of me to single him out. In order to be hurt, your confidence must be placed there, and, as I say, talking about Norman is very painful, very difficult for me.

MARY MOWERY My sister-in-law, Fay, met Roger Donoghue that summer when Norman brought him by and Fay was painting on the deck. From then on I got to know Norman better, saw him more socially. Before that my relationship was more as landlady when he rented apartments from me and Eldred at the Waterfront, which had started, I think, as early as '57 or so.

I used to see him at parties and it would bother me. Toward the end of the evening he'd often become aggressive and unpleasant. He'd want to spar with Roger, and he'd end up jabbing hard and cutting him. Since Roger was a boxer, he wasn't going to unleash what he could do, he was only fighting defensively, and usually he'd get him to stop by jollying him out of it.

Roger used to give Norman lessons, but there was also talk that Norman was teaching Adele how to fight, to get her to fight with other women. At one point he also strung a tightrope on the beach, three or four feet above the sand, and was trying to walk across it. He got nowhere, but the kids used to do it.

I never talked to Norman about all this, probably because I kept wanting him to pull back. But he didn't want to be conventional or square. He was afraid, maybe, of aging, but I felt he was making a mistake the way he did it—all the idiocy of running around with those violent people, being almost out of control. The amazing thing is that he protected his time to work. Party hour wouldn't start until later. He'd never get up in the morning and start drinking.

DR. JACK BEGNER Eldred and Mary Mowery were part of the gang, also Barbara and Rick Carrier. Carrier was a photographer and had done one film documentary on Puerto Rico, and he was always trying to interest us in putting up money for a film. But I don't think Norman ever put money in, because he must have seen that the guy was insubstantial.

Eldred was a silent graduate of Harvard. How the hell he ever graduated I don't know. He'd been in a lot of trouble when he was a kid up on the Cape. But Rick was going to make a movie and Eldred was going to be the hero. It was as if Eldred was always doing Norman one better. He left Mary for a young chick and put an earring in her belly button, through the skin, which he was very proud of.

There were a lot of drugs around. That Rick was a bad influence—so was that guy named Dutch. Mark Robinson was a tough egg then too, though now he's respectable. They were all drinking, they didn't know what was going on, and then there was the idea to make that dumb movie.

RUTH E. FRIEDMAN   Socially Norman was an animal, a bully. There was a fight in '60 up in the big house on Miller Hill Road about who was the toughest, the most macho, biggest prick in the world. I was dancing with my husband, and Norman cut in. My husband refused to let go, and Norman started swinging. Jan Muller jumped in. Challenges like "You're not a man"—that sort of shit. For Norman it was his whole business of keeping people in thrall.

ROGER DONOGHUE   Things did seem to be pretty heavy that summer. There was an Irish guy, a writer, now dead, who Norman used to box with. They'd use gloves, but then they'd get furious at each other, get in wars, and end up fighting barefisted. One time I saw Norman get busted up a bit, and his nose bled, and so forth. I was also working out with him when I was up there, but in a professional way, not this other shit.

JILLEN LOWE   I had met Barbara Mailer on Fire Island, and through her Norman and Adele since we lived around the corner from each other on Perry Street, and I went up to the Cape for an extended stay with them. I remember one dinner party that was grand, truly baronial, with Norman holding forth at one end of the long table and Adele at the other. Lots of people, lots of talk, lots of wine flowing. Norman and Jimmy Baldwin totally engaged in bright and rapid banter, not at all hostile. A give and take of ideas, high energy.

I didn't know everyone who was around. The group was a very amorphous collection of characters, and it changed; names were dropped here and there, all around. Everybody thought they were somebody for five minutes. Of course there was Roger close at hand, and a woman named Mitzi Morris from New York. A couple of poets—Bill Walker and Bill Ward. Of course Bill Walker wasn't middle-class, but Norman was always attracted to both the ruffians and the duchesses. With me, at first he was very impressed with the fact I lived in a four-story brownhouse with a young, very successful husband. He used to introduce me with "This is Jillen Lowe, you should see her house." And it was funny. This Jillen didn't know she had a house until Norman kind of planted me in it.

But when I went up to P-Town my marriage was breaking up. Until then I'd been very much Jacques' wife. When I met Barbara I was deciding to make a life of my own, and Jacques wasn't part of it. I was just a nice little Catholic girl trying to keep it together, even though I was falling apart. Still, I was quite straight. I wasn't into orgies or dope, I wasn't doing a lot of things they were involved with. Norman, though, was like a magnet; wherever he went, people gathered, especially the young poets and writers. He was a brilliant conversationalist, a pugilist verbally as well as physically.

And then I failed him miserably. I remember the evening very well. We went out with Henry Geldzahler to a club. Adele and I were sitting opposite Norman and Henry, and it was like watching a tennis match. Norman would make a brilliant remark, Henry would parry, and they were going back and forth. I don't think either of us said three words the whole night, just listening to the two brains. But at the end of the evening, walking down a midnight street, we ran into some wild and woolly Irishman who knew Norman. His name was Tom Curran, a very attractive guy whom Norman often boxed with, and off I danced into the night with him to become his house guest. I virtually leapt into his arms, and Norman became very angry.

In a sense, I suppose he felt betrayed. He wanted me to be very much one of the group, and suddenly I'd moved out of their house to be with another man—an Irish boxer, no less. They'd treated me like family, he said, and I'd left them, all of which was true, since they *had* treated me like family, and it was something I was to miss very much. I felt closer to Barbara and Norman and Adele than to my own family, but Adele was also flabbergasted at how I'd responded to this guy, my dancing off down the street. I thought it was fun in the midnight light, but apparently watching from a few feet away it was quite startling. She called me Madame Bovary. Leaping into the arms of an Irishman was out of script; those lines hadn't been written for me.

The irony, of course, was that everyone's marriage seemed rocky that summer. Birds of a feather, I suppose, flocking together. Norman and Adele's marriage included, although they may not have acknowledged it to themselves. There was boozing, fighting, a lot of fucking. There were phenomenal undercurrents of attraction, everyone was sort of semi in love with everybody else. Because of my friendship with Barbara and Adele, though, I valued the whole thing too much to blow it by having an affair with Norman. Still, it wasn't a matter of whether their marriage was in trouble, because it seemed that *everybody's* marriage was in trouble, and everyone was behaving outrageously. But it didn't necessarily seem a portent of things to come, that people were going to get divorced because they were being outrageously unfaithful. We were all terribly Scott Fitzgeraldish, very dramatic and romantic and having high times. It didn't occur to me that anybody was really going off the wall.

It's true, though, I was the first of the group actually to go get divorced, and I haven't the foggiest if this had an effect on Norman's thinking about himself and Adele. Part of Norman is the tender Jewish boy with a need for order and propriety, and up until the explosion over me and my Irishman I was really trying to live the straight and narrow. On the other hand, my feeling was that there was a tempest brewing, and I was afraid to be embroiled because it was so seductive.

Norman was writing—at a separate place—which always amazed me, that he could keep going—and Adele was throwing these little gatherings, keeping the house together, her children and her guests. They were never alone until they went to bed, and the energy between them was very high. Norman was electric. Adele matched him, a fiery lady, gorgeous and seductive. After I went off and got a place of my own in Truro I heard a lot of stuff, though I wasn't around. I heard about Norman getting beaten up by three black guys, and I thought that was the kind of energy surfacing. It was confirming. Try tasting blood, you know, and it just doesn't seem to stop. But again, I wasn't interested in being involved in that—it scared me.

At the end of the summer my husband was up with our children, and it was Jacques, in fact, who had arranged for Norman's interview with Jack and Jackie Kennedy, because he was Kennedy's photographer. I guess it was a couple of weeks after Norman covered the convention, and I remember Adele was petrified because he drove at ninety miles an hour down the Cape highway to Hyannisport. I don't remember hearing anything about the interview itself, how they were received by the Kennedys, because Norman was still angry at me for going off the way I did; it wasn't disapproval of the affair itself—that would have been terribly square—it was more like we were all behaving on a five-year-old level.

Although I hadn't seen much of them after that, I did go to one huge party they gave up on the hill with lots of people, like Eldred, who was always around, sort of silent but appealing and attractive and, like the rest of us, boozy and crazy. Bill Ward too. Ward was definitely a mover in those days with the *Provincetown Review*, and he was going around with Harriet Sohmers. I wasn't a writer, so Ward didn't have any clout with me. He seemed a little pimply and vague, but I was intrigued with him and his lady-with-mile-long-legs. My God, Harriet was enormous, and I used to imagine them in bed together. That's what they were to me, what a lot of the people were—images floating into a party, very flamboyant, very colorful, and always drunk. The party lasted well into the night, long after I left. That was what everyone was doing that summer, having dinner, going out to drink at the Old Colony or the Ace of Spades or the A-House, where you'd listen to Gerry Mulligan or sometimes Mose Allison, then winding up at some impromptu party until dawn. That Norman also managed to do his work was amazing.

BILL WARD   How do you characterize a place? P-Town was a lark. The mixture of people, the painters, the writers, the hippies. Kline and Rothko, Hofmann, Edwin O'Connor in Wellfleet, Kevin McCarthy. Henry Geldzahler was up there too, and Norman sort of protected him in the bars, made it clear that no one was to fuck with him. Reggie Cabral's A-House, one of the places to go for your cocktail hour since Reggie had shows there—Gerry Mulligan, Mose Allison, Eartha Kitt, they'd all be around.

Bill Walker, Danny Banko, a whole bunch of us worked at the Lobster Pot. We'd serve the appetizer, then slip out the side door to the Old Colony and have a drink, then come back and serve the main course—back and forth between the Pot and the Colony. After work there'd be parties, mostly bring-your-own, except for the O'Haras, who'd throw big bashes up on their hill, and John Frank, who threw fantastic parties too, let-it-all-hang-out-type parties back on Atkins Mayo Road, where one night Adele and Harriet Sohmers got into some kind of to-do and it was real fighting. The two of them rolling down an incline outside in the woods—fists, pulling hair—nobody breaking it up and Norman egging them on.

Still, a lot of work *was* getting done. You'd party till two or three, sleep till ten, then get up and do your thing. Nobody had any money, but it didn't matter, and sometimes Norman would pick up the tab for dinner. He also gave us some stuff for the *Provincetown Review*, poems and then that piece "Eye on Picasso."

I remember I heard about the fight he had with those three black guys out on Shankpainter Road. The cops tried to take him home in order to protect him, but he wouldn't leave. Those situations he'd get into, it was a shame. I was always talking to him about his great novel and I remember him saying that he had to pay his overhead, but he was still going to write it, *the* book.

Dabney once did an article on Walker and an all-night scene up at Norman's. Supposedly Norman gave Walker some kind of advice that he always remembered—"Do things that frighten you," but Dabney himself always seemed to be hanging back. Walker was the star. Then Dabney wrote about "the very famous writer, a man's man, who met Bill and his girl at the door and served them cold daiquiris in the living room." The writer's wife then supposedly appeared at the head of the stairs clad only in a black garter belt: "As she descended the stairs, she described in graphic detail what she wanted done to her." Nothing unusual for Provincetown, but it shocked Bill.

It was very odd. I couldn't believe that was supposed to be Adele, although there's no question that Walker was mooching off people. He and I kept our distance, walked around each other. A couple of times we came close to a fight, but for whatever reason he never pushed it. Walker could've walked all over me. He was a bull. But I always felt he was also a bullshit artist. I know Norman loved him, but I never trusted the man. Maybe it was the macho thing between them, but all I saw was take, take, take. Walker attached himself to Norman, then afterwards to Rip Torn. In New York, Torn had rented a loft on the lower East Side, and Walker was supposedly doing a movie script for him. I mentioned some criticisms of it to Rip, who was paying the freight, and he said, "Yeah, those are good. Why don't you help Walker?" Walker turns around and says, "Hey, back off! This is mine!"

CLAY FELKER   The Kennedy assignment had come about in the early spring at the Five Spot, the jazz club on the lower East Side in Manhattan. I'd known the owner, and since it was a crowded night he put me at Norman's table, assuming that the two of us were friends. Norman was with Mickey Knox and Knox's wife, Joanne, as well as Adele, who was very angry about something and trying to start a fight, trying to bait Norman, who was just sitting there with a kind of beatific smile on his face. She'd been drinking, and at one point, out of sheer embarrassment, I suppose, I asked if he'd be interested in writing about politics for *Esquire*.

We talked about it and he said he didn't know much about political writing, which was when I suggested the Democratic convention in Los Angeles. Within five minutes the assignment was nailed down. It was completely unpremeditated, brought about by this crazy scene, except that it fitted into the way we were thinking at *Esquire* at the time—namely, to compensate for our long lead-time by leaning on a writer's style and unique point of view.

The following week the two of us got together for a conference. As I recall, we were going to give him thirty-five hundred dollars for the piece, but he repeated that he didn't know the political world and didn't have any entrée. I told him not to worry, that I'd go out to Los Angeles and introduce him around, since I knew political types from my days as a political reporter for *Life*. This seemed to solve the problem, and we went ahead and made the arrangements.

The convention was midsummer. He'd been in Provincetown, and he flew out in advance and picked me up at the airport. On the way into town he started telling me again that the only style of political writing he knew was Marx. What he was saying, in effect, was that he didn't know how he was going to do the piece. I told him I wanted whatever his version was, whatever hit him.

Over the next three or four days I moved around the convention hall with him and took him to parties, including a bash given by Gore Vidal at Chasen's. There was also a big party at Jules Stein's. What I didn't do was go with him step by step as he was interviewing people. I just helped him however I could, like making sure his credentials were okay, and later, I think the night after Kennedy was nominated, the two of us had lunch with Arthur Schlesinger, Jr.

But I still didn't know how he was going to do the piece. At the airport one of the first things he'd said to me was "My tubes are rusty," which was the worst thing I could have heard, because I didn't want him chasing girls. No matter, because it was obvious he was constantly on the move, working hard. He was listening and learning. Remember, his career was at a low point. He was very gratified that people knew who he was. Max Lerner, for example, came along and kind of gave him some help. Then, toward the end of the week, we all went to dinner at the Beverly Hills Hotel. He was with Shelley Winters, there was a lot of good-natured badinage—this was the night before we were leaving—and at one point he said, "I think I know how I'm going to do it." I didn't press him. He didn't want to explain. He just wanted to let me know that he'd solved the artistic problem.

MAX LERNER   I must have taken Norman around to various press conferences. I know I was interested in his being at the convention because he was playing the role of the outsider, in effect saying, "And here I am. I'm new at this, but I got things to show you."

What he was talking about was a fresh voice, a new vision. His demeanor was that of an initiate, but a brash initiate, as though in his own mind he was in L.A. to take us all on. He was talking very vividly, also meeting people vividly, and being a little oppositional on all kinds of things, even though he'd acknowledge that everything out there was new to him and that he was feeling his way.

I'm afraid I can't remember specifically, but I must have introduced him to a number of my fellow correspondents, since at a convention these are the people you become part of, a little cluster or group. So it would have been people like Jimmy Wechsler and Scotty Reston. Also, the second group would be delegates, and the third would be political people, candidates' staff, that kind of thing. My memory, though, is that Norman was working very hard and not being shy about it. You got the feeling of freshness but not knowledgeability, and what interested him most of all was power—he was basically power-fascinated and, I think, enjoying this possibly for the first time.

MARTIN PERETZ I don't think I went out there with Max. He was there, I was there. But through Max and Norman and Shelley Winters I got invited to a lot of parties.

When I saw Norman and Shelley together I had a sense they had a history—that was fairly obvious. She didn't weigh as much then, but neither was she the woman you would've thought Vittorio Gassman fell in love with. She was a Hollywood personage who cared about politics, a hanger-on but with a ticket of her own, unlike me, who was a hanger-on on someone else's ticket. She was also very much for Stevenson and she couldn't stand the Kennedy crowd, and the socializing split sharply along those lines.

I'd probably known that Norman was going out to the convention, that he was on assignment for *Esquire*. Maybe he didn't know a lot of the political or reporter types, but at the parties he was an absolute personage. Wherever he was, he was at the center of the group. I don't drink at all, almost, so everyone looked like *shikurim* to me, but my visual image of Norman was that he always had a glass in his hand—bourbon, I believe.

I remember him and Max having a verbal joust in the middle of another party which lasted about forty minutes, with Norman heckling Max and Max defending himself. I don't remember what it was about specifically, but Norman was baiting Max with remarks like "You're the old-fashioned liberal." His attitude was that Max was a philistine and represented all the safe and tried views, so it was a conflict of generations. Norman was also going after Max in competition for the stars, because Max had a history with Hollywood. I remember Phyllis Kirk was there, a beautiful woman who played in *The Thin Man*, and there were Shelley and Gina Lollobrigida, plus people who hung around the Kennedys.

I never know when Norman feels uncomfortable, so I don't know how he felt at the convention. But he was coming on. He was pugilizing. The physical movements were that of a boxer, and the words were sharp jabs. I remember talking to Marian Schlesinger, Arthur's now ex. I guess she'd never met Norman before—she was very taken with him, and she said something to the effect that he was so "lithe." I remember thinking that as long as I'd known him, lithe he'd never been, but he did have that kind of elegance that maybe looks lithe—the elegance of a jab, an elegance of movement.

We never discussed what he was going to write, though. Norman never discusses his work in progress. But I had the feeling that he was absorbing everything, taking notes, talking to people to get a sense of the event. I have a visual image of him chatting with Eleanor Roosevelt. This was her and Herbert Lehman's last gasp, the last hurrah. Let's call it what it was: they were trying to prevent this Catholic kid from being made President. They hated Joe Kennedy. They thought he was an anti-Semite, a papist and a fascist, and they had Adlai Stevenson. She gave a big press conference to talk about Stevenson, a last-gasp effort to keep the nomination from going to JFK.

CLAY FELKER   When Norman returned he went back up to Provincetown and started to write, at which point the luncheon was set up with Jack Kennedy in Hyannisport. The assignment was quite unusual to begin with, and I think the meeting originated within the Kennedy camp, largely through Pierre Salinger, who had been asking questions about Mailer. Peter Maas had told him that Norman's favorite book was *The Deer Park*, Salinger told Kennedy, and of course at the lunch Kennedy very cleverly said that his favorite book of Norman's was *The Deer Park* too. In fact there was some doubt whether Kennedy had ever read anything by Norman—nobody really knows; he was being a politician, and remember too, at that point Jack Kennedy was very aware of the power of magazines. *Esquire* didn't have the mass circulation of *Life* but it had great impact on opinion leaders, and Kennedy was aware of our interest. We'd done earlier pieces on him, I'd been in touch with Salinger, who was a good friend of mine, and they knew Mailer was quite likely to turn in a long, possibly very important piece.

ADELE MORALES MAILER   We had the dark green Triumph roadster and I remember we drove very fast to Hyannisport, like 100 mph maybe. Why? Because Norman was in a rage that I'd forgotten to send the laundry out and he didn't have a clean shirt. But I also think he was a little nervous about the interview, so he came down very hard on me and we started screaming at each other. That's what made us late, looking for that shirt. He finally found one and I ironed it up quickly, and then he drove like a madman to get there for his three o'clock appointment. I cowered in the seat, terrified.

When we arrived in Hyannisport, though, he was very cool. Remember, we knew people from every level, from top to bottom. Lyndon Johnson was out on the front lawn with the press. Pierre Salinger was there, maybe Peter Maas... Arthur Schlesinger too, I think. Then I met Jackie. I was wearing black velveteen pants and a beautiful purple sweater with a cowl neck. She said, "Oh, what a beautiful sweater. I used to have one just like it and I loved it." So we made some woman talk. Eventually she explained she had a sailing date and left, but I thought she was nice and gracious, not phony gracious.

I don't remember what I did while Norman was talking to Kennedy. I think it was a private meeting, for about an hour. I met Kennedy too. He took me on a little tour upstairs. Showed me paintings, either his or maybe they were

Jackie's. He knew I was a painter, though I'm not sure *how* he knew, and of course he asked me about my work.

ARTHUR SCHLESINGER, JR. My first real meeting with Norman had been back in '52, I think, when Mary McCarthy, he, and, God help us, Norman Podhoretz and I participated in a debate at Columbia. Mary and I were attacking the thirties—the politics and culture—and the two Normans were defending it. Norman M. and I, both being young and vehement, lashed out at each other rather ferociously, but also good-humoredly. That was the first time I met him, though we'd overlapped at Harvard without knowing each other.

Then in the fifties we were on the Cape in Wellfleet. There were a lot of interesting people there at the time—Dwight Macdonald, Mary and Kevin McCarthy, Montgomery Clift one summer at Kevin's, Edmund Wilson, Edwin O'Connor, Dick Hofstadter, Francis Biddle, who'd been attorney general, and his brother George, the painter. So I'd see Norman from time to time, and he'd come to dinner with Adele. He was drinking a good deal, the evenings were rather contentious, but they were fun. I suppose he regarded me as an awful liberal, but I think we talked more about writing than politics, and I didn't identify Norman with any particular political tendency, except a romantic quasi-nihilistic leftism.

The next time I saw him was when he came to Hyannisport the summer of '60. Kennedy and his people were quite curious about Norman and didn't know how the interview would turn out. Both the Kennedys were amusedly apprehensive but also sort of pleased that he was doing it—apprehensive because Norman is totally unpredictable and they had no idea what he was likely to say. I wasn't present for the interview, but my impression was that Norman was a little apprehensive himself. He was very much on his good behavior, very soft-spoken, and he comported himself with great courtesy. Of course most of the time I've seen him in the last twenty years he's been a man of distinguished manners.

Kennedy had great confidence in his ability to deal with people, and he was a man of infinite curiosity. He said he'd read Mailer, and he supposedly made the famous remark "So you're the man who wrote *The Deer Park*." Whether he'd actually read it, I don't know. Kennedy read a lot, mainly biography and history, not fiction, but he was a great reader, so it's possible. On the other hand, he pulled the same thing on a couple of other writers, praising books of theirs that he knew they thought were neglected.

I have a vague memory that Kennedy was rather pleased by the piece when it came out. There was some kidding about Norman's calling him an "existential hero," and Kennedy's reaction was one of skeptical pleasure—skeptical because he wasn't quite sure what an existential hero might be and whether he actually qualified. Jack's charm, his imperturbability, his self-possession and indestructible composure, though, all had a kind of social fascination for Norman, who liked the style and would rather have liked to have had that same kind of imperturbable, good-humored urbanity himself. That was perhaps more of the attraction than anything specifically political. Later Norman and I talked quite a lot about Robert Kennedy, whom he knew less well but whom, in a way, he came to feel great sympathy for, a certain identification with, because in a way he was more "existential" than Jack, I guess.

Norman found their Irishness important too. We've talked about his fascination with the Irish, whom he regards as kind of honorary Jews. He finds the Irish dramatic; they're romantic, they're outsiders, they're oppressed and they live by words. They're also tough, and I think he responded in part to the machismo, so it's possible that Jack Kennedy came along at a useful time for him. That piece was a far cry from Malaquais' politics. It was his first "mainstream" political essay, and perhaps it gave him direction for the next ten years.

CLAY FELKER   Soon after the Hyannisport meeting I got a call from Norman and flew up to Provincetown to read what he'd done so far. This was the first time I'd seen it—what he said was about half the piece—and although I was very pleased I still didn't say anything. I knew it was going to be long, since what he was showing me must have been 5000 or 6000 words, and we gave him an outside deadline, meaning that the finished article had to come in exactly the day stipulated. The date was predicated on its coming in that very morning, since with quick editing we could get it out by noontime and make the November issue, which would appear the fifteenth of October, just a few weeks before the election.

This was the same summer that Norman was supposedly drinking a lot and also after he'd been arrested, which was one of the reasons I made the trip, not just to read the piece but to see how he was getting along. But I found he was perfectly sober and focused on his work, just as he had been in L.A.

The piece came in just when he said it would. (Norman subsequently wrote a number of pieces for us and never missed a deadline, not once.) Still, we didn't have an awful lot of time. I was the one who wrote the subheads, and I had only a few hours. The title of the piece, "Superman Comes to the Supermarket," was changed by Arnold Gingrich—"Supermarket" became "Supermart." Gingrich hated the piece, thought it was just blather. Except for the fact we had left space in the issue, he wouldn't have run it, and he told me so. And this was why he decided to change the title, just to show that he was editor. I argued with him, but he wouldn't budge. Norman later wrote a letter to the magazine and was furious. He thought it had been a cabal, and even though I wasn't involved, he held me partly responsible.

Looking back on the whole thing, I remember two things. One, that on my way out to L.A. I was afraid Mailer was going to explode on me. That was what attracted me to him as a writer, that explosive talent that was so unpredictable, and because of this I was determined not to let myself get too close to him; I wasn't going to risk whatever authority I had by going out and getting drunk with him. The other thing was just how rewarding it was. The greatest thrill an editor can have is to pose a question and then have the writer come up with insights that you yourself could never have thought of. You know a piece is only going to be mediocre if all the writer does is give you back your own level of perception, so what you want is somebody who can break through to new levels of understanding. And that's why all of us except Gingrich were so excited about Norman's essay: he understood the meaning of Kennedy as opposed to what the rest of the political journalists were writing about, which was just the mechanics of politics. But that isn't what elections are really about, the mechanics. They're about how politics touch people, their deepest aspirations and fears and hopes, and that's what Mailer articulated more brilliantly than any other writer at the time.

There was nothing to indicate that he was going to come up with these insights, and, in fact, it seemed he was a bit intimidated by the whole process. But he did, and he even came away suggesting that his piece may have gotten JFK elected. Who knows? It's arguable. He articulated an appeal to young Americans, and *Esquire* had an audience of young Americans. Just as those of us who were the editors were reflecting that change—we were not Eisenhower-age people, we were a new generation—here was a new political figure for whom Mailer more than made the case.

NORMAN PODHORETZ   I was slightly surprised by Mailer's sudden interest in the Kennedys, but then I realized it was a little like his attitude toward the Beats. Now, I'm notorious for my belief in success, and I don't apologize for it, but I have never confused success with intrinsic virtue or merit. Norman, though, is different. It isn't that he goes in for fashion. Fashion is transitory, and when something's just a passing fancy, it's not likely to interest him, but when the fashion is really taking, in other words, when it acquires power, that's when he gets interested. The Kennedy business, his interest in Castro, both were examples of the same thing. Anything that could conquer had to be substantial and seemed to him worthy of respect, even reverence.

NORMAN MAILER   Maybe at some point during our conversations I said to Felker, "I think I've figured out how to do this," because I do know that I had an epiphany the day I saw Jack Kennedy arrive at the convention. He was in the back seat of his open car, his face suntanned, and there were a crowd of gays on the other side of Pershing Park, all applauding, going crazy, while the convention itself was filled with the whole corrupt trade-union Mafia Democratic machine. And I could feel these two worlds come together, both juxtaposed to this incredible guy who looks like a movie star. I'd found my image, and at that moment it was almost as if I saw it like a great painting. In fact, out of all the pieces I've written, that one's probably more like a huge mural in my mind than almost anything I've done. Maybe "Ten Thousand Words a Minute" is like that too, but in those days I couldn't write unless I saw a large image.

My feeling about JFK was that while I was quite excited about him, I was also very worried, and I hoped I wasn't blowing smoke. Never have I written anything where I'd felt so provisional, even though I was writing for a national magazine, a mass audience, which of course was why I got so agitated afterwards with the Castro business and the Bay of Pigs.

But I can't begin to indicate how existential it is. You simply are not taking your pulse as you write these things. You're doing your best and you're dealing with the fear that the piece isn't good; no matter what I've written, whenever I have the feeling something is good *while* I'm writing it I get very uneasy. And that's the feeling you should have. Because if it's worthwhile, something is being forged out of the deepest reflexes in yourself, and for precisely that reason you're not in command of it. You're not adjusting a motor on a car. You're doing your best. Very often you're bewildered, and all I ever claim to have had in those years was that I'd come to depend upon my literary instinct as such. In other words, if this was the stuff that was coming out, then it was wiser than the stuff in my conscious mind, which was really trying to keep up with it.

So all the while I was writing the Kennedy piece I was worried that it was superficial and propagandistic, that I was phony, that I was making too much of JFK's personality and too little of the objective political strengths. After all, I did have my good friend Jean Malaquais always saying, in effect, "You are a ridiculous sentimentalist, you're taken in by all this *qvatch*." And that worried me. But looking back on it, what I'm impressed with is that it was right. Kennedy did make a profound change, he altered the country forever and as a result was one of the most important Presidents we ever had. Also, the piece left me with a feeling that the one thing I must always count on is the navigator at the center of my unconscious, which knows more than I know. I take this for granted now, but back then I wasn't as sure.

Maybe some people thought that my enthusiasm for Kennedy came from being a sucker for fashion. But most of the people who make that charge aren't noted for the fecundity of their original ideas. I certainly wasn't being co-opted. The Kennedys didn't spend any time with me. Still, I'm the guy who's said that we only do something good when both our best and our worst motives are involved, so it's perfectly possible that the allegation is well founded. I'm not the man to defend myself, because what was worrisome, in fact, was that I was going from a radical position to a liberal one. I was worried whether I was reversing my field in fear or on an honorable tack. I find in sailing that tacking is far easier for me than running with the wind.

ART D'LUGOFF Norman and I got together back in the city during the Lord Buckley protest that Doc Humes was organizing. Humes was the sort of guy who in the late fifties got people together, like George Plimpton, Podhoretz, a lot of people. He was sort of a catalyst character, a brilliant guy, very friendly, very congenial.

The problem was that Buckley had been denied a cabaret card. They'd done the same thing with Billie Holiday, Stan Getz, Gerry Mulligan, and a number of other people—whoever had a criminal record or whoever the cops knew through informers were involved with drugs. They ran it like a kangaroo court, so we came up with this project to end the fingerprinting of artists who worked in cabarets. Wagner was mayor, and he tried to act tough with us, so we decided to do an appeal to intellectuals and writers, because the musicians' unions didn't give a damn and the lawyers were delighted at having clients whom they could make a fortune off of. Charlie Mingus, for example, had to pay two hundred dollars just to have somebody represent him. These great big civil libertarians in those days, doing him a favor!

This was a time when jazz had started stirring in the Village, at the Five Spot, the Village Vanguard, the Jazz Gallery, the Village Gate, and so forth. There was also the poetry thing, the beatnik thing, and there was some attempt to cross over and explore the relationship between the two—what they called jazz-in-poetry. The Five Spot and the Gate, therefore, were gathering places, and I met Mailer a number of times here at the Gate when he was with Charlie Mingus, who was also a good friend of Humes's. I liked Mingus and never had any problems with him, even though there were all sorts of distorted ideas that he was a terror.

But there was something racist about the cabaret-card thing as well. It seemed to touch blacks or Puerto Ricans in particular. When Mulligan or Getz needed a card, even with all the problems they had, they got it. Either you paid somebody off—and then you got the card right away—or you had to get a lawyer to try and put in a fix. So we started the committee and demanded time with Mayor Wagner. There was a meeting at Humes's place uptown with Mailer and Podhoretz, while Wagner was chasing me and Humes and everybody else with subpoenas. They tried to get us to say that we gave some local policemen a shot of booze or some crazy thing, because we claimed we knew graft was involved, then there were threats against my license. We got the front page of *The Times*, though, and the *World-Telegram* gave us such a spread that they never touched me again.

<u>H. L. "DOC" HUMES</u>   That whole period around November '60 has to be looked at in terms of pathology. It was crazy beyond belief—the cabaret-card scandal centering on Lord Buckley, the trouble the Village coffee houses were having, and of course the big folk singers' riot in Washington Square Park, which was the first time anyone saw the TPF, the Tactical Police in fatigues instead of uniform. I was chairman of the Citizens Emergency Committee, which was attempting to deal with the repressiveness being brought down on Buckley. Norman was a member, so were a lot of other literary and artistic people. Since the days of Prohibition the New York police had been mugging and fingerprinting artists before they could do club work; any prior arrests and you couldn't perform until you'd paid a week's salary. A lot of musicians were losing their cards, Thelonious Monk had to pay ten thousand dollars to get his card back, and it was a real racket, out-and-out harassment. Willy-nilly, Norman himself was a target.

What happened was that Norman was busted at Birdland the night before the famous Lord Buckley confrontation at the license bureau on November 15. It was a setup, no question. He had wanted to pay his bill of $7.60 with a credit card, and then the next thing people were jumping him out on the sidewalk and he was arrested for disorderly conduct. I went down and bailed him out at seven in the morning, with the result that he couldn't go to the license hearing because he was too pooped, and it threw everyone off their stride because Norman was expected to be there. He had been active on the Citizens Emergency Committee, and there must have been two hundred or three hundred people involved, protesting the "Buckley assassination," as I called it.

Norman's interest in power is a superficial feature of his personality and makeup. Perhaps he's now inclined to think that truth is the motivating force if he's become more religious or spiritual—everybody has traversed that landscape—but then he was very involved in political power and the whole Kennedy thing. He was even thinking about running for mayor, and I was supposed to be his campaign manager.

This was only the tip of the iceberg, though. Kennedy had just been elected. Nobody knew what the new administration was going to do, and the corporate Establishment was very uneasy. The difference between Eisenhower and Kennedy was like night and day, and the craziness reached its apogee just after Kennedy was elected, between November and the inauguration in January. Repression filtered down from everywhere. Manhattan was awash in alcohol. Everybody was moving, uprooting themselves, which may have been why Norman took an apartment in my building on Ninety-fourth Street, one floor above me.

All of this exacerbated Norman's personal situation. He and Adele had been coming out to our farm in northern New Jersey, and he'd be perfectly balanced, relaxed, and humorous. The minute he got into the city, though, the pressure cooker started to work on him. The change was almost instantaneous. He was a completely different human being. So was Adele. Several people commented on it, it was that phenomenal. Now, twenty years later, looking at his extraordinary transformation, I'm seriously wondering whether he wasn't the target of some kind of psychotropic warfare—psychoelectronic possession.

This isn't as bizarre as it might appear. At the time I figured it was the trees and the surf that made the difference. He would get cranky to the point where he himself would comment on it, on the fact that he was being impossible, that he was in a heavy depression and having rapid mood changes. When he'd arrive in Red Bank it would take him six hours to unwind—you could actually watch the process. He'd get out of the car, stretch his legs, lie out in a chair outside the house. We'd crack a jug of cheap red vino, maybe smoke some of my good home-grown. Decompression. Two, three days later, though, back in the city, you'd get a lot of bizarre conversational turns. He'd be talking about one subject and suddenly veer off on a completely different tack and would still be talking as though there were some connection you just didn't see. He tended to ascribe this to being the victim of an occult influence. He wouldn't use the term "devil," it was more shadowy. A little bit like *Barbary Shore*, that "presence."

In '58 and '59 he'd begun to explore grass. He'd smoked it before but hadn't experimented, like me. I remember sifting grass with him, separating the stems and leaves and seeds, showing him various ways of rolling a joint. By experimentation I mean smoking it every day and experimenting with different parts of the plant, consciously monitoring its effect on mood. He had been heavy into Seconal, stuff like that. But out in the country he was his own man. A person. In the city he transmogrified into a personage: the public persona, a projection of the media. I think he even described it once as a Dr. Jekyll-Mr. Hyde type of thing, with the city driving him mad.

I've always picked up on the odd statements that creative people make, because you don't know where the stuff comes from. And during this period it was as if somebody was trying to isolate Norman. It was as though the deck was being stacked so that no matter how he played his cards, he was going to wind up more or less cut off from all sources of psychological support. He talked about what was happening to him quite openly, quite objectively, much like the form of *Advertisements for Myself*, and sometimes he would speak in the third person, which again is another anxiety symptom.

BARBARA PROBST SOLOMON   That year on the literary scene in New York it was all in fashion to go crazy, like Doc Humes. Humes had an apartment underneath Norman in the same building on Ninety-fourth Street. He'd written a big, important novel about Europe, *The Underground City*, then went nuts, violently manic-depressive. It was the fashion to push things to their ultimate extreme— all kinds of sexual and drug experimentation. Once, at a party—not at Norman's—someone put LSD in my drink, and I went home and woke up seeing things. I thought I was going crazy until someone phoned later in the afternoon and asked how I liked my acid trip. The literary world thought they had dibs on it, that it was their baby, until they noticed that the rest of America was out on a binge and that it looked dumb. It was the beginning of the sixties, really, and I used to say to Larry Roose, a Freudian friend of mine, that it was all very violent, that I didn't like being part of it. I certainly didn't see it coming with Norman, but one sensed that it was *all* getting out of hand.

ADELINE LUBELL NAIMAN   I suppose I should've seen it coming, but I never really thought about it because I don't like to deal with violence. Perhaps the whole scene was just falling apart. But how funny it is to look at something as if it had a formal shape, with historical and literary hindsight, putting a form on a universe that had a certain amoebic quality when you were living in it. I'm giggly about it because it's like my senior thesis when I wrote about Scott Fitzgerald in the context of the twenties. It was very neat and tidy, all those names bubbling like distinct notes on a musical score, clear, crisp, though in fact it must've been a real mess, just like life itself. In the midst of it you're never able to say with any clarity that this world is ending and another era beginning.

JILLEN LOWE   When I went back to the city from the Cape it was a mad time, a freeing time for myself in a way but also quite hysterical. We were all sort of square, middle-class, hardworking kids from hardworking environments; a few goof-offs here and there, but generally from very straight environments and hard workers. Then suddenly, *whoosh*, it didn't work. The pressures were building, and we all exploded, each in our own way. Norman went farther out, but then again, Norman was the role model.

ALAN KAPELNER   I suppose I was partial to Adele. I always liked her and would have loved to have made it with her. I know she and Norman had an orgone box on Perry Street in 1959, and she was using it more than Norman. You'd sit in there, there's a light and you could read. You can have sex in it too, according to Reich. They had a one-person job, but if you're inventive I suppose you don't need a big box.

I used to go to the Cedar, hanging out mainly with painters, but Norman was generally over at the White Horse, which was a rougher place, and you'd hear about fights, brought on by the laborers and longshoremen who were taken up as clowns by the literati, something which I found revolting. Everyone knew Mailer, he was a celebrity. Jackson Pollock and I were good friends, and I tried to get Norman to buy a Pollock for a thousand dollars, but he refused. Since he obviously didn't understand Pollock's work, I sent him two postcards explaining it. Then I tried to bring the two of them together in Southampton, but it never came off, though if it had I don't know what might have happened. Pollock wasn't an alcoholic, he was one of those periodic drinkers. He was a very quiet man, a most ungarrulous person, a listener.

After a while I'd had it with the Village scene, and I guess I wasn't seeing Norman and Adele so much. I cut off the whole scene, like I cut off cigarettes. But once I ran into Adele's sister, Joanne, who told me things weren't going well between them. Then a few times I bumped into Adele and she looked pretty bad, so once I asked what she was doing about the situation. She never really answered me. In retrospect, maybe I should have pressed. But then I thought, What good can it do?

The problem was a psychotic condition—Norman's need for publicity. He'd always seemed extraordinarily self-conscious, aware of how to create controversy, but now he'd become a publicity junkie, and it affected our relationship. I wasn't alone in that. Seymour Krim spoke about it, Vance Bourjaily too, and Vance was a good friend of Norman's. We all felt that he was diminishing himself. By the time of the stabbing I wasn't seeing him at all.

MICKEY KNOX   I had first met Joanne Morales when Norman invited me out to Adele's parents' for Thanksgiving in 1951. She was only fifteen then, an extraordinary-looking creature who never said a word all through dinner. Norman or Adele then brought her to Joe Abelson, their friend at Talbot Studios, to be photographed, and as a model she did covers for *Vogue* and *Harper's Bazaar*. She was extraordinary, one of the few models to get a hand when she'd come out on stage, because she had this attitude, "Fuck you, I don't give a shit." You know, she was a spic from Brooklyn. By '59 she'd separated from her first husband, I fell in love with her a year later, and I think Norman liked the idea. It was also a terrible time for him, though, that's for sure. The stabbing didn't just come out of the blue. He was strange, and I was worried. Adele, I don't think, had that much to do with what was happening to him, like I really don't think she was the catalyst. Norman's inner life seemed to be burgeoning. It was necessary for him to have these intense periods of self-examination even if he sometimes seemed strange, like a zombie.

ADELE MORALES MAILER After that crazy summer we had moved uptown from Perry Street to Ninety-fourth Street because Betsy had been born the year before, September 28, and we needed more space. It was a sublet. Maybe Humes had told us about it, because he lived in the same building.

It was when we moved that Norman began to develop those mannerisms, the accents, which he had never used before with me. He became a different person. Something was happening that was very, very, very wrong. . . . But I can't talk about the thing, what happened. It's too painful. And it did . . . well, it changed my life. I've had to learn to let go of the past and concentrate on today. There are certain things, no matter how much therapy, that are painful, that even with a therapist arouse too much when you dredge them up. I can't go into it. It stirs up too much, that's all.

H. L. "DOC" HUMES The party was on a Saturday night, November 19, in their apartment on the twelfth floor. The occasion was Roger Donoghue's birthday, but Norman was also testing the waters to see if he should run for mayor. There may have been two hundred people, a crazy mix including some guys off the street. I was Norman's campaign manager, and at one point in the evening I had told him, "Norman, you gotta run to lose," and he hit the ceiling. He was caught up in the machinery without knowing anything about it.

GEORGE PLIMPTON I remember the date very well because it was the day of the Harvard-Yale football game, a Saturday. I was watching the game on television and Norman kept calling throughout the afternoon. He had given me a task and he wanted to be sure I'd fulfill it. He had some odd idea I could persuade the "power structure" to turn up at his party. You'll remember that his campaign was based on the rather interesting idea that he was truly suited to represent the disenfranchised of the city—Bowery bums, deadbeats, bag women, prostitutes, pimps, victims of police brutality, outcasts, runaways, and so forth—and if he could convince this marginal if large group that he had solid connections with the "power structure" of New York City, he'd get their support in his quest for the mayoralty. It was a huge constituency, he felt, if they could be corralled. So my job was to get the "power structure" to his apartment so he could show its representatives off to the disenfranchised. Among these worthies, I recall, were the fire commissioner, the police commissioner, Tammy Grimes and Brendan

Behan (representing Broadway, I guess), and Sadruddin Aga Khan, the publisher of the *Paris Review*, who at that time had a position with the United Nations and was thus supposed, I presume, to represent that organization. Or perhaps the Ismaili sect. Who knows? There were some other people on his list. I can't recall now who they were. David Rockefeller of the Chase Bank. Dignitaries. All of them spokes in the "power structure." And do you know what is extraordinary? I *tried* all these people. Absolutely. While that football game was going on (Harvard got lambasted, incidentally) I had a telephone balanced on my shoulder trying to reach the fire commissioner, or whoever, to invite him to Norman's party! I can't believe what I would do for that fellow. The only time I can ever remember turning him down was when he would knock on my apartment door at one A.M. and ask me to go campaigning with him down through the Third Avenue bars or wherever. He had this tremendous black hound that came with him, standing there in the doorway with this long red tongue lolling down, and I would say, "Oh God, Norman, it's one in the morning and I'm tuckered."

In a way I'm sorry I didn't go. It would have been interesting.

But I would just as soon have skipped that damn political-rally party. I went with Peter Duchin. He was the only one on my list I'd been able to persuade to come. He was in a happy mood that evening because Yale had won and he had gone to Yale. In Norman's mind he must have represented New York musical circles in some way. The party was dreadful. The disenfranchised had turned up in alarming numbers. Crazies. I saw a man hobbling around in so many bandages he looked like a mummy. "A victim of police brutality," I was told. Everyone looked terrified. The disenfranchised looked terrified, very likely because they probably thought they'd all been gathered in one place to be swept up in a vast police dragnet—a trap. The other guests looked terrified because the disenfranchised were a rather forbidding crew. C. Wright Mills, the socialist philosopher, was sitting on a sofa. Everyone else was standing, milling around. Mills looked horrified. One tiny vignette I remember was the hound-dog face of Leonard Lyons, the columnist from the *New York Post*, appearing at the front door—just for an instant. One look and he was gone!

No sign of Norman.

Peter Duchin and I didn't stay very long. We went down in the elevator. Norman was out on Ninety-fourth Street. He was not in good shape at all. He was carrying a rolled-up length of newspaper, a manifesto perhaps, and he came up and hit me alongside the face with it. I could not have been more startled. He was furious. He wanted to know where the "power structure" was. How was I to answer that? I may have pointed feebly at Peter Duchin—I don't remember. Norman has said since that I hit him back—with a good stiff left jab that he quite admired—but that's just not so. The only people I have ever hit with a left jab were sparring partners when I was getting ready to try to hit Archie Moore with a left jab. What I do remember was a police car across Columbus Avenue and two cops watching us, one of them outside the car, staring at the scuffling going on at the entrance of Norman's apartment house. Would that they had come over! Or that one of the other guests coming down—Roger Donoghue, for example, who had been a professional boxer—had, facing Norman's rage at the failure of his party, the lunacy of the whole thing, had taken him out with a good punch. As it was, he got cuffed around, but he survived it.

Everyone knows what happened then. He went back upstairs—the party ground just about deserted—and in the kitchen Adele looked up, a glance at this disheveled figure, his coat torn, bleeding at the corner of his mouth, and she commented, I guess somewhat acidly, that he looked like some bum who had been rolled by a bunch of sailors in the port of Marseilles, something like that, and that was when he picked up the kitchen knife.

BARNEY ROSSET   I was there with a girl who was crazy, certifiably insane. A very beautiful girl, half black, half Jewish, who had tried to commit suicide right around that time, slitting her wrists with a razor, and as soon as we arrived at the party she started to pick up the vibrations. She got very agitated in a way that I was afraid she was going to do something.

I had never seen such a bad combination of people in my life. There was one guy Norman had supposedly picked up in Times Square. Also a couple of cops, Allen Ginsberg, and George Plimpton, whom Norman supposedly hit or pushed off the sidewalk downstairs, saying, "Get out of here, this is my turf." There was another guy in combat boots, a total stranger. I react to certain types, especially cops, and I got a very bad feeling about the police being there. The hostility was all-pervasive, the closest thing I can think of to the antiwar demonstrations later on in the sixties, exactly like Lincoln Park in Chicago in '68. The violence wasn't only Norman, it was *everybody*. I was aware of the cops in the room and kept asking myself, "What are they here for? To arrest somebody? Are they here to get me?"

ALLEN GINSBERG   I got into a fight with Podhoretz. He had already written his attack on Kerouac and what he called "the know-nothing bohemians," this big chunk of leaden prose which people took very seriously as a statement of civilized values. It was in *Partisan Review,* but then the idea spread like trench mouth and finally wound up filtering down to *Life* magazine and the Luce empire, those illiterates who don't know the Chinese classics, calligraphy, improvisation, spontaneous haiku writing, not even Christopher Smart. They thought if you rhyme or something, that makes it classical, and it was Podhoretz's own lack of literary experience that led him to mistake Kerouac's form for a lack of discipline or formlessness.

Kerouac's response was "This is really too bad. That guy's article will probably wind up confusing a lot of people, and he himself is confused. Why don't we have him to tea?" So we called up Podhoretz and invited him over. Now, he may have justifiably resented me because when I was twenty and editing the *Columbia Review* I'd published a poem of his by cutting it in half to the good part without asking him, which was a mistake, a very juvenile stupidity on my part, but he took the trouble to come down anyway. He was a little stiff but polite, and Kerouac tried to talk to him. We brought out some grass, but he seemed worried about drugs, so he didn't want to turn on, and we couldn't make a dent with him. Eventually he went home, and that was the end of it.

But the night of Norman's party he came over to me. I'm paraphrasing but it was about five sentences in a row, to the effect: "Ginsberg, you really have some talent and I realize that you're an intelligent writer and really gifted. You could have a career in New York, be part of the larger scene with us if you'd only get rid of those friends of yours like Burroughs and Kerouac. You have much better taste than they, why aren't you working with us instead of these people that are so nowhere?"

To my eternal shame, I lost my temper. I suddenly saw myself in a B movie out of Balzac, with me as the distinguished provincial being tempted by the idiot worldly banker—"We'll give you a career if you renounce your mother and father and your background." It was so corny, like being propositioned by the devil or something, Blake's devil who is ignorance, so I started screaming at him, "You big dumb fuckhead! You idiot! You don't know anything about anything!"

Now, true to his particular nature, Podhoretz thought I was going to get violent, because that's all he thinks about. I was violent-tongued, I admit that—in those days I'd go into towering rages over literary matters because I was in the middle of a big fight with the whole New York Establishment, not only over Kerouac but Creeley, Charles Olson, Denise Levertov, Gary Snyder, Philip Whalen, Michael McClure—the whole gamut of poetry that was being rejected—and I was on my high horse.

Podhoretz yelled, "He's going to get violent," and Mailer came over and took my arm, so I had to reassure him I wasn't going to hit anybody. I'm sure I contributed to the tension by my grating voice, but I had no intention of hitting him, and soon I left with C. Wright Mills and got into a conversation with him in the elevator. He had made a breakthrough in history and economics parallel to ours in poetry, and I was wondering if he was being treated as badly up at Columbia as those of us who were breakthrough poets.

I remember the incident as an epiphanous moment in my relation with Podhoretz and what he was part of—a large right-wing, protopolice surveillance movement. I saw it in political terms as an individuality-versus-police state. Like the people in the Congress for Cultural Freedom, like Irving Kristol, whom I saw as a Dostoevskian conspirator involved with murderous politics. After having gone over too far on one side toward the Stalinists, they rebounded too far the other way, while the Beat group was more or less based on Vachel Lindsay, Whitman, populism, and individuality.

BARBARA PROBST SOLOMON I left about an hour before the stabbing. Fanny was the one who invited me. Norman had given her a list and she was doing the arrangements, and she was there early on in the evening. It was a very mixed crew, everybody from all walks of Norman's life, plus a real motley crew toward the end, when Harold, my husband, said, "I don't like the look of this, I'm going home." I was talking to Norman Podhoretz, and he said that he didn't like the look of things either. Norman M. was in an odd mood. Earlier he'd come up to me and said, "Now, don't you talk to me, stay away from me. I could really let fly tonight"—something like that. Then when I left, around one-thirty or so, he was very rum-murky, cloudy, surly. Maybe thirty or forty people were left, but others were coming in off the street.

FRANK CORSARO   You couldn't move. The place was packed wall to wall, mobbed with the wildest, most heterogeneous group imaginable. Really straight-out street bums too, and I remember saying, "What the fuck am I doing here? I'm not enjoying myself, let me get out of here."

I had talked to Adele and she had been drinking, and when she was drinking she got very abusive. Between the two of them they used to abuse each other endlessly. I remember having a funny feeling when she began acting lessons with me that she was probably ambivalent sexually. That would do it, wouldn't it? It was probably bouillabaisse time all over the place.

BILL WARD   Aside from Podhoretz, I remember Tony Franciosa because he was sitting with his floozy girl, obviously expecting people to admire him. King shit. I didn't get into any fights, so to me the party seemed pretty orderly, but there were a lot of kooks there. Norman was getting drunk—I guess bourbon-drunk—and there was a lot of booze.

I remember trying to get into the bathroom. Adele was in there with this girl. They were very cozy. . . . That's possibly what might have triggered Norman.

H. L. "DOC" HUMES   I had left the party and gone back to my apartment, one floor below, with C. Wright Mills. We'd been talking, trying to ignore what was going on upstairs, and he left just before Adele came to the door. I didn't realize she was hurt until she told me. Her face was pallid, she was in shock, but she was remarkably lucid. I brought her inside, pulled the mattress off the bed in the guest room, put her down on it and called a doctor I knew—Connie Rosenberg, an old friend from the Village. He told me to keep her quiet, that he'd be right up.

Adele was scared and also angry. But she was boozed, which kept her quiet and probably saved her life. The point of the knife had punctured the cardiac sac, but she was fully conscious, thinking about what had to be done. As we waited for Rosenberg she explained that it had happened in the dining room, in the presence of witnesses—five or six people, I don't remember who. What she wanted me to do was keep it out of the papers for the sake of the children.

The precipitating factor was alcohol. Norman was so in the bag that he was reeling, on the verge of passing out. Zombielike. On a scale of 1 to 10, about a 9, and I don't think he was fully aware of having stabbed her until after it had happened.

Rosenberg got uptown fairly quickly, bringing an ambulance with him, and he immediately took her down to University Hospital. Why there? Probably because he had entrée and the surgery she needed was extensive. He advised me to stay at my apartment.

After they'd left we went up to check on Norman. I wanted to see if he was still alive, that he hadn't done any damage to himself. By this point the maid may have split, and I think she was down in my place. She was a middle-aged woman—Hetty, I think, was her name—and she had her wits about her. Not like *An American Dream*, 'cause I would've had some inkling of hanky-panky.

I wasn't in Norman's apartment more than a minute. I didn't want to provoke any outbursts, just make sure he wasn't about to dive out a window. He was lying down, resting. When I asked if he was all right, he sort of came up with a drunken "Ahh, get out of here" kind of thing. I said, "Fine, I'll split."

I think he stayed in the apartment until the next afternoon. I would've been told if he'd left the building, since everybody was alerted—the doorman, the super, everyone. Sunday and Monday, things were quiet all day. The cops didn't come around until after he showed up at the hospital Monday night, which was when it hit the papers too. I found out about Connie Rosenberg's note to the

[Nov. 21, 1960
      To Adm. Psychiatrist:
          In my opinion Mr. Norman
Mailer is having an acute paranoid
breakdown with delusional thinking
and is both homicidal and suicidal.
    It is felt that he has committed a
felonious assault on Sunday, Nov. 20th
and his admission is urgently
advised.

                    Conrad Rosenberg, M.D.
                    41 Park Ave.
                    MU 5-1960]

hospital psychiatrist later, and obviously he was laying the groundwork for protecting Norman. We hadn't known whether Adele was going to live or die, then we found out it was serious, and everybody was worried about his being sent up.

That evening, though, was a culmination of a whole sequence of events, commencing with the arrest at Birdland a couple of weeks earlier. When you get to know Norman you find that the case-hardened exterior is very much a defense structure, since there's a very tender, sensitive soul underneath. In those days he was afraid of admitting it because it was equated with weakness, with "the nice Jewish boy from Brooklyn."

What's peculiar is the way the tensions mounted in the month prior to the stabbing. I noticed small stuff, fleeting impressions while running into him in the building or while walking the dog. He'd sometimes come out with something that was like a false note in music, it would bring you up short. It didn't seem to be Norman. Usually he exercised a certain amount of restraint with booze, but that night I'd never seen him so drunk, and it was as though an occult influence were operating. Not supernatural or ghostly but just as he intuited, a shadowy influence at work that was deliberately trying to make him into a madman. And certainly his crack-up came too quickly. Like any disease, anxiety neurosis has a developmental course over a period of time, with certain marked stages—it'll generally take six months to a year—but with Norman the last stage was as though somebody had speeded up the movieola. By the end of October his anxiety had skyrocketed.

The symptoms were all over the place. He was showing more and more tendency to drink. He had periodic outbursts of paranoid ideation, referential thinking—namely, that everything somehow related to him. His physiognomy too. He was hunching his shoulders as though in expectation of a blow—what I call the Chicken Little syndrome. Also he was lapsing into his weird Texan accent, another characteristic of depersonalization.

Plus he was having a lot of problems writing. He'd come and sit in my living room and be morose, just clean his nails and talk idly about unrelated subjects as though he was trying to flee from the things that were really bugging him. It was like watching somebody with severe constipation. He couldn't get his mind focused. He badgered and nagged himself about undone work. He saddled himself with needless daily deadlines, something I'd never seen him do before.

The whole period was so bizarre I can't even begin to describe it. Afterwards the literary scene in Manhattan was shattered, whether because of the stabbing or just contemporaneous with the event I'm not sure. But the hiatus between Kennedy's election and his inauguration was the period when the hammer came down. The stabbing seemed like a turning point, and people became genuinely terrified. Everybody pulled in their horns and stopped talking to each other, and in fact there's been very little communication in the quality lit biz ever since— just the way a public execution or a hanging will have a chilling effect. Some people tried to dismiss it, some tried to explain it away as just Norman's craziness. But even his enemies realized that he wasn't functioning at his normal level,

and, indeed, a fair number of people saw what was ailing him as ailing themselves.

But I look upon the years of '59 to '62, with the Bay of Pigs, as some kind
of watershed of evil. You can't underestimate this. Even the weather was weird—
an Indian summer with clammy days. It was almost as if somebody had been
out to totally overturn the applecart before Kennedy ever put foot in the White
House, and here was one of America's finest writers literally cracking up in front
of our eyes.

LARRY ALSON   Barbara and I stayed very late, until three in the morning or so,
and in many ways it was just as bizarre as people claimed. Two gentlemen who
may or may not have had Mafia ties offered Norman a job as a color commentator
for the Yankees' radio broadcasts. Leonard Lyons was there, and the next day
in his column he wrote, "I knew something was wrong when I asked the elevator
man, 'What's going on up there?' and he said, 'A lot of strange people.'" And,
of course, this is as accurate as everyone else's account. It was a self-service
elevator.

I also remember Roger Donoghue, heavily in his cups, seizing a rectangular
table about eight feet long where all the liquor was laid out, glasses, appetizers,
whatever, and heaving it up in the air.

After Barbara and I went home, Doc Humes called us about five-thirty and
told us to get dressed and come uptown in a cab; he was concerned because the
baby was still in the apartment with Norman, who may or may not have been
maniacal, he wasn't sure. He was talking about going in with a baseball bat and
rescuing the child. At the time I didn't know anything about Doc Humes's way
of viewing the world, and he announced, "The phone is safe, we cleared it
through Central." Now, if I'd known him and his later history, I would've
understood some of the bizarre surroundings. Doc Humes, with his mind working like a computer, begins feeding information, giving it out the other end,
analyzing what's going on and what should be done.

Barbara's reaction was "Oh, my God," and she didn't call Fan. We just headed
straight uptown. It was already getting light, and when we went to Norman's
apartment, he had already left, and only the maid was there with Betsy. Adele
had been taken to the hospital and we went down there right away. Knowing
Norman as I did, I was sure he'd show up sooner or later, and in fact I discussed
this with Barbara: "What's our obligation, our loyalty? Is it first to Norman? To
society? What?"

When we arrived, there were no police. To our utter astonishment, though,
we saw Norman approaching the hospital, strutting down the sidewalk, looking
like a wooden marionette with his arms swinging stiffly at his side, and inside,
no sooner had we spotted the surgeon when Norman said, "You're the doctor
who's gonna do the operation?" The surgeon said, "You understand I'm under
some time pressure here, I've got a lengthy operation ahead of me." Norman's
response? "Since I know more about the condition of this than anyone, I think
you should know . . . you'll discover an incision of such and such a nature and

such a depth." The surgeon was very cool and handled it the best way he could: "Thank you, Mr. Mailer. I must get into the operating room." And Norman said, "Good luck, do a good job."

BARBARA MAILER WASSERMAN   Norman stayed until Adele came out of surgery, the three of us just sitting there grimly. It was probably the most horrible day of my life.

LARRY ALSON   The next I saw Norman was with Roger and a friend of Roger's, a retired detective, someone with police background; it may have been later on Sunday or the following day in Norman's apartment. I was called up there, and it was like a council of war. The advice of this ex-policeman: "Norman, we'll give you a car, you go out into the New Jersey countryside, register in a hotel under a phony name and stay there until this whole thing cools off." Norman didn't follow the advice—wisely. Subsequently I was called into Joseph Brill's office, Norman's attorney. Whether Brill was recommended by Cy I'm not sure, though initially, at the arraignment, Norman was represented by John Cox. The best part about Brill was that he said, "This is a talent that must be protected."

I was aware of Norman's having trouble with his work in the latter fifties. I felt that *Advertisements* was sort of when he gathered his forces, but when all his writing was tinctured with those little white spots of cancer, when he kept talking incessantly about cancer, it bothered me very much.

He said he had to stab Adele to "relieve her of cancer," but I didn't believe that was what it was about at all. The night of the party she was with somebody in the john, that's what I was told. I knew the woman she was with, and she's totally expunged from my mind.

RHODA LAZARE WOLF   I always had the feeling that Adele was Norman's puppet. A very tough one, who finally turned on him. It was like Pygmalion, who turned on the maker. It's horrible that he became violent, but the thing that's amazing to me is that while on a global level the hostility Norman created was enormous, on a personal one-to-one level Adele created much of the hostility herself. We all have extremes, highs and lows, but what was dangerous about Adele was that hers were higher and lower than most. She didn't realize that Norman was in another league from the people she was used to, and I suppose she was perfect for him at the time because she was a girl who didn't have an ego and she needed one.

ROGER DONOGHUE   They had been fighting for six months. One night, I remember, we were up at a party on the West Side—Jason Robards was going with Bacall, we were all together, and Adele and Norman ended up in a fistfight. Part of it, I guess, was that he was fucking around a lot.

But the night of Norman's party—which was to celebrate his mayoral candidacy and my birthday—the dignitaries didn't show up, and that depressed him. He'd also invited guys from a neighborhood bar, tough street kids, and then a lot of people who'd heard about the party—like at the Lion's Head, via the Village grapevine—they showed up too, hangers-on, masses of creeps. There'd been scuffles in the living room. People coming in off the street drunk, getting drunker, they'd make a grab at somebody's girl. There were more guys than girls too, and I don't think Norman and Adele were much together.

I left about three A.M., went downstairs, and out on the street he was trying to fight with a couple of these kids, then he tried to pick a fight with me. I chased the punks away, then pushed Norman away and left. I found out about the stabbing Sunday when I called the apartment at noon just to see if he was all right. Cy Rembar answered the phone. He said they were all trying to find him. Barney, his mother, Barbara and Cy, a regular family sit-down, they were all deciding what to do, talking to all his friends, trying to find him.

MARJORIE "OSIE" RADIN   Somebody in the family must have called. My husband and I ran into New York and went to Norman and Adele's apartment. Fan and Barney were staying with the kids, and we went up there to be with them. No one else was there. My mother had died in 1957, and I remember Fan saying, "I keep praying to your mother, she would've known what to do." Barbara was the one who was running around for lawyers and everything else. Cy isn't a criminal lawyer, but I'm sure he must have referred them to Brill.

Maybe he should have gone to a shrink; he doesn't believe in them, but maybe it would've helped. Since I hadn't seen him, I had no notion that he'd been deteriorating. Fan hadn't said anything, but would Fan ever say anything? She just praises him. Every day I speak with her, it's the same thing over and over again.

FAY DONOGHUE   On Sunday, after Roger had phoned me about the stabbing, Norman himself called and said he needed a place to stay. He showed up wearing a dark suit. We didn't talk about what had happened but rather about what he should do. He wanted to go on the Mike Wallace show since it was scheduled for Monday morning—which was really why he wanted a place to stay, so the police wouldn't find him and prevent him from going on TV. I'm not completely sure, but as I reconstruct it, I told him it was better to go to the police than act like he was running away and then turn up on some TV show. But he insisted. He said it would prove he was in his right mind. I said that it would be a far sight better if they didn't think he was in his right mind—which was his family's point of view too.

ROGER DONOGHUE   What he was worried about was that if he turned himself over to a doctor who declared him nuts, then anything he'd write in the future would be questioned. I remember he told me that the next day—"If I turn myself in, it'll affect my work." That was the same phone call—it must have been Monday—when he said, "You should have flattened me," meaning that during the party I should have taken him out right there on the street.

FAY DONOGHUE   When he first came to my apartment he was just how he is, very tense and talkative. Maybe we had a drink. He stuck to his point of view. He wasn't out of his head, there was no question of his ability to express himself, his logic, his reason, or sincerity. I told him that Mike Wallace would try to put him in the worst possible light, because Wallace always does that, and that he'd be the worst person for him to talk to. Me, I had to get up early in the morning for a business trip, so I went to bed in the back bedroom. Norman stayed in the living room. When I got up he wasn't sleeping, and I gave him an extra set of keys in case he needed to come back during the day, when I had to be in Boston, but when I got home that evening he wasn't there. Then, after a while, his poor, darling mother appeared. She was very intelligent and reasonable, and it was pathetic. She had a taxi waiting, and we stood at the door as I told her that as far as I knew he'd gone on the TV show, that he had a key but that I didn't think he'd come back. She said how much they wanted him to go to a doctor. I said that I knew he didn't want to, but she really begged me in the most touching way to call her or to urge him to get in touch with them directly—to see it their way if he did come back. I assured her I would. I also assured her that I wasn't protecting him from her or conspiring with him to avoid her. I was terribly, really deeply touched by her conducting this search alone on foot. It was a mother looking for her son.

ROGER DONOGHUE   In the midst of this, I think he talked to Dick Devine, who'd been with us at the party and was with me the following day. Devine was a restaurateur, a character off the West Side docks—the kind of guy Norman had never met, Irish, second-generation, big and rough, all the Irish mob stuff. Norman had met him six months before the party, and he may have been the one who said Norman should go away for a few days till things cooled down.

LARRY ALSON   After the Wallace interview Monday morning, Norman had come to our apartment at 395 Bleecker Street. By then the police were looking for him, and that's when Barbara said, "Go see so-and-so, who's an analyst." Norman said "Sure," and he saw the guy—after he'd done the interview and the police were looking for him. The analyst reported back to us that this was one of those instances that was totally hopeless, that the defenses Norman had built up were of such intricacy that there was no way to demolish them—in effect, that Norman was doomed.

Throughout all this he was using his southern accent. Whenever he got into tight spots he'd always use the southern accent, or the Irish one, or a combination of both. We saw him Tuesday morning when he was arraigned in court. Everybody was there, Fan and Cy too.

NORMAN MAILER ("OPEN LETTER TO FIDEL CASTRO," *THE PRESIDENTIAL PAPERS*)
"In Cuba, hatred runs over into the love of blood; in America all too few blows are struck into flesh. We kill the spirit here, we are experts at that. We use psychic bullets and kill each other cell by cell. . . . We all knew that the best of us used up our memories in long nights of drinking, exhausted our vision in secret

journeys of the mind; our more stable men and women of some little good will watched the years go by—their idealism sank into apathy. . . . You were aiding us . . . in that desperate silent struggle we have been fighting with sick dead hearts against the cold insidious cancer of the power[s] that governs us . . . giving us hope they would not always win." . . .

The letter to Fidel Castro was written in short sessions of manic work over several weeks, writing usually when drunk and late at night. But it was gone over in mornings when sober, and . . . was made finally as good as I could make it, which may not be that good, for I was in a state of huge excitement at that time, I was running for Mayor of New York, I had just begun my campaign, the Presidential election was upon us and then over, and I was going to announce my campaign two days before Thanksgiving with a press conference. There I would read the Open Letter to Fidel Castro. That was to be a Tuesday, and on the preceding Saturday night I threw a big night at my apartment. It was a combination of a birthday party for my friend Roger Donoghue, and an unofficial kickoff for the Mayoralty campaign. The evening ended in fights on the street, debacle, disaster, a stabbing—my wife. What my friends were later so kind as to call The Trouble.

MICKEY KNOX I didn't hear about the stabbing until Monday when Norman telephoned, and we drove all around the city. One thing he was concerned about was that his "open letter" to Castro was still in the apartment. He couldn't go up there since he thought the place might be covered by cops, so after he'd done the Wallace show I went to get it. He stayed in the car, waiting, two or three blocks away.

I don't know why he thought the letter was so important. Of course he wanted to have it published, but I remember thinking, What's with this stupid letter when all the rest is going on? I suppose he'd given it a great deal of effort and thought, and at that time the Castro thing—Castro had just come in and was having a lot of trouble with the American government—was foremost in everybody's mind and there was a lot of press on it. He must have felt the letter would make a real splash, hence the need to retrieve it.

While we were driving around I took the knife away from him. I said, "Norman, that's the one thing you shouldn't have on you," but then he took it back. He insisted, saying, "I'm not going to use it, but I need it for personal reasons." I knew he'd been carrying a knife, but so were a lot of other people. It was a little penknife, otherwise Adele would have been dead. The blade was very short, so I didn't understand how the medical report and court testimony indicated that the wound was three and a half inches deep.

While we were driving around he talked about refusing to see a psychiatrist. He was very rational, certainly calmer than I'd ever seen him. And sane, not only in his behavior but also the tone of voice. He just seemed more reasonable, more collected than he had in a long time. Later, when it was already evening, I drove him to the hospital. He said he wanted to see Adele alone, so I just dropped him off. It was at that point he was arrested.

MIDGE DECTER   By this time the two Normans had become very close, to the extent that when Mailer went into hiding, Norman P. was one of the people he got in touch with. He called, saying, "Meet me." He was going to give himself up. He was going to the hospital to see Adele late Monday, and that's where they were supposed to meet.

They hadn't seen each other on Sunday, but Norman P. had had a conversation with Norman's sister, Barbara, and either directly with Norman's mother or with her through Barbara that afternoon. Mailer's family wanted him to turn himself in and go off to a nuthouse. Norman P. said: "Absolutely not. I'm against it, against his saying, 'Here I am, I need psychiatric treatment, I'm crazy.'"

His position was that Mailer wasn't crazy. In fact, he'd known what had happened before Norman M. called. Norman P. saw it as part of the madness in the air, because that very Sunday morning there was a meeting of the citizens' committee about cabaret licenses. It was at somebody's house—I don't remember whose—and Doc Humes appeared, terrifically agitated, and told us what had happened with Norman. We were absolutely flabbergasted, but then it became apparent, not from his agitation but from the things he said would follow from the stabbing, that Humes himself was in the midst of a kind of paranoia. He said the cops would get us all. He came up with a tape recording of a phone conversation with somebody that was going to prove we really had the goods on the cops, that "we've really got them now." He said, "Let's play this tape." Real *meshugge* stuff. In any case, Norman P. didn't at that point make any effort to find Norman M. I think maybe he called the hospital to ask about Adele, but I'm not sure. I don't think we sensed that she might die, but it was shocking. We went home, and shortly after that, I guess, Barbara called.

Then Norman M. phoned Norman P. on Monday. They met at the hospital, and Norman P. went to the police station with him afterwards. He was also at the arraignment the next morning. But that night, Monday, when he came home he said, "It's fascinating to me that when you're wearing your middle-class uniform, your blue suit, the cops will talk to you in a certain way no matter what you've done or who you are." He was referring to Norman M.

My own feeling about the marriage was that it wasn't bizarre so much as it was the first time I noticed the funny trick that Mailer continues to have, which I once described in an interview: He invents a lady character and then marries someone who has to play this role. Adele was cast as the primitive Indian when in fact she was actually a girl from Brooklyn who wanted to be a painter. I always assumed that the clue to the marriage was in *The Deer Park*, that Adele was Elena and he was Eitel. Eitel was a fierce snob, and while he fucked her and said "I'm in love with her," he felt Elena was beneath him. I witnessed Norman's rudeness to Adele and a good deal of hers toward him, just as I remember what Fanny said to Norman P. after the stabbing: "I told Adele that Norman was no ordinary man and that being married to him was not for an ordinary woman."

NORMAN PODHORETZ   I have a memory of Norman telling me that early Sunday morning he'd come to our place on One Hundred-sixth Street between West

End and Riverside and called up to us from the street. The apartment was on the second floor, and we must have been asleep and didn't hear him, so I have to assume that he changed his mind and went elsewhere.

But later in the day he called, and I met him downtown in a coffee shop or bar near the hospital. I think he then went with me to the hospital Monday night when I went in to see Adele, who was scared and crying but told me she wasn't going to press charges.

At some point, either before we went to the hospital or maybe it was on the phone, Norman asked me to promise to do whatever I could to stop them from having him committed. He wouldn't tell me exactly what had happened, and I remember his saying that this was to protect me—what I didn't know I wouldn't have to lie about—and I agreed because it was my feeling that he wasn't crazy. I agreed with him too when he said that if he were committed his work would always be judged by that. I thought he had the right to make the decision for himself and that if he preferred going to jail to being institutionalized, then he should be allowed that choice. In fact, he must have asked me to make that promise earlier, maybe by phone on Sunday, because I was at the family powwow in his apartment that afternoon, Sunday. Cy Rembar was there, John Cox, and maybe Barbara. I'm not sure any of them wanted him committed, but I think Barbara had been wanting him to get psychiatric help.

On Monday, though, he told me he was going to go to the hospital to get arrested. I was there at the time of the arrest, and I went with him to the police station up on One Hundredth Street. They booked him up there because that was the precinct where the crime took place. I remember he was rather quiet, although I don't trust my memory enough to say that it was a spacey kind of quiet. The cops, I remember, were very polite, and I was struck by that.

Eventually some sort of deal was made. I never knew what it was, he never told me. But Monday night he definitely wanted to be arrested, and he definitely didn't want to be packed off to Bellevue.

APRIL KINGSLEY HOPKINS   I was a nurse at New York University Hospital, which was then on Twentieth Street and connected to Bellevue, and I saw Adele on Sunday when I came on at three in the afternoon. People knew who she was, they knew what had happened.

When I came on for my shift she'd already been operated on and was awake. She was in the front room, close to the door of the three postoperative intensive-care rooms on the first floor, to the right of the stairs, and she asked me to move her because she was afraid Norman would come back, though she didn't say what she thought he'd do. We didn't usually do that, but she seemed agitated, so we moved her to the little postoperative cardiac room, which was more secluded. Only immediate family would have been allowed to see her since she was on the critical list, and the procedure was that everyone was checked in at the front by the ward secretary anyway, so we tried to reassure her that no one could just walk in.

At nine on Monday night Norman came in alone. He looked very concerned and depressed—dazed, not agitated. He wanted to talk to her and sat down in a chair to wait, in front of the desk. There was a glass partition behind the desk, so I was able to see him, and I remember he was wearing a lot of gray, probably a gray suit.

We all had been given orders to call the main office if and when he showed up, so realizing what the situation was, I went out to tell him that Adele didn't want to see him. It took me a few minutes to work up the courage, not because I was scared but because by telling him to get out of there I'd be doing something illegal. On the other hand, I didn't want to be the one responsible for his being arrested. We were supposed to detain him, and Miss Poole, the ward secretary, had already notified the police, so I went out and sort of tried to get him to go. I had told Adele that he was there and she'd said she didn't want to see him. She was scared, in an anxious state, and I told him, just as I told him that the police were on their way. He sat there for ten or fifteen minutes before getting up, and I suppose he was arrested on his way out.

City Magistrates' Court of the City of New York

640

.....Felony.........COURT, BOROUGH OF.....Manhattan.........

CITY OF NEW YORK
COUNTY OF New York } ss.:

Detective Francis Burns   24th Squad ...., police officer,
name of officer   assignment

being duly sworn, says that as a result of information received and investigation made, he arrested .

........Norman Mailer...

on a charge of Felonious Assault...

which he believes the defendant   committed on November 20th   5:00 A.M. 1960

at ....in premises 250 west 94th Street Apt. #12IH

in the City and State of New York, County of..... New York

in that the defendant did feloniously cut and stab one Adele Mailer
in the abdomen and back with a knife which he held in his hand, inflicting
injuries for which the informant was treated at University Hospital
where she is now confined.

[the defendant did feloniously cut and stab one Adele Mailer
in the abdomen and back with a knife which he held in his hand, inflicting
injuries for which the informant was treated at University Hospital
where she is now confined.]

Wherefore deponent prays that defendant   be held a reasonable length of time to enable deponent to

produce complainant or to complete the evidence in the case.

Francis Burns

Sworn to before me

....November 21......................... 19..60

Chief Magistrate of the City of New York

SEYMOUR KRIM Tuesday morning I went to the arraignment, when he made the speech to the judge, "If you put me in Bellevue, it will be an indictment of my work as the work of a crazy man." Lester Blackiston was with me. I didn't see Norman's father, but his mother was there and who could fail to note her concern?

I couldn't talk to Norman, I was in the audience and he was off to one side, but he looked shaken and strained, white-faced, haggard, I suppose because the whole thing was very intense, although it took no more than twenty or twenty-five minutes. In defending himself he was very articulate, very controlled, and it was quite an eloquent speech, speaking for literature as well as for himself.

The talk in the Village afterwards was that it was a terribly sad business. Maybe a few people vindictively said, "Norman's been going off the rails for some time," but everybody I knew had compassion for him and was hoping he'd get out of it. There was the example of Delmore Schwartz, of course, who always somehow got off the floor to do good work, and you hoped that Norman had the same recuperative powers. I just remember this general sadness.

IRVING HOWE People felt it was a tragedy, that a man had been driven to do something that he didn't really want or intend to do, that he'd lost control. Among the "uptown intellectuals" there was this feeling of shock and dismay, and I don't remember anyone judging him. The feeling was that he'd been driven to this by compulsiveness, by madness. He was seen as a victim. Nobody I knew thought that Norman was simply or coldly acting out some idea. And certainly no one was saying, "He's been talking about violence—it serves the SOB right."

CHANDLER BROSSARD I'd read about it in that morning's *Daily News*. There was a picture of Norman being booked, and I thought, Oh, how creepy, how strange, how awful. I thought of getting in touch with him—I don't know, to comfort him or something—but I realized that this was all too far out for me. I remembered the trouble I'd had with Adele in Connecticut, my telling him that someday he was going to do something awful to this woman.

Norman, as far as I'm concerned, is the most successful mind in the literary world, but my theory about him was that he had no central sensibility. He's a kind of intellectual hermit crab, looking for the cast-off shell of other animals to throw himself into their house. You take people like Michaux or Genet, each has a sensibility that remains consistent throughout his work. Norman is incapable of such a vision, though. Only if he puts on the clothes of Hamlet can he say "To be or not to be"; he cannot say it as Norman.

Why? Because in a terribly paradoxical way there's a very usable emptiness in Norman. The fact that he assumes these various accents—the Texas sheriff accent, the English accent—I mean, wow! What just happened? He's just turned the corner on two wheels and he's talking like Clive Bell. Or there's the Irish accent. And then he's got the Chandler Brossard one too, which at one point made me think: You, Norman, really are an unemployed actor looking for a big role, and if you imagine yourself as somebody else while writing a book, you are not Norman Mailer in your own head. This is funny, the first time I've ever seen anybody make emptiness walk on two legs. If you had a fundamental sensibility, you couldn't do this.

That was the scary thing about him. When you were with Norman, whether it was drinking or just bullshitting, you thought, Ohhh, he's bought a one-way ticket. He was willing to become a victim of ecstasy. He was capable of the ultimate act for his own purposes, without thinking of the effects on other people. And it wasn't just irresponsibility, because Norman was so involved in the adventure called Norman that it wouldn't have surprised me if he decided to kill himself. He was prime for it because, goddamn, anybody who metaphorically goes into a black bar and shouts "Nigger" has to have some final trip in mind. Because they'll be killed. And Norman, you see, the same guy who equated sexual turn-on with violence, was going for something that was bound to consume him.

I'd told him this, that same weekend in Connecticut. "Norman," I said, "you really do puzzle me. You think that violence leads to intimacy. But this is so fucking Nazi-like, so scary about you, because I think you really do believe it, and I don't. I think it means some terrible Land of the Dead, taking that trip, going to that place. You're toying with the notion, aren't you, Norman, that other place over there?"

"Yes," he replied. "But I'm very afraid of it."

DR. JACK BEGNER   Art Dishman, a friend, was Norman's doctor for a while and was called in to treat Adele. I think Art blamed it on Adele, and so did Fay and Roger Donoghue, who told us about the party. Roger said Norman was getting worse and worse, and Adele, instead of calming him down, was making it worse. She started talking about his masculinity, making fun of him, and that's the one thing Norman can never take, someone denigrating his sexual vigor.

After he got out of Bellevue the presiding judge permitted Norman to see Dr. Phil Wexler, head of psychiatry at Presbyterian, who would then make a recommendation to the court. There were limitations set—whether this included no drinking I'm not sure—but he abided by them. It was also at this time that I wrote an affidavit, a character reference, I think, at Art's request.

EMMA CLARA "ECEY" GWALTNEY   We hadn't seen Norman for four years when we found out about the stabbing from the newspaper. We hardly knew what to do. Fig sent him a wire, which he answered from Bellevue, because I remember the envelope was stamped "Censored." The note read:

Thanks for your telegram. It was good to get it—I suppose. I wish we'd made it earlier when one of us wasn't sitting around in a disaster area. But this is ungracious. I was glad to get the message from you, and I'll look forward to seeing you when this is over. Norman.

Fig filed the note away, writing across the face of the envelope:

Letter written in psycho ward after he finally did to Adele what should've been done years earlier.

RHODA LAZARE WOLF For Fig Gwaltney to say Adele deserved it was quite something, because Fig was a very mild, totally nonhostile person. But also, whatever his reasons for not liking her, I think that he saw Norman as an incredible genius, and because they were so close and did things for each other there may have been anger at anyone who aggravated him. A lot of people felt that way.

GLORIA JONES We were in Paris, and someone woke us up, saying, "Oh, my God, something awful has happened. Norman has stabbed Adele." Jim was very sad, very upset, even though he was still mad at Norman because of *Advertisements*. He tried to call him but couldn't get through. Nobody in New York seemed to know where he was.

Later in the day people like Eileen Finletter began to tell us what they'd heard too. We all saw each other, sort of clustered, and I think everybody's reaction was sadness, that it was such a terrible thing. Nobody had had a clue, though, that it might have been coming.

EILEEN FINLETTER When I heard, I didn't have much sympathy for Adele, because I didn't like her. I don't know why, there's absolutely no reason. I thought she was absolutely beautiful and stunning, but I thought she was like one of Saul Bellow's wives, absolute hell. I was right about both of them. Adele was impossible. A yenta, the kind who would put Norman down in one way or another. So my first reaction was "How terrible! What did she do to push him that far?" Instinctively I felt it was her fault, even though I knew Norman had probably been drinking, taking drugs, doing the whole bit.

My personal impression was also that if Norman had not lived in New York, what's called Norman's violence—which is something quite different from his intensity—would not have occurred. The stabbing, the fistfights, the whole thing. Everyone said it was in him and he had to get it out, but my own feeling was that it had to do with the world of the city. Had they stayed up in Connecticut, I'm not sure it would have happened.

JEAN MALAQUAIS I read about the stabbing in the Paris papers and sent Norman a telegram to say I was standing by him. Of course I was aware of his drinking and pills and marijuana. He'd tried to make me smoke pot too, just as he was always trying to make me drink. His purpose in smoking, he said, was to clarify his mind. He felt brilliant, he stated, capable of thoughts he didn't know he had in him. In fact, he claimed he switched from Marxism to his pataphysics of an embattled god when he started with marijuana. From that time on, the time Mailer "discovered" Theos and karma via pot, the liveliness of our discussions gradually petered out. A god engaged in a thumb-wrestling contest with the devil in some cosmic bar for the possession of our souls—no, it is far beyond my intelligence. We do go on, but rather out of habit and, yes, much affection.

BARBARA PROBST SOLOMON I went to see Adele in the hospital. She looked gorgeous, I'd never seen her look so gorgeous. After that she started seeing analysts, but at the time she didn't seem particularly angry at Norman. She was mostly angry about the people who'd let her bleed. She had been baiting Norman most of the night, I think, and I definitively heard her make some remark that he wasn't as good a writer as Dostoevsky.

LARRY ALSON While he was in Bellevue for seventeen days the family was gnashing their teeth. Fan always believes in him, so all she was concerned about was gaining his freedom. Barney too. But as usual Barney was serving as an auxiliary, a subsidiary, whatever. Later, when Norman got out, his demeanor was that of somebody with a frontal lobotomy—flat affect, sort of disconnected.

But thank God for Joseph Brill, the lawyer. Brill was extremely thorough. He knew this was one of the most important cases he'd ever handle, and part of his preparation was sitting with the family.

SHIRLEY FINGERHOOD Cy, I assume, was the one who found him. I knew of Brill because he had an excellent reputation as a top criminal defense lawyer in the city. He had a beard and a swagger.

MICKEY KNOX I visited Adele in the hospital, but I also visited Norman when he was in Bellevue after the arraignment. He was calm, subdued. He talked about what it was like being in Bellevue. There was something between us, as I recall, a door or screen or something, and they let us talk for only about five or ten minutes.

After the stabbing things were very unpleasant between Joanne and me. Once she got over the shock of it, she was absolutely vitriolic about Norman, whom she'd adored up to that point. There was always a coldness between her and Adele, who is ten years older, but now she was totally on Adele's side and blocked Norman out from then on. She couldn't understand why he'd done it, it was beyond her comprehension.

Al, Joanne and Adele's father, was just saddened by it, oddly enough, when I thought he could have been hostile and dangerous. He always liked Norman, and still does. Adele's mother was crazy and violent and probably wanted revenge, but I tried to avoid her.

I was unhappy because it was such a fucking mess, but I wasn't confused and I thought I even understood it. I knew Norman, I knew Adele, I knew the potential for violence was enormous, so the explosion didn't surprise me.

MIDGE DECTER Norman P. hadn't been able to visit him in Bellevue, but Mailer then came over for lunch the day he got out. He was absolutely himself, very calm, and definitely not tranquilized. After his obviously heated state, for all I know it was a time for reflection. Norman had always had a "court," and when he got out he turned up with the doctor who'd been examining him, which was quite remarkable. The doctor had been converted into another courtier.

At lunch, though, he didn't talk about the stabbing. He said he had to be on his good behavior, but he didn't specify how things were being worked out with Adele's lawyers. I remember too that after she got out of the hospital there was a short-lived attempt at reconciliation, that or a brief pretense that they were going to go on as before, or they hadn't yet made public that they were breaking up. I remember we went over to their place—they were still on Ninety-fourth Street—and it wasn't the same between them.

DIANA TRILLING   Norman telephoned me from Bellevue just as I was writing him a letter. I told him I had a letter to him in the typewriter, and he said, "Read it to me," which I did. Mostly I had been explaining that I had to write to him because I had been talking about him and his situation. How not? It was the universal subject of conversation. But I didn't like talking of him behind his back without his knowing what I was saying, so I wanted to tell him what I had been thinking and saying to other people about the stabbing.

Now, I'm very matter of fact and clinical about such things, not literary. I was very worried for Norman: I thought he had had a psychotic break and that he needed psychiatric help. But Lionel wholly disagreed with me—it's an interesting example of how wrong people were who thought we were always of the same mind about everything. Lionel insisted that it wasn't a clinical situation but a conscious bad act; he said Norman was testing the limits of evil in himself, that his stabbing of Adele was, so to speak, a Dostoevskian ploy on Norman's part, to see how far he could go. My position was that I thought he should see a psychiatrist, and I remember Lionel saying, "He's your friend, you'll have to say to him what you want to say, but it isn't what I would say."

I hadn't had any inkling that Norman would do anything like this, and I'm kind of bright about such things. We'd been invited to that party, by the way, but hadn't been able to accept. And, indeed, when I heard about it I was terribly upset. He could easily have killed her. He was within a fraction of killing her, and he didn't have control of himself—I don't care what he said or Lionel said.

Well, I read him my letter on the phone. He listened closely, but he didn't comment on it, except on one sentence. In explaining why I was writing, I had written, "Silence is its own form of communication." He said, "That's a good sentence. I want that sentence." His tone was very quiet and serious, nice. He wasn't at all excited. I found that very reassuring.

That was the period in which Lillian Hellman and I were friends, and we were on the phone quite often while Norman was in the hospital. She was worried too. I think she assessed the situation clinically, much as I did. When he got out of the hospital he called and asked me if he could come over; we made a date for the next afternoon. That evening I mentioned on the phone to Lillian that he was coming to see me.

She got quite agitated about that. She said, "Diana, you can't do that. You can't let him into the house. Are you going to see him alone?" I said, "Yes, of course." She said, "No, that's dangerous. You can't do that. You're taking a terrible chance. You can't be alone with him." This was very odd. Compared to Lillian I'm tissue paper, she was so much tougher than I am in every way. I thought, This is really strange. I, who am afraid of my shadow, am unafraid to see Norman, but she's afraid. It was all very funny. I kept saying, "He's never done anything the least bit out of control in my presence, Lillian. I'm not the least bit worried about being alone with him." People have often asked me, with our politics so different, how I came to be friends with Lillian. I know the answer to that. So many women are only home-bound, limited in outlook. I've always looked in my life for bold, brave, large-spirited women to be friends with. Long before women's liberation Lillian had been out there in the world, living what I thought must be such a handsome, independent life. It was a great disappointment to me to discover that she kept small scores on people.

Well, Norman came to see me, and I felt very sad for him, even though he didn't agree with me that he needed medical help. Anyway, I've come perhaps to agree with him that there isn't all that much useful psychiatric help to be got. What he said to me almost immediately was how awful it was always going to be, "because people will just gently move knives away so they're out of my reach." There was no question in my mind but that he felt guilty for what he had done. Maybe not guilty enough, but guilty.

LILLIAN HELLMAN   I've never told anyone this story, except a psychiatrist. When the stabbing happened I'd been in Rome and read about it in the newspaper, then I came back to New York in January.

Shortly thereafter I had a telephone call. It was Norman's voice and he said, "I'm speaking from a phone booth in Bellevue and I haven't got much time. I'm very broke. Would you come down and bring me five hundred dollars?" I said, "Okay, I'll bring it down."

This was during the last months of Hammett's life; he was very ill in bed. After I got the money I went into his room to say goodbye for the afternoon. He asked me where I was going. I said, "I'm going down to give Norman Mailer five hundred dollars because he needs it. He's in terrible trouble, as you know because you read the newspapers."

There was a long pause, and he said, "Lillian, you're not going to do any such thing. You're a sucker and often a goddamned fool, and you're not going out of this room."

Dash was among the most generous people I had ever met and so this puzzled me. I said, "My friend's in trouble, I'm going down with five hundred dollars. That isn't so much money." He said, "I'm not talking about the five hundred dollars. You're just not going to meddle in this business."

Then Dash got out of bed. He could barely walk, but he made it to the bedroom door. The house was a beautiful old mansion and had wonderful brass locks with great big brass keys that nobody could ever move, but Dash locked the door, put the key in his robe, and went back to bed, saying, "Now, take your hat and coat off and sit yourself down." I said, "Have you gone crazy? Give me the key right away." I went over to the bed, but he said, "Lillian, you know I'm very, very weak, but I'm strong enough to break your arm if you try it. You're not going down there." I began to cry, and he said, "Please leave me alone now. I'll open the door when you promise not to go down there."

I went and sat on the couch. About an hour later I said, "I want to get out of the room. Dash, unlock the door." So he unlocked the door and I walked out. We never mentioned the episode again. To this day I remember Hammett's anger. It was so unlike him to deny anybody money, but he wouldn't answer my questions.

What I'm not going to tell anybody is why Hammett was so opposed. He used a sentence that I'll never repeat because it was very anti-Norman. And Dash liked Norman.

Many years later I told Norman this story, but he denied it ever happened. Which might show Norman's good nature and sweetness.

BARBARA PROBST SOLOMON   I had drinks with him, just the two of us. He was giving me advice about the publication of my book. I remember feeling I'd always been his friend and that I would have died had he known that I was afraid of being alone with him, but the fact is I was very scared. He was visibly changed, more low key and going out of his way to be courtly. I remember vividly my sense of the meeting: he was testing me, testing how his friends were reacting to what had happened.

Later, life was hard on Adele. She was something of Norman's creation, after all. When he needed an F. Scott Fitzgerald creation, he took a rather fiery, beautiful person, put the spotlight on her—"I'm macho, you're my Zelda"— and he wound her up like a clock. Afterward she was left hanging. Adele was always fairly malleable, like the young actress the director makes into a glamorous star. In contrast, Bea was the immovable object. No Zelda she.

JUDY FEIFFER   Adele was angry, I'm not saying she wasn't, but she was a lady, and her behavior towards Norman was admirable and loyal. I don't know how or why or in what way she loved him, but she felt Norman was a major American genius, and that was important to her. In a sense she was his creation, like in *The Deer Park*. He was the man in her life, and she's a passionate woman, so it had to be one of the most intense and convoluted and strange relationships to this day. But even so, months after the stabbing, when life was normal again, I visited her, and she told me she was going to try to make the marriage work.

DR. JACK BEGNER   I've always admired Adele because she left him like a lady. She could've ruined his life, destroyed him, but she chose not to by refusing to press charges and agreeing with the conditions the lawyers set out.

MARIA IRENE FORNES   What I saw of her was always a person that was rather good-natured, even after the stabbing. Afterward she would say, "I guess you know what Norman did," and she would laugh.

Norman I saw about two months after the stabbing. I wasn't close to them anymore, but he told me that at first they said that Adele had fallen on something, on broken glass, but then he'd decided the next day, "After all I couldn't hide behind a woman's skirt." To me that was really so sad and ugly. I mean, he stabbed her. An ordinary person commits a stabbing, he doesn't have this choice, whether to hide behind this or that. I'm talking about Norman's privilege, that even in a moment of despair he is reacting in a privileged manner. As a human being, when you have almost killed someone, anything but total humility is unacceptable. Or total self-defense. Or total craziness—"What am I gonna do? What am I gonna do?" And what I find objectionable in the reaction "I will not hide behind a woman's skirt" is that it's neither one nor the other. It's like saying "I won't go to jail in Alabama, I'll go to jail in West Newport." After what had happened he was in no position to bargain.

I suppose she was willing to protect him because she is a jerk, but the fact that she's willing allows him to think he's in a position to set the conditions of his release. I don't know what they worked out, but it involved the public fact that they were supposedly together, while they weren't when I saw them. I'm not saying she was a fool to go along with the conditions, but the thing is that Adele was a person who would go along with anything. Sort of like the way Genet says in *The Balcony*, "You are the Queen, you are this, you are that." It's the same thing as her going to be an actress, then going to be a painter. These were her assigned roles.

BARBARA PROBST SOLOMON   Mrs. Mailer took the helm after the stabbing. She made the great remark, "If Norman would stop marrying these women who make him do these terrible things..."

FANNY SCHNEIDER MAILER   He stabbed Adele because of anger. She drove him to it, and she could drive anybody nuts. I'd seen the anger, but I didn't attribute much strength to it because I thought it would wear off. But after it happened I placed my faith in prayer. I thought it would work out, I never gave up for one minute. Maybe the way I was brought up made me tough, but you can only place your trust in God. . . . Sunday night I guess I was up at the house— I don't remember what happened. I just prayed that he wouldn't be put in jail, that he should be free to live his life from then on. What else could I do? I was helpless. Every human being is helpless when it comes to a real crossroads.

JAMES BALDWIN   When I finished writing "The Black Boy Looks at the White Boy" it was exactly when Norman encountered his disaster and was in Bellevue. The piece was for *Esquire*, but I refused to turn it in before showing it to his sister, Barbara. I left the typescript with her and said, "I want to show it to you before anyone else. I don't want to betray Norman."

RHODA LAZARE WOLF   Norman has written things that are great, but he's still not the great novelist, and back then he was so confused. What's remarkable is that in spite of what was going on underneath—all of which came out of his relationship with his parents—he had this marvelous rationale about art and life—and he actually did it, he lived it. And it wasn't just something that he did half-ass. It almost killed him—or actually Adele—but he was compelled to go through with it.

When we heard about the stabbing—Dan heard and called me—it didn't surprise me, but there was nothing for us to do. We had already pulled back by then, and Dan had been saying, "He's out of his mind, he's impossible." His looks had changed, everything. So we couldn't possibly get involved, and it just seemed cheap at that point to try. Dan doesn't cry, but I do . . . and I did. And despite everything that had happened I continued to love Norman. Yes. Oh, my God, yeah . . . I was peripheral in all this because at that point Norman had no use for me. He'd made certain overtures, but I just couldn't accept them. I thought of Adele, but really all I could think of was Norman and Barbara, and I felt that Adele had provoked him, very much so. I'd heard all kinds of stories— that she wouldn't leave him or let him leave even though the marriage was finished, that she was doing all kinds of awful things, and so after the stabbing, even when I'd moved away from Norman, my feelings were . . . well, Whatever Norman does, you protect him, you back him up.

Barbara very quickly saw the whole thing, the tragedy about Adele, the tragedy with Norman. She was overcome. She knew what he was going through but couldn't speak to him, and when Barbara can't talk, it's because she's angry. Mrs. Mailer, though, went crazy. The day after, when the police were looking for him, she was terrified that they'd take him away from her.

Still, one of the biggest surprises was that despite everyone's prediction that the stabbing was going to be the end of Norman, it wasn't. Joe Coleman, who worked at *The Voice* and was a crazy genius himself, did a brilliant analysis of why it wouldn't hurt Norman—the psychopathology of the time, people needing a hero, notoriety becoming an entertainment for the masses. And it's turned out that he was completely right.

VIII:
DEATHS
FOR THE
LADIES,
PRESIDENTIAL
PAPERS,
AND
AN
AMERICAN
DREAM
(1961-65)

HENRY GELDZAHLER I'd talked to Norman during the year after the stabbing, and the following summer I was staying at the Waterfront when he and Lady Jeanne Campbell first got together. What amazed Norman was that first Adele had liked me, and now Jeanne was crazy about me too. I met her at a party at the beginning of the summer, but we already had friends in common, so right away she and I plugged in, and I suppose Norman found it useful psychically that there was a continuity between Adele and Jeanne in me.

That summer Jeanne was writing columns for the *Evening Standard* and was going to do a story about a fat farm up Cape, a kind of inside look at a real American phenomenon. She asked if I wanted to come along—"Let's go look at the fat girls." "Wait a minute," I said, "I'm not exactly a skinny boy, I'm not sure that's so funny." She wasn't exactly trim herself, though, and finally I agreed to go, and we took Norman's car, the little two-seat Triumph. We had lunch with the girls, saw them weighing in, but afterwards, when we came back to the car, all the fat girls were sitting on it. We got hysterical, imagining how we'd have to return the car to Norman and explain why the springs or whatever were totally flattened.

I liked Jeanne, but I also felt she was suppressing much of her energy, sub-verting it to his energy. She was also positioning herself to become the wife in a way that made it clear that once she achieved it, she wouldn't be Little Miss Priss. Remember, she's a Beaverbrook or Argyle, and not to take that seriously—both in herself and her daughter—would be to miss a fundamental part of her character.

NORMAN MAILER (OF A FIRE ON THE MOON) *Norman, born sign of Aquarius, had been in Mexico when the news came about Hemingway [July 2, 1961]... and had one full heart-clot of outraged vanity that the* Times *never thought to ask his opinion. In fact, he was not certain he could have given it. He was sick in that miasmal and not quite discoverable region between the liver and the soul. Hemingway's suicide left him wedded to horror. It is possible that in the eight years since, he never had a day which was completely free of thoughts of death.*

Of course, he finally gave a statement. His fury that the world was not run so well as he could run it encouraged him to speak.... Besides, a British lady columnist passing through Mexico with him thought it would be appropriate to get his remarks on the demise. This, after all, was special stuff—the reactions of one of America's best-known young novelists would certainly be appropriate to the tragic finale of America's greatest living writer....

MARY MOWERY I was awfully busy with children and running the Waterfront that summer, so Eldred probably did more socializing. Norman still had the group of Washington friends around from the previous summer—the Carriers, Bill Ward and Bill Walker, Lester Blackiston, Dick Dabney, a couple of others that Eldred had to run out of the house with a shotgun once because they got drunk and were threatening him.

Even though later that summer he was with Lady Jeanne, he'd been up alone earlier in May or June, staying in one of the smaller apartments. Some of the Washington punks had driven Norman's car up from New York, and I called the police because they dumped it over at the Patrician and threw the keys away or something. By the time the police arrived, Norman came walking from somewhere in the East End, and I had to explain what had happened. I could see he was annoyed by the whole thing—he'd come up alone and was trying to get down to work.

Even when he was with Jeanne, though, he still liked wild and mean people, but I don't know what she thought of them. I liked Jeanne, she was a very friendly person, although I didn't understand her. She had one of the apart-ments—the one above us—and early on she was with her cousin. My mother was staying with me that summer, visiting from Kansas, and since Jeanne didn't have a phone we let her use ours. She'd get these transatlantic calls from famous people, but after she'd hung up she'd sit down and talk. My mother isn't easily fooled, she doesn't like people who try to charm her, but Jeanne took an interest, and what impressed me was that a woman with her background had that ability. I don't know if she was writing, but she knew a lot of people. There were calls from India.

Mailer, Mary Hemingway, and Lady Jeanne Campbell.

I also saw her dancing the twist quite wildly at the A-House, and I'd never seen anyone dance as freely. She was a true English eccentric. Norman isn't an eccentric, really, but she was an original. Once we were all at a party at Jay Kurtz's, and the group included one of the guys from Washington, a huge guy, a monster. They called him Big Foot or King Size or something, and he and Kurtz got into a big fight and Kurtz knocked him out. Then they were all going off to another party, and they were dragging King Size into the taxi with them. They decided they'd better have something to pacify him with if he came to, so Jeanne took a toilet plunger along in the taxicab.

FAY DONOGHUE   I think maybe she was in Provincetown to interview Norman. She'd just been interviewing Yuri Gagarin, the Russian astronaut, and there was a rumor going around that she'd had an affair with him. Plus there was the glamor of who she was—Lord Beaverbrook's granddaughter and all. I first met her at a party given by some crazy sculptor who went mad finally. He used to live in the woods in back of Bradford Street in a trailer—the doorstep was an old radiator. It was one of those typical P-Town parties—a drunken brawl started. Jeanne entered the fracas armed with a toilet plunger and went around pounding everyone with it.

ROGER DONOGHUE   The great thing was that she helped Norman tremendously after the Adele thing. He had been very depressed, and I think she raised him out of it. I remember a party she gave when they were first going together. Jimmy Reardon, a tough-guy friend of mine, was there. So was Jeanne's mother, who asked Reardon what he did. He said, "I'm into meat, I'm a meat purveyor." And Jeanne's mother replied, "Is your veal tit fed?" I nearly fell off the chair waiting for Reardon's reply. He just nodded, speechless.

Jeanne was very intelligent and strong. With that English accent of hers she could have been flighty, but she's a smart lady. She helped Norman by taking him to a whole different set of people, not only in London but the social European group living in New York. She was more independent, more in control than any of Norman's women.

DIANA TRILLING I don't know how to explain Norman's recent interest in that ragtag world we call "society"—charity balls, that kind of thing. He's not Proust and America isn't that kind of country; this part of the century isn't Proust's part of the century. It's the world of money and fashion and overnight celebrity, an Andy Warhol world. Norman's too good for that, it disturbs me. But I suppose it started further back than I realized. I remember an amusing episode when he was first with Jeanne Campbell, and her mother, the Duchess of Argyle, came to America on a visit. They gave a party for her in Jeanne's apartment. The room was jammed, it was worse than the worst subway crush. As soon as we arrived I was introduced to Jeanne's mother, and I talked to her for a minute or two, then I made way for somebody else.

After a while I couldn't stand the crush and I told Lionel I wanted to go home. He was glad to leave too, so we started to go, sort of waving goodbye to Norman. "No, no, wait," he called. He came over. "I want you to meet Jeanne's mother." I told him I'd met her, but he kept insisting that I had to come and talk to her some more. He nagged at me about what an interesting person she was until I heard myself say, "No, I don't think so." I meant to be rude to Norman, not to Jeanne's poor mother, about whom of course I knew nothing. But Norman was shocked. He said, "I always thought I could count on your good manners."

You see, that was an important part of our relation. Norman thought I was polite enough even to be counted on in a situation with a duchess. He didn't seem to realize that part of good manners is being able to be rid of them—or not rid of them so much as being able to use them independently, like his own behavior the night we first met. I think he often confuses manners with propriety: it had to do with some basic misapprehension of people in society.

FANNY SCHNEIDER MAILER With Jeanne I stayed at a distance. Her mother once came on a visit, and I went up to Norman's apartment and fixed dinner for her. It was like touching ice water; you don't stick your hand in, it's uncomfortable. I was at a respectful distance and she was at a respectful distance, but I wasn't overcome with the fact of her royalty, not a bit. Perhaps Norman was impressed with it. But he found it was nothing, it was *poof*.

NORMAN ROSTEN He once brought the English lady, Lady Jeanne, over to meet us, which was an unusual thing for him to do. He just pushed the buzzer and came up. This was before they were married, and I think he wanted to show her off.

HEDDA ROSTEN Partly to show her off, yes, but also to get our reaction. I didn't know who she was, but when I saw her, I thought, laughing to myself, My God, what hath Mailer wrought this time?

<u>NORMAN ROSTEN</u> She was stunning—a little heavy, yes—but I think Mailer said something terribly complimentary, like "Isn't she gorgeous?" It was clear he was quite taken with her.

<u>ADELINE LUBELL NAIMAN</u> It was the fall of '61 when he called out of the clear blue sky. We hadn't spoken for a half dozen years, since the night of our fight about Adele. He was with Jeanne and wanted me to meet her, and he asked if they could come and visit. I was shaking all over, just as I had the night of our fight, but I said, "Sure, come on."

When they arrived, Norman and I didn't sit down and talk about it. First, because I knew I couldn't ever trust him again, that I couldn't talk intimately or personally or openly any more; he may have been mending fences, but he had Jeanne with him and he was trying to please her. Also, I recognized in Jeanne another me in some ways. I didn't think it was important to him to sit down and say "I'm sorry." But I don't know. Recently it startled me when he admitted he'd driven me out. Of course I know he never forgets anything, but I hadn't realized that he was aware of how central it was to our relationship.

<u>WALTER MINTON</u> I was sort of astounded that all of a sudden she now turned up with Norman. I figured he must have looked at her and said, "Jesus Christ, if I was a girl this is what I'd look like." Given the fact that she has the same kind of bushy hair as he does, it was almost like you wanted to screw your sister.

<u>ARTHUR SCHLESINGER JR.</u> I knew Lady Jeanne before she was married to Norman because she was a correspondent here for the *Evening Standard*. Charles Winter, the editor of the *Standard*, was a friend—we'd been at Cambridge together, in England, before the war. I met Lady Jeanne through him; either he sent her to see me in Cambridge—Cambridge, Massachusetts, that is—or I looked her up once when I was in New York. When she and Norman were together, '61, '62, I was in Washington by then and was rather surprised to hear they were married.

<u>EILEEN FINLETTER</u> I wasn't around, although I'd known her from before, and when I heard about the marriage, my response was laughter. I thought it was rather cute.

<u>RHODA LAZARE WOLF</u> Norman's had many love affairs, and I wouldn't be surprised if he fucked Diana Vreeland. One of the things he used to talk about was the "wicked ladies"—"getting in with that group, with those wicked ladies." By "wicked lady" I assumed he meant a shitty society dame, and then he wanted to fuck one after another of them, and I'm sure he succeeded. He wanted so much to be a part of the ugly Oscar de la Renta thing, so it didn't start with Jeanne; it was germinating earlier, when he was playing with the tape recorder— like his old high school trick of blowing smoke rings, standing there and tapping his cheek—the same concentration of self-masturbatory fantasies. It all had to do with his desire to conquer the world. He doesn't want to be the boy from

Crown Street, he's always wanted to be his own creator, and what can be more narcissistic than that?

NORMAN MAILER (LETTER TO FRANCIS IRBY GWALTNEY, APRIL 14, 1962)

Dear Fig:

Thanks for the review. At the present moment, it's one of two I have seen, and since the book has been out for two weeks and no more in the offing, maybe Deaths for the Ladies *will go down in the records as having its worst review written by* Time *and its best by Don Francisco Gwaltney. Anyway, I thought it was a well-written review, i.e., I wouldn't know how to write a review of that book in the space you had, and get an equal number of notions in.* . . .

NORMAN MAILER (EXISTENTIAL ERRANDS) Deaths for the Ladies *was written through a period of fifteen months, a time when my life was going through many changes including a short stretch in jail, the abrupt dissolution of one marriage, and the beginning of another. It was also a period in which I wrote very little, and so these poems and short turns of prose were my lonely connection to the one act which gave a sense of self-importance. I was drinking heavily in that period, not explosively as I had at times in the past, but steadily—most nights I went to bed with all the vats loaded, and for the first time, my hangovers in the morning were steeped in dread. Before, I had never felt weak without a drink—now I did. I felt heavy, hard on the first steps of middle age, and in need of a drink. So it occurred to me it was finally not altogether impossible that I become an alcoholic. And I hated the thought of that. My pride and my idea of myself were subject to slaughter in such a vice* . . .

One modest reality used to save such hours from dipping too quickly into too early a drink. It was the scraps of paper I would find in my jacket. There were fragments of poems on the scraps, not poems really, little groupings of lines, little crossed communications from some wistful outpost of my mind where, deep in drink the night before, it had seemed condign to record the unrecoverable nuance of a moment, a funny moment, a mean moment, a moment when something I might always have taken for granted was turned for an instant on its head.

Some of those curious little communications which came riding in on the night through an electrolyte of deep booze were fairly good, many were silly, the best were often indecipherable. Which would feel close to tragic. Almost always the sensation of writing a good poem in the dark of early morning was followed in the daylight by the knowledge I had gone so deep I could not find my eyes. My handwriting had temporarily disintegrated in the passion of putting down a few words. Somebody had obviously been down in the rapture of the depths.

It was not so very funny. In the absence of a greater faith, a professional keeps himself in shape by remaining true to his professionalism. Amateurs write when they are drunk. For a serious writer to do that is equivalent to a professional football player throwing imaginary passes in traffic when he is bombed, and smashing his body into parked cars on the mistaken impression that he is taking out the linebacker. Such a professional football player will feel like crying in the morning when he discovers his ribs are broken.

Deaths for the Ladies, and other disasters: *"I was drinking heavily. . . . Most nights I went to bed with all the vats loaded, and for the first time my hangovers were steeped in dread."*

I would feel like crying too. My pride, my substance, my capital, were to be found in my clarity of mind or—since my mind is never so very clear—let us say found in the professional cool with which the brain was able to contend with the temptations and opportunities each leap of intuition offered. It was criminal to take these leaps like an amateur, steeped in drink, wasteful, wanton . . .

I would go to work, however, on my scraps of paper. They were all I had for work. I would rewrite them carefully, printing in longhand and ink, and I would spend hours whenever there was time going over these little poems, these sharp dry crisp little instants, some of them no more and hopefully no less possessed of meaning than the little crack or clatter of an autumn leaf underfoot. Something of the wistfulness in the fall of the wind was in those poems for me. And since I wasn't doing anything else very well in those days, I worked the poems over every chance I had. Sometimes a working day would go by, and I might put a space between two lines or remove a word. Maybe I was mending. As the sense of work grew a little clearer and the hangover receded, there was a happiness working mornings on Deaths for the Ladies *which I had not felt for years. I loved* Deaths for the Ladies, *not because it was a big book—I knew my gifts as a poet were determined to be small—but because I was in love with its modesty. The modesty of* Deaths for the Ladies *was saving me. Out of the bonfire I seemed to have made of my life, these few embers were to be saved . . . Every line was placed on the page by me. The spaces were chosen with much deliberation, the repetitions of phrases were like images in a film. The music of the poem as a whole—if it had any—was like the montage of a film. I felt that all of* Deaths for the Ladies *made up one poem, not at all a great poem, never in any way, but still a most modern poem about a man loose in our city . . .*

Of course, if you fall in love with a book, you may be certain it will drown, suffocate, or expire all alone on an untended bed. Deaths for the Ladies *came out in modest edition and sank without a sound. It was only reviewed three or four places, and the one good review it received (the Sunday* New York Times) *was six months late. Poets, for the most part, resented it. Why should they not? I had dabbled in that life for which they were willing, if they were good enough, to starve and to lose love. They had studied their craft, I had just skipped about in it. They were dedicated to poetry. I was dedicated to climbing out of the hole I had dug for myself, and poetry was offering the first rung . . .*

But to end on a note less altruistic to the interests of art, let us look at one review. I had had secret hopes, I now confess, that Deaths for the Ladies *would be a vast success at the bar of poetry. The hopes got bounced. Here is the review in* Time, *March 30, 1962:*

Ever
see
a drunk
come on
daring
I mean
drunk
like
daring
was a
sloppy
entrechat?
Mr M
comes on
with fourbucks
of poems
about sex
not love
that run
down
like this
only
not
lined up
neat.
Having less
than
fourbucks
fun
a reader
counted
the words

and concluded
Mr M
is making up
for his
first book
which had
too many.
You
didn't
score
this
time
M
a
n
.

But hell you know that.

In a fury of incalculable pains, a poem was written in reply, sent to Time
magazine's column of letters, and printed there.

POEM TO THE BOOK REVIEW AT TIME
You will keep hiring
   picadors from the back row
   and pic the bull back
   far back along his spine
You will pass a wine
   poisoned on the vine
You will saw the horns off
   and murmur
The bulls are
   ah, the bulls are not
   what once they were
Before the corrida is over
   there will be Russians in the plaza
Swine some of you will say
What did we wrong?
and go forth to kiss the conquero.

Now, on the comfortable flank of this reminiscence, I think I may have been
fortunate to get so paltry a reception on Deaths for the Ladies. For if I had been
treated well, I might have kept floating in a still little pond, and drowned my
sorrow for myself in endless wine and scraps of paper and folios of further poems.
Instead, the review in Time put iron into my heart again, and rage, and the
feeling that the enemy was more alive than ever, and dirtier in the alley, and so

one had to mend, and put on the armor, and go to war, go out to war again, and try to hew huge strokes with the only broadsword God ever gave you, a glimpse of something like Almighty prose.

MIDGE DECTER   Lady Jeanne's not an East Side lady, she's a British aristocrat, and that's a very different kettle of fish. They're far more formidable, the real thing; there was a streak of craziness, of wildness, with no sense of consequences, which only a true aristocrat would have. And Norman was not unaffected by the fact that she'd been Henry Luce's mistress, either.

We spent some time with them after they were married and living in Brooklyn. Her grandfather disapproved of the match, and at least at that point she was cut out of her inheritance. Mailer said, "She'll give up ten million dollars for me, but she won't make me breakfast." After they split up she said, "Here I married this terrific, powerful, dynamic, romantic literary man, and he turned out to be a guy who had to go see his mother every Friday night for dinner."

So each of them was pursuing some idea and obviously hadn't really seen the other. I assume she's the wife who's strangled in *An American Dream*. She was one of those people who could be absolutely straightforward with you and then, in a second, suddenly become the duchess. She was also drinking a lot.

BOWDEN BROADWATER   He'd changed greatly. There was an enormous expansion of personality. He had quickness, a sort of tough, ambitious way about him, and he'd put on stature. As one friend remarked after he married Jeanne, "He's become more ducal," which sort of sounds nasty but wasn't meant that way. It had to do with his becoming almost patriarchal.

JUDY FEIFFER   It was a high-velocity marriage, with energy and sparks. Jeanne's fascinating in the way that only English aristocratic women are—a kind of high bohemia. There is the intellectual sparring, the sexuality, the sense that she'd been around. And Lady Jeanne had been around. She was smart and interesting. She was a correspondent with a life of her own, and she was fascinated by him too. I'm sure they turned each other on sexually.

DIANA TRILLING   But there had always been Norman's insistence on propriety and rules with his daughter Susan. She and my son Jim were about the same age. She was up here on a Christmas visit when they were twelve or thirteen, and Norman said they should meet, so it was arranged. Jim had to go out to Brooklyn and pay a call, and then he was allowed to take her to an afternoon concert—I think it was in Carnegie Hall. Afterwards Norman and Jeanne met them, and then they came back to my house and we all had tea. The next vacation, or perhaps when Susan moved up from Mexico, Norman said to me, "Susan's back." I said, "Great, I'm sure Jim would be delighted to see her. Tell her to call him, he'll be so pleased." He said, "My Susie doesn't call Jim, Jim calls Susie." I loved it. "My Susie doesn't do the calling."

EDITH BEGNER   That same summer in P-Town Norman and Lady Jeanne were living in the Sinaiko house. Jeanne was very pregnant, and I guess Kate was born that August. Josiah Child had a party for us, we were all out on the screen porch, and we see the two of them coming down the street, Jeanne looking like a fat nun. She was a funny-looking dame anyway, but she was wearing some sort of *shmatte*, with her belly out to here. Then along comes Norman, practically in evening clothes—a dark suit, white shirt, and tie. Norman! In Provincetown! Suddenly, because he was married to Lady Jeanne, he was nobility. He was very polite, the perfect gentleman, and like everybody else, I was at a loss for words.

ROGER DONOGHUE   He'd already bought the house in Brooklyn Heights, and I planted a tree in the backyard when Kate was born. "A tree grows in Brooklyn," we said, for his new daughter. The goddamn tenant who took the apartment four years later cut it down.

JEAN MALAQUAIS   I had an argument with Mailer after his marriage to Jeanne. It wasn't really serious. I said he had a way of exploiting his women. He became angry: "What do you mean? I work like a horse for them." None of his wives ever had to make a living, so how could I reproach him with being their exploiter? I reminded him of the time Elisabeth, my wife, and I were invited to dinner, about eight days after Kate was born. Jeanne had just gotten out of the hospital and left bed to prepare the meal. When we were finished, it didn't even dawn on him he might clear the table. As I recalled that evening, he countered, "What's the big deal? Jeanne was perfectly all right." I guess he has no feelings for such trifles. It's not even a question of upbringing or anything like that. He just sits, talks, and eats.

ANNE BARRY   In the fall of 1962 I was hired by Norman. This came about because in '61, my senior year at Radcliffe, I'd taken Erik Erikson's course, and for the final big paper we had to look at someone's works, their letters and autobiographical writings, and analyze them. I chose Mailer, using *Advertisements*, and wrote a galumphing, huge, pretentious, wonderful sophomoric paper, 52 pages long, on Norman Mailer's identity crisis at the age of thirty-nine.

In the service of this paper I'd written Mailer asking if I might come down and interview him. I felt very daring, thinking I was the only college kid ever to write such a letter, yet he wrote back, astonishingly enough, and said, "I usually don't say yes to letters like yours but I liked your handwriting." Of course I had framed my letter carefully with my italic pen.

I didn't get to see him until spring vacation. I met him at his sister's place on Bleecker Street—I think he was living there—and we went to a bar, but he didn't like the atmosphere, the vibes weren't good, so we got up and went to another bar. The meeting went into the evening, and we had a lovely time laughing and joking and talking about everything under the sun. I thought it was the nicest, funniest, most bubbly time I'd ever had. I adored him. Eventually we went back to Barbara's, and I was dimly aware of Jeanne Campbell there, in the background, I guess to look me over.

Anyway, I came to the horrid realization that Norman Mailer was not having an identity crisis at the age of thirty-nine. What I'd misunderstood was that he was a very funny man, yet I had written this totally humorless paper, and while I can laugh now, I went back to Radcliffe in despair. I couldn't rewrite the thing—I had to hand it in two days later—but I kicked myself for being so stupid.

Norman had said that I should get in touch with him and that maybe I could do some typing when I came back to New York, so I went out to Brooklyn Heights, where he'd bought the brownstone, for an interview.

Norman and Jeanne were living on the ground floor, the garden apartment, since they hadn't yet redone the apartment upstairs. Kate had just been born, and Jeanne had brought Sadie, her own maid, who was very old, to live with them. Jeanne was downstairs, Norman and I upstairs in the small studio, but she came up at one point to dictate some thank-you notes. I realized afterward that the point of this, like at Barbara's, was to study me carefully. I guess she found me no danger and soon went away, and then Norman, apparently thinking he'd already asked me to work for him—which he hadn't—said, "Well, when do you want to start?" We discussed salary, and he proposed something munificent like fifty dollars a week. I was so green and grateful and dumb that I took it.

So I began working in September of '62. My day was walking Tibo, making Norman breakfast and lunch, taking the laundry to the laundromat, typing, and filing. I typed a lot of stuff for *Presidential Papers*, some poems, although *Deaths for the Ladies* was already done, magazine articles, and a lot of stuff like his columns for *Esquire*. I had the impression of Jeanne always sleeping late. She also had a cable thing to London, a Telex or whatever it's called, for her political commentary, but if there was some reason for me to go downstairs, she was either sleeping or sort of trailing around in her housecoat. I remember her dropping clothes on the floor as she undressed. If she took off her coat, it went on the floor. I don't think she thought I'd pick up her clothes—I doubt she even considered whether anyone would.

Things were pretty tempestuous, but usually I never ran into her. There were whole aspects of Norman's life that I don't think she was particularly interested in or didn't have any use for. She had her own life, and she seemed totally out of key with the pace of his. For example, she'd had a wonderful, fey, fashionable interior decorator decorate the downstairs apartment; he'd covered the walls and ceilings in a god-awful flowered-print cotton fabric so it looked like a French bedroom, and it was all padded underneath the fabric. It was incredibly expensive, but it was so comical and incongruous because it didn't exactly reflect the Mailer sensibility. I think once Norman made a joking remark about the walls, but basically his behavior was correct.

And, of course, upstairs there was nothing that fitted that kind of woman. That's when Norman had Ray Brock come in and build the crow's nest and catwalk, and there was a rope ladder up to the loft area. Ray and Norman consulted at great length when they were building the lofts. Ray was unmarried then, though he later married Alice of Alice's Restaurant, and now I've heard he died quite young.

This was not long after the Adele business, of course. In fact, one time his parole officer came by. Awkwardly they shook hands, then they chatted, made small talk—"How have you been? What have you been up to?" It seemed a courteous conversation, but at that point I walked out of the room. Later Norman made a remark, something like "Whew, these things are terrible." He was embarrassed, I was embarrassed. I mean, how does one cope with that kind of thing? It just seemed incongruous and inappropriate to all parties concerned.

Still, despite the differences between Norman and Jeanne, I thought she must have been very comforting to him after the Adele business. After all, they'd lived together in that tiny, oh, maybe ten- by fifteen-foot studio, where I later had my office. I couldn't imagine how they'd managed it with that sofa bed, because there wasn't room enough to walk around when it was unfolded. I hadn't seen them at that stage at all, but he told me they'd lived in that tiny space until the downstairs apartment was fixed, so they must have been very content with each other. By the time I arrived they were fighting, though, and the whole house wasn't big enough for the both of them.

Norman once made a rueful remark about how marriage is what ruins it all. He was sort of nonplussed by this, by how odd human relationships were, that with the same person you could have such different responses and that the two of them could have been so happy in that little space and then be fighting when they had all the room they needed. And to me that fancy flocking on the walls and ceilings in the apartment showed how out of sympathy they were—that she'd had the house decorated that way seemed a very ladylike but incredibly aggressive and hostile act, just imposing that décor.

The first entry in my diary—which I began promptly after starting work for Norman—was October 11, 1962. It's quite early on that I began musing about the devil, so he and I must have been talking about it. My diary reads like a very poor parody of Norman Mailer. Actually I didn't really understand him, but it seemed to make perfect sense to me then, and I prided myself on my mystical streak.

It was also late that fall—my diary dates it November 27—that Susie came to live with them. She was thirteen. Danielle and Betsy would come on weekends to visit, often with Hetty, their maid. Susie was going to live with Norman because she'd be with Bea during the summer and vacations, but she had to go to high school and start thinking about college. So she went to Elizabeth Irwin. I don't know if there was any acrimony about this with Bea, but I think Norman was very happy to have her there. She arrived before Jeanne left, I think, though I can't remember them ever in conjunction with each other.

The atmosphere of the house during that year—well, everything was very lively: deliverymen, messengers, agents, crackpots, and fans, even convicts wandering in and out. I don't know if that was special to that year, whether Norman was dissipating himself; all I know is I walked in and there it was.

At first I was mainly typing his poems. Day after day he would take pieces of paper out of his pocket and explain their importance to me. He would have me type them, then sometimes retype them, even though he didn't necessarily rework them. I suppose it's true—it makes sense what he says—that this was partly the first step toward climbing out of the hole he felt he was in.

He did these poems for a long time, and sometimes they were meaningless drivel to my twenty-two-year-old eye, and I'd often sneer at them and correct his punctuation and grammar. His response was to call me "Mrs. Mark Twain," an affectionate teasing, because Mrs. Mark Twain dumped on her husband's work and criticized it, and I don't know but she may have been a nagging censor, his unofficial editor. But this was joking, a name he came up with. It was part of his humor. He also used to tease me about what he perceived as my prissy New England uptightness and WASP mannerisms, because I had told him about my growing up in New Hampshire, my father going to Amherst and becoming the business manager of Phillips Exeter, and my going to Radcliffe. Even when he was depressed, really down in the dumps and very quiet, he'd still joke with me and often tell jokes in which he was the butt, like when he had to make lemon meringue pie in the army.

From time to time the household was empty, and we had wonderful talks. I'd arrive in the morning and make breakfast—always scrambled eggs. I'd also make lunch. Not tuna fish then but sixteen-ounce shell steaks from the Bon Ton meat market. The steak had to be precisely done—first onions fried, then the steak, pan-fried, medium rare—though eventually that sixteen ounces of steak became a little too much even for Norman. I didn't realize it then, but I suppose it's possible that he was on a drinking person's diet, the protein to burn up the booze. Certainly he was drinking a lot, but, as I say, I was so green that I was in a surreal world.

I suppose that's why he was protective, warning me about mistakes I might make, explaining the world to me. I felt he was someone I could trust with my life, and even though I was young and awkward and gauche, I could ask him questions or disagree. Our talks got as personal as you could get, I used to discuss my lovers with him, and he was aware of my being involved in things and walking through situations, and maybe I was a little crazy then too. For example, I was involved with some people from the Living Theater and went to a party in a loft which lasted three days, and I remember flicking my cigarette into a piece of tin foil; the host flinched and with a pair of tweezers picked my ashes out of about five hundred dollars' worth of cocaine. But the code of the time said you didn't scream at people when they made blunders like that. Years later the guy resurfaced and visited me. His mind was blown, his eyes were dead and cruel, he was a drunk and dangerous. He was into S&M, which he had been before, but I hadn't known, even though there'd been whips all over his apartment. It's as if I went through that whole period as an innocent, walking in and out of weird situations, and I missed immense amounts of information. Which is why I confided in Norman, of course, and why he'd get so avuncular with me.

NORMAN PODHORETZ   I found his marriage to Jeanne Campbell quite comprehensible, even obvious—she was Lady Jeanne Campbell, the daughter of the Duke of Argyle, the granddaughter of Beaverbrook, the mistress of Henry Luce, all of which fascinated him.

I quite liked her, liked her better than some of the other wives, actually, and I think she was very fond of me, at least for a while. But as with all Mailer's marriages, I began to find the fighting tiresome. Once they had a huge fight in my house, and Jeanne ran into our bedroom and jumped under the covers of our bed, literally hiding from him and refusing to leave. She spent the night in our bed, while Norman, Midge, and I stayed up the rest of the night in the living room, talking, waiting for her to come out. That was another thing about being Mailer's friend. He never understood that people had to get up in the morning and go to work; if he came over to your house it was impossible to get him out before five in the morning, and he simply wouldn't take a hint.

It was a rocky period for him, no question. He was writing those little poems that he knew I never thought much of, but I was also aware that the poems were his way of keeping himself alive as a writer. He was looking for things to do, marking time. He wasn't blocked in the usual sense—I don't think he was ever blocked in the sense of being unable to write at all, though for a long time he certainly had trouble writing fiction.

But I didn't think he was crazy, and I've known a lot of ambulatory psychotics in my life. He was unstable and volatile, but I was never afraid that he was going to crack. You knew he'd come out of it. It was just a question of time, of waiting for this thing to pass.

DIANA TRILLING   I didn't speak to him at all while writing my essay, "The Moral Radicalism of Norman Mailer," and he didn't know what it was going to be like. He knew I was writing it, and he offered his father's services to give me such biographical material as I might need, but after the piece was finished I asked him if he wanted to read it. He came to the house to read it, and I could feel something strange was happening. He finished reading and then sort of made a move as if he'd had a lot of air stored in his lungs. He asked me if I would mind if he went for a walk, so I told him to go ahead. I was troubled too. Before he went out he said, "I didn't expect such a formal piece." I acknowledged that it was formal literary criticism. But what had he expected—some kind of "My friend Norman" piece? He said, "No, I don't know what I thought, but I wasn't prepared for this."

It was obvious that he was disconcerted, and while he was gone I thought, I've treated him the way I would treat a major writer; he ought to love the piece. If he's not smart enough to know what I'm doing with it, then that's too bad. I'm not going to let myself be upset.

So when he came back I wasn't all aflutter: "Oh, dear Norman, have I not written a good piece? Do you not like it?" Precisely what he said I don't remember. If it had been memorable I'd have remembered it. He never mentioned it to me again. His word about it was "formal." I suppose by that he meant that I had written a masculine essay—probably that wasn't the part of me he cottoned to. On the other hand, it should have been nice for him to feel that I was putting my best force of intelligence so largely on his side. Not that at the time I was aware that he particularly needed legitimization. Thank God I didn't think about that one way or another or I could never have written the essay to begin with.

That piece was the second serious essay ever written about Norman, the first being Podhoretz's in '58. Norman was still not being given his literary due: I got very little feedback on that essay in the literary community. The psychoanalytic community was something else again. They hated it. I gathered they were violated by the fact that I said that Mailer, without knowing it, was really more a Freudian than a Reichian. That's too complicated an idea. Anyway, their real objection was that I took him seriously. They could only think of him as a case. Now, I suppose, they think of him as a troubled artist. As a celebrity. They've become more alert to celebrity than they used to be. Everyone has.

On the literary front, I think it had something to do with me that Philip Rahv and William Phillips got to know Norman and became friends. They of course had always been aware of him as a literary character, but I think I brought them together a bit personally. I don't mean to overestimate my own intimacy with Norman. I think there was a time when the relationship was important to both of us, but I don't want to make it oversized. Still, when Phillips gave me a party for the publication of *Claremont Essays*, he asked only six or eight of my closest friends, and Norman was one of them. And if I may say so, I think that perhaps Norman got something from me for his reportage from my piece about Ginsberg, "The Other Night at Columbia." He admired that piece and wrote about it a bit in *Partisan Review*. One influence at least I do claim: for good or bad, I think I introduced Norman to the uses of smell. It was a sense he had neglected in his previous writing.

LIONEL ABEL I'd see him at parties, like *Partisan Review* parties at Phillips' on Eleventh Street. There would be the same gang—Susan Sontag, Hannah Arendt, Mary McCarthy if she was around, everybody—and the thing I noticed was that everybody wanted to *touch* Norman. People would go over and literally touch him. Later, in '65, I met Moravia in Rome and I mentioned this. Moravia said, "Maybe they feel that he's more real than they are. That's why they want to touch him, to hang onto reality."

WILLIAM BURROUGHS There was no ostensible central issue at the Edinburgh Writers' Conference in 1962. Norman was there, along with a number of other writers—Rebecca West, Mary McCarthy, Stephen Spender, Lawrence Durrell, Richard Hughes, Angus Wilson, plus various Europeans—and the conference split into factions. Alex Trocchi, Mary McCarthy, Norman, and myself were on one side, as opposed to Spender and Hughes, who were, shall we say, the more conservative element. This was the first time I'd met Mailer, and we saw each other a fair amount during the conference.

I remember Hugh McDermott, a frosty old Scots poet, quite a local celebrity, said that people like us—not Mailer, but me and others—belonged in jail instead of on the lecture platform. Mary McCarthy countered by speaking of my work and also Nabokov's in very high terms, which went down very, very badly with Spender, and it got fairly acrid. Norman was very much in the center of things, in the thick of it. He wasn't being hostile or anything, but he asked questions; he asked a Yugoslavian Communist a lot of questions the man didn't want to hear, like about so-and-so, who'd been imprisoned. But I wouldn't say there was all that much hostility toward Norman so much as it was directed toward me and Alex Trocchi—with the exception of Rebecca West, who was standoffish towards all of us.

I hadn't been that aware of Norman throwing in with Ginsberg and Kerouac in '57 or '58, but I did sense some kinship because of "The White Negro." I think he had a sense of shared values and felt this was where the action was. I don't think he was ever involved with drugs the way a number of us were, and I think I read somewhere that he felt he'd been naïve about homosexuality, that he hadn't wanted to think about the question, so he hadn't faced it. Even so, I thought of him as an ally, a friend. For both Mary McCarthy and him to come out for me was a great help. And it's possible that when he saw the hostility toward me it only strengthened his allegiance.

RHODA LAZARE WOLF   Barbara and I were together a lot during this period when she was breaking up with Larry. She was looking gorgeous. Because of the aggravation, she'd slimmed down and had the most beautiful figure you ever saw, and her hair was just starting to turn gray. The breakup, though, took a while. I suppose she talked to Norman a great deal, although Norman was going through his own *tsuris,* and eventually Larry moved out of the Bleecker Street apartment. But Barbara was already involved with Harry Jackson, the painter. They never lived together, but their thing went on for a year or two.

ALAN KAPELNER   Harry was a painter, a dear friend of mine and also Jackson Pollock's closest friend. They both came from Cody, Wyoming, and Harry was an authentic cowboy. He'd come to New York right after the war—in his boots and cowboy hat—to get into Hans Hofmann's school. He was tough and aggressive and macho, the same type as Norman, maybe with equal intelligence but not as brilliant.

The problem, I suppose, was that she was more into Harry than Harry was into her. He was a womanizer and always loved to be seen at a party or just walking down the street with very good-looking women. He wasn't a beauty himself, but women were attracted to him because he was aggressive, full of temper, extremely eloquent and literate. Not like Vance or Norman, but he had a good mind, and his wisdom had a stiletto sharpness to it.

BARBARA PROBST SOLOMON   It wasn't until after breaking up with Harry that she realized she didn't have to seek that kind of self-dramatizing male. Suddenly she existed in her own aura, not just as Norman Mailer's sister, and she didn't have to seek a romantic object who was some knock-off of Norman.

TULI KUPFERBERG   We took the name "The Fugs" from *The Naked and the Dead.* I thought it was funny, I wanted something outrageous, and maybe that's the word we thought we could get away with.

We'd all been reading at the Metro Café, on Second Avenue between Ninth and Tenth. Culturally a very important place, 'cause in the early sixties that's where almost all of what was going on on the East Side was happening. Every poet of consequence read there or passed through, people from the West Coast included. Ginsberg, Burroughs, Gregory Corso, and Ed Sanders and I used to meet there, though actually Ed and I had first met at the *Fuck You* thing, the magazine. We also used to meet in front of the Avenue B theater, where people sold their poetry books, but Ed would be handing his stuff out free. The Avenue B theater was where Jonas Mekas would run avant-garde films.

Then, also, there was a Polish Ukrainian bar on St. Mark's Place, the same place as the Electric Circus, and they had a sort of club with a jukebox. We used to go there after readings and watch these fat-assed Poles trying to dance to the Beatles and the Stones—the whole scene had a lot of vitality, so I got the idea of combining poetry and the music. There was one other person, Ken Weaver, who was from Texas and dishonorably discharged from the air force, plus me and Ed.

The Fugs was just a goof at first, then Ginsberg got involved and occasionally did a gig with us. Mailer might've come to a couple of performances, and maybe Ed gave him some of our albums. He was also at parties, usually the high-class parties, not the ones in the dumps. He was always detached, because he was an established artist, which was probably a drawback. He couldn't come to the Metro and just sit there, it would've disrupted the whole thing, and I'm sure he knew that. But we were cynical about the whole "Camelot" atmosphere of those years, and one of the things we did was make up a deck of playing cards—designed them and had them printed. Jack Kennedy was the King of Hearts—the whole Kennedy family and Pierre Salinger were in there. Every card in the deck was a person in America, a cross-section of the famous people, and Norman was the joker, which may have been kinda stupid on our part.

CLAY FELKER   At *Esquire* we loved to start fights, which was why we assigned Norman to write about Jackie Kennedy. This was after he stabbed Adele, remember. There we were, having this guy who'd stabbed his wife going to write about the First Lady. The assignment was obvious.

NORMAN MAILER ("THE FIFTH PRESIDENTIAL PAPER—THE EXISTENTIAL HERO-INE")   *"An Evening with Jackie Kennedy" was begun in Villefranche in March, 1962, continued in Paris, and finished in New York in May, 1962. Since one had stopped smoking in January, the writing went slowly. [It was] published in* Esquire *in July, 1962.*

HAROLD HAYES   Mailer's relationship with *Esquire* had begun years earlier, and in fact I'd seen an announcement for *Advertisements for Myself*, and having liked "The White Negro," I called Putnam's and asked to see the manuscript. Instead I got what Mailer thought we should have, which was "The Mind of the Outlaw," along with a very complicated series of stipulated constraints, eight or ten in number, which I negotiated with Charles Rembar. These included top billing on the cover, with nobody else's billing larger than his own. I don't recall whether the other conditions included no editing of the piece, but at that time *Esquire* put great emphasis on not editing arbitrarily anyway.

Mailer had sent us a letter in January 1961 about the change in the title of "Superman Comes to the Supermarket." The magazine took the position that it would title its own material and subtitle it however it wanted to. He complained that we had changed "Supermarket" to "Supermart," and also took great exception to the comments in italics which were a sort of summary of each section, like chapter headings. Clay Felker wrote them—they weren't changes in the piece, they were insertions, which we referred to as "call-outs." They were not in Mailer's voice, they were in the magazine's voice, and we inserted them because the piece was quite long.

Even though he was as pissed off as his letter indicates, he and I were on amicable terms. He was not on amicable terms with Clay Felker, and his animus was toward the whole magazine. He felt he'd been fucked over.

Still, Norman initiated the idea of doing a column for us in '62, and we were pleased to have him. The magazine has always been committed to getting the best writers, first with Hemingway and Fitzgerald, and so on, and we were also very much absorbed with the writer-as-personality. The writer was central to many of the events of the sixties.

After "Superman" I was dealing directly with Norman. There was "An Evening with Jackie Kennedy" in July '62, then the Liston piece. His column, "The Big Bite," started in November '62, and he turned it in to me directly. Later there was the essay "Some Children of the Goddess."

The Liston piece, "Ten Thousand Words a Minute," also dealt with the Benny Paret-Emile Griffith fight and was a very important piece in the evolution of Mailer and *Esquire* because it demonstrated his capability of making metaphor of anything he wanted to look at. Of course he was always interested in boxing, and the Liston-Patterson bout was a big fight. It was hyped, and everybody was watching it, but all the papers would be on top of it, and we were stuck with a three-month lead time. Hence the need for metaphor. Not that he spun out metaphors—he didn't just find some fancy way to write. It was that he saw something in the event that would have application to all our lives, so even with the three-month lead time, the piece wasn't dated or redundant.

NORMAN MAILER ("TEN THOUSAND WORDS A MINUTE")   *And Paret? Paret died on his feet. As he took those eighteen punches something happened to everyone who was in psychic range of the event. Some part of his death reached out to us. One felt it hover in the air. He was still standing in the ropes, trapped as he had been before, he gave some little half-smile of regret, as if he were saying, "I didn't know I was going to die just yet," and then, his head leaning back but still erect, his death came to breathe about him. He began to pass away. As he passed, so his limbs descended beneath him, and he sank slowly to the floor. He went down more slowly than any fighter had ever gone down, he went down like a large ship which turns on end and slides second by second into its grave. As he went down, the sound of Griffith's punches echoed in the mind like a heavy ax in the distance chopping into a wet log.*

HAROLD CONRAD   Norman's description of the Griffith fight was absolutely right, I was there. It was a terrible fucking scene, frightening. You saw that Paret was going to die, everybody knew it, but the referee, Ruby Goldstein, was frozen, just standing there immobile, and didn't stop it.

Later I was putting together the Patterson-Liston fight with Roy Cohn and Tom Bolan and their company, Feature Sports, and they didn't know anything about the fight business. Fugazy, the limousine guy, was involved, but they dumped him. I hooked up with them because my partner had been Al Bolan, Tom's brother, a nice guy. So I got the thing going, I was handling the press, and it hit me, "I'll try to get all those writers out there. Shit, I'm gonna give this fight racket a little style." Even Jimmy Baldwin got an assignment and showed up. Also A. J. Liebling, Jimmy Cannon, and Nelson Algren and, of course, Budd Schulberg. Budd I'd known longer than any of these guys. We'd been kids together, we'd go out drinking. I'd take him down to the gym, so he knew about boxing.

As for Norman, I'd only met him once before, when I wrote for the *Brooklyn Eagle*. But out in Chicago we got to be friends. I hustled the Buckley thing for him—he was debating Buckley two days before the fight, on Saturday—and we were drinking all the time, hanging around together at the Hefner mansion, though there were all kinds of beefs, bullshit between Budd and Norman—I suppose because Norman was drunk most of the time.

I set up a press room in the grand ballroom of the Sheraton, a hundred typewriters, wires clicking, the whole thing. Three days before the fight I get a wire, "Must have credentials to cover fight," and it's signed Ben Hecht. A day or so later I go into the press room and I see a bunch of young guys standing by the wall, looking at this guy typing away with a cigarette in his mouth. It's Hecht, and these guys are creaming. We've all been raised on Hecht. So I go over to say hello, and he stops typing and looks up. I see that all the lines on the page are even, about eight lines: "All good men come to the aid..." over and over again. He's been doing an act for the young reporters. He says to me, "Jeez, I'm glad to see you. I don't know what the hell's going on here." I tell him I'll get his credentials. "Who are you covering it for?"—I think of Ben Hecht, he'll be covering for *Life* or *Time*. But it's the *Hackensack News*. "I had to come," he says. "This is my town, the biggest story. I had to be here."

Everybody was going bonkers—they always do at a big title fight, but this is more than just a fight. It's a scene, a promoter's dream.

The Buckley-Mailer debate in the Medinah Temple was packed. College kids, the Cohn and Bolan set, and about two hundred newspaper guys. Norman started, and then Buckley came up with that shit, that syntax of his, and Mailer came back with his great line: "Mr. Buckley, you want me to lie down on the railroad tracks, tie my hands to the rails, and wait until the engine of your logic gets around to riding over me?"

I also threw a party for friends in the penthouse. Everyone got into beefs, I needed a referee. Norman had Baldwin in tears. He was rough on him. I don't know what it was about, but I had to go placate Jimmy, and then I became a kind of father figure for him. Then there's the big postfight party at the Playboy mansion. It's a smash, six hundred people, action on all three floors, and in the midst of it Norman takes me aside and says he's got something to say to the press. I tell him to be in the press room at ten in the morning. I was as drunk as he was, so I forgot all about it when we moved Liston's press conference from noon to ten.

The next morning I get to the ballroom and it's packed, the cops are bringing Liston down from his room, and there's Norman, he's up on the stage sitting in Liston's chair. I got the cops with me in the wings now, and I'm thinking, How do I get the son of a bitch out of Liston's seat? Norman had been up all night, probably two nights running, so I stop Liston and go out to Norman and say, "Norman, Liston's here. You're fucking up my press conference, so get the fuck out of the champ's chair." He says, "Fuck him, I ain't moving." I says, "Those cops'll kick the shit out of you." "Fuck the cops," he says.

Now, I'd seen a picture of the president of Sears, Roebuck being carried out of a board meeting in his chair, so I say to the cops, "Don't lay a finger on him. Just pick up the chair and carry him out." Which is what they do, depositing him backstage. Norman, he's like a Chinese mandarin, with that stupid grin on his face.

Ten minutes after the press conference started there's a voice from the back of the room. It's Norman. He's come back in, and everyone starts booing. "Throw him out!" they're yelling. But then Liston—who was a boozer himself— says, "Leave the bum be. He's just drunk." And Norman comes up and they shake hands. They're pals. Catastrophe averted.

PETE HAMILL   It wasn't until the press conference the morning after the fight that I realized there was something bizarre going on, and it was just as bizarre to everybody else. This was really before Ali and all that, and nobody was used to that kind of crazy stuff. I had spent my time trying to find Patterson before he got out of town, so I got there late, just when the thing with Norman happened, and it happened very quickly. I was concerned, because I didn't want anybody to beat the shit out of him. Everybody thought he was off the deep end, like "Jesus Christ, what the fuck is this?" There was talk that this was the Mailer who had stabbed his wife, people thought he was flipping out again, that it was all consistent. My reaction went a little further: I could imagine myself sitting down and writing "Superman Comes to the Supermarket," but I couldn't imagine myself pulling that kind of caper where I crossed the line into participating in events instead of observing them.

But the whole week it was one of the last great boxing scenes. Because of Conrad all sorts of writers showed up who wouldn't ordinarily cover that kind of thing, like Norman, Schulberg, and Baldwin. What made it magical were all those personalities, some of whom had never been to a fight before, and the sensibility was pure Conrad. I wasn't the *Post's* main guy at the fight. Milton Gross, or maybe Al Buck was there, and I was the supplementary guy writing sidebars whenever they came up. I was twenty-seven, just a reporter, and I hadn't written any columns or novels yet.

Anyway, I hadn't known Mailer in New York and I think I just introduced myself. We had breakfast at the hotel one morning, just the two of us. He was sober, and he wasn't pulling rank either. He was encouraging, maybe because I was from Brooklyn or maybe he knew my work and thought I had the beginnings of some kind of talent. I really have no idea why, I didn't ask him, though it might also have been that he was more of a boxing novice than I. I had known Patterson since the fifties, both personally and as a fighter from the Gramercy Gym, Cus D'Amato's gym, where my kid brother Brian used to box as an amateur. I knew more about Patterson than most people, just as Jack McKinney from Philadelphia knew more about Liston, so to some extent maybe Norman was interested in the way I saw Patterson, since I'd written about him when he took the championship back from Johansson, I guess in '60.

My interest in Mailer, though, was not simply in the boxing context. What was important to the newspaper guys of my age was what he'd done in his *Esquire* piece, "Superman Comes to the Supermarket." I was already working at the *Post* in '60, and I remember that suddenly most of the younger guys were talking about this amazing piece. There was Ed Kosner, now editor of *New York*, Don Forst, who later was at the *Boston Herald American* and then the *Los Angeles Examiner*, Gene Grove, Norman Poirier, and Al Aronowitz, and the piece had an amazing impact. It showed us that there was a way to do journalism that was not as rigid as we had thought it was. It was as if Mailer had taken the form and expanded it, shoved it around, and said, "Okay, here's what you can do with this fuckin' thing." I'd read *The Naked and the Dead* and *The Deer Park*, but here was the Mailer who seemed to satisfy both your journalistic and literary instincts at the same time. Of course there were other guys doing good work, like Gay Talese, who was also working for *Esquire*, and Tom Morgan, who was writing really good profiles, but Mailer had come along and put himself at the center of the action.

So in Chicago I think he was flattered that the so-called professional journalists, as compared to critics or some other kinds of shitheads, respected what he did. There was probably some sense of running with the real guys, and in a sense he was an amateur in the best sense of the word: he loved what he was trying to express. I don't remember if he'd done any journalism between the Kennedy piece and the fight, but I think the scene in Chicago was the first time he was getting this kind of feedback from younger guys like me and Larry Merchant and Stan Isaacs. I don't think the older guys, the Jimmy Cannon-Red Smith generation, respected him all that much, because they didn't know the novels, and to them Mailer was simply the guy that stabbed his wife.

I don't know if his pleasure at our reaction was bittersweet, in the sense that while the Kennedy essay was a triumph, he might have had the nagging feeling he was through as a novelist. I didn't know him before, remember, and I'd be the last to say that writing "Superman Comes to the Supermarket" was a fall in his literary fortunes. Besides, I've always thought that literature-as-the-National Football League, with team standings and all that shit, was ridiculous. I thought it then, I think it now, since the whole point is just to write as well as you can, whatever it is you're writing.

As we talked Norman wasn't trying out his piece on me as a guy like Murray Kempton will. He was just absorbing, not spinning out metaphors or talking about the politics of the fight business, just absorbing. He was for Patterson, but he also had amazing respect, as everybody did, for Liston. We talked about the Paret-Griffith fight, which I'd covered—and in fact that's one of the reasons the Post had sent me to Chicago, because I'd done this job on the Paret-Griffith fight that nobody could touch because I speak Spanish. I knew Jose Torres, and Jose had boxed Paret in Puerto Rico in '59 or something, so I knew how to write that story.

As for Norman, what can I tell you about his work habits? He carried around a little notebook, but his notes weren't the kind that a reporter takes. I know that because he and I went to a bar with Gene Courtney, a boxing writer from Philadelphia—a scene he actually mentions in his piece. The two of us made a bet on whether Patterson would win, and I think I gave the bartender the money to hold. What I remember is Norman taking out his notebook and noting a line of conversation. I was sitting on a stool, Mailer and Courtney were standing, leaning against the bar, and Norman turned away, right there, and wrote himself a note. That's when you see that funny look on his face—a kind of out-of-focus expression when he throws the thought down, then snaps back in again. This is different from the way most other guys work, myself included. I tend to take more notes than I'll ever use because I want to make sure I've got the name of the street, what kind of trees were over the entrance, who said what to whom, and I write down exact quotes. But Mailer wasn't trying to reproduce dialogue. I think it was probably a scrap of language or an image that drifted through his head, and he just took out his pad.

WILLIAM F. BUCKLEY, JR.   It was terribly funny, really absurd. Each of us was to be paid $1500—$1250 or $1500—and Norman demanded cash in advance. He wouldn't mount the stage, he said, unless he was paid beforehand, and the poor producer had to run out and somehow round up the money.

NORMAN MAILER ("TEN THOUSAND WORDS A MINUTE") *The night before, at Medinah Temple, before thirty-six hundred people (we grossed over $8000) I had had a debate with William F. Buckley, Jr. The sportswriters had put up Buckley as a 2½-to-1 favorite before our meet, but I was told they named me the winner.... [Then] on Monday morning the New York Times had ... called the result a draw. I did not take it well....*

I had been [at the fight] with half a body from half a night of sleep for too many nights, and half a brain from too many bouts of drinking drinks I did not want that much, and dim in concentration because I was brooding about the loss of a friendship which it was a cruel and stupid waste to lose. And Baldwin too had been brooding. We had sat there like beasts of burden, empty of psychic force to offer our fighter.

Now, too late, in the bout's sudden wake, like angels whose wings are wet, we buried our quarrel; this time it might stay buried for a while. "My Lord," said Jimmy, "I lost seven hundred and fifty dollars tonight."

Well, we laughed. I had lost no more than a paltry twenty-eight.

CUS D'AMATO I don't recall how, maybe through Roger Donoghue, but my feeling is that when Patterson became champion, I believe in '56, Norman was already around boxing. I remember that he and I were talking quite a bit—we always talked—and we spoke several times in Chicago, with him asking me questions. He understood a lot more than he heard—he'd really look and see, whereas the other guys either were getting paid off, that or they'd just go around and get a consensus of opinion from people who were mostly incompetent. I was fighting the Organization then, and a lot of newspaper writers, the old-timers, were on the payroll, and used to go and get their envelopes every week. Norman was aware of this, I think, so he never bought the company line. He was perceptive enough to ask the right questions, the most revealing questions.

But the newspaper writers were working for the people I was fighting. They used to blast me every week 'cause I was the only serious person confronting them, and they tried to make me a bad guy. I mean, there were a lot of tough guys around. The International Boxing Club controlled boxing all over the world, and from the time Patterson had been fighting a year or so—figure '53, '54— they were trying to put me on ice. They had the money and considerable political influence, and they also had TV locked up, plus the press in all the big cities.

By '62 in Chicago, it's true, just like Norman wrote in his article, I tangled with Fat Tony—Fat Tony Salerno, the gambler. But he wasn't part of IBC. The guy I really tangled with was Frankie Carbo. Contrary to what people assumed, Carbo wasn't Mafia, but he was the tough guy who controlled the fight managers by using the Managers Guild, which had been a good organization, but then when Joe Louis retired, IBC tied up all the top contenders so they weren't permitted to fight anyone else. They got control of all the titles, not just the heavyweights. For example, Nat Fleischer, who ran *Ring Magazine*. He may have been innocent, but maybe he was intimidated by IBC, because he would never rate Jose Torres, my fighter, in spite of the fact he knew Jose was the best fighter around. He'd say, "But he hasn't fought any contenders," which of course was because IBC controlled the contenders, and you couldn't get a fight without their say-so.

Norman was aware of this, I know, because we spoke about it. Harold Conrad was aware of it too. It had gotten to the point where I slept in the back room of the gym with a police dog. Not that I thought I was going to be shot—things didn't happen that way—but the boys could have found a means to take care of the situation to make it appear an accident. Like I stopped riding the subways because they're crowded and it's very easy for a guy to shove you off the platform.

Also I knew they were politically powerful enough to get the cops to frame me, so I always safety-pinned my pockets so nobody could palm off dope on me; if you got caught with drugs, you were barred from the fight business for life. I just anticipated all the possibilities, and this had gone on for more than four years. I was on television, exposing what was going on behind the scenes, and I refused to let anyone control my fighter or the decisions I was making for him. They wanted to control everyone, all contenders, all champions. They controlled every champion except Sugar Ray Robinson, because Robinson was already established, but they tried to work on him too.

So when Norman wrote his essay, and talked about me and the mob and the psychology of boxing, he knew a lot of this background. His mind and emotions were very different from the usual newspaper guy. But also it was partly his genius. When Norman Mailer wrote something, people read it, and the perception penetrated to even the average person. The only people who wrote the truth about what was going on were *Sports Illustrated* and Norman, and that's how my side of the picture was becoming public.

MARA LYNN CONRAD   That whole crazy scene in Chicago! Harold was handling the press, keeping everything in his head, but we didn't know what to expect. We were just geared up, ready for whatever came next. What I remember most is, after the fight we went to Hefner's party, and you could feel the friction between Norman and Budd.

HAROLD CONRAD   Yeah, he and Schulberg got in terrible fights. They were both drinking, and they're both kind of aggressive when they get drunk. They'd known each other and hadn't liked each other, then they're put together as roommates in the mansion! Before the bout they'd had a fight in my suite when I had all the heavies up—Jimmy Cannon started on Schulberg with the Communist shit—"Your father was no fuckin' good"—and Norman got into it. Then Norman went to work on Baldwin, and Baldwin was almost in tears. Mara took him into the other room and he started to cry. He was in love with Norman, and Norman had been very salty to him—"Fuck you," that kind of attitude.

But I don't really know if there was a specific beef between them—Norman and Budd, I mean. Everybody was so drunk. At one point they threatened to get physical, but it got stopped before they went outside. Schulberg kept coming to me saying, "I ain't gonna stay with that s.o.b. at that fuckin' place." Norman had been on his ass, the way I saw him do with a friend of mine, a black girl. This was at a party at our place in New York. The woman's kind of an ex-hooker, very tall, very beautiful, very knowledgeable, and he was calling her a "cancerous broad." Maybe he really wanted to fuck her, or maybe he just wanted to insult her, to let her know he knew where she was at, because she comes on very grand.

Mara says Norman wasn't that bad in Chicago, but I know Roger got fed up with him. We were all drinking, but he was drunk all the time—I mean, impossible.

MARA LYNN CONRAD   It's true, Norman was drinking, but maybe he was also drunk with victory after the debate. That got him charged up. But "impossible," no way. Most folks are lucky—they fall down and pass out when they get drunk. Not Norman, though. But I don't think his judgment ever left him, even at the press conference when people thought he went ape. Because when Norman goes ape he's always got a little reserve that tells him exactly what he's doing and whether he can get away with it. At the press conference he knew Harold would handle it.

But it just broke me up when they carried him offstage in the chair and into the hallway out front. That's how he got up out of the chair and came back in through the front doors of the room again. He was smiling, he wasn't obstreperous. Liston was up on stage already, and Norman started shouting from the back about some idea he had. We never found out what the idea was; I don't think even he knew, but later he said it was a promotional scheme, something involving the Mafia.

There were at least two hundred press guys there, and they all thought Norman was crazy, so they started yelling at him. But Liston looked up and said, "Let the bum talk." Liston enjoyed him—he's a street guy and knew what was happening.

HAROLD CONRAD   Norman was fuckin' up my whole press conference, and I don't think he had any sense of what was going to happen when he pulled that stunt. It was Liston's chair, see. If I hadn't told the guards to carry him out, they would've beat his ass. And Norman couldn't have known I'd come up with that.

Being ejected from Sonny Liston's press conference, Chicago, 1962: "He said, 'Fuck 'em, I ain't moving.' I says, 'Those cops'll kick the shit out of you.' 'Fuck the cops,' he says."

Tom Bolan and I were thinking more of saving the press conference than Norman, goddamn it.

Later on he was worried and angry that Red Smith blew the whistle on him. Smith wrote something about the press conference, and Norman said, "The son of a bitch is gonna ruin my parole." That's why Norman hated Red Smith. He's the only guy that ever hated Red Smith, all because Smith stuck in something about him in his story for *The Times*.

The interesting thing was that Norman had gone out to Chicago rooting for Patterson because he loves Cus D'Amato, Patterson's trainer. Also Patterson was the underdog. But Liston became champion, and they yelled back and forth at each other at the cocktail party, and that's when Norman became a big Liston booster. He later interviewed him one-on-one, which is rare, 'cause rarely do you get those guys alone.

ROGER DONOGHUE   For twenty-four hours at Hefner's mansion we never saw daylight. There were two heavies at the door who wouldn't let you in unless your name was on the list, and at one point I got a phone call in my room—it's this Brockton voice, namely, Marciano, and they won't let him in. The fucking heavyweight champion of the world! So I ran over to one of the bodyguards and said, "You'd better get on the phone and let Marciano in or you're going to be minus two doormen down there." Archie Moore was there. And Joe Louis too. But no broads. The bunnies were locked on the top floor for Hefner, who'd come down in his bathrobe for a peanut butter sandwich and then disappear. It was the most sexless hangout I've ever seen.

What flipped Norman was the debate with Buckley. He took me back to meet him, telling me, "Send out psychic darts into him." Bullshit stuff. He was boozed but managing to hold his own until Talese's review in the next day's *Times* claiming it was a draw. Then there was the press conference, and I called Jeanne Campbell and said, "You'd better protect yourself, he's flipped." He was in the same kind of mood he'd been in with Adele. I told her to find some head people to talk to him. He was paranoid, and I gave her the number of a psychiatrist friend. Then I didn't see him for a while after that. I was mad at him—"Fuck you, you're acting like a jerk, embarrassing me in front of my fight friends, and I don't need it." I didn't abandon him, I just told him it was too damn depressing.

NORMAN MAILER   The idea I wanted to present at the press conference was demented—namely, that the psychic forces that had surrounded Floyd Patterson had made it impossible for him to fight against Liston because he had been knocked out by a psychic vortex. The Mafia had so surrounded the ring, so surrounded Liston, who was their candidate, that they had established the evil eye, and in his vanity Patterson had separated himself from Cus D'Amato, who knew more about warding off the evil eye than anyone alive, and so it was the evil eye that got Floyd, not Liston. Liston was the most amazed man in the house when Patterson went down.

My idea was to publicize all this. I was still thinking in terms of movie scenarios, and the notion was to bring back Cus D'Amato, with Patterson winning the rematch. That's why I say it was demented. As far as I was concerned, I had seen it all — it was absolutely true, there was no question in my mind — and in "Ten Thousand Words a Minute" that's why I said that at the press conference I had picked Patterson to win by a knockout in the sixth round and I was still right. You see, it was just that the true scenario hadn't had a chance to enact itself, because Patterson was knocked down in the first round. Two minutes. And nobody ever was quite certain what knocked him out, so at the press conference I was going to attribute it to witchcraft, which in my grand and demented theory was going to build the greatest gate in history.

RHODA LAZARE WOLF   I had a feeling that the period after the stabbing, when Norman was with Lady Jeanne, was even worse than the period before. The marriage was very short, and he "kills" her in *An American Dream*, but if they hadn't split she would have killed him.

Dan and Norman were still not talking, so I only went to a couple of things where Norman read or gave a talk. It was pathetic. He acted kind of psychotic, saying one thing and then suddenly switching to something else, with no connection. I think it was when he gave something at Town Hall or Carnegie Hall, a poetry reading, and Jeanne was there, even though I think it was after they had separated. She was quite slim and lovely-looking but with all her AC-DC boys in tow.

I couldn't believe what I saw, and it was kind of overwhelming, because I was always defending Norman. I was annoyed that he was making a fool of himself. I listened to him because I felt that he had a peculiar kind of sensitivity to what was going on, that in some part of his brain he knew what was happening to him and why people were reacting the way they did. But I don't think he could have taken those perceptions and used them differently, because, in fact, he wasn't in control. Not then. Some of his perceptions were so crazy and inaccurate, he wouldn't have known what to ignore and what not to ignore. He was sick, and the form it took was an extreme kind of detachment.

I didn't talk to Barbara or anybody else except Dan. Norman was a great victim, a scapegoat for a lot of people, so a lot of them weren't saying nice things about him. I didn't know any of his friends in such a way that I could have talked to them about it, and I avoided talking to Barbara because Dan and Norman were still enemies. Not that I'm that loyal a wife, but Barbara feels that everyone should love and support her brother no matter what, so I felt caught in the middle. Barbara and I didn't suspend our friendship, we just didn't talk about Norman.

PETE HAMILL   Probably a month or so after the Patterson-Liston fight I took Norman to the Gramercy Gym to meet Jose Torres, thinking he ought to get to know a fighter instead of staying on the outside. I wasn't worried that he'd be taking up the cudgel for Jose because I knew Jose: Jose is not a sycophant, never was, and, in fact, nowadays he thinks of Norman as *his* friend rather than the other way around.

At the same time, I got to know Norman. He was with Jeanne, and from the little I saw of them in any kind of intimate way, I think she enjoyed him and there was a kind of rowdy attraction. It's hard to explain if one hasn't been there, but I think what she must have found attractive was the total unpredictability, which was unlike anything she'd ever encountered. The combination of Brooklyn hoodlum, which was a role Norman could don from time to time, and an obviously brilliant man. The dangerousness too—and I'm not talking about physical danger so much as just not knowing what is going to happen next. It's like when you go up the Amazon, there's a sense of danger because you don't know what's around the bend, or the sense of danger in combat, that for fourteen straight hours nothing happens, then somewhere up the block there's someone suddenly shooting, and you don't know when it's going to arrive. . . . It's like the sense I have of Norman in conversation, that he's trying to really talk and figure something out. It's the same pattern. Norman's mind is moving, bobbing, and it must be the same in a relationship, since there is a totally unrehearsed, spontaneous, unconventional part to him that makes bizarre and brilliant leaps.

DIANA TRILLING Secretly I used to drink more when I was with Norman than I usually did, just to see if I could keep up with him. I'm not a good drinker, far from it, but I have periods in which I do better, especially with brandy. It has to do with how I'm feeling, how life is going for me. I remember one night when Lionel and I and Jeanne and Norman went to see some Egyptian belly dancers, then we went to a little place on the East Side that Norman knew about. There was a piano player and a half dozen beautiful hookers, college-graduate hookers, but you could sit quietly and talk. We drank an awful lot, but we weren't at all smashed. It was rather marvelous, really superior chitchat we talked. I never thought of Norman as someone with whom you could have an extended speculative conversation; he always made it too rarefied for me, and I tried to bring it back by talking about what kind of supper I was going to cook. That night, for example, he started talking about God and the devil, and I remember I asked him how he felt about chop suey.

ANNE BARRY My diary should help get this straight, so let me see if I can find a date for Jeanne Campbell leaving. . .

Ah ha!–"January 27, 1963: Jeannie is gone for good. She took off in an aristocratic snit, leaving a legacy of old black Sadie."

Then on February 23, 1963: "Moved in: Jeanne Johnson." She may have been around before that, but there wasn't much overlap at all.

Sadie was Lady Jeanne's maid, a little old black lady. She was sixty-eight but could've been a hundred—as spry and ageless as anything, and with little bright eyes. She was as big as a minute. Her legs were swollen, she was retaining water and was sure she had cancer, because she was going to some healer up in Harlem. She got sicker and sicker, and so she stayed behind when Jeanne left.

Norman moved upstairs at this point but kept the downstairs apartment for her to live in. I remember I once went into the downstairs apartment and found her there with all that flowered crap on the walls, and Tibo, the dog, had peed on the floor. Sadie said she couldn't get up to let him out the back door, so obviously he'd been incarcerated for hours and was dying and finally couldn't stand it anymore. He was so embarrassed and humiliated that he was licking it up.

So about this point Norman finally persuaded Sadie to see a new doctor, who said it wasn't cancer at all but heart trouble. Norman kept her on, paid all the medical bills, and then finally had to break down and say that he couldn't afford to keep that wonderfully decorated apartment for her, so Sadie lived upstairs for a while, only then she couldn't take the four flights of stairs either. Norman carried her up and down every time she went out. I love that man for that. But still, this obviously wasn't a workable solution.

By now Jeannie Johnson had turned up, and we all decided that Sadie should go on welfare. We had this lovely idea that she should be self-sufficient, have her own little place and cook pork chops, and we would all go over and visit. We were all so green and naïve, but that green soon wore off. Getting Sadie on welfare turned into a horrible, Kafkaesque torture. Norman was making phone calls, writing letters, and I'd go down to the welfare office all the time, until finally we managed to work it out.

Norman and Jeanne had been fighting that fall, but I don't remember that there was a decisive fight. But after she left he wasn't in good shape. He was awfully depressed, and fucked his brains out mostly. I have a picture of us that winter sitting in the living room without the lights on. It's like a snapshot in my mind. It's dusk, it's dark, it's depressing. Norman isn't talking, he just looks beat. Maybe we'd been talking before and he's stopped to think. But there were long stretches of gray, sad silence, and I was just there. Ten, twenty minutes of the kind of silence when you just sit, you don't want to be bothered, but you want another body around. I wasn't confused by this, the reasons were pretty obvious: his life was insane, his emotional relationships in chaos. I'd seen the end of his marriage to Jeanne, and as impossible as the marriage might have been, the breakup was still devastating.

So I was brought into this innermost turmoil of his life. I suppose another person might've been kept at arm's length, but I guess I was loyal. I was hardworking. I cared about him. We got along together, and what was supposed to be a nine-to-five job turned out into a nine-to-midnight job, qualities he needed. It was a very bad year: Susie arrives, Jeanne departs, Jeannie Johnson arrives, and then Norman meets Beverly—all in the space of only seven months.

NORMAN MAILER (LETTER TO FRANCIS IRBY GWALTNEY, MARCH 8, 1963)

Dear Fig,

The weeks have gone by, and I still haven't gotten clear to take that trip I wanted to take, and visit you. The trouble is that my personal life has been on a roller coaster. I've been breaking up with my third wife Jeanne Campbell and getting together with her, and breaking up again, and it's been a kind of bloodless hell, the sort I deserved, I fear, as a first payment on my sins, and then on top of that, I've been scuffling to make a living because I have a lot of alimony to

meet, and so the two weeks so far have not presented themselves. . . .
   Give my best to Ecey,

Best,
Norman

NORMAN MAILER   I told my daughter Betsy about the first time I fell in love with her sister Susie. I'd split up from Adele and hadn't seen Susie for over a year because Bea felt I was too crazy, telling Susie I was in jail for a year. Bea is as generous as they come. Then Jeanne and I were together and had a house, so I asked Bea to send Susie to live with us. She was having her own romance, so she agreed. But then Jeanne and I split up. It was orderly, we liked each other, and had too much respect for each other despite our fights, to do it any other way. Still, I was in a deep depression. Here I was on my third divorce, and I hadn't thought about myself that way. I mean, with *my* mother? Originally I'd thought I'd be married once, conceivably twice.

Anyway, each day another piece of furniture went from my apartment to Jeanne's new one. Susie was thirteen at the time. One day I came home and she was sitting in the living room sucking her thumb. She used to suck her thumb, even at thirteen, even though she was otherwise poised and cool. So it grated. She sucked it in the most obscene way, jabbing it up into her mouth. I said to her, "Why don't you take your thumb out of your ass and go do your homework?"

She gave me a look—I've never seen her look more Mexican or Puerto Rican—a kind of surly, macho grimace. Then she said, "Poor man. His woman took the dishes today."

I thought, Jesus, she's tough. If half of it comes from me then I know I'm tough, I can get through this. That's when I fell in love with her.

After I told Betsy this story I said, "Now you know the trick. Except since you know it, it won't work for you. Like the old story about the two women who go to the rabbi to get pregnant. The first one walks two hundred miles to see the rabbi and he blesses her and she comes back and gets pregnant. Another one from the same village goes on the same visit, and the rabbi says, 'It won't happen to you. You know what is supposed to happen.'

ANNE BARRY   I remember going to a party at Podhoretz's house. I can see him vividly, sitting in a chair, and there seemed to be a kind of jousting between them, intellectual jousting. Competitive. Little ripples. Posturing, rooster behavior. Not only intellectual, though, but mixed up with the personal.

I knew the two Normans were close, and they would do funny things together, like letters they'd put into newspapers, and there would be great discussions of the wordings. They'd get involved in little projects, and there'd be lots of telephone calls, arguments about someone misunderstanding or not having the right interpretation or not taking the correct line. It was mainly lit-business stuff. If Podhoretz says that Norman would call him at all hours of the morning, I suppose in a way that was true too, since there were many nights when Norman was sitting around drinking.

How Midge fitted into all this I'm not sure. I think she's brighter than Podhoretz. I think she's terrific, wonderful. But Podhoretz was considered a heavy hitter in those days, and I got the sense that Norman considered him in no way his inferior. My impression was that their relationship had to do with discussing the nature of what is a Jew, what is a radical, what is a political person, a writer, an artist—all those questions you debate vigorously, the kind of stuff you stay up all night discussing in college.

When Norman was doing the stuff on the Hasidim, they would talk and argue, and Norman, I recall, came away very impressed with the Hasidim, with their toughness. He talked to me about it. He was really involved in these spiritual questions, wrestling with problems of cosmology. He'd give me all this half-baked philosophy, which I'd probably appreciate a lot more now, having something stronger to come back at him with. Then, though, I didn't have any complex theory about why he was into this stuff; I was just a kid and assumed it was because he was Jewish.

NORMAN PODHORETZ   He'd been reading Martin Buber, talking about God and the devil, and I had a vague notion of what he wanted to do for the *Commentary* column, using Buber as a focus or anchor. To a certain degree, though, I was nervous about the reaction I'd get—I was afraid that I'd be laying myself open to charges of being intellectually irresponsible. Another problem was that he wanted to do the column on a monthly basis, while I wanted him to do it every few months. He got very ugly about this. One night we were discussing it in a bar, and he started attacking me, calling me "a delicate bureaucrat" and trying to bully me. He didn't understand that I was apprehensive and had every right to be apprehensive since I wasn't sure he could do the kind of thing that would work for *Commentary*. Anyhow, I felt that all he really wanted was to win.

In any event, he asked me to take him to a synagogue on Yom Kippur because he wanted to see Hasidim in the flesh. We met on the afternoon of Yom Kippur eve in Crown Heights, actually not far from where he'd grown up, which is the headquarters of the Lubavitcher Hasidim, and the synagogue was in a little basement, very unprepossessing. I was a little on edge because I had grown up among the Hasidim and I knew that things would get ugly if Norman didn't behave himself. I'd told him to wear a hat, and to my relief he showed up wearing a fedora, all dressed up in a blue suit.

We got to the basement room early, before sundown. There were wooden benches, and as is common in that kind of setup, there were young men, students, smoking and dropping cigarette butts on the floor—Orthodox Jews, especially Hasidic Jews, don't treat synagogues like churches. Nobody paid much attention to us, and the room began to fill up until it was as crowded as the subway at rush hour. Then the *rebbe* was announced, and suddenly, as though by magic, the crowd parted and the two of us were almost decapitated as the benches were hoisted up to make room for the *rebbe* to walk down front. The services started, then after a short while Norman announced he'd had enough.

Outside, he said he thought the Hasidim were "mean and tough"—his characterization. Their attitude, he said, was "Out-of-my-way-motherfucker." He was also fascinated by the Jewish mystical tradition, surprised to discover that there was such a thing. We talked about it quite often, and in a certain sense I was his mentor, even as he was doing the column, which we'd finally compromised on when he agreed to do it on a bimonthly basis.

Still, the older I get, the more peculiar I think he was—and is—in his whole relationship to Jewishness. That a man of his curiosity and energy should show so little interest about something so close to him, something that is in his blood, is extraordinary. Just the fact that he's never gone to Israel is in itself suspicious. In those days, though, I was quite tolerant. If he wanted to have nothing to do with being Jewish, I felt, Okay, that's his choice, whatever the reason. Now I see it differently.

Perhaps he didn't want to be perceived as another Jewish writer; that's fair enough. But it's still extraordinary that someone who regards himself as a fearless spiritual adventurer avoids and evades what is perhaps the most relevant spiritual adventure in his life. I know he wants to see himself as the existential hero without ties to the past. But we all come from somewhere, and Norman Mailer, obviously, does not come from ancient Egypt.

PAUL KRASSNER After I'd started *The Realist* I'd approached him to do an interview, and eventually, in '62, he contacted me and said, "Hey, let's do it. I'm ready." We started at his place out in Brooklyn, only right away my tape machine wasn't working, so I felt stupid. But, lo and behold, he proved totally opposite to his image—very kind and thoughtful, showing a lot of empathy for my discomfort, and what he did was arrange another meeting. Not me, him.

A week or so later we finally got going, and it was a two-way street. It's one of the interviews I've done that has stayed with me the longest, in terms of trying to maintain my own balance between rationalism and mysticism. I asked about birth control, and it was like he got into a boxing position sitting down. I'm almost Catholic in my own attitude toward birth control, but we went at it with me taking the opposite side. It was partly my feistiness that then led him to come to see a show I did at the Village Gate, which probably led to his speaking at Carnegie Hall. He saw that there was a whole different kind of forum you could have, because I remember he reacted when I talked about fighting back against the telephone company and Con Edison, doing little tricks like putting an extra hole in the IBM billing cards, things like that.

In '63 I was doing a lot of these stand-ups, and at Town Hall in February I introduced various people in the audience—Dr. Albert Ellis, Joseph Heller, and then I called out for Norman too. He was supposed to be there, but Jeannie Johnson stood up instead. She was with Susie—she'd already started working for Norman, taking care of Dandy and Betsy—and she announced, "I'm a friend of Norman's. He couldn't come tonight." "Well, that's the story of his life," I cracked. Some people thought she was a stooge, a straight man, but later she came backstage and introduced herself. I remember she had an incredible quality. We shook hands. Women didn't shake hands then, but she did it with a sense of authority, with confidence, and she looked like a Moroccan princess. Norman,

I found out later, suggested that she might ask me for a job, which she soon did.

I started going out to Brooklyn for dinner. Just Norman, Susie, Jeannie, and me. Jeannie was like a member of the family, she knew Norman's idiosyncrasies—grapes in the eggs and all that stuff—and after a while I started staying there, in the room right above the fishnet hammock as you enter and look up, right above the kitchen. Beverly had just moved in too, and Jeannie would give me details—from Beverly's point of view—of how the romance was developing.

The courtship developed because by then Jeannie had started working for me. Her official title was "Scapegoat." She was my managing editor at *The Realist*. She'd call up and say, "I majored in scapegoating at the University of Alabama." This was in early '63. Five or six months later we got married—June 30, 1963. Did Norman arrange things? Sure. But he did it subtly. He trusts people to make their own choice. Ironically, the two of us had gotten into a discussion of this in our interview when he spoke about "falling into relationships," and it was almost prophetic. He had told Jeannie she'd enjoy my show, then recommended her to me for the job, so whether it was matchmaking or not, he was there behind the scenes working out a vision of what he thought was appropriate. Jeannie and I were on such a wavelength that he would've been irresponsible not to introduce us.

ANNE BARRY Jeannie Johnson had been in Bellevue for three months when she arrived at the house in February, right out of the hospital, looking very shaky, wearing a little short skirt and red stockings.

I don't know whether Norman adopted her legally, but he had Jeannie under his wing and was protective after she had been in the hospital. There were a lot of jokes about her being his daughter, and her calling him Daddy and fooling around. I think she was sleeping upstairs, and Susie slept in the loft, because Ray Brock hadn't yet built the crow's nest. I don't know if Norman had an affair with her—he was having sexual relationships with everybody. They both had a joking, irreverent view of life and shared the friendship of a lot of oddball, East Village characters. Both appreciated the whimsical and offbeat, and Jeannie was also a prankster, fooling around with funny notes, funny presents, hiding things.

The main thing for Norman was her energy and irreverence. It's very difficult to live your life with a lot of ass kissers, and he liked to have people around who didn't come across as adulatory, hence his matching her up with Paul. Paul was like a kid brother to Norman. When he got too crazy or out of line, Norman would shake his head over him.

SANDY CHARLEBOIS THOMAS Later on, after the Kennedy assassination, Norman's reaction to Paul's *Realist* piece was that it was "tasteless"—specifically, the conceit of LBJ fucking JFK's throat wound aboard *Air Force I* while returning to D.C. from Dallas. But Norman was obviously mad at Paul for the "Impolite Interview" they'd done earlier. He'd wanted Paul to take certain things out, but Paul refused, so it was hard for Paul to do anything right in Norman's eyes thereafter. With Norman, if you crossed him you were out, eighty-sixed.

But his relationship with Jeannie was interesting. The adoption, I mean. And with Walker it was the same generosity. Norman paid bail money, and I know he never got it back. This was later, in '67 or '68. Walker had come across the Mexican border with a sixteen-year-old pregnant tomato—an American—and the trunk of the car was loaded with pot. He was charged with dope dealing and statutory rape. Five thousand dollars' bail. Norman had me wire the money. I was horrified, and just as I predicted, Walker never showed up for trial.

But when Jeannie was living in Brooklyn, Norman saw Paul and her as a couple, I think, and when they decided to get married he insisted on putting on the wedding in Brooklyn Heights—cakes, people, the whole business. Paul told me later—years later—and I think it's okay to say this now—that they were never really married, though. They didn't have a license and they used an unordained minister. It was a gigantic charade, a typical Krassnerism. After he and Jeannie split up, I asked him about their divorce, and Paul said, "Don't tell Norman, but we were never married."

The two of them lived in an incredibly messy loft that Paul had on Avenue A. The place was stacked with newspapers, and one day the Fire Department came around to check on their illegal living space. Paul told them to come in and look around, then asked, "Do you think anyone could live in this?" They said no and left.

ANNE BARRY   One of my jobs was to write to various convicts, like a guy by the name of Raimondo and also Arnold Kemp, as well as to several others. They wrote to Norman because they wanted help with their writing. But Raimondo would write these somewhat masturbatory letters to me, beginning with, "Hi, Sweet Face." He was in prison for assorted burglaries, breaking and entering—we didn't quite know what—and he was one among several who said he'd known Norman in Bellevue. What's Norman going to say—"No, he's lying"? Because by definition he's crazy, he's in Bellevue, so how could he deny what these people said?

Anyway, I wrote to Raimondo for a year, and he proposed to me regularly. I would say to Norman, "I can't do this, I won't do it anymore," and he'd say, "Look, just do it." I said, "What if he gets out?" "Don't worry," Norman said, "he'll never get out." And then, God help us, he did get out, I think in the fall of '63. He came to Norman looking for work, and Norman had him doing odd jobs, like washing the windows, and suddenly I'm supposed to help him with his writing. I didn't find him particularly charming, but he did do one nice thing—he came to my apartment and gave me advice on how to burglarproof it. Another time I got locked out of the office downstairs and he got in for me. He also took up with Norman's maid. She was always falling asleep on the job because she had bought furniture and was paying for it by having a job at night, on the streets. I gave her seventy-five dollars because I felt so bad that she was resorting to a life of sin.

Then I was alone in the house one time with Raimondo when Barney called up asking about one of Norman's checks, which, it turned out, Raimondo had forged for fifty bucks, and I had to confront him with it. I was afraid because I was alone with him, even though he supposedly wasn't violent—but still, here's a guy whose life was terrible, and everyone was away. But he was wonderful. "What, me, forge a check? That's not my line. Don't you realize that everybody has a specialty? Mine's breaking and entering!"

Norman confronted him, and Raimondo took off with the maid. He took off with a few other things too, like a radio, and then eventually he left the maid and disappeared. Norman, I think, was more wounded than angry, mostly disappointed.

I'd ask him why he got involved with this *meshugas*, and his response was that since he'd managed a certain success in the world, he had a general obligation to help others. It wasn't any Dostoevskian idea that criminals had more experience than the rest of us—no, it was charity. Only I was the one who would mostly get them. Norman would write occasionally, go over some of the letters and then say, "Now Anne Barry is going to criticize your manuscript in detail." I'm laughing, because I had to write Raimondo every goddamned week, and he'd write these letters wanting to know when his man Norman was going to write, and meanwhile he's pining for me and dreaming about me every night without ever having met me.

The other guy was Arnold Kemp, a Chinese-looking Negro. Big and strong, a shaved bullet head, the kind of guy you wouldn't want to meet in a back alley. He'd done a lot of time, I think for armed robbery. I'm not sure, but maybe Norman might've done something for him with the Parole Board. But I had less to do with Kemp than Raimondo. Raimondo turned into a pain in the ass, and I guess Norman was more directly involved with Kemp because he wrote less often and had more talent and was the more interesting. He actually ended up getting a book published. Norman said it was pretty good—I don't know whether it was pretty good for a convict or just really pretty good—but Norman helped him and advised him, and maybe he gave him a blurb. I don't know whether he actually helped him find a publisher.

WALTER MINTON We had a contract, but I think there was also a contract for Dell to do the paperback of *The Presidential Papers*, which may have come first. I don't know, therefore, if that collection was something Norman decided to do on his own. The idea may have come from Dell originally.

NORMAN MAILER (DEDICATION TO *THE PRESIDENTIAL PAPERS*)
This book is dedicated to some ladies
 who have aided and impeded
 the author in his composition

They are
 Beverly Rentz Sugarfoot Bentley
 Jeanne Louise Slugger Campbell
my daughters

Susan
Dandy
Betsy
Kate

my adopted daughter   Jeanne H. W. The Invaluable Johnson
my secretary   Anne Morse Towel-Boy Barry
my sister   Barbara Jane Alson

   and Sadie
   and Hetty Diggs
   and Every-Mae

CHARLIE BROWN Beverly originally came to New York as part of Arthur God-frey's troupe in the early fifties, and she was real young, seventeen or maybe even younger. She'd been working in a restaurant in Pensacola, where Godfrey was a navy pilot in the reserves at the big flight school down there, working in a sandwich joint, when he came in, spotted her, and picked her up.

Beverly and I had the same mother, different fathers. My father is "Brownie." Her father was Burks Rentz. Our mother's name was Marguerite, maiden name Brown; she married my father in 1943, whose real name is Charles C. Brown, Jr. Caused a lot of confusion.

Beverly's maiden name was Rentz. Beverly Rentz, then Bentley, but Bentley was a stage name.

My father was in the Army Air Corps. He's originally from Pensacola. Marguerite is from Atlanta, which was where Beverly was born. There were five kids total. I'm the only one by Brownie. The others were Connie, Gordon, Beverly, and Margie. Gordon died a few years ago. Connie's the oldest, now in Newport News, Virginia, working for the Civil Service. Margie's in Delaware, married to a fellow named Sam Burrows, and they have a restaurant. Me, I just play the guitar.

So Brownie walked into this whole passel of kids, and he didn't know what to do with that. He didn't get along with either Beverly or Margie very well, he tried to dictate too much of their lives, he had never had a family before and was real young. I think also—just my personal opinion—he wanted to fuck all of them. And he didn't know how to deal with that: he's fucking my mother and you've got a bunch of pretty little girls running around. And Beverly was a fox, man.

She was very strong-willed, the only one who ever stood up to my father. Like when my old man would come in drunk, doing his army bit, there were heavy-duty fights, and they used to drive me nuts. Beverly's a scrapper, always has been. I was only about seven, and it scared the shit out of me.

My father disapproved of her life-style and thought she was fast and that there was something wrong with her ambition. I would imagine her leaving home with Godfrey created a big issue with my mother too, who never had any sense of Beverly's drive, nor mine either. When Beverly was a kid all she wanted was to be an actress, all she talked about was becoming a star.

Anyway, when Beverly hit New York she was a "little Godfrey." She wore funny little short skirts and would hold up signs like "We're going to break for a commercial," or she would sell cigarettes. She was also a hand model for a while on several TV shows: they would shoot her hands turning the pages of books, holding perfume bottles, and things like that.

So New York was it, the big time. When she first went there she was living on Sutton Place, a walk-up, which she was only paying sixty-three dollars for, but it was an unbelievable spot. She had some pretty fancy boyfriends too, like Orson Bean, Eddie Fisher, Andy Griffith. Later she did a movie with Griffith, *A Face in the Crowd*.

She had started doing TV shows like *The Big Payoff* with Bess Myerson, where she walked contestants in and out of the isolation booth. She may have done *The $64,000 Question* too, but I don't remember. We went backstage at *The Big Payoff*, my mother and father and myself, then Beverly took us all around the city, like to the Museum of Natural History, all the places in New York to go with a GI family. Before this she'd been writing to us, sending us clippings and stuff on what she was doing. She was in Broadway plays, or she'd be up for this and that, and would send us all her résumé pictures.

In '58 or '59 she wound up making a movie in Spain. It was Smell-O-Vision, something called *The Scent of Mystery*, a strange movie. Peter Lorre, Diana Dors—and Mike Todd, Jr., directed it. Good idea, big bucks, lousy story. I think it was then that she was involved with Papa Hemingway. I don't know whether she met him there in Spain or went over with him or what.

I know of two movies she did; maybe she did more. There were a couple of Broadway plays too, one she got some nice reviews for, *The Heroine*. It came to Broadway during *The New York Times* strike, and the damn play closed—'62 or '63, I think.

So in the late fifties, early sixties, she really did seem to be making it. She may not have been the most talented actress in the world, but she was reasonably hot and working. Also, she had money. During the fifties, I think, we borrowed from her a couple of times. If anybody wrote and asked for money—we need this or that, I remember my folks did that once or twice—she was always generous.

She told me about her relationship with Miles Davis in letters first, and I knew about it long before anybody else in the family. She wouldn't have told them. I mean, these people were from Georgia, right? One night—much later, when I was in New York and playing at the Bitter End—she came down to see me. Miles was driving around the Village in a white Dino Ferrari. Beverly and I were standing outside talking between sets, he pulls up in front, and she said, "My God, there's Miles," and went over and had a long, intense conversation with him. The next time I saw him he came to a show I was in, invited me to see him play somewhere, and was real nice to me. I know literally nothing about their relationship except that she was probably in love with the man. They seem to have spent quite a bit of time together, actually living together for a number of months. She talked about his human frailties and never told me about any viciousness between them, only talked about him in terms of how afraid he was of living and what a good time they had together. Obviously she thinks he's a genius. Sometimes I do, sometimes I don't.

ROGER DONOGHUE   I'd met Beverly in '56. A beauty. She could smile and show both rows of teeth, so they gave her one of the first big Colgate TV commercials. I used to see her every now and then at P. J. Clarke's, and that's how I came to introduce her to Norman.

At the time he'd just separated from Lady Jeanne and was very depressed and the two of us were slumming. We were in P.J.'s, standing at the bar, when Beverly came by with Jake LaMotta, quite high. We were half bombed ourselves, and I introduced them. Beverly made the crack, "Well, if it isn't Norman Motherfuck Mailer!" and I guess it was love at first sight.

I don't know what happened to LaMotta that night, but a couple of years ago, in fact, I ran into Norman and asked how the divorce from Beverly was going. He says, "Jesus Christ, she's gonna jump on my grave. It's goin' tough." Then we got talking about the movie *Raging Bull*—it had just been released—and he cracked, "Maybe I shoulda married Jake LaMotta."

About a week after I'd introduced them I called Norman and asked if he wanted to go with Fay and me to Café 72. He said, "Beverly doesn't want to go there, she wants to go some other place." "Beverly?" I said, "Beverly who?" He said, "Beverly Bentley," and I said, "The hell with Beverly. It's my invitation, and we're going to Café 72." So Beverly came, and she pouted, and then the next few times we went out together, we had to go where she wanted. Finally I said to him, "What the hell are you doing?" He said, "I'm in love." "Oh, for Christ's sake," I said, 'cause if I broke up with somebody I'd date five girls for four months or just go out with the guys to fights. But some people, you know, *bang*, the next day they're in love.

FAY DONOGHUE   That's right. Very quickly Norman fell in love with Beverly. She always wanted to go to restaurants where she was known and make a fuss and order something a certain way known only to herself and the proprietor. I said something in my usual snippy way about it once, and Norman said, "Be careful what you say because I'm crazy about her."

ANNE BARRY   Norman used to sleep in front of the bookcase in the corner next to the kitchen—in the living room, in other words—and I remember letting myself into the apartment one morning and finding him asleep with this blond woman, her head on the pillow beside him. That was my first glimpse of Beverly, and it was the morning after they'd met, I think. I was kind of amused and bemused by all these events because even though I knew he was fucking his brains out that winter after he split from Jeanne, he didn't do it so much at home. But he did say to me something like "I really like this girl." And, indeed, my impression is that after that she never left.

I can't say that I noticed a brightening of his mood, because everything was so hectic all the time. I didn't see anything in common between Jeanne and

Beverly, but his jump from one to the other didn't make me ask questions either. In my diary I report that Beverly arrived March 17, 1963. On April 1, I write that I was talking to her while making breakfast for them both. I didn't say what we talked about, but I seemed to like her okay and I thought she was nice, sort of easy.

In the beginning Fan liked her a lot too. There was something very fresh about her, very warm. She was somebody a mother would like and would think good for her son because she seemed supportive—not just that she was a good cook or housekeeper but that she was a *nice* girl. And she looked corn-fed— you can see it in her pictures, a freshness, an openness that isn't really New York.

She wasn't so nice when she was drinking, though. She wasn't drinking as much as she did later, but they'd go out to parties, and she was on the same schedule of staying up all night, then not rising before noon. But things happened fast that spring, and then they took their car trip to visit Beverly's parents in Georgia; first they went to see Ecey and Fig, then drove out West to Las Vegas and San Francisco, and on the way back they visited Beverly's folks.

NORMAN MAILER (LETTER TO FRANCIS IRBY GWALTNEY, APRIL 18, 1963)
Dear Fig,

I don't want to get your expectations up with stop-and-start stuff, but there's a small chance I can come down for a week or ten days about the 12th of May and I thought I'd write and find out if the time is good or if it isn't. . . . If I come down in May, I think it will pretty damn sure have to be incognito, as far as the good people of Fayetteville are concerned. Odds are I'll be taking a girl along with me. She's a Southern girl named Beverly Bentley, an actress who was born in Georgia and grew up in Florida. I think she and Ecey will get along fairly well, what with their Southern manners in common, and I'm sure you'll like her. In fact, you've probably seen her on television because she's been making a decent living doing commercials for the last ten years and if you ever saw a horrible movie called Scent of Mystery, *the Mike Todd Jr. Smell-o-vision, well, Beverly played the lead. From what she tells me about it, the picture was even worse than* Between Heaven and Hell *or* The Naked and the Dead. . . . *Actually, my hope is to spend a quiet time in Fayetteville, because I want to get going again on my novel and so a quiet room in an air-conditioned motel, or ideally, a couple of rooms in a rooming house would do us fine, and we could get together each evening for supper and a couple of drinks, and maybe you and I could go off for an overnight trip into the Ozarks. . . .*

My best to Ecey and the kids,
Norman

EMMA CLARA "ECEY" GWALTNEY   I always had the feeling that Norman made up the rules as he went along. Which is maybe the way to be, but he's a puritan about some things too. When he and Beverly came to see us he got after me because I introduced them as "Norman and Beverly Mailer." He came out in the kitchen and said, "Her name is Bentley. You ought to introduce her as Beverly Bentley." Yet, before, he'd written Fig and instructed us otherwise, just like he'd let us know that Adele would be wearing a wedding ring "for our friends."

Anyway, that trip was the same kind of thing as a lot of his other trips—being in the country, relaxing, fishing and swimming, only Beverly also got a pregnancy test. That came about because our friend Andy Nettleship and his wife, who were pathologists and had their own lab, were over one night, and Andy said to Norman, "You write a lot about death, I want to give you a challenge: I'm doing an autopsy tomorrow morning at eight; I want you to come and watch." Since it was already late I wasn't about to get up and watch an autopsy, but Norman was real determined to do it. Fig didn't want to go either, but he didn't want Norman to know he couldn't take it, so he steeled himself, even though he thought the whole thing was silly.

The next day, when they came back, they said it was something else. The man had died of peritonitis—a ruptured appendix—but what Fig remembered was the hardened arteries, that when they cut into an artery it was like calcium, and he said the smell was incredible. Norman said the same thing: "I'll never get the smell out of my sinuses." He seemed shattered by it, perhaps the cutting. He talked about what a nice-looking old man it was and that the scalpel hitting the hard deposits in the arteries sounded like a knife scraping chalk. That night we went out to Andy's for dinner. They raised their own cattle, so they were real proud of these great big gorgeous steaks they were serving, but Norman said, "I don't want to offend anybody, but after that autopsy I can't eat a bite of the meat."

Before dinner Andy showed us around his lab, and I overheard Beverly asking him if he could do a pregnancy test. Fig and Norman were off somewhere, and Andy said, "Oh, sure." Beverly and Norman didn't make any effort to hide the fact, and Andy did the test the next morning—I don't remember, maybe Norman took her out there—and later he called up and confirmed it. Beverly wasn't surprised. She was two months pregnant and said, "I knew it, but I just wanted to be sure." But Norman seemed totally out of it. Women do him that way a lot. But it was no big deal. We didn't turn to them and say "Congratulations." In fact, we thought it best not even to talk about it since they weren't married and maybe they thought it was an inconvenience.

I don't think she had told her parents—I mean, just the idea of them not being married. They were going to see them on the way back from Las Vegas and San Francisco, and later Norman described arriving at Beverly's parents' because he thought it was so funny. Again, his interest in southern customs. He said they walked across the yard, met her folks, and as soon as they were inside they said, "Would you like to take a bath?" He said he didn't know whether to be insulted or not, so he'd replied, "Well, do I smell or something?" He thought it was hysterical, but I understood immediately. To the southerner, with no air conditioning, the most refreshing thing in the world is to have a bath. They knew that Beverly and Norman had been on the road, so it was hospitality: "Come in and have a good, refreshing bath."

That was the first time I'd met Beverly, and I thought she was very agreeable. In fact, Norman had written to me and said, "Ecey, I think you'll like Beverly. She's a southerner too, from Georgia, so I think you'll have a lot in common." I felt she let Norman have the spotlight entirely, totally. Two years later, though, when I next saw her she was a whole lot different.

HAROLD CONRAD   They came out to Vegas to see the Liston-Patterson rematch. Beverly loved the fight scene, the macho shit, and she fitted right in there. She was tough, and I remember once I grabbed that broad's shoulder, and she was hard, like a fucking rock.

MARA LYNN CONRAD   We all spent about a week together, going out to dinner, stuff like that, and right after the fight we were in the Thunderbird Lounge. I was at a table with Buddy Rich's wife, Marie. Liston had won, I think, but everyone's surly after a fight, and Norman was alone at the bar. I don't know where Beverly was—I think they'd had a fight. Two guys came up to Marie's and my table and one of them punched me on the shoulder and said, "I think you dropped this." He held his hand out and there was a big screw. It was an insult—these guys are coming on like we're prostitutes. So I stand up to go look for Harold. I see Norman at the bar. The two guys—heavy, redneck guys, real trouble—are still hovering, so I show Norman the screw and say, "Those guys are really bothering us." He says, "I can't get into it." He was still on probation, so he really couldn't, but I shoved him—"You're not gonna help? Nuts to you!"— and I stalked out to find Harold in the lobby.

He's finished with the fight, he's finally taking his first deep breath in six months, and he says he doesn't want to deal with it either. But at least he comes back with me. The two guys have taken the next table now, and they're still throwing lines at us. I said, "Harold, say something to them," but he shakes his head. The guys don't let up, so I say, "Harold, if you don't do something, I will." I had no idea what, but when he still wouldn't do anything, I stood up. I had a triple vodka on the rocks, one of those big glasses, and I'm a softball pitcher, see, I can hit anything, so I take several steps back from the table, then whip around and pitch the glass right into the guy's face. I'd held the glass at the bottom so it wouldn't spin, and it went straight at him. His legs went out, he went over backwards, and everybody jumped up screaming. I turned around and started out, and I could hear all this crashing and shouting, and then I see the cops coming. In Vegas nothing much happens very long without eighteen six-foot-four cops moving in, so I say to them, "Uh-oh, must be some rumble," and I keep walking. Then I decide I'd better look—it's mayhem, like a movie-set fight scene, with everybody around those two tables hitting each other and picking up chairs. And there's Harold and Marie in the middle. And Norman too, because you couldn't escape it.

So I figured I better go get Buddy Rich. He was playing at the Tropicana, so I took a cab over and said to Buddy, "I've done a terrible thing. I kind of overshot my mark and started this terrible fight. Your wife's in the middle of it, you better come get her 'cause nobody else wants to do it."

Buddy and I jumped in his Maserati, and even though the Tropicana was quite a way from the Thunderbird we made it in thirty seconds flat. Buddy's a karate expert, so we're walking through and he's getting ready! But when we got to the lounge it's already been ironed out. They've gotten rid of the rednecks, apologies have been made, and nobody got hurt too bad except the guy I'd hit with the glass, who'd been cut a bit.

Then I saw Norman in the parking lot. He was walking somewhere alone. So I said, "Norman, what happened in there?" He said, "Oh, it was all right. The cops came and nobody got into trouble." I was all apologies. Maybe I had made him feel bad when I'd shoved him, I don't know, but I think it was that night that he went and kicked some guy's door down. I don't really know why he did it—I heard the guy had bugged him, and he wouldn't open his door, so Norman kicked it in. I don't know if they exchanged blows, but Norman paid for the door.

HAROLD CONRAD   Norman didn't kick the door down, the other guy did. The other guy was Wid Watson. Big, looked like Errol Flynn. He was a playboy type. He was a friend of mine and I introduced them. For two days he had wanted to be friends with Norman, but Norman couldn't stand him, so that night in the lounge Norman called him a faggot, told him to fuck off. Very late, four in the morning, Norman's in his room with Beverly—I think they were in bed—and Wid went up there and started banging on the door. Norman yelled at him to go away, so Wid kicked in the door. Norman slugged him. Then the hotel people came and stopped it.

MARA LYNN CONRAD   Then there was the episode when we all went to hear Don Rickles, another night. Rickles always made Jew jokes. He'd call out to the waiter across the room, "Hey, you Jew, I'm gonna make a lampshade outa you." That kind of shit, and I could see Norman starting to get steamed. Beverly yelled something at Rickles, then Norman started hollering louder than Beverly—"It's guys like you who make it tough for everybody," which brought the cops running.

HAROLD CONRAD   I don't know what the hell he said, some stupid thing, but I'd gotten Norman on a TV show the next day to talk about the fight. We're over at the studio, and it turns out that Rickles is supposed to be on the same show. He's an old friend of mine, so when he saw Norman he ran over to me and said, "Never bring that son of a bitch around to my show again!" Then he ran out of the place, real scared.

MARA LYNN CONRAD   Then the day after the fight I ran into Norman in the lobby. It was like five in the morning, dawn was just coming up. This was after the thing with the two rednecks. He said, "Beverly's out walking someplace." We started driving and there she was, walking along the road toward the desert, crying her heart out. So I got out of the car and persuaded her to get in with us. She was so unhappy she wanted to die, she was that miserable. Norman had told me she was pregnant, but she didn't know that I knew, and I didn't say anything to her. I waited for her to tell me.

But I told them they should go out to the desert to hear silence. "Drive to Death Valley, turn off the motor, and listen," I said, and she wanted to go. We started out, and then she decided she wanted to go back to the hotel. There was no shouting or fighting, just Beverly's tears. It was like she was all wrapped up in her problem.

HAROLD CONRAD   They later drove out into the desert, though, just the two of them, and it was an intense thing. They were like a newly married couple, young, in love, sometimes fighting, although not in front of us. She was sort of taking a back seat to him, but she got in the spirit of the fight scene, and everything Norman did, she was right behind him. But I also think Norman was still suffering from the last few years—the Adele thing, Lady Jeanne, all of it.

MARK LINENTHAL   I hadn't met Beverly before, but I noticed that Norman was being supersober when they arrived in San Francisco. They were planning to get married, and both of them were determined to make it work. Beverly and Frances, my wife, went out shopping while Norman and I talked. He was engaged in a straight man-to-man assessment of his life and was ready to say he'd been dumb about a lot of things. He proffered this, a *mea culpa* evaluation, which wasn't extended but pointed. Without my eliciting it, he said something like "I've been so crazy," and he assumed I knew what he was talking about. The point was: "What you've read about me is true, but that's not the way it's gonna be in the future. It's a closed chapter."

DON CARPENTER   They'd come for a couple of weeks, and they'd brought the dog with them, Tibo, a wonderful dog, and Norman was resting and relaxing and walking the dog more than he was writing. Friends of mine would see him on the street in North Beach and did the wonderful thing of not recognizing him in order to give him his peace. We'd corresponded, but this was the first time we met.

He asked me over to dinner and I went alone, without my wife, and I was really stupid, because I'd drunk a lot of wine before arriving, then kept making social gaffes, saying the wrong thing. Motor mouth. Overimpressed, finding myself in the presence of the master. When I first got there he was on the telephone to New York, talking business: a thousand dollars he wanted for a book review for the *New York Herald Tribune*. I was in the kitchen with Beverly and the dog. She and I were getting along very well, not only then but in every subsequent meeting, but inadvertently I called her "Baby." Soon Norman comes in and sits down, puts those peepers on me and says, "Listen, you don't call my girl friend 'Baby.'" I just melted through the fucking floor. I felt terrible.

We had cantaloupe with prosciutto, and he fried steaks for us. He's one of those guys who comes on hard, then goes soft and tries to relax you, and as we finished dinner he told me about falling off a landing craft in the war, explaining that when they were landing in Japan on one of the islands he'd been the only soldier to fall into the water out of the LCIs. He told this as a joke on himself, which is one of the ways he tests people, but I failed the test. I said, "You must have been the worst soldier in the Far East." And he said, "Mumble, mumble." Now I know you're just supposed to laugh and slap him on the back appreciatively, because the story is ended.

After dinner we went down the hill for espresso, and I took him to the Jazz Workshop. That's where it went foul. We couldn't talk—not about books, not about politics. I asked him about James Baldwin, who was hot at the time, and he looked down at the floor and said, "I kinda hoped you'd be different"— meaning, let's not have the "whether James Baldwin sleeps in the nude" conversation.

The next morning I woke up with a terrible fucking hangover and realized how dreadful I'd been, so I sent him a telegram—a very good telegram, very funny. The night before we'd talked about the phrase "Mickey Mouse," and in my telegram I said the phrase was very useful because you can say things like "That's a pretty nice Mickey Mouse watch you've got there"—which is a double trip. Anyway, the point of the wire was not Mickey Mouse but me wagging my tail and saying, "Can we be friends?" He called up right away and said, "Good wire, good wire. Let's meet." So it was set up for five at Tosca's, a bar on Columbus, just off Broadway, with opera on the jukebox.

My wife and I got there and were waiting when Mike McClure walks in. We talked, and then I mentioned that Mailer was in town. "Oh, that's very interesting, ha, ha, ha," he said. "Have you seen him?" I nodded, and then he asked when and where. "In fact," I said, "I'm gonna meet him in two or three minutes." "Bullshit," he says, then turned around, and there was Norman coming in the door.

So we all sat down. Tosca's was kind of a hangout, and a couple of other friends joined us, including Lawrence Ferlinghetti. I took a back seat and basically just listened. Tell the world, redemption lies in keeping your mouth shut.

Norman seemed current and really knew what was going on, and he and McClure and Ferlinghetti talked about the whole West Coast scene. I don't think Norman was deferring to them because San Francisco was the spearhead. It was more acknowledgment—like a guy from Dodge City doesn't lord it over anybody but admits there are things going on in Tombstone as well. He was— as he can be—tremendously polite. There was the sense of "Some of us in New York and you guys out here are brothers"—a confederation of *Ausländer*, all of us against the straights. At the same time, though, there was the sense—a sense that's been borne out by history—that he was King Arthur and the rest of us were the Knights of the Round Table; the table was for the purpose of equality, nobody sat higher or lower than anybody else, but there was only one King Arthur. Norman never gives that up.

ALICE ADAMS   Beverly was incredibly pretty, also very funny. I was sure she was lying about her age—I couldn't believe she was as old as she said she was. And she was really practicing to be a good wife, meticulously ironing Norman's shirts. A friend of mine and I did things together with them, like looking around San Francisco and having a great picnic up in Napa, the wine country, and Norman was wonderful. One of his most appealing qualities is his intense curiosity about anyone and anything that's happening. My friend was very unliterary, an architect, so Norman geared his questions appropriately, asked him about things he would be expected to know. We also talked about Herb Gold, whom Norman had never liked. In *Advertisements* Norman had described Gold's writing as being like that of an old lady, so Herb would say Norman had accused him of being homosexual. Herb was obsessive about Norman, and because he knew we were friends, he'd always bring him up, once describing him as a pale imitator of Jack Kerouac.

But what I most remember about that visit was what fun it was. It seemed to be an extremely happy moment in his life.

CHARLIE BROWN   Beverly called, telling us she's coming down to Georgia to see us with her ace new boyfriend, a famous writer named Norman Mailer. We said, "Who?" "Norman Mailer. He wrote *The Naked and the Dead*." I said, "Yeah, I saw that—damned good war picture. But who the hell is *Norman Mailer?*"

At the time I'd finished school and was hanging out, playing music and teaching guitar at the Muskogee Conservatory of Music. They said they were going to drive from the West Coast because they were taking a trip across the country. My vision instantly was this fancy New York writer, he's got lots of money and he's gonna be coming through in a red Maserati. At the worst, he's gotta look like Steve McQueen, getting out of this beautiful car with my beautiful sister. But they arrive in a '61 Falcon convertible, and of course what we saw was this overweight, short, little Jewish guy with a lot of hair and big ears. Norman's got startlingly blue eyes—like Paul Newman's—but I still couldn't believe it. Only those blue eyes—they were his one saving grace. Also, they've got Norman's dog, Tibo. Jesus, what a disappointment.

That first evening was very strange, like a test of who this guy was, and I was laying for him. You don't say "fuck" in my house; you don't say "fuck" in any southern household. And there he was telling a story at the dinner table, which was probably a very funny story, but I wasn't listening. I was waiting to see what would come out of his mouth, because I was ready to pounce on his ass—and I did. He said "fuck" a couple of times more, and I told him he didn't belong there, he belonged with the boys. I said something real hostile like "Shut up! You're saying this stuff in front of my sister and my mother, and I don't like it." But he didn't even acknowledge it. The man is very bright, he knows what to do with a fat redneck—leave him the fuck alone, namely—and within half an hour I was in love with him.

I don't think he drank heavily, even though I know those were his heavy bourbon days. He did his whole thing with my father, talking army, and Brownie loved him instantly. He was totally in awe of the guy, and Norman had my mother wrapped around his little finger too. She had cooked a turkey, it was just family because Beverly had said not to invite anybody, and we're all sitting around the table, and I could see that for my mother he could do absolutely no wrong. He was such a charmer. A real winner.

They didn't stay more than two days. Beverly was at the house while Norman got himself a goddamned motel room, and I remember that was an issue. They wouldn't stay in the house together.

When the two of them finally left, my mother and father and I sat around the table talking. We hadn't seen Beverly since '57, and the first thing was "She sure is fat." It never occurred to me she was pregnant, although she'd told my mother, I think. But no question, Norman had definitely made a good impression. Most people from New York were sort of strange to us, and we thought he was too in that he cursed a lot and said funny things. He had a forceful way of talking, even when he was joking, and you had to listen, 'cause he talked about mystical things like energy, and I'd just never met anybody like that before. Also, we didn't know about Adele until later. If my mother had known, forget it. She would've thrown him out of the house. Stab! Who? What? My daughter with this maniac? I didn't find out until I got to New York, and the way my mother found out about all that weirdness was through Beverly, but only after they were married.

ROGER DONOGHUE   When Fay and I got married that fall, in November, Norman was my best man. I think he was still trying to get the business with Jeanne cleared up, but for our wedding he gave us a lunch at an Italian restaurant we all loved and had a sculptor friend make a little bronze wedding cake on top of which were little male and female boxer figures. He was playing the grand patron, being gracious as hell.

I remember we ended up getting married in a Unitarian church at Seventy-eighth or Seventy-ninth and Madison. The minister was Dr. Crane, big on television talk shows, and he took us—all eight of us—into the chapel and was telling us how, when the Crash came, the Christian Scientists had tried to steal the church from the Unitarians. Norman turned to him and said, "It wasn't very Christian of those scientists, was it, Doctor?"

From the start, though, I don't think Beverly was ever passive or starry-eyed. She was always the "I'm the actress" type, always full of juice, with her own ideas.

EILEEN FINLETTER   Norman and Beverly had gotten married themselves in late December, I think. I'd just come back to the city, a friend of mine was giving a party, and I was happy because she said that he was coming and I hadn't seen him for several years. But then he walked in drunk, weaving around like a boxer. There was somebody there he was mad at, whom he was taunting, "C'mon, get me." Later I went up to him and said, "Oh, Norman, how marvelous to see you." And he said, "My God, you've spent too many years in Europe, you look like one of those Parisian bitches." I was left breathless. But a week later Barbara, his sister, called and said, "Norman told me you're in town. We're having a family dinner out here in Brooklyn and we'd like you to come." I went, and Norman couldn't have been more adorable. He didn't remember anything about that evening. At the party he had been dead drunk, but at home I saw the Norman I always knew.

ALICE ADAMS I noticed a change the following fall, though, in November, when I went to New York. He was very bad.

The first night he had a huge party for me. Then he and Beverly went away, I think up to P-Town, and I stayed at his place for five or six days. I had the flu and felt so rotten that I wasn't drinking, but when they got back they took me to a party to celebrate the inauguration of *The New York Review of Books*. It was a party I didn't feel like being at—a New York intellectual party. At ten-thirty or eleven, I wanted to leave, but Norman physically restrained me. It was some sort of power play. He doesn't like people to get sick, especially women, and he insisted we go to another party, given by musicians Beverly knew, in a penthouse downtown, and again I was physically kept from leaving. The next morning Beverly apologized. But Norman told me how wonderful he felt, said that he always felt good when he behaved in a certain way. He wasn't apologizing, he was overriding my situation with his assertion.

CHANDLER BROSSARD Norman and I had stopped seeing each other because I couldn't take him around other people—he behaved in a very macho, fake way, which I found offensive.

But I knew Buzz Farbar—Bernard, I won't call him "Buzz"—at Pyramid Books because my wife, Sally, worked there. There were two people Bernard wanted to meet very much, Norman and another friend of mine, Bruce Fried-man. Bernard was on the make. He was a celebrity fucker—he's that kind of person—and he imagined himself an ex-heavyweight boxer, a bullfighter, and all that bullshit... Oh hell, what a bore these fantasies are. It was like Lana Turner wanting to be in the movies; she stopped being the girl on the street corner and got to be a film star. That's what Norman did for Bernard, put him into pictures.

BERNARD "BUZZ" FARBAR Norman and I met at the annual Christmas party given by Rust Hills, the fiction editor of *Esquire*, in '63. The two of us, I remember, broke up a fight between Shag Donahue, a writer, and Hills. We'd said hello, made a couple of jokes, and went about our ways earlier in the evening—measured each other, as it were, since Norman was doing a lot of that in those days. But at four-thirty or five in the morning we sort of realized what a nice relationship was starting, maybe because we were breaking up a fight instead of starting one.

Part of the substance of our relationship as it grew was because most Jewish guys didn't play football, aren't built the way I am, and don't take chances. But Norman makes you better. For example, I used to be somewhat lazy. He made me stretch a bit. Things had come easily to me, then I realized that even if you've been lucky you still have an obligation, like noblesse oblige, to jump on things.

I went to CBS in '64 and was director of something called CBS Legacy Books, and two years later Norman did a book for me on bullfighting, also a twelve-inch long-playing record with interviews, music, people talking about the bullfight. It was a new packaging idea, vastly expensive to produce, and the great thing about Norman was he offered to take fifteen hundred dollars because he knew I was trying to show CBS I could bring these things in for peanuts. Scott Meredith was angry—he was just beginning as Norman's agent and wanted to show him he could get a lot of money—and he insisted that Norman couldn't do it for so little. But Norman held firm, claiming that he'd already agreed, though I think I finally gave him $2500. It was a favor. Something he was doing for a friend.

Subsequent to this I became a senior editor at Trident Press, Simon and Schuster, and wanted to bring Norman over. Call it a campaign. I told Herb Alexander of Pocket Books and Leon Shimkin at S&S that if any writer was worth a million bucks it had to be Norman. But they insisted on a physical exam so they could have insurance on him, and I realized that Herb Alexander was unsure of Norman's mental state and what he really wanted was a psychiatric exam. I was incensed. I told Norman about the physical exam, not the other, and because I hate bearing bad news I sort of let it die. Norman would ask, "What's going on?" and finally I handled it by saying, "Look, this sucks." What he deduced was that they were tendering the offer as their way of showing that Pocket Books was in the running, because they were getting attention in the newspapers, so we dismissed it as a publicity ploy. I didn't have the heart to tell him that they'd been asking me about the stabbing.

DON FINE   Scott Meredith as Norman's agent? Scott told me the story once when we were driving to an Ali fight. He said he initiated it by asking Norman to send him everything he hadn't been able to get published. He said, "I'll tell you in two weeks what I can and cannot place—short stories, whatever." Norman sent the material over, Scott called him almost immediately—"These I can sell, these I can't"—and indeed he went ahead and sold what he said he could. "Now," he said, "I want to be your agent," and Norman said, "You *are* my agent." I repeated the story to Norman and he confirmed it.

E. L. DOCTOROW   I had met Scott Meredith earlier, when I was at NAL, and I felt that his relationship with Norman did him a lot of good; maybe it gave him a sense of possibilities behind the contracts, behind the deals. He was hard-nosed, and maybe Norman liked the fact he'd chosen an agent who was known as tough and not entirely respectable. Scott's attitude was, it's all money: "If you guys can come up with the money, Norman's yours. If you can't, take a walk."

ANNE BARRY   I can't quote him accurately, but Norman thought Meredith would make him a lot of money, and he was going to go for that. What the hell, he was going to do it.

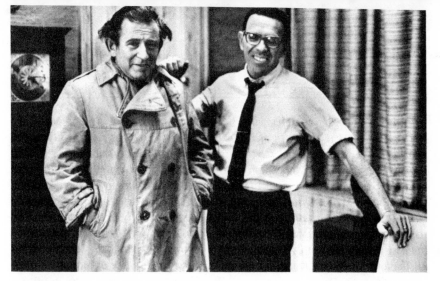
With agent Scott Meredith.

Eventually my salary went up to sixty-five dollars a week, but periodically Norman was hurting for money. He didn't communicate panic, but before *An American Dream* he was worried, I know that.

The incoming checks went to Barney. I had a checkbook, Norman would sign a batch of checks, and I'd fill them out to pay the grocery and electric bills, the household expenses. Cy was managing the money as well as investing it, because every now and again they'd talk, just day-to-day stuff, and like if his account was running out, I'd call up Cy and he'd put more money in. It was obvious that Cy was almost like an older brother and seemed very fond of Norman, concerned for his welfare. Again, the Jewish family. I didn't sense any competition between them, because they had such different styles: Cy seemed more laid back, urbane, very well groomed, and his suits were always well pressed and he never needed a haircut. And Norman, of course, was Norman.

NORMAN MAILER (LETTER TO FRANCIS IRBY GWALTNEY, NOVEMBER 9, 1963)

Dear Fig,

I really enjoyed the hell out of your last letter and have taken a month and a half to get around to answering it only because I've gotten caught up in a job of work which could be killing if it gets going wrong. I decided the only way out of my financial hole was to take a jump, and so I contracted with Esquire to write a novel in eight parts, each installment (ten thousand words) will appear in a successive month, and since I didn't have anything behind me when I started, it comes down to writing a book in eight months, which has a finished draft good enough to make it a good novel. I did, however, succeed in selling it to Dial and Dell before I started for a price so large it's crazy, and what's good about this is that I'll have economic freedom for a couple of years and may be able to do my big book in relative calm.

Incidentally, the agent I had who brought this deal off was a real live wire who accomplished a hell of a lot for me—his name is Scott Meredith—and so if you're dissatisfied with John when the time comes to get a new book published, maybe it would be worth your while to let Scott take a crack at it. . . .

NORMAN MAILER (LETTER TO FRANCIS IRBY GWALTNEY, DECEMBER 20, 1963)

Dear Fig,

...I don't want to moralize, but the difficult thing about writing well when one is angry is that the truth of it tenses up one's whole body physically so you tend to lose the cool sense of each moment passing into each new moment in your book. That sense of knowing when you're right and when you're getting off your balance. I know when I'm mad, I tend to accelerate not only in the physical speed with which my hand writes down the words but I also telescope the progression of the ideas and so something which makes sense internally to me is hysterical in its external manifestations. If it weren't for this difficulty I think anger might be the best single emotion to write out of, for it firms up one's balls and burns out all the half-shitty half-loyalties to people we don't really like or admire.

I'm working sixty days ahead of publication (that's my automatic deadline); I've now finished the first three installments of the serial. Everything is fine so far except that I can't describe a screw as thoroughly as I might like to, and I ain't moving quite as fast as I should be moving. In the first three parts I don't think I've gone a quarter of the way. It's a little like giving a course and taking too long on the earlier writers so you find you have one lecture left for Stendhal, and a half lecture for Proust, a half lecture for Joyce. But writing the serial is in itself fun. It makes me work. Since it's been eight years since I've set out to write a novel and finish it, I think I would have taken forever to get somewhere if it weren't for the fact that I have to make my decisions in great haste and stick by them. It's a little like playing ten-second chess. You have to take the bold choice each time, because you know you can depend on getting something out of the bold effects—the subtler choices may prove too subtle and fail to come to life in the speed with which you have to write. I don't know how good the book will be, but it's interesting writing a serial. I'm not so sure I'll say when I'm done: I swear, never again. Since I, like you, used to be very much of a second, third, or even fourth draft novelist, it occurs to me that much of the possibility in this may have developed over the last twelve months when I was writing against a deadline once or twice a month and so formed the habit, for better or worse, of having my first drafts become the basic body on which the final result was clothed.

Anyway, that much for shop. Bev is coming along nicely and should have the baby by the middle of March. She hasn't put on any weight since this summer except around the middle, and we're both looking pretty good, although I am definitely on the plump side. If I get any fatter I'll need an old skinny gal like Ecey to shake some life into me. But now you tell me Ecey's getting plump too. God Almighty...

And love to Ecey, Yee Yee, and Frank, Jr.

Merry Christmas,
Norman

HAROLD HAYES *An American Dream* was his proposal, and I threw my hat in the air. Very risky, and you always wonder if something's going to come off, but what he was doing was unique to my experience. Nobody had done that that I knew of, at least not in our time, and the example he gave, when he set the whole thing up with me, was Dickens and Dostoevsky in the nineteenth century.

WALTER MINTON   After *Advertisements* Norman hadn't been supporting himself with fiction, and sometime after that he signed a contract with us for a big novel, 150,000 words or so, for a $50,000 advance. The book was the big autobiographical novel, beginning with the essence of Norman Mailer—with a gene, a sperm in the testicles of an ancestor. I can't swear to it, but I think it was the beginning of his Egyptian book. The story was set a long time ago. I don't remember whether or not it was Egypt—it could have been the plains of Russia or Poland. I saw about 70 pages of it.

But at the time, Dick Baron at Dial offered him a contract for *An American Dream* for $100,000, which didn't make me very happy, but I decided to step aside. Dick said we could have a piece of it, but whatever he was offering didn't seem equitable, and I remember telling him, "You know, we've got the contract— don't throw me any bones."

In my mind it wasn't a total rupture. Norman was having problems with Adele and alimony money, and what he and I hassled about was strictly business. The problem was that I wasn't ready to match Baron's offer. I didn't have the money. The book itself, though, was being referred to as a novel about Las Vegas, not the big novel we'd contracted for. But even though it ends in Vegas, it's not the book Norman set out to write, and the arrangement with *Esquire* came about after Baron had commissioned it.

RICHARD BARON   We offered him a hundred thou plus. He'd been at Putnam's since '55, was still under contract to them for one more book, and in '67 he had to go back for *Why Are We in Vietnam?* Walter Minton's position was that *An American Dream* was not the book he had under contract since it was a smallish book. But later, in fact, *Why Are We in Vietnam?* turned out to be the smaller of the two. He settled for it because he felt that was probably all he was going to get.

I had been a big fan of Norman's ever since *The Naked and the Dead* and wanted nothing more than to publish him, and in fact I had even asked Jim Silberman, my editor in chief, to visit him in the hospital in 1960. I was independent then, and later when I got in touch with Dell I was always checking to see if he was free or not, if there was any hope of moving him even for a single book, which is all Minton thought was going to happen. The opening came in a conversation that Don Fine had picked up and brought to Al Meyer's attention. I don't know if he got it from Scott Meredith or where, but I backed him a hundred percent. We were only buying a single book, but I was hoping for more.

But I think he left Putnam's because he wanted to get the hell away from Minton. Minton had him sewn up contractually, and it implied a limitation of money, subject matter, freedom. By becoming a free agent he could go out and raise dough to pay off that $100,000 nut a year he had to carry with his three ex-wives. Minton, by and large, was very tight with the dollar.

In the mid-sixties we were all wheeling and dealing. Everything was changing. Publishing went from the Maxwell Perkins-Thomas Wolfe tradition to dollars and bright lights—a combination of Hollywood and the sports world.

DON FINE   I got a phone call from Scott Meredith. He said, "How'd you like to publish Norman Mailer's *An American Dream?*" He told me exactly what he wanted, hard- and soft-cover deal. It was $100,000, maybe $125,000. Originally it was bought for Dell and Delacorte, not Dial. If Dick Baron claims he bought the book, I'm afraid his memory is askew. I was the one who made the deal, and then—nobody believes I could be so selfless—I said, "Listen, it would be really nice for Dial in its new arrangement with Dell to have a Norman Mailer novel." So I gave it to them. Ed Doctorow was Dial's editor, and Dick was just preening, he was so proud to have a Norman Mailer book.

MARA LYNN CONRAD   After Vegas we'd started seeing him and Beverly in the city, and Harold arranged for Norman to meet Ali. Muhammad really loved Norman, and after their first meeting they'd see each other here in our apartment, at the fights, or in hotel suites, often when there were other guys around.

Muhammad is a very bright guy, but many of the same lines he uses over and over. Norman, though, would always come back with an original line, so it was verbal play back and forth, and he wasn't scared of Muhammad, which was the important thing. There were very, very few guys around who weren't— like newspaper guys would come up to meet him and their hands would be shaking—so Muhammad really appreciated Norman's cool. You could tell from their banter, the way they'd go back and forth with each other.

I think I was there at the training camp when Norman visited and was first introduced to Ali. Muhammad turned to Boudini Brown and said, "You oughta pay attention, 'cause this is the writer champ like I'm the fighter champ. This guy makes a million a book, so listen to him."

HAROLD CONRAD   Actually, Ali really doesn't even know who the fuck Norman is, even to this day. He doesn't know writers. If I brought in Shakespeare, Ali wouldn't know who the guy was. I had to give Norman a big buildup in order to give him some juice, so I told Ali, "Pay Mailer respect. He gets a million a book." You say "a million dollars" to Ali, that's it—Norman's in. Otherwise he wouldn't have known Norman from Adam.

JOSE TORRES   Pete Hamill had introduced us in '62, but it wasn't until '64 that Norman and I became close and I began to read his books. Gay Talese, Dick Schaap, and Pete were my American friends. Pete was instrumental here, really took me around, and I suppose started my education, which Norman later finished. For example, the first time I saw a group of people using marijuana was when Norman invited me to a party in a loft in Manhattan. It was after the

"Muhammad really appreciated Norman's cool. You could tell from their banter, and at one point Muhammad turned to Boudini Brown and said, 'You oughta pay attention, 'cause this is the writer champ like I'm the fighter champ. This guy makes a million a book, so listen to him.'"

Olson fight but before I became champion. He went out of his way to warn people not to offer me any of that shit, as well as alcohol. When somebody did, he went after the guy.

Also they were very politically influential in my life. I came from a very conservative town, also from poverty. I had the colonial mentality, the whole thing, and anyone I saw smoking grass was a Communist. But Norman and Hamill radicalized me, and Norman was like the first person, the only guy, who could measure me intellectually and emotionally. Plus he's never used me. Like, for example, he'd never get in a fight when I was around because he knew I would come to his aid and he didn't want to get me involved.

Once, though, I almost got into a thing myself. Around this time Tom Wolfe started calling me "Mailer's pet primitive." Norman and I were at Elaine's one night, and I saw this guy wearing a white hat and suit and asked Norman if it was Wolfe. Norman said yes, but then when I said I was going over to him he said, "Don't."

I went anyway. Wolfe was standing at the bar, and I grabbed him by the shirt and said, "My name is Jose Torres. Do I look like a fucking pet primitive to you?" He didn't have a response, wouldn't talk to me, so I said, "Fuck you," and walked away. Norman was laughing, but he had to ask me what had happened because he wouldn't look.

But at places like the Lion's Head or Elaine's and P. J. Clarke's, the conversation was different from anything I'd heard, and for the first time I realized why I'd hated the army. I realized that I felt more intelligent than the bunch of dummies and racists who'd been telling me what to do, so looking back at when I first met these writers, I'd been totally unaware of any intellectual feeling. I was the hottest fighter in New York at the time, but Pete and Norman never flattered me. We talked, they struggled with me. It was real. You knew we were going to be friends for life.

FANNY SCHNEIDER MAILER   I didn't like it when Norman started boxing, that Torres got him involved. I know he likes it, but I hope it doesn't hurt him.

CUS D'AMATO   He claimed that a writer had to have discipline, that it was just like a fellow going into a fight, and he was right, 'cause discipline is the whole thing: you make yourself do what needs to be done no matter how you feel. He said that once he begins to write, his instructions to his wife are not to accept any calls while he's putting in his eight hours. Nothing is allowed to interfere, which is the same professional discipline a top fighter has. Both have to be able to get themselves to do whatever has to be done no matter how frightening or intimidating.

NORMAN MAILER (TESTIMONY BEFORE THE SUPREME COURT OF MASSACHU-SETTS, ATTORNEY GEN. OF MASS. V. A BOOK NAMED *NAKED LUNCH*)   *William Burroughs is in my opinion—whatever his conscious intention may be—a religious writer. There is a sense in* Naked Lunch *of the destruction of soul, which is more intense than any I have encountered in any other modern novel. It is a vision of how mankind would act if man was totally divorced from eternity. What gives this vision a machine-gun-edged clarity is an utter lack of sentimentality...*

Just as Hieronymus Bosch set down the most diabolical and blood-curdling details with a delicacy of line and a Puckish humor which left one with a sense of the mansions of horror attendant upon Hell, so, too, does Burroughs leave you with an intimate, detailed vision of what Hell might be like, a Hell which may be waiting as the culmination, the final product of the scientific revolution. At the end of medicine is dope; at the end of life is death; at the end of man may be the Hell which arrives from the vanities of the mind. Nowhere, as in Naked Lunch's *collection of monsters, half-mad geniuses, cripples, montebanks, criminals, perverts, and putrefying beasts is there such a modern panoply of the vanities of the human will, of the excesses of evil which occur when the idea of personal or intellectual power reigns superior to the compassions of the flesh.*

We are richer for that record; and we are more impressive as a nation because a publisher can print that record and sell it in an open bookstore, sell it legally. It even offers a hint that the "Great Society," which Lyndon Johnson speaks of, may not be merely a politician's high wind, but indeed may have the hard seed of a new truth; for no ordinary society could have the bravery and moral honesty to stare down into the abyss of Naked Lunch. *But a Great Society can look into the chasm of its own potential Hell and recognize that it is stronger as a nation for possessing an artist who can come back from Hell with a portrait of its dimensions....*

EDWARD de GRAZIA   The *Naked Lunch* case had come to me through Barney Rosset, the publisher of Grove Press, after I had been asked by the American Civil Liberties Union to write an amicus curiae brief for the *Tropic of Cancer* case in Maryland. Cy Rembar was calling the shots, supervising the lawyers handling the various *Tropic of Cancer* cases nationwide, but Grove was having difficulty bearing all the legal expenses. Barney had said to me at lunch, "I've got half a dozen published books in the warehouse that I'm afraid to sell because of potential legal expenses"—among these being John Rechy's *City of Night* and a Genet book, though he was mainly concerned about *Tropic of Capricorn* and *Naked Lunch*.

Rosset had more or less terminated his relationship with Cy Rembar, and my understanding is that while he thought Cy was a great lawyer, he was afraid that he wasn't able to control costs. Rembar was opposed to ACLU involvement, even on an amicus curiae basis. He felt that it confused matters, and also, Barney has since told me, Cy wouldn't defend *I Am Curious Yellow*. Why he wouldn't, I don't know. Maybe he felt it wasn't important or that it was actually obscene. Cy isn't as radical or as pure in his view of First Amendment scope and meaning as some other lawyers.

I don't think there were any hard feelings. There were a few cases of *Tropic of Cancer* still floating around which Rosset asked me to take over. I got the Florida case to the Supreme Court, which "quietly" summarily reversed the Florida Court's determination that the book was "obscene" and freed *Tropic of Cancer* effectively for the whole country. It was a 100-to-1 shot, and we won.

So it was under these circumstances that I was running the *Naked Lunch* case in Boston. Norman and Allen Ginsberg were the big-gun, celebrity witnesses— Dwight Macdonald maybe, and I think I tried to get Mary McCarthy but couldn't. Then we had some local Harvard people. I think I'd probably discussed who might be good witnesses with Barney, and it may be that he suggested Norman.

Norman was excellent. He came in well dressed, wearing a three-piece suit, and he was very sure of himself, confident that what he had to say about the book was valid and important. The strategy was to have witnesses attest to certain social values, so I wanted Norman to testify as a writer not only as to the book's literary merit but its moral ideas. Beyond this, though, there was no coaching. With Norman there was no need to.

Aside from getting into a fight in the hotel bar the first time we met, we got along, and obviously he was one of my heroes. I had been impressed with *Advertisements for Myself* because I felt he had something revolutionary in him that was authentic and good and important and that inspired people. Our fight was really sort of playful—I was teasing him. My suitcase had been lost on the train from Washington and I'd been talking to Allen about needing a tie. Norman had a colorful tie, and so maybe I made a grab for it, and he sort of said, "You want to fight?" But it was jocular, and I remember the tone of it more than what specifically happened.

Norman stayed for the whole trial—two or three days—though it was Allen who helped me plan strategy. He knew Burroughs and the book very well, far better than Norman, obviously, and I kept him as our last witness. Barney had suggested having Burroughs there, but I thought that was taking a risk. Burroughs was sort of spacey and odd. I'd met him at a party and liked him, but he looks like an accountant or an undertaker, or both, and this was '64, remember. There was the homosexuality aspect and Burroughs' confession of heroin addiction and killing his wife in Mexico, and so it seemed better to let the book speak for itself. In fact, we also had some misgivings about putting Allen on because of his involvement with homosexuality, but I didn't think anything would come up in that area. Plus he knew the book so well—better, I think, than Burroughs himself. I do remember, however, that his hair was very long, very uncouth, and even though he had a tie on, the judge looked down at him and cleared his throat with a kind of suppressed anger or disgust and said, "Straighten your collar." Allen just said, "Yes, sir," straightened it, and went on to do a beautiful job.

WILLIAM BURROUGHS   I was in Tangiers during the trial, but because of Norman's willingness to testify, to take the time out from his own work, I began to think of him as a real ally, truly helpful after his support at the Edinburgh Writers' Conference.

EMMA CLARA "ECEY" GWALTNEY   When Mike was born in March he called to say he'd finally stopped smoking. In the past he'd tried to quit several times, but he said that it got to be that he hated it so, just like a woman you hate, and that going cold turkey was the only way he'd been able to do it. But this was another example of his power: Beverly was quite a smoker too, and when he quit she quit.

NORMAN MAILER   Michael was about six weeks old in April, and we went up to P-Town so that I could finish *An American Dream*. Beverly was in a postpartum depression, overly worried about Michael, as most mothers are with their first-born, and I had absolutely no idea how I was going to end the damned book.

NORMAN MAILER (LETTER TO FRANCIS IRBY GWALTNEY, MAY 15, 1964)
Dear Fig,
    I can't make this as long a letter as I'd like to, because I've just been working on installment eight—I've managed to clear five weeks for it, and it may turn out to be the longest of them all, because I have to go on until the book is done. It's not that hard to write a hundred thousand words in eight months—I know you've done it often. But the trick here is to make them one hundred thousand finished words, and that makes for strain, because it's hard to relax and get swinging away. So you don't get many bonuses. It's a little like an actor having to memorize Shakespeare. He can't really relax in the part because of the demands of the language. So here you can't relax into the serial because of the pressure of time. Anyway, let's see how it all turns out.
    . . . we're going to Provincetown for four months, June 1 to September 30, and with any luck I hope to get a house with four bedrooms. If I do, will you and Ecey consider coming East for two weeks this summer? Dandy, Betsy, and Susy are going to be with me for June and part of July, so things will be a little cramped during that period. But from August 1 on, I'm sure we'll have plenty of room,

and if you want to, you and Ecey can bring the kids. Provincetown is a fishing village three miles long and two streets wide, population three thousand in winter, fifteen thousand in summer, but I'd match it in beauty against any European fishing village I've seen, and it's a marvelous part of the East. Around then it will be getting pretty hot in Louisiana or Arkansas, and the nights are cool in Provincetown. So don't argue with me. Find time and find a way to come up and be our guest for a couple of weeks. You'll have the best time you've had in years, or I'll consider the trip a failure. And Frank and Mary Lee will go out of their minds swimming in salt water. (If my plans work out right, we'll have a house on the beach.)

Mike is now a couple of months old, and his head has slimmed down from a banana to a lemon. Much to his mother's lack of delight, I insist on calling him Lemon-Head Boiks, since that is indeed his middle name: Michael Burks Mailer, Bev's father's name being Burks Kendrick Rentz. Anyway, Mike looks three-quarters like Beverly, one-quarter like me. He's got my head, my upper lip, and a nose which gives promise of being just as fat. He looks like a squirrel and he's got a prick on him which makes little girls' eyes open with wonder, carries it in a state of constant erection, as far as I can see. Can you imagine that—a squirrel who's hung? . . .

ANNE BARRY He was both tense and stimulated by the writing, but I don't remember him being particularly difficult or wrapped up in himself. Of course,

First-born son, Michael, and Beverly in Brooklyn Heights.

once in a while he'd be in a mood where he'd snap, but I didn't think these were necessarily related to the book. Beverly was pretty good during this period, except she couldn't get along with the help. There were scenes, and either she'd fire the person or they'd quit. They'd come and go, maybe five or six that one year, but, oh God, it seemed like even more than that. The problem was she was sort of arbitrary, hysterical, and uneven. There was something about her way of dealing with those women that made them sullen and uncommunicative, sloppy and unwilling to work.

I don't think Norman talked to me about keeping the book a secret as he was doing the installments, though. I suppose my WASP discretion meant he didn't have to. But I felt free to give him suggestions, and he never felt I was interfering. There wasn't much, but once in a while I'd say, "Norman, I've been typing this for so long, and your hero hasn't had anything to eat for days." Then he'd write in scrambled eggs or something.

There were also funny dilemmas that arose. For example, in one installment he already had the corpse cooling, the body of the woman thrown out the window, and it was only then that he had me call up the coroner's office to find out if it's possible to prove that a corpse has been moved. They told me about dependent lividity—that the blood will go to the lowest point, leaving bruises on the body where it has been resting. I told Norman, and he turned white. Whatever the plot he had in mind, it was important that it not be obvious that the body had been elsewhere as a body, that the corpse had not been moved. I don't remember the exact phrase, something like "Well, back to the drawing board"—only it was better than that—and he went and closeted himself for several days to work himself out of the hole he'd inadvertently written himself into.

With the final installment, though, I let him down, and it was terrible. It was the very last day, the last minute, and I'd been typing all night. At five in the morning I fell asleep. But then he wanted to rewrite the whole chapter or the ending or whatever. I had my head down and I couldn't be roused. I think he pecked it out himself, but he was very disappointed in my lack of stamina.

HAROLD HAYES I didn't see him during this time, but as far as I could tell, he was holding up fine. Given the usual problems with time, it's possible that the eighth and final installment was late and longer than we expected and that we had to make adjustments to fit it in. I wouldn't describe it as ripping apart the magazine, that would be hyperbolic. But we had to make adjustments and concessions to space, no question.

WALTER MINTON He definitely did have problems with the last installment. *Esquire* was ready to go to bed, they'd left space for the ending, which came in long after deadline, and finally they set it in six-point type. It literally had to be squeezed in, because that's all the room they'd left.

RICHARD BARON After he delivered the completed manuscript in August I told Norman I wanted the definitive novel, the big one. I thought he already had it, in fact, if he wanted to put in more time and develop *An American Dream*, but he said he didn't think so—it would require at least another year or two of work, and that would mean more money. I said I'd be happy to give it to him, and at the same rate he was already being paid. I was serious, and in fact would have traded what I had for double the amount, so I offered to put him on a yearly retainer.

NORMAN MAILER Later, when Baron suggested that I take another year, that he'd pay the bills so I'd be able to turn it into *the* big book, he was being extraordinarily generous. He had the idea that it was a publisher's role to help talented writers in all sorts of odd ways, so he made the offer because he'd heard me say at one point that it could have been a much larger book if I'd created Rojack's intellectual powers: to wit, his studies of magic. In other words, do the sort of thing that Saul Bellow might do with such a character. But since I'd written the book the other way, now if I were to give Rojack a lot of intellectual baggage, it wouldn't work. Because, remember, the hero has attainments we have to take on faith. Like Robert Jordan, who's a teacher from a far-western university. When he tells us he's a teacher, fine. Do I know to this day what he taught, was it English or what? Or Gatsby's being a gangster. Rojack's of the same ilk. I decided to leave it at that.

After the serial I spent four months doing a lot of work polishing it the summer of '65, and that was when I stopped smoking, which I'd first taken up at seventeen, in college. I do think stopping affected the metaphors in *An American Dream*: my writing became more sensuous, less articulate. When I smoked I would always have the word, the precise word I wanted. After I stopped, it was the rhythm and the sound of the word that gave me more.

ANNE BARRY He'd been talking a lot about writing "the big book," and several times he made brief forays into it. I don't recall whether it was set in ancient Egypt, but I remember certain pieces of subject matter, like it began before the hero was born. But these brief forays seemed to come to naught. He and Beverly had an intense relationship, he had intense relationships with everybody, and I think he was conscious of frittering away energy—though I wouldn't call it dissipation, that's too pejorative a word. I suppose, like many men, he might have been aware of his age and diminishing physical capacities. Men have it hard, don't they? We women just get better and better.

RICHARD BARON By this time Norman and I began to recognize there was a bit of simpatico between us, and he would refer to me as Baron. The tough-guy stuff. We became close, which was why, at the beginning of the summer, I had gone up to Provincetown. He thought I was crazy, the same way some people think he's crazy, and things happened where I may have been a little too heavy with people even by P-Town standards.

We'd rented a place on the water next to Norman and Dorothy Zinberg. Norman and Beverly had all the kids, not only their son but all the others, and Adele was somewhere else in town. One night we were at a party, Norman was boxing, I was doing a bullfighting thing with a cape, dancing with Zinberg's wife, and suddenly the chandelier fell down and cut her. I was petrified. I'd had a few drinks, but even after I'd apologized there was talk all over town about this awful guy Baron.

I wasn't boozing as much as Norman, but a few days later we were over at Motherwell's, and Zinberg comes up and starts berating me all over again about hurting his wife. We were standing at the bar, he was going on and on, and I raised my arm in some conciliatory gesture and knocked over a full bottle of ginger ale, which hit him on the foot. He cried out, "My God, you've broken my toe!" And I had. His retaliation consisted of not letting their kids play with ours. What could I say? That his wife was enjoying herself and leading me on?

NORMAN MAILER   There was a gathering at our place a couple of weeks later, both Baron and Zinberg were there, and it was funny as hell. Baron *had* broken Zinberg's big toe, and that night he did it *again*. He was boozed and he stepped on Zinberg's foot.

JACOB DRUCKMAN   At the time he was building his own Sailfish out of a kit. It was up on sawhorses, and since I'd built one myself, I'd sometimes stop on my way down to the beach and make comments. Probably I was coming on as very knowledgeable, because I remember feeling, Jesus, this guy doesn't enjoy having someone around who knows more than he does. He seemed *uncommonly* competitive, particularly when it came to a so-called macho activity like making something with your hands.

I didn't know who he was, and we didn't actually meet until one afternoon when I was out sailing and it suddenly grew very dark. A storm was starting to blow up, and I was off the beach when I suddenly saw him. To the west of the beach there are some old pilings, 12 by 12's, part of the foundation of an old house that had once been built out over the water, the ledge standing ten feet up at high tide. And as I'm watching, I see this guy walking up and down the pilings, shadowboxing in the wind, almost as if he's shadowboxing the storm, like King Lear on the heath. At that point I was starting to get nervous, and I tried to get the sail down, but the damned halyard had stuck at the top of the mast, so I figured that if I could sail over to the bulkhead, this guy could reach the top of the mast and free it. Which is what happened. I quickly pulled the sail down and said "Thanks very much" and introduced myself, and he said "Hi, I'm Norman Mailer."

NORMAN MAILER (THE FIGHT)   *Once, sailing in Provincetown harbor on nothing larger than a Sailfish, he had passed a whale. Or rather the whale passed him. . . . He had recognized at the moment that there was nothing he could ever do if the whale chose to swallow him with his boat. Yet he felt singularly cool. What a perfect way to go. His place in American literature would be forever secure. They would seat him at Melville's feet. Melville and Mailer, ah, the consanguinity of the M's and the L's—how critics would love Mailer's now discovered preoccupations (see Croft on the mountain in* The Naked and the Dead) *with Ahab's* Moby Dick.

RICHARD BARON   He put a raised seat on the Sailfish. He'd figured it out perfectly from an engineering point of view, but it disturbed the boat's balance, since a Sailfish is very light, little more than a surfboard with a sail.

Norman didn't know how to sail, but he knew I was a sailor, so we took it out in the bay one afternoon. I was at the tiller and he was enjoying himself immensely when I started smelling something strange and shouted, "It's whale shit! There's a whale coming at us!" Norman was facing me, I'm pointing behind him, and he says, "Come on, Baron, cut the crap." He thought I was kidding him about *Moby Dick*, since we'd just been talking about his doing his big novel, and I said, "No, Norman, there really is a whale coming at us."

We were far out, past the point. It was just gliding by, not twenty feet away, and, my God, those goddamn Sailfishes weigh nothing, they just turn over. But Norman thought it was just the funniest thing ever. We'd always referred to "the big novel" as "Moby Dick," so he started saying, "My God, if I'm swallowed by the whale I'll be famous, and the whale will be known as another Moby Dick."

ANNE BARRY   During that summer Barbara visited with her son, Peter, so too Beverly's English friend, Valerie Danby-Smith, who'd worked for Hemingway and Brendan Behan. She married Gregory Hemingway, "Papa's" son who's a doctor. I'd once met Brendan Behan at one of Norman's huge parties in Brooklyn; he was singing the most hideous songs about nuns that went on for twenty-two verses. There was also a son who visited in Provincetown, although there'd been a paternity dispute because Behan's wife said that the baby wasn't his. But once you saw the kid—he walked like Behan, looked just like him—you knew she had to be wrong.

Bill Walker was also around, and Buzz Farbar too. Buzz was always around, in Provincetown and Brooklyn, and I never knew why. Norman was involved in some business ventures—maybe it was the movies they eventually made— but I never saw any substance to this relationship, unlike his friendships with Jose and Roger Donoghue. I liked Jose a lot better, so that colored my view. He seemed to have more sweetness and—that old-fashioned New England word— more character than the others, while Roger was really a close friend.

A lot of the people around Norman adored him, and he liked the adulation. Some of them, though, I viewed with asperity and WASP disdain. They were hangers-on who liked the free booze and the excitement and glitter. Norman had enormous loyalty toward these people, and once in a while I'd nag at him— "Norman, how can you stand it? These are terrible people. Don't do this." His response was that I didn't understand and should get off his back.

RHODA LAZARE WOLF I was always amazed at Beverly, that she could cook for twelve people at a time. Not only the kids but so many friends whom they'd have for dinner. Fan seemed to like her the best of all the wives because in the beginning she was acting like a mother to all those kids, feeding them, building a home. And it was very impressive, just getting all those kids to pitch in and work.

CHARLIE BROWN Beverly and I had had a running correspondence, and I told her I wanted to go to music school. She said, "Juilliard's it, you gotta come to New York." So the door was opening a little wider, and I went north in the fall of '64, by bus, to check things out. I stayed with them in Brooklyn. Michael was just a baby, and I was supposed to do some baby-sitting.

I'd never seen anything like that incredible apartment before. It was strange. The ceiling was curved. What the hell is this, something wrong with your ceiling? At first Norman wouldn't pay too much attention to me. I kept trying to make conversation or find something to talk about, but he made me nervous. I was afraid of him. I still am. You don't know quite what the man's gonna do from minute to minute. He really pissed me off, because his attention span was so short. I just thought, Well, he's one of them New York writers.

My impression was that Beverly had gotten exactly what she wanted. She was running the household and being the queen bee, and there was also the amazing social scene. They'd have parties, they'd go out constantly, and the amount they drank, you couldn't believe it. And, oh God, was Beverly keeping up with him. I didn't really consider if she had drunk that much in the past, I just figured that's what you do in New York.

I met some of their friends at their dinner parties. Buzz Farbar was there a lot, Jose Torres I loved, and we became fast friends immediately. Donoghue I liked too. Every time he'd talk to me he was too drunk to make much sense, but at least he was talking to me. Also Paul Krassner. I liked Paul, though I couldn't understand why a man who lived in New York and who obviously had some money dressed in army pants all the time. Now I realize I was mistaken about the money, but at the time I thought everybody in New York had money.

Obviously Norman was a major power on the social scene, and I started meeting all these people—political people, the hierarchy of the literary world, major writers. There were also some Kennedy people around. The Javitses too. In fact, I played a party for them. I don't remember specific names, but I remember thinking, My god, Norman knows so-and-so. He's a heavyweight— this joker could be President or something.

I'd never seen Beverly act the queen bee before—you know, like throwing maids out. There's the famous story of her going through five maids in one year—and it may have been one week for all I know. I walked into the house in P-Town once and got hit with a peach square in the kisser. She'd gotten frigged out at some housekeeper and was throwing things just as I happened to walk in. I got the peach in my face, then some black woman comes flying out the door.

Beverly wanted everything to be perfect, but since she couldn't do all the housework herself, she kept hiring people. But then she'd discover that these women weren't perfect, so she'd get pissed, scream at them, then throw them out. I don't know how much it had to do with Norman. Probably a lot. When she was living on Sutton Place she didn't behave that way, but then again she didn't have a home and kids to bring up, and she didn't have all those ideas of the perfect American situation, the American dream, to deal with.

But she had figured she was tough enough to handle Norman's history with women. She thought she was tougher than the other ones, had more street sense, and that was what Norman was after, a woman with balls. Then, when she had the kids, it got in her way and it was too much for her to handle. With the household and the whole social environment, it looked to me like she was headed for a nervous breakdown. That was it, life with Norman. "It's too much, I can't handle this," she'd say, but in the meantime she's doing it, she's handling it, and making it far worse by being the maniac.

Hetty was the constant retainer then, in addition to the others, and of course Annie Barry was around too. As for me, I was expected to do odd jobs, handyman things, and I thought that was as it should be. Carpentry, mainly—building little things in the apartment, straightening out the catwalk, some nails here and there.

I remember that during that first fall Norman was revising An American Dream. I stayed in the little room up where the catwalk goes around, the room below the tower. He worked in the tower, and I'd hear him doing dialogue, talking it out, saying it aloud to himself. Then when the book came out in March, I read it and realized that part of it was about my sister and Miles Davis, though the figure of Cherry is really a composite of Beverly, Jeanne Campbell, and Carol Stevens. Cherry is a singer, Carol is a singer, and, in fact, when I met Carol later on, she said she'd known Norman for a long time.

RICHARD BARON His mood was very positive while he was revising An American Dream, and he was putting in at least four hours a day in his studio. So far as I was concerned, the Esquire serialization had been great. Maybe he'd needed the goad, maybe he didn't. Either way it had helped the book.

What he chose to do was an impossible task to begin with—his literary ideas for An American Dream—and he did the best job possible within the limitations of time. When it was done he then got involved with the book's promotion, marketing, even advertising. There wasn't anything he didn't want to see—his photograph, flap-copy ads. He'd sit down and argue with Sussman of Sussman and Sugar, our ad agency.

He has an absolutely keen marketing sense. He's more aware of the mass market than most writers—the effect of a photograph, the nuance of a single word—and obviously because he knows what motivates people. Specifically, he knows the value of shock. Where I might be inclined to say, "This isn't good because it's offensive," he'd say, "Baron, you don't know your ass from a hole in the ground. I'm showing you something that's going to sell an extra five or ten thousand books, and you can't even see it." Like the jacket photo. I thought it was too unusual; it didn't make him good-looking or virile, it made him look all crazy. He said, "That's just what they want." And he was right. He also brought in his own sketches for the cover. It was his idea to stick Beverly in there—her face off to the right of the American flag motif within a white circle. It wasn't just a gift to his wife; he thought some of the "in" people, like reviewers, would pick up on it, and, again, he figured it perfectly.

What he balked at was appearing on TV. I'd ask him and he'd say, "Come on, Baron, would you ask Tolstoy to go on television? I'm not going to lower myself to tout my own book, I'm not going to whore."

E. L. DOCTOROW   I went to Dial from New American Library in the autumn of '64, just as An American Dream was being published—too late really to have any effect, since the manuscript was already in galleys. My first professional experience with him was when I told him that I felt the book suffered from the reader knowing without doubt that the guy had killed; I thought if that information had been deferred, it would have created tension and made the story snap together a lot better. His response was, "Why didn't you come here six months ago? Where were you when I could have used that?"

Baron had started to recruit me in the late summer. I was unhappy at NAL and I was looking. Baron called me, and I went up to Dial for an appointment with him. He was late, and I waited in the anteroom for twenty minutes. Then I left, telling the secretary, "The next time Baron wants to talk, tell him he can come to see me." It was just the sort of spirit that intrigued Baron. In a subsequent conversation the more negative I became, the higher his price got. So I eventually went there. Baron was a good promoter, and I think one of the reasons he and Norman hit it off was because they're both kind of combative personalities. Norman appreciated Richard. He had no illusions about him, and he liked that feistiness.

I remember Norman was very careful about the design of the jacket, the copy on the flap, the type face, as he was on every other book of his I edited. I think I wrote the flap copy on An American Dream, and then I think he took a whack at it, especially the last paragraph. The "frontier of unexplored territory which lies far out in that land between . . . "—I think that's probably a Mailer metaphor. The flag on the cover was his idea too—reversing, misapplying the colors on the American flag so that the stars are black on red and the stripes blue and black. The picture of Beverly, the postage-stamp inset, that was his too. Also the cover photograph. He chose that picture. Anne Barry took it, and then subsequently, in '66 or '67, she came to work at Dial—I think on Norman's recommendation.

ANNE BARRY   I snapped the photo when he was shadow-boxing with me. But when it was reproduced in the papers he looked drunk and crazy. Norman was furious. We tried to find out what had happened but of course got nowhere.

JOSE TORRES   I don't know if it was Beverly or Norman who invited Miles Davis to the Village Vanguard party for *An American Dream*. At the time I didn't realize Beverly had been involved with Miles, or even that Norman had used him in the book—the Shago Martin character.

But there was an incident with Miles that night. He came in looking slick and went over to Beverly. "Hi," he says and starts playing with her hair, straightening it out, caressing it. Norman sees this and comes over and says, "Hey, stop that." Miles didn't stop, so Norman grabbed his hand and pulled it away. People around them got very quiet, and there was a staring contest for about thirty seconds. Then Miles did an about-face and walked away.

GLORIA JONES   It seemed that Norman and Jim weren't as mad as they'd been before, because we went to that party too. Both Norman and Beverly seemed to be extremely pleased that we had come, and she took me aside and said, "Thank you for coming." Norman seemed pleased, very happy too, but I don't think it was a real rapprochement. I don't know if they ever saw each other again, though maybe they did once more in the seventies.

For Jim, going to the party was a gesture. He sort of felt people were picking on Norman in the reviews, and at the time Norman didn't seem in such good shape.

NORMAN PODHORETZ   We had a long session in a restaurant on Third Avenue, around the corner from *Commentary*, and while I don't remember specifically why I thought *An American Dream* was such a bad book, I do remember thinking that in those years he had ambitions that were unrealistic and that bore little relation to what his most authentic talents were pressing for. His fixation on "the big book" was born of a kind of Joycean idea of the artist-hero. It was a willed, made-up notion rather than a dictate from his nervous system, or, if you like, his soul, and as such it was impossible of achievement. The issue wasn't writing the book in installments. *The Brothers Karamazov* was also written in installments. This issue was the book itself, whether or not it was forced, whether or not it was any good.

NEWSWEEK   *An outpouring of all-consuming ego... Hipster, faith healer, dour diagnostician, Norman Mailer serves up in* An American Dream *the purgative for an American nightmare. For Rojack, the prescription may be suitable. But for the public, one wonders whether the operation would be successful without the patient dying.*

TIME   *... this sounds like a ride on a hobbyhorse. But because Mailer is a born writer, it is a heady ride—a bit absurd but, like all of the latter-day Mailer, somehow disarming because it has been attempted by a man who knows all along that the bystanders may laugh.*

TOM WOLFE, NEW YORK HERALD TRIBUNE, BOOK WEEK   *... Once the first fourteen and a half pages of the book are out of the way, Mailer exhibits much of the
best things he has going for him, his drive, his pace, his gift of narrative, his
nervous excitement, things Cain and Raymond Chandler had, but not too many
other American novelists. Using the serial form—ending each chapter cliff-hanger
style—Mailer creates excellent suspense—in fact, in much of the book Mailer
moves, probably unconsciously, in the direction of Cain and shows great promise.
In the context of a Cain adventure, Mailer's gothic attitude toward sex—which
Cain shares—a great deal of new-sentimental business about how making love
to a broad is all mixed up with death and fate and how you can tell your fortune
by the quality of the orgasm—all this is not embarrassing in the context of a
Cain novel like* The Postman Always Rings Twice.

*Of course, Mailer cannot match Cain in writing dialogue, creating characters,
setting up scenes or carrying characters through a long story. But he is keener
than Cain in summoning up smells, especially effluvia. I think Norman Mailer
can climb into the same ring as James M. Cain. He's got to learn some funda-
mentals, such as how to come out of his corner faster. But that can be picked
up. A good solid Cain style opening goes like this:*

"They threw me off the hay truck about noon..."

PHILIP RAHV, THE NEW YORK REVIEW OF BOOKS   *The trouble with Mailer, to my
mind, is that he has let himself become a victim of ideas productive of "false
consciousness"; and these ideas are willful, recklessly simple, and histrionic. He
has too many ambition-fed notions and he does not sufficiently value the artistic
function.... Salvation is not to be seized by force of heroics or diabolics. Life's
cruel and inexorable processes can be arrested neither by the brain nor by the
phallus, least of all by the phallus. But if Mailer ever extricates himself from his
entanglement with the hocus-pocus of power and the glamor-dream of the romantic
domination, both physical and psychic, of existence, he might yet emerge as one
of our greater talents.*

STANLEY EDGAR HYMAN, THE NEW LEADER   An American Dream *is a dreadful
novel, perhaps the worst I have read since beginning this column, since it is
infinitely more pretentious than the competition. Mailer's novel is bad in that
absolute fashion that makes it unlikely that he could ever have written anything
good.*

RICHARD POIRIER, COMMENTARY   *Of course* An American Dream *isn't good or
bad simply because it deals with aspects of life seldom treated with candor in
serious literature, and even less frequently with Mailer's relish of detail. It is in
fact an introspective novel, and in reading it... I was most often reminded, for
comparison, of the recent poetry of Robert Lowell. Mailer and Lowell are alone,
I think, in having created the style of contemporary introspection, at once violent,
educated, and cool. Their language substantially extends the literary resources*

of English, and people will later turn to them in any effort to determine the shapes our consciousness has been taking.

HARPER'S *Like an ancient tragedy,* An American Dream *is a work of fierce concentration, with such pressures behind each scene that it risks (and occasionally achieves) absurdity. It is an American dream as Oedipus the King is a Greek dream: not the fantasying of a personal or communal ideal but the acting out of personal and communal guilt.... The states of mind are extreme, not rendered by psychological explanation but with an extraordinary, almost unbearable immediacy.... In its earlier serial publication,* An American Dream *seemed to be hardly more than a series of cheaply lurid episodes in which the middle-aged bad boy of American literature was trying too hard to shock a bourgeoisie.... But now that the novel can be seen as a whole, the episodes come together in a pattern of remarkable imaginative coherence and intensity.*

CONRAD KNICKERBOCKER, THE NEW YORK TIMES BOOK REVIEW *In* An American Dream, *his first novel in 10 years, Norman Mailer burns his remaining bridges. He tells a sometimes bizarre, always violent, absolutely contemporary story of evil, death, and strange hope. Reading it is like flying an airplane with the instruments cross-wired... Unwise, irresponsible, devoid of the charm that now passes for literature, it diagrams the pentacle around which so many of us dance with such fateful urgency.*

JOAN DIDION, NATIONAL REVIEW *... An American Dream is one more instance in which Mailer is going to laugh last, for it is a remarkable book, a novel in many ways as good as* The Deer Park, *and* The Deer Park *is in many ways a perfect novel...*

In fact it is Fitzgerald whom Mailer most resembles. They share that instinct for the essence of things, that great social eye. It is not the eye for the brand name, not at all the eye of a Mary McCarthy or a Philip Roth; it is rather some fascination with the heart of the structure, some deep feeling for the mysteries of power. For both Mailer and Fitzgerald, as for the tellers of fairy tales, there remains something sexual about money, some sense in which the princess and the gold are inextricably one...

They share a couple of other things, Mailer and Fitzgerald. The notoriety, the devastating celebrity which is probably in the end at least as nourishing as it is destructive. The immense technical skill, the passion for realizing the gift. The deep romanticism. And perhaps above all the unfashionableness, the final refusal to sail with the prevailing winds. Fitzgerald was "frivolous," and Mailer is "superstitious." Philip Rahv has spoken for the rationalist establishment: An American Dream *lacks "verisimilitude." Rojack "hears voices." His suicidal thoughts seem induced by the moon, and "appear to have nothing to do with guilt-feelings or remorse." Mailer is entangled with "the hocus-pocus of power." Had Mailer not been so "entangled" he might have sent Stephen Rojack not to that telephone booth on the desert (not a "credible experience," Rahv chides) but to a good Morningside Heights analyst. Had Fitzgerald not been so "frivolous" he might have gone not to Hollywood but to Spain, and written* For Whom the Bell Tolls. *If only. Mailer thought to preface* The Deer Park *with this line from Gide: "Please do not understand me too quickly." There seems little danger of that, and the loss is entirely ours.*

IX: THE AGE OF AQUARIUS (1965-69)

CLAY FELKER When I was at the *Herald Tribune* I suggested to Norman that he go to Vietnam and do a series for us. I initiated talks between him and Jim Bellows, the editor, who liked the idea. Mailer, though, was not happy about the assignment and really didn't want to do it, perhaps because he felt too old for combat, but at the same time he felt challenged. What Bellows wanted was *The Naked and the Dead* writing, vivid reporting of a bunch of ordinary GIs, a look at the war from up close. After starting here in this country, Norman would go to Vietnam and pick up a combat unit. He would file regularly, every week or so, and the whole thing was planned for two or three months. It was all set, the money was arranged, then Jock Whitney turned it down because he didn't like Mailer's attitude toward the war.

RICHARD BARON When they were in the talking stage Norman called me up and said, "Hey, Baron, I may get a chance to go to Vietnam. You wanna come? You're the one guy I can count on." He knew about my experiences in the army, and while it was a little too macho perhaps, I said, "You bet your life."

NORMAN MAILER I didn't do it, and there was a very detailed history to it. First, I was scared right through—you know, one of those true fears, as if someone says to you, "Hey, why don't you race a Grand Prix car?" But I said, "Okay, I'll do it on two conditions: one, that my pieces be printed *in toto* or not at all; and second, they run only on the front page." The reason I wanted the front page was that I felt I'd be going into a real hornet's nest: Green Berets, CIA, Saigon profiteers, Communists who'd see me as a Trotskyist—all the crossroads were going to run through me and I'd be a sitting duck. I wouldn't be going over like another writer, I'd be under crossfire, and therefore the greatest protection I could have was to be on the front page, since if I got offed, there would be a lot of attention paid to it.

So I made my goodbyes to Beverly, took a last look at my children, and was all set to go when the deal fell apart. The *Herald Tribune* folded.

Then a couple of years later, maybe about '68, I was over at Abe Rosenthal's house one night for dinner and I told him about what the *Herald Tribune* had once offered and said, "Why doesn't *The Times* send me over?" Abe said, "Nah." I said, "C'mon, Abe." He said, "Nope, we're not gonna send you." "You think about it," I said, "it might be very exciting stuff." He said, "No." I said, "Why not?" Then he leaned forward—it was an incredible moment—he said, "You'll get killed." He said it like "You won't know where the bullet's coming from either." I was very impressed with that protective instinct in Abe Rosenthal. I think he cared about me and still does. That was his assessment of the situation, and he's a realist, which meant that my own assessment hadn't been inaccurate.

JERRY RUBIN In the spring of '65 we formed a committee to plan two days of nonstop protest against the Vietnam War to let the whole world know about Berkeley. We were going to get every important intellectual in the country, so I wrote out a list of everybody I wanted to speak, including Norman Mailer. But the Trots and the CPers—the official left—didn't want him to come and didn't want him identified with the antiwar movement because he'd stabbed his wife. They said he was too unpredictable, his reputation too mixed, and I threatened to resign.

I phoned Norman anyway, introduced myself, since he didn't know who I was, and I asked him to come. "It's gonna go thirty hours, we're gonna have people like Ben Spock, Bertrand Russell, and I. F. Stone, and you're gonna be one of the featured speakers," I told him. "We're gonna have over 20,000 people." I remember him saying, "I've never spoken to 20,000 people before..."

As promised, he called me back in a week and said he was preparing a speech on Lyndon Johnson and that, yes, he'd like to do it at Berkeley. I went back to the organizing committee, and although the Trots remained opposed, the CPers came up with a compromise: they'd agree as long as they knew in advance what line Norman was going to take. I told them that wasn't good enough, that I wasn't going to screen a speech by Norman Mailer. "The whole idea," I told them, "is that anybody who's against the war can speak from whatever point of view they want. And besides, Norman Mailer speaks to the unconscious of this country." I was holding a gun to their heads—I told them I'd blow the whole protest if they didn't go along—and eventually they had to agree.

So finally Norman came out. I was too busy to meet him at the airport, but he had friends out there—Don Carpenter and Michael McClure, who brought him to campus. Never having met before, we said hello just as he was going up to the platform to speak.

The rally itself was unbelievable, like a Nuremberg rally, there was so much energy. One o'clock in the morning and "Yay for Communism"—10,000, 15,000 Berkeley students standing up and cheering, people hanging off the rooftops, and you knew that the times were going to be strange when something like this could happen. During the spring the campus had been at a standstill, the mass movement had collapsed because of the Filthy Speech Movement coming out of the Free Speech Movement, and all of it was now being funneled into this protest. And when Norman got up and gave his speech—an extraordinary speech—the crowd went crazy. It was the first time anybody had made fun of the President, and here he was telling the country to take LBJ's photo and turn it upside down, doing this in the theater we'd conspired to create for him.

PAUL KRASSNER   I was emceeing when Norman got up, and when he finished, the response began to build rhythmically, getting louder and louder. The cheering was so powerful I just waited. I couldn't go on while he was still out there, I didn't want to interfere with that moment. Besides, you just had to let it run its course.

Then as I passed him—he was coming off, I was going back up to the podium—he said, "How'd you like to print this in *The Realist*?" I hesitated for a moment, only because I couldn't say anything but yes. He realized the impact he'd made. He was on cloud nine, flying. What are you gonna do, go like Rocky? And even though he'd been appalled by some of my earlier material in the magazine—like the thing on the JFK assassination—he obviously wanted the speech to reach beyond Berkeley, and he knew I'd print what he said without changing a word.

I don't remember if he gave me the speech then and there or mailed it to me. On the cover of that issue I put Lyndon Johnson's picture upside down, yet it so happened that this was when there was a water shortage in New York, so I took one of those Water Department signs and put it over Johnson's picture in the place where *The Realist* typeface usually went. The cover read "Don't Flush for Everything," then there was Johnson's picture, with *"The Realist"* printed at the bottom. The post office held up the issue because I hadn't officially applied for a change of title, and they were claiming I'd renamed the magazine *Don't Flush for Everything.*

DON CARPENTER   I hadn't been able to figure out why he'd decided to come until we got to the campus and I saw this fuckin' soccer field covered with human beings. Then he gets up on the podium—it hits me: it's his insane prescience. Over the years Norman's said many things to me that were like extra real, and although he may not always be able to verbalize it, he has an extraordinary sense of what's going to happen. He *knew* it was going to be a big thing that night. He *knew* that by telling everyone to turn LBJ's picture upside down he was going to make political history. Thank God—but I remember that when Norman finished and the crowd was going ape, Dick Gregory turned to me, saying, "I ain't gonna follow that shit." He wouldn't even go on.

WILLIAM PHILLIPS   Around this time *Partisan Review* ran an anti-Vietnam War statement signed by Norman Mailer, Eleanor Clark, Martin Duberman, Alfred Kazin, Malamud, Marcus, Podhoretz, Poirier, Richard Schlatter and myself. I don't know who the other commentators were, but Norman began his contribution by saying, "Three cheers, lads, your words read like they were written in milk of magnesia," making it clear that he thought we weren't in the forefront of the antiwar protest.

We didn't oppose the war the way the left generally opposed it, granted, and, in fact, there were contradictions in our opposition which Mailer was smart enough or intuitive enough to catch. He himself had no contradictions—he went all out.

Norman had identified himself with the Movement in the sixties, and had chosen allies like Jerry Rubin and Abbie Hoffman, which I wasn't angry about, but I thought it was going too far. My feelings about the counterculture were ambivalent in that I could approve of some of its aims but couldn't sanction the extremes. I don't think his support of the counterculture was self-serving. I've never thought of Norman as self-serving, he is too complex. His drives to associate himself with extreme movements, with extreme figures, with anti-Establishment figures, have always been very strong. It's part of his person to identify with these things, and I don't think the identification is ever calculated. Two years later he expressed his reservations about the Movement, and I wasn't surprised. The situation had changed. People were becoming aware of its deficiencies.

DIANA TRILLING   After the publication of *An American Dream*, for some reason Norman seemed to be staying away from me. We'd been friends for such a long time, and when he came to England for the publication of that book, he and Beverly came to stay with us overnight in Oxford. The only person he wanted to meet there was Iris Murdoch, so I invited her to the dinner we gave for him, but they got on badly. It wasn't Norman's fault—I'm afraid she wasn't very nice to him. She snubbed him when he wanted to talk about existentialism, and she wasn't very nice to him about playwriting. She didn't realize that he wasn't probing into her life as a playwright but that he was very much interested in dramatizing his own work. But as far as we were concerned it was a lovely visit.

Then suddenly he began drawing back from me a few months later. I've never known why, and I've always suspected that someone must have made some creative trouble between us. Lillian Hellman once told me that after the stabbing—whether it was several months or a year or more later, I don't recall—Norman had come to her house quite drunk one night and, despite her resistance, made a terrific pass at her. She described it as an assault, really; she said he tried to break down her bedroom door. Over the years that story traveled around the city. I heard it from several people. It occurred to me that maybe someone had heard that story and, instead of thinking that it came from Lillian, had thought that it was a story that I had told and had passed it on to Norman that way. I'm always having my best jokes credited to other people; maybe that unhappy encounter was credited to me. Please understand that I have no evidence of this whatsoever, I'm just speculating, because it would be the kind of thing that would certainly have driven a wedge between Norman and me—he would be bound to think I was some kind of person who had sick fantasies. Actually, I don't know what turned him away from me at that point. Maybe there wasn't even any general estrangement, but it felt like it.

NORMAN PODHORETZ   My own friendship with Lillian Hellman pretty much paralleled my friendship with Mailer. She had known him longer, of course, since '49. They were involved with each other politically when he was in his Stalinoid phase, and then there was a further connection when Lillian wanted to dramatize *The Naked and the Dead*.

Political alliances aside, though, he always flirted with her. She flirted with him too. Up through the late sixties I was very close to her, much as I was to him, and there were all sorts of episodes involving the two of them when I was either an observer or participant. She had no particular role in my own relation to Norman except that I met him through her, and the three of us, sometimes with Midge and whoever Norman was married to—either Adele or Jeanne or Beverly—would spend time together. Hammett, though, never made an appearance, even when we all visited Lillian up on the Vineyard. But I think Hammett never wanted to meet Lillian's friends. Why, I don't know.

JOSE TORRES   I became world champion on March 30, 1965, and a lot of it was thanks to Norman.

My business manager was then Cain Young, a black guy who'd made a lot of money "blockbusting" in Crown Heights, and he was going to put up $100,000 to guarantee the fight. Then at Ali's first important fight in New York he heard my wife giving an opinion on Ali, and he became very annoyed, making comments about her "expertise." She told him she'd learned a lot from Cus D'Amato, at which point I took Ramona's side, told him not to mess with her, and we took a cab right over to Norman's in Brooklyn. It was eleven or eleven-thirty at night, and I explained what had happened. Norman says, "Wait a minute," and calls his father, his accountant. He's got Barney on the phone, cups the mouthpiece, and says to me, "How much money can we lose if the worst happens?" I said, "I don't know. But maybe the most, $90,000." "Okay," he said, turning back to the phone, "I can lose $90,000."

What had happened was that Cain Young had wanted me to release Cus from his contract if he was going to put up the money, so when Norman offered the $90,000 I phoned Cus to tell him we had a solution. Cus refused: "We could

lose. I don't want you to fuck up your head worrying about your friend's money."
Three weeks later Young apologized and put up the money.

But that wasn't the end of it. In the midst of training, Johnny Manzanet, my
trainer, got into a big argument with Young and blew the whole thing. He's a
Puerto Rican, a tough guy. He said to Young, "In case you didn't know, Norman
Mailer, who's a real man, a friend, was gonna put up the money, but Cus was
too decent to let him do it." Young was so humiliated he wanted to walk out.
It was Cus—whom he hated—who'd decided. But Young finally came around,
we went ahead with the bout, and I became champion.

For four months I'd been training, killing myself. The fight lasted nine rounds,
and from the Garden I went to Toots Shor's with Cus, Cain Young, and my
wife. I saw Gay Talese and went over to him and said, "What the hell are you
doing here, Gay? There's a party for me at Norman's." He said, "I wasn't invited."
I says, "So what? I'm inviting you. I'm the main guy, you're gonna go." He still
says no, so I get on the phone: "Norman, I'm here with Gay Talese. Can he
be invited?" Norman said, "Of course." Gay was very sensitive, very Italian, and
since he was my first friend before Pete, he was hurt that I became closer to
Pete and then to Norman and not to him.

Anyway, I think everybody knew I was going to win, so there were about a
hundred people at Norman's, and they had a band. There was also a Japanese
moviemaker doing a documentary on me, and he was lucky enough that I won
so he could end the movie with the party. Archie Moore came, Peter Falk,
James Baldwin too, but I was exhausted and left at about four in the morning.
The following day I woke up drunk. Usually I didn't drink, but here I was drunk,
so I went back out to Brooklyn, and the party was still roaring. There had been
a fight, also somebody fell from the parapet, and there was also a fight between
two women. Incredible, the whole thing.

CUS D'AMATO   I've always felt that Jose was the most underrated champion we've
ever had. I remember when he won the championship, there were a lot of
newspapermen at the camp talking about the beating a fighter takes, and I said,
"You're all wrong. If the fighters got hit as much as you people think, everybody
would quit. They'd never need to abolish boxing. Now, take Jose Torres. I'll bet
that he hasn't been hit more than six solid blows in his whole career." "Impossible," they said, so I called Jose over and asked him how many solid blows
he'd been hit in his professional career. He said, "Two." Two! Why? Because
Jose was one of the few guys who mastered the ability to anticipate a punch.
Like the gunmen in the old days who could look into their opponents' eyes and
see the second they were going to draw. That's the way Jose was as a fighter.
Close up, in the confrontation, he could in a split second anticipate a punch.

JOSE TORRES   I'm sure Cus says my friendships with Pete and Norman affected
my boxing. He used to have talks with me: "Jose, this isn't good for you, you've
gotta cut this shit out."

But I always felt that boxing was a temporary thing for me. I wanted to get involved in other things, and the idea to be a journalist came from Pete. He wanted me to be a writer in '61, '62, even before I began talking with Norman. When he switched from sports to doing his column, he used to send me to do interviews and to describe the scene, how the guy looked, the ambience. Then, when I was training in Jersey, there was a guy who used to come and see me, and one day I asked him who he was. He explained he was a migrant worker from Buenos Aires and San Juan. They were making fifty cents an hour in those days, so I wrote a piece about migrant workers in Jersey for *Diario*, the Spanish daily in New York, and it was sold as the cover story for *Weekend* magazine. But nobody believed that I wrote it—they all figured it was Pete Hamill.

Pete, in fact, wanted me to quit when I became champion. He said, "Stun the world, quit now. Fuck this shit." I said, "Pete, I gotta make money." He said, "Fuck the money." I considered quitting, but then told myself I still loved boxing, even though when I became champion I started losing interest because I couldn't go higher.

But I fought for two more years before losing the championship in '67 to Dick Tiger. Norman felt I still had the potential to regain the title and that I didn't have to quit. This was a week after the fight, and we were talking. He thought I'd really won the fight; it was a decision by only one point, and both Cus and I felt I'd lost because we'd had problems with the Garden.

But I talked to Norman about retiring. I told him Pete had wanted me to quit and was now pushing me to make the decision. Norman told me he'd help me if I wanted to be a writer. So my original mentor was Pete, but in terms of seriousness in writing, it was Norman.

CUS D'AMATO   Norman and Jose Torres admire each other a great deal, and I think Norman likes him because Jose's really a spontaneous person. If he's in a group and somebody says something funny, Jose will go into a roar of laughter, roll off his chair, roll on the floor, no matter where he is.

Jose is never Norman's flunky. He thinks of Norman as a very brilliant person, but he's without the pretense most people have, and he'll stand up to Norman. What he's learned about the mind and emotions in boxing he's learned from me, but there are times he thinks I'm wrong, and he'll stand up to me.

The only change I noticed in Jose after he became friends with Mailer was a definite loss of interest in boxing. Jose would go out to bars, stay out all night, and so forth. I didn't like it, and I told him. But Torres, of course, didn't think of it in those terms. When a person feels he's good, sometimes his ego gets so great he feels he can overtake anybody. Like Muhammad Ali, who has the same terrible ego and was going to defend his title without training. Torres used to do the same thing but in a much more minor way.

I assumed it was a psychological thing that was inhibiting his efforts, because his sense of anticipation, all those things, weren't completely intuitive. When you're used to seeing a man perform in a certain way, and you know the type of thinking that makes the performance possible, then a very, very tiny, almost immeasurable difference in his performance means that something mental or emotional is involved. I landed on him for this, recognizing that Norman wasn't the only one; it was all the writers Torres used to meet when they'd go and drink—Hamill, Budd Schulberg, Harvey Breit, Gay Talese. And since Jose was interested in writing, he looked up to these people.

PETE HAMILL   From 1958, or whenever I first met him, Jose has not altered in any substantial way, even after becoming world champion. He wouldn't be in awe of Norman, and as they became friends I certainly wasn't worrying that he'd be corrupted by the literary life. Jose is incorruptible. He couldn't give a rat's ass if he sat next to Bill Paley at a party—he doesn't give a fuck, and half the time he forgets and doesn't show up anyway.

EMMA CLARA "ECEY" GWALTNEY   The summer of '65 Fig and I, our daughter and son drove to New York. We were going to see the World's Fair, then drive up to Provincetown with Norman. Beverly was already up on the Cape, and Norman announced that we were going to his folks' for dinner. His sister Barbara was there, Fan had herring and onions in sour cream, which was delicious, but I wasn't used to it and said, "Oh, this is rich." He said, "What do you mean? This is the kind of food I grew up on." Then he engaged his mother in some conversation about old Jewish practices. He was asking her questions, and she'd reply—it was a general conversation—but all the while Barney was keeping it more personal, and he wouldn't let up. He'd say, "Ecey, you look just the same, you look wonderful. But Fig, there's something worrying you. You've changed some way." It was as if he was putting down the husband to charm the lady. Norman tried to change the subject, but Barney kept getting back on it and just dominated the table, and I thought, Here's one little bantam rooster of a man. What struck me was how much like Norman, almost a carbon copy, and there was something really ironic about Norman's discomfort, since I've seen him go on exactly the same way.

Two days later, after the World's Fair and after Norman had taken us on a walking tour of Brooklyn, we all piled into our car and drove to Provincetown, with Norman driving because he wanted to take back roads, not the Interstate, so he could show us things. Beverly had the place all fixed for us, and we stayed in the room next to theirs on the second floor—I remember we could hear them talking—and the kids stayed in the little tiny room across the hall.

She had made dinner—a big striped bass and lobster and a wonderful sauce for the rice of Dijon mustard and butter. There were two black women working for her, Hetty and Alice Bradford, and Alice and I made friends. I'd go into the kitchen and visit with her, but Beverly didn't like me talking to her, which I thought strange, because even though I didn't grow up with a lot of help, I knew how you should treat people. Now I realize it was maybe because she came from a family that didn't have help and she didn't know beans about it.

Beverly usually didn't get up until ten or eleven. But she also seemed a whole lot different from when I'd met her two years earlier. She was much more assertive. She was being very efficient and running things, and very proprietary too. Like at one of their parties—it seemed as if there was a party nearly every night—I was in the kitchen with a man named Harvey Dodd who said he was hungry, and since Beverly was flying around, really drunk, I said, "Let's look in the refrigerator and see what we can find." Beverly then came in and demanded, "Where did you get that cheese? I don't want you going in my refrigerator!" I said, "Oh, Beverly, I'm sorry. It's my fault. I did it," and she quickly said, "Oh, well, then it's all right."

Norman was also particular about his cooking. He'd always had to have it just right, even back in 1948. During his first visit to us, he was going to peel potatoes for me, and he insisted on using a scraper. I do it with a knife, but he'd used a scraper in the army, so he insisted that was the only way. Now it was the same thing. One night he was going to stir-fry in his wok. Of course it isn't really Oriental at all—he just takes leftover roast and puts some vegetables in—but I said, "I'll help you cut up the celery." I should've known better. I went ahead and did it, and sure enough, he said, "Uh-uh, that's not the way to cut celery. You have to cut it on the diagonal." I was cutting it crosswise, and so I got myself a little lecture.

The two of them, though, had already started having quite a few fights. I remember Beverly stayed up after one party, after everybody else had gone to bed, and she was playing the kazoo, saying, "Here I am, two months pregnant and playing Bessie Smith records. Here I am, thirty-six years old, I don't know what I'm going to do." Then, after another party, when everyone had left, when it was just Norman, Beverly, and me downstairs, she was furious at him and was jumping up and down, with her long blond hair flying. Norman was standing with his arms crossed, rocking on his feet like a big Indian, watching her real coldly. She was saying, "You treat people worse than niggers in Georgia. You're just a bully! I want a divorce. I want it right now!" He said, "Put it in writin'." "I will," she said, and he said, "You're gonna have to have a witness, you know." She said, "I've got a witness—Ecey." I was standing over in the door, and I guess we just don't take things that seriously, 'cause I said I'd be her witness, so she wrote, "I, Beverly Rentz Mailer, want a divorce from Norman Mailer. Witness——" I don't know what happened to that note, but if Beverly remembers this incident—which she may not—I'll bet she could kick herself.

Then there was another party, when Norman got hit by a young black fellow, right in the eye. He had to have a little butterfly stitch, which maybe Beverly did for him. I remember she was screaming at the guy, "Don't hit him in the head! Don't hit his head!" I mean, all those parties seemed so utterly different from a southern drinking party: there was no wild fun, no redneck good-ol'-boy horsing around. It was just tense and tight, with a lot of one-upsmanship—which was what made Norman so aggressive.

That summer Richard Baron, the publisher, was in Provincetown too—his second summer up there, I think—and Norman had been trying to help Fig by getting Baron interested in one of his novels. I was standing with Norman and Baron at one of those parties, and Norman said to him, "I don't know whether Fig really wants to go with you. He may or may not. He hasn't decided yet," then he turned to me and asked, "What do you think, Ecey? Do you think Fig'd be happy?" I said, "I would think so," but then later Norman told me, "You said the wrong thing. You're not supposed to be eager like that. You've gotta stand up a little bit." I knew what he meant, but it irritated me because I thought: I'm so tired of this one-upmanship. Fig'd be thrilled to get the book published, so let's cut it out, huh?

During those days there were all kinds of little tests. Like one night Norman jumped up, stuck out his stomach, and said to me, "Hit me right here."

"Why?" I said.

"Just hit me as hard as you can with your fist," he insisted, and pointed to a certain place with his thumb. So I drew back and hit him.

"You didn't hit me where I said," he said. "You hit me where you wanted to, so you must have some hostility."

Again it made me mad, and I told him, "The trouble with playing any kind of game with you is that you make up the rules as you go along."

"You should do that more often, Ecey," he smiled. "You're just too polite. It's bad for your blood." So he'd changed the rules again, just making that comment. He'd do that, and it would just turn into an eternal contest that went nowhere.

We went out a lot to eat, or to the A-House for music. One night just the four of us had dinner in Truro at a New Englandish sort of restaurant where college boys were the waiters. They brought the chowder in little cups, and we ate that. Then they brought the salad, but we couldn't find the salad dressing. Norman called the waiter over and said, "Young man, where's the salad dressing?" The poor waiter looked over at Fig's place, saying, "The gentleman there . . . ," but he didn't know how to finish, he couldn't go on. The salad dressing had come in a little bowl like the soup dishes, and Fig had eaten it because it was thick and very good, in fact even better than the chowder. Suddenly Norman got hysterical and said, "He ate the fuckin' salad dressing!"

Later we went to hear Bobby Short play. We were right on top of him at a little itty-bitty table, and Fig was sitting with his feet sprawled out. I saw Norman look at him and say, "Fig, maybe you better pull your feet back. People have to walk there." Fig said, "Oh hell . . ." He'd speak that way to Norman, and sometimes with others he'd put on the gruff, but Norman was always chiding him for being rude to waiters and waitresses, and I could tell it made him uneasy. But it cracked me up. I found it endearing, because for all the outrageous things Norman's done, there were all these little things that worried him, like manners and being proper.

We often walked with Norman on the beach, and I did have the sense of Provincetown, not Brooklyn, being his "hometown." He could get away from the city and it was comfortable. Also, he had a nice place to work where he went every day, almost like clockwork.

Still, I would've gotten depressed living there. There's a kind of starkness to the place, with the sea roaring in, and the wind, and the mournful sound of the buoys and the gulls. We also had the feeling that while there were serious people there like the artists, most people were more serious in their fun, in their boozing and screwing around. Fig did his best to understand it, but he really couldn't. He couldn't connect it at all with any kind of literary effort or real work. He also thought the macho fighting business was stupid, and because he realized that Norman was getting into a lot of fights, he thought he was out of line.

ANNE BARRY All the parties and people blend into each other, but I do remember that it was at one of those parties I saw Norman get into a fight, and despite all the stories about his fighting, this was the only time I actually saw it.

It was so stupid, an awful fight with some black guy who turned out to be something like a welterweight or Golden Gloves champion. It started inside the house, then the two of them went outside. Everybody was screaming, "Stop it," and I remember Beverly stoically not saying a thing, loyally knowing the code, which I thought was shit. Here was this middle-aged man running to fat, drunk, up against this young guy, and it was crazy. At moments like that I found myself thinking, This man, these people, this life—it's insane and dangerous to self and others.

JOSE TORRES My wife and I were up there too for the first time in 1965, which was the summer they'd bought the house, and Beverly was pregnant with Steve. Norman always showed respect to my wife, who's Spanish, and he never used words like "shit" or "fuck" in front of her. But one night while we were eating, he and Beverly got into an argument, and Beverly screamed at him, "You know why you need me? You need my cunt." Norman was shocked because my wife was there, but Beverly went on: "If we keep arguing, I'm gonna hit you in your mother's cunt." Norman stood up and yelled, "I'm gonna pick you up and throw you through the window." Ramona was watching, I'm shaking, so I said to Norman, "Excuse me, can I see you for one second?" If he'd tried to throw her, I'd have had to hold him, so instead I said, "Let's take a walk." Which is what we did, just so he'd cool off.

JACK KEARNEY That same summer Shirley Smith got knocked down the stairs at a party at Joe Acker's, where Al Wasserman had an apartment. Al and Barbara weren't married yet, but they were pretty much together. I was on the ground floor and heard a commotion, then I saw a woman hitting Shirley. Everybody had been drinking, and my first reaction was not to get between the two women but to protect Shirley from falling and breaking her back, because the stairs were so steep. Stair by stair I braced my shoulder against her till she was down on ground level. Beverly and Connie Banko meanwhile were slugging her from above. I asked Shirley if I could help her, and she said, "You can take me home," so I got her into the car—there may have been one or two other people with me—but then she started screaming, "They're trying to fuck me, they're trying to fuck me." I was pretty out of it too, but I sobered up fast and went straight to the police station, where I told the cop there, "Look, this woman's very distraught, she's been at a party"—I didn't mention the fight—"and she's yelling obscenities out the window. I'll tell you where she lives and you take her home, or I can take her home, but you radio the other cops that I'm being a good Samaritan." So they said, "Go ahead, you take her," which I did, out to Lee Falk's, in Truro. The next day I got a call from Lee, who was furious and wanted to sue everybody for assault and battery. He'd left her at the party, but no one had wanted to phone him to come get her because he would've blown his top.

BARBARA MAILER WASSERMAN   That same night, while Beverly had the fight with Shirley Smith, Norman had a fight with Lane Smith, who later turned up in his film *Maidstone*. But I think Norman had been in a fight the night before too.

AL WASSERMAN   I don't know what Jack Kearney's thinking of. He had nothing to do with driving Shirley Smith home. The party was at my place, my big social gesture of the season. Jack might have been there, but Shirley was very drunk and obnoxious, and Lee Falk, her boyfriend, had gone home in disgust. I was taking Shirley outside to calm her down, but she kept coming back inside and attacking people, stomping on their feet with her stiletto heels and walking up to women and grabbing their nipples. Finally Beverly and Connie ganged up on her. At about five A.M. practically everyone had gone, but Shirley still refused to leave. Fig Gwaltney helped me put her in the car. Fig was driving, and I stayed in the back seat trying to wrestle her down and soothe her at the same time. We went to the police station and threatened to deposit her there if she wouldn't give us some other destination. The tactic worked. In between laments about her wasted life she managed to direct us to Truro. The last I saw of her was at dawn, hobbling up Falk's driveway, wearing one high-heeled shoe. The other shoe I found in the apartment after Fig and I got home. She never came back for it.

BARBARA MAILER WASSERMAN   Right, and I remember Al and Fig were gone an hour and a half or more, Ecey and I were cleaning up after the party. The sun was already coming up, and we looked at each other. "Boy," I said, "that woman's crazy as a fox. She's got our men, and we're here doing the dishes!"

EMMA CLARA "ECEY" GWALTNEY   A lot of funny things happened that night. I remember Al chewing somebody out, really intense, but he stepped back on somebody else's foot and said, "Oh, excuse me," so polite, and then went right back to his diatribe.

The whole thing was bizarre, not my kind of party. There was a great big tall woman dancing. I thought she was gawky and awkward, but Norman argued with me, saying, "Well, in a kind of animal way she has a lot of grace." It was Shirley Smith. Beverly thought she was being too familiar with him because she had asked him something about *An American Dream*; that's when Beverly flew at her, screaming, "If you want to know about it, I'm Cherry. Who do you think Cherry is? *Me! I'm* Cherry!" She wasn't making a whole lot of sense then, and the next thing, she went over and socked Shirley on the cheek. It was sickening, the sound of flesh hitting flesh.

JOSE TORRES   In the fall Norman had a custom-made Mercedes-Benz that had belonged to Pedro Domecq, the brandy guy, which I borrowed one night, and got stopped for running a red light. Even though I told the cop I was Jose Torres and the car belonged to my friend Norman Mailer, they wouldn't believe me. Norman was at the Garden watching a fight, so I gave the cops the phone number of his mother. They called her, and Mrs. Mailer says, "My son wouldn't give his car to anyone. The guy has to be lying." I was stuck there until one of the station house cops recognized me, but I had to leave the car.

The next morning I called Norman, who started laughing, and we went down with two copies of *An American Dream* which he'd signed, plus I gave them pictures of myself, and finally they released the car. A week or two later I was training in Jersey, and Norman decided to put his mother on, so he said, "Listen, I want you to meet the guy you almost put in jail. These Puerto Ricans are tough and a little crazy, so don't expect my help if he gets a little rowdy with you." She came anyway, with Beverly and Barney and the kids. I went over to her and said, "So you're Norman's mother. Do you know what you did the other night? Well, I just wish my own mother would do the same for me!" She was visibly relieved, also flattered, I think, by what she took as my gallantry. Once she met me, I was okay. And I was very nice to her—I would kiss her, be very

Mr. and Mrs. Barney Mailer.

polite. The one thing she'd get pissed off at was when Norman would mention Malaquais as one of his mentors. She'd say, "What? How do you compare that old, no-goodnik with yourself?"

FANNY SCHNEIDER MAILER   I was sitting and reading, and it was around eight in the evening. "We have Norman's car," the police told me. It was a car he'd just bought. Was it from Jean Malaquais? Yes. Of course, Jean would push it on him. So I said to the police, "Take good care of the car. What you do with Jose Torres is your business." I hardly knew Jose. I cared only about the car, because Norman just got it.

CHARLIE BROWN   I was in on the ground floor of his big project in the fall, building that crazy Lego city. Norman had this architectural idea, he was looking for a way to create a model, and he asked me and Eldred Mowery to do it.

I think someone had given Michael a set of Lego blocks. Norman saw the damned things and realized what he could do with them. At the same time he hated them. He didn't want to touch them. They were plastic, and they made— he said, and I quote—"an obscene noise when clicked together"; therefore I had to be the one who clicked them together. I remember going out to the Lego factory in New Jersey in that damn '61 Falcon of his with the top down, buying crates of these things, I assume at discount. I'd just go out there and they'd load up the car—something like ten thousand Lego blocks—two or three trips back and forth across the Verrazano Bridge, always alone, because otherwise there wasn't enough room for the crates.

We had so many cases of red ones, so many of blue. The people at the factory would always ask, "What's he gonna do with all these things?" Norman gave me instructions to be "discreet," so I was tight-lipped about it, just smiling, and would say, "It's an architectural project." Who knows, maybe he thought somebody would steal his idea.

Eldred and I would unload the crates and bring them up to the apartment. To give Norman his due, he'd occasionally come down and carry a box. We put them in the living room, all the furniture shoved aside, which created an absolute mess. Beverly was beside herself, and there were a million people there all the time, friends who came visiting. All in all, we were at it for two months, though it felt like years.

There was no actual design, only a basic concept. We built the frame out of aluminum, with five-foot legs, on a four- by eight-foot sheet of plywood, having first tried blocks of wood glued together. Eldred had originally been hired to do some major work around the apartment—specifically, to make a tightrope in the living room, but then Norman put him to work on the city. Norman's got all these crazy ideas about what he wants to do—Norman the engineer—and at one point he wanted Eldred to put all these strange trapdoors in the model city. He'd make an appearance and say, "No, no, you've got it all wrong," or "Make me something that looks sort of like this," and he'd pick up a few blocks. "Now put these together, glue them, and I'd like them to go here." He was constantly appearing with a sheaf of papers in his hand, and his secretary, Annie, would be running around making phone calls and taking dictation. He would pop in for fifteen minutes, supervise, then disappear.

Eldred has a much finer structural sense than Norman. He doesn't talk very much, but he did have a few words to say to me about Norman's ability to design things. But he'd never say straight out "Norman, you don't know what the fuck you're talking about." Instead it was "Well, I don't know. How about if we do so-and-so, because otherwise it will fall over?" Beverly meanwhile was always yelling, "I can't stand this shit in my living room." He didn't pay any attention, though, and they'd just throw things at each other.

I think he finally determined it was done when somebody from the Museum of Modern Art came out to see it, took pictures, and wanted to display it at the museum. Norman said, "Great, we'll get it over to you." Then he discovered there was no way to get the son of a bitch out of the apartment. Guys came with cranes, he had all sorts of people doing research: Should we take the glass out of the front window? Can we cut the door? He refused to disassemble it because we couldn't have reassembled it exactly the same way, and he wanted it precisely the way it was. Finally he says, "Eldred, build a fence around it. Fuck it, that's it. It stays." And there it still stays, despite the fact that he's always hurting for room with all the kids. The thing takes up a third of the living room. Of course he also put it on the cover of *Cannibals and Christians*.

E. L. DOCTOROW   Although Norman later inscribed my copy of *Why Are We in Vietnam?* with "To Ed, in recall of the fine editorial times we had on *Cannibals and Christians*," there was actually no great contention about the ordering of the pieces in the collection that Dial published in '66. I've always taken the position that in any collection there was some structure to be found, some way that things balanced and came together so that something emerged that was greater than the individual pieces. I've always had a very organic idea of these things, and Norman had this feeling too and was very clear about what he wanted.

I don't think we talked specifically about the 100 or 150 pages of the imaginary interview in which he discussed God and the devil and redemption. Still, I learned something from him that I value. He took a professional attitude toward all his work, in the sense that he was able to stand back and judge it as something separate from himself—in effect, play audience to it. He saw his writing as something out there by itself that deserved to be judged on its merit, so that he could accept the fact that something was not as good as it might have been. Relative to other writers, I found him far less defensive, less vulnerable. He could say, "I did it, it's out there, I know its faults, I know it might've been better. But now I'll go on to the next thing." He was always free of that self-destructive tormenting most writers go through. It was almost as if each book was a round in a fight: some rounds he did better than others, while in some he took some bad shots. But he was able to judge it and go on. That takes distance between you and the work, and the fact that Norman can do it and knows when to stop writing, when to stop worrying a book, is probably one of the reasons he's one of the most prolific, if not *the* most prolific of the major writers since World War Two.

So there never was any temperament on his part. In those drinking days I'd see him get into really mean, drunken fits, take a swing at someone. That was his public presence. But I remember first being surprised by and then relying on his absolute courtesy. When you talked, he listened. He was not bellicose or difficult. I had far more problems with lesser writers than I did with him. Professionally his conduct was irreproachable.

As with *An American Dream*, the cover of *Cannibals and Christians* was his idea—he wanted to use the photograph of his Lego city. I think *Saturday Review* was doing a story on him, and he was going to have his picture taken in color. Maybe the photograph of his Mile High City was Baron's idea. If Norman wanted it, Baron wouldn't have objected. He would do anything to keep Norman happy—a future Dial writer as well as a present one.

ANNE BARRY   After I left Norman I spent three months copy-editing in the Harcourt Brace College Department, then I went to Dial. Richard Baron had asked me to come and see him, so I assume Norman had called him. But I'd met Richard Baron up on the Cape the previous summer. He loved Norman, wanted to be with Norman, in fact wanted to *be* Norman. So his point of view was that anybody who could handle Norman Mailer could handle him.

SANDY CHARLEBOIS THOMAS   I was going up to Provincetown the summer of '66, and I asked Roz Garfield, who had rented us a house, if anybody might need secretarial help. She mentioned Norman, and I wrote him, addressed "Norman Mailer, Provincetown," saying, "I'm a secretary. I can type 120 words a minute, take shorthand, and I have a yellow belt in aikido." He wrote back, in pencil on unlined paper—a style I soon became accustomed to—and said that yes, he could use someone, was also fascinated by aikido, and that I should stop by and see him.

He invited me out on the deck. Stephen was in a playpen, he'd been born that March, and Norman was wearing cut-off blue jeans and a sleeveless shirt. He offered me a drink, then walked the tightrope set up on the deck as he talked. What he wanted me to do was pick up manuscript pages in the afternoon, then bring them back the next day, when I'd pick up the next batch. I was to do the work at home. He'd already started *Why Are We in Vietnam?*, and he asked me not to talk about it or let anyone see the material. It was going to be a trial period, because, as he said, "I write in longhand and pencil. It's hard to read, and this is a very strange book."

He would give me 15 or 20 pages at a time, and I never retyped the same page. Norman wrote, I typed. He wasn't editing typescript for *Why Are We in Vietnam?* There was some crossing out on the handwritten pages—a word here, a word there—sometimes a sentence running off the page and over the top and across the back, and from time to time he'd ask me if it sounded all right—I think because it was such a peculiar book and he was interested in whether or not it read well.

Sometimes he'd wear the same T-shirt for days without washing it or the jeans either. I don't think it was superstitious, just easier. He had several raggedy old outfits like that, and it never changed, but even his proper clothes were always horrible. When he and Beverly had gone to England he'd had a three-piece pinstripe suit made, a ghastly thing. If memory serves, he had one or two suits, never a lot of clothes, and back in the city he'd send me to Saks Fifth Avenue to buy a hundred percent cotton socks and a hundred percent cotton underwear. And believe me, it's hard to get boxer shorts with a button fly. This was one of the jobs that drove Madeline, his other secretary, absolutely bullshit.

Initially he paid me by the hour, but by July 1 I was doing more than simple typing. Norman gets pots of mail, and he would stack it on the dining room table in neat little piles according to priority: "This should be answered soon, this can wait." He was planning to fly Madeline to Provincetown to do the correspondence, but I started doing it, first taking dictation, then, as time went on, he'd say, "You can answer this" or "This is what I want to say to this person." The whole thing sort of mushroomed. All in all, I typed *Why Are We in Vietnam?*, the play version of *The Deer Park*, *The Armies of the Night*, *Miami and the Siege of Chicago*, *Of a Fire on the Moon*, and *Prisoner of Sex*, and I think I did the *Maidstone* transcript. I also did some transcripts from his talks when he was running for mayor. But it always used to drive him nuts when I'd quit, which I did with some regularity. He likes being used to somebody, having things ordered, and he used to get upset over typos I'd make too. I seldom made typos, but when I did they'd be hard to catch because I'd turn one word into another, like "the *shit* came into dock" instead of "ship." These would annoy him no end, because he'd miss them in copyreading too. He used to accuse me of trying to sabotage him, which always made me laugh.

I know he did some research for *Why Are We in Vietnam?* For example, he sent Madeline to find the name and specs for every gun and their cartridges. But when you did research for Norman, you'd hand it to him, and that's the last you ever knew. It just sort of disappeared.

On the domestic scene, though, I think "passionate" is the best way to describe Norman and Beverly during this period, rather than "love" or "romance." I don't know how much love was lost there, but there certainly was a great deal of passion. Beverly comes right out of the old Baptist tradition. Her religious superstitions were equivalent to wearing an amulet, something to protect you from demons, and she talked about putting curses on people. She said she had a great aunt who was Cherokee, but she showed me a picture of the woman once, and if she's Cherokee, I'm Israeli. She's black, baby. And, of course, the southern black community brought over a lot of the demonic stuff.

Norman had one superstition too, that copper bracelet he's been wearing since the sixties. Somebody told him it was good for arthritis and, in his case, gout. He and I also talked about dope. By then he had a philosophical view—maybe it was a medical position—that to smoke dope was to borrow on the future. His line was that it's playing footsies with the devil: that there are real spiritual experiences on dope (including acid), but they may occur at a time when the person isn't ready for them. Therefore he wasn't going near the stuff, just drinking a tremendous amount. Beverly, on the other hand, disagreed with him, and to complicate matters further, Norman was presenting himself as a cultured man, stiffly, even pompously as an "Edwardian," to use his very term.

So over that summer I got to know him well. He worked in the mornings, and then we'd get together afternoons and do correspondence. He always ate tuna fish at lunch. Best tuna fish salad I've ever eaten. No variation. Five days, seven days a week when he was writing. Just tuna fish, rye bread and butter, sliced tomatoes. Cole slaw only on special occasions. I once asked if he'd like something different; he said that he didn't want to change. Again, during working hours everything had to be totally structured, which also meant that usually I was the only person who could eat with him. He never drank coffee, always tea. Now that he drinks coffee he drinks instant coffee as opposed to good coffee, and I suppose here too because the outcome is predictable.

I was also the one who ordered the booze. Lots of it—cases. In general the parties were Norman's idea, but Beverly loved them. Obviously there was a lot of drinking, and the two of them kept pace with each other. In succeeding years, usually when Norman went to P-Town to write, he and Beverly would go on a diet and quit drinking. Soltonoff, a chiropractor on the lower East Side who was a friend of Beverly's, had a clean-out diet consisting of fresh green vegetable salads and lemon juice, and that's all they'd eat.

But that first summer I got involved with a lot of the family shit, like shopping. How can you avoid it? At the time there was a lot of money around, they were running a lot of guests through, and they had a lot of help. There was a full-time young white girl from the south who took care of the kids, a black cook, plus a Portuguese cook's helper for a while, though she didn't last very long.

I ate dinner with them quite often too, and at the dinner table the two of them were enough to give anyone ulcers. She gave as good as she got. She was his equal, a real match, and often it could be vicious. The poignant part of it is that Beverly is an injured person—there are some people who just are. For example, she told me one night about going to hear Dizzy Gillespie when she was still involved with Miles. Dizzy came over at intermission and said, "Oh, did you hear? Miles got married today."

She was very vulnerable—still is—despite the anger and apparent strength, and I knew right away that the social scene that summer was insane, which both intrigued and repelled me. Michael Todd came once for lunch with the whole family, oodles of children. Ditto for Vance Bourjaily and his wife. Bob Lucid, Norman's archivist, Bob Lifton, and Kevin McCarthy too. Also Richard Baron brought around Rod Thorpe, the writer, because he wanted Norman to introduce him to the high-art types. Ed Doctorow was around for a few days too. Norman liked his writing very much; Norman very seldom recommends any writer, but he suggested I look at *Welcome to Hard Times*, which is a wonderful book. And Norman liked his editing. Cy Rembar was up and back, Scott Meredith, Roger

Donoghue, and Mickey Knox too. Allen Ginsberg and his coterie. The Conrads. Father Jacobs. Eddie Bonetti, of course, and Jeannie Krassner came up with Holly, Paul's and her daughter, who was about Stephen's age. Jeannie stayed with the Mailers, but then she fell in love with that guy Bob Costa, who ran the Playhouse, and stayed with him.

One night Norman was doing a reading at the Art Association, either from *The Deer Park* or *Cannibals and Christians,* and Jeannie came dressed in an incredible costume—a royal blue sequined bikini, over which was a full-length, orange felt belted coat, the belt bright blue to match the bikini. And, of course, she wore the coat open to make the whole thing work. The party afterward was, as usual, a zoo. Leo Garin, the director, was there, being perfectly ghastly. Jeannie and Bob Costa got into a fight very late—it was almost dawn—and she poured her drink on his boot. Costa, being very vain, just flipped. He was beside himself and said he was going to leave her; they'd known each other all of four days. Jeannie decided she couldn't bear it, and for her part she was going to commit suicide, so she headed out to drown herself, walking off the deck in her high heels and bikini. Everyone's shouting, "Oh God, Jeannie's going to drown herself! What'll we do?" Connie Banko turned around, saw that it was low tide, and laughed. "It'll take her a week to get out to where it's deep enough!" Jeannie eventually came back to the party, but it was wonderful seeing her out there striding across the flats in that crazy sequined bikini.

At another party, Madeline and I were at the door. Norman had a fight with some young guy, and then some chick walked the tightrope and split her head on the deck. That was the only party when there was a guest list, because he expected it to be so big, yet somehow he got into a paranoid snit about gate-crashers. Norman hates gate-crashers.

He once wrote, "I showed a talent for getting into stunts and worse, much worse," and it's a reasonable description. One small thing sticks in my mind because it was so pitiful. One of the local fishermen in P-Town came by for drinks. He wasn't a brilliant guy but pleasant enough, just out of his depth, and while they were talking he put his feet up on the coffee table. Norman went ape, launched into an incredible diatribe about how people don't put their feet on his table. "Proper behavior," "boors," the whole thing. I told him what he'd done to the guy was horrid, but he got stubborn, just couldn't let it go. Which was odd, because here he was picking on a weakling, when ordinarily he always went after someone physically stronger or at least his own size.

That same summer I also saw him in a fight with a young, handsome brute who beat the shit out of him. Norman had invited the guy over, then all of a sudden they were out on the street. The guy really had to do it, Norman left him no choice. Everybody was jumping up and down, screaming, and Beverly was shouting, "Don't hit him on the head! Don't hit him on the head!" Norman wound up with a cut across his forehead.

RICHARD BARON   One night we were at Mailer's house—twelve of us, maybe—and some guy came in off the street and there was a fight. I got very frightened, upset. I didn't want this guy breaking my writer's fingers, so I grabbed him and threw him out of the house. Fifteen minutes later—it was so typical—the guy came back and he and Norman had their arms around each other. They'd had a fight the night before too. Later I heard that this guy had fought Norman out on the street and hurt him. But here they were fifteen minutes later hugging each other.

JACK KEARNEY   A neighbor had said, "Come on, Norman's having a party," and when I arrived, there was a ruckus with a guy named Black—a white guy who was black Irish—and Norman was having him thrown out. Three or four guys were manhandling Black, so I walked over and asked if he needed any help. Black said that he could handle it, but they threw him out anyway. I walked over to Norman and said, "That's a strange way to treat your guest." He didn't get angry with me, although, as I learned later, he'd been right to throw him out, since Black was being obnoxious and had caused a disturbance. Even so, I guess Norman felt guilty, because he went outside and invited Black back inside.

Apparently Norman appreciated my forthrightness, because that's when we started to talk. There was another party a week or two later, maybe it was only days. He had a black eye—the one he had in the photograph on the back of Why Are We in Vietnam?—and this guy Black was there again, being obnoxious. In order to make amends for my misjudgment the previous time, I stepped between them and said to Black, "Why pick a fight? What kind of triumph would that be? Look, he's already beat up." Norman had a funny look on his face—maybe he was angry, maybe amused. But Black said to me, "Okay, any way you want it. How would you like to try to take me out?" I said arm-wrestling, and I clobbered him, and he left. There was no violence, just arm-wrestling, and I've never been in a fight in Provincetown or anywhere else. I'm not a violent person.

There were numerous parties that summer—usually starting at midnight and going on till dawn. Lynn, my wife, is not a late-nighter, so I'd frequently take a nap in the early evening and go alone. Norman's style was always to stand in the corner. He had a kind of imaginary bubble around him, and he didn't like people to come inside that bubble unless he invited them by initiating a conversation, usually with wit and satire. People would come up and talk to him and then walk away; the only time he'd respond with what you could call violence was when someone was egging him on or goading him into a situation by violating his space.

I think a number of his close friends knew that he'd never hit you, and it was an article of faith. On several occasions I know I told him I didn't want to hurt him. We would be having words, and I'd remind him that I'd been a hard-bitten bosun's mate in the navy and had had many a bare-knuckle fight on the fo'c'sle of a ship. Also that I'd grown up as an Irish street fighter, and wouldn't want to be responsible for injuring a great artist. We'd both be bombed, I'd deliver such a line, and he'd laugh. Lynn, I don't think, was ever concerned about my being at those parties because of him. She was concerned about some of the hangers-on, some of whom were pretty rough, but coming from a blue-collar Irish background, I didn't find them unusual, and I knew Norman liked to talk to them. In fact, Norman always reacted to my Irishness. He was very complimentary, admiring the spontaneity and fearlessness of the Irish. It's something I'm neither ashamed of nor proud of, since the Irish are a little nuts in that respect. I can remember relatives pointing to a brick and saying, "That's called Irish confetti."

That summer we used to go sailing. My son was just going into his teens, and I was concerned about the war—wondering if it would sweep away the whole generation—and I worried specifically about my son being drafted. So we were talking about the Vietnam War, and Norman said, "I know what to do, but those bastards in the Pentagon won't listen to me."

"What's that?" I said.

"You just gotta make the soldiers eat everything they kill."

I laughed a little nervously at that, and he said, "Seriously, what we've gotta have is an international War Olympics." He then went on in great detail: that each nation would have three hundred soldiers, who would fight it out on an equal basis; thus the generals and professional military types would get promoted without killing civilians.

DR. JACK BEGNER   I treated his eye the summer of '66 when someone hit him as they were sparring.

EDITH BEGNER   That's right. We hadn't seen him much. He'd come to a party at our house the winter before, and I'd asked him to autograph his new book, maybe *An American Dream*. He wrote "To Jack and Edie, greedy but stand-up guys." We thought it was offensive, and so did Blanche Manso, who grabbed the book and tore out the page. She gave him hell, said he had a helluva nerve. He was nonplussed and said, "I thought it was a nice thing to say." So that and other things had changed our relationship. We weren't friends anymore—we'd broken it off.

Then that summer the telephone rings and I hear a hesitant voice, "Is the doctor home?" I knew who it was, but I said, "Who is this?"

"Norman Mailer, and I wondered when the doctor's having office hours."

"What do you mean, Norman? You know Jack doesn't practice when he's here in P-Town. But if you're sick, he'll be glad to help. What's wrong?"

"Well, another eye. I've got a bad eye."

DR. JACK BEGNER   It was a terribly bad eye, and I saw that he was scared. He'd caught a right hook that had taken the brow off plus the skin on his nose. I didn't stitch it, I used butterflies, and later, when it was healing, I said, "Let's take a picture of it." It had been much worse before, but that's the photograph he used the following year on the jacket of *Why Are We in Vietnam?*

NAT HALPER   We hadn't spoken for several years because of our words over Adele's painting. I don't remember how it came about, but we slid back into it slowly—not as friendly as before, though, because there was wariness on both sides.

One evening, though, they were at a party at our place, and later that night I was sitting in the gallery when Beverly came in, alone and quite drunk. We had a large picture on the wall—I forget who'd done it—and Beverly wanted to buy it as a present for Norman. It cost five or six thousand dollars, which in those days we considered a big amount. I thought, Jesus Christ, I can't sell this to her when she's drunk, so I said, "Check it with Norman and come back tomorrow." Then she says, "Okay, but let's go down to see Charlie Brown after you close." I thought she meant a Peanuts movie, so at ten we went down to the Gifford House, and there was this guy named Charlie Brown playing guitar who turned out to be her brother. During the performance she begins yelling at me, "I want that picture." She's boozed and carrying on and people are turning around, so I said, "All right," just to shut her up. But no, she wants me to write out on a piece of paper that I've agreed to sell her the painting at such and such a price. So I did, but I signed "Hans Hofmann." She must not have actually shown the piece of paper to Norman, because the next day I ran into him on the street and he said, "I understand you're becoming quite a businessman." I couldn't register what the hell he was talking about, then I realized that he actually believed I'd tried to sell her an expensive painting when she was dead drunk and that she'd let him believe this to stir up trouble. Neither one of them ever mentioned the painting again.

DIANA TRILLING   That summer Beverly and Norman came over from Provincetown one night to have dinner with Lionel and me in Wellfleet. They'd both been drinking—Beverly much more than Norman—and there was the most horrible scene. She spent the entire time after their arrival taunting him. You could see that Norman was getting very upset but keeping himself in control. All Lionel and I could think of was, My God, and finally Lionel put his arm around her and said, "Let's go for a walk," and he took her outside and got her to vomit. Meanwhile I challenged Norman to a card game that I'd just invented: it was a kind of double solitaire, but it also had a relation to poker. I bet him five dollars a game that I could beat him. It was a lot of money for me to gamble, but I wanted to distract him. Well, the first game was just a demonstration— he watched and listened. The next game he won, and he won all the rest. I was furious. I had challenged a dozen people to that game, and everyone had floundered. Not Norman—he got it at once, just out of the blue.

When Beverly got back the atmosphere was so thick you could see that they weren't finished with the fight at all. We talked about it after they left. "My God, she's going to start it up again—he'll drive off the road and kill them both." Her behavior was truly intolerable—she was telling him about the other men she'd known. I know Norman was always on good behavior at our house— people used to comment on it—but I don't know how he could have stopped her that night. Maybe by hitting her, but I'm not sure. That might only have set him off. It scared me for both of them, but I was also scared for myself too. It was frightening to realize that I was associating with someone of whom I could think that he might drive off the road and kill her even if it meant killing himself.

JOSE TORRES   Beverly was doing Act IV, and they had Al Pacino up to do *Conerico Was Here to Stay.* There was a party in my apartment, she was drunk, and Norman picked her up and started walking her down the stairs, just to get her out of there. She started shouting, "He's going to kill me, please come down! He's gonna kill me." In fact, she fell down the stairs by herself. She had a lump like a baseball, and we took her to the doctor with a bad contusion.

LYNN KEARNEY   At the time they organized Act IV, Al Pacino, who was then an unknown, was up, and I think Leo Garin was directing him. One afternoon they were rehearsing a scene that was supposed to be a Wild West shoot-out. I was painting scenery, Jack was building a kind of stage, and all of a sudden tables started turning over, chairs were flying around, and there were Pacino and Garin in a knock-down, drag-out fistfight. Norman was there too—he was at most rehearsals, because even though Act IV was Beverly's baby, he was very interested, especially when they put on *The Deer Park.* He stayed out of the fight, though.

JACK KEARNEY   This was the summer I built the "meshuggene machine" in collaboration with Jake Druckman. I was working on kinetics at the time, and Jake asked me if I could build a machine that composed music and never played the same tune twice. So, using a fifty-five-gallon oil drum, an old washing machine motor, and assorted spring-steel strips, plus a bunch of tennis balls, I built it, and then we had a challenge with Charlie Brown, who was still the lead guitarist in *Hair.* The machine sounded like kabuki. It would go "*de-bomp, bomp, bong-boom,*" and Charlie had to improvise on that. The audience was mostly friends down in that small cellar, and Jake said it gave the electronic musicians at Harvard and Yale a lot of new sounds, saved them six months. Norman was fascinated too. He would laugh heartily at it, speculate as to where all these sounds were coming from, and of course he was there when Charlie was trying to beat the thing, all of us laughing our heads off.

JACOB DRUCKMAN   Our socializing really began only when he and Beverly had moved into the house they bought at 565 Commercial. He was cordial, but I felt there was always a little competitive edge, although he would talk to me about my music, my compositions, and we felt a certain amount of togetherness in that.

In fact, the year after I'd met him I'd asked if I could set some of his poems to music. I had a commission from the Walter W. Naumburg Foundation to write a set of songs for Elizabeth Mosher to perform at Town Hall. She didn't choose me, the committee did, so it was like a marriage arranged by a *shadchen,* and we had rather a stormy session when I first told her I was going to set Norman

Mailer's poetry to music. She said, "Oh no, not that *dirty* man!" She was worried I was going to give her four-letter words to sing.

I chose the poems from *Deaths for the Ladies* because I'd admired them. I proposed a 50/50 split if any money were to come of it, and then, very generously, he said, "Make the split 40/60," signing a letter of agreement I sent him, but there was no discussion of which poems I'd chosen or how I'd set them. He didn't come to the Town Hall recital but heard them performed by the Provincetown Symphony, and afterward he came up with some wonderful criticism, very gentle but strong. He admired what I did with the poem "I Know a Town," which is a very beautiful poem about Provincetown, but he didn't like what I'd done with the satirical poem, a string of nouns, like "lobotomy" and "psychiatry." He said, "Forget doing anything humorous, it's not part of your personality." And he was right—I shouldn't have touched that poem, because the music came out heavy-handed, not anywhere close to the biting wit of the original. The more mellifluous, seductive, sentimental, almost ironic sentiments I could handle—not the others. I've had great composers look at my music, Aaron Copland among them, but Norman's one little comment was huge and important in that it clarified my thinking about *myself*. He knows little or nothing about music, but it was a gut reaction and absolutely right in its perceptiveness.

He responds very strongly. The summer of '66 I did my first piece with electronic music, a piece for trombone on tape. It was of a violent nature, really tragic, violent sound, and Norman was crazy about it when I played him the tape. That summer they had a benefit for the Art Association—Norman and Act IV, a reading from *Cannibals and Christians* and a scene from the play of *The Deer Park*—and he asked me if he could put the trombone piece on the program, with the result that we brought in the trombone player who had premiered it in New York.

What I'm trying to suggest is the incredible collaboration among people up in Provincetown doing their work. I was looking for it, but it just seemed to come about naturally out of our socializing, our eating and drinking together. There was a lot of booze connected with it, doubtless, but the real work happened without booze. Take Jack Kearney's and my music machine. The concept started in the late evenings, talking and drinking, when I told him about electronic music and complained that his kinetic sculpture never made nice sounds. So he started to work on the machine, and found a sound source that was much more beautiful than the original idea by welding rods of various lengths and pitches to one end of a drum, which acted like a sounding board. Pebbles were supposed to fall randomly through the grate and pluck the tines. But the stones made such a rumbling noise you couldn't hear the sound of the tines, so one day he came to my studio in Sinaiko's garage and asked me to help him tune it. I lined the drum with foam rubber and replaced the pebbles with Ping-Pong balls, and presto! we got this wonderful sound.

We had the idea of using it somehow in a theatrical way, and since Norman was excited about it too, we decided to have a performance at Act IV's cellar at the Gifford House. The machine was put on a riser, and we asked people from the audience to stand up in the dark and work it by remote control. Then we'd bring the light up on their faces as they'd react to the sounds. Just wonderful.

That summer I also helped with the music for Act IV's production of *The Deer Park*, although I didn't compose any music for it. Act IV was certainly Norman's baby; he was running the show. Because Norman's fame colors everything, he was the man with the clout, and he could suddenly turn from being very cordial and formal to the street fighter—there was that kind of unpredictability, which I took as one of his inner necessities.

You'd see this at parties. If it was late enough he and Beverly tended to get very violent, and sometimes it would lead to third parties getting black eyes, bloody lips—the women too, because Beverly was very much part of it. Everyone would be in high spirits, drinking, carousing, dancing and wildly flirting, and then around three in the morning somebody would begin to say terribly insulting things. Often Beverly and Norman would create these situations. In fact, they seemed too close in that, almost replicas, and if anything, she could be more pugnacious than he. She was certainly a very sexual woman, everything about her was sexual, and I tended to think of them as partners. Baiting someone, they were on the same wavelength, totally in concert—the heavyweight champions, as it were, looking for competitors. Beverly usually went after women; Norman after men.

A few times he started with me—sometimes joking, sometimes insults, usually "manly" insults, as though I were being put on my mettle, like "What are you, a faggot musician?" He would want to arm-wrestle or throw punches to see who'd flinch, and often when it got that way I wouldn't stick around.

DR. JACK BEGNER   One night Norman went over to John Cox and hit him with his elbow. They used to get into that—oh Jesus, elbow bangs. Cox fell over their little dining room table in the foyer. Then Norman fell over that goddamned railing and broke it off. Then both of them fell on the table and crushed it to pieces. Still, they got up and kept banging at each other. I couldn't separate them. Norman practiced that on all his friends—it was a regular routine—just like he got into head-butting a couple of years later.

E. L. DOCTOROW   That aspect of Norman—his private side of drinking and fighting—I found foreign to my own temper and personality, and some of it I used to find childish and didn't particularly respect, because I thought he was too much under the spell of Hemingway. Now I'm not so sure I was right. It's too easy to find the childishness without understanding the connection between this and the work, since writing itself is an act of courage. For most writers there's a constant and insatiable act of self-judgment that has to be placated and mollified. No matter how many books you write, there's a voice that says you're not good enough. The issue is self-censorship, and for a writer one way of coping is by getting into the habit of tearing off your shirt and facing the bullets; it tones up the whole person in terms of pain and danger and elicits that ability to overcome whatever resistance there is in yourself to writing well and truly. Whatever the resistance—fear, hesitation, self-censorship of any kind—it can serve as a tonic.

But Norman's competitiveness may also be generational. Even though I'm only seven or eight years younger than he, I have the sense of Norman and others, like Vidal, Styron, and Jones, as being of a totally different generation. I read *The Naked and the Dead* when I was in high school, and there was an enormous distance between me, a kid at Bronx High School of Science, and the combat-veteran author of *the* novel of World War Two, who was already a mythical presence in the mind of any aspiring writer. Norman and these others came out of the war battling. They all went through the same thing and then came out and fought among themselves. Very competitive guys, all of them, and I think it has something to do with that background, while my own generation is made up of loners who just didn't have a common experience like World War Two.

SANDY CHARLEBOIS THOMAS   Norman is an intense cook with a few specialties. One of them he calls Hache de la Poire, which consists of canned roast beef hash sautéed in a big frying pan in which he distributes pear halves, grapes, various fruits, maybe sliced apples. Sometimes he'll drop an egg on top of it. It's almost inedible.

Once he told me about making lemon meringue pie in the army when he was a cook. The pie pan was something like three feet long by two feet wide. He was supposed to separate five dozen eggs. Of course he'd never watched his mother and didn't know how to do it, but he put his mind to it—after all, he had a degree in engineering. And he came up with a system. He'd break the eggs on a board, then quickly take a knife and push the yolks to one side. Now, egg whites if they have any yolk in them at all won't beat, and of course his system wasn't perfect, so he wound up with a mess. What his company had for dessert that night was lemon pudding, and the point of the story as he told it was, "Boy, what an idiot I was."

Still, he considers himself something of a cook, and on special occasions he would make his other specialty—mushrooms stuffed with *duxelles*. This is his *real* French number, and in all the years I worked for him he made it no more than two or three times. It was a big operation, a tremendous amount of chopping and sautéing, and he would give lectures on each and every step, all the while dashing around the kitchen telling everyone what to do. It was the only time I've seen him swear at his mother. She was in the kitchen trying to be helpful, and he went into a rage and ordered her out.

MIDGE DECTER   Norman P. and I visited P-Town in '66, and it was crazy. He was writing *Why Are We in Vietnam?*, working most of the day. They'd hired two hippies, a couple to help around the house, but they were certainly no help, more like extra houseguests. There was another visitor besides us, plus the baby, and Beverly was like a *Yiddishe mama*, trying to make the kids chicken soup. She was running all around town, I remember, looking for a parsnip or a turnip, because Fanny had told her that's how you make chicken soup, and her fuse was getting shorter and shorter.

One night there was a big dinner party—Ben and Hilda Sonnenberg, who lived next door—I don't remember who else, but P-Town people. Norman had spent the whole day fixing his stuffed mushrooms. At the end of the party—which was no doubt drunken, because we were usually quite drunk most of the time—Beverly finally cracked and exploded at one of these two useless hippies. She picked up the platter that still had a few mushrooms and *shied* it across the room at the hippie kid, screaming. Mailer then exploded, furious with her. He's always had this dream of living a decorous life, at the same time he's always using these women, and he yelled at her, "You don't treat servants that way!" He was especially mad that she'd thrown the mushrooms he'd spent all day preparing—"My labor! My time!" Everybody said good night, off they went, but Norman and Beverly continued screaming, possibly for close to an hour. We were sitting there, a captive audience, and finally Norman P. says, "Please, stop!" At which point we had no choice but to go off to bed too.

I'd heard that Beverly met Norman in P. J. Clarke's. The story was that he walked in, there was this gorgeous blonde at the bar who said to him, "Norman Mailer, motherfucker!" But she never struck me as a prima donna, she struck me as having a head full of quasi-mystical nonsense. I thought she was a nice girl who was given a role to play that she was simply not up to; like Adele, she was supposed to be the primitive, albeit the southern redneck variety. All the wives had to be something, and if I was made uneasy by Norman, whom I understand and know something about and have thought about, if he made me anxious when he'd look into my eyes, saying, "Be this, be that," what must it have been like to be married to him?

PAUL KRASSNER He enjoyed being with Beverly whenever I saw them, but that doesn't mean they didn't fight. Norman was in love with every woman he was involved with. Each had a different style, but Beverly bore him two sons, which added a few points.

CHARLIE BROWN When Brownie—my father, Beverly's stepfather—visited P-Town, he and Norman seemed to get along fine. There was a kind of distance—Brownie, usually a wild man, was obviously in awe of Norman, while Norman went out of his way to curb his seven-second attention span, because I think he was kind of fascinated with Brownie—the army, the South, that stuff, plus his being Beverly's stepfather.

I remember a night we were all together and ducked out of a party still in progress. Peter Manso took us for a ride in his Porsche, running maybe 130 mph down Route 6, and my father, stuffed in the back, was screaming, just loving it. That night he and Norman were best friends. Norman wasn't condescending, which was what I'd been afraid of, nor did he get into any of that physical shit with Brownie, which could have been disastrous.

EDWARD BONETTI I'd just done five months in the Brockton State Hospital for acute depression and was staying at Danny Banko's. Norman came by and Danny reintroduced us. He was friendly—no airs, no bullshit—and he invited me to dinner. I couldn't go that night but went over the next day for a drink. I was doing a lot of drinking then as well as writing a lot of poetry.

So I went over to 565 and met Beverly. She was doing Act IV and asked me if I would come by some Monday night and read my stuff. I was a little shy, but I said I'd give it a try, only I thought that since I'd never given a reading before, they should first look at the things I'd written—prose pieces but with a kind of poetic flair. After Norman had read them he said, "You've got something here," so the following Monday I read at the Act IV theater. They didn't have plays on Monday nights, so I began reading every Monday.

I'd write a little bit each time, work on it, and then Norman and I would talk about it. It wasn't like he was grabbing a pencil or taking notes, but when he had the time he'd look at something I'd given him and we'd rap about it—like "Maybe that section is too long, you may not need it." I trusted him.

Then I started taking him bits and pieces of everything I was working on. The fact he was famous affected me that way—I'd finish something and run right over there. Finally he said, "You can't come here like this, Eddie. You'll be banging on my door every fucking day. The next thing you show me, make sure it's finished." So he broke that habit by telling me I had to stand on my own two feet, get enough together, and then we'd talk about it. Which, whether by design or not, was how I got a lot done. He was always very honest, sometimes painfully so. There's one short story I did, and after he read it he said, "Either you're too dense or I'm too dumb."

The rest of the time we were seeing each other socially, at each other's houses— great dinners. One time Norman Podhoretz and Midge Decter were visiting. I didn't like Podhoretz. He seemed weary and arrogant. I liked his wife, though. Also Jose Torres and his wife were around, and Rip Torn and Ann Wedgeworth, his wife before Geraldine Page. Plus Sandy, Norman's secretary. We'd have great dinners in the dining room, that little room off from the kitchen, and in those situations Norman wasn't the famous writer. He'd laugh like he was a man having a good time, and Beverly was beautiful and loud.

Otherwise he was working on *Why Are We in Vietnam?* all the time, and I never saw him really staggering drunk. He's kind of a sipper. But I've seen him in situations I don't think any living man has ever seen him in. I suppose it's because he doesn't have many close friends. I told him that once when he was having a nasty scene with Beverly and wanted to draw me into it. I liked Beverly, I still do, but I didn't want to get caught in the crossfire, so I told him I wasn't going to take sides and possibly become a fucking enemy because he was having a family problem. He said, "Well, you're *my* friend, aren't you?" And I said, "Yeah, I'm your friend, and you don't have that many." He mumbled something, let it go by, but I still remember it as a bad scene.

CHARLIE BROWN   She may not have been aware of losing her career, but that's in fact what happened. She gave it up in order to marry him and to have a home. Only what happened was she got a short circuit. It drove her crazy. But Norman set up the theater for her, Act IV. I don't think he did it purely out of the goodness of his heart—he did it under duress, because otherwise his life would've been miserable. She wanted to have her home and her kids, but she wanted her career too, so she put tremendous pressure on him. I would watch it go on, unravel in front of me. She was constantly talking about wanting to do this part, act in this or that, so Act IV brought up guys like Pacino, and if Norman hadn't said, "Okay, I'll do it for you," then it would've been even worse around there.

The impression she tries to give that Norman forced her into sacrificing her career—maybe out of vanity or competitiveness?—it's bullshit. She just walked into a situation she didn't have any way of understanding. She assumed she could be Mrs. Mailer, have the home *and* the career. She figured at some point down the line the marriage was going to be an alliance of power and she was going to be able to have everything. Boy, was she wrong.

SANDY CHARLEBOIS THOMAS   While she was rehearsing *The Deer Park* she was already into her schedule of staying up all night, then sleeping until noon. You didn't talk to her until one, two in the afternoon. If somehow she was awakened by the phone too early, it would poison the rest of the day.

DIANA TRILLING   Norman always wanted to put me into the play production of *The Deer Park*. He wanted me to be Marion Faye's mother. But even before that he'd wanted me to act. He'd got the idea lodged in his mind, even though I kept saying, "I've never acted, Norman, I'm not an actress." Certainly I wasn't Marion Faye's mother, for heaven's sake. I've never understood this. Actually, maybe he was being very smart. I'm rather a good actress.

SANDY CHARLEBOIS THOMAS   Right after the opening of *The Deer Park* in P-Town I was sitting next to Fanny at the family table at the Gifford House, where we were celebrating. She turned to me and said, "I shouldn't boast, because he's my son, but he's a genius." I smiled. I'd heard her say it a hundred times. Her pride in Norman was grotesque. Just the way she looked at him. She's tiny, so she always looked up at him, but she always looked up *to* him. She was in awe of him. The same wasn't true of Barney, though, and while Fanny and Norman would sometimes get into fights, I never saw anything between Barney and Norman. Norman treated his father rather tenderly. Both parents tried hard to stay clear of Norman's disputes with the various wives. When they were on the scene it was as if they'd come to be with the grandchildren, like that was the ostensible reason for the visit.

By September, when *Cannibals and Christians* was out, he was off on his new projects—not only *Why Are We in Vietnam?*, which he'd been writing, but also the play of *The Deer Park*, which he decided to do in New York. Leo Garin had come up to P-Town to do a dry run of the play, and there were all sorts of groupies around. Adele was up too.

In September, as soon as we came back to the city, an office was rented near Times Square, where Norman and Buzz Farbar were doing the casting. Madeline

Belkin and I were working fifteen hours a day to get the script out because they had to have it for casting calls, and that's when Norman put me on salary, a hundred fifty dollars a week. I was at the Broadway office, Madeline out in Brooklyn.

BERNARD "BUZZ" FARBAR   I'd flown to P-Town, and when I got off the plane wearing a white linen suit, looking very tanned, Norman says, "My God, it's Don Beda!" They were already staging the play that night, and I played Beda, reading from the script, in the same white suit. The next night Mara Conrad told me to wear a blue polo shirt. Norman was angry about it. "Never change costume without telling the director," he said. I knew nothing about the theater — it was a terrible breach.

That fall in New York I read for the part at the Riverside Plaza Hotel. Obviously Norman had thought about it, then asked if I'd be in the play even though Leo was adamantly against it. Me, a nonprofessional.

Opening night, Rip Torn showed up late. The first scene we were all supposed to be in tuxedos; Rip didn't have black socks, so he took some lampblack and smeared it on his ankles. Mickey Knox and I were going crazy laughing. Crazier yet was that I got terrific reviews, like "Brilliant in cameo role was newcomer Bernard Farbar," which made everyone upset. Here were Marsha Mason, Hugh Marlowe, Rosemary Torres, and I get the good notice.

The feeling I had was that ultimate decisions were made by Rip and Norman, and Leo was just responsible for coordinating costumes and scenery. It's true that Rip was fighting with Norman because a lot of the actors felt that Norman was being too intrusive. The others knew they couldn't go to me or Mickey or Beverly with their complaints, so it fell to Rip. Norman was up in the balcony once, Rip onstage, and they were shouting back and forth. Beverly took Rip's side, which figures. The fight should've cleared the air, but nothing concrete was ever resolved.

MARA LYNN CONRAD   I found Leo Garin, the director, pompous, one of those directors who inspires everyone to scream at him, which everyone did. Most of the problem was that there were opportunities in the script to be highly imaginative, but Leo wasn't using any of them, and everyone knew it. Rip Torn is a depth actor who'll reach as far as it goes, but there was competition between them.

RIP TORN   When Leo Garin called and asked if I'd do *The Deer Park* I told him, "I can't, I don't get along with Norman." The Marion Faye role was very difficult to cast, but somehow Leo prevailed, and later Norman told me I hadn't been his first choice. "I'm not usually that wrong," he said. "How could I think you were an off-off awful actor?" He was referring to a skit Burt Reynolds and I had done at the Sanctuary Theater: I played Rip Reynolds, Hollywood stud, and he played Burt Tone, off-off awful actor. So when Norman said, "How could I be so wrong about you?" I said, "Because you didn't like me personally."

Anyway, once things got rolling we had a dispute when he wanted to cast

Adele. Adele's a very good-hearted and talented woman, but I didn't think she had the training to do eight performances a week, which is quite different from being a movie actor. That's a mistake people make about acting, and I think Norman thought he knew a lot more about it than he actually did. She gave a very good reading, was made understudy to play Elena, and I argued with him about that too. He said, "What? You're taking Leo's side?" I said, "All I got to say is, with Beverly and Adele both in it, you want the critics to review your life as a circus or do you want them to review your work?" He said, "Fuck you," then thought about it and realized I wasn't taking Leo's side so much as talking about what was best for the play. Adele did play the role, I think, for a week, and she was just tremendous some nights, but other nights she didn't have the stamina to come up with it. What Norman was doing was trying to give her a break, and he was willing to go all out for her.

As things progressed, everybody was going crazy because they were all afraid of him. It's been my dumb lot in life to think I'm a leader, so everybody came to me and said, "You've got to tell him to stop rewriting, to stop changing it." I said, "Bullshit—the minute I start, you guys will all hide behind a rock, and Norman's gonna think it's just my temperament."

Norman got wind of this, and he posed himself up in the balcony, puts his foot on the railing, and says, "Now, who wants to talk to me?"—like he's on a mountain up there—and I said, "Blah, blah, blah, and this is how we all feel." He said, "I don't think anybody else feels like that." I turn to the others. "You feel that way, don't you?" Silence. Beverly turned on them then. "You fucking assholes. Rip's the only one who's got any guts. You all put him up to it, and now you're hiding, just the way he said you would." Marvelous. Look, Norman wouldn't have stayed with Beverly all those years if she didn't have certain qualities.

During the three or four weeks of rehearsal you knew it was an exciting play. So much of American theater is what I call "Blame It on Mom," or "How to Get Through an Illness and Die Easier," but here was a guy writing about things that were germane to American society. We used to argue about acting, though. He thought it was a bag of tricks, and I'd say, "But with me it's always a different bag of tricks, different from time to time." He has more respect for actors now than he used to. Paul Austin, who was our stage manager, now a director, used to say Norman was a great actor but a great one-time actor. There were people in the play who were very skilled, like Hugh Marlowe and Will Lee. They had experience, and Mickey Knox had worked in film and was good too. Others had little experience, and, in fact, Buzz Farbar had never done anything before.

Leo Garin wanted to fire Buzz because he wasn't getting anywhere with him during rehearsals, but I said, "Let me work with him. I'm a director, let me see what I can do." So I proposed that instead of having him standing and walking, I'd have him sit through the scene. All he'd have to do was get up, shake my hand, and go out. Norman said, "What the hell's so difficult about standing onstage?" I said, "It's the most difficult thing to stand there and look relaxed." He said, "Anyone can do it." So I said, "Then let's see you do it." He got up on the stage and stood there for a minute. We all looked at him. The hands went right in the pockets. I said, "Amateur actors, number one: pocket pool!"—that's what actors call it. We have our own toughness, and that's what we call a guy who has his hands in his pocket: he's playing pocket pool. In fact, I always have my pockets sewn up unless it's a character role.

Anyway, everyone laughed at Norman, he flushed and took it good-naturedly, because I'd kind of suckered him. So I worked with Buzz, and he got a rave review—"Brilliant in a cameo role." After that we always called him "Buzz Cameo."

Norman's a very good improvisational actor, as Paul said, a great one-time actor. He used to say to me, "I don't know how you do this every night. You were probably best the first week of rehearsal." I said, "Come on, Norman, I get better every night." He said, "Repetition causes cancer." "I don't repeat it the same way," I said. "It's like going out playing a ball game every night—it's the same game, but the moves are different."

There was always friction between everybody and Leo. For all his talent, Leo would turn on you the minute you showed you cared for him. Somehow he didn't feel worthy, he thought you were bullshitting him. He also had the uncanny knack of stepping in and stopping us just when we'd get things cooking. I told him he had to let us finish a scene, not pick, pick, pick and continue interrupting us.

There were probably people warning Norman against me, and they likely thought we'd knock each other off. It frightened people, I think, that Norman and I were close. He'd get down with me, practice his Texan accent. I was born in Temple, in the heart of east Texas, which is a tough place. The people are just hardscrabble. It's difficult to get by unless you strike oil. I knew Norman's accent came from being in a Texas division in the army, but there were also people who had a theory, a lot of literati—"Norman thinks Rip is Sergeant Croft." Part of my reputation was also that I was an outlaw, which came, I suppose, from going down south to work for civil rights in the early sixties. After Kennedy was killed I was what we call "gray-listed."

Norman liked a lot of actors, unlike some directors, who have very little compassion for them. They don't understand there's very little work—80 percent unemployment. I've always said the acting profession is like the Appalachia of the arts. But I think Norman felt most comfortable with me when he found that I was a regular guy. I liked to go out and raise hell and have a good time. I wasn't particularly interested in talking show biz.

Although I wasn't involved in any of the craziness of those years of the mid-sixties and Act IV, I still have a crazy reputation, but it's basically because people believe the roles I play. For *The Deer Park* I went to McNulty's next door, smoked about sixteen different teas to get one that smelled like pot, and everybody believed I was really doing grass onstage. When Buzz exited he kissed my hand, and people freaked over that. And then, with Elena, I would come up behind her. I had on leather pants, she was bending over, and I would pull her to me. In the audience's mind they thought I was really giving it to her, right on stage, never mind my pants and her towel.

Still, for all the problems with the play, by the time it was finished, after close to a hundred fifty performances, I'd won an Obie.

MICKEY KNOX   Norman and Leo Garin had been fighting, and one day Norman threw him out, announcing that he was taking over and was going to direct the play himself. Leo, though, wouldn't leave; he just sat in the back row. Norman had insulted him in front of everyone, cut him down, and no one dared say a word, but Leo was playing on his sympathies. Norman stormed around for a while, then relented.

Norman's understanding of acting and actors came with the Actors Studio production of *The Deer Park*, but once we started doing the play at the Theatre de Lys, it was total immersion. It made me think of something he'd said back in '49 in Hollywood, his comment that "actors have no center." He, having a definite center, as most writers do, saw this quite sharply—an artistic type *not* centered in terms of character, personality, or behavior. And he was right. Actors are like jelly. They present a mask, which may be what intrigues him. If nothing else, an actor doesn't have to lock himself in a fucking room four or five, maybe eight hours a day. You're free. You play a role, it lets you experiment with your personality.

ADELE MORALES MAILER   Norman wanted me to be in *The Deer Park*, so I went and read for Leo Garin. They called me back several times, but finally Leo decided not to give me the part. Both he and the producer felt Norman shouldn't have two wives in the production.

Norman felt I'd be good in the role, and he also knew this was a way for me to get my Equity card. I was asked to be Rosemary Torres' understudy for Elena, and I had the part for a couple of weeks after she got into a car accident. I also filled in for Mara Conrad, which was not a role I'd studied. I'm not a quick study anyway, but I went out on stage and went completely blank. It was a long speech about broccoli and cabbage or something, and I just made it up. Everyone thought I was brilliant, but afterwards Norman was furious because I'd changed his words.

WILFRID SHEED, LIFE   *Norman Mailer, the well-known pitchman and lay missionary, has brought his new circus to town: a play called* The Deer Park, *for which he has already beaten his own drum to shreds and toted his own sandwich board. . . .*

The hoopla does not stop at the play's edge, either. For no sooner do we enter the theater than we find the author at it again, in the person of an interlocutor called Sergius O'Shaughnessy, telling us one more time what the play is all about and how significant it is . . . to the point where the decoding and unraveling of Mailer seems to become a whole art form in itself. In a sense, the advertisement is the play.

At least, there isn't much else. Dramatically speaking, Mailer himself gets off the ground splendidly, but his vehicle doesn't move an inch.

WALTER KERR, THE NEW YORK TIMES   *I don't suppose "cute" is exactly the right word to apply to Norman Mailer or to his works and pomps, but at the Theatre de Lys the author is busy being so earnestly, so innocently, so endearingly wicked that one wants simply to grin, to give in, and to pat somebody.*

As a playwright, Mr. Mailer does certain things exceptionally well. Curiously, they are the conventional things — the stereotypes of Hollywood that every man, woman and child from Erich von Stroheim forward has already had a whack at, the leering, soft-spoken, leather-booted young sado-masochists that Tennessee Williams and Rip Torn together have long since carved out of quiet ice . . .

Mr. Mailer can keep a scene moving (the scenes are literally urged forward by a ringside bell and a lighted scoreboard that clocks them off), he can keep your attention by using terse words instead of clotted ones, he can chat on the stage without letting the temperature fall too low . . .

If the play was as candid about its real content, and didn't go straying as pretentiously as it does, Mr. Mailer might be still more fun.

BARBARA LONG, VOGUE   *The Deer Park is not a good play but it is entertaining in a peculiar way, an uneasy gift from the mind of an uneasy man, a strangely dated piece, strangely sweet, from the last of the innocents.*

SATURDAY REVIEW   *Unfortunately, the novelist appears to have been more interested in describing the whole spectacle of Hollywood at its worst than he does in committing himself to a deep exploration of any one of his major characters . . . Nevertheless, Mailer's wild swings at a sordid segment of our society are welcome in a theater that has been too much confining itself to jabbing and clinching.*

GERALD WEALES, THE REPORTER   *The art, the politics, and the sex in the play are no more believable than the characters.*

EDITH OLIVER, THE NEW YORKER   *Mr. Mailer may have adapted his novel but he has not dramatized it, and he has drowned it in words, even filling the chinks between scenes with narration, so that very little registers—and the busy, fussy production is no help at all. . . .*

Much of the rest of the show is immensely forgettable . . . As for the dirty words (and they are dirtier than any I've ever heard on a stage)—well, that is the way Hollywood conversation goes, I guess (or went; Mr. Mailer's Hollywood doesn't exist anymore). . . .

There is a good deal of talk about truth and reality and guilt; at times the air is filled with guff.

HAROLD CLURMAN, THE NATION   *Norman Mailer's* The Deer Park *(Theatre de Lys) is a good show. There are pretty ladies in it, attractive clothes, handsome men, a hint of Hollywood glitter, some silken writing and several ideas. It provides a more absorbing evening than most uptown drama. It is not a good play . . .*

E. L. DOCTOROW   Norman was very attentive to the reviews, and as usual was involved in promotion. He's always foreseen the benefit of things like television and advertising, and in the composition of an ad for our publication of *The Deer Park: A Play* he wanted to select the quotes. There were a lot of favorable ones and a lot of violently negative ones, and his idea was to have an ad pitting the two schools against each other, a "Which can you believe?" kind of ad, obviously a repeat of what he'd done in *The Village Voice* with the novel years before.

PAUL KRASSNER   Norman and I had a falling out in '67, when I was society editor for *Ramparts* and reviewed his opening-night party for *The Deer Park*. I intended it as an affectionate treatment. Norman felt it was an invasion of privacy.

But it came on top of other things. I had published some of Norman's poems in *The Realist* and run a dumb headline, "*Short Hairs* by Norman Mailer, with which the editor does not necessarily agree." Also, in doing a stand-up at the Fillmore East or the Village Theater, somebody from the audience had asked if Norman Mailer had ever taken LSD. I said, "No, he's afraid his cock will fall off." I wrote him about this—I didn't want anyone telling him I was making cracks behind his back. Then Emmett Grogan, who was one of the best bull-shitters around, a real con, told me that Norman had called him a pacifist, and he'd said, "Come here, I'll bite your nose off." I printed the story without checking with Norman. Understandably, Norman was quite pissed off. He thought I was treating him as a media object more than a friend, and he didn't want to have anything to do with me.

It was painful, but I had to understand. I mean, where do you draw the line between reporting and snitching? Maybe I did violate a certain ethic, especially in writing about the party, but there *were* bizarre things going on. A fistfight broke out, also someone invited a couple of bums in off the street, who came up mixing with Hal Conrad and Mailer and everyone else, bums with snot all over their faces, dipping their hands into the ice bowl. How could I not write about that? I didn't invent them. That's not my style of a practical joke. Norman was furious, though, and called my column "mungy."

What it boils down to was a very real difference in style between us, going back to my piece on the JFK assassination, where I speculated that power-hungry Lyndon Johnson may have fucked Kennedy in the neck aboard *Air Force I*. Norman's line was that it was going to make it rough for the serious researchers. Also, he didn't want somebody at my wedding who was going to wear sandals, a friend of Jeannie's. And it had come out earlier too, in the interview we did. I had written something about how, when I was in Cuba, I'd gone to a prostitute, and in talking about it I used the word "fellatio." He insisted I should have used the word "cocksucking." We had a whole little dialogue about it, the propriety of one term over the other.

CHARLIE BROWN   Norman was pretty blatant about Carol Stevens. One night he asked me to go over and entertain her because he'd forgotten he had a date with her when he had to do something with Beverly. Like he got between a rock and a hard place, and who was around? Brother-in-law. This was when I was doing the music for *The Deer Park*, and I was already aware that maybe there were a couple of other women in the picture. Carol had nothing to do with the play, but Norman was constantly hanging out with her.

All I knew was that she was a singer, so as requested, I went over to her place on the East Side, a dinky little place but nice. I went over to hang out simply because some woman's going to feed me dinner and I'm supposed to pacify her for a while. And that was what it worked out to be. I got drunk, smoked some dope, and got sick. If she thought it was strange that the brother-in-law was a stand-in, she didn't let on. But what choice does she have, right? She was, and possibly still is, totally enamored.

BERNARD "BUZZ" FARBAR   During the run of *The Deer Park* Norman, Mickey, and I had been hanging out at the Charles IV restaurant on Thompson and Fourth Street, and that's where the idea for the film came from—*Wild 90*. We were all very funny, a lot funnier than in the movie. We'd start insulting each other, each of us coming back with more, and it was Norman who said we ought to film it, and I suggested Leacock and Pennebaker.

There were three films in all, and Supreme Mix was founded with the second, *Beyond the Law*. Norman was the major stockholder, I was producer and was paid a salary, but if we'd been successful I was to have a piece of it. Norman wasn't worried about the risk. He has great faith in his ability to make money, so he didn't mind being in a corner, and, in fact, he seems to turn out his best work when he's under pressure.

D. A. PENNEBAKER   My partner, Ricky Leacock, had graduated from Harvard with Norman, and while *The Deer Park* was still running at the Theatre de Lys, Norman called to ask if I'd be interested in making a film with him. Initially I thought he wanted to do a live-action documentary about the Gallo brothers. I assumed he wanted to be accurate, though I understood the poetic possibilities since I'd spent time in bars with him, Buzz, and Mickey and heard their repartee in all their accents—Italian, Irish, Negro.

Then I had a meeting with Cy Rembar and Norman at the Algonquin. Cy really didn't like the idea and was putting a damper on it, and my position was, "Norman puts up the money, we put up the labor, and we split 50/50 whatever comes of it." But Cy didn't like that; he thought all profits should go to Norman. I said, "Fine, but then you're going to have to pay us something along the line."

When we got going, though, he stripped down a loft of mine, not worrying about the technical aspects. It was a kind of experiment—no script, no notes. The film was to be ninety minutes long and the cost—oh, ten to twelve rolls of stock. He was determined to turn it into a real paying movie. Maybe he got the idea because our film *Don't Look Back* was making money. I think he thought, Pennebaker may have it, because he's done a big media hero, Dylan, but I'm gonna crack the movie case on the strength of my sensibilities, what I know as an artist. "Wild 90" was a phrase he'd picked up, meaning the firebomb's gone off, the shit's hit the fan. He claimed it was a Mafia phrase.

Fundamentally it was Norman, Farbar, and Knox, but he was determined I was going to be in the film too, so he made me into a Protestant policeman. Why Protestant, I don't know. It was as if making me part of the film—part of the crime, so to speak—would keep me from claiming innocence later.

The money part was never crucial. If someone comes to me about shooting a film, if it's at all intriguing we'll shoot it. Some of the best films I've made have been done that way. Dylan and his manager had come to me and said, "Make a film," so I did. Norman was paying for our time, just a couple of thousand, no great stakes, but he always gives you the sense that underneath he's a businessman: he'd decided to do something, and it wasn't anybody else's business what the market for beads was in Budapest.

Still, while he learned a lot between *Wild 90* and *Maidstone*, his third and last film, none of it was very useful because he resisted learning how to edit. I'd told him that if he was going to get into this he'd have to crack editing, learn to use the movieola. But I don't think he really believed me, because he hired someone, which is not how films are cut. He went through a lot of agony and only later on began to see all the things he'd done wrong.

Anyway, we'd shot *Wild 90* basically in the course of one night. He would say, "Let's try a little something," and *bang*, we did it. In front of the camera Norman's like a professor who's coming into class ten minutes late and has to make it all up very fast out of the sheer force of his personality. He dominates the camera, not letting it go anywhere else. He needs to control the audience. He has the idea that he can look at a camera and take it away from the person who's running it, as if he's got the control and is photographing himself. It's like a dream, his own dream. It's similar to the way he talks to people from a public position, as if he's talking to somebody directly *behind* you. Even when he jokes, it's as if he's doing it for the record—it's as if he's saying, "I can figure out how to make the camera talk back." It's where the energy is, where he learns what he has to learn to get on with it.

WILLIAM BURROUGHS   I haven't read *Why Are We in Vietnam?*, so I don't know if there's a connection to my cut-ups, which is simply an application of the montage method and already old hat in painting. It's closer to the facts of human perception than any sort of linear construction because life itself is a cut-up: you walk on the street or look out your window and your consciousness is being caught by random factors. That's the premise of a cut-up, and we made this process explicit by actually cutting up the work, using a scissors.

I guess the analogy in Norman's work might be his movies, where he gave his actors the barest outline of a story and assigned a camera crew to film groups as they improvised. At the time, '66 and '67, a lot of this stuff was going on, and Norman is always aware of what other people are doing. Anything is grist for his mill. He's constantly trying things to find out which of them is true or real, and it's an approach that I can see as quite valid.

JONAS MEKAS   Norman had first gottten interested in films as early as '61 or '62, probably by coming to the Charles Theater, which was on Avenue B on the corner of Twelfth Street. For a year or two it was a very, very busy place for independents. Stan Brakhage, Ken Jacobs, Ron Rice, Patty Smith, even Joseph Cornell, everybody began there. Kenneth Anger and, of course, Andy Warhol too, because that's where we presented the *Sleep* and *Eat* and *Kiss* series. Allen Ginsberg and Michael McClure and all the poets came also, and across from the theater was a bar, called maybe Stanley's, where everybody went after the shows.

It was a very exciting time, like a seed period, germinating in various directions. Of course it became much more visible after '63, but the beginnings were between '57 and '63, which was when the term "underground" came in. Ultra Violet was around, but she wasn't in films until Andy did his. She was part of Salvador Dali's entourage, and he used to come too. Also Christo. He had just arrived, and we gave him his first introduction to the New York art scene. Rauschenberg and Johns, they were there, and most of Pop too.

I'd probably met Norman before, either at *The Village Voice* or parties, where we'd just bump into each other, but somehow no close friendship developed, even though I respected him and he knew something about me. But in '61 and '62 he was interested in films and would come when I was setting up these showcases. I was always there, often running the projector, so I'd see him usually once every two months or so. I think he asked me questions about the new forms of cinema, and in fact once gave money to Ron Rice, whose work he'd seen and liked, to help him make *The Queen of Sheba Meets the Atom Man*. I think he also was around in '66 when we showed a lot of Warhol films in screenings at Lafayette Street.

Leacock and Pennebaker had been straight arrows, doing documentaries for big corporations. We showed some of the early work of each, although Leacock didn't get interested in independents and avant-garde until later, when he broke away from television. I think perhaps the fact that Jean-Luc Godard had used Leacock as a cameraman—maybe both Leacock and Pennebaker for the film he shot in New York, *One American Movie*—led Norman to the possibility of using them for his films. He wanted to make a conventional film, not an avant-garde film. He likes narrative with people, with protagonists. And, of course, he became the center of the films himself, so in the first two films, since he couldn't use expensive Hollywood production, he chose the cheapest way available—conventional independents like Leacock, who could be trusted to give a professional look to the films.

I have no doubt that he was inspired by Andy Warhol and Bob Downey. Warhol had been coming to our screenings for years, but I hadn't met him in the early days because I was always too busy to pay attention. Downey was a theater person who went into making outrageous political satires, like *Babo 73*, *Chafed Elbows*, and later *Putney Swope*. In fact, I think Norman had seen his films and helped him financially. But it was really Andy's whole concept of using friends, everybody, which was not early but the later Andy Warhol and Paul Morrissey style. Norman used some of the same people Warhol did, and the style and lessons of Warhol are also there—not having a script, just outlines, and having the people in the film create their own characters. They improvise, and of course it's an old method that Stanislavski and the Actors Studio used too.

The slow drawn-out style of Warhol's movies was not part of the Method itself but more the mood of the factory or Andy's life-style: no rush, everything takes its own turn, there's nowhere to go. And he was also against editing, he just strung pieces together. *The Chelsea Girls* was in '66, and I'm sure Norman had seen that film, which was the last of Andy's directing. After that Morrissey made all the films, and they were edited.

But what Norman got most from Andy, I think, was the confidence to do films—kind of "If Andy can do it, so can I." He was probably excited at the possibilities of working that way, to get out of the system, to work with certain scenes, like the one with the police chief in *Wild 90*. His association with Rip Torn when they did the production of *The Deer Park*—that was an influence too, perhaps. I think Norman's films are the most underestimated and most neglected independently made films. Part of the problem was that since he was already a well-known, successful writer, people were expecting something on a comparable level, but the style Norman chose for his films—which was the only approach he could have chosen—was too private, too independent to have that kind of appeal. He may have had false expectations by wanting wider distribution. But once you have that kind of distribution, people go into theaters expecting a more conventional, more Hollywood type of film. In contrast, Andy's films never left certain theaters and certain audiences, and Morrissey's films never made big money, never went into real commercial successes.

So Norman may have had false expectations. He wanted to make money from the films, but if he'd really wanted to succeed he would have approached it differently. Perhaps because he is Norman Mailer he thought he could change the terms, push through even with that style.

Even though later I didn't really like *Maidstone*, I felt he succeeded, because there was always something original. He was still bringing more Norman Mailer to the people. It's like going to see a film with Garbo. There's actually no great film with Garbo, but it doesn't have to be great cinema, because the main value is Garbo, and that comes through. And I felt the same was true of Norman. His films are not great, but there is this presence, his mind and his temperament, an undeniable presence, very strong and always there. He couldn't make a film about somebody else. He has to talk, he has to provoke. Without his presence he'd have to be a filmmaker and know the craft of cinema, which he doesn't.

But Norman was not unique in his expectations. It was part of the sixties mood, the common feeling that anything was possible, and many independent filmmakers deceived themselves by thinking that suddenly their work would be shown everywhere and would be in every film library across the country. But no, that wasn't true. They were still working within a limited form whose content appeals only to a minority. It's not identical or a pure comparison, but it could be compared to the fact that narrative forms of prose are published in editions of millions whereas poetry sells maybe two or three thousand copies—so independent filmmaking always fell within the same minority.

DON CARPENTER   Norman and I talked about it, but I didn't say what I wanted to say, which was "Don't put your own money into a picture."

I had done some work in television and on movies for television, so Norman called me up and asked me to handle the distribution of *Wild 90* on the West Coast. I hoped to get various campuses in the state system, so I showed up at SF State. I didn't get much feedback, but then Ralph Gleason got interested, so we took it down to a place in Oakland and showed it. Lenny Lipton, a film critic from the *Berkeley Barb*, hated Norman and didn't like the picture either, so we got nowhere. That was the end of it until Peter Manso and Tom Luddy, who now works for Francis Coppola, showed it at Berkeley. There were no other showings.

Later I came east, and Norman had set up Supreme Mix with Buzz Farbar. I didn't like Buzz, I thought he was an acolyte, like the guys I'd seen in Hollywood. Rip tried to convince me he wasn't, and then later, when I was back on the West Coast, Buzzie called me and asked me to come to New York for a series of meetings about a movie he and Rip wanted to do about cocaine smuggling. This was after *Easy Rider*, so you wonder where they got the idea. They wanted me to write it, so I said, "Sure, send me a ticket." Buzz said, "Huh?" He couldn't come up with the plane fare, so I thought, That's the end of that. It was also the end of my association with Buzz Farbar.

During my visit in '68 I stayed away from Norman when Buzz was around. I didn't want to see him with his entourage, and I certainly didn't want to be part of it. Anybody who kisses my ass, tells me what a great writer I am, I'm immediately suspicious. Norman isn't the only person I know whose ego flourishes with that kind of flattery, yet I doubt Norman could face himself if he admitted that he's often surrounded by second- and third-rate people.

HAROLD CONRAD   I'm in all of Norman's movies, including *Wild 90*, which opened January 7, 1967, at the New Cinema Playhouse. God knows what happened to it after that. Norman set up Supreme Mix to distribute it. I said, "You don't need a fucking office for one picture." But no, it was going to be a business. He had an office, he was paying rent, all that shit. Buzz had no other income at the time, he was on his ass, so Buzz was going to get paid, and Norman kept him on payroll for his second movie, and his third too.

TOM QUINN   I was supposed to have been in *Wild 90*, but then I had to miss it—and there's a real story there:

After the Ali-Zora Folley fight at the Garden, Eleanor Kane, who wrote a book called *Pro Football Broadside*, and I went over to Toots Shor's to meet Norman, Jose, Farbar, and Brian Hamill, Pete's brother. Eleanor was about the only girl at the bar, and some guy started to make the move on her. Normally this kind of thing doesn't bother me. If I'm with a date I say, "Come on, why don't we move?" No big thing. But it was such an atmosphere I really couldn't do that. All these guys, my pals, want to see a fight, and suddenly I realized that the other guys, the friends of the guy coming on to Eleanor, they're pushing it too.

I always do this, always show how noble I am—I walk out first, which means you turn around and you get hit, right? So as I turn around, the guy hits me over the eye. Ah, shit, the guy knows how to fight. So I get to work. I'm throwing body punches, moving around, really setting him up for a good left hook in the chops. Finally I take out his teeth. But I got the eye, I got to take care of it.

I'd been working on Wall Street about a year now, so the next day I go into the office with this egg. "Mr. Quinn, what in the world...?" asks one of the senior partners.

"I'm just mortified," I explain. "I've been working out at the gym, and this kid wanted to fool around a bit."

"You should never do that with an amateur, Mr. Quinn."

Wonderful. Only about two weeks later Larry Merchant, the sportswriter for the *Post*, does a piece about a proposed elimination tournament for heavyweights since Ali has refused to go into the army. He mentions the names of all the characters he knows, the would-be contenders, then finishes by saying, "You could add Tom Quinn, who recently punched out some guy in front of Toots Shor's for saying not nice things to his girl."

Of course my boss sees it and says, "Mr. Quinn, that story you told me about your club and that boy's elbow, it's not exactly true, is it?"

"No, it isn't, Mr. Lewis. I was too embarrassed to tell you what happened. Is my work satisfactory?"

"Oh yes, indeed it is."

"Well, thank you," I said. "I wish you and all my associates here the best of everything. I hope we all enjoy whatever we want to get out of life. But I have one thing tucked away in my heart now forever, which I doubt if any member of this firm will ever have."

"What is that, Mr. Quinn?"

"Mr. Lewis, I don't think you're ever gonna hear Jose Torres say to you like he said to me, 'Man, that was some fuckin' left hook, baby!'"

That's how I missed Norman's first movie. I had to go home and take care of my eye.

But around this time everybody was starting to get into the movie thing, and a while later Norman asks me to come to dinner at Pier 52 late one night. At the table are Jimmy Reardon and Roger Donoghue and about seven other fat Irishmen, plus Norman, who announces, "We're making a movie tonight. It's called *Beyond the Law,* and you're the cops. So eat and drink all you want 'cause that's all you're gettin' paid."

We went over to a loft, and there's Joe Shaw and Torres as well as some other people. Norman says, "I know all you guys and I know you spend most of your lives talking yourself into situations or out of 'em. And that's what I want you to do tonight. Get together with someone."

So I got together with Shaw. I'm a moralistic cop and he's a rape suspect, black and mean and evil. I addressed the lineup, making this little speech: "You gotta go in there, do this, and think about what you've done!"

Norman liked the line and asked me how I came up with it. "Parris Island," I said.

"No, it wasn't Parris Island," he argues. "That was out of Our Lady of Victory grammar school in 1943."

Well, I could have fallen over, 'cause I actually went to a school called Our Lady of Victory. I know I'd never told him that, so it was just a little weird. The whole night was weird, in fact, but only a prelude to *Maidstone* a couple of months later.

GEORGE PLIMPTON   Norman called and asked if I'd be in *Beyond the Law*. He explained that he'd tell me what my role was once I got there. I agreed, which wasn't surprising, since if Norman asked me to jump off the Brooklyn Bridge I have the awful feeling I might actually think about it. Anyway, I got down to the shooting, and he explains to me, "Now, you're the mayor of New York. You're going to walk through the door there into the prison and look through these jail cells for victims of police brutality. All right, you're on!"

I'd just got there. I said, "Wait a minute. I've gotta think about this..."

He said, "You're on!"

So I went in through the door into the glare of this little camera crew, a number of extras—or they may have been stars (how was I to know?)—standing around in what looked like a deserted apartment. A few of them were crouched against the wall. I took these to be the prisoners. I went in among them. It was great fun. A parlor game, really. I got carried away, creating imaginary mayoralty aides and calling out comments to them about what I was looking at, and "growing" swiftly in the part. I began to hog the set. They couldn't stop me. In fact, I've always accused Norman of leaving big chunks of me on the cutting-room floor because he thought I might overshadow him in the film.

D. A. PENNEBAKER   There were too many people in it, too many things happening, with everybody doing their little Christmas gig, and Norman lost control. It was funny, though. The funniest was when we got our elevator man, a sweet guy who'd been a boxer, to play the child molester in the lineup. Mailer's doing this bullshit detective thing—"We know what you did to that little kid!"—and George, the elevator man, was horrified. He didn't know what to do. All these people he assumed were the lords of the manor were getting off on it, and Norman loved it, because he knew it was working, that the cameras were picking up this guy going through hell itself.

ROGER DONOGHUE   In 1966, maybe the beginning of '67, Pete Hamill had put together the Joe Shaw thing and then brought me in on it. Harvey Breit and George Plimpton and Norman were involved too, and I brought in Charlie Addams. I said, "Each of you guys gotta put up a thousand"—or whatever it was—"to remove all your black guilt."

Shaw was a real talented welterweight who'd been managed by Cus D'Amato, but Cus paid more attention to Jose than Shaw. So Shaw was a fighter no one wanted to fight. Originally Pete had taken me down to the Fourteenth Street gym to see him, and I said, "Jesus, the kid looks dynamite." Setting up the whole sponsorship deal was Pete's idea, and since I didn't want to get involved with managing, I made Tommy Quinn the manager of record. Quinn was still a stockbroker, but as an amateur boxer in Georgetown he'd won the intercollegiate light heavyweight title. He'd been into boxing in the marines too.

We had about a $10,000 package, then it probably went to $20,000, with each of us putting in more, and then Tommy put up a lot of his own money too. Norman and I and Plimpton were involved in PR. We got Shaw a lot of press, and he was rated number four in the welterweights, and would have had a shot at the title if he'd won his fight in New Orleans. It was the night Martin Luther King was murdered—April 4, 1968. Quinn, Freddy Brown, Norman, and I were probably the only white people in the arena, which seated eight or nine thousand. But Shaw blew it. He had the guy on the floor and let him go.

The same thing happened when we got him a fight in the Garden with Luis Rodriguez. With all the publicity and me doing the matchmaking, we got him to the point that if he won the Garden fight he would've still had a shot at the title. But he blew it. He just didn't have what it takes to finish a guy off. If he knocked someone down he'd say, "Okay, I'm boss now," and just stop. He was a real good fighter, but he didn't have it in the ticker. By the summer of '68 it was over with.

TOM QUINN   I had become friendly with Fay and Roger Donoghue in '63 or '64 when I was working on Wall Street after moving down from New England. I'd just got talking to them in Clarke's one night. There are seventeen ways to spell "Donoghue" and they're all wrong, but Roger spells it the same way as my grandmother and they're both from the same part of Ireland. Fay's willing to agree that we're related, so I am too. Lot of mouth, like the fights, bullshittin'.

So Roger kind of dragged me into the good New York saloon scene. Now, one thing about Roger, he treats everybody the same. He can be talking about Bang Bang Bell, who was a cop he knew, or Jimmy Reardon, or Norman, and it makes no difference. A lot of people perform for Norman, but Roger, never. Mailer was just a guy he knew who was a pain in the ass sometimes and wonderful sometimes, so the two of them were good friends. I knew that, so I'm not surprised one day in '66 when I come out of the IRT on Fourteenth Street, bump into Roger, who says, "We gotta go over to the Gramercy Gym and look at some busted-wing fighter. You're my cover story. I gotta look at this guy 'cause he's one of Norman's reclamation projects."

We walk into the gym and Roger says, "Norman, you remember Tom?" Then he introduces me to Pete Hamill, whom I don't know about. But Joe Shaw, the fighter, I do know about from my boxing in the Marine Corps in '56.

Some background: I was eastern intercollegiate heavyweight champion in '55 at Georgetown, then went to Quantico. In Olympic years the military allows officers to box, and they kind of steer your career very cautiously. Me, I was a second lieutenant, commissioned officer, the only officer on the team, a team that included Terry Downes, who became middleweight champion of the world. They wanted me as a light heavyweight, tried to get me to make 178, and I was selected for the Olympic trials. But I got sick. I was undefeated at the time, 25 and 0, but I knew I wasn't going to get past a round or two, so I never fought for the Marine Corps, even though I trained and was on the team.

The best guy we had, though, was Joe Shaw. I never knew what happened to him, so when I asked, Hamill says, "That's the problem. Nobody's heard of the guy."

Now Shaw's a welterweight, a small welterweight, 143-144 pounds, and he's in the ring with a light heavyweight, and as Roger and I are watching, he hits the guy with a left hook and flattens him. And Roger, who wants to get out of there, who's there really only as a gesture to his pal Norman, now suddenly he's very interested. Me, I'm extremely interested, but I still don't know what the hell is going on.

A half hour later we're over at Pete's Tavern. Norman, Roger, Pete, and myself. "Okay, Roger, here's the plan," Norman says. "We got Plimpton. We may have George C. Scott. I talked to Bruce Jay Friedman, but I don't think he's coming in. There's Harvey Breit, and of course you and Tom." Suddenly I'm included. Norman's throwing names all over the place, Roger says he's interested, but there's no specific plan. Obviously Norman's talking about promoting the guy, but it's still pretty vague, like we're putting in two hundred bucks apiece just to get it started.

Then Pete stepped in and said we'd get Freddy Brown to train him. Freddy Brown, the great trainer. It starts to evolve now that we're going to manage a fighter, and someone says that we've gotta have a manager of record. Roger proposes that I do it, using the impeccable logic that I'm the Wall Street guy. So I said, "Sure, I'd love to do it."

I can't tell precisely what happened at our later meetings, but the next time we got together it was up at CBS, with Buzz Farbar. We also had a number of meetings at A. G. Becker, the Wall Street firm where I was still working, and it was fun because these guys would arrive at five as the partners are leaving, and in comes Mailer.

Soon Charlie Addams shows up. Then we got a letter from Walter Matthau saying, "Roger, great to hear from you. The fighter sounds great. My accountant says, 'Walter, don't be a *shmuck*.' He won't let me in." Budd Schulberg is contacted too, and he says, "Hey, I've done this six times already. Count me out." Plimpton or Pete—one of them—had talked to Sinatra. And Woody Allen too. Larry Merchant, the sportswriter, he doesn't want in but he'll support us, and he took eighty-five tickets for Shaw's first fight out at Sunnyside Gardens in Queens.

So we have this fight out at Sunnyside Gardens. Joe Flaherty does a real bitchy *Voice* piece—"If you can afford human toys, you should be able to play with them," something like that—but still everybody came. There was a limousine from the Lion's Head—Joel Oppenheimer in a limousine! Nobody quite believed we were serious, but we were. We'd decided to pay Shaw on a weekly basis and also let him continue with his job as a bouncer at the Dom, the disco. Norman had this great line—it's impossible to quote Norman exactly, but something like "There's an electricity, an atmosphere at the Dom that I think is very good for him. Competitive vibrations, a cosmic infection. On the other hand, he's got all these hippie broads who want to chomp his crank, and he doesn't feel like doing road work the next day!" Quintessential Mailer. He'd have all this incredible theory and the practical aspect of it too.

Nonetheless I was working out with Shaw. I'd pick him up at four-thirty A.M. when he was through with work, we'd drive up Third Avenue and see people we knew coming out of Clarke's trying to get a cab, and just as it was getting light we'd do sprints around the lake in Central Park. This went on for the whole summer, with me showering afterwards and then going off to work.

As far as physical gifts, Shaw was as good a fighter as I'd ever seen—his speed, punching, defensive ability. But as Roger later said, there was a little something wrong with that left tit. In fact, Joe Flaherty once said one of the nicest things anybody ever said about me: "Shaw's the only fighter I ever saw that needed a heart transplant. They should give him Quinn's heart." That's because I got so into this thing. I mean, I vomited after a fight one time, I was so pissed off, so upset. Shaw had so much talent, but he'd go out and box and pose and pose and pose, and nothing would happen. He'd figure the guy out in the second round, throw a left hook, throw a right, knock him down, say to himself, "I got him," and then stop fighting. He had three opportunities at a title shot. He won two of them, then in New Orleans he should've destroyed the guy but didn't. That's the one where I went home and puked.

We ran our syndicate this way: Pete had the connections; Roger and I did the footwork, the phone calls, the arrangements, the contracts. And that was killing me. I just got splayed. It was a schizophrenic existence, dealing with Wall Street and then the literati. I'd get a call from Norman to have dinner at midnight, and I'm supposed to go to work the next day, so it got to the point where I was the best stockbroker in the Lion's Head and maybe the best storyteller on Wall Street—and that's not the way it's supposed to work.

But this was also my first break into the New York scene, and I loved it—the Lion's Head, the Village, Plimpton's parties. I was single, and I have what Pete Hamill calls that great gift of Irish moderation. Which is none. It was kind of "Thank God, I have a chance to catch up on this." I was from a conservative background, with sixteen years of Catholic schools, and suddenly it's nice to have George Plimpton, Harvey Breit, and Norman Mailer listening to what you have to say, listening to your opinion and accepting it. Jules Feiffer, David Amram, Nora Ephron, Al Capp, Dwight Macdonald. It was kind of like that explosion you get in college when suddenly there's a new fact, a new bit of knowledge on every page—and there was also the whole media thing. The girl next to me at work, Victor Navasky's fiancée, told Victor about Shaw, Victor told Jack Newfield, and Newfield came up and did something for *The Voice*. It was marvelous, and I figured this is what you came to New York for.

Our contract with Shaw was for three years, but the interest was gone after the first year or so. It took six months to get things going, and then about twelve months later it became an obligation, a chore. But what finally won me over to Norman, the thing I found I really loved about him, was that he's the most loyal guy I think I've ever met. He was the only one who came down to the New Orleans fight, whereas none of the other guys got around to it. Not to knock Pete, but Pete set the thing up and then only saw Shaw fight twice. Pete had other things to do. He was busy. Norman found the time. Why? Because he'd made a commitment.

But, in fact, after the New Orleans debacle one of the best things Norman said was "From now on I'm a dilettante. I'm not going to participate anymore. That's up to you and Roger. You're the boxing guys, I'm not." He accepted the limits of the situation, just as he had earlier when Shaw fought a draw in Philadelphia. After that fight Norman made some speech. The Philadelphia papers loved us as a group, but Norman was saying it was an outrage, a classic Philadelphia situation—what was wrong with the fight game, with the town, whatever. I told him, "Norman, for Christ's sakes, let's have one spokesman, okay? Besides, I thought we were lucky to get a draw," and he said, "You're absolutely right."

I was always intrigued why Roger was around, why I would be around. What did we have to offer Norman? And here's my theory: With all his genius, with all his ambition, Norman knows there are two things he would like very much to be that he can't. One is Irish, and the other is a fighter. So there was this vicarious thing, and Roger was perfect, because he is so totally without pretension—so obvious, so transparent. Chesterton, G. K., was the only one to really understand it: "The great Gaels of Ireland are the men that God made mad/ For all their wars are merry and all their songs are sad."

PETE HAMILL   I'd known Shaw for as long as I'd known Jose. Both of them were in the Olympics together. Jose knew how good Shaw was, and he was upset because Shaw couldn't get fights, wasn't going anywhere, so I think I had the idea and asked people to do it. With Norman there was no big struggle. He had some bread at the time, and he said "Yeah." Jose also talked to Cus, so we made sure he knew what we were going to do. Cus had already pulled out of the city and was living upstate, and he had no objections.

Nobody did any real work except Quinn. I think Harvey Breit was a friend of Roger's, or perhaps the connection was Budd Schulberg, because he and Breit had written a play called *The Disenchanted*. Harvey certainly wasn't a Lion's Head guy, and I'd met him only once or twice before. I don't know who brought in Plimpton and Charlie Addams. It might've been Quinn. What we had, in effect, was a group of amateurs who got Shaw up from nowhere to rank number four in the world. But then he boxed Luis Manuel Rodriguez in Madison Square Garden and couldn't get off, didn't do anything, and got outpointed.

HAROLD CONRAD   I wasn't involved, but I was very well aware of it. Shaw could've been a good fighter, but he had no discipline, and those guys ruined him. They treated him like he was a fucking literary gem—pampered him, gave him money, bought him suits. He's coming to parties, you'd have thought he was one of the executives. You don't do that with a fighter. You have to keep a guy hungry.

JOE FLAHERTY Mailer and the others had been claiming that their guy was another Sugar Ray Robinson. They arranged a deal that if they could sell out Sunnyside Gardens, Teddy Brenner would then put him into Madison Square Garden. So I trucked out to watch the fight. Shaw had a terrible evening. If you looked at him in a stance, he looked classic, standing straight up with the jab out and everything cocked. But he never threw anything. He was in constant training to be immortalized in marble. They were all furious about the piece I wrote because it meant some financial loss. Still, years later Tom Quinn told me I was right.

I went after them because it seemed it was a lot of uptown literary types jerking off. It was Plimpton I was really after, though I subsequently became friends with him. But he'd been saying that Shaw was so good that everybody was afraid to spar with him, so I asked, "What's the solution if nobody will spar with him?" And Plimpton got very arch, cutesy-pootsy, and said, "Perhaps Norman and I will have to spar with him." That's all I needed. After that quote I ended the piece, "If you can afford human toys, you should be entitled to play with them."

RICHARD BARON As soon as Norman had satisfied his Putnam's commitment with *Why Are We in Vietnam?* I went to work on him to write the big book for us, and I went after him hot and heavy for about a year. Norman's ambition was to be able to say that he got paid a million bucks. It wasn't just the money—which was a lot in those days—it was the effect. He knew he could get it from me, and we went along, only then Helen Meyer, who was running Dell, said no. Her position was that Norman was a drunk and had stabbed his wife—all that crap. She was a little Jewish lady who looked like she ran a delicatessen someplace, and although she was very bright, she didn't want to risk a million dollars on a guy she called "a crazy *meshuggener*."

So Ed Doctorow and I were up there doing battle with her. We laid it on the line: "Norman's entering his most prolific period, this is a very serious thing. He's going to go down as the writer of this epic." We believed it, both of us, and we told her the money wasn't at risk. I'd secured the business end of it, and Norman, in fact, didn't give a shit if he only got $10,000 up front. He just wanted to be able to say he had a million-dollar contract.

Earlier, my sale of 60 percent of Dial to Dell was to raise money, and what was driving them crazy was that they had to furnish sufficient working capital for Dial's needs without having any say. I had $200,000 worth of contracts when I came over there; within three months I'd upped it to two million. I'd turned it into a major house immediately.

We worked on Helen for a year, and I got Don Fine to help, even though Dell was fucking him over by having us read everything he wanted to buy first.

Meanwhile I'd been hanging out with Norman. I went to London with him, which is when he finally said, "Okay, I'll do it, Baron. But you gotta get the million." I went back and worked things out so it was a good deal for Dial, and we got the contract made up—this is late '67. Then Norman himself starts fucking around a little bit, giving me a hard time about "Delivery—satisfactory in form and content," which was all I needed to get into another fight with Helen. Here I was buying a major writer, and, my God, with the paperback sales of *An American Dream* behind us, with Norman himself, only the sky was the limit. So I told him to go easy, cool it.

So we come to the big signing in Helen Meyer's office, a few floors over mine at 750 Third Avenue. Norman, though, hasn't given in on form and content. Helen bought it from me that there'd be no problem, she had agreed to take a go, it's the culmination of more than a year—trips to Europe, my working on Norman, my working on everybody, breaking Dell down, the whole bit. Now, at the fucking final closing, Helen won't budge on the form-and-content line. Obviously she's looking for a way out, she's gotten cold feet.

Norman's not stupid, so right away he knew what was happening, and he walked out. "Goodbye. Sorry we can't do business." He saved face. Helen also saved face. And nothing happened. From that moment our paths parted. Norman doesn't know that, or maybe he does. He knew it meant a lot to me, but he doesn't know that's what soured me on Dell. And the worst part of it is that we'll never know what it could have meant for his work if at the time he'd been able to sit down and really take a run at it, concentrating all his energies on writing the big one.

Subsequently NAL made him a big offer—$800,000, I think—although that pretty much came to naught. The friction continued between Dial and Dell, between me and the management of Dell, and it was at this time that I was told to fire my then wife; she had called Helen a liar at a board of directors meeting and everything went to shit, my marriage included. The way things turned out with me out of there, though, he may have been right. He wouldn't have been well published at Dial.

JOE FLAHERTY   The summer of '67 Harvey Shapiro at *The Times* asked me to do a profile of Norman, "At Play in Provincetown," so I approached him. He didn't remember me, but he remembered the piece I'd written about the mammoth pro-war parade mounted by the fire commissioner in which Abbie Hoffman and I marched as reporters and saw a couple of flower children get stomped. So Norman said to me very kindly, "I enjoyed your piece; I found it extremely scary. But Provincetown is a special bastion where I go to play, and I don't like to expose it to the press. My close friends are there. But I hope you know I'm not putting you down on this."

I'd been anxious about approaching him, he was a mythic figure for me, and his "Superman Comes to the Supermarket" and the piece about the Patterson-Liston fight had awed me. They were breakthroughs, because the usual Scotty

Reston journalism, with all that weight of responsibility, was antiquated and had nothing to do with me, nothing to do with the way government or sports worked, and because I grew up hanging around bars, where the talk is so funny, so darkly perceptive about what really goes on, I'd always wished it could filter into public consciousness. Mailer, using his own persona, had done it. His perceptions were high-risk, and even if I didn't want to believe them all the time, the gambles were astonishing. I'd once seen Jack Kennedy in an open limousine, tanned, air force shades, the sandy hair blowing, the smile, the teeth; women were jumping up and down, and it hit me—"Motherfucking good! He *is* the President. I can't believe it." Mailer, I felt, had known that something was afoot that was going to let us all out, allow people like me to have that kind of feeling.

So his piece on Kennedy and the fight made the biggest impression on me of any of his books, many of which I've admired, and approaching him, naturally, I was a little frightened. Having no formal education and what not, I thought I'd be over my head a little. There was no strategy for the piece, but I would've loved to be near him for a couple of weeks, put my head on his head and see what I came up with. Half your life you have these fantasies—you read something you love or see somebody perform, you say you'd like to talk to him. Like dreaming of tossing a ball around with DiMaggio. And perhaps Harvey Shapiro, a little puckishly, also knew that I, as an Irish longshoreman, could blow the whistle if Mailer and the other guys were playing pseudo tough guy. He knew my affection for prizefighting, had admired the piece I'd done on Shaw, and he had heard that Jose Torres would be up there too. But then Norman nixed it, politely but for the obvious reason—to maintain his privacy. He didn't want anybody looking over his shoulder when he was up on the Cape.

WALTER MINTON   It was only after Norman signed the contract with New American Library that we had words. The book in question was the one he had under contract with us after *An American Dream*, and when he delivered *Why Are We in Vietnam?* he claimed that it was the book he owed us. I said, "Horseshit, it's a very short book." The upshot was that we took it and paid him $25,000, half of what the contract called for. I told Cy that Norman could fulfill the other half of the contract with another short novel or a political book. Cy said, "What if he does something off the NAL contract—which he has a right to do because of your contract—and it runs to more than 50,000 words?" I said, "Let's go back to the good old-fashioned days of pulp magazines. We'll pay him by the word. If it runs over 50,000 words, we'll pay him fifty cents a word." It wasn't put quite that way, but that's how it came out—such that if the book ran 75,000 words, we'd advance $37,500 and put a ceiling on it of $50,000. So we signed a letter of agreement. Later I ran into Cy and he said to me, "You're always talking about wanting to be a lawyer. You pulled a pretty goddamn smart one on me—in effect you've got a contract for his next book." I said, "Do we really?" However, we never did publish another Mailer book. NAL had the contract, they ultimately gave up on it after publishing the political books, and Little, Brown bought it from them.

<u>GRANVILLE HICKS, SATURDAY REVIEW</u>   Why Are We in Vietnam? *strikes me not as a hoax but as a lark, a book that Mailer, in his perhaps perverse way, got a kick out of writing.*

...I am confident that the proportion of the once forbidden Anglo-Saxon monosyllables to other and more conventional words sets a record. ...I might suggest that he had set out to put an end to the literary use of four-letter words by making the reader everlastingly tired of them....

Mailer has grown a great deal in power of language since he wrote The Naked and the Dead. *Why, then, has he been writing trivia and tripe for the past ten years or more?...He wanted to be and believed that he could be not only the best novelist of his generation but a decisive influence on generations to come.... So he has devoted himself to nonliterary matter and to fiction that can hardly be taken seriously. If he had been able and willing to do the best he could without worrying about being President, he might have made a contribution to American letters commensurate with his abilities.*

<u>LIFE</u>   *Is it worth reading? Only because the 16-year-old behind it is a 44-year-old named Norman Mailer committing atrocity on his talent.... Mailer fails repeatedly because anything is possible in fiction except joking people to life with puns, doggerel and dirty words.*

<u>THE NEW YORK REVIEW OF BOOKS</u>   *Coarse, violent, scatological, [the book] often sounds as if it were the text of an underground LP, but there is no bad faith in it. On the contrary, it is a book of great integrity. All the old qualities are here, Mailer's remarkable feeling for the sensory event, the detail, "the way it was," his power and energy. Among the new qualities there is a certain directness, a refusal of fuss. In the canon of Mailer's works the new book is a departure: it has little or nothing in common with* The American Dream *[sic]; rather, it has the angular integrity of* Barbary Shore *and more verve than anything by Mailer since* The Naked and the Dead.

<u>NORMAN MAILER (THE ARMIES OF THE NIGHT)</u>   *So after years of keeping obscene language off to one corner of his work, as if to prove after* The Naked and the Dead *that he had many an arrow in his literary quiver, he had come back to obscenity again in the last year—he had kicked goodbye in his novel* Why Are We in Vietnam? *to the old literary corset of good taste, letting his sense of language play on obscenity as freely as it wished. ...it was the first time his style seemed at once very American to him and very literary in the best way, at least as he saw the best way. But the reception of the book had been disappointing...what was disappointing was the crankiness across the country. Where fusty conservative old critics had once defended the obscenity in* The Naked and the Dead, *they, or their sons, now condemned it in the new book...*

<u>DOTSON RADER</u>   In the winter of '67 Norman spoke at one of the earliest antiwar rallies at the Fillmore East. He got up and told a joke I've heard him tell at least fifteen times at public gatherings, the joke about the forty-year-old woman

who leaves her husband and takes up with a twenty-year-old stud. The husband sees his wife and the young man in a restaurant and says to the young stud, "My God, you're still with her? How do you like sticking it up her worn-out old pussy?" And the wife says to her ex-husband, "He likes it fine once he gets past the worn-out part."

So he tells this joke in '67 to an audience of Yippies and hippies, and suddenly he has a terrible, hostile group on his hands. People were throwing things at the stage, calling him a pig and a fascist. The more they screamed and yelled the more hostile he became and the more he incited. There he was, ready to take on the war, but in a way that alienated his audience, just as the language of *Why Are We in Vietnam?* put everybody off as well.

NORMAN MAILER (THE ARMIES OF THE NIGHT)   *On this morning in September, 1967 . . . Mitch Goodman [told] Mailer that there was going to be a March on Washington in about a month, [but] when Mailer [said] . . . no, he did not think he would go to Washington, Goodman interrupted by saying, "This is going to be different, Norman. . . . Some of us are going to try to invade the corridors of the Pentagon during office hours and close down some of their operation" . . .*

"All right, Mitch," he said, "I don't know what I'm arguing for, I'm sure you'll need all your strength to melt some of the real hard heads. . . . Mitch, I'll be there . . . but I can't pretend I'm happy about it."

JERRY RUBIN   The Pentagon demonstration of October 21, 1967, was sort of my idea, since Dave Dellinger had asked me to come to New York to coordinate a national day of protest. After running for mayor of Berkeley I wasn't sure what

National Guard Troops at the Pentagon, 1967: "He may have called himself a left-conservative but in the end The Armies of the Night *became the bible of the Movement."*

I wanted to do, so I agreed and flew east. There was your usual coalition of Trotskyites and CPers and pacifists and SDSers, and what they needed was a coalition figure, so they hired me as the project director for a hundred dollars a week. That was when I first met Abbie Hoffman, and I remember he said, "Let's have an exorcism at the Pentagon." Dellinger's thinking had been to march on the Capitol, but I said, "What's wrong with people meeting to pass bills? What's wrong with the Capitol? What we want to do is go after the war machine." There was some objection that the bridges could be shut off and the protesters would never get to the Pentagon and the demonstration would die, but finally I won. We had the demonstration, and of course later Norman wrote *The Armies of the Night*.

E. L. DOCTOROW I had lunch with Norman just before the October weekend of the Pentagon march. I was going down to Washington too, and he said something very uncharacteristic: "I feel I'm all washed up. I feel I'm out of it now, it's passed me by." He meant this in terms of his grasp of things, and he was really quite morose. It was such a ludicrous thing to say that I tried to jolly him out of it. Maybe the feeling was something as mundane as "Life has passed me by, I'm out of touch." It could have referred to anything—perhaps his personal life—but it was the only time that I'd heard him make that kind of statement. On the other hand, I know enough writers, myself included, to realize it's usually a good sign when a writer feels like that; you may have to hit bottom to find what you need, in order to come up from that kind of depth.

As I recall, part of the genesis for *The Armies of the Night* was a report in *Time* magazine about what happened to him during the march. I've always felt that he's often at his best when he feels under pressure, in some way embattled, and as a writer he rises to his own defense by creating a rationale for what he's done. The idea of himself as an adversary fuels him certainly, and I don't know of anyone who's quite used himself this way so productively. It's a literary strategy and also the reason he's terribly underrated in this country as a writer. To use Trilling's distinction, he's thought of as a "writer-figure" to the detriment of a real, serious response to his work. What people call his journalism, his collections, aren't read as they should be, yet the test is to ask what the literary culture in this country would have been like for the past thirty-five years if he'd simply withdrawn. It's inconceivable, isn't it? But it's still characteristic that throughout his career people have been counting him out, even though Mailer should never be counted out, because just when it looks the worst for him he'll find some new propulsion for his work. By nature he'll find the utmost in something and go for it, and here what started out to be an article became a book-length classic.

RICHARD BARON At the beginning he wasn't boozed at all. The first day was very serious; though it's strange about Norman, he can drink like a fish and still remember every single thing that happens. But I walked out of his so-called "pumpkin" speech, and his description in *The Armies of the Night* is dead accurate: the place was a mob scene, nobody was listening, and people were there for the show, for the celebrities.

EDWARD de GRAZIA   I'd organized something called Artists of Conscience, which really didn't do anything except put together the evening at the Ambassador when Norman and the others spoke the night prior to the march. Also, I was involved in organizing volunteer lawyers to defend demonstrators, but the purpose of the Ambassador thing was to raise bail money, which we knew we were going to need the next day. There were two parties—a dinner before the speeches and another party afterwards. The dinner party was a block from the Ambassador—that's the party Norman describes in *The Armies of the Night*, where there were a lot of academic liberal types—and, in fact, some of my more puritanical antiwar friends didn't like the idea of having a celebration before the march, of getting high, happy, boozed, and then going over and talking against the war. Nonetheless all of us were drinking except Paul Goodman. Norman was maybe a little bored. None of us was particularly close to each other, just individuals there in a common cause, and I remember Goodman kept saying, "Ed, we've gotta get out of here, we're due over at the Ambassador," where I was supposed to be the master of ceremonies. So finally he got me to get everyone out, and Norman, Paul Goodman, Dwight Macdonald, Robert Lowell, and I trooped over.

Norman, I think, was carrying a big mug of bourbon, although I may be remembering the *Time* magazine account more than what I actually saw. There's no question, though, that he was pretty drunk. Everyone was. Lowell too, and he practically passed out onstage.

The Ambassador was a wonderful old ex-movie theater on the corner of Eighteenth and Columbia Road, the intersection of Washington's bohemia. It's since been destroyed, but in the mid-sixties it was a psychedelic rock palace. I remember all this sort of through a haze, but the place was full, a thousand people maybe, and everyone was a little bit pissed because we were late. Things were kind of up in the air, chaotic—which was characteristic of the whole Movement—but the situation onstage was . . . well, everyone was just going to do his thing. Norman had gone off to take a leak, and we started without him. I did the introductions, then Paul Goodman went on, because he was the soberest.

Next, Norman came on and took over. That's when he and I had that dialogue in which he sort of threatened to punch me out. He started his speech, imitating LBJ with his southern accent, and there were some catcalls from the audience. He's funny that way: it's almost as if he feels the need to provoke antagonism towards himself in order to get his dialogue going. Still, booze fuels some of his genius, and, indeed, he was a genius up there. I don't remember him lapsing into tedious abstractions at all, and the act he was putting on, what he was communicating, definitely succeeded in driving up the energy level. Dwight Macdonald was sort of hissing at him, like he ought to finish up, and Norman responded as if he were brushing off flies. Eventually, though, Macdonald got up to speak. Lowell was just trying to stay awake enough to do his bit, which he later did, very much to my surprise.

The next day at my apartment people were still coming over with money for the bail fund, then I was at Legal Central, and finally I went out on the march myself. The soldiers, the gas masks, the bayonets and tear gas—there's no point in describing it since *The Armies of the Night* does it better than I ever could.

I hadn't seen Norman since the night before, though, and Sunday morning I got a call from, I think, Phil Hirschkop, a Virginia lawyer who was supervising the Virginia legal defense. The Pentagon's in Virginia, and they'd taken the demonstrators to a compound also in Virginia. Hirschkop said something like "Mailer's been busted, and he wants you to come down."

Yet I'd had no intention of going out to those barracks. I wasn't Mailer's lawyer, I wasn't anyone's lawyer, I was organizing the lawyers. In fact, we'd had some discussions about this because some of the demonstrators, the artists I'd met, had been worried and liked the idea that if they got busted there'd be someone they knew who could get them out. Everyone kind of wanted to be in that position, and obviously Norman felt he had some claim on me. Since I was head of this group of lawyers, he probably figured I had clout.

Anyway, I went out. Hirschkop had everything under control; a number of our other lawyers were going around talking to people, interviewing, doing what was necessary. I went in and found Norman—I think in the area they'd set up as a courtroom. There was a judge or magistrate, whatever he was called, sitting with the U.S. attorney; it was a kind of assembly-line set-up, and at some point I became concerned that they were going to treat Mailer as special. I talked to Hirschkop about it because he had helped set up the processing system with the U.S. attorney, and he sort of pooh-poohed the idea but said, "If it's necessary, let me know, and I'll come. But let's see what happens to him."

Soon enough, however, it became evident that Norman was going to get special treatment. Everyone else was being released, sentence suspended. The deal had been worked out for everyone to plead nolo contendere, but Norman told me he wanted to plead guilty—he was refusing to take a nolo because he wanted to say he had done it, that it was an act of civil disobedience. This shouldn't have made any difference to the court, but in Norman's case it might, so I told him I'd prefer that he do just what everybody else did so he wouldn't be singled out. He refused.

TULI KUPFERBERG   He was being treated worse than anyone else in jail—in fact, worse than he later reported in the book.

They kept him to the last to be arraigned, so he had to wait an extra day, and it was obvious that they were gonna make an example of him. Mailer and Chomsky, I think, were the only ones of that famous front line who got busted, and I definitely felt that Norman had done the right thing. I'm not saying now that his or my position was a lot more consistent than it seemed then—in fact, I was very confused, and Norman didn't know that I'd actually decided to take the plea deal, then changed my mind when I appeared before the judge. I said, "I want a lawyer," and the judge said, "Take him back!" Everyone was getting off by pleading, but suddenly I knew I didn't want to just leave.

No one was urging Norman to stay. Very few people were gonna stay, and I didn't know what he was going to do. We had a conversation about it, as he reports in the book, but I wasn't sure. He doesn't say he told me he wasn't going to take the deal, does he? Because I don't think he knew what he was going to do at that point either.

It was a huge room we were in, with hundreds of people, a very dramatic place to be, like the guy he describes, the sociology professor who was the firebrand. Then someone else got up and made a speech, and there were political discussions, arguments about what was the right thing to do. I don't think Mailer made a speech, but he probably participated, and I think he had a dialogue with the white guy whose father was in the Defense Department—Teague, that's it, Walter Teague. Mr. Militant. He had the Vietcong banners. But Mailer and I didn't have any extended discussions about what we were going to do, and, actually, he overstates my role considerably. I didn't convince him to reject the nolo deal. You could see that he was picking up on what was happening, then made the decision on his own.

EDWARD de GRAZIA   I didn't know if there were any other real die-hard types. I wasn't representing them, and I never talked to Tuli Kupferberg. I had the impression the government lawyer was telling the judge what to do, and the judge was more or less doing what the prosecutor, who was from the Justice Department, wanted. And what the prosecutor wanted was for Norman to go to jail for five days, so Norman got sentenced. We filed an immediate, handwritten appeal, but then Hirschkop persuaded them to let him out on personal recognizance; in fact, I think we talked about his being released to me or to others, but Norman said he didn't want that.

I had a car and was going to take him back to the airport, just as I'd picked him up when he first arrived. But he had a couple of guys hanging around making a film, so when he was released the filmmakers were there taking pictures as he made his grand exit. That's when he said, "They're burning the flesh and blood of Christ in Vietnam." I ignored all the showboating, I didn't like it. The filmmakers were sort of saying, "Come out with Ed, walk this way..." There was a crowd—police, people in charge of the correctional institution, some reporters—and Norman's speech, which I'm sure was extemporaneous, really seemed off the wall. We didn't know what the hell he was talking about. I still don't know why he did it.

Hirschkop was the attorney of record for the appeal, but I didn't think jail was the only issue. I didn't get my head busted or have to do time, so I have some hesitancy about criticizing people, but I thought we ought to give his appeal special attention because it involved some good First Amendment freedom issues, since he was the only one, or one of the few out of hundreds, who had been given a jail sentence. One of our objectives in all the work we did was to make it impossible, or at least very costly, if the authorities used the kind of People's Park violence on demonstrators. In fact, I remember Norman was very worried when we found out there were going to be paratroopers there, not just police but the military. Unfortunately the appeal was eventually lost. They finally let him off, I think, with time served.

I didn't realize Norman was writing a book until his secretary or somebody called me from Provincetown to ask about the legal situation. She also said, "Oh, Norman likes you. You can tell from the book." I was aware he was doing some research, but other than that one phone call, that's all I heard about it until I read the *Harper's* excerpt.

SANDY CHARLEBOIS THOMAS   I was in California the fall of '67 with Emmett Grogan, but I came back a week before the march when Norman asked me to drive his Corvette down to D.C. so he'd have the car if he needed it. It was an exercise in futility, of course, since there was little chance of my finding him, but eventually I did; then, when he didn't get out of jail until Sunday, I'd already gone back to New York. He was a little pissed off, for which I didn't entirely blame him. He'd wanted me to hang out and be there to drive him back to New York, only it was such an open-ended situation that there was no way of knowing when they'd spring him.

As for the book itself: I don't know whether I was aware of its naïveté—not then. Any person on the street could have told you more about what was happening in the sixties, of course, but it was still something extraordinary. I've always been seduced by Norman's writing, just fall into it like a pig in shit, and it really didn't matter to me what he said. I can't remember specific questions, but he used to grill me about where things were going on, what was happening, who was doing what. Street politics. The action. I'd met Jerry Rubin and Abbie Hoffman through Paul Krassner, and he knew that I'd been at Abbie's apartment when we came up with the name "Yippies." Norman may acknowledge that Jerry tutored him for hours, that *The Armies of the Night* could never have been written without his help, but in fact I was the one who interviewed Jerry initially. Norman sent me over to check him out. Norman didn't see Jerry until later, when he was writing Part Two of the book.

JERRY RUBIN   A week or so after the event Norman's secretary, Sandy, called me and said he wanted to send her over for an hour's interview; then, after taping me, she called back and asked if I'd come out to the house in Brooklyn for lunch. I think I eventually went out there about five or six times, for two- or three-hour sessions—Mondays, Wednesdays, and Fridays, very concentrated. Norman and I spent about ten to fifteen hours together. He was interviewing me himself at that point and took notes in longhand.

What he was interested in was the behind-the-scenes of the demonstration, our manipulation of people, because this was really the first radical demonstration where it was the activists, not middle-of-the-road types, who determined what happened. It was the first outburst of people saying, "We're willing to make this commitment," and the whole thing was engineered to be as confrontational as possible. Our isolating the Pentagon was designed to inspire young people to fly Vietcong flags and to show that the so-called enemy wasn't really the enemy at all—in effect, to have them question the assumptions of the cold war. Previously, with the exception of Stop the Draft Week in Berkeley—and remember, Berkeley was always six months ahead of the rest of the country—people would march and then leave at three o'clock to be back in time for a good weekend.

All this—our state of mind, our strategy—was a revelation to him. He had no idea that there was such a plan or even that we had factions. I explained how we chose the Pentagon, our attitude toward the middle-class peace movement, the importance of young people, the use of the media—all those ideas of the sixties. What he found fascinating was the way we'd manipulated Lyndon Johnson to become our public adversary, brought the President down to our level: by making an outrageous claim that we were going to "shut down the Pentagon," we forced LBJ to oppose us, which in turn created our demonstration.

Still, as we talked, Norman and I disagreed. My position was that when a country is engaged in a genocidal war, people have a responsibility to disrupt and stop the country from operating. Norman didn't see it that way. He was kind of preliberal on the subject. The reasons for his stance were obvious: there was the age difference, and second, the security difference, insofar as he had more to lose. And at the same time I was fanatic enough and self-righteous enough to say, "Well, I'm superior to you because I'm willing to make a greater commitment."

Which, of course, goes right to the heart of it. In '67 a lot of us concluded that Norman was middle-class, that basically he liked our society and wanted to live in it and wasn't about to become an outlaw. He might write favorable things about outlaws, he might understand them, but he wasn't about to become one himself. Emmett Grogan got into this with him, sometimes unpleasantly, and so I was excited when he got himself arrested, that he'd lent his name and personage to what we were doing. I was excited he was writing a book about it, and there was a part of me that knew he would have lost his effectiveness if he'd become a Yippie. Norman was better being Norman Mailer. He was an important author, and his genius clearly was that he was going to give me back our position in a better way than I was giving it to him to begin with. He may have called himself a left-conservative, but in the end *The Armies of the Night* became the bible of the Movement.

PAUL KRASSNER   Jerry may claim that Norman picked his brain for *Armies of the Night*, but I also know that for any oral history everybody makes themselves come out looking good. It's very funny, and the reason is that Jerry is the professional brain-picker. Norman writes his books. Jerry brain-picks his.

MIDGE DECTER   Norman went to the demonstration, got himself arrested, and then a day or two later he called up *Harper's* and said, "I'd like to do a piece on it." I ran into Willie Morris' office, and the only question was whether we could raise enough money by putting together a book deal. We were talking about an ordinary piece, maybe a little longer; he thought he wanted to do 20,000 words. Mailer talked to Willie, and Willie, I knew, was afraid that we would lose the piece. In the meantime Scott Meredith sold it to Bob Gutwillig at NAL and worked out a deal that *Harper's* could afford. Mailer hadn't discussed money with us. All he did was set it in motion, then Scott stepped in.

Norman had never written for *Harper's* before, and within two days Scott called and said, "Here's the deal. NAL will publish it. You'll have to provide them with a manuscript by such and such a date." Meantime Mailer's up in Provincetown, and he's writing. I don't know whether he started in Brooklyn Heights, but at some point—it was plenty fast, I know that—I received a phone call saying, "It's getting long." He had to set himself up in that impersonal persona, working in the third person, but when we first discussed the piece there wasn't any indication that he was going to use it.

I know that he was always in need of money and certainly needed money then. NAL, I think, had paid $25,000. We paid $10,000. What they had bought was only a little pamphlet. But when Gutwillig phoned I said, "It's big, it's marvelous, it's a book."

Willie and I then went up to P-Town to edit it. It was winter, Beverly was there, and Sandy was typing. Willie was reading, and when he'd gone through 20 pages, he'd give them to me. Mailer meanwhile was still finishing the tail end, up in his room on top of the house.

The typescript was pretty messy, especially given the conditions under which everything was being done. Mailer was going over Sandy's typing with the emery board, you know, and since I had no trouble with his handwriting I was in some cases erasing his interpolations and printing them neatly so pages wouldn't need to be retyped. There wasn't much editing; Mailer edits himself. The kind of editing one does with him is to say, "In this part here you really should explain a little more. You go over that a little too fast—it's hard for the reader to follow the point you're making." That kind of stuff, but that's not editing, and he was never testy about any of these suggestions. Mailer's an absolute pro.

Back in New York, Gutwillig called to ask when he'd get to see it. I told him, "It's extraordinary. Absolutely marvelous. You guys are so damn lucky." "I'm relieved," he said, and I said, "Why should you be relieved? There's no writer who gives better value for the money." He said, "Is that so?"—something disparaging—and I thought, Yeah, you little twerp. Why did he even bother to sign with you?

The elapsed time was probably about six weeks. As soon as we knew that the manuscript was close to completion, Willie instantly wanted it for the next issue, and there was about two seconds' worth of discussion about breaking it up. I said absolutely not, which was Mailer's position, and we didn't rip the issue apart, we just didn't put anything else in it.

The result was that the piece put *Harper's* squarely on the map. It didn't do what the *Prisoner of Sex* issue did later, which was sell more copies at the newsstand than any single issue in the magazine's history, but it was clearly something extraordinary. An event, an editor's dream come true. The only sour note was a new copy editor who was a complete idiot; she thought it was outrageous, this ridiculous prose, and she said something like "I wonder what he writes like when he's sober?" Willie was fuming and said to me, "As soon as this is over, we're getting that girl out of here." And we did; she was fired.

SANDY CHARLEBOIS THOMAS   Norman was putting in ten-, twelve-, sometimes fourteen-hour days, and we worked over Christmas and New Year's. Midge and Willie Morris were editing in the kids' bedroom while I was typing, and there were times when they'd be hovering, literally just grabbing finished pages out of the typewriter.

Norman would go in the morning and write, sometimes to the studio behind Banko's, the one with the oil stove. It must have been colder than hell. In the evening he'd go over the editing when I'd crash because I was so out of it with the flu. Beverly was there too. It was a perfectly ghastly Christmas. On top of everything else, the two of them were fighting.

MIDGE DECTER   It was bleak as hell. Late one afternoon we were sitting in the living room totally exhausted, and Mailer said, "Let's go out and get some air— I'll show you P-Town in the wintertime." There was a light dusting of snow down, he had a jeep, and we went over the dunes and then to the only place open where you could get a beer, the local VFW Post.

Afterwards we went back to the house since we still had work to do, but as soon as we walked in, Beverly starts saying to Mailer, "You're evil." Now, Beverly is the third wife of Norman Mailer's I've lived through, so to have a wife of Mailer's saying to him "You're evil" and give some spooky reason for it—that I was used to. I didn't even notice it, but Willie, who was a southern innocent and had literary fantasies, was quite bewildered.

Beverly had been listening to records—evidently she was spending the winter doing this on their broken-down stereo—and something had happened to the needle. She was drunk and repeated, "You're evil. The minute you left, the needle fell out. You hate this record player. You worked your voodoo on it, and now I can't get it back in, I can't even find it." We were having a conversation about the manuscript, and she's crawling around the floor, still muttering and mumbling. I couldn't stand it, and since I'm fairly handy, I said to her, "Let me see if I can do it." I took the needle, looked at it, then told her, "It's broken. The reason you can't fix it is because it can't be fixed. You have to go buy a new one tomorrow." And she's saying, "Dammit, I'm gonna fix it!" Meantime we're trying to have our conversation, but she's still over in the corner on her hands and knees muttering, "Norman, you're evil." The next morning Willie and I flew out very early with Sandy, and Willie leaned over to me and said, "Midge, if I'd had three hundred dollars in my pocket, I'd have bought the woman a new stereo." Norman was self-controlled through it all. He wasn't particularly patient with her, he just ignored it.

TULI KUPFERBERG   The sixties was a movement from below, a movement of the naïve—not naïve in a pejorative sense but a movement of the children, young people in their twenties new to politics and undeveloped ideologically. So Mailer was above this. He was more developed, not only in the ordinary terms but because he seemed to have formulated a position and stood for something definitive. There was "The White Negro," plus a lot of positions he defended, even if they may not have formed a totality. Paul Goodman was someone else on that level, but he always dragged his feet as far as the sixties went, although he began to be impressed after a while.

Someone who writes a book like *Armies* is not truly the participant observer, but I loved it and think it's probably the best book out of the whole period. There was always the question of where you go from there, but *nobody* had the answer. A few years after *Armies* came out I met Norman in London. He was going to Malcolm Muggeridge's TV show, and he introduced me to Muggeridge. Muggeridge, referring to the conversation Norman and I had in D.C. about not accepting the nolo plea, said, "Oh, you're the one who was morally superior to Norman Mailer." So I said, "Yeah, for about five minutes." And that's still my answer. We're all brave at certain times, and we're all weak too. In the long run, you can't hang it on Mailer. It's a perpetual dilemma, every day, any day, right now, as to whether we're not doing what we could be doing. For a radical that's a real issue, and at least Mailer raised it and didn't simply make himself into a hero.

In certain ways Mailer may have been conservative, most conspicuously about dope, but I probably was too. He also wore a suit, so you'd never call him a hippie. He wasn't really in the mainstream of sixties radical activity. He was probably too old, too off on the side. On the other hand, we didn't really care. He wrote his book, and because he's brilliant he was able to see more than people who had been involved with the Movement for years. So maybe I'm talking about the withdrawal of the artist. I'm sure he thought of himself as an artist first, and if he thinks of himself as *homme engagé*, then maybe there's a contradiction. The French did it better. They got themselves killed in World War Two.

I don't know if Jerry Rubin is responsible for his political attitudes, or to what degree. But if you reflect on it, whatever Jerry's faults were, a lot of them were the faults of the sixties. The Movement collapsed, Jerry collapsed. The Movement "sold out," in quotes; Jerry sold out, without the quotes. But actually he didn't really sell out. He never bought in. So in a way he's typical of a whole stream of the sixties—the superficiality.

Jerry also knew how to work the media, and when I consider that, it throws a frightening thought into me—that the whole sixties thing was a media event. Maybe that's occurred to me once or twice, but I didn't really want to believe it. It wasn't uncommon that the media influenced plans for a demonstration, almost in the same way that *The New York Times* sets the agenda of American politics. Reagan picks up the paper—"What does *The Times* say? What did I do right or wrong, what should I do now?" One can say, "Of course, obviously," but it's still upsetting. There's the little song I sing, "It's only a media world..." Real upsetting.

MICHAEL McCLURE   I think I understand Norman's so-called bourgeois side. I was at People's Park in Berkeley when Richter was shot. I was there participating, getting real good at breathing tear gas. I'm a kid from Kansas, and I know those fifteen-year-old Berkeley street kids could tell me a lot about the politics of the immediate situation that I wouldn't ever be able to begin to formulate and express. Still, those kids couldn't have written the play I had running in Berkeley that same night. So fuck the kids. If I can learn anything from them, great. I may be an irreducible bourgeois, but I cared about my play, not what the fifteen-year-olds were saying.

DIANA TRILLING   If Norman wants to analyze graffiti, that's a legitimate exercise, because it's a phenomenon of some social interest and importance. But he seems not to be adequate to it. It's a matter of what you can do with a subject, and the only time he has really transcended himself with an actual social subject was in *The Armies of the Night*—that and, of course, a great deal of the reportage. He was in the very midst of what I call the revolutionary Establishment, and yet in *The Armies of the Night* he was able to get above it and look at it. When he undertook to mock himself and Macdonald and Lowell, when he described those kids baring their breasts and trying to seduce the guards in front of the Pentagon, when he bothered to tell us that those great armed guards were in reality only little boys who were being knocked for a loop by the sexual taunting, and then complicated the scene by implying that those armed boys on the steps of the Pentagon were nevertheless power, and that those girls were the spirit of the future, he was soaring well over the left-wing Establishment. *The Armies of the Night* was his greatest book without any question.

ALFRED KAZIN   Before my *New York Times* review of *The Armies of the Night* there was a party at the Park Avenue duplex of Ellie Frankfurter, now Ellie Munro married to Jack Kahn. Although I like Ellie well enough, I've always thought Kahn was a mediocre imitation of Norman.

Anyway, this party was before Ellie was married to Jack, but it was at the same duplex where the winding stairway goes up into the middle of the second-floor living room. I walked up the stairs, and Norman was standing there sort of receiving people. You couldn't get into the party without passing him. I made some joke about it to him, and to my absolute amazement he said, "Let's go down and fight." My reply was, "Come on, Norman, don't be silly. Do we walk or take the elevator down to the street?"

Then my review appeared—in which I spoke of Mailer as another Whitman, using the self as a litmus test of democracy—and Norman told friends of mine how generous I was even after he had insulted me. He said, "I behaved like an ass to Alfred, but he writes this long review." I thought to myself, He *is* an ass. Did he really think (a) that I took it seriously? and (b) that if we had fought, I'd allow my judgment to be tarnished?

ALFRED KAZIN, THE NEW YORK TIMES BOOK REVIEW   *"I am the man," said Walt Whitman. "I suffer'd, I was there."... Whitman staked his work on finding the personal connection between salvation as an artist and the salvation of his country.... I believe that* Armies of the Night *is just as brilliant a personal testimony as Whitman's diary of the Civil War,* Specimen Days, *and Whitman's great essay on the crisis of the Republic during the Gilded Age, "Democratic Vistas." I believe that it is a work of personal and political reportage that brings to the inner and developing crises of the United States at this moment admirable sensibilities, candid intelligence, the most moving concern for America itself. Mailer's intuition in the book is that the times demand a new form. He has found it.*

ALAN TRACHTENBERG, THE NATION   *... a permanent contribution to our literature—a unique testimony to literary responsiveness and responsibility.*

RICHARD GILMAN, THE NEW REPUBLIC   *... one of the most fascinating and instructive episodes of our recent cultural history. More than any other of our writers Mailer has intervened in the age so that he has come to count, more securely as time goes on, and if it isn't exactly in the way he wants, if it still seems ridiculous to call him the* best *American writer, he nevertheless matters in a way that only a man with so mighty and precarious an ego as his could find disappointing. He long ago made it out of niceness and Jewishness and Brooklyn; with this book he makes it into a central area of the American present, where all the rough force of his imagination, his brilliant gifts of observation, his ravishing if often calculated honesty, his daring and his* chutzpah *are able to flourish on the steady ground of a newly coherent subject and theme and to issue in a work more fully in our interests than any he has ever done.*

Mailer's subject, as it has always been in some measure, is himself, but this time a self balanced between objective events and private consciousness in a riper way than ever before... In writing about his participation in the anti-Vietnam demonstrations in Washington last October (most particularly the march on the Pentagon), Mailer has finally succeeded in laying hands on the novelistic character he has never quite been master of before, and at the same time succeeded in finding a superbly viable form for his scattered, imperfect and often greatly discordant gifts...

In The Armies of the Night *Mailer's talents come more than ever into working agreement and, moreover, move to ameliorate his deficiencies. Antinomies are resolved: the artist who has to invent and the observer who has to prey on facts merge into the same person; the transcendencies of art and the imminences of action move toward each other's replenishment; the excesses of personality find a new and strangely valuable use in the face of the opaque excesses (and history has come to be almost nothing but excesses) of our public days and years.*

This is the central, rather wonderful achievement of the book, that in it history and personality confront each other with a new sense of liberation. By introducing his ego more directly into history than he ever has before, by taking events which were fast disappearing under the perversions and omissions of ordinary journalism as well as through the inertia we all feel in the face of what is over with, by taking these events and revivifying them, reinstating them in the present, Mailer has opened up new possibilities for the literary imagination and new room for us to breathe in the crush of actuality . . .

The important thing is that Mailer had refused to leave history, actuality, to historians and journalists. Writing as he can, as part-inventor, part-observer, part-intervener, writing with gusto and vigor and an almost unprecedented kind of honesty, writing very badly at times . . . but writing always with a steady aim: to do for our present situation and by implication, all our communal pasts and futures, what our traditional instrumentalities of knowledge and transcription haven't been able to do—place our public acts and lives in a human context— Mailer has put us all in his debt. In the light of that, whether or not he's the best writer in America, the best novelist or the best journalist would seem to be considerations out of a different sort of game.

ELIOT FREMONT-SMITH, THE NEW YORK TIMES *. . . the best analysis yet of the politically and generationally splintered spectrum of the protesting Left, from the Old Left with its adherence to "the unbreakable logic of the next step" to the existential, antiauthority New Left, every shade of which was present in Washington that weekend.*

CONOR CRUISE O'BRIEN, THE NEW YORK REVIEW OF BOOKS *Mr. Mailer's autobiography—in which we may hope "The Steps of the Pentagon" is but a chapter— will constitute the Confessions of the last American.*

IRVING HOWE The time of the greatest tension between us was during the late sixties when I was critical of the New Left. Norman did many foolish things, like signing appeals for SDS fund raising. He simply didn't see that there was a deeply authoritarian side to the New Left.

Jerry Rubin was never dangerous, but Norman got involved with the levitation of the Pentagon, all sorts of things like that, and some of my objections I expressed in *Dissent*. I thought he might very well break with the magazine insofar as it was a very sharp attack, but he didn't. He never said a word. He saw it, I'm sure, but he took it in reasonably good spirit that there were differences between us.

But *The Armies of the Night* was an irresponsible book. He didn't take into account that those kids were brought down to a confrontation that they weren't prepared for, that the leaders were not just against the war—which I was too, of course—but in many cases actively supported the Vietcong. Some had a deep authoritarian streak in their political views, romanticizing the Third World, and there was really semifascist violence to the New Left, especially the Weathermen. And about all this Norman had nothing to say, though occasionally in *The Village Voice* he'd wonder if he really wanted a revolution, since he'd met some of the leaders, who were dumb as well as not tough enough.

There's a distinction, a tremendous and tragic change, between the kids of the early sixties and the late sixties. Hayden represented some continuity. The *Dissent* board and SDS had a meeting in '62 or '63, and I remember liking all of them except Hayden, who I thought was a commissar. And you know, Norman is smart enough to see this. If he met Hayden, he couldn't help but see it. Or more generally, the atmosphere of the time—the Molotov cocktail on the cover of *The New York Review of Books*, for example—you can't hold Norman responsible, but he didn't dissociate himself either. Some of us did, at considerable discomfort and pain, because it meant being isolated from the dominant trend in the intellectual world.

There was tremendous power that came from being looked upon as a spokesman or leader of youth. I always admired Paul Goodman for this. He'd been one of the gurus for the Berkeley people in the earlier stage, and then he published an essay criticizing them, and he was finished. But there's a tremendous allure to getting up at a meeting like Vietnam Day and being wildly cheered because you're on the side of progress. Intellectuals have always felt isolated, and I think Norman was swept along like a lot of other people. He'd been looking for this for fifteen years. But he was also a little scared, because I think there's always in Norman a rational, Jewish son who has his wits about him.

I put Norman O. Brown, Marshall McLuhan, and Norman, all of whom were avatars of the sixties, into what I call "the psychology of unobstructed need." The idea that if you need, you go out and get. It's the psychological equivalent of extreme economic individualism, of social Darwinism or, for that matter, of Reaganism. It's ahistorical, and it doesn't take into account that as soon as you have a relationship with another human being you're obstructed necessarily, that there is necessary friction and limitations simply because the other person exists.

I remember when Norman endorsed an SDS fund-raising appeal in '67 and I said, "Norman, what the hell are you doing? Don't you know what these people represent?" He wouldn't say I was wrong, but, characteristically, he put forward—from his point of view—a deeper, more fundamental consideration—namely, that it was not their opinions but their energy that mattered, that the SDS was in the forefront of history, and what counted in a moment of historical crisis was that they'd push through. He wasn't Lenin, I wasn't Trotsky, but there was an analogy here, that in a historical crisis qualifications and criticism have to be pushed aside. He knew it wasn't a question of age. In effect, what he was saying was, "Sure you're right—this one is stupid, that one I wouldn't trust with a gun, but what you don't see is the deep energy, the upheaval. You're too concerned with surfaces." He thought of it as a goad to the historical process.

JERRY RUBIN   There was a confrontation between Emmett Grogan and Norman at some point, and Abbie was there too. Emmett believed that stealing was okay—I didn't, and still don't—but Grogan wanted to check out whether the author of "The White Negro" and *Armies* was hip enough to take that stand. Norman just stonewalled him. Emmett went around afterwards saying that Mailer was as radical as the middle class could go, which created some pretty bad vibes, which I don't think ever went away.

PETE HAMILL   Generally, it was at parties with literary types that Mailer made you nervous. I always felt it was some sort of "hoodlum goes to college" or "Peck's Bad Boy" kind of thing that was operating, but he had no particular beef with me or Jose or anybody else from that part of his life. The booze and the audience were intimately connected. Depending on the audience, he'd drink in certain ways, and the drinking would unleash things that were maybe there anyway. This was generally at parties at his house, so it was *his* guest list. God knows what he was anticipating when he'd put a guest list together, although drama may have been the criterion, and, I think, depending on the way things turned, the unrehearsed part was where it would go.

JOSE TORRES   Bruce Jay Friedman, the writer, was leaving a party in Brooklyn Heights, and he was pushing and ruffling Norman's hair. Norman butted him with his forehead and said, "Let's go downstairs." I was on crutches, just getting over an Achilles tendon operation, so I'm coming down because they're going out to fight in the street. Beverly yelled down, "Fuck 'em, let 'em fight. Let that fucking bastard get killed by Norman." Friedman had gotten into his black Jaguar sedan in front of the house, and Norman was punching at the windows, so Friedman got out, and they started arguing face-to-face. Norman put his head in Bruce's chest and went *boom!* Then I saw Friedman hit Norman in the body. Friedman was too big, so I stepped in and said, "Wait a minute," and told him to get in his car, which he did. Norman started punching the car again, but Friedman took off. Norman came back to me, didn't say much, so I said, "Are you hurt?" He said, "No," so I said, "It's four in the morning, I'm very tired, I'm going home."

The next morning at six or seven the phone rings. It's Norman. "Jose, I'm sorry, I embarrassed you. I shouldn't have done that." He was apologizing because up till then it was the only time he got involved in a fight when I was there. He knew I could lose my license, even be charged with a felony.

TOM QUINN   I was Norman's favorite opponent at head-banging. It's something I had done with my pal Joe Loughran, back in law school, two ex-marines out drinking. Norman told me that some marvelous black guy named John "Master" Bates, a bouncer, taught him. You didn't butt heads with Bates, Mailer said, you put your hand in front of your forehead.

What you have to learn is not to flinch, also where to hit your opponent. You use the upper part of your forehead, not lower down where it's soft, which is of course where you try to hit the other guy, where it hurts the most. What happens is you'll be sitting around after a couple of drinks, you grab the other guy—you reach your arm around and grab the back of his head—and you say, "Ah, you bullshit. You wanna?" And it just happens.

You bang heads—seven or eight times sometimes—until one of you just can't take it. And with Norman I never lost, which would make him furious. Once he wanted to take me outside and fight because I beat him in Clarke's. "Come on outside, I'll tear your fuckin' head off. I'll kill you." I said, "No, Norman. We did it here, that's it. I'm not gonna fight you." Then a week later he's on Dick Cavett's show talking about it—"I was sitting back at Clarke's with my friend Tom Quinn banging heads..."—and lo and behold, suddenly everyone's calling me, telling me I've been mentioned on TV, and for all things, banging heads.

But it's the dumbest thing, really. I haven't done it for years, not since I last saw Norman. To do it successfully you just gotta... well, *bang!* Until the tears start to come. It's a bad headache. It hurts, and I guess you've gotta be boozed. I don't know how the hell I could do it under any other circumstances.

But I never really sparred with Norman. With Roger Donoghue a couple of times, yes, but I never wanted to get into one of those things with Norman, because it was inappropriate. I would have almost had to patronize him. You'd have to let him use you, so to speak, otherwise I'd probably hurt him or embarrass him. I didn't want to be a challenge, I didn't want to be a conquest, so I wasn't going to let it happen, and the only way you don't let it happen is to avoid it. If I were of the stature of Jose Torres, I could do it. Jose can handle that, he was world champion.

JASON EPSTEIN   I've talked to Gore Vidal a lot about literary reputation because he's also concerned about it as an issue, but it seems to me that there's no context of social or cultural values in which to have one. The world's not the same. We take writers seriously as celebrities but not as writers. The mechanisms for evaluation and establishing reputations don't seem to be there anymore.

Related to this is that Norman likes to startle people and keep an audience paying attention, so that his best books are acts of theater as well as whatever else they may be. *The Armies of the Night*, for example. It was a manifesto, a piece of work meant to rally or produce a political reaction. And as a performance, an event, it's a perfectly legitimate thing for a writer to do, especially a writer like Norman, who needs to be in direct touch with his audience.

SEYMOUR KRIM   I wrote my essay "Ubiquitous Mailer vs. Monolithic Me," responding to *The Armies of the Night*, because the book acts out themes that had been obsessing me for years, ideas about the literary artist being in the center of history and shaping it with his voice. But I also said that Norman's books were an extension of his presence in New York life, which was bringing to the surface raw, competitive emotions among writers, quite apart from literature itself. My original piece, the unedited version, starts off with me trying to fuck a girl who, with her clothes off, suddenly begins yapping about Norman, like there was no escaping him, which I attributed to Norman's outrageous publicity hunger. This was an oversimplification, granted, but his grabbing of the spotlight and developing a persona change from shy Eagle Scout to a kind of literary Frank Sinatra made me and a hundred other writers out there wince. His hunger in this department was unique, and the only precedent for it, as he himself would have said, was Hemingway.

It may also have had to do with his Jewishness. Jews have a native theatrical streak, and even though Norman never made much of his Jewishness, unlike Bellow and Roth and Malamud and so on, I take him as a great Jew. What interested me was that he was the first American Jewish writer since Clifford Odets to really identify himself with America. He wanted to avoid the parochialism of many Jewish writers, as I did when I started off wanting to be a novelist and was bugged by the idea that as a Jew I should write about the goddamn righteous Jews pushing carts on the lower East Side to send their kids to college. I mean fuck all the piety. We wanted to get into the mainstream of American life, not the side streets, and obviously this has something to do with Norman capturing people's attention as a public figure.

I admired Norman, but I resented the hell out of him too. I used to hear other writers fret and fume and curse Norm for dominating the stage. Somewhere in his sharp head he realized that scribblers as such are usually impotent to change the course of events, but as a proud literary man he was going to be damned before he'd submit to being emasculated by the philistines, who think that the word on the page is impotent or doesn't count. It was like his remark to Allen Ginsberg when they appeared together on a John Crosby TV show in the late fifties—he said that while he respected Allen and the Beats, he'd never wear long hair and dungarees, never go around in such a fashion as to permit corporate rednecks to make fun of him. He'd wear his three-piece suit and cordovans to show he was traveling in their league, a suit of armor, so that they couldn't put the rebel down because of his surface. Likewise, he felt that he could influence institutions by becoming a big shot in the media. Vidal and Capote had similar *chutzpah*—they've been shameless too—but Norman has done it with more boldness, lung power, and even with more mistakes—he wasn't elitist when it came to falling on his face.

FANNY SCHNEIDER MAILER When I heard that Norman got the Pulitzer Prize for *The Armies of the Night* I said, "*Umbashrien Got tsu danken!*"—which, freely translated, means "Keep the evil eye away." I was very thankful. I'm always thankful for good things—it's a habit from my father, who told me that when you're impressed with something important you shouldn't get carried away. I had hoped he would win the prize, and then when he got two prizes, the National Book Award too, I said it again, a double *Umbashrien*!

Still, I couldn't understand why he hadn't gotten the Nobel Prize. I figured he had a few enemies. I think he might've hurt somebody's feelings, and that went against him.

RICHARD WEINBERG I was in charge of the activities for our Harvard twenty-fifth reunion in June of '68, and there was a big brouhaha when Norman was proposed as a speaker. Of course this was the year after *The Armies of the Night* and right in the midst of anti-Vietnam War protests, and, in fact, in the reunion book he referred to America burning women and children in Southeast Asia. So there was definite opposition to his speaking. The stuffier element in the class felt that he was just a touch out of order. George Goethals was sort of an intermediary, I guess, as part of his championing the underdog.

GEORGE WASHINGTON GOETHALS As Class Poet, I was involved and wanted Norman to be one of the speakers. The Brahmin types all screamed, "Oh, he'll be dirty, he'll offend the children." I pushed it as far as I could and finally persuaded Morris Gray, marshal of the reunion, to rethink it, and at the last minute they relented and asked him. Norman called me up and said, "I feel I've been fucked over. They didn't want me at first, and now they want me. What the hell should I do?" I said, "There's been a lot of shit and I know you've been through it, but we really want you." His reply? "I hear you, but I don't know if I hear the rest of the goddamned crowd." And he decided not to do it. He showed up but didn't speak.

RICHARD WEINBERG We didn't talk about the rejection, but it was evident that he was fascinated by the WASPs. I suppose that as he went through Harvard he got more and more into that group, as I have. Ever since I graduated I've lived on the fringes of it, and there's no other group like Harvard WASPs; they're really a culture unto themselves. I'm both amused by and also understand why Norman goes sailing and socializes with Louis Cabot. On the other hand, Louis Cabot has spent a lot of time trying to understand how the non-Harvard WASPs live. He's been—how shall I say?—developing his own consciousness. That Norman later decided to spend summers in Maine isn't unrelated to this either.

MIDGE DECTER When we spent a weekend in P-Town the summer of '68, Norman P. brought along the manuscript of *Making It* for Norman M. to read. Mailer read it then and said, "This is a marvelous book. I learned more about American sociology from it than anything I've read in a long time. But I think you're too nice to people."

NORMAN PODHORETZ By the time I'd finished writing *Making It* there was already a prepub scandal, and Norman insisted I bring the galleys up to the Cape. I said, "Wait," because I wasn't eager for him to read it in my presence. I have a thing about people reading my work before publication, and also I was worried that he might not like it, and if he didn't like it, I didn't want to know about it. But he pressed me, and I finally agreed to spend a weekend in Provincetown while he read the book. Norman's a slow reader, so it was a day or two before he came back with his reactions: first, that he was puzzled and couldn't understand what everybody was carrying on about, but secondly, that he liked the book very much. I was delighted and relieved, and we talked about it at great length.

Four months later I was on a promotional tour and arrived at my hotel in

Washington, D.C., to find waiting for me the galleys of Norman's review for *Partisan Review.* I couldn't believe my eyes. I was flabbergasted, incredulous. What he was now saying had no relation to what he'd said up in Provincetown. The next morning I phoned him.

I don't remember my reply when he said, "I reread it and changed my mind, so I had to say so," though in retrospect what I should have said was, "Then you shouldn't have written about it." Here I was, being beaten up all over the place, and instead of helping me when I was down, my great friend was giving me another kick in the ribs. To make matters worse, I'd known that Norman was doing the review, and since he'd spoken about the book in such favorable terms, I was counting on his support.

Still, we didn't break over *Making It.* We got together and talked. He was uncomfortable, embarrassed about the whole thing because down deep he knew what he'd done. What he was telling himself, I think, was that he'd written the piece for my own good—he said as much in the piece itself, though not to my face. His position was simply that he'd had to do it and that he would have to live with the consequences.

Still, I couldn't believe that he'd simply reread the book and changed his mind. A "change of mind"? That's circular. I mean, what caused him to change his mind? I couldn't believe there was any pressure put on him directly, but there was pressure put on him by the atmosphere, by the real poison in the air. Under those circumstances, to have backed the book would've taken guts, and doubly so because he was my friend.

Now, there had been times prior to this when I thought Norman wasn't sufficiently appreciative of things I had written, and I also thought he never began to understand *Commentary*—what kind of magazine it was, how good it was. His review of *Making It* was another matter, though. More and more I began to see that despite his reputation for recklessness he never overstepped a certain line. He couldn't defend *Making It* without overstepping that line, and he couldn't attack *Making It* without betraying a friend. The choice he made spoke for itself.

In some ways the sixties was Norman's period, when he more or less came into his own. The moment met the man. In the end I was repelled by the sixties. Mailer saw it as a saving moment in American history, the great Golden Age. For me it came to represent a living experiment that tested the radical hypothesis, with results that were dangerous and destructive. If Mailer had never reviewed *Making It,* I would have been spared a very unpleasant episode, but I suspect the break between us would have occurred anyway.

WILLIAM PHILLIPS   I don't know why Mailer shifted; I've always wondered about it. But it was very embarrassing to get this piece about Norman P. which so upset him. Whether it was justified or not is another question, but it was unpleasant because I was friends with both of them.

DIANA TRILLING   Norman Podhoretz's *Breaking Ranks* distorts his life because he writes as if he were the sum only of the ideas to which he was now giving name. He leaves out completely the part that was played in his development by his sexual ideas. The sixties were a very subversive time for him: the politics were subversive, but so were the sexual attitudes. All this home-and-family line of his today postdates the debacle of *Making It*. But it was my impression that even by the time of *Making It* he and Norman were no longer the close friends they had been. It was Norman Podhoretz to whom Norman Mailer turned after the stabbing of Adele. Let historians take note of that, because the character of whom you read in *Breaking Ranks* isn't exactly the same person to whom Mailer would have gone, and actually went, in that troubled situation. God knows that all of us change, but an autobiographer ought to at least be able to suggest what were the chief connections or chief breaks between his personal present and his personal past. Podhoretz could have written a wonderful sexual autobiography, by which I mean a sexual *and* political-intellectual autobiography, if he had committed himself to self-knowledge and if he'd had the courage.

LIONEL ABEL Podhoretz had had no idea what the response would be, since two years earlier the book might have been a success. By the time it was published, though, the term "Establishment" had become a dirty word. The culture had been radicalized. *Making It* assumed stability and values of success that people were by then questioning, hence the outpouring of reaction. Later, with his swing to the right, Podhoretz was more or less excluded from the literary community as someone who had disgraced himself.

Still, I don't think of Mailer's review as altogether unfavorable, though for Podhoretz it was an outright betrayal. There was also the break with Lionel Trilling when Lionel had told him not to publish the book, not because he hated him but because he valued him and wanted to protect him. Podhoretz also broke with Jason Epstein because of a review in *The New York Review of Books*. So he broke with three friends—Mailer, Trilling, and Epstein—because they didn't see the book the way he did.

But afterwards, and with his switch to the right, it wasn't just that he and Midge decided to cut people. People didn't want to see *them*. In the old days he and Midge used to give enormous, wonderful parties when they lived on West End Avenue, then suddenly nobody would come. There was a political atomization of the literary world, and it was exacerbated by the rhetoric of the mid-sixties, the violence over the Vietnam War. The kids marching in the streets chanting "LBJ, LBJ, how many kids did you kill today?" created very violent feelings, feelings that were unheard of.

NORMAN MAILER There's something so judgmental and narrow about Podhoretz now. He was merrier in the old days. He talks too much now of how he took care of me in those old days. I also took care of him. How many people I argued with, saying, "No, no, Norman Podhoretz is not really as middle-class as he seems. He's really a great guy, and stand-up." Today he couldn't stand up without having his arms around a missile. He's just as brave and tough as all those other military-industrials. What I find most distressing is that he never asks himself whether he didn't lose his nerve living out on the left during the sixties. Think of all those ongoing years of alienation, all those simmering fears of the ultimate wrath of the authority. How dull and righteous he is today.

But let me go back to my review—that famous review!—of *Making It*. In Provincetown I didn't say it was a great or a marvelous book, not for one minute. I said it was a good book and that it was being treated unfairly, so I was going to redress the balance.

Now, there was some background to my shift in the review. Norman P. had had a dinner party for Jackie Kennedy about a year or two before. It had been very, very important to him, and one of the little conditions Jackie Kennedy made was that I not be invited because she was still mad at me for that piece I'd written, "An Evening with Jackie Kennedy." So Norman, my good friend, didn't invite me, and told me later, in effect, that her presence at the party meant more to him than my bruised feelings. Fair enough.

The first part of my review of *Making It* was, in fact, an attack on the reviewers who had been doing him in. Now in the course of writing, I was rereading the book, and after my indignation at what they'd done to him had been expressed, I began to discover another indignation working its way forward: I felt he'd injured a promising book. At a certain point I probably crossed the line from friendship. You can keep friendship and objective criticism together—you can do a severe review of a friend's work—but I think I crossed the line from objective criticism to self-serving criticism in that I began to enjoy pointing out what the faults were. I no longer was necessarily writing in sorrow. I was also taking pleasure in attacking the book, just as his detractors had. It is sad to say but *Making It* had a subtly awful quality. It's like that joke: If Podhoretz were whining to the Lord, "Why, Lord, do you not reward me? I work so hard, why do you reward others and not me?" And God replies in a voice of thunder, "Because you *bug* me!" That was the fatal vice of *Making It*. One's teeth got on edge. The second half of the book on second reading is unbelievably soft, even smarmy—and my annoyance became more important to me than my friendship.

Norman P., however, had had these high hopes that my review was going to turn the day, and so it was a bitter disappointment for him, maybe even crueler than all the others. From his point of view I had betrayed him. And from my own point of view I did betray him to a degree. Yet I also felt, This is fair—he betrayed me with the Jackie Kennedy party. Because not only had he not invited me, he invited Bill Styron, who was then my dire rival. Betraying Podhoretz, therefore, wasn't the world's worst thing to me. Maybe it was my way of saying, "Fuck you back." I'm diabolical enough in my own small way that I could've set him up by telling him I was going to redress everything. Deep in me I could've been saying, "All right, now we get you for that Jackie Kennedy party." Who knows? I don't ever pretend to know. I'm no angel. I guarantee it. So it could have been a double cross. But at the highest level, *Making It* on second reading was truly a meretricious work. I would never have written that half-favorable, half-mean review if I thought it was a fine job. Literature must come first. That's the only Gibraltar we have.

SANDY CHARLEBOIS THOMAS   Norman was always transferring funds. His father kept the money and I had power of attorney for a household account. I'd write out the checks and ask Barney for funds month by month. In '66 there was a lot of money around. But over the years I was aware of enormous financial ups and downs. Before every book contract it would be bad. When it was especially bad he would go and do something like *The Armies of the Night* for *Harper's*, just to get himself out of a hole. *Why Are We in Vietnam?* didn't make much, although as usual he'd gotten big money up front. The only residual I knew he counted on, year after year, was from *The Naked and the Dead*, maybe $10,000 yearly. Cy was handling the big money, income-tax stuff and the like. Barney had a desk in Cy's office and was handling the cash. The house on Columbia Heights was in Fanny and Barney's name, as they were the "officers" of the 142 Columbia Heights Corporation. When Barney retired he was handling Norman's accounts out of his own apartment in Brooklyn, but Cy was still very much involved. I would see Barney once a week or so. He lived around the corner from Norman and would come over.

The grocery bills on the Cape used to come to $700 a month or so, and probably half of that was liquor. Today the bill would be $2500. Norman knew how much he was running through, but I don't think he's ever realized what it means *not* to have money. Still, I don't see Norman's having so many kids as crippling. His expenses are high and he's got to produce, sure, but he once said to me that without the kids he wouldn't work, because essentially he's lazy.

FANNY SCHNEIDER MAILER   He didn't mean to throw the money away. He was always groping for something different, something exciting, something he could feel was his, and I think he was really trying to do something with his movies. The problem was he didn't know how to approach it. He trusted everybody around him, and they all took advantage of him. I wasn't there, but I heard about it. I thought to myself, All that money gone under the bridge. It was a case of, if he did something, it had to be real, whether or not it cost him his fortune. But he never once, I could almost swear to it, stopped to think, Where is this leading me? Even though I wasn't there, don't think for one moment I didn't understand. I understood everything that was going on. I had a big heartache about it. But I didn't talk to him, because I felt it would be words lost.

SANDY CHARLEBOIS THOMAS   I think Norman first sold some of his shares in *The Voice* to finance *Maidstone*, the third film. Then it became very expensive, and when *The Voice* was sold he got his money out, and I guess a lot of it went for setting up the editing office.

ED FANCHER   I can't talk about the sale of *The Voice* to Carter Burden because that's confidential. But we did have to talk to Norman about it, he was part of the deal, so Dan and I flew up to Provincetown and stayed overnight. Again, I can't comment on the rumored figure—$250,000 or $500,000 or whatever—

that Norman got and then sank into his movie and then the mayoralty campaign. I can't talk about that. Just say Norman was satisfied with what it was that was worked out. And he was perfectly friendly to Dan and me during our visit.

TOM QUINN   The first I heard about *Maidstone* was when my wife and I visited them over the Fourth of July weekend, '68, in Provincetown. His idea was that this time he'd multiply the cost of the previous films and finally do it right. But I was a little worried because my wife, Marcia, is a nice, twenty-four-year-old sheltered Jewish girl from Long Island, she's pregnant, and that May or June my best pal was killed in Vietnam. For the first time she's seen Irish sentimentality. Marine emotionalism. And it almost flattened her. She'd just dissolve in tears, it was too much for her, and then the spectacle up in Provincetown... Well, seeing it over Norman's shoulder was something else. The Fourth of July weekend was a carnival. We're out eating Friday night, it's crowded, we can't get any service. Beverly is wearing a full-length Indian headdress, feathers down to the floor, and she gets up on the table and does an Indian wine dance so we'd get drinks. I'm like a one-eyed cat peepin' in a seafood store—I just can't get enough of it. But Marcia—here she is six months pregnant, Bobby Kennedy has just been shot, my best friend killed in Vietnam, and suddenly she's about ready to collapse. I didn't even notice it, but Norman did, and he stopped the whole circus, which is what he did two nights later at a big party at his house when, again, he sensed Marcia just wasn't going to make it. It was one of the most incredibly sensitive and generous things, and the next day he took us into town, where we just sort of walked around eating ice cream cones. Still, that weekend should have warned me about *Maidstone*.

So later that month we're out in the Hamptons for the film—Marcia and me, Roger and Fay. I think I'm going to be a star. A couple of days pass, I haven't seen much of Marcia because she's off with Roger and Fay while I'm in front of the camera. But then there's a brawl at the hotel. She gets knocked down by some guy with a shotgun—the townies have had enough of Norman's freaks—so we just took off without a word. I hadn't been in the office in three days. Nobody knew where the hell I was. I have a pregnant wife and here are all these wackos. Enough was enough.

I had been on camera sixteen hours that weekend, and yet I'm not in the film for a minute. Totally cut out. I guess Norman kind of saw me as the quarterback who quits the team just before the championships because he has to study. So I was there at awards night—at the film's screening—but didn't get my letter. I just sat there. Then Norman came over to me and said, "What do you think, isn't it the best damned thing?" I said, "Norman, keep at it. You oughta keep doing this." To which he had no response, not then. But three years later I wrote a couple of screenplays, and I sent them to him. One was lousy. He wrote me back, "Keep at it. Keep at it." I knew exactly what he meant. He had saved the line for years. Finally at a party he said to Marcia, "I've decided to forgive Tom for walking off my set." And she said, "Fuck you, Norman. Do you have any idea what I went through?" And she told him the story. He'd had

"Maidstone," Gardiner's Island, 1968; Tom Quinn (arms folded, left rear), Jose Torres (seated, right middle), and director Mailer.

no idea all this had taken place—that I hadn't seen her for days or that she'd been knocked down by the guy with the gun.

D. A. PENNEBAKER Different people made the arrangements for Gardiners Island, one of our locations. Bob Gardiner is not a very attractive person, but he's the real thing, a tenth-generation type, and what Norman did was brilliant, casting him as the head of the CIA. Or casting the richest man in the world, John de Menil, as an *agent provocateur*. And the fact that Norman was out there really turned people on. Everybody felt they were at the center of something.

Beverly was of course really pissed at Norman, but she also wanted her crack at the big time, so there was this duality of purpose she never resolved. Everybody was bugged because the whole thing was capricious. Nobody was running the show, and they were at the mercy of the cameramen and didn't know if the cameramen were any good. Actors working their way up don't know what a scene looks like and want to be protected by a director. Norman was saying, "That's your tough luck," so the ones that had anything at stake were nervous. The others, who were just hanging out for the free booze, were fucking up the works for the pros, which was pissing everybody off.

BARNEY ROSSET There were a number of locales being used, including my place, but chief among them was the Ossorio estate. Alfonso Ossorio was a

At Ossorio's house amidst the Pollacks, Dubuffets, and objets bruts.

painter, a strange one, and very, very wealthy. Philippine sugar plantation money, went to Harvard. After the war Ossorio became a painter full time and used his money very creatively, chiefly to promote his own career. He implants things in his paintings—buckles, bones, marbles, found objects—and he's also been a great helper to other artists. He bought a lot of Pollocks very early, right at the beginning, and Dubuffets too. He also has one of the world's great collections of French *la brut*, insane art, art taken out of insane asylums. He's very much a Catholic as well, and I don't mean vaguely Catholic, since there's a chapel right in his house.

Anyway, the house is like one incredible set, and I proposed that Ossorio let Norman shoot some scenes there. He's now very sorry he agreed. It ended our relationship. There was a good deal of small theft, not on a major scale—nobody walked off with a Pollock—but overall they messed up the place, and Ossorio was furious. He has seventy-eight acres, and there was no way he could control things.

To make matters worse, my own house is right next door. From the start I locked the place up. Thus the famous episode with Lane Smith took place at Ossorio's. What happened was that Smith was to be in a scene that took place in Ossorio's mammoth living room, which you enter by going down a flight of stairs. The dwarf who used to be on *Fantasy Island*, Herve Villechaize, was playing the piano, and Smith was drinking and was competitive. Norman ordered him out of the house in front of a hundred or more people, so he was humiliated. He came outside where I was sitting on the patio with my then wife waiting for the scene to be shot, and he was so furious he started threatening Norman. Soon Norman came out and told him, "Ah, shut up, you old cigar butt," and went back inside.

I'm listening to Smith rant, and now he's lying in wait for Norman. After a half hour, when the scene breaks up, Norman comes outside, and Smith grabs him. Norman turned around—he'd been facing the other way—and hit him on the jaw, just one shot, which flattened him. Then Norman turned back and went on with his conversation.

If you said this about anybody in the world except Norman you'd think it was totally insane, but I'd seen this sort of thing happen several times during the past few days. Another actor had been punched, Norman had been attacked too, and there was a prizefighter, not Jose Torres, who was attacked, supposedly as part of a scene, but the man turned around and just clobbered someone in the face, I mean really took him out. And of course this was all before Rip came at Norman with a hammer. With Lane Smith, though, it didn't just end. Norman had hit him, knocked him down, but then Smith got up. Norman's back was turned, and Smith jumped on him and threw him to the ground.

Smith subsequently claimed that it was Jose who hit him, but that can't be right because I called to Jose to help and he said, "No, no, I can't do that," and walked away. Smith was still on top of Norman, and Michael McClure staggered by. I asked him to help. Again no deal. So then I said, "Where's Buzz Farbar, our bodyguard?" Somebody said, "He's asleep, drunk under a table." So I jumped on top of Lane Smith and grabbed him by the throat to drag him off. I grabbed him so hard that I got him into an upright position, and then, incredibly enough, Norman somehow sort of disappeared. It was ludicrous. I'm trying to hold Smith, nobody's helping, and then a few people came up and socked him in the jaw two or three times. Who? I don't know, just some of the nameless freaks. And that's what broke Smith's jaw. There were two shots to his face which were real smashers.

This still wasn't the end of it, though. Jose's friend, the fight trainer, really wanted to kill Smith and had to be stopped. He had gotten ahold of the guy and pushed him thirty or forty feet over against my house, screaming, "You can't do this to Norman," and he was crying. There was also a small black guy who was going to hit Smith on the head with a bottle. And my wife, who's five feet and weighs about eighty pounds—I was told this was filmed, it's marvelous—this guy's swinging the bottle back, and she came up behind him and wrested it out of his hand. At that point I just let go of Smith, and he disappeared into the dark. I talked to Cy Rembar as soon as I read that there was a threatened lawsuit. Cy was concerned, and I said I could guarantee that Jose Torres didn't hit him, because the son of a bitch had refused to get involved, and as for Norman, although he'd hit the guy, he wasn't the one who'd done the damage.

JOSE TORRES   Norman hadn't been drinking, he was working, and, in fact, he'd only drink on weekends, the night before the day off. But Lane Smith left the scene, then came back where the shooting was, and started shouting, "Mailer, you can take your crew, your equipment, your camera and shove it up your ass." Norman walked up to him—*boom*, one shot right in the jaw. Smith went down and was unconscious for five or six seconds. Then he got up and looked around and says, "Who hit me?" Norman says, "I hit you." Smith says, "You didn't hit me. That was a nigger punch."

There were two black guys there, and one of them went *whoosh*, right into Smith's head. I held the guy back, someone else pulled Smith away. Smith says to Norman, "You didn't hit me, Jose hit me." I said, "If I'd hit you, sucker, you'd still be on the fucking floor."

A week later I'm kidding around with some Puerto Rican or Mexican soldiers in Vietnam, I was doing a tour, and one of them asks, "Who hit Lane Smith, you or Norman Mailer?" They'd read about it in *Stars and Stripes*, a headline story, which they showed me: Mailer and I were being sued by Smith for a broken jaw. The hospital bill was three thousand dollars supposedly, and I didn't get the details until I got back to the city. Norman had already begun to negotiate with the bastard. "I'll pay the hospital expenses only if you sign a paper saying I hit you, not Jose." Which is what the guy did.

FAY DONOGHUE   What irritated us was that everyone was so clearly taking advantage of Norman's generosity—eating, drinking as though there was no tomorrow. We'd gone to the first meeting, cocktails and dinner. But the next morning was beautiful, and we said "Screw it" and went to the beach instead. Tommy Quinn came back and told us you couldn't breathe the air on the bus without getting high. He said they all acted so badly over at the location that they got thrown off the property.

SANDY CHARLEBOIS THOMAS   It wasn't as crazy as the Haight in '67, but it was more interestingly crazy. He had everyone out there at a big hotel we rented, one great big old wooden beachside hotel and part of another, both of which were jammed. There was lots of booze, because I had it shipped out, but the strategy wasn't to get everyone drunk and let them go apeshit. Norman's thesis was that you can build a movie like a novel—incrementally, letting characters fulfill themselves—and he didn't want people fucked up.

He began by explaining the basic plot, then told everyone to get their groups together, design a subplot, and snatch one of the four camera crews to film it. There was no script, nothing in writing. Leo Garin, I think, was to decide on which groups got which camera crew. He's another one of Norman's sycophants.

At one point I think I asked Norman why he was throwing away $200,000 on this thing, and he said he had the money to test his thesis—so it was "a scientific endeavor," to use what I recall as his phrase.

One group was fucking a lot. There was something really sleazy, slimy about it, and a lot of it went on in Barney Rosset's bathhouse. There was a very handsome actor, actually a scene of him screwing somebody. I heard that Barney Rosset's mother-in-law came out and saw Herve, the midget actor, floating on his stomach in the pool, freaked out, about to drown. She called the hotel, and Jose and a couple of guys came over to pull him out.

BARNEY ROSSET   The shooting went on for five or six days, and it was clear that this thing was out of control and quite insane. It was obvious the first day, the first hour, which was why I locked up my house.

Take the people who showed up. There were a few normal ones, like Jose and his fight-trainer friend. But the groupies and the rest of them . . . I mean, like that dwarf, Villechaize. And Ron Hobbs, a literary agent I know, who's very tall and skinny, chasing a black girl—she's in the film, black and very tall—chasing her across the lawn, these two forms going, running, disappearing. Pennebaker was a little off the wall too, plus Ricky Leacock, who was very calm and detached but still in a way *too* detached. Also McClure, who can be very crazy. There was even a lion's cage, which came from the circus on a flatbed truck. It was deposited in my driveway, where it stayed for five days. Our house was sort of sunk into the ground and I had a window that looked out over all this, and there I am looking at this cage, me, my wife, and mother-in-law. These people were running around at our head level and we're getting a weird view of it. People by the dozens, running around, chasing each other, fighting, fucking, acting insane.

I was terrified of the violence, which was so thick you could feel it. After the first or second day these people had finished shooting, it was still light, and they'd gone back to where they were staying, in Bridgehampton, five miles away. My mother-in-law went outside, then came back into the house screaming, "There's a midget in the swimming pool!" My wife and I go outside, and sure enough, there he is, floating. Somebody had thrown Villechaize into the pool, and he was drowning. I was able to reach over the edge and pull him out. My reaction was sheer rage, sort of "What right do they have to put this thing in our pool and then go home, just split?" Here we were in our house, this Quonset hut sunk in the ground, with the swimming pool and a lot of trees; the place has been vibrant with maniacs one minute, and suddenly they're all gone. My poor mother-in-law hasn't been out all day, she's been barricaded inside, then she comes back in screaming. What I said to my wife was, "Goddamn it, we're gonna get Norman!" I wasn't worried whether the midget was dead or alive. I didn't even call the rescue squad.

I got in my car and raced the five miles to the Bull's Head Inn, where they were all staying. I went up to Norman's room and pounded on the door. "Norman, you've gotta come back and get your midget!" And Norman? He and Jose went back with us and scooped up the guy, and I was told later that they took him to the hospital, where his stomach was pumped. Whether he was suffering from booze or drowning I don't know, probably a mixture of both. The next day, though, to my utter amazement he was back playing the piano in the Lane Smith scene.

HAROLD CONRAD   You would not have believed the scene during that dopey movie. Listen, Norman's my friend, I love him, and I don't want to be the one to say he does *shmucky* things, but *Maidstone* is one of the things, when you talk about it, that makes him look like a *shmuck*. Leacock and Pennebaker had six cameras going. You know what color film costs? But some camera guy would say, "Take this guy over there and let him say something." Hour after hour with the cameras rolling. I'd worked in Hollywood, and it killed me to see all this waste. Pennebaker should've said, "For Christ's sake, Norman, this is costing," but I don't think he or Leacock gave a fuck.

Norman must have enjoyed it, because he was running around being a big man. We were using this beautiful house, the artist's house, and there was also that midget. He was having a ball and got really drunk, so we put him in the pool, put his arm over the rail, and left him there. Everything was supposed to be improvisational, everyone was boozed and stoned, and while all this craziness was going on the cameras never stopped rolling. A black guy and some broad are doing it on camera, also some dame was sucking a guy's cock there in the bushes. So Norman says to me, "You're going to be one of the studs in the male whorehouse." I said, "Not me, not with these fucking idiots. Whatever happens to this film, I ain't going to be on film as a male whore for anybody."

MICHAEL McCLURE   In short order, Norman and I had a big falling out. I got the camera crews together and had them filming me giving a lecture to Norman's girl friend, Carol Stevens. I used his name from the film, and said, "Norman T. Kingsley is really a great novelist, a deep-feeling individual, and making this

Norman T. Kingsley, Presidential candidate marked for assassination.

With Michael McClure and Jose Torres.

film is undercutting his enormous talent." I was drunk and was doing it out of frustration as the only way I could tell Norman what I felt. But Norman went apeshit. He said the film was costing him $100,000, and who the fuck did I think I was—on and on.

But unlike *Beyond the Law*, *Maidstone* was some kind of psychotic pigout. I didn't think so when I first heard about it, but by the second day, when I saw the setup, what the involvement was, the laxity with which it was conceived, the impossibility of the people confronting one another in a hopeless situation, then I was sure nothing was going to come together. Pennebaker's involvement looked pretty vague around the edges too. I knew that the first twenty minutes. It just wasn't like Norman, it wasn't like anything I'd ever seen before.

I was supposed to have a big part, but then I ended up with no part at all because of our fight. But I hung around. I got schizzed out, got myself in a state where I drank a bottle of vodka and screamed filthy words at the top of my lungs until I passed out and woke up in a state of existential horror. I can't blame it on anybody but myself. I was the one who brought it on. Still, I could imagine it happening to *anybody* given the brooding violence out there.

BARNEY ROSSET The finale, of course, was the attack on Norman with the hammer, and Pennebaker never stopped filming. Beverly was yelling at him, "C'mon over here, *do* something!" But it was like with Lane Smith. No one lifted a finger. It's self-serving of Penny to say, "Well, I was making this great shot, how could I stop?" There are times when one has to stop, and besides, the scene didn't save the film. It's weird, almost a setup.

By the time they'd gone to Gardiners Island I'd had enough and refused to go. Rip was pissed off at the sheer amateurishness, the ego-tripping, and I think he felt quite hurt personally, really let down. Norman was supposed to give him more of a directorial role than he was getting, and being quite an ego-tripper himself, he had been growing angrier and angrier. I spoke to McClure, who's a very gentle person, and he wouldn't go either. I suppose he sensed what was happening. He told me that Rip had come up to him and said, "Let's go and kill Norman"—kill him, that is, within the action of the film. McClure liked Rip very much—he sort of tried to give himself a macho image, the two of them used to ride around on motorcycles together—but he still wouldn't go. I said, "Michael, this is terrible. You have to go. It's your duty to be there to stop him." His response was, "No, thanks," so I mean, he knew what was gonna happen.

Did Norman sense it? I have no idea. The assassination had been discussed, and Rip, I know, was extremely angry. On the other hand, if he was really going to kill him, he would have done it a lot more efficiently.

HAROLD CONRAD   The owner of the place, Gardiner, took us out in his forty-eight-foot motorboat. Beverly and Mara and the kids and I, and also Rip. It was a beautiful day, a beautiful forty-five-minute trip across the water. Gardiner's a bore, so I'm watching Rip sitting all alone in the front of the boat. I don't know if he's pissed or stoned, but he's deep into it. Nobody knows what the scene is going to be, since everything was ad lib. But there was something about Norman being killed at some point in the story—that was Rip's idea anyhow. Norman hadn't wanted a fucking script, his line was "Do what you want to do," and Rip's thing was that Norman had to be killed.

So we get to the island and go off to tour the beautiful old house while the others are off to shoot the scene. Mara and I soon hear this screaming. I run over, forty feet away, and I see Rip trying to hit Norman on the head with a hammer. At first I didn't believe he was really hitting him. I thought he was faking it, which was probably what he meant to do. But he really did hit him. I could tell by Norman's reaction, he was going apeshit. And Torn's got this crazy, maniacal look in his eye. They're tussling, the kids are screaming, Beverly's screaming, then Torn's bleeding, because Norman's almost bitten his ear off.

SANDY CHARLEBOIS THOMAS   I arrived just as Norman was climbing off Rip, and there was blood all over the place, mostly from Rip's ear. Beverly was there with the children—Michael and Stephen, Dandy and Betsy too—and they were terrified, screaming, so Roberta Swafford and I put them in the truck and just took off.

Norman put plaster on his head. Rip's ear was a mess, but he didn't go to the hospital until the next day, because I saw him that night. He felt terrible because he'd misjudged so badly. He hadn't meant to hit Norman. In the plot he was supposed to try an assassination attempt, but either he didn't pull the punch or Norman moved, and he clipped him. I suspect it scared the shit out of Norman, which is why he lost his temper and nearly took off Rip's ear. Rip was devastated. He knew Norman was never going to forgive him—ever—and Norman really did stay tear-assed for quite a while; perhaps he'd gotten so involved with the movie as to really think Rip was trying to kill him. Could be. It was quite mad. That night everyone was at the inn, there was an attempt at a party, but it was very, very tense.

HAROLD CONRAD Gardiner took us off the island in his boat, and we all went to dinner at a Chinese joint. I remember it was me, Lady Jeanne, Mara, and Norman and Beverly, maybe a few others. Norman was like a guy who'd been in an earthquake and it doesn't really hit you until two days later. He wasn't hurt that bad—cuts, a little blood, bruises, but he was still up. He was just exhilarated with the whole thing. On and on he'd talk about Rip, and saw it as a betrayal. He was pissed off at the stupidity of Rip's using a fucking hammer, and it was quite a shock—this great peaceful setting, untouched out on that island, and all of a sudden there's kids screeching, Beverly screaming, and blood.

MICHAEL McCLURE I took Rip to the hospital in New York. His ear was swollen bigger than my fist, and I thought it would have to be amputated. He wasn't exactly *compos mentis* either. Anybody who'd been involved in *Maidstone* wasn't *compos mentis*. He was trying to tell me it was a toy hammer, a ten-ounce hammer, but I didn't care; I thought Rip had it coming, Norman had it coming, everybody had it coming. I was just glad nobody got killed. After seeing what happened to Lane Smith, I thought anybody could've done in anybody.

RIP TORN The last ten minutes was kind of the loaded gun of the thing, and of course there were people out there who had real guns.

Norman must've told twenty or thirty people to set up a phony assassination attempt, because the film was supposed to be about assassinations. I don't know anyone who was dumb enough to go for it except me, although I wouldn't have done it without help. The night before, Leacock and I—I was associate director—went over everything that had already been shot, and everyone was saying to me, "You gotta save this film, you gotta do something." I said, "Oh, no, whatever I do, everybody'll think it's a personal kind of thing." And they said, "Oh, no, everybody'll back you up." Sure, just like the time during *Deer Park* rehearsals. In fact, the film was supposed to be over, I was supposed to be in Stockbridge, but I agreed to stay another day.

Also, I was worried because there really was a plot, I mean for real. Ten or twelve guys were so angry at Norman they wanted to catch him and literally stone him. He'd made people very, very angry, and he'd done it deliberately, insulting them, demeaning them in the style of his character. It wasn't his own style; he likes to have fun, but he doesn't go out to bully people. But the more he played his character, the more he became the fascistic Norman T. Kingsley. But nobody was going to face him one-on-one, except for dummy here, and I thought I was doing it for the film.

Anyway, the night before, everyone had argued that we had to save the film, especially because Norman had sold his interest in *The Voice* to make it. Also, I had an interest in making films with him because he was giving me a chance to create characters in a way I wasn't usually allowed to, and in fact I'd turned down *Easy Rider* to do *Maidstone*. Nicholson tells the big story that I walked off *Easy Rider*, but it ain't so. You gotta be in a film to walk off it. I wasn't in New Orleans walking off *Easy Rider*, I was wrassling around with Norman.

It was my idea to use the hammer, granted. But if I'd gone in with a blank gun, I probably would've been shot to death. I've had a lot of experience with guns, hunting as a boy, then in the military, and I know that close up you can kill somebody even with a blank. Also, I didn't want the assassination to involve a group. The atmosphere was too crazy. With a hammer I'd have control, and in fact I went to Norman and showed him the hammer because I wanted him to know what I was going to do.

People were talking all kinds of garbage afterwards, like it was a rubber hammer. It wasn't a rubber hammer. On the other hand, I definitely pulled the shot. He was so paranoid that he got frightened when I said, "Norman T. Kingsley, you've got to die." I didn't say "Norman Mailer," but he must have taken it that way— I didn't know that Kingsley's really his middle name. And then he turned around and bit my ear.

Now, growing up in Texas, nobody ever thought of biting as unmanly. Guys are rough-and-tumble, they're not Marquis of Queensberry, but biting is what they use as a last resort. If a bear has got you, you clamp on its ear or something. So when Norman did that, I didn't know what to do. I talked to him calmly— you can hear me saying something in the film, like "Hey, Dad, I need this ear to work with." It was as cold as that. He says, "Okay." I says, "Let's back off and start over." Then we started wrassling and choking each other. That's when Beverly rushed over, screaming. Norman tried to say I'd done it right in front of the kids, but they were two hundred yards away.

But, shit, let's get down to what nobody seems to realize—the only direction I had was when Norman first told me his idea: "I want you to play my half brother. I want you to set up this group, kind of like the rat pack, and we'll call it Cashbox. Don't make a lot of conflicts with me in the beginning, let it build. I'll do some things that will irritate you, and we can ricochet back and forth. Then I want you to set up a phony assassination attempt." That was the whole idea, the only direction he gave me, and the way it worked was, he'd set up a kind of military perimeter. I'd left his perimeter, and he thought I was gone. But I put on a pair of sneakers and waded up through the swamp, so mysteriously that all of a sudden I just reappeared. I thought it was an obligatory scene, that he was gonna play dead. Like *bang*, you're dead. Only he didn't, and the joke was on me. But once the thing went down—despite the meeting the night before—I was all by myself. Everyone else was so afraid of Norman.

The funny thing was that at first Norman was furious at me, but then he seemed to calm down. He called when I was in the hospital in Stockbridge to tell me about the Lane Smith suit, then asked, "What are you doing in the hospital?" I said, "I'm on IVs, my ear is terribly infected." He said, "You trying to tell me my bite is poisonous?" I said, "I'm not taking it away from you, but your bite isn't any more poisonous than anyone else's. The human tooth is more infectious than a dog's." That's when the freeze set in.

He called me, though, when they were releasing the film and told me that the scene was in it. He said he hated to admit it, but it was the best one in the film, and in fact it made the film. I said, "Yeah? So why'd you put me in purgatory for two fucking years?" He said, "Just building the gate."

BERNARD "BUZZ" FARBAR   We kept going because we had Norman's enthusiasm. Sam Cohen, an agent from ICM, saw a rough cut and promised Cy Rembar over lunch that he'd give $300,000 of his own money because *Maidstone* was so terrific. Of course the deal never came through.

D. A. PENNEBAKER   We were sort of producing the film, so I went back to New York and assigned someone to do the sound sync. That took a month, then Norman began to edit, which took six months. I gave him some advice, but I didn't edit it, because then it wouldn't have been his film. Norman still assumed that editing was shit-assed, dirty work, which is often true in a feature film but in this kind of project the conceptual work doesn't come in until the editing. It's lonely work, and I don't think he understood that film had *any* lonely work other than the initial conception; he assumed you hired a person, hopefully the cheapest you could find, and let him put it together while you come in once in a while to give suggestions.

His difficulty was sticking with it. Toward the end I think he was desperate and he started putting in a fair amount of time, but by then maybe it was too late. It's gotta be fresh, like a concert. What he needed was an extraordinary putting together, so that it always moved unexpectedly on you. Instead it moves so deliberately that you begin to anticipate things, and the surprises get fewer and fewer. It loses the quality of something constantly flowering. I had hoped that with his three films he'd say, "There aren't any rules," because that's what's wonderful about Norman, he has no rules. I'd hoped he'd bring that possibility into filmmaking and explode it. Documentary filmmaking is so hidebound, it really needs somebody with Norman's arrogance to come in and shove it around. Unfortunately that's not what happened.

ANDY WARHOL   Norman did it wrong. He thought filmmaking was easy. I thought he'd be smart, and since he was so famous I thought he was God. People are wrong when they think you can just throw actors in front of the camera. When we put them in front of the camera they turned on for us and they'd come alive, like kids in a family movie. But in Norman's films this didn't happen. Why, I don't know. Maybe it was the editing. Maybe if he'd done them as a video novel it would have worked. Maybe he used too many people. When we tried to use fifteen people it didn't work either, because there was too much to look at. Still, it's true anything could have happened. If *Maidstone* had come off, it would have been magic.

JONAS MEKAS   Although there hadn't really been an audience for *Wild 90* and *Beyond the Law*, that doesn't mean the films are no good. They weren't expensive, but they were much more real than the attempt of *Maidstone*. They were writers' films, so afterwards there was some hope that he would insist upon and intensify the direction he'd taken. But then *Maidstone* was an attempt to go beyond Warhol and Morrissey and to make a commercial film, because he saw that his earlier films weren't reaching people. But to do that you have to be a filmmaker, and lessons like that are expensive. If I'd had any idea he was going that big with that kind of money, with a corporation and distribution, I would have told him, "It's a mistake, don't do it." But nobody asked me. Then I went to the screening, and Norman came in in his velvet suit, and there was this Hollywood atmosphere to it.

The reaction among independent filmmakers wasn't very favorable. I don't think anyone had ever spent that kind of money making an independent film. He was no longer part of our cinema, he was going somewhere else. But no one felt that it would distort what the independents were doing. It was just something passing, and the whole movement was already established, with its classics and direction.

SANDY CHARLEBOIS THOMAS   The first time I became aware of Norman's affairs was after the filming of *Maidstone*. We were sitting at the kitchen table in P-Town, Norman, Beverly, and I, and quite innocently I remarked, "Do you remember that woman, so-and-so, in *Maidstone*? Well, I just heard she has the clap."

The reaction was instantaneous. Beverly wheeled on him and started screaming, "You're not bringing that into the house, goddammit!" Norman was livid; it was one of the few times he lost his temper with me. All I could say was, "Norman, I didn't know!" It was the first time it dawned on me that he'd probably screwed every woman in the cast, and I was able to slide out of there only because the two of them really got into it.

MIDGE DECTER   Over the years we talked to him frequently about his children— not why he's had so many but specifically his hatred of birth control. I always translated that into my own formulation—namely, whatever else he is, Norman Mailer is the enemy of sterility. Everything he does and likes—being the way he is, carrying everything to extremes, and making his life a kind of scenario of his ideas—it's all part of it, so naturally he'd go around knocking up every woman he gets mixed up with. Almost on principle.

The price he pays is needing lots of money month to month. On the other hand, there is all this life, Mailer with all his progeny and all his women, and he never gives up on any of them. When I saw *Maidstone*, there they all were— Adele, Jeanne, this one, that one. And clearly there was some other lady he was balling, whoever she was, so by the time I saw the movie I knew well enough to watch and say, "Oh, that's interesting. Who's that?"

SANDY CHARLEBOIS THOMAS   Norman has to have children with every woman he's with. Why? I asked him once, since I consider it reprehensible. "What is it with you?" I asked, particularly since in *An American Dream* he had been talking about pulling the diaphragm out. What he said was that the sexual act didn't have real meaning for him unless there was the risk of having a child, that in modern society we tend to make the sex act much less than it is. In the Bible it says "becoming one flesh," and it seems to me that Norman was saying that unless there's the possibility of becoming one flesh, you might as well jack off.

SENATOR EUGENE McCARTHY   I had thought at the time that his perceptions of the '60 convention were much better—not just interesting but objectively better— than the obvious stuff of Teddy White and that crowd. Also I think the speech I made for Stevenson out there in Los Angeles had moved him, so later we talked about it at a big reception for Mark Lane when he was running for assemblyman.

Anyway, at this party in New York Norman gave his speech before me, very rapid, and as we passed, I said to him, "Fella, you have to learn how to breathe." He had liked that and put it in his book *Miami and the Siege of Chicago*. But he also said that my speech at a primary fund-raiser didn't convey the passion I'd had at the '60 convention in Los Angeles. But, as I told him, "That was *then*."

There were a lot of liberals in that literary and artistic world who'd jumped in with Bobby Kennedy. Norman might've said Bobby was the existential politician, but some of the others wouldn't have been that intense about it. But there was the pragmatic issue of how his coming in would inevitably divide the antiwar people. The idea I was presenting was that first we try to win on an issue, then we compete for the power of the group. Norman and many of the others should've understood that. Perhaps his image of the politician-as-existentialist prevented him from seeing it. Plus Bobby had a kind of machismo, taking on Hoffa, confronting Wallace on the race issue. But I don't remember Norman as someone who went over to Bobby from me. He jumped in because Bobby gave him the incarnation he was looking for. There was no defection, like with Arthur Schlesinger, Jr., and some of the others. Norman came in with Bobby.

Despite what some people were saying, I don't think Norman's politics were frivolous, his candidacy for New York mayor notwithstanding. His support of Bobby was psychological, personal with the Kennedys, and my guess is that it was Bobby's style that attracted him. In politics you can have what you often see in religion: people look for an incarnation of their search for meaning, which may be why Norman has sometimes seemed very erratic and desperate. It was the same sort of thing on a somewhat different level with Robert Lowell—you saw him leaving his WASP, puritan thing, becoming a Catholic, and then looking for the answer in the Greeks. Yeats did the same thing, trying mysticism, testing Catholicism, going back to ancient Ireland, and finally he just said, "Who knows?"

Anyway, in Chicago, the day after Humphrey's nomination, we had gone to the Blackstone for dinner, across the street from the Hilton on Michigan Avenue. That's the same night Norman came over to our table to talk to me. I was still in Chicago because the Secret Service had warned me, "Don't leave town. If you do, the police will arrest everybody with a McCarthy button." The Secret Service boys, you see, were pretty good to me. They said things like "We can't promise your room isn't bugged, so don't say anything on the telephone." They didn't tell us *who* was tapping our phones, only "We can tell the phone's bugged because you get a clearer signal, which means they put extra power on it."

Norman wrote that he was surprised I was having a quiet meal with these guys who weren't big pols the day after I'd lost. But it shouldn't have surprised him. We had two whole months to get ready, and we realized that we were going to lose. Aside from the antagonism that had developed between the Kennedy and McCarthy people, which got worse after Bobby's death—as if we were at fault, somehow responsible for it—we also realized that a lot of Kennedy people weren't committed against the war. So what Norman didn't realize was that I could be reasonably quiet and restrained because losing wasn't a shock. I hadn't lost what I had expected to win.

He seemed pretty subdued himself, though. Perhaps it had to do with his recognizing what all that violence meant, and maybe he had a deeper sense of it than I did. Perhaps we should have refused to go to the convention unless the National Guard agreed to stay out of there, but we hadn't known the measure of police and military force that was going to be enlisted. On the other hand, a lot of my delegates weren't ready to die for the issue and were ready to support the party nominee once it was over.

We'd been warned, but we hadn't expected the raid on my headquarters at four-thirty that morning. In fact, I didn't know what had happened until I got up at four-thirty, looked out the windows at the park where people were camped out, and decided to go over there to talk to them. The Hilton has a desk on each floor, and when I went out I saw that at the desk on my floor, the twenty-third, there was a kid with his head bandaged. He was still bleeding, and he told me what had happened at our headquarters on the fifteenth floor. The police had gotten keys from the hotel, gone into rooms, and thrown people out of bed. I went down—then I went down to the lobby, where they had about forty people sitting on the floor like prisoners of war. There were about thirty cops around with masks on. I asked, "Who's in charge?" Nobody was.

Dick Goodwin arrived, and God, he was as white as a sheet. We decided to send our people back upstairs, four and five at a time. Dick was watching, he thought the end of the world had come. He was a sort of double agent. Originally he was with me, then he went over to Kennedy, then he came back when Bobby was shot. But I think he was in on trying to get Teddy to run, so he was trying to work with the Kennedy people too.

Looking back, I'd say Norman was right: in terms of Chicago and the police, it was essentially fascist. That's why the Secret Service had told me not to leave town—the word was out that the police were going to use a "loitering" or "disturbing the peace" charge to arrest everybody. In fact, they picked up Murray Kempton for loitering.

I don't criticize Norman for going over to the park and giving speeches. I went over myself once, but to quiet people down, not stir them up. Going over there was something Bobby Kennedy might've done, and Norman would've liked that. Or perhaps he was deeply moved by what was happening and thought that this was the only way to face up to events.

Still, it was hard to conclude after Chicago that fascism would sweep the country. I see it as a much more subtle force—like the power of the IRS over people is essentially a fascist power, because fascism is essentially the power of bureaucracy. Liberals think you can bureaucratize freedom. You can't. The danger of fascism isn't the police taking over so much as the subtle internal stuff, like the IRS defining religion, how you're going to live, what's family life, or the FCC controlling what everybody hears, or the Federal Elections Commission controlling elections. They're more dangerous than the FBI and CIA because they "break and enter" all the time, psychologically and electronically. Norman, however, sees fascism more as storm troopers, whereas if I were ever to run for office again, I'd campaign basically against those three bureaucracies.

JOSE TORRES   I was covering the convention for *Diario* and the *San Juan Star.* Norman and I were sharing a room at the Hilton, and he was very protective of me. For example, we were in Lincoln Park and a guy from the National Guard came up and said, "Hey! It's Jose Torres." I shook hands with him, but Norman was checking, checking, checking, and told me, "Let's go back to the room," where he wanted me to wait while he went down again. I was watching TV, he didn't show up, then they announced he'd been arrested. Actually he'd only been detained, but later he explained that he'd wanted me back in the room because he was afraid that since I'd been recognized they'd go after me once the trouble started.

The next night, very late, there was the tear gas, and again he says, "Let's go into the hotel." We go upstairs, we're watching from our room, then we went into a suite of rooms where I knew some guys. It turned out to be a Republican hideout—Bob Dole's suite, in fact. We could see four guys hitting a girl down below on the street, and I got very emotional. "Those motherfuckers," I said, so some Republican guy says, "Yeah, yeah, those damn kids..." I was shocked. The whole scene was crazy, so unbelievable.

MURRAY KEMPTON   The convention was nearly over, Humphrey had been nominated, the cops had been coming down all week, and somebody invited all the delegates who thought they'd been fucked over to march on Convention Hall. I said that I thought the idea was ridiculous. "I'm supposed to march on Convention Hall and demand admittance to something to which I already have a ticket?" This guy said, "It might not be a bad idea, because it could keep the police from clobbering people."

My son and I then went over to see McCarthy and ran into Norman and Cal Lowell. Norman's position was, "We've got to raise the ante on Daley. I think we should go on this march." I laughed and said, "I've always thought that until you make up your mind you're one of the dumbest people I've ever known." Cal was in one of his moods, but he said, "He's not dumb at all." I was being horribly condescending, which was the parochialism of the delegate—I was a McCarthy delegate—but Norman, as an outsider, was proposing an overview. I'd been on the streets and thought that kind of savagery lasts about two days, that on the third day everyone was after reconciliation, but I was totally wrong. Norman then said, "If you get me permission to address the New York caucus"—the McCarthy caucus, although there were some Kennedy delegates—"I'll say that if more than half of them will march, I'll march. Otherwise, no."

He was treating me as though I was a total pro, with deference for my knowledge of how the system worked, and I was saying, "You're perfectly safe if you want to make the speech." But there were problems. The regulars were furious at us, and Paul O'Dwyer, who's the most wonderful guy on earth, was running for the Senate, so they wouldn't be marching. Although I didn't want to do it, I then made a speech to the delegation saying that I could understand the problems every delegate had but that I thought it would be a calming influence if a group of us joined the demonstration.

Norman was the only sane person at the convention. I think he halfway wanted a confrontation, or was at least toying with the idea. That's his temper artistically. He would've been perfectly happy to get hit over the head and end up in the hospital. But not jail—there are no second acts for that kind of thing, and he'd already ended his previous book by getting busted.

TULI KUPFERBERG   I'm not sure I even saw Mailer. If I did, I don't remember, perhaps because I guess I'd started to resent his appearances as a reporter. He'd been a participant in Washington, but now he seemed to be moving back. I wanted him to be more with us rather than being a reporter. I never discussed this with him, never got a chance, and I don't know if I would've had the courage.

Still, after Chicago, whatever Movement was left was Yippified, and Mailer was definitely not a Yippie.

PAUL KRASSNER   There was still the rift between us, but when I saw him in McCarthy's suite the chill seemed to be off. Again, though, I screwed it up. We shook hands, he was being cordial and all, and instead of just accepting it graciously I said, "I thought you weren't speaking to me?" He gave me a quizzical look and said, "I don't think this is the time to discuss that."

Still, despite our disagreements, he's never really come out and expressed horror at my so-called labyrinthine turn of mind—perhaps because he's shy about giving compliments!

Was he aware that Sandy Thomas and I were seeing each other after Jeannie and I broke up? Sure. In fact Time magazine was going to do a cover story on him in '68, and they asked to interview me. I got the word that Norman didn't want his friends to cooperate, so I wrote Time a note: "He doesn't trust you, I don't trust you, and besides I'm too busy fucking his secretary."

ABBIE HOFFMAN   In Chicago he got up on a barrel in Grant Park and gave a little talk, then I got up and spoke, but we really didn't spend much time together, and not until later in Provincetown did we talk. His misgivings about the Yippies destroying the culture were correct on an abstract level, but he wasn't talking as

The Democratic National Convention, Chicago, 1968.

an organizer. Counterculture was the way you got troops in Vietnam not to fight.

Three weeks later I went up to Provincetown to see my first wife with the two kids. I'd just finished *Revolution for the Hell of It*, I was kind of proud of what I'd done and I guess I wanted to brag. I was manic of course; I hadn't slept in twenty days and had just been through the most apocalyptic moment of my generation—the Chicago police riots—and I was on my way to tell Norman "I finished my book!" But a maid in uniform—a black maid, which of course was a shock—said, "Mr. Mailer doesn't want to be disturbed when he's writing."

I'd heard the rumors about the rituals of his writing, and I shared none of it. My identity is not as a writer, I'm an organizer, so I started yelling, "He won't see me? Well, tell him I finished my fuckin' book way ahead of his, goddammit!" And I ran out. They must have told him, because later that afternoon, as I was getting on the plane for Boston, he appeared at the airport. He said, "I'm sorry I didn't see you this morning, but I was working, and I get lost in my work. Where are you going?" He was being gracious, gentlemanly, and had come out to apologize.

SANDY CHARLEBOIS THOMAS In the fall of '68 someone broke into the Brooklyn Heights apartment through the crow's nest. Nothing was stolen, but it looked like papers had been gone through—household mail, bills, stuff like that. Norman was up in P-Town, and when I called him he told me not to phone the police since he thought they might have been the ones who'd done it. We were all paranoid in those days and later found out that we had every right to be.

DON CARPENTER I met Barbara when I came to New York for the first time and stayed at Rip Torn's. My first novel, *Hard Rain Falling*, had done well, and my second, *Blade of Light*, was just published, so I was a king at my then publishing house, Harcourt Brace Jovanovich. I'd met Torn at Michael McClure's and I'd vowed to do a movie for him, which I eventually did. The first thing Rip did was take me down into the subway system, then he ran off and left me. He was laughing his ass off, like it was the funniest thing in the world to lose this poor kid from Berkeley in a crowded subway. Perfect Rip Torn. I was in a total panic.

Anyway, during that trip Norman invited me to dinner, just me, and there were his parents and Barbara, Beverly's brother, Charlie, and Charlie's girlfriend.

His mother liked me, but I had to pass a test there too. I was offered chopped chicken liver, which I politely refused. I'd never eaten chicken liver before and didn't want to start. But it was forced on me by Norman. His mother was sitting next to me, and I had a feeling it was more for her than me. But the liver was terrific. We didn't talk much, nor did I say much to his father, but I knew Mrs. Mailer liked me because she invited me to her birthday party a week or two later.

In front of his parents Norman was the absolute patriarch, the generous soul for whom every guest is a diamond. Attentive, really in his wit, seeing to it that everyone participated. Like sometimes you go to a party and they talk about Jerry and Booboo and what happened in P-Town last week? None of that. He was the perfect host. He made me his absolute equal. He and I were going to eat the same amount, drink the same. In fact, when he asked me what I would have to drink, I told him bourbon and water, and he gave me gin and tonic, which I despise but which I drank anyway. Why? Because he was drinking gin and tonic. The whole point was to relax me and make me feel good, with none of that pushing me into saying stupid things. Aside from feeling complimented, it was a delight, because Norman didn't feel constrained to be a shit. Ever since, I've always felt that the best kept secret in American literature is what a nice guy Norman Mailer is.

The disparity between him at home with family and him in the public eye was sharp, though, because after dinner we all piled into Beverly's Citroën and drove to a party given by some fat countess. There were bartenders, and small, crowded, cluttered rooms, and a lot of young arrogant guys who thought they were something because they were there. On the make. The New York phenomenon, which I didn't recognize as such until I'd been back to New York a couple more times. But I got into a brush with one of these guys when I dropped an ash on his jacket, brushed it off, and apologized. He gave me one of those "You soiled my jacket, what the fuck is going on?" numbers. I said, "Hey, I said I was sorry," and he gave me some more shit. So I was forced to look the guy right in the eye and say, "Fuck you." And he just completely cooled out. In San Francisco we would've gone out in the street. It's not New York's fault, but these types infest the city.

As for Norman, though—he was a dignitary, in the sense that he was sitting in an easy chair, with Beverly at his side, receiving people. He behaved in an excellent manner, but it was not the same as at home, not the same friendly man as he'd been at dinner. This was an imperious man.

During this trip Norman also gave a big party, and I saw him do his rope trip, climbing up this rope he's got hanging from his living room ceiling. He also asked me if I wanted to visit his office, which at that time you could only get to by climbing the rope and crossing a two-by-six. I share something with Norman which is absolutely clear in *The Naked and the Dead*, and it was also clear from the office setup: we both have a terrific fear of falling. If I'm in a situation where I could fall, I fall, so I fear heights, and so does Norman. Only his attack on the problem is different from mine. I don't go anywhere where I can fall. He does, and constantly. Like in *An American Dream*, walking the parapet.

Anyway, I've worked out a way of dealing with his challenges, from high-walking to head-butting. I refuse them all: "No, thanks." One night, at another party, he'd been butting around, and he came up to me with that little-boy-bull look on his face. He took hold of my shoulders and started to incline his head. I fixed him with my gaze and smiled, just looked him right in the eye and continued to smile. And he knew from that I was not going to butt him back, and he just backed away. There was no problem and I was spared the headache.

At the first family dinner I realized that Barbara was sort of my date. We were in the kitchen at one point, both reaching for beer out of the refrigerator, and we talked irreligiously about Norman. We put him on a little bit between us, kind of winked and made saucy "We love him, but he's not a god" kind of remarks.

Barbara and I got along fabulously and developed a relationship that was totally independent of Norman. She was willing to meet me for lunch and dinner, take me places, show me what New York was like from the point of view of someone who is not famous or guarded. We had a wonderful time for about two weeks, just a fantastically good time, and we got to be real pals, which we are to this day. But it was and is separate from Norman's umbrella. In fact, Norman and I have never spoken of it.

But the strangest thing was that we were followed by a detective. We caught him at it in midtown—a black guy with a raincoat over his arm who'd stop when we'd stop, look in shop windows when we did. Very straight-looking, looked like Malcolm X. It took me years to figure out why. It had to do with the paranoia of the time, but I was never into that paranoia. Ralph Gleason had turned a lot of people over to me—Mario Savio, Jerry Rubin—all of whose phones would've been tapped. But it never occurred to me that mine was tapped too and that I would have a file or I'd be written up collaterally because of my associations. Now I realize that was probably the case, as well as for Norman Mailer's sister—she was probably being written up collaterally too. I suppose they wondered what secret information was being passed. I'm sure we were identified by our associations and followed as subsidiaries, maybe in the hope that we'd go into a door they'd already marked.

JOHN LEONARD I didn't meet Mailer until '67 or '68, but before then, when I had a book review program on KPFA in Berkeley in '62, I'd reviewed his poems *Deaths for the Ladies* and said they were lousy. When I came to New York in 1967 Christopher Lehmann-Haupt—who was responsible for bringing me here as well as getting me the job at *The Times Book Review*—invited me to a party, and there was Mailer. I hadn't been in New York long, I'm in awe, circling around the celebrity. Finally I screwed up my courage, introduced myself, and asked him, "What are you working on now?" He gave me a baleful look, went into his Texas accent, and said, "Well, Leonard, I'm doing a new collection of poems since I know how much you admire my poetry." It was incredible. He'd heard my review on WBAI in New York and remembered it five or six years later. When I got to know him a little better I realized he's able to recall every review he's ever gotten.

SANDY CHARLEBOIS THOMAS   Norman's public self was not dissimilar from his TV personality, but at a small dinner party with friends he could be perfectly delightful—self-critical, charming, funny, thoughtful, and courteous. More times than not he wouldn't be, but he *could* be. It might have been connected to the booze, because as an evening would wear on, the charm wore off. There was also his personality with his wives. In private he can be either wonderful or a horror show.

His private personality has to do with the people who work for him, those in a weaker position. He was always wonderful to me and to Madeline Belkin and Anne Barry—to all of us who worked for him. He'd lose his temper occasionally, but rarely was he rude.

But before going on those TV shows he always went somewhere and drank. Once in a while he'd say, "Watch me, let me know how I do." I think he liked doing these things, but he was nervous, which is perhaps why he drank. And ten times out of ten his performance was ghastly. He would become contentious and unpleasant, do his finger-pointing routine, and come across as a dreadful boor, and almost stupid to boot. The next day he'd ask for my reaction, and I'd burst into tears. His response was "That bad, huh?"

He should never have gone on TV, and I think perhaps he knew that some-where deep in his heart. He's a writer, and I don't understand his fascination with actors—or with actresses, either. Beverly was an actress, he turned Adele into an actress, and now Norris too. If few people know his tender, generous side it's because becoming vulnerable is painful, especially becoming vulnerable to a large group of people who want to suck you dry. He admitted to me once that being famous had some real drawbacks, but at the same time I think he felt the trade was worth it. However complicated or ambivalent he was about TV, he sure as hell used it. The Merv Griffin show, Carson, Cavett, he went on them all.

IRVING HOWE   One sensed the terrible waste of time with the whole media thing. He'd be on one of those TV shows, and I'd say to myself, "What's he doing there?" It didn't matter whether he was good or bad. The real point was why go on them at all? Perhaps it was because he was frustrated about not being able to change history, like a Dickens or a Tolstoy.

NORMAN PODHORETZ   It was either '68 or '69, my daughter Ruthie gave us a surprise party for our anniversary, and Norman was there. We hadn't seen each other for a while and there was a bit of strain, not because of his review but because we were drifting apart politically. After everyone had left he stayed on and said, "Let's talk."

What he wanted to talk about was my pro-American politics—my so-called move to the right. "I don't understand the position you're taking," he said, and demanded I explain myself. This was the one occasion when he allowed himself to enter into my terms sufficiently to understand what I was saying. He wanted to understand, but as things proceeded he got so upset he said he couldn't go on. He didn't just get up and leave—it wasn't that abrupt—but he did put an end to the discussion. Maybe he hadn't realized how serious I was up until that point. He may also have been upset because he wasn't able to answer my arguments about the nature of the country, the nature of the middle class. Toward the end of the sixties, as my political views began to change, I knew very well that it was going to cost me a lot of friendships. I was trying to prevent this from happening, though, especially with Mailer. I knew Mailer and I couldn't be as close, but if there were going to be a break, I was determined not to be the one to initiate it.

NORMAN MAILER ("A PARIS REVIEW INTERVIEW") . . . *at best you affect the consciousness of your time, and so indirectly you affect the history of the time which succeeds you. Of course, you need patience. It takes a long time for sentiments to collect into an action, and often they never do. Which is why I was once so ready to conceive of running for Mayor of New York. I wanted to make actions rather than effect sentiments.*

CLAY FELKER One morning Peter Maas, Gloria Steinem, Jimmy Breslin, and I were sitting around in a restaurant around the corner from *New York* magazine and talking about the upcoming campaign. I don't remember the exact conversation, but it has been said by people who were there that I suggested that Breslin run for mayor and then write about it. Jimmy said, "No, no, no. We should get Mailer to run." So when this took fire, I got Mailer and Breslin together in a photographer's studio, we shot a picture of the two of them, and used it as our cover picture. What we had was an inside track.

JOE FLAHERTY Between '67 and the campaign Norman and I had no sustained conversations. I'd heard from Dan Wolf that he said some nice things about my work, and sometimes at *Voice* parties we'd see each other to say hello, but I was never at any of his wild bashes in Brooklyn. So when I was dubbed to run his campaign I was a little shocked.

At our initial meeting we started by talking about the legitimacy of a Mailer candidacy, since it was in the air that Robert Wagner was coming back. I knew that Mailer had flirted with the idea before, but none of us knew the history. If we'd known that the party when he stabbed Adele was connected to his earlier "candidacy," then we'd have said, "Put a fucking ice bag on his head, he's off again. It must be an every-decade madness."

It was the first time I'd been in Norman's apartment, and I thought it was spectacular—the low-slung ceiling, curved like a bow, the panorama looking over lower Manhattan. My God, I came out of railroad flats—this was William Powell. I was in love with it all, saying to myself, "This is a good enough reason to have a literary career." In retrospect, it was a very selfish evening on all our parts. We never considered Breslin as the candidate—that must've been *New York* magazine arrogance. But we were looking to send somebody's ass into the breach.

I thought it was absurd, me running the campaign, even though I'd been involved in local politics in Park Slope. If we were going to be taken seriously, we needed some respectable organizers, but Norman, on the side of the angels, said, "I won't hear of it. I don't want the campaign polluted with professionals." Later, however, he agreed with Jimmy and met with Adam Walinsky.

I felt bitter about never seeing Norman's friends involved. Torres, of course, couldn't break with Badillo, nor could Hamill. But the others, all they wanted to do was star turns—go to parties or appear on talk shows—people like Peter Maas and Jack Newfield. The people in the office were canvassing, doing the shit work, breaking their fucking asses, but Mailer cronies like Farbar I never saw except at parties, though I was just as happy I didn't have to deal with them. I wasn't smitten and couldn't figure out why Mailer was.

JOSE TORRES   Norman had promised me he was ready to back Badillo, and I told Badillo that. One night I'd driven my sister to the airport, but then, because of a huge snowstorm, I couldn't get back to the meeting Jack Newfield and company were having at Norman's, when they convinced him to run.

The next day I called him to find out what had happened, and he told me, "Before you say anything, I know you have to support Badillo. You can't support me." He also said, "I double-crossed you," but I felt it was performing at a high level to say he didn't want me to be embarrassed, and he knew I had to support Badillo. But Badillo never forgave him—he's told me that. He made Norman his grudge.

Badillo and I had a good relationship because he was the top Puerto Rican in the U.S. and was then the Bronx borough president. He wasn't typical in terms of the stereotype Puerto Rican. He was tall, he was white, he was articulate, and he'd been married twice, both times to non-Hispanics. But he has never

With Campaign Manager Joe Flaherty at Coney Island.

forgiven Mailer, because he thinks Mailer cost him his defeat. I don't believe it; the numbers don't prove it. But with Herman the numbers are not clear proof. What he insists is that more people would have voted for him if they thought he had a good chance to win, but then when Norman came in they thought it would splinter their vote, so they went with Wagner.

FANNY SCHNEIDER MAILER   Running for mayor was a mistake, and I told him, "You don't understand all the spiteful things people do to someone who's running for mayor. You don't need that. That's the last thing in the world you need. Your mind doesn't work as mean as these people are, they're going to take advantage." We didn't really have words about it, it was just that I expressed my opinion. And I figured it's a losing fight, because he doesn't know all of the underhanded things you have to do as a politician, the disagreeable things you have to think up to win out. I said, "It's not a clean business. You don't work that way. You won't do well."

Also, I took it for granted that Breslin was riding on Norman's coattails. But even though Breslin was a mistake, it wouldn't have made any difference in the outcome, and frankly, I didn't want Norman to be elected. I figured it would ruin him. He wasn't following what was good for him. He just liked the thought of being a candidate. He wanted to be a leader, to have the sense of authority and power. He wouldn't misuse that power because he was sincere in wanting to help the city, but it wouldn't do him any good. . . . He was naïve. He didn't act mature in understanding what would be demanded of him. He always aimed high, but it's different in his books because that's his genius. He doesn't have a mean, conniving plan in his head at any time against anybody, he just doesn't, so he never realized what that world was all about. Barney didn't express what he felt about it in so many words, maybe because he himself would've liked the idea of power, but he didn't want Norman to lose any prestige either.

JOE FLAHERTY   Norman is a rabbi in the sense that he really believes that if you come out with the right ideas, you'll prevail. He's also a patriot in the best sense of the word, a Paul Revere on horseback, and he was having a love affair with what he presumed was the decency of the New York electorate. He always appealed to the best in people and thought they would respond in kind. I had no such illusions, which didn't make me any smarter, just more bitter, but Norman's premise sustained him throughout the campaign, unlike Breslin, who, I thought, ran the race on one leg at best, cynical and hedging his bet. My heart was much more with Mailer, because he gambled like a Dostoevsky character, a bit of a fucking fool, if one would have it. Lost, but took your heart with it.

TOM QUINN   I was working for a money-management firm, commuting 110,000 miles yearly back and forth between New York and the West Coast, when I called him and said, "Gee, I'm really disappointed that you didn't ask me to be comptroller." It was just a joke, but at the time he was furious with Breslin because Jimmy was doing his slob routine, never showing up to campaign, so

"I never saw him pander. The constant liberal talk about people being shaped by their environment, he thought that was the last liberal robbery. It took away people's souls, the line that blacks had no chance coming out of the slums."

suddenly the notion must have appealed to him. The way I figured it, it must have occurred to him: What the hell, all these fat Irishmen look alike anyway. If I'm up making a speech and Quinn's sitting in the background, half the people won't notice that it's not Breslin. That was the only reason he asked me—I really think so.

But there was the problem of the required number of signatures to get me on the ballot—25,000 or 50,000 signatures. The campaign was already two weeks old, so it was really out of the question. More important, I remember standing there at Mailer's bay window looking over at Wall Street. He had gone off somewhere, and I was saying, "Okay, pal, this is it, really. Enough. You had a wonderful time. Even if they can somehow get you into this thing, don't." Here I had driven myself crazy, one foot in Wall Street, one foot in Madison Square Garden, one foot in the Lion's Head, one foot in the literati, one foot in the movies. How the hell was I going to get anything done? I'm working out of California, where those guys haven't heard of Louis L'Amour, let alone Norman Mailer. I'm gonna try to explain to them that I'll be commuting between L.A. and New York, running for comptroller of the city of New York with Jimmy Breslin and Norman Mailer?

GLORIA STEINEM   I'd promised Jimmy Breslin that while I wouldn't run for comptroller—which he wanted me to do but which frightened me because I'd never spoken in public before—I'd help with the campaign. This was when Breslin had first been approached by Norman, and I think he wanted to make sure who else would be involved. I remember him taking me off to a bar near *New York* magazine, and there was the implication that he was worried about Norman as a running mate. About that time Tom Quinn came in.

I never considered it a serious effort in the sense they'd win, but I thought it was a creative way of inserting ideas into the campaign. Later on I saw a lot of flakes involved. Norman seemed to have a penchant for surrounding himself with substantially less experienced, less intelligent people than himself providing they had credentials from the sports world or were of another race, black or Puerto Rican, preferably street kids. This prompted me to invite a variety of young people, black and Puerto Rican, but politically smart ones, to a meeting at my house. Norman expressed surprise and kept saying, "Where'd you find these people?"

Basically, you see, he equated the highest and the lowest with the whitest and the blackest. That was his problem and also one of the reasons I left. The same with women. His basic response to women of any race and men of color is that we're close to the earth and have this instinctive knowledge of which he is envious, an instinctive grace or athletic ability or sexual ease, but we don't have his intellect, his sense of strategy, political power, or ability to make things happen. It's not Norman's fault. Norman was born into a society that believes that white men are human beings and everybody else is a "special interest."

The only really hopeless argument I had with him—he was really angry, and there was no resolution—was about a guy who was around all the time, a hanger-on, who, it seemed to me, was using Norman for his own purposes. He'd just beaten up a homosexual in Elaine's in a very unpleasant, sadistic way. I argued that this guy was symbolic of the people who weren't helping the campaign; I told him he deserved better, that he should surround himself with people who had ideas, who would give him guidance rather than hinder him. He defended his friend, though. He said, "I'll be devoted to this guy the rest of my life because I once saw him in a fight, he was getting knocked down again and again, and he kept getting up." I said, "Norman, anybody who's grown up in a poor neighborhood could tell you he should have stayed down." And he never forgave me for that because I had questioned his ethic of what was admirable. I think he'd remember that because it was severe and emblematic of a lot of things.

Still, I can't think of any other woman who was involved with the campaign on a policy level, which maybe shows that I was the only one with poor judgment. I was also fund-raising. I remember going on Jimmy's behalf to collect money from Lawford or one of the Kennedy people—five thousand dollars, I think. There was also a big fund-raiser at some plastic surgeon's house on the East Side. Mary Hemingway and David Merrick were there, and I might have helped with that. Basically my role as fund-raiser was a residue from not having run for comptroller, which was a little ironic, since it seemed to me one didn't need much money to do what we were going to do, namely, publicize ideas. You're out on the street and having press conferences, and of course there were Manso's position papers. I suppose it's inevitable that you get sucked in after a while, but it wasn't that in the beginning.

There was never really a blowup between us. That's not how it ended. I just kept asking myself what was I really doing, was it worth while? Norman and I had dinner at one of those Aegean fish places, and I explained that I thought it was more important for me to be an outside organizer and press contact for the California farm workers' march to the Mexican border. It was a fine, amicable conversation, and then I sort of just drifted away.

JOE FLAHERTY   Everything Mailer had set out to do in his life he'd achieved— the nice Yiddish boy from Brooklyn who went to Harvard, brought in a war novel at twenty-four, stood the world on its ass, had a bevy of beautiful women. He must have thought that if you kick down that much in the ethereal world of the arts, why not take on something as mundane as politics? He was always the risk taker, and the risks had paid off. But don't forget, the more middle-class you get—middle-class in your security, money, tastes, what not—the more you're going to be cut off from experience, and from what I gather, Mailer was never a street kid. He was always the student, and he wanted to escape that. He once wrote, "The last thing I want to be in life is the nice Jewish boy from Brooklyn." Joyce said, "I lived all my life to be a bad Catholic." These bugaboos work on both ends. I think he constantly sought out experiences in both his personal life and in his work in order to break out. I don't think they come naturally, nor do they become natural for any writer, so it was as if he was running for mayor to recharge his batteries. Like running with the blacks when he wanted to do his essays on hip and cool, or getting turned on by meeting cops during the campaign, the new exposure to tough guys on the right.

Still, when he'd weaken at times during the campaign, it was not to play the "orthodox" candidate. He may have told people to cut their hair or shave their beards—I wouldn't shave mine for him, which put me in limbo—but these were only cosmetic things. Otherwise he never made a decision that was a sellout. I heard him take positions that were patently absurd, but I never saw him pander. Malcolm Muggeridge said that he was never a liberal, and that appealed to me in Norman. The constant liberal talk about people being shaped by their environments, for example—we both thought that was the last liberal robbery. It took away people's souls, the line that blacks had no chance coming out of their particular environment.

MIDGE DECTER   Norman P. wrote him a letter and said, "I'm not supporting you," and explained why. He wasn't supporting anybody else, but he was against what Mailer stood for. He didn't think his candidacy was serious, and if it was serious, then it was bad news.

Specifically? Well, I think Norman M.'s a radical—as radical on the right as he is on the left, but I don't call that conservative. When he ran for mayor he advocated all sorts of radical things, actually right-wing radical, if indeed not fascist things. For example, the notion that every neighborhood should be autonomous. He said to Norman P. after the race was over, "People don't understand, you don't understand. I was serious when I was running for mayor."

Or once, sometime later, some lunatic at the Israeli Consulate asked us if we would have an evening for Rabin, the prime minister of Israel, to introduce him to leftist intellectuals so that he could make the case for Israel. I told him it was a dumb idea. The man insisted. So Rabin came to our house with a couple of assistants. Cal Lowell was there, Dwight Macdonald, all the enemies. And Rabin, who's rather a dull fellow, was answering their questions. At one point Mailer said, "Why don't you break off relations with the United States? It's not good for you, it doesn't help you in the world's eyes to be a dependent of the U.S. You guys could probably take on the Russians." Well, I know Hebrew, and Rabin was incredulous. He turned to one of his assistants next to him and asked, "Is this man serious?" The night was a disaster.

DIANA TRILLING   Norman ran for mayor, I suppose, because he wanted to make a statement about the modern consciousness. But being mayor of New York means you have to know about collecting the garbage, keeping the transportation going, getting your share of state and federal funds, learning how to allocate your money among the variety of clamoring factions, each of them representing an important vote, and, my God, none of that is a metaphor.

Take the university uprisings of '67 to '69 or, at any rate, the one at Columbia in '68, which I knew best. Dwight Macdonald was all for it; he said it was a way of "shoving society." That's a figure of speech. But it wasn't shoving society, it was shoving a university, and that's a different thing and no figure of speech. Universities are actual and fragile. In addition, they are among the very best things we have in our faulty world, and they're still profoundly showing the damage they suffered in the disturbances. It was a grievous and irresponsible thing to ruin a university in order to make a statement about society, and just so, you don't run for mayor in order to make a statement about the modern consciousness. You could ruin or at least harm a whole city for the sake of that poem.

The trouble with Norman—and, heaven knows, he's not alone in this—is that he doesn't know what he wants to do in action and what he wants to do as a writer in terms of metaphor. It's one of the central problems in his kind of writing, much worse even than it was for D. H. Lawrence. He doesn't know where the practical universe and the universe of figurative language meet or do not meet, should not meet.

ROGER DONOGHUE   Jesus, the Village Gate fund-raiser for Norman's campaign was a disaster. The only person who didn't think so was Tommy Quinn.

JOSE TORRES   The Village Gate thing! Norman was dead drunk and told the worst fucking jokes I ever heard in my life, like the cunt joke, which had a sophisticated woman next to me stuttering. That's the worst I'd ever seen my friend Mailer.

HAROLD CONRAD   Kenneth Tynan was there, and Norman insulted the shit out of him, told him to get the hell out. That's when Breslin and everybody got pissed off. It happens over and over again, yet with the right kind of direction, combined with his reputation, he could've been the darling of the press. He's a rebel, always was. He knows what he *thinks* he's doing, but he's not always right. The Gate thing was like the Liston thing in Chicago: some harebrained scheme came out of alcohol and he thought he'd seen the light.

PETE HAMILL   Maybe the process of running from one joint to another turns your head into mush, but what I heard was that halfway through the campaign Norman began to take things very seriously, actually thought he had a shot, and I think what happened was he worried too much about style instead of what he was talking about. The object should have been to bring in ideas, particularly when he was in those debates with the other candidates, which was a chance for him to show the difference, to show what a really intelligent candidate could be like, somebody who didn't go by the conventions. But he didn't. He got jogged a lot, and then they hit themselves in the head with the fuckin' microphone that night down at the Village Gate. I wasn't there, but I think Breslin's line was "I found out I'm running with Ezra Pound."

JOE FLAHERTY   Maybe in most artists there's a self-destructive bent, and it was almost as if he walked in and suddenly felt a lack of courage. These were the people he was supposed to win over, and I have the feeling he thought, I can never win them. So the only answer was to fall back on his worst self and become boorish—"Before you reject me, I'll tell you a cunt joke"—that sort of thing, or telling them about their tight little anuses. It was one of his few failures of will, as if he was reverting to the Brooklyn kid. "I'll never own you even though I move among you," and the defense is "I'm going to be so obscene, so unsightly, you're not going to have a chance to reject me or refuse me a check for my campaign." It's done without wit or grace, and I think he damages himself psychically. And he was ravaged by it the next day. He was crushed, sitting stunned in a chair, tears in his eyes. I'm making an analogy: Even though he hadn't consumed that much alcohol, it was as if he had a DTs kind of hangover and was shattered by what he'd done.

HAROLD CONRAD   Things also seemed pretty bad with Beverly. I was out with them at a restaurant, and a smart-ass black guy was trying to make her, so Norman wrestled him, and the guy went down. He was a real nasty black guy, but he's lying there, so I put my hand down to help him up. Norman says, "What are you helping that cocksucker for?" I'd gotten him about a foot off the ground and just let go, which got a chuckle out of Norman. But he was still pissed at Beverly, like it was her fault, so the two of us got into a cab, leaving her to go her own way.

FANNY SCHNEIDER MAILER   During the campaign Beverly just wasn't around. I don't know where she was, but I had to come every day from my office to cook dinner for Michael and Stephen. She knew how much I wanted the boys to have a good meal, so she just put it in my lap.

JOE FLAHERTY   What surprised me about Beverly during the campaign was that she was coming on as a health-food enthusiast. She was always screaming about the air. One day one of their kids was throwing up. I'd diagnosed it as the flu, but she was going on and on—"It's the fucking air! Look at the air outside!"

One night we were all at a bar near Madison Square Garden, a place owned by Quinn and Hamill, that group. We'd gone to a fight after campaigning, and Beverly was flying in from Florida. One of the campaign people picked her up and brought her to the saloon. Obviously she'd had a couple of drinks on the plane, and we were no better. Boudini Brown, Ali's mentor, had been baiting Norman, breaking his balls, taunting him about the mayoralty with race put-downs, and when Beverly came in he became that kind of flirtatious southern black to the southern white girl, and it was all bad vibes. I've hung out in enough bars to know when a scene is about to go down, so I got them out of there, saying, "It's been a rough day, we've had some rocky press, let's go."

Our driver was some young college kid. I was in the front, Norman and Beverly in the back, yelling and screaming all the way to Brooklyn. Here was the poor child's chance to get next to the modern Scott and Zelda, and they're sounding like Archie and Edith Bunker. Norman went into his lament in his broad southern accent: "Ah bin workin' my ass off all over the streets of New York, Ah been here, shakin' my tail, gettin' shit upon by the press. You tell 'er, Flaherty, you always fuckin' Dutch-uncle me, you bully. Now you tell 'er. She shows up, the candidate's wife, half drunk." Then he says to Beverly, "You ain't doin' shit in the campaign. You come into that bar, that motherfucker is puttin' me down, and you're jive-ass. Don' you know he's fuckin' Satan, he's the devil?" He's going on and on, and the poor kid in the front seat, his eyes are popping. Finally I say, "Norman, would you calm down?" He's reduced her to sobs. We arrive at the house and I get out, furious. But then he tried to make up. "What's wrong?" he asked, still in the southern motif.

Now there's this strange transformation. Out of this domestic fight they're both trying to woo me. He says, "You're always kickin' mah ass, everyone in the campaign says you never leave me alone. Now, ah'm jus' askin' you to kick her ass for showin' up drunk in public and fuckin' around."

I finally said, "Fuck you, fuck the press. If there's one thing I hate, Mailer, it's a bully. You reduced this woman to tears for no good reason. We were out drinking too. Who's going to report us? James Reston is gonna be in a fight saloon?"

He says, "You don' understand, ah bin workin'—"

"We've all been working," I said. "This kid driving us doesn't even have a place to sleep. I'm tired of your 'working' . . ."

He was horrified by my outburst because it was really felt. "Well, Joe," he said, "you don't understand what probably triggered my anger. I love this woman, but the one fucking thing I can't stand about her is that goddamn rebel accent!"

It was so absurd I fell on the hood of the car in laughter.

He says, "What are you laughing about?"

I said, "That fucking corn-pone accent just drives the shit out of me too."

Even so, they still didn't realize what was so funny. They'd played this game of Big Daddy and Maggie the Cat so many times they weren't aware of it. So Norman says, "Come upstairs, you could stand another draft," and Beverly is cooing, "You're upset, Joe. Come up." I swear to Christ, they took me up, poured me a couple of belts of first-rate whiskey, and now they're holding hands. I'm sure they went to bed and fucked their brains out, but I'm sitting there looking at them and thinking, Am I going crazy? When I went downstairs the poor kid was waiting, and he had that look—If this is the adult world, you people can stick it up your ass. I'm going back to college.

Beverly had gained weight, but certain women reach a degree where they look Ekbergesque. Beverly wasn't yet soft fat, just kind of hard, farm-girl heavy. She wasn't around that much, except at parties or the night we were on TV—Mailer/Breslin, live on Channel 11. It was a disaster, but afterwards she came over to me and said, "At least Norman wasn't plastic." "Neither was Disraeli," I said, and walked out.

That appearance was similar to other times I've seen him on television, like the time he walked out from the Green Room with a glass in his hand, and I turned off the set. On the other hand, when he rose to the occasion, when he was being baited, there were never better moments in the campaign. The one time I remember was when he gave his speech at *Time-Life*. He was dazzling. There was a history of *Time-Life* people baiting him, and, of course, he was constantly screaming about "Luce morals" and "*Time* cancer." He could've gone in drunk, saying "Fuck you, you don't even sign your articles"—whatever—but instead he took the high ground and creamed the joint. That's the one time I had the feeling that across the board—from my mother to cab drivers to the guys in the Melody Lane Bowling Alley—they would've all listened, and we could've won. He soared. He took you to the gates of heaven, as if he could say, "I've got the ear of the Lord." He let you know what was possible. That day I had this mad fantasy of kidnapping Mailer and for the rest of the campaign never letting him out but just replaying a tape of that *Time-Life* speech.

Once during the campaign Norman warned us about reporters who would try to interview his mother, condemning them as trappers and leeches. He was furious about a piece someone had done for *The Times* on mothers of famous sons. Mrs. Mailer had been interviewed, and there was a quote from her saying that Norman was "precocious." Norman bellowed at us, "My mother never used the word 'precocious' in her life."

I also knew about Barney's gambling because Breslin told me that Barney used to use Fat Thomas, a pal of his, as his bookie. This might be an apocryphal story, one of Jimmy's golden oldies, but he said he once brought Fats with him to meet Norman, and Barney was there and looked in shocked horror when Fats walked into the apartment. According to Breslin, Barney thought he was coming to collect.

The night of our defeat there was a party at the Plaza, Norman had rented a suite, and the two of us went into the bedroom alone. I told him, "You gave it your best shot. You were totally honest." But he still had the naïve sense that

With running mate, columnist Jimmy Breslin, conceding defeat, June 18, 1969.

we'd just missed a couple of tricks—maybe it was the Gate, maybe something else. That's the nice side of Mailer, his absolute belief in America, his romance with the American people. He never understood that unless you're some packaged shit lawyer they don't take you seriously. But "naïve" puts him in the realm of *shmuck*, and I don't mean that. He was a romantic, and even as the returns were coming in he was looking for reasons—the Village Gate, the Newfield interview with Mary McGrory, when Jack got his jollies comparing Norman to Ezra Pound. He was looking for all those things that chipped away his credibility, but he never had the conception of what people perceived as a candidate, even though I'd thought that the disastrous *Daily News* polls would've brought that home to him. He just never realized that the electorate wasn't going to perceive us as anything but writers.

He was deflated and dejected, not angry. Our only concern was Procaccino, that maybe we'd forced the worst possible scenario on the city. And also Badillo. Badillo ran a close third, and Norman said, "We're going to be crucified, we're going to be blamed for taking away the votes Badillo needed to win." And to this day Herman still blames Norman for that loss.

But never in my life did I think we could've won. From the day we started I thought we were going to get our ass kicked, but I also thought we would ventilate the party, put ideas on the town, give them some light. I felt we were sending a message: "You motherfuckers aren't going to get away with it any more. We're going to have somebody after you, regardless if it's a Mailer or somebody else, who's going to snap at your heels, call you buffoons, assholes, embarrass you with witticisms, insights, ideas, and expose you for what you are."

NORMAN MAILER (OF A FIRE ON THE MOON) *It was a decade so unbalanced in relation to previous American history that Aquarius, who had begun it by stabbing his second wife in 1960, was to finish by running in a Democratic Primary for Mayor of New York....*

He was so guilty a man that he thought he would be elected as a fit and proper punishment for his sins. Still, he also wanted to win. He would never write again if he were Mayor (the job would doubtless strain his talent to extinction) but he would have his hand on the rump of History, and Norman was not without such lust.

He came in fourth in a field of five, and politics was behind him.... He had in fact been left with a huge boredom about himself. He was weary of his own voice, own face, person, persona, will, ideas, speeches, and general sense of importance.

EDWARD "EDDIE" BONETTI   They were arguing a lot the summer after the campaign, when he was doing the moonshot book, after he'd come back from Houston. He was in a rage, dispirited, overweight. After seven weeks of campaigning he hadn't caught his breath, and Beverly was fucking that French kid whom I didn't like at all.

In *Of a Fire on the Moon* he says we went to one of the better, more respectable restaurants, which it wasn't. It was the Governor Prence, essentially a tourist trap. Nor was I as drunk as he says. We had a bet that I couldn't get through dinner without using the word "fuck," but I didn't feel there was any put-down in his saying I was betting money my wife had earned as a waitress. I just felt he was hostile and preoccupied, that there was something burning in the back of his brain. He was working on a book he couldn't resolve, and he knew it. He just packed it up in the end with the stuff about Provincetown and burying the car. He later told me, "I wish I hadn't written all that stuff in the end. I didn't need it. I had to pad it."

Still, that evening was memorable. We went out from the Prence to the Coachman to hear Anita O'Day, and our banter continued. He and Beverly were going at each other in spurts—some joviality for a while, then the mood would change and they'd look at each other with hatred. We saw the show and went back to his house, where we got drunk. Beverly and my wife Kay were inside, and Norman and I were standing out in the street with a bottle—Jim Beam, which was what he used to drink then. At one point he says, "Eddie, you're either a genius or the biggest phony to come down the pike." Then he turned around and walked into the house. I'll never forget it.

JACK KEARNEY   In the late sixties Provincetown was really in the vanguard of "happenings." It was all very loose, spontaneous, and playful, and the first real happening was when I made a huge yellow metal woman riding a bicycle. I was doing a lot of kinetic sculpture then, welded steel and electric motors, and I was going to wheel it—*The Emancipated Woman* she was called—down Commercial Street, to put on the lawn at the Chrysler Museum. It was about eight feet tall, and the figure had a small washing machine motor in her left hand, which was driving her through the navel, and her boobs would swing in opposite directions. Chrysler wanted it on the lawn so the public could play with the

Beverly's Citroen, the summer of 1969, Provincetown.

electric button. It was so big we couldn't get it in a car, though, so we had to get a police escort down Commercial Street, which became a carnival, with hundreds of kids and adults trailing after us. We got to the lawn with this huge entourage, set the thing up, and an elderly woman in her seventies stuck her head out of the upper window of the house next door—she was wearing an old-fashioned nightcap and a long flannel sleeping robe and was screaming down at us, "That goddamn thing—shut it off. My television won't work!"

Another "happening" came about because Beverly wanted me to make a piece of sculpture out of her old Citroën. I detected a little spark in Norman's eye at that moment, and we had the car towed from Hyannis to the Provincetown Auto Body Shop, where I told them to cut the motor and frame away, leaving the body and everything smashable off to one side. About fifteen people showed up, and we smashed it with a thirty-ton bulldozer. The bulldozer operator got into the spirit of the thing and made a speech, something to the effect of "On this auspicious occasion, with all these dignitaries present, I consider it a great honor to crush this car." It was always that way—everybody got involved. Like the Florsheims were there—Dick, now deceased, and Helen—and even though they were rather conservative they were in the thick of it too, enjoying it like a festival.

When the bulldozer had flattened the Citroën, though, we cut it up into pieces and gave them away to friends; pieces are probably still hanging on walls all over town. The two rear fender guards, the skirts around the wheels, had popped off, and I immediately realized they were shaped like the pointed head of Charles de Gaulle. At that time de Gaulle, in an outburst of patriotism, had just prevented Fiat of Italy from taking over the Citroën Company, so I proceeded to make a de Gaulle caricature out of the fenders.

We mounted it on a steel post on the deck at 565, and to our astonishment it would turn in the wind. Norman was in Houston for the moonshot, I was putting ball bearings on it when he phoned, and Beverly called down from the third floor, "Norman wants to know what you're doing with his de Gaulle."

"Tell him I'm putting it on ball bearings to make it turn like a weathervane."

She yelled back, "Pick up the phone. He wants to tell you something."

Norman says, "Boy, you could make the best fucking ball bearings on the moon because the moon is a perfect vacuum. Think about that, why don't you?"

I said, "Right. I forgot you were an engineer before becoming a writer."

But the smashing of Beverly's car was what led to the biggest happening that summer, the one that served as the conclusion to *Of a Fire on the Moon*. Danny

Banko had wanted me to take his car and do something with it like I'd done to Beverly's. "The car's about to croak," he said, and my response was, "Why don't we bury it if it's dead?" I told him we should get a bunch of guys, dig a hole, and put it in his backyard.

Norman was fascinated. As he said in *Of a Fire on the Moon*, "My friends in Provincetown would take a lawn mower apart to make a salad." Which really says it all. The car burial became a protest against lousy craftsmanship. Word spread like wildfire, and at the appointed hour three hundred people showed up. We passed the hat and got a lot of beer. The only problem was that we had only three shovels, so we were having a hell of a time digging a big enough hole. Somebody got the idea of hiring a backhoe, phoned, and found out that it would cost seventy-five dollars, so we passed the hat again. Soon, coming over what is now Suzanne Sinaiko's orchard was this snorting monster, what looked like a dinosaur, and everybody cheered.

The problem was that every time the backhoe hit the water level the hole would fill up, and it kept getting wider and wider but no deeper. After a great debate we all decided that a half-buried car was better than a no-buried car. Danny drove the Ford up on the lawn, coming in like Napoleon, and he wanted to drive it into the hole. I talked him out of that, and instead we pushed the car in backwards. A mighty cheer went up. Then suddenly, as the car began to settle at its weird angle, something happened on the dashboard and the windshield wipers went on, and everybody shouted, "It's not dead yet!" So we had to kill it, and then we had the benedictions: Heaton Vorse was wearing biblical robes and he read from *Scriptures for the Dead*, Victor Manso, Peter's brother, intoned some lines from Virgil, and then Eddie Bonetti, otherwise known as "Bonzo the Poet," showed up in a striped mechanic's costume carrying a great crescent wrench. He made the sign of the cross with it over the car, chanting, "Ashes to ashes, and dust to dust. If obsolescence don't get you, attrition must."

NORMAN MAILER (OF A FIRE ON THE MOON) *Aquarius was in a depression which would not lift for the rest of the summer, a curious depression full of fevers, forebodings, and a general sense that the century was done—it had ended in the summer of 1969. . . .*

His wife and he were getting along abominably. . . . She was an actress who now did not work. An actress who does not work is a maddened beast. His lovely Pisces, subtle at her loveliest as silver, would scream on nights of the full moon with a voice so loud she sounded like an animal in torment. They were far and away the noisiest house on the street . . .

[During the burial of Banko's car] Aquarius watched his wife at the other end of the lawn and knew . . . that their marriage was over . . . He broke up with [her] on Labor Day night . . . In the morning, after a night of no sleep, he was on a plane to Houston.

CHARLIE BROWN I know her career was a big issue in the divorce, and I want to be fair-minded about it, but I think those two were made for each other. I don't know when things came to an impasse, but she would have continued to hang around and put up with most anything if Norman had just suffered her. She wasn't keen on his running for mayor. She was very overweight, and begged him to come up to Provincetown for the summer, to give up the moonshot book, and probably during the campaign itself she was frightened of losing him. She certainly was afterwards, in July and August, when he was at Cape Canaveral and then in Houston.

Carol Stevens wasn't the only woman Norman was fucking—there was some stewardess in there Beverly told me about. But then over the summer she started fucking that twerp Philipe, the French kid. She was such a jerk. She could've done so much better than that; she could've made Norman jealous if she'd wanted to. She didn't have to pull that shit. I hated that kid. I used to have visions of my fist going into the guy's face, turning him into putty. I hated everything about him. What he was really getting off on was fucking Norman Mailer's wife.

I was in and out of P-Town all summer, and she was becoming unraveled, irrational. Just the way she would talk about what was gonna happen in her career—"I'm going back to do this and this, and I'll show him." Then in the fall she told me about her affair with François Cevert, the Grand Prix driver, Jackie Stewart's teammate. She met him at the Watkins Glen Grand Prix, and I'm sure she imagined she'd go off to Paris, the whole bit. But she had only four or five days with him total. She went down to Mexico to join him, but then he explained that his fiancée was arriving the next day. What a sucker. Beverly sometimes doesn't think clearly. She never did.

JOSE TORRES   Norman called me up—I was either in New York or Puerto Rico—to ask my advice. He often confessed very personal stuff to me, and he said he was having trouble with Beverly. I said, "I'm from a different culture, Norman. I'm too strict with women. I can have twenty girls, but my wife with another man—no way."

He'd told me right away, saying, "I told her to take a trip with him to find out if she's really in love."

"Norman, what kind of bullshit is this?" I said. "I don't care what happens. When she comes back, as a friend of yours I'll never see her, never talk to her again. Don't blame him. It's her. If she intended to cheat on you, you can't trust her."

He said, "Well..."

"Norman, we're different. You may feel she's right because you had girl friends. But with me that doesn't matter."

SANDY CHARLEBOIS THOMAS   She knew what she was getting into when she married him, no question. But the fall after the campaign Norman went back to Houston and Beverly got involved with that race car driver. That's how I came to type Of a Fire on the Moon. She called me and said, "I'm going to the Mexican Grand Prix. Roberta Swafford, the housekeeper, is here, but I don't know her well, so will you come and help with the kids?" Which is what I did, staying out in Brooklyn and typing for Norman after he'd returned, when I'd go back and forth to Provincetown.

He was still in the midst of his affair with Carol, which had been going on for years. There was another tomato in there somewhere too, but that fall Carol came to dinner at 565 Commercial, and Norman's aunt and uncle from South Africa were there too. He'd known Carol for years, from when she was a jazz singer. He'd told me about her long before she showed up on the scene: "There's this woman I was involved with—"

While Beverly was away in Mexico he was coming apart, though. Carol was visiting off and on, and at some point when he and I were alone he said, "The funny thing about all this is that I'm probably going to grow old alone."

BARBARA PROBST SOLOMON   I'm sure Norman was upset when the marriage was coming apart. In '66, even though I'd been living with other men, I went bananas when Harold, my husband, wanted a divorce. Norman said, "You're like me; it has nothing to do with living with somebody else. You think marriages are forever, and your whole universe crumbles when that structure is shaken."

What he was saying was that marriage had to be central, and he said he remembered how I'd cried when Bea and he got divorced. He said people think it's the writing of books that is central, but they're wrong—which of course is totally contrary to what most people perceive in him. . . . That's why he said I had a total right to be hysterical, that it was a perfectly normal reaction. He argued with my family that they shouldn't have me hospitalized. Everybody felt I hadn't a leg to stand on, but what struck him was that my reaction was reasonable—you make a pact that somebody is going to be your savior for life, and, indeed, you come to depend on it. In his case the real marriages were Bea, Adele, and Beverly. Barbara once said that she thought the trouble with Norman was that he tended to overinvest his wives with what he wanted them to be— in effect, that he idealized them. And here too there's a lot of misunderstanding, because however sympathetic to his own sex, he recognizes that divorce can be equally shattering for the woman.

SANDY CHARLEBOIS THOMAS   Norman told me, "This is one fence you won't be able to straddle," and what he was saying was that I had to choose between him and Beverly. I continued to see Beverly, though, and I saw him too. He did the same thing with Eddie Bonetti. Eddie refused to agree to his terms, saying that Beverly was also a friend of his.

But I always thought that his relationship with Beverly was one of the great love affairs of the world. There was a strong bond, a real attachment, which is why the disattachment was so agonizing for both of them. It's been harder for her, though. He's found a replacement and all the cards are on his side of the table. She didn't fuck around before Philipe, and he was obviously out of the question, really harmless. She should have cut loose much earlier.

The number of things Beverly didn't know, though, it's pretty incredible. She really thought that the house in P-Town that he bought in '66 was in her name. I'm the one who went to Town Hall and had to tell her it wasn't. That was when they were separating, after she came back from Mexico. In a way it was probably Norman's figure of speech. He told me that when he and Adele had a house in Connecticut it drove him nuts to deal with maintenance, so when Beverly wanted a house he said, "Okay, but it's yours. You take care of it and it's your house." That's what he said; he told me he'd said it, and she told me too. So she always believed the house was hers, only she didn't take care of it. When the bills came—like the tax bill—they went straight to Barney.

JOHN LEONARD   In 1969 I was coming back from the University of Pennsylvania and found myself getting on the Metroliner in the Philadelphia train station. It was midnight. Mailer was in the luxury car and, to my astonishment, he recognized me. I think he was tired, yet he wanted to be expansive and didn't have anybody to talk to. "Sit down, I'll buy you a drink," he said, and then spent a lot of time looking at me, waiting for me to ask the interesting question, whatever it was, which I didn't. Soon we started talking about Barbary Shore, and he explained his feeling that he wouldn't know how to finish it even today. He was at his best, setting out to charm me, which he did quite successfully. He'd been around the country, had a lot of luggage, including a briefcase full of the manuscript of Of a Fire on the Moon, and I was privileged to carry it. It was snowing as we were looking for a cab outside Penn Station, and he said, "If you're mugged, you die before giving that up, because there's no other copy."

X:
THE
PRISONER
OF SEX
AND
MARILYN
(1970-75)

<u>DOTSON RADER</u> After he and Beverly had split up, Marion Javits gave a party at her Park Avenue apartment. Norman came in with a tall woman—taller than him—whom he introduced as a model. She had very thick, dark hair and was Semitic-looking, with a bobbed nose and big nostrils. Rather common-looking, but the most noticeable thing about her were her legs. Norman would say "Kick," and she would kick all the way up to her shoulder and knock the drink out of your hand. This amused Norman immensely, and she did it several times that night, and once later at the Whitney Museum.

In any case, Norman was later sitting in the living room having a kind of desultory political conversation with Senator Javits. He wasn't getting any re-action, so I sat down next to him, and we started talking. He wanted to know what was going on in SDS and the antiwar movement. Of course he'd already written *The Armies of the Night*, and while I wouldn't say he was naïve, he'd had only a glimmering of the factionalism on the left. Also, he was only just coming to the question of the connection between the Vietnam War and the uprisings in the cities, between Vietnam and the Hispanics and blacks at home. Our conversation, therefore, turned to "The Days of Rage," which had taken place the year before in October. I had been there and broken with SDS over the Weathermen, and he wanted to know what had happened.

I had first gotten involved in SDS when I was an undergraduate at Columbia and had attended the SDS conference at Princeton, although I had also been involved in the civil rights movement. But in '68 I'd also begun to have a sense of the totalitarian aspects of the New Left. My first impression of this occurred when we took over the buildings at Columbia. I was in the mathematics building, renamed "The Red Chameleon," which was where Tom Hayden was, and two days before the bust came we had a big debate about what we were going to do. The crazies, Mark Rudd and the others who ended up as Weathermen, were debating whether to stockpile gasoline; the jocks, the straights who were against the occupation, were threatening to take over Low Library, and there were people who were pushing to burn the place down. They also wanted to burn Mathematics Hall when the police attacked, and I suddenly realized I was in the midst of a bunch of people who had lost their minds.

Then in October about four or five hundred of us ended up in a Lutheran church in Evanston in connection with "The Days of Rage." We were kept up day after day, night after night, without any sleep, listening to one harangue after another. The paranoia grew and grew, and the talk went further and further into terrorism. People were standing up and making the most insane proposals: that we arm ourselves, get bombs and Molotov cocktails, and blow up the Cook County jail, because they had arrested people. If anyone stood up to raise an objection, someone would start shouting "Pig! *Provocateur!*"

Rudd had become a sort of generalissimo at that point. He had a "blood" bodyguard, a number of whom I thought were practically mentally retarded thugs, who'd given pledges in blood that they would die before they'd let Mark's person be attacked. They were the KGB of our little gathering. At one point a hysterical girl got up and pointed at a twenty-year-old black fellow and said, "He's an undercover agent." Other people joined in, Rudd's bodyguards dragged him away down to the church basement, while the rest of us sat there for three or four hours listening to the screams of this poor pigeon being tortured. The consensus was that he shouldn't be "offed"—that was the terminology then— but knocked unconscious, tied up, and put in the trunk of the car, driven over the state line into Indiana, and dumped in a cornfield. Which was exactly what was done. The irony is that it turned out the guy actually was an undercover agent, but all I could think of listening to him scream was, here were white middle-class revolutionaries, acting in the name of the oppressed, tormenting a black. That's effectively when I got out of the Movement. The remnants of the split in SDS, whom I sort of tailed along with, just went up to Chicago the next day and toured through the Loop smashing windows.

JERRY RUBIN In January 1970 Norman testified at the "Chicago Seven" trial— mainly, I think, for Abbie and me. This was in connection with the '68 Dem- ocratic convention, of course, and we'd gone over the whole thing the night before, with Norman being coached by Bill Kunstler, because Bill wouldn't let a big fish be handled by anybody else. In those days Bill wasn't an ideologue. He was still discovering, we were pushing him, and, like Norman, he was middle-class.

Norman was on the stand maybe three hours, and like everything else with him, you put something in, it always comes out better. He described us as satirists of society, that what we were doing was theater of the absurd. He said, "They're not criminals, they're not irrational, they're good people who believe in America and who think America's gone wrong and want to alert people." Every sentence was quotable. Like *The Armies of the Night*, it was a statement of what the Movement was all about. He sanitized us—which was exactly what the lawyers wanted. He presented us as theorists, people with a philosophy.

There was also the father thing there, that we were the children of Norman Mailer's writings. In '65 the father figure had come out and said, "I approve of you." In '66 he was challenged by Emmett Grogan. Norman probably did a macho thing, but Abbie told me that Emmett had one-upped him. I said to Abbie, "What is this, one-upping Norman Mailer? So he doesn't say stealing is right. Okay, so we're hipper than Mailer, hipper than our father, so what?" Then came *The Armies of the Night*, and father says, "Hey, these people have something to say, they're going to influence the future of our country." And when he testified he told the jury, in effect, "I may be crazy, but I'm a writer. These people are a little crazy too, but it's the crazy people who tell you where sanity lies. Listen to them, their craziness has the ring of truth."

JOE FLAHERTY After the campaign I'd told Norman and Jimmy I wanted to do a book. Both of them said, "Go ahead," but then when I sent Norman the galleys I got reports that he was upset with it. Finally he called me at the Lion's Head, I think from Provincetown, and said, "I'll be quite honest—I was furious with your book, but many of my friends who've read it say it's wonderful." He thought I'd had a little too much fun with it, that I should have given the campaign more portent, but then he said, "I guess they're right. But did you have to tell everything?"

"I thought I told everything on everybody," I replied.

Suddenly his voice softened: "Why were you so harsh about yourself and your personal life?" (I'd discussed fighting alcoholism and my first marriage breaking up.) And I said, "I was going through a bad period, and that affected the campaign."

"Take it out," he said. "We paid you no money and we abused you."

I said I wouldn't feel comfortable doing that, but then he said, "Well, would you take something out for me?" Immediately I think, Uh-oh.

"You've got me crying the day after the Gate performance..."

You see, the next day when we went to his house and he realized how bad it had been, I was raging at him: "I don't give a fuck about the liberal money types who've got their noses up their ass and walked out. But it was the first time your workers"—meaning the kids, the troops up on Fifty-seventh Street—"had a chance to get near you. You ignored them. They were looking forward to this, and it should've been their evening." He said, "Oh, it wasn't that bad," but I recounted it, and as I did, tears came to his eyes. "We fucked it, we blew it." And then, of course, I liked him again and felt like a shit, and I said, "No, we'll bring it back."

But then, reading the galleys, he said, "You have me crying there, then you also have me with tears in my eyes when we're driving down Queens Boulevard and I got angry at the shoddy housing. So I sound like a crybaby."

I said I'd take out the tears on Queens Boulevard, adding "And?" "Nothing more," he said, "but I want to say something to you. All the time I said I went into this only to run for mayor, I said I'd never write about it. But you know writers—it was always in the back of my head that somewhere I'd use the material. Now I have no need to do it. You did." Then *my* eyes filled with tears. He said, "It's a fucking tough, honest book. Look, when's the pub party? I'll be down." I was ecstatic. The only other attempt to change something was his suggestion that I could make more of the ending. I said, "No. The opening paragraph says only a fool makes drama where there is none."

So when *Managing Mailer* came out he was fantastic, absolutely super at the publication party at the Lion's Head. He came as he said he would, and naturally he was the star, but when people wanted to talk to him he'd put his arm around me and say, "Hey, this is the guy who wrote the book."

Breslin, though, tried to censor the book by making a deal. He didn't come to the party, but back when the book was in galleys there was a going-away party for him before he went to Ireland. He came up to me and said, "I haven't read the book, but somebody told me there's a mean passage on Adam Walinsky." I said, "Well, Jim, since you haven't read it, I can tell you it's an accurate account of what happened at our meeting with Adam." He said, "I'll tell you what: you take it out and I'll give you some real funny stuff when you weren't traveling with me, stories about the times I fucked up. I'll be the buffoon." You see, he was worried about the Kennedy throne if Walinsky was knocked, because that was his connection, and he didn't want anything that hurt the throne. I looked at him in horror. "Breslin, three years ago if somebody made the same suggestion about your work, you'd've hit him. Let's drop it before I reach the same conclusion." He was shocked, and I just walked away. Twenty minutes later Jeff Greenfield, another Kennedy princeling, who was at the party with John Lindsay, came up to me and said, "Got the galleys, John loves the book." I said, "Who?" "Lindsay—he loves the book. He'd love to blurb it, but he has one problem: Adam Walinsky was the first Democrat to endorse him, you see, so if you could drop the Walinsky stuff, John'd love to write a big blurb for you." I looked him right in the face and said, "That scumbag couldn't pick up snow in Queens, how's he going to sell my book?"

NORMAN MAILER (THE PRISONER OF SEX) *After a time he thought of himself often as the Prisoner. He did not know why, nor what he was prisoner of. It was simply that his ego did not rise very often these days to the emoluments of the Prizewinner. His mood was nearer to the dungeon. For his battered not-so-firm ego was obliged to be installed in Provincetown through a long winter to go through the double haul of writing a book about the first landing on the moon while remaking himself out of the loss of a fourth wife. It was a winter to offer all the excitement which comes from dredging the liver. He spent cold months of meditation on the rivets that hold a rocket together, and in the late spring of '70, time of deliverance, his long work was done, he went up to Maine with five of his six children (the oldest would be in Europe for the summer) determined to get some idea of what it might be like to raise a family, for it was on this point that his last marriage had begun to wallow, then had sunk: his fourth wife, an actress, had seen her career drown in the rigors of managing so large a home. . . .*

The question therefore was not so much answered as honored by his summer experiment; his ego, at least, was rested. The Prisoner had not contemplated his ego in weeks. He did not have to when his dungarees were dank with the water of pots and he knew at last what a woman meant when she said her hair smelled of grease. In fact, he now possessed an operative definition of remarkable banalities. "The children almost drove me mad" was rich in context to him, and he could hardly have done without the lament of the truly wasted, "I didn't have a thought to myself all day." They were clichés. They were also paving blocks at the crossroads of existence. Who could deny after an experience like his own that all the big questions might just as well originate here.

MIDGE DECTER The idea for *The Prisoner of Sex* came out of a conversation that Norman and I had at a dinner party. I'd been interested in Kate Millett and asked Irving Howe to review *Sexual Politics*, and I was talking about women's lib when Mailer said something like "I oughta write about it." I said, "God, you certainly ought to." Then I dragged Willie Morris in, and we signed Norman up to do his essay, resulting in the biggest-selling issue in the history of *Harper's*.

The trouble at the magazine happened just before the issue came out. It started when Bill Blair, the publisher, wanted to prepare a paragraph for the advertisers in case they were upset by Norman's language. "That's ridiculous," I said. "All we have to say is that this is the major issue facing us now, and Mailer is the major writer in America, and *Harper's* magazine is grateful and proud to have him writing for us." "Would you just write that down on a piece of paper for me?" he said, so I went to the typewriter and wrote some piece of PR bullshit, three sentences long, and gave it to him.

Then there was our mass resignation. But the story that *The Prisoner of Sex* was responsible is nonsense. That's the line Willie sent out to *Newsweek* and *Time*—"the man of business against the man of literature"—and that's what they wanted to hear, so that's what they wrote. But it was all a lie. Willie was in trouble with the ownership over money, over the success of the magazine. Bill Blair had hired some young bullshitter as his assistant, and they began to piss away a lot of money on stupid advertising and promotions. Now, a magazine like *Harper's* cannot make big money, but the owner of the magazine was a dope who had this fantasy about large profits. Willie played his cards very foolishly by agreeing with him, then he got into a fight with Blair over who was responsible for the bad balance sheet and went traipsing off to corporate headquarters in Minneapolis for a showdown, saying, "It's me or him," meaning Blair. They said "Blair." Then he came back and announced, "They're pushing me out on account of Mailer."

But then Mailer bought Willie's story too. Out of what? Vanity? It's irresistible. So Willie stormed off the magazine, like in an hour, went to a bar, and called me down to announce "I'm quitting." He wasn't fired exactly, he was told to fall into line about money, but he'd escalated it to the point where he had nothing left to do but walk out. He told me he was leaving, and I saw the story taking shape when he said, "It's Mailer. That's really why they're doing this to me." Then he told Mailer, and pretty soon everyone else bought the story too. For me not to have walked out would have been the end of me with Mailer as well as the end of my good reputation in the literary world. What was I to do, walk around like the ancient mariner, saying to people, "It's very complicated— please, you don't understand"?

DIANA TRILLING   The Theater for Ideas was organizing a debate for March 31, 1971, and when they called to ask me if I'd speak, they said that every woman they'd asked other than Germaine Greer had refused to be on the same panel with Norman. They regarded him as a male chauvinist pig and they wouldn't give him the opportunity to debate with them. *The Prisoner of Sex* had just been published or was about to be published, and I think it was Mailer who himself originally proposed the evening, but Germaine Greer was set. Her book *The Female Eunuch* was just coming out too, and I accepted with the one condition that I be the last speaker. I realized that Greer was much more the star of the evening than I was and that therefore she should speak last, but those were my terms, and she pleasantly agreed. I wanted to be last because I hadn't the faintest idea of what might be said and I wanted to be able to change my prepared speech if necessary.

But as the evening got closer I saw a piece in *The Village Voice* by Jill Johnston about Greer having helped some poor girl prepare for her first sexual intercourse, apparently getting her into proper shape for a sexual entrance, and I went into a panic. I thought, My God, what am I doing in this company? By that time I knew that Jill was going to be one of the panel too. Lionel was wonderful in that situation. He kept saying, "You are what you are, you'll do what you have to do. Stop worrying about what kind of situation you're in—it won't matter." So tempted though I was to back out, I didn't back out, but I was truly scared. I saw myself as the token straight, the sacrificial lamb of the evening. Maybe Norman had come to see himself that way too, except he was the one who had set the whole thing up.

When I got to the Green Room at Town Hall, there was Norman posing with Greer for the photographers. I thought, What's he doing standing there holding Greer's book up to the cameras? Why should he lend himself to that kind of promotion? When he came over and kissed me hello, I thought this wasn't the man I usually kissed hello. I suddenly didn't like him. Greer looked at me malevolently but never said a word. She was wearing a floozy kind of fox fur that trailed over her shoulder to the floor. It was mangy. I expected moths to fly out of it. Wasn't it Orlovsky—or was it Ginsberg?—who said that if he shaved, the moths would fly out of his beard? Then a little girl from the provinces walked into the Green Room carrying a box containing a gardenia for Norman. It was a token of love; she was offering herself to him. Could anything have been more inappropriate at that moment? And between this little girl and Germaine Greer, the situation was plenty inappropriate for me too. I certainly didn't belong there.

We went out on the stage but we had to wait forever before the curtain could go up. The audience was very restive but we couldn't start because Jill Johnston had disappeared, and when she finally did come back, carrying a paper cup with some kind of weird liquid in it—she kept offering me a sip, but I refused to sip—she announced that she wanted to speak last. She was wearing dungarees, Jackie Ceballos of NOW, the fourth speaker, was wearing a slacks suit with big gold embroidery on it—the trade unionist of the liberation movement with gold embroidery. What a collection we were! Norman said it was all settled that I was to be last. There was good reason Jill had wanted to come at the end, as we later discovered, but Norman prevented that.

I was sitting onstage on one side of Norman, Germaine Greer on the other, and you couldn't miss what was going on between them. She was publicly out to get him, and obviously he was aware of it—how could he not be? He was very self-conscious about it.

I don't buy that avenging-penis talk of his in *The Prisoner of Sex*. What avenger? A penis can go limp—then it's avenging the avenger. Norman should have taken that into account.

Anyway, whatever the embarrassments or complications of his situation with Greer, I didn't feel tender toward him as I ordinarily might because I didn't like the way he was acting to me. We had a much more intimate and trusting relationship than he seemed willing to demonstrate in front of Greer. It was as if he was suddenly casting me in the role of visiting family—something like that—and I didn't like it a bit. I don't like people who treat me differently depending on who's watching.

Finally we began. The curtains opened, and as I looked out over the audience I was blinded by the klieg lights. They were making a movie—something else I hadn't expected. Still, I could see it was a mob. The jet-setters were downstairs at $25 a ticket; I don't remember whether it was $10 or $15 in the balcony. Jammed. Both Adele and Jeanne Campbell were there, but I didn't see Beverly. I don't know how many seats there are in Town Hall, but all week people had been calling me to ask if I could get them in. God, what an evening. I'd of course read Norman's book carefully and written a paper—I never speak in public without writing out my speech. The only ground rule was how much time we each had. It was either fifteen or twenty minutes—I forget which—maybe it was even less.

Ceballos spoke first, Jill second; Greer was third. Jill allowed Germaine to finish, then she put on her show. Two lesbian friends in dungarees charged up the steps from the audience, and all three of them embraced—three pretty solid women embracing with more ardor than aim. The scene had been prepared, but they lost their balance and fell over on the stage, which I don't think had been prepared at all. So then the three just sort of rolled around, off and on each other, hugging and kissing. Norman was furious, and he made the most unbelievable remark I've ever heard. He called to Jill to get up and act like a lady! Could anything have been more perfect? These three lesbians are rolling around on the stage and Norman commands, "Jill, get up and act like a lady!" But actually it was worse than that, because I could sense that he was going to get up and try to pull them apart. I just hissed at him, "Don't touch them!" I don't know if he heard me or not, but he didn't move. If he had laid a hand on one of those women there would've been a riot.

Everybody in the audience had been whooping and cheering all evening, and the yells and shouts had been full of obscenities, most of them directed at Norman. He was on the hot seat, a little rattled, I think, but he managed fairly well. He wasn't boozed. He gave as good as he got, matching obscenity with obscenity—if that's managing well, which I suppose it was. When Jill and her friends were on the stage he said something like "You can get as much prick and cunt as you want around the corner on Forty-second Street for two dollars and fifty cents. We don't need it here"—which was sound enough, but nothing was every effective. Jill and the others, though, finally got tired and walked away. What else was there to do, rip off each other's pants?

JOSE TORRES   I was sitting in the third row, and what got people upset was when the women were hugging on the floor and Norman said, "Hey, c'mon, get out of there. Nobody's come here to see dirty jeans rolling on the floor. If they want to see fucking, they can go to the corner." Then he was booed for calling Betty Friedan "a lady."

DIANA TRILLING   Okay, so now it's time for me to talk, and I read a very serious piece. I'm going along, standing at the podium, but as if I have eyes in the back of my head, I'm perfectly aware that Greer is doing a job of upstaging me. I'd read somewhere that she tried to do it to Hildegarde when they appeared together. Hildegarde had supposedly turned to Greer and said, "I've been upstaged by the best of them. You don't get away with it."

I felt Norman was conspiring in it. Afterwards my friends in the audience told me that Greer was passing him notes while I was speaking. Certainly I knew he wasn't paying attention to what I was saying, and I was getting into a rage. Either Norman pays attention to what I say or he's not a friend of mine.

Then the last straw: I wasn't allowed to finish. I thought I was still within my time limit and had about five minutes to go, but Norman said, "Time's up!"— very peremptorily, like that. I frowned and said, "Just a minute." I quickly summarized what I had left to say.

My piece was serious; Greer's was serious too. I guess we were all serious. Norman was as serious as he was in *The Prisoner of Sex*; it was on that level.

But for me the important fact of the evening was that he had treated me not with *dis*respect but with lack of respect, and I was conscious at the time of reappraising him, of suddenly seeing him in a new light. I felt I was being somehow misused, or at least mistreated as a friend. I had been addressing his work straightforwardly and with the greatest seriousness, but he wasn't responding that way.

The next day when he read my speech he called me up. I suppose in a way he apologized for how he had acted the previous evening, but not really. He said he hadn't realized what a serious speech it had been. But doesn't he know me well enough to know that any damn thing I do is done seriously, the best I know how?

I didn't press him or tell him I was angry, but I must've said something that implied the question, "Did you go to bed with her?" because he managed to tell me that he hadn't. He indicated that he was kind of fearful of her—as well he might have been because later on she wrote a piece about the evening saying that she had never thought he would be any good in bed anyway.

But even if he didn't go to bed with her, he was terribly taken with her. But you don't desert a friend, sort of slough a friend off, because you're taken with another woman. Nobody's allowed to do that to me. I've had it done to me two or three times in my life, and I don't readily forgive it. If somebody wants to make Mary Jane, okay, let him make Mary Jane, but he mustn't misuse me in the process.

Later, when I too wrote about the occasion, I said that though its calendar date was 1971, the sixties had come to a close with that evening. What I was referring to was the fierce improvisation of the evening and its particular kind of sexual license.

JOSE TORRES   I met Germaine Greer at the party afterwards, a big party in the Village. Then I saw a guy go up to her and ask a question. She said, "Next?" I asked somebody, "Who was that poor guy?" "Anatole Broyard," was the answer, the culture critic from *The Times*.

JULES FEIFFER   I thought the Theater for Ideas events were wonderful. You could watch all of those powerful egos at work, elucidating absolutely nothing, and everybody had his or her own style. Susan Sontag would always rise and ask a question, and I don't think she's ever spoken an unparsed sentence in her life. Lizzie Hardwick would get up and be the southern girl who wasn't very well educated and didn't know much. She'd present all her lack of credentials, then, pausing for a moment, she'd proceed to give a withering, brilliant dissection of everything everybody onstage had to say, proving how weak everyone's argument was but her own, which I think she did that night with Norman and Greer, because I remember giggling to myself.

That evening was show business, just as most of those evenings were. But that doesn't mean they weren't worth while. They were great fun and got a lot of attention. It's ego-tripping at a very high level. You're getting a lot of intelligent people saying interesting, amusing, and even sometimes perceptive things, complex people working off each other, playing off each other, even though a lot of what they're saying is pure bullshit based on the moment. Certainly anything that went on between Greer and Norman had an enormous subtext, so the overt stuff was wonderful to watch.

There's no doubt that Diana Trilling was offended, though, and mainly because you can't be with Diana more than thirty seconds before she'll talk about something called "the intelligentsia." She takes a very aristocratic view, as I suppose Lionel did, of a very special group in society, as if this is the rabbinate. I was never a part of that group, so the very people she thought were so highly serious were often hilarious to me. Philip Rahv, for example, when he was having his fights at *Partisan Review*. I'd read those letters and think, This is a joke. I was too lazy to do it, but one of my fantasies was to write a satire of the letter pages in *Partisan* or *Commentary*, because you have all these people writing cool, reasoned, scholarly rebuttals to each other which are really filled with such rage and personal venom. It's jockeying for position. "I'm right, you're wrong," "It's my ball," "It's my turf." Underneath the civilized tone are murderous fantasies. They're supposedly arguing about something, but they're really saying, "I disagree with you. Therefore there's only one thing left for me to do and that's kill you!"

D. A. PENNEBAKER   I was interested in the idea of filming the Town Hall event because I knew there'd be a lot of energy to it. It's like what everybody dreams about—the New York intelligentsia having at each other. In the back rows there was an extremely hostile, basically lesbian-oriented, very anti-Mailer group. Norman could feel it from the beginning, and he went at it like a torero, sort of excited. You don't see these people in the film, but you hear their shouts and screams. You feel this sinister quality, like an edging to the film. It's as if they're going to get shot going out the door and it's their last chance to say what they think.

KATE MILLETT   I'd been asked to be in the Town Hall debate, in Germaine Greer's place, but I'd refused because the topic was supposed to be whether women should have their rights, which for me is not a debatable subject. It was sensationalism, making a kind of pugilism out of the whole issue of feminism. I didn't know if it was a publicity stunt for Greer's book and also Norman's, which was just about to come out, but that's how it appeared to me, a hype, and despite my telling the person who ran the Theater for Ideas that I wouldn't do it, she drove me crazy, calling every day.

Then I read *The Prisoner of Sex*. I'd read all of Mailer's work because, after all, I did part of my doctoral thesis on him—that's what *Sexual Politics* was initially, a doctoral thesis—so *The Prisoner of Sex* seemed to me very inferior to his usual stuff. It was mean-spirited and vitriolic. It made a great noise, and a lot of people read it, but I don't think he did himself a service with that book. If you're an important writer, as he surely is, it's a tragic error to pit yourself against any progressive movement or any movement for human rights.

That's an interesting thing about Mailer—he always seems to understand what's the matter with masculine arrogance, but he can't give it up. He's locked into the system. He's not really a progressive person, he's so much more a conservative than a liberal. Especially in *Why Are We in Vietnam?*, where he's so conscious of what's twisting those lads to become killers and soldiers, but there's an inability to withdraw, to participate no further. But in *The Prisoner of Sex* there isn't even that ambiguity. It was just a tirade, bombast, a scratching for old patriarchal grips someplace.

ARTHUR KRETCHMER *The Prisoner of Sex* is the one Mailer piece *Playboy* didn't publish which I still wish we had, one of the most important pieces of intellectual writing ever done in America, a phenomenal piece of work.

GLORIA STEINEM Norman and I ran into each other at an enormous anti-Vietnam War rally at the big church up by Columbia in December '71. I had already spoken, he was just coming in, and we were approaching each other in this long, dank, cavernous Gothic hall. I'd become more publicly identified as a feminist because I'd written pieces and taken part in demonstrations and so on, and from about fifty feet away he said, "Oh, Gloria, how are you? I'm glad to see you. You know, we ought to get together. Your people and my people ought to have a talk." I said, "What do you mean by 'my people'?" He said, "You know—women, women." To be funny, I said something like "Norman, I can't do that until you stop thinking your sperm is sacred," only he took the remark straight and, looking crestfallen, said, "I can't." Then he just walked on by. There was something wistful about it, not angry or hostile, and that was the last time I saw him for a long while.

JOSE TORRES Burt Sugar, the editor of *Ring Magazine*, and I were doing a book about Ali, going half-and-half—he'd do the research, I'd do the writing—and I took about seven or eight months working on it before asking Norman if he'd do the introduction. He said of course, but he'd have to read the book first. A couple of days later he phoned and said, "You can do a really good job with this, but you've got to rewrite the whole thing." I was a week from deadline and didn't have money, but he said, "Don't worry, I'll get you more money and more time." So he called the publisher and said, "If you give Jose three months and five thousand dollars extra, I'll write the introduction." The editor said, "Are you kidding?—he can have a year!"

Norman and Carol Stevens were living in Vermont, so that summer of '72 I rented a house next to theirs. Norman says, "You'll work every day and I'll check it. You teach me how to box, I'll teach you to write. But I'm gonna teach you my way, and I don't want nobody interfering. Pretend I'm a tough, strict manager. I want you to listen to me. I know this business. And I don't want you to write a history of Muhammad Ali—that's already been done."

The first thing he did was start throwing pages away, *bang, bang, bang*. "Take these pages, put them into one page. Use this here, that there. Okay? Here's one chapter of your book. Now, I want you to write two chapters—your opinion, very subjective. Not bullshit history, not statistics, but the way you saw fights, what you know about this guy, what he spoke to you about." I had tapes, his secretary transcribed them. He told me to work and sleep in his office. The schedule was get up at seven, have breakfast, work, work, work until one o'clock, then go to Norman's place, box with him, have lunch and discuss the book for an hour. Then I'd go back to the office and work, work, work till six o'clock, when I'd show him the manuscript. He'd say, "What are you trying to say here?" I'd explain, and he'd say, "That's not the way to put it" or "This doesn't make sense. Make it clear." I'd come back, he'd say, "Still no good." I'd come back again, he'd say, "Still no good. Take two days off." Then finally I'd come back, he'd be smiling and say, "That's what I want."

He was in Vermont on vacation—planting stuff, gardening. In fact, I remember one time he was planting garlic. I said, "Norman, you're doing this fucking wrong." He said, "Well, I may not be a genius at *everything*." And he wasn't just kidding. He is a genius, of course, but his mother started telling him that probably before he could walk. But what he was most involved with that summer was learning how to box, and he learned fast. He said, "I want you to teach me to box because these people don't have the money to pay me for helping you with this book."

As we progressed I remember telling him I was amazed at the effort you need to write a book. Fighting was something I controlled; with writing it was different. English isn't my native language, and it was fucking hard work, so it was such a relief when he said finally, "You've finished, you can go home. I'm going to read the whole thing." Later he phoned and said, "Jose, it's really a good book."

CUS D'AMATO   Jose had invited me up to watch him teach Norman and to make suggestions because sometimes when you're teaching somebody you're not aware of everything. They were boxing on a summer porch which had a roof over it. They didn't wear headgear. My fighters never wear headgear because I think it gives them a false sense of security and no benefits, and watching Norman, I had the impression that he was very serious. He'd get a little frustrated because Jose was naturally too advanced for him, and he'd want to do certain things that he couldn't do—at least not with Torres—certain combinations which didn't work. Jose, naturally, couldn't open up and hit him because he feared he might hurt him. Norman would say, "Jose, c'mon, don't hold back"—that's the way Norman is—but Jose would never do it. He's a professional, and besides he loves the man.

Boxing is a very misunderstood sport. People have the idea that if a person sticks out his left hand and just taps a fellow and runs like a thief, then that's boxing. But to me boxing is when a person hits but theoretically doesn't intend to get hit. A slugger, as opposed to a boxer, accepts that he's going to be hit, so he's willing to take a punch in order to deliver one. If you allow your temper

Publicizing Torres' book, Sting Like a Bee, *on the Dick Cavett show.*

or your fear to get involved, then you become a slugger and you're gonna get hit, and because you're competitive, you're gonna punch back. Which would sometimes happen with Norman. He'd get frustrated and walk in and try to really hit Torres and end up sort of flailing, because the more he tried to hit him, the more difficult it would become.

Jose would laugh and say to me, "Norman comes at you with such feeling"— meaning that Norman really went at him in a serious way—"and when he doesn't hit you, he gets very frustrated." Norman, you see, hadn't arrived at the point where he was impersonal and could do it intuitively, and the only way you do it intuitively is by getting a solid foundation. Your emotions are involved if you're not experienced. I constantly create competitive situations by letting my fighter box certain people in order to build his character and strength. I'm not only testing him, I'm compelling a confrontation, but one within his reach, so that he rises to the occasion.

Jose was doing that for Norman, and Norman wasn't embarrassed that I was watching when he'd make mistakes. Mostly he would get irritated with himself. He was driving himself, demanding performance. I would make minor but basic corrections along the lines of "You're dropping your hand, your head's coming up," things like that, which was fine. All fighters have fear, but with the two of them I don't think it was an issue because Jose was trying to teach without letting Norman suffer the usual consequences. Learning to fight in a gym, a guy is always gonna get hit.

What I thought was unusual was that Norman believed he always had to test himself. Most people are willing to carry a bluff, like a number of writers I've met, like Hemingway, who was supposed to be a great fighter but was really a bluff. A bluff picks his spots and projects an impression that really doesn't exist. With Hemingway, if he got in an argument that would come to a fight, he wouldn't go outside, he'd just sneak-punch somebody, that kind of thing. But Norman isn't like that. If he's gotten involved in something, he carries it to its conclusion. Other guys won't get involved unless they have the advantage, but Norman, even if he doesn't feel totally confident, he's aware of the fear and compels himself to see it through and to fight.

JOSE TORRES You cannot be reasonable and intelligent when you're fighting. Fear isn't something you conquer, it's something you control and work with. But I don't think Norman feels that way about it. His ego is so strong that he just wants to block fear completely, to push it aside.

He has a problem in the way he sees boxing because he thinks you can have a plan. He makes it too complicated, and in the heat of battle that doesn't work. If I teach a fighter, I teach him how to throw punches to specific areas. I teach him to throw a lot of punches very, very fast, since the punch that knocks you out isn't the hard punch but the one you don't see, so the faster you can throw punches, the less the other guy can anticipate. Norman's problem is he intellectualizes. He'll start saying, "If I throw this jab, he might come up with this..." He starts controlling himself too much, relying on thoughts.

On the other hand, he can deal with pain very well, maybe even better than me, because I think I became a narcissist when I became champion—looking at myself, my figure, worrying about anything that happens to the body. But Norman doesn't even take aspirin. He goes to a chiropractor more for back movement than for pain, and I know he's not afraid of getting marked. If he was boxing with me or some other professional I think he'd even be proud of it.

I think learning how to fight helped him in not being so crazy. He always had confidence in his intellectual ability, and suddenly he had more confidence physically. In Vermont we trained for three months, and after the summer he thought it would be wrong to get into fistfights because he knew he'd have the advantage.

Another thing was, he'd never get in a fight when I was around. He felt the other person would think he was doing it because of me. That, or he was sure I'd get involved, which worried him. He'd start the arguing—I saw it several times—but he would never throw the first punch, so I had to tell him, "Norman, if you get into a fight, you *have* to throw the first punch. You fight to win fucking fights." But that's the conflict in Norman. . . . There was also the alcohol— because when he was getting into fights he was drinking. He once told me that his real self came out when he was drunk. It's part of that idea of himself he sees allied with the devil. The way he wanted to deal with it was to learn how to fight, to be able to take care of himself for real.

BERNARD "BUZZ" FARBAR   My wife and I drove up to see Norman and Carol in Vermont, and one day he and I boxed, Jose was the referee, and since it was still the period of Supreme Mix, we had a lot of anger towards each other, for a lot of reasons. I was really working hard on Norman, fighting like a street fighter, and Norman fetched me a terrific blow right across the head. But he broke his thumb in the process, and while he was soaking it in ice Fanny came over to me, furious: "He broke his hand!" I said, "How about my head? What do you figure he broke it on?"

JOSE TORRES   I said "Fine" when Buzz wanted to get in the ring with Norman because I trusted them to behave. I told Norman that I wanted him to do this and that, hit him on the chin, the jaw. But when they started I got scared. I looked at Buzz and knew he wasn't playing around. He was there to try to take Norman out. It was that pseudo ego shit, and I became overprotective of Norman since Buzz knows how to fight a little bit and he's stronger than Norman.

Norman wasn't wearing headgear, and I saw that Buzz was throwing KO punches. I wanted to believe that Norman was making him miss, but there was the possibility that one would land. I wasn't sure, because I didn't know how much Norman had learned. They boxed three rounds, and not one of them connected, even though Buzz was trying so hard to take him out. I was proud of Norman, but that situation clued me in that Norman and Buzz were on a different wavelength from mine and Norman's. I don't compete with Norman intellectually, and in the ring I have never competed outside of my actual fights.

CUS D'AMATO   Later, after that September or October, when Norman was just moving into the house in Stockbridge he'd bought, I visited him, and we talked at length and probably more deeply about the mind and emotions in boxing than we had before. I gave him my definition of a real pro: a man who can be completely impersonal, who doesn't allow his emotions to get involved with anything he does, who's able to be constantly objective. I don't like to say a lot of these things to just anyone, because people say, "He's some kind of screwball." But with someone like Norman it's okay.

Anyway, while we were talking he suddenly excused himself and came back with a book, *Zen and the Art of Archery*. He asked if I'd read it, and I told him, no, I'd never heard of Zen. He said, "Are you sure? Because you don't know it, but you practice Zen." Later, having read the book several times, I realized that the principles I use do involve that kind of thing, developing an impersonal state without interference from any emotions.

It wasn't that either Norman or I was the student or teacher. I thought of him as a friend and as someone who was very curious not only about boxing but also about people's minds. We talked about fear, because when you become impersonal you control fear, separate it from your mind and body. Because of my concentration I've been hit blows and never felt them. I was there but outside my body: I could see myself throwing punches, just like I was watching somebody else, and it happens automatically, intuitively.

But that night Norman never argued with me. He just asked me questions. He wanted to get information. That was his method, asking questions. He felt I knew something, so I was the one doing the talking and explaining, and when Norman wants to know something he can become very, very patient.

ANNE BARRY Although his relationship with Carol had been going on for a while, I didn't meet her until I went up to visit them in the house they bought

With Carol Stevens, New York, 1972.

in Stockbridge. I was there just for a weekend or so—Maggie had been born in March '71, there were a lot of kids and people around, and I couldn't read Carol very well. She was quiet, and either she walled me out or there was nothing there. She was a singer, but I remember she sang in a rather sweet, tenuous sort of voice. She puzzled me, she didn't fit in with the rest of his wives. It didn't seem to me that it would last, although I couldn't put my finger on why.

Nor could I tell if Norman was restless with the situation, although it was obvious he didn't like the house. I kept reassuring him that it really was quite an adequate house, that it was certainly big enough, and so forth, though I admit it wasn't my type of house either—in fact, I thought it was terrible—a hideous new-old-fashioned house. It was a great big place, and upstairs off the long hallway were lots of rooms that were just cubicles, cookie-cutter, boxy little rooms. And downstairs there was something painful about the parlor. Carol had gotten it up with Victorian furniture, little loveseats and the lady's chair and the gentleman's chair and the rosewood medallion frames and Victorian "anti-ques." It was so stiff no one would dream of sitting there.

ADELINE LUBELL NAIMAN I liked Carol but couldn't understand why Norman continued to get himself into these insane relationships in which his fantasy was to shape the woman. I don't mean a Pygmalion complex exactly, because when Norman fell in love it was very real and genuine and bound him in some ways. But he'd always make more out of the recipient of his affection than the simple fact that he was in love with her for herself.

RHODA LAZARE WOLF Barney died of cancer in the fall of '72. I think he'd been sick for a year or so. Dan and I went to the funeral parlor, where the coffin was uncovered, I think, and I wouldn't go up. When we walked in, most everyone had already left, and Norman said to me, "Be happy. My father loved a party. Don't feel sad."

JOSE TORRES Norman didn't tell me that Barney had died until two months afterwards. I'd been in Puerto Rico, and when I came back I asked how his father was. He said, "He died." "When?" I asked. "Two months ago." "Shit," I said, and I felt bad that he hadn't told me. But I don't think he was that upset. He said, "He was in no pain, there was no suffering."

BERNARD "BUZZ" FARBAR Barney died the year before my own father died. I was thirty-eight, and it's a hard time to have your father die, and mine died suddenly, so I was pretty upset. I'm a private person and I didn't really have anyone to talk to about it, so I talked to Norman. Norman's the only person I can speak to about such things, such problems of life, of that enormous or deep meaning. So far he's given me the right answers, or at least in talking about it he'll say when he doesn't have an answer. But he's always there.

When we talked he didn't give me cheap comfort or say, "Oh, you'll get over it." Barney had died the year before, and Norman said, "It's like having a hole in your tooth. It's a pain that can never be filled. Not a day goes by that you won't think of your father." Some people say you outgrow it, that the memory just sort of fades. But not Norman. He said, "There's always that slight hole there—it can never be made whole again."

JOE FLAHERTY   I didn't pay the fifty dollars to go to Norman's fiftieth birthday party on January 31, 1973, at the Four Seasons because my friend from the Lion's Head, Frank Crowther, organized it. Wall-to-wall people, and I kept thinking of the Groucho Marx line, "Why would I join a club that would have me?" You couldn't move, you couldn't get a drink, the din was terrible.

There had been a press release that Norman was going to make an important announcement, which turned out to be something called the Fifth Estate, a group he was organizing to monitor the CIA. But it was no place to try something like that. I doubt there was a serious brain in the room, what with all the celebrities, and Norman stood up and went into this convoluted entrail of philosophy, prepped with a bad joke that had something to do with a cunt. I broke out in a sweat. It was the Village Gate *redux*. Oh my fucking God, I thought, the CIA oughta kill this rambling idiot up on the stage. I couldn't look at him. I never can when he does things like that. Because of my affection for him, it mortifies me. I grabbed Jeanine, my lady, and got the fuck out and never looked back.

SANDY CHARLEBOIS THOMAS   That birthday party! The East Side friends, the limousines, they were all there. The food was great, but Norman made a *shmuck* of himself.

JULES FEIFFER   It's always interested me that two people I venerate very much, Norman and Izzy Stone, seemingly take occasions when people are there to honor and adore them and make certain that the crowd ends up hating them. They make speeches that seem designed to turn the room against them, then they seem surprised by what has happened. Izzy, I think, really knows what he's doing, but I'm not so sure about Norman. I've seen him on at least three or four occasions deliberately provoke a crowd, then, out of some sense that he's gone too far, he'll try to win them back, which only makes things worse. He's never seemed to be in charge of his insult comedy, and the audience's antagonism always seems to come as a surprise to him.

Which is exactly what happened that night at the Four Seasons. I was still with Judy then, my ex-wife, and what I remember was the celebrity glow. Everybody you'd want to see was there, and everybody was very happy to see each other. There hadn't been a party like this in a long while, you hadn't seen so many familiar faces that had become unfamiliar, and it was very nice to be out, hanging around and talking to people. Partly it was a fashion show, but I don't like fashion shows, so I mean it was glittering but not glitzy. It was also relaxed. People were there to mix, to really enjoy themselves.

Then Norman got up to talk. He went up to the dais kind of jovial and spunky

Mailer's fiftieth birthday party at New York's Four Seasons—$50 a ticket, the Fifth Estate, and Mailer's faith that his daring would win.

but quickly became aggressive and pugnacious. His technique is almost a perversion of the public speaker who opens with a joke to relax the crowd, since he opens with a joke to tense up an already relaxed crowd. In this case he told a joke about the disposition of Oriental cunt, which is a stupid joke, and you have to wonder, Doesn't he know it's stupid, certainly not a joke you tell at the Four Seasons? So he tenses the crowd and polarizes them, as if he feels he operates best as a public figure not even by dividing the room but by turning the room against him. He doesn't work to be adored, he works to... I don't know how to finish that sentence, but he's certainly not working to be adored.

I wasn't irritated that I'd gone so much as I was irritated that he had fucked up his own party. I was very fond of Norman, sorry for him, sorry that he had to engage himself on that level. Maybe he even walked out thinking he'd had a wonderful time. But I felt bad for him, because it was a wonderful evening that had stayed wonderful until the guest of honor got up and made a mess of it.

JOHN LEONARD I got Max Frankel to approve *The Times* paying for the fifty-dollar ticket, and I went with Jill Krementz because Vonnegut refused to pay. Afterward I wrote an article for the Sunday *Times Book Review* saying I felt that people had wanted him to make a fool of himself, that it was almost willed by the audience, that they wanted him to get drunk—and this was at the time when he certainly had a desperate drinking problem. There was also the feeling that he could get away with it, that his daring would win. But then disaster strikes... and I now suspect he wills the disaster as often as he wishes it wouldn't occur. It was a very ugly audience. Famous, yes—but they came to see Norman make a fool of himself.

After my article appeared I got an anguished phone call from him saying, "It wasn't the audience's fault, it was mine. Would you let me try to explain what I was doing?" I agreed and told him I'd need his copy by the following Monday to make the next issue. There proceeded a couple of late phone calls from Mailer—I think he was in Stockbridge—and then on Friday night he phoned to say "My daughter's typing it, our maid's going to New York by bus tomorrow, and she'll give it to the person I can trust to get it to you by the time you go to work. What time are you in the office?" I told him, and goddamn it, at nine o'clock—I'm the only one at the *Book Review*, the office doesn't open until nine-thirty—this little old woman comes in and says, "Here's Norman's story. I hope you like it." I couldn't believe it—it was Norman's mother! The piece wasn't particularly good, but she was so pleased—she was exactly *the* mother, and somehow he needed her. I loved it.

LAWRENCE SCHILLER   Although *Marilyn* was published in 1973, the story behind my involvement goes back to 1971, when John Bryson, a photographer, called me and said, "David Stuart, who has an art gallery, is going to have an exhibit of Marilyn pictures and I'm going to give some of mine. How about you?" I thought about it, and being a little commercially minded, I suggested that we get all the photographers who photographed Marilyn—really do something and make some money. I was also working on the Lenny Bruce biography that Albert Goldman was writing, which had been sold to Random House, so I went back to them and asked Jim Silberman if they would be interested in doing a Marilyn Monroe book. Jim said yes, but he wondered whom we could get to do the writing. He wanted someone who was well respected, who knew something about Monroe, so we talked about Loudon Wainwright of *Life*, Pauline Kael, and Rex Reed. But Silberman wasn't offering me a lot of money and kept saying, "What kind of success can this exhibit be?" I kept saying, "It's gonna be big, and I want fifty grand for the photographers, not a penny less."

I don't remember how I got to Bob Markel, the head editor at Grosset and Dunlap. But soon I was in his office with Harold Roth, Grosset and Dunlap's president, and Roth's seeing the commercial possibilities. They offer $25,000. I'm saying, "What do you mean, $25,000? I've got fifty offered by Random House," even though I've really only got twenty on the table.

I went back to California, the Random House contract's still on my desk, and Roth called again. He was the only one pursuing me, but I insisted "Marilyn is alive, we've gotta make her bigger than life. If you really want this book and you want me to take less money, then get me"—and I threw out a string of names—"Get me so-and-so, get Gloria Steinem, get me Norman Mailer."

When I hung up, those two names rang a bell. *Ding dong.* Norman was looked upon by feminists in a certain way, and I said to myself, "Jesus, what if

Gloria Steinem wrote part of the book and Mailer wrote the other part? They're adversaries, right?" So I called Roth and/or Markel back and then went on my merry way putting the exhibit together and printing a program. Then all of a sudden Markel called. "We've got Norman Mailer. I've spoken to Scott Meredith, he's spoken to Norman. Nothing is in writing yet, but we believe Mailer will write 25,000 words."

"Let me speak to Harold," I said, because I knew Roth was the money man. Harold got on and said, "Well, we don't really have Norman yet—you'll have to show him the pictures—but Scott Meredith has told us privately that Norman needs the money."

I said, "How much are you paying Mailer?"

"Fifty thousand," he said, and I said, "Then you gotta give me fifty thousand because the photographers aren't going to take second seat to Norman Mailer. You're dealing with ego, the war between writers and photographers." Harold, I knew, had no place to go. He didn't have me under contract yet, but he'd already committed himself for fifty thousand to Scott.

So he sent me a draft contract, and although there were a lot of things I didn't like, I called him and said, "All right. I'll fly in at one A.M., I'll shower in your office before you come in, I'll go over the contract with my lawyer at breakfast, we'll meet at nine-thirty, and by the end of the day if we have a deal you'd better have a check ready."

Airplanes are like a little cell for me, I'm isolated from all outside influences and I can start to think, so flying east I realized what Harold had in mind. Obviously it's a big, controversial thing, Mailer writing on Monroe, so I say to myself, "This is going to become a Norman Mailer book. The only way it's going to work is if I hammer out a contract where I retain total control. Otherwise I'll have been bought off, the photographers will have been bought off, and Roth will run the show." Also, I know I have to have total control because Roth may not even realize how big it can be, that this is a *Time* cover, this is *Life* magazine, this is headlines all over the fucking world.

ROBERT MARKEL   It was my idea to use Norman, not Harold Roth's or Schiller's. When Larry first came to us I didn't think the Marilyn book was a particularly good idea, and I felt that without a significant text it wasn't interesting commercially. I'd said this to Harold before we went off to Europe for the Frankfurt Book Fair, and at one point Harold, who was in Italy, called me in Paris and said, "Schiller is pressing us for a final decision on his Marilyn album." I said, "I don't think it's a good idea at all, but let's talk when we're back in New York."

By the time we'd returned, Schiller had called again and was using Random House as his leverage. I repeated that I didn't think the project was worth bothering with unless we found a really terrific writer. Harold asked, "Like who?" and I just blurted out, "Norman Mailer." I called Scott Meredith, we had a meeting, and he told me that Norman was on a lecture tour in Texas and that he was hoping to hear from him within twenty-four hours. He thought Norman would be interested, although he'd have to speak to him directly. At the time we were talking about a 25,000-word sort of introductory statement, and Scott must have viewed it as a month's work. Figuring $50,000 for Norman, $50,000 for Schiller and the photographers, Harold and I felt that $100,000 for world rights would make sense. Anyway, within two days I spoke to Norman, and although he'd never heard of Schiller, he was quite warm on the idea immediately. I told Harold, and I reported Norman's interest to Larry, who then flew into New York on a redeye to hammer out the contract.

I didn't know Schiller either, or even his reputation, but almost immediately my impression was that his point of view and ability to do negotiations were really West Coast. There were clauses he wanted in the contract that I'd never heard of, like favored-nations clauses, plus he was demanding contractual equality with Norman. He was very shrewd, very quick of tongue, and quick on his feet to understand a whole variety of ins and outs.

But it's absolute nonsense that Schiller demanded a check on the desk. What did happen was that we agreed to the deal and shook hands, and Larry, with that little childlike grin of his, said, "I guess I'd better call Jim Silberman at Random House." I offered him my office so he could phone privately, but he wanted to speak to Silberman in my presence, like "I've got Norman Mailer for my project, so I'm turning Random House down." He was quite polite about it, but I sensed that he thought this was a wonderful deal he was pulling off. It was no longer just groveling around in the Hollywood Hills. This was the big time; he'd hit in New York and was now going to be associated with a real literary talent. It never occurred to me that Schiller would challenge Norman's over-all authority in the project. Which, in fact, he did—repeatedly and virtually from the start.

LAWRENCE SCHILLER   I went back to California. The exhibit opened, and in the meantime—this is November now—Mailer signed the contract. Then Markel called to say they'd set up a meeting with Mailer and wanted me to bring the photographs to New York.

Now, there are two versions of this first meeting: one the fantasy version we later gave the press, the other the real version—and to be honest, at this point both are mixed together in my mind. The fantasy version was that I took all the furniture out of a hotel room, pinned the photographs all over the walls, put a chair in the middle of the room, and invited Norman to step in, at which point, we said, Norman sat there and fell in love with Marilyn.

What actually happened was that I went up to see him at his house in Stockbridge. I was carrying the photographs in two big artist's cases, which must've weighed forty or fifty pounds. Carol Stevens was there, I remember, because Norman told me she was a jazz singer, and that night he played me a tape or a private record he'd made of her singing. One of his sons was there, also the baby, Maggie. I placed the photographs around the room, laying them on the floor, propping them against chairs, wherever they could be seen.

I slept there that night and went home with the understanding that he was going to do the book. Meanwhile I hired Allen Hurlburt, the art director of

Look magazine, to design it. I'm also having discussions with Markel and Roth about the paper and printer we were going to use, as well as negotiating in Japan and doing the exhibit.

During this time I'd been aware of the research Norman was doing, because my office had been helping him get stuff he needed. Also, he called me three or four times to ask questions about Marilyn during my relationship with her. His secretary called my secretary to get copies of her old films, which he was watching in 16 mm in Stockbridge, plus he saw a couple at the Fifth Avenue Screening Room.

ROBERT MARKEL   The contract was signed in November. At the time, Norman and I had a meeting in my office. Larry had sent the photographs in huge crates from the Los Angeles exhibit, and I pointed out things he'd told me, like the photograph taken of Marilyn after she was told Gable had died. What struck Norman most was how different she looked from one photograph to the next, and he talked a little about chronology and Marilyn's moods. But then he sat down opposite me at my desk, and after a few polite remarks, looked at me directly and said, "What are we gonna do about Bobby Kennedy?" Of course there'd been a lot of discussion in general about a possible relationship between Bobby Kennedy and Marilyn Monroe, and I'd done some homework, pulled out the Fred Guiles biography of Monroe, so it was not surprising that he should be focused on this as an area where we'd have to make certain decisions. Perhaps he was testing me, but I think I just mumbled, "I don't know." At this point all I had in my stewpot was Norman Mailer sitting in my office, and he's gonna write, ostensibly, a 25,000-word introduction to this collection of photographs. How he was going to handle Kennedy wasn't my main concern.

He didn't start writing until December 9. That was the official start date, because first he was going on that Holland Line cruise. He and Isaac Asimov and Katherine Anne Porter were going to be on a ship to watch the launching of a satellite from Cape Canaveral and were to give lectures to the passengers. I'd hoped he could begin earlier, right away in November, because I thought time was terribly short, but he said he couldn't do it until he got back from the cruise.

During the next month and a half of writing he'd call me at home to report his progress, usually in the late evening, and I remember the night—I think in early January—he called and said, "Well, I've completed the first 65,000 of the 25,000 words, and I'm not even up to Arthur Miller yet." I laughed, he laughed, and I said to myself, "Your gamble is going to work, Markel. Obviously Mailer can't confine himself to a mere 25,000 words. He's gotten the bit between his teeth."

Meanwhile Larry had gotten the former art director of *Look* to design a book to accommodate 35,000 or 40,000 words in a single-column format. But Larry's first reaction when I told him we now had 65,000, 70,000 words was "Terrific," even though it meant scrapping the dummy. He realized it was a different kettle of fish, a full-fledged Mailer book as opposed to a photograph book with a Mailer introduction. He loved the idea—the combination of Mailer and Monroe. On the other hand, he hadn't yet seen the text.

Also, during this period Norman wanted to see as many of Monroe's films as possible and asked me to set up showings for him, which I did. In fact, I obtained a print of *The Misfits*, which I don't think he'd seen before, and I watched it with him and Norman Rosten, who was writing his own Monroe book and whom Norman had invited to come along.

NORMAN MAILER (MARILYN) *The new candidate for biographer now bought a bottle of Chanel No. 5—Monroe was famous for having worn it—and thought it was the operative definition of a dime-store stink. But he would never have a real clue to how it smelled on her skin. Not having known her was going to prove, he knew, a recurrent wound in the writing, analogous to the regret, let us say, of not having been alone and in love in Paris when one was young. No matter how much he could learn about her, he could never have the simple invaluable knowledge of knowing that he liked her a little, or did not like her, and so could have a sense that they were working for the same god, or at odds . . .*

NORMAN ROSTEN Norman had never met Marilyn, and I know he'd very much wanted to when he was living in Bridgewater back in the late fifties. Marilyn was just over the hill, in Roxbury, with Miller, and because I was a friend of both Arthur and Marilyn, Norman told me a number of times that he wanted an introduction.

But Miller didn't want to set anything up with Mailer. He just didn't like the idea. Miller is a rabbi, and he didn't want this strange guy powering in. He wasn't a buddy of Mailer's, and they'd always had a vague sort of animosity toward each other ever since the late forties in Brooklyn Heights. Also, Marilyn and Arthur were already married, and at that time it made a difference, especially since Arthur was a very proper guy. I'm one of his oldest friends, but if I danced with Marilyn at a party and maybe held her a little too tight or whispered in her ear, he'd look at me and get a little nervous. It's his temperament. It wasn't just directed towards Mailer.

It was amusing because Norman used to say to me, "Here I am in Bridgewater, here's this prick Arthur who won't even invite me over for a cocktail so I can meet Marilyn." He wanted to meet her just as he wanted to meet all those historic women, like Jackie Kennedy, and of course Mailer was also one of those guys who felt that beautiful women would want to meet him. I suppose it has something to do with glamour wanting glamour. Why did Arthur Miller want to marry Marilyn? Same thing.

But I didn't need Arthur to get in touch with Marilyn. Both Hedda, my wife, and I knew her very well apart from him. A year before she'd married Arthur I'd met her through a photographer friend who'd known her in Hollywood. One day he was filming her in Prospect Park and they got caught in the rain, so he brought her over to our house. We didn't know who she was at first, she looked drenched, and Hedda gave her a change of stockings and some coffee. After that

Arthur would come over when she came to see us. We didn't introduce them— that's a myth. He'd already met her when he was out in Hollywood working on *On the Waterfront*.

Then it got into the gossip columns that the two of them were getting married. Mailer knew that we were friends with both of them, that we saw Marilyn off and on at our place, and it was just after the marriage, I think, that he started telling me he wanted to meet her. Once or twice I tried to set it up, and I remember once she was coming over, so Mailer was going to come over too, but then one or the other of them didn't show up. It was a time when she was drifting all over the place.

Later, when Arthur and Marilyn were in Roxbury, I told her that Mailer still wanted to meet her, so if there was ever anything happening, a party, then . . . But I left it at that, and nothing happened. She certainly knew who Mailer was because she said to me, "Oh yes, I know about him," but she just didn't seem to want to go out of her way.

HEDDA ROSTEN   No, she didn't want to meet Mailer. She said, "One writer is enough for me."

NORMAN ROSTEN   Well, she never said that to me. She just giggled the way she would and shrugged her shoulders and intimated maybe they'd meet some-time. What bothered Mailer was that Arthur never invited him when they were living so near. He grouched about it, and I suppose the animosity between Mailer and Miller started when they were both working for Wallace back in '48. Arthur was more liberal all along the way. Mailer quickly got very cynical through Malaquais and others. He didn't hew to anything organized. He was a maverick, and although I've never thought about it this way before, it's the two Jewish traditions: one, Miller as sobriety; the other, Mailer as rebellion. That was the temperamental difference between them. Miller didn't want to risk his bride being contaminated by Mailer or—while I didn't say it then—maybe getting fucked by Mailer. Arthur is that kind of guy. And I think Marilyn herself was just staying out of any problem. She had enough of them.

Now, this was well before Norman wrote his book about Marilyn, and when he started writing he had to rely on watching her films. In fact, one night he called and asked if I wanted to come with him. He'd been screening all her movies, and we went to a screening place in midtown. I remember he sat there with a yellow pad taking notes, but we didn't talk about the film or Marilyn either. He never said, "I'm doing this book for the money," he just said he was doing it, but he was absolutely straight with me about my own book. Both of us had begun writing about Marilyn around the same time, and he didn't try to pick my brain. I think I told him he could read my book when I was finished, which in fact he did. I know there were later lawsuits about his using other people's material, but he'd asked if my project was a biography, and I said no, it was a memoir. He wasn't doing a biography either. It was an interpretation, but still so different that my book wouldn't challenge his. Also, I trust people, and Norman is a friend, and I couldn't imagine that he'd run off with anything. So I let him read it in manuscript, and afterwards he asked if he could use a couple of excerpts, one of which he claimed was a good ending for him— Marilyn's near drowning, which happened at Miller's place near Port Jefferson, on the North Shore of Long Island Sound.

NORMAN MAILER (MARILYN)   *Once in Brooklyn, long before anyone had heard of Marilyn Monroe . . . he had lived in the same brownstone house in which Arthur Miller was working on* Death of a Salesman *and this at just the time he was himself doing* The Naked and the Dead. *The authors, meeting occasionally on the stairs, or at the mail box in the hall, would chat . . . each certainly convinced on parting that the other's modest personality would never amount to much. In later years, when Miller was married to Monroe, the playwright and the movie star lived in a farmhouse in Connecticut not five miles away from the younger author, who, not yet aware of what his final relation to Marilyn Monroe would be, waited for the call to visit, which of course never came. The playwright and the novelist had never been close. Nor could the novelist in conscience condemn the playwright for such avoidance of drama. The secret ambition, after all, had been to steal Marilyn; in all his vanity he thought no one was so well suited to bring out the best in her as himself, a conceit which fifty million other men may also have held . . . It was only a few marriages (which is to say a few failures) later that he could recognize how he would have done no better than Miller and probably have been damaged further in the process. In retrospect, it might be conceded that Miller had been made of the toughest middle-class stuff—which, existentially speaking, is tough as hard synthetic material.*

ROBERT MARKEL   He turned in the text in late February '73. His official word count was about 105,000, which, after my suggestions, he pared down to about 95,000.

When I received the draft I wasn't bothered by what some people characterized as his "lack of research." I'd started out with a 25,000-word intro, and it was never meant to be a full-fledged biography. Norman was venturing out, "free-lancing out," as Robert Lowell put it, along the razor's edge, and I felt that between his text and the photographs we had a potential winner. Nor was I anticipating any legal problems with the books he was basing his text on. But the shit began to hit the fan, I guess, when Larry flew into New York and first saw the text.

LAWRENCE SCHILLER   After my first meeting with Mailer I had known that his words would tend to dominate; I accepted the reality of that because in the contract I had ultimate control. Before, when I'd heard the text was running long, I'd gone to my designer and said, "Allen, you've designed the book for 20,000 words. How will we accommodate a longer text?"

Allen knew Mailer often wrote long, so he had a plan: he'd left the columns to run high to accommodate an extra 10,000 words. We also decided that if it ran even longer, we could put in pages of text without pictures. But I had no idea that "long" meant 100,000 or 125,000 words. We had accommodated for maybe 15 percent or 20 percent extra, so when Markel called and said the text had come in at 100,000 to 125,000 words, virtually five to six times the original length, I phoned Hurlburt, and he went into a panic.

Markel wanted me to see the text, so I flew into New York. Then I went up to see Mailer in Stockbridge. Having hit the ceiling with Markel, I used a softer voice with Mailer, and as an introduction to the real issue I showed him the book's layout.

Then I told him, "Norman, I'm not a writer, I'm not presumptuous enough to tell you what to do, but the first chapter seems too long to me." He didn't show any pique at this, didn't come back with "You're fucking with my text," because I was being very soft about it. He was just listening, and the unstated assumption on both our parts was that it was just a draft and he was gonna be polishing it.

I then showed him the pictures and gradually moved to what I considered the real purpose of my visit—the Bobby Kennedy thing. Right away, though, I saw him getting a little upset, so I backed off. I asked instead, "What do you think the text will finally come in at, because we've really gotta plan the design?" Since I'd brought sample pages, Norman starts to become an art director—"We can set in this size type here and that size type there . . . I always specify in my contract the type faces used." Of course I know that his contract doesn't specify that, so I think maybe there's gonna be friction. But for the time being I got an answer to my question: he tells me the text is going to come in at 110,000 words.

So I left it at that and went back and started to lay into Grosset and Dunlap. Either Markel got upset or he communicated my objections to Norman, because in my next conversation with Norman I feel the friction starting to surface. I was also trying to figure out how to counteract the Kennedy thing, maybe by using a picture not in the exhibit, the photograph of Joe DiMaggio and his son at Marilyn's funeral. I didn't want the last thought in the reader's mind to be, Did she sleep with Kennedy, and was she killed, and who killed her?

Norman's estimate on length was pretty close, so while I was staying at the Chelsea Hotel editing the film *The Man Who Skied Down Everest* I was working with Hurlburt at Grosset and Dunlap to finish the design. After a trip back to California to see my wife, I was prepared to lock the book and set the text in dummy type, cheap linotype right off the press, so we could paste it up to see where everything fell. Then I brought my cover to Markel. It was just a photograph, and Markel said, "It's a beautiful picture, but where's the type on it?" I said, "I'm not putting Mailer's name on the cover." "What!" Markel says, and I explain: "Everybody's gonna know it's Mailer's book. That's gonna be headlines. You want a cover that will draw people in the bookstores so they'll go and pick it up. What do you want to smear type all over it for?"

"But we've already advertised it with a dummy cover that's got both Marilyn's and Mailer's names on it," he explains.

"Who's bigger than life? Not Norman Mailer. People can see him every day— they can't see Marilyn." Then I took a pencil and smeared "Marilyn" and "Mailer" on the front cover. "Now, you want to fuck it up like that? I'll put the names on the spine but nowhere else." Markel is beginning to see what I'm talking about, but he says, "My God, Mailer's gonna have a heart attack. He's never had a book without his name on it."

Then we decide we'd better set up a meeting immediately so I can show Mailer the layout and the cover because we're running late and we've gotta go to press. But Mailer's flying here and there, I've got to go to California, so Markel said we'd have to do it at the airport. I said, "Fine, we'll do it in one of the airline lounges." Little did I know Markel would get the United Airlines Friendship Lounge—which I always thought was pretty funny, given what happened.

I arrived earlier than Mailer. Who knows what Grosset and Dunlap had told him? But as soon as he came in I had the impression that he was feeling tremendous friction, as if he was worried that his text was going to be tampered with. Besides Norman and myself, there was Markel and a girl from Grosset and Dunlap. Before we started, though, I asked to take a picture of Norman walking outside.

I didn't tell them why I needed the picture. In fact I wanted it for the cover of *Time*. I'd told my wife and everybody else, "This book will be so big, I'm gonna get the cover of *Time* magazine." Everybody laughed, they just didn't believe me, except maybe Harold Roth. But I didn't tell Norman. I just took the picture, and he gave me a dirty look. He didn't like having his picture taken, especially outside, because it was March and pretty cold.

Then we went back into the Friendship Lounge, where the boards of the book were laid out on six banquet tables. Norman went up and down, looking, stopping here and there, saying things like "I don't like that picture" or "Larry, why don't we take little teeny pictures and put them between the columns and the margins?" Of course he was justifying it all philosophically, but I wasn't listening. What he's doing is redesigning the book, even though the book is already designed and we're about to go to fuckin' press! And Markel is saying, "Oh yes, Norman. I agree, Norman. Don't worry, Norman."

We got to a certain point and Norman says, "That picture doesn't go here. It doesn't match the text. I'm talking about Norma Jean here—you should put in an earlier picture." I said, "This isn't like a rainbow, it doesn't have to match." Then, to make my point, I picked up the bound edition I'd put together and I thumbed through it from the back, saying, "You see, Norman, when people pick this up they're looking at the photographs first. The pictures are laid out so that there's a panoramic view. The text and photographs don't have to match, because when someone's sitting in bed with the book on their knees they're not gonna look at the text right away, they're gonna look at the pictures. They're gonna read the text second." My God, at first I don't realize what I'm saying, what I've done, but his face is getting redder and redder. Actually, he was getting white, that ashen look he gets when he's angry.

But meanwhile he's still saying, "I want this moved here, I want a small picture there," all the while getting Markel's support. Markel's saying he'll do everything, and he looks back at me, and finally it hit me—I realize what I've done—so I start to compromise a little: "All right, we'll put in a small picture here." Then

Norman said, "I want a picture of her when she was married, I want—" I said, "I'm not putting all those pictures in, but I'll use a baby picture, okay? But you're fucking up the book!"

Now, what followed is clear in my memory, although I'm not sure of all the dialogue, that it's actually verbatim. But when I told him he was fucking up the book, Mailer said, "Don't tell me about book publishing. You've never published a book before." Then he said something like "Larry, you don't know a damn thing about laying out books." So I said, "Well, what do you know about Marilyn Monroe?" He said, "And what the hell do you know?" And then I said, "At least I fucked her and you didn't." I probably didn't use the word "fuck," but that's what I was saying, and he was apoplectic. We were standing about a foot apart, and while he didn't raise his fist, he was ready to take a swing at me, just barely controlling himself.

At that point Markel was shitting his pants, and he took Norman out of the room. I don't think he'd even told him what had been true from the beginning—namely, that I had total control. Me, I never would've said to Norman, "Fuck you, I'm gonna cut your text," and I never did. But I didn't want him redesigning the book either. My feeling about the text was, Okay, it's there, we're gonna fit it in, we're gonna make it work. I'm gonna have to live with the first chapter—he never did adjust it—and I'm gonna have to live with the Bobby Kennedy shit too. I realized I had Mailer and I had to live with him. But basically I felt that the meeting was the end of any relationship between the two of us.

ROBERT MARKEL   At first I'd thought Mailer would be dominant, but as soon as I saw the two of them together I realized otherwise. Larry was going to go nose to nose with him, and I remember worrying, because I saw that Schiller was a fresh, uncontrollable force and just kooky enough to ruin my project.

I'd taken Nancy Brooks, our chief copy editor, out to the airport, and it was a four-hour session. Norman was saying, "We should have pictures of Marilyn as a baby so people will know what she looked like at various times in her life." Larry was saying, "No, that's not what I have in mind." Norman would go over some copy, and Larry would jump in screaming "No, goddammit." Norman's shouting "I won't take this anymore. I quit." Larry's yelling "If you don't do what I want, I'm withdrawing the whole project from Grosset and Dunlap." It was a tremendous dustup, with ebbs and flows and peaks and valleys—Italian opera at its finest.

Nancy Brooks was just observing, but I was trying to act as a referee, the Arthur Donovan of this major heavyweight fight. All the while I'm realizing that Larry's taking on Norman all the way. I was amazed at Schiller, this upstart, this West Coast *macher*, and I was thinking, Who is this kid? Here we have a veteran editor, myself. We have the illustrious Norman Mailer. We're getting the project together, and the likes of Larry Schiller is telling us what to do? I just wanted to hold things together until five-thirty, when Larry was supposed to board his plane. So when I took Norman outside, that's what I told him, that we'd fix it the way we wanted as soon as Larry got the hell out of there. I took

Larry outside too and told him, "For God's sake, Larry, don't blow this."

The major conflict was over the design, which left big margins both in the gutter and on the outside edges of the pages. Norman wanted small black-and-white photos—news photos, anything—to be put in the margins so that the reader could be oriented to the specific happenings as he'd related them chronologically. Larry felt this would only compromise the design of the book: "This isn't a biography in the ordinary sense. We don't have to illustrate your text. I'm not going to compromise the beauty of the photographs and the way they're laid out to illustrate your text. And that's just the way it is." Norman said, "That's not the way it is. This is a biography of Marilyn Monroe illustrated with your photographs."

Norman, though, was really quite patient and sort of amused by Larry. He admired Larry's hubris, was amused by Larry as the wheeler-dealer, as someone who gives no quarter and who'd stood right up to him in a way that few men do—stood up to him not only on business matters but on literary and artistic matters too. But meanwhile I'm made desperate by it. I wish Larry would just go away and stay away and let me make this book for better or worse. I want to get the bloody thing out, so I'm relieved when Larry finally gets on his plane, although I continue to worry that the meeting has put the whole thing in jeopardy.

LAWRENCE SCHILLER   After the meeting I began to see that Grosset and Dunlap didn't know how to handle prepublication publicity. "Look," I said to them, "we've got the American Book Association meeting coming up. What are you gonna do, a little black-and-white brochure? A dummy cover like every other publisher? No way. You gotta do a twelve- or fifteen-page color portfolio." I convinced them to redesign a whole booth at ABA of Marilyn Monroe, and I designed a beautiful color poster that folded out. They paid for it; I wasn't paying for a goddamned thing. But I was starting to fight with the PR people at Grosset, and every time they'd pass something off by saying "Don't worry, we're doing it" I'd threaten to withhold publicity photos.

I thought the book was gonna be big, but I was a little nervous, so I showed the dummy to a couple of people. Then I did crazy things, like test-marketing the dummy by displaying it in a Doubleday bookstore on Fifth Avenue where I knew the manager. After all the screaming about not putting Mailer's name on the cover I wanted to see if it was really gonna work. But then we got the real confirmation that it was going to be big when Grosset made the sale to the Book-of-the-Month Club on the basis of Mailer's unedited text.

ROBERT MARKEL   Initially we'd scheduled publication for late August since we saw it as our major title to come out early in the fall. The Book-of-the-Month Club was reading and selecting its summer and fall selections, and for the first round of consideration we weren't going to let any of the book clubs see the dummy and the photographs except in my office. Larry was partly responsible for the idea, so I set up a meeting with the Literary Guild as well as the Book-of-the-Month Club, and I made a dog-and-pony show at each of these separate sessions. Schiller's position was, you have a precious object and you make it a big deal and you make people come to you. I even had people flying in from England when we were selling foreign rights. Also, with magazine people, I'd refuse to leave it with them overnight. I was shooting for the moon, taking the big risk and throwing the dice. It's not something that comes to me naturally, I'm not the type to do flamboyant things, but in this case it struck me as appropriate.

Anyway, the Literary Guild came in and found the dummy very impressive, but a week later said they weren't interested, maybe because their committee was all women. But I didn't tell anyone except Harold Roth, since, to get the bidding up, I wanted the Book-of-the-Month Club to think they were in a hot contest. They took it as an "A book," which meant they would offer it in some form or other, but they hadn't decided whether to make it a full selection, which would have meant a difference of a half million dollars.

So I prepared packages for the judges. We still didn't have an edited text, and I gave them Norman's manuscript complete with his pencil marks and the Bobby Kennedy stuff unfinished, because we were still investigating that whole business even after the goddamn thing was typed. Although I hadn't even had time to read it myself, I sent a covering letter with the manuscript: "Please forgive me, dear judge, but you must understand this is not completed, we haven't had the time." I was bending over backwards trying to get us a main selection.

My hope was that BOMC would choose it as a September full selection, but as things turned out, they said they had already slotted stuff for September and October, two big novels, one by Michener, and to make the case worse from Norman's point of view, the other by Gore Vidal. If we wanted a full selection we had to move up the publishing date to no later than June 10 or risk not having it happen at all. So that's why Norman suddenly had an unalterable deadline. He had to finish so we could publish the book in time for BOMC to get their copies.

I called Norman and Scott. I think Scott was very concerned about Larry doing Norman damage by running wild, but then when he saw things were moving well he was buoyed up because it meant that Norman was gonna get some dollars.

In fact, right in the beginning when we were starting to sell off foreign rights Scott called me up and said, "Norman needs $25,000." I think he said he had to pay the government. I spoke to Harold Roth, Harold said, "Give it to him," and we sent the check over that afternoon as an additional advance. We were going to worry about a lousy $25,000? No way, not with Mailer, and that kind of behavior impressed both Norman and Scott tremendously.

So when BOMC came through, I called them. I wanted them to know the book looked like it was going to do well. But I also had to tell them that it moved up our publishing date.

During this time *Marilyn* was taking up a majority of my time, but I was also dealing with our sales conference, which was coming up in May in Las Vegas, plus the forthcoming ABA scheduled for Los Angeles. Things were moving very rapidly because of the BOMC decision, which was related too to *Time's* cover piece.

Schiller was extremely important in arranging the *Time* cover story, I'll grant him that, although I also felt he was becoming a pest. He was attempting to direct our sales of the book in foreign lands, attempting to be our art director and the designer of our ads, and was insisting that he read all the press releases and monitor all phone calls. I don't know whether he saw this as his main chance, but he was basking in this extraordinary event he'd helped to produce and was going around town virtually saying that he'd invented Norman Mailer. In fact, several people reported back to me, "This Schiller who signed up Mailer...," and once or twice I let him have it. "Listen, let's get this straight, buddy boy: I thought up Norman for this project, not you. You'd never read a word of Mailer until this project, and I seriously doubt whether you still have." He would laugh good-naturedly but seemed impervious to insult, certainly impervious to any insult I could muster.

Still, at any hour of the day he could be found talking to our publicity department, telling us how we should talk to the press, because he knew about the media. He was also talking to magazine and newspaper people, he was all over the place, a terrific one-man band, and there's no question that he was partially responsible for getting us the *Time* cover. The only problem was timing. We wanted the cover postponed because we thought it was coming out too early to be of significant help in terms of over-the-counter sales, as we wouldn't have books in the bookstores in sufficient quantities. So after Schiller briefed me as to what was happening at *Time*, I took the risk and did something one never does: I phoned Henry Grunwald and told him our dilemma, asking if he could postpone the cover piece for a month. Watergate was breaking over our heads and Grunwald said, "Ordinarily I'd understand and try to accommodate you, but in this case I've got a problem. If I yank the *Marilyn* cover story, then I can't guarantee I'll ever run the piece, because Watergate is breaking so rapidly. So decide what you want." I said to him, movie style, "Henry, run the piece."

What other decision could I have made? I went back and told Roth, and we ordered triple overtime in our warehouse to get 17,000 copies out in one weekend.

LAWRENCE SCHILLER Even though Grosset had lots of outside confirmation that *Marilyn* was going to be big, they still didn't know how to do PR. They tell me they're just gonna mail a copy of the book to *Time* and hope to get a review. I'm screaming "Send the book in dummy form. We're gonna get a cover when they see it." But no, they said they couldn't do that, so I told them I was sending the dummy. We were having big fights, and meanwhile Mailer isn't talking to me either.

I'd already shown the book to a few people, and one of them was a guy at *Time*. Then he called—"You got your cover, Larry. But you've got a problem. Your whole credibility is gonna be lost on the Bobby Kennedy thing. Everybody's gonna have to attack it. Mailer's got no credibility."

Now, I'd been worried about the Kennedy stuff all along, but I hadn't really pushed him on his research or checking facts. For example, during my second trip to Stockbridge, after the first draft was done, I'd realized he hadn't interviewed Joe DiMaggio, and I offered to set it up. What Norman said to me, though, was "Larry, I have my image, I know what I want to write about DiMaggio. DiMaggio is renowned for saying very little in interviews. I'll just lose the comfort of being able to write about him without owing any favor for the interview." So I left it at that. But now with the Kennedy stuff, I'm nervous, so I checked back with Norman because I realize that the shit is going to hit the fan with the reviewers. I said, "Norman, look, I know some of the stuff about Bobby came from me, some came from Los Angeles, but do you have confirmation of these things as fact? For instance, did you call Eunice Murray, Marilyn's last house-keeper, who reportedly found the body?"

He said he hadn't, and I asked why not.

"She's dead," he said.

"Who tells you she's dead?"

"I got this private investigator, Stratton, who checked it out."

At the time I had no idea that Rick Stratton was just a friend of Norman's, so I believed him. I took his word that he'd hired a real private investigator who'd checked it out. I didn't yet have an inkling that he might have been winging it.

But after my conversation with the guy from *Time*—a conversation that I never told Norman about—I called Roth and again raised holy hell about the Kennedy stuff. "I've got it from a reliable source that that stuff may blow the *Time* cover story, or we're gonna get crucified. You better go to Mailer and make sure that stuff is backed up." Subsequently they did, in fact, but what I'm not smart enough to realize until afterwards is that they're laying it all on me: Markel is saying, "Schiller wants this and that," not "Grosset wants credibility and confirmation."

Meanwhile I'm getting set for ABA and making arrangements for a *60 Minutes* segment. I'm scheduled to do the taping of my interview with Mike Wallace in his suite at the Beverly Wilshire. The book wasn't out yet, but they were going to film the opening of our ABA exhibit, plus interviews with me and Norman, and I'd worked out a release date with them to coincide with the book's publication, two months away. But I hadn't realized that Wallace had already interviewed Mailer in New York before coming to L.A. So I went up to Wallace's suite. He was lying on the floor in his bathrobe, but he's a good street reporter, and he started asking me things like "How much did you pay Norman?" I said, "That's something only Mr. Mailer can tell you." He said, "Well, I was told $50,000 and that he writes for money." So I start to get paranoid because suddenly I realize he's already interviewed Norman.

Then he got into the Kennedy stuff. I said, "Norman's a fine reporter, he's done his research and has had an investigator on it. Eunice Murray is the only person who could corroborate it, and, of course, she's dead."

Wallace pauses, looks up at me, and says, "She ain't dead. She's living out here in southern California. She's in the phone book."

It was like being hanged—when they drop you, everything comes out the bottom. I didn't know whether Wallace had talked to her—he certainly wasn't telling me—but I saw it coming. So I ran downstairs to find Norman, who's surrounded by photographers in the lobby or someplace, and I realize he's mad at me because he was getting all these bad vibes. That's when he first used his line with me, the one he uses so often but that I'd never heard before: "Once a philosopher, twice a pervert." Years later I quoted it back to him and added something of my own: "Once a philosopher, twice a pervert, three times a historian."

But that night was all hell. Norman wouldn't stand next to me unless he was forced to, and then he made it clear he didn't want to associate with me. All of us, including Roth and Markel, saw what was happening. Norman wouldn't admit it, though, not until 60 Minutes ran the promos for the segment, calling it "Mailer, Monroe and the Fast Buck."

Meanwhile I've gotten a call from Time confirming that they have the book on the cover and they'd like us to send this and that photo. I said, "I'm not sending you any photographs because we want to design our own cover." The Time guy in effect says, "Fuck you, Schiller," and hangs up on me, like I'm not playing the game right. But I went ahead and did a design anyway, using the photograph I'd taken of Mailer outside United's Friendship Lounge, where he looks like a bull. It's in black and white, showing all his antagonism, but the rest of the cover was Monroe in color. I knew that when Norman saw it he'd hit the fuckin' ceiling because of the photo, and two, the first time he gets on the cover of Time he's gotta share it with Monroe. On top of that, she's gonna upstage him because he's in black and white and she's in color and sitting on his head. But I also knew what I was doing, because if Time used the picture, I'd own the cover and could market it to magazines all over the world. So I sent in our design, and two weeks later I got a call from their art department asking where they could get the transparency of Monroe and a better print of the Mailer photograph. So I knew they were using it. But, as I had predicted, when the cover came out Mailer was ready to kill me.

Obviously the book had been getting lots of exposure, and I was still thinking we had a huge winner until the 60 Minutes story was aired. Wallace is very smart—he divides and conquers: I was horrible on the show and so was Norman. The final note was Norman defending the Kennedy stuff by saying, "I thought it was important enough to get the book out there half finished rather than not to get it out at all." And I think that after the show we lost more than half the sales of the book. Thank God for the Book-of-the-Month Club, the Playboy Book Club, and the foreign sales, which had all happened before, like the sale to the London Sunday Times for $75,000. Scott wasn't involved; he was just taking his agent's percentage from Norman's share of the sales. My contract and my control was only with Grosset and Dunlap, and the only big fight I had with Scott was when he advised us to sell magazine serialization rights to Playboy and I insisted on Ladies' Home Journal. I said, "You already have the Playboy market, but you don't have the women's market. Marilyn never offended a goddamn woman. Why are you afraid to sell to women?"

Kretchmer, I realize, was disappointed not to get it, but I think he knew that I was responsible for that and understood my reasoning. Also, even though *Ladies' Home Journal* was offering $40,000 as opposed to *Playboy's* $50,000, Grosset finally sided with me.

ARTHUR KRETCHMER   I felt there were segments of the book about DiMaggio, Miller, Marilyn's agent, and two other men in her life that when taken together offered a portrait of Marilyn that really held, a portrait of somebody growing up, changing, being full of the myths of American culture. So I said to Scott Meredith, "I'd like to edit the book so that I get these five men as a series of portraits." But I got word back that Norman didn't want to do that, so we dropped out of the bidding. Months later I told Norman that I'd been disappointed not to get *Marilyn*. He said, "You would've taken the whole book if you'd done those excerpts, and I couldn't give that much."

ROBERT MARKEL   After the book came out Norman had the idea of holding a press conference, which he scheduled for July 18. I was opposed to it, Schiller was opposed to it, but Norman went ahead anyway, again putting himself on the spot.

LAWRENCE SCHILLER   I begged him not to do it. *Begged* him. "You're throwing yourself to the lions," I said, and he replied, "No, I'm gonna hold it at the Algonquin. That's the writers' hotel—they'll respect me as a writer."

My feeling is that Norman doesn't understand the press because he hates them so much. He claims he knows how to talk to AP reporters, because they only write 250 words, and he knows how to give a statement that is condensible. That's his theory. But in fact he goes on a tirade, he goes on and on as if he's giving the Gettysburg Address, and he gives them so much information that the press takes the worst of it, because that's what sticks out.

So I couldn't persuade him not to go ahead with this thing, although I'd told Markel, "If he's doing it at the Algonquin, make sure it's in a big room, because in a banquet hall, even if you've got fifty members of the press, it's gonna look like a small press conference, and I don't want this to look important." I said I'd been a member of the press, I'd been on the other fucking side, but I was also remembering what happened to me when I gave a press conference to release the Capitol record of the Jack Ruby tapes. I knew that Ruby was dying, so I reserved a big banquet room at the Americana in New York, just anticipating the worst. So when a reporter, in the middle of the press conference, pinned me to the wall with "What do you have to say now that Jack Ruby is dead?" the question came from ninety feet back and wasn't heard by half the people in the room. In a small room, though, there's always momentum, everything builds on everything else.

Anyway, I forced myself to fly into New York when he told me he was going

ahead with it, my thinking being: I've gotta direct the press away from him. Let them go after me or we're gonna destroy the book.

The two of us walked into the Algonquin, and it's a teeny little room, a suite or a small conference room, with the press and TV cameras packed in like sardines, and I was furious. I turned to Markel and said, "You're a fucking idiot. I told you to get a large room. You still don't know how to handle the press." As usual, he didn't reply. Just the poker face.

We had to squeeze to the front of the room, and I pushed myself to sit next to Norman. But it was still a fiasco. Norman came on as if he were fighting Carmen Basilio in Madison Square Garden, only he was Art Aragon, the boxer who every time he lost had a good explanation of why he'd really won. He let the press bait him. He exploded. He was raving, and it was a gang bang, only in a gang bang, at least, the victim gets tired. Norman never got tired.

Throughout it all I'm thinking, Oh, my God, we're losing our sales. But all the while Norman was challenging the press to go out and get the real scoop, that Marilyn was killed by right-wingers in order to frame Bobby Kennedy.

ROBERT MARKEL   It was a shambles, just terrible. I was standing in the back of the room with John Leonard, who was there as *The New York Times* representative, having recently been appointed the *Book Review* editor. He had come to see the fun, but he had also played a role in Pauline Kael's front-page review in the *Book Review*, which was published four days after the press conference, on July 22, but which, of course, comes out to people in the trade the week before. Whether this was one of Norman's reasons for scheduling the press conference I don't know, but it's a possibility that might bear scrutiny because there was a history there.

Naturally, I'd thought it extremely important to try to orchestrate a Sunday

Times Book Review in which the least damage would be done. But most of all I wanted a front-page review, which you can sometimes arrange with a major book by calling it to the attention of *The Times* well enough in advance.

Earlier, though, when Norman had been writing the text, he was asked by *The New York Review of Books* to review *Last Tango in Paris*. He'd read Pauline Kael's review and was licking his chops. He was in our office one day—I guess in from Stockbridge to work on captions or something—and he asked if I'd lend him a typewriter and an office so he could get his piece in. And what he did was call Kael "the first frigid of the film critics."

Now, unbeknownst to me, John Leonard had been trying to get Kael to review for him. I don't know why, but she'd been turning him down regularly. Norman's review of *Last Tango* was published in May, and as I learned after the fact, when John saw Norman's attack on Kael, he said to himself, "I'll capture Pauline by giving her the opportunity to get her hooks into Mailer." And lo and behold, that's exactly what happened.

DIANA TRILLING   Writers are always suspicious of other writers who make money, so there was nothing special in their suspicion of Norman. All the "advanced people"—the *Partisan Review* types, the *Commentary* types—they are none of them immune to the desire for money. This attitude of suspiciousness existed even in the thirties: until we make the money it's wrong to make the money. But starting in the seventies people began to call Norman to account—with some basis, I think—for dissipating his energies and writing so many different kinds of things, obviously *just* for money. *Marilyn*, I suppose, is the prime example.

ROBERT MARKEL   None of us understood the degree to which Norman's text was derived, or, as he later put it, "based in the main" upon other texts. I hadn't read his manuscript line for line against either Fred Guiles's *Norma Jean* or Maurice Zolotow's *Marilyn Monroe*. He'd used their books to develop the chronology, but that wasn't unusual. Also, he didn't have time to screw around, and he probably figured that Grosset would get the permissions and that would be the end of it.

We weren't aware of a serious problem until we applied for permissions by sending galleys to the various people. Guiles was presumably shown a set— "Here's what Norman Mailer's doing"—and he hit the ceiling. We weren't committed to press at that point, and I think Guiles's claim of plagiarism came in first, then Zolotow's, but they were virtually back to back.

Norman considered it simply a permissions problem that had nothing to do with him. He was nettled by the fact that the issue had been raised at all and seemed to feel that it was an administrative matter that hadn't been handled properly. For our part, we didn't disabuse him of that notion because we were uncertain ourselves. It was quite ambiguous until we did what, quite obviously, it had never occurred to us to do before—that is, make a careful line-by-line reading of those other books against his. This was precipitated when we sold the book to Hodder and Stoughton in England and they in turn disposed of the serial rights very advantageously to the London *Sunday Times.* Hodder's had applied for permission to Mark Goulden because his house, W. H. Allen, had published Guiles in England. Goulden's now dead, but he was a difficult fellow at the best of times, and he indicated to Hodder's that he thought there was a problem of plagiarism. This was back in April or May, I think, but I thought we'd be able to smooth things over both here and in England by going beyond permissions departments and making it a matter between publisher and publisher. In fact, Harold Roth and I made a personal visit to the office of Harold McGraw and said, "Please, nobody has done anything terrible here. If Norman literally drew upon Guiles's book and Guiles is having a fit, you as a publisher understand his sort of behavior and you can bring him to his senses. Please, we certainly don't want to pit publisher against publisher, so don't allow Guiles to use you."

We then settled with McGraw-Hill for nine hundred dollars, I think, but then Goulden claimed he wasn't going to give permission at all, which would blockade the English publication. The folks in London were looking to us for relief because the deal there was being threatened, so Cy Rembar called a meeting in his office on behalf of Norman, who by this time was really hot under the collar. He felt his publisher had not come to his support, and while he didn't seem personally angry at me, he was giving the impression that Grosset hadn't known what it was doing, and he was holding us responsible. We all agreed that a meeting was necessary, so it was going to be Norman, Cy, Scott Meredith, Harold Roth, and myself. We had lots of discussion too, though, about whether Schiller should come, and at first we tried to stop him. We thought we'd simply inform him of the meeting after the fact rather than risk his disrupting things, but as it turned out, he was into it with all fours and came anyway. We also had Don Engel, Grosset and Dunlap's lawyer.

Cy was siding with Norman all the way, trying to find a way to contain the matter so that Norman's reputation wouldn't be injured. That was the key issue, for him as well as for Scott and Norman. This didn't come up directly with Norman and Cy, but it was definitely in the air, because I confided to Don Engel that Norman's concern might go beyond our considerations of timing of publication or loss of revenues.

We'd essentially separated the English situation from the one here, and the real problem was how to deal with Goulden, who had become intransigent in his demand for a major piece of the action, so we hired counsel in London. There was some discussion of who would assume the legal costs, as well as the monies to be paid off, and I think then we settled on the sum of $17,500. We paid our attorneys ourselves, though, without passing that along.

The settlement to Zolotow was also small potatoes, under $10,000 and perhaps even as low as $3000. Norman had discussions with him, and he got off his high horse when Norman agreed to give him a nice salute of indebtedness. In fact, Norman rewrote the galleys also to thank Guiles, whose "admirable portrait," blah blah blah. All of those acknowledgments were constructed after the fact to satisfy these guys' rapacious desires to be paid off one way or another.

We also did some last-minute work on the book because there were other potential threats, one from Elizabeth Taylor's attorney, the other from Arthur Miller. The thing with Elizabeth Taylor was quite amusing. In his initial draft Norman described a meeting between Taylor and Monroe in the Polo Lounge of the Beverly Hills Hotel and quoted an unidentified witness who reported Taylor saying, "Get that dyke away from me." The galleys were circulating in Hollywood, and Taylor's representative called and said, "Elizabeth is wild and furious and is going to sue the publisher and author for six million dollars." We quickly checked through the book for the only reference she could conceivably be talking about, and I called Norman, who said that Eli Wallach was the unidentified witness and that when he'd talked to him about *The Misfits* he'd sworn that's what Taylor said. Norman then double-checked with Wallach and told me to let it stand. Having checked with our counsel, and knowing that I could find twelve witnesses in fifteen minutes who could claim they'd heard Taylor say a lot worse about a lot of people, I didn't think it was a problem. Unless Norman wanted to remove it from the book for his own reasons, I felt we could stay with it.

The problem with Arthur Miller came about because I told Norman that I felt it would be useful and appropriate to send him a set of galleys. Norman said okay, I sent them out, and then Arthur called and said that he very much resented the passage in which Norman implied or virtually stated that he'd lived off the earnings of his wives—that he'd been supported by his first wife and then later had lived off and invested Marilyn's earnings. I passed this along, and Norman said, "No, it's true. He's failed to refute it in the statements he's made to you. But even if it isn't true, what's libelous about that in this day and age?" Arthur's attorney called and said he felt Arthur wanted to bring an action. I said, "Would you mind telling me what course of action?" He said, "Libel," and I said, "Would you mind citing any passage in the book which you consider libelous?" And that was the last I heard of it, although in fact Norman did modify a sentence or two.

NORMAN ROSTEN Norman had been so straight about using excerpts from my book as well as giving it such a nice plug that I was amazed when those lawsuits were brought. I didn't know the details, but with me, Norman or the publisher had gone to my agent and paid a permissions fee. I also didn't understand what he was supposed to have taken when so much was in the public domain anyway.

At first, though, I thought Arthur Miller would be the one to sue. Mailer says some terrible things about Miller, really cruel, gossipy stuff. On the other hand, my answer to Arthur is, "Don't become famous and people won't pick on you." When I read what Mailer wrote I realized, Jesus Christ, he really didn't like the man.

ROBERT MARKEL After the meeting at Cy's I was still feeling quite unsettled. I knew that Cy's allegiance was to Norman, and that concerned me because Norman's interests and Grosset and Dunlap's interest might not necessarily be in tandem very much longer, and already the question of monies, the prospect of having to make payoffs, had come up. We realized we were going to have to pay off Mark Goulden in order to keep the whole British deal in place.

In July or August, after the book was published, a story appeared in *The Times* saying that Zolotow had filed a five-part complaint, based on ninety-six passages of Mailer's allegedly taken from his book. I don't know what Norman's response was to that specifically, but I do know that when Harold Roth said he was a reasonable man and was quoted in relation to the Guiles claim as saying, "I wouldn't rule out a settlement down the line," Norman's position was, Goddamn it, don't you realize that by settling, in effect you're admitting guilt? He was very sensitive about that, even though it was in his best interest to get the thing over with. The stench of the situation had begun to rise earlier, but in late June and in July Norman had made public statements, quoted in *The Times*, denying that he'd plagiarized, even though we thought we'd settled the matter before the book had come out. Finally, in November, Zolotow retracted his charge of plagiarism and apologized.

LAWRENCE SCHILLER The potential problems with Zolotow and Guiles had come up right around the time of the ABA. I hold Scott Meredith totally responsible. He represented Zolotow and obtained a copy of his book for Norman because the book wasn't easily found. He'd told Norman, in effect, "Don't worry, I'll get you permission. There's no problem with Zolotow." With Guiles, I think Norman felt that since he'd made a point of giving credit, and since Grosset had gotten permission from his publisher, there would be no problem either. The other thing was that we were running so late, Grosset and Dunlap's lawyers hadn't looked at the text.

All I know is that Norman wanted to go to the mat, while everybody else, of course, wanted to settle. Roth kept saying, "Larry, a drop in the bucket. That's the least of our worries." Norman was quite upset with this and perceived it, justifiably so, as a sellout. He was really mad at Roth and may have talked about suing, but I think Cy dissuaded him. You could never tell Cy's true feelings, though. He was coming across publicly as the voice of moderation, but while he didn't say it in so many words, his attitude seemed to be, Shut up, Norman, you're lucky to get out of this.

ROBERT MARKEL We printed 100,000 copies of *Marilyn*, the first printing in hard-cover, but I honestly don't remember how many copies we printed *in toto*. There were at least ten different foreign-language editions, including Greek, Portuguese, and even a Serbo-Croatian edition, and those foreign sales included not only the book itself but also the magazine serial rights. It was a big payday. We had world rights as part of the contract, and originally Scott let us have them because he thought he was selling just a 25,000-word foreword to Larry Schiller's collection of photographs. I don't think he anticipated what was going to happen—namely, that those foreign rights brought us at least a half million dollars, only half of which went to Norman and Schiller.

I don't know if Mailer was worried about sales, and, in fact, that November or December the book was still selling well when he came in with his idea of a full two-page ad. Since he was now more or less in the hands of Harold Roth, there was a big meeting in Harold's office. What he wanted to do was exactly what he'd done with *The Village Voice* ad for *The Deer Park*: present all the positive and negative reviews, including Kael's, setting the two in opposition.

Harold was very much against it. He thought the two pages would be a stupid waste of money, but more, it was the adversarial nature of the ad as Norman conceived it. Harold didn't feel it was the proper way to sell a product, and after being extremely patient with Norman, he virtually said this. Then he became quite transparently patronizing of Norman and said, "Norman, please, I didn't tell you how to write the book. Don't tell me how to make up the ad."

It got to that, but how Norman finally persuaded him to do it, I don't know. Harold just finally gave up and said, "Okay, but you'll see. No good will come of it." Norman, though, was really quite serious. He implied he'd made a study of this kind of thing and knew what he was talking about—like what made the people in our fancy-shmancy advertising office think they knew better than he how to create an ad for the book-reading public?

DON CARPENTER   Norman was in San Francisco for his *Marilyn* publicity tour, and I went to a party for him given by Grace Warnecke, a rich society lady, George Kennan's daughter. He was in the hands of a young, attractive PR girl whom I was talking to when Bob McNie, Alice Adams' architect boyfriend, started making points by punching him flat-handed on the left shoulder. Bob's about three or four inches taller than Norman, heavyset, a tough-looking guy, and he was leaning on Norman—punch, punch, making sarcastic points. Norman, like a bull, was starting to lower. He was looking at the ground and his mouth was getting tense and his shoulders were hunching. I put my hand across the front of the PR girl and said, "Step back, step back," because I knew trouble was gonna happen and I didn't want to get a spare fist in the face.

We were three feet away, Bob was still at it, as if saying, "You have to take this because I'm so much bigger than you are." Then he got really stupid—he slapped Norman's cheek, just a light slap but the kind a big guy would give a little guy, and it occurred to me immediately that what was going on was that Alice had told Bob about knowing Norman in Paris.

Instantly Norman reached down and took Bob between the legs with one hand, grasped his neck with the other, then lifted him up over his head, whirling him around, and threw him to the rug. Bob jumped up and offered to shake Norman's hand, like "Hey, that was really good." But Norman wouldn't have anything to do with him. He just growled and turned away.

I don't know what Alice did—she was in the other room. But Norman's right when he says his only guilt is that he happened to be there. Unlike other fights you'd read about in the past, he didn't cause the trouble, he ended it. Poor Bob was drunk and obviously very, very jealous.

ALICE ADAMS   I wasn't sure what happened because my back was turned. But Bob is extremely good-looking, six feet tall, well built, with very broad shoulders. He and Norman were talking to a very beautiful woman, and I turned around

Norman's idea of a two-page ad.

briefly and saw Bob get up from the floor, enraged and making gestures of going after Norman, but John Warnecke restrained him.

Various witnesses say that Norman picked up Bob, twirled him around in the air three times, and dropped him on the floor. That's impossible. Bob weighs 195, and besides, there wasn't enough time for Norman to do that. What started it I don't know, although everybody was drinking a lot. I don't think it had much to do with this woman, because neither Norman nor Bob was seriously interested in her. But Norman didn't look good. He'd been traveling, he was tired, and he looked old and seedy. He had on a dark blue blazer that was dirty and stained. Bob also had on a dark blue blazer, but it was clean, and he was looking great.

Afterwards we all went out to a Chinese restaurant for dinner, and the two of them shook hands sort of drunkenly. But what makes me mad is it's such a trashy demise to a long friendship, and I say "trashy" because every day for a week afterwards there'd be one more version of this ugly, stupid incident. People like Don Carpenter kept saying how wonderful Norman was twirling Bob McNie around. He says that's what he saw, but I don't believe it. But there were several people who were dying to be good friends of Norman's, trashy people who put out that garbage in the newspapers.

JOHN LEONARD I'm on the board of directors of the MacDowell Colony, and they asked me to head the committee to choose the 1973 recipient of their literary medal. Thornton Wilder had gotten it, also Lillian Hellman, and I chose Mailer because, even though he was younger than most, he'd written about twenty books or so. Then all hell broke loose when Mailer brought out *Marilyn*. All hell in the public-relations sense, because Arthur Miller had always been one of the significant contributors to the MacDowell Colony, and there was a lot of talk about maybe we should rescind the award. But the MacDowell people were wonderful, saying, "No, we've made a decision and we'll go ahead with it." I'd lined up Elizabeth Hardwick to make the presentation that summer—this was '74—then she got invited to spend two months in a villa in Italy, so we didn't have anyone to make the speech. I said I'd do it and make it a brief defense.

I'd spent a good part of the summer working on the speech and convincing Norman to come. Eventually he drove up with Carol Stevens, and, as I had promised, we put them up at our house. There was a big party, then he and I sat up drinking until two in the morning, when he came out with "You're gonna get me tomorrow, aren't you?" I said, "What do you mean?" He said, "You've never written anything about what I've written, so you're gonna use this occasion to get me." I was thunderstruck, my sense of civility really offended. I mean, he didn't realize that I had made the choice and argued for him. So I told him he was being ridiculous. "Go to bed," I said. "I'll get you down there in time, and then you just listen."

I couldn't even figure out how to be mad enough, see? I think he wanted to read what I was going to say, but he didn't ask. He just said, "You're out to get me" and gave me his gremlin, Munchkin grin. He went off with a glass, but I didn't fall asleep for a half hour, saying, "Son of a bitch—why the hell would he think I'd ever do that to him?" My reading of it was that he'd spent too much time in the New York literary community. I don't know—it so violated everything I would've expected of him. But I think he was actually anxious about it. He was the youngest person ever to receive the award, and he was getting it for a career, not an individual book.

I had to wake him in the morning, and he would hardly talk to me as we went over to the ceremony.

There were five hundred people gathered outside in the open for the presentation, the largest gathering MacDowell had ever had—local people, guests, the media, *The New York Times*, *The Boston Globe*. Mailer always attracts a larger crowd than other people; they all want to see "the wild man." So I got up and introduced him, and later my then wife told me that as I went on with my speech Norman had become more and more benign. In fact, as he passed me on his way to the podium he said, "If you'd write the same thing against me, it'd be fine criticism." He was trying to make a compliment, something like "Review my books and tell me what I do wrong. I'll pay attention now."

As he began he thanked me and the audience and then spoke for about fifteen or twenty minutes without cards. He proceeded to introduce four different ideas— one was about Watergate, the other this and that—and then at the end he tied them all up. It was very coherent, brilliant. By the end the crowd was standing, screaming, and all the little old ladies came up to lick his hand, and he didn't want to leave, he got so much adulation.

Never did he once say anything about the night before, though, and I've never brought it up. My father was a drunk, and I'm very aware that there are conversations you never want to remind anybody of. I think I know him well enough now to ask him, and I'm certain he'd remember, since he remembers everything.

The odd thing, though, is that several months later, in the fall, I told him that if he wasn't going to write fiction, he had to do something on Hemingway. I said I could get him $60,000—what we would ordinarily pay for an entire issue of *The Times Book Review*—or that I'd talk the publishers into giving him a special section. He said, "If I ever do it, I'll do it for you."

Let him write whatever he wants. Still, I got very annoyed at the *Marilyn* project. I felt his whole set of ideas about death belonged to another object. I have no objection to journalism or any of the stuff he does, although I still want him to write novels; but if he's going to do this stuff, then take it head on. Everything he thinks about revolves around some larger and more interesting target, and I'd be far more interested in reading about Hemingway than Marilyn Monroe or any other subject he chooses to visit with his apprehensions.

Why? Because Mailer could've been the greatest literary critic of our time, though obviously that's not going to pay the freight. What he said about Salinger, Styron, Vidal—even though it was nasty, bitchy, all that stuff was marvelous. When he decided in his anger at Kate Millett to talk about D. H. Lawrence, it was the best stuff I'd ever read on Lawrence. What he does is consume a book and regurgitate the writer that he thinks was there. He's also prepared to cope with the writer's intentions. His sympathies are broad because he's confident enough in his own talent to extend his sympathy and make the best possible case for what the writer is trying to do, how he perceived the world, how he went about doing it. These are wonderful, ideal credentials, and obviously why I'd like to see him put together his fear of death, his ambiguous relationship to celebrity, and his literary criticism in something about Hemingway. In fact, in the aftermath of *Marilyn* I remember saying to him, "Now you'll do your *real* suicide book."

I admit I was appealing to his ego by saying, "This has never been done before. I'll give you the whole issue of the *Book Review*—we start you on page one, run all the way through to whatever length you want. If it goes longer, I'll sell ads. The only handicap is that I can't get dirty words into *The Times*." He'd be paid accordingly—whatever I'd have to pay to fill up the magazine—and he could then publish it as a book. He liked the idea, he could see it. But then nothing happened.

LAWRENCE SCHILLER   It was really during the 60 *Minutes* segment on *Marilyn* that I became aware of Norman's financial situation, which was why, a year later, I thought of him doing *The Faith of Graffiti*, even though he wasn't talking to me at that point.

A designer had brought me pictures that had been done by a New York photographer; they were going to be published as a book in England, and the designer wanted to know if I'd publish it in the United States. While the photographs were interesting, I thought it wouldn't sell as a book without a good text. But I was smart enough not to call and ask to speak to Norman directly. I knew Molly Cook, his secretary in Provincetown, so I phoned her and said, "I'd like to send this book of photographs to you. Please show it to Norman because I'd like him to write a text, and I'll pay him $35,000."

A couple of days later Norman phoned me. The conversation was strained, and he said, "Look, I'm interested. I can write something, but I don't want any interruption." Then he said I should phone Scott to discuss money and make the deal.

With *Marilyn*, when I'd signed the contract with Grosset and Dunlap, Harold Roth had mentioned that they had to get Little, Brown's permission since Norman was under a multibook contract with them. Now I was more aware of the situation, so I discussed it with Scott, who said there really wouldn't be a problem because Norman would write the essay very fast. I agreed and said, "Good, I want him to make some quick money here."

And that's what it was, a short essay.

More important, by the time he was done I knew I could phone him and he'd speak to me. Whether or not either of us believed we'd be doing another book together, the ice had been broken for *The Executioner's Song*.

NORMAN MAILER (THE FIGHT)   *Months ago, a story had gotten into the newspapers about a novel he was writing. His publishers were going to pay him a million dollars sight unseen for the book. If his candles had been burning low in the literary cathedral these last few years, the news story went its way to hastening their extinction. He knew that his much publicized novel (still nine-tenths to be written) would now have to be twice as good as before to overcome such financial news. Good literary men were not supposed to pick up sums. Small apples for him to protest in every banlieu and literary purlieu that his Boston publisher had not been laid low with a degenerative disease of the cortex but that the million was to be paid out as he wrote five to seven hundred thousand words, the equivalent of five novels. Since he was being rewarded only as he delivered the work, and had debts and a sizable advance already spent and five wives and seven children, plus a financial nut at present larger than his head, so the sum was not as large as it seemed, he explained—the million, you see, was nominal.*

ARTHUR KRETCHMER By '72, when I became executive editor of *Playboy,* Norman had already often appeared in the magazine—on panels, the Buckley debate in '62, a '67 essay on bullfighting, then the '68 interview with him. Still, my impression is that the first real piece we commissioned was "The Fight" on Ali-Foreman in Zaire, which was initiated by Scott Meredith and mostly handled at this end by Geoffrey Norman, with some assistance from me.

Norman and Geoffrey had a great relationship, and I know that Norman thought the world of Geoffrey as an editor. The two of them were flip sides of a rednecked coin—Norman a New York-New England redneck, Geoffrey a Gulf Coast redneck—and while both are basically serious intellectuals, they're both tough guys. Norman appreciated Geoffrey's work, his feedback. However, when he handed in his manuscript, it was twice as long as anybody could deal with, and, of course, Scott charged us more money because we were faced with publishing it in two parts.

I was annoyed and even considered not running it. We couldn't devote an entire issue to the piece the way *Harper's* had done with *The Armies of the Night* and *The Prisoner of Sex.* In fact, before the assignment I'd told Geoffrey, "You want to publish Mailer, the magazine wants to publish Mailer, and we want to have a strong relationship with him. But this piece could come in very big, and we don't want anything big. We want something in the realm of 8000 to 10,000 words." Then it arrived—28,000 to 30,000 words on a goddamn prize-fight. I had seen a filmed version of the fight, so I decided there was a graphic solution, that this thing made sense as a drama in two parts: first Foreman's power, then Ali's comeback. With the captions and illustrations, which are very rare for us in nonfiction, the solution made sense and would keep the thing intact.

But after the piece came out we had a legal problem. Norman had described a whole bunch of people riding in a car, jiving each other, and he quotes somebody saying, "Well, that Elmo Henderson"—a sparring partner of Ali's— "that Henderson, they got him out of an insane asylum." Norman had picked the line up, didn't think about it, and although we questioned it, we were rushing to close and left it in. Henderson, though, had never been in an insane asylum, and he sued for a million dollars, claiming libel.

Norman-the-journalist, was tremendously upset about having made such a mistake, such a bonehead journalistic play, so what had been a fairly peripheral relationship between us suddenly got fairly intense. We sent him to Dallas for the trial, and he got to know David Krupp, one of our most intelligent and literate lawyers, because they spent a lot of time together.

From our point of view the case came out all right. We settled out of court for not very much money, although Krupp's time is very expensive. While Scott Meredith had a fairly straightforward and mercenary attitude—dictated by Norman's life-style—Norman's attitude toward us changed from then on. He and I flew from Chicago to New York together—this was later, when he was writing *The Executioner's Song*—and he alluded to the Henderson thing, saying how seriously he took his function as a journalist. He wasn't merely saying "I fucked up" but rather "I'd like to think that I wouldn't have made that kind of mistake." He was chagrined, and also apologizing.

But the only way you can afford Norman is to publish him more than once, which is what we've done, obviously. The dynamics of it are interesting, and Norman's right when he calls himself a "loss leader." We don't publish him for direct sales, as opposed to other writers, like Le Carré and Joseph Heller or Woody Allen. Norman's a funny character this way—he's not a commercial writer. He is simply the most interesting writer, a writer you want to publish if you're editing a magazine, and whether or not all of *Playboy*'s readers are going to line up eagerly to buy the issue doesn't really come into play.

But there's another side to it that *is* commercial. The magazine I want to put out has to reflect what's going on in America and be the best it can be every given month, and that magazine has to have Norman because it's a different world without Norman. *Playboy* with Norman is a magazine of the moment, of impact. Powerfully, incontestably, Norman has tried to express our era. He looks through infinity and says, "Who are we? What have we done? What can we be?" For example, there was the piece he wrote in *The New York Times Magazine* years ago about the high-rise he wanted to build where people with the guts lived on the outside, on the edge of cables, and the people who didn't have guts lived in the interior. That image or idea tells you a lot about our society. If I knew my Greek history better I'd tell you who he is, but he's our chronicler, our Thucydides or whatever.

So we've published Norman because he's a long-run investment. Our magazine doesn't function on pornography or *Enquirer*-like sensationalism. It functions on the fact that people who read *Playboy* have a certain sense of upscale events, and Norman's part of that psychology. Also, for Norman himself, other magazines have really lost the franchise to do what he needs. Norman's a cosmic character with cosmic money needs, and they came together in *Playboy*, plus the fact that he keeps offending the intellectual establishment. This obsession of his—What are we reaching for? Who are we? Finally he runs out of places like *Dissent* or *Commentary* or even *Harper's* because he plays in the mirror of reality, and that's a very, very strange place.

XI:
THE EXECU-
TIONER'S
SONG (1975–79)

NORMAN MAILER (LETTER TO FRANCIS IRBY GWALTNEY, MARCH 26, 1975)

I'm going to be lecturing at Loyola in New Orleans on the 26th of April, and what I thought is I could go on from there to Little Rock the next day, and if there's a connection, fly to Russellville. Or, if not, maybe you could pick me up. But in any case, if that time is agreeable to you, I'll plan to do it that way and also plan to stay through on Monday and not go back to New York until Tuesday. The beauty of it is that my lecture tour will be over in Loyola—seven lectures in ten days—so I will feel like celebrating.

As for my drinking habits, we have been apart for too long, my friends. I no longer drink bourbon. The congeners are too rich for this man's fifty-year-old blood (fifty-two-years old). I now like a light Bacardi rum, pale as can be, with good Schweppes tonic. That ought to be easier to find.

Incidentally, Fig, you say you lost thirty pounds? I've gained them. Hélas! Hey, I'm looking forward to seeing you all.

*Love,
Norman*

562

FRANCIS IRBY GWALTNEY (LETTER TO NORMAN MAILER, APRIL 3, 1975)

... We're set for your visit. I've even told my booze dealer to find me a couple of quarts of LIGHT rum (Bacardi) and I've located the Schweppes (the local tonic is Canada Dry). When you get to New Orleans, call me and I'll pick you up at the airport in Little Rock ...

We're making no plans, but if you're willing, we might have a few (20) of our more articulate rednecks over for a swallow and then run them off. ... My fifteen creative writing students want to meet you. We have a seminar and most of the time we sit around and shoot the shit, not at all the way Lt. Shedler would have had it, although there is a regular army captain in the group (I habitually call him Corporal), but Karl and I are in charge. If you would like to amble in, there would be no speeches, no fucking around—just chatting. Your veto of that would be easily understandable because, by that time, your ass will be dragging your tracks out. (I'm going to sit you down and give you my standard lecture on frugality because there's no reason why you should have to work so hard or travel so far to support your establishment.). ...

What the fuck does helas mean?

JOSE TORRES   In the spring of '75 I was up in Stockbridge, and he told me, "I met this girl Barbara," and he showed me her picture. Then he said, "I think Carol knows because she found this," meaning the photo.

BARBARA NORRIS CHURCH MAILER   We met in the spring of '75, almost by chance, when he was visiting Fig and Ecey after a lecture tour in Florida and New Orleans. I wasn't self-conscious about meeting him, even though our backgrounds couldn't have been more different.

I grew up an only child in Atkins, Arkansas, population 1391. I was loved, I was told I was beautiful, and everything my parents could do for me they did within their means. My mother was a hairdresser and still is. My father worked on construction jobs running a crane, or on the interstate highways leveling the roadbed with the big blades. He was a terrific blademan, and because he was a minor officer in the union and popular in the union office, he always got work.

In high school I was in all the clubs and the president or secretary or something of all of them. There were only forty-four kids in my class, and about six of us girls were the "in" crowd who did everything, like putting out the newspaper and school annual. I was gung ho, basically Miss Goody Two-Shoes, with straight A's and all these extracurricular activities. I didn't smoke, didn't drink, didn't even fool around until I met Larry, my first husband.

I also went to church three times a week. Both my parents took it seriously and still do. Freewill Baptist. I was terrified my whole adolescent life because I thought I was going to die and go to hell, since in our church everything was a sin, even going to the movies. When I was seven or eight the preacher got up at the Sunday night service and said he'd seen a girl in our congregation coming out of the theater. She was the daughter of a deacon, about fifteen, and the preacher called her by name and made her kneel at the altar. Everybody was in tears, and they all went up and prayed for her. It was the most traumatic experience, and I thought, Oh, my God! And she just went to the movies!

Then at eight I got saved. It's kind of obscure what that means, but you kneel at the altar, you cry, and everybody comes up and prays with you. You pledge your life to Christ and beg forgiveness for your sins. I don't know what an eight-year-old kid can possibly do to sin, but the preacher would describe hell, the actual colors and the density, and the congregation would sing songs, like "If I Could Hear My Mother Pray Again." They were trying to scare you into being good, and, in fact, I had nightmares from seven until thirteen, and I was sure I was going to die and go to hell before I was seventeen. Seventeen was the magic number for some reason.

Still, I didn't have the feeling of being boxed in when I was in high school. About fifteen of us went to college, but most of my class is still living in Atkins or Russellville, and I'm the only one to come to New York. Russellville is the metropolis, about twelve miles from Atkins, with movie theaters, a bowling alley, and Arkansas Polytechnic College, which is where I went to college. Little Rock is sixty miles away, the real city, where the ballet or an art show would come, but it was only later, when I was divorced and on my second social go-round, so to speak, that I'd go over there.

My high school didn't have an art department, but I could draw well, so I did illustrations for the paper and the annual. Then when I went to college, in '67, I took an art course and after nine weeks switched majors to art.

Tuition was only about a hundred dollars a semester, but I worked summers. I picked beans one summer, but that was hard work out in the sun, so I went to the Atkins pickle factory, worked there when I was sixteen, seventeen, and eighteen. They bottle under different names—Vlasic is one of the many labels—and at first I did piece-packing. You have to get so many in a jar nice and neat, and you have to get so many jars done in a day. People who have been working there for twenty years are real swift, like the fifty-year-old lady next to me who'd been doing it all her life. You were supposed to get fast, but I was all thumbs, so then they let me squirt the brine into the jars, until I got bored squeezing the gun and just held it open and sort of filled the jars and in between too.

So they took me off that and put me on the hamburger-slicer—the machine that cuts pickles into hamburger slices—but one day the girl on the slicer across from me and I started throwing pickles at each other. The boss saw us, so I was finally put in the onion room, which is the lowest level of hell. You peel big, fat, fresh onions. For the first few days you cry and cry, then you get used to it, and to this day I still don't cry when I peel onions—maybe my tear glands were destroyed forever. Besides that, I smelled. Six weeks after I finished that job I still slept with my hands under my pillow because I couldn't stand the smell.

In August of '69, when I was twenty, I married Larry Norris, who was two years ahead of me in college and majoring in wildlife biology. The plan was that I'd work for a year while he finished, and then when he went into the army I'd go back to school.

I went to work as a secretary for Russellville Steel. I'd been there for about three months when one day I was at the file cabinet and one of the men I worked for came up to me, put his hand on my rear end and said, "Since you're married now, you know all about... and so how about you and me?" I said, "Get your hands off me" or something equally original, and I pushed him out of the way, real hard. That afternoon I was fired for making too many typing errors.

So there I was, supporting my husband through college, newly married, with a little apartment and no job. But I'm usually lucky, and just the next day I got another office job at a shoe factory, the lowest on the totem pole of twelve people. Then, through a fluke, I was picked to be an assistant manager. But it still was a horrible, horrible job, and as soon as Larry graduated, in January, I went back to college.

Larry was a first lieutenant at Fort Knox for six weeks of armor school. Tanks. Then he was moved to Fort Campbell, Kentucky, where we lived for five months before he was shipped out to Vietnam. It was a rocky road during that period, because while he'd been gone at Fort Knox I'd decided that I really shouldn't have gotten married in the first place. I hadn't dated anyone but him between sixteen and twenty, and I felt I just wanted to go back and be a kid again.

Eventually I got on the bus and went home to my parents, who supported me, but all my friends said, "You've only been married three months, go back and give it another try." Meanwhile Larry was calling, asking me to come back, and then he drove all the way to Atkins to get me. Five months later he left for Vietnam, right after Christmas, 1970, and just before he left I got pregnant. He didn't even know until he arrived in Saigon, and the baby was born while he was there.

He was right in the midst of things when Da Nang was hot, and he wrote me marvelous chronicles of the war, drew diagrams and sent me pictures. He was there eleven months. I was living with my parents, going to school, pregnant, and very unhappy. I think I decided to leave him right after he came back. One day I came back home and found him burning all the letters he'd written to me. I think he wanted to get rid of everything we had together, but I managed to snatch the pictures and all his medals out of the fire so I could give them to Matthew. He was also burning up Matthew's baby pictures—he was just going nuts with a big bonfire.

When I'd been in college and pregnant with Matthew I'd seen Fig Gwaltney in the English Department. I remember once he was standing at the end of the hall and I was walking toward him. This was the year of the miniskirt, and I had real long legs and long hair, a skirt that came up to *here* and a belly out to *there*. I got to the end of the corridor, and Fig had a big grin on his face and made some comment. I don't remember what, but it was obvious he was very interested in me from whatever angle, and we started to talk. After that we'd have conversations in the hall, but I never took a class with him.

I'd known who he was before I met him. Around school the kids liked Fig. He wasn't easy or up front so much as irascible, which can be appealing too. At one time he'd been heavy, then he had to lose weight because of high blood pressure, but he was still big and handsome. The students knew that he had published ten or eleven books and had a big New York agent. He was the star of the teachers in that respect, and we all knew that he was friends with Norman.

By this time I was divorced and teaching art at Russellville High School. Fig and Ecey weren't people I called all the time, since I was much younger and had my own circle, but we were friends, and in 1973, after I got to know them better and Fig had seen some of my work, he asked me to illustrate his novel *Idols and Axle Grease*.

My meeting Norman came about because one day I'd taken my art class over to see a workshop given by a young filmmaker. Afterwards somebody I knew came up to me and said, "Guess who was in our class today—Norman Mailer!"

He was visiting Fig, so I thought it would be terrific to meet him. I called up Fig and said, "I hear you're having a cocktail party for Norman Mailer. Can I come over?" I don't think he really wanted me to come, a foreboding or something, but finally he agreed, and I went over to their house.

EMMA CLARA "ECEY" GWALTNEY Fig virtually discovered Barbara Norris. I'd first met her when Larry was just back from Vietnam and in my Black Lit class. Barbara came in to see me because he'd missed a couple of classes and couldn't get his paper in, and she said, "I hope you'll be patient. Larry will get his work done, but we're having problems right now." I gave him an extension because I could tell he was down, although I didn't really know him.

Larry was the only boy she'd ever gone with, and after her divorce she dated a lot of men, including our present governor, Bill Clinton, before he was married. She was very pretty and always ambitious. And she wanted to get out of here; she often said there's nothing for women to do here but teach school or be a secretary. I remember when she was teaching, she caused a little stir at Russellville High School because she wore jeans to her art class. The stupid principal got after her about it, but she said she sort of enjoyed the fuss, and I can believe it. In fact, she can handle controversy better than any human being I ever saw.

BARBARA NORRIS CHURCH MAILER At the cocktail party I walked in the door, and there was Norman sitting by the window. It was a bright sunny day, so there was light behind his head, and his white hair was like a halo. He smiled, I smiled, and he got up immediately and came over to me. He was wearing patched jeans. I had on jeans too and a shirt tied around my waist and big "bear trap" sandals that made me about six feet two, so I had to look down at him. I said, "Hi, how do you do? I'm—." "Hello," he said, and turned around and walked out of the room. I thought, Well, I guess he really hates tall women. Forget it.

There were twenty guests there—English teachers, the local literary establishment—so I was talking to other people when a little while later Francis came up to me and said, "Why don't you stick around and come out to dinner with us?" I said, "Oh, gee, Francis, I don't think I should. I don't think Norman liked me very much."

"Liked you? Hell! *He's* the one who wants you to come, not me."

So then Norman came back in and sat next to me on the couch and we

With Barbara Norris, wife-to-be, in Americus, Ga., near Plains, home of Jimmy Carter, 1976.

talked. I'd read some of *Marilyn*, which I had gotten from the Book-of-the-Month, though only in bits and pieces as I flipped through the pictures.

Anyway, people began to leave, and we went to friends of Fig and Ecey's and mine, Van Allen and Ginny Tyson, who live out in the woods in a wonderful house built over a brook. Norman and I stood out on the porch with the brook flowing underneath and talked for about an hour. I don't really remember what we talked about, but he was giving me a pretty heavy line about how beautiful I was, just on and on and on. I was pretty used to that, so I quipped, "Well, it's a wonderful line, Mr. Mailer, but, then, I've always bought a good line if it's well presented." It was that kind of banter back and forth. I wasn't thinking anything, I had no plans. I liked him and he was fun.

It wasn't even a decision about that night, because at ten I was supposed to pick up Matthew, who was then three, from his father, and I was planning to bring him back out to the house in the woods. But Norman insisted on going with me. He was so tender, holding my hand in the car, and he waited when I went in and got Matthew, then we drove back out to the Tysons'. Matthew was sound asleep, Norman carried him inside, and we stayed another couple of hours before going back to my place. Eventually Norman went back to Fig and Ecey's and left the next day.

I don't remember if he was using his southern accent that first evening. He doesn't have a real southern accent, he has what he *thinks* is a southern accent. Besides, he talked awfully fast—which sure ain't southern.

He'd given me a post office box in Stockbridge so my letters wouldn't go to the house, because he'd told me about Carol. He'd signed my copy of *Marilyn* with a sweet, wonderful inscription, so a few days later I wrote him a funny note and put in some pictures from the local modeling I'd been doing because I wanted him to remember me.

And did he! He phoned me when he got the pictures and said he was coming back down, and I thought, Terrific! Wonderful! It wasn't an issue where all this was leading. I just took our relationship as it came, I never worried that he was or wasn't going to see me or whether or not he'd call.

So I left Matthew with my mother, and Norman and I spent three days together at the Sheraton in Little Rock. What did we do during those three days? Mostly stayed in bed. But I also took him to the Marriott Hotel, where all the politicians hang out at lunch, and to a wonderful Cajun place down by the river where you get all the shrimp you can eat. We talked and talked, and let's say he charmed me. Like when he first walked off the plane, he was carrying a great big red-and-white stuffed dog. It was so outrageous to see him come off the plane with this dog—he'd decided to get me a present, and I liked that. It was endearing. I'm sure he delivered a line, but I can't remember it. It's been so long and he's given me so many lines in between.

But he was always self-effacing. I knew he was a famous writer, but I had only the vaguest notion of how famous, and I really didn't know too much about him. Of course, Francis had filled me in on how many times he'd been married, but I didn't care. I just wanted to see him again. When we parted in Little Rock it wasn't "Well, goodbye, this has been fun, I'd like to see you again." Something had happened and we knew we'd be seeing each other. It was almost like "We're gonna get together very soon and I'll call you." Which he did.

Meanwhile I hadn't told Fig and Ecey or anyone about Little Rock, and I sensed that Fig was resentful. I knew that Norman was his friend since the war— I knew the bare bones of the story—so I sensed that there was this feeling on Fig's part that Norman was his, like I was usurping something. Before Norman had met me in Little Rock I'd run into Fig in the supermarket and asked him, "Have you heard from Norman?" He said, "Oh, yes, he wrote me a letter soon after he left." Then he said something implying "Don't expect him to call you again, because he's not going to." There was an edge to it, and even though he didn't say so, the message seemed to be "Little girl, you're in over your head. Get out of this or you're going to get hurt."

But I knew he and Ecey were upset when they heard from someone else that I had gone to Chicago in June. That summer I was taking an American Lit course from a girl, Ruth Harrison, who was a friend as well as my teacher, and I let it slip that I was going to Chicago to be with Norman and would be out of class several days. I suppose I wanted to tell somebody, but Ruth immediately told Ecey.

Norman was doing publicity for his Ali fight piece for *Playboy*, so I flew up to Chicago, which was the first time I'd ever been on an airplane. Norman was doing TV, radio, that sort of stuff, and I was with him. Was I self-conscious? Again, no. Even though you're suddenly in the big city, you don't suddenly lose your self-confidence. If you're used to being loved and admired and in charge, these things don't suddenly stop.

Obviously by now it was no longer a one-night fling, but we still weren't making any plans. I knew that he had at least four steady girl friends, so from the beginning there was no lying. The only thing was I had to let my parents know where I was in case they needed me, and that was really traumatic. At that point they didn't even know I was seeing him. They vaguely knew Norman was a writer, a friend of Fig's, and that I'd met him. So I called them and told them I was in Chicago. Dead silence on the other end. Then, I think, tears and upset and "How can you do this to us?"

The next step was several weeks later when he asked if I'd like to visit him in New York. He came into the city from Stockbridge, and we spent a week together in Brooklyn Heights. I'd already told him my plan of working for my MFA at the Rhode Island School of Design or in Boston, but now he said, "I want to see you more often. Why don't you come to New York and try modeling instead? You can always do your MFA. This'll be more fun. You'll get a good job, you'll get your own apartment." I can't say why, but I really wasn't uneasy about all this.

Norman then set up a luncheon for me with Amy Greene at the Algonquin to talk about modeling. She knows a lot about the beauty business and has this place in Bendel's called Beauty Checkers, plus a string of them in other cities too. Both Amy and Milton Greene, the photographer, said I had a real shot at modeling if I'd go home and lose twenty pounds. Amy said that when I came back she'd call Wilhelmina for me.

So I went back to Arkansas and starved myself. By the end of July, a month later, I weighed one hundred seventeen. Larry wasn't resentful about my new plans because he was newly married, and Matthew was going to stay with my parents. At that point I wasn't telling them what I was doing because I wasn't sure what the final outcome might be; I just said I was going to New York to start modeling, would see how it worked out, and if I was successful I'd get my own place and send for Matthew.

Norman hadn't been with Carol full time even before he met me. He'd spend two weeks with her and then two weeks in New York, where he always had this other life. I just turned into the other life. But it wasn't easy for Carol. It wasn't an easy time for anybody. I spent two weeks of August by myself. Norman went up to Maine with Carol and the kids, then when he came back to New York at the end of August, he'd already made his decision to leave Carol. Me, I knew I wasn't going back to Arkansas.

I'd always had the dream of being a model in New York. It was such a glamorous thing—the fun, the money. I'd modeled locally for department stores, and I'd read articles about models and thought, Gee, I could do that. Painting was always a part of me, it was something I did and had to do, but I didn't have grand ambitions or see it as a career. Still, while the decision to go to New York had to do with the modeling, it was mostly Norman. If Norman had lived in Boston or Saskatchewan, I would have gone there. It happened to be New York, though, and so much the better.

Obviously I felt I had a lot of options. It's also true I attach myself to people who are on the move—exciting, interesting people like Bill Clinton back in Arkansas, who wasn't yet governor but who had a terrific personality, charisma, and possibilities. So, undeniably, New York and the glamor were part of it too.

I wouldn't be content to move now to Connecticut or Stockbridge, say. I love the swim of New York. I can't live in the country and just paint and walk around in blue jeans. I never liked that, even when I was back home. I confess I liked being a winner, I liked getting my picture in the paper.

So it's true, in a sense, that everything I am today is because of Norman. But when I decided to go up to New York there were no conditions, no promises. All he said was, "Don't bring any of your Arkansas polyester clothes." I didn't think he had to take responsibility for me, even when I finally brought Matthew up. There was no big discussion of our living together or getting married—it just evolved.

EMMA CLARA "ECEY" GWALTNEY   When Barbara came over to our party that afternoon he was immediately taken with her. Then, on the way out, they discovered they had the same birthday, January 31, which absolutely blew Norman's mind. In fact, later they had their horoscopes read and found they were born one minute apart—twenty-six years difference but one minute apart. That night, though, I think he got back to our house at about four, and then Fig drove him to the airport later in the morning.

He was still with Carol at that point. I had no idea what she was like, but, in fact, the afternoon he was here he called her to check in and say hello. "I'm behaving myself," I recall him saying, "I really am. Here, I'll let you talk to Ecey." I'd never met her, I didn't know her, but I said, "Carol? Really, he's behaving himself so well it's disgusting. He's gettin' boring." I was just joking. But the irony was that it was that afternoon that Barbara came over and met him. Not that Carol would even remember, but I always wondered if she thought, Sure, Ecey knew all along. But I didn't.

It got complicated during the next few months, and even though he wouldn't admit it, I think Fig was hurt that Norman hadn't told him, hadn't just said, "I've fallen for this friend of yours." I'm talking about Little Rock and then, afterwards, the meeting in Chicago. Apparently Barbara swore Ruth Harrison to secrecy, but she called us and kept saying, "Have y'all talked with Barbara or Norman lately?" We said, "No," and she said, "Well, I think you need to."

Soon Barbara resigned from Russellville High School and told them she was going to live in New York and try to get back into modeling. I think she did this on instinct. It wasn't just businesslike or ambitiousness on her part either, because she was truly crazy about him. Norman's a dazzling man. He talks so well and is so charming, maybe he'd do the same to anybody. But when everyone heard she was going up to be with him, people around here were saying, "Considering Norman's track record, she's very foolish. He'll get her up to New York, set her up, then walk out on her the next week." Of course I knew this was nonsense, since Norman's nothing if not responsible, but Barbara herself said to me, "Suppose in five years he's tired of me? I'll already have made my own friends and I'd be all right. I'll survive." She'd figured it all out. I think she told her parents she was staying with Barbara Wasserman, but eventually she took her own apartment in Fan's building and made friends with Fan.

*Barbara Norris Church
Mailer, New York.*

<u>BARBARA NORRIS CHURCH MAILER</u> That first week in New York I met Norman's mother and sister. Neither really knew what the story was, but they knew I was a friend of Francis' visiting New York and I think they thought Norman was being sort of a godfather to me.

I liked Barbara immediately. I knew she and Norman were very close, but the real shocker was that they looked so much alike. The reason Fan got me an apartment in her building was that she wanted me near her. We'd spent a lot of time together in August, when I'd first moved to New York, while Norman was in Maine. I was by myself, and we'd have lunch and go out to the Promenade or she'd come over to have dinner with me at Norman's apartment. She was really agile in those days, and we became very close.

Norman was the first Jew I'd ever met, and even though Fan may be the quintessential Jewish mother, I'd certainly met people like her in the South. But during that month I got to know her I didn't think she knew I was with Norman. She just thought I was a friend of Francis'. She always liked Francis, especially because he wrote books, and also he'd won her heart because she'd heard the story about his sticking up for Norman in the army.

But she was also very curious about me because she'd never had a friend really, even when she was a kid. She'd had her sisters, but she'd certainly never had a gentile friend. So she was very curious about what we did, our religion and all that. In fact, I'd go with her to temple.

I think Norman finally told her about us that fall when we were going away to Manila. He phoned or went over to see her, and I think she had mixed feelings. On the one hand, she was not close to Carol. On the other, she thought,

Oh no, here's Norman breaking up another family. She came over and said to me, "Darling, I want you not to go." I guess she was saying in effect, "Don't get involved in this." But I said, "No, I'm going." I don't know whether she was looking out for me or Norman, but eventually she resigned herself.

When we came back from our trip we were just as close as ever, and that's when she found the apartment for me. Every morning she'd call me, and I'd go upstairs and zip up her dress or help her find her contact lens if she'd dropped one. We'd have coffee and talk. It was nice for her because she had someone to see all the time.

FANNY SCHNEIDER MAILER I knew Barbara was involved with Norman the minute I laid eyes on her! I don't know how she can say she thinks I didn't know. And it's funny... I knew because she's pretty and pleasant and has a personality that warms you up to her very quickly. Norman was still with Carol in Massachusetts, so almost every day Barbara would see me, and we got to know each other. She was easy to be with, and, like Norman, she has a very honest personality. She's unique, very different from Norman's other wives. She has character. She knows when to overlook things and she doesn't fight and scream.

I knew she'd never met a Jew before, and we laughed about it. She thought Jews had horns. She was what Norman needed, though, in looks and knowledge and character—a true person. The age difference didn't bother me. I figured he'll be able to measure up to it. And it didn't bother me at all that she wasn't Jewish, because I wasn't dealing with anyone who was so church-going that she couldn't live without it.

BARBARA NORRIS CHURCH MAILER We were in the Philippines for ten days, and immediately afterwards we went to Rome and stayed at a ritzy hotel at the top of the Spanish Steps. We were there a month while Norman was working on a film script for Sergio Leone. I don't know what happened, but Leone suddenly one day said, "Forget it, I don't want the script," and he didn't want to pay Norman either. They were waffling. They kept saying things in the press like "He wrote it on a napkin." Norman wanted to buy the script back because Billy Friedkin wanted to make it, but Leone wouldn't sell it either. Later, after about six years of litigation, we got our money, $75,000, which at that point had deteriorated to practically nothing—ten thousand, I think—because of the legal expenses.

We didn't even really know what had happened until we got home. Cy was handling it, and Mickey Knox had been very much involved—either he'd generated the project or was a go-between for Norman and Leone. Anyway, while we were still in Rome I met Mickey, and we got along terrifically, going out to dinner with him and his girl friend every night. It was also in Rome that I got my first big break. One day I wandered into a beauty shop where I'd seen a cosmetics display and struck up a conversation with the owner, who then asked if I'd pose for some pictures if they did my hair. It was on the basis of these photos that Wilhelmina took me on. This was December '75 and really the start of my career.

Then I started to use my professional name, Norris Church. I had never liked the name Barbara Norris, and in the old days I just used to sign my paintings "Norris." So I told Norman I wanted to keep that, and for a while I thought I'd use just the one name, except it got so complicated when I was introduced to people—"This is Norris," and they'd say, "Norris what?" I would've taken back my maiden name, but "Norris Davis" didn't sound right, so one day Norman came up with "Church."

That December, after we got back, I was going down to fetch Matthew from my parents, and Norman insisted on going because he didn't want me to deal with it alone. My parents knew we were coming, but this was the first time I was going to deal with the situation face-to-face.

We stayed at Fig and Ecey's because it was easier, and Fig had a talk with Norman—"Do you know what you're getting into?" sort of thing. I think he felt sorry for Norman and was giving the old pep talk: "She's a lot younger than you. She'll probably get to New York and meet somebody else." They all thought I was just using him.

Anyway, the first night we went over to my parents. They were upset I was taking Matthew back because they thought it would be better for him to stay with them. Norman was very cool, very gentlemanly. He and my father didn't talk privately, and as far as I know he didn't make any promises to them. Besides, we really weren't living together, which let my parents have this charade of saying I had my own place.

Of course I'd heard what people were saying back in town. My friend Jean Jewell used to tell me, because I kept in pretty close touch with her. When I first signed with Wilhelmina, for example, I told friends I was a model and was going to be in magazines, which immediately meant girlie magazines to them. The story went around that I was a *Playboy* centerfold, and everybody ran down to buy the issue. Then, of course, my picture came out in *Vogue*, and they had to change their tune. It was the same with the movie role I got the next year. I had told friends that I was making a movie, and it was these same people who spread the rumor that I was in a porno film.

EMMA CLARA "ECEY" GWALTNEY   Her parents still didn't know about them, because Barbara called and said, "We'll be coming down on December 20." I said they could stay with us, and she said, "I was hoping you'd say that, because it would be awkward to stay with my folks. Norman's going to talk to them."

It was a big occasion, very awkward and tense. I remember Norman brought his blue velvet suit and a nice tweed, and they were going to take her folks out to dinner. He changed into his tweed suit and said, "Do I look all right?" I said, "Yes," but we were also teasing him. One thing he's always enjoyed about the South is our bantering insults, although he never really got used to it. Like we kept saying, "Norman, try not to talk too fast, so that these people can understand you. We realize you're an intellectual, but try to slow down." He said, "Are you kidding? As fast as Barbara talks...!"

Anyway, I guess it went all right. The Davises are good solid Baptists, and I was amazed. I asked Barbara how they could reconcile it. She said, "They had to." What a choice! Accept it or just give up their daughter. And remember, Barbara is their only child. The mother was the one whose feelings were more on the surface, and she's more stolid in her beliefs, so maybe she was upset. I'm sure they hadn't heard about Norman, and I gather her father went out and bought a book about the Jews, because he'd never met a Jew before. He's a nice guy and was probably eager to win Norman's good wishes.

But during that same trip there was a wonderful moment for Barbara, and it couldn't have worked out more perfectly. She'd dated a lawyer here, Dick Gardner, who married somebody else. On the way in from the airport I said, "There's a party at the Russellville Country Club. You want to go?" Norman said, "Sure."

We weren't members, so I made arrangements with friends, and we all had dinner there Friday night. Norman wore his blue velvet suit and Barbara had on a black velvet jump suit and looked really stunning, absolutely gorgeous. Dick Gardner just happened to be there, so Barbara got up very casually and said, "Oh, hi, Dick. How are you? This is Norman Mailer." And Norman rose and turned on the charm—"I understand you're quite a golfer..."

Barbara was triumphant in a subdued way, but we laughed about it later. It was the perfect little coup, and it couldn't have fallen into her lap any better. There was a sense of the prodigal daughter returning, looking gorgeous, really shining after having lit out for New York.

Later, when Barbara sold her house, I was over there buying some large lamps from her. She said something about getting pregnant, because "Norman said I'm gonna have to quit taking the pill." I know Norman doesn't believe in birth control—he's written about that—but the way she said it seemed so strange to me, even though she'd said it with a little bit of pride. In the same conversation she asked if I liked "Charlie" cologne. I said, "Sure," and she said, "Take this, then, because Norman won't allow me to use cologne. Once we were going out and I'd put on some cologne, and he made me come back and take a bath."

BARBARA NORRIS CHURCH MAILER   When we came back from Arkansas I moved into the apartment that Fan had arranged with the superintendent of her building. Initially Norman hadn't wanted me to take the place because it was unattractive, but I took it mainly for Matthew and my mom and dad. I wanted my parents to know that I had my own place and wasn't just living with Norman.

While we were in Italy he'd decided he wasn't going to tell Carol he was leaving until after Christmas, so he went back to Stockbridge. He promised me he'd be back for good on New Year's, which he was.

That first year in New York I started meeting Norman's friends, like Buzz Farbar, Jose, and Harold and Mara Conrad. My meeting Harold and Mara—that's a wonderful story. Norman told me he wanted to put them on because he'd never put them on before. Like they were too hip. So he called them to say that he had a new girl friend and wanted their opinion because he was a little nervous. I wore a very low-cut, sexy red dress and a cheap blond wig I'd bought at A&S, and I put on a lot of makeup. When we arrived, Norman introduced me: "This is Cinnamon Brown from Waco, Texas, and she wants to be a porny star." Then he said he wasn't too sure about the idea, because I was fresh out of Texas, and that it would be a terrible career for me. Me, though, I'm insisting—"That's what I want to do. I can make a lot of money"—and the two of us stage a big fight. Norman's screaming "You can't be a porny star, you don't have any tits." I say, "Oh, tits, what're tits? I got a terrific pussy"—that kind of thing, back and forth. Mara and Harold are looking at each other in dismay, not knowing what to do. Mara takes Norman out of the room and says, "Look, let the kid do it. She's cute, she's terrific, she might be a big star. If that's what she wants, keep out of it."

In the meantime I went to the bathroom, took off the wig, put on a wonderful, high-necked black dress that I'd bought at Saks, redid my makeup and combed my hair, which was then shoulder length, straight and classic. When I walked back into the room Mara said, "Who are you?" Truly, she didn't recognize me, so I said, "I'd like to introduce myself. I'm Barbara Norris." Norman rolls on the floor, Mara sputters, "Well, whoever you are, welcome," and Harold is laughing and laughing, just dying.

The next week they invited us over again. We're standing in the hallway, still laughing about that first evening, and Mara opens the door. She's standing there stark naked! I'm in hysterics, and she says, "You're not gonna get one up on *me!*"

MARA LYNN CONRAD   I've known all of Norman's wives except Bea. He married all of them because he's gallant, old-world, and has a kind of courtesy to him. But he still hadn't found the right woman until he found her in Norris. Oh God, she's what he was looking for all that time.

Why? Because she embodies everything he thinks a woman should be. She's very feminine, soft, affectionate. She's ambitious but not in an unpleasant way, and she's willing to work for whatever she wants. And on top of this she loves *Norman* first, she genuinely loves him as a man.

She was also very funny, and I thought, Yes, he needs humor in his life. And she had courage, the courage to wing it for whatever comes next, to handle whatever might happen. That sounds heavy, I know, but people who live by principles have some kind of security that people who don't never have, and her calmness was something Norman was keenly aware of.

JAN CUSHING OLYMPITIS   I met Norman and Norris at Pat Lawford's, just after Norris had arrived from Arkansas. There were about twenty people, nobody interesting, so I said to her, "What do you do?" She replied, "Well, I'm living with Norman Mailer."

She was much hickier than she is now, not sophisticated but still secure. She'd brought a copy of Norman's *Genius and Lust*—it was just out—and the first thing she did was show me the sketch of Henry Miller on the jacket and ask what I thought of it. I looked at the drawing and told her I didn't think it was very good. "Well, thanks a lot," she said, "I'm the one who did it." We laughed. I thought she was very candid and handling herself beautifully.

At dinner I was seated next to Norman. Norris was at another table, and at one point Norman interrupted his conversation with Pat to ask me, "What do you think of my girl?" I thought this was interesting, because he didn't really know me, and I told Norman, "She's a good egg." Later he went back to Norris and said, "I don't know this girl, but I've gotten a lot of comments about you and I think this is the most sincere. She didn't say 'beautiful' or 'glamorous,' she said 'good egg.'" From that moment on Norris and I were friends. She called me from Wilhelmina the next day to have lunch.

During the rest of the evening she handled herself perfectly. I didn't get the impression that she'd trotted over to Saks or Bendel's to get herself outfitted as soon as she'd hit the city. She explained she'd fallen madly in love with Norman but didn't know how long she was going to stay, although obviously she hoped it was for a long time.

I'd read enough about Norman to know that she might just be another quick fling, and my first feeling was that it wasn't going to last, so at lunch I said to her right off, "I know what it's like to be with someone as difficult and well known as Norman"—years before I'd been dating Peter Maas, also Henry Kissinger—"and so if you need help in New York and you want me as a girlfriend, I'll be there for you." I felt that if I could take her around and introduce her to enough people, it might make Norman like her more as a person. I thought she needed a girlfriend, someone to make him think, Well, here she is in New York, and she's got her own group—she's not dependent on me.

DOTSON RADER   As early as 1973, '74, one had begun to see Norman in places one wouldn't expect to see him—say at the Heinzes' or at a fashion-show opening or at the Buckleys', in a wide variety of circles where he was by nature an outsider.

Norman is essentially a leftist, but his intrigue shifted from oppositionist groups on the street to the people who actually run the nation. I'm not saying he joined the East Side; he simply shifted the route of the tour bus so he began to be seen with people like Peter Glenville, Marietta Tree, Jerry Zipkin, and Slim Keith. Of course he's always been fascinated by power, and also by people like Plimpton and Buckley.

I realized that he was seeing new people when I gave him and Norris a joint birthday party when I was living in Bridgehampton. He'd met Norris, I guess, about six months before, and when I'd met her, we became like brother and sister, terribly close. So I told Norman I wanted to do a buffet for about a hundred fifty people and asked him to send me a list of those he wanted me to invite. I had assumed, wrongly, that he would want the people I'd seen around him for a long time, a lot of intellectuals and writers, like Dick Goodwin and Doris

Kearns, who, in fact, did come. But a good half or more of the guests were socialite types, like Peter Glenville and Jan Cushing.

Two people refused to come, however. One was Lally Weymouth, who said she wouldn't come if Jan was going to be there. I told her that Jan was on Norman's list and so was she, but since Jan had already accepted, I couldn't withdraw the invitation. The other one was Truman Capote, who lived down the road from me. There was already a lot of snow that year, and Truman, joking, said, "Oh-h-h, Dotson, there's going to be a blithard; we're going to be thnowed in at the houth and I know what's going to happen. I'll be trapped in the little bedroom upstairs, and in the middle of the night Norman's going to come in my room and rape me. I just can't chance it. Give my regreth."

GEORGE PLIMPTON   I enjoy Norman's company as much as that of any man I know, but I'm still ill at ease with him. Why, I'm not sure. I was recently looking at some kind of X-ray photographs of human beings showing auras of electrical currents coming off them, electrical vibrations, and there's definitely a very large electrical field that comes off Norman. Even sitting with him when he's absolutely at his ease, the energy is there, something almost palpable, and I've never known a person who had it to such a degree.

Some examples: Several years ago Norman was anxious to talk to me about my writing, specifically about my book *Shadow Box*. He wanted to tell me why he hadn't felt more strongly about it, why he hadn't supported me more with a comment or a puff. He arranged a lunch. It was like a doctor's appointment. I told him I thought it was the best thing I had done, that as a writer I have a certain level I can write to, no more. I explained this, even though it's difficult to talk about. But it didn't satisfy him. He wanted me to have let myself go more. He was much more bothered than *I* was. More than anybody I know, Norman never stops measuring you. He does it constantly, and it's part of what I mean by that electrical current.

Another time I gave a stupid, silly toast at a dinner at Jan Cushing's. I thought I was going to be the only speaker so I made it too long, and I just got stuck, and it turned out not to be very funny. And there was Norman, saying, just to let me know, "George, that was the longest damned toast I ever heard in my life." He was disappointed. He wanted me to be better, which, again, is part of his competitiveness.

Paradoxically, I think we're both New Englanders in a funny way. We don't talk about innermost feelings. When we discussed *Shadow Box* he said I had a lot more to say, that there was something locked up. True. He feels there's a reticence in me, and that is precisely how I feel about him. Maybe he really wanted to be a great prizefighter or get a good punch in on Jose Torres, be the mayor of a city, the thumb-wrestling champ in the room, but these things always seemed to me to be a type of veneer—poses, guises. When you see Norman reading from his work, explaining what he's up to, with those little spectacles on, that's another Mailer entirely, and the true and the best one.

GLORIA JONES   I think the last time before his death in '76 that Jim had seen Norman was at Christmas at Pat Lawford's, in '72 or '73. They were very polite with each other. I don't think Jim would've taken any shit from Norman, but he'd also grown out of all that; in a sense, I suppose he grew bigger and bigger because he was facing a sure death. I don't know whether he knew it or not, but certainly his character was kinder and more mature. Wouldn't you have believed there was affection in spite of the breakup? I mean, these two men, they're probably the two best of what are really the six best of that generation. I think Norman knows Jim was really good, and Jim, I know, right to the end felt exactly the same about Norman.

DOTSON RADER   I provided the link for Norman with the Carters. Norman has never called me and asked to meet someone, but I have a pretty good perception of the kind of people he's going to take to, so I got him to meet my friend Ruth Carter Stapleton, and he took to her like a duck to water.

But his interview with Jimmy for The New York Times was a disaster. Plains is about as southern . . . goddamn, it's about as far up the asshole of America as you can get. Norman was out of his element. He loves southern accents but just doesn't understand southerners. In fact, later, when he read the piece I'd done on Carter, he said he thought I'd captured Carter better than he had. I asked why, and he said, "Because I could never shut up. I never let him talk." I said, "Norman, the key to dealing with southerners is to let them talk. They love to talk, and if you let 'em, they'll tell you everything."

LAWRENCE SCHILLER   November 11, 1976, I was cutting the film The Trial of Lee Harvey Oswald with David Greene, who'd won an Emmy for Roots, when I read about Gary Gilmore. I knew there was a movie there, that I had to go out to Utah, and after I met Kathryne Baker, Nicole's mother, and read Nicole's letters to Gilmore I knew there was also a potential book. I wasn't yet thinking of a writer—Mailer or anybody else—because there were more important things to be done, like gaining access to people and locking the thing up. I wanted to make sure the story didn't get fractured into several stories with several people, and I was drawing on my past experiences and saying to myself, "Now, make sure you don't make a mistake, Schiller."

One of my concerns, which I quickly realized after reading the letters, was whether I could handle Gilmore's mysticism, so I decided to bring in Barry Farrell, who'd written an article on Gilmore for New West. I wanted someone who could work as my cornerman in this boxing match, someone to say, "Hey, you're missing this" or "Why don't you discuss that?" So I asked Farrell to come aboard, telling him straight out that it was a limited situation, with no promise of a book or anything else. Then, when ABC pulled out—they'd given me seed money—I had to do the Playboy interview to give myself working capital, so I asked Barry to edit it, and he did a very, very good job.

ARTHUR KRETCHMER   Before Norman's involvement there was the magazine's involvement with Schiller on the Gilmore interview. That story is in The Exe-

cutioner's Song. Barry Golson, our executive editor, and Schiller hated each other from the very first minute. Schiller put on great, phenomenal, antagonistic performances in Utah. He had the material, and Barry contacted him, and then Schiller did all those things one heard about, manipulating around the sale of every piece of it. The ultimate irony is that Schiller ultimately behaved very creditably and didn't cheat anybody. I could be wrong—but he didn't cheat me for sure. Abused me a little bit, certainly abused Golson a lot. And misled Rupert Murdoch. In fact, he misled everybody by allowing them to function on the notion that Schiller was a snake and would therefore do anything, letting everybody get involved in this unique competition for the material, with Barry Farrell as his anchor.

The antagonism was never between Golson and Norman but between Golson and Schiller. Golson wasn't wonderful. He later made a terrible mistake by writing negatively about Schiller in a "Playbill," our monthly coming-attractions column. I let him make that mistake, so ultimately I'm responsible. But Schiller felt wronged, because he couldn't do anything about the text, so he never quite forgave us.

Golson never could bury any of it either. He hated being the audience of Schiller's show, and I don't blame him. Anyway, at the time it was quite a game with those three—in fact, they called it "the Larry, Barry, and Barry game." They teetered into my office, literally after deadline, after all our discussions about space, and Schiller asked that the interviewer not be designated "Playboy" in the interview and other outrageous shit.

LAWRENCE SCHILLER   Between November 16, when I first saw Nicole's letters, and January of '77, when Gilmore was executed, I'd interviewed people and had a pretty good feeling where the windows were for a book, how someone could tell the story and lay out this part of the country. All the while I had a feeling there was a best seller here, and the idea of getting Norman to write it was like a little pebble under my mattress, something that's making me turn over and over. I'm saying, "Jesus, Norman's the writer for this—he could take the material and really fly with it. But he's still pissed at you, Schiller, and for this thing to work he's gotta respect you."

I'd thought of Norman for two reasons. Somewhere somebody had told me he'd had a violent relationship with his father; I didn't know whether it was true, though I did know about his father's gambling, so it got me thinking. Then I remembered that Norman had stabbed his wife, and I also sensed his great passion for women. What I knew but no one else realized, not the press, not anyone in the world, was that the underbelly of the Gilmore story was Nicole. When I'd met her and sat on the floor with her and looked into her eyes I saw the magic there, and I knew that, figuratively, this was another marriage for Norman.

First, though, I had to get him to meet her.

I collected Gilmore's interviews and some of Nicole's material and again sent a package to Molly Cook in Provincetown, who then called me, asking for more material. Even though Norman hadn't yet talked to me, I sent it, because I

Mailer, Lawrence Schiller, and the makings of The Executioner's Song.

knew that somebody was reading it, eating it up, and it wasn't Molly. Then Norman called and said, "This is the best interview I've ever read." I don't think he considered the material as the basis for a book yet, but I told him, "Look, I've got this girl out here in Malibu. She's gonna be the key, the other half of the book. I want to bring her to New York so you can meet her."

After the execution Nicole had been in the nuthouse. It had taken me a while to get her out, and then it took me a while to make sure she wasn't going to try to kill herself again, so I was shepherding her. I was like a Spanish chaperone. But she was in a daze and didn't know who Norman Mailer was. I gave her *Marilyn* to read, but I don't think she got through fifty pages.

So, Stephie, my then fiancée, now my wife, and I brought her to New York. She was a space cadet—she'd never been to a major city in her life, so she was like Alice in Wonderland. We took her ice skating in Central Park, then we met Norman at Trader Vic's. Over lunch Norman asked whether she played chess. I'd already bought her a chess set, and the two of them went up to her room. Half an hour later Norman emerged, and just the two of us went for a walk down Fifth Avenue. It's then that he said, "You're right. There's a book there."

A lot of people felt the project was "beneath him." They saw it as a Gilmore book, and Gilmore had dirtied himself with his suicide attempts, made a mockery of his right to die, and the public's perception, based on the AP and UPI type journalism coming out of Salt Lake City, was that this was a trashy *National Enquirer* story. Plus there was my involvement, the sense that Schiller wasn't Norman's road back to the Nobel Prize for literature. Norman himself never said anything, but others had.

In the trade he was being characterized as someone who wrote essays as an excuse for serious literature. I ran into this when I went out to sell the book. Marc Jaffe at Bantam insisted that Mailer guarantee openly and in front of another editor that he would write a narrative. They were afraid he'd write a long article and force them to publish it as a book. They didn't want a replay of the fight book or another long essay like *Of a Fire on the Moon.*

That's why, after he said he'd like to do Gilmore, I set up a meeting with

Scott Meredith. I walked in and told Scott how the deal was going to go down: "I'm gonna deliver x dollars"—I think I said $500,000 or $600,000—"if Norman will do this book." Scott kind of laughed at me, because Norman had gotten a reputation and wasn't saleable for that kind of money. I'm not talking against Norman, but this was a period when he was in an odd place. He'd signed with Little, Brown to write "the big one," which he'd been talking about for ten years but hadn't produced.

I then went out on the street. I knew I could deliver Norman and I was seeing about four people a day, looking for the best deal. Scott, I'm sure, being the tough agent, is thinking, "Let's see if big-mouth Schiller can deliver..."

Finally I put together the deal with Warner Books, which is the best deal I can make. I don't think Scott believes me, but twenty-four hours later he has no choice because he's reading the contract. Still, he finds it unbelievable considering Norman's situation. *He* couldn't go out and get half a million dollars. Plus I was prepared to deliver the first $250,000 to Mailer. I would take the second $250,000 and pay third parties out of my end. That's a deal Scott can't refuse—Mailer's got a quarter of a million in his pocket. So I walked into Scott's office confident that I'm making the best deal I've ever made under every term and condition. I'm also confident that I can work with Mailer again in a situation that really challenges me. I say to myself, "I'm gonna be able to prove myself as a good journalist, I'm gonna get all those interviews and collect material, and the book's gonna allow me to do it."

Then I started doing the research and sending him stuff to read. This was before Norman's first trip to Utah, and I was insisting more and more that the mother was a key element of the story, while Mailer wanted to go more in the prison direction, the whole penal thing. Basically the question was whether he was still going to do just a love story or whether there was something as large there as what I was plowing out of the goddamned desert. Because I was just plowing away, every week throwing bunches of stuff Mailer's way, and I can tell by the way he's talking to me that he's falling more and more in love with the research and, I think, getting a little scared that the cut into the material is opening up bigger and bigger.

He'd anticipated a six-month project, but he's not the type of guy who shies away. In fact, he'd once said to me when we were talking about *Marilyn*, "You gave me $50,000 to write 25,000 words. I delivered 100,000 and never once asked you for a penny more," so I knew that it was the quality of the material that came first for him, not the business deal. I was going into my research totally, jumping into a well without a bottom, and I knew that if I gave Norman ten million facts, he'd be smart enough to see their worth and not rely on his bravado, as he had with *Marilyn*. In fact, he later acknowledged this to me. We were flying back from Oregon and he showed me the first 15 or 20 pages he'd written, and I said, "Jesus, you're not using your own voice." I probably didn't say it as nicely at the time, but I was reacting out of everybody's worry that he wasn't going to write a narrative—and, of course, I'd felt that his voice was in every goddamned line of *Marilyn*. So he looked straight across at me and said, in effect, "You've given me so much material, so much fact, I don't have to rely on my own ego."

This was one of the reasons he didn't fall back and go with a short love story. It was also his way of saying to *me*, "You earned your place in this work." I think he knew all the mistakes he'd made with *Marilyn*—certainly I knew all the mistakes I'd made—and here was a big chance. We'd gained mutual respect, so why were we gonna fuck around again? Mailer was no longer going to tell me to stay out of it, and for my part, I had more guts to tell him what I was feeling, both about him and what he was doing with Gilmore. That was true even though I wasn't gonna have my name on it, either in a collaboration or coauthor title. But Norman was saying I'd earned my place by doing all that research and giving him the material. As things turned out, he went a step further by putting me in the book, which took me by surprise.

DIANA TRILLING After Norman's visit with us in Oxford and the Town Hall meeting, we started to drift apart, but the real break didn't come until '77. It's a very unhappy story what happened then, a truly unhappy story, and I've wondered whether I want to talk about it. I think I should. But this is an interview about Norman. I'm not trying to give an account of my life, so I'll try to keep other people out of it as much as I can. Of course, I can't keep Lillian out entirely; the story doesn't make sense without her part in it. But I'll be as minimal as possible.

After Little, Brown canceled my contract for my volume of essays We Must March My Darlings, I took it to Harcourt Brace Jovanovich. They'd been my earlier publishers for my book *Claremont Essays*, and when Lionel died, Bill Jovanovich told me he'd be glad to have anything of Lionel's or mine. But their publicity department didn't know me, and they asked me for a list of people whom they could ask for blurbs for We Must March. I included Norman in the list. He read the book very promptly and gave it a blurb. It wasn't exactly my idea of a stirring promotional statement, but I didn't give it very much thought, because in the next week or so they decided that they weren't going to solicit promotional material to put on the jacket. Then one day—I don't remember the exact lapse of time—they called me from the HBJ promotion department and told me that Norman had revised the comment he'd given them, and they read me his new statement. I couldn't believe my ears. What he had done was to downgrade his blurb to the point where it was manifestly unusable. I'd never heard of a thing like that. It was conceivable that someone might want to withdraw a comment that he had given, but to downgrade it so that it wasn't usable, that was something that had no precedent in my experience.

Well, there had to be an explanation, and pretty soon I had one. You know what New York is like. I was told that between Norman's first and second blurbs for my book he had been at some kind of party at Lillian Hellman's house, a lunch or a dinner or something, where Lillian had been talking about me rather unpleasantly, and Norman had mentioned that he had just given me a blurb for a new book. It seems that Lillian had been outraged. She was reported to have said, "And you dare to sit at my table and say that!" And after the meal she had taken him off into another room. He was said to have emerged from that conference very red in the face.

This story came to me from several different sources, and so I wrote Norman a letter asking him if it was true that he had altered his comment on my book in obedience to Lillian's command. I don't mean that these were the words that I used, but in effect that was what I accused him of, and of course he wrote back indignant at the idea that I should think he could be bullied into acting in so unmanly a fashion. He said that what had happened was simply that he had examined my book again and realized that he didn't agree with my politics. The fact is, however, that my politics in 1977 were no different from my politics at any time I had ever known Norman. Before Lillian had delivered her ultimatum, or whatever it was that she did deliver, no difference in our politics had ever come between Norman and me.

So there we are. I've tried to put the incident from my mind, but I'm afraid that I haven't succeeded. I'm also afraid that Norman hasn't made much effort to help me forget it. Somewhere in these intervening years I recall that he did indeed once invite me to a party at his house in Brooklyn, but the party didn't even start until ten o'clock, and no one was going to be there whom I could count on to bring me home.

Oh, there's something I perhaps should bring in here. In early 1976, just a year before the publication of *We Must March My Darlings* and the situation about the blurb, there was a celebration in Norman's honor at the Gramercy Arts Club. Lionel had just died a few months earlier, so I wasn't up to making a speech, but Norman had wanted me to be the main speaker of the evening. If our political differences were so important to him, why did he want me as his chief celebrant at that dinner? I attended it even though I didn't speak, and he had me put next to him on the dais.

LILLIAN HELLMAN Diana's up to her tricks again. I am convinced she knew perfectly well that I never had anything to do with Little, Brown's turning down her book, never saw the book, never was told about the book, never spoke to anybody about it, and don't believe they ever said that I would object to anything in it. I became the cover for what was a simple turndown by a publisher who evidently did not like the book well enough to publish it. And I don't believe Roger Donald was so foolish or such a liar as to say I had anything to do with it. Diana saw a chance for a publicity story and took it. *The New York Times* was a patsy in giving her the front page without checking with me. But even they, with a front-page story, could not sell what was basically an uninteresting book.

Now this is where Norman comes in. Norman had given a blurb without reading the book, and he happened to be here for dinner shortly afterwards. I did not know he had given the blurb, and I was shocked when I found it out.

I said, "Norman, I am shocked that you would endorse a book that attacked me. This is the second time you've done it. The first time was a book by Meyer Levin—I've forgotten which one." Norman said, "What book?" I said, "Diana Trilling's." He said, "Look, I read half of it and liked it. But I shouldn't have endorsed that book or any book that is against you. I didn't write very much of a blurb in any case, but I will certainly take care of it. And I wish to apologize. I think you are right."

LAWRENCE SCHILLER   Norman started working on *The Executioner's Song* in May '77 and first went out to Utah in June, with the notion that he would stay in Gary and Nicole's house in order to pick up "their vibes." I figured, Norman doesn't tell me how to do my thing, I'm not gonna tell him how to do his. By then I'd given him about 9000 pages of what eventually was over 16,000 pages of interview transcript. He had formed his images and didn't want them fucked up. He just wanted to soak up the place like a sponge. He wanted to touch it, smell it.

My method of interviewing is to spend the first hour or two talking about the person's parents and grandparents. Then we talk about everything except what I've come to talk about—the person's life-style, car, house, furniture, clothing. I'm always circling until the person has forgotten there's a tape recorder, and then I get to the area I'm really after. I don't think Norman had seen interviews done like that—the unpeeling-of-the-orange interview. Part of it comes from my insecurity as a journalist. I'm not Mike Wallace, to walk in and say "This is what I want." Besides, I believe that you can only perceive how people act in certain situations by understanding their heritage, the context. By asking for a simple narrative you don't get emotions, you get facts. The emotions are woven in by talking about background—"When was the first time you had a fight with your wife?" "What's your first memory of your grandfather?" I don't think that's the way Mailer would interview. But he wasn't going to compete on that level because he realized my method was effective.

During those nine months I think Norman made six or seven trips, also two or three to Oregon, and one to Marion, Illinois, to see the prison. I didn't go with him to Marion, but I did go to Oregon, because Nicole was there, and I also went back with him when we did Bessie Gilmore, Gary's mother. Norman Mailer was a nonentity to Vern Damico, Gary's uncle, but he has a way with people and really built a relationship with Vern. He also got along with Brenda, and in fact on several occasions I told him I thought the two of them were getting too close and Brenda might become too paramount in the book. He actually did spend a night at the house where Gilmore and Nicole had lived, and at one point even decided to write the book in Provo and was looking for a place to rent.

Since I was with him I saw how he operated in the field. He dressed casually in old Levi's or corduroy pants. He became a man of leisure, because he wasn't under the pressure of collecting facts, and for the first time I saw a different man. His speech was slowed down, he was very relaxed. He was taking notes, but not heavily, and there were times when I'd say, "Don't you want to use a tape recorder?" He'd say, "No, no, everything's all right, Larry." We'd go out together. We'd drink—he introduced me to rum sours, a light Bacardi and a twist—and it was different too from when we'd once been on tour to sell *Graffiti*. Then we'd get to a strange town and it was still chasing chicks, like the two nurses we bumped into one night. But that wasn't the case with *The Executioner's Song*. Neither of us needed that.

I think a lot of it was due to Norris. She made one trip out with him, but I didn't see her. I'd already met her before, though, in Manila, and then, of course, when I'd go to New York I saw her more and more. But Norman never told me she gave him the voice for the book. If he wants to say that, he's giving Norris a gift. But she was certainly responsible, at least in part, for his being so relaxed.

There was also collateral research. We did a lot of it, like supplying him with microfilms of all the newspapers. We got Utah television stations to open up to him, trading off with promises of interviews with us when the book came out. I was handling that, and Norman had Judith, his secretary, and another researcher organizing the stuff as we were funneling it in.

Now, as for my role in the book as subject: I suggested that Norman interview me because I felt he should have the whole story. It wasn't ego. I just said, "I'm the one that put the package together, and it's eventually gonna get known. I have to come clean, because the reviewers will go at it. I want you to know everything, and then you decide how much you want to use."

So we began interviewing on airplanes. After the first interview, Norman said, "You have to be in the book. When Nicole goes into the nuthouse and Gary is in prison there's no central character who can serve as the link between them. You're that character."

At first I suggested that Earl Dorius, a lawyer for the state, could be used. Norman went and had dinner with Dorius alone. He came back and said, "Dorius is good, but I can't get into his head. The character has to be you, Larry."

I said to him, "If it has to be me, then you've gotta lay me out the way I really am."

"You're sure you can take it?"

I said, "This book is my dream, Norman—I'm willing to take the gamble."

I told Stephie, whom I'd married by then, and she got very, very upset. What I said to her was, "If Norman writes this as I think he's gonna write it and goes all the way with me, then this book will win the Pulitzer Prize." She said, "You're stupid. How can you say that?" I said, "Look at the goddamned historical novels they pick for Pulitzers. They don't have the detailing. When it comes to non-fiction, the Pulitzers are given for detailing, and even *Blood and Money* didn't have the detailing. We've got it, and we're gonna win it, so I'm gambling with Norman going all the way with my character."

Of course, Stephie walked out of the house for a week when she eventually read a draft of the book and saw how far I'd gone—the whole thing of my diarrhea and all that. She loves me, but at the time she didn't understand that I, as a dramatist, a filmmaker, know what's needed to make a character work.

When Mailer interviews, though, he confounds the public myth. He's not competitive or pushy, he's more like a sponge. He says very little and doesn't go after anything except what a person says. If you don't give him an answer he doesn't become an adversary, unlike my technique of dividing the interview into several separate sessions so I can become pushy in at least one of them.

The prison research was always going to be part of the foundation of Gilmore as a character. Norman talked a lot about convict life, the behavior and values in prisons, with a kind of philosophical overlay to it. He'd have long conversations with Warden Cupp and a few others. But in fact I think he realized that all the stuff he'd gotten about prisons wasn't as good as what we'd found out about Gilmore from people in Utah, so he decided not to use it, because the book was already too long.

Gilmore's letters and poems were merely edited to force the reader to look with tunnel vision, to accentuate the mood or situation Mailer thought was pertinent. He didn't want the reader to have to search out and define. But the letters were the most edited of all the material. There were about 600 to 700 pages on legal-size yellow ruled paper, written on both sides, and many letters weren't used at all. Mailer did a little cleaning up of the grammar once in a while and also edited some sentences to remove hesitations and pauses—the "ahs" and "ums"—but he didn't go out of his way to highlight Gilmore's stuff about karma. In fact, it's there in the over-all letters more than in the book.

But most of his research was being done out in Utah, driving around, seeing people. I can't stress this enough. It seemed that he could spend five minutes with someone and have enough to write 50 pages. He just soaked it up.

ARTHUR KRETCHMER   It was during the period he was doing the interviews of Nicole that Norman and I happened to end up on the same plane to New York out of Chicago. I'm sitting there next to the literary giant of my time and I'm figuring out whether to sleep or be intellectual, which I thought were the only two alternatives. Norman, though, abruptly turned to me and said, "You guys at *Playboy* ruined my life." I said, "How's that?" He said, "You ran a piece by some Greek guy on how to bet sporting events. I read it, took it all very seriously, and, though I'm not totally committed, I've got little bets in every day." Then he pulls out these ledger sheets covering every pitcher, every act in the baseball season and sits there trying to figure out whether Jim Palmer was a good bet that afternoon.

BARBARA NORRIS CHURCH MAILER   When I moved in with Norman, Beverly and I were sufficiently friendly that I could talk to her about things like cleaning out the apartment. I think she may have figured I would come and go and maybe felt she could get Norman back.

Norman had just started work on *The Executioner's Song*, and he asked me to marry him, because now the divorce had been filed, Beverly had been friendly, and the two of them were talking amicably about a settlement. Nobody was pressuring anybody, so we thought it would all come about. In fact, that summer we stayed in the Provincetown house for Beverly's convenience, because she was doing summer stock in Connecticut. So things were still cool between all of us. She would call, and we'd talk about how Michael and Stephen were doing, since they were living with us, and one night we piled all the kids in the car and went down to see her in her play and had dinner together.

I got pregnant that July. I wasn't using birth control because we wanted a baby, and I remember coming out of Rosy's bar after we'd been drinking and telling Ellen Hawkes I thought I was pregnant. Actually, I think I asked them when she and Peter were going to have kids, and she guessed why I was asking. She'd met Peter at about the same time I'd met Norman, and since we very much wanted John Buffalo and I was so happy about it, I guess I wanted her to be happy too.

I asked Norman to phone my parents and tell them, which he did because he didn't want to duck out on his responsibility. He just phoned and told them how much he loved me and that we were going to get married as soon as we could, as soon as the divorce from Beverly was settled.

But our cordial relationship with Beverly ended when she heard I was pregnant. We were back in Brooklyn, and she was parked up on the sidewalk in front of the apartment. I was upstairs and Norman was talking to her in the Citroën, and apparently she went berserk. She screamed and yelled and carried on. He got out of the car but then leaned back in to say something, and she tried to take off while he still had his head in the car.

I assume it was horrible for her that I then had a son, John Buffalo. Up until then, of course, of all Norman's wives she'd had the *only* boys. Her whole thing—and she said so in court—was "Norman gave me the Provincetown house because I had the boys." Her attitude was "I'm the important one"—then here I go and present him with another son. So it became clear that the divorce wasn't going to be easy and that she was going to take it to the newspapers. Beverly wanted $1000 a week, plus taxes, plus the house in Provincetown, plus money for her acting lessons. There was also medical and life insurance. Plus, plus, plus. There was no way in the world Norman could have taken care of his other seven children if Beverly had been given all she asked for. That's when it all started, in '77, and the divorce dragged out for the next three years because of procedures and appeals.

GLORIA STEINEM I've talked with Beverly once or twice over the years about the divorce. She called me, we discussed her problems. I don't remember her asking me to do anything—I think she perhaps wanted to share the situation, find solace of some kind. The catastrophic part of divorce is what leads women to marry men who don't think women are human beings. It happens too often— less and less so now, but still too often. So the initial problem was not the divorce but the marriage. Doesn't everybody marry Norman for the wrong reasons? I suppose I'm saying that in terms of healthy, well-adjusted, conscious, aware women, Norman is unmarriable.

I know Norman and consequently I feel sorry for him. I find it almost impossible to be angry at him . . . so his force in the world should therefore probably be judged by people who don't know him at all. The issue, though, is that what unites his public and private personas is his idea of what a man should be, which, in a larger, anthropological sense, dictates that men should be aggressive, take chances, and father many children. It's an exaggeration of a patriarchal ideal that in and of itself is impossible to achieve and has enormous penalties, more so for women but also for men, who are under stress, have heart attacks, then go off to war, get killed, do a whole lot of destructive stuff to live up to this code.

For Norman the division between his public and private selves is minor compared to the compulsion to live up to this masculine image. He's in a prison. Many people have shared similar beliefs, but he pushed it further: more children, more violence.

GORDON LISH I came to *Esquire* in September 1969, and even though I was the fiction editor I worked with Norman on his piece about television. The idea was initially mine and came out of a trip west I'd taken with my family. One of my boys was a collector of fossils, and we went to some crazy town—Hurricane, Utah—where we entered a little house where fossils were being sold out of the cellar. Three or four generations of the family, eight or nine people, were all watching a midday quiz show, with the shades drawn against all the outside splendor. It was a phenomenon of a whole higher order than I had heretofore encountered. I had an image of people all over the USA plugged into their TV sets at midday, fixated, comatose. It suggested a new plateau in a kind of Huxleyan world, so when I came back from the trip I suggested that *Esquire* have writers look at TV as an all-encompassing phenomenon, devote an entire issue to three major essays.

Tom Wolfe agreed to write a piece for $10,000, but Norman's agent said he'd only do it for $20,000. Tom is probably my best friend—he may have heard Norman was getting $20,000—but he was reluctant to proceed, probably because it would look like a *mano a mano*; and the third writer, William Gaddis, who was supposed to write about Johnny Carson, reneged as well.

Twenty thousand dollars wasn't all that much considering some of the other fees we'd paid at the time, so over the next two or three months Norman worked on it, and, by God, there it was, on the very day he'd promised. He hadn't skimped; it was a sizable piece and earnestly executed, but it didn't speak to the ideas I was interested in. It was more anecdotal, more personal, and somehow my original notion had been lost in the wash. Still, I was tickled to have it, and we decided we'd edit it together at the house he had on Mt. Desert later that summer.

So my wife and I and our sons went up to Maine in August. The house Norman was renting was quite large, built out over rocks at the end of a fjord, really quite spectacular, and this was the first time I'd seen him deploying himself as host, and he was as accomplished and graceful in this respect as he is in all others. He had his daughters and sons with him, and while I was out on the deck taking home movies of my boys playing on the rocks with his sons, he went inside to get his motion picture camera and started photographing too. He was just terrific, very *haimish*—and there's no more agreeable trait in my book. Instantly warm, a decent human being, but at the same time there was a certain sense of old-time honor too, a sense of "You are in my home and you are my guest and I'm proud to have you here"—a commitment to ceremony which I love.

Later his daughters cooked dinner, and we drank heroically. I'm virtually a competitive drinker, and Norman can drink rather heroically himself. I'd been asking him during the day, "Shall we get to work?" and he'd been putting me off—"After dinner, after dinner," and by the end of dinner I was pretty swacked. But I operate fairly well when drunk, and Norman does too, so we repaired to his study and pulled out this long manuscript, at least 25,000 words, and began plowing through it.

Now, I'd heard tales that Mailer was difficult to edit, but to the contrary, I found him singularly civilized, and among all writers I've dealt with no one has been more professional. Me, I tend to be rather exacting and not so easy to get along with as an editor, but Norman proved himself admirable in all respects in bringing about a text that would be agreeable to both of us. There were things I wanted worked on further, certain sentences that I thought one could drown in and not be happy for the death, so we started line-editing at eleven, a bottle between us, and went on until about four in the morning. My wife and kids— I didn't know where they were. I simply lost track by then.

I was saying things like "Let's get this out, let's do this to it." He'd argue eloquently for those elements he wanted sustained, and his arguments were usually impressive. I got my first look at the astonishing intelligence of the man, which is often displayed in print but was altogether surprising to see in person— that on his feet he could launch himself into one of his wonderful intuitions, trip out on it. The circuitry of his thinking was spectacular. He'd defend a sentence in relation to all its amplitude and even as a strategy in dealing with the reader, as if to say, like an editor, "We need this kind of mechanism here." Not that many writers have such a palpable sense of the necessary dialogue between writer and reader, the tacit relation between the writer and an *intelligent* reader. Norman, though, expects some kind of concord at a certain level of intelligence that is unusual and he positions himself to achieve it, first stylistically, then editorially.

The way we worked was like a dance: when Norman wanted to dip, I relaxed whatever muscles were required to allow us to make a graceful dip, and ditto too when I wanted to dip. I came away feeling that Norman Mailer, even in extreme situations—I think we put away two bottles in the course of dinner and afterwards—well, that he's an incredibly diligent worker, something that requires a tough connection with one's consciousness, with one's poise and sense of one's place in the world. It's the opposite of preciousness. Not giving up, saying at three in the morning, "I'm exhausted, let's finish it off another time." I didn't have to leave with an edited manuscript in hand. In fact, I think at one point I said that maybe we ought to pick it up another time. But no, he was going to finish the task and finish it with great grace and correctitude. I was immensely impressed, not only by the physical and intellectual performance but by its moral dimension too. We were proving to ourselves we could get the work done under those circumstances as well as any other circumstances, which I suppose is precisely what he means by an "existential" task. And finish it we did, so that the piece came out in the October '77 issue.

BARBARA NORRIS CHURCH MAILER   All the while Norman was writing *The Executioner's Song* he was in serious financial trouble, and we were borrowing money every month to live on. The house in Provincetown was taken, and one month they even seized our bank account, so I tried to make order out of chaos by managing the finances.

At first Norman hadn't discussed money with me at all, so I hadn't realized what the situation was. After I got pregnant, though, I got pushier and pushier, and around Christmas Norman hired a new secretary, Judith McNally—it was a new regime. After going through all the records and bills, I realized what idiocies had been committed by his financial people. They always filed his taxes late, which meant he spent thousands and thousands in late fees and penalties, and they also weren't taking all the possible deductions. I just went berserk. But Norman didn't care. He just didn't want to be bothered.

Between '72 and '77 the situation had rapidly deteriorated, such that in the spring of '77 he sold the brownstone in the Heights to raise cash for his taxes. By the following fall the debt was around $300,000, mostly owed to Scott Meredith, who was supporting Norman with monthly loans. Plus there was a big chunk still owed to the IRS, and the penalties every month were getting fatter and fatter. Norman also had to borrow about $90,000 from his mother, since a chunk of the monthly money from Little, Brown was going to Scott to repay the loans, with interest. The nut was about $1000 a day, a staggering figure. Broken down roughly, it included a secretary, plus part-time secretaries when Judith couldn't get all the work done, as well as Myrtle, our housekeeper, and I think there were seven kids in private school and college at that point. There were also Carol, Beverly, and Adele. Meanwhile we had the apartment, plus taxes, and a $600- or $700-a-month phone bill, most of it on business— Norman's calls to Utah and to Larry in California.

I was concerned about Norman having to work under that pressure. But while he worries about money, it doesn't depress him. After *The Naked and the Dead* he'd always had a lot of money and always spent it. So it's a given—owing x number of dollars a year—and he's got to work like crazy to pay for it. If we have to economize, what do we cut out? The housekeeper? Then we're slaves to the house. The secretary? How can Norman work without a secretary? And the kids are going to be in school for the next twenty years. The wives are always there too. So what do you cut out? We can take subways instead of taxis, sure, but that'd be laughable given our over-all situation.

EMMA CLARA "ECEY" GWALTNEY Lord, what a talker Norman must be. I'd love to have been a fly on the wall listening to how he told Barbara's parents she was pregnant. Barbara phoned me later to tell me, and I think she said that he'd told them how sorry he was that the situation was the way it was, also that it would be very different before long. I'm sure he convinced them he's an honorable man, which of course he is.

When John Buffalo was about eight months old they brought him down. They still couldn't get married, but they stayed with her parents. I asked Barbara, "What if your parents had said, 'We love you, your life is your own, but we don't agree with what you're doing'?" I was making up a hypothetical situation— that her parents had used the only power they had and said, "It's against our principles. You can't sleep together in our house." Barbara's answer was, "Well, they knew we wouldn't have come." And she was right. They'd know that was their choice. But what if they'd decided to sweat it out? Would Norman have capitulated to their principles? He might have. I suppose it would have depended on Barbara too.

BARBARA NORRIS CHURCH MAILER Norman was working on *The Executioner's Song* when John Buffalo was born, April 16, 1978. Where his name came from is Norman's and my secret. Maybe someday I'll tell John Buffalo. Maybe never.

EMMA CLARA "ECEY" GWALTNEY When Barbara had first gone to New York, Matthew was four and stayed down here. I had the impression he was going back and forth for a while, and then finally he went up to stay. Barbara, I'm sure, had prepared him. She has a way of accepting things herself, of not making a fuss over 'em which communicates itself—"This is just what we're going to do"—that sort of thing.

Maybe it was hard at first—like it seemed to me he was totally cowed by everything that was happening. Then, after John Buffalo was born, it was like Norman adopted Matthew. He didn't treat him any differently from any of the other kids. Norman's an incredibly good father, good with all the kids, and he wound up looking after Matthew just like the others.

BARBARA NORRIS CHURCH MAILER Matthew didn't go to St. Anne's when he first started school, because he and Maggie started at the same time and we didn't have the money. Maggie and Carol were living in New York that year, and we couldn't send one kid to private school and not the other, and we couldn't afford both. So Maggie started at P.S. 6 and Matthew went to P.S. 8.

Whoever says Norman would spend the money on his own kids but not on Matthew is just wrong, plain wrong. We were broke, and neither kid went to private school. The next year, when things eased up a bit, I put Matthew in St. Anne's; Maggie was again in public school, but it was because she was living in Stockbridge and didn't want to go away to boarding school.

But there was never an issue of Norman assuming responsibility toward Matthew. Neither of us ever hits the children, but if Norman wants to discipline

Matthew, he yells at him or has a talk with him. From the beginning he's tried to relate to Matthew as he'd relate to one of his own kids.

LAWRENCE SCHILLER Norman was sending me 100, 150 pages at a time, and as I was reading these chunks I said, "We've got a great book here, it's brilliant. But if you can get more time from the publisher, would you go through it again?" "Sure," he said, "if I had five years, I might go through it a couple of times. But I can't do that. I've gotta publish now. It would take me three months to do what needs to be done, and I'm stuck for money."

"If I can get you the money, will you do it?"

"Of course," he said. So I went to Kaminsky at Warner's and got him another $100,000, which brought us up to $600,000. But the things I had to do to get that $100,000 were unbelievable, including life insurance policies. They were scared. First, that Norman might die and they'd be out the money without a publishable book. But they also wanted me to make sure, irrespective of Norman, that if something did happen, there'd be a person who might finish the book or someone whom Norman could coexist with. Norman's still unaware of all the measures I had to go to simply because I never told him. I just worked it out.

But I knew the money was the real problem. He owed Scott Meredith $175,000 or $200,000, he owed his mother, and I knew the New York State people were attaching the money from Kaminsky. What the exact tax figure was I didn't know, but I was also getting attachment notices in California, which I was embarrassed to tell him about. I was even trying to figure a way of getting him this money without it being income—in effect "lend" it to him, because I didn't need the tax advantages. He was very reluctant to do this, so then I tried to convince Scott of ways to avoid the tax problems, but he was telling me to stay out of it.

Anyway, that hundred thousand dollars gave him three months, and he reworked it. There's hardly a sentence he didn't do something to. This was February, March, April of '78, and he was sending me pages every couple of days. And because Norman didn't have the money to type it, I was taking it to CBS at night, where I could have it secretly typed by the script typist, sneaking the cost into a movie budget.

We were talking every day on the phone. He wasn't on edge, he was confident, and so was I. I was reading it installment by installment, sometimes reading it as it came out of the typewriter. Now I was sure it was gonna win the Pulitzer Prize, and I was always telling my wife Stephie that. She kept saying, "How can you talk like that?" "Because the detailing is there, the flatness, and Mailer doesn't exist in the book. They have to give him the award."

ARTHUR KRETCHMER I'd seen the book in typescript in Los Angeles. My Los Angeles editor and I stopped by Schiller's apartment, and he handed me the first draft, which no one had seen at that point. I went home and read it and called Schiller: "Listen, Norman has done an incredible thing here. He's changed his voice. The voice is flat, midwestern, uncolored, intentionally repetitive. It's the manipulation of an American idiom that no one will understand, but it's phenomenal—as dry as that air out there, colorless, so intentionally held back. Those are the most real people in American nonfiction that I know about. The exercise here is spectacular."

Five hours later Schiller called me back—"Norman says *Playboy*'s the only magazine in the country that should even see the book. You're the ones to publish it because you've understood so well what he was doing. No one will fucking understand it, no critic in New York will get it." This is Kretchmer on a pedestal, right?—"What a great editor you are, you've got this vision of the book, Norman wants you to have it." Fine, only then Larry reminds me it'll cost only $100,000.

He'd given me the hundred thousand-dollar figure before he handed me the book, saying, "Norman is in debt up to his eyeballs. Scott has lent him well over a hundred thousand to keep going, and he has to be made whole by this publication, otherwise there's no reason to do it." What he was getting at was Norman's feeling—which I was aware of and could understand—that publishing in *Playboy* would probably cost him book sales, so the argument was "You have to give him the incentive to do it... blah blah blah."

At some point I gave him a counteroffer, and Schiller refused to negotiate. I said something like "That's not very sporting of you, Larry. What am I supposed to do here?" And he said, "You bought the fucking interview, and I let you steal it because I knew that interview had a function for me in *Playboy*. But you can't steal this."

All along he'd been thinking of trying to sell it elsewhere of course, and now he began to threaten me with who else would publish it if we didn't. I told him that another magazine wouldn't have near the money we'd been discussing, and he came back with "I'm not saying I'm going to give it to anyone else." Then he got angry and said, "I'm not shopping this thing. If you don't buy it, nobody buys it."

What happened then was that once I'd made the decision to lay on the hundred thousand for three installments, the negotiations got easy. It wasn't hard to justify that kind of money, even though we'd never paid that amount before; also it was easier back then to okay a hundred thousand without going to Hef. At the time, Hef didn't know what we paid for it; only Nat Lehrman, my publisher, knew. In fact, though, I never had to justify the decision because by the time we actually published it our participation was so logical, so much a part of our culture, that nobody ever asked. Hef was impressed with the figure and made reference to it at a later meeting, saying he hadn't known we were such a good market that we could afford to pay a hundred thousand dollars for a book. It was a snide remark, but I don't think it was critical.

Still, Norman hadn't been involved in any of this—nobody had wanted him in on it—but after the deal was cut he called me and said, "I'm really glad you're going to do it. A couple of people have seen the book, but you're the right place for it because you understand it."

This was an allusion to what I'd initially said to Schiller about his voice. I kept referring to it as a "plains voice"—"You've got the fucking plains in your text. It's right there." He said, "I picked it up from Norris. If the book has any feeling for small-town life, I guess I picked it up from Norris."

Then while we were essentially out of the money negotiations, except for the foreign rights, we started to do the excerpting. Each of the three installments was to be 7000 words, for a total of 21,000, and we sent Norman the first excerpt, which our articles editor, Jim Morgan, had done. Norman looked at it and said, "This is crazy—what's going on? You can't take from one place and then another and butt them together. It's got to be continuous. This is not the definition of an excerpt." It was essentially the same protest he'd raised earlier over our proposal to excerpt *Marilyn*: he felt that by taking parts of a book that don't follow chronologically and pressing them together you're giving a condensation of the whole book rather than excerpts from it.

I said, "We have to do it our way. This is the only way this thing can work. If we can't do it, there's no deal." There was no signed contract at that point. In fact, the contract doesn't get signed, the checks don't get written, nothing gets done until we're shipping magazines. So then he called me back at home, and said, "I have to come out and see you. We can work this out."

He knew it was all coming apart, so he said he'd pay his own way out, because . . . I can't remember the specifics, but the gist of it was that he had a concept of how to do it. I had reminded him on the phone that the contract called for x number of words and that one of the reasons we had to condense it our way was we couldn't go with any more than that. He'd thought about that, obviously, and when he arrived in Chicago he said, "Look, I realize what the problem is. I want you guys to have it, but I don't want to harm my relation to my eventual reader of the book. So I don't care about the number of words. Give me more words and I'll give you excerpts you can use." Money didn't enter into it. He said, "Forget all that—just give me more space so that I can create the context for it."

He gave me examples to support his concept of why you're cheating the reader if you take things apart and put them together in ways different from the book. First of all, he objected to our beginning. He said, "I know why you're beginning where you are in the excerpts." We had opened in a particularly dramatic spot, leaving out the book's opening and going right to the first night's murder; there are two murders and the execution of Gilmore, a great deal of other stuff, and one excerpt took all of it. So he said, "How can you do that to me? There'll be no book left. It'll look like all I did was write a book with these violent highlights. It doesn't establish the environment, the context that I worked so carefully to create at the opening. You can't have it."

"Well, what can I have?" I said, and we talked about what we could use in terms of the first murder and the execution. In fact, when our deal was first cut, the negotiations had broken down over Norman saying we couldn't have the execution at all. I remember laughing about it, but now he went on about all this in terms of "Here's why I need to create a context . . . I need an opening, I need to do this. I'll give you the installments, let me take care of the words. No one will ever call you on the words if you let me show you how to do it." So I finally agreed to his proposal. He went home and worked on it a couple of weeks, then sent in the excerpts when he'd finished them.

He'd really come in like a traveling salesman—come in the night before, slept over, was in my office at ten o'clock in the morning, spent till four o'clock in the afternoon with me, and by the time he flew home we'd made a deal that was completely independent of all the other deals that had been made. That was one of the wildest things about it: there were thousands of pieces of paper already in existence on the exact terms of this deal, and Norman and I had just violated them all, in every sense. To this day I'm convinced that Norman was ready to say, "Let's do six chapters, let's do ten, but let's do it right." He was convinced that a number of people were only going to read the *Playboy* version— that's what was obsessing him, that the *Playboy* editors looked upon it as the excerpts of a novel, while he was beginning to look at the installments as a work in and of itself. In fact, he said to me, "Some people will think it's better than the book."

In a funny way that may have been true. The book was too long, too patient, and if there's a tremendous flaw in it, it's the story of Schiller's negotiations, which are nowhere as interesting as Mailer decided they were. To have Schiller in the book was to demonstrate the intensity of the media business, but Norman approached it with the same patience that he approached setting up Gary Gilmore at the beginning. But the book didn't need the origin and history of Larry Schiller. Also, I'm not so blind that I didn't understand why he wanted to make a public justification of the relationship.

Given the really positive feedback we got, the serialization may actually have helped book sales, yet I thought the way Norman talked to me was very revealing. At the end of that wild day in Chicago he said, "Look, I know this is a hassle, but I'm not sorry. I know how much pressure you've felt, but none of this is a lie. I'm telling you the absolute truth when I say I'm seriously in debt, and I'm never out of debt." I said, "Okay," but he said, "No, seriously, I've gotta keep working. I can't take seven years to do a book. Styron has the discipline to take seven years." A rich wife, whatever the reason, I don't know—but Norman said, "Besides, I don't know what I'd do if I had seven years. Maybe I'd never finish."

With *The Executioner's Song* I suppose he had a choice to do a shorter book— say, the 300-page love story. The irony is he did do that book, but he used 1000 pages. It's like Truman Capote's answer to the question "Do you polish and polish and polish your work?" He says, "No, of course not. Someone comes and takes it away." You hit the deadline, they take it away. That was Norman's point as I walked him down from my office and put him in a taxi for the airport to go back to New York: he functions to the day of the deadline, and knowing there's a finish to that day, he then goes on. Not that he doesn't rewrite, but there's a limit to what he will be able to do to make it perfect. Then there's no looking back.

LAWRENCE SCHILLER   At Little, Brown, Norman's editor, Ned Bradford, had been very sick, and by the time the book was done he'd died, so I don't think he was ever consulted on it at all.

But I'd also been screaming about Little, Brown. They'd only put up a token

$25,000 but were getting a third of all the paperback money! It was only after *The Executioner's Song* was successful that Scott got the contract on Norman's big novel rewritten, that $300,000-a-year deal, but that included a piece of his share of the movie rights to *The Executioner's Song.*

Earlier, when I'd had my meetings with Thornhill and the other guys in Boston, they were polite, but I was this little Jewish guy from California, and they didn't even dare look at me across the table. Then, when Norman delivered his 1250-page book, they had no confidence in it. They didn't understand it. To them it was still Gary Gilmore, an unpleasant, undignified subject, not what they wanted Norman Mailer to write about, and they probably figured it wouldn't help the big book Norman still had under contract to them.

Roger Donald was not yet on the scene when I started having fights with the head of the sales department about the cover, and I finally hired my own designer to move them in the right direction. I was pushing a photograph to convey the feeling of the West—the isolation, the sparseness. But they wanted Mailer's name in big letters, and some of the designs were unbelievable, including one that was blood-red, dripping. I kept screaming, "Don't you understand? When you have a Rolls-Royce, it's known by its cover, not by its name. This is gonna be a great book. You don't need Mailer's name at the top—put it at the bottom."

Norman was laughing through all of this when he'd be at the meetings. He couldn't believe it, because I'm saying, "You know, I'm The New Ingot Company, and I have stockholders too!" The Little, Brown people are shuddering—they're never gonna publish another book with me—and I'm thinking, big deal, 'cause it's obvious that Kissinger is more important to them as a Little, Brown author than Mailer.

ROGER DONALD   I don't think of Norman as a "loss leader" for Little, Brown— never did. We paid him large advances because we expected to get our money back, otherwise we wouldn't have done it. But I won't discuss money; it's simply Little, Brown's policy not to talk about money or numbers of copies sold. I don't know where the newspaper figures come from, and I've yet to see anyone get it right. But I won't say, because we consider it ungentlemanly to discuss other people's money.

What I can say, though, is that *The Executioner's Song* was a success in every sense of the word, in terms of both its critical reception and its commercial rewards. I guess other publishing firms have loss leaders, but I don't think Little, Brown does. We're a very smart publishing house, and that's been our history for a hundred and forty years. In the modern period of the Thornhills there's been an improvement in the list and a kind of aggressiveness that's added a lot of important authors and made money in the process. Norman was no exception. He made money for Little, Brown.

With *The Executioner's Song,* I took on the book just at the point of the jacket decision. Larry Schiller presented some ideas, our people presented others, but nobody liked any of them. Then one of the design assistants found a lovely picture of the Utah sky, and somebody up in Boston said, "Gee, that's wonderful" and sent it to me. I thought it would make a sensational jacket, so I showed it to Norman, and he said, "Yeah, it's terrific." There was a solitary truck—a semi, not a pickup truck—in the original photograph, which he thought was wrong and should come off, although I thought it conveyed a nice sense of loneliness. But that's not the kind of thing I'm going to fight over. We went through half a dozen jackets, I think, and Norman was looking at the sketches as they were proposed.

He also worked closely with the publicity person. The marketing people and I sat down and decided what kind of publicity we wanted, what the house thought would be absolutely the best use to make of Mailer, whether he should do a tour or not, whether he should do network shows. There were obvious difficulties—Gilmore and the kind of person he was—and also the problem of everybody on the talk shows wanting to talk to Norman only about either capital punishment or Larry Schiller's involvement and not the book itself. So we came up with a plan to have a very limited tour, to provide people with lots of information ahead of time, along with some very gentle but firm guidelines about not having discussions about Norman's personal life.

We presented this to Norman and he said it sounded good, so we went through the list of shows we thought were right. He knocked off one or two of them, saying, "Those guys come after me" or whatever, and added a couple. So we had a plan that everybody—the publicity people, the marketing people, Norman, and myself—agreed to.

Larry Schiller did very little of the publicity himself, mostly in Utah and some in Los Angeles. But he was involved in the planning and was tremendously helpful with his connections. Larry's a difficult character—he'd be mad at me if I said he wasn't difficult—but he's also tremendously bright and fabulously energetic and was very good at seeking people out and promoting the book.

Larry had also been heavily involved in the publishing process, so he absolutely did not take the money and run. There had been a fair amount of quite understandable friction between him and various members of the staff at Little, Brown, though. Larry wanted things done a certain way, and obviously Little, Brown felt they were the publishers. There were lots of lumps and bumps in the process, so one day Larry came into town, and Norman called me and said, "I want you to have lunch with Larry. He's having a tough time getting what he wants from the people in Boston. He thinks they're mad at him, and maybe they are. But he's got a lot to offer, so I think it would be awfully good if you two guys can get together." That was Norman seeing himself in the role of paterfamilias or mediator.

<u>JAMES ATLAS</u>   The first I heard that Mailer didn't like my *New York Times Magazine* profile was from Phil Nobile. Phil had spoken to him for an item for *New York*, which I suspect Mailer himself had initiated, since I don't think it would have occurred to Nobile to call him up and ask what he thought of my article. What Mailer declared was that I had stabbed him in the back, that I'd come to him in friendship and then concentrated on his past excesses by referring

to the fact that he'd stabbed his wife and that there'd been a dispute with Styron. What the personal dispute was about he'd never tell me, and that's what I should have said in the piece.

The *New York* item was headed *"Times* Irks Mailer, Atlas Shrugs," and went on to say: "The lengthy portrait was mean-spirited in its delectation in past excesses. He feels that Atlas merely pretended great friendship and sympathy during months of interview... He's specifically incensed by Atlas' remark that he convinced Little, Brown at the last moment to label *The Executioner's Song* a novel."

I found his reaction shocking because I thought my piece was objective. I've written just as objectively, I like to think, about Roth and Updike and other people. But the point is that I don't expect these people to be friends. But Mailer really is a very naïve fellow. He expects to be praised by a reporter. We weren't friends—I didn't go to him as a friend.

He had read my Delmore Schwartz biography and was very keen on the project, and in fact he was the one who brought up the issues he later complained about. We were sitting in a Chinese restaurant in Brooklyn Heights one day and I asked, "When did you decide to settle down?" or some question like that. He said, "After I stabbed Adele." Then he gave me the names of all his wives and others to see. Adele wouldn't talk to me, but I spoke to the British one, Jeanne, although not to Beverly. I also saw his mother, and she said something to the effect of "Norman's a bad boy at times." I got the impression she was a very shrewd and powerful woman.

It was my idea to time the piece with *The Executioner's Song*, and he made every effort to be very open with me. He was also very curious to know what I thought of *The Executioner's Song*, so I went to his house with a suitcase, as he'd instructed, picked up the manuscript in typescript, and read it right away. He was trying to show himself at his best. He was aware of my being someone from *The Times*, and he's in great awe of *The Times*, which is another facet of what I mean by his naïveté.

But then he was furious about the piece and persistent in going after me. A few months later I wrote about Thomas Wolfe for the *Book Review*, a reconsideration of Wolfe, and I quoted from Mailer, purely as a literary critic, a remark he'd made about Wolfe in one of his essays. Mailer wrote a letter to the *Book Review* about all the mistakes I'd made, how I was a good writer but tended to distort the facts, and I was amazed at this. I wrote a little reply saying that I thought he was just annoyed because I didn't mention him more—I was just making fun—but it was as if our roles were reversed, as if he wasn't the powerful one and me the young man.

Still, when I was with him I was aware of how publicity-conscious he was. He and Bellow are the greatest writers of our times, but Bellow handles it quite differently. Mailer's more manipulative, more conscious of being in the public eye, more the celebrity. I don't object as such—it's created a kind of adventure for him—but I think he can be unprincipled about it. For instance, after he sent his letter and I gave my little rejoinder in the *Book Review*, he called up the *Book Review* editor to complain, and I don't think you do that. If you're going to be in the public eye, you have to be a little tough about it. After all, he has such a great reputation. It's a reputation that's often argued over, but still, why should he even care about such minor matters as reviews?

I grant you, there were faults to my profile. One was I didn't say enough about *The Executioner's Song*, which I think is a really great book. Also, I didn't say enough about his career, lit-crit stuff, which I wish I'd done more of, because I didn't make sufficient argument for how great I really think he is. But he's still oversensitive, a very oversensitive person with a lot of megalomaniacal ideas, a fascinating person but very childish and vindictive, and now I'd be afraid to run into him. Maybe he wouldn't hurt me, but that that should even cross one's mind . . . I'm not quaking in fear, I just feel it would be a very unpleasant experience.

<u>NORMAN PODHORETZ</u> There was never a decisive break so much as a slow drift, and I saw him less and less, and when I did it was awkward.

Our drifting apart was the same as what happened with Lillian Hellman. By the time I wrote *Breaking Ranks* I hadn't seen Lillian for a year or two. Even though we never actually had a fight, I realized that it was all over, so I took advantage of the freedom to open up on her and say what I thought. With Norman, he was still phoning, but less and less frequently. Then, when he had

Norman Podhoretz, East Hampton, 1978.

finished *The Executioner's Song*, I'd finished *Breaking Ranks*, and he invited us to dinner in Brooklyn Heights. There was one other couple—Mike Arlen and his wife, I think—and I told him he probably wouldn't like what I was saying about him in my book. He said, "Well, you owe me one," a reference to his review of *Making It*, and I laughed and said, "Well, we'll see if you still feel that way when you read what I've written."

I never heard from him again, only through third parties—my son, Jack Richardson, Buzz Farbar—all of whom reported that he was very angry. I haven't spoken to him since, so although we'd been drifting apart, he was the one who broke with me, plainly as a result of *Breaking Ranks*.

But the fact was that I'd been trying to avoid any kind of ultimate confrontation with him. I was writing things that Mailer couldn't possibly agree with, like my "hawkish" foreign-policy piece in the Sunday *Times Magazine*, but I was still trying to avoid a break because of affection and shared experiences. I knew that the days of great intimacy were over, but I still didn't want to break entirely.

I don't regret the events that led up to the writing of *Breaking Ranks*, because for me the book was a major event, a coming out of the end of a block. The freedom to say what I really thought about a lot of people, including Mailer, was a freedom that I had purchased, as one might say, in blood, and the book redeemed all those difficulties, because in the end it's more important to be able to speak one's mind. And I certainly couldn't have done that if Norman and I were still friends. I couldn't have and wouldn't have. There are things you can't say about your friends, not if you want them to be your friends, and if you do, you can't expect them to forgive you.

MIDGE DECTER   When Norman P. finished *Breaking Ranks* we'd drifted apart from Norman M. because to see him was to have arguments and quarrels, and we didn't want arguments and quarrels. He understood that. The night we had dinner in Brooklyn, Norman P. had made his position clear, and when we left I said, "Well, that was nice," and Norman P. said, "He'll never forgive me."

BARBARA NORRIS CHURCH MAILER   Norman hadn't really been living in New York the years before I'd met him, he was just in and out, so he was never on the social scene until I came along, and after '76 we became part of it bit by bit. I met Pat Lawford, I met Jan Cushing, and we'd meet people who'd later invite us to their houses. So it sort of pyramided. People like Mort Janklow, Mark Goodson, the TV producer, the de la Rentas. A lot of it, I think, was my doing, because I enjoyed the glitter, the back and forth, the small talk. I'm not in awe of these people, nor do I think they necessarily have false values. I like them. They're famous because they have a lot of interesting things going on, they're moving and doing, whether it's film or television or writing or business.

ALICE MASON   With each of his wives, going back to Carol Stevens, Norman was a client of mine. He was always looking for an apartment in Manhattan, looking in a haphazard way for something special. Whoever the woman was would say she'd like to move in from Brooklyn, and he'd say, "Go look for something."

I think one of the Kennedys, maybe Steve Smith, referred him. He always wanted to rent, not buy, but even so, I remember when Norris called and asked if I had anything I sort of laughed, because they need space, and rentals in Manhattan are very high.

In any case, it was around this time I started inviting them to my dinner parties. Norman had stopped drinking, and his reputation for getting in quarrels was completely contradicted by his new manner. He had mellowed. He was always a considerate, even gentle guest, even though I always have a variety of people with whom you can really get into a big discussion. But Norman's always in character, never changes no matter whom he's with, though of course you never see him with reactionary, right-wing Republican types, or Waspy Social Register types either.

I talk about "Social Register types" because my business, of course, has made me aware that co-op buildings are often very stuffy. To a certain extent those types definitely exist, and since Reagan they've come out of the closet. They're like they were twenty years ago—anti-everything that's not in the Social Register. Anti-Irish, anti-vowels—meaning anyone with vowels in their name, so it's not just anti-Semitism. They just cut coupons and have nothing to say. They're boring, and Norman wouldn't be caught dead with them.

Achievement, not success, is my criterion for dinner guests. Someone can be very rich, worth a hundred million dollars, but no one wants to talk to him. People know how hard it is to achieve in New York, so every achiever recognizes other achievers. Money per se is not the issue. Take Henry Grunwald. He's a very intelligent man, the head of Time, Inc. Who cares if it was handed to him? He's doing something, he's an achiever. You can say JFK had it handed to him, but he too was an achiever. And Norman certainly fits this standard.

Beyond this, though, Norman has mellowed, and people recognize that. Certainly I do, just as I recognize that Norris has played a real role here. She's a very unspoiled girl. Granted, somebody like Marietta Tree isn't going to invite Norris without Norman, but more to the point, I think she has made him a different person. He's come out into the sunshine with her. Every other woman he's married, the thought was, I'm marrying Norman Mailer, I want this and that. They were all competitive. They wanted everything, and they didn't get any of it. Norris, though, wasn't demanding and even paid her share. So I find her a very unusual woman. For example, she does things the plainest Jane would do, and she brought these qualities up from Arkansas with her. Some women are prima donnas, but not Norris. I can seat her next to anyone at a dinner party—it doesn't have to be Henry Grunwald—anyone, and she's perfectly happy.

JAN CUSHING OLYMPITIS   I'd invited the Mailers to a dinner about two weeks after first meeting Norris. I also invited Pat Lawford because I love her and she was the one who introduced us, also Arthur Schlesinger, Jr., and his wife, Alexandra. There were some people from *The New York Times* as well. I can't remember exactly who, but it was the kind of dinner I usually give—sort of like *Face the Nation* or *Meet the Press*—and ever since then I often invite the two of them to these dinners. I find discussions boring and would rather have an interesting fight—something where Arthur, for example, says, "Well, that's perfectly ridiculous."

Norman, though, I always regard as an asset. With Norris he's rather placid, terribly gentlemanly and polite, and also very kind. There's never been any vivid temper, nothing like the fight at Lally Weymouth's with Gore Vidal. I like excitement, but I wouldn't have the two of them together any more than I'd put Truman and Pat together, because of what Truman's written about Joe Kennedy.

But Norman's history doesn't matter to me. I don't care about it. To me he's a star and a genius. I admire his creativity a lot more than Norris', certainly, but put to the test, I'd take her side. There are a lot of friends who wouldn't, because of his power, but here again I'm talking about my response to people for what they are, not their reputations.

There's a larger question too. I think society knows that Norman is dabbling in our world, just as we're having him because we find our situation basically boring. It gives him insight into a world he's never known, and one that he's perhaps wanted to understand for years. In a sense, he's on the outside looking into this zoo full of animals. Some of them are rather exotic, and he enjoys it, being part of it without being locked in.

KURT VONNEGUT   A year or two ago there was a poorly researched piece in *New York* magazine called "Good Old Parties," which mentioned us as well as Norman and Norris. The fact is, we don't go to a lot of parties. It's bad for your health, it makes you feel terrible. Jill, my wife, is out scrambling all day, she leads a very athletic life carrying all that photo equipment, and when she comes home she just wants to watch the telly. But I'm aware that Mailer belongs to a social set we don't belong to—the Kennedys, that whole scene, although we know it marginally because of Pat Lawford. Still, my move to the Hamptons in contrast to Norman's staying in P-Town isn't emblematic. His social situation is different from mine. I had been living in Barnstable, really a village on the Cape, all year round and knew every single soul to nod to, most of whom took a very dim view of divorce. In their eyes I had disgraced myself, and I no longer felt welcome. P-Town, on the other hand, has always been much more bohemian and, I suppose, accepted Norman's presence more easily.

RHODA LAZARE WOLF   It took me years to accept what everybody accused Norman of doing—that a lot of times he behaved the way he did with an eye toward publicity. I think part of it is true, and I find it offensive, but I also think the explanation is much too simple.

But really, the only time I began to have negative feelings about Norman's behavior was when he started going around with that shitty crowd that gets listed in all the columns. I found that so upsetting. I hadn't seen it in the fifties, although I was aware he always wanted to be with what he viewed as wicked ladies. In the late fifties and sixties attention was more on bohemianism, the artists and writers of the Village, whereas now it's the East Side types and movie stars, so I suppose it's a broad cultural shift and goes beyond Norman. But Norman is ambitious and wants to be where the action is. He's always the explorer and always has to conquer. He likes to feel he's a star, so he started moving into the society group. Marion Javits was important in all that kind of shit, and it really began in the late sixties, snowballing in the seventies, when the East Side really took to him.

PETE HAMILL   One of the things missing from the public perception is his sense of humor. While I hardly think of myself as one of Norman's friends, it's been apparent to me that there is a kind of merry Norman—not one-liners, but when he's in the mood, he's at his best.

I see him around town socially, and what you've got to remember is that there's no intimacy at these things. There's a huge difference between having dinner with just four or six at his house and being at a dinner party at Alice Mason's, say. At one Norman is basically focused, whereas with the other it's hard for anybody to be focused. Fundamentally, Norman likes to take a subject and try to shoot it through a hoop. That's his MO. He likes the sense of continuity, of building, and it's almost like there's a process to his talk and the process itself is exciting to him. He's as amazed by the convolutions of the process as some of his listeners are. He doesn't sit there with a script, it just begins to go. At big parties, though, there are so many interruptions—hellos, goodbyes, how are you—that there's no flow. It's a series of jagged encounters, and Norman functions much better when he can take something to its conclusion. Why? Because he's essentially a storyteller. He's also an actor, a performer, which I'm sure Dickens and Dostoevsky and other novelists were too. He'll respond to his audience, just as they'll respond to him, and a Jan Cushing responds differently from a Jose Torres.

So I get the sense that a lot of these parties are sheer entertainment for him. I don't think he uses them the same way Henry James did. You can see that in James's notebooks: he'd go to a party, come home and note that he'd talked to two or three people; three pages later in the notebook he's got *The Turn of the Screw*. Norman does not do that, as far as I know. He's certainly not writing a book about the East Side or turning out short stories or anything that might use that material. It's entertainment—like some people go to the movies.

Certainly Norris is a factor, but she's no social climber, saying, "We must go to so-and-so's." Obviously he really cares for her and wants to make sure she has an interesting life with him, but that life only happens after he finishes work. She's working too, so there's no life together until after sundown, and that's when they wander around and are entertained. As a matter of fact, I like Norris. Among all the various women who have been in and out of this saga she's clearly superior.

MICKEY KNOX The same thing started happening to me with Gore Vidal as had happened with Jim Jones. He would harangue me. The drunker he got the more I would have to defend Norman, only at one point he gave me one of his screenplays to produce, and he gave it to me for nothing. I asked Norm if he had any objections. He and Gore, of course, were feuding, and I felt I had to get his okay.

"No," he said. "If you can get a picture produced, for Christ's sake, go ahead," which was what I'd hoped he'd say, because otherwise I'd have had to make a choice and give up the project.

A few weeks later, though—it must have been close to the fight at Lally Weymouth's party and then the Cavett business—I called from the airport to say goodbye on my way back to Rome. He said, "I want you to give a message to Gore. Tell him I said he's scum."

"I'm not a fucking messenger boy, Norman. You tell him."

"How much are you making on this screenplay deal?" he said. "Twenty-five thousand dollars? Is that what our friendship is worth?"

I said I didn't know what he was talking about—I still don't—and then he hung up on me.

I wrote him in 1980, but he never answered, and I was deeply hurt. Buzz was also upset, because the three of us had always been together, like when we made those movies. Then, two years later, Buzz called when I was in the city, and he said, "Come over and meet with Norman." I said, "I'm not gonna get a lot of shit from him or get into a fight. If he just wants to get rid of all the bitterness and hate he feels for me, all his anger, then fuck it."

"I swear he wants to see you. It's okay."

"You're sure? Don't bullshit me."

"Mickey, you got my word."

So I went to dinner at Nicola's with Rip and Buzz and Norman. We hugged, and I said how hurt I'd been because over the years and years... He said, "I know, I know." He didn't come right out and say so, but he regretted it, felt that it was really his doing. He'd been my closest friend for so long. We were like brothers and we'd always talked to each other.

LIZ SMITH Gore will always say to me, "Oh, I'm so glad to see you, the woman who thinks Norman Mailer is the greatest living writer." I reply, "I think you've written one of the best books ever written in America, so fuck off, Gore." Then he'll say, "Imagine, Norman Mailer calling a gossip columnist to give his side of the story."

One of the things that made him so angry was that I printed Norman's remark that he wanted his kid to take on Gore's boyfriend—this was at Lally Weymouth's the night of their fight. Gore thought it was beyond the pale, a pointedly antigay remark, and certainly from Norman's point of view it was—the suggestion that a fourteen-year-old could lick a pansy. I thought, Well I ain't perfect either. Every day I have to figure out how far I'm gonna go, so one time I handled it by saying, "Gore, maybe you're right. Maybe it *was* a rotten crack. I think it was almost as bad as your calling me a 'cunt' in public for using it."

"What's the difference?" he demanded.

"None," I explained, "because to call a woman a 'cunt' is a terrible thing, a sexist slur where you're insulting the dearest part of her."

He stayed angry, though, and finally I had to say, "Look, I never said I was right. I have to go with what I get sometimes, and that was just too good not to print." It's taken him years to get over it.

BARBARA NORRIS CHURCH MAILER Jan Cushing once gave a dinner party that I went to alone because Norman was with Dick Goodwin sailing down from Maine.

It was an interesting evening, everybody was giving crazy toasts, and I got up at one point and gave a toast to Norman, "To my husband, who's not with us tonight. Here's to you, kiddo"—something like that.

I was sitting next to Ahmet Ertegun, who remarked, "Since we're giving toasts to writers who are not here, I'm gonna toast Gore Vidal." This was right after Vidal and Norman had had their little tussle at Lally Weymouth's. I said, "Ahmet, I really wish you wouldn't do that. You know how I feel about Gore."

"I'm going to do it anyway," he said, and I said, "If you do, I'm going to pour a glass of wine on your head." He laughed and gave his toast.

I got up and said to the room, "When Ahmet told me he was giving a toast to Gore, I said, 'I'll pour a glass of wine on your head.' Apparently Ahmet doesn't believe I'm a lady of my word." At which point I turned and did it. The whole room clapped and cheered.

I hadn't had much to do with Vidal, but I'm not going to smile when someone defends a man I know Norman detests. Ahmet was being intentionally provocative.

JEAN STEIN One has to deal with the myths about Norman, and part of becoming his friend is adjusting oneself to the true Norman as opposed to the public Norman. I probably have never seen a greater disparity between the public image and the real person anywhere.

He is a fine human being. He listens to you, he's there for you, he's helping every second. Sometimes he spins off on some idea, but it's always fascinating and original, even if it might be slightly off the wall. With men he is competitive, and he has a tendency to surround himself with people who don't talk right up to him. With women, though, it's completely different; there are no rules, and with women he can have friends who are more substantial. But his loyalty to old friends is something I've rarely seen. It may well be a way for him to stay in touch with what he knows is real.

LAWRENCE SCHILLER While I was directing the TV movie *Marilyn* I heard from a press guy that *The Executioner's Song* had won the Pulitzer. I called my wife right away, then Norman. The book was a huge success.

WALTER KARP, ESQUIRE *For years Mailer has been carrying on a passionate romance with crime and violence. For years he has been telling us how much he* admires the recklessly abandoned and how much he despises the rest of us. Had Mailer discovered in Gary Gilmore the ultimate weapon to bash in our brains with? Were we to learn in 400,000 superheated words why Gilmore, the wanton killer, is morally superior to the vast horde of "creeps"—a favorite Mailer word—who inhabit what he calls "Cancer Gulch"? The answer, surprisingly, is no. The Executioner's Song is an extraordinary book precisely because it contains no creeps, no Cancer Gulch, no romantic contempt for the common life, and most important, no Norman Mailer. At long last, Mailer has used his immense narrative powers, a true gift of the gods, the way they are meant to be used: to tell a story that is not about himself.

TIM O'BRIEN, NEW YORK   No gimmicks, no tricks, no Advertisements for Myself. The prose is spare and dry and clean. Most important, Mailer does not inject his own personality or judgments into the narrative, doesn't sermonize or philosophize, and doesn't attempt to force his material into any preconceived analytical molds. . . .

THE NEW YORKER   This inordinate length in relation to the squalor of its subject—the aimless crime, the familiar journalistic smash and grab, the all-American legalistic wheeling and dealing, the preening of the professional moralists, the tawdry character of Gilmore himself, the pathetic lives of his family and friends—is a fault and a serious one, if only because it demonstrates a lack of values, a lack of selectivity, an assumption that more is more . . . Mr. Mailer reports with some satisfaction that he wrote his book in a mere fifteen months. That would seem to explain the trouble with The Executioner's Song—its long-windedness, its uncertain credibility, and maybe even the portentousness of its title.

JOHN GARVEY, COMMONWEAL   A remarkably compassionate work . . . The Mormon families whose lives were torn open by Gilmore's murders are decent people whose hopes were modest and good, and Mailer is able to write about them without condescension. What I mean by that is the tendency of some writers who deal with criminality to see in the victims a naivete or smugness of stuffy respectability which draws violence, almost justifiably. What Mailer shows us is the horror which occurs when decent people happen on a man like Gilmore at the wrong moment. But Mailer is also fair to Gilmore and Nicole, Gilmore's lover, and this romance—exploitative, manipulative, also complicated and true—is the center of the book.

. . . This is the best thing Mailer has done in years, and considering the good books he has given us that's saying a lot.

JOAN DIDION, THE NEW YORK TIMES BOOK REVIEW   It is one of those testimonies to the tenacity of self-regard in the literary life that large numbers of people remain persuaded that Norman Mailer is no better than their reading of him. They condescend to him, they dismiss his most original work in favor of the more literal *and predictable rhythms of* The Armies of the Night, *they regard* The Naked and the Dead *as a promise later broken and every book since as a quick turn for his creditors, a stalling action, a spangled substitute, tarted up to deceive, for the "big book" he cannot write. In fact he has written this "big book" at least three times now. He wrote it the first time in 1955 with* The Deer Park *and he wrote it a second time in 1965 with* An American Dream *and he wrote it a third time in 1967 with* Why Are We in Vietnam? *and now, with* The Executioner's Song, *he has probably written it a fourth.*

What Mailer could make of this apparently intractable material was unclear. It might well have been only another test hole in a field he had drilled before, a few further reflections on murder as an existential act, an appropriation for himself of the book he invented for An American Dream, *Stephen Rojack's* The Psychology of the Hangman. *Instead Mailer wrote a novel, a thousand-page novel in a meticulously limited vocabulary and a voice as flat as the horizon, a novel which takes for its incident and characters real events in the lives of real people.* The Executioner's Song *is ambitious to the point of vertigo . . .*

I think no one but Mailer could have dared this book. The authentic Western voice, the voice heard in The Executioner's Song, *is one heard often in life but only rarely in literature, the reason being that to truly know the West is to lack all will to write it down. The very subject of* The Executioner's Song *is that vast emptiness at the center of the Western experience, a nihilism antithetical not only to literature but to most other forms of human endeavor, a dread so close to zero that human voices fade out, trail off, like skywriting . . .*

. . . When I read this, I remembered that the tracks made by the wagon wheels are still visible from the air over Utah, like the footprints made on the moon. This is an absolutely astonishing book.

<u>JOHN LEONARD</u> I think the putative literary community is so thin-skinned— so quick with the insult and ready to take offense—and the reason is that it's been so hard to arrive at a situation where you're taken seriously as any kind of intellectual in a country that doesn't respect intellectual values. There's a sense of beleaguerment, that you're holding out against the vulgarization of ideas. And Norman, what does Norman do? He does things that are obnoxious to that community. He becomes a celebrity and he swims in the media. Sometimes he does it very well, sometimes he's awful. But it's not "high culture," and this particular culture doesn't understand why a writer might enjoy it.

Yet Norman doesn't understand limitation. He lusts for greatness and wants to be very nineteenth-century, he really does want to be the kind of novelist Dickens was and at the same time be a Darwin, a Freud, a Marx, to know everything and to compel us to understand what it is he knows. It's an incredible, imperial ambition, with that substratum of "I'll always go against your expectation," and so there's the need to work on the edge, the fear that unless there's a deadline, a terrible financial burden that needs to be discharged, he can't operate at all. He liked writing *An American Dream* to deadline. He *needed* it. Panic is almost his condition. . . . But it's not the idea of the writer today. The writer today is somebody who has a cushy job at a university, has a private income, and only occasionally does journalism. There's the notion too that there's something wrong with journalism, that the mere fact you have to produce a certain number of words by a certain time for a certain frame means there's something wrong with you. We're stuck with a weird Flaubertian notion. Bellow, Styron, the late John Cheever, all were richer or poorer depending on the flow of the advance. They do not stoop to the marketplace. But hey, the marketplace is terribly dynamic, no different from the culture itself.

XII: ANCIENT EVENINGS AND ONWARD (1980-84)

ROGER DONALD Norman took time off from the Egyptian book to do *Of Women and Their Elegance* for Simon and Schuster. It had, in fact, been under contract a long time, at least predating *The Executioner's Song*. I don't know precisely why he decided to finish it then—whether it was for financial reasons or whether Milton Greene asked him.

LAWRENCE SCHILLER Norman often falls back into the pit, and that's what I thought when he did that Milton Greene book, *Of Women and Their Elegance*. He had me read it, and I said, "Norman, you're crazy. You're gonna get crucified." He said, "I've gotta do it for Milton." I said, "Well, go out and interview twenty models, then. Don't write about Marilyn Monroe again. You're not gonna be able to fuck her—why're you still writing about her?"

Maybe it's his fixation on Monroe, I don't know. But he got a quick sixty grand from Simon and Schuster, and it was an opening wedge to Dick Snyder, the firm's president. In fact, I'm the one that started the whole thing, the possibility he might leave Little, Brown for S&S. Yet even if it was a quick sixty grand, Norman didn't realize he was falling back into the goddamned pit. Later he was bitching that S&S had screwed up the design, but that was nonsense. The problem was that the book was a piece of shit. The pictures and Mailer's text don't match the title, so the reviewers crucified it.

JEAN STEIN   About two years before my book *Edie* was published, the first draft was completed and I thought it was pretty close to the end, so Norman said he would read it. He just volunteered, so I left the manuscript with him and went out to California, knowing that there would never be a tougher critic and that the book needed criticism. But out there I was paralyzed with terror. Norman was so sensitive. He kept calling with bulletins to let me know where he was in the book, so I wasn't sitting in a total vacuum.

When I returned he said, "Let's have lunch," and he sat down and warned me, "It's better you know now the kinds of things that are going to happen to you, because I didn't learn until after *The Naked and the Dead*." To compare my book to *The Naked and the Dead* is ridiculous, but what he told me was that after his first important book people had put him in a niche and when he fell out of that niche, it disoriented them. He said that *Edie* would have an impact and that people who had categorized me were going to feel threatened.

Then he said, "The book is fine as it is, you don't have to do any more work, but you could make it 25 to 30 percent better." It wasn't a question of doing more interviews but of reorganizing parts of the book. He also felt the book needed line-by-line editing, which I, Miss Naïveté, didn't know anything about. He literally sat me down like a teacher and showed me what I should do. He said, "You don't have to do it, it's just a suggestion," but he was right.

I had already worked eight years on the book, and George Plimpton came in for three of those years to collaborate with the editing. But what Norman was saying was, "You've come this far, go for broke," and it was a challenge in the sense that he wanted what was best for the book. So I continued to work on it for two more years because I felt I had to live up to its potential. If the book wasn't good enough, it had better get good enough—that was the challenge. It energized me. Norman really gave me the courage.

DIANA TRILLING   It was presumptuous of Norman and very unthoughtful to have written that letter of his to *The Times* calling on Lillian Hellman and Mary McCarthy to stop quarreling and behave like nice little girls. Who called on him to adjudicate between them, and in those terms of male superiority? It was really insufferable. A most serious issue is involved in their dispute. It's the issue of freedom of criticism in relation to money. If a critic cannot voice her judgment of another person's work without risking that she'll be sued for libel and go bankrupt even before the case ever comes to court, then obviously freedom of criticism belongs only to the rich. Mary and I have never particularly been friends, but she's a very distinguished critic, in quite another literary league from Lillian's; you'll remember that was the point Meyer Shapiro made in his statement he gave to *The New York Times*. To be sure, Mary spoke hyperbolically and even theatrically of Lillian that night on the Dick Cavett show, but it was a theatrical occasion; she was part of a show. As a dramatist Lillian should appreciate that. And the question Norman should ask is, how Lillian justifies bankrupting Mary as her way of replying to criticism. When Lillian undertakes to punish Mary for what she believes to be a libelous statement about her, all she's really punishing Mary for is not being rich. If Mary were as rich as Lillian, what difference would it make if Lillian sued her and even won?

What a patronizing letter of Norman's that was! Its tone of condescension was really intolerable.

NORMAN MAILER ("AN APPEAL TO LILLIAN HELLMAN AND MARY McCARTHY," *THE NEW YORK TIMES BOOK REVIEW*) *In January, on the Dick Cavett show, Mary McCarthy called Lillian Hellman "a bad writer and dishonest writer," then added, "I said in some interview that every word she writes is a lie, including 'and' and 'the.'" Lillian Hellman then filed a defamation suit against Mary McCarthy.*

A number of writers were asked for their opinion of this case by The New York Times *(March 18, 1980), but I chose to be among the missing. The quarrel was between two of the American writers I most respect—on the other hand, the awfulness of the attack was matched, I thought, by the recklessness of the lawsuit.*

Yet, as another month has gone by, I wonder if it is not now possible to address a letter to both these authors. It is, at the least, an opportunity to pay them critical homage: They are both splendid writers. They are, however, so different in their talents that it is natural for them to detest each other. Writers bear this much comparison to animals: The giraffe and the anteater walk together no more than the lion and the lamb. We have all purchased a different piece of the universe, and it is natural to think that our piece—which is to say our perception of reality—must be defended with savagery. After all, a vision opposite to our own can destroy those nuances we have spent our lives working to protect. Anyone who knows literature, or who has worked in literature for his or her life, is not going to be surprised that Mary McCarthy and Lillian Hellman do not like each other. McCarthy's work has been a constant illustration to us that honor is a pose, a kind of scaffolding for identity—and identity is the central spiritual problem of our time. Who of us has any? It is possible that Mary has had more to say about the shifting nature of that most personal possession, our identity, than any American writer.

Lillian Hellman, on the other hand, has spoken to our disappearing sense of honor, our individual and our national honor. She is the only artist of the 1950's whose remark before the House Committee on Un-American Activities is unforgettable. "I will not cut my conscience to fit the fashions of our time," she said at a time when everybody else was saying a good deal less. She was also in effect saying, by the force of her person and her work: "Forget identity. You have it or you don't. There is only honor, or lack of honor."

Such differences are profound. They produce mortal insults and lawsuits. I think the latter is a disaster. If Lillian wins, then every American writer will have to feel that much more tongue-tied at daring to criticize another American writer without qualification. So I wish Lillian Hellman would drop the case. But I do not know if she can. The insult has been too personal. Men used to kill each other in duels, now women try. To say what Mary McCarthy said, knowing with her critical sense that her words had to be deadly to Lillian's honor, was a barbarity and a brutality. Lillian is not a mature woman in the full command of her powers, eager to defend herself; she is an honorable and much-damaged warrior who could not raise a pistol since she can no longer see.

Mary McCarthy has an absolute right to detest Lillian's work, but not to issue the one accusation against which no writer can defend himself or herself. To say that Lillian Hellman is dishonest is blarney. No writer worthy of serious consideration is ever honest except for those rare moments—for which we keep writing— when we become, bless us, not dishonest for an instant. Of course, Lillian Hellman is dishonest. So is Mary McCarthy, Norman Mailer, Saul Bellow, John Updike, John Cheever, Cynthia Ozick—name 500 of us, Willa Cather, Edith Wharton, Henry James—we are all dishonest, we exaggerate, we distort, we use our tricks, we invent.

After all, it is almost impossible even writing at one's very best to come near the truth. Given my respect for Mary McCarthy, I must say then that it was a stupid remark to utter on television and best left unsaid.

To Lillian Hellman I would plead: Forswear your suit, drop it. That suit can bring censorship and self-censorship on writers. Perhaps, with your high standards, you have not noticed how endangered a species we are.

At any rate, to both women I say: I have learned so much about writing from each of you that your quarrel is as painful to me—and to many others, I expect— as a quarrel between the nearest and best of one's relatives, one's dearest, one's friends.

GEORGE PLIMPTON   The fact that Norman should write as a peacemaker, and lecture and plead with those cranky women, is absolutely appropriate and right. It could only be done by somebody who sits at the top of the heap. Actually, Lillian has been quite sweet to me, but then I got on her bad list for publishing a piece by Martha Gellhorn in the anniversary issue of *The Paris Review* which took her to task for trafficking with facts—what Gellhorn called being an "apocryphier." Hellman said I should've given her the piece and let her reply to it in the same issue. But of course that's not the way it's done. I offered her the whole next issue for her reply to the charges, but she never took up the invitation.

DAVID PLACE   In the late sixties and early seventies we'd started to socialize with Norman, both in Maine and Provincetown. Then the summer of '80 he started renting our family barn, because once I was visiting him in the other place he rented, the Thomases' at Soames Sound, and he said their stay was coming to an end as the place was being sold. The house near the barn belongs to the Parkmans; Francis Parkman is my mother-in-law's brother, so he's my wife's uncle. He was the head of St. Mark's School for years, an educated man, and also his oldest son, Harry, was in Norman's and my class at Harvard, so he made it his business to make Norman feel at home.

In the last ten or twenty years I guess he would look upon me as one of his half dozen best friends in our class, and often in the summer we've gotten together, gone on picnics, sailed together. I know he's sailed with Lou Cabot too. I can't quite figure it out, but after Lou remarried, about eight or nine years ago, he and Norman befriended each other. I've known Lou and sailed with him since he was ten years old. He's an interesting guy and interested in different kinds of people, and so several times he's persuaded Norm to take the two- or three-day run down the coast from Maine.

MARA LYNN CONRAD As far back as the early sixties I'd suggested to Norman that he try Maine. He'd been in P-Town for years, and I'd just come back from the camp I'd gone to as a child, about twenty-four miles north of Augusta— very remote, no telephones—so I told him, since he was looking for a place to disappear to.

He drove up there—how he actually found the camp I'll never know—but the owner, who was a very peculiar fellow, wasn't having visitors. But Norman found someplace else to stay, and the next year he looked around and found a house, the farm he bought with Dick Goodwin.

Then later he took the houses on Mt. Desert—the first one on Soames Sound, then the barn—and I went up there for a week. The last night he gave a big party, and some of the society folks, the WASPs, came, what I call the mayonnaise people. And once again it was obvious that he doesn't act differently around these types—he's just a great host at work, going from group to group, seeing that everyone has drinks, that they're introduced to each other. When I'd flown up, I met people on the plane and they all gave me cards—"I have a yacht, come over . . . ," and of course when they found out I was visiting Norman, it was "Oh? You must bring him." Naturally I tore up the cards as soon as I got off the plane, since he would go up there to be with his kids.

I sometimes had the feeling he was testing me. I'd been ill, and he was pushing me, putting me in a do-or-die situation to show me I'd come through. Like when he had me climb the Beehive. The Beehive is a 500-foot rock formation, like a small mountain. There are narrow trails and these iron rungs set in the face of the rock, and on top of that no one told me what to expect. All the kids are with us, everyone has passed me, I'm on the iron rungs, and *bam*, I freeze. I can't go forward, I can't go back. I'm in a chicken state, all alone, trembling and exhausted. Then I hear a voice going "Oh-oh-oh," and I realize, "Jesus, that's me." I'm whimpering. Then I start getting angry—"Fuck you, mountain, watch this!"—and somehow I forced myself to get going and made it up to the top.

They were all there, sitting in a semicircle, watching me come up the last slope, and they gave me a big hand. The kids were already rested and wanted to go down, but I said I had to rest and needed a cigarette. Norman waited with me, saying I wasn't allowed to smoke—"Park rules'"—but I had one anyway. I was still quivering. I didn't tell him, but he insisted on carrying my bag down, so I think he knew.

I wasn't pissed, even though initially I said I'd just walk partway up. Maybe it would've been fair to warn me, but afterwards I wouldn't have missed it for anything. If Norman had told me how tough it was, it would have been boring.

JAN CUSHING OLYMPITIS   In '76, when I first met him he was still drinking, but he stopped in the spring of '80. Why? Animal instinct, I think. He may not have admitted it to himself, but he knows his entire personality changes when he drinks. Alcohol turns him into a madman the same way cocaine turns people into paranoiacs. I know it wasn't easy. One night at dinner he was seated next to Marvin Davis' daughter, Patti, who's very sweet but not exactly what he's used to, and it was obvious he'd have loved to have a drink. He didn't, though. I watched him. He was smart enough to know what could have happened.

BARBARA NORRIS CHURCH MAILER   Beverly and I never had a direct confrontation except in the courtroom when the case finally went to trial up on the Cape. At one point she was testifying and I was watching her and giving her the dead eye, which I think made her nervous. After she got off the stand I continued to eye her, very coolly, and when the judge left she started screaming at me, "You're a witch. You're trying to put a curse on me." I stood there and kept looking at her until she said, "You're very happy, aren't you?" I said, "Yes." That was the conversation. That fall the divorce was granted and Norman and I could marry.

MONROE INKER   I wasn't Norman's lawyer until two weeks before the trial. He'd been referred by Dick Goodwin, my wife's cousin, and I couldn't reorganize the case because the pleadings were already frozen, so what I concentrated on was putting together the proper financial statements from Ed Lucci, Norman's accountant, Scott Meredith, and Cy Rembar, since I didn't think the ones that had been filed were proper under the rules. The rest of the work was talking to Norman about his life, his background before Beverly, his marital history. His reputation, I figured, wouldn't mean a damn thing, and as a matter of fact the other side raised the issue of the stabbing, and the judge ruled it inadmissible.

From the outset the problem was money. This lady had insatiable demands, yet Norman's net earnings aren't impressive at all. It's like with each marriage another floor of his house gets taken. Eventually he sold the goddamn house, hence the analogy: every week another floor. Money was once plentiful, say in the sixties, but then he just pissed it away. He squandered a fortune on that movie *Maidstone*, and then all the deals he's made with ex-wives... I mean, if you look at his financial history, to maintain his standard of living and all his children, he's had to cut away at his capital year after year. It's crazy. He had the feeling he could always turn around and write another best seller, so until I asked him to put his financial records together I don't think he'd paid much attention at all.

But Beverly's demands were irrational, impossible to meet. I had talked to her lawyers, Brooks Potter and Ruth Budd, and said, "You're asking for the moon. Is there any way of settling it?" They'd say, "Those are her demands," so it was senseless to try. My sense of Beverly was that she was a very vengeful, angry woman and there was no placating her.

The kids, however, were a nonissue, so the easiest part of the case was the custodial arrangement. They were not in court and weren't asked to be. Norman was able to tell them this was no game, and in fact, at one point he let them in on the proposal he made to Beverly about the Provincetown house. He wanted to stop the IRS from auctioning the house to a stranger; his idea was to buy it back, then sell it and split the proceeds with her, putting his half in trust for the kids. The IRS made a fair offer, Norman flew down from Maine, but Beverly never showed up. She wouldn't agree to it. She was still saying "I want the house" when in fact he no longer owned the house.

Norman was angry and also not angry. He was angry at some of her lawyers, their strategies, but he never seemed angry at Beverly. He wasn't even angry about the stunt with *People* magazine when she had them come to her $800-a-month apartment to photograph her apparent "poverty." But he was angry at her lawyers, at some of the questions they asked about writing and writers and their interpretation of certain events.

Since Beverly was arguing that she'd given up her career, we explored the possibilities of her earning money, and I thought her saying that she was still going to be a Broadway star was pure fantasy. But Norman was very solicitous of her. He said, "I don't want to make fun of her or demean her." There were questions I wanted to ask—questions that would cast light on her character and personality—which he wouldn't permit me to go into.

As for the publicity, with a public figure it's inevitable. Nor did I worry about Norman talking to the press. A couple of times I tried to stop him in the corridor. Sometimes I could, sometimes I couldn't. But basically you couldn't stop him, not him. It's like saying you're going to dry up the Mississippi.

Beverly was awarded $575 a week for seven years, plus child support, tuition, and health insurance. But now she's claiming she's still Mrs. Mailer. The divorce was filed, but she's appealed on the grounds that there was a conflict of interest, even though the court had a hearing on this at the beginning of the trial and thrown it out. The so-called trigamy issue—that Norman was never legally divorced before he married Carol Stevens, divorced her, and married Norris—well, it's completely irrelevant and just more fantasy. The other issue she's appealing on is the money. Her new lawyer—her third now—is saying they shouldn't have limited the alimony to seven years, that the $575 a week should be extended indefinitely.

BARBARA NORRIS CHURCH MAILER   I wasn't there when Shirley Fingerhood married Norman and Carol. It was on a Friday, about five. Then he came home, changed clothes, packed a little bag, and flew off on a seven o'clock plane to Haiti for the divorce. From the outside the arrangement seemed ludicrous, but it wasn't laughable to me. I was torn ten different ways. I realized he was doing absolutely the right thing as far as Carol and Maggie went—it was as difficult for Carol having Maggie out of wedlock as it was for me to have John Buffalo.

But I didn't know if she'd actually go through with the divorce; she could've pulled one of those "Now that we're married, I like it."

She was being given the same amount of alimony and child support he was giving Beverly. Norman initiated that. He didn't think of giving her a lower amount since, unlike Beverly, she'd been so decent about the whole thing. Beverly was kicking and screaming, demanding more, Carol wasn't. It was a point of honor.

Anyway, he went along to Haiti and came back the next day. We applied for the marriage license the day after, on Monday, and since you have to wait twenty-four hours, we got married on Tuesday, November 11. Ed Koch had somebody call up the marriage license bureau and tell them to let us in the back door so we wouldn't have to stand out front for the press. Ed and Dan Wolf both came to the wedding Tuesday night.

My parents were happy, although it was sort of anticlimactic for them. I wasn't sure we were actually getting married until Monday, so they couldn't come up for the wedding. It happened too fast. We just pulled the wedding together, and I didn't invite anyone until Tuesday morning because I didn't want to put a curse on it. Tuesday morning, about nine o'clock, I called Jan and Pat and said to each of them, "We're having a wedding today." Jan ran out and got the cake, Pat got the champagne, and Judith and I were on the phone inviting people. We wanted Father Pete Jacobs to marry us, but the Catholic Church wouldn't allow it for the obvious reason that neither of us was Catholic and both of us had been married before. A rabbi from the local temple, David Glazer, did it. After the party we just split, left the apartment full of people, and caught our night flight to London, where Norman was acting in *Ragtime*.

SHIRLEY FINGERHOOD   I make up my own ceremonies, and since Norman and Carol were getting divorced the next day, I couldn't say the sort of things I'd say to the ordinary couple, like "Do you plan to cherish each other?" Instead I said that the marriage acknowledged these people's desire to give Maggie the same inheritance as the other children and to acknowledge the love that had been between them. Maggie was there, and whatever I said, Norman was impressed, because he asked me to marry him and Barbara. I couldn't do it, though, because I was going to be upstate, and, as it turned out, this was just as well. One of the papers said I married him twice in two days, so when people asked me if it was true I could honestly say no.

LIZ SMITH   I called Norris on the story that Norman was going to marry Carol in order to legitimize their child. She said, "Liz, I don't dare to talk to you about this, Norman would kill me."

"Well, look, it's not your fault that I'm calling. Just tell him I already know and I'm calling to ask him about it."

After a moment or two Norman got on the line. "Norris tells me you already know?"

"Yes. Don't you want to explain? It's very bizarre, and you know they're just going to crucify you." He agreed but said he didn't know what he could do about it, so I said, "Well, let me write the story, and that'll take the edge off it."

Which is what I did. I called *The Daily News* and told them, "I'm gonna give you this story and it's an exclusive, but if you put some shitty headline on it or make fun of him I won't ever do another news story for you again." They didn't, and apparently Norman was satisfied.

GEORGE PLIMPTON   That same year Norman came to the preview of *Reds*. I have a small role—you look into your popcorn, I'm gone—but I play a foppish, fatuous editor (typecasting?) who tries to put the make on Diane Keaton. Norman came up to me at intermission and said, "You rascal. You actually created a role there." He was impressed that I hadn't just been George Plimpton. He was pleased but also a little bit—what—envious? He hadn't done that in *Ragtime*. In *Ragtime* he's Norman Mailer. Wow! That was infuriating to Bobby White, Stanford White's grandson, an artist and a great friend of the Styrons. He was just infuriated that it was Norman who played his grandfather. I saw him practically walk into a tree at a lawn party, he was so upset. I don't know why. I

Mailer as Stanford White and Norris in Ragtime, *London, 1980.*

thought Norman was fine, although, of course, I knew it was Norman on the screen and not Stanford White.

EMMA CLARA "ECEY" GWALTNEY   Fig and Norman had little estrangements over the years, but the worst—and it was very sad—began the latter part of '79.

Fig had written a combination review of *The Executioner's Song* and a profile of Norman for the *Arkansas Gazette,* making a sort of flip remark referring to Norman's eight children, his four wives, and his "present live-in companion." I didn't say so, but I thought it was questionable myself, although I could also see that he was using it to introduce a discussion of how Norman seems to the public in order to lead into saying that *The Executioner's Song* would become a classic for showing what's wrong with society. Barbara, though, was terribly offended because he hadn't named her by name.

Well, it was a comedy of errors, a tragedy of errors. I didn't even know about all this, so for Christmas, '79, I just wrote Barbara a light Christmas card note— "Are you holding up for the South? Are you cooking greens?"—and then got a hot letter back from her. I think she's now sorry she wrote it, but what she said was "It was good as always to hear from you, but you failed to mention one very important thing—Fig's review. Either you didn't read it or you must agree with it or you must be very slow-witted . . . I can't believe he didn't mention me. Am I not a person? You introduced us, for God's sake."

It was really nasty, I was crushed, and she said she'd be in Atkins in a week or so if I'd like to talk. Unlike Fig, who was very visceral and had a gut reaction, I like to talk things out. So I went to Atkins, and, as Norman says, "in my polite way" I confronted her with the discrepancy: How could she complain that we'd introduced them but then hadn't used our names when I'd seen interviews with her where she'd say, "Norman and I met at the home of an old army friend"? I suppose I might have been more assertive about being "slow-witted," but I didn't mention that. I just pointed out the contradiction. She said, "I know I mentioned Fig's name. The interviewer just didn't put it in." I could see it playing out in front of me, so then I said, "Another thing—as you say, we introduced you, but it was odd for us to get the news about you and Norman from Ruth Harrison." It was only then I told her we'd been hurt by that. Still, she did say she was sorry she'd said what she'd written in her letter.

My problem was I could see it from more than one side. From my vantage point, outside of it all and just watching people I loved get into all kinds of a mess, I felt I could step in and straighten it out. But you can't do that, so it was all very sad, because the falling-out happened before Fig died in February of 1980.

BARBARA NORRIS CHURCH MAILER   From what Ecey told me I gather that when Francis died it was a special occasion, like an anniversary, and they were having steak for dinner. He choked on a piece of meat and they took him to the hospital, but the choking had thrown him into a heart attack or stroke, and he died the next day.

It was never resolved, and in fact it's a very sad ending to the story. Francis' review of *The Executioner's Song* talked about me as though Norman had gone through Russellville, sort of like "There's a girl in this town who had a kid by Norman Mailer." It wasn't just the omission of my name, as Ecey might have it, it was the way he said it.

I think Fig took it very hard that we hadn't sent him a copy of *The Executioner's Song*. Norman got only ten copies from the publisher, which we immediately gave to the kids, to Vern, Gary Gilmore's uncle—that sort of thing. The other straw was an interview I gave to *The New York Times*. I told the interviewer that I'd been introduced to Norman by an old friend of his, Francis Gwaltney. I even spelled the name, but Fig thought I'd deliberately slighted him.

But I think there was more to it, because I can't believe Francis would be so petty as to build all of it on that one thing. What it came to was that the two of us had gone off and left him. He'd never come to New York, despite Norman's urging over the years. He had plenty of chances to leave, like writing TV scripts for the Alfred Hitchcock shows, but I think he was afraid to.

Anyway, after the review Norman and I both wrote him harsh letters, and we didn't speak for a long time. Then, when Norman and I were getting married in November, I thought, Well, that's enough, I'd like to make up. I wrote him a note and said, "I think we should end this. Norman and I are getting married now, and it's all your doing, et cetera, et cetera," and "Please call or write if you see it like I do." I never heard from him. I hadn't talked to Ecey either, and then, two months later, either my mother or someone in town called to tell us he'd died.

After that I called Ecey and said, "At least I feel good that I wrote Fig that letter and tried to make up with him." She said, "What letter?"—so I'll never know if he ever got the letter or whether he threw it out and didn't tell her.

Then in March of '81 my father had his heart problem and we went down to visit. We sat down with Ecey and talked it over and buried the hatchet.

Norman, of course, had told me stories about Fig in the army. Francis was his oldest friend, and Norman is very loyal to his friends. He really likes to hang onto the past, which is why he was always going down to Arkansas before he met me. To see Francis, pure and simple. Nobody was the star in that relationship.

JOE FLAHERTY In 1980, '81, Norman started giving "soirees" at his place over in the Heights, the first of which was to raise money to keep Carl Oglesby and his group in Washington studying the Kennedy assassinations. What he needed, though, was an old Mafia maître d' from the Copacabana to throw out three quarters of the guests.

There was a horrendous woman there who'd written a piece for *McCall's* or something, coming on like the big expert—she'd found the smoking gun, she had proof that the CIA was behind the JFK assassination. Other people who'd studied the assassination, like Robert Sam Anson, who's intelligent and responsible, kept trying to bring it back to the point of proof, but this woman kept going on—"I did this, I did that." Finally I said, "Yes, madam, but what is *this?*"

"Who are you?" she yelled at me, and I said, "Who the hell are *you?*"

"I'm so-and-so, and I had this big article in"—whatever. I said, "Well, you didn't pull down the nation with it, we're all here tonight," and I went on, trying to bring it back to the reason we were there, to raise money for Carl, not to prove who killed Kennedy. Norman came up to me, put his arm around me, and said, "Pull this fucking thing together, it's gone mad."

Then Dotson Rader provided comic relief by going into a litany about his social calendar, how he'd driven all the way in from Long Island, given up going to this and that, and then he turned to me and said, "You've been wonderful, keep yelling at them." But the same horrible woman kept screaming, "I have the proof. I printed it!" It was such a glum bunch of fucking leftists. You look at them at these meetings and you realize why the left always loses. Anyway, Bob Anson said, "Look, I'd love to prove the CIA did it"—that was the woman's theory—"but we've never been able to." Then Dotson stands up and says, "Of course, everybody knows the CIA was involved. What has that got to do with it?" Somebody else said, "We don't know that, Dotson." But he objected by announcing, "But when I was having lunch with King Constantine, he said to me—"

It broke me up. "Who?" I said, laughing at the whole thing. It ended in a shambles. It was the kind of group you'd never send out for pizzas with various toppings; the anchovies would be on top of the sausages.

Later Norman threw the same kind of evening for Abbie Hoffman when Abbie was coming out of hiding and had to face the cocaine charges. It too was chaos, with people screaming and accusing each other of being CIA agents.

ABBIE HOFFMAN   He was chairman of my defense committee and also agreed to do the introduction to my book *Soon to Be a Major Motion Picture*, which came out in '80, just when I started to surface. I think Jerry Lefcourt, my lawyer, must have asked him. It's not me that would say that, and I don't think he came forward, 'cause he doesn't think as a political organizer. With him it's all instinct.

Then he gave that meeting for me at his house. Not my best hour. I choked as a speaker, maybe because Clay Felker was in the room and *The Daily News*, which he was then associated with, was trying to put me in prison. And also because Norman was there. When I'm with someone I really admire, my act falls apart, I'm off stride.

Earlier, though, I saw Norman once when I was underground, right before I was coming out. I had dinner at the house in Brooklyn. The two of us hadn't talked for six or seven years, and he offered me money, which I didn't take; but underground, if I needed bread, I knew he was there.

I saw in the Sunday *Times* that a student asked Senator Hayakawa, "What do you think about the FBI framing Abbie Hoffman on a cocaine transaction?" And Hayakawa responded, "What's wrong with that?" So this is where we're headed, which has been Norman's view for a long time. He swayed me a little towards a kind of pessimistic outlook because I'm the ultimate optimist.

NORMAN MAILER (INTRODUCTION TO JACK HENRY ABBOTT'S *IN THE BELLY OF THE BEAST*) *Sometime in the middle of working on* The Executioner's Song, *a note came from Morton Janklow, the literary agent. He was sending on a letter that had been addressed to him for forwarding to me. He assumed it was because our names had appeared together in a story in* People *magazine....*

This letter... offered instruction. Abbott had seen a newspaper account that stated I was doing a book on Gary Gilmore and violence in America. He wanted to warn me, Abbott said, that very few people knew much about violence in prisons.... If I were interested, he felt he could clarify some aspects of Gilmore's life as a convict....

Abbott's letter... was intense, direct, unadorned, and detached—an unusual combination. So I took him up.... I don't think two weeks went by before I was in the middle of a thoroughgoing correspondence. I felt all the awe one knows before a phenomenon. Abbott had his own voice. I had heard no other like it.....

JACK HENRY ABBOTT When I'd first heard there was to be a book on Gilmore, I didn't know who was writing it. Then I read it was Mailer—maybe in *People* magazine, I don't remember. I'd been through a lot of the same shit as Gilmore, and my feeling was that no one ever said anything for us, our type of prisoner, the worst kind they've got in prison, so I thought it could be important for him to have an idea of what to pursue. I also had an axe to grind against the Utah prisons.

Actually, I wrote to Mailer thinking I was going to die. I couldn't keep anything down, I was losing a lot of weight. They had me scheduled for an emergency operation at Springfield, the federal prison hospital in Missouri, and I'd been there three days when my mail caught up with me and I had an answer from Mailer.

I started writing him with a little pencil stub—that was all I was allowed—on funny pieces of paper, and I was analyzing the prison system. All those letters were completed by the time my operation was over—I took a long time recovering. I was then sent to Lompoc, and at that point Mailer started telling me I had a gift, that I might not have the skills, but I had my own voice.

At the same time I put in a request to see the Parole Board at Lompoc. Mailer didn't write anything to them; I didn't ask him to. They gave me a date, said I'd already served too much time on another sentence and that they'd turn me loose unless I picked up a new federal offense. Then I got involved in a work strike and got sent back to Marion, which is worse than any place on this planet. Instead of taking apart psychopaths and nuts, like they do in Vacaville, they go after people with strong political or religious beliefs. They don't use drugs—they control your behavior. They've got every day of my life computerized, so if they want to show I'm insane, they push a button and get information that supposedly indicates as much. They can also turn that information around to prove I'm an incorrigible criminal.

After *The Executioner's Song* was published and Norman was on the Donahue show in Chicago, he came to visit me in Marion, bringing a signed copy of the book. I met him in a visitors' room. I'd always pictured him from his younger days, when he had black hair and would wear a black turtleneck shirt. I'd never seen any recent photographs, so he looked completely different. He was very gentle at first and seemed nervous. I don't know at what point when we were talking, but there was a long span of silence—I caught him looking at me and saw the expression on his face, a real compassionate expression, like he'd seen something that made him real sad.

He was showing his gratitude and also being supportive by bringing the book. Then he said, "I showed my agent your letters." At that time I figured Meredith had literary judgment; now I know he doesn't. But Norman said, "You have a book here," although he advised me I shouldn't try to do something like a book of letters until I was out because otherwise they wouldn't release me. I said, "I don't care when it's published." He said, "I'll send you the letters, you go through them and edit them, and we'll go from there." Then I got the contract from Random House after *The New York Review of Books* published my letters and Erroll McDonald saw them.

ERROLL McDONALD   After the publication of Abbott's letters in June, I called *The New York Review of Books* for Mailer's number because his introduction mentioned that their correspondence was voluminous. I was given the number of Norman's assistant, Judith McNally, since they said she was the one who actually edited the piece, with Abbott's assistance. She told me to deal with Scott Meredith and Russell Galen, and Galen sent me approximately 20,000 words of letters, most handwritten, some the typed material that Judith had been working with. I made an offer of $12,500, and it was accepted immediately.

Early August '80 I'd decided to go out and see Abbott in Marion with Judith, since she was the sort of go-between. Then the two of them had a falling-out over letters Jack claimed either Mailer or Judith had lost—volumes and volumes, he said, though Judith questioned whether he had in fact written them. She never said she was frightened of Jack, but she thought he was a little bit off. Jack was the one who brought up magic—that Judith was a lapsed nun and into demonology and had written him really weird letters.

In Marion, though, Jack received me with suspicion. He'd expected Judith to come along despite their disagreement, and then, although Judith had told him I'm black, he wanted to know why a young black who wasn't corporate in his appearance—I was wearing blue jeans, a Lacoste T-shirt, a tan linen jacket, and cowboy boots—was being sent to work with him. Why not Jason Epstein? Why not one of the big-time guys? By this he meant that I was a flunky and that he was being shafted. The only hint I'd had about Abbott's racism was in a letter he'd written to Bob Silvers at *The New York Review of Books*, which was chiefly about women and black people; his attitude was totally repulsive—he talked about women as "niggers."

Anyway, as we discussed the shape of the book, he was worried that Random House wouldn't publish his Communist-Marxist views, and I told him not to worry, that the issue was how the book was to be structured.

By the middle of December I tried to get permission from the prison to go back out and show him the manuscript for approval. I had taken it upon myself to cut and paste, to structure the book—I had a manuscript to show him. But my request was denied. I went anyway, having secured a lawyer from Carbondale, Illinois, who'd represented Jack. The lawyer took the manuscript in as confidential material, and Jack went through it with him sitting there.

The man who had denied me permission was in charge of the control unit, which is the part of the prison reserved for troublemakers, people who are incorrigible, where they monitor their every movement. I then got in touch with the warden, who said that due to a "change of conditions" I wouldn't be given permission to see Jack. The Federal Bureau of Prisons upheld his decision, and that's when I asked the lawyer to take the manuscript in. I knew something was going on, but I didn't know specifically about the strike or Jack's participation.

When the lawyer came out he said there were weird things going on, and he'd heard rumors that Jack was in trouble. He was vague. I didn't press him because he obviously didn't want to talk about it and he'd done me a favor by taking in the manuscript.

I never accepted the image of Jack as the stand-up guy, the existentialist who stood against the world saying "Fuck you." All through his letters there were hints of weakness and vulnerability, but, initially, when I went out to Marion I wasn't worried that there was something that could backfire. I was only thinking about the book. Plus I was worried about my own safety; they don't like blacks or Jews in Marion, and it was a weird place to be. I thought I'd just get Abbott's approval and come back and put the book into production. Also, when we'd first decided to publish the book I'd had no idea he would ever get out; the possibility of his release was so remote that it wasn't even a consideration.

JACK HENRY ABBOTT (IN THE BELLY OF THE BEAST)   *I do not want to be in prison so long that I come to gaze up at the sky and curse the stars for my misery. I do not want ever to come to the upside-down conclusion that "no one is to blame," as the saying goes. Or that this state of affairs always has been and always will be in our world. Or that I turned the key on myself. . . .*

How I wish this would end! How I wish I could walk free in the world, could find my life again and see and do things other people do.

I don't see how that would be possible now, though. Too much has happened, for too long, to me. But I want to try. It is my right . . . , at least, to walk free at some time in my life even if the odds are by now overwhelming that I may not be as other men.

ERROLL McDONALD   He was released June 5, 1981, Friday, and the next day, Saturday, he phoned me at eight-thirty A.M. from a coffee shop at Lexington and Ninetieth. I couldn't figure out why he was up there at that hour of the morning since I knew his halfway house was downtown. I went to the coffee shop right away, not because I had any thought of having to mother him now that he was in New York but because I wanted to find out what was going on, what he and I could expect from each other. Then I went with him to Macy's. I didn't want to take him to discount places on Fourteenth Street, so Macy's was halfway style, halfway economy. He'd obviously thought about clothes; he knew exactly what he didn't want—no hiphuggers, no bell-bottom pants.

JACK HENRY ABBOTT   Norman had met me at the airport at about one A.M., and we went to his place. Because his wife and kids were asleep, we went out on the terrace and talked for about an hour, then I took a cab to the halfway house. When I got there everything was closed down. I couldn't sleep, so I sat up until daylight looking out the window. There was like a real fine dust of soot everywhere. All I could smell was garbage. Out on the sidewalks old winos were stumbling around, people who looked like they were hallucinating, people just lying in the gutter. I wondered, What the hell is this? Then I went downstairs to get a cup of coffee, and as soon as I got outside all these people started running up to me begging for money. There wasn't much traffic at that hour and newspapers were blowing across the streets. . . . All the people looked like they were in a state of death. Dead but upright.

I knew that this was the lower East Side, that's all. People say my release gave me a chance for a new life, what Dante calls "the *vita nuova*," and they ask why I fucked up. Well, the answer is I didn't get delivered to Paradiso. They delivered me right back to prison. I didn't start walking around with a knife until after I saw what was going on around me. Like one night I came out of a deli on the corner of Fourth Street and Second Avenue and saw somebody get stabbed. Then I also learned that there was a men's shelter across the street with thousands of crazy patients turned loose, and there was also the Slasher, who was arrested about half a block from the halfway house. Another time I was standing on the corner of First Avenue and a car got firebombed—they put gasoline on it, *kaboom*! So after that either I went out with someone else or I never went anywhere alone in that neighborhood without the knife—to the laundry and back, to the deli, whatever. I was stuck in that hell, the most violent and bombed-out area in New York City.

In fact, the first day I grabbed a cab and told the driver, "Get me out of here. It doesn't matter where, just keep driving and I'll tell you when to stop." He thought I wanted to get away from the blacks, so he took me uptown to the Yorkville district, the Eighties on the East Side. He said there's nothing but whites up there. The guy tried to help me, and he took me to a café, a little dump, and I ordered some eggs and phoned Erroll McDonald. I hadn't wanted to call him originally, but now I did, about eight in the morning, and told him where I was and that I'd probably need some help. I went back and sat down at the counter; soon the phone on the wall was ringing and ringing. The owner, a big Pole, answers it, and I hear him scream, "It's for you." I'm looking around at the other people in the café, waiting to see who's going to come and get the phone. He keeps screaming, "It's for *you*." So I take the receiver, but McDonald's already hung up. I sat back down, and the Pole's glaring at me—I don't know why, I guess he didn't like me, but he acted real crazy and wouldn't serve me. So I waited. I was going to stand outside, but then Erroll came in. We talked and then he showed me Central Park.

We also went shopping for clothes at Macy's—a pair of shoes, a shirt, a pair of pants. Erroll said I could have the pants altered. I know Erroll's been quoted saying I blew up and demanded a pair of scissors, but that isn't true. What happened was we were at the desk, and the salesman told him it would take three days for alterations, and Erroll said something like "Well, the guy can't buy them then, because he needs them immediately." I only had a suit, I didn't have any other pants, so I told Erroll I'd just cut off the bottom of the pants so I'd have something to wear. Erroll asked the guy if he had a pair of scissors, then went over to another salesman and asked him. This second guy looked kind of surprised and probably thought we were crazy. Then he said he couldn't do it because it would look like Macy's made their customers do their own alterations. I thought this was too much, and Erroll had two or three of them jammed into the corner, talking to them. I'm standing there embarrassed and disgusted but not angry. Finally a tailor came out and cut the pants for me.

Anyway, the halfway house and the neighborhood were getting to me right off the bat, and I was conscious of the possibility that somebody would jump me, that there would be a little bit of blood somewhere and I'd probably be sent back to prison. I told Erroll that it was bad down there and that I was packing a knife. I also told Bob Silvers. I went to see my parole man and told him too, "Look, you've got to get me out of this halfway house." But he said that it would take at least three weeks of paperwork to get me transferred and by then my time would be up anyway. So I had to just sit it out.

BARBARA NORRIS CHURCH MAILER   I first became aware of Jack when he started writing to Norman, but there are so many who write to Norman that to me he was just another guy. I hadn't had anything to do with cons before, but I didn't feel threatened because he was still in prison and I didn't think he was going to be getting out. Still, I hadn't wanted any part of it. My attitude to Norman's involvement all along had been, "You wrote the book about Gilmore—didn't you learn anything? It's not gonna work, these guys don't change." Norman is the eternal optimist and said, "It'll be fine, this guy's different, blah blah blah," and later he didn't tell me that Jack was actually getting out. He told me only when Judith let it slip, and then I didn't realize he was going out to the airport to pick him up until he was walking out the door: "I guess I'd better tell you now—I'm going to pick up Jack."

That night I was already in bed when the two of them came back to the apartment, so I didn't meet him until the next night when he came to dinner. I'd said to Norman, "I don't want this man in the house, I don't want him around our kids." Norman said, "Please have him for dinner once, and then you'll never have to see him again." So I agreed. And when I met him I was totally taken with him. He was very sweet, very touching, because he was nervous and almost like a little boy. Norman, I think, had decided to give us time alone and was still working when the bell rang. I answered it, and there was Jack in a three-piece navy pinstripe suit, a white shirt, little round glasses, his hair neatly combed back. It's June or something, and he'd bought a winter suit just like Norman's, paid four hundred dollars for it in Utah.

The ice was broken by John Buffalo, who immediately went over to Jack, took his hand, and said, "Let me show you my room." Buffalo was about three, and I think Jack thought he was this funny little creature—he didn't know what to do exactly, so he was just following him around, kind of grinning. After that he was madly in love with him.

At dinner Jack didn't do much talking. He was nervous because he thought he was supposed to be back at the halfway house at eight. He didn't want to call himself so he had Norman call, and it turned out he wasn't supposed to be back until ten. But he was still nervous he'd be late. He didn't say much about the lower East Side, but a week later his suit was stolen, which was very, very traumatic for him.

I can't pretend I knew the old Jack at all, but one of the reasons I was full of trepidation was his crazy business with Judith. He'd turned on her and accused her of losing some of his letters. I'd thought he was really flippy about it, but then when his suit was stolen I saw this same Jekyll-Hyde thing. He said he was gonna go to all the pawnshops, track down the guy who'd stolen it, and kill him. Then a few days later he called up in an absolute rage because his new shoes had disappeared.

Actually, he didn't call up in a rage, he called to tell me about being in a rage. He'd come back to his room, and his shoes weren't there, so he'd slammed his hand into the wall and broken one of his fingers. Then he'd gone out in the street and just walked and walked to walk off his rage. When he came back he remembered he'd taken his shoes to his counselor to keep them safe. He started laughing about it, and that's when he called me. I think he was conscious of his anger and trying to cope with it.

At that point I was having a lot of conversations with him on the phone because he liked me, but also he was having these logistical problems like "Where do I go to buy toothpaste?" "Where do I get my clothes cleaned?"—stuff like that which he didn't feel free to talk to Norman about. He was very timid about it and not sure he was doing things the right way, like ordering in a restaurant. We went out once, and he looked at the menu and it was as if it was almost too much to grasp the variety of things, the money and everything, so he just said, "I'll have what you have." That was easier than dealing with it. So his neediness very quickly became clear to me. He was saying, "Help me, I'm lost." And because he was a little in awe of Norman, and since I was more accessible, the softer presence, he'd come to me for advice.

He also told me wild stories about stuff he'd done or seen in prison, and I had the feeling he was boasting—very Gary Gilmoresque stories, like in the prison movie theater when someone stabbed the guy next to him, leaving him sitting next to a corpse. But I never turned to him and said, "I don't believe you," because I just didn't feel like getting into an argument. If I heard even a note of criticism directed at me, though, I'd answer him, and he'd back off immediately. But basically, I have to admit, Jack won me over. I'm not easily touched, not normally soft about people who've had hard breaks, but Jack has the ability to touch you. He's very intelligent, but there's still that little boy inside him who was sent away to reform school years ago.

JEAN STEIN   There were people who criticized Norman because of Abbott, but poor man, he'd only tried to help. He told me off the record that he didn't know until later that Abbott had given names at Marion to get released. But Norman is so honorable that he has never in any way acknowledged that publicly.

DOTSON RADER   I first met Gilmore—I mean Abbott, I can't keep them straight—at a dinner at Norman's.

I love to go there when it's just Norman and Norris, the children, the grandmother, because I'm rarely in a family situation and it feels like I've come home, and Norman's as different as night from day in those situations. So when Norris asks me over, I normally ask—which is rude, I know—"Who's going to be there, is it going to be just family?" In this instance she said, "Just the family and a couple of friends of Norman's." Then she asked if I could bring Pat Lawford, so Pat and I went together, and when we walked into the apartment, there was this individual—Jack Abbott.

I had never heard of Abbott and didn't know he'd just gotten out of jail, so Pat and I didn't know what the hell was going on. The other guests were a Jewish fellow whom Norman calls his mentor and the mentor's daughter. I know Norman loves Malaquais, but he's an asshole; I found him pompous, pretentious, and out of touch, as well as a bit of a commissar.

The minute I walked in the room and saw Abbott, though, I had a sense of threat. He's lean, he never blinks, he stares. While Pat went over to talk to Norris, I shook his hand and said, "How are you? Are you from New York?" I didn't know what to say because I didn't know who he was. But he knew who I was as a writer, and he said, "Why did you become a pig?" I said, "I beg your pardon?" He said, "Why did you become a fucking pig? I read your books in prison, and now you're running around with the rich." I asked which books he'd read, and he said, I Ain't Marchin' Anymore and Blood Dues, repeating, "Why'd you become a pig?" I proceeded to tell him about some of the things I'd felt during my experiences with the antiwar movement, but he didn't smile, he didn't change his expression. He talked in an absolute, quiet monotone that reminded me of the tone morticians use. Then he told me he'd been in prison writing a book, and he showed me a copy of In the Belly of the Beast.

Dinner was a disaster. It's the only time I've ever seen Norman lose control of his own dinner party. He made the fatal mistake of seating Pat next to Abbott, at which point Abbott proceeded to attack the United States as a fascist country, and then Malaquais joined in. Pat demanded to know if either of them was registered to vote, and both said they wouldn't besmirch their political integrity. Norman had his head sort of down but was eyeing me once in a while, as if giving me a cue to calm Pat down. But Abbott continued his attack. It wasn't a Marxist-Leninist line, it was essentially Trotskyist, and Pat went into an absolute rage—I've never seen her angrier. She was loud, pointing her finger, talking about her brothers, and she just exploded: "One of my brothers was President of this country, my brothers gave their lives for this country, so how dare you criticize when you don't even take the goddamn time to vote!"

Norman tried to calm her and everybody else by changing the subject. But nobody wanted to change the subject. Everybody was in a rage, including me. But Abbott sat there cool and calm. Finally Pat said, "Well, if you don't like it here, why don't you move somewhere else?" Abbott said, "I want to." She asked where, and he said, "Cuba." "Good," she said, "I'll pay for your ticket," and she literally grabbed for her purse. Abbott didn't blink, but at that Norman got up from the table and started collecting the plates, something I've rarely seen him do.

Pat is glaring at me, giving me these looks—"It's time to leave." But we then sat through about twenty-five minutes of talk from Malaquais, who had just been in Poland and was going on about how Solidarity was a crypto-fascist movement set up by the CIA to bring the Soviet Union into Poland so that Poland wouldn't default on its forty-billion-dollar loans from American banks. He also started calling the Catholic Church a CIA front. All the while Abbott was staring at me with his cobra eyes. He wasn't looking at anyone else, just me, and I thought, I'm just the kind of guy he wants to kill.

Pat and I finally walked out, and we were both in such an absolute rage that when we got in the car to go back to Manhattan we just looked at each other in amazement. We both love Norman, and we couldn't understand how he could get caught up with these people. Then I said to Pat—and this is the absolute truth—"I don't know what the hell he was in jail for, but I'll bet you a thousand dollars he'll kill somebody within six weeks. I've seen killers twice before in my life, and he's the third.

JEAN MALAQUAIS If there was any moment when voices were raised, it was between Pat Kennedy Lawford and myself. I pay no attention to names; I have no memory for them. So I was introduced to her but didn't retain her name. At a given moment during dinner she asked, "Whom do you vote for?" Maybe the question didn't come out of the blue, maybe we spoke about Reagan, and I said, "I don't vote for anyone, neither a Democratic nor a Republican fraud." At some point, because she'd raised her voice, I said, to cut it short, "Now, look here, lady..." I am afraid it made Norris squirm and Norman swallow hard.

I know nothing about the check Pat Lawford supposedly offered Jack for passage to Cuba. Jack didn't say a word to her in my presence. He's very subdued, and that was, I think, his first social dinner at the Mailers'.

I believe Pat Lawford may have thought I was a Commie. I'd been in Poland in March, and she had questions. But when I briefly analyzed the Solidarity movement and the attitude of the Polish workers, I guess she was somehow reconciled to the idea that I wasn't a full-blooded Red bastard. She must have left before we did because I took Jack down to the halfway house about one in the morning.

BARBARA NORRIS CHURCH MAILER Nothing happened. The problem was between Jean and Dominique and Pat. Jean was going on about Solidarity and talking about America as a repressive country, and of course Pat was bristling at this. Dominique is a little version of Jean who doesn't believe in voting or any of the things Pat vehemently believes in, and she was jumping in and backing Jean, which drove Pat crazy, because here's this kid mouthing all these platitudes and she's—what, fifteen? Jean was showing off, perhaps for Jack, probably for everyone. He was going on in excruciating detail about Poland, and all for a trapped audience. In fact, Norman said a few times, "Would you get on with the story?" Pat was getting angrier and angrier, and Norman was trying to calm things with humor, but that didn't work. Jean was really on center stage that night. It was a wonderful arena for him—Jack on one side, Pat on the other.

EMMA CLARA "ECEY" GWALTNEY During my visit in early summer of 1981 Norman had wanted to have a dinner party for Jack, but Barbara objected. She didn't think it was such a good idea, so Norman said, "Okay, we'll just have him come here to dinner then." I didn't care either way. I was in an emotional shambles after Fig's death and I just wanted to keep busy and forget everything.

So it was just Norman and Barbara, Dandy, Matthew and Buffy, and I, with Jack, who seemed totally different from the man I later saw on *60 Minutes*. I found him rather charming in a way but really shy and quiet, with a nice dry, timid handshake. We sat next to each other, and I thought, Well, what to talk about? So finally I just busted in and asked if he could watch television in prison. "Who picks the shows?" "Are you censored in any way?" "Do you see any movies?" He said he got to see movies, and I asked which ones he liked, and he said, *Bang the Drum Slowly.*

That sort of stopped me, and I said, "That's one of my favorite movies too"—which it is—and I asked him, "What did you like? Which character?" He said, "I liked the guy who was so caring with the DeNiro character." DeNiro plays a kind of goofy ballplayer, not very good, who's dying, and the other fellow is the star of the team, and even though he hates to get involved, he can't help it, he's compelled to befriend him. So I had the feeling that Jack was identifying with the DeNiro character. I don't know whether he'd remember me, but I said, "Listen, what are your plans?" He said, "Well, I don't know."

JACK HENRY ABBOTT Another inmate, a middle-aged white guy who was in protective custody because the inmates called him a rat, sent a letter to *The New York Review of Books*, and Bob Silvers gave it to Norman just after my release. The letter accused me of being a snitch at Marion.

I was over at Mailer's one day, and he said, "Let's go downstairs." We went down to the office, and he hands me the letter and says, "You're a snitch." I says, "So what? It's what I told you." I'd given statements against some attorneys, but the letter said I'd snitched on strikers, given names, and I'm saying, "That's not it. Fuck, no. That's completely out of context."

I'd told Mailer about the strike in my letters. And when I was on the hunger strike, they used to tell him I was on a fast. He'd have Judith call up to check on me, and they'd say that nothing was wrong, yet I almost died after sixty days. I wrote him about it, also Bob Silvers. But I'd talked to Mailer on the phone from Marion when I was fighting with the guards and being beaten and all during the strike. Random House sent me the contract right after I'd been beaten. That's when the stink started, when it started getting thick. There were five of us beaten as leaders. We were all white. They didn't beat blacks, Indians, or Mexicans, and it had to do with my book. They weren't going to let me walk away from that. I'd had to cooperate, there was no way around it. Things had come to a head, and the administration knew exactly what they were doing.

ERROLL McDONALD   I found out about it in June, and I think Peter Matthiessen knew some of the American Indians at Marion whom Jack had implicated. I don't know what Matthiessen's role was, but I know Jack talked to him a couple of times by phone. Anyway, toward the end of June, not Silvers but Abbott told me about the letter from the guy at Marion, and he also told me that Norman had confronted him with it.

JACK HENRY ABBOTT   In July I took the bus to Provincetown, the last stop, and Norman picked me up at the station. It was the first time I'd been out in the open because I'd gone straight from prison to Manhattan, and Norman took me for a walk across the dunes. I'd never seen sand dunes like that anywhere.

BARBARA NORRIS CHURCH MAILER   Although he liked Provincetown much better than New York, Jack wasn't that different when he came to visit us and stayed two days. We had one lovely afternoon together when the two of us went into town, had lunch, and climbed the Pilgrim Monument.

Then there was a dinner with Peter and Ellen at the Flagship. Danielle was with us, and what we talked about was Jack's going to MacDowell after he was allowed to leave New York, or to the Provincetown Fine Arts Work Center. Norman and I were going to Maine in August, and if it could be worked out we planned to find a little place for him to stay, a cabin or something. He wanted to go to the woods by himself, he so hated the city, and in fact when it came time for him to take the bus back to New York, he didn't want to go. I think he would truly have been happy as a hermit.

We had several talks about it, especially the day the two of us went out together. He said how much he hated New York and how he couldn't control himself and was "gonna blow." I thought what he meant was that he was going to break parole and just take off, and I kept saying, "Don't do it, you only have"— whatever it was—"a month left, and then you'll go to Maine."

During our last weeks in New York and then up on the Cape I realized he was getting increasingly short-fused, and after he went back to the city I was on the phone with him practically every day. He'd call and say, "I'm gonna blow, I can't stand this," and go over all the things that had been happening to him, all the imagined insults, like when he bought cigarettes and the guy at the counter gave him a dirty look and slammed the money down. I tried to reason with him, but he'd say, "It's no good. People are like that in New York," and at one point I almost called his counselor because he was so crazed and agitated. But I thought he meant he was just going to get on a bus and leave. If I'd realized he was going to kill somebody... Well, Norman and I discussed it and didn't feel the situation was that bad. We kept saying to him, "You only have a month left, then we'll go to Maine."

But it wasn't just the lower East Side, it was the city. Random House offered him a room to work in, and he also took the ferry to Staten Island, where he'd gotten a dog through a friend from prison who had since gone straight and raised Dobermans or something. He would go out there to play with the dog. He had the puppy spayed, her ears and tail clipped, and he was talking about finding an apartment out there because he thought Staten Island was calmer than Manhattan. I remember he kept calling it "country."

JACK HENRY ABBOTT   I was back in the city, and I'd been with two girls at the Great Jones for about four or five hours, drinking and talking and listening to music. Then we decided to go to a club, a disco, so I went over to the halfway house and told the guy at the desk I was going to be out all night and said if he'd cover me I'd pay him. Then, later, about three A.M., the girls wanted to get something to eat. I should have known better, but we went to the Bini-Bon café. We start to order, and Adan, the guy who gave us menus, puts his hand on my shoulder and says, "I don't take orders. That's the guy who takes orders"— pointing to another waiter.

After a while we're eating and I see Adan looking at me and he says, "What are you looking at?" I turn away from him, trying to ignore him. But then I hear him again: "What are you looking at?" He starts to step over, so I get up and walk over to him and ask, "Have I done something to you?" "No, no," he says. "Then what did you say that for?" I ask. "Say what?" he says, adding, "What's wrong with you?" "Nothing's wrong with me," I reply. "What's wrong with you?" Soon I got tired of it, and I turned and walked back to my table. I'm thinking, Well, it's nothing. If I'd been alone I'd have walked out the first time he said anything.

But as I'm walking back to my table Adan's talking loud, and people in the room are watching. So I turn back around to him. You see, I keep thinking that he's going to come over to the table and upset us. So I say, "Look, if you really got a problem, let's talk about it someplace besides the middle of the floor." Adan says, "Do you want to go outside?" That's when I looked at him and started thinking, *He's really coming on. He's really too aggressive.* Meanwhile another waiter walks by, and I figure he knows Adan and can talk to him, calm him down, so I say, "Look, we've got a problem here." I'm thinking that if I talk to him nice, then he'll see I'm not acting aggressive, that I don't want any trouble, and he'll cool Adan off. I say, "Is there anywhere we can go to discuss this? What about a cloakroom?"

"We just throw our things on the floor in a corner when we come to work," he says. I see a door to the kitchen, so I ask, "What about in there?" He then says, "Customers aren't allowed to use the rest room."

All this time Adan was standing there, mimicking and taunting me, and then he says something about how the customers aren't sanitary. I said, "Look, I don't want to use the rest room. That isn't the point," but Adan turned around and reached behind the counter, like to put something in his pocket, and then turned around and hit me in the chest. He jarred me, and I took a step back and told him, "Okay, then, let's go outside." I didn't think he'd do anything. He was acting like he's got a knife in his pocket, and I was taking it that he's bluffing. I've seen a lot of people do that, so I'm not paying much attention to it.

I get out the door but pause to say something to him, and he says, "Go over there," pointing towards the street corner. Now, I'm trying to talk to this guy, and I turn back to say something to him, but before I can turn all the way around he says, "Around the corner." He's walking right behind me, and I'm thinking, Well, he's playing a game like I see kids playing all over New York. They talk like they're in the movies. They talk real loud and say that they're going to hurt somebody. He was like acting, trying to scare me. He was putting it on.

When we stopped walking, that's when I started getting worried. It was dark and there were broken bottles and garbage all over the place. When I turned around I could see he was about ten feet away from me. I'm thinking he's going to dive into me, take a shot at me with that knife and just jump back out. I hollered at him not to come any closer, and I pulled out my knife. I held it up so he could see it. I'm thinking that this guy is fucking nuts, and I'm just trying to get out of there. But I'm also going to defend myself if it comes to that. So I shout at him again, "Now stay where you are," and I'd just started to say "Don't come any closer" when he came right at me. There's no question in my mind that he came at me. No question whatsoever. He charged me. He dove at me.

I was still yelling at him when he stopped dead on the end of that knife, when he said, "You didn't have to kill me . . ."

DETECTIVE WILLIAM MAJESKI   I was on the scene right after the stabbing, about twelve minutes later. I've seen a lot of bodies, but this was different. Although Adan was twenty-two, he looked younger, and his face, the expression, was angelic. Also there was a tremendous amount of blood. The knife had gone to the heart, and apparently just about every drop of blood in his body had been pumped out. There was literally a pool going from the body across the sidewalk to the curb and out into the gutter.

Later that Sunday we visited Malaquais and talked to him for about fifteen or twenty minutes. He didn't tell us to get a warrant; he was very receptive, in fact, although he didn't want to accept the reality of what had happened because

Jack had been with him earlier that morning. He was upset, almost to the point of collapsing. His wife too—I could see it in her eyes. He invited us to search the house, which I thought was unnecessary. After we left I phoned Mailer in Provincetown.

BARBARA NORRIS CHURCH MAILER   Norman and I were in shock. It was low tide, and we walked out on the flats, talking. Neither of us thought Jack would show up in Provincetown—that was too obvious. We were wondering where he was but figured he'd probably get caught right away in the city.

We were both in shock. Before I'd met Jack I'd had the feeling that this was Gary Gilmore all over again, but after I'd met him I changed my mind, thinking, Well, maybe he'll be the one to make it. But both of us knew that we weren't responsible for getting him out. I don't remember which month—I wasn't involved then—but I know Norman had been surprised that they were releasing him when they did. Neither of us knew why he was getting out that early. Norman had simply written a letter for him, so it was ludicrous that people kept saying to us, "Didn't you learn anything from his psychiatric records?" We weren't privy to his psychiatric records. Nor did we know that Jack had talked at Marion until later. He insists he'd told Norman about it, but the way we found out was that letter a con wrote, and before we'd come up to P-Town Norman had

Jack Abbott (center), Det. William Majesky (holding Abbott's arm), with attorney Ivan Fisher bringing up the rear; Federal Courthouse, New York, 1981.

confronted him with it—"I want you to be aware of the story that's going around. Is there any truth to it?" And of course Jack denied everything.

<u>LAWRENCE SCHILLER</u> I remember I spoke to Jerzy Kosinski at one point and he explained to me all the people who had been involved, including himself, saying, "They're going to come after me because I'm the public figure." Maybe a day or two later I said to Norman, "They're going to come after *you* because *you're* the public figure, so you'd better decide whether you want this. Because if you don't, there are ways around it." He said, "No, I have to stand up for what I believe." I said, "There's a way of standing up but not standing up in public. You don't have to be abused."

I wasn't saying he should disappear. I was saying that you can handle it with certain press statements at proper times, taking a certain attitude, watching your words very carefully. You can go and be a witness for Abbott, but you don't have to hang out at the trial. You can stand beside him, go visit him, and make a public statement as to your feelings. You can discuss the act of murder as horrendous but still express a deep understanding of what Abbott's gone through. In effect, I was saying, "There are ways of walking the tightrope." But Norman doesn't believe in walking the tightrope. He believes in being on one side or the other.

<u>DETECTIVE WILLIAM MAJESKI</u> When I'd talked with Norman on the phone he'd said he was coming in to New York, so on Tuesday night we had dinner at an Italian restaurant on Forty-fifth Street. A U.S. marshal was with me, and the two of us had worked out our ground rules very early, although after the first three weeks things deteriorated because he started to comply with the wishes of his superiors instead of mine.

Anyway, this was the first time I'd met Mailer, and as we talked he seemed uptight. There were bodily manifestations, moving of utensils, moving of plates. Perhaps a slightly higher pitch in his voice, more rapid verbalization. Also he was lapsing from one accent to another; I remember there were two specific accents that came into play, and I thought it kind of peculiar. But I had been forewarned by people I'd contacted earlier, initially attorneys, then people in the literary world, plus one of the detectives involved when he had stabbed his wife. What I wanted was a better feel for what his position might be, whether he might be harboring Abbott, whether he would he helpful to the investigation or would try to mislead us.

I probably alluded to the fact that Abbott would be captured with or without his help, but I asked that he give serious consideration to contacting me if and when Jack ever got in touch with him. For his part, I think he was looking down the line on this thing—down the line, around the bend, back a few miles. He was exploring and re-exploring, re-evaluating, probably on a daily basis. He could have said, "I don't want to cooperate with you," which I wouldn't have accepted, although in some small measure I would have understood. I still would have pursued him, and I could have held a gun to his head. In fact, at one point I was ordered by a sergeant to work up a conspiracy case to arrest Mailer, which almost led to a fistfight; it was nonsense, but those were the kinds of things I had to deal with on my side of the investigation.

After that first meeting—which wasn't that long, perhaps an hour and fifteen minutes—I walked away feeling confident that Mailer wasn't harboring Abbott and that at least he was considering cooperating. He was, I realized, caught in a dilemma—whether to side with Jack, whom he had personal commitments to, or to side with us. Most people in this situation don't choose, they simply drop out of the picture entirely. What Mailer was trying to do was follow a very delicate path, maintaining a commitment to Jack yet maintaining his responsibility to society.

I wouldn't say he was naïve—that isn't the appropriate term. But I think what Norman failed to do was make a separation between the man's literary ability and his personality, his capabilities outside the literary realm. Abbott's whole personality is based on the premise of prison society, and in his mind he was justified in killing Adan because any time you're posed with a threat or an imagined threat in prison you eliminate it—you eliminate it, because if you only wound or maim a guy he'll come back and kill you. That's Abbott's whole inner structure, his moral standard. It's been established over twenty-five years in prison and you can't take a lifetime of that and suddenly adjust it to society.

Throughout this time I was talking to Norman, and within several weeks I was confirmed in my feeling that he was walking a narrow line. There was no way for me to be assured of what he'd do if push came to shove, and I don't think he knew either. I'd met Norris, and clearly there was a difference in point of view. My evaluation of her was that she was very uncomfortable with the situation but also strongly loyal to Norman. Her loyalty and respect for him were probably what gave her the strength to put up with all of it. I think she felt that Jack should be put away forever, whereas Norman, although he didn't want Jack back out on the streets, still thought he should have a defense.

JILL KREMENTZ   When Jack came to New York I had an assignment from *People* magazine, and I called Norman and said, "I'm not going to show up at ABC-TV at seven-thirty in the morning and have you get mad. Do you mind if I do it? Either you agree or I let them send somebody else to stand outside the building and get you walking out." He was anxious for Jack to have the story in *People*, so he agreed but with the condition that "the piece not focus on me." I said I didn't have any control, but I'd been told it was a story on Abbott, and I felt certain that the most they'd use was one picture of the two of them together—which was exactly what they did, the one with Norman and Jack doing research at the Forty-second Street Library.

Then, of course, when the whole Adan thing happened, people became interested once again, and I sold a great many copies of that picture. Mailer, much to his credit, never got angry or tried to suppress them or said I was violating our friendship.

KURT VONNEGUT Abbott came to our house because of Jill's assignment, and the day he came over she took the most damaging photograph of me, stripped to the waist, in short pants, with Abbott in a suit. I'd been working upstairs—it was a hot day—and she said, "Come on down, I've got somebody I want you to meet."

I only saw him that one time, but she saw him a lot. In fact, her photographs were used on the "Wanted" posters, and then, when he was in the clink, he said she was the only person who could photograph him. She also became friends with Ivan Fisher, Jack's lawyer, and Detective Sergeant Majeski. Majeski's very nice; he stops by here just for a cup of coffee and talks. Fisher's a Groucho Marx-style defense attorney, except he's very bright, and we've had dinner with him. Jill was sort of a double agent. They both liked her. She knew what the defense was but wouldn't tell Majeski, and at one point she had a pretty good idea who the prosecution witnesses were but wouldn't tell Fisher. All of this, of course, was after Jack had been caught in Louisiana and was awaiting trial here in New York, a period of three or four months.

LAWRENCE SCHILLER When we were just starting to make the film of *The Executioner's Song* in the fall of '81 I wanted Norman to come to Utah to listen to the actors so that he could adjust the dialogue. During the summer he'd been calling me with ideas for casting, and some of them were unbelievable—like Michael Caine to play Gilmore. Or he'd call and suggest Clint Eastwood, forgetting that he'd already called me five other times about Eastwood. The irony was that the day of the readings was the same day Jack Abbott was caught. I heard the news on the radio, and Norman said, "Thank God he wasn't killed."

DETECTIVE WILLIAM MAJESKI After Abbott had been brought back from New Orleans on September 23, I spoke to him in the federal courthouse and then in the city courthouse during his arraignment. Initially he was reluctant to have any kind of discussion with me. He had the option of not saying anything, but soon he started responding, and at one point he definitely felt comfortable with me—although later, during and after his trial, things changed because he came to realize just how much responsibility I had in bagging him. At the beginning, though, he wasn't sure. He knew of me as a detective but nothing more.

I think my police experience lends a lot of credence to my view of Jack—I've dealt with ten, fifteen murderers, done polygraph tests, tested two professional mob hit men, and also done a lot of organized crime and narcotics investigations. I had read Abbott's book a half dozen times, and that's one of the things I confronted him with. He asked me if I'd read it, and I said, "Yes, and although I think it's well written, I must tell you I think it's bullshit."

He looked very taken aback at this, and I pressed it: "Honestly, I mean you're talking to a professional. I'm telling you that you're full of shit on most of what you wrote." I was referring to his descriptions of his experiences—the cockroaches in his cell, the beatings he received—all of which I thought he vastly exaggerated. But then I got an interesting response from him. He just looked at me, smiled, and then said, "Let's talk about something else."

Later we had another exchange during one of those periods when Jack had decided to hate Norman. I was waiting for his attorney to show up, and he was saying he felt that Norman was the person giving the media all the information about him. He felt that Norman was capitalizing on him, even making a lot of money off him. To a degree I defended Norman, but not overly so, because I wanted more of a feel for where Jack was coming from. Then he started espousing his views about being in prison—"Why should Mailer get all the credit and fame out of this when I'm the one doing the time?" When I pointed out that it wasn't Norman who had stabbed Adan he didn't respond at all.

JACK HENRY ABBOTT I've never spent more time thinking about anything in my life than Adan. When I was a fugitive I was thinking that if I got caught, all I'd have to do is get a good lawyer and show exactly what happened, and even though I'd probably be sent back to prison, there wouldn't be any question that I did what I had to. Then I got back and started hearing all these strange things about him, which put into question what I had seen him do that night, and I couldn't believe it. I needed answers—like who he was, what his past was—the answers to the questions I was reading in the newspapers. But now I have to take great care in talking about Adan because he is dead. Because of this and because of my past and because the press was coming down so hard on me, nobody wants the responsibility of saying that perhaps Adan might have . . . uh . . . asked for it because he made a movement at me.

I can't answer to what *The New York Times* says. Those people are flat liars. They have middle-class lives and have never had to be questioned about anything, so it's easy for them to take positions. They don't like my book because I'm a Communist, and they don't have a right to be angry because Adan was killed. They don't got the right for a fucking thing, because they haven't paid their dues. Simple as that . . . They don't got the right to tell me all this shit when they've done all that they did to me. And the thing that is outrageous is that there's a stubborn refusal to understand what really happened: I serve nineteen years in prison, I get out and they throw me in the lower East Side, I get into a fight with a waiter and he gets killed, and now they try to cast this Adan into an angelic mold.

IVAN FISHER The Abbott case was never *pro bono*. The second day I met him we discussed fees, and $100,000 was the beginning figure; then I agreed to reduce it to $75,000, with a $25,000 retainer. Random House was pushing another lawyer, Jerry Lefcourt, who represented Abbie Hoffman. Meanwhile 1400 lawyers, famous names, managed to locate Abbott in the holding area; Bill Kunstler was one of them, and he offered to represent him for nothing.

Initially I'd seen Abbott half an hour after he got off the plane from New Orleans, and my reaction was positive. I wasn't expecting to see a maniac, and he certainly didn't look like one. He described the incident, the death of Adan, and I explained to him what was about to happen out in the courtroom: we'd say "Not guilty" and make no bail application. I recall saying it was a very good fact for us that there was only one wound, because most intentional slayings have more than one. Then I told him his book was a hit. He'd had no idea of this, and he was surprised. On the phone from Louisiana he'd been talking about some kind of political defense, and I begged him to keep his yap shut. Then he said he'd chosen me over Lefcourt because I was known as someone who would represent him personally, not some belief or cause or issue, which is the kind of thing Jerry seems to be associated with.

The day after the arraignment I called Meredith to ask about the financial situation. He said, "We've got $500 or $5000, but money is coming in." I asked if he was willing to advance Jack funds for my retainer. He said yes. I asked how $25,000 sounded, and he said, "Okay," and some papers were drawn up.

He advanced Abbott the money, charging him interest at a fair rate. Initially Meredith was easy to deal with, but later on it was difficult because Jack began to feel that Meredith was more interested in Meredith than in Abbott. Jack is very sensitive to people treating him like a child—understandably so because of how guards treat prisoners—and he certainly didn't want this from someone he thought was working for him. He was particularly upset when he heard Meredith was negotiating a movie deal without his approval. So was I. It was very, very poor from a public-relations standpoint, and Meredith hadn't simply leaked it, he'd almost held a press conference and grandly announced a deal with a Manhattan film company. Page Six of the *Post* called me for confirmation, and I said, "There's no such deal." The woman at the *Post* said, "If there was, how would you divide the money?" I repeated again and again, "There is no deal," but they went ahead and printed the goddamn thing as if they hadn't talked to me. So Abbott wrote off a note, firing Meredith. This was well before the trial, of course.

Within a few weeks I set up appointments to speak to people who knew Abbott because I wanted to get an assessment of him before the event to see whether I should interpose a psychiatric defense. I met with Silvers, McDonald, Russell Galen from Scott Meredith, and Malaquais, as well as Abbott's sister and brother-in-law, whom we'd flown in. I also met with Norman and Norris.

Norman's immediate concern was to help Abbott's defense, but I was very struck by Norris' hostility. She was horrified, and vehement that Jack should never again be released because he was an outrageously dangerous man. I said, "Hold it, hold it. He said the guy came at him with a knife. What are you talking about?" Later both of them told me that Norman had criticized her privately for the way she'd acted. He was fine but slightly ill at ease, although my impression is that he's never at ease. But he was also patriarchal—protective of Jack, protective of Random House, protective of Silvers.

Still, his basic position was that he wasn't prepared to have Jack back out on the street. He raised that issue immediately and wanted to know what my defense intentions were. I was imbued with positive feelings after having spent a week or two with Jack, sincere feelings, so I said that despite the anti-Abbott media wave, I hoped to get him a fair trial and establish the truth of his claim that Adan had a knife, that he'd seen something sharp and pointy coming at him. I told them I hoped to get him out. Norris was crazed—"Ahhh!"

"Won't he have to do the parole time?" they asked, and I told them no, we'd already worked out a scheme to beat that.

"What about the escape?" they asked, looking for something to keep Jack in, and I was getting angry. These are supposed to be his friends, and they're looking for something to keep him in prison? I wanted him out, and I said, "It's my intention that within six months Jack Abbott should be back at your house."

Norris says, "Not in mine he isn't."

BARBARA NORRIS CHURCH MAILER   Ivan was going on about "We're gonna do this, we're gonna do that, get the back sentence taken out, the back years he still owes for breaking parole. We'll get rid of that, and we'll have Jack back out on the street."

I just sat there listening, and then practically the first thing out of my mouth was, "I can't believe you're this stupid and naïve that you want to get this man back out on the street."

Ivan's eyes bugged out. He was aware that I'd been friends with Jack, and he was bowled over, and I went on: "I like Jack, he's been a friend, but he's crazy and he'll do it again. He doesn't need to be back on the street, and I think you'd be nuts to try to put him there."

Norman was a little embarrassed that I was being so strong about it, and he was trying to shut me up, but I'm not shutting up. His position was sort of middle of the road: he wanted Jack to have the best defense, but he also wanted Jack in jail, but not forever. I was saying, "Forever!"

JACK HENRY ABBOTT   Before the trial, when I was in the Queens House of Detention, I called Norman and said, "Let me tell you what happened," because all the time I'd been fleeing I was thinking about it. I figured Adan was just some smart asshole, and I was mad that the press was saying he was an actor and all, and I couldn't believe it, because he didn't strike me as anything but a tough guy. But the press was already citing my book and everything. So I told Norman, "It couldn't have been intent to kill, because I meant to nick him in the arm, and when I stood back I still thought I'd hit him in the shoulder, not the heart, until he brought his hands up." Norman said, "You try to convince a jury of that. If you were using cocaine..." I said, "I'm not trying to convince a jury, I'm trying to convince you."

Still, I couldn't find reasons for Adan attacking me. I had arguments with Fisher about it and fired him twice. The investigators said Adan didn't have any record of prior violence, but it wasn't until during the trial that I discovered that he was taking me around the corner to piss. Then I had to reevaluate all my recollections. For about two days before I went on the witness stand I was in a daze. Up until then I wouldn't let Ivan use it, but then I said, "Okay, add 'extreme emotional disturbance'." I went over it and over it. . . . But I still think it has nothing to do with psychology. If anybody had invited me outside like that, I wouldn't have thought it was to use the rest room. The guy was taunting me. So when I called Norman again, I told him I felt it was fated. That's when he told me about stabbing his wife. He said that he'd felt that compulsion of fate when he'd stabbed a woman, even while he was doing it—that it was irreversible, the logic of events. For me with Adan, it was communication, his body language, the way he was standing, directing his voice, his tone, the words he was using.

Before that I had stopped talking to Norman because I didn't think he believed me. It didn't make sense to him that a waiter would take a stranger outside and try to kill him. Then I called him and said, "Now I know why he took me outside. That's where customers use the toilet. When he was standing in the corner looking up and down, he wasn't looking out for witnesses, he was looking out for my privacy."

Norman came to the trial the next day.

Norris thinks I'm crazy, a little unhinged—but not in a bad way. She's real easy for me to talk to, I find. She's more open than Norman. But there's a lot of things wrong with being open. You make hasty and incorrect judgments, things of that nature. She never came to see me when I was awaiting trial, but she once asked me on the phone if I was around other prisoners. I said yeah. She said, "You don't have any problems with them?" I said, "I'd better not." She said, "Just don't kill anybody, Jack." She said it real serious. "Don't kill nobody again."

IVAN FISHER   Norman didn't see Abbott for quite some time while he was awaiting trail. Abbott had very changing views—sometimes he said he didn't want to see Norman, sometimes he did. The two of them had had a phone conversation one night about Adan and about the incident at Marion where he supposedly snitched. Jack insisted that Norman had known about it well before his release. Norman disagreed and told him, "Look, I don't care what you say, you killed a decent guy. You keep talking about what a crazy he was, but I checked him out. That kid was sweet as hell. Admit you did a lousy thing, admit you're gonna have to pay for it. Reconcile yourself to what you did at Marion. Stop lying to yourself."

The upshot for Jack was that Norman became persona non grata. This didn't frustrate me, because Mailer, I thought, was a liability, as he added emphasis to the rage surrounding the case. Also I think, What the fuck good can he do for us? I search my soul, I can't find a goddamn good thing. So I can't use him, what difference will it make?

Then there was a rapprochement. Norman and Norris began speaking to Jack by telephone, and Norman and I had a meeting—I picked him up when he had to go someplace with a manuscript, and we talked in the limo. I told him I was considering a defense involving a form of diminished capacity, and he reiterated that he didn't want anything to do with a defense that would attempt to get Jack out scot-free. He said he'd help under certain conditions—if the defense addressed the issues that I was talking about. He also wanted to make the condition of his assistance that Norris not be involved. At some point—I think at that meeting—he got upset and said, "Wait a minute, I hear you're just out to spring him." Again that bothered me. Who is Norman or anybody else to decide what should happen to Jack? I'm thinking, Fuck you, I'll go subpoena you. Because what people kept losing sight of was that I was representing a man for murder. My case is looking impossible, the circumstantial evidence is lethal, and I can't establish self-defense without putting Abbott on the stand. Abbott believed—and he was right—that he couldn't get a jury who'd never heard of him or who could understand that having been in jail all his life had changed his reactions. Also, for me there was the thought that he'd be a bad witness, blow up on the stand and thus reveal the answer to the basic question, "Why would you kill him?"

Then, during the pretrial, Jack had a burst of recollection one night. He realized he'd been all wrong, that Norman hadn't been a rat, and he called him. Then Norman called me and said that he would like to see Jack and was ready to support him in court. I explained my pretrial strategy, that it was a bluff: we'd open strong and scare the prosecutor. I thought Fogel, the prosecutor, was bright but inexperienced. Also, his wife had just given birth to their first child, and I figured they were staying up nights. I'm good at voir dire, and I felt if we opened strong and suggested we were going to win, we'd hook our wagon to all the enormous fear of Abbott, make the prosecutor so afraid of letting him out that he'd take a plea for something like ten or fifteen years. I would have taken such a deal in a flash.

When Norman called I was in bed, working. It felt neat to hear him, he was so excited. He'll be horrified to hear this, but I actually made the final decision to put him on the stand maybe only an hour beforehand. I wasn't lying when I said I intended to put him on, but I hadn't made the final decision until that day. My other theory was that I'd be able to destroy the prosecutor's chief witness, Larsen, but I couldn't come close. Larsen destroyed me.

BARBARA NORRIS CHURCH MAILER   I think I told Fisher that I didn't want Norman involved in the trial, and later Norman and I discussed it. I was vehemently against his testifying. I thought the whole thing was a totally useless maneuver. Jack himself didn't call me. I never visited him, and he didn't get in touch with me until a long time after. The first time I saw him was the day Norman testified, the first time I went to the trial. He smiled and waved and that was it.

IVAN FISHER   At one point Jack wanted to fire me because he felt I'd been too nice to the girl he'd been with the night of the killing when I'd put her on the stand. So Jean Malaquais, who'd been operating as a mediator all along, came in and cooled him out. Malaquais was someone Jack could trust. From the beginning he had seen Jack as a victim, another Genet, the French existentialist hero whom Jack loves. That's why Jean and Norman have to get credit. Not because Norman testified but because Norman and Jean were there to hold Jack together. Jack's state of mind was terrible, with extreme swings of mood. He sent me a letter at one point, apologized and thanked me for tolerating him, then the next day he fired me again. The guards were on his case, saying, "Hey, hotshot writer, you're gonna fry for this one" or "You can write the longest book ever written after you're convicted." Also they wouldn't get him back to his cell until three A.M., then they'd wake him at six, never letting him shower.

DETECTIVE WILLIAM MAJESKI   I did a very thorough investigation because I knew that Fisher's people were looking for incriminating things about Adan, so I paralleled their investigation and found nothing damaging, nothing derogatory, not a damned thing. Adan never carried a weapon, never drank heavily, didn't use narcotics, not even marijuana. He was the type of person who always interceded when other people were having problems, and he certainly didn't belong in that neighborhood and he didn't belong in that job.

Nor was he homosexual. I checked into that because I thought that was a possibility. The urination story was also garbage. It was a theory hypothesized by a waiter who worked across the street, who initially sold it to the DA. My feeling is the reason that Adan went outside was to try to calm Abbott down.

ERROLL McDONALD   The district attorney, Fogel, phoned me to ask if Abbott was the author of everything in the book. I haven't heard who he was claiming actually wrote it.

DETECTIVE WILLIAM MAJESKI   There was a tremendous pressure built up in Norman the day he testified. From day to day he wasn't sure if Fisher was going to use him, and I can only guess at what was going through his mind, thinking that once he got on the stand he was going to be ripped apart. The DA asked my opinion of doing something like that, and I said it wouldn't accomplish anything for our case. After Fisher finished, Fogel asked me again if he should ask any questions, and I said no. When he said, "No questions," the expression on Norman's face was priceless, a combination of surprise and relief—but also a little disappointment, I think.

THOMAS HANRAHAN   What I found most repulsive about Abbott's trial was that it became so chic, with coverage by *The Village Voice, The Soho News, The East Village Eye*—what I label as trendy journalism.

My sympathies were with the kid, Adan. I'd talked to his father-in-law but not the wife, since I find it the most distasteful part of my job as a reporter to have to talk to people who are really shattered. So during the trial I felt I'd rather have been elsewhere, like covering a good old plain murder trial rather than this, which was such a circus because of Mailer's presence.

There were all sorts of other things. Like that little French Communist sitting there, Malaquais. I disliked him because I felt he was a no-good creep with nothing meritorious about his intellect or his personality. And to have him, with his ponderous, pretentious bullshit, sitting there as if he's mulling over the great existentialist problems of Jack Abbott—I just didn't like it, and if that makes me a reactionary, so be it.

I also found it disgusting that Susan Sarandon and Christopher Walken showed up. Several reporters asked them why they were there. Given Walken's resem-

Mailer, Jean Malaquais, and Abbott confer during a recess in the trial.

blance to Abbott and the fact that a story had appeared that Abbott had sold the movie rights to his book, it was natural to speculate that he was doing research. I went up to him in the courtroom, and he said, "I don't think it's appropriate to talk about it." Then, when we were waiting to come back in for the second session, I was first at the door, and he and Sarandon were pressed very closely next to me. Someone again asked her why she was there. She said, "I'm here for the same reason as everyone else." "What particular aspect of it?" the reporter asked again, and she said, "Oh, just generally." So I made a crack—"Could you be more general? You're starting to edge toward specifics. Be more general." Now, I don't believe in pushing people around if they obviously don't want to talk, but I made that crack because I really felt like saying, "You stupid bitch, you're not here for the same reasons as everyone else. You're not the average person. You're a public figure, you're a goddamned Hollywood movie star."

JEAN MALAQUAIS After Henry Howard was expelled from the courtroom for his outburst—yelling at Jack and Norman—he was out in the hallway. I had to make a phone call, and he came over and said something like "There is no anger left in me since my son-in-law was killed. But I saved a bone so you could carry it as a pendant." I guess he meant a bone of Adan's corpse. I suppose he'd seen me in the courtroom speaking to Jack, patting him on the shoulder, things like that. I'd tried to avoid the television and newspaper people, but of course they immediately surrounded us like paparazzi. I said to Howard, "What gives you the right to hustle me? Am I supposed to ask your permission to be with Jack?" After a while he said he'd like to have lunch with me to talk things over. Well, no, I wasn't game—not with a symbolic pendant around my neck. Then somebody, maybe an official, called me away, so I said, "I'll be back," and I left.

Later I found him again and said, "Don't think I was running away from you." "That's what I thought," he retorted. "I'm glad you came back, though." He shook hands with me, but the next day he raved on television about Mailer's having blood on his hands.

<hr />

THOMAS HANRAHAN   There were about thirty-five or forty reporters at Mailer's press conference. He agreed to talk to the press after he had testified, later that same afternoon.

Mike Pearl of the *New York Post* asked the question, "Mr. Mailer, you say 'Culture's worth a little risk.' Specifically, what elements of society are you willing to risk? Cubans? Waiters?" That was what triggered Mailer off, the beginning of the brawl. But there'd also been one prior question about Abbott being a candidate for psychotherapy, and Mailer said, "Abbott and I are almost cousins in that we both feel superior to psychiatry." Then came Pearl's implication that Mailer was a racist. And then I blew up, screaming that Mailer was full of shit.

I've worked the lobster shift, midnight to eight, at the *Daily News* for about a year. What you do is mainly look at stiffs—murders, plain and simple. I've also done stories in Northern Ireland, so I'm accustomed to violence, and I've spent night after night seeing people freshly killed and getting to know the detectives who do nothing but late-night murders. I'd also once lived very close to the Bini-Bon restaurant, and I'd get off work at three A.M. and have to walk home across Fourteenth Street while all sorts of shit was going on—like heroin sales and whores being beaten by their pimps.

I guess what first affected me about the Adan murder was that he was an aspiring artist and a newlywed, so at the press conference I became enraged with the way Mailer was handling it. I'd been aware of his reputation as a loudmouth, but I could also understand his relationship with Abbott, his interest in a person like that, so I didn't find that difficult to deal with. But what bothered me was his callousness. Instead of starting off by saying, "I'm really upset about the death of this kid," it seemed all I was hearing about was Jack Abbott and his problems. I wasn't hearing anything about the poor bastard who'd been cut up, and to me this was such a typical cheap street murder that there was nothing glorious or interesting about it. Then Mailer started saying that if you felt Abbott should have the book thrown at him—which is exactly how I felt, that he should've been convicted of murder in the second degree—you were a Nazi or neofascist, a reactionary law-and-order type.

It was a matter of style, really, and that night when I thought about it I realized he must've been loaded for bear, because he'd really set himself up. Like his comment "What did you do today to make yourself so self-righteous?" That was a jab. It was a combative situation, sure, but I was interested in hearing what Mailer had to say, since earlier he'd imposed a news blackout. I know some elements of the press have had it in for Mailer, but I didn't have anything against the guy. For example, I had a drink with one of my girlfriends after the press conference, and she was very anti-Mailer, as a feminist, but I hadn't had any of those preconceived notions.

So I walked out of the press conference shouting, "Mailer, you're full of shit." I'd sensed that he was really getting pissed, and I knew that I was pissed, and I didn't want to get involved in any physical confrontation. Also I looked at my colleagues in the press corps, whom I like to a great extent, and I saw their looks of incredulity—"What the fuck is going on here, where is this guy coming from?"—and that fueled my animus. I was reaching the point of getting very hot, so I decided it was time to split.

The next day Mailer and I actually had a short conversation. I'd seen him years before at the Golden Gloves, which I cover for the *News*, and also at fights with Hamill and Jose Torres. Also, I'm a friend of Al Gavin, who's the boxing coach at the Fourteenth Street gym, and Al had told me about "Stormin' Norman" down at his gym. So, despite my anger, when Mailer came over to me with his hand extended, I figured I'd just let it lie. He said, "You know, we got pretty hot yesterday, didn't we?" I agreed we had and said, "I was going to hit you, but I know you studied under Al Gavin." Then we had a five-minute, small-talk conversation about the Gloves and Vinnie Shomo, a famous, superb Harlem knock-out artist. It was one of those situations when small talk is a way of negotiating after you've had a beef with someone. Then the day after that he came up to me again and said, "You're Hanrahan, aren't you? I want to thank you for your writing." He thought my *Daily News* piece was fair, in contrast to the coverage in the *Post*.

LIZ SMITH   Norman is used to dealing with the press, just like Truman Capote and Gore Vidal. But of the three of them, Gore is by far the strongest in terms of saving himself, while Norman isn't afraid to put himself on the line. And that's what sets him apart. He isn't self-protective. He doesn't lie. He's honest— too honest maybe, because we live in a world of terrific bullshit. The popular thing was to attack Norman for Abbott, but it was far more complicated. On television he was asked by Gabe Pressman if he didn't have "blood on his hands." Norman's reply? "Yeah, people who say that are right. I do." He didn't miss a beat, and largely, I think, because he's what the French call a *naïf*. He's totally uncynical, not messed up the way I think a lot of people are, especially writers who want to be celebrities.

IVAN FISHER   Jack read through all the clippings and saw how much heat Norman was taking, and then I think he regretted how hard he'd come down on him. He'd get very angry at the press and say, "Shit! Damn! They know Mailer had nothing to do with getting me out." On the other hand, he didn't say he felt responsible for getting Norman into it.

For Norman and Norris it was a difficult time, and it seemed to be common knowledge that they were upset with each other. Norman said that Norris was extremely upset at the whole situation, especially the press conference, and he indicated it was a big problem. They were not talking to each other for a while, stuff like that.

<u>JOSE TORRES</u>   When I called, Norris answered, and I said, "I want to talk to Norman because I'm concerned about this shit that's going on. This guy Abbott killed was Hispanic, and the Hispanic people are saying Norman's crazy. They hate him."

That was the feedback I was getting, all negative. People coming up to me on the street, calling me on the phone—"Your friend is crazy," that sort of stuff, and there I was, defending Norman, and I told Norris that. Then a minute after we'd hung up, the phone rings and it's Norman. I said, "People are saying you approve of this killing. That's the way you're perceived—as a guy who approves the killing because Abbott's a special guy, a good writer, who shouldn't be wasted in jail. That's bullshit, Norman. The problem is, the way you look at the world and your explanations are so complex people don't understand. Realize that, will you? And reporters are no different, because they just write what people can understand."

<u>BARBARA NORRIS CHURCH MAILER</u>   Until all the publicity I hadn't realized people hated Norman as much as they do, which was a shocking thing to discover— the extent of it. That's why I didn't go to the trial until the day Norman testified, the same day he gave the press conference. I couldn't deal with it, and I was going through a very bad time. I'm usually a calm person, I don't get rattled, but during that period I guess I came close to having a breakdown because every day there was something new in the papers, some new lie. The press is like a blob of jelly; there's no way to fight it, and the more you protest, the worse it gets.

So that whole period was full of tension for both of us. Norman was on edge, going to the trial every day, facing the crowds, and it culminated in the press conference. The reporters kept on with their insane questions and then took what he was saying and totally twisted it. Like his statement "Culture is worth a little risk" or "I've never been a believer in an eye for an eye"—interpreting them to mean that Norman felt nothing should be done to Jack. Which was simply not true.

But when Norman erupted I was surprised. I'd never seen that in him before, and I more or less thought, My God, this is the Norman of twenty years ago. I'm still not sure what triggered it, but it was the closest I've ever come to being bowled over.

Afterward we took a taxicab home. I was in tears, and I was in tears for the next few days, especially the next day when the *Post* story came out. But being in tears didn't seem to do any good. At one point I thought of taking the kids to Arkansas, just to get them out of the city until things cooled off. But then I realized I couldn't leave because I didn't want Norman to have to face it by himself.

My parents, in fact, wanted to know if all of us wanted to come down to Arkansas. The case wasn't getting as much press down there, although it was in *Time* and *Newsweek*, so they were upset, although they'd also been through so much with us before. It was almost like every other month I was calling and saying something like "I'm calling to tell you before you read it in the papers."

There were also our friends, who stood by us. They'd call to offer support, and then most of them left us alone so as not to bother us. If there was any ostracism, it was subtle, and I don't remember any from any particular quarter, including the East Side. I don't think we were on any "Don't invite" list, although we didn't go out much. Some people might have had a "wait and see" attitude, but they didn't banish us, and at least to our faces they were saying, "We understand how horrible this is."

JACK HENRY ABBOTT The publicity about the trial was part of the right-wing elements out there, the Moral Majority wanting to get the liberals. They got them in the fifties, but not in the sixties and part of the seventies. Now they're attacking them again in the eighties.

But the liberals too were against me; it's like some of the staunchest Nazi ideologues were ex-Communists. For example, Robert Sam Anson's article in *Life* said that my relatives took me for a Mongolian idiot, that I had a Mongoloid expression on my face. Anson is a racist son of a bitch. The guy did a real number on me, and it's eating on me. I can see it was also a mistake to do the interview with *60 Minutes*. When the interviewer asked how I felt about the outcome of the trial, I told him, "I'm not guilty of manslaughter. It was an accident that I killed him." He kept saying, "But Adan's dead." I had to tell him, "Remorse doesn't have anything to do with guilt before a court of law for murder. I didn't murder that guy. The remorse—I feel sorry for having done it—is between me and Adan's family. But as far as the law goes, I'm not guilty of murdering Adan." He kept harping on that. Every time his arguments ran down he would make a general remark and say, "But he's dead." People are dying every day, intentionally being chopped up and all that other shit out there, and it happens. It's like they keep trying to play on my sensitivity, until they make me out to be callous about the whole thing.

Several times I'd told Norman that I didn't want him to speak to the press and that I hadn't wanted to put him on the stand. Also, in his introduction to my book he cited the passage in the book which describes one inmate killing another in a cell and identified it as something I'd done. I corrected it in the galleys because, I told him, he'd made it sound like I'd done it, which I hadn't. But it came off the presses that way. I talked to Erroll about it, and he says, "We could stop it." Then I talked to Norman and decided it was no big deal, then later at the trial they used that same passage to convict me.

I like Norman as a person, but he's of the bourgeois class, whereas I'm of the proletarian class and you can't put my story in a middle-class context. It's a different language, and Mailer can't understand it if he translates everything into the counterparts of his middle-class world. For example, the way he sees policemen is naïve. He isn't analytic, he thinks some are good old Joes, and he can see a guard as a regular guy when in fact he's a Gestapo agent.

Still, I feel real bad for Norman. Not only for Norman but also Silvers and McDonald and Epstein. But I feel more sorry for Mailer in this whole thing because the consequences on him are more important than those on a normal person—on him as a force. So for a real long time I didn't know what to do. I didn't know whether to chase him off by telling him a lot of crazy things— like James Cagney in *Public Enemy*, the movie where he's screaming, really breaking like a punk or something. Still, I didn't want him to break with me thinking that I was guilty of murder. But I also didn't want him to get burned.

JAN CUSHING OLYMPITIS   The East Side didn't regard it as an embarrassment that Norman continued to support Abbott after he'd killed, but people were shocked and surprised. Initially there was no reaction when they got the guy out—that was typical Norman—but afterwards Pat Buckley told a friend of mine that she thought he'd flipped his lid, quote-end-quote. Most people didn't know *what* to say. Probably every ex-wife was thrilled, particularly Beverly, but his friends were concerned for his mental stability and they were worried. I mean, how is the Kennedy family supposed to feel about it? Let's suppose it was Sirhan Sirhan who had written a book in prison before killing Robert Kennedy and Norman had taken the same position. They've had two brothers assassinated. Pat was in a state of shock. She called me. She said, "Kid, I feel for Norris."

Also, when you see a press conference like that on TV, with Norman so adamant, there's an element of fear. People were frightened. And there weren't that many people around town who were thinking of picking up the phone to say "Norman, can we help?" I know I didn't.

SENATOR EUGENE McCARTHY   I called him and said, "Look, Norman, you can't have all that guilt. You've got to share it." Some people had told me he was feeling very guilty, but I think he carries a lot of guilt *in general*. It's part of his religious sense—personal and social guilt. Like Yeats and Lowell, carrying the burden of guilt. The same thing.

DOTSON RADER   I don't think it's true that Norris felt caught between Norman and negative reactions from Pat Lawford. In fact, when the *Post* piece came out, Pat hadn't yet seen it, and I brought it into the bedroom, where she was putting on her earrings, getting ready to go out. I read it to her, and she stopped and looked at me and said, "Read it again." I reread the pertinent passages, and she said, "I don't think so." That was her only comment. But I've also been with her on a number of other occasions when the subject of Abbott has come up, and she's always defended Norman's intent.

GEORGE PLIMPTON   In the midst of it all I wrote Norman a letter saying I felt for his difficulties vis-à-vis Abbott, that what I had read about his behavior had been exemplary of how I thought he should have behaved, and that's how I continue to feel. It would've been so easy for him to back away and hide up in Maine or wherever. I thought for him to put himself on the line and to admit that he was indeed partly responsible, but wasn't going to cop out, took a great deal of courage. I wrote something to the effect that I especially valued his friendship after seeing how he had behaved.

Of course, I do think that one of the reasons Norman felt compelled to stand as close to Abbott as he did was that he'd come within a millimeter of being exactly in the same cup of soup himself. That kind of blind idiotic rage is very much in the makeup of everybody. Norman recognizes that. He'd picked up a kitchen knife. He won't again. I think the great thing that's happened to Norman has been Norris. My God—Norman at peace.

ALICE MASON   There *was* talk in East Side circles. No one said anything directly to me, but people were astounded and critical of what he'd done, the chance he took, because they could never do it themselves. Norman went where they wouldn't dare to tread. He took a stand on something he believed in, and he has far more integrity than most liberals.

ABBIE HOFFMAN   After the stabbing I went over to break bread, as he says, and I was trying to cheer him up. "Hey, Norman, look at it this way. I'm a convict, I'm a writer, my first name's Abbott. You're batting 500. That ain't bad these days."

BARBARA PROBST SOLOMON   Norman's always believed in trying to help people in prison. The first time, in Spain in '48, he was successful. This time he wasn't. I think he saw himself releasing the artist from prison—the good guys being the ones who get locked up.

BERNARD "BUZZ" FARBAR   Norman has to follow through what he's started. He's always done that. He'll see it through to the end, and even if he knows that each step is going to get worse and worse, he'll go to the last step. It's his morality. It's in Rojack in *An American Dream*, walking the parapet right to the end, even though he doesn't have to.

IRVING HOWE   He not only took responsibility but he knew he'd have to live with it, so I made the decision not to say anything about it in public, even though several magazines asked me to write about it, including *The New Republic*. Marty Peretz and, in fact, one of our own editors at *Dissent* felt that we should split with him. But I didn't agree, since one has to have loyalty to people when they're in trouble, and even though I think Norman behaved foolishly in many ways I'm absolutely sure that his initial response was based upon good faith. My guess is that I wouldn't think Abbott's as talented as Norman does, but it's not criminal to make a mistake.

GLORIA JONES   When I first married Jim he also had a prisoner he was interested in, so it could've happened to us. Peter Matthiessen has a writer he's trying to get out, Shana Alexander is trying to get Mrs. Harris out. I'm sure Bill Styron was also sympathetic, because he once took a guy in and then the guy went out and raped a girl—and in fact I was there at the "Y" when he talked about it in the middle of Abbott's trial. So it must have been very sad for Norman. Jesus, how would you know that letting a guy out, he's going to stab somebody?

ALFRED KAZIN The biggest thing in my life is the Holocaust, and the basic fact about it is that a great many people killed without having any interest in whom they killed. And for my money, Mailer has done exactly the same thing with his obsession with murderers.

That's why, even before the Abbott thing, I'd hated *The Executioner's Song*. I wasn't impressed with the book's style. For me it's very simple: I'm opposed to murder. And I don't see how anyone coming from a Jewish background, with this terrible history of the Holocaust murders, can defend murderers or be that interested in murder.

It's all very well to speak about the Jews being timid and for Norman to say he doesn't want to be a nice Jewish boy. I know all that—I've been through it. But the big change in the last few years is that Jews themselves have become killers. It's one of the reasons why people like me are not friends of Menachem Begin. I remember when I went to Israel for *Harper's*, the great days when Willie Morris gave me a check for four or five thousand dollars and sent me there to write an article. He really wanted Norman to go. Well, Norman never did go, and over the years my impression is that he's become more and more snotty about the Jewish issue in general. Certainly the vast number of *shiksas* he's married is no guarantee of any commitment.

My feeling is that his idea of courage has only to do with aggressiveness— nothing else. It's all aggressive. I don't think his writing ten or twelve hours a day has to do with courage. He's obviously one of those writers who loves to write, who would be unhappy if he didn't. That's not courage. There's no will needed. The will is not to do it.

I'm not blaming him for the killing of Adan, I'm not saying that. I'm trying to define the cultural and social linkage—and, put very simply, Mailer thinks he's a great rebel. But I believe that if I reviewed the whole postwar history, I'd find that he's riding the waves exactly like a surfboard. It's fashion and show biz. He doesn't think differently. He's too self-conscious, too cockily brilliant. And what lies behind it is a great personal trauma, as with most Jews. Norman's not the prisoner of sex, he's not the prisoner of Jack Abbott. He's the prisoner of Jewish history, and no matter how gifted you are, how courageous, you always feel you're under wraps. Carrying what happened to us in the Second World War, we've felt this restraint very bitterly. So I understand it when I see him break against that restraint, only there's also a positive side to being Jewish, which he hasn't begun to acknowledge.

MIDGE DECTER By the time of the Abbott crisis I'd lost interest. I came to feel that we were all getting too old, and it was really too dangerous, and the matter is far too serious. Part of my political shift has to do with my own children, the two oldest of whom got out of high school in the late sixties and were therefore of the radical counterculture. One of them resisted it, one of them flirted with it. Both had a very hard time. All their friends were destroyed in one way or another. Drugs. Breakdowns. I thought, Well, okay, philosophy is philosophy, but one's kids are one's kids and we're no longer just manipulating ideas.

DIANA TRILLING   Four or five years had gone by after Norman's and my break, and then he got himself tangled up in that terrible Abbott affair. He went on the Dick Cavett show to try to explain his position, and he handled himself so well, so gravely and with such quiet dignity that I wrote him a note of sympathy and compliment. I felt that no matter how he felt about our relationship, it still might mean something to him if I gave him this bit of support, and indeed he answered gracefully.

The press acted badly to Norman in that situation. I happen to think that all the literary talent in the world doesn't forgive the fact that Abbott's a criminal. But on the literary front mine is a minority opinion. The literary imagination has always been fired by the idea of the prison, the criminal, the outlaw—and not only the literary imagination, the popular imagination too. How else do you account for Robin Hood and Genet and the undying appeal of gangster films? Of course, Mailer did lead with his chin in the Abbott affair. He got badly hurt. I felt very sorry for him, and let's keep it in mind that the parole officers were far more to blame for Abbott's release, and they're supposed to be trained in judging whether or not a criminal is dangerous. Their practical intelligence is not supposed to have been deformed by romantic illusions.

Looking back to *Advertisements* and Norman's example of the three kids who stomped an old man to death, I think that although he truly believed what he wrote then—that that was their moment of love—that certainly wasn't his position in the Abbott affair. He didn't say that he had got Abbott out of jail so that he could kill yet another person to know yet another moment of intense love. God, no. That was a million miles away from what he said on the Cavett show.

LIZ SMITH   Just after the Abbott business I ran a story saying that *The Executioner's Song* was going to be released on NBC television rather than as a feature film in theaters. I'd tried to reach Norman, but neither he nor Norris was home. But since I was pretty sure the story was accurate, I printed it. Then Norman called me, very upset: "This isn't right. Why didn't you call me?"

"I tried," I said. "But look, it's no big deal, I'll run a correction."

A couple of weeks later, though, I heard that my original version had been right, and I called Larry Schiller. "Norman's just a little confused about this, Liz," Larry explained. "It will be released as a feature film *overseas*."

So I printed that, and again Norman called, again upset.

"Look, Norman," I explained to him, "it's not me jerking you around, I think it's Larry. I would never do anything to hurt you, you know that."

"I know, but you keep saying this. You've done it twice now."

"Because you're wrong, Norman, and I was right in the first place. Talk to Larry."

Another few weeks passed, and I saw Norman at the premiere of *Ragtime*. I was standing there with my arm around him, photographers are taking pictures of us, and he said, "Liz, we should make a bet: when they release the movie as a feature, you're gonna lose."

"Sure," I said. "I'll take you and Norris to the greatest dinner any place in the country if I'm wrong. But if I'm right, the shoe's on the other foot. Okay?"

He laughed, and that was the end of it. Why was he so convinced he was right when he wasn't? Because essentially Norman's not a tough guy at all. He believes what people tell him, in this case Larry Schiller. He has his theories of honor, which are absolutely antediluvian but so trusting and romantic.

ROGER DONALD   What Little, Brown did for Norman when *Ancient Evenings* was delayed wasn't unique. When somebody gets in scheduling trouble, somebody we've worked with and believe in, we back them up. I don't see it as being tremendously generous so much as smart because good publishers publish authors rather than books.

In '78 I'd read *Ancient Evenings*—what was finished then. Ned Bradford, Norman's original editor, had died, and subsequently I saw more manuscript as the stuff came in. I was enormously enthusiastic. The book was exceedingly unusual, and in my editorial report I remember writing, "This book is unlike anything I've read before. It has such power that even when I get lost in places and do not quite know what's going on, I am compelled to keep turning the page by just the power of the language."

Norman and I talked, basically with me asking questions. What he wanted at that point was to get to the end, so he suggested that rather than me slowing him down, I just keep my suggestions to myself until he was at the end, and then we would start back at the beginning and go straight through. He had been on it, I guess, for eight years and wanted to finish.

Over the next year he was sending stuff in, and I'm reading it but not responding to it. I'm taking notes, and eventually, when he completed the draft, we talked. There was no blue-penciling. I wasn't going to fix his prose because I can't fix his prose. What I hoped to provide was an intelligent reading, so I'd tell him where something wasn't working or where I was confused or something seemed slow or repetitious. This was done at a fairly general level, since he said he didn't want me to get into great detail. I'd done my homework, I knew the manuscript well, so that when he made reference to something or wanted to sit down and talk about it, I could. It quickly became apparent to me that I didn't have to worry about hurting his feelings. What he wanted to know was what I thought, and I could tell him.

Norman and I are friends. I've gone out with him, gone to his house in Brooklyn, and since I live in Park Slope, not far from him, on weekends it wasn't uncommon for me to hop on the subway and go to his place, where we'd spread out the manuscript and work on the dining room table. He was more anxious at the end than he was at the beginning. In part this was time pressure because we had set a deadline, a cutoff date, and toward the end he was scrambling very fast, trying to get everything done he wanted to.

GEORGE PLIMPTON   I went to the reading Pat Lawford arranged when Norman read from his Egyptian novel, and I've never loved him more. I thought how lucky I was to know him. He was so *good*, and you saw the great depth of the man—the studying, the focus, the discipline, the concern, the artist. I've always liked him, but when he's wearing his spectacles and is concerned about his craft there's no effrontery, none of those geysers; there's something very vulnerable and touching about him too. That's when, without striving to impress people, he suggests to us what his true gifts are, and that's finally how he'll be judged— by the work. Which is how he wants to be judged.

ARTHUR KRETCHMER   Perhaps our publication of *Ancient Evenings* followed as a natural consequence of *The Executioner's Song*.

I can't speak for my fiction editor, Alice Turner, who made the decision to take it and pulled the excerpts, but I don't think the decision was affected by the idea of losing Mailer if we didn't. I know Scott very well—his office was a constant stop for me among the many agents I saw when, as the magazine's articles editor, I would routinely go to New York. Obviously Scott's role is to look for money, to get the best deal for Norman, so it wouldn't have shaken him if we hadn't bought *Ancient Evenings*. Also, there's no way I'm going to shut down the relationship with Norman by saying, "This is too difficult for our readers." He'd understand that, and I could've talked my way out of publishing it just by explaining that the novel wouldn't work for us.

The negotiations weren't complicated. In fact, the deal for two excerpts from Arthur C. Clarke's new novel, which also appeared in *Playboy*, wasn't any different; Scott said, "Here's Mailer's new novel. Do you want it? We're talking serious money." And we paid serious money—fifty grand. Still, I repeat: I knew I wasn't going to lose Norman on a continuing basis if I didn't publish *Ancient Evenings*. Maybe Alice or Barry Golson had that thought, but not me. There's a predilection for Kretchmer to publish Mailer, so I'm not worried that he'll turn around and go elsewhere. Part of the reason may be loyalty, but never mind loyalty. How about codes? If you take somebody else's million dollars, you've been bought. I never bought Norman. Norman is a *mensch*, and he knows there are things you don't do. Besides, he isn't going to rush to take a million dollars just because he's in debt. One of the charming things about him—and even the IRS finds it charming—is that he's not afraid of being in debt. Norman functions best from the bottom of the well.

VICTOR NAVASKY   I won't comment on the identity of Frank Page, but whoever he is, he came to us at *The Nation* some months earlier with a piece about "Belles Lettres Magazine." It was a very funny parody, with first names of real people, so we said, "Yes, we'd love to publish it. In fact, do more." A second one came out, then a third, then he wrote his parody of people at *The Times Book Review* trying to decide who should review *Ancient Evenings*. I know zero about whether Benjamin DeMott was prodded by Page's description of him as "soft," so I have no way of knowing why *The Times* assigned him to review it. Still, knowing DeMott as little as I do, I'd be astonished if he could be prodded to do anything. He lives in an isolation booth. I don't think he leans backwards or forwards, which makes him quite an amusing character.

BENJAMIN DeMOTT, THE NEW YORK TIMES BOOK REVIEW *Ancient Evenings turns out to be neither magnificent nor a masterpiece. What is more, describing the book simply as a failure—a near-miss earning respect for noble ambitions and partial triumphs—will not do. The case is that, despite the brilliance of those first 90 pages, this 700-page work is something considerably less than a heroic venture botched in the execution. It is, speaking bluntly, a disaster...*

BENJAMIN DeMOTT I teach at least one of Mailer's books, *The Executioner's Song*, with reasonable regularity, and I've also taught *The Armies of the Night*, and I haven't missed very many of them, so I didn't feel any anxiety about doing the review. I can't imagine that someone situated as I am would. I'm not operating from the publishing center of reputation-making in New York—I'm outside that. I read what I read, and look to be entertained or instructed or amused without much sense of the ramifications. I don't mean to paint myself as an innocent, but the thought of reputation didn't enter my mind since I don't cross the paths of people who think in those terms.

I've had a lot of very interesting letters about my review, but I can't speak about them because they're personal. Like correspondence about any review prominently played, you get a mixed range, and some readers immediately thought about the piece in terms of literary politics. But that world I don't know much about. Nor did I even see the piece in *The Nation* under the byline of "Frank Page" in which I was described as "too soft." Either I have nice friends who don't mention things like that or else I'm really living in a highly isolated warren of the world.

I'd like to think they assigned me *Ancient Evenings* because they thought they'd get a good, truthful piece. Or maybe they thought they'd get a voice that wouldn't be as involved in the currents of publishing and reputation-making and gossip as somebody a little bit closer to the scene. I believe I wrote a thoroughly responsible, careful review. I didn't have in mind other considerations, and it seems to me that the only difference between this assignment and my others for *The Times* was that I hadn't been offered this much space before.

JOHN LEONARD One of the reasons I admire *Ancient Evenings* more than a lot of other reviewers is that in that novel Mailer's obsessions are deliberately abstracted and put into a context that forces the reader to contemplate how he would imagine a society (in this case ancient Egypt) entirely apart from the

Enlightenment and its eighteenth-century ideas of progress, ideas that Mailer has never believed in. All the abstractions, all the things he's argued before, he's put in this ancient culture. Then we get down to the whole theory of dung, and we're back to smell—back to the naturalistic gift that he's had more than anything, and that's as real as going into the streets; that's not another society at all.

In one sense, Mailer's close to the whole German romantic anti-Enlightenment movement. There's the anger, the simultaneous fear of excess and attraction to excess, the smell of blood and feces, a similarity inasmuch as the best prophets of the unconscious are also appalled by the powers of the unconscious. But I think Mailer's an anthropologist too, a zoologist as well as sociologist. In an odd way I trust what I call his sense of smell. If there are certain demented features of the culture he sniffs them out before other people, and not in terms of stereotypes. For example, if he feels uneasy about blacks, we know there's going to be a crisis of liberal confidence about blacks some ten years later and other people are then going to be expressing it. He's somebody who can detect shit through history and biology, ransacking any particular discipline and then applying his insights to produce brilliant metaphors. He's more a creature of metaphors than ideas; he puts on ideas like adhesives—"intellections," as I think he said in *Pieces and Pontifications*. But all the while I have a sense of passionate connections being made, of his suspicion of rational systems and his search for alternatives. I consider myself a real child of the Enlightenment, and Mailer's important for me as somebody who represents the anti-Enlightenment. That's why *Ancient Evenings*, whatever the variousness of its reviews, was an important book for me.

PUBLISHERS WEEKLY *Following a beautiful retelling of the Isis-Osiris myth (a superb novelette in itself) the reader is immersed in the daily life of 19th and 20th dynasties Egypt and the fate of one, Menenhetet, through his three reincarnations... The inextricable connection between the Egyptians, nature and their strange gods is brilliantly depicted. Since the pharaohs and their consorts are considered to be gods, the reader is treated to the most portentous and monumental copulations in all of literature. Pharaoh Usermare's desire for women is insatiable, but he also has a strong taste for "the buttocks of brave men," and one of the most memorable scenes in this magnificent novel has the victorious army of the pharaoh engaged in mass rape of Hittite prisoners after the battle of Kadesh. Although sex is very much in the forefront throughout, the most impressive aspect is the way Mailer conveys the exquisite sophistication of the court and the beautiful, if morbid, preoccupation of the ancient Egyptians with the afterlife. This great work concludes with an awe-inspiring account of a journey through the Land of the Dead. Mailer, a bold gambler, wins all the chips with this one.*

ELIOT FREMONT-SMITH, THE VILLAGE VOICE *Maybe too much has been riding on it—the "big novel" with promises going back at least 12 years, and about five books produced in-between. It contains, here and there, real splendors of charm, insight, craft, and yearning thought. It is also hopelessly clotted. I fret he may have found a god he cannot express to me, and it's this impasse that careers the book into boresville...*

MARY LEE SETTLE, LOS ANGELES TIMES   *I know of no other modern works that so successfully evoke the pre-Judeo-Christian era before magic yielded to morals except Marguerite Yourcenar's* Hadrian *and Fellini's "Satyricon" film... Ancient Evenings goes beyond them into a language and a world that is more alien, but alien only until we consent to go there, and when we do the reward is great. Every object is permeated with magic. That glimpsed area is evoked where changes of images, faces, places are as familiar as the nightly approach of dreams... Huge in scope, magnificent as fiction, luxuriant and wise, this is Mailer's finest and most courageous book.*

CHRISTOPHER LEHMANN-HAUPT, THE NEW YORK TIMES   *Something has gone wrong. It may be that 10 years was too long a stretch of time to spend on the book, especially when its writing had to be interrupted by the production of three other books. Or perhaps Mailer worked with too much determination to prove that he could finally deliver the big novel he had promised for so long and thus used too much muscle when he should have relaxed.*

RHODA KOENIG, NEW YORK   *Ancient Evenings is a turgid book, and revels in guts and gore, but the most offensive thing about it is the vanity that permeates the entire work, an immense, suffocating vanity that pushes the reader away from any identification with the main character.*

HAROLD BLOOM, THE NEW YORK REVIEW OF BOOKS   *Mailer is desperately trying to save our souls as D. H. Lawrence tried to do in* The Plumed Serpent *or even as Melville did in* Pierre. *An attentive reader ought to bring a respectful wariness to such fictions for they cannot be accepted or dismissed, even when they demand more of the reader than they give... Mailer, until now, has seemed to lack invention, and so after all to resemble Dreiser more than Hemingway, a judgment that* The Executioner's Song, *an undoubted achievement, would sustain.* Ancient Evenings *is an achievement of a more mixed kind but it is also an extravagant invention, another warning that Mailer is at home on Emerson's stairway of surprise.*

GEORGE STADE, THE NEW REPUBLIC   *In* Ancient Evenings *we get the fullest workings-out so far not only of Mailer's psychosomatics, but also of his poetics ... The architectonics of this novel, the many intertwined chains of linked imagery, prove once again what we sometimes forget, that Mailer is an artist as well as a mind. And he succeeds very well in solving the most difficult of the problems he set himself—how to present fully and rigorously a form of consciousness that will seem at once alien and familiar to the modern reader... Mailer's somber excavation of our aboriginal and buried human nature, I believe, is a new and permanent contribution to the possibilities of fiction and our communal efforts at self-discovery.*

FREDERICK BUSCH, *CHICAGO TRIBUNE*, "BOOK WORLD" *Of* Ancient Evenings, *and the volumes rumored as successors, I must sadly say, with Menenhetet's spiritual father, "I could not trust Your ambition. I can, however, honor Your genius."*

SATURDAY REVIEW *Probably the most ambitious fiction undertaken by any American writer since* Gravity's Rainbow *a decade ago. I'm sure that Thomas Pynchon, wherever he is, will like this gutsy, risky book; I think Melville might have admired it.* Ancient Evenings *has been worth the wait.*

PEOPLE *... clotted with words, tortured images, half-baked ideas, pretentious dialogue... Of course, anything that Mailer writes is of interest and this was a daring project for the best journalist in America. Too bad that reading it is so unrewarding.*

WALTER CLEMONS, VANITY FAIR *Mailer is sure to catch hell for this demanding book. It's partly his own fault. He has so repeatedly told us that he will one day write a great novel—sometimes to the extent of becoming a windbag on the subject, to keep his spirits up—that we can't read* Ancient Evenings *without asking, Is this it? I will not be suckered into making that kind of pronouncement. Mailer has been counted down and out, and has sprung up again, as many times as Menenhetet I. The* Executioner's Song *was very, very good, and so is* Ancient Evenings. *He's undertaken a huge act of imagining and carried it out with the most delicate (and indelicate) craft. He earns the description he applies to Menenhetet I, who has "that look of character supported by triumph which comes to powerful men when they are sixty and still strong."*

NORMAN MAILER Look, if a book is rich enough, it really shouldn't be unanimously received. . . . I won't turn on the fact that I was very competitive for years, because it keeps you working. It's a lovely instinct if it doesn't poison you. And I'm a little rueful that I'm not as competitive as I used to be. But you have to ebb a bit as you get older. What I'm concerned with now is how many books I have left to write. It's no longer a question of Is one the champ? I'm a writer like other writers, either better or less good than I think I am. But in the meantime I have a life to work at. And how do I want to lead that life in the time remaining to me? In other words, no more stunts. . . . There aren't that many authors who do marvelous books after seventy, are there? I figure I've got about ten years left. If I'm saving something tremendous, I better get started on it.

THE NEW YORK TIMES ("MAILER AND RANDOM HOUSE SIGN A CONTRACT FOR 4 BOOKS," AUGUST 2, 1983) *Norman Mailer, the 60-year-old novelist who has been a major literary force since publication of* The Naked and the Dead *when he was*

25 years old, has signed a four-book contract with Random House. According to an industry source, Random House will pay Mr. Mailer more than $4 million for all publishing rights to the books.

The contract, which becomes effective at the expiration of the author's current contract with Little, Brown, is considered to be among the largest multibook contracts in publishing history. It is also the most important switch by a major American literary figure to another publishing house since Saul Bellow went to Harper & Row in 1978 after 30 years at the Viking Press. . . .

Scott Meredith, Mr. Mailer's literary agent, confirmed that his client had been angry that Little, Brown tried to sell paperback rights to the author's current best-seller, Ancient Evenings, before Mr. Mailer and Mr. Meredith thought it advantageous. "We were furious," Mr. Meredith acknowledged. "But that's not the reason Norman left. All families have feuds. He left because as much as he loves Roger Donald, who is one of his closest friends in the world, he knew some of the other Little, Brown executives only slightly, and the decision was made that he ought to have a New York publisher. It probably would have happened sooner except for Norman's friendship with Roger."

Mr. Donald, Mr. Mailer's longtime editor, is executive editor of Little, Brown. The company, owned by Time, Inc., has its headquarters in Boston but maintains a New York editorial office, headed by Mr. Donald. William A. Guthrie, Little, Brown's director of advertising and publicity in Boston, said that the publisher "has no statement at this time." Mr. Mailer, who has published seven books with Little, Brown, said in a statement released through Mr. Meredith, "I have had a long relationship with Little, Brown, and for the most part an agreeable one."

Random House, owned by Newhouse Publications, has its headquarters in Manhattan. Jason Epstein, editorial director of Random House, will be Mr. Mailer's editor. One more book remains on Mr. Mailer's contract with Little, Brown; a short novel, it is scheduled to be delivered on Sept. 30 for publication next year. The first novel under the new Random House contract, which calls for four novels to be delivered within the next nine years, is due within 36 months.

Little, Brown initially showed Ancient Evenings to paperback houses in advance of its April 25 publication date "to see if we could get an offer we couldn't refuse," according to Mr. Guthrie. When the best offer turned out to be $130,000, with clauses that could have earned the author considerably more, depending on sales, Little, Brown decided to withdraw it temporarily from the market. In May, by which time the novel had climbed to No. 6 on The New York Times best-seller list, Warner Books paid $501,000 for paperback rights. The book is currently in its 15th week on The New York Times best-seller list and has sold to publishers in 12 foreign countries for advances totaling more than $750,000. . . .

JASON EPSTEIN I forget the exact dates, but over the summer of '83 Scott Meredith initiated discussions with Random House about a contract for Norman. I don't know why he came to us rather than, say, Simon and Schuster, but I know that Scott wanted us to publish Norman, and, I suppose with Norman's compliance, he came here.

None of us at Random House had had any idea that Norman wasn't happy at Little, Brown. We don't like to pursue other people's authors, we don't raid other houses, so neither in this case nor in any other would we have made an overture to someone's agent when we knew he was committed elsewhere. The first question we asked Scott was, "Are you free to discuss this as far as Little, Brown is concerned?" Scott told us that Norman had already broken with them. My impression at that point was that despite his closeness to Roger Donald, the trouble may have stemmed from his having no one up in Boston whom he could deal with in an easy way.

Whatever, Norman wanted to get these problems off his mind. Maybe he wanted to work with me—I'd heard something to that effect too—but most of all he wanted to get the rest of his working life arranged in an orderly way, it didn't look possible at Little, Brown, and that's why they were coming to Random House. Scott never said it in so many words, but I sensed that what Norman really wanted was to clear the decks and have nothing to worry about financially for the rest of his life.

Bob Bernstein, the president of Random House, also told Si Newhouse that Scott had come over. When it involves that kind of money you obviously talk to the guy who owns the company. We knew that Si wanted to publish Norman, and it made it a lot easier to go ahead when Si said, "Yes, do it." Bernstein and Tony Schulte—he's the vice-president who looks after all the various trade departments—and I handled the negotiations. We didn't see Norman until it was all done. There were no stumbling blocks, but it's a long contract—15, 20 pages—and there were a lot of things to discuss.

We arrived at a contract for four major novels over nine years. If there are other books that turn up along the way—if Norman decides to write another Pentagon book, for example—that's subject to a separate agreement. But when we sign a four-book contract for nine years we don't expect the author to be a mechanical object. We improvise. We're flexible, and we know we'll have to figure out how much time each book will take and what it would do to the rest of the contract. Still, the contract as it stands isn't specifically for his projected trilogy that began with *Ancient Evenings*, and I don't even think specific novels are named.

But the contract, running for nine years, is unusual, since most authors don't want to be committed for that long. Here, though, Norman's okay until he's seventy. And if these four books are any good, if they pay off, he'll be okay after he's seventy too. The four million dollars—that's the figure *The Times* reported—was based on our hunch that Norman would pay out—and, indeed, not only is he one of the best writers in the world, my feeling is that he may be in his prime. I have the feeling that something has happened, that he's gotten less complicated, much more direct. I've known him for many years, going back to the late fifties, and he's a lot stronger than he's been in the past, a lot freer of complicated, nonliterary ideas. The *meshugas* stuff, like running for mayor—all that's behind him. Somehow he's come through intact, and the energy's very much there.

WALTER ANDERSON   Shortly before Si Newhouse named me editor of *Parade*—I had been managing editor for a few years—we discussed what I wanted to do with the magazine. It was my feeling that quality would work, that Americans respond to quality if that's what you offer. I'd had an idea about Norman for some time, I'd never met him but after reading *The Executioner's Song* I wanted to know how he felt about capital punishment. Since he hadn't answered the question in the book, I told Si I wanted Mailer to do a piece on the subject, and Si got very enthusiastic about it. I then negotiated with Scott Meredith, and subsequently I made it clear to Norman that I didn't care which side he took, whether he was for or against. My assumption was the piece would be a benchmark, and, indeed, when he turned it in it was beautiful.

As for Si Newhouse's role, though: Condé Nast owns both *Parade* and Random House, and while I've never discussed Norman with Bob Bernstein or Jason Epstein, I don't think that Si told them, "Let's buy Norman Mailer." Here at *Parade* the capital punishment piece was my idea, which I presented to Scott Meredith. I discussed it with Si, yes, but Si Newhouse doesn't *allow* me to do quality work—he demands it. I consider Norman *the* quality writer of our time, and Si shares that opinion, absolutely. He's extremely high on Norman, but he's high on William Styron too, who's also at Random House, and I'm certainly not aware that he had an acquisition plan to get Norman. He wouldn't discuss that with me anyway. We do not discuss Random House. It's an ethical question—just as Si never asks me what something costs.

JOHN LEONARD   Mailer's Random House contract sounds like Isiah Thomas' contract with the Detroit Pistons. Essentially it stipulates "my working life." But if we are to believe what Mailer has said about his work, then the circumscription of the nine years also gives him enough pressure to produce; they didn't have to put a time limit on it, so maybe he felt he couldn't deal without a time limit.

On the other hand, I think we're all far too tied up, maybe even obscenely so, in Mailer as a public figure, a performer, to be able to recognize "the great novel" that all the reviewers keep talking about waiting for. Finally "the great body of work" is not going to be judged in the lifetime of the writer who writes it anyway, and if Mailer talks about a body of work, or about changing the world, then that must be a useful source of energy for him. And he continues to produce. I can't conceive of him not writing. I don't think he could live without writing—that's his identity. So I can't accept the consensus that now, with his family and his financial concerns settled, with his new contract, he's sitting pretty to turn out "serious" work. I mean, what else has he been doing? He's *always* been a serious writer, even when he's been absurd.

THE NEW YORK TIMES ("LITTLE, BROWN REJECTS NEW NORMAN MAILER NOVEL," OCTOBER 6, 1983)   Tough Guys Don't Dance, *the novel completed just last Friday by Norman Mailer, was rejected yesterday by Little, Brown & Company, the publisher that Mr. Mailer is leaving in favor of Random House, with which he recently signed a $4 million contract.*

That contract, calling for four novels to be delivered within nine years, was to become effective at the expiration of the author's current two-book contract with Little, Brown. The contract with Little, Brown called for delivery of the final novel by last week.

Yesterday, in a prepared statement, Roger Donald, executive editor of Little, Brown, said, "Since Mr. Mailer's future works will not be published by Little, Brown & Company, discussions between Mr. Mailer, his agent, Scott Meredith, and Little, Brown have concluded that it would be more appropriate for Mr. Mailer to change his publisher now. As a result, his new novel, Tough Guys Don't Dance, *will not be published by Little, Brown."*

One source at Little, Brown said that the publisher had "turned down" the new Mailer novel. But Mr. Donald refused to go beyond the official statement except to acknowledge that he "had seen the novel."

Mr. Meredith said: "We had asked Norman's new publisher to read the manuscript just simply out of friendship, and they loved it and are most anxious to publish it. Little, Brown was aware of this and aware that we would consider it a courtesy if the book were released rather than published by them."

Mr. Meredith added that events had happened so fast that Random House had not yet had time to offer terms for Tough Guys Don't Dance, *a psychological thriller, but that it apparently was going to do so today.*

The novel will be offered by the Meredith agency at the Frankfurt Book Fair in Germany next week, the largest international book fair, and Mr. Meredith said it had already been sold to the French and Swedish publishers of Ancient Evenings *for more money than they paid for that recent best seller.*

Whatever the reason for Little, Brown's rejection, officials of the company are known to have been upset by Mr. Meredith's statement, at the time of the announcement of Mr. Mailer's contract with Random House, that he and Mr. Mailer "were furious" that Little, Brown tried to sell paperback rights to Ancient Evenings *before the author and agent thought it to their best advantage.*

In reply, Arthur H. Thornhill, Jr., chairman of Little, Brown, said: "Although we were all disappointed with the initial results of the paperback reprint rights auction of Ancient Evenings, *the decision not to accept any offer was sound, for later, Warner Books bought the rights for an excellent sum, and we believe they will be very successful. Moreover, the strategy was fully discussed with the author and agent and at no time was there any indication of their being 'furious.'"*

JASON EPSTEIN We bought *Tough Guys Don't Dance* after our contract had already been negotiated. Scott had told us about the book, and I said, "Terrific, I look forward to reading it," and Scott said, "Well, it's certainly Little, Brown's book, but there's no reason you can't read it." I said, "It's Little, Brown's book, and you understand that and we understand that. Fine."

So Scott started sending it over as Norman was writing it, and by the time I finished the first chapter I knew it was going to be terrific. There was no way to miss it—you can tell from the first sentence of these things—and then to my great surprise Scott said, "I think we can leave Little, Brown." I didn't expect that, but then we made an offer. Scott was the middleman, and I assume he took our money and gave it to Little, Brown.

I think *Tough Guys* is unlike anything else Norman's ever done. It's got tremendous, uncomplicated energy, which comes out in a big, unmediated rush. There are no theories, no politics, and the book doesn't attempt to be anything more than just a piece of literature. He wrote it under enormous pressure, and it really surprised me, because the first time through I thought the plot was entirely improvised, that he didn't know from one moment to the next where he was going with it. But when I read it again I realized that everything had been planned for. He wrote it in something like two months, and, despite the pressure, he knew where he was going from the beginning. He had to know. He didn't have time to go back and do it any other way. It's like a Shakespearean comedy. People are nothing but coincidences and false identities. He told me that he'd put himself on "automatic pilot"—that's the phrase he used. But when I read it again I realized it wasn't so automatic. Everything is there.

LEO LERMAN My involvement with the book started earlier, though, before Thanksgiving. I was talking to Jason, and he said that the new novel was quite wonderful, so I rang up various parties and got the manuscript on a Friday, and by Sunday I had finished it. And I liked it, yes indeed. It has some of Norman's best writing in it, especially the descriptions of Provincetown in the winter, which are absolutely wonderful. I've been to Provincetown only in the summer, but I've been to Nantucket off-season, and I know he got the atmosphere and the strange characters up there. It was as if after his many years on the Cape this was all stored up and just gushed out, something that had been growing in him that was now emerging.

I also enjoy thrillers, and when they're good I know that they are literature. Here was someone for whom I had enormous regard playing with the genre, playing with it marvelously while letting me know he's having fun. Even the title and the story it comes from are part of the joke. It's like an opera: the dead are strewn on the field—some have heads, some don't. It's baroque, and here it becomes bizarre; and it's as if Norman trusted himself, let himself go and didn't work the book to death. In that sense, I suppose, it's a mature *American Dream*.

So upon reading the manuscript it was my idea, purely mine, to buy it for *Vanity Fair;* I thought it would be marvelous for the health of the magazine. I had intended to publish it in four parts, perhaps condensed here and there but not less than 40,000 words. Several people thought it was ridiculous to commit four issues to Norman Mailer, but I'd decided to do it anyway. I already had the Eudora Welty lecture and a Saul Bellow novella, so it wasn't that I needed something to fill four issues. *Tough Guys* took me, and I took it.

WALTER ANDERSON The summer of '83 Norman wrote his Clint Eastwood piece for us, and sometime afterwards, maybe in October, he had Scott Meredith send me the manuscript of *Tough Guys Don't Dance*. He'd previously shown me the manuscript, not the galleys, of *Ancient Evenings*, and again with *Tough Guys* he asked for a critical reading.

When I had read *Ancient Evenings* I thought the battle scenes were the finest I had ever read, that they alone were worth the price of admission. I also felt that the conflict between the boy and his grandfather, the question of whether the boy can make it through the River of the Dead, was an extraordinary device to create tension in the book. But I could forecast fairly well what the criticism of the book would be because I didn't think the plotting technique would be recognized. And it wasn't. The criticism was that he couldn't tell a story.

Then I read *Tough Guys*. I began at five one Saturday afternoon and finished at one in the morning—I couldn't stop. It was as if Norman had set out to demonstrate that he too could write a page-turner, as if responding to the criticism of *Ancient Evenings*. "Oh? I can't tell a story? Then I'll tell a story that's never been told before." Like a boxer, he was compensating, hitting with the right, coming back with the left. Even when he wasn't sure how he was going to end it—it was just coming out of him as he was writing—he wasn't worried; and then he took the plot and twisted and opened it up with the wonderful father-son stuff, keeping it tight, moving page after page, and creating a character that could be any of us.

JASON EPSTEIN   As he was finishing *Tough Guys* I suggested to Norman that he take a trip to Russia. The idea had occurred to me when I was rereading some of his journalism and was struck by how fresh and durable *The Armies of the Night* still was after all these years. Suddenly, without reflection, it crossed my mind that if he went to the Soviet Union he could write a book about what it's really like over there, and it occurred to me too that he might have unique access because he's Russian, I mean his family is Russian, and he's spiritually connected to that country in some deep way. Although he's totally American, and among our writers the one whose life has been most committed to America as the place where he lives and works and which he thinks about, his exuberance and energy are obviously not American Protestant. It's something else, and it struck me that somewhere lurking in Norman there's a Russian, maybe a nineteenth-century Russian but a Russian nonetheless.

His first response was fairly positive—not an immediate click, because Norman has to think about how he uses his time very carefully—but after he had talked to Scott Meredith they both came over and we discussed it. Finally he decided to go the last few weeks of March '84. The plan was to visit Moscow, Leningrad, and then Vilna, Vilna being the place where his family comes from. My thought was that he might be looking for his roots, in addition to the journalism book I had in mind, also reconnoitering for what would be the third and final volume of the projected trilogy beginning with *Ancient Evenings*. At the very least, I was sure he'd discover something there, something immensely surprising and invigorating in ways that I couldn't even begin to anticipate.

WALTER MINTON   I can't swear to it, but I think I saw maybe 70 pages of the big novel that eventually became *Ancient Evenings* many, many years ago, sometime around 1964. The story was set long ago, and I don't remember exactly, but I think it was not Egypt but the plains of Russia or Poland. It literally began with what was the essence of Norman Mailer—with a gene, a sperm in the testicles of an ancestor. I remember I was amused because I didn't know where he was going. Peter Israel, also at Putnam's, thought it was absolutely awful, which Peter now seems to have forgotten, because he's told people he liked it.

Still, with *Ancient Evenings* Norman may have written a book different from what he'd set out to do initially. I think it started as one book planned at Putnam's, went to NAL as one or two books, and then became the projected three-volume novel at Little, Brown. Perhaps one of the next two volumes of the trilogy will go back to his original idea about Russia.

NORMAN MAILER   The 50 pages Walter saw were from a novel that starts in a hospital in a small town in New Jersey. A child is being born. *Ancient Evenings* did, in fact, have its beginning of all beginnings as the saga of the Mailer family back in Russia with my grandfather as I imagined him; the 50-page manuscript went from Long Branch, New Jersey, back to Russia. But then I came upon the writings of Isaac Bashevis Singer, and I thought, Oh Lord, there is absolutely no need for my book. Still, there is an attenuated connection between what I gave them at Putnam's and the scheme for *Ancient Evenings*. What I showed Putnam's is part of the same trilogy, but potentially the third volume, which takes place in the near past and the present, as opposed to the first one in the ancient past.

WALTER ANDERSON   Before he left, Scott Meredith called and told me that Norman was interested in doing a piece on the Soviet Union. I told him, "I'd rather not talk about it with Norman. There'll be focus later, after he gets back." My reasoning? That wherever you have Norman Mailer, you get Norman Mailer in that place. Someone like Theodore White is like a pane of glass: if you send him, you see through him; you get a sense of the place without necessarily seeing the writer. The thing about Norman is that you get his personality, and because of this it's a mistake to try to focus him too tightly, to restrict his creativity. He's like a sponge, and in talking to Scott my thinking was, simply, that we'd squeeze the sponge and see if there was something for *Parade*.

What will Norman be like ten years from now? All I can say is that I know our readers respond to him. From the first slap on our behinds to our last heartbeats, we all struggle and identify with struggle. But some, as Faulkner said, do more than endure, they prevail. These are the best among us, our real leaders, and Norman is one of them. He's broadened our culture, made us less afraid to be ourselves. He's caused us to ask questions, to think about who we are and what we are doing, forced us to become better than we have been. But above all there's his energy, his enormous energy. And he has more energy now than ever before, probably for three reasons: one, he recognizes he's not going to live forever and wants to get the work done; two, he has so many people dependent on him that he has to make a lot of money; and number three, which is perhaps number one, Norman is never predictable. He always likes to stretch the rules, and maybe he's going to prove that as you get older you don't have to get slower.

LEO LERMAN   Norman and I had a very long lunch in the barroom of the Four Seasons, sitting against the window. We talked about lots of things—about our childhood and our Jewish mothers, about all those things that two fellows coming out of similar worlds talk about when they're telling what's happening in their lives. And it was then that Norman had told me he was going to Russia. It probably was rooted in my question "When will you have time to write for me?"

We didn't talk about Vilna or Lithuania specifically, and he never used the word "roots," but he certainly mentioned "going back," so I remember having an impression of his wanting to look at where his family came from, wanting to find that past. I cannot think of the word in English, but we have a *mishpocheh* feeling—a kind of cousinish sense that there's an awful lot of ground we don't have to cover—and my feeling was that the trip was part of his infinite curiosity. Sometimes you can't tell whether his energy comes from the curiosity or the curiosity from the energy, but it's self-generating, the whole thing.

Also, as we talked I found a new Norman—somebody of a certain measured consideration, a certain mellowness, always bearing in mind that when I say he's mellowed I don't mean he's slowed down. There is the same will that seems to grow—the absolute power to sit down on your *tuchis* and work. There's always been that industriousness—it's the air Norman breathes—and in this sense he's the personification of the immigrant's golden dream. But now the rhythm has changed. His back is to a different wall, and that wall is time. I'm not saying he's frittered his time away; if he sometimes thinks so, that's placating the gods or a Yiddish conscience. But I think these next years could be the pressure cooker for those past years, because he's had enormous experience, both in life itself and in technical experience as a craftsman. So now, granted time and granted fewer worries, the pressure must come from knowing that these are the last years—"This is it, now"—and he has to produce.

JEAN MALAQUAIS   For all Mailer's visibility, his almost compulsory striving to remain in the public eye—and he has many a trick in his bag—I think that deep down Norman is very much a private man. It is as if the noise-cum-minor-scandals he stirs up in his wake were a camouflage, were false colors beneath which he protects the integrity of his inner self. It is my experience, in almost four decades of friendship, that he is a man of considerable discretion; I can't remember him ever prying into my personal life or, for that matter, confiding about his own. I was struck by the quality of self-deprecation one could sense amidst his *Advertisements for Myself*—a misnomer, if any. Still, in my view he is a third-rate psychologist who tries to unravel Mailer's persona in the light of his overt manifestations. Neither is he to be sized up in some little pseudo-dialectical artifice a contrario: he would act aggressive because shy, violent because cowardly, bombastic because modest, and so on. Nothing could be more misleading; he is a man of too many moods to be cracked open with a tin key. No, the manner to probe in depth a writer of his abundance, scope, and multiformity is to address his work as though one didn't even know his name. Norman Mailer is nowhere to be found except in the substance of his literary output.

To the question of Mailer's place in American letters my answer would be that he stands out as the most gifted and by far the most versatile writer of his generation. Since I have expressed more often than not my reservations about several of his books and essays, I could hardly be suspected of partiality. Let me say, then, that his *Armies of the Night* (a unique example of Rabelaisian Americana), *Why Are We in Vietnam?* (a minor masterpiece), *The Executioner's Song* (a devastating portrait, clean of any sociological blah-blah, of death-thirsty White Christian Teetotalers), and even the much-flawed *Ancient Evenings* (an epic saga in its own right) will assure him an inexpugnable niche in the annals of literature.

Though Mailer didn't tell me the reasons for his recent trip to Russia and Lithuania, it would seem that he is in quest for his ancestral roots; an autobiography—the age is ripe—is looming in his mind. But since he has an uncanny talent for ever renewing the fount of his pen, he may still produce the elusive "great American novel." After all, cancerous America is the one mistress to whom he remains faithful in a perennial love-hate affair. Reading in typescript his *Tough Guys Don't Dance*, I came upon the following pot of gold, which could epitomize—and indeed fulfill—Mailer's gargantuan literary ambition: "She [Patty Lareine] was as insatiable as good old America, and I wanted my country on my cock."

LIZ SMITH, NEW YORK *DAILY NEWS*, APRIL 5, 1984 *Norman Mailer, world champion writer, called to give me this statement: "When it comes to lying, Larry Schiller makes Baron von Munchausen look like George Washington!"*

The author was steamed at a story obviously leaked by his pal Schiller to the effect that Norman had gone with Larry to Russia recently and would write the TV miniseries of "Peter the Great," taking the money and running and eschewing screen credit.

Mailer says he might do something stupid like that if his children were starving, but he really wouldn't. "I don't take the money and run. I happened to be in Russia for my own reasons, deciding if I might write something about the country. Larry asked me to read a script for his production and I agreed and made a few suggestions. But when he began to talk about my doing a polish job on it, I told him, 'I don't do polish jobs; that's not the way I work.' Larry knows I am not going to do this script for him!"

By the by, the role of Peter the Great requires a very tall man for the job, but actor Donald Sutherland has already turned Schiller down. Seems Donald's wife

Michael Mailer the summer before
entering Harvard, Provincetown.

Matthew Norris, Provincetown.

Susan Mailer Colodro, Maine.

With Norris and son,
John Buffalo.

Maggie Mailer.

Stephen Mailer

Elizabeth and Danielle
Mailer.

Kate Mailer.

Myrtle Bennett, who joined the Mailer household in 1971 and continues to preserve order.

Mrs. Fanny Mailer, Provincetown, 1983.

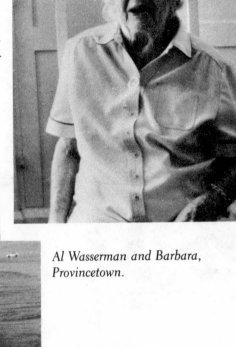

Al Wasserman and Barbara, Provincetown.

didn't care to spend the time required behind the Iron Curtain. So far, Schiller is said to have spent a lot of NBC's money on this enormous project and it isn't even inches off the ground yet.

More Mailer: We'll be seeing two excerpts from Norman's finished novel Tough Guys Don't Dance *in the May and June issues of* Vanity Fair. *The book portions were rumored purchased by former editor Leo Lerman for a whopping $80,000. Actually, the figure was only $50,000 (still not chopped liver), and despite tales that new editor Tina Brown feels "stuck with it," she is saying, on the contrary, she believes it's one of the best things Mailer ever wrote. Well, the Literary Guild thinks so, too. They took the book for August when the hard cover is published by Random House.*

JOHN LEONARD   Basically, it doesn't interest me to prescribe which direction Mailer should go in, whether he should write fiction or nonfiction, or what his animating principle may be. That's less important than the books themselves.

What's amazing to me, instead, is his buoyancy. What he's doing now—who knows?—anything could happen. The two of us did an interview just before his trip to Russia and he said that he no longer believes that he can fulfill his earlier announced role of changing consciousness. But I think that modesty is temporary. If some idea excites him and something comes up, then he could change completely, and the great huge ambition would occur again.

So I have no real sense of where he's going, and I expect I will only be able to figure it out after he's told me. Certainly he's not going to seek approval in any way that the culture would specify. I used to think that maybe he went *against* such specifications as a way to win approval out of perversity—"I'll do the opposite and prove that I can do anything." But when he's produced the books that he has, I don't think it's been calculated at all.

I suppose in his mind, recently, there has been a fencing with the notion of an orderly career progression, like that of John Updike, whom he's come to admire and about whom he now has nothing but pleasant things to say. But it doesn't work that way. I admire Updike too, but I look to him for certain confirmations brilliantly rendered of stuff that I already know or should have known, but I've never found discoveries there. While Updike confirms, Mailer changes your life. And when he told me he no longer aspires to change the consciousness of the race or whatever, I looked at him with bewilderment, because I think he's changed the consciousness of lots of people in a way that most writers don't. That's why I'm so attracted to Mailer and always have been.

Among his contemporaries, Styron goes on writing what he writes—morally earnest and, to me, largely unfelt contemplations of the big issues. Bellow finds his animating principles in the goddamnedest places, sort of like Mailer, but then—to his recent detriment, I think—he takes them too seriously and seldom loses his head. Some of his new collection of stories and novellas is stunning, and I do consider him a genuine comic genius, although he hasn't produced as many books as Mailer.

I suppose what I'm talking about is the notion of "a body of work." By this I mean the energy in a writer to keep producing, the challenge the system under-goes. The constant feeding on your psychic yard goods is the highest drain, and what is amazing is that Mailer has produced—what, twenty-five books?—in the most difficult of public and personal lives imaginable. Nowadays his personal life has probably never been in better order, and it seems to me that he's less panicked, less looking over his shoulder—but whether this is good or bad for him I don't know. But he's still going to find something, notice something, and he's going to write. And whatever it is, it's likely to surprise me. It's comparable to when I read science fiction: if the alien life form presented is too recognizable, then I'm a little disappointed. I can imagine everything Bellow and Updike and other writers are telling me, but what's so characteristic of Mailer is that he's finding something, telling me something I couldn't have imagined beforehand. Which is why I trust him. He continues to astonish. Sometimes I'll like it, sometimes I won't, but there is no other writer, with the possible exception of Günter Grass, whose next book I feel the necessity of reading immediately to find out whether I'm going to be changed again. And I require that, I require the risks that Mailer takes on my behalf and on the behalf of all intelligent readers, as if he's always insisting, "Let's go too far."

LEO LERMAN   Does it matter whether it's fiction or what we used to call non-fiction or verse? No. Whatever it is, it will be a summing up. Norman has been part of an extraordinary experience: he has managed to be at the center and also, somehow, to write about the center while sometimes in opposition to it, so in summing up he'll cast light over what this has all been for. I'm not talking about autobiography as an outgrowth of his Russia trip, specifically. I think his next work will be less self-conscious, less abstract, perhaps less grandiose in concep-tion. However, while I don't know whether I'll be here to see it, whoever is may ultimately realize that the work Norman does in the next ten years, time and circumstances permitting, will be the richest work he's ever done, the fullest and the most filled with wisdom.

LILLIAN HELLMAN   I'm not so certain this will be Norman's best period but I hope to God it is. I think the failure of the Egyptian book has been good for him because it will teach him not to be larger than his pants. You don't write the grandiose novel by trying to. You write a grandiose novel because you've done it, not by starting out and saying, "I'm now writing the great novel," which I think is the way he probably began that book. No matter. I have a kind of instinct that Norman's now going back to the naturalistic writing of The Naked and the Dead.

DIANA TRILLING   Norman had sent me a copy of Ancient Evenings and asked me to read it and tell him whether or not the book had succeeded. His note said that he knew that he could count on me to tell him the truth. It was extraordinary. I mean, it was an extraordinary request to make of someone to whom you had hardly spoken over the last six years. It happened to come at a time when my eyes had been giving me great trouble; that's an awful lot of book to read—it's all I can manage to keep up with my own work. I think I wrote that to Norman. But even were my eyes not bothering me, I couldn't undertake to meet that request. What I'm trying to say is that he didn't have the right to put such a large burden of proof upon me. There had been too much failed faith between us.

I suppose that in a sense I had always thought of Norman as someone who could free me from the excesses of my own strictness of standard, introduce me to or at least allow me some new kind of personal authenticity. Yet, of course, at the same time I would be countering his influence with its opposite. These were the two sides of my nature that existed in conflict. He was to speak his side in my interior dialogue. Whoever doesn't understand that dialogue isn't worth bothering about.

My superego friends could use the correction in Norman just as Norman needed the principle of control which they might teach him. He is not, in my view, the writer he could and should be for that very reason, because he has never achieved that delicate balance. Still, though he has had so uneven a career, I continue to feel he is the best writing artist of our time. I have never read *The Executioner's Song*. I was afraid to read it when I was doing my *Mrs. Harris* book because its style was so insidious: I was afraid I would try to imitate it. And now, as I say, my reading is very restricted. But friends whom I trust tell me it's one of his best works. Whether or not, I still think of him as having far and away the most literary talent now going. Actually, I once asked him when he was going to write his *War and Peace*. He wasn't thrown by the question, nor by its elaboration: I went on to say that his *War and Peace* should be a novel of middle-class life, firmly rooted in established society, but that where Tolstoy had made his excursions into history, Mailer should make his excursions into dissidence.

Which, of course, is what I'd really like him to do, and it doesn't necessarily have to be a novel; it could be another *Armies of the Night*, or even autobiography. When you can see that somebody has the capacity to do something so uncommonly good, then you have to hold onto that and say, "Oh boy, please, please come through."

CONTRIBUTORS

JACK HENRY ABBOTT, the author of *In the Belly of the Beast*, is now serving a prison term of fifteen-years-to-life for the killing of Richard Adan.

LIONEL ABEL is the author of *Meta Theatre* and *The Intellectual Follies*, and has been a longtime contributor to *Commentary*, *Dissent*, and *Partisan Review*.

ALICE ADAMS' fiction frequently appears in *The New Yorker*, *Atlantic*, *McCall's*, *Redbook*, *Paris Review*, and elsewhere. Her books include *Rich Rewards*, *Families and Survivors*, and *Superior Women*.

JOHN ALDRIDGE was the book critic for the New York *Herald Tribune Book Week* and served on the staff of *Saturday Review* from 1970 to 1972. He is currently professor of English at the University of Michigan in Ann Arbor; his books include *After the Lost Generation*, *Critiques and Essays on Modern Fiction*, *In Search of Heresy*, *The Party at Cranton*, *A Time to Murder and Create*, *In the Country of the Young*, and *The Devil in the Fire*.

LARRY ALSON, editor and writer, now lives in Ossining, New York. He was married to Barbara Mailer from 1950 to 1961; they have one child, Peter Alson, twenty-nine, a writer based in New York City.

WALTER ANDERSON, an ex-marine, is the editor in chief of *Parade*, the Sunday magazine with a readership of fifty million. "Norman is the most loyal friend anyone could have, and there is nothing I couldn't discuss with him, no question, no confidence I couldn't share. His discretion is absolute. When we talk about boxing, however, he's invariably wrong and I'm right—something he hasn't yet accepted."

JAMES ATLAS' work has appeared in *The New York Times Book Review*, *The New York Times Magazine*, *Harper's*, *The Village Voice*, *The New Republic*, *Commentary*, and many other journals. His *Delmore Schwartz: The Life of an American Poet* was nominated for the 1977 National Book Award.

JAMES BALDWIN, the well-known novelist and essayist, makes his home in St.-Paul de Vence, France. *Go Tell It on the Mountain*, *Notes of a Native Son*, *Giovanni's Room*, *Another Country*, *The Fire Next Time*, *Going to Meet the Man*, *Tell Me How Long the Train's Been Gone*, *No Name in the Street*, *Just Above My Head*, and the play *Blues for Mr. Charlie* are among his many published works. He is a member of the National

Institute of Arts and Letters, and his awards include a Guggenheim Fellowship, the Martin Luther King Award, and the George K. Polk Award.

RICHARD BARON, president and chairman of Dial Press from 1958 to 1968, is now president of the New York Publishing Company.

MARVIN BARRETT: Professor, School of Journalism, Columbia University; author of *The End of the Party*, a novel, as well as many other books, including *Moments of Truth?*, which won the Sigma Delta Chi Award in 1975. Harvard, class of '42; *Advocate* president, 1941.

ANNE BARRY worked as Norman Mailer's secretary after graduating from Radcliffe, from 1962 to 1966, when she went to Dial Press as an editor.

EDITH BEGNER: A New Yorker, she has published eight novels and often spends her summers in Provincetown.

JOHN "JACK" BEGNER, M.D.: Urologist; Provincetown and New York resident.

EDWARD "EDDIE" BONETTI, fiction writer and poet. His published works include *The Wine Cellar*, a collection of short stories, and *Apple Wine*, a collection of poems. He is also a contributor to literary journals such as *New American Review* and *New Letters*, and lives on Cape Cod.

SEYMOUR BRESLOW: Currently practicing dentistry in Stamford, Connecticut. Harvard, class of '43.

BOWDEN BROADWATER: Harvard, class of '42; *Advocate* staffer, Signet Society.

CHANDLER BROSSARD's novels include *The Bold Saboteurs*, *Wake Up, We're Almost There*, and most recently, *Raging Joys, Sublime Violations*. After several years of travel throughout Europe he is now resettled on Manhattan's West Side.

CHARLIE BROWN, songwriter and musician; Beverly Mailer's half brother. He played lead guitar in *Hair* and now, in addition to his songwriting and recordings, composes and performs television jingles.

WILLIAM F. BUCKLEY, JR., is William F. Buckley, Jr.: Novelist, essayist, columnist, political pundit, host of the nationally syndicated TV show *Firing Line* and editor in chief of the *National Review*. His books include *God and Man at Yale*, *Up from Liberalism*, *The Unmaking of a Mayor*, *Cruising Speed*, *Inveighing We Will Go*, as well as his Blackford Oakes spy novels, the latest of which, *The Story of Henri Tod*, appeared in 1984.

WILLIAM S. BURROUGHS: Cultural guru for several generations of the American avant-garde; his best-known work was the "banned-in-Boston" *Naked Lunch*. Other titles include *The Exterminator*, *The Soft Machine*, *Junky*, *Nova Express*, *Cities of the Red Night*, and his most recent novel, *The Place of Dead Roads*. He was elected to the American Academy and Institute of Arts and Letters in 1983.

DON CARPENTER's published fiction includes *Hard Rain Falling*, *Blade of Light*, *Getting Off*, *The True Life Story of Jody McKeegan*, *A Couple of Comedians*, *Turnaround*, and a collection of stories, *The Murder of the Frogs*. His credits as screenwriter include *Payday*. He lives in Marin County, California. He claims, "I love Norman's writing because he's a Kit Carson for writers; he's been to some strange and wonderful places, and he loves to show the way."

HAROLD "HAL" CONRAD: Sports writer and columnist at the *Brooklyn Eagle* and New York *Daily Mirror,* publicist, prizefight promoter, and associate of Muhammad Ali. Author of *Dear Muffo* and *Battle of Apache Pass,* as well as a contributing editor to *Rolling Stone.*

MARA LYNN CONRAD: Dancer and actress whose Broadway shows include *Body Beautiful, Amazing Adele, Touch and Go,* and *Inside U.S.A.* Her television credits include *The Taming of the Shrew* and the *Colgate Comedy Hour,* and she has appeared in such movies as *Last Train to Gun Hill, The Confession,* and *Let's Make Love,* with Marilyn Monroe. She also appeared in all of Mailer's three films. She continues to act and dance and makes her home in New York City with her husband, Hal Conrad.

FRANK CORSARO: Director of on- and Off-Broadway theater, musical theater, opera theater, and television productions. A leading figure in Actors Studio, he directed its production of Mailer's *The Deer Park, A Hatful of Rain,* and *The Night of the Iguana.* Director for the New York City Opera at Lincoln Center, he continues to teach acting in New York City.

PATTI COZZI: Married to Ciro Cozzi, proprietor of Ciro and Sal's and the Flagship restaurants in Provincetown. Active in the Provincetown Art Association.

CUS D'AMATO was born in the Bronx in 1908 on January 17, the same birthday, he reports, as that of Muhammad Ali. Manager and trainer of world champions Floyd Patterson and Jose Torres, he now teaches boxing at his training camp in Catskill, New York, and says, "As a result of my many years of fighting the International Boxing Club, they have finally dissolved and relinquished their control of the sport."

HOPE GORHAM DAVIS lives in Cambridge, Massachusetts, where she holds a Bunting Fellowship at Radcliffe to write a memoir about her experiences during the thirties, when she was an underground member of the Communist party and worked for the New Deal in Washington, D.C. She writes regularly for *The New Leader* and other publications and is married to Robert Gorham Davis.

ROBERT GORHAM DAVIS reports that he is writing "a combined autobiography and family history of a highly imaginative sort," adding that in 1983 he wrote an unfavorable review of *Ancient Evenings* for *The New Leader.* Formerly a professor of English and creative writing at Harvard University, 1933–43, he had Mailer as a student during the latter's "decisive" sophomore year.

MIDGE DECTER: Author and critic. As an editor at *Harper's* she published Mailer's "Steps of the Pentagon" and *The Prisoner of Sex.* Her own works include *The Liberated Woman and Other Americans, The New Chastity and Other Arguments against Women's Liberation,* and *Liberal Parents, Radical Children.* At present she is director of the Committee for a Free World and is married to Norman Podhoretz.

EDWARD de GRAZIA: Leading New York City civil liberties lawyer who successfully defended the film *I Am Curious, Yellow* and William Burroughs' *Naked Lunch.* Legal adviser and organizer for the march on the Pentagon in 1968. Most recently the author of *Banned Films: Movie Censors and the First Amendment.*

ORMONDE DE KAY, JR., is a free-lance author who writes primarily on historical and biographical subjects. Harvard, class of '45; *Advocate* staffer.

BENJAMIN DeMOTT was a columnist for *Harper's* and the *Atlantic*, as well as a contributing editor to the *Saturday Review*. His novels are *The Body's Cage* and *A Married Man*. He is currently a professor of English at Amherst College.

ART D'LUGOFF: Founder and owner of the Village Gate, New York City's leading jazz club.

E. L. DOCTOROW, author of *The Book of Daniel, Ragtime, Loon Lake*, and *American Anthem*, was an editor at Dial Press, 1964–69.

ROGER DONALD: Editor in chief, Little, Brown and Company.

FAY MOWERY DONOGHUE: Known professionally as Fay Moore, she is an artist noted for her portraits of equine thoroughbreds and has recently completed a mural for the Meadowlands in New Jersey, a reproduction of which appears on the cover of six million 1983–84 telephone books. A resident of New York City, she was introduced to her husband, Roger Donoghue, by Mailer in Provincetown, where she often visited her brother and sister-in-law, Eldred and Mary Mowery.

ROGER DONOGHUE, a world middleweight contender from 1946 to 1952, has coached and sparred with Mailer over the years of their friendship. Currently he is sales representative for Tsingtao and Raffo beer companies. "We wandered through the night in the late fifties and early sixties. His fascination with boxing had come from Adele's father. We went to training camp in Summit, New Jersey, where Norman boxed with Ralph 'Tiger' Jones and Yama Bahama. He did well for an intellectual. Sometime later I taught him to hook off a participle. Tough writers *can* fight."

JACOB DRUCKMAN: Pulitzer Prize-winning composer and professor at Yale University School of Music. He is associated with the Columbia-Princeton Electronic Music Center, has composed music for the Joffrey Ballet, and has received Guggenheim and Fulbright fellowships, as well as an award from the American Academy and National Institute of Arts and Letters, of which he is now a member. While summering in Provincetown he was a contributor to Act IV and later set Mailer's poetry to music.

ARNOLD "EPPIE" EPSTEIN, childhood crony and high school classmate of Mailer when both lived in the Crown Heights section of Brooklyn, is now a liquor distributor living in Englewood, New Jersey.

JASON EPSTEIN: Publisher, editor, and vice-president of Random House after working at Doubleday and Company from 1951 to 1958. At present he is Mailer's editor. Director of *The New York Review of Books*, he is also the author of *The Great Conspiracy Trial*, 1970.

KINGSLEY ERVIN has taught English in Athens, Greece, and is headmaster of Grace Church School in New York City. Harvard, class of '45; *Advocate* staffer.

EDWIN FANCHER: A psychologist practicing psychotherapy and psychoanalysis, he was cofounder with Dan Wolf and Norman Mailer of *The Village Voice* and was its publisher from 1955 to 1974.

BERNARD "BUZZ" FARBAR: Free-lance editor and filmmaker, formerly fiction editor at *Saturday Evening Post*, senior editor at Trident Press, Simon and Schuster, and then director of CBS Legacy Books. He has appeared in Mailer's films and served as vice-president of Mailer's film company, Supreme Mix.

JUDY FEIFFER: Photographer and author, formerly a senior editor at William Morrow, publishers; she was also vice-president for East Coast Productions, Orion Pictures. Her books include A *Hot Property* and *Love Crazy*.

JULES FEIFFER: Cartoonist, writer, and contributing cartoonist, *The Village Voice*. He has received an Academy Award for animation as well as a special George K. Polk Memorial Award in 1962 and the Outer Circle Drama Critics Award in 1969 and 1970. He is author of *Sick, Sick, Sick, Passionella and Other Stories, Harry, the Rat with Women* (a novel); his plays and screenplays include *Little Murders, Grownups, Carnal Knowledge*, and *Popeye*.

ISADORE FELDMAN: Army buddy, who first met Mailer at Camp Stoneman, California, in early 1944, was with him during the Luzon campaign, and later recognized himself in the character of Goldstein in *The Naked and the Dead*. Employed as a welder by McDonnell Aircraft for thirty years, he is now retired and lives in St. Louis, Missouri. He and his wife have four children.

CLAY FELKER: Editor, *Esquire*, 1957–62; consulting editor, Viking Press, 1963–66; founder and former editor and publisher, *New York* magazine.

DON FINE: Vice-president and editor in chief at Dell; subsequently publisher and editor at Arbor House until 1983, when he formed his own publishing company. Harvard, class of '44; *Advocate* staffer.

SHIRLEY FINGERHOOD is a civil court judge, New York County, and lives in Manhattan.

EILEEN FINLETTER, who has maintained her friendship with Mailer since meeting him in Paris in 1948, currently makes her home in London.

IVAN FISHER: Noted New York trial lawyer who represented Jack Henry Abbott.

JOE FLAHERTY: Author of *Managing Mailer, Chez Joey, Fogarty & Son*, and, recently, the widely acclaimed novel *Tin Wife*, published shortly after his death in the fall of 1983. A native of Brooklyn, where he worked as a longshoreman, he became a staff writer for *The Village Voice* and was a frequent contributor to many publications, including *Esquire, The New York Times Sunday Book Review, Sport*, and *Penthouse*. He was Mailer's mayoral campaign manager in 1969.

MARIA IRENE FORNES, Off-Broadway dramatist and director, is the author of *Tango Palace, Promenade, The Successful Life of 3, Dr. Kheal, Sefu and Her Friends, Mud*, and *Sarita*, among others. She is the recipient of four Obies, one of which was for Sustained Achievement.

RUTH E. FRIEDMAN is the fictionalized name of a painter who has requested anonymity. She currently lives in New York City.

HENRY GELDZAHLER: The former curator of twentieth-century art at the Metropolitan Museum of Art, he also served as New York City's commissioner of cultural affairs from 1978 to 1982. He is now writing, lecturing, curating exhibitions and advising corporations and collections.

ALLEN GINSBERG is the author of *Howl, Kaddish, The Fall of America: Poems of These States, Mind Breaths*, and *Plutonian Ode*. He was elected to the National Institute of Arts and Letters in 1973 and received the National Book Award in 1974. A resident of New York, he is codirector of the Poetics School at Naropa Institute in Boulder, Colorado.

GEORGE WASHINGTON GOETHALS is professor of clinical and personality psychology at Harvard University. Harvard, class of '43 and Class Poet; *Advocate* staffer.

EMMA CLARA "ECEY" GWALTNEY is associate professor of English, Arkansas Polytechnic Institute, Russellville, Arkansas. She is the widow of Francis Irby Gwaltney.

FRANCIS IRBY "FIG" GWALTNEY, a native Arkansan, was among Mailer's closest friends for almost forty years. The author of the novels *Yeller Headed Summer, The Day the Century Ended, A Moment of Warmth, The Numbers of Our Days, A Step in the River, The Quicksand Years, Destiny's Chickens,* and *Idols and Axle Grease,* he was professor of English at Arkansas Polytechnic Institute until his death in February 1981.

NATHAN "NAT" HALPER, critic and noted James Joyce scholar, owner and director of HCE Gallery, Provincetown, was a member of the board of directors of the Provincetown Art Association until his death in 1983.

PETE HAMILL was born in Brooklyn in 1935, left high school after two years to become a sheet-metal worker in the Brooklyn Navy Yard, later studied painting on the GI Bill at Pratt Institute and Mexico City College, worked as a designer, and started writing for newspapers in 1960. A columnist for the *New York Post,* the New York *Daily News,* and other papers, he is currently a contributing editor to *New York* magazine. He is the author of *A Killing for Christ, Irrational Ravings, The Gift, Flesh and Blood, Dirty Laundry,* and *The Deadly Peace.* Both *The Gift* and *Flesh and Blood* have been produced as CBS-TV specials. His latest novel, *The Guns of Heaven,* was published in 1984.

THOMAS HANRAHAN: Reporter, New York *Daily News.*

ROBERT C. HARRISON: Co-owner of Hargood House, Provincetown. Harvard, class of '43; *Advocate* staffer, Signet Society.

HAROLD HAYES, former publisher and editor of *Esquire,* is now vice-president of CBS Magazine Division.

HAROLD HECHT: Film producer who, with Burt Lancaster, optioned the screen rights to *The Naked and the Dead.* He lives in Beverly Hills, California.

LILLIAN HELLMAN's plays include *The Children's Hour, Days to Come, The Little Foxes, Watch on the Rhine, Another Part of the Forest,* and *Toys in the Attic.* She has received the New York Drama Critics Award twice, several Academy Award nominations for her screenplays, and the Gold Medal for Drama from the National Institute of Arts and Letters. In 1969 she was given a National Book Award for her memoir *An Unfinished Woman,* and her second memoir, *Pentimento: A Book of Portraits,* was nominated for the same award in 1974. *Scoundrel Time* appeared in 1976 and *Maybe* in 1980. After a long illness she died on Martha's Vineyard early in the summer of 1984.

ABBIE HOFFMAN: Cofounder of the Yippies, "Chicago Seven" defendant, author of *Revolution for the Hell of It* and *Soon to Be a Major Motion Picture.* He spent six years underground, and, after serving time on a highly questionable drug charge has returned to community organizing.

APRIL KINGSLEY HOPKINS, free-lance curator and art critic, is married to Budd Hopkins, the painter. Formerly she was a nurse at New York University Hospital.

IRVING HOWE: Critic and writer, as well as professor of English at the Graduate Center of the City University of New York and at Hunter College. His books include *The Critical Point, Decline of the New, Steady Work, Thomas Hardy, Politics and the Novel, William Faulkner, Sherwood Anderson,* and *World of Our Fathers,* and he recently completed a study of literary "modernism." He was founding editor of *Dissent,* and is also a frequent contributor to *Partisan Review, Commentary, The New Republic, The New York Review of Books,* and other publications. He has received the Bollingen Award, a National Institute of Arts and Letters award, and a Guggenheim Fellowship.

H. L. "DOC" HUMES: Cofounder of The *Paris Review,* author of *The Underground Man* and *Men Die.* Currently he lives in Cambridge, Massachusetts, where he runs a drug rehabilitation clinic.

MONROE INKER is a leading Boston attorney with White, Inker, Aronson, Connelly and Norton, P.C.

GLORIA JONES, the widow of James Jones, is an editor at Doubleday and Company and currently lives in Bridgehampton, New York, and New York City.

ALAN KAPELNER's novels include *Lonely Boy Blue* and *All the Naked Heroes.*

ALFRED KAZIN: Writer and critic, the literary editor of *The New Republic* and a contributing editor to *Fortune,* 1943–44. A member of the National Institute of Arts and Letters, he is the author of *On Native Ground, A Walker in the City, The Inmost Leaf, Contemporaries, Starting Out in the Thirties,* and *Bright Book of Life.*

JOHN "JACK" KEARNEY is a Chicago and Provincetown sculptor. Formerly vice-president and trustee of the Provincetown Art Association, he is a member of the board of the Art Institute of Chicago.

LYNN KEARNEY: Runs the Contemporary Art Workshop in Chicago with Jack Kearney, her husband. She is currently a trustee of the Provincetown Art Association.

GENE KELLY: Leading dancer, choreographer, film actor, director, and producer. His best-known roles were in *Time of Your Life, Pal Joey, An American in Paris, Singin' in the Rain, Les Girls, Marjorie Morningstar, Let's Make Love,* and *Forty Carats.* He received the Cecil B. De Mille Award in 1981 and is the author of *Take Me Out to the Ballgame.*

MURRAY KEMPTON has worked for the *New York Post, The New Republic,* and the *World-Telegram and Sun.* He was a delegate to the 1968 Democratic convention and is a member of the American Civil Liberties Union, Committee for Cultural Freedom, and League for Industrial Democracy. He has received numerous awards, including a George K. Polk Memorial Award and the 1974 National Book Award in contemporary affairs for *The Briar Patch.* His other publications include *Part of Our Time: Some Ruins and Monuments of the Thirties* and *America Comes of Middle Age: Columns, 1950–1962,* and he is a contributor to *The New York Review of Books, Commonweal, Life, Harper's, Atlantic Monthly, Esquire,* and *Playboy.*

MICKEY KNOX: Film producer, whose credits include a number of spaghetti westerns made in Italy. As an actor he recently appeared in *Hart to Hart* with his friend Lionel Stander, *Archie Bunker's Place, Quincy,* and the ABC-TV miniseries *Winds of War,* as well as in numerous feature-length films. His last stage appearance was in the New York production of *The Deer Park*. He was married to Joanne Morales Betay, Adele Morales Mailer's sister, from 1960 to 1969. Currently he lives in Rome.

PAUL KRASSNER, editor of *The Realist* from 1954 to 1974, has published numerous articles in such varied magazines as *Co-Evolution Quarterly, High Times, Mother Jones, National Lampoon, Penthouse, Playboy, Playgirl, Rolling Stone,* and *The Village Voice*. His books include *Impolite Interviews, How a Satirical Editor Became a Yippie Conspirator in Ten Easy Years,* and *Tales of Tongue Fu*. He lives in San Francisco, where he is completing his autobiography, although he often takes his stand-up comedy act on the road.

JILL KREMENTZ is a well-known photographer and author of children's books.

ARTHUR KRETCHMER: Editor in chief of *Playboy* since 1972, who says: "I have never negotiated with Norman. I have only negotiated with people who negotiate on his behalf. When you hear Scott Meredith or Larry Schiller say, 'Arthur, Norman would never try to pressure you, but you know he *really* needs the money,' then you know how shrewd the man really is."

SEYMOUR KRIM: Writer, editor of *Nugget Magazine*, 1961–65, consulting editor of *Evergreen Review*, and reporter for the New York *Herald Tribune*. He has taught at the University of Iowa Writers Workshop, New York University, the University of Puerto Rico, Penn State, and has been teaching at Columbia University since 1978. He is the author of *Views of a Nearsighted Cannoneer, Shake It for the World, Smartass, You & Me,* and the editor of *The Beats,* an anthology.

TULI KUPFERBERG: Poet, political activist, and cofounder (with Ed Sanders) of the sixties rock group The Fugs.

JOHN LEONARD's works include the novels *The Naked Martini, Wyke Regis, Crybaby of the Western World, Black Conceit,* as well as the collections of essays *This Pen for Hire* and *Private Lives in the Imperial City*. He was *The New York Times* book and culture critic from 1967 to 1983, television critic for *Life*, 1969–73, and often writes about television for *New York* and other magazines. He is currently completing *The Glee Club,* a novel.

LEO LERMAN: Well-known editor, writer, cultural critic, and arbiter of taste. He has contributed pieces to *Vogue, House & Garden,* the *American Scholar,* the *Saturday Review, The New York Times Book Review,* the *Herald-Tribune Book Review,* the *Atlantic Monthly,* the *Saturday Review of Literature*. For ten years he wrote a column for *Dance Magazine*. He became contributing features editor at *Mademoiselle,* features editor at *Vogue,* children's book editor at the *Saturday Review of Literature,* editor in chief at *Vanity Fair,* and is now editorial adviser to the Condé Nast Publications, internationally. His published books include: *Leonardo da Vinci: Artist and Scientist, Michelangelo: A Renaissance Profile,* and *Museum: 100 Years of the Metropolitan Museum of Art,* for which he received the Lotus Club Award. Lerman appears in one rambunctious movie: *The Troublemakers*. He has always, angelically, made trouble.

MAX LERNER: Author and lecturer, an editor of *The Nation* as well as a columnist for the *New York Post* and the Los Angeles Times Syndicate. His books include *It Is Later Than You Think, Ideas for the Ice Age, The Age of Overkill, Education and a Radical Humanism, Tocqueville and American Civilization,* and *America as a Civilization*.

HARRY LEVIN: Educator, writer, and, since 1939, professor of English and comparative literature at Harvard University. He was a Guggenheim Fellow, 1943–44, and has received several awards for his literary criticism. *James Joyce: A Critical Introduction, The Power of Blackness,* and *Hawthorne, Poe, Melville: Ground for Comparison* are among his many published works.

MARK LINENTHAL: Poet and professor of English and creative writing at San Francisco State University, where he was also director of the Poetry Center for many years. "Norman is famous and faraway now, and we rarely meet, but we were close friends. He was important to me. Recalling significant episodes has been overwhelming, a little like a series of psychoanalytic sessions in which forgotten parts of myself have been unearthed and encountered."

GORDON LISH is the former fiction editor at *Esquire* and is currently senior editor at Alfred A. Knopf. A lecturer at Columbia University, he received a Guggenheim Fellowship in 1984. His books include *English Grammar, The Gabbernob, Why Work, A Man's Work, New Sounds in American Fiction, Dear Mr. Capote,* and, most recently, *What I Know So Far.* He is also the editor of *The Secret Life of Our Times* and *All Our Secrets Are the Same.*

JILLEN LOWE is a poet and journalist, many of whose articles on cultural events and personalities have appeared both in Cape Cod and in national publications. She is now writing a novel in Wellfleet, Massachusetts, where she makes her home.

EUGENE McCARTHY: Former United States Senator from Minnesota and 1968 Democratic presidential candidate. He is also a poet, educator, and writer whose books include *Frontiers in American Democracy, Dictionary of American Politics, A Liberal Answer to the Conservative Change, Limits of Power, The Year of the People,* and *Other Things and the Aardvark.*

KEVIN McCARTHY: Stage, film, and television actor, known for his roles in such plays as *Winged Victory, Death of a Salesman, Two for the Seesaw, Brecht on Brecht, The Night of the Iguana, Cactus Flower, The Three Sisters, Happy Birthday, Wanda June,* and *Equus.* He has made many films, including *Death of a Salesman, The Best Man, The Prize, Invasion of the Body Snatchers, Hotel,* and *Kansas City Bomber,* as well as frequent television appearances. A member of the Actors Studio since its founding in 1947, he appeared in its production of Mailer's *The Deer Park.*

MICHAEL McCLURE: The author of two novels, *The Adept* and *The Mad Cub,* as well as many books of poetry, including *Dark Brown, Star, September Blackberries, Antechamber and Other Poems,* and *Fragments of Perseus.* He is the playwright of *The Beard,* which he describes as "a much reviled dialogue between Billy the Kid and Jean Harlow in a blue velvet eternity." His dramatic adaptation of Franz Kafka's "Josephine the Mouse Singer" won the 1979 Obie for best play. A poet "who deals with the area between biology and vision," he continues to live in the Haight-Ashbury district of San Francisco.

ERROLL McDONALD is a senior editor at Random House.

NANCY MACDONALD has been the director of Spanish Refugee Aid, Inc., from 1953 to 1984. She is currently working on a book about that organization.

JOHN "JACK" MAHER: Harvard, class of '41–'43, '45–'46; *Advocate* staffer.

ADELE MORALES MAILER is a painter, designer, actress, and writer. She was divorced from Norman Mailer in 1961; she has two daughters, Danielle "Dandy" and Elizabeth "Betsy."

FANNY SCHNEIDER MAILER continues to live in Brooklyn Heights.

BARBARA NORRIS CHURCH MAILER: Actress and painter, whose oils have most recently been shown at the Central Falls Gallery, Soho. Currently studying at the Herbert Berghof Studio in New York, she was last seen on ABC-TV's daytime drama *All My Children*. She is the mother of two sons, Matthew Norris and John Buffalo Mailer.

WILLIAM J. MAJESKI holds the rank of detective in the New York City Police Department and is currently assigned to the Brooklyn District Attorney's squad.

JEAN MALAQUAIS: Philosopher, teacher, translator of *The Naked and the Dead*, and the author of the novels *Man from Nowhere*, *War Diary*, *World Without Visa*, and *The Joker*, as well as the critical study, *Sören Kierkegaard, Foi et Paradox*. He has remained one of Norman Mailer's closest friends since the two first met in Paris in 1947.

ROBERT MARKEL was editor in chief of Grosset and Dunlap and the editor of *Marilyn*.

CLIFFORD MASKOVSKY went through basic training at Fort Bragg, North Carolina, with Norman Mailer, and the two subsequently served together in the Luzon, Leyte, and Japan theaters. He now lives in San Diego, California.

ALICE MASON: New York City real estate broker and a leading hostess who once a month has a dinner "in the salon manner for sixty of New York's achievers." She adds, "Norman's one of my few regular guests because my dinners are all about conversation, and he's one of the best at it."

JAMES MEADS is Chief of Police, Provincetown, Massachusetts.

JONAS MEKAS: Filmmaker and leading spokesman for the American underground cinema; editor of *Film Culture* and film critic at *The Village Voice*. His best-known film, *The Brig*, was voted Best Documentary at the Venice Film Festival in 1964.

KATE MILLETT: Leading feminist, sculptor, filmmaker, and author of *Sexual Politics*, *Flying*, *The Prostitution Papers*, and *The Basement*.

WALTER MINTON, now a practicing lawyer, was president of G. P. Putnam's Sons, Mailer's publisher from 1955 to 1963.

MARY MOWERY continues to live in Provincetown, where during the sixties she and her then husband, Eldred, owned and operated the Waterfront summer apartments.

ADELINE LUBELL NAIMAN: Writer and editor, as well as an authority on computers in education; Radcliffe class of '46 ('45) and roommate of Phyllis "Sliver" Silverman, Bea Silverman Mailer's sister. As an editor at Little, Brown she read the first 200 pages of *The Naked and the Dead* in manuscript draft and urged publication. "Norman knows what he's doing when he writes. He was a pro to begin with, not simply an intuitive, inspired, or imitative aspirant like the rest of us. His intellect is formidable. He's also one of the sweetest men I know and a loyal friend. I love watching him with his kids— he's such a great father. It all comes from his mother's adoring him and believing in him, which frees him to care for others. That probably also accounts for his being so uxorious and philoprogenitive!"

VICTOR NAVASKY has been editor in chief of *The Nation* since 1978. A graduate of Yale University Law School, he was the founder of *Monocle* and an editor at *The New York Times*. His books include *Kennedy Justice* and *Naming Names*.

GLEN NELSON is now a research chemist in product development for a corn-processing company in Indiana. Originally from New York, he served with Mailer in the Philippines.

JAN CUSHING OLYMPITIS: Born Jan Golding, whose grandfather owned Sterling National Bank and Essex House. A graduate of Briarcliff, she built "an impressive reputation as a hostess," according to Enid Nemy of *The New York Times*, after she returned from several years in Paris and was divorced from Frederick Cushing. Worked at *Vogue* and Wells, Rich and Greene, then set out to "create a life for herself" and became known for gathering "intelligent, stimulating men and pretty, vivacious women" in her home. She and her third husband, Manoli Olympitis, from whom she is now separated, have one child.

D. A. PENNEBAKER began his collaboration with Ricky Leacock in 1959 in Leacock, Pennebaker, Inc., whose best-known documentaries include *Don't Look Back, Monterey Pop, Town Bloody Hall*, and Mailer's three films, *Wild 90, Beyond the Law*, and *Maidstone*. He recently finished *Rockaby*, based on Samuel Beckett's play of the same name.

MARTIN PERETZ: Journalist and educator. He has been editor in chief of *The New Republic* since 1974. Previously an assistant professor and department chairman at Harvard, as well as master of one of the houses, he continues as a lecturer in social studies. He is a trustee of Brandeis University, an overseer of the Bard College Humanities Center, and the honorary chairman of the Jerusalem Foundation. He was awarded the Jerusalem Medal in 1982.

WILLIAM PHILLIPS: Editor, *Partisan Review*, 1936– ; former consulting editor, Dial Press, Criterion Books, and Random House; professor of English, Rutgers University and Boston University; author, *A Sense of the Present* and, most recently, *Partisan Review: Life Among the Intellectuals*; editor, *The Best American Short Novels, Art and Psychoanalysis, Short Stories of Dostoevsky*.

DAVID PLACE: Class agent, Harvard, class of '43.

GEORGE PLIMPTON: Author, critic, and editor of *The Paris Review*. His books include *Out of My League, Paper Lion, The Bogey Man, Mad Ducks and Bears, One More July*, and *Shadow Box*. He collaborated with Jean Stein on *An American Journey: The Time of Robert F. Kennedy* and *Edie: An American Biography*.

NORMAN PODHORETZ has been the editor of *Commentary* magazine since 1960 and has written numerous essays, as well as *Doings and Undoings: The Fifties and After in American Writing, Making It, Breaking Ranks: A Political Memoir*, and, most recently, *Why We Were in Vietnam*.

NED POLSKY: Professor of Sociology, State University of New York at Stony Brook. He is the author of *Hustlers, Beats and Others*. He continues to live in Greenwich Village.

TOM QUINN is currently vice-president of Provident Capital Management, Inc., an investment management firm in Washington, D.C. A former stockbroker, he managed the prizefighter Joe Shaw, himself having been an intercollegiate heavyweight boxing champion for Georgetown University. He appeared in Mailer's film *Beyond the Law*.

DOTSON RADER is the author of *I Ain't Marchin' Anymore, Blood Dues, Miracle, Government Inspected Meat and Other Fun Summer Things, The Dream's on Me*, and *Beau Monde*. He was a contributing editor to *Esquire* from 1971 to 1979 and is now a contributing editor to *Parade* while at the same time working on a memoir of Tennessee Williams and a book-length essay about runaway children.

MARJORIE "OSIE" RADIN, Norman Mailer's cousin, is the daughter of Beck Schneider Shapiro (Fanny Mailer's older sister) as well as the sister of Charles Rembar. She now makes her home in New Jersey.

CHARLES REMBAR is a leading New York literary and constitutional lawyer whose *The End of Obscenity* received the George K. Polk Memorial Award for Outstanding Book of 1968–69. His other books include *The Law of the Land* and *Perspective*, and he has been a contributor to *Antioch Review, Atlantic Monthly, Evergreen Review, Life*, and *Esquire*. He is a graduate of Harvard, class of '35. "Norman," he says, "has written about my own influence on him. I have nothing to add except to say that the feeling on both sides has easily survived some sharp disagreement on practical questions and some fundamental conceptual differences. Of course, it is entirely possible to value and to enjoy the writing of an author whose ideas conflict with your own, and in Norman's case the writing is so good that it's impossible not to. He's extraordinary, in my judgment one of the all-time best."

BARNETT "BARNEY" ROSSET, JR.: Publisher and founder of Grove Press and one of the leading campaigners against literary censorship with his courageous publication of such books as *Naked Lunch*.

HEDDA ROSTEN: A writer for radio and television, including scripts for such TV dramatic programs as *Studio One* and *Alcoa-Goodyear*. Her play *The Happy Housewife* was produced on CBS-TV and published in *The Best One-Act Plays of 1951–52, Best Television Plays*, and *Anthology of Plays 2*. Another of her plays, *Footfalls*, appeared on CBS and in the anthology *Prose and Poetry in America*.

NORMAN ROSTEN, poet, playwright and novelist, has received a Guggenheim Fellowship as well as an award from the American Academy of Arts and Letters, and his publications include *Under the Boardwalk, Over and Out, Marilyn: An Untold Story, Selected Poems*, and, most recently, *Love in All Its Disguises*.

JERRY RUBIN: Co-organizer of the 1968 march on the Pentagon after becoming widely known in the Berkeley antiwar movement. Cofounder of the Yippie movement and a "Chicago Seven" defendant, he is also the author of *Do It!* and *Growing (Up) at 37*. Later a venture banker on Wall Street, he pioneered the concept of "networking" to bring together professional men and women in social settings, which has led to his present project, a restaurant-type salon in midtown New York City where "financial and creative energies can gather."

LAWRENCE SCHILLER: Photographer and book producer (*Marilyn* and *Faith of Graffiti*), he is also a film producer and director whose works include *The Man Who Skied Down Everest, Marilyn*, and *The Executioner's Song*.

ARTHUR SCHLESINGER, JR.: Historian, political theorist, writer, and critic. Former adviser to John F. Kennedy, he is now the Albert Schweitzer Professor of the Humanities at the City University of New York Graduate Center. His books include *The Age of*

Jackson, The Imperial Presidency, A Thousand Days: John F. Kennedy in the White House, and *Robert F. Kennedy and His Times.*

LIZ SMITH, syndicated columnist, New York *Daily News,* also makes regular appearances on the NBC-TV news hour *Live at Five.* A native Texan, she can be counted on for finding both the hottest items and the spiciest ribs in Gotham.

BARBARA PROBST SOLOMON: Novelist and journalist whose books include *Short Flights, Arriving Where We Started,* and *The Beat of Life.* Her essays on political and cultural topics have appeared in leading American and European periodicals, including *The New York Times, The New Republic,* and *The New York Review of Books.* She divides her time between New York City and Europe and is now at work on a novel.

JEAN STEIN: After her interview with William Faulkner appeared in *The Paris Review* in 1956, her extended interviews with artists, writers, and prominent personalities, published in numerous magazines, have set the standard for cultural histories. Most notably, she perfected this form in *Edie: An American Biography,* which she completed in 1982 with George Plimpton. Her previous book was *An American Journey: The Time of Robert F. Kennedy,* also with George Plimpton.

SOL STEIN: Novelist, playwright, publisher and editor; in 1957 one of ten founding members of the Playwrights Group of the Actors Studio. He is the author of a number of novels, including *The Magician, Living Room, The Childkeeper, Other People,* and *The Resort.* He is the founder of the publishing firm Stein and Day.

GLORIA STEINEM, the leading feminist spokesperson, writer, journalist, and activist, was a cofounding editor of *Ms.* Her first book, *Outrageous Acts and Everyday Rebellions,* was published in 1983.

WILLIAM SYLVIA: Patrolman (retired), Provincetown Police Department, a.k.a. "Cobra."

JERRY TALLMER, cofounder with Ed Fancher, Norman Mailer, and Dan Wolf of *The Village Voice,* was not only its associate editor from 1955 to 1962 but, as its drama critic, originated the Off-Broadway Obie Awards. He is currently with the *New York Post,* where he writes on the cultural scene.

SIDNEY TEITELL, originally from New York, was assigned to the same barracks as Mailer during the course of basic training at Fort Bragg, North Carolina. At present he lives in New Jersey.

SANDY CHARLEBOIS THOMAS: Mailer's secretary from 1966 to 1970, she now runs a business and secretarial service in Stowe, Vermont. "Having had it with the New York hassle," she says, "I moved to the country and found a replacement for Norman Mailer: God."

RIP TORN: Civil rights activist, stage, film, and television actor best known for his roles in *Sweet Bird of Youth* and *Tropic of Cancer.* He played Marion Faye in the 1967 New York production of *The Deer Park* and also appeared in Mailer's film *Maidstone.* In 1984 he was nominated as the Academy Awards' Best Supporting Actor for his performance in *Cross Creek.*

JOSE TORRES, the former light-heavyweight boxing champion of the world, is now a columnist for *El Diario-La Prensa* in New York City, contributing editor of *Penthouse,* and the Commissioner, New York State Athletic Commission.

DIANA TRILLING has been fiction critic for *The Nation* and columnist for *The New Leader* and has contributed numerous articles to such magazines as *Partisan Review, Commentary, Harper's, Atlantic, Redbook, McCall's, The New York Times Book Review,* and *Vanity Fair.* The editor of the *Viking Portable D. H. Lawrence, The Selected Letters of D. H. Lawrence,* and the *Uniform Edition of the Works of Lionel Trilling,* she has received a Guggenheim Fellowship and a Rockefeller National Endowment for the Humanities grant and is a fellow of the American Academy of Arts and Sciences. Her books include *Claremont Essays, We Must March My Darlings, Reviewing the Forties,* and the best-selling *Mrs. Harris: The Death of the Scarsdale Diet Doctor.* She is now writing her memoirs.

KURT VONNEGUT's most well-known books include *Player Piano, Cat's Cradle, God Bless You, Mr. Rosewater, Slaughterhouse Five,* and, most recently, *Dead Eye Dick.* With his wife, the photographer Jill Krementz, he divides his time between Manhattan and the Hamptons.

BILL WARD: Editor, the *Provincetown Review,* 1959–68. He is currently education officer in the New York City Board of Education.

ANDY WARHOL: Pop artist, filmmaker, author, and magazine publisher. He has received the Film Culture Award and the Los Angeles Film Festival Award. He produced the rock group Velvet Underground, is well known for his experiments in filmmaking, and now publishes *Interview* magazine. His books include *From A to B and Back Again, Popism: The Warhol '60's,* and *Andy Warhol's Exposures.*

ALBERT "AL" WASSERMAN has been a producer, director, and writer for NBC News and president of Wasserman Productions, Inc., writer and director for NBC White Paper programs and for *The Search,* CBS public affairs series. His work has won numerous awards, including two Lasker medical journalism awards, the Sylvania TV award, the Robert Flaherty film award, an Academy Award, and a Peabody Award. Now a producer for CBS News *60 Minutes,* he has been married to Barbara Mailer since 1968.

BARBARA MAILER WASSERMAN, writer and editor, is the younger sister of Norman Mailer. A graduate of Radcliffe, class of '48, she edited the anthology of women's writing, *The Bold New Women.* She and her husband, Al Wasserman, make their home in Greenwich Village.

RICHARD WEINBERG is the owner of Rix Stores, a Boston area pharmacy chain. Harvard, class of '43.

SHELLEY WINTERS made her Broadway debut in 1941 and was brought to Hollywood by Columbia in 1943. Nominated for an Oscar for her role in *A Place in the Sun* in 1951, she has won Oscars as Best Supporting Actress for *The Diary of Anne Frank* and *A Patch of Blue.* She was nominated in the same category for *The Poseidon Adventure* and has since appeared in numerous films as well as stage productions.

RHODA LAZARE WOLF: "I wish to be identified," she says, "only as a close friend of Barbara Mailer."

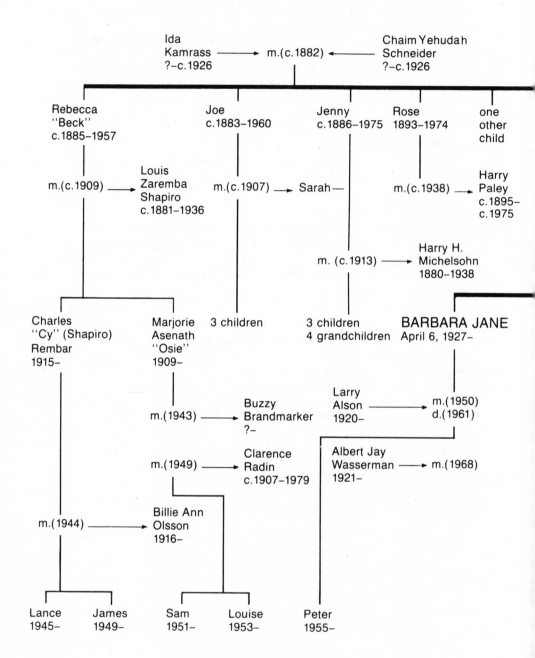

MAILER FAMILY TREE

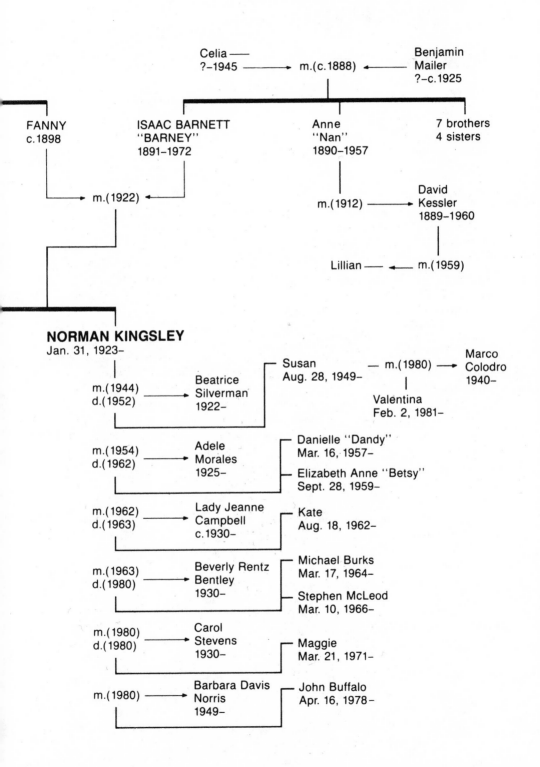

Celia —— ?–1945 —→ m.(c.1888) ←— Benjamin Mailer ?–c.1925

FANNY c.1898

ISAAC BARNETT "BARNEY" 1891–1972

Anne "Nan" 1890–1957

7 brothers 4 sisters

m.(1922) ←

m.(1912) —→ David Kessler 1889–1960

Lillian —— ←— m.(1959)

NORMAN KINGSLEY Jan. 31, 1923–

m.(1944) d.(1952) —→ Beatrice Silverman 1922–

Susan Aug. 28, 1949– — m.(1980) —→ Marco Colodro 1940–

Valentina Feb. 2, 1981–

m.(1954) d.(1962) —→ Adele Morales 1925–

Danielle "Dandy" Mar. 16, 1957–

Elizabeth Anne "Betsy" Sept. 28, 1959–

m.(1962) d.(1963) —→ Lady Jeanne Campbell c.1930–

Kate Aug. 18, 1962–

m.(1963) d.(1980) —→ Beverly Rentz Bentley 1930–

Michael Burks Mar. 17, 1964–

Stephen McLeod Mar. 10, 1966–

m.(1980) d.(1980) —→ Carol Stevens 1930–

Maggie Mar. 21, 1971–

m.(1980) —→ Barbara Davis Norris 1949–

John Buffalo Apr. 16, 1978–

AFTERWORD:

Alas, Poor Norman (1985–2007)

It came out a week before the publication of *The Castle in the Forest*, a three-page article in *New York* magazine titled, "Mr. Tendentious: Norman Mailer has a Bone to Pick. With you. And you. And. . . ." The article began with the observation that "whenever Mailer puts out a new book . . . eager profilists find it compulsory to mention that the famous pugilist has 'mellowed.' It's hard to dispute, given his two canes and near blindness," the story went on, "but if the reviews for *Castle* are bad (and the buzz ain't good), don't be surprised if the old lion roars yet again . . . Below, a necessarily much-abbreviated dossier, Mailer's All-Time Enemies List."

There followed the names of novelists William Styron and Truman Capote; Mailer's second wife, Adele Morales Mailer; Lyndon Johnson's national security adviser McGeorge Bundy; and then, there, splat among them in the number five spot, yours truly, Peter Manso. Germaine Greer, Kate Millett, Gore Vidal, and *New York Times* book reviewer Michiko Kakutani all followed.

Each entry was formatted in the same way, and in my case the text read:

> **Crime:** Writing a biography of Mailer in 1985 that, despite being authorized, was not to Mailer's liking.
>
> **Action taken:** Cut off relations when the bio was published and thereafter referred to him as a confirmed enemy.
>
> **Blowback:** In a 2002 book about Provincetown, Manso wrote—among many unflattering things—that Mailer had a doctor's wife procure psychedelic drugs for him. Mailer fired off a letter to a local paper asserting that "P. D. Manso is looking for gold in the desert of his arid inner life, where lies and distortions are the only cactus juice to keep him going."[1]

Perhaps my editors missed this piece, or just did not deem it relevant since the decision to reissue the biography had been made months before. But with the decision to republish *Mailer: His Life and Times*, they asked for an afterword that would carry Mailer's life forward from where I'd left it in 1985. I was forced to explain that I no longer had access to Norman's world. By that I didn't mean I was now an outsider so much as an apostate in relation to the Mailer family and many of their friends, even though Norman and I had jointly owned a house in Provincetown for almost three years; that I had comanaged his 1969 New York City mayoral campaign;[2] had been instrumental in getting him financing for the movie version of *Tough Guys Don't Dance*; and had also introduced him to his future financial angel Roy Cohn[3] who later factored Mailer's contract at Random House, which is still in effect today.

In a word, I'd been Norman's protégé and pal for more than three decades, as well as his housemate and authorized biographer.[4] But now I was on the outs and could not deliver the fresh material my publisher wanted. What to do?

The *New York* magazine piece was right on with most of its details; wrong on several others. My Provincetown book, *Ptown: Art, Sex, and Money on the Outer Cape*,[5] was not nearly as unflattering as suggested: among other things I asserted that Mailer had made the town "as mellow as Jell-O" by standing up to the local bully-boy cops in the early '60s, plus I couldn't (and still don't) see that saying that someone is using psychedelics is nearly as damaging as the chemicals themselves. The real issue was that my problem with Norman, and his with me, was far more complex than could be explained in a short magazine piece, revolving, as it did, as much around our communal house[6] and the interaction of our families as around my book. The problem was not my biography, *per se*, or my Ptown book, at least not in any straightforward, literal sense.

Norman, of course, never made any of this clear; on the contrary, publicly he'd tried to hide our true connection as much as possible by asserting I'd double-crossed him in my role as biographer. This, like so much else that came out of Norman Mailer's mouth during his later years, was a calculated lie that ultimately pointed more to Norman and what had happened to his career—not to say his sense of moral balance—than to anything about me, as can and will be demonstrated shortly.

But first let us turn to the letter he "fired off to a local paper" on which *New York* magazine's description of our floundering relationship was based. Mailer's nasty little screed appeared in the *Provincetown Banner* on May 16, 2002, more than seventeen years after publication of *Mailer: His Life and Times*. The time lag here is of central importance, and the letter must be quoted in full for its artful slurring of past and present:

> Some years ago, when Peter Manso did his oral biography on me, I heard countless complaints from the people he interviewed once the book came out. He had put all kinds of words and speeches into their mouths they never uttered. When I asked Manso to see the transcripts, he refused.
>
> I will now state that every remark or action he has attributed to me that I have read about in the *New York Post* and in Sue Harrison's review of his latest book in *The Banner* (May 9) is wholly and totally untrue. For example, I have never called any woman ever a "cancer-hole." I must say, however, that Manso is psychic if somewhat skewed, for as I came to know him well, that

became my private term for him. I do not know if that is accurate. A label closer to the vein might be "poison drip."

I have my faults, my vices and my unattractive side, but P. D. Manso is looking for gold in the desert of his arid inner life, where lies and distortions are the only cactus juice to keep him going.[7]

Perhaps I should say that I, too, have my faults—my vices and unattractive side—but backstabbing is not among them. My arrangement with Norman was from the outset that in exchange for access, I would allow him to review the manuscript before I turned it in to the publisher. As things turned out, he reviewed two drafts of the book, not one.[8] Each of these he covered with his marginalia that, collectively, runs ten or fifteen thousand words or more. Why so much commentary, aside from Norman's well-known tendency toward long-windedness? Because in addition to his "right of review for accuracy," I'd vouchsafed that if there was material in the manuscript that he found offensive or repellent, the removal or alteration of which would not upset the book's structure or alter meaning, I'd be willing to discuss making changes; hence, laying the foundation for later demands.

Let me acknowledge right off that the idea was to accommodate him, a gesture for which I feel no need to apologize. This was not an unreasonable approach for a biographer lucky enough to have the cooperation of a subject like Mailer, not to mention the help of the many luminous figures who agreed to be interviewed on Norman's say-so. But if this quid pro quo was mandated by a professionalism on my part, there was also my personal relationship with Mailer to reckon with—which was no simple thing. Our first contact had been when I went to him as a snot-nosed teenager seeking advice on "being a writer." That was the summer after my second year of college, and I distinctly recall donning a certain hat-in-hand attitude, which I now look back on with some chagrin since it later came back to haunt me at the time of our breakup. My enthusiasm was real enough, though, to stay with me through grad school and beyond, since I was to mix in Norman's life through four of his six marriages, beginning with Adele. I wrote position papers for his New York mayoral campaign, and then edited the book *Running Against the Machine*[9] in 1969, at which time he was still married to Beverly Bentley. It was in the fall of 1983, after he'd segued to Norris Church following his brief marriage to wife number five, Carol Stevens, that we purchased the Ptown house and lived *en famille*—Mailer, his wife Norris, and a fluctuating number of children, along with me and my partner, Ellen Hawkes, for two long summers that seemed more like six. The summer before the house purchase, we'd been together, too, although on a more reduced basis: I provided Norman with a spare workroom in the place Ellen and I were renting, since his own rental, a block or two up the street, was overflowing with his kids, making it impossible for him to work there. That was the summer of Jack Abbott, it should be noted, and to have Norman around was to field the many collect calls from Jack, who was then on the run, fleeing the murder charges that eventually brought the cops to my door. As luck would have it, Norman was off in New York doing his mea culpa with Dick Cavett on TV when the cops showed up, and I was the one taken downtown to deal with the FBI.

The living situation at 627 Commercial Street in Provincetown was to prove problematic, indeed terminal for our relationship. But going in on the deal, I'd refused to accept even the possibility of a bad outcome. How else to put it? Given Mailer's stature as a literary figure, the potential of our sharing a house was hugely attractive, in fact irresistibly Boswellian. Norman was my mentor, my godhead, really, and I was going to get "up close" and produce a book unlike any other—more thorough, more intimate and smarter than Hotchner; more authoritative than Carlos Baker. And by embracing the oral biography format, I sought to remove myself from the narrative and ensure objectivity,[10] plus avoid any problems with my housemate-subject. Besides, the plan was to divide the house within the first year, then live side by side in our separate units, which struck me as eminently sensible. In the interim, we'd make do. We'd share the kitchen and other common areas of the 6,000-square-foot waterfront manse, each of us would have his individual bedroom and private bath, and we'd even agreed to buy two refrigerators—originally Norman's idea since he foresaw, as I did not, the wildly ravenous appetites of his teenage sons.

Many people would have run the other way, but not me. Not even in the face of dire warnings from my partner, Ellen, whose track record for common sense was always far better than my own. We moved in during late April or early May 1984, by which time it was clear that the condoing process, involving surveys, permits, and all sorts of municipal filings, was going to take us into the next year. And then, by the time Norman arrived on the Cape several weeks after Ellen and me, he had got it into his head that his particular karma in this process was to play architect, which led to his setting up a drafting table in the middle of our communal living room and talking about his days as an aeronautical engineering student at Harvard. He needed, he claimed, a view of the bay to dope out "the stresses." He needed access to the deck in order to go outside and look upward to "conceptualize in three dimensions." And rather than do any substantive writing work, he began to churn out a series of renderings for what the final, renovated structure was supposed to look like. One concept had a flat roof; another, a series of high-peaked, barnlike dormers. The most overstated, baroque version was his Russian dacha—there on Provincetown's beachfront, not two miles from the pilgrims' original landing spot, a structure that would have made Yuri Andropov or, better, Tolstoy, feel completely at home. Where had this cockamamy idea come from? Earlier that spring Norman had gone to the Soviet Union on a magazine assignment, and when he got back, all he could talk about was Russia—Russian writers; Lee Harvey Oswald in Russia with his Russian wife, Marina; borscht even; as well as his own Russian-Jewish background. And of course architecture.[11]

In the meantime, as the condo process inched forward in millimeter-like increments, we all managed somehow to coexist in the large house that suddenly was no longer so large. We ate dinner together, sometimes breakfast and lunch, too; shared the *New York Times*, which we passed around the table section by section; and we talked endlessly. Seated at the dinner table would usually be Mailer's kids, six or seven in number, from all his marriages, plus Matthew, Norris's son from her first marriage. Norman's mother was with us, too. She was then in her eighties, not well, and had started conversing out loud with her sister Rose, who'd been dead for ten years. There was also Norman's sister Barbara and her husband, Al Wasserman, a surprisingly tranquil man amidst our high-strung menagerie, and occasional guests like Dick and Doris Kearns Goodwin and, once or twice, Pat Kennedy Lawford, whom the ever gallant Norman treated like royalty. We were also joined now and then by the third entity of our little community, Roy Cohn, who, with several of his bronzed young New York staffers, was renting our garage that had been turned into a two-bedroom beach cottage not fifty feet from the main house.

This was, of course, *the* Roy Cohn, the man who'd helped execute the Rosenbergs and put Dashiell Hammett away in federal prison while working as special counsel to Sen. Joseph McCarthy. Mailer and Cohn yammering away at each other was something to behold, since Roy was easily Norman's equal as a talker.[12] He was also, I became convinced, a true psychopath, which made things all the more interesting. Originally, I'd balked at having him join our little real estate venture, even though I was responsible for introducing him to Mailer in the first place, but Norman had other plans, as became evident when Cohn telephoned from New York several weeks before our scheduled closing, saying he'd "fixed things" by getting his buddy Si Newhouse, the publishing magnate, to put up a $300,000 interest-free loan for "all of us." I had to tell Mailer this, I couldn't just bury it, and Norman's response when I relayed the information was to say, and I quote with total recall, "It's about time I had a patron."

It was surely one of the most grandiose lines of all time— ". . . *about time I had a patron.*" And it was no mere throwaway; he meant it. Several days after Roy's call, a check with all the requisite zeroes arrived via FedEx, followed by a momentary frisson when Norman didn't want to collateralize his share of the loan with his Brooklyn Heights apartment. But Cohn fixed that, too, and, *shazzam*, Roy Marcus Cohn, Esq., he of the Blacklist, Reagan supporter and consigliere to the Gambino crime family, was attached to our project. Later, when our in-house barrister succumbed to AIDS, Norman and Norris would be compelled to sell the cottage to Roy's lover,[13] although by then I was gone. Good riddance.

But to return: in connection with the biography, the understanding was that Norman had "right of review for accuracy," just as his only restriction on me was that I was not to interview his children, although with all of us under the same roof there was no way he could separate me from the kids' daily chatter, harmless or otherwise.

But there was no need to. Over the three years it took me to finish the book, he came through near 100 percent, as did I. Routinely, in New York and up on the Cape, I was keeping him abreast of my progress, and whenever I needed something—a date, an anecdote, a detail to fill a hole in someone's story or to provide context—I'd call and usually he'd make himself available. He'd okay me to people like Lillian Hellman, who ordinarily would have hung up if I cold-called her.[14] The first of four times I interviewed his mother, Norman walked me over to

Mrs. Mailer's apartment on Pierpoint Street and prompted her to talk after a lifetime of telling her never to speak to reporters. Another gift, though one we'd planned on from the start, after I was done interviewing most of my "witnesses," he sat still for what had to be twenty hours of talking into my tape recorder, then went through my two typescripts, making his detailed written comments.

At the very end, when we sat down shoulder to shoulder for our bartering session, most of the time he got his way, and when he didn't, he knew why. The text that emerged was word-for-word the text that was printed. Michael Korda, my editor, made no changes whatsoever except to cut one overlong quote from Norman's early novella, "A Calculus at Heaven." Otherwise, the manuscript received only copyediting—commas, periods, that sort of thing.

Nevertheless, seventeen years later Norman claimed I double-crossed him, and his letter to the *Provincetown Banner* revealed what had evolved as the new Mailer, not to say how this new Norman Mailer fit into the new Provincetown where he and Norris had moved permanently in 1995. At the time, *Ptown: Art, Sex, and Money on the Outer Cape* was several months from release but nonetheless being circulated around town in the form of hot Xerox copies that had been made from a galley the publishers had sent to a local arts magazine for review purposes. The reason for this *samizdat*-like stealth was that the book was saying out loud what others had dared only to whisper—that the nation's most legendary arts colony had been taken over by increasingly wealthy "separatist" gays who, for the most part, cared more about real estate than abstract expressionism. The traditional Portuguese fishing community was gone; likewise, the young poets and painters, forced out by the runaway housing costs. And so dire was the situation that a number of old-guard lesbians I'd known for years had started to complain that even they were being squeezed by the new majority that was succeeding where the puritans failed; namely, in homogenizing a town long famous for its unabashed diversity.

Norman, who had first fallen in love with Provincetown while still an undergraduate, had been talking about these changes ever since the mid-1980s, which was when the new guppyization, as we came to call it, first took hold. In 2002, though, he was in another place. Publicly, he had joined the new majority, which was not a silent majority at all. PCism was the new lingua franca, most noticeable in the tendency to *carp, carp, carp* about persecution and slander, and Norman chose to echo this new idiom, indignant years later over an anecdote in my book where someone claimed he'd used the term "cancer-hole" to describe a member of the opposite sex. Another problem was my suggestion that he'd once used drugs (God forbid!), but his protest was ridiculous, referring, as it did, to things that took place during the late 1950s and early 1960s, that period when he stabbed Adele, and most people, including his own sister, thought he was having a paranoid breakdown and could have said *anything*.

But his protest rang hollow for another reason: it was designed, pointedly, to please the new Queen of Provincetown, a fiftyish woman by the name of Alix Ritchie who was reputed to be worth 200 to 300 million dollars. Since arriving on the Cape, Ritchie had coopted almost every important cultural institution in town, from the local newspaper, *Provincetown Banner*, which had published Norman's letter, to the Provincetown Art Association and Museum, the Fine Arts Work Center, Provincetown International Film Festival, Provincetown Repertory Theater and Seamens' Bank, just as she supported the Provincetown Business Guild, our local gay chamber of commerce. Ritchie and her partner, a younger woman "artist," sat on the governing boards of practically all these groups, thanks largely to Alix's relentless networking, plus her frequent contributions that, reportedly, ran to $500,000 and more.

For Norman, who had always gravitated toward money and power, an alliance with Ritchie was inevitable, but there was also a more immediate connection. Norris, fifty-three, had been undergoing chemo almost since the couple had started living full-time on the Cape. She was still active, even if she'd been driven to wearing a wig and her prognosis was uncertain, and the well-connected Ritchie had helped get her appointed interim artistic director at the Ptown Rep Theater, a position that promised to keep her out of the house as well as fend off depression.

Thus, a bond had been forged. At the same time, only the month before Norman's letter appeared, Ritchie had mounted a campaign to discredit my Ptown book—a holy war, as it were, to defend the town's new gay majority against what she took to be slander. The real engine of her wrath, though, was that I had written, quite accurately, that despite her great wealth, Ritchie herself was "without a past that qualified [her] as bohemian, artist, or intellectual," meaning that, despite her local power grab, she had no understanding of the traditionally hardscrabble, often bellicose, and wildly eccentric qualities of our genius-filled Provincetown. And in response she branded me homophobic, confusing the issue completely. She billed herself as a progressive, of course; Ritchie had financed the new *Ms.* magazine in New York, contributed heavily to liberal candidates, and counted Gloria Steinem among her friends—yet despite her forward-thinking persona, she tried to have her attorney pressure Simon and Schuster into canceling my book.[15]

Disturbing as this was, it went further. Her publication of Mailer's "poison drip" letter served, as it was intended, to sanction what evolved into an ongoing Ritchie-organized telephone campaign designed to pressure my sources into claiming— you guessed it!—that my about-to-be-released book falsified what they'd said in our interviews. And amazingly, a number of people went along with it. One local, a bearded doctor who had treated my family for more than thirty years, and whose own father was, reportedly, a veteran of the Abraham Lincoln Brigade, stated in his own letter to the *Banner* that not only had he been misquoted but I'd gotten him drunk during our interview. Another of my sources threatened legal action if her quotes weren't excised from my text. The editor of the local arts magazine canceled his scheduled excerpt of *Ptown*, claiming that my material hadn't been cut to his exacting standards, even though *Vanity Fair* had had no problem serializing my previous two books.

Even the Provincetown Fine Arts Work Center joined in and banned me from their premises, as did the Provincetown Art Association, which canceled my scheduled reading and kicked me off a panel on the topic of "Censorship and the

Arts" that had been planned ten months earlier, with me as the chair. The two local bookstores, which were also pressured, might have caved in and refused to carry my book were it not that *Ptown: Art, Sex, and Money on the Outer Cape* debuted on the *Boston Globe* bestseller list in the number two spot, quickly rose to number one, and stayed on the list that whole summer. Money, it goes without saying, overcomes all.

New York magazine missed all this since Provincetown's new elite had not exactly put its new McCarthyism out on the national wire any more than Norman acknowledged the true facts of our relationship. What he had not wanted known in particular was that a major element of his resentment stemmed from our communal living situation of two decades earlier, which was by no means simple. Here, our problems had peaked during our second summer. There were a hundred little issues, some insignificant, some not. The crowning event took place in early June when my partner Ellen's two declawed house cats were let out of the house by Norman's son Stephen, then nineteen, who'd been having a hard time of it emotionally all spring because of his parents' vitriolic divorce, or rather, how the publication of my biography had, regrettably, reawakened his mother's pain. This was a deliberate act of cruelty on Steve's part, as he later acknowledged,[16] and it led to a confrontation between Norman and Ellen from which there was no pulling back. I was out of town at the time and things were certainly not helped by the fact that Ellen had been stewing all winter over the increasingly high-handed way Norman had been making it plain that he regarded the house as his and Norris's, not all of ours jointly. With the cats' disappearance and recovery, Ellen had a heart-to-heart with Steve that left them both in tears, then she went downstairs to get herself a drink. In the living room, which was located directly under our bedroom, where she'd bawled out Steve, she found Norman glaring at her. He was "white-faced," she later told me, and right off he barked at her, "You don't call my son an asshole!"

"I'll call him whatever I want when he pulls a stunt like that!" she replied.

"Don't you know that you could destroy him forever? How old are you? You don't have kids so you care more about your damn animals than my son's life!"

On and on he went about "teen suicides" until finally Ellen, who was only three weeks from deadline on the book she was writing, replied, "Oh, Norman, why don't you stuff it?"

"Where would you like me to stuff it?" he sneered.

Knowing full well that the writer who loved obscenities would find the word *asshole* offensive when applied to himself or to one of his sons, she now said, "Since you've been walking around here talking about your farting all the time, I'm sure you can figure out where to stuff it."

The reference to farting and to Norman's habit of talking about same had a basis in fact, most surely, and this so outraged the father of nine that he started all over again about why should his kids be expected to watch out for Ellen's cats, let alone be quiet all the time? Here, he was referring to our complaints over being awakened at one and two in the morning when Mike or Steve would get in from the bars, or when they'd be whooping it up out on the deck while we'd be trying to work. "You and Peter expect this to be something out of *Brideshead Revisited!*" he yelled.

"No, Norman," she replied. "I'm just tired of coming down to the kitchen every morning and finding gridlock with all the dishes stacked in the sink, or finding wet bathing suits and towels all over the living room and stairway. I put up with it last summer but I don't intend to anymore."

"You'll put up with me and my kids in exchange for the privilege of living in my house."

"*Privilege? Your* house? We'll see about that. Paying half the mortgage and half the expenses hardly makes it *your* house!"

Early the next morning, from upstairs in our bedroom she could hear a hungover Norman holding forth to his two sons about how the house was *his* house — he paid all the bills and he wasn't going to let this hysterical bitch yell at them. She also heard him going on about how the house wasn't "good for women," because when he and fifth wife Carol had rented the place years before during his split from Beverly, Carol would "get hysterical, too."

When Ellen descended, lugging file boxes out to her waiting car, she found two empty bottles of Irish whiskey in the barroom. Norman, nursing a cup of coffee in the nearby kitchen, wheeled around and glared at her once more, his eyes redrimmed. Nothing was said. Ellen simply turned and left.

"I felt driven from the house," she later explained. "We'd entered into this arrangement with the understanding that we'd go through one summer *en famille* and then the house would be divided . . . The first summer was hard enough, with all the compromises and concessions made from our side. When Norman arrived in the spring of '85, it was obvious — and so stated — that he was both furious about Peter's book and quite ready to treat Peter and me like shit. With his two sons there with him, he was playing king of the hill."

In retrospect, it became clear that it had taken me far too long to realize that my pal was not my pal at all. The situation may not have been that bad the first summer, but I'd been too caught up in my little project to say anything. Now, once I got back from my out-of-town trip, Norman attempted to apologize the only way he knew how, which was with a series of ifs, ands, buts, and on-the-other-hands, just like Steve had tried to use to justify letting the cats out, telling Ellen his mother was going through a breakdown. Here, I told Norman his bullshit wasn't good enough and followed my partner out the door to a friend's at the other end of town, where Ellen, against all odds, managed to get her book out on time.

Several weeks later I was compelled to return to 627 to pick up some papers, and Norman and I had our final confrontation. Earlier that same day "Page Six" of the *New York Post* had quoted me as saying that life with the Mailers had turned out to be a nightmare — "a circus, a lunatic asylum," is how I put it, I recall, and having taken in my comments, Norman was furious. He stopped me at the bottom of the stairs as I was on my way down from the attic where we had our work areas. He had his chin tucked in, his teeth clenched, and he was glaring at me from less than a foot away, standing with feet spread, shoulders set.

"It is what it is, Norman," I said almost matter-of-factly in answer to his demand I explain my "disloyalty." "It's as simple as that, no more, no less."

I was in no mood to compromise and was staring back at him, resolved not to look away. His face had lost all color, gone that same deathly white he'd used on Ellen, and it occurred to me that he might try to throw a punch.

"You're too small to squash!" he hissed.

It was laughable but I didn't laugh. "Go ahead, Norman. Take your best shot," I said. "Do whatever you want. I just *do not care.*"

He began to sway slightly as if he was becoming light-headed. I could feel his breath on me, he was that close. But it made no difference.

"You know, Norman," I said, "they would've put you in the booby hatch years ago if you didn't have your family-support apparatus."

That ended it. I turned and walked past him, and we never talked again except to settle up on the house and after that to grunt at each other once at an embassy party in New York and to stare across the small lobby at the Provincetown airport. I think he may have been more uncomfortable than I was, although there was more behind his "poison drip" letter than either the blowup with Ellen or his need to please Norris, who, I decided, had wanted the whole house for herself as soon as we'd all moved in.

There were several things, in fact. One was Norman and his son Michael, or rather Michael and me, for there had been a strange, undeclared contest on his part for Mike's attention. First after Mike had turned to me, not to his father, for advice when he got jammed up with a girlfriend, then again when Mike went down to Connecticut one weekend to watch me drive a race car at Lime Rock, and again when he accompanied me to a book signing for *Mailer: His Life and Times.* It was foolish. Michael was his son, not mine. But Norman had to compete for something every day of his life and in this case he may have felt he was losing authority, perhaps on the back of the problems he'd been having with Steve. Was it guilt? Jealousy? Or just the usual Normaniac competitiveness? I do not know. Whatever it was, it was there. Constantly. As Ellen observed, Norman used the boys as his sounding board, his built-in audience or applause meter, and it was certainly telling that later he was to haul in Mike to bear witness at our final settlement session on the house.

The other element was Norris's appetite, or rather my response to it. This was a woman from the sticks who had forty or fifty sweaters stacked in her closet and multiple vials of cosmetics, perfumes, and emollients in every part of the house. Not a day went by when there wasn't a FedEx or UPS delivery from Saks, Nordstrom, or Williams-Sonoma, or wherever, since she was, without question, the consummate shopper. She was also the supposedly dedicated painter who would use roll after roll of double-ply Bounty to clean her brushes instead of reusable rags as did the many professional artists, including my father, I'd known all my life—which I saw as emblematic of the same self-indulgence that lay behind her desire not to split up the house.

But first and foremost there was the book, no question. Before the project got under way, Norman had warned me that in the end he might respond to the bio the same way aborigines are said to respond to having their photo taken—with a sense of having been violated, as if the process had robbed him of his soul. Was this just hocus-pocus on his part, another way to give himself the edge so later on he could say, "I told you so"? I do not know, just as I do not know that Norman ever really believed all the quasi-spiritualistic nonsense he spouted, whether in print or to dumb TV interviewers too timid to challenge him. It doesn't matter, though. At the start I had rejected the idea that the book would create problems, relying on the idea that fairness, simple equity, and intelligence would keep us both on an even keel.

The first thing Norman did after the bio was published was to plunk himself down at our dining room table to go through the stack of reviews the publisher's clipping service had sent up to Provincetown. For an hour or more he sat there soberly going through the clips, a number of them the lead reviews of the Sunday book sections from major newspapers across the country—Dallas, LA, Boston, Philadelphia, Chicago, and so forth. He was the picture of concentration here—pursing his lips, shaking his head, tapping a finger against the tabletop—and it was soon evident that it didn't matter to him that Rhoda Koenig of *New York* magazine, for example, had wound up her review by affectionately calling him "nice but meshugge," or that my book was being treated as the life of a major writer, if not *the* major writer, of his generation. What mattered was that his mother, wives, and friends had all talked about him publicly, "fixed" him, as it were, and this was something altogether major, since for so much of his life he'd come to rely on masks as his way of dealing with reality. "I became an actor, a quick-change artist," he'd told us in *Advertisements for Myself*, "as if I can trap the Prince of Truth in the act of switching a style." Now anyone with twenty bucks for a copy of *Mailer: His Life and Times* would have a handle on when he wasn't performing in the interests of "trapping the Truth" so much as being the Prince, pure and simple.

As Saul Bellow observed, one of my hero's darkest secrets was that a large part of him belonged more to the performing arts than to literature. What Bellow, and also Gore Vidal, who first brought the Bellow comment to my attention,[17] did *not* know was that Norman wrestled with this endlessly, perhaps because he never believed that his writing could stand on its own. Or perhaps he fundamentally misunderstood people like Camus, Sartre, and Malroux, not to say Hemingway, who never had the luxury of confusing art and "action," faced, as they were, with Nazi SS in the streets of Paris or Falangist firing squads in Spain. Maybe he just knew more than the rest of us about the new age of TV, who knows? Whatever it was, being stripped of his masks was a major threat to him, since artifice, which is the wealthy cousin to lying, had long been his survival kit. Anyone who doubts this would do well to consider Norris's feelings hard upon her famous husband's death when a mistress nobody had ever heard about (except me and, I'm sure, Buzz Far-bar) appeared out of the woodwork to announce she was selling to Harvard her diary that detailed how Norm the changeling performed in bed and had had her stashed on the side, starting in the early 1980s, for a dozen years or more.[18]

How though, two decades later, to turn his penchant for secrecy into the lie that I made up quotes was another matter. We settled up on the house at the end of the summer, 1985, and I vowed to move on. That fall, back in New York, I began to hear from people like Arthur Penn, Sondra Lee, Frank Corsaro, and others at the Actors Studio that Norman and Norris were working a tag-team routine, going around the Studio, urging people not to cooperate with me for my new biography of Marlon Brando.

His performance in New York was relatively benign in comparison with what he did later because the *Banner* letter, being an item in print, could be picked up online and easily reused by any reporter looking to juice his story, which is exactly what happened with the release of *Ptown*. Another element that was new was the charge that I'd refused to show him "the transcript," an accusation after the fact so patently fabricated as to suggest that now he meant business, as if he'd dug in his heels and was blind to the consequences, since he was leaving himself wide open to a lawsuit.

The notion that Mailer of all people would take the time to review 35,000 pages of transcript filled with all the *ahs* and *uhms* and other detritus of spoken speech, or even spot-check such material, was preposterous. His impatience with clerical stuff was legend. But even had he been so moved to exert himself, his considerable strategic or lawyerly intelligence would have told him this was a waste of time and that he had to listen to the tapes instead, for if I was under suspicion for altering quotes in my manuscript, who's to say I hadn't altered the typed transcripts, too? The audiotapes, not the transcripts, were the only way to be sure.

The truth was—and I have to repeat this if only because Norman was right to calculate that his "poison drip" tag was going to hurt me for a good long time to come—that he never asked me to produce the transcript, or the tapes, either. Starting in late winter 1983, he read the first of my two manuscripts, the semifinished version that lacked an ending, then six months later reviewed and commented on the final draft, which he signed off on in June. Leave aside the fact that his marginalia shows I didn't hold out on him, his comments put him in the rather incongruous position of being my accomplice if, as charged, I really "put all kinds of words and speeches into [people's] mouths," since they are *prima facie* evidence he approved of the text from which Simon and Schuster set type.

Now there are two kinds of premeditated duplicity, commonly known in the church as *lies of commission* and *lies of omission*. The first involves advancing a false or misleading account of events. The second, which is usually more complex, means that somebody is trying to obscure or bury something that *is* true, sometimes by destroying documents or other evidence, or by defaming the person who knows the truth and poses a threat to the liar. What Mailer was doing was an amalgam of both, but principally he was smearing me in order to nullify me, since a nonfiction writer being perceived as dishonest can be fatal: if the characterization sticks, the writer's readers will never again be able to believe in his work; his publishers may decide not to publish him again (which may encourage his agent to dump him, as well); and, most damaging, if he manages to continue in his profession, his all-important sources will almost certainly flee every time the journalist approaches, tape recorder or notebook in hand.

All of this, I have no doubt, is exactly what he had in mind when he sought to capitalize on the controversy swirling around my Ptown book. But rather than continue to talk *around* the problem, let us consider his charge as if this were a court of law. Defense Exhibit 1 will be the notes of support I received from members of the Mailer family. Sister Barbara Wasserman, ex-brother-in-law Larry Alson, several ex-wives, two cousins, and Norman's mother, Fan, each of whom had been offered right of review and been allowed to go over his material before publication.

From cousin Osie Radin, July 15, 1985: "The book is fascinating, and once begun, difficult to put aside . . . The sequence is exactly right, and the narrative flows. I am grateful to have been included in this enormous work and am sure it will add much luster to your already well-launched career. I wish you the greatest success . . . PS, May I submit the following corrections for additional printings? . . . I am sending this page at Barbara's suggestion."[19]

Cousin Charles "Cy" Rembar, then one of the most able intellectual property lawyers in the country, also wrote. His letter was dated May 22, 1984, when I was still putting the book together: "I keep recalling things. I know you have a deadline but this may be short enough to insert in the galleys. . . ."

A second communication from Rembar, dated May 2, 1985, came after publication and addressed the subjects of my family time line and Rembar's immigrant father's adoption of the name "Shapiro": "I trust corrections can be made in future hardcover printings (of which I wish you a great many), and in the paperback, book club, foreign and any other editions."[20]

The longest response came from Barbara Wasserman, who asked that she have access to the whole manuscript, not just her quotes. Herewith, some items from the running critique she wrote:

- p. 10. "Mother's wrong. Norman had the name Kingsley from as early as I can remember. Middle names were somehow important to me as a child, and I'm sure of this."
- p. 17. "Rhoda's nuts. My mother took me to Kleins most of the time, and that was a lot lower than A&S [Abraham and Strauss]."
- p. 51. "What does Norman mean, a failed Cy Rembar? Cy's no producer type."
- p. 126. "Adeline's got it wrong—I didn't meet her until after I got to college."
- p. 182. "My mother, Rhoda and Adeline are full of shit, and the inaccuracies I want to go over with you."
- p. 459. "Ginsberg a bit long, no?"
- p. 626. ". . . on the whole Larry's account [of the stabbing] is pretty accurate, and more than I remember myself. But I do remember talking with Norman in the hospital. I said something like, 'Norman, you've flipped out,' and he got absolutely furious with me. I also remember Adele reaching out to me as she was being wheeled off to the operating room."
- p. 891. "Doctorow awfully good."

- p. 953. "Diana [Trilling] should know better than to open up her mouth like this. You're all going to get sued."
- p. 1077. "My mother's really senile—my father stopped smoking after his hernia operation around 1946."
- p. 1306. "Jean [Malaquais] will probably call Dotson [Rader] for calling him a Stalinist."

In the end her comments filled almost a whole legal pad. Nowhere was there the suggestion I'd "put words into [her] mouth."[21]

Norris was less relaxed, however. She had insisted on reading both manuscripts and wound up demanding a number of cuts based on the scenario that she was the most stabilizing thing in Norman's life—the down-to-earth, level-headed ex–Arkansas schoolteacher who'd domesticated the world's wildest genius writer. On page 1161 of the first manuscript, for example, her description of first meeting Norman at the Gwaltneys' in Fayetteville read: "I wasn't nervous about meeting him, but later he told me that he'd walked into the other room because he was overwhelmed and didn't want to say the wrong thing and alienate me right away." Her marginal comment read: "This is too self-serving—could you cut here?"

On pages 1164–67 the text read, "Norman was doing publicity for his Ali fight piece for *Playboy* so I flew up to Chicago, which was the first time I'd ever been on an airplane . . . Was I self-conscious? Again, no . . . If you're used to being loved and admired and in charge, and if you're also competent, these things suddenly don't stop. In fact, when I walked into *Playboy*, everybody said, 'Oh my God, let's get her for the magazine'—da, da, da. Why wouldn't I have self-confidence? Norman adored me, everybody adored me." She cut the last four sentences, commenting, "Oh, Peter—don't put all of this crap in about me saying how wonderful I am."

Understandable as that was, she next crossed out the line "Norman had made it clear to me from the beginning that he wasn't in love with Carol, but he never promised he was going to leave her," commenting disingenuously, "Do I really bullshit all the time?"

Another cut follows: "Maybe the sex was so marvelous it eclipsed everything. They're [sic] other things in life but not when you're starting a relationship!"

Then another: "My summer school course was shot to hell, but I wound up with an 'A' anyway."

And still another: "I liked being a winner, I liked getting my picture in the paper . . . Norman was my main chance."

Then, finally, she did it, she stepped over the line. Referring sweepingly to the previous cuts, she scribbled in the margin, "Stop putting these self-serving words in my mouth! . . . Peter, I never said that!"[22]

Now, wherever on God's green earth Barbara Davis, aka Barbara Norris, aka Norris Mailer, aka Norris Church, grade-school art teacher and part-time Fayetteville, Arkansas, Vlassic pickle factory worker, got the idea she could throw her weight around like this I will never know. But the assertion that I'd "put words into her mouth" left me no choice, I had to go back to the transcript. And what I came up with was that syllable-for-syllable, word-for-word all my excerpts were dead-on. Everything she claimed she'd "never said" was there, the same syntax, the same context. Even her tone of voice had been carried over.

What to do?

My response, shameful or not, was to accommodate her. I had no choice. As much as I resented the accusation of inaccuracy, her arrogance, I knew, would be sanctioned by Norman and the last thing I needed was to get between Norman and his young wife. I consoled myself with the thought that the material Norris wanted cut wasn't saying anything that any half-alert reader wouldn't get from the remaining text, anyway.

I'd also agreed to give Mailer's friends and fellow writers the same right of review, and with the exception of the notoriously self-absorbed Lillian Hellman, and also Jean Malaquais and Diana Trilling, whom I was seeing socially and didn't need written confirmation from, most of these people wrote me back to express their satisfaction: Arthur Schlesinger, Seymour Krim, Norman Rosten, *Vanity Fair* editor Leo Lerman ("an extraordinary book"), Norman Podhoretz ("You did a very good job of transcribing and editing"), and the ever gracious George Plimpton ("Let me know if you want me to do anything more").

All of them were happy. Even Liz Smith, the columnist for whom Norman could do no wrong, weighed in with an unsolicited note of appreciation and praise.[23] Call these endorsements Defense Exhibit 2.

Exhibit 3 in our mock tribunal would have to be Norman's marginalia that I herewith present in order to clear my name, to undo damage done wrongly and without cause, and to shed some light on the subjects of Norman Mailer's vindictiveness and fakery. To paraphrase Jimmy Baldwin, the difference between Mailer and most people is that Norman always imagined he had everything to lose,[24] which was the source of his lying as well as the unfortunate assumption that he had to dominate the world around him. This was his innocence, really, since not even children are granted the luxury of believing they possess such control, and in Norman's case, there seems little question that the motivating belief came from his mother, not to say his later string of compliant women, his mates who let themselves be shaped and bullied, and served as "codifiers." Whatever its origins, though, his need to micromanage and have others play assigned roles in his little pageant pointed to one thing: Norman lived all but totally inside himself, sometimes even in a past that was close to illusory. His marginalia, in its frankness and impatience, illuminates this as much as anything he ever wrote, I believe, just as it echoes the *New York* magazine observation that he always had "a bone to pick. With you. And you. And . . ."

A bibliographic note: the first typescript Mailer read lacks an ending and runs 1,403 pages; the second and tidier final draft, which he had in his possession for almost a full week in June 1984, consists of 1,142 pages. His comments in the early draft are written in green and violet ink as well as in pencil; in the second, in pencil alone. The final draft contains many notations, more than the early draft, which include heavy rewrites of his own blocks or "testimony." Individual comments vary in length from the aforementioned single-word expostulations, "Bullshit" and "Lies!" to long grape-arbor tendrils of argument that climb up and down the margins and run over to the back of the page.

His commentary begins on the very first page of the finished manuscript where, ever the litterateur, he complains, "This title is really a subtitle," indicating he wants the book to be called *Norman Mailer: His Life and Times*, not the more colloquial, arguably more commercial *Mailer: His Life and Times*. Next he jumps into the text proper by objecting to the report of one of his cronies that when he was a teenager his mother refused to let him play ball in the streets because she was afraid he'd get hurt. A page later, he adds, "Is this for art, physics, philosophy or to sell three more books?" in response to the recollection of another pal that their gang was heavy into masturbating: Humor? Forget it. He's lost to self-seriousness, just as he is several pages later when he responds to Rhoda Lazare Wolf's account of his "big brother" relationship with Barbara, who, as an adolescent, was self-conscious about her zaftig figure. "This is in danger already of becoming a most unpleasant book and Rhoda is certainly one of the reasons," he snaps.

Already his tendencies as a reader are clear and it isn't prudishness that's pushing him, as we find out on page 54, where he introduces the abbreviation, "TE," that will serve him throughout the manuscript. Here, the abbreviation is written out in large block letters followed by an equal sign, which is then followed by the coda "Too expensive for its value." Too expensive? When I later asked *who* such items might be too expensive for he looked at me as if I'd suddenly lost 20 IQ points and replied, "*Me.* Each of us must look after himself in this life, don't you agree?"

Woody Allen, as someone pointed out to me, had one of the characters in *Sleeper* deliver the line that Norman's ego deserved to be donated to Harvard Medical School. Had Allen known what was going on here, he might have changed the recipient institution to Bellevue.

The marginalia, I must admit, was also of some real value to me, since Norman couldn't keep himself from making changes to my text, which meant that he caught mistakes in dating and chronology. There were his legal catches, too, as when he warned me about Sandy Charlebois Thomas's account of the sexual shenanigans on the set of *Maidstone*. In one instance Sandy had singled out several women by name, including the Warhol superstar Viva, and here Norman drew an arrow to "Viva" and wrote, "I don't believe she was there. Be careful. Sandy will sink you yet." A dozen pages later, when Sandy identified someone who purportedly had "the clap," Norman jumped in again, writing out the woman's name in full and cautioning, "She'll sue you quite properly."

Aside from the utilitarian value of his comments, they lent a sense of enterprise to the project that in my lonely writer's journey I found encouraging, bracing. They also established my book as "the authorized bio," which I knew was going to be meaningful when it came to advertising, a fact not lost on my publisher. Even so, the majority of Norman's responses were revisionist, disgruntled, and dictatorial, if occasionally charming. It didn't matter if the issue was Stalinism, the New York theater, the makeup of the editorial boards at *Dissent* or *The Paris Review*, say, Norman always knew best, which, time after time, could get more than a little irritating.

Herewith, a sampling, mostly from the final typescript: [25]

- p. 102 (I). Classmate George Washington Goethals speculates that Mailer "protected" himself from WASP anti-Semitism at Harvard by going out of his way to announce his Brooklyn Jewish background in advance. NM: "To be Jewish is to harbor a psychic defect and thereby be gifted with instincts for transcendence. It's a blessing and a curse to be a Jew. You takes your chance."
- p. 145. Fan Mailer's description of their Brooklyn Heights neighborhood as "not really a Jewish neighborhood, but I wasn't exactly looking for a Jewish neighborhood . . ." NM: "I think we've got the point by now. What are you trying to do—start a pogrom?"
- pp. 186–87 (I). Norman block reading "until I started going nuts in the '50s" changed to "until I started going off my own tracks in the '50s."
- pp. 195–97. Emma "Ecey" Gwaltney recalls Bea telling Mailer he looked "more Jewish with his glasses on." NM: deletes, "TE."
- p. 236. Actress Shelley Winters claims that Norman, recently arrived in Hollywood after the success of *The Naked and the Dead*, invited the show-biz in crowd to come to his party by sending out wires. NM: "Total shit. Everybody was invited by phone. And *they all came*."
- p. 323. In a 1954 letter to friend Fig Gwaltney, Mailer says of Truman Capote, "He's got such a little pretty talent. One of these days he'll fly like a butterfly right up his own asshole." NM: deletes.
- p. 345. Barbara Forst recalls that during the late 1950s, Mailer was secretly tape-recording friends at the dinner table. NM: deletes, "TE."
- p. 374. Rhoda Lazare Wolf on how Mailer "brought on his own psychosis" that led to his stabbing Adele. NM: deletes, with the comment, "Crude! Do I really have to put up with her?"
- p. 391. Irene Maria Fornez recalls that once in the middle of sparring with Mailer she realized he wasn't playing around, that "it was something hostile." NM: deletes, introduces a second abbreviation, "TAP"—Twice a Pervert—that he puts side by side with "TE."
- p. 398. Novelist Chandler Brossard remembers Mailer describing William Styron as "the kind of guy who'll end up winning the fucking Nobel Prize . . . He plays all the angles"; also that Mailer referred to wife Adele as "that cunt" and boasted that he wanted to "beat the shit out of her [in order to] cool her off." NM: deletes, with the comment, "Brossard ought to marry Malaquais . . . This is all uniformly *shit*."
- p. 404. Nat Halper reports that Mailer spoke of his father, Barney, as draining the family coffers with his gambling debts and that to save appearances Norman would slip him money on the side. NM: deletes.
- p. 445 (I). Mailer comments that he and James Jones had always been competitive, that Jones became irritated at one point because Mailer beat him at arm wrestling, and that Gloria, Jones's wife, "was so fuckin' upwardly mobile." NM: deletes, with the comment, "I can live without this. You create a

context with your questions that forces the reality. Naturally one responds to the question, but what of the reality? The feud or distance with Jones had roots far deeper than the arm-wrestling. You work too hard at fulfilling your a prior [sic] hypothesis. In law it's called *leading the witness.*"

- p. 485 (I). Jean Malaquais, talking about "The White Negro" and James Baldwin's response, "A Black Boy Looks at the White Boy," insists that Baldwin "was right, Norman *doesn't* understand black people." NM: "Whereas, Malaquais does. It's good we have Jean around—otherwise we wouldn't know how to think. Don't go to Fanon, go to Malaquais."

- pp. 516–17. Alan Kapelner, talking about the craziness that was Greenwich Village in the 1950s, describes Jackson Pollack's habit of urinating on people while drunk, adding, "He probably would have peed on Norman . . ." NM: deletes, with the comment, "Do I have to sit here and be pissed on?"

- pp. 528–29 (I). Putnam's publisher Walter Minton claims that *Advertisements* "proved to be pretty much of a bomb." NM: "It sold 9,000 copies hardcover and went into paperback. I would guess Walter recovered his money and a little more."

- p. 533. Brother-in-law Larry Alson claims Mailer stabbed Adele out of the belief she was involved in a lesbian affair and she had taunted him with "You fag, you can't get it up." NM: deletes, "TE."

- p. 545. Seymour Krim recalls Mailer's court arraignment after the stabbing: "I didn't see Norman's father, but who could fail to hear his mother? When reporters asked her, 'What do you think of your boy now?' she said, 'My son's a genius! You have to understand!' " NM: deletes, "TE."

- p. 601. Harold Conrad recalls the feud between Mailer and Budd Schulberg at the Liston-Ali fight, where the two were assigned to bunk together at the Hefner mansion in Chicago—"Schulberg kept coming to me, saying, 'I ain't gonna stay with that cocksucker at that fucking place.' " NM: suddenly the wallflower, deletes the word *cocksucker*, adding "TE."

- p. 613. Norman Podhoretz claims that Mailer was ignorant of the Jewish mystical tradition. NM: "I didn't need Norman P. to discover the mystical tradition. He's inaccurate. I had been reading Buber for years."

- p. 642 (I). Dr. Jack Begner, Norman's "summer" doctor in Provincetown, recalls that Mailer's court sentence for stabbing Adele included seeing a psychiatrist "on a weekly or bi-weekly basis for one year." NM: "Not so. Begner is the most dependable contributor to this work. He, unlike the others, is always wrong."

- p. 644. Secretary Anne Barry recalls that Mailer was embarrassed at taking on the "commercial" Scott Meredith as his new agent—"that he would ever come to such a point." NM: deletes, "TE."

- p. 690 (I). George Plimpton claims that Mailer and third wife, Lady Jeanne Campbell, "had a very strange relationship . . . full of violence and beatings, one of which I semi-saw." NM: deletes, with the comment, "This is not so. I've never been a man for whips."

- p. 717 (I). Harold Conrad on Mailer's anger at sportswriter Red Smith for writing that Mailer broke up the press conference at the Liston-Patterson bout in Chicago. NM: "Unlike everyone else I always thought Red Smith was a shit-head. This is because he kicked me when I was down. Ditto A. J. Liebling."
- p. 750 (I). Emma "Ecey" Gawltney on the early days of the Norman-Beverly affair, when, with Beverly pregnant and the two of them about to visit Beverly's parents, Norman seemed "totally out of it." NM: "This is interesting. You're leading witnesses again. I visited Beverly's folks after all the other visits. I'll elucidate when I talk to you."
- p. 796. Fanny Mailer gives thanks, in Yiddish, for her son's winning the Pulitzer Prize for *The Armies of the Night*. NM: deletes, with the comment "Do you never tire of putting my mother in for comic relief? It's getting to be a one-joke book."
- p. 797. Midge Dector recalls Mailer reading the galleys of *Making It* and advising Podhoretz that he was being too nice, and complimenting George Plimpton for being "charming." NM: "Not accurate. She is fulfilling political needs to do damage." On the next page, Norman inserts a new opening paragraph in his "reply" to Podhoretz, justifying his turncoat review of *Making It*: "There is something so judgmental and narrow about Podhoretz now. He was merrier in the old days. He tells too much of how he took care of me in those old days. I also took care of him. How many people I argued with . . . It is sad to say that *Making It* had a subtly awful quality . . . One's teeth got on edge." Mailer's comment here runs the equivalent of two typescript pages and then, as if he cannot leave well enough alone, the argument gets picked up again on page 19 of the manuscript's footnotes section.
- p. 831. *New York Post* columnist Murray Kempton quotes Mailer as saying at the 1968 Democratic convention that Chicago mayor Richard Daley "must be made to hit the face of decency." NM: "Totally inaccurate. You know I never speak that way. It's anathema to me."
- p. 844. Tom Quinn quotes Mailer's rant about his New York mayoral campaign running mate Jimmy Breslin: "Was the guy raised in a beer barrel?" NM: deletes, with the comment "I never said it." (He did, though, not once but several times. As one of the campaign's principal figures, I was present when he used the line after Breslin arrived nearly an hour late for a press conference, and another time when Breslin failed to show up for a meeting at campaign HQ.[26]
- p. 885. Kate Millett calls *The Prisoner of Sex* "mean-spirited and vitriolic." NM: "She is parti-pris here and not entitled to judge without rebuttal." (In his reading of the first manuscript, on page 1,061, Mailer had written, "It's the standard speech and hasn't changed in ten years. I would point out, however, that *Prisoner of Sex* is not 'mean-spirited and vitriolic,' not even as a mirror image of *The Politics of Sex*. What Millett did in her book that was intellectually unforgivable was to quote out of context to the point

where she was altering meanings. On an intellectual level that [is] equal to kicking people in the head once you've got them down in the alley. . . .")

- p. 894. Secretary Anne Barry observes that Mailer and fifth wife Carol Stevens "didn't seem like [they had] a terrific relationship." NM: deletes.

- p. 903. Mailer is quoted talking about *Marilyn* to *The Washington Post* (July 19, 1973), on the virtues of writing a book quickly. NM: deletes.

- p. 921 (I). Sandy Charlebois Thomas's description of the development of *The Armies of the Night*: "I can't remember specific questions but he used to grill me about where things were going on, what was happening, who was doing what . . . I'd met Jerry Rubin and Abby Hoffman through Paul Krassner . . . Norman may acknowledge that Jerry tutored him for hours, that *The Armies of the Night* could never have been written without his help, but in fact I was the one who interviewed Jerry initially . . . Norman didn't see Jerry until later, and they may not have really talked until Chicago." NM: "She's in absolute error. Jerry and I talked for many hours while I was writing Part II of *Armies* . . . Sandy may not have been around while I was talking to Jerry. She was smart and did terrific work but she was a free soul. So, many of the times you really needed her, she was off exploring some aspect or another of that free soul."

- pp. 933–38. Grosset & Dunlop head Robert Markell on Mailer settling a plagiarism charge arising out of *Marilyn*: "I think I even had a private discussion with Scott [Meredith] in which he said that Norman's hope to someday receive the Nobel Prize might founder on this potential reef of plagiarism." NM: "40 pages on a book written in two months with the aid of a couple of psychotic liars [Markell and Larry Schiller]??"

- p. 948 (I). Tom Quinn, the big ex-Marine boxer who was Norman's favorite opponent in butting heads, states that "with Norman I never lost, which would make him furious." NM: "Tom is in error. We only did it once and in the middle I asked if he'd accept a draw. . . ."

- p. 962. Norris acknowledges that Mailer installed her in a nearby hotel in Maine at the time he was living with Carol Stevens. NM: deletes.

- p. 975. Dotson Rader on a birthday party he threw for Norman and Norris in Bridgehampton that Truman Capote refused to attend, saying, "Oh-h-h, Dotson, there's going to be a blitthard, we're going to be thnowed in at the house and I know what's going to happen. I'll be trapped in the little room upstairs and in the middle of the night Norman's going to come in my room and rape me. I just can't chance it. Give my regrets." NM: deletes.

- p. 999 (I). *New York Times Book Review* editor John Leonard comments that Mailer "has memorized every review he's ever gotten from anybody." NM: "No, not memorized, merely able to recall. It's a healthy faculty since it keeps most working writers from losing their memories altogether."

- p. 1016. Critic James Atlas on how Mailer was incensed at Atlas's *New York Times Magazine* profile: "Mailer is a very naive fellow. He expects to be praised by a reporter. We weren't friends, I didn't go to him as a friend." NM: deletes, with the comment, "Cut!! *He pursued me.* Lies—cut."

- pp. 1020–21. Norris on how her love for New York's East Side set showed Mailer "the glitter, the back and forth, the small talk." NM: deletes, with the comment, "TE. *Cut.*"

- p. 1023. Jan Cushing Olympitis on how Mailer was "very intrigued by WASPS." NM: deletes.

- p. 1031 (I). Brother-in-law Charlie Brown recalls that Norman "beat the shit out of her [Beverly] in the middle of the night in Ptown . . . I wrote a couple of songs about it. I knew it was the end of it [the marriage]." NM: deletes, with the comment, "This is absolutely untrue. I didn't touch her that summer of '69 when we broke up. I was afraid to. We were murderously enraged at one another." (Again, Norman lies. He came to my house early the morning after their blowup, bleary-eyed and filled with despair, like he *needed* to talk. In the course of the conversation, he acknowledged, ruefully, he'd "lost it.")

- p. 1035 (I). Mailer acknowledges that he has left a wife every time he finished a book or a designated sequence of books, and also that during the 1960s, he was "at the height of my powers" and that Beverly is to be blamed for keeping him from writing "the big one," because she "kept me so boozed and brawling." NM: deletes.

- p. 1044. Lawyer Monroe Inker comments on the dire state of Mailer's finances resulting from his many divorces: "Money was once plentiful, say in the '60s, but then he pissed it away like a baby." NM: deletes the phrase "like a baby."

- p. 1046. Inker again, pointing out that even with their divorce settlement consummated, Beverly "always has a shot at him for more money . . . She could still go back to court if she became a public charge, if she had to go on welfare . . . It's Norman and I, not Norman and Beverly, who are married forever." NM: deletes, with the comment, "Very TE. It's a road-map."

- p. 1082. New York City police detective William Majeski's claim that Norris regarded Jack Abbott as "a monster," changed to "I think she felt that Jack was a monster" and then to "I think she felt Jack should be put away forever. . . ." NM: marks passage "TE."

- p. 1098. New York *Daily News* reporter Tom Hanrahan's account of the press conference where Mailer called anyone who felt Jack Abbott deserved to have the book thrown at him "a Nazi or neo-fascist." NM: "When did I say that? You were there. How come you didn't query Hanrahan more closely?" (I was present at this press conference and Hanrahan's, not Norman's, version is the correct one. Norman woke me with a phone call at fiveish the next morning to say that Norris was about to leave him after being barraged by outraged calls from her East Side society friends.)

- pp. 1111–12. Diana Trilling explains her thoughts on the need to draw a distinction between what she'd always called "the psychotic stuff" in *Advertisements*—the delinquents who kill "to experience love"—and Norman's involvement with Abbott, which was a different thing altogether: "He didn't get Abbott out of jail so that he could kill yet another person to know yet another moment of intense love. God, no. That was a million miles away from what he said on the Cavett show." NM: "Never once is she brought to gaff with this egregious misinterpretation . . . I wonder if Diana feels—as well she might—responsible for Lionel dying of cancer. Her 'kill for love' is an unruly tic."

- p. 1122. *New York Times* article of August 2, 1983, quoting agent Scott Meredith as saying Mailer had switched to Random House because he was "angry" at the way Little, Brown marketed *Ancient Evenings*. NM: deletes the line but leaves the body of the article intact, with the comment that this is "all lies. Why institutionalize factoids?"
- p. 1200 (I). Diana Trilling again, observing that Mailer's greatest drawback as a writer and moralist was his difficulty distinguishing between metaphor and reality; also, that Mailer had always preferred Lillian Hellman's politics to her own. NM: "Here we go again! Diana is finding love by stomping on me . . . I'm not in the least near to either lady's politics. In fact, Lillian and I never discuss politics. We're too far apart. Ditto, Diana."
- p. 1235 (I). Editor Roger Donald on how the press has usually been inaccurate about Mailer's sales, and how Donald and others at Little, Brown "consider it ungentlemanly to discuss other people's money." NM: "How right he is! There are many reasons I'm properly considered not to be a gentleman and most of them are my fault, but the first is that everyone is aware of every cent I make whereas who would dare to ask about Updike or Bellow?"

In general, his comments struck me as petulant and self-protective. His greatest scorn, however, was reserved for Lawrence Schiller, his partner on *The Executioner's Song* (1979), *Marilyn* (1973) and *The Faith of Graffiti* (1974). By 2002, however, they had become close to indivisible entities as a result of almost *ten* collaborations on books and films. "I respect Larry's sense of reality—I think he might respect mine," Mailer acknowledged at a press conference for their TV miniseries *Master Spy* the same year as the *Banner* letter. "There are times when we have quite a bit of fun and there are times when we're ready to punch each other out. We argue back and forth" a lot.[27]

Schiller, who certainly wasn't Norman's equal in any sense of the word, made his living as a photographer, book packager, filmmaker and all-round hustler. Born in Brooklyn in 1936, he had, according to one of Mailer's stories that may or may not have been wholly reliable, started his professional life while still a teenager with a police scanner and a 4x5 Speed Graphic given to him by his father, the manager of a local Davega sporting goods store. With the first piece of equipment he used to find auto crashes in the greater New York metropolitan area, day or night, it didn't matter; the second, to snap pictures of the victims of these wrecks, which he'd then allegedly sell to the victims' relatives or to interested insurance companies, depending on which of them paid best. From these ghoulish entrepreneurial prowlings he moved on to freelance photo assignments with *Life* and the *Saturday Evening Post*, and eventually in 1966 published his first book, *LSD*, on the then hot subject of drugs.[28] Another book, a bio of Lenny Bruce, followed, and not long afterward he got lucky as only paparazzi get lucky once or twice in a lifetime when he snapped the famous swimming pool photos of Marilyn Monroe in the nude when the actress, like Bruce, was at the end of her tether. This was emerging as his trademark, people on the edge or over it. He stormed his way into Jack Ruby's hospital room to record Ruby's death-bed "confession" for Capitol Records, later released as an LP, and also bought the confessions of Manson gang-member Susan Atkins, a tabloid coupe that cemented his reputation as one of the leading purveyors of the literary rights of convicted killers.[29]

By the early 1970s, when he and Mailer made contact, Schiller was openly reviled as a master of checkbook journalism and a ruthless wheeler-dealer—what one reporter later called "one of the most unsavory and insensitive opportunists ever to crawl from the sewer of the American media."[30] Between 1976 and 1978 he produced and/or directed three network TV movies, including the potboilerish *The Trial of Lee Harvey Oswald*, then outbargained David Susskind and others for the exclusive book and film rights to the Gary Gilmore story for what would become *The Executioner's Song*. Over the next fifteen years he continued to churn out product, including not one but *two* O.J. books: the first was Simpson's sanctimonious bestseller, *I Want to Tell You*; the second, embarrassingly titled *American Tragedy*, was the story of the O.J. defense team, which was paid for by the first book even though there were conflict-of-interest issues and charges about ethics.

Schiller's forte, obviously, was to find headline-making material and turn it into money, and although his website today boasts of a number of Emmys, his books, movies, and miniseries were anything but synonymous with "class." *The Plot to Kill Hitler*, *Murder: By Reason of Insanity*, *Her Life as a Man*, *Marilyn: The Untold Story*, *The Real Story of Flight 93*, even the bestseller *Perfect Murder, Perfect Town* (billed as "the uncensored story of the JonBenét murder and the grand jury's search for the final truth")—all were written and/or directed by Schiller with a variety of coauthors, among them LSD advocate Richard Alpert, *Time* correspondent James Willwerth, who had covered the O.J. trial, showbiz empressario Albert Goldman, and a slew of moonlighting reporters from newspapers and wire services across the country.[31]

Mailer was far and away the most distinguished of these collaborators, and at the time the two joined forces he'd never been in as bad a place, financially; for he was foundering under the weight of federal liens for nonpayment of income tax,[32] private school tuitions, and alimony to ex-wives, and his credit worthiness was near nil as a result of the bank foreclosure on the Provincetown house he'd shared with Beverly. Originally assigned to write a series of extended photo captions for what Schiller had sold as a picture book, Mailer expanded his text and *Marilyn* turned into a major box office hit. Another quick infusion of cash came with *The Faith of Graffiti*, and with *The Executioner's Song*, there was a $500,000 advance, the first $225,000 of which went to the cash-starved Mailer directly, Schiller agreeing to take his cut almost completely at the back end.[33] The book remained on the

New York Times bestseller list for twenty-five weeks, besting the competition from Vonnegut, Styron, Wouk, and even Ludlum; it won Norman his second Pulitzer Prize, and led to the four-hour, two-part Tommy Lee Jones NBC TV movie of the week, which represented Mailer's first mainstream scriptwriting job since going to Hollywood for Sam Goldwyn on the back of *The Naked and the Dead*.

It was less than a year after the success of *The Executioner's Song* that I interviewed Schiller. I knew him by reputation, but we'd also met briefly at Norman's in Brooklyn. Physically, he was, and is, an unkempt man in a wet, walrusy sort of way, with a mouthful of protruding teeth and a beard that I can only guess was meant to give him a certain Hemingway dash that no one would otherwise remotely associate him with, just as he also wore Hemingway-style bush jackets and khakis. Like most hustlers he was smart, full of nerve and combativeness, and what was most obvious was that he enjoyed his reputation as an independent who refused to play by other people's rules.

The other thing, and I remember reminding myself of this at the time, was that in setting up our initial interview—there were three sessions in total, on September 11, 12, and 13, 1983, all on the phone—I was careful *not* to offer him right of review, nor did he ask for it. I did not tell him that his partner Norman, of all people, had reminded me that during the writing of *The Executioner's Song* the two of them had had a number of very heavy fights, and despite the book's success had not talked for more than a year afterward. In dealing with Schiller, Norman warned me, "Watch out."

As we got going something took place that did not entirely surprise me: Larry was a terrific interview. A lot of this was due to his own skills as an interviewer, which was evident in his understanding that you have to "layer" stories with shadings and detail, as opposed to settling for a straight, untextured narrative, or just a throwing out of facts. He was informed, analytical, and had unusually detailed, almost painterly, recall; he was also an animated personality, which helped considerably. But the real driving force was that he *wanted* to talk, was in fact bursting to talk, and I found myself listening, not having to prompt him at all as he'd launch into these long bursts of monologue on what it was like to work with Norman that included times, places, names, and even patches of dialogue. Money and their dealings with publishers were part of it, too, such as the story of how he had outmaneuvered the networks to get the Gilmore story in the first place, and later, how it had been him, not Norman, who'd camped out in "that fucking desolate hellhole" of Utah to interview Gary, Gary's girlfriend Nicole, Uncle Vern, and the other principles in the story.

As I slipped one cassette after another into my Sony, he just kept going. Norman had come west for a total of only three days, he claimed. He, Larry, was the one who'd gone to Gilmore's execution, then strong-armed Howard Kaminsky, their publisher, to come up with an additional $100,000 to buy Mailer three extra months to polish his edit—a rewrite that was *his* idea, he insisted, because he knew "what it was going to take" to turn the book into a bestseller. The two of them had fought over the title, even over Norman's prose and whether to have the book marketed as nonfiction or as a novel.

Listening to him, it gradually hit me: what he was claiming was that he had contractual say-so; that in the end Norman wasn't in charge of the *The Executioner's Song* at all.

This was pretty heady stuff, to say the least, so after our last session on September 13, when I had him repeat his claims, I went back to check them against a copy of *The Executioner's Song* publishing contract. As it turned out, his payout figures were spot-on. Likewise, the primary parties to the contract were Warner Books and Lawrence Schiller in the guise of two corporate entities, the New Ingot Company, Inc., and Charles Fries Productions of Los Angeles. Norman Mailer was party only to a collaboration agreement between himself and New Ingot; the Warner contract did not list him as the owner of the book, only New Ingot, just as New Ingot was obligated to deliver "the novelistic nonfiction book . . . about the life of Gary Gilmore" to be written by Norman Mailer with whom New Ingot had "a valid and subsisting" agreement.

Mailer's secondary status was further defined by the Warner payout arrangement: "All compensations due Author for said writing services," the contract read, "shall be the sole obligation of Owner and that Warner shall have no responsibility therefore." [34]

Very few people I'd interviewed had come close to talking like this, or rather, revealing information of such density, and it did not matter to me that the book packager was bragging, or that what he was saying may well have stemmed from his resentment that he'd done almost all the research for the project without receiving coauthor credit, or that Norman, hogging the spotlight, had excluded him from the Pulitzer ceremony when their book got its award. Pure and simple, what it added up to was that Mailer was a hired hand, and beyond that, for all his PR skills, during this period very much the guy in a quandary: he needed the cash Schiller was bringing in but loathed being indebted, which made him the compromiser who couldn't walk away, or kick his well-connected partner out the door, either.

Mailer wanted everything—the cash and the class both—which made him into the liar as well, since he would never admit his dependency. There was no question, I had to use Schiller's material, and later Norman's response turned out to be exactly what I should have expected it to be. "Here's the cutting edge," he ranted, upon reading Larry's remarks, "every time Schiller makes a self-serving statement, you can count on it: 5 to 1, it's false." [35]

Below, more of his responses to Schiller's "fabrications," many of which were not fabrications at all.

- p. 911. Schiller asserts that he "almost threw up" when he read the first chapter of *Marilyn*; that, contractually, he had "artistic and creative control" over Mailer's text; and also that Norman's "conspiratorial" writing about Bobby Kennedy and Marilyn Monroe was "vulgar and obscene." NM: "This is pure lying. He helped me with research on the possible murder all the way, day by day . . . Impossible bullshit." Specifically, his response to Schiller's dismissal of the Kennedy material as vulgar and obscene: "How would Schiller know?"

- pp. 914–18. Schiller recalls his dispute with Mailer over the cover design of *Marilyn*. NM: ". . . all horseshit and hopelessly mixed with truth and self-serving for Schiller."
- p. 924. Schiller recalls that, in an early version of *Marilyn*, Mailer asserted that the facts pertaining to the RFK-Marilyn relationship could not be checked with Monroe's housekeeper Eunice Murray because Murray was dead. Challenged on this, Mailer defended himself, saying he had hired "a private investigator" to look into the matter. The PI, it turned out, was Mailer pal and later convicted dope smuggler Rick Stratton, who was not a professional investigator at all, which left Schiller with the sense that Mailer "might have been winging it." NM: deletes, with the comment "TE and horseshit."
- pp. 929–30. Schiller claims that Mailer would not budge on the RFK material "and to this day he probably still believes it. Why? Because his ego won't allow him not to." NM: deletes.
- p. 966. Several times Schiller makes reference to "our strained period." NM: deletes all such references.
- p. 982. Schiller claims that he "laid down conditions" for *The Executioner's Song* after promising to put $500,000–$600,000 in Mailer's pocket. NM: deletes, with the comment "This is ridiculous."
- p. 989. Schiller claims that Mailer wanted the two of them to interview as a team for *The Executioner's Song*. NM: "Horseshit!!"
- p. 990. Schiller claims that he wanted Mailer to interview him before drawing him as a character in *The Executioner's Song*. NM: "God, what a *maniac.*"
- p. 1003. Schiller recalls that he felt the early manuscript of *The Executioner's Song* was "unpublishable" due to the writing. NM: "He's incredible."
- p. 1004. Schiller claims that at the time of *The Executioner's Song*, Mailer was indebted to agent Scott Meredith for $175,000–$200,000 in addition to what he owed his mother and the New York State tax people, and that he, Schiller, squeezed the extra $100,000 out of their publisher to "buy" him three months to edit the book. NM: "Ridiculous. I cut it in those three months the way you have yet to cut this work. . . ."
- p. 1013. Schiller recalls that he wanted to call *The Executioner's Song* fiction, not nonfiction. NM: deletes, with the comment "LIES—I wanted to call it fiction, not Schiller."
- p. 1036. Schiller calls *Of Women and Their Elegance* "a piece of shit," then points out that Mailer "keeps falling back into the money pit." NM: "What is he—my guru? You're making the same mistake with him that I did."
- pp. 1083–84. Schiller recalls Mailer's visit to the Utah film set of *The Executioner's Song*, where he had to tell him, " 'Norman, I'm directing this film, not you. I won't have a writer around when I'm directing.' We had a fight, he got mad at me and went home." NM: deletes, with the comment "I'm not going to be lied about and pissed on by liars."

- p. 1193 (I). Schiller pats himself on the back, claiming that *The Execu-tioner's Song* was "the best deal" he'd ever pulled off, adding that he is con-fident he is going to prove himself as a journalist and "work with Mailer again." The reason for his confidence? "I know Norman's fallen for Nicole!" NM: "Schiller has nothing if he does not have a manic sense of history. I was moved by Nicole. It is not often that you see an attractive sev-enteen year old who is wandering through space after a tragedy. But I had no designs on her. Assuming she was drawn to me—which I doubt—I still have a professional bias against mattress journalism. I was certainly in love with the fact that she had had a genuine and not sleazy romance with Gilmore."
- p. 1195 (I). Schiller insists that Mailer's show of gratitude for all the re-search he had done was to say, in effect, "I didn't do my homework on *Marilyn*, and I wouldn't be doing it for this book either if it wasn't for you, Larry." NM: "I hate to see Larry Schiller become so self-serving. When I interviewed him for *The Executioner's Song* he had more humor about himself. As for *Marilyn*, it is not a book I apologize for. But for the last chapter, which suffers from the haste to finish on time, I think it's among my better books. The glossy packaging, however, I could have done with-out."
- p. 1207 (I). Schiller on their relative contributions to *The Executioner's Song*: ". . . in fact we realized that all the stuff he'd gotten about prisons wasn't as good as what we'd found out about Gilmore, so we decided not to use it because the book was already too long . . . I'm not gonna say how much of the book is from my tape transcripts, how much his own material, but using my transcripts was all cut and paste and I was amazed at his re-straint . . ." NM: "I hope he's using the editorial *we*. There wasn't one seri-ous literary decision made on that book by Schiller. In fact he was very upset with the style I chose and only came around to liking it months later when other people began to feel enthusiastic for the manuscript. Schiller made an immense contribution to *The Executioner's Song* with his inter-views. His technique was rich and it also enabled me to re-interview the principals, knowing in advance what he'd covered and what was worth pursuing instead of having to decide on the spot. Larry, however, has very little instinctive literary taste. He thinks, lives, breathes best-seller so while I had many conversations with him, I rarely took him seriously. I did, how-ever, respect him other ways. His energy and his productorial drive, his urge for comprehensiveness left me working harder than I might if left on my own, for when all is said and done *The Executioner's Song* was a prodi-gious task and I was tired in those years. His notion, however, that he was in on the creative process is vainglory. The book is hardly cut and paste. The interviews he did were often wonderful but they bore the same rela-tion to the finished product that maybe sap does to maple syrup."
- p. 1208 (I). Schiller recalls that for *The Executioner's Song*, Mailer talked to Joan Didion as there is "no better writer on the West than she . . . I once

dropped him off at the Beverly Hills Hotel to meet her." NM: "His stories are about as accurate as Ronald Reagan's. Norris and I once had a social lunch with Joan and John Dunne. I never consulted her on the book . . . Larry should carry a sign saying, 'Watch out, all historians. I am a walking factoid.' "

- p. 1378 (I). Schiller recalls that Mailer announced that *The Executioner's Song* was being made into a theatrical film even after it was announced that it was a made-for-TV movie. NM: "Larry is doing the cover-up. He lied to me all the way on this to keep me content and working on the script."

There is considerably more of this, and Norman's tone needs no explanation. Schiller's response to Mailer's vitriol does, however. My dates are fairly precise: Mailer's review of the first of my two typescripts took place in February 1984. Two weeks later I got a letter from Schiller demanding he be allowed to review what material of his I was using. A second note from Schiller's secretary in LA followed, and deciding to nip the problem in the bud, I replied by sending Larry his edited quotes on March 9, 1984, via certified mail, even though he had not been given right-of-review. A fortnight later he got back in touch again, calling me on the phone. He wanted transcript. His inference was that he'd been misquoted.

"Dear Larry," I responded on March 26, "Apropos your request for transcript: this is something I never promised, and would never promise . . . It sets an unwieldy precedent for the book, and in no case when I have agreed to right-of-review has this involved review of transcript . . . I will, as a courtesy, consider any emendations you may ask me to make . . ."

Going to the heart of the matter, I then added, "I assume you have now had the opportunity to discuss with Norman those passages which you wanted to review with him before inclusion in the final manuscript . . ."

At the time I was still editing the book, and communication between us was complicated by Schiller's departure for the Soviet Union to work on his movie *Peter the Great.* My letter included the directive, "Via express mail, Certified, for immediate transmission via telex to Lawrence Schiller in the U.S.S.R., telex copy of same to Peter Manso." [36]

Despite my precautions I was wary: this was the same Schiller who had once gone out to the Grosset & Dunlop printing plant in New Jersey, I think Norman told me it was, to physically inspect the counters on the presses to ensure that he and Mailer weren't being short counted on their *Marilyn* royalties. This was an unheard-of move, but as always, Larry hadn't given a damn about publishing protocol. Now that there was palpable tension in the air that involved Norman, I wasn't sure he wouldn't try to lay his problem off on me.

And he did have a problem, plainly. As anyone who ever witnessed Norman Mailer in a dither can attest, when he got bothered, he could get dangerous, and I don't mean physically dangerous as in his early years; I mean dangerous in the sense that he could become totally inflexible, intractable, and all but impervious to reason. He'd seize up, go rigid emotionally, like the only response possible was either a thumbs-up or a thumbs-down, Sicilian-style. And here he had responded to Schiller's testimony by scribbling "Horseshit!" and "Liar!" up and down the margins of my manuscript, so angry that he'd actually gouged through the paper several times with his soft No. 2 Ticonderoga, his usual writing instrument.

Thus, when Schiller found himself confronted, he must have known he was in a bind—a double bind, really, since the material Norman read the *second* time around included some of the corrections Larry had sent back to me. The problem was that Larry's vanity had kept him from rewriting the material as much as he should have; at the same time, he knew that a lot of what he'd said originally was true and should never have been changed at all. Now he was being forced to grovel, to accept Norman's whipping.

The simple truth was that he needed Norman as he'd always needed him— for his class, brains, and respectability. Norman was Harvard and other such fantasies often harbored by the uneducated, whereas Schiller had attended Pepperdine University in Los Angeles, far from the Ivy League. Likewise, Larry the photographer had never been able to put himself on the level of Cartier-Bresson, or even Weegee, any more than without Norman he could hope to be seen as a bona fide journalist, which was something later events would show he wanted ever so desperately.

But there was a still deeper issue that made the situation volatile, which was that each of them saw in the other everything they had in common: greed, stubborn-ness, opportunism, and the unrelenting need to win. Under the skin the two were twins. Their only difference aside from talent was who needed what most at any given point in time—which is to say who had the greater leverage or clout. Char-acteristically, they'd fight, go through periods of communicating through their wives, then make up only to fight anew.

Given this symbiotic whip of egos and dependencies, can there be any question that Schiller had felt pressure to recant when Norman leaned on him? Then to re-sent it, and everyone associated with what was happening? And if there was a sin-gle source behind the accusation that I withheld transcript—if Norman hadn't just created the whole idiotic accusation out of thin air—didn't it have to be Schiller and no one but? Larry was the only one with motive, as they say, just as he was the only person out of the two hundred or so interviewed who'd demanded to see transcript and who I told to go fuck himself.

Unavoidably, it was *New York* magazine's contention all over again, that Mr. Tendentious had to have "a bone to pick. With you. And you. And. . . ." The real blunder was mine, though, unambiguously. I'd turned Schiller down on the basis of Norman's say-so, trusting in my good old buddy, my mentor, my partner, who then used Schiller's accusation to punish me two decades after he'd finished pun-ishing Schiller himself.

Two decades! That's what separated the two events and the gap says as much about Norman's capacity for vengeance as about the changes that came over him as an old man victimized by his vanity, not to say by Schiller and a figure we have not yet discussed, the academic J. Michael Lennon, who came to play an increas-ingly instrumental role in Norman's life. The changes showed mostly in his work, though, as they always do and took the form of an impossible balancing act, as if, in Norman's mind, by going "big" with books like *Harlot's Ghost, Oswald's Tale*, and that last all-but-impenetrable brick called *The Castle in the Forest*, he could stay in touch with his native voice and energies while at the same time producing schlock with Schiller. *The Executioner's Song*, though not as deeply felt as Capote's *In Cold Blood*, is nonetheless very special and may well be the last sustained piece of memorable writing Mailer did; whether or not Norman was able to acknowledge this is an open question but many of his readers thought so and said so, which for an ego like Norman's is always the last stop on the line, not to say something exceedingly difficult to handle.

To me, the first telltale sign of what was happening was the 1984 publication of *Tough Guys Don't Dance*, which was the first of his scheduled four books for Random House. *Tough Guys* sold surprisingly well given the fact that the noirish tale of pot, blow jobs, and brutal physical dismemberments on the Outer Cape was cranked out in less than two and a half months. Unfortunately, it also opened the door to a movie version that pricked Norman's fantasy that he could be another Bergman. Produced by the Israeli team of Golan-Globus, the men behind such opus works as *Bolero, The Happy Hooker*, and *Death Wish 4*,[37] the film adaptation, which Norman directed as well as wrote the script for, chewed up more than two years' time, then proved a bomb at the box office. The critics savaged it with the 1987 Razzie Award for Worst Director of the Year, as well as nominations in the Worst Actor, Worst Actress, Worst New Star, Worst Picture, and Worst Screenplay categories. The mainstream reviews were just as embarrassing: "Not the high point of Mailer's career" (Vincent Canby, *The New York Times*). "Befuddled and paranoid" (Roger Ebert). "Incomprehensible" (*TV Guide*). And from *The Washington Post*, "This is Norman Mailer in full homosexual panic . . . lunatic . . . over the edge. . . ."[38]

The other problem was that he got somewhat carried away doing PR, claiming he was ready to give up writing for a second career in film.[39] With typical resistance he bounced back, however, and produced *Harlot's Ghost*, which was his first big book since *Ancient Evenings*. "Big" hardly described it: at 1,200 pages, the encyclopedic CIA tome had to be priced at a record thirty dollars per copy, five dollars more than the closest priced work of popular fiction of the time, and sales were so disappointing that not even Jason Epstein, Mailer's friend and editor, could sugarcoat the pill when the book clung to the next-to-last spot on the *New York Times* bestseller list for four frustrating weeks, then sank like a rock. It was too long, too dense.

But the real crisis lay in the fact that *Harlot's Ghost* was only the second of the four books Mailer owed Random House, and it was already 1991, the last year of his seven-year contract. He was two books behind. The answer, as in times past, was Schiller, who over the past ten years had directed and produced a half dozen network miniseries, and now, as Schiller would later recall, Norman phoned "as if we'd never had an argument," wanting to get something going.[40] *Oswald's Tale*, a psychography of JFK assassin Lee Harvey Oswald done up as a novel, was the product of their reunion. Between the writing and research, it used up another four precious years, but like *Harlot's Ghost*, it wasn't the runaway success the folks at Random House had hoped for; in fact, *Oswald's Tale* failed to make the *Times* list altogether.[41]

Feeling the pressure, Norman took extraordinary measures. He was now seventy-two, had been diagnosed with angina and was wearing a hearing aid, and in 1995, the year the Oswald novel was published, he pulled out of New York to embrace a "monastic regime" of living full-time on the Cape. The objective was to focus on his work, abjure Park Avenue cocktail parties, and get down to it in the time he had left. But even with the comparative economy of living in off-season Ptown, the Mailers were forced to pull money out of the 627 Commercial Street property, the house Norman and I had owned jointly. This took the form of a series of equity loans and refinancings, starting in April 1994, even before they moved up to the Cape, when Norman and Norris took a $358,000 mortgage. Public records[42] show that they then took out a $190,000 line of credit in the form of a second mortgage; since my departure in 1986, they had also pocketed almost $200,000 from the sale of the cottage to Peter Fraser, the late Roy Cohn's boyfriend. In June 2006, they would refinance once more with a loan in the amount of $510,000, which represented anything but a pay-down on the property Norman and I had originally purchased for $302,000 and financed at $200,000.

Plainly, by the late 1990s Mailer was once more on the skids financially, so again he threw in with his guardian angel, now to write out-and-out TV hackwork, starting in 2001 with *American Tragedy*, where he served as coproducer in addition to writing the teleplay based on Schiller's second O.J. book. ("It'll be a dignified treatment of a sensational story," said CBS movies and miniseries chief Sunta Izzicupo in announcing the project.)[43] Even with his quick payday, though, Norman couldn't keep his mouth shut, maybe because that elusive thing with Mailer—his conscience—had started bothering him.

"I found the advertising for it repugnant," he told the *New York Observer*, accusing CBS's marketing of being overly sensational in its promotion of the film. "The emphasis of the movie was not on whether O.J. was guilty or not guilty because there was so much evidence on each side. What I was interested in . . . was how a defense team works, especially how a Super Bowl defense team works. . . . When they ran that thing—*See the picture that O.J. tried to stop*—I thought it was as cheap as shit."[44]

Who cared, though? He should have only complained as strenuously about Schiller, who soon pulled him into another four-hour miniseries, *Master Spy: The Robert Hanssen Story*, which turned out to be his most self-destructive commitment to date. Here, Mailer didn't just write the screenplay but did the research for Schiller's *Into the Mirror*, the book on which the film was based. It was mind-boggling—Norman Mailer, the two-time Pulitzer winner and recipient of the National Book Award, researching someone else's book? The only explanation was that this was the price he had to pay to get the scriptwriting gig, what else? Both of them must have been disappointed, though—*The New York Times* called Schiller's text "cartoonishly simplistic" and "painful," and in its pan of the miniseries adaptation the *Times*'s Caryn James added insult to injury by observing that Norman had penned his script "apparently without breaking a sweat."[45]

Oh, the loss of face! During the seven year period from 1995 to 2002, Mailer had collaborated with Schiller on four projects. Seven years, four collaborations! There was nothing quite like it in the annals of the post-WWII American lit business, certainly no parallel involving anyone of Mailer's stature, and the full sadness of this becomes evident only when we pull back to carefully review Norman's overall output during the last two decades of his life. To wit, from 1991 on, Mailer published four "real" books as distinguished from ephemera like *Portrait of Picasso as a Young Man: An Interpretive Biography* (a rehash of an earlier essay with near plagiaristic borrowings from John Richardson's Picasso bio, 1991); *Why Are We at War* (a recycling of Mailer speeches with a dialogue between Norman and old friend Dotson Rader, 2003); *The Spooky Art: Some Thoughts on Writing* (a cut-and-paste anthology assembled from decades of interviews, essays, and lectures, 2003); two Q&A books, *The Big Empty: Dialogues on Politics, Sex, God, Boxing, Morality, Myth, Poker, and Bad Conscience in America* (undertaken with Mailer's son John Buffalo, 2006), and *On God: An Uncommon Conversation* (a self-billed "platonic dialogue" between Mailer and his archivist J. Michael Lennon, 2007); and a volume entitled *Modest Gifts*, made up of Norman's incidental poems and drawings (2003).

For the most part, these titles were designed to keep the author's name in the news, mollify needy dependents, and bring in a few more dollars. The "real" books, by which I mean books that were thought out and written, original pieces created from whole cloth, were 50 percent fewer in number: *Harlot's Ghost* (1991), *Oswald's Tale* (1995), *The Gospel According to the Son* (1997), and *The Castle in the Forest* (2007). There was also *Into the Mirror: The Life of Master Spy Robert P. Hanssen* (2002), the project on which Norman served as "investigator." But of these "real" books, almost 50 percent of Mailer's titles were Schiller collaborations, a calculation that does not count the two Schiller-Mailer TV miniseries, *American Tragedy* and *Master Spy*.

The relationship between the two becomes all the more distinct if you go back to *Marilyn*. From 1973 on there are nine collaborations—five books and four teleplays—which, startlingly, represent more than one third of Mailer's *total career output*, posited on my count of twenty-five original "written" works starting with *The Naked and the Dead*.[46]

Seventeen versus nine! Presented in cold numbers, the figure is no less staggering when it is remembered that Schiller did not partner with Norman until the early 1970s, when Mailer had done easily 60 percent of his most memorable writing.

A numbers game? I don't think so. The irreducible truth is that the partnership all but took over during the last third of Mailer's life, largely because Norman had trapped himself with a lifestyle of too many wives, mistresses, and kids. The once defiant author of such breakthrough works as *Advertisements for Myself*, *Cannibals and Christians*, *Miami and the Siege of Chicago*, and *The Armies of the Night*, as well as *The Naked and the Dead*, *The Executioner's Song*, and perhaps also *The*

Deer Park—yes, that's the canon in a nutshell—had gotten himself in and out of a number of relationships during his lifetime but for sheer longevity none had hooked him like his marriage to Schiller. And the worst thing was, he knew it, just as he knew that his tie to the self-promoting book packager was likely to keep him from ever getting the Nobel Prize—over Philip Roth, Styron, and half a dozen others he'd been competing with for as long as anyone could remember.

Schiller was not merely Norman's business partner; he'd worked himself into the grain of Mailer's life. This was evident, say, less than a year before Norman's death when he appeared at the University of Texas's Ransom Center to celebrate the university's acquisition of the Mailer archive for a neat $2.5 million.[47] Norman, the guest of honor, had brought sister Barbara, son John Buffalo, and also Schiller, who sat opposite Gay Talese on the panel, "A Conversation with Norman Mailer." It was like putting the head of an oil conglomerate at the helm of the *Exxon Valdez*: Lawrence Schiller, he of the police-scanner radio and flash camera, suddenly a cultural historian? A scholar of American letters, or just Mailer's buddy harvesting the perks of the relationship?

Even stranger was his involvement in the Norman Mailer Society, a group of 150 or so professors and grad students that was founded in 2002 to "perpetuate and study Mailer's work." The society's inaugural program listed Schiller as a benefactor,[48] which certainly pointed in the right direction: in 2004 he donated $2,000; in 2005, $15,000; and then in 2006, as though to guarantee himself an evening in the Lincoln bedroom at the Mailer White House, he made another contribution of a whopping $20,000 while continuing to serve on the executive board with John Buffalo Mailer, Barbara Wasserman, and Jack Abbott defense lawyer Ivan Fisher.

Was he a personal friend or a business partner, a benefactor or a pretentious self-promoter? It took no great insight to see that if Schiller was Norman's angel, it had to be that he was an avenging angel. He was Mephistopheles. With his TV docudramas and Hanssen books and O.J. rip-offs he had lured Mailer away from doing what Mailer needed to do most, which was to follow through on that promise he made in 1959 to "change the consciousness in our time." However bloated his ambition, Mailer was thirty-six back then, filled with all the impending force of a thunderhead, and it had looked to many of my generation that he was one of our culture's very best hopes. But the job had been left undone. Norman's life was now passing him by, sucked up by this toothy parvenu from Hollywood who, like the far more attractive Gatsby, needed a little culture to accompany his worldly success.

But if Schiller couldn't keep away, then Norman had not been able to suspend his own temptations, either. I have no way of knowing how many times, if ever, he turned down Schiller's blandishments, but the informality of their arrangement was something made-to-order: "Norman, I've just signed up so-and-so. You interested?" Schiller might offer, operating as a one-man production office, talent agency and cash register, and if it was a *Yeah*, the high-energy deal maker would scurry off to take care of all the details. Then *boom*, there it was, a new project on the table. How could Norman resist? He'd kept Larry's name off the spines of their books just as he'd blown up and called his partner a maniac and a liar, but they were wedded. By the new millennium they were in fact old marrieds who'd been together so long, they couldn't acknowledge what was happening, least of all Norman, who'd marooned himself up in Provincetown where he needed all the energy and attention he could get.

But his collaboration with Schiller was not just about money, the point has to be made over and over. This was not Hammett grinding out stories for *Black Mask* or Martha Gellhorn financing her novels by writing pieces for *Colliers*, or Fitzgerald running off to Hollywood. It was a dependency. Schiller was a fan. In Oprahspeak he was the *enabler*, a supporter in addition to a money supply, and Norman needed every bit of support he could get. There were his health issues, plus how many of his readers and reviewers were now looking backward to his last "important" book, jumping over *Ancient Evenings, Harlot's Ghost, The Gospel According to the Son*, to go back to *The Executioner's Song* and *The Armies of the Night*, leapfrogging a gap of almost thirty years, which, according to Webster's, is all of a full generation?

Granted, like so many other American writers, Norman was a victim of the changes in our culture and changing reading habits. To his credit, he had continued to publish in small, low-paying, high-brow venues like the *New York Review of Books*, but his loss of readership was not a market phenomenon alone. People were not listening. He'd stepped back and begun to repeat himself by recycling the same tired tropes he'd been using for forty years. Who would have known? "Cancer" and "plastic"? Lee Harvey Oswald's chromosomes? Hitler gestating inside his mother's womb? Who cared? And in the howling, wintry bleakness of off-season Ptown, what did he have to fall back on? The privilege of sitting there in his big house on the water, listening to the February wind and trying to evade having to live with his failures, which is the fate and destiny of any sincere artist? He was surrounded by the fawning of quasi-sophisticates like Alix Ritchie, plus there was the occasional visit of a reporter or photographer up from New York or Boston, but otherwise he was alone, and his isolation made him all the more vulnerable to the backslappings of Schiller and J. Michael Lennon, the eager president and founder of the Norman Mailer Society, who'd also learned how to capitalize on Mailer's worst vanities, the neediness and fears of his senior years.

And that was the real problem, *his vanity*. "This is Norman Mailer," I can recall him intoning into the phone in that pompous clipped baritone of his, as if the conversation could proceed only after his correspondent had been set straight. Long-distance operators, secretaries, even the local plumber Bob Meads, all were expected to know who they were talking to. Meads, a wonderfully droll Portuguese whose brother was the town's police chief, was so taken by Mailer's affectedness that he built a monument to it: anyone walking into the Meads Brothers plumbing shop off Shank Painter Road was greeted by a discarded toilet seat tacked to the wall to the left of the register, its lid labeled in black Magic Marker, NORM SAT HERE.

His role-playing found fullest expression in the local restaurants. I'd seen it countless times, but by the 1990s he was the grand old man, the *patron* hobbling into Pepe's or Sal's Place on his two canes, making a show of acknowledging the tourists' stares and stopping to chitchat with the owner as he struck a godfatherly

pose. Stardom suited him, as it always had. Watching his routine one night after
our break, I thought back to how he used to grab the check, but not to buy you a
meal so much as to calculate your one-third share. *One-third?* Yes, his explanation
was that for a person in his tax bracket, it didn't make sense to go fifty-fifty, since if
he took the meal as a deduction, the government would end up paying a third
which benefited both of you. It was all very droit du seigneur. What he didn't
make clear was that he was the one taking the deduction in addition to pocketing
your one-third of the tab in cash and that, on a dollar-for-dollar basis, the arrangement was singularly to his benefit, not yours.

There was little question that the show was more important to him than the finances, that has to be understood. But either way it pointed to the same majester-
ial sense of self that never thought twice about using Caswell-Massey Verbena, the
expensive lime-scented eau de cologne, for his daily underarm deodorant while
others used Right Guard. Nor, to my knowledge, did he ever question his habit of
feasting on lobster tails and mashed potatoes—his favorite summer meal—that,
perforce, meant leaving behind all but the easily accessible tail meat for Myrtle,
the family's Jamaican housekeeper, to wrestle with and turn into the next day's ef-
fort-free lobster salad. Sometimes his demonstrations of self-love could spill over
into the operatic, as when he burst into the dining room one fine sunny morning,
beside himself at finding a single white rose lying on the doorstep, which signified
that someone was trying to put a fatal curse on him. Whether he really believed
this nonsense didn't matter; he went so far as to accuse me of withholding the
identity of the rose-leaving stalker, why I had absolutely no idea, not that he bothered to explain. In another episode, early on after he first arrived from New York at
the time we were all moving into 627, he grabbed a screwdriver and started furiously digging the wood filler out of the desktop his son Mike and I had prepared
for him. We had sanded and painted an old door we'd found in the basement,
then filled in the hole where the knob had been with Plastic Wood and set the
door atop two filing cabinets; it was your standard student-type desk, totally functional. But rather than say thank you, Norman went a little crazy, once more operating on inner impulses he seemed powerless to resist.

"Goddamnit, don't you guys know by now," he shouted, "I can't work on a surface that's *plastic*."

His whole cancer-gulch speech came next, the standard lecture on disease and
synthetics and the end of civilization as we know it, which was as boring as it was
stupid. He was treating us like strangers, thank you, and then and there I was reminded of the little number he'd pulled a half year earlier when he got cold feet
about going through with the house deal: I'd put up the down payment of $30,000,
which was now about to be forfeit, and he wanted me to know he'd pay half "our"
loss. *Half?* Yes. Only it hadn't occurred to him that since he was the one breaking
the contract, maybe there was no reason for me to be out $15,000 for the privilege
of having him as my ex-partner.

I could talk about his superciliousness when, not long after his mayoral campaign, I'd tried to turn him on to Hunter Thompson with a copy of *Fear and
Loathing in Las Vegas*, or how, in Ptown, he responded with barely disguised dis-

interest to a surprise visit by a pal of mine from Berkeley who was maybe the only young black writer to snare a Fulbright who'd also jeopardized all by going out and burning his draft card. The simple truth was that reality, for Norman, had to be a mirror of his celebrity, his and his alone. Philosophically, he approached things in a way that might properly be called autotelic, as in self-generating, self-justifying, and self-advancing, and his relationship with Roy Cohn illustrated how far this could go. There was the classic "It's about time I had a patron" line, but later on, when Roy asked Norris to paint his portrait, all Norman could do was grouse, "What are you doing to me?" Cohn had arranged for Norman's house loan and factored his publishing contract, and once even flown daughter Dandy back to New York in his private plane; but none of that mattered now. Now he complained to Norris, "I don't want to be publicly identified with this man. It's bad enough he's living next door . . . How are you going to sign it?"[49]

This was Norris's "society" period when she was signing her work *Norris Church Mailer*, trying to make a name for herself among some of New York's richest and best-connected. Her technique, not exactly in the tradition of Vermeer, consisted of photographing her subjects, then projecting the image onto a blank canvas, tracing the form out in pencil, then coloring it in. The process usually took less than a week. When she was done with the Cohn portrait, we all gathered in the living room for the unveiling. Roy was there with several of his minions, sipping his favorite drink of Dom Perignon seasoned with two saccharin tablets, and soon he slipped her $3,000 cash. "Will that be okay, Norris—three thousand dollars?" he asked. Later on, Norman fumed, "We can't take his three thousand dollars. With his troubles with the IRS, it will come back to haunt us."

Norris, the ex-Wilhelmina model, kept the money and the summer rolled on. Norman's need to have it both ways resurfaced, reportedly, at Roy's fifty-ninth birthday party that fall at Basha Szymanska's apartment back in the city, where he and Norris found themselves surrounded by Cohn's usual jet-set crowd of Si Newhouse; Cohn's law partner and New York City councilman, Stanley Friedman; Lee Iacocca; Donald Trump; Helen Gurley Brown; Sen. Alfonse D'Amato; Reagan strategist Roger Stone; and Marie Lambert, often called the most powerful judge in New York. Mike Wallace was also in the room with a 60 *Minutes* cameraman, shooting a piece on New York's most feared lawyer, and he wanted a comment from Norman on why the famed leftist writer was celebrating Roy Cohn's birthday surrounded by some of Manhattan's best-known Republican businessmen and politicians. Stand-up Norman averted his face and fled the camera, ducking into the crowd.[50]

It was similar to his early behavior with Schiller, having his cake and eating it, too. The following year at Cohn's memorial service in 1986, there was a subtler but more significant sequel: eulogies were delivered by Roy's law partner, Tom Bolan, Reagan Administration U.N. delegate Jeane Kirkpatrick, Barbara Walters, and Mailer's old antagonist William Buckley, Jr., among others. Donald Trump sat in the audience weeping with Cohn's lover, Peter Fraser, and the ubiquitous Si Newhouse. Norman and Norris, however, were nowhere to be seen, just as neither of them ever spoke publicly of their relationship with Cohn again.

But to return to Norman's slide after he started living full-time on the Cape: if Schiller had become indispensable to him during the 1990s, so did J. Michael Lennon, who billed himself as dedicated to preserving Norman's literary legacy. He, too, was a feeder, albeit of a different order. Bearded, with perennially down-cast eyes and the featureless face of an aging insurance salesman, Lennon had appeared in Provincetown in the early 1980s when he was teaching at Sangamon State, a small Midwest university nobody had much heard of. In due course he moved on, in the manner of secondary professors, to a place called Wilkes University, in Wilkes-Barre, Pennsylvania, where, as a faculty member of the English Department and part-time administrator, he prospered by editing anthologies and reference books, setting up student workshops, and, eventually, establishing a writing program even though he himself was not a writer.[51] In fact, his publishing record, then as now, showed that with the exception of the occasional academic article, Prof. Lennon's publications consisted of anthologies of others work, Q & A compendia, and, with his wife as coeditor, a thorough, not to say obsessive, privately printed encyclopedic bibliography of everything Norman Mailer ever wrote—letters to the editor, speeches, fragments, even Norman's grade school compositions.[52] Lennon's whole life was Mailer. On his limited academic salary, he'd even bought a condo in Provincetown to be near Mailer. He did research work for Mailer. He appeared with Mailer at the Provincetown Rep Theater to do stage readings. He accompanied Mailer to parties and gallery openings and even tagged along when Norman made his periodic éminence grise appearances at the Fine Arts Work Center.

Lennon served as a complement to Schiller, assembling and sorting old writings into new. It was he who dreamed up the templates for the several anthologies and Q&A collections—the "nonbooks" that filled Norman's last two decades. For any academic, the relationship would have been a golden opportunity, a definite career boost, but for Lennon it became a franchise. He prevailed on Wilkes to award Mailer an honorary doctorate and had him put on the board of the school's new MA writing program. He organized Mailer's papers in advance of their sale to the University of Texas. He also founded the aforementoned Norman Mailer Society, for which he served as president, and if there was any sure evidence that Norman had let himself fall into the pit of his own ego, it was here, with this group that proved less an academic society than a fan club. The society was made up of 150 or so professors and grad students (many from good ol' Wilkes), who met annually in Provincetown or Brooklyn so as to be close to its namesake, usually for three days taken up with the reading of papers with titles like "The Grammar of God and the Contingency of Evil: Mailer's *Castle in the Forest* and the Boundaries of Courage" or (more racily), "Daddy's Girls: Phallic Power and Perverse Paternity in Mailer's *An American Dream*."[53] Panels, symposia, and discussion of the society's business and finances were also part of the program. At the end the participants could look forward to a reception at 627, where Lennon operated as a sort of master of ceremonies, a regular Ed McMahon who led the group in paying obeisance upon the stoic Norman, who would look on, vodka in hand, ensconced in his favorite chair like a geriatric Buddha.

I attended the 2007 gathering for the purpose of this afterword. The society was meeting once more at the Provincetown Inn, where the first thing to greet my eye as I walked in was a ten-foot floor-to-ceiling banner in the main ballroom, emblazoned with, so help me, the likeness of Norman. The background was bright orange, Mailer's bushy eyebrows delineated with heavy slashes of black, and, as Lennon explained to the group, the wall hanging had been gifted by the Ransom Center at the University of Texas, the buyers of the Mailer archive. He joked about it the way academics usually joke, which is by trying to sound light-heartedly ironic, but he also was the one who had schlepped the huge pennant all the way from Texas, then gone to the trouble of hanging it, showing forth Norman as Mao, Che, or perhaps Orwell's Big Brother.

Score another point for slavish devotion. Another was scored by the applause Lennon elicited with his introduction of keynote speaker Lee Siegel, Manhattan lit critic and he of the faked emails in fulsome praise of his own New Republic blog several years before. Siegel had recently published a 5,000-word panegyric praising *The Castle in the Forest* for the *Sunday Times Book Review*,[54] and his speech likened Mailer to Dostoevsky, extolling "the vastness of Mailer's ambition." When he was done finally, Lennon led the group in more applause. Siegel sat down, waving, to his new fans as if he had pitched a no-hitter. Then came the clencher: the society's membership, it was announced, was not reappointing Lennon to another term but making him president for life!

It was stupefying, the sheer banality of it. Norman had written of a "journey back into the self" in 1955 when tepid reviews of *The Deer Park* had threatened to finish off his career at the top, and he'd acknowledged that "for the first time in my life I had worn down to the edge, I could see through to the other side of my fear, [and] I knew a time could come when I would be no longer my own man, that I might lose what I had liked to think was the incorruptible center of my strength. . . ."[55] Well, that time *had* come. It was now, and it was here at an academic conference in Ptown of all places, where numerous creative types had long taken their stand, believing they were protected by the ghosts of O'Neil and Tennessee Williams. Now these minor professors had come on pilgrimage from the University of Virginia, Falls Church; Florida State; and Lennon's Wilkes University, where Norman, with his archivist's help, had recently established the Norris Church Mailer Fellowship in creative writing! And more! The conference, in addition to its learned papers, was offering a Mailer family art show as well as a "literary" walking tour, highlighting Mailer's Provincetown residences and work places that included the site of the old jalopy burial depicted in *Of a Fire on the Moon*.[56] All this in the only place on earth that could lay claim to such diverse, wildly talented originals as Peggy Guggenheim, Billie Holiday, Sinclair Lewis, Al Pacino and Robert De Niro, John Dos Passos, Edna St. Vincent Millay, Alan Dugan and Mary Oliver, as well as almost every significant American painter from Hawthorne and Hopper through Kline, Rothko, and Motherwell. It was the place where a younger, fiercer Mailer took on the cops and fought censorship battles. He'd swapped three or four wives here, put on happenings, directed stage plays, given readings, and hosted some of the most raucus midnight-to-dawn parties anyone could remember, all in addition to crafting some of the best English language prose of the twentieth century. But now, courtesy of Provincetown's Visitor's Service Board and the efforts of J. Michael Lennon, an ossified Norman Mailer had become the centerpiece of his own MLA meeting.

With typical diffidence, Gore Vidal would have split a gut laughing at the incongruity of it all, for on top of everything, the conference was taking place the same weekend as the start of the annual Women's Week, one of the town's premier off-season gay attractions. Budweiser dykes, lipstick dykes, and just plain horny dykes filled Ptown's narrow streets, and there was little question that these visitors weren't fighting among themselves over whether to spend Saturday afternoon listening to treatises on Mailer or hang out at the Back Room or the Vixon disco. The booze was flowing; these academics, with Norman's blessing, were yakking.

But if this juxtaposition was surreal, doubly surreal was that Norman was still in the hospital, at New York's Mount Sinai, where he'd been for more than a month. During the past half year, he'd been through several major surgeries for a variety of problems and now the word was that the prognosis "wasn't good." Scheduled to preside over the conference, he'd had to cancel and send his regrets. Sister Barbara and several of the kids were subbing for him. He was, in fact, dying. And thinking about it, I couldn't help wondering how he was coping with the knowledge of everything that had happened to him. My other thought, which was one that kept coming back to me, I could not help it—a number of people I'd known had quite sensibly swallowed a handful of pills when the time had come, and Hemingway of course had used his shotgun, so what was Norman doing, at eighty-four, hanging on, all tubed up and stripped of his dignity in a tony East Side hospital?

It had always been the case that because he rarely listened, there was little or no dialogue with Norman, which meant that my effort in our relationship, one that purported to be a close one, was huge. On the simplest level, he had to be the one in charge and you were expected to accept that. Whether it was a discussion of military strategy or the U.S. State Department, or deciding which restaurant to go to and who had to sit where, it didn't matter, he was setting the tempo. Sometimes this was amusing, sometimes not. I have heard him lecture his sons Michael and Stephen on how they had to take sides between their mother and himself, an ultimatum that left both kids terrified: Michael, the oldest, developed a tic at the age of nine or ten, where he'd blink and chew on his lower lip whenever his father came to visit. This was at the time when the boys were living with Beverly at the 565 Commercial Street house before Norman had them all evicted, kicked them out into the street, literally, as an act of spite after Bev had dared to stand up to him in court. On his assigned days he would arrive in his beat-up Loden coat, always in a rush, and right off he'd start to complain to the babysitter that the kids weren't dressed and ready to go; at other times he might lose it at the dinner table, and witnessing these outbursts I had to wonder if there and then the kids weren't being scarred for life, as their mother had charged. They may well have been. A sad fact of life is that in many a divorce, the kids will go with the money, which is what seemed to happen here except the specie was more Norman's celebrity than hard cash; later, I heard that Norman had made a deathbed apology (of sorts) to his oldest son, saying he never would have been "so good a writer" if he'd been "a better father." Mike, basically a soft personality though he's chosen to throw his hat into the ring as a producer of movies, tried to let his dad off the hook by telling reporters he preferred "quality" to "quantity," which left me thinking, How stupid and wasteful. Norman, I am sure, meant his words as a consolation. But for who? His statement assumed that a child would rather have a famous artist for a father than a parent who had been there, alert and supportive and giving all along.

So even with his last breath the great mythomaniac had reached for a sound bite, and, regrettably, his oldest son followed in his footsteps with a catchy quote of his own. So did most of the other kids, too. On the day of Norman's death, John Buffalo, twenty-nine, self-identified actor, writer, journalist, and playwright, announced he was going to produce a Hollywood remake of *The Naked and the Dead* based on a screenplay he'd written that had been approved by his father;[57] a week later he apologized, saying he was "appalled at the timing" of his press release, which was "an accident of fate."[58] Son Stephen talked to the press, too, offering up an account of being at his father's bedside at the moment of the great man's passing: it was "like he was seeing something amazing," he said. "It was a good way to go." He added that he and brother Mike had smuggled "a rum and OJ" into the hospital for the old man's last drink.[59] Dandy, fifty-two, Mailer's second oldest daughter, cooperated for a feature story on her painting and work as an art teacher at a private school in rural Connecticut, and benefited from the billing in the *New York Times*.[60]

And then there was Norris, who despite her grief and the return of her cancer may have talked more than all the kids put together. After the burial in Provincetown, where she was photographed holding an American flag given to veterans' widows,[61] she announced (through Sue Harrison, the *Banner*'s arts editor, whose review of my book Norman had used as the occasion for his "poison drip" letter) that the family would be holding its major memorial in January in New York's Carnegie Hall.[62] How she came up with Carnegie Hall at that point was puzzling, unless Norman himself had planned his own send-off, which was a possibility not to be overlooked. But her strangest comments came out several days later in a *New York Post* story, "Widow Defends Mailer, Says He 'Loved Women.'" Norman, she claimed, was widely misunderstood, indeed unfairly judged. "Most people who said he was a male chauvinist didn't know him and didn't read his work . . . A lot of the most inflammatory things he said were comments taken out of context," she explained, adding that she remembered a "calm and simple man," especially in his time away from New York. At the end, she added, "they had to put a ventilator in . . . to have that powerful mind and not be *able to talk* was just horrible."[63]

Though she also spoke of how much Provincetown had meant to him and his work, several weeks later she contacted Cape tip Realtors for an appraisal of 627, explaining that she might be putting the Commercial Street house up for sale.[64] Then, once into the new year, came the real news: *Publishers Weekly*, the *New York Observer*, and several other outlets announced that Norris Church Mailer had signed to write a memoir of her life with her writer husband and their extended families. "Mailer has been the subject of several biographies over the years," the *PW* story read, "but this is the first significant book deal struck since the two-time Pulitzer winner's death in November . . . Church Mailer, a former model, is the author of two novels . . . She was Mailer's sixth wife and was married to him for 32 years."

No purchase price or pub date was mentioned. The book was being published by Random House and edited by David Ebershoff, who had edited Mailer's last four books. Agenting the property was superlawyer John Taylor "Ike" Williams of Fish & Richardson in Boston, who, in addition to Norris, represented Larry Schiller and *Provincetown Banner* owner Alix Ritchie.[65]

The level of unabashed, craven feeding was simply too great. Writers are said to be extremely self-centered people, and Norman, I think, was second to none in this department; but what of these people around him, including Mike Lennon, who, operating as family spokesperson, had needed to inform the AP wire service that he was Mailer's new authorized biographer in the same breath he announced Norman's passing?[66] Why couldn't these people shut up? Decorum, what in better times used to be called proper timing, where had it gone to? And where, oh where, was that independence of spirit, that individualism Norman Mailer more than anyone on the cultural scene had once embodied as something like a noble grace? Had none of it trickled down? Were Mailer's offspring all so molded that their greatest reality was the sound bite, much as it had been at the end for Norman himself?

At the burial the photographers caught Beverly alone after Norris, the kids, Barbara, and the others, including Lennon and Schiller, had left. She stood looking down at the freshly filled-in grave, grieving, even though Norman in the end had left her penniless, an aging actress of seventy-seven. Adele, who did not attend the funeral (like all the ex-wives except Bev), had also been left in penury, even though one of her daughters, I'd heard, made a last-minute appeal to Norman while he was still in the hospital to leave her some money.

In November 1960, Adele had lied to keep him out of jail, then foolishly taken next to nothing in their divorce settlement and lived ever since in a dilapidated walk-up. But never had she talked to the press. Now she was keeping quiet no longer. On the day of Norman's death she let herself be interviewed by the *New York Post* and for the first time addressed the stabbing. The *Post* story read:

> A boozy Mailer stabbed his second wife, Adele Morales, with a dirty penknife during a party . . . and she almost died . . . Morales, now 82 and living in poverty, told the *Post* yesterday that Mailer never apologized and she is still angry about it . . . "He never made an attempt to make it right," she said.[67]

In April, five months later, the memorial service took place at Carnegie Hall, as previously announced. Notices of the event were posted online and in the *New York Times*, with tickets handed out to the public gratis as if it were a sneak preview of some Hollywood blockbuster, not a tribute to a writer. Two thousand people showed up. Once more Mailer's children spoke of their dad as loving, provocative, a philosopher, a friend, and a joker. Stephen, who had embarrassed his brother Michael with a rendition of "Candle in the Wind" at the burial in Ptown, stole the show by announcing he would "channel the spirit" of his father and then dramatically fell to the floor of the stage, got up, and delivered what the *Washington Post* called "a not bad Mailer impersonation," opening with "Carnegie Hall, Carnegie Hall. *Well, why the fuck not?*"[68]

Charlie Rose, the TV host, served as MC. The celebrity speakers were Joan Didion, Don DeLillo, William Kennedy, Tina Brown, and Sean Penn, who, to my knowledge, had never had any real connection to Norman. Norris stood to receive a round of applause but was too weak to speak; over the past few months her cancer had returned and the week before she had been in Sloan Kettering, and was, I learned, about to check herself back in the next morning after the evening's party, being put on by Random House.[69]

At the end, after all the encomia—DeLillo called Mailer "not just a voice but a force" while Didion spoke of him as "a great and obsessed stylist"[70]—there was an announcement from Lawrence Schiller: the Mailer home in Provincetown was being turned into the Norman Mailer Writers Colony. It would serve and support writers of fiction and nonfiction alike, as well as those working on scripts for stage and film. Norman's work area on the third floor was to be preserved as a museum, the five bedrooms below used to house visiting writers and scholars, and the first floor living room was slated for lectures and conferences.

"Distinguished scholars in residence will be invited to assist those who have been selected for fellowships at the college level," Schiller said, noting that several universities had already expressed interest in partnering with the colony.[71]

"He didn't want it lost to history," the ex–book packager and TV miniseries producer told reporters, explaining that months before, when Norman was in the hospital and "could hardly breathe with tubes all over," he had spoken about dedicating the house in which he'd written his final books to "an arts-related purpose." A charitable foundation had then been established, Schiller said, and since the project was first put in motion, Didion, William Kennedy, Doris Kearns Goodwin, and Günter Grass had consented to be on the board.

"Schiller hopes the colony will be launched soon," said the *Cape Cod Times*, one of the many non–New York papers covering the Carnegie Hall event.[72]

Added Schiller a week later, "The house will be the center point. As the foundation grows we may buy other properties, motels and the like."[73]

As spring turned into summer, the Mailer industry rolled on with Schiller, Lennon, Norris, and assorted Mailer offspring greeting attendees at an open house at 627 that was designed to raise between $12 million and $14 million for the planned writers retreat. Forty percent of this money was to be used, their expensively printed four-color brochure read, "to buy the residence from Mrs. Mailer at fair market value."[74] What the tax benefits might be for the state or the cost to the town was not mentioned, although the trusty *Banner* spoke of Mailer's "vision for helping writers," and quoted Lennon on how the retreat would embody Mailer's "church work . . . his giving back."[75]

Also not mentioned in May; the appraisal figure for the house had been $4 million and $4.5 million, which was, presumably, its fair market value.[76] How Lennon could thus refer to charity or "church" work on the part of Mailer or his family was anybody's guess.

Lennon then resurfaced the following week in Alex Beam's *Boston Globe* column, speaking of "the freebooting scribes" who were writing, or were bound to write, future Mailer bios in competition with his own. The University of Texas archive was a treasure trove, he said, then pointed out that these competitors "are not going to get access to the copyright permission that I am going to get." Any fellow scholar was welcome to write on Mailer, it seemed, but was going to have trouble quoting from letters and manuscripts.[77]

So there it was. Not only was Norman's legacy going to be made secure but Schiller and Lennon were now the official guardians of the flame—this schlockmeister and the professor. The museum plan struck me as absurd; Norman's final vanity. The house at 627 Commercial Street as the new *Finca Vigia*, a reenactment of Hemingway's residence in Cuba even though Papa had never envisioned a museum or monument named after himself, that it had been wife Mary's and Fidel's idea after the writer's death? Another Alfoxden, the Wordsworths' grand retreat in Somerset? Emerson's cottage in Concord? Or Robinson Jeffers's Tor House in Carmel, where the overtly egomaniacal Jeffers, unlike Hemingway, had most surely planned his own reliquary?

It was Alice in Wonderland time now, and stunned as I was by Norman's death—which I was, for despite my disappointment, I'd always cared about him deeply, hoping that he'd wake up, cast off the philistines, and get back to work for real—I found myself less and less able to avoid the most pressing question: How could I have swung from identifying myself as one of his most ardent advocates to being so disillusioned? Once upon a time I'd happily let myself be dubbed "Mini Mailer" by my fellow Mailer-Breslin campaign worker Joe Flaherty,[78] yet during the past year I'd been willing to allow one of my dearest friends, the novelist and Oscar-winning screenwriter Jeremy Larner, quoting Lionel Abel in a long-ago issue of *Partisan Review*, who was quoting an expression from *Finnegans Wake*, to refer to Mailer as "Norman Mindbad," a descriptive that grew on me more and more as I wrestled with the shortcuts and simplifications of Mailer's later sensibility.

The answer to such a question is, of necessity, complex, since it rests not only on Mailer and the changes he underwent but the changes that have swept over me, too. Perhaps the closest parallel is the generic, "Why have you swung to the right? You've been a leftist all your life." David Mamet, Norman Podhoretz, and any number of other serious souls have undergone that particular conversion, but, fortunately, the paradigm does not apply to me. But I cannot betray who I was any more than I can deny who I am today. I have both changed in my response to Norman and what he came to represent just as I have remained constant in believing that a large body of his work remains irreplaceable. Granted, his vices were tolerable to me when I served on his mayoral campaign staff and also when I reaped the rewards of being his housemate and biographer. But that, I'd like to think, is because his work justified it. We forgive bad behavior on the part of artists all the time. Maybe we shouldn't but we do. But when an artist's work degrades, falls away and betrays that which has come before, it is like finding oneself aboard an inflatable rubber raft that has suddenly sprung a leak, or driving along with the fuel gauge dropping to empty: you may try to say No to what's happening but eventually you must acknowledge that things ain't what they used to be, and whether you like it or not you had better reorder your priorities plenty quick.

This is what happens also when someone you have had a relationship with tries to destroy you or abuses you in order to better their own situation. Call it a bad divorce. One would be superhuman not to respond. Honor may demand it, not to say one's sense of survival.

The bottom line? Norman, for as long as I knew him, was always aggressive, self-indulgent, carnal, secretive, and vain—*un monstre sacré*, as only the French know how to describe great artists like Picasso who lack the graces that make day-to-day existence harmonious and possible. Now, Norman was never Picasso, but perhaps he had to have been all these things, just as he had to have come from the womb of Fan, who we know stroked and cosseted and indulged him from infancy on. And, equally, he had to have his string of pliable women just as his chemistry mandated a retinue of male pals, all of them, in greater or lesser measure, ready to abide his self-deifying—of this last I know whereof I speak, believe me. But most writers, we know, do not escape unscathed from their creative journey and Norman was no exception. He gravitated to the East Side of Manhattan, which is a state of mind as much as a place for someone of Norman's political instincts, and as a craftsman he retreated from the world of naturalism, which had always been his first and best palate. This left him to write novels that were not novels at all, making the questions he raised early on all the more troubling; I refer specifically to the question of courage and originality, since the terrible truth is, and I do not believe I am wrong here, that Norman, from the late 1970s on, gave us very little that was new and vital. He got caught up in pretentious nonsense. It was as if he'd stopped feeling. He'd stopped *seeing*. He'd stopped experiencing in a way that meant that the humility required to render a portrait of anything outside oneself was no longer available to him. So he had grown stale; he'd withered. Call it age, call it corruption, but he never again had the voice he found for himself in *Advertisements*, or the originality of his essays on JFK, the Democratic and Republican conventions, and his account of the October 1967 march on the Pentagon, not to say the courage to take the stylistic risks of *The Executioner's Song*.

Now let it be utterly clear: I am aware that time does things to us all, just as I know that my original infatuation with Norman had to do with things that were pushing him in ways I could not see were likely to do him in in the end. But taking a quick if inexpensive look at the talent in the room today, it is clear to me that a number of Norman's contemporaries (or near contemporaries) have managed to keep their antennae intact. Peter Matthiessen, Jim Harrison, Cormac McCarthy, Robert Stone, Russel Banks, Harry Crews, Tom Wolfe, the aforementioned Vidal, Didion, and DeLillo, and certainly Philip Roth, who just gets better with age, not to mention a good twenty others in this country and abroad—all have stayed the course. Norman, with the help of Dokter Schiller, drowned in a pool of Norman.

I imagine this pained him greatly, because he had to have been aware of what had happened to him. I was, certainly—aware and pained both, that is—and this left me in the same place as the actor Billy Redfield, who suffered similar feelings about his good friend Marlon Brando, another genius who abused his gift. About Marlon, Redfield wrote:

> "Brando was the American challenge to the English-speaking tradition in the classic roles . . . an artistic, spiritual, and specifically American leader." As a pioneer he was "not only truthful but passionate—not only Greek handsome but unconventional . . . illiterate but unaccountably sophisticated." But he came to the point where "he no longer cared—which is the last stop on the streetcar. To try may be to die, but not to care is to never be born . . . He is a movie star . . . Brando is not to be blamed, merely regretted. The money he commands is irresistible, while important roles alarm him. As an actor, Brando must be either forgotten or fondly remembered."[79]

Norman is not to be blamed, merely regretted . . . either forgotten or fondly remembered.

For Mailer, as for Brando, it came down to character. Whatever their differences in education or cultural habitat, Norman was no less self-absorbed and angry than his theatrical counterpart, even though Marlon, whatever his *mishegoss*, would never, not in a million years or more, ever have dreamed of having a museum named after himself.

NOTES

1. Kachka, Boris, "Mr. Tendentious," *New York* magazine, January 7, 2007.
2. Manso, Peter, ed, *Running Against the Machine: The Mailer-Breslin Campaign*, New York: Doubleday, 1969; Flaherty, Joe, *Managing Mailer*, New York: Coward-McCann, 1970.
3. Roy Cohn to Norman Mailer, October 15, 1980 (author's Norman Mailer archive). Cohn wrote this letter after meeting NM in early September, 1980, in Provincetown. The reference to *Playboy* magazine is that the author had met Cohn the previous spring in the course of interviewing him for *Playboy*, which ultimately killed the piece for reasons that were, as Cohn states, political. The letter was Cohn's way of embracing a fuller relationship with Norman, just as he later sought to ingratiate himself by arranging Mailer's contract at Random House. It read: "Dear Norman, Out of every experience—including *Playboy*'s liberal intolerance—something worth more seems to emerge. In this case—that something is your fairness and friendship—for which I am very grateful. My respect and deep appreciation. Roy." The letter is undated but its envelope is date-stamped Oct. 15, 1980.
4. cf. Brinkley, Douglas, "Mailer's Miscellany," *The New York Times*, April 25, 2005.
5. Manso, Peter, *Ptown: Art, Sex, and Money on the Outer Cape*, New York: Scribner, 2002.
6. Probate and Family Court Department, Barnstable Division, Barnstable, MA, Bk. 4499, pp. 113–15, re. 627 Commercial Street, Provincetown.
7. Norman Mailer letter, *Provincetown Banner*, May 16, 2002.
8. cf. Norman Mailer marginalia, typescripts (2) of *Mailer: His Life and Times* (author's Norman Mailer archive).
9. Manso, *Running Against the Machine: The Mailer-Breslin Campaign*.
10. Manso, Peter, *M:HLAT*. New York: Simon & Schuster, 1985, p. 690.
11. Norman Mailer architectural renderings (4) re. renovation of 627 Commercial Street, Provincetown, MA (author's Norman Mailer archive).
12. Von Hoffman, Nicholas, *Citizen Cohn*, New York: Doubleday, 1988.
13. cf. Probate and Family Court Department, Barnstable Division, Barnstable, MA, Bk. 5497, p. 98, re. sale of property at 627A Commercial Street, Provincetown.
14. Lillian Hellman to author, March 12, 1982 (author's Norman Mailer archive).
15. Manso, Peter, *Ptown: Art, Sex, and Money on the Outer Cape*, pp. 206–8, 282, 283, 292; cf. Ritchie to Simon & Schuster correspondence, spring 2002.
16. Stephen Mailer to author, March 12, 1985 (author's Norman Mailer archive).
17. Gore Vidal to author, 1984 (author's Norman Mailer archive).
18. Yi, Esther I., "Mailer Sex Stories Arrive at Harvard," *The Harvard Crimson*, April 24, 2008; "Mailer's Lust Goes to Harvard," *New York Post*, April 23, 2008; Neyfakh, Leon, "Mailer Mistress Makes a Move," *The New York Observer*, April 23, 2008.

19. Osie Radin to author, July 15, 1985 (author's Norman Mailer archive).
20. Charles "Cy" Rembar to author, May 22, 1984 and May 2, 1985 (author's Norman Mailer archive).
21. Barbara Wasserman notes to author, n.d. (author's Norman Mailer archive).
22. Norris Church Mailer marginalia, mss. I and II, *M:HLAT* (author's Norman Mailer archive).
23. Arthur Schlesinger, Jr., to author, May 14, 1985; Seymour Krim to author, March 13, 1984; Norman Rosten to author, n.d.; Leo Lerman to author, n.d.; Norman Podhoretz to author, March 23, 1984; George Plimpton to author, n.d.; Liz Smith to author, n.d. (author's Norman Mailer archive).
24. Baldwin, James, *Nobody Knows My Name: More Notes of a Native Son*, New York: Dial Press, 1961, p. 172.
25. Norman Mailer marginalia, mss. I and II, *M:HLAT*.
26. cf. Flaherty, Joe, *Managing Mailer*, New York: Coward-McCann, 1970.
27. "Master Spy: The Robert Hanssen Story," Behind the scenes, CBS.com, www.cbs.com/specials/master_spy/scenes.
28. cf. "Lawrence Schiller," Wikipedia, www.wikipedia.org/wiki/Lawrence_Schiller; Lawrence Schiller website, www.lawrenceschiller.com/biopage.html; "Lawrence Schiller Biography," www.filmreference.com/film/42/Lawrence-Schiller.html.
29. cf. *Dialogue: Assassination*. Broadcast no. 16, October 13, 1971, Transcription, www.maebrussell.com; Burn, Gordon, "Dead Calm," *The Guardian*, June 5, 2004.
30. Ott, Chris, "Various Artists: Why Did Lenny Bruce Die?" Shallow Rewards, February 6, 2006, www.shallowrewards.blogspot.com.
31. cf. Lawrence Schiller website, www.lawrenceschiller.com/biopage.html.
32. cf. Probate and Family Court Department, Barnstable Division, Barnstable, MA.
33. cf. Collaboration agreement between Norman Mailer and the New Ingot Company, Inc., February 15, 1977.
34. Publishing agreement between Warner Books, Inc., and the New Ingot Company, Inc., and Charles Fries Productions, Inc., March 4, 1977.
35. Norman Mailer marginalia, ms. II, *M:HLAT*, p. 914.
36. Lawrence Schiller to author, March 7, 1984; author's receipt for certified mail, March 9, 1984; author to Lawrence Schiller, March 26, 1984 (author's Norman Mailer archive).
37. "Golan-Globus Productions," The Internet Movie Database, http://www.imdb.com/company/co0206391.
38. "Awards for *Tough Guys Don't Dance* (1987)," The Internet Movie Database, http://www.imdb.com/title/tt0094169/awards; "Tough Guys Don't Dance (1987)." Rotten Tomatoes. www.rottentomatoes.com/m/tough_guys_dont_dance; Ebert, Roger. "Tough Guys Don't Dance." Rogerebert.com. September 18, 1987. http://rogerebert.suntimes.com/apps/pbcs.dll/article?AID=/19870918/REVIEWS/709180306/1023; "Tough Guys Don't Dance." TV Guide. http://www.tvguide.com/movies/tough-guys-don't/review/121059; Hinson, Hal. "Tough Guys Don't Dance." Washingtonpost.com. September 18, 1987. http://www.washingtonpost.com/wp-srv/style/longterm/movies/videos/tough guysdontdancerhinson_a0c934.htm.
39. Barber, Bonnie and Gregory Katz, "Camera Angels Reporters on the Set of 'Tough Guys.'" *Provincetown Arts*, Summer 1987, pp. 18–21, 116–17.
40. Severs, Jeffrey, "The Untold Story Behind *The Executioner's Song*: A Conversation with Lawrence Schiller," *The Mailer Review*, vol. 1, no. 1, Fall 2007, pp. 81–117.
41. cf. Hawes.com, "*New York Times* Bestseller List, 1995."
42. Equity loan documents re. 627 Commercial Street, Barnstable County Registry of Deeds. Bk. 21113, p. 23, June 15, 2006; Bk. 12389, pp. 76–81, June 30, 1999; Bk. 12389, p. 68, June 1999; Bk. 12389, pp. 73–74, June 30, 1999; Bk. 5497, pp. 98–100, December 31, 1986; Bk. 5497, pp. 92–93, December 31, 1986.
43. cf. "Schiller, Mailer to Recreate The O.J. Simpson Trial," The Internet Movie Database, April 26, 2000, http://imdb.com/name/nm0771659/news? year = 2000.

44. Gay, Jason, "Norman Mailer to CBS: You Blew It! . . ." *The New York Observer*, November 26, 2000.

45. Maslin, Janet, "Books of the Times; The Churchgoing Dad Who Turned to Treason," *The New York Times*, May 9, 2002; James, Caryn, "TV Weekend; The Dream Team for an American Nightmare," *The New York Times*, November 10, 2000; cf. Genzlinger, Neil, "TV Weekend; A Spy's Puzzling Tale: Was There More to It Than Money?" *The New York Times*, November 8, 2002.

46. The figure of twenty-five original works does not include the collections, anthologies, and interview books or the non-Schiller-affiliated film script for *Tough Guys Don't Dance*, Mailer's script doctoring for Sergio Leone's *Once Upon a Time in America* (1984) or other incidental film writing.

47. "Photos of Norman Mailer from the Flair Symposium," Harry Ransom Center, http://eupdates.hrc.utexas.edu/site/PageServer?pagename=Photos_From_Flair.

48. Conference program, the Norman Mailer Society, November 1, 2003, http://www.normanmailersociety.com/old/2003_conference_prog.htm.

49. Von Hoffman, Nicholas, *Citizen Cohn*, New York: Doubleday, 1988, pp. 445–49.

50. Von Hoffman, Nicholas, *Citizen Cohn*, pp. 22–23.

51. cf. Spearie, Steven, "J. Michael Lennon: Former SSU Professor Glad for Opportunities," Sj-r.com, November 5, 2007; "J. Michael Lennon," Wikipedia. http://en.wikipedia.org/wiki/J._Michael_Lennon; "New Collection of Norman Mailer Works Edited by J. Michael Lennon," *Wilkes Creative Writing Program Faculty & Student News*, August 12, 2005, http://www.wilkes.edu/pages/1195.asp#lennon%20headline.

52. Alibris.com, "Norman Mailer Works and Days," J. Michael Lennon & Donna Pedro Lennon, Sligo Press, 2000.

53. cf. Tentative program schedule, the Norman Mailer Society, October 11–14, 2007, http://www.normanmailersociety.com/conference_prog_07.htm.

54. cf. Siegel, Lee, "Maestro of the Ego," *The New York Times Book Review*, January 21, 2007.

55. Mailer, Norman, *Advertisements for Myself*, Signet paperback ed., New York: The New American Library, 1960, p. 218.

56. cf. "The Fifth Annual Conference of the Norman Mailer Society," *The Cape Cod Voice*, September 27–October 10, 2007, p. 57.

57. Calabrese, Erin, "Pals Shed Tears for 'Gracious' Mailer," *New York Post*, November 13, 2007; Mayberry, Carly, "Mailer's Son Gets 'Naked' Pic Rights," *The Hollywood Reporter*, November 12, 2007; *The New York Observer*, November 20, 2007.

58. Neyfakh, Leon, "Mailer's Son to Liz Smith: *Naked and the Dead* Movie Not a Cash-In on Father's Death," *The New York Observer*, December 6, 2007.

59. Calabrese, Erin, "Widow Defends Mailer, Says He 'Loved Women,' " *New York Post*, November 19, 2007.

60. Nash, Margo, "A Woman With a Rich History, Making Art and Teaching Children," *The New York Times*, March 11, 2007.

61. Marquard, Bryan, "Norman Mailer, Writer and Icon, Buried in Provincetown," *The Boston Globe*, Local News Updates, November 13, 2007, http://www.boston.com/news/local/breaking_news/2007/11/r_writer_norman.html.

62. Dziemianowicz, Joe, and Dave Goldiner, "Cape Cod Pals Mourn Norman Mailer," NYDailyNews.com, November 21, 2007.

63. Calabrese, "Widow Defends Mailer, Says He 'Loved Women.' "

64. Author interviews (2) with anonymous source—Provincetown Realtor, December 6, 2007 and May 12, 2008.

65. Thornton, Matthew, "Mailer's Widow to Write Memoir," *Publishers Weekly*, February 26, 2008; Neyfakh, Leon, "Norman Mailer's Widow Memoir for Random House," *The New York Observer*, February 26, 2008; "Novelist Norris Church Mailer," *Publishers marketplace.com*, February 26, 2008; Fish & Richardson P.C. website.

66. Pyle, Richard, "Pulitzer-Winning Author Mailer Dies," Associated Press, November 10, 2007.

67. Williams-James, Brigitte, and Andy Geller, "Requiem for Mailer," *New York Post*, November 12, 2007.
68. Segal, David, "For a Public Provocateur, A Center-Stage Farewell," *The Washington Post*, April 10, 2008.
69. Author interview with Jan Amory, April 10, 2008.
70. cf. Getlin, Josh, "Champion of the American novel," *Los Angeles Times*, April 10, 2008; Cohen, Patricia, "At Tribute, Mailer Children Recall a Family Man," *The New York Times*, April 10, 2008.
71. Neyfakh, Leon, "Mailer Family Establishing Writer's Colony at Late Author's Home in Provincetown, MA," *The New York Observer*, April 9, 2008; Cohen, Patricia, "At Tribute, Mailer Children Recall a Family Man," *The New York Times*, April 10, 2008; capecodonline.com, April 18, 2008.
72. Forman, Debbie, "Writer's Colony a Tribute to Mailer," *Cape Cod Times*, April 18, 2008.
73. Sowers, Pru, "Mailer's House on Course for New Life as Writers Colony," *Provincetown Banner*, April 24, 2008.
74. The Norman Mailer Writers Colony, A Prospectus (c/o Lawrence Schiller at the Norman Mailer Writers Colony), p. 4.
75. Harrison, Sue, "A Writer's Retreat," *Provincetown Banner*, June 12, 2008.
76. Author interviews (2) with anonymous source—Provincetown Realtor.
77. Beam, Alex, "Biographers Start Your Engines," *The Boston Globe*, June 17, 2008.
78. Flaherty, Joe, *Managing Mailer*, p. 201.
79. Redfield, William, "One Might Have Played Hamlet, the Other One Did," *The New York Times*, January 15, 1967.

ACKNOWLEDGMENTS

This book does its best to be accurate to the events of its subject's life. More than two hundred people were interviewed over a period of forty months, some interviews filling more than ten hours of tape. Follow-up sessions were routine, especially when earlier testimony was unclear or ambiguous. The transcript totaled close to twenty thousand pages. Secondary materials such as news stories, magazine profiles, and Mailer's autobiographical writings were used in preparing for interviews and as well as for corroborative purposes.

My premise has always been that memory is fragile. Recollection is everyone's second chance. A book like this must continually "triangulate"—compare multiple versions of a single event, taking as the truest the approximation woven by all. To the extent that the writing of a history is a reconstruction—and here the reconstruction of a personality most complex—one can assume there is more truth in a montage than in a monolith.

And so with the editing. Fatigue, tears, laughter (likewise, the ill-timed phone call, or the need to change a spent cassette)—all served to butcher syntax in the course of taping, and thus I have taken the liberty of smoothing what would otherwise be objectionable. The aim was not to refine people's speech but to make their testimony accessible. To catch the feel of Mailer over the run of sixty years—not just the trajectory of his personal growth but his impact on an entire culture—I needed to allow witnesses to speak in their own voices. Yet the transition to print called for something more, and thus the necessity of trimming, tightening, tuning. In certain instances, participants requested the right of review; in most, not. I have taken care to ensure that their substance and attitude have not been lost.

Plainly, a book of this kind cannot happen without the participation of many, and I owe a debt of gratitude to all those who gave of their time and energy. Their contributions are self-evident, yes, but nonetheless, formal acknowledgment is still called for, and so profound appreciation to: Jack Henry Abbott, Lionel Abel, Alice Adams, John Aldridge, Larry Alson, Walter Anderson, James Atlas, James Baldwin, Richard Baron, Marvin Barrett, Anne Barry, Edith Begner, Dr. Jack Begner, Edward Bonetti, Seymour Breslow, Bowden Broadwater, Chandler Brossard, Charlie Brown, William F. Buckley, Jr., William S. Burroughs, Don

Carpenter, Harold Conrad, Mara Lynn Conrad, Frank Corsaro, Patti Cozzi, Cus D'Amato, Hope Gorham Davis, Robert Gorham Davis, Midge Decter, Edward de Grazia, Ormonde de Kay, Jr., Benjamin DeMott, Art D'Lugoff, E. L. Doctorow, Roger Donald, Fay Mowery Donoghue, Roger Donoghue, Jacob Druckman, Arnold Epstein, Jason Epstein, Kingsley Ervin, Edwin Fancher, Bernard Farbar, Judy Feiffer, Jules Feiffer, Isadore Feldman, Clay Felker, Don Fine, Shirley Fingerhood, Eileen Finletter, Ivan Fisher, the late Joe Flaherty, Maria Irene Fornes, "Ruth E. Friedman," Henry Geldzahler, Allen Ginsberg, George Washington Goethals, Emma Clara Gwaltney, the late Nathan Halper, Pete Hamill, Thomas Hanrahan, Robert C. Harrison, Harold Hayes, Harold Hecht, the late Lillian Hellman, Abbie Hoffman, April Kingsley Hopkins, Irving Howe, H. L. Humes, Monroe Inker, Gloria Jones, Alan Kapelner, Alfred Kazin, Jack Kearney, Lynn Kearney, Gene Kelly, Murray Kempton, Mickey Knox, Paul Krassner, Jill Krementz, Arthur Kretchmer, Seymour Krim, Tuli Kupferberg, John Leonard, Leo Lerman. Max Lerner, Harry Levin, Mark Linenthal, Gordon Lish, Jillen Lowe, Eugene McCarthy, Kevin McCarthy, Michael McClure, Erroll McDonald, Nancy Macdonald, John Maher, William Majeski, Jean Malaquais, Robert Markel, Clifford Maskovsky, Alice Mason, James Meads, Jonas Mekas, Kate Millett, Walter Minton, Mary Mowery, Adeline Lubell Naiman, Victor Navasky, Glen Nelson, Jan Cushing Olympitis, D. A. Pennebaker, Martin Peretz, William Phillips, David Place, George Plimpton, Norman Podhoretz, Ned Polsky, Tom Quinn, Dotson Rader, Barney Rosset, Jr., the late Hedda Rosten, Norman Rosten, Jerry Rubin, Lawrence Schiller, Arthur Schlesinger, Jr., Liz Smith, Barbara Probst Solomon, Jean Stein, Sol Stein, Gloria Steinem, William Sylvia, Jerry Tallmer, Sidney Teitell, Sandy Charlebois Thomas, Rip Torn, Jose Torres, Diana Trilling, Kurt Vonnegut, Bill Ward, Andy Warhol, Richard Weinberg, Shelley Winters, and Rhoda Lazare Wolf. Thanks also to those people who were interviewed but whose voices do not appear in the text; despite the length of the manuscript, the demands of narrative, as well as limitations of space, required leaving certain material, however marvelous, on the cutting-room floor.

Even more, the author wishes to thank members of the Mailer family: Barbara Mailer Wasserman, Al Wasserman, Charles Rembar, Marjorie Radin, Adele Morales Mailer, Barbara Norris Church Mailer, and most of all, Mrs. Fan Mailer who, at about eighty-six years of age, continues to give as good as she gets. To Norman himself, I say that I'm glad our friendship seems to have survived this, and hope that the book has justified the trust.

For their advice, enthusiasm, and support, my gratitude to my editors, Michael Korda and John Herman, as well as to Richard Snyder, president of Simon and Schuster. Throughout the course of this project our relationship has been marked by a spirit of collaboration, and I daresay no author could have had it better.

Similarly, no author could have a better agent than Lois Wallace, of the Wallace and Sheil Agency. From the beginning, when I first proposed this book, she has been a source of reassurance and encouragement. Without her confidence in the project I would have been less patient and thorough, and would have produced a lesser work.

For logistical support in various forms, thanks also to: Ellen O'Donnell and the Provincetown Art Association; Jane Hutchings Peters and John Roderick, officers at the Cape Cod Bank and Trust Company in Provincetown; Sanford Tamarin; Charles Frazier, my Irish *consigliere* on the Cape, and also to Frank Curtis, his opposite number in New York City. To Will and Rhoda Rossmoore, my love and gratitude for the idyll of Stamford.

For assistance in research, transcribing and typing, I owe a special debt to Alice Ruckert, who stayed with the project through thick and thin. Her role was immense and, true to her word, she never wavered in giving the book her fullest efforts, her first priorities. Likewise, thanks to Sandy Thomas, Mona Vold, Mersh Lubel, Lisa Yost, and Elise Mallison, who burned the midnight oil to process the manuscript at the end. To Adam Weisman for his scurrying around the Columbia University library, both kudos and thanks.

Finally, my greatest debt is to Ellen Hawkes, my companion and my love. She not only put aside her own writing to help with the editing, she served as my balance, my inner ear. With her special intelligence, she has been my severest critic and also my surest prop. This book is dedicated to her.

PETER MANSO
September, 1984
Provincetown

INDEX

PHOTO CREDITS